D0208098

THE ENCYCLOPEDIA OF THE NEW YORK STAGE, 1940–1950

THE ENCYCLOPEDIA OF THE NEW YORK STAGE, 1940–1950

SAMUEL L. LEITER

Greenwood Press
Westport, Connecticut • London

Library of Congress Cataloging-in-Publication Data

Leiter, Samuel L.
The encyclopedia of the New York stage, 1940-1950 / Samuel L. Leiter.
p. cm.
Continues: The encyclopedia of the New York stage, 1930-1940.
Includes bibliographical references and indexes.
ISBN 0-313-27510-6 (alk. paper)
1. Theater—New York (N.Y.)—Dictionaries. I. Title.
PN2277.N5L365 1992
792'.097471—dc20 92-7397

British Library Cataloguing in Publication Data is available.

Library of Congress Catalog Card Number: 92-7397
ISBN: 0-313-27510-6

First published in 1992

Greenwood Press, 88 Post Road West, Westport, CT 06881
An imprint of Greenwood Publishing Group, Inc.

Printed in the United States of America

The paper used in this book complies with the Permanent Paper Standard issued by the National Information Standards Organization (Z39.48-1984).

10 9 8 7 6 5 4 3 2 1

For Benito

Contents

Preface

This is the third volume in a series that began as an attempt to provide a description of every legitimate production--play, musical, revue, revival--given in the New York professional theatre for each decade from the 1920s on. There are several methods of computing the beginning and end of a New York theatre season; the previous volumes in this series followed that used by Burns Mantle in his annual *Best Plays of the Year* series, by which a season ended on June 15 and began on June 16. In the 1945-1946 volume of *Best Plays*, that system was revised; Mantle began his 1945-1946 season on June 16 but ended it on May 31. Thereafter, he (or his successors) counted June 1 as the beginning of a season and May 31 as the end. To keep the present series relatively consistent, and because the 1930s volume of this series ends on June 15, 1940, I have decided to begin coverage with June 16, 1940, and to end all seasons on May 31. Only works produced in Manhattan are given, and these works are restricted to the theatres of Broadway and Off Broadway. There was minimal activity in the other boroughs, none of it in any way exceptional.

The listings are not restricted to English-language productions; every known foreign-language production visiting the city and reviewed in the English-language press has been chronicled. Non-English-language offerings were not as extensive in the 1940s as previously, being restricted chiefly to the Yiddish theatre, which was itself in a decline. Almost all such activity described in the English-language press is included, provided there was sufficient information available to warrant inclusion. Small numbers of titles of Yiddish plays not covered here because of a lack of information are available in the pertinent sections of the Burns Mantle series.

Often it was difficult to determine whether a given production was amateur or professional. A number of works that might be called "semiprofessional" are included. These sometimes were included because a participant went on to become a major theatrical (or other media) figure. The fact that a company was occupying a Broadway playhouse is no guarantee of its professional status, as the Dramatic Workshop of the New School for Social Research, a group made up in its later years mostly of student actors, played regularly at Broadway's small President Theatre. Because of the ambivalent nature of the company, press coverage of its activities was sporadic, and a number of productions went unreviewed. Again, only those that were reviewed are included here. On the other hand, as its name implies, the Equity Library Theatre, which was founded in the decade, used professional actors belonging to the actors' union, but offered so many productions (in strictly limited runs of several performances each) that the great bulk of its work was uncriticized, and even the dates and theatres (usually unconventional spaces, such as library auditoriums) of these performances are sometimes problematical. The titles (and little else) of many of these works are mentioned in the Burns Mantle series and in the *Theatre World* series begun by

Daniel Blum in 1944. If the available reviews provide sufficient information, such productions are included. In many cases, these shows received just one review (usually by George Freedley, who happened to have been a sponsor of Equity Library Theatre). When such solitary reviews provide the basis for an entry, that fact is duly noted.

The book describes nearly 1,150 alphabetically listed productions (although, because of revivals and return engagements, the number of titles is less). In cases where a play received multiple productions, these are listed chronologically.

The following types of offerings are not described in the *Encyclopedia*, except as noted:

1. Vaudeville shows. Some revues were very much like vaudeville and some vaudeville presentations were similar to revues, but the designations of previous historians and of contemporary critics have been followed in determining which was which.
2. Ice-skating revues, except those given in a regular theatre, for example, the series produced at the City Center.
3. Circuses.
4. Nightclub and cabaret shows. As with vaudeville, some nightclub shows were similar to revues.
5. Benefit productions, except for certain cases. There were some highly elaborate wartime revues designed to raise money for various war-related causes. These normally were given only once. However, those few shows--such as Irving Berlin's *This Is the Army*--whose main purpose was to earn money for war-related funds, but which were given in regular runs, receive full entries.
6. Operas and ballets. In those few cases where a primarily dance or operatic work was staged in a legitimate playhouse and reviewed by theatre (as opposed to music or dance) critics, it has been included. There were a few such operatic or semioperatic works on Broadway in the 1940s, including the works of Gian-Carlo Menotti, Marc Blitzstein's *Regina*, and Kurt Weill's *Street Scene*, and part of their interest stemmed from the controversy over their operatic status.
7. Productions not reviewed in the press, or reviewed so briefly or unsubstantively as to prevent effective description. As mentioned previously, some productions that received only one review have been included provided that review contained substantive information about a production.
8. Children's theatre productions. There were several interesting children's theatre offerings with future actors of importance such as Jason Robards, Jr., Tom Poston, and Lilia Skala, but their numbers are small, and they have not been included here.
9. Puppet plays.

HOW TO USE THE ENTRIES

Titles that begin with the abbreviations *Mr.* and *Mrs.* are considered as if these words were fully spelled out: *Mister* and *Mistress*. Titles beginning with contractions such as *It's* and *I'll* are considered as if they were spelled without the apostrophe. Titles that begin with articles such as *A*, *An*, *The*, and foreign equivalents have these words placed at their ends; for example, *Big Knife, The*. Each listing is headed by specific information concerning the respective offering. Credits are given wherever available, which is not the case for a handful of shows for which such data as directors, designers, producers, dates, or lengths of run may not be provided.

The following are typical examples of entry headings: The types of data included in the entry headings and their respective abbreviations (where applicable) are noted after the examples:

ALL MY SONS [Drama/Business/Crime/Family/Marriage/Small Town/ War] A: Arthur Miller; D: Elia Kazan; S/L: Mordecai Gorelik; C: Paul Morrison; P: Harold Clurman, Elia Kazan, and Walter Fried i/a/w Herbert H. Harris; T: Coronet Theatre; 1/29/47 (328)

SOUTH PACIFIC [Musical/Military/Race/Romance/Tropics/War] B/LY: Oscar Hammerstein II and Joshua Logan; M: Richard Rodgers; SC: James Michener's book, *Tales of the South Pacific*; S/L: Jo Mielziner; C: Motley; P: Richard Rodgers, Oscar Hammerstein II, Leland Hayward, and Joshua Logan; T: Majestic Theatre; 4/7/49 (1,925)

(1) MACBETH [Dramatic Revival*] A: William Shakespeare; M: Lehman Engel; D: Margaret Webster; S: Samuel Leve; C: Lemuel Ayers; P: Maurice Evans i/a/w John Haggott; T: National Theatre; 11/11/41 (131)

1. **Title:** Most works are listed under the title by which they were advertised or reviewed; in some cases this title was in a foreign language, but the work, being well known in English, may be entered under its English name with the foreign title in parentheses. When known, earlier titles by which a play had been called before its New York production are given in the text of the specific entry. Any question about a title may be resolved by checking the Index of Titles. All entries in the text are arranged alphabetically. When there is more than one entry (production) for a title, the entries are arranged chronologically. Each production is preceded by a number to designate its place in the chronology; thus, the *Macbeth* example above was the first of several productions of the play.
2. **Categories:**[1] Following the title, and placed within brackets, are the categories to which the play has been found to correspond. Each new work (works determined not to be revivals) has been designated, for example, for the sake of simplicity, as a comedy, drama, comedy-drama, musical, revue, or miscellaneous. The genre words *tragedy*, *melodrama*, *farce*, *operetta*, *comic opera*, *musical comedy*, and so on have not been used in the category listings but will often be found within the entries. If a production is a revival, it is termed either "Dramatic Revival" or "Musical Revival." An asterisk (*) follows these terms for all plays or musicals described in previous volumes of *The Encyclopedia of the New York Stage*. Asterisks also are printed whenever a title is mentioned that may be found in an earlier volume of this series. Following the genre designations are various categories appropriate to the work. Terms such as those given in the examples should provide a bird's-eye view of the nature of the play. This subject categorization is as thorough as possible, although these categories are meant as a guide and should not always be accepted literally. A play may only be indirectly related to war, for example, but the word *war* in the heading may signal that this is indeed a "war play." Perusal of the specific entry should make clearer the reason for inclusion of the word. Some plays are also categorized by the language in which they were presented, if other than English. Appendix 2, where all such categorizations are compiled into lists, provides further background on the category listings. In most cases, the listings are self-explanatory. Titles designated as "Dramatic Revivals" or "Musical Revivals" have not been further categorized, aside from whether they were presented in a specific foreign tongue. This is also for "Revues," which are further categorized only if they are of foreign origin or were given by a predominantly black cast.
3. **Author** (A): The name of the playwright(s) of a straight (nonmusical) play. When the author serves in other capacities as well, such as director, producer, and so on, a slash (/) signifies this; for example, A/D

(author/director). When the same individual functions alone in one capacity and with someone else in another, the slash is not used and the name is given separately according to the specific function. This holds true for all of the artists listed below.
4. **Sketches** (SK): The author of sketches in revues and similar productions.
5. **Translator** (TR) or **Adaptor** (AD): The person who translated or adapted the work from one language to another.
6. **Revised By** (REV): The person who revised a script before it was produced; a rare credit.
7. **Book** (B): The librettist(s) of a musical or revue. ADD.B. is for those who provided additional material to a book.
8. **Conceived By** (CN): The person responsible for conceptualizing a show; used mainly for revues.
9. **Music** (M): The composer(s) of a musical or revue. Also, the person who composes incidental music for a straight play. ADD.M. is used when additional music is supplied by someone else.
10. **Lyricist** (LY): The lyricist(s) of a musical or revue; used occasionally for songs interpolated into a straight play. ADD. LY. is used for persons who supplied lyrics in addition to those credited to the main lyricist.
11. **Source** (SC): The source--novel, play, story, poem, idea, and so on--upon which a work is based.
12. **Director** (D): The director.
13. **Choreographer** (CH): The person responsible for creating the dances in musicals and straight plays.
14. **Set Designer** (S): When the set designer was responsible for all elements of a show's design (sets, costumes, and lights), the abbreviation DS (designer) is used. In many cases the set designer designed only one other element, so S/C (set designer/costume designer) or S/L (set designer/lighting designer) are often used.
15. **Costume Designer** (C): The costume designer, sometimes the same person who designed lights (C/L) or sets (S/C).
16. **Lighting** (L): The lighting designer, sometimes the same person who designed the sets (S/L) or costumes (L/C).
17. **Producer** (P): The individual or company acting as producer. When multiple producers are credited, their participation is designated by such forms as b/a/w (by arrangement with), u/t/a/o (under the auspices of), b/s/a/w (by special arrangement with), i/a/w (in association with), and so forth.
18. **Theatre** (T): The theatre where the production opened. Occasionally, the names of subsequent theatres at which a production played are given, but this practice is not followed consistently. When the theatre's name is followed by (OB), it signifies that the theatre is Off Broadway. In a few cases, theatres that operated under what would eventually be recognized as Off-Broadway terms (as defined by the unions as well as by their location), are designated as Broadway here. For example, the President Theatre was a small theatre in the Broadway area, but was used for the productions of the Dramatic Workshop, a semiprofessional group. Similarly, Madison Square Garden, the sports arena, was used for a Broadway-type revue called *Funzapoppin'*, and the City Center of Music and Drama, a Broadway-sized house on the outskirts of the Broadway area, was used under special arrangements with the unions that allowed it to operate outside of Broadway economic constraints. For purposes of this book, such theatres are designated as "Broadway." A list of all theatres used by the shows in this volume, broken down into Broadway and Off Broadway, is given in appendix 10.
19. **Opening Dates**: Following the name of the playhouse is the date on which the production officially opened, given in the following form:

7/20/40. Apart from dates mentioned in quotes, all dates are given in this form.

20. **Length of Run**: The figure in parentheses that ends most headings signifies the number of performances attained by the work. These figures are not always known in the case of minor Off-Broadway or Yiddish theatre productions.

The text that follows each heading offers a fairly comprehensive view of the work described. It attempts to give the important historical background, a summary of the plot, and an idea of the critical reaction to the play and the performance. Representative quotes of the critics are incorporated verbatim or in paraphrase. Footnotes are not used, and the name of the reviewer is often provided within the sentence by enclosing it in parentheses. When a critic's name appears, it is followed by an abbreviation of the newspaper or journal for which he or she wrote (for example, *NYT* for *New York Times*). A list of such abbreviations is found in appendix 8. In cases where a review is anonymous, only the abbreviation of the source is given. In addition to critical quotes, hundreds of anecdotes culled largely from biographical and autobiographical accounts have been incorporated. Since footnotes are not used for documentation, enough information is given in the entries (author's name or title of the work cited) so that the appropriate source may be located in the bibliography.

Many plays described in this volume have not been included in earlier accounts of the period. Almost all such works were in the Off-Broadway theatre, which had a number of manifestations--including the Yiddish theatre--during the period. Many more might have been described but, as mentioned earlier, these either were not reviewed or were reviewed by one or two critics whose accounts are insufficient to provide adequate source material. An example is the work of the Equity Library Theatre, which often gave over forty productions a season. The chief source of reviews for *The Encyclopedia of the New York Stage* is the abundantly well documented annual clipping scrapbooks of the research division of the Lincoln Center Library of the Performing Arts. These include reviews from the *New York Times*, *New York Post*, *New York Herald-Tribune*, *New York World-Telegram*, *New York Journal American*, *New York Sun*, *PM*, *New York Morning Telegraph*, *New Leader*, *Christian Science Monitor*, *Newark Evening News*, *Women's Wear Daily*, *Brooklyn Eagle*, *Variety*, *New York Daily News*, *New York Daily Mirror*, *Daily Compass*, *New York Star*, and, less frequently, *Billboard* and *The Daily Worker*. These have been supplemented in the present work by reviews from such sources as *Theatre Arts Magazine*, the *Saturday Review of Literature*, *Catholic World*, and the annual collections of George Jean Nathan called *Theatre Book of the Year* (begun in 1942-1943). Thus the entry for an important production is likely to be based on nearly two dozen reviews.

At the end of the volume are ten appendices and a selected bibliography. The appendices include a chronological calendar of productions, a listing of plays by category, the major play awards of the day, a listing of novels and plays providing the sources for plays and musicals, a list of institutional theatres and their offerings, a list of visiting foreign troupes and their repertories, a listing of the long-run hits of the period, the abbreviations of the newspapers and periodicals cited in the text, a season-by-season statistical breakdown of production totals, and a list of all Broadway and Off-Broadway theatres used by the productions in this book.

I would like to thank Bill Gargan of the Harry Gideonse Library at Brooklyn College, CUNY, for his always-enthusiastic help. Other Gideonse staff members were also helpful, as was the staff at the Lincoln Center Library for the Performing Arts. Since only a compulsive workaholic would undertake a project such as this, it is absolutely necessary that such an individual have the support of a loving and caring life partner; for being that person, I tender my wife Marcia my deepest gratitude.

NOTE

1. Category listings for all Yiddish-language plays not produced by the Yiddish Art Theatre contain only the genre and language of production.

Introduction

The Depression was over, but depression remained a worldwide ailment as the 1940s barrelled their way into history. At the decade's onset, the big question tearing at the nation's guts was whether or not it would become actively involved in the ever-hotter foreign conflagration. On December 7, 1941, the answer came when the Japanese bombed Pearl Harbor; America immediately declared war and dug in for the duration.

The New York theatre already had had its share of plays related to the imminent encounter, but these were relatively few in number. Most war-theme plays of the thirties took a definitely pacifist view toward the possibility of renewed hostilities. But as the situation worsened, a small number began to take a more militant stance; the most outstanding example was *There Shall Be No Night*, produced at the end of the 1939-1940 season and still running when the theatrical forties proper began. War plays inspired by our actual participation were, at first, a bit slow in coming; before long, however, it would be a rare play or musical that did not have some connection--no matter how tenuous--with the conflict. The war brought years of excitement and prosperity to Broadway, but there was a sharp turnaround in the postwar period. The hedonistic "there's no tomorrow" outlook rapidly faded into a concern with the harsh realities of forging a new future for the country and the world in an era dominated by national and international fear and distrust.

THE THEATRE AT WAR

Broadway donned its most patriotic colors, not only in the types of plays and musicals it displayed, but in its active and enormously successful participation in war bond and other war-related fund-raising campaigns, including the presentation of spectacular benefit productions at the city's biggest theatres and sports arenas; in the performances in veterans' hospitals; in the provision of free or reduced-price seats to members of the armed forces (over nine million seats were thus provided); in the free matinee seats given during one fundraising drive to bond purchasers; in the junk-salvage campaigns that were important homefront activities; in the creation of outstanding hit shows--Irving Berlin's *This Is the Army* and Moss Hart's *Winged Victory*, not to mention a special revival of *Candida*, with Katharine Cornell--designed specifically to raise money for the war effort; in the trips to the front made by theatrical artists under USO auspices to play for the troops (a number of performers died or were injured in plane crashes); in the large number of enlistments registered among theatrical figures; and so on. Most notable of the legitimate theatre's demonstrations on behalf of the armed forces overseas was the tour to Europe's combat zones of Katharine Cornell's famed production of *The Barretts of Wimpole Street*; Americans serving in the Pacific got to see Maurice Evans's brilliant version of *Hamlet*, later called *The GI Hamlet* when he brought it to postwar Broadway. Over twenty other shows also played at army bases in the United States and abroad.

One of the most popular close-to-home manifestations of the theatre's assistance to the men and women in uniform was the Stage Door Canteen. This was a cabaret established in the basement (formerly known as the Little Club) of the Shubert-owned Forty-fourth Street Theatre (provided rent-free), serving American and foreign soldiers and sailors. It was staffed by Broadway hopefuls as well as stars, who often entertained, danced with the men in uniform, or worked in the kitchen. The Stage Door Canteen, which had branches in Washington, Philadelphia, and Hollywood, was set up by the American Theatre Wing, so called because it was originally a wing or branch of a British service organization created during World War I.

The physical act of attending the theatre was affected by wartime cutbacks, rationing, and potential danger. Air-raid threats led to the nightly dimming of marquee lights and the use of special traffic-light covers with slits. Tire and gas rationing made it difficult for anyone not resident in town to get to see a play. (These obstacles eventually impacted on touring shows as well.) On Thursday nights from 9:00 to 9:20, blackout tests were conducted, making the usually vibrant Broadway area resemble a cemetery. Paper shortages required that the number of programs given to spectators be reduced to one for every two spectators. Many of these conditions found their way into jokes purveyed in Broadway musicals, revues, and comedies.

Despite the hardships, however, the wartime economy, fueled by the huge defense industry, as well as by black marketeering, put cash into many hands eager to spend it visiting (or even producing) amusements. New York overflowed with free spenders, including not only the masses of workers pouring into the city for war-industry jobs, but the hordes of military personnel stationed in the region. Theatre--as well as hotels, bars, nightclubs, movies, restaurants, and related businesses--boomed as it had not since the roaring twenties. Summertime, traditionally a period of slow business, could not be discriminated from the rest of the year as far as the new theatregoers were concerned. Travel was limited by wartime restrictions, so people were practically forced to remain in town, which definitely helped the box-office take. The habit of dressing for the theatre vanished in the crush of new audiences who had been weaned on movies and had rarely, if ever, seen a live stage performance. Male spectators were as likely as not to attend a Broadway play--often ignorant of what they were paying to see--tieless and in their shirtsleeves. Crowds of thrillseekers thronging Times Square helped speed up the process by which Forty-second Street between Seventh and Eighth avenues, once a proud theatrical thoroughfare, descended into carnival-like sleaze.

The thirst for entertainment as an antidote to the horror overseas was responsible for increasing annual production totals, and these went hand in hand with a never-before-seen number of long-run hits. There eventually was so much activity that, with only about thirty-four theatres (totalling around 40,000 seats) available, it led to that *rara avis* known as booking jams. When *The Red Mill* was revived in 1945, its desperate producer, in order to get into the Forty-sixth Street Theatre, owned by the Shuberts, agreed to pay the avaricious landlords five percent of the gross; such an arrangement never before had been known on Broadway. Despite the crush, no new Broadway theatre was built during the war (or immediate postwar) era. Nevertheless, while a lot of money was made on a good number of productions that in other times might have faltered, the overall ratio of hits to misses remained roughly one in three, with some seasons doing a bit better, and others a bit worse. (After the war, one in four became more usual.)

Few serious plays of lasting significance appeared during World War II because the overwhelming emphasis was on escapism, but some outstanding lighthearted entertainments were birthed. These included several pathbreaking musicals (especially *Oklahoma!*) that not only expanded the range and altered the style of the conventional musical theatre, but also managed to inject a heretofore unfamiliar strain of cynicism and irony into plot-lines that normally might have been content solely with frivolity.

AFTER THE WAR WAS OVER

When the war ended and the military traded in its uniforms for civvies, the artificial excitement that thrilled the Great White Way from 1942 to 1945 rapidly paled. War-generated incomes slumped and business slackened, hitting a definite recession by 1948-1949 and--because of the fabulous sums now needed to put on a show--reaching record low production totals a year later. Summers were once again deadly seasons for most Broadway shows. Unemployment levels among actors, which dropped remarkably during the war, when there were jobs aplenty, rebounded to levels of over ninety percent, as in the previous decade. Before long, Broadway would be so burdened with ailments that alternative means of production would assume an importance not acknowledged since the teens and twenties, and Off Broadway would begin to make the strides that soon would bring it to national prominence.

Meanwhile, the nation was struggling with the vast array of problems strewn in the wake of the great conflict. The euphoria of victory quickly faded before the onrush of readjustment difficulties confronting the demobilized military; the growing demands of racial minorities for a fair slice of the national pie; the threat of nuclear annihilation made palpable by the detonation of the A-bomb over two Japanese cities; the reconstruction of war-ravaged nations; the complexities of establishing world peace through the newly created (1945) United Nations; and, among other things, the nightmare of a cold war that pursued suspected Communists with the zealousness of Transylvanian mobs hoping to plant a stake in Dracula's heart. Much of this was reflected--sometimes sharply, sometimes dimly--in the theatre of the time.

The anti-Communist mania had especially painful effects on the entertainment industry. It had begun even before the war, as witness the demise in 1939 of the Federal Theatre Project following the suspicion by a congressional subcommittee of left-wing infiltration. The fear of Communists in the theatrical woodpile continued into the following decade, including a 1940 brouhaha in which the actors' union, Equity, was believed to be under Communist influence. Such accusations were put on hold during the war, when the nation banded together to fight the fascist menace, but in 1945 actor Frank Fay raised the issue again, charging that the union's leadership was Red. Similar headaches were brewing for those whose liberal politics stood behind the USSR during the war, when it was our ally and it was acceptable to be pro-Soviet, or those who--no matter how patriotic their motives--had been involved in what later were determined to be left-wing causes. In the wake of Allied military victory, the FBI began to investigate those in the public eye suspected of having anything to do with a list of organizations determined to be subversive, regardless of how innocent of such subversion participants may have been. In 1947 the House Un-American Activities Committee--then led by J. Parnell Thomas--began a relentless pursuit of suspected left-wingers in the media, a pursuit that would not end until the mid-1950s and that dragged not only the "guilty" but the innocent through the slime.

The brunt of the attack was on Hollywood, and ten screen writers were jailed for contempt of court; all had belonged to the Joint Anti-Fascist Refugee Committee, created to oppose the policies of Spain's dictator Franco. (One of them, Dalton Trumbo, authored the 1949 Broadway comedy *The Biggest Thief in Town*, but, in a show of the producers' cowardice, his name was removed from preopening publicity for fear of damaging the play's chances.) Because they were also connected with Hollywood, some of Broadway's most outstanding figures, including Fredric March and Florence Eldridge, John Garfield, and José Ferrer, not to mention émigré dramatist Bertolt Brecht, were questioned about their activities. The situation grew horrific in the next decade, when the careers and lives of important theatre talents were actually destroyed. Related to the Communist witch-hunt was an incident in 1949 when Arthur Miller, desiring to travel to Belgium to view a staging of his *All My Sons*, was denied a passport by the State Department because of his perceived political beliefs.

THE COMMERCIAL THEATRE

Broadway in the 1940s was the domain of a smaller number of outstanding producers than in the past. The major producing organizations, such as the Theatre Guild and the Playwrights' Producing Company, remained active, but less so than before. Some formerly successful producers (such as Jed Harris, Richard Aldrich and Richard Myers, Courtney Burr, and Rowland Stebbins) were fitfully active but not consistently effective during the decade. A number of veterans, however, did contribute importantly to the commercial theatre. Their names and samples of their best work include Dwight Deere Wiman (*By Jupiter* and *Street Scene*); Herman Shumlin (*The Corn Is Green* and *Watch on the Rhine*); Brock Pemberton (*Janie* and *Harvey*); Max Gordon (*Junior Miss*, *The Doughgirls*, and *Born Yesterday*); Gilbert Miller (*Dear Ruth*, *Antigone*, *Edward, My Son*, and *The Cocktail Party*); Eddie Dowling (*The Glass Menagerie* and "Hello Out There"); George Abbott (*Pal Joey*, *Best Foot Forward*, and *Kiss and Tell*); Alfred de Liagre, Jr. (*The Voice of the Turtle* and *The Madwoman of Chaillot*); John Golden (*Claudia* and *Counsellor-at-Law*); Vinton Freedley (*Let's Face It*); Guthrie McClintic (*Medea* and *The Velvet Glove*); Katharine Cornell (*The Doctor's Dilemma*, *The Three Sisters*, *Antigone*, and *Antony and Cleopatra*); John C. Wilson (*Blithe Spirit*, *Bloomer Girl*, *O Mistress Mine* and *The Winslow Boy*); Billy Rose (*Clash by Night* and *Carmen Jones*); and the Messrs. Shubert. The latter, however, although remaining the monopolistically powerful theatre owners of yore, were only peripherally involved in production during the decade, providing several operettas (such as *My Romance*) and revivals (including *Blossom Time*), but confining most of their nonlandlord activities on Broadway to frequent investments in other producers' shows.

The Shuberts' monopolistic proclivities, however, became the subject of a 1949 federal investigation launched by the attorney general's office. The brothers Shubert, Lee and J. J., had their money in seventy-five percent of the shows; ninety percent of those that did not benefit from Shubert investments were forced to play in one of the seventeen Shubert-owned theatres (they also controlled the booking in another). Their control of out-of-town theatres and booking made it even likelier that they were guilty of restraint of trade. If you did not play in a Shubert theatre out of town (provided you could find one), you might not get a Shubert theatre in New York. (The Shuberts were also accused of malefactions in the ticket-speculation maelstrom of the late forties.) An antitrust suit was brought by the government against the Shuberts, who denied the charges, but who were eventually forced to dismantle much of their empire.

A number of important new producers were moving into the limelight during these years, although several had begun to produce in the 1930s. They (and samples of their best work) included Howard Lindsay and Russel Crouse (*Arsenic and Old Lace*, *The Hasty Heart*, and *Detective Story*); Cheryl Crawford (*One Touch of Venus*, *The Tempest*, *Brigadoon*, and *Love Life*); Kermit Bloomgarden (*Deep Are the Roots*, *Command Decision*, and *Death of a Salesman*); Leland Hayward (*A Bell for Adano*, *State of the Union*, and *Mister Roberts*); Richard Rodgers and Oscar Hammerstein II (*I Remember Mama*, *Annie Get Your Gun*, *Happy Birthday*, *South Pacific*, and *The Happy Time*); Robert Whitehead (*Medea*, *Crime and Punishment*, and *The Member of the Wedding*); and Michael Todd (*Star and Garter*, *Mexican Hayride*, *The GI Hamlet*, and *Up in Central Park*). On the cusp of their brilliant producing careers were people like David Merrick, Alexander H. Cohen, and Jean Dalrymple, whose major contributions would arrive in the 1950s.

These producers were operating in an increasingly manic environment; that they accomplished as much as they did is a tribute to their fortitude and aggressiveness. Some of them, like Todd and Rose, were among the most colorful figures of their times, and their activities and lifestyles (frequent subjects of the gossip columns) were followed with avid interest by countless citizens, which only served to provoke additional interest in their stage productions.

Following the war, Broadway theatres, of which there were never enough during the boom years, were often dark, and many had to convert to other purposes, such as movie theatres or television or radio studios. The only theatre to be added to the otherwise decreasing number available (thirty-three by the last year of the decade) was the 1,600-seat Mark Hellinger (named for a Broadway columnist) on West Fifty-first Street, remodeled in 1948 with producer Anthony Brady Farrell's money out of a 1931 movie palace first called the Hollywood and then the Warner (and sometimes referred to as the Warner's Hollywood Theatre or Warner Brothers Hollywood Theatre). (Brady was a multimillionaire from Albany who tried to make it rich on Broadway in the late forties; his series of mediocre shows met with disaster, and he soon retreated with a dented bank account.) He paid $1.5 million for the theatre (it originally cost $3 million) so as not to have to accept any other landlord's terms for attractions that he sponsored. Brady joined a tiny number of producers still owning their own theatres, as by now most producers merely rented an available space.

Theatre ownership was (and remains) a risky venture, as these structures stood on vastly expensive real estate, but employed economically unfeasible schedules that allowed for profitable activities for only a few hours a day; moreover, most theatres lacked the kind of air conditioning that would have allowed them to remain profitably open in the summer. The building code--mindful of the danger from fire in playhouses lacking appropriate fireproof materials--forbade the construction of more economically sound enterprises overhead. A vigorous campaign to revise the building code was instituted toward the close of the decade by theatre investor Howard Cullman, but although he eventually succeeded in his aims, it would be many years before the new code prompted anyone to build a Broadway playhouse. (Also sought, but years from realization, was a change in the laws that prevented alcoholic beverages from being sold in theatres.)

A major part of Broadway's problem stemmed from skyrocketing production costs and a consequent rise in ticket prices that made theatre going too costly for the average consumer. One significant reason for the higher costs was the prices paid during the war for hard-to-get materials and labor. Another was the inflated salaries of stars, presumably emulating the demands of their Hollywood and broadcasting brethren. Playwrights were also seeking a larger cut, including a share in the subsidiary rights of their plays. Still another cause was rampant unionism and its featherbedding requirements. When Margaret Webster staged *The Tempest* in 1945, her use of incidental music led the American Federation of Musicians to deem the show a musical; although only twelve musicians were used, the union demanded that sixteen be hired, each earning ninety-two dollars a week. Several subsequent revivals ran into similar obstacles. The stagehands' and designers' unions could be equally troublesome, especially when it came to transferring a noncommercial production's sets to a commercial engagement.

No longer could one produce a modest play for $15,000 or $20,000. Prices were now three or more times as high as in the previous decade. The Kaufman and Hart hit, *You Can't Take It with You*, cost about $16,000 in 1936, while Hart's *Christopher Blake* tallied up a sum of over $180,000 a decade later. *Life with Father* had cost $23,000 at the Empire Theatre in 1939. A similarly sized cast appeared in the same theatre with *Life with Mother* in 1948; the original scenic design was supplemented by only one additional setting, but the new show cost over $85,000. Musical costs were much, much worse. A first-class musical of the thirties may have cost in the vicinity of $60,000, but in the forties some shows went as high as $350,000; the average first-class musical had to cough up a minimum of $150,000 ($200,000 to $225,000 was normal) to raise the curtain. No small number of such shows lost every penny.

There had been a hit-or-miss syndrome prevalent since the twenties, but never had the odds against creating a hit seemed quite so overwhelming. All sorts of devices were used to stimulate business, including the flourishing of Sunday performances, which had become legal in 1941 (although not without a fight). Another increasingly used option, especially late in the decade, was the two-for-one coupon known as a "twofer." Since the full tax had to be paid regardless of the discount, a pair of four-dollar tickets cost the twofer buyer $5.60. A hopeful idea of the 1948-1949 season was that of the "show trains," specially scheduled trains--averaging one a month--headed for New York from scattered Connecticut towns and carrying 300 to 500 playgoers holding tickets to specific shows and paying a twenty-five percent discount on their transportation fee. A "show plane" concept was also briefly tried for Albanyites, but did not last long.

Awards have always been a potential stimulus for movie and theatre ticket sales. Until 1947, the chief awards were the Pulitzer Prize and the Drama Critics Circle Awards, but these recognized only plays. Selection by Burns Mantle as one of the ten best plays of the year in his annual compilation was another important coup. The Pulitzer only acknowledged American plays (and an occasional musical), and the Critics Circle gradually provided awards for both musicals and foreign plays. On occasion, the Pulitzer and Critics Circle could not decide on any winners. Apart from certain awards presented by non-theatrical organizations, or the annual lists of bests in the trade papers *Variety* and *Billboard*, actors, directors, producers, and designers were not recognized by widely publicized awards.

On April 6, 1947, a ceremony at the Waldorf-Astoria Hotel was held that, in time, would become the commercial theatre's equivalent of the presentation of Hollywood's Academy Awards or Oscars. This was the first annual granting of the Antoinette Perry Memorial Awards, the Tonys, named after one of Broadway's rare women directors and producers (1888-1946). Perry had worked untiringly to help talented young players find work in the theatre; had been, as president of the National Experimental Theatre, Inc., extremely active in the search for new playwrights; and had devoted countless hours to the war effort under the auspices of the American Theatre Wing, of which she was chairman of the board and secretary. The award was created as a tribute to her selfless devotion to the theatre and was to be chosen for their own by theatre people, not the "outsiders" responsible for most other prizes. During the initial years, the concept of "bests" was replaced by one recognizing important contributions. On occasion, this allowed for several people to share in a specific category or for one individual to receive an award for several contributions. To downplay the competitive aspect of the award, no public mention of the nominees was made until 1956, and the deliberations of the award-granting committee were kept secret.

The award categories were designed to remain flexible, and have undergone various alterations. Most are listed in appendix 3. There also were "special awards" (quickly abandoned) given to a theatre treasurer, a famous pair of first-nighters, a prolific backer, a theatre editor, a scenic technician, and a restaurateur. At first, articles like money clips and compacts were given as awards, but in 1950 the Tony medallion was designed.

Although the Tonys were not specifically created as a spur to box-office bonanzas, and the effect of the Tonys on ticket sales was not yet discernible, Broadway needed any such shot in the arm it could get. Shows that ran for months, even those that far surpassed the one-hundred-performance mark that formerly designated a hit, frequently failed to pay off or even to break even. *Allegro*, for example, played to near capacity in a large theatre for ten months but paid back less than two-thirds of its $250,000 investment. Because it took so long to recoup, careful investors were more leery of putting their money into musicals than straight plays. A good example of a straight play hit that paid off quickly is *A Streetcar Named Desire*. This one-set show cost about $85,000, recouped its "nut" in thirteen weeks, and earned a 225 percent profit during its first year. Considerably more money was to come in when a second company took the play on the road. At the same time, those musicals, like *Oklahoma!* and *Kiss Me, Kate*, that enjoyed long and profitable runs usually earned their investors considerable fortunes, making the risk of Broadway investment increasingly fascinating, for all its obvious pitfalls. *Kiss Me, Kate* had trouble finding financing, but once confirmed as a success, it earned over $10,000 a week in profits on a $150,000 investment. Records were being set by the big musical hits in their annual grosses, one example being the $2,635,000 grossed by *South Pacific* in its first year. This could be compared with the $2,500,000 grossed by *Abie's Irish Rose* throughout its 1921-1927 run or the $4,300,000 grossed by *Tobacco Road* from 1933-1941 in what was then the second-longest run in history. Nevertheless, while these hits were raking in the profits, fabulous sums were being lost, the flops of 1948-1949 alone taking with them $4,535,000.

When the decade began, Broadway's reporters bemoaned the fact that there were only 69 new productions (including revivals) on the Great White Way during 1940-1941. The totals rose somewhat a year later, fell off a bit in 1942-1943, jumped nicely in 1943-1944 to 97, declined a tad in 1944-1945, and then dropped but remained fairly stable in the next few years, hovering between 76 and 79, before declining to 70 in 1948-1949 and to a half-century low of 57 in 1949-1950. Behind these figures were others, however, that demonstrated that the number of new American works produced was actually shrinking, and that the season totals were inflated by visiting companies, revivals, and foreign plays. The average rate of failure to success remained around three to one for the first part of the decade and came closer to four to one--or worse--during the latter part.

The hit-or-miss philosophy fed the development of the long-run phenomenon, which also was partly promoted by the decrease in the overall number of shows available. Long runs had never been as common as in the forties, as can be seen by comparing the number of forties shows with over five hundred performances (appendix 7) to the similar lists in this series's volumes covering 1920-1930 and 1930-1940. Fifty-one such shows originated in the decade (not counting *Life with Father*, which enjoyed most of its extraordinary run in the forties), compared to eighteen in the thirties and twenty-four in the twenties.

The cost of tickets was exacerbated in 1944 when the ten percent federal admission tax was doubled, and when an outburst of ticket speculation made the available tickets that much further out of reach to the general public. Probably the highest-priced ticket of the decade was the $24 charged by Billy Rose's *Seven Lively Arts* on opening night, but the average prices were much lower. Straight plays averaged $4.40, including tax, and musicals averaged out at $6.60. ("Popular-price" attractions normally ranged from $1.50 to $2.50, although there were variations at either end.) This was not much more than what it had cost to see a Broadway show toward the end of the twenties, although prices had descended considerably during the Depression. Tickets in the forties, however, were considered excessively dear, and it was feared that many prospective playgoers were being lost as a result.

Ticket speculation or "scalping" had plagued the theatre in the past and was to do so again in the forties. It often proved impossible to purchase seats for hit shows at the box office, but scalpers with access to tickets could sell them for whatever they could get. Ticket brokers could legally charge--in addition to tax--only a seventy-five-cent surcharge for orchestra seats and fifty cents for the balcony. But at one point late in the decade, well-heeled theatregoers were paying up to $125 for a pair of ducats to shows like *South Pacific* or *Kiss Me, Kate*. An investigation was launched, and it was discovered that most of the brokerages were ignoring the law, but the difficulty of getting customers to bring charges made it hard to prosecute. Also culpable but difficult to punish were the "office-in-his-hat" scalpers, who used whatever means they could, including bribery of box-office personnel, to gain access to tickets. The speculation problem had not been solved by the end of the decade. Some even wondered (and continue to do so) why, in a free-market economy, the practice of charging whatever the traffic can bear for an item in short supply but great demand should even be questioned. With such legalized, deregulated, but accounted-for trade, it was argued, the writers, performers, and producers might benefit as well as the ticket sellers.

Because of the enormous production costs, there were very few producers left--among them John Golden, Michael Todd, Vinton Freedley, and Dwight Deere Wiman--who could still handle all the financing for their own productions (even if it meant taking loans to do so). John Houseman noted in 1948 that "there may be ten producers capable of financing their own productions and less than half that number who are willing to do so."[1] It became imperative that the risk be lessened and that other means of raising money be found; the decade, as a result, saw a large-scale invasion of small investors anxious to gamble on a Broadway hit and to share whatever profits accrued. (Several producers even advertised for backers in newspaper ads.) An early example was 1941's hugely successful *Arsenic and Old Lace*, which paid handsome dividends to twenty-three investors. The old-time producer who put his money where his mouth was and became an active participant in the creative work of putting on a show now succumbed to the businessman-producer, who ignored the creative angle and concentrated on raising the funds, promoting the show, and handling all the legal problems, often without a penny of his own involved.

Instead of producing a string of shows under his own continued corporate sponsorship, the new producer treated each production as a separate business venture. In this arrangement, which still prevails, the producer controls fifty percent of the show, while the other fifty percent is divided up among the backers, or "angels" as they came to be called. (Part of the producer's share, of course, may have to be chipped away in the nitty-gritty reality of getting the show on.) Producers welcomed this new way of relieving themselves of risk (and of the excessive tax bite when they earned too much by being the sole profit-taker on a megahit). The name of the arrangement is the limited partnership, and it first became the law of Broadway in the early 1940s, following the 1939 imposition of an excess-profits tax on corporations that would have required producers and investors to divide not one hundred, but only sixty-two percent of a show's profits, the rest being paid to the government in taxes. The legitimacy of the limited partnership as a tax-saving device was recognized by a Treasury ruling of 1948 that accepted it as a partnership lacking the taxable nature of a corporation.

To interest potential investors, producers of the forties had to arrange backers' auditions, normally involving the show's creators and several specially hired performers, including a piano player (often the composer). These individuals would provide capsule versions and explanations of the shows, usually at some fancy apartment (but hired spaces were also used) where drinks and hors d'oeuvres were served. Many shows had to audition over fifty times (several shows actually reached one hundred auditions) before raising the necessary lucre. For most of the decade, only musicals went this route, but several plays were beginning to hold backers' readings by the end of the era.

A principal source of income for several years came from the Hollywood studios, ever alert for possible film properties. The studios needed strong script material to shore up revenues weakened by the loss of important film stars to the war. There was some West Coast investment in production, but in amounts far less significant than those paid for movie rights. Playwrights and producers could walk away with a healthy chunk of cash, even if the work was never made into a movie. *Harvey* earned the top prize of the decade with the sale of its rights for $750,000. At one point in mid-decade, Hollywood dumped $9 million into the Broadway arena over a three-year period, but by the late forties, when Hollywood was forced by declining revenues to retrench financially, these sums dwindled markedly. In 1948-1949, for example, Hollywood bought the rights to only two plays, for which it paid a mere $90,000.

Another vital source of income for Broadway that shriveled during the decade was the road. In the past, a hit show could practically be guaranteed to continue hitting the jackpot as it toured the hinterlands, either with its original cast or with well-known replacements. There had been a boom for road shows in 1941, but gas shortages and travel restrictions proved devastating in 1942 and

1943. As the forties progressed the touring option became increasingly less available to all but the most highly publicized musicals and a handful of the most popular stars. Even the Theatre Guild, with its established base of 200,000 subscribers in thirty cities, began to suffer serious problems in sending out its yearly series of plays. By the end of the decade, the Guild was forced to make up the gaps in its touring season with already-proven successes presented by other managements rather than with works of its own devising. The expenses of touring, combined with a decreasing number of available theatres and a populace that had gradually lost the theatregoing habit because of the ever-increasing dearth of touring attractions, meant that except for rare instances, the road was dead. Only stars such as Tallulah Bankhead, the Lunts, Helen Hayes, Katharine Cornell, or Maurice Evans had the power to lure spectators out of their homes to see a straight play. At the decade's close, the word on many lips was subsidization, some form of government support that would make it feasible to provide first-class theatre outside of New York City, even if no profit was being made. The enormous rise of college and university theatricals was one form of such subsidization, but these productions, even with talented students, were only rarely of professional stature. However, the seeds were planted in the forties at a handful of places for what would arise in the fifties as the resident or regional theatre movement; in time this movement would develop into the nation's number one play-producing generator, while New York increasingly would become the show window for work first created elsewhere.

Those who found Broadway too rich for their blood did have a major new attraction to keep them home nights. It was in 1948 that the electronic marvel of television--its development suspended because of World War II--began to invade American homes in awesome numbers. That year saw seven hundred thousand sets in use. A year later there were two million sets, and two years after that there were fifteen million. Television would also provide some respite from the unemployment lines for many who would have preferred to be earning their living on Broadway. Television's impact was predominantly on the movie business and on radio programming. Jack Gaver wrote in 1949 that the theatre world did not think TV a menace because there was no replacement for the experience of a live theatre event:

> Broadway anticipates that television will have no great effect on it and may even prove a friend. The feeling is that mechanical entertainment already has done about all of the harm it can to "live" entertainment. Broadway producers and actors have been among the first in the television field, and the best of television's dramatic material has come out of Broadway hits. The argument is that once the novelty and convenience have worn off . . . , people will realize that, after all, they are merely looking at pictures. . . . If they want to see actors in the flesh, they will still have to patronize theatres.[2]

BROADWAY'S INSTITUTIONAL THEATRES

Not all of Broadway's producers were individuals or groups of individuals billed by their personal names in programs and on posters. As before, several important organizations attempted to provide quality theatre that combined commercial attractiveness with artistic excellence. The two best established, as previously mentioned, were the Theatre Guild and the Playwrights' Producing Company. In addition, the decade saw brief but significant contributions from the American Repertory Theatre and Theatre Incorporated.

Producer Cheryl Crawford and actress-directors Margaret Webster and Eva Le Gallienne were the brains and talent behind the American Repertory Theatre (ART), which premiered in Princeton, New Jersey, in September 1946, opened in New York two months later, and closed in June 1947 with heavy losses. The ART sought to provide a high-quality repertory program for

Broadway, but soon learned that repertory on a major scale is an impossibility without sizable subsidies. Even the $350,000 subscription base with which it began proved insufficient for its needs.

The ART leaders would have liked to create a three-city plan, each city with its own company. The productions would be rotated with those of the other cities, thereby providing a wide variety of plays for each. They hoped at first to avoid New York entirely, but lack of support forced them to change their minds, and they settled into the 1,100-seat International Theatre on out-of-the-way Columbus Circle.

From the start they ran into innumerable obstacles, financial and artistic. The unions were of little help, refusing to make the crucial concessions required by repertory. For example, since the ART's most elaborate production had a large number of stagehands, their union demanded that the same number be retained even for the company's smallest shows, which had only minimal technical demands. Another major hurdle was finding enough good actors willing to play at reduced salaries for the joy of doing the great plays. An all-American company was sought, irrespective of the general lack of classical training then prevailing in the United States. Among the best-known players were Walter Hampden, Philip Bourneuf, June Duprez, Ernest Truex, Richard Waring, and Victor Jory. Newcomers included Eli Wallach, Anne Jackson, Julie Harris, Efrem Zimbalist, Jr., and William Windom.

The productions were Shakespeare's rarely done *Henry VIII*, Barrie's *What Every Woman Knows*, Shaw's *Androcles and the Lion* (with O'Casey's "Pound on Demand"), Ibsen's *Ghosts*, *Hedda Gabler*, and *John Gabriel Borkman*, Kingsley's *Yellow Jack*, and, the only commercial success, *Alice in Wonderland*, in Le Gallienne's familiar adaptation. The choices were not widely approved. A solid but not exceptional company, expensive tickets, and negative reviews--both for the repertory concept and for the individual shows--seriously undermined the company and forced it out of business before it had time to learn from its various setbacks.[3]

The ART was designed as a profit-making enterprise, but Theatre Incorporated was not. It had begun in 1945 as an effort to create a "people's theatre" on Broadway, with the aim of doing a repertory of new plays, experimental productions, and classical revivals. The inspiration came from Beatrice Straight, Penelope Sack, and Robert Woods, who took over the nonprofit, tax-exempt charter previously granted to a group called the Michael Chekhov Studio and used it to found their idealistic new organization. Norris Houghton joined the board of directors, and Richard Aldrich agreed to become managing director. Because Aldrich also happened to be wed to star Gertrude Lawrence, that charismatic actress convinced Theatre Incorporated to start its project by reviving Shaw's *Pygmalion*, with herself as Liza Doolittle. *Pygmalion* was an immediate hit and the star earned a windfall but the play's long run killed the repertory theatre idea. Theatre Incorporated proceeded to capture another brass ring by importing Britain's Old Vic (discussed later), which illuminated Broadway with a series of remarkable classical revivals. Several millionaires guaranteed the company against losses, but the Old Vic was a complete sellout and not a cent was lost. Theatre Incorporated next provided a flat revival of *The Playboy of the Western World*, starring Burgess Meredith. In 1947 the organization helped produce a brief run of *The Wanhope Building* for the Experimental Theatre (discussed later) and vanished from sight after its importation in 1948 of Houghton's British production of *Macbeth*, starring Michael Redgrave, a hit in London and a flop over here. The company's main acting find, discovered during open auditions it held for eight hundred actors, was Julie Harris, then without professional experience. To season her, she was given small roles with the Old Vic and in *Playboy*, which included another newcomer, Maureen Stapleton, discovered by director Guthrie McClintic.

There was definitely a zeitgeist at the time about somehow establishing a nonprofit, art-oriented theatre on Broadway. Another example was the City Center of Music and Drama, a name given to the former Mecca Temple on West

Fifty-fifth Street after the city took it over in 1943 for nonpayment of taxes. This was a huge, 2,800-seat auditorium that Mayor La Guardia thought would make a perfect people's theatre and would thus serve the city better than if it was auctioned off. The sum of seventy-five thousand dollars was raised from interested citizens to make the playhouse presentable. The City Council agreed to let it be leased for a token fee to a private group for operation as a popular-priced institution offering the best in theatre, dance, opera, and concert music. The first play produced was a revival of Rachel Crothers's *Susan and God* with its original star, Gertrude Lawrence. It was followed by a return engagement of *The Patriots*, recently seen on Broadway. The unions agreed to allow concessions in order for the cost of tickets to be held down (three dollars was the top price reached during the decade), and all productions were given limited runs, usually lasting two, but sometimes three, weeks. Most of City Center's theatrical offerings, however, were return engagements of Broadway hits (including *Porgy and Bess*, *Harriet*, *Othello*, *The Cherry Orchard*, *Medea*, and *A Streetcar Named Desire*), a number of them playing there after completing a tour or before going out on one. The place suffered from serious acoustical problems, and plays that required low-keyed acting were often destroyed, either because the actors shouted or because they could not be heard. Thus musical entertainments--especially opera and ballet--fared better than drama.

The most important contributions made by the City Center to the art of theatre came, first, when José Ferrer and Richard Whorf organized a stock company there--the New York City Theatre Company (sometimes known as the New York City Center Theatre Company)--in 1948, and second, when Maurice Evans ran a similarly titled company there in 1949. The companies were allowed only two weeks for rehearsal, and the players were given minimal salaries (fifty dollars a week), regardless of their reputations. Among those in the first group were John Carradine, Fred Stewart, Phyllis Hill, Lou Gilbert, Robert Earl Jones, Uta Hagen, and Paula Laurence. The offerings included *Volpone*, *Angel Street*, an evening of Chekhov one-acters, *The Alchemist*, and *S.S. Glencairn*. Under Evans's management, the Center produced *She Stoops to Conquer*, *The Corn Is Green*, *The Devil's Disciple*, and *The Heiress*. *The Devil's Disciple* was so popular (aside from Evans's delivery of the prologue in the first play, it was the only piece in which he himself had a role) that it moved to Broadway. However, the unions would not allow a simple, inexpensive move and required that it be recreated from scratch, which cost its commercial management forty thousand dollars. Evans's company was not a stock company, and, although some actors appeared in more than one production, most casts were chosen especially for each work.

The Theatre Guild and the Playwrights' Producing Company, while committed to quality theatre, were economically less altruistic. The Guild's golden decades were the twenties and thirties; by the forties, the kinds of challenging plays on which it once had taken risks were being produced more and more by the independent managements. During the early forties, its wavering strength placed it on a precipice when it had only $30,000 left in its treasury. Had its next show failed, it would have been bankrupt. However, that next show turned out be 1943's blockbuster musical, *Oklahoma!*, which allowed the Guild to make an astonishing comeback. Many people had refused to invest in the $80,000 show; a $10,000 investment would have returned $250,000 within half a decade.

The Guild proceeded to offer a series of fine (and not-so-fine) works throughout the period. It continued to provide a seasonal subscription series to cities around the country, expanding its subscriber base to the West Coast, although, as mentioned earlier, an increasing number of plays it sent out had first proved their saleability in productions originated by others. In New York its subscription audience remained around 19,000, because a larger number could not comfortably have been accommodated. The Guild also began to produce radio dramas, in 1945, with a weekly series of hour-long broadcasts. In 1947 television began to see Theatre Guild presentations.

By 1939 the organization had outgrown the 984-seat Guild Theatre, whose capacity did not allow the income necessary to pay stars the kinds of salaries they were coming to demand. The company eventually sold the theatre and produced its plays in whatever playhouses were available. Throughout the period, the Guild's artistic policies were in the hands of only two managers, Lawrence Langner and Theresa Helburn, the old six-member board having been dismantled in 1939.

From 1940 to 1950, there were forty works produced on Broadway under Guild auspices (sometimes "by arrangement with" or "in association with" independent producers), an average of four a year (a dropoff from the earlier average of six a year). When the Guild had no production of its own for local subscribers, it would offer one produced by someone else, such as when the Shubert-sponsored *My Romance* was put on the season's list for 1948-1949. Only four plays produced under Guild auspices closed on the road before making it to New York. Gaver reported in 1949 that the company's record since *Oklahoma* had been "one success out of every two and a half productions, an enviable mark."[4] One way the Guild learned to cut costs was to try out some of the productions at the Westport Country Playhouse, owned by Langner and his wife, Armina Marshall.

Its productions included noteworthy revivals such as *Ah, Wilderness!*, *As You Like It* (with Katharine Hepburn), *He Who Gets Slapped*, *Twelfth Night* (with Helen Hayes and Maurice Evans), *The Rivals* (with Bobby Clark), *Othello* (with Paul Robeson), and two imports starring John Gielgud, *Love for Love* and *The Importance of Being Earnest*. Several of these turned out to be commercial successes. While many of the new plays were disposable, some were hits and others proved of critical value: The most distinguished new plays included *Come Back, Little Sheba*, *The Iceman Cometh*, *Jacobowsky and the Colonel*, and *The Winslow Boy*. Popular, if not critical, acclaim, was granted to new works such as *The Silver Whistle*, *The Pirate*, and *O Mistress Mine*. Guild-sponsored musicals, in addition to *Oklahoma!*, included *Allegro* and *Carousel*. So, despite various economic factors being responsible for the Guild's gradual slippage during the decade, it contributed some of the finest theatre then available and added considerable distinction to its reputation.

The Playwrights' Producing Company, founded in 1937 (its first production was in 1938) by top playwrights Robert E. Sherwood, S. N. Behrman, Elmer Rice, Maxwell Anderson, and Sidney Howard (who died soon afterwards) to produce their own work, faltered in the forties. It suffered from internal problems (Behrman resigned, shifting his allegiance to the Theatre Guild in 1946, and was replaced soon after by Kurt Weill) and a lack of sufficiently successful works generated by its membership. The glue that held the company together was its sole nondramatist member, attorney John Wharton, who eventually wrote a book about it (*Life among the Playwrights*).

During the decade, the company presented its Sidney Howard Award ($1,500) as a memorial to the playwright. Some years saw no prize given. Among those honored were Tennessee Williams for *The Glass Menagerie*, Garson Kanin for *Born Yesterday*, and Arthur Laurents for *Home of the Brave* (Kanin and Laurents divided the award). At other times, worthy groups, such as the Authors' League Fund, the Experimental Theatre, or the New School for Social Research, were the beneficiaries. Sixteen plays were offered in the forties under the company's leadership, several with the cooperation of the Theatre Guild or independent managers. During two seasons, 1944-1945 and 1947-1948, there were no productions. Anderson was the most consistent contributor, with eight plays, including the successful *Anne of the Thousand Days* and *Lost in the Stars*. One of his plays, the unsuccessful *Truckline Café*, was coproduced with Harold Clurman and Elia Kazan, an arrangement that caused very bad feelings within the company. Rice provided four works, including *Dream Girl*, *Flight to the West*, and the musical version of his *Street Scene* (with Weill). Behrman wrote two plays for the company, the unsuccessful *The Talley Method* and *The Pirate*, the latter's popularity being mainly attributable to its stars, the Lunts. Sherwood, busy writing political speeches, film scripts, and a major political biography, provided only the flop, *The Rugged Path*, notable for bringing Spencer Tracy back to Broadway (he never returned). The remaining entries were the products of outsiders, Garson Kanin and Sidney Kingsley, the latter offering the distinguished historical drama *The Patriots*. Although there were some fine plays produced under the Playwrights' aegis, not enough were commercially successful. The lack of confidence in the company shown by playwrights who now and then sought outside sponsorship also was a serious blow to morale. Following Weill's death in 1950, the company's standing began to slip seriously. Nevertheless, it remained active until 1960.

The Playwrights' Producing Company was at the heart of one of the bitterest controversies of the decade concerning the critical establishment. It developed following the devastating pans rained down on Anderson's 1946 turkey, *Truckline Café*. The morning following the appearance of the reviews, the newspapers carried a wordy advertisement signed by coproducers Kazan and Clurman. The ad noted the decision to close the play in a week because of the pans. The authors went on to attack the critical establishment as being largely unfit for their jobs and for ruining the commercial theatre by their opinions. They defended their decision to do Anderson's drama, noted its best features, and concluded by lamenting the fact that the critics were driving the best writers from the stage by their failure to recognize thoughtful dramaturgy. This was followed by an advertisement from Anderson, and then, a few days later, one from the company itself in support of its writer. It castigated the critics for their vituperativeness while praising Anderson for the power and quality of his plays. Anderson's ad is probably the best remembered because in it he wrote:

> The public is far better qualified to judge plays than the men who write reviews. . . . It is an insult to our threatre [*sic*] that there should be so many incompetents and irresponsibles among them. There are still a few critics who know their job and respect it, but of late years all plays are passed on largely by a sort of Jukes family of journalism, who bring to the theatre nothing but their own hopelessness, recklessness and despair.[5]

Soon the letters to the editor columns were filled with debaters on one side or the other. For all the publicity generated, the audiences stayed home and the play closed after thirteen performances. (Anderson never gave up in his distaste for the critics and published other blasts against them in the future.)

Actually, the critics were at the center of controversy on a number of occasions. Playwrights other than Anderson occasionally took up the cudgels, as did Ben Hecht when *Lily of the Valley* was speared; both Hecht and Charles MacArthur, following the death of *Swan Song*; Irwin Shaw, after *The Assassin* was assassinated; and Joseph Hayes, following the debacle of his *Leaf and Bough*. Producer Herman Shumlin stepped into the ring to debate the response to *Jeb*. And actor-director-librettist Orson Welles not only attacked the press on his weekly radio programs for savaging his *Around the World in Eighty Days*, but threatened them with voodoo. Sometimes controversy stemmed from attempts to bar from theatres critics who were considered especially negative. No critic may actually be prevented from reviewing a play, as a state law passed in 1941 specifically forbids such exclusion, so the best a producer could do was to cut the critic's name off the free list, forcing him (or his employer) to pay for tickets. The Shuberts were especially inclined to these practices, and, at various times, did what they could to prevent Louis Kronenberger of *PM* and Robert Garland of the *New York Journal-American* from their theatres. The Shuberts even sought to sue *Variety* for its pan of *The Student Prince*.

The chief daily critics of the forties were Brooks Atkinson (spelled during the war by Lewis Nichols) of the *New York Times*; John Mason Brown (succeeded by Burton Rascoe, then William Hawkins) of the *New York World-Telegram*; Howard Barnes of the *New York Herald-Tribune*; Louis Kronenberger of *PM*; Wilella Waldorf (succeeded by Richard Watts, Jr.) of the *New York Post*; Richard Lockridge (succeeded by Ward Morehouse) of the *New York Sun*; John Anderson (succeeded by Robert Garland) of the *New York Journal-American*; Arthur Pollock (succeeded by Louis Sheaffer) of the *Brooklyn Daily Eagle*; Burns Mantle (succeeded by John Chapman) of the *New York Daily News*; Robert Coleman of the *New York Daily Mirror*; and George Freedley of the *New York Morning Telegraph*. Each of these was backed by one or more second-stringers. Reviewers for other newspapers, such as the *Brooklyn Citizen* (Edgar Price), *Women's Wear Daily* (Kelcey Allen, succeeded by Thomas R. Dash), the *Christian Science Monitor* (John Beaufort), the *Daily Worker* (Ralph Warner), the *New York Star* (John Lardner), and the *Newark Evening News* (Rowland Fields), also covered the theatre regularly. *Variety* and *Billboard*, the weekly trade papers, provided wide coverage, employing a staff of reviewers; their weekly box score of critical reactions disturbed the New York Drama Critics Circle, which sought to end the practice. There were also the weekly and monthly reviewers: a partial list would include John Mason Brown of the *Saturday Review*; Euphemia Van Rensselaer Wyatt of *Catholic World*; Rosamond Gilder of *Theatre Arts*; Joseph T. Shipley of the *New Leader*; Wolcott Gibbs of the *New Yorker*; Joseph Wood Krutch of the *Nation*; Stark Young (succeeded by Irwin Shaw, then Harold Clurman) of the *New Republic*, Louis Kronenberger of *Time*, Thomas F. Wenning of *Newsweek*, and so on. One of the most famous critics was George Jean Nathan, who published a weekly notice in the *New York Journal-American* and a monthly one in the *American Mercury*, and collected his reviews annually from 1942-1943 in a series of fascinating volumes, where he expanded on his original comments. (Many, but not all, of these critics are represented in this book's entries.)

OFF BROADWAY

Those wishing to produce theatre in New York free from Broadway's economic hassles had the option of putting on their shows in venues off the beaten track. What in the early thirties came to be called Off Broadway had a distinct history dating back to 1915, when the Provincetown Players, the Washington Square Players, and the Neighborhood Playhouse gained the public's interest. Off Broadway remained an active alternative to the commercial theatre in the twenties and thirties, although the vast majority of the work produced in its unconventional locales, few of which were originally designed as theatres, was amateur or semiprofessional. Except in special circumstances, Equity actors were not permitted to act in such productions, although some probably did so under assumed names. Occasionally, one comes across a name in an obscure production of the twenties or thirties that later became well known.

During those decades, a few works were deemed interesting enough to be transferred to a commercial staging on Broadway. For the most part, however, Off Broadway by the early forties had become a barely noticeable distraction from Broadway's professionalism. Off-Broadway playhouses were scattered around the city, both uptown and down; the list of theatres in appendix 10 demonstrates the great number of venues employed (most for only one or two productions). Reviewers visited these places only sporadically, and their responses generally ranged from patronizing to acrimonious. While Off Broadway remained consistently available to hopeful new groups, it was hardly ever used by independent producers seeking a cheap launching pad for what might attract the big-time interests. Independent productions were more likely than not to be vanity productions. Off-Broadway works that made it to Broadway invariably were the products of established groups. For most of the period, the theatre's unions kept a wary eye on Off-Broadway productions that employed union members (usually in a blend with nonunionists), but interfered whenever they suspected exploitation. This meant that, some exceptions apart, Off Broadway remained mired in mediocrity.

The actual meaning of Off Broadway at the time is open to discussion. Technically speaking, most Yiddish theatre of the period should be considered Off Broadway, although several Yiddish works were done on Broadway itself. A few small theatres that once were part of the Broadway scene, such as the Princess, the President, and the Roof Theatre of the New Amsterdam Theatre, were actually deemed by critics of the period as Off Broadway, and will be so considered here. In other instances as well, fuzziness prevails when separating Off Broadway from Broadway. Certain productions at the City Center were not counted in the annual statistics compiled by some sources for Broadway because such statistics only included commercially produced works. Thus, in one sense, they were Off Broadway, even though they used professional actors and stagehands (under reduced wages through special union dispensations). A similar lack of clarity surrounds the example of the Experimental Theatre, described later. While it was nonprofit in structure, and its productions were usually seen on an Off-Broadway stage, some of its productions employed Broadway theatres. Its philosophy, however, was definitely more Off Broadway than on.

The most important Off-Broadway activity of the war years stemmed from two groups, one more amateur than professional, the other more professional than amateur. The former was the Dramatic Workshop, a program founded in 1940 by Erwin Piscator at the New School for Social Research on West Twelfth Street in Greenwich Village. This émigré director had been one of the most outstanding figures in the German theatre of the 1920s and was the creator of the epic theatre concept that influenced Bertolt Brecht, who developed his own unique vision of the style. Piscator, who spoke of "theatre as a tribunal," had a leftist-slanted, political approach to the art. The plays he produced at the Dramatic Workshop, however, while always of a boldly liberal temperament, were rarely polemical.

Casts at first were made up of students in his school's program (many, like Marlon Brando, Elaine Stritch, Gene Saks, Rod Steiger, and Tony Curtis, became famous) mingled with professionals (including such talents as Sam Jaffe and Dolly Haas). Piscator's productions--which he either directed or produced--frequently included such mechanical devices as a revolving stage, minimal furnishings, unusual lighting effects, actors entering and exiting through the aisles, and so forth, but his workshop theatre was tiny, which made his accomplishments that much more remarkable. In 1942 the Workshop produced Dan James's *Winter Soldiers* (which Burns Mantle selected as one of the season's ten best plays) and ran into union difficulties. Piscator was required to pay the actors Equity rates, but pressures from Equity and the other unions necessitated a shift to all-student companies. Budgetary motives forced the company to leave the New School auditorium in 1945 and move into the 299-seat President Theatre on West Forty-eighth Street. Because it was an amateur operation, only selected dramas were covered by the reviewers. Piscator's principal work during the decade included *King Lear* (with Sam Jaffe), his adaptation of *War and Peace*, Jean-Paul Sartre's *The Flies*, Armand Salacrou's *Nights of Wrath*, Robert Penn Warren's *All the King's Men*, Wolfgang Borchert's *Outside the Door*, and a version of Franz Kafka's *The Trial* called *The Scapegoat*.

The other important Off-Broadway venture originating during World War II was the Equity Library Theatre (ELT). This concept, which began as the Library Theatre Project in the 1943-1944 season, was largely subsidized by producer John Golden. For several years, it was run under the cochairmanship (for the New York Public Library) of George Freedley, critic for the *New York Morning Telegraph* and curator of the library's theatre collection, and (for Equity) actor Sam Jaffe. (Freedley resigned after the 1946-1947 season.) Most productions were offered in small auditoriums of Manhattan libraries, with Golden providing a starting base of $1,000, to which he subsequently contributed additional funds. Other persons and institutions also donated money. Frequently used libraries were the Hudson Park branch, the Fort Washington branch, the George Bruce branch, the Hamilton Grange branch, the 115th Street branch, and the Muhlenberg branch. Admission was free, there were only a handful of performances, and the actors--at least eighty percent of whom had to be Equity members--were not paid.

The productions, which were predominantly revivals ranging from the classics to Broadway hits, allowed actors and directors a showcase for their talents. A number of productions were staged by famous actors, among them Mady Christians and José Ferrer. Established directors such as John O'-Shaughnessy also got involved. On occasion, well-known actors, such as Herbert Berghof, Gene Barry, and Kurt Kasznar, were cast in challenging roles. Outstanding young talent was given excellent opportunities, as when the still-unknown Kim Stanley played the lead in *St. Joan* in the 1949-1950 season. Occasionally, a classic never seen before in New York, like *Mandragola* or *The White Devil*, was given a production. Some presentations consisted of scenes from several plays. Reviewers were actually discouraged from attending, but a number of productions were covered by Freedley himself, and his sometimes sketchy notices are often the only record of what transpired.

The annual number of productions generally ranged from twenty to forty or so, and the 1946-1947 season saw a decade-high total of fifty-six. In 1947 the name Equity Library Theatre became a misnomer when it was discovered that the public libraries had no legal authority to allow their premises to be used for a union's activities, and the actors had to find other venues. Those used at first included the Greenwich Mews Playhouse, the Lenox Hill Playhouse, several high school auditoriums (which brought the productions to student audiences), the Society of Illustrators, and the Guild for the Jewish Blind. A new offshoot of ELT arose in 1949-1950; called Equity Community Theatre, and situated at a Bronx community center, it offered four performances each of four shows for an admission charge of fifty cents, with actors, directors, and technicians paid at a per performance union rate. The same season saw the intimate Lenox Hill Playhouse (331 East Seventieth Street) become, for the time being, the regular home of ELT. By the decade's close, ELT had been incorporated as a nonprofit organization, and a drive to raise $25,000 for it was begun.

One of the inspirations leading to the ELT was created, largely under the influence of director Margaret Webster, in 1940. It was called the Experimental Theatre, Inc., and was an earlier version of the showcase idea for actors in need of opportunities, as well as for unusual but uncommercial new plays (although the premiere production was a revival). The Experimental Theatre had to overcome resistance from the unions, especially Equity and the Dramatists Guild, who looked askance at their members working for nothing, although the public was intrigued by the project. But the unions finally accepted the notion, and the first season, which saw three productions, opened in the spring of 1941 with Webster's production of Euripides' *The Trojan Women*; it contained a new prologue by Robert Turney that emphasized the play's topicality and satisfied the Dramatists Guild regarding the involvement of one of its members. These productions were offered for a single matinee on the stages of Broadway theatres currently being used for other productions.

The war put a temporary end to the Experimental Theatre after its first season. Most sources declare that it returned after the war, but there were actually two productions given under its aegis during the war, both of them about Abraham Lincoln and both given at matinees on the Shubert Theatre stage. The first, in 1942, was *Yours, A. Lincoln*, with Vincent Price (then starring in *Angel Street*); the second was *The War President*, in 1944. In 1947, the Experimental Theatre returned on a more stable basis, under the sponsorship of the nonprofit service organization called the American National Theatre and Academy (ANTA). ANTA was founded in 1935 under a national charter granted by Congress, but had no money to carry out its grandiose schemes of developing a national theatre. It eventually became an advisory, information-gathering and -propagating organization for theatre people nationwide and also expanded its interests to encompass international theatre concerns through becoming the American representative of the International Theatre Institute

(ITI).

Under the banner of ANTA (using money from a national fund-raising drive), and with the cooperation of the Theatre Guild, the American Repertory Theatre, Theatre Incorporated, and the Playwrights' Producing Company, the Experimental Theatre offered a subscription season of five new works for five showings apiece at the intimate Princess Theatre. The Princess proving too small for the burgeoning subscription audience (who paid fifteen dollars for the entire series), the disused, 900-seat Maxine Elliott's Theatre was leased for the six-play 1947-1948 season. Each work now had six showings. The increased seating allowed for a leap from 1,500 subscribers to 5,400 (the group fell only 200 short of this goal), each subscription costing from seven to eighteen dollars. By the time the project ended in 1950 (with a fifty thousand dollar deficit), several of the Experimental Theatre's twenty-two productions (not counting those of 1941-1944) had proved intriguing enough to be moved to commercial auspices on Broadway, although none succeeded there. Among them were Brecht's *Galileo*, in a now-famous, six-performance production starring Charles Laughton, and John Garfield in Jan de Hartog's *Skipper Next to God*. These stars (whose presence was resented by some as a commercial ploy that took jobs away from needier actors) accepted salaries, respectively, of eight and ten dollars a performance. A controversy erupted because the company had rejected Barrie Stavis's *Lamp at Midnight* about Galileo (picked up by Off Broadway's New Stages group) in favor of Brecht's play in order to benefit from Laughton's fame. There was also anger over the Experimental Theatre's choice of several foreign plays over native ones. Other Broadway-bound works of interest were *Ballet Ballads*, which combined ballet and drama in three short pieces, and a one-act by Richard Harrity, "Hope Is the Thing with Feathers," seen on a three-play program called *Six O'Clock Theatre*. When produced on Broadway, the other plays were replaced by different ones. Union regulations required that when the shows moved to Broadway, their original sets or a duplicate be destroyed, so long as a new one was built at union costs.

Late in the 1947-1948 season, the company's activities were revised to allow only what were called invitational performances. First offered at the Lenox Hill Playhouse (occasionally referred to as the Lenox Hill Settlement House), these began with a series of plays given minimal stagings in a special series of four performances each for invited audiences only. Because financial problems stemming from poor management and overly elaborate sets had come to plague the project, these invitational showings were limited to $150 budgets; the results were often surprisingly imaginative. Under the terms of a special contract, the actors (all Experimental Theatre actors belonged to Equity) received five dollars a performance. The following season, the invitational plays given were granted a $500 budget but only allowed two showings each. Several other Off-Broadway locales were now being used, including Brander Matthews Hall at Columbia University, the New Stages theatre on Bleecker Street, the Master Institute on Riverside Drive, and the Educational Alliance on East Broadway. Two invitational plays--both commercial failures--made it to Broadway, *Seeds in the Wind* and *Uniform of Flesh* (its title changed to *Billy Budd* in its 1951 commercial staging).

As pointed out, the Experimental Theatre was theoretically an Off-Broadway concept, even though six of its productions were staged in a full-scale Broadway theatre. More consistently Off Broadway was the Blackfriars' Guild, a Catholic organization that came to public attention in 1942, most of its works directed by former Broadway actor Dennis Gurney, and all of them offered at the intimate Blackfriars' Theatre one flight up at 320 West Fifty-seventh Street. This group began by mingling professionals and amateurs but eventually had to succumb to union demands and eliminate the professional component. A few later-important players, such as Eileen Heckart, had their early New York stage experiences here. The Blackfriars provided a steady diet of plays, many of them with a Catholic religious orientation (plays about miracles or saints, for example), or with a socially conscious theme (*Caukey* was about a black-dominated society in which the white people were oppressed), but a good portion of their plays were regular comedies and dramas, albeit with morally unobjectionable subjects and treatments. One of their works, *Career Angel*, was moved to Broadway, but it failed. Several representative Blackfriars' offerings were by priests, most notably Father Urban Nagle (*Savonarola*, *Lady of Fatima*, *City of Kings*, and *Armor of Light*).

Between 1941 and 1943, a group of actors called the American Actors Company (or Theatre) was active at the Provincetown Playhouse and the Charles Weidman Studio (also known as the Humphrey-Weidman Studio), a dance studio at 108 West Sixteenth Street sometimes used for Off-Broadway plays. Steeply banked bleachers faced the studio floor, which had no proscenium or curtain; staging plays in such an environment was decidedly experimental at the time. Only five of the company's plays were reviewed, but three of them were by Horton Foote, who would become a respected writer. Foote contributed *Only the Heart*, *Texas Town*, and *Out of My House*, all of them concerned with small-town life in Texas. *Only the Heart* was revived at Broadway's small Bijou Theatre in 1944. The troupe was also responsible for giving regular work to Mary Hunter, one of the few women directors active during the decade. Will Hare was one of the company's most successful acting products.

A much more vital Off-Broadway organization active during the war must be mentioned. This is the American Negro Theatre (ANT), founded in 1940 by playwright Abram Hill, Frederick O'Neal (who was later elected president of Equity), Austin Briggs-Hall, Hattie King-Reeves, and others, many of them formerly active in Harlem's Rose McClendon Players. From their ranks would one day spring into the mainstream such outstanding actors as Sidney Poitier, Earle Hyman, Ruby Dee, Hilda Simms, Alvin Childress, and Harry Belafonte. When the group began, it was so poor that the only free space it had available for rehearsing was a local funeral parlor. A cooperative arrangement allowed all expenses and profits to be shared. ANT members worked without salary, except for part-time salaries to three company officers during a three-year period when a grant was received. Fifteen new scripts were fully produced during the troupe's less-than-a-decade existence, and a smaller number of works were given studio presentations. Production costs for the tiny theatre ranged from $750 to $1,500. Audience members paid three dollars annually for a three-play subscription. A training program was developed as well, and over two hundred students received a solid basis in all aspects of theatre technique. The ANT sought to provide a home for plays that would enhance the image of black people as individualistic, three-dimensional human beings, and negate the usual demeaning stereotypes.

After being situated for several years in the tiny basement auditorium of the 135th Street Library in Harlem, the company was dispossessed. It moved to larger quarters in the Elks Building at 15 West 126th Street, where, unlike at the library, it had to pay rent and electric bills, which began to put a serious dent in its finances. Its biggest success had been its production of white author Philip Yordan's play, *Anna Lucasta*, originally written about a Polish family, but transformed into a black drama that became so popular it moved to Broadway (with several cast changes) for almost a thousand performances and was played on the road for years. Because of legal maneuverings, the ANT received a pittance of only one and a quarter percent of the royalties, but this was enough to provide it with $20,000 that kept it afloat until it was forced to leave the library. However, the commercial success of *Anna Lucasta* proved destructive to the ANT, as actors began to view it as a springboard for their own Broadway careers, which deprived it of its character as a community-oriented experimental company.

The ANT produced plays by blacks as well as whites, the former group comprising such works as Hill's own *Walk Hard* and *On Strivers Row*, Theodore Browne's *Natural Man*, and Owen Dodson's *Garden of Time*. White-authored dramas included Curtis Cooksey's *Starlight* and Phoebe and Henry Ephron's *Three's a Family*, produced under special arrangement at the same time as this play was being given with a white cast on Broadway. Eventually, the inability to find enough worthwhile, profitable scripts led to the company's demise in 1948. There were other black groups active in the forties, including the short-lived Negro Playwrights Company and the Harlem Showcase, but the only one to gain attention outside of the black community was the ANT.

The real outburst of Off-Broadway activity occurred following the war, when the Broadway theatre began to shrink and to offer less and less opportunity for serious new plays. Many young people, fresh out of college or the military, flocked to the city in search of artistic careers, and discovered that they had to invent the opportunities for such careers themselves. The heart of much of their activity was located in that hitherto congenial home of the avant-garde, Greenwich Village. There, two tiny old theatres, the Provincetown Playhouse and the Cherry Lane Theatre, had remained hospitable to aspiring thespians and would continue to do so for decades to come. More and more Off-Broadway groups began to crop up in the Village and around the city, although the general public came to know of only a handful. Much of their activity took place during the summertime (generally between June and October) because of lower rents. Plays were done in cellars, churches, halls, garages, brownstone living rooms, studios, and so on. The troupes were mostly non-Equity; the union pretended that it did not know that some Equity actors were involved with them. A new twist in actors' program bios was offered when many of these fledgling thespians proudly mentioned the teachers with whom they were studying. Most teachers were Stanislavskyites of one stripe or another.

While, on the surface, the theatre seemed dead, these actors and their multifarious activities gave proof that the art was actually on the verge of a resurgence. Arthur Pollock noted in June 1950, for example, that

> More and more groups . . . are springing up. The city was alive with them last summer. And you may be sure that when the Broadway theater slows down in the coming spring more of them will appear all over town. The professional actors will scatter into the summer theaters, but here in New York there will be a vigorous summer season. . . . This is annoying for those who have to cover their doings, but they can not be ignored. They matter very much.[6]

The new wind blowing toward the increased professionalism of Off Broadway arose in late 1947 when a group calling itself New Stages, founded by David Heilweil and Norman Rose, began operations. Made up mostly of radio actors seeking to expand their horizons so that they could move into television work, this company took over a former movie theatre at 159 Bleecker Street (the same place eventually was turned into an arena theatre and became famous as one of the homes of the Circle-in-the-Square before that company moved to Broadway; it still exists as their downtown playhouse). Because fire laws prevented a license being granted to a theatre of 300 or more that had no proscenium or asbestos curtain (as here), the number of seats was reduced to 299, which subsequently became the union-recognized standard for Off-Broadway houses. At first, a lack of funds led to the actors being paid in company stock rather than in cash. Various concessions were allowed by the unions to help the fledgling group get on its feet. The company gained instant attention by producing Stavis's play about Galileo, *Lamp at Midnight*, provoking an intriguing debate regarding the quality of the play and production in contrast to the Experimental Theatre's staging of Brecht's *Galileo*. It made an even greater demand for attention by producing Sartre's long one-acter, "The Respectful Prostitute" (on a bill with another play as curtain raiser), soon after; "The Respectful Prostitute" generated so much excitement that it moved to Broadway for a successful run. New Stages managed to provide four more productions, including another Sartre play, *The Victors*, and an interesting revival of Lorca's *Blood Wedding*, before fading away.

Meanwhile, other groups were being born, although the critics only rarely covered them. Among those that came along soon after New Stages were Originals Only, Playcrafters, Associated Playwrights, and Interplayers.

The last named moved into the Provincetown in the summer of 1948. Its roster of starving actors--working cooperatively and sharing menial tasks--included future leading figures Gene (then Jean) Saks, Beatrice Arthur, Kim Stanley, Michael Gazzo, and Anthony Franciosa. Among the company's half-dozen or so productions were *him*, *The Infernal Machine*, *The Silver Tassie*, and *Within the Gates*.

Some of the same people were involved in On-Stage, Off Broadway, Inc., and the New York Repertory Group. (Such groups often formed as splinters when dissension arose among the members.) On-Stage, managed by Robert Ramsey, was active in several theatres, including a large room in a brownstone at 6 Fifth Avenue. Its shoestring repertory included one summer season of forgotten American plays, including *The Contrast*, *The New York Idea*, and *East Lynne*, and it also introduced New York to T. S. Eliot's *The Family Reunion*. On-Stage's revival of Strindberg's *Creditors* at the Cherry Lane was considered excellent; it was staged by future great Frank Corsaro, who was the company's leading director. Darren McGavin was first seen locally in an On-Stage production. Off Broadway, Inc.,'s principal contributions were Gertrude Stein's *Yes Is for a Very Young Man* (which placed Kim Stanley in the spotlight) and Robert Hivnor's *Too Many Thumbs* (with Stanley and Nehemiah Persoff). The New York Repertory Group offered barely noticed presentations of *The Adding Machine*, *Hamlet*, and *The Taming of the Shrew*, among other works.

Located way uptown, and far from the turmoil of the Village, was an acting school called the Abbe Practical Workshop, founded by Robert O'-Byrne and his wife, Gloria Monty. Like the Dramatic Workshop, it provided an outlet for its student players by producing mostly new dramas. It was housed on Riverside Drive at what was generally known as the Master Institute Theatre, a place that would later do lengthy duty as the home of the Equity Library Theatre. With Monty doing most of the directing, it offered a series of plays in the late forties, giving each only about three performances, but often attracting a critic or two. Although it was lauded for fine work in advancing experimental theatre, few of the ten or so reviewed plays it did during the period excited much attention. One of its regular actors, Richard Venture, eventually had a successful career.

The proliferation of small Off-Broadway troupes toward the end of the decade was amazing. There were 264 such groups known during the 1949-1950 season, and another fifty or more were believed to be in existence. John Chapman wrote at the time, "Since most of these bands offered several productions apiece, it is obvious that the number of off-Broadway plays verged on the appalling."[7] In 1949 a quintet of such troupes--Off Broadway, Inc., Studio-7, the Interplayers, We Present, and People's Drama--banded together under an umbrella they called the Off-Broadway Theatre League. They sought safety in numbers as a way of combatting Equity's decision to forbid its members from participating in their activities. The League argued, "The obvious inability of the existing commercial theater to provide a place for serious young theater people is generally recognized as being the precipitating factor for the off-Broadway theater movement."[8] After some haggling, Equity permitted its members to work in the League's plays provided they obtained a temporary work permit; they made up no more than forty-nine percent of the cast; they were paid at least five dollars a week; the nonunion actors registered with Equity; and the profits above specific guideline figures for each theatre were shared among the Equity actors.[9]

According to a 1949 article in *Theatre Arts*, the typical Off-Broadway company expressed its ideals in a manifesto and was ultimately concerned with doing the kind of play that Broadway could not afford to do. Most of the plays were not truly experimental, but were drawn from the established modern and ancient repertory. The few daring new plays produced were flops. Social commentary seemed a necessary ingredient in any new play debuting Off Broadway. Companies rarely lost money, however, because they required only a modest investment. When the Provincetown or the Cherry Lane were used, the company had to put up about $3,000 for its season (the break-even point was about $700 a week), but when it performed in places like settlement houses, the rent was rock bottom. One of the more expensive rentals was a small theatre in Carnegie Hall used at one point by the Interplayers. Funds were normally supplied by the company members themselves; this created an artistic danger since the democratic structure of these groups allowed all members an equal voice in policy, including casting.

Before departing from the subject of Off Broadway, it might be noted that during the forties there was an increasing interest in what is called arena staging or theatre-in-the-round. The work of Glenn Hughes at the Penthouse Theatre in Seattle and of Margo Jones at her Dallas theatre was being written about and discussed. Arena staging--with its minimal settings--offers an opportunity to provide imaginative productions at only a fraction of the cost required by a proscenium arrangement, so it was natural for producers worried about the rising costs of production to consider it as an alternative. A number of barely noticed arena stagings transpired in tiny Off-Broadway venues throughout the decade, an early example being a 1943 revival of *Hotel Universe* at the Barbizon-Plaza Hotel. The first New York arena staging in what was deemed a commercial offering was also Off Broadway, in a converted garage at 212 Eldridge Street on the Lower East Side. The play was *John Brown*, the company and theatre were People's Drama, and the director was Gene Frankel. Rod Steiger, then unknown, was in the cast. Produced on May 3, 1950, it was followed in less than a month by a much more polished arena staging of George Kelly's *The Show-Off*, presented in the ballroom of the Edison Hotel and considered a Broadway-level production. A permanent home for arena staging in New York arrived in the early fifties, when Off-Broadway's Circle-in-the-Square was established.

FOREIGN-LANGUAGE PRODUCTIONS

Foreign-language plays were rarer than ever on Broadway. Apart from a Spanish revue that was mostly music and dancing, a Yiddish-language production starring Molly Picon, and the visit of the Hebrew-speaking Habimah Theatre, Broadway audiences found their non-English-speaking theatre Off Broadway. However, the only companies regularly reviewed were those of the Yiddish theatre. Even an interesting group of German-speaking refugees called the Players from Abroad, who played Off Broadway at the Barbizon-Plaza Hotel, and whose actors included such outstanding figures as Elisabeth Bergner, Herbert Berghof, Albert Bassermann, and Uta Hagen, was practically ignored. This volume offers entries on only three of their half-dozen or so productions, and these descriptions are restricted by the sparse commentary available in English sources. The most regularly covered company was Maurice Schwartz's Yiddish Art Theatre (YAT).

The YAT began in 1918 and ended in 1949. It celebrated its twenty-fifth anniversary in 1943. Year in and year out, except for brief periods when the company was playing elsewhere, the YAT provided interested audiences with the most culturally elevated examples of Yiddish theatre. Most frequently, it could be found at a Lower East Side theatre on Second Avenue, but in 1941 it occupied Broadway's Jolson Theatre and in 1944 it was at the Adelphi. Its plays were frequently adapted by Schwartz himself from novels, and he served in the capacities of producer, star, and director for every play. YAT productions were elaborate, colorfully acted, episodically constructed, melodramatic, and sentimental. Audiences without Yiddish were given detailed English synopses. Most reviews of the company's work stressed the flamboyance and versatility of Schwartz's larger-than-life performances.

The decade saw twelve YAT presentations. While some were period plays set among Jewish characters in Europe during the past, a good number were set in the near present and had political themes related to the Jewish community. (Political themes, however, were not uncommon among the history plays, which often treated the topic of anti-Semitism and pogroms.) Among them were *Dr. Herzl*, a biographical drama about the founder of Zionism; *The Family Carnovsky*, concerned with a German-Jewish family during the time of Hitler's rise; and *The Voice of Israel*, an anti-British play about the struggle to establish Israel, produced in the year that that nation was officially born. The period dramas included works like *Herschel, the Jester*, which gave Schwartz a chance to show his skill at buffoonery; *Shylock and His Daughter*, which provided a revisionist look at Shakespeare's treatment of the moneylender of Venice; and *Yosele, the Nightingale*, in which Schwartz got to sing, and which was a romantic comedy based on a Sholem Aleichem story set in a nineteenth-century village.

For those inclined to the lighter sort of throw-away Yiddish theatre, called *shund*, there were several charming pieces starring Molly Picon (who also ventured onto Broadway in English-language roles). Even more regular appearances were put in by comedian Menasha Skulnik, who produced a string of amusing Second Avenue musical comedies in which he played his typical role of a bashful, awkward nebbish pursued by the man-hungry Yetta Zwerling. *Be Happy*, *The Big Shot*, *Good News*, and *I'm in Love* were the titles of some of these formula concoctions. Skulnik's popularity expanded even further through his TV appearances, and he moved onto Broadway in English-language comedies during the fifties.

There were other Yiddish offerings during the decade, but few attracted much English-language attention.

VISITING COMPANIES

The forties were not a very comfortable time for foreign companies to be journeying abroad, what with the problems of the war and its aftermath. Thus there was a sharp dropoff in visiting troupes during the decade. Only five important groups arrived, and four were from the British Isles. Donald Wolfit, who was known for his devotion to touring the English provinces with a company of classically oriented players, arrived in 1947 with a five-play repertory, four by Shakespeare and one by Jonson. Although the notices gradually improved during his stay, Wolfit was considered a ham and his actors depressingly mediocre.

Numerous homegrown revivals of Gilbert and Sullivan were produced, as in previous decades, most of them in the care of second-rate companies who offered a series of shoddily decorated works from the canon. But Gilbert and Sullivan lovers took heart from the visit in 1948 of the masters of the genre, England's D'Oyly Carte Opera Company, with a repertory that ran a total of 136 performances. Martyn Greene and Darrell Fancourt were, as in past visits, the mainstays of these famous Savoyards.

Micheal MacLiammoir and Hilton Edwards were the leaders of Ireland's Dublin Gate Theatre, founded in 1928 and devoted to a wide-ranging classical and modern repertory, as well as Irish plays; this program was meant to contrast with that of Dublin's Abbey Theatre, devoted principally to plays of Irish life. But when the Gate visited Broadway in 1948, it brought three plays by and about the Irish, Shaw's *John Bull's Other Island*, Johnston's *The Old Lady Says "No!,"* and MacLiammoir's own *Where the Stars Walk*. Audience and critical reaction was dreary.

The most brilliant visitors were the members of London's Old Vic Company, who, in 1946, made their first visit here. Sponsored by Theatre Incorporated, they were the first troupe from abroad to come to these shores following the war. There was a warm outpouring for these Britons because of the sympathy felt for those who had recently been in harm's way. But sympathy aside, the classical revivals offered by this company, led by Laurence Olivier and Ralph Richardson, were widely considered absolutely superlative. The two parts of Shakespeare's *Henry IV* (rarely seen together) benefited from Richardson's unforgettable Falstaff and Olivier's fiery Hotspur in Part I and hilariously decrepit Shallow in Part II. In *Oedipus* everything faded before Olivier's wrenching, Greek god-like hero (Richardson was Tiresias), made more memorable yet by his radically contrasting performance, on the same bill, of the ridiculously foppish Mr. Puff in Sheridan's eighteenth-century farce, *The Critic*. Olivier's feat was jokingly called "Oedipuff." Both Richardson and Olivier further displayed their great craft in *Uncle Vanya*.

The only other visitors were the Habimah Theatre from what was then called Palestine but would, while they were playing here, be renamed Israel. These actors nearly failed to get out of their country in one piece, as fighting between Jews and Arabs was going on at Tel Aviv's airport. They escaped by ship to Cyprus and arrived for their New York engagement mere hours before their first performance. The Habimah offered a four-play repertory, including the seventeenth-century Spanish play, *David's Crown*, Tyrone Guthrie's staging of *Oedipus Rex*, and its famous productions of *The Golem* and *The Dybbuk*, based on Jewish folk materials.

PRODUCTION OVERVIEW

Despite the occasional appearance of protest drama during the forties, the theatre was no longer as committed to serving as a weapon for social progress as it had been in the previous decade. During the war years, the ominous cloud of world events made it imperative that the theatre provide a means to put one's worries on the shelf for a couple of hours. Both the musical and straight theatres were primarily a place to laugh at funny comics, ogle attractive performers, wallow in spectacle, indulge in romance, and otherwise escape from the harsh realities outside. When creative inspiration waned, revivals of old favorites took the place of new plays. This is not to say that there were no attempts during the war to provide serious drama dealing with contemporary concerns; even before Pearl Harbor, during the 1940-1941 season, there were *Flight to the West*, *Watch on the Rhine*, and *Candle in the Wind*; moreover, *There Shall Be No Night* was still running from the 1939-1940 season. But the thrust of most productions during the war was to make people happy.

Looking at the decade as a whole, rather than in halves, it can be said that there probably has never been a period when so many plays were influenced by a war. The plays ranged from farce to tragedy and every mixture in between. Some put spectators on the front lines (*The Eve of St. Mark*, *Storm Operation*, *The Rugged Path*, *A Sound of Hunting*, *Command Decision*, and so on); some found Nazis and fascists on the home front (*Watch on the Rhine*, *Tomorrow the World*, *Decision*, and son on); some examined the Nazi threat in conquered or threatened territory (*The Wookey*, *The Barber Had Two Sons*, *Candle in the Wind*, *The Winter Soldiers*, *Jacobowsky and the Colonel*, *The Moon Is Down*, and so on) or showed what we were doing when we restored democracy to such places (*A Bell for Adano*); some looked at life on domestic military bases (*Winged Victory* [using an all-military cast and designed specifically to raise funds for the air force], *At War with the Army*, and so on); some anguished about soldiers with psychological problems (*Home of the Brave*, *The Hasty Heart*, and so on); others tackled the problem of psychologically troubled veterans (*Foxhole in the Parlor*); a few worried about how homecoming soldiers would be received by loved ones (*Soldier's Wife*) or created amusing homecoming crises (*John Loves Mary*); others concentrated on veterans confronting racial problems (*Jeb*, *Deep Are the Roots*, and so on); several focused on dead servicemen returning as ghosts (*The Wind Is Ninety*); others laughed at the foibles of servicemen and women (*The Doughgirls*, *Strip for Action*, and so on); still others thrilled vicariously to their romantic adventures while on leave (*The Voice of the Turtle*); or simply put one or more of their characters in military uniforms because that is what so many young men of the day were wearing. All such plays were unquestionably patriotic in motif, and never was American participation in the conflict questioned. Almost every branch of the armed forces was represented. Most plays were preoccupied with the war in Europe, only a couple bearing on the Pacific conflict (*South Pacific* [both the play and musical of that name], *Mister Roberts*, and so on).

The musical stage did not shirk its chance to glorify the military. One revue, Irving Berlin's *This Is the Army*, created just to raise money for the war effort, earned millions. But most musicals with uniformed personnel were preoccupied with what went on when soldiers and sailors had spare time on their hands (*On the Town*, *Something for the Boys*, *Let's Face It*, and so on) and were not engaged in military duties.

Related to all such works were those plays on the periphery of the war; these investigated the complacent attitudes that led to the Nazi rise (*The Searching Wind*); dug into America's past to reassert the values that were being threatened by the holocaust (*The Patriots*); reassured us that we would endure (*The Skin of Our Teeth*); excoriated American greed for endangering our fighting men (*All My Sons*); and so on.

The best of the war plays, as is usually the case, arrived once the fighting was over and there was time to reflect on the experience. Most would agree that *A Bell for Adano*, *Command Decision*, *Deep Are the Roots*, *Home of the Brave*, and *Mister Roberts* were the finest dramas of the decade to reflect the war experience.

Although there was a dearth of truly significant plays that had the legs to outlive the decade, the 1940s will always be remembered as the era that first saw the plays of Tennessee Williams and Arthur Miller produced. Williams had flopped with his first big play, *Battle of Angels*, which closed out of town in 1940 (but was later produced as *Orpheus Descending*); he returned, however, with such portentous dramas as *The Glass Menagerie*, *A Streetcar Named Desire*, and *Summer and Smoke*, each of them still being regularly revived five decades later. Williams's plays, noted for their Southern settings and lushly poetic atmosphere and dialogue, were typically concerned with psychosexual problems, especially among neurasthenic women; mendacity was a favorite theme. Miller was more interested in problems of ethics; his plays suggested the social realism of the thirties, but his subjects were treated in universal human rather than narrowly political terms. His first major effort, *The Man Who Had All the Luck*, was a promising flop, but he overcame its rejection with *All My Sons* and *Death of a Salesman*. *Salesman* and *Streetcar* are, in the eyes of many critics, two of the finest plays in American theatre history.

Another work deserving of such praise is Eugene O'Neill's *The Iceman Cometh*, which arrived in 1946 after O'Neill's twelve-year absence from Broadway. This searing, wordy, four-hour-long drama, set in 1912 and dealing with a group of derelicts surviving on their pipe dreams in a seedy waterfront bar, was the last of his plays to be done during his lifetime. (Like Williams's *Summer and Smoke*, it would have to wait for a brilliant revival by Off Broadway's Circle-in-the-Square Theatre during the next decade before its value was fully appreciated.) These three plays represent the pinnacle of American dramatic achievement during the forties.

Another new playwright, who never quite achieved the esteem of Miller and Williams, but who was to provide a string of important realistic plays about everyday, lonely midwesterners, was William Inge, who contributed *Come Back, Little Sheba* in 1950. The number of other new American playwrights of note is not great. They include (along with their most successful plays) Norman Krasna (*Dear Ruth* and *John Loves Mary*), Arthur Laurents (*Home of the Brave*), Arnaud d'Usseau and James Gow (*Tomorrow the World* and *Deep Are the Roots*), Garson Kanin (*Born Yesterday*), Jerome Chodorov and Joseph Fields (*My Sister Eileen* and *Junior Miss*), Ruth Gordon (*Over 21* and *Years Ago*), Joseph Kesselring (*Arsenic and Old Lace*), John Patrick (*The Hasty Heart*), Mary Chase (*Harvey*), and Carson McCullers (*The Member of the Wedding*).

Despite the critical or commercial fame of the plays listed, only a few have held up, and most of the playwrights did not achieve many subsequent stage successes. Several of these works, though, hit long-running jackpots that earned fabulous sums. The biggest moneymakers among straight American plays (all over a thousand showings) were the comic fantasy about an invisible rabbit, *Harvey*; the political satire, *Born Yesterday*; the sexy romance, *The Voice of the Turtle*; the farce about old ladies who poison people, *Arsenic and Old Lace*; and the comedy-drama about the navy during World War II, *Mister Roberts*.

The majority of the best-received plays were by members of the old guard (like O'Neill), but their plays, too, were mostly of momentary interest, and few have lasted. These playwrights (and one or two of their chief contributions) include Maxwell Anderson (*Joan of Lorraine* and *Anne of the Thousand Days*), S. N. Behrman (*Jacobowsky and the Colonel* and *The Pirate*), the naturalized citizen John van Druten (*I Remember Mama* and *The Voice of the Turtle*), Rose Franken (*Outrageous Fortune* and *Claudia*), Paul Green and Richard Wright (*Native Son*), Moss Hart (*Winged Victory* and *Light Up the Sky*), Lillian Hellman (*Watch on the Rhine* and *Another Part of the Forest*), George S. Kaufman (*George Washington Slept Here* [with Moss Hart] and *The Late George Apley* [with John P. Marquand]), George Kelly (*The Deep Mrs. Sykes* and *The Fatal Weakness*), Sidney Kingsley (*The Patriots* and *Detective Story*), Emmet Lavery (*The Magnificent Yankee*), Howard Lindsay and Russel Crouse (*Life with Mother* and *State of the Union*), Clifford Odets (*Clash by Night* and *The Big Knife*), Paul Osborn (*A Bell for Adano*), Elmer Rice (*Flight to the West* and *Dream Girl*), William Saroyan (*The Beautiful People* and "Hello Out There"), and Thornton Wilder (*The Skin of Our Teeth*). The new plays of Philip Barry and Robert E. Sherwood were nowhere near the quality of their earlier writings. In later years, the most highly respected of the works enumerated was Wilder's satirical cartoon about man's ability to survive by the skin of his teeth, and covering history from the ice age to the present day. Most of the other plays, including the once greatly admired *Watch on the Rhine*, have dated more or less badly. The only play by one of these veteran writers to receive more than five hundred performances was *Detective Story*.

Plays about black people were evolving--but very slowly--from the triter, stereotypical works of earlier years into mature treatments in which black characters were more sharply individualized and their social problems more sensitively handled. An increasing number of white plays provided good roles for black characters, and not simply the menials so familiar in the past. It remained common, though, for black characters to be cast as servants in white households, often for comic purposes.

The most successful black drama, *Anna Lucasta*, was by a white writer, Philip Yordan, whose Polish characters were transmogrified into black ones in one of the era's biggest hits. In fact, most of the best-known Broadway plays about blacks were by white writers, such as Robert Ardrey (*Jeb*); Dorothy Heyward (*Set My People Free*); Lillian Smith (*Strange Fruit*); Arnaud d'Usseau and James Gow (*Deep Are the Roots*); Maxine Wood (*On Whitman Avenue*); and Paul Green (*Native Son*, based on black author Richard Wright's novel). In the black community, these plays were sometimes considered well intentioned but ultimately insulting as treatments of their world, although a few were appreciated for their insight and honesty. There were, however, several striking works by black writers, including Abram Hill's *On Strivers Row*, Theodore Browne's *Natural Man*, Owen Dodson's *Garden of Time*, and Theodore Ward's *Our Lan'*. Several productions also followed the practice of taking a famous white play and reviving it with black actors, including *Lysistrata* and Gorky's *The Lower Depths*, called *A Long Way from Home* in its black version. (See also *Carmen Jones*, described later.) The black contribution to the decade's theatre was most pronounced on the musical stage.

Foreign plays were less in evidence than ever before, although several important works originated abroad. The British remained the most active foreign source, with smash hits by Noël Coward (*Blithe Spirit*), T. S. Eliot (*The Cocktail Party*), Patrick Hamilton (*Angel Street*), Robert Morley and Noel Langley (*Edward, My Son*), Terence Rattigan (*O Mistress Mine*), and Emlyn Williams (*The Corn Is Green*). Germany offered little, although Brecht's *Galileo* held some interest, but France came through with some truly worthwhile plays. They were not all successful, but their reputations have, to a good degree, lasted. Among them were the plays of Jean Giraudoux (*The Madwoman of Chaillot*), Jean-Paul Sartre (*The Flies*, *No Exit*, *The Red Gloves*, "The Respectful Prostitute," and *The Victors*), and Jean Anouilh (*Antigone* and *Cry of the Peacock*). In terms of its contemporary reception, Giraudoux's *The Madwoman of Chaillot* was probably the most noteworthy of these Gallic entries.

An interesting phenomenon of the period was the several plays that attempted to capitalize on the popularity of famous movies. Since the traditional pattern had been for the movies to adapt stage plays, the tendency suggests a spirit of desperation among producers unable to find promising new scripts. *Laura*, *Rebecca*, and *Wonderful Journey* (the play which, under its original title, *Heaven Can Wait*, had been the inspiration for *Here Comes Mr. Jordan*), were the three such attempts, all of them flops.

Themes and topics of the period, in addition to the war, ranged from escapist fantasies, often about life after death, to serious concerns with American values, which often were called into question. A number of plays went back into American history to contrast the nation's ideals with the present reality, and the theme of incipient fascism (occasionally stirred by issues of academic freedom) was a frequent visitor. It was, indeed, the basic issue of Kingsley's *Detective Story*. Civil rights was another theme of increasing importance, especially with regard to racial bigotry and anti-Semitism. Political satire was sparse, but there were several valuable plays that employed it in good measure, most notably *State of the Union* and *Born Yesterday*.

Censorship continued to be an issue hovering over Broadway, although the number of plays officially forced to close was small. At the start of the decade, Mayor La Guardia made a much-publicized decision to close down the city's burlesque houses, charging them with immorality. Several Broadway shows then provided burlesque under the guise of legitimate theatre entertainment, but one of them went too far. This was the Shubert-produced *Wine, Women, and Song*, which prompted the authorities to invoke the Wales Padlock Law (section 1140A of the criminal code), close the Ambassador Theatre for a year, and send its ailing producer to prison. The most questionable use of censorship was the case surrounding the 1945 drama *Trio*, about a lesbian relationship. Homosexuality remained a subject that inspired fear and hatred among officials and religious figures. Like the similarly themed *The Captive* of the twenties, *Trio* was widely deemed a strong and honest presentation of its subject, but, two months into its run, License Commissioner Paul Moss (relying on hearsay about the drama) invoked wsection 1140A--which prohibited plays dealing with sexual per version--and shut it down. An outcry was raised by many in and out of the theatre (including the American Civil Liberties Union), but his decision stood. The small number of other forties plays with homosexual characters (such as *Outrageous Fortune* and *Proof Thro' the Night*) managed not to provoke the authorities as much as *Trio* did and were not threatened with legal action.

In the 1940s, Broadway's musical theatre made enormous strides forward. Rodgers and Hammerstein led the way with their brilliantly integrated show, *Oklahoma!*, which, because of its period flavor, Americana motif, and romantic story, has been called "folk operetta" to distinguish it from the more conventional musical comedies such as *Panama Hattie* or *High Button Shoes*. Some prefer to call the more dramatically sound musicals of the day, with their solidly constructed and emotionally satisfying librettos, "musical plays," although the latter is perhaps more suitable for works set in the present and dealing with contemporary issues. Whatever the designation, Rodgers and Hammerstein continued to show the way with their resoundingly successful *Carousel*, the less effective *Allegro*, and the enormously popular *South Pacific*. The musical play genre was further enhanced by *Pal Joey*, written when Rodgers was still a partner with Lorenz Hart, and which was the first major musical to have a louse for its hero; *Up in Central Park*, Herbert and Dorothy Fields and Sigmund Romberg's Currier and Ives salute to the period of Boss Tweed and his gang; *Bloomer Girl*,

Sig Herzig, Fred Saidy, Harold Arlen, and Yip Harburg's memento to the nineteenth-century inventor of female pantaloons; Alan Jay Lerner and Frederick Loewe's *Brigadoon*, set mostly in a mythical Scotland; and Harburg, Saidy, and Burton Lane's *Finian's Rainbow*, a socially conscious fantasy in which a bigoted white senator is turned black. More conventional musical comedies, although nonetheless memorable, were *Kiss Me, Kate*, a splendid treatment of Shakespeare by Bella and Samuel Spewack and Cole Porter; Ogden Nash, S. J. Perelman, and Kurt Weill's *One Touch of Venus*; Moss Hart and Weill's excursion into psychotherapy, *Lady in the Dark*; George Abbott, Phil Silvers, Jule Styne, and Sammy Cahn's nostalgic trip back to 1913 in *High Button Shoes*, made memorable by Jerome Robbins's dances; another Robbins dance fest, *On Your Toes*, by Betty Comden, Adolph Green, and Leonard Bernstein, about three gobs on leave; the Fields and Irving Berlin's *Annie Get Your Gun*, scoring a bull's-eye with Ethel Merman as the famous sharpshooter; the Fields and Porter's *Mexican Hayride*, a festival for Bobby Clark; Abbott and Frank Loesser's *Where's Char ley?*, based on *Charley's Aunt*; and Joseph Fields, Anita Loos, Jule Styne, and Leo Robins's paean to the roaring twenties, *Gentlemen Prefer Blondes*. As this very small selection demonstrates, Rodgers and Hammerstein were the new and reigning kids on the block, but veterans Porter, Harburg, Weill, and Berlin were in the thick of things, and newcomers Lerner and Loewe, Styne, Bernstein, and others were no slouches either.

Conventional operetta, with its soaring melodies and romantic locales, remained a viable, if ever more old-fashioned, musical medium. Leading examples included *Song of Norway*, *Rhapsody*, *Music in My Heart*, *Gypsy Lady*, *My Romance*, and *Marinka*. Several of these tried the method used by the old perennial, *Blossom Time* (which reappeared during the decade), by which a famous composer's music was borrowed to provide the background to a pseudobiographical treatment of his life. Edvard Grieg and Peter Tchaikovsky were among the composers so graced.

Also notable during the forties were the shows that tried to bring opera and Broadway together, with dramatic critics usually covering the shows along with their music-specialist colleagues. Whether these works were operas or musical plays was hard to say, but they served to advance the Broadway musical toward a time when librettos would disappear and all the words would be sung (if not always in operatic registers). Shows of this sort included several outstanding works by Gian-Carlo Menotti, "The Telephone," *The Medium*, and *The Consul*. Others were Benjamin Britten's *The Rape of Lucretia*, Kurt Weill's *Street Scene*, and Marc Blitzstein's adaptation of Hellman's *The Little Foxes*, *Regina*. Several of these works were later revived by full-fledged opera companies.

The most popular operatic musical was an expert, updated adaptation by Oscar Hammerstein II of Bizet's *Carmen*, made over into *Carmen Jones* and played by an all-black cast. It was the most successful of the various black-oriented musical shows of the decade. More traditional, but interesting nonetheless, were such black-dominated shows as *Cabin in the Sky*, with music by Russian-born Vernon Duke; *St. Louis Woman*, composed by Johnny Mercer with Harold Arlen lyrics; *Beggar's Holiday* (a racially well integrated show--quite unique at the time--based on *The Beggar's Opera*), with music by Duke Ellington; and the moving Kurt Weill-Maxwell Anderson opus, *Lost in the Stars*, about the problems of apartheid in South Africa. This work was another in the list of dramatic musicals then coming into their own.

Black performers were also very evident in the nonbook musical shows called revues, especially dancer-choreographer Katherine Dunham, who was responsible for a number of them. She led her troupe through various ethnic dances from the Caribbean and Africa in such terpsichorean spectacles as *Carib Song*, *A Tropical Revue*, *Bal Negre*, and *Blue Holiday*, not all of them successful. The majority of the revues, of course, were not ethnically oriented. Irving Berlin's big army show *This Is the Army* was one of the best revues; others of note included *Inside U.S.A.*; *Star and Garter*, with which Michael Todd made the outlawed form of burlesque legitimate and charged top prices to see it; *Wine, Women, and Song*, a burlesque-type revue that ran afoul of the law; *Ziegfeld Follies of 1943*; *Seven Lively Arts*, which cost and lost $350,000 for Billy Rose; *Three to Make Ready*, the third in a series that had begun in the thirties; *Call Me Mister*, composed solely of people who had served in the war; *Angel in the Wings*, one of several revues featuring Paul and Grace Hartman, comedian-dancers; *Make Mine Manhattan*, which made Sid Caesar a star; *Small Wonder*, which had Tom Ewell as the MC; *Lend an Ear*, a launching pad for Carol Channing; and *Touch and Go*, created by Jean and Walter Kerr, who would become, respectively, a hit dramatist and a major critic. A couple of madhouse comic revues starring comedians Olsen and Johnson--who had originated the concept with their *Hellzapoppin'*--also were offered during the forties, but the formula soon paled.

There was also a series of shows that tried to bring back vaudeville, but did so only briefly. They had names like *Priorities of 1942*, *Keep 'Em Laughing*, *Harlem Cavalcade* (which had a black company), *Show Time*, and so forth. A type of musical show that did very well, however, was the ice revue or "icetravaganza," a series of which was produced by Arthur Wirtz and skating champion Sonja Henie at the huge Center Theatre in Rockefeller Center. These shows were differentiated critically from the spectacular ice shows done at Madison Square Garden, which, unlike those at the Center, starred Henie herself. Perhaps the fact that the Center was a regular theatre and the Garden was a sports arena gave theatre critics the feeling that they were two different--if related-- species.

No recent decade had had to depend as much on revivals to fill stages as did the forties, with the war, the Hollywood talent drain, and the high cost of production operating to reduce the supply of new plays. During one season, 1947-1948, there were approximately thirty revivals on Broadway, which, for all the interest such things have for theatre buffs, is not a sign of creative health. Some of the revivals seen during the decade were of the historically significant sort, especially those of Shakespeare's plays. The best of these included *Twelfth Night* with Helen Hayes and Maurice Evans; *Macbeth* with Evans and Judith Anderson (the Michael Redgrave-Flora Robson *Macbeth* flopped); *Hamlet* (the GI version), once more with Evans; *Othello* with Paul Robeson; *The Tempest*, imaginatively cast with black actor Canada Lee and Norwegian ballerina Vera Zorina; *As You Like It* with Katharine Hepburn; *Antony and Cleopatra* with Katharine Cornell; and the two parts of *Henry IV*, as perfectly done by the Old Vic, with Olivier and Richardson. Worthy failures were two *Richard III*s, with George Coulouris in one, Richard Whorf in the other. As this list reveals, Shakespeare could be a perfect vehicle for the right stars in the right roles.

Shakespeare's self-styled modern rival, Shaw, was represented by some brilliant resuscitations, too, including *Man and Superman* with Evans; *The Devil's Disciple*, also with Evans (the leading classical actor on the American stage at the time); *Candida*, in a couple of Cornell revivals, one with Burgess Meredith as Marchbanks and one with Marlon Brando; *The Doctor's Dilemma*, again with Cornell; *Pygmalion*, a hit with Gertrude Lawrence; *Androcles and the Lion* with Ernest Truex; and *Caesar and Cleopatra*, sparkling with Lilli Palmer and Cedric Hardwicke. Greek tragedy was ably presented, with two fine productions of *Oedipus*, one with Olivier, the other in Hebrew. Equally towering was the Robinson Jeffers adaptation of *Medea*, with a scorching portrayal of the heroine by Anderson. There were two dazzling Wilde revivals, *The Importance of Being Earnest*, with John Gielgud, and *Lady Windermere's Fan*, with Cornelia Otis Skinner. Chekhov found a niche with a distinguished *Three Sisters*, including Cornell, Anderson, and Ruth Gordon, and *The Cherry Orchard*, starring Eva Le Gallienne. Strindberg fared well in an Off-Broadway version of *The Father* with unknowns, but failed badly on Broadway soon after with stars such as Raymond Massey. José Ferrer slashed his way further into stardom as the hero in *Cyrano de Bergerac* and rolled them in the aisles in *Charley's Aunt*, two of the best revivals of the period. Not quite on a par with them was his *The Alchemist*. More recent plays that received notable treatment included *Burlesque*, played for laughs and tears by the great Bert Lahr, and *Counsellor-at-Law*, with Paul Muni repeating his old role to great acclaim. (Muni flopped, though, in a revival of *They Knew What They Wanted.*) Another hit revival of not too old a play was Molnár's *The Play's the Thing.* Molière was given his hilarious due in the wild-eyed antics of Bobby Clark's version of *The Would-Be Gentleman*, and Clark also contributed his irrepressible services to a new staging of *The Rivals.* An even older English comedy, *Love for Love*, with Gielgud, was too precious for Broadway. These are but the most interesting of the many straight-play revivals in a period when the New York stage seemed devoted to them.

Musicals, of course, were occasionally revived, but nowhere near as often as straight plays. There were only four musical revivals that deserve mention, two of them operettas by Victor Herbert. One was the 1906 *The Red Mill*, the other the 1913 *Sweethearts.* The remaining revivals of note were of the great 1927 Kern-Hammerstein collaboration, *Show Boat*, and the 1935 Gershwin masterpiece, *Porgy and Bess.*

ACTORS, DIRECTORS, CHOREOGRAPHERS, AND DESIGNERS

With the war raging for most of the early forties, there was a consequent demand for manpower that scooped up many talented players who might otherwise have been advancing their theatre careers. Numerous men and women of the stage fought at the front, but many more utilized their talents by entertaining in the special service units designed to raise the morale of the nation's combat forces. Another vacuum, but one that did not cease with the end of the war, was the one caused by Hollywood, which was quick to offer lucrative contracts to any vibrant new talent appearing on Broadway. Frequently, however, the stage regained, if only momentarily, the services of an actor or actress who was already established in films. Often this was simply a play for increased attention from the studios on the part of a performer whose movie career had momentarily (or permanently) cooled.

Movie stars attempting to recapture the thrill of live performance, if only in one or two appearances, counted among their number Richard Arlen, Jean Arthur, Mary Astor, Jean-Pierre Aumont, Charles Boyer, Madeleine Carroll, Melvyn Douglas, Henry Fonda, John Garfield, Katharine Hepburn, Paul Kelly, Charles Laughton, ZaSu Pitts, Anthony Quinn, Luise Rainer, Basil Rathbone, James Stewart, Margaret Sullavan, Gloria Swanson, Franchot Tone, Spencer Tracy, and Orson Welles. A handful picked hits; even their names did not help the others. On the other hand, Ralph Bellamy appeared in three plays, hitting a home run each time, while Boris Karloff did four plays, coming up roses half the time.

The younger generation of forties actors who made a notable contribution included June Allyson, Eve Arden, Gene Barry, Barbara Bel Geddes, Marlon Brando, Yul Brynner, Montgomery Clift, Richard Conte, Alfred Drake, Kirk Douglas, Betty Field, Uta Hagen, Julie Harris, June Havoc, Julie Haydon, Charlton Heston, Judy Holliday, Celeste Holm, Kim Hunter, Anne Jackson, Henry Jones, Danny Kaye, Arthur Kennedy, June Lockhart, Dorothy McGuire, Gary Merrill, Cameron Mitchell, Patricia Neal, Barry Nelson, Jack Palance, Gregory Peck, Margaret Phillips, Vincent Price, Maureen Stapleton, Barry Sullivan, Eli Wallach, David Wayne, Richard Widmark, Shelley Winters, and Irene Worth. Most debuted in the forties, but a few had started during the previous decade. Although their stage work was not especially notable at the time, being confined to minor roles or out-of-the-way productions, such players as Eileen Heckart, Tony Randall, Burt Lancaster, Jack Gilford, Martin Balsam, Darren McGavin, Beatrice Arthur, Gene Saks, Walter Matthau, Kim Stanley, Nehemiah Persoff, Rod Steiger, and Lauren Bacall were getting their theatrical feet wet during the period.

Leading stage actors--a good number of them movie actors as well--past the first blush of youth and topping their previous accomplishments during the forties included Brian Aherne, Shirley Booth, Mady Christians, Audrey

Christie, Lee J. Cobb, Eddie Dowling, Tom Ewell, Judith Evelyn, Arlene Francis, José Ferrer, Dorothy Gish, Ruth Gordon, Miriam Hopkins, Victor Jory, Jessie Royce Landis, Eugenie Leontovich, Karl Malden, Raymond Massey, Elliott Nugent, Natalie Schafer, Dorothy Stickney, Jessica Tandy, Vivian Vance, June Walker, Richard Whorf, and Jane Wyatt.

Among established character players who offered notable work were Luther Adler, Stella Adler, James Barton, Sidney Blackmer, Mary Boland, Joseph Buloff, Billie Burke, Louis Calhern, Morris Carnovsky, Leo G. Carroll, Donald Cook, Melville Cooper, George Coulouris, Frank Craven, Hume Cronyn, Clarence Derwent, Dudley Digges, Mildred Dunnock, Frank Fay, Will Geer, Grace George, Ethel Griffies, Edmund Gwenn, Walter Hampden, Josephine Hull, Walter Huston, Otto Kruger, Sam Levene, Philip Loeb, Myron McCormick, Burgess Meredith, Thomas Mitchell, Arnold Moss, Mildred Natwick, Joseph Schildkraut, Lee Tracy, Estelle Winwood, Peggy Wood, Roland Young, and Blanche Yurka.

Several substantial actors who were Central European émigrés provided meaningful performances, including Albert Bassermann, Else Bassermann, Herbert Berghof, Elisabeth Bergner, Dolly Haas, Paul Henreid, Oscar Homolka, Oscar Karlweis, Lotte Lenya, and Lilli Palmer.

The most respected and admired stage stars remaining active were Judith Anderson, Tallulah Bankhead, Ethel Barrymore, Katharine Cornell, Maurice Evans, Helen Hayes, Gertrude Lawrence, Eva Le Gallienne, Alfred Lunt and Lynn Fontanne, Fredric March and Florence Eldridge, Paul Muni, and Mae West, but Ina Claire, Jane Cowl, Pauline Lord, and Laurette Taylor were closing out their careers (Claire would reappear once more in the fifties).

Visits by top English stars allowed audiences to indulge in the finely honed abilities of Peggy Ashcroft, Gladys Cooper, John Gielgud, Alec Guinness, Cedric Hardwicke, Rex Harrison, Wendy Hiller, Martita Hunt, James Mason, A. E. Matthews, Robert Morley, Laurence Olivier, Michael Redgrave, Joyce Redman, Ralph Richardson, Flora Robson, and Donald Wolfit.

Hilarity reigned when the great Broadway clowns, declining in number, put in their appearances. Most prolific and wide-ranging were the portrayals of Bobby Clark, but considerable laughter was provoked--usually in revues--by the cavorting of Milton Berle, Sid Caesar, William Gaxton, Jackie Gleason, Bert Lahr, Beatrice Lillie, Victor Moore, Zero Mostel, Olsen and Johnson, Martha Raye, Phil Silvers, Ed Wynn, and, among singing fools, Eddie Cantor and Al Jolson.

On the musical comedy stage, there were many brilliant performances. Gertrude Lawrence went from straight plays to musicals with ease, but Ethel Merman did only musicals and was the reigning queen. Her rulership was challenged, however, by the appearance of the somewhat younger Mary Martin, while Nanette Fabray won many hearts in one musical role after the other. Another talented star was Scottish singer-actress Ella Logan. Betty Garrett came into the limelight in several shows, and dancer Joan McCracken displayed outstanding musical talents in musicals and ventured into straight parts in regular plays. Dancer Vera Zorina showed her physical graces in a couple of musicals; she, too, expanded into straight plays, even playing in Shakespeare. Bambi Linn and Japanese-American Sono Osato were among the most charming dancers in the decade's many dance-dominated shows. Katherine Dunham, as described earlier, brought her presence to many shows she also choreographed. Gene Kelly was terrific in *Pal Joey* before being swallowed by the movies. But the slack was taken up by long-legged Ray Bolger and the exotic Jack Cole. One of those Cole influenced, Bob Fosse, made his maiden voyage as a Broadway dancer during the decade. Gower Champion was also making a name for himself, both as a dancer and a choreographer. Carol Channing began her Broadway career playing a lesbian in a war drama, but made a sensational mark in musical comedy at the end of the period. Another young attention-grabber was comedienne Nancy Walker. Ray Middleton came into his own as a singing star, Ezio Pinza moved from opera to Broadway, and John Raitt began his starring career, but Alfred Drake reigned as the king of forties musicals, demonstrating a first-class ability in drama and comedy as well.

Black actors made important notches in the theatre of the decade, the most significant newcomers (although this was not necessarily apparent at the time) being Pearl Bailey, Harry Belafonte, Vinie Burrows, Alvin Childress, Ossie Davis, Ruby Dee, William Greaves, Gordon Heath, Eartha Kitt, Canada Lee, Frederick O'Neal, Sidney Poitier, Muriel Rahn, Lloyd Richards, Frank Silvera, Hilda Simms, Muriel Joanne Smith, and Duke Williams. Others who made vibrant contributions during the decade included singers Richard Huey, William Marshall, and William Warfield. More experienced black stage artists doing significant work included Osceola Archer, Alonzo Bosan, Todd Duncan, Juano Hernandez, Avon Long, John Marriott, Paul Robeson, Ethel Waters, Dooley Wilson, and Frank Wilson. Waters was able to make the transition from musicals to serious drama effortlessly. This was a period when black actors made some important breakthroughs on Broadway. Robeson's *Othello* was the first in the mainstream New York theatre with a black in the title role, and Canada Lee was given a chance to play classical roles traditionally given to whites. He played Caliban in *The Tempest* and Bosola in *The Duchess of Malfi*, using whiteface makeup for the latter.

The Yiddish stage had but three actors known to the world at large during the forties, Molly Picon, Menasha Skulnik, and Maurice Schwartz. But there were many supporting players who had their followings.

The single most important development for New York's actors during the forties was the establishment in 1947 of the Actors Studio by Elia Kazan, Robert Lewis, and Cheryl Crawford. All were products of the Group Theatre of the thirties, which had demonstrated the usefulness to the American stage of Stanislavsky's acting theories. The Studio was created as a workshop for professional actors to develop their skills in a supportive environment. It was not a school for beginners and required an audition before one could be accepted. Membership was strictly limited, and auditions were difficult to pass. Fees were not required, the Studio subsisting instead on contributions from members and nonmembers alike. When the demands of their professional lives made it impossible for the original triumvirate to give the Studio their undivided attention, Lee Strasberg was invited to assume its leadership.

Strasberg, another Group alumnus, was a scholarly actor-director who had evolved his own approach to Stanislavsky's ideas, an approach that, in the thirties, had caused a schism with another leading member of the Group, actress Stella Adler. She had a rather different notion of the meaning behind Stanislavsky's theories; these had undergone considerable revision over a lengthy period. At the Studio, Strasberg had a powerful forum for implementing his interpretation, and it was not long before this interpretation--commonly called "the Meth od"--became a household word. The proponents of Method acting included some of the greatest talents of that decade and later ones, but various mannerisms--such as sloppy speech, careless physical behavior, and self-indulgent emotionalism--associated with the worst excesses of the technique gave critics a pile of rocks to throw at Method actors. The Actors Studio remained unfazed and eventually expanded into playwrights' and directors' units. Years after Strasberg died (1982), it remained a going concern. At times, it engaged in production, including once in the 1940s, when its actors demonstrated their techniques in Bessie Breuer's poorly received *Sundown Beach*.

Kazan not only cofounded the Actors Studio; after abandoning his acting career, he became the leading stage director of the decade. His astonishing string of forties successes--marred by only a sprinkling of flops--included *The Skin of Our Teeth*, *Harriet*, *One Touch of Venus*, *Jacobowsky and the Colonel*, *Deep Are the Roots*, *All My Sons*, *A Streetcar Named Desire*, and *Death of a Salesman*. The directing field remained male-dominated, but several important females made something of a dent. Chief among them was Margaret Webster, following through on the promise she had shown in the thirties, especially with the classics. Her frequent coworker, Eva Le Gallienne, did some directing, but was busier as an actress. Margo Jones codirected the hit play, *The Glass Menagerie*, for which she did not receive as much credit as she was due, and also did a couple of other dramas, including *Summer and Smoke*, but the travails of Broadway convinced her to concentrate on her burgeoning arena theatre in Dallas. Choreographer Agnes de Mille ventured into directing, but did not build up a heavy résumé in this guise. Another woman director of note was Mary Hunter, who worked mainly Off Broadway; her New York directing career ended with the decade. Catherine Littlefield found a special niche in directing the annual ice-skating revues that filled the Center Theatre.

Among the male directors, the veterans continued to reign, among them George Abbott, Harold Clurman, Jed Harris, Arthur Hopkins, Robert Lewis, Joshua Logan, Guthrie McClintic, Rouben Mamoulian, Max Reinhardt, Lee Strasberg, Orson Welles, John C. Wilson, and Bretaigne Windust. Younger directors included Morton Da Costa, José Ferrer, and Garson Kanin. A few important directors were confined by circumstances to Off-Broadway venues, including the young Frank Corsaro and Germany's Erwin Piscator.

Several playwrights tried their hand at directing their own plays. John van Druten and Sidney Kingsley were quite proficient at the art, and George S. Kaufman was so good that he was usually busy directing someone else's work when not doing his own. However, Clifford Odets and Lillian Hellman were cautioned to stick to writing and to leave the staging to others.

The art of choreography was growing by leaps and bounds as the idea of infusing ballet into musicals took root, especially following the success of the idea in *Oklahoma!*, whose dances were created by de Mille. She was responsible for several distinguished musicals during these years. George Balanchine, who was the first to use thematically related ballet in a Broadway musical (1936's *On Your Toes*), choreographed a number of musicals before turning his full-time attention to ballet. Helen Tamiris offered some of her unique terpsichorean ideas to musical staging, as did Felicia Sorel, Hanya Holm, and Anna Sokolow. Katherine Dunham's contributions have already been mentioned. Among the men, veteran Robert Alton did some important work during the early forties, but the bulk of the decade's greatest dances came from newcomers. One was Michael Kidd, responsible for four shows. Another was Gower Champion, who usually appeared in his own routines. Also commonly showing off his own dances was the idiosyncratic Jack Cole, whose work was influenced by Eastern styles. The man who generated the most excitement among Broadway dance aficionados, however, was the inventive Jerome Robbins, whose choreography was sometimes the most memorable thing about the five shows on which he worked. These artists were responsible for moving the musical theatre into an increasingly dance-oriented direction, with dance and acting blending as seamlessly as possible in the direction of complete integration. In the best shows, dance was invariably related to character and plot.

Some of those who had established themselves as leading set and costume designers in the thirties remained active. Most powerful and respected were Boris Aronson, Watson Barratt, Howard Bay, Stewart Chaney, David Ffolkes, Frederick Fox, Jo Mielziner, Motley (who also did costumes), Donald Oenslager, Oliver Smith, and Raymond Sovey. Still brilliant, but not as active, were Norman Bel Geddes, Mordecai Gorelik, Robert Edmond Jones, and Lee Simonson. Once-prolific scenic artist Aline Bernstein did only one set, but designed costumes for many shows. The major young set designers were Lemuel Ayers, Ben Edwards, Harry Horner, Leo Kerz, Samuel Leve, and Paul Morrison. Horace Armistead and George Jenkins were not quite as active, but their sets were admired. This small number of designers practically monopolized Broadway scene design during the forties. Some of them did their own costumes, and most did their own lighting. A few designers, such as A. H. Feder, Moe Hack, and Peggy Clark, however, specialized in lighting.

Among designers who specialized in costuming, the best and busiest of the period were Lucinda Ballard, Rose Bogdanoff, Alvin Colt (not yet as busy as he would be), Raoul Pène du Bois, Paul du Pont, Grace Houston, Helene Pons,

Emeline Roche, Ernest Schrapps, Irene Sharaff, Julia Sze, and Miles White. As in previous decades, it remained the practice not to credit a costume designer when the garments worn by the actors were purchased at local retail establishments. The principal exceptions were when an actress's gowns or ensembles were the creation of a famous fashion designer, such as Mainbocher or Valentina, both of whom regularly provided striking outfits for Broadway's leading ladies. In fact, one reason that Mary Martin agreed to do *One Touch of Venus* was because Mainbocher said that he would design her clothes.

CONCLUSION

The forties was a fascinatingly divided decade, beginning with a nation just emerging from the Depression and then plunged directly into a catastrophic world war. Broadway's theatre was there to do its job, and it did so nobly, engaging in practical war work as well as attending to the duty of cheering up the populace at large. That entertainment is desperately sought as a crucial form of escape from worldly troubles was never more in evidence than during the conflict, when lighthearted presentations dominated the Great White Way and every night--despite the blackouts--seemed like New Year's Eve. Then the war ended and the citizenry were forced to take stock. Business declined, although some of the most exceptional plays in American history were produced. Television, projected as being of minimal potential damage to the theatre, was now every American's dream. One nightmarish view of reality it soon would offer was of what could happen to those who had seen a pink-shaded destiny for the nation. How that reality was to affect the stage during a period that began with renewed military conflict, moved ahead into an ever more chilling cold war, and cast a shadow of fear over would-be dissenters will be discovered in the plays described in volume four of this series.

NOTES

1. John Houseman, "There's No Business like Show Business," reprinted in John Houseman, *Entertainers and the Entertained; Essays on Theater, Film, and Television* (New York: Simon and Schuster, 1986), 58. Houseman's is one of the best surveys of the economics of producing in the forties and has been invaluable in the preparation of this essay.

2. Jack Gaver, *Curtain Calls* (New York: Dodd, Mead, 1949), 310.

3. The material on the ART is adapted from my *From Belasco to Brook: Representative Directors of the English-Speaking Stage* (Westport, Conn.: Greenwood Press, 1991), 123-124.

4. Gaver, *Curtain Calls*, 154.

5. Reprinted in John F. Wharton, *Life among the Playwrights, Being Mostly the Story of the Playwrights Producing Company* (New York: Quadrangle, 1974), 134.

6. Arthur Pollock, "Healthy 'Underground' Seen in *Plough and Stars*," *Daily Compass*, June 2, 1950, clipping file, New York Public Library at Lincoln Center.

7. John Chapman, *The Burns Mantle Best Plays of 1949-1950* (New York: Dodd, Mead, 1950), 382.

8. Quoted in Stuart Little, *Off-Broadway: The Prophetic Theater* (New York: Coward, McCann and Geoghegan, 1972; New York: Dell, a Delta Book, 1974), 42.

9. Lawrence Kane, "Five Minutes from Broadway," *Theatre Arts* 33 (December 1949), 43-47, 97-98.

THE NEW YORK STAGE, 1940–1950

A

ABI GEZUNT (***As Long As You're Healthy***) [Musical/Yiddish Language] B: Jacob Kalich and Sholom Perlmutter; M: Joseph Rumshinsky; LY: Molly Picon; D/P: Jacob Kalich; CH: Lillian Shapero; S/L: Michael Saltzman; T: Second Avenue Theatre (OB); 10/8/49

Molly Picon, doyenne of the Yiddish theatre, celebrated her quarter-century reign by appearing in this hit musical comedy that displayed her multitalented charm. The show was in the Second Avenue sentimental formula tradition, "slow, obvious and stereotyped, with old-fashioned scenery and some fairly hideous costumes," according to Brooks Atkinson (*NYT*); it was still very enjoyable as quaint family entertainment. A large percentage of the show's success was owing to the petite star, who played a double role that displayed her versatility. The fifty-one-year-old star even learned to roller skate for one of her routines. While most of the dialogue was in Yiddish, English phrases were scattered throughout.

The setting is a kosher hotel in the Catskill Mountains, the only place where one can enjoy oneself without having a good time, as one character remarks. Tzirele (Picon), a naive, religiously orthodox displaced person from Poland, marries the half-owner of the hotel (Muni Serebrov) and learns that he has been carrying on with the flirtatious wife (Mae Schoenfeld) of the social director (Julius Adler). The piously orthodox Tzirele's plan to trap him involves her inventing a sexy identical twin from Paris named Mirele, who arrives at the hotel as a French chanteuse and immediately wins the hearts of all the male guests, including her own spouse. The husband eventually realizes the truth and sheepishly returns to the fold. At the show's end, Picon's husband, actor-librettist-director-producer Jacob Kalich, appeared before the curtain to recap Picon's long career, made especially piquant by the fact that her American debut had been in the same theatre.

Picon's role gave her numerous chances to win the audience's hearts. One of her best songs was "Mama Loshen," in which she had fun listing various comic Yiddish expressions and insults. Whitney Bolton (*NYMT*) declared, "Miss Picon was only wonderful 25 years ago when I first saw her and she is only wonderful now, a fascinating expert comedienne who has her own kind of way on a stage, and an entrancing way it is, too. She is surrounded by an expert company but nothing is ever as good as when she is on stage, joshing the plot, sky-larking, making acid jokes or singing in that way that only Molly Picon can sing."

The cast included Irving Jacobson, Max Bozhyk, Henrietta Jacobson, Sylvia Feder, and Miriam Feder. The Feder sisters, a harmonizing duo, had a show-stopping number in "The Tzimmes Polka."

"ACCORDING TO LAW" (see *A Strange Play*)

(1) "ACROSS THE BOARD ON TOMORROW MORNING" and **"THEATRE OF THE SOUL"** [One-Acts] P/T: Theatre Showcase (OB); 3/20/42

"Across the Board on Tomorrow Morning" [Comedy/Barroom/Fantasy/Gambling] A: William Saroyan; D: William Boyman; C: Helen Hecht; "Theatre of the Soul" ("V Kulisach Dashi") [Dramatic Revival] A: Nikolai Evreinov; D: Bernarr Cooper; C: Charmion de Ved

A small theatre with a postage-stamp-size stage in a brownstone at 341 West Forty-seventh Street was home to these two one-acts. The curtain raiser was Evreinov's "Theatre of the Soul," a 1912 "monodrama" set in the soul, the heart, and the nervous system (shown as a noisy telephone) during the split second before a man commits suicide. The work dramatizes a battle between the allegorical forces of the Emotional and the Rational as represented in the central character, a professor. The professor gives a lecture on the principles involved, using a blackboard and chalk, the issue being the Rational's attempt to get the Emotional to give up a dancer with whom the married professor is in love, thus threatening his family life. When the emotional side kills the rational side and then is rejected by the dancer, he shoots himself, and ribbons representing blood come out of the heart on the blackboard. Meanwhile, the real man, represented as a subliminal force, continues on his way. In this version the emotional forces had such names as Emotional Entity (Bernarr Cooper), Rational Entity (Sterling Mace), Emotional Concept of the Dancer (Maia Gregory), Rational Concept of the Dancer (Anne Selby), and so on. The work failed to impress.

Saroyan's fanciful play with metaphysical overtones was the major draw, but it proved a disappointment because of its inadequately acted and staged production. Brooks Atkinson (*NYT*) enjoyed the offbeat writing, which he called "boogie-woogie drama played on a piccolo." Wilella Waldorf (*NYP*) thought it "as crazily philosophical, as amusingly imaginative, as meaninglessly fascinating as some of Saroyan's earlier and longer works." George Freedley (*NYMT*) loved it, thinking it "an amazingly good play about life," but declared it to have been ruined by the director's tampering. Others thought it unnecessarily loquacious and repetitious. Arthur Pollock (*BE*) panned it by saying that the author "hasn't a useful idea in his head and if he had he would get it twisted trying to write a play about it."

The piece, which is reminiscent of later absurdist drama, is set in Callaghan's, a bar and restaurant on East Fifty-second Street, in which Thomas Piper (Anthony Jochim), the philosophical waiter, notices the audience watching and starts talking to them, which the other characters, with some embarrassment, begin to do as well. Young Harry Mallory (Bernarr Cooper) enters and engages in conversation with the other customers. He then makes the waiter sit down while he waits on him; when the waiter acts aggressively, Harry fawns on him. Rhinelander 2-8182 (Betty Bartley), Harry's girlfriend, arrives by cab and gives birth to her child by Harry (a Filipino dishwasher midwifes it), and the cabdriver (Leonard Yorr) remains to join the talkfest. The child, named Callaghan Mallory (Clement Brace), grows to manhood instantly, appearing with the next day's paper announcing the end of current reality. Various topics purporting to be about contemporary concerns are bruited about as the confusion between illusion and reality is explored. It is revealed that all of the characters are dead and that the street outside no longer exists. Then they are alive again, and the street too returns. Near the close, the bartender tells the taxi driver about a horse named Tomorrow Morning, which the taxi driver says he'll play across the board.

(2) "ACROSS THE BOARD ON TOMORROW MORNING" and **"TALKING TO YOU"** [One-Acts] A/D: William Saroyan; S: Cleon Throckmorton; P: Saroyan Theatre; T: Belasco Theatre; 8/17/42 (8)

"Across the Board on Tomorrow Morning" [Dramatic Revival]; "Talking to You" [Drama/Blacks/Crime/Invalidism/Romance/Sports/Youth]

William Saroyan started his own producing company to put on this revival of "Across the Board on Tomorrow Morning" and a new one-act, "Talking to You." The first was characterized by Brooks Atkinson (*NYT*) as "a comic, spontaneous stage gambol that Mr. Saroyan has neglected to bring to life in the theatre." Black actor Canada Lee took the part of Thomas Piper, Callaghan was played by Edward F. Nannery, Harry was played by Irving Morrow, Rhinelander 2-8182 was acted by

Lillian McGuinness, Callaghan Mallory was played by William Prince, Lewis Charles was the cabdriver, and Maxwell Bodenheim (a well-known Greenwich Village poet who now seemed a wreck of his former self) played the Poet, reading one of his own works, "Jazz Music." The play was too intimate for a full-scale Broadway theatre, thought some, while its inconclusive ending proved widely disturbing. Louis Kronenberger (*PM*) commented, "Saroyan is trying to show that there is no life left in people, that they merely repeat one another and bask in the illusion of living. But he says it in a mere spate of words, words that not only make no sense, but that contain no poetry."

"Talking to You," which Kronenberger characterized as "a maudlin and melodramatic piece of drivel about the goodness and evil in the world," again starred Canada Lee, this time as a prizefighter named Blackstone Boulevard. Blackstone is a champion boxer, but his abilities are marred by a streak of integrity that prevents him from harming decent people. He adopts as his brother a deaf, white runaway (Jules Leni). There is also a blind man named the Tiger (Irving Morrow), who is in love with a girl named Maggie (Lillian McGuinness), and who provides Blackstone with philosophical advice. The play contrives a miracle by which the deaf boy finds the gift of speech, which brings ecstatic happiness to the pugilist. A dangerous ex-con named Fancy Dan (Lewis Charles) threatens the fighter with a gun but is pursued by a goosestepping, German-speaking midget (Andrew Ratousheff). When Blackstone goes to the aid of Fancy Dan and tries to protect the boy, the midget kills him.

Howard Barnes (*NYHT*) characterized the plays by noting, "At times they are vibrant with eloquence, meaning and humanity. As often, they are the product of an undisciplined exuberance which becomes little short of embarrassing." There was considerable confusion about Saroyan's metaphysics, which seemed pretentious and even meaningless. Most agreed that the plays were ineptly directed and needed cutting, especially the first with its several tiresome monologues delivered by the waiter. Rosamond Gilder (*TAM*), for example, wrote that both "were badly directed and poorly cast; but, as with everything [Saroyan] touches, they had a saving grace of imagination and of a kind of joyous playfulness."

Lee received accolades, John Mason Brown (*NYWT*) declaring, "The evening's only recommendation is Canada Lee. He is an admirable actor, possessed of a versatility which his fine performance in *Native Son* did not suggest."

ADDING MACHINE, THE [Dramatic Revival*] A: Elmer Rice; D: Robert Eley; S: Janet Owen; L: Dey Urban; P: New York Repertory Group; T: Cherry Lane Theatre (OB); 11/48

A barely noticed Off-Broadway revival of Rice's 1923 expressionist drama about the fate of Mr. Zero (Arthur Lewis), a dully conventional white-collar worker, done by a new company. William Hawkins (*NYWT*) praised the group for its "highly interesting" production, which allowed some of the action to spill over into the tiny playhouse's aisles and which made use of interesting lighting effects to create ominous shadows. The acting, however, was flat and unnuanced, although future star Beatrice Arthur turned in a good job as Zero's shrewish wife.

AFFAIRS OF ANATOL, THE [Dramatic Revival*] A: Arthur Schnitzler; AD: Harley Granville-Barker; D: Mady Christians; S: Gerhard Henshke; L: Hans Sondheimer; P: Herbert Kenwith for Equity Library Theatre; T: George Bruce Branch of the New York Public Library (OB); 6/5/46 (4)

The last revival of Schnitzler's *fin de siècle* tale of the eponymous Viennese Casanova had been in 1931, with Joseph Schildkraut. It was now given in a showcase presentation directed by Mady Christians, a leading Broadway actress who also happened to have played Lona (played now by Barbara March) in the 1924 Berlin revival directed by Max Reinhardt. Only George Freedley (*NYMT*) covered it for the press, and he wrote, "This is certainly the most expert production which E. L. T. has had in its three seasons' existence."

The interesting cast experimented with mingling some highly experienced actors and some rank novices. The veterans were involved because the piece gave them a chance to play roles for which they would never have been considered in the commercial theatre. Carmen Mathews, a respected actress of somber roles, proved "a brilliant young comedienne," Tonio Selwart was strongly approved as Anatol, Henry Jones was "as droll a comedian as [Freedley had] ever seen" as Max, and good work was offered by Eleanor Anton and Barbara Anderson.

AFRICAPERS [Revue/Blacks] P: Jimmy Payne; T: New York Times Hall; 5/14/44 (1)

A familiar assortment of black revue numbers produced on a Sunday evening at the former Little Theatre. The most notable feature was a preponderance of frankly erotic dancing, greeted with warm enthusiasm by the audience in the balcony. George Freedley (*NYMT*), apparently the only critic attending, could not make out the program well enough in the dark to note the names of most of the performers. He did remark that a quartet of pretty females introduced four new songs by Robert Hugh Cloud. "They fixed their eyes and keyed their performance to what appeared to be a 'dead' mike without any consideration of the audience. . . . It was an altogether ridiculous affair." The program included Juano Hernandez, the well-known actor, doing an outstanding job as a dialect comedian. Songs, drumming, dances, and storytelling filled out the bill.

AH, WILDERNESS! [Dramatic Revival*] A: Eugene O'Neill; D: Eva Le Gallienne; S: Watson Barratt; P: Theatre Guild; T: Guild Theatre; 10/2/41 (29)

The first New York revival of O'Neill's popular 1933 comedy about young love in small-town New England in 1906 was generally approved. It was the first of a series of low-priced ($.55 to $2.20) revivals staged this season by the Guild. George Freedley (*NYMT*) said that the passage of time "had not dimmed its virtues," Brooks Atkinson (*NYT*) thought it "the best play of the season so far," and Richard Lockridge (*NYS*) declared, "The play is there in all its gentle warmth and all its quiet laughter." It proved a refreshingly nostalgic reminder about a decent America for those frightened by the heated state of world affairs. Some thought it even an improvement over the original. Its major drawback was a too-leisurely pace; many thought that the work was overlong, and that the scene on the beach, in particular, needed cutting.

The new cast was a first-rate one. To a few critics, William Prince's Richard was a bit too self-assured and mature, but others thought him outstanding. Freedley commented, for example, "His youth, honesty and common decency shine forth through his modesty, through his wind-blown poetic moments. It is a deeply felt and keenly satisfying performance." Although the critics differed on individuals, it was generally agreed that expert work was contributed by Harry Carey as the gruff Nat Miller, a role in which Carey, with a manner more Montana than Connecticut, could not quite erase the memory of its creator, George M. Cohan; Ann Shoemaker as Essie, his wife; Tom Tully as the drunken Sid Davis; Enid Markey as the spinster Lily; Dennie Moore as Belle, the tart; Dorothy Littlejohn as Muriel; Victor Chapin as Arthur; Virginia Kaye as Mildred; and Zachary Scott, not yet a star, as the bartender.

When this revival was in the casting process, actress Ruth Gilbert applied to the Theatre Guild and asked producer Theresa Helburn to consider her for the role of Muriel. According to George Jean Nathan's *TBY* (1942-1943), Helburn exclaimed that Gilbert was "altogether too young for the part!" the producer completely ignorant of the fact that the same actress had played the part in the original production eight years earlier.

ALCHEMIST, THE [Dramatic Revival] A: Ben Jonson; M: Deems Taylor; D: Morton Da Costa; S/L: Herbert Brodkin; C: Emeline Roche; P: City Center Theatre Company; T: City Center of Music and Drama; 5/6/48 (14)

One of the plays offered in the series initiated at City Center by actor-producer José Ferrer. Jonson's then rarely seen 1610 ribald romp was the second of his plays to be offered by the company, which earlier in the year had shown *Volpone**. Although not a total success, this worthwhile but difficult comedy bested *Volpone* in critical esteem because of its superior production. The play itself, however, was deemed less important than *Volpone* because its satire on greed was not as incisive and its targets not as impressive. Its five acts were compressed into two, some discernible chunks were taken from the text, and a prologue was provided to clarify the exposition.

Brooks Atkinson (*NYT*) found its plot "tedious." Richard Watts, Jr. (*NYP*), de clared that the presentation, "for all its essential richness and vitality, lacked bite and power" and was marred by too much "antic" fooling on the part of the cast. But Robert Coleman (*NYDM*) said that the company played the piece "to the hilt, with such gusto and style as would have pleased an Elizabethan audience." Euphemia Van Rensselaer Wyatt (*CW*) concluded that "this is . . . the consummate production of a text which could be immensely tedious were it not for the cast's appreciation of every shade of wit and their expert characterizations." George Jean Nathan (*TBY*), responding to critics who faulted the production for guying the action for easy laughs, had no similar objections because he agreed that it was necessary to rid the play of its library odor.

The tale concerns what happens when Lovewit (Bert Thorn), the master of a house, places it under the protection of his unscrupulous servant, Face (Ferrer), the latter then taking up with a quack alchemist named Subtle (George Coulouris) who says that he can turn base metals into gold. The pair, along with Subtle's wench of a mistress, Doll Common (Nan McFarland), undertake to use Subtle's alleged skills to fleece the gullible townsfolk, which they do until the master returns and Face discards his acquaintances and manages to put a good face on things.

Ezra Stone was the credulous, licentious Sir Epicure Mammon, Ray Walston (in a widely praised performance) was shopkeeper Abel Drugger, Phyllis Hill was Dame Pliant, Leonardo Cimino was the Second Officer, and Hiram Sherman was the foolish but well-heeled Kestril.

ALICE IN ARMS [Comedy/Military/Romance/Sex/Small Town] A: Ladislas Bus-Fekete, Sidney Sheldon, and Mary Helen Fay; D: Jack Daniels; S: Frederick Fox; P: Edward Choate and Marie Louise Elkins; T: National Theatre; 1/31/45 (5)

A tripartite team of dramatists were too many cooks for this romantic comedy about the love life of a returning soldier who happens to be a WAC. "Mechanically put together and with dialogue so wooden as to splinter, it defeats the usually charming talents of Peggy Conklin . . . , and ambles along as a sort of sophomoric grade-B show," grumbled Lewis Nichols (*NYT*).

Alice (Conklin) returns from three years of military service in France to her small home town of Linwood, Pennsylvania. Walter (Roger Clark), a local engineer to whom she was formerly engaged, expects to marry her, but his hopes are dashed when Sergeant Steve Grant (Kirk Douglas), with whom Alice spent a romantic furlough in Paris, shows up, followed by another amorously inclined serviceman, the colonel (G. Albert Smith) for whom Alice was the secretary overseas. After some complications concerning who will win the prize, it goes to the handsome Steve.

Kirk Douglas, still ascending the steep road to fame, did not make a great impression, nor did any of the others trapped in this flop. Florence Shirley, Judith Abbott, and Tom McElhaney were among the victims of this piece that George Jean Nathan (*TBY*) termed "a knock-kneed paraphrase of *Dear Ruth* and without the slightest infection of merit."

ALICE IN WONDERLAND [Dramatic Revival*] A: Eva Le Gallienne and Florida Friebus; M: Richard Addinsell; D: Eva Le Gallienne; CH: Ruth Wilton; S: Robert Rowe Paddock, C: Noel Taylor (masks and marionettes: Remo Bufano); P: Rita Hassan and the American Repertory Theatre; T: International Theatre; 4/5/47 (100)

A very well liked revival of the popular and faithful 1932 adaptation of Lewis Carroll's *Alice in Wonderland* and *Through the Looking Glass*, with the sets and costumes cleverly adapted from the original John Tenniel drawings accompanying the texts. The tour de force role of Alice, who is practically never offstage, was played by dancer Bambi Linn, the White Rabbit by William Windom (who also played the Gentleman Dressed in White Paper) alternating with Julie Harris, the Mouse and Humpty Dumpty by Henry Jones, the Duck and 2 of Spades by Eli Wallach, the Red Chess Queen and Cheshire Cat by Margaret Webster, the March Hare and Eaglet by Arthur Keegan, the White Queen by director Le Gallienne, Tweedledum by Robert Rawlings, Tweedledee and the Gryphon by Jack Manning, the Duchess by Raymond Greenleaf, the Mad Hatter by Richard Waring, the Queen of Hearts by John Becher, the Mock Turtle by Angus Cairns, the King of Hearts by Eugene Stuckmann, and the White Knight by Philip Bourneuf.

The production, said Brooks Atkinson (*NYT*), proved "to be a little masterpiece of humorous fantasy, . . . freshened by a new production and acted with originality and relish." John Mason Brown (*SR*) noted, "Dramatically, it does not build or try to build. It merely continues, going forward almost in the Red Queen's fashion. But, unmade as it may be as a play, it is well-packed as a trunk." On the other side of the fence was George Jean Nathan (*TBY*), who failed to find the material worthy of rejoicing and suspected that it would not go down well with contemporary youths, who liked their entertainment expressed in more violently melodramatic terms.

Bambi Linn stole many critics' hearts with her sylphlike dancer's grace, long, blond hair, and innocent charm, yet Nathan insisted on referring to her as "a hearty ballet dancer with limbs approaching the contours of the jeroboam," unlike the "fragile and dreamful little creature" of Tenniel. More common were opinions like George Freedley's (*NYMT*) that "she makes all others who have essayed the role before mere tintypes. Hers is a lovely, spirited, tenuous, limpid, graceful and incredibly beautiful Alice." Almost every one of the other principals in the large cast was singled out for much praise, with special attention going to director-coadaptor Le Gallienne herself for her "thoroughly disorganized and fluttery White Queen" (Euphemia Van Rensselaer Wyatt [*CW*]).

The tuneful score, providing not only several fine songs but a nearly continuous underscoring of the action, and the lavish decor were loudly applauded as well. Still, there was some feeling that the piece erred on the side of overproduction, that some of the scenes could have been omitted as not being especially necessary to the story, and that ten or fifteen minutes could have been edited out. The railway carriage scene was considered a major offender. There was also a problem with audibility, particularly for those characters wearing the brilliantly designed masks created by Remo Bufano.

The short-lived American Repertory Company offered five other productions during the season. *Alice in Wonderland* was the company's most successful production and shifted to the Majestic Theatre in 5/48.

ALIVE AND KICKING [Revue] SK: Ray Golden, I. A. L. Diamond, Henry Morgan, Jerome Chodorov, Joseph Stein, Will Glickman, and Michael Stuart; M: Hal Borne, Irma Jurist, and Sammy Fain; LY: Paul Francis Webster and Ray Golden; ADD.M/LY: Sonny Burke, Leonard Gershe, Billy Kyle, and Sid Kuller ("special music and lyrics": Harold Rome); D: Robert H. Gordon; CH: Jack Cole; S/C: Raoul Pène du Bois; L: Mason Arvold; P: William R. Katzell and Ray Golden; T: Winter Garden; 1/17/50 (46)

A talent-packed musical and comedy revue that was more dead and rigid than alive and kicking and lasted less than two months. Its cast included comic actors David Burns, Carl Reiner, and Jack Gilford, singer-comedienne Lenore Lonergan, Jack Cole and his dancers (including Gwen Verdon--in her Broadway debut--and Bobby Van), and Jack Cassidy.

A commonly shared opinion was Howard Barnes's (*NYHT*): "There are occasional interludes of amusing satire, agile dancing and attractive chanting. . . . Generally they serve to emphasize the show's over-all lack of style and design." "This is a rather lack-luster carnival handicapped by uncommonly dull sketch materials and tunes," offered Rowland Field (*NEN*). Even the usually imaginative choreography of Jack Cole, meant to be the major contribution of the show, was not enough to salvage it. "Cole's dance style," lamented Robert Coleman (*NYDM*), "pseudo-Hindu embroidery on the modern dance form, becomes a bit taxing after many viewings." But Brooks Atkinson (*NYT*) declared, "Every step and movement . . . is bizarre and graphic. . . . Mr. Cole is a superb dancer. His is like a macabre manikin out of a decadent show-window, with sharp features, spectral eyes and a bullet head. When he dances he is all unearthly fire and flickering motion--his fingers dancing as wildly as his feet." Verdon, Cole's assistant, also received some critical attention.

The best numbers were "Meet the Authors," a fast-paced spoof of a literary luncheon, with Reiner, Lonergan, and Burns, the latter as an angry writer lecturing on urbanity; Lonergan's singing of Harold Rome's "Cry, Baby, Cry," backed up by Rae Abruzzo and Laurel Shelby; Cole's dance routines of "Abou Ben Adham," "Calypso Celebration," "Propinquity," and "Cole Scuttle Blues"; "Hippocrates Hits the Jackpot," a burlesque of doctors in which Burns performed an operation for a radio giveaway show called "Stop the Operation"; "French without Tears," a routine in which Lonergan burlesqued French chanteuse Edith Piaf; a bit starring Reiner as an Elizabethan actor auditioning for a part in a Shakespeare play; and a skit in which Gilford quit smoking but could not resist swallowing the smoke from his neighbor's cigarette and even had to shoot a pistol in order to inhale its fumes.

ALL FOR ALL [Comedy/Business/Friendship/Labor/Romance] A: Norman Bruce; SC: Aaron Hoffman's play, *Give and Take**; D: Harry Green; S: A. A. Ostrander; P: A. L. Berman; T: Bijou Theatre; 9/29/43 (85)

A revised version of a 1923 Broadway comedy about capital and labor. Norman Bruce was a pseudonym for a team of adaptors who chose to keep their names secret. They updated the old farce by inserting contemporary references to rationing and the draft. It starred dialect comedians Jack Pearl and Harry Green (who also directed) in what proved to be a "piece of theatrical shoddy" (Howard Barnes [*NYHT*]) that could not sustain interest all evening, despite the actors' best efforts. It was Pearl's debut in a legitimate play. He and Green were often very funny as Potash- and Perlmutter-like characters, but the evening seemed like a vaudeville sketch stretched beyond endurance to fill up three acts.

More a revival than a new play, the piece concerned John Bauer, Jr. (Lyle Bettger), newly graduated from college and filled with progressive labor ideas. His father (Pearl), who owns a California fruit-canning company, puts the firm in his son's hands. The latter, in consort with his father's friend, Albert Kruger (Green), the dimwitted foreman, sets up an "industrial democracy" in the plant. Bauer, Sr., and his foreman end their friendship, and the new plan practically wrecks the business, whose mortgage is on the verge of being foreclosed until an eccentric millionaire (Loring Smith) appears with a scheme that saves the firm. The old friends are reunited, and the romantic complications of the son with the foreman's daughter (Flora Campbell) are ironed out.

"Dialogue, plot and style are all so old-fashioned as to be quaint," scoffed Arthur Pollock (*BE*). The production marked the return of the intimate and renovated Bijou Theatre to the Broadway ranks (there was then a theatre shortage) after a seven-year period.

ALL FOR LOVE [Dramatic Revival*] A: John Dryden; D: Iza Itkin Caden; S: Douglas Barton; P: Equity Library Theatre; T: Fort Washington Branch of the New York Public Library (OB); 5/27/46 (4)

A rare revival of Dryden's Restoration period retelling of Shakespeare's *Antony and Cleopatra*, given a very low budget showcase presentation with unknown actors. Roland von Weber was Antony, Judith Wister was Cleopatra, Susan Roy was Octavia, Joel Marston was Dolabella, and Joel J. Thomas was Ventidius. The sole critic attending, George Freedley (*NYMT*), thought that "the old play makes an extremely interesting performance on the stage," that Wister acted "with conviction and inspired belief," and that Weber's "Antony was authoratative and remarkably persuasive."

ALL FOR LOVE [Revue] SK: (editor) Max Shulman; M/LY: Allan Roberts and Lester Lee; D: Edward Reveaux; CH: Eric Victor; S: Edward Gilbert; C: Billy Livingston; P: Sammy Lambert and Anthony Brady Farrell; T: Mark Hellinger Theatre; 1/22/49 (141)

This uninspired musical and comedy revue was brightly designed but dully written and wasted the performances of Grace and Paul Hartman, the comic dancers who headlined the show. Another star involved was comic Bert Wheeler. None came off well, a sign of the show's poor planning being the inclusion of barely any dance material for the Hartmans.

The show was the first to play at the Mark Hellinger, a newly rechristened theatre (named after a figure well known in the Broadway area) formerly called the Warner Brothers Hollywood Theatre and up to now a movie house. Its owner, a wealthy Albany businessman named Anthony Brady Farrell, had paid $1,500,000 for it and another $250,000 to renovate it. The revue that opened the theatre cost an additional $200,000, money that most critics thought unwisely spent. The sketches were considered inadequate and tedious, the music and lyrics consistently uninteresting, and very little else original or worthy of note.

Among its mediocre sketches was a parody of the play *Edward, My Son* called "Morris, My Son," while a big production number set in 1899 was about the Hudson River day steamer the *Benjamin B. O'Dell.* Slightly better were a pair of sketches featuring the Hartmans spoofing television and deep sea diving (Paul fished up a mermaid in the latter), and forcing Paul to contend with various comic props. Wheeler's most commented-on bit was his description of a female wrestling match in which, with falsies, he imitated one of the combatants. Leni Lynn and Dick Smart were featured singers and June Graham and Milada Mladova the chief dancers. Dancer-singer Patricia Wymore was appreciated by a few for her contributions.

Brooks Atkinson (*NYT*) found little to praise, blaming even the Hartmans: "Paul always carries that dismal face around with him, looking sullen, stupid, fatuous, bewildered, and resentful by turns; and Grace always retains that embarrassed, toothing giggle. . . . [However,] they have not mastered either the props or the timing. They have never looked like such shoddy workmen as they do now." Ward Morehouse (*NYS*) said that this was "A production of unlimited expenditure, overpowering ineptitude, and unfathomable dullness."

ALL IN FAVOR [Comedy/Romance/Sex/Youth] A: Louis Hoffman and Don Hartman; D: Elliott Nugent; S: Samuel Leve; P: Elliott Nugent, Robert Montgomery, and Jesse Duncan; T: Henry Miller's Theatre; 1/20/42 (7)

A group of adolescents in a Washington Heights boys' club decide that to increase their revenues and provide themselves with money to pay their $30 rental arrears, they will allow some girlfriends to join the club. Three girls arrive, leading to complications. Wack Wack (Raymond Roe) finds himself falling in love and spending the night--innocently--with the Brooklyn girl, Cynthia (Frances Heflin), when she loses her purse and finds herself without funds to get home to Sheepshead Bay. Both are aspiring musicians. Wack Wack's twelve-year-old brat brother Peewee (Tommy Lewis) blackmails him so that he, Peewee, can get into the club. After various other developments, the club's treasury is saved when Peewee wins some money on a radio quiz show.

The characters were all stock types, many of them offensive, none of them honest; the language was considered unpleasantly profane; the acting was raucous; and the principal importance of the piece resided in its opportunity for Frances Heflin (sister of actor Van Heflin) to shine. Ralph Warner (*DW*) wrote, "She reveals a talent which makes it certain that she will rise to the front ranks of the current ingenue crop. She is an actress with depth, charm and sincerity."

The play also provided Arnold Stang as Weasel a role for his Broadway debut, and veteran J. C. Nugent (father of the director) was one of the few adults in the cast. Said Richard Lockridge (*NYS*) of the play, "It is scatter-brained comedy of adolescence, full of toy emotions and kiddie-kar humor."

ALL IN FUN [Revue] SK: Virginia Faulkner, Charles Sherman, Everett Marcy, and Howard Barse. M/LY: Baldwin Bergersen, June Sillman, John Rox, Glen Bacon, Irvin Graham, Will Irwin, Pembroke Davenport, and S. K. Russell; D: Edward Clarke Lilley (dialogue), John Murray Anderson, and Leonard Sillman; CH: Marjery Fielding; S: Edward Gilbert; C: Irene Sharaff; P: Leonard Sillman; T: Majestic

Theatre; 12/27/40 (3)

As Rosamond Gilder (*TAM*) observed, "Bill 'Bojangles' Robinson, rolling his eyes, relishing his lines, murmuring encouragement and surprise to his incredibly agile feet, exuding ebony gaiety and the joy of life, was the high water mark of" this otherwise pedestrian musical revue costing $110,000. Robinson's numbers included a trademark staircase dance and a highlight that showed how he would be dancing forty years hence.

The work was composed of an ill assortment (in two acts and twenty-five scenes) of sketches, songs, and dance numbers. Impish Imogene Coca had weak material that allowed her to score only sporadically. Her best numbers showed her spoofing modern dance ("Afternoon of a Faun"), portraying a frazzled shopper during cocktail hour, and garnering laughs with Pert Kelton as a pair of erotically inclined traveling saleswomen enticing their boyfriends to their hotel room. The best comic material, however, belonged to burlesque comedian Red Marshall, who moved freely in and out of the show to revive it whenever it began to suffer palpitations. His best sketch, "A Matter of Principle," with Pert Kelton and David Morris, revealed him as a lunch-counter man arguing ferociously with a customer over the cost of a biscuit. He was also funny in a Pullman car sketch and as a dental patient. Others on hand included roller-skating comedian and MC Paul Gerrits, dancers Don Loper and Maxine Barratt, singer Marie Nash, who sang the best song, "How Did It Get So Late in the Morning?," dance team Anita Alvarez and William Archibald, and Wynn Murray, an energetic comic singer known for her ample girth but whose new streamlined figure seemed to rob her of both fun and personality. Kelcey Allen (*WWD*) spoke for many when he said, "*All in Fun* turned out to be a noisy and mediocre musical, with an undistinguished score and not too well supplied with comedy."

This show had encountered considerable trouble in the tryout period when comic Phil Baker, who was not only to star, but was coproducer and a heavy backer, pulled out because of disagreements over certain cast members and a dislike for some of his material. The show then underwent considerable alteration and remained on the road for a few extra weeks before coming to New York and being immediately trashed.

ALL MEN ARE ALIKE [Comedy/British/Marriage/Military/Sex/War] A: Vernon Sylvaine; D: Harry Wagstaff Gribble; S: Frederick Fox; P: Lee Ephraim; T: Hudson Theatre; 10/6/41 (32)

A "heavy-handed" (Rosamond Gilder [*TAM*]) British farce memorable solely for the comic antics of master clown Bobby Clark, who appeared in glassless spectacles instead of his trademark eyeglasses painted on his face. The piece, produced as *Women Aren't Angels* in London, where it was a hit, was set in Alfred Bandle's (Reginald Denny) country residence, where the lounge hall contained eight doors--four leading to bedrooms--that came into frequent and violent use in the course of the frantic action, especially when Clark was bounding in and out of them in the chase scenes. He even made an exit through the one large window by clinging to a hanging vine. The helter-skelter plot allowed the comedian to appear in kilts, in a union suit, in a rug held in place with a belt, and in his wife's naval auxiliary uniform.

In the summer of 1940, with London being blitzed, married marmalade manufacturer Bandle retreats to his Surrey country home for a rendezvous with sexy Frankie Marriott (Lillian Bond), not knowing that she has married, only to discover that his simpleminded American business partner, Wilmer Popday (Clark), has arrived as well in order to give his partner the company ledger. A bizarre assortment of other characters--including a Scottish deserter in kilts (Ian Martin), a brat (Milton Karol) evacuated from war-torn London, a beautiful spy (Jeraldine Dvorak), a Scotland Yard detective, and various military officers--also turn up on the premises. The principal action develops when the wives of Bandle and Popday (Cora Witherspoon and Velma Royton, respectively) and the French husband of Frankie (Rolfe Sedan) appear, with the husband the jealous type who runs after would-be seducers of his wife with a loaded pistol in hand. Some of the business required members of the cast--especially the more attractive female members--to run around in their underwear, and there was considerable humor of the blue variety, to which several critics objected.

The bulk of the reviews focused on how funny Clark was even in this clinker. Supporting him were several respectable troupers, including A. P. Kaye, Ethel Morrison, and, for several performances, director Gribble as Sidney Butch when the original actor, Eustace Wyatt, could not open because of illness. Concerning the play, George Freedley's (*NYMT*) was typical: "It became so incredible and so bad that I laughed in sheer annoyance and unbelief that anything like *All Men Are Alike* could still be produced."

ALL MY SONS [Drama/Business/Crime/Family/Marriage/Small Town/War] A: Arthur Miller; D: Elia Kazan; S/L: Mordecai Gorelik; C: Paul Morrison; P: Harold Clurman, Elia Kazan, and Walter Fried i/a/w Herbert H. Harris; T: Coronet Theatre; 1/29/47 (328)

This bombshell of a thesis drama represented Arthur Miller's first success. He was immediately heralded as a great white hope of the American theatre by some, while others had serious reservations. It was selected as the best American play of the season by the Drama Critics Circle and was one of Burns Mantle's ten best. Miller was inspired to write his play when he heard during the war of a war profiteer's daughter who, despite her love for her father, had exposed him and then left home. Its original title had been *The Sign of the Archer*.

Set in the backyard of the Keller home in a small town and transpiring in a single Sunday, it pictures the Keller family of Joe (Ed Begley), son Chris (Arthur Kennedy), and mother Kate (Beth Merrill). Larry, another son, has died in the war, although Kate finds this hard to accept and keeps believing that he is alive. Chris, a former army captain now in business with Joe, is in love with Larry's bereaved fiancée, Ann Deever (Lois Wheeler), but Kate opposes the match. It soon develops that Joe may have escaped imprisonment for the manufacture and sale to the air force of defective airplane cylinders, a crime that led to the deaths of twenty-one flyers. Joe's betrayed partner--Ann's father--took the rap for the deed and went to jail. When the truth--revealed in Larry's last letter to Ann--comes out, Joe claims not only that he had placed loyalty to his family--for whom he had to provide a living--ahead of patriotism but that he was driven by the profit motive. The idealistic Chris--previously convinced of Joe's innocence--confronts him in horror at the revelation. Joe discovers that Larry, racked by guilt when he learned of his father's complicity, killed himself. Joe realizes that "in sinning against other men's sons, he has sinned against his own" (Euphemia Van Rensselaer Wyatt [*CW*]), and deals with his moral irresponsibility by shooting himself.

Some believed that the Ibsenesque play's dialogue was biting and authentic, its characters sharply individualized, its structure dramaturgically sound and lifelike, and its theme of vast significance. Brooks Atkinson (*NYT*) hailed the new arrival, saying that Miller "brings something fresh and exciting into the drama. . . . It is a pitiless analysis of character that gathers momentum all evening and explodes with both logic and dramatic impact." "It has an urgency," wrote Rosamond Gilder (*TAM*), "an originality that augurs well for [Miller's] future . . . for he sets authentic characters in a situation that is sharply individual yet broad and vitally important in its implications." To Ward Morehouse (*NYS*), the complexly plotted play was "occasionally . . . fitful and spasmodic," but when dealing with its central issue had "extraordinary poignancy and power." But George Jean Nathan (*NYJA*) was unimpressed, believing the theme familiar and the treatment equally conventional. "It seems to me to be just another in the line of exhibits which misses out because it says what we already all too well know in a manner we already know as well, and in terms and language that are undistinguished." Howard Barnes (*NYHT*) reported that Miller "has an acute feeling for the theater and a certain sense of form, but he has not blended them in a satisfactory drama." He felt that the characters were more like puppets than self-motivated personages and that much of the action was contrived.

The production itself was lauded by most for its pulsing direction and vividly intelligent and emotional acting, especially that of Merrill, Begley, and Kennedy. Expert work also came from Karl Malden (as the partner's embittered son), John McGovern, Peggy Meredith, and Eugene Steiner.

According to Kazan's *Elia Kazan: A Life*, coproducer Clurman himself had wanted to direct the play and was very upset when Miller chose Kazan. This led to what Kazan called abominable behavior by Clurman at rehearsals. "His discipline . . . was that of a naughty child." Clurman would sit with a secretary, presumably giving notes, but laughing and talking loud enough for others to hear, or would be dallying sexually with another woman at his side. In these and other ways he made his presence unbearable for Kazan. Clurman also kept insisting to Kazan that the character of Mrs. Keller be made responsible for part of Keller's guilt, although Kazan resisted these suggestions. Kazan said Miller was influenced by them and tried rewriting the part, only to give up the attempt. However, in *Timebends*, Miller's autobiography, the playwright disclosed his belief that Mrs. Keller definitely shares her husband's guilt. That year was the first for the Tony awards, and Kazan won as best director.

ALL THE COMFORTS OF HOME [Dramatic Revival] A: William Gillette; REV: Helen Jerome; D: Arthur Sircom; S: Harry G. Bennett; C: Paul du Pont; P: Edith C. Ringling i/a/w Mollie B. Steinberg; T: Longacre Theatre; 5/25/42 (8)

An unsuccessful revival of Gillette's 1890 farce, based on Karl Lauf's German work, *Ein toller Einfall*. Its last revival had been in 1901. The original version starred Henry Miller and Maude Adams in the roles of Alfred Hastings and Evangeline Bender. These parts were now taken by Gene Jerrold and Florence Williams.

All the Comforts of Home seemed dull, dated, and unfunny in 1942. The staging was in the frenzied door-slamming mode. Richard Watts, Jr. (*NYHT*), commented, "A laborious farce, full of mechanical complications and misunderstandings, it goes its hoary and quavering way, reminding us that the Gay Nineties may not have been so hilarious after all."

Its story was about how Alfred, an impecunious young doctor, and his friend Tom McDow (Oliver B. Prickett) decide to cash in on Alfred's position as guardian of his uncle's (William David) home by turning it into a rooming house while the uncle, thinking that his wife (Grace McTarnahan) is deceiving him, leaves home for the Continent with her and his daughter (Peggy Van Vleet) in tow. Alfred takes in a wild assortment of screwball lodgers, various complications ensue, Alfred and his fiancée call it quits, romance blossoms for Alfred and Evangeline, daughter of a produce dealer (Nicholas Joy) lodging in the house, and all else is put to rights when the uncle returns.

Dorothy Sands did well in the role of Josephine Bender, nagging wife of the produce dealer, and Celeste Holm was noticed as Fifi Oritanski, a flirtatious opera singer.

ALL THE KING'S MEN [Drama/Crime/Journalism/Marriage/Politics/Sex/Southern] A: Robert Penn Warren; D: Erwin Piscator; S: Willis Knighton; L: Hans Sondheimer; P: Dramatic Workshop of the New School for Social Research (OB); T: President Theatre (OB); 1/18/48 (21)

Normally preoccupied with foreign authors, Erwin Piscator's Dramatic Workshop, operating on a minimal budget, produced a new American play with *All the King's Men*. Although based on the author's 1947 Pulitzer Prize novel (itself an outgrowth of an earlier attempt at a blank-verse play called *Proud Flesh*), it was not a commercial success, but it did lead to an important movie.

Warren's dramatization never came to life, and its presentation seemed to George Freedley (*NYMT*) "more like a reading of the novel than the acting of a play upon the stage." Joe Pihodna (*NYHT*) thought that the play's twenty-three scenes moved "along rapidly and with sustaining interest," although he faulted Warren for being more of "a philosopher than a dramatist." Louis Kronenberger (*PM*), who argued that Piscator's direction had actually drawn attention to the drama's flaws, called the event "a sound experiment" but not "a sound play." Piscator's epic staging--making use of a revolving stage and projections--reminded some of the "living newspapers" of the 1930s. The competent but uninspired cast (except for Robert Osterloh in the lead) was composed of students and faculty of the Workshop.

Warren's drama concerns the rise and fall of a Huey Long-like Louisiana governor, with the politician's involvement in fathering an illegitimate child and being betrayed by his wife a significant but extraneous part of the story. The governor is Willie Stark (Osterloh) and he has risen from backwoods poverty to political demagoguery, but, his ruthless, fascistic behavior aside, he gets things done, including the building of bridges and the creation of hospitals. Still, he hurts too many people in his thrust to power and is eventually slain by one of his victims. To clarify the philosophical dimensions of the play, two choruslike figures on the apron--an apologist journalist (Dan Matthews) and a professor (Claude Traverse)--debate the arguments for and against dictatorship. The author's attitude toward the demagogue was ambiguous and seemed to take a sympathetic stance toward dictatorship under certain circumstances. Several critics noted Warren's questionable theme that the end justifies the means.

The story of the play's genesis is discussed in Maria Ley-Piscator's *The Piscator Experiment*. She revealed that Warren had not wanted the play to be directly political. "He wanted the facts of a man's life dressed up as poetic images. He did not want any lesson for society, any criticism of it. He wanted his play merely to interpret a world in which all paths lead to corruption, not to attack that world." Nor did he consider the play a biographical account of Huey Long. "Willie Stark was to him purely fictional." But, as shaped in Piscator's hands, the work became political theatre, wrote Ley-Piscator. She noted that Piscator realized that the play was dramaturgically flawed but was nevertheless the exemplification, although indirectly expressed, of a great moral truth about "the reality of a human being who in adversity capitulates."

ALL YOU NEED IS ONE GOOD BREAK [Comedy-Drama/Family/Gambling/Illness/Jews/Mental Illness/Prison/Romance] A: Arthur Manoff; SC: a short story of the same name by Arthur Manoff; D: John Berry and J. Edward Bromberg; S: Samuel Leve; C: Paul du Pont; L: Peggy Clark; P: Monte Proser and Joseph Kipness i/a/w Jack Small; T: Mansfield Theatre; 2/9/50 (4); 2/20/50 (32)

This is one of the rare cases where a play opened on Broadway to devastating pans, was quickly closed, was revised, and reopened shortly afterwards. The results the second time around were not better than the first, and the play was removed after a month.

Arthur Manoff's first play was considered earnest but unskillful and garrulously tiresome. It had thematic points in common with *Death of a Salesman* and stylistic suggestions of Clifford Odets's plays, but was clumsy, shallow, and burdened by a tedious central character who would not stop talking. Rowland Field (*NEN*) said that it "is a crudely composed and acted exhibit that carries on interminably about the character deficiency of a worthless social and economic misfit." Howard Barnes (*NYHT*) considered it "a pother of words which are equally devoid of meaning and emotion."

Martin Rothman (John Berry) is a pathological Bronx daydreamer whose dreams are built on shifting sands. A victim of self-dramatizing illusions, this shipping clerk earning $35 a week believes that he is somehow different and destined for success and wealth, the only thing preventing him from achieving his goals being the elusive lucky break. At home his failure of a father (Reuben Wendorf), invalid mother (Anna Appel), and teenage sister (Ellie Pine) look to him to support them. Gambling debts begin to choke him. He tries to make a fortune by playing--with money borrowed from a druggist (J. Edward Bromberg)--the number 623, seen by his mother in a dream. He also has a romantic interlude with a girl (Lee Grant, the playwright's wife) he met on the beach, his ulterior motive being to gain access to her brother's money. But all his dreams come to nothing, and after a disastrous final stab at finding his break in a crap game, he lands in jail, his mind crushed, while his mother lies in the charity ward of a hospital in need of a gallstone operation, with the rent unpaid and the electricity about to be shut off.

Martin's daydreams often came to life through the use of revolving stages and fanciful lighting effects, giving the show some technical, if not artistic, finesse. When tried out on the West Coast, the play was in a single act, but was expanded for Broadway. Comedian Milton Berle, present at opening night, quipped at the expense of the title, "All you need is one good act." The cast included Gene Saks, Shimen Ruskin, Phil Carter, Lee Krieger, Salem Ludwig, Lucille Patton, and others.

ALLAH BE PRAISED! [Musical/Politics/Romance/Sex] B/LY: George Marion, Jr.; M: Don Walker and Baldwin Bergersen; D: Robert H. Gordon and Jack Small; CH: Jack Cole; S: George Jenkins; C: Miles White; P: Alfred Bloomingdale; T: Adelphi Theatre; 4/20/44 (20)

The Adelphi Theatre (originally the Craig) on West Fifty-fourth Street was brought back into service during a Broadway theatre shortage to house this "second-rate" and "drearily slow" (Lewis Nichols [*NYT*]) musical comedy. Apart from its highly effective sets and costumes, and some distinctive dance routines, the show had little to offer. Smutty humor, a shoddy and totally unbelievable libretto, out-of-context jokes about Lindy's, Broadway, and Hollywood, and a forgettable score doomed it to oblivion.

A sample of its humor was when, during a discussion of finances, one character said, "How did you get such an odd figure?" and the other replied, "I eat too much." Another went, "She's got a big asset," which fed the punch line, "Her face is all right, too." A number of fine performers could not praise Allah for their material. Among them were comic Joey Faye, nightclub comedian John Hoysradt (who dragged out his satire on a trio of famous radio commentators), singers Patricia Morison (whose voice was panned), Edward Roecker (in his Broadway bow), and Mary Jane Walsh, statuesque beauty Jayne Manners, and dancers the Kraft Sisters (Evelyne and Beatrice), Anita Alvarez, and Milada Mladova, among others.

The story, set a few years in the future in 1948, was about an emir (Hoysradt), a graduate of Dartmouth College, who returns to Persia, where he runs a harem with American girls, one for each day of the year. The ladies have come here because they are bored with life in America. He will have to give up the harem unless a lend-lease arrangement with America can be concluded. The nationality of the inmates brings on an investigation by a pair of U.S. senators, Tex O'Carroll (Roecker) of Texas and Marcia Mason Moore (Morison) of Maryland, who fall for one another. Tex's sister Carol (Walsh) is there as well, having been chosen to be the emir's 366th spouse, allowing her to wife it once every four years. Finally, the needed money comes from some suddenly discovered oil wells.

During the show's tryout period, producer Bloomingdale (of the department store Bloomingdales) asked play doctor Cy Howard what could be done to rescue the troubled production. Howard's reply, as reported by George Jean Nathan (*TBY*), was, "Throw it away, and keep the store open nights."

ALLEGRO [Musical/Family/Marriage/Medicine/Romance/Sex/Small Town] B/LY: Oscar Hammerstein II; M: Richard Rodgers; D/CH: Agnes de Mille; S/L: Jo Mielziner; C: Lucinda Ballard; P: Theatre Guild; T: Majestic Theatre; 10/10/47 (315)

This ambitious musical--selected as one of the ten best works of the season--by the most successful composer-lyricist team of the decade was widely hailed for its grace, simplicity, and originality, but it had many detractors as well. *Allegro* was the first Rodgers and Hammerstein musical stemming from a script not based on an earlier play. The idea for the show--a biographical account of a fictional doctor's life, meant as an allegory of modern life--had come from Hammerstein, who had a close relationship with his doctor. Rodgers liked the story idea because his own father and brother were physicians. According to his *Musical Stages*, he also appreciated the questions raised by the tale: "How does a doctor maintain his integrity when tempted by an easy practice of wealthy hypochondriacs? How can he avoid compromising his principles when he is caught up in the politics of a large hospital?" They revised the original notion of a cradle-to-grave story to end it in the doctor's mid-thirties. Rodgers and Hammerstein were so busy with their various shows--they had become producers as well as a writing team--at this high point in their careers that they welcomed the chance to have the Theatre Guild relieve them of producing headaches by putting on this show. The show's relative failure, the first such of the Rodgers and Hammerstein collaborations, was something Hammerstein never forgot, and he was writing a revision for a television production when he died.

Music and dance were so closely sewn into the fabric of Hammerstein's seriously intended libretto that some thought it difficult to prophesy which numbers would outlast the show; among those that did were "A Fellow Needs a Girl" and the blues tune, "The Gentleman Is a Dope." (During the New Haven tryout, when Lisa Kirk was singing the latter number, she fell into the orchestra pit, was caught by a pair of cellists, was hoisted back onto the stage, and continued as if nothing had happened.) The unconventional format of the work led some to believe it a pioneer in the melding of music to a serious drama.

According to the program, "The story starts in 1905 on the day Joseph Taylor, Jr., is born, and follows his life to his thirty-fifth birthday." The plot, mingling humor (not enough) and sentiment (too much), was structured around the life of this everyman American character (John Battles), born in a small college town to country doctor Joseph (William Ching) and Marjorie Taylor (Annamary Dickey). Joe's early years are reported by his father, mother, and grandmother (Muriel O'Malley), and he does not appear until the age of sixteen. A shy youth, he goes to college while his sweetheart Jennie (Roberta Jonay) impatiently waits for him. After graduation he marries the grasping Jennie, whose cruel behavior causes Joe's mother to die of a heart attack (her ghost returns to advise her son). The young couple moves to Chicago after the 1929 crash, and Joe practices medicine at a large hospital, making a lot of money, but Jennie, who has become caught up in the social whirl of cocktail partying, cheats on him. Emily (Kirk), the nurse who loves him, is aware of the affair. After he discovers Jennie's infidelity, he divorces her and, turning down an impressive new position, returns home to fuse a romantic relationship with Emily.

To capture the show's essence as a legend, it was presented in a seemingly minimalist style that recalled *Our Town** for some, although a surprising amount of machinery (including loudspeakers, a revolve, treadmills, and background projections) was used. Hammerstein eventually realized that he had betrayed his own dream for the show in allowing it to become so complex. The artfully symbolic scenic units were shifted on rolling platforms without any waits for changes. Instead of *Our Town*'s Stage Manager, the action was accompanied by the narrative and editorial comments of a Greek tragedy-like singing and speaking chorus.

It was the need to have a director who could fuse all the elements of the show, narrative, songs, and dances, into a unity that led to the hiring of Agnes de Mille. De Mille perceived many book problems, observing that Hammerstein had not fully realized the work he had set out to write. According to Rodgers, she proved unable to handle her many chores, and Hammerstein ended up directing the book portions and Rodgers the songs, although neither was credited for these tasks. The rehearsals--which also involved much rewriting--were a horror. "It was not a satisfactory solution by any means," wrote Rodgers.

The reviews were interestingly mixed. Brooks Atkinson (*NYT*) considered it a work of "great beauty and purity" throughout its first act and lauded it for exquisite taste in manner and execution; he found, however, that it had a relatively "commonplace" second half that, because of the unhappy events following 1929, was an emotional letdown. Euphemia Van Rensselaer Wyatt (*CW*) saluted the show: "*Allegro* is full of understanding of the best and the cheapest in American life. The story is simple and so is the setting--to the eye--although the cost was fabulous. The values are sound; the sentiment rich; the music integrated and expressive."

Most agreed that the piece was staged with exceptional imagination, but some, like John Mason Brown (*SR*), argued that the book was "uninspired" and too schmaltzy to swallow, especially in its pitting the purity of small-town life against the corruption of the big city. George Jean Nathan (*TBY*) thought it "as pretentious as artificial jewelry, and just about as valuable."

Rodgers himself later agreed that the material was "too preachy." Among notable songs were "So Far," the capitalist satire, "Money Isn't Everything," and the cocktail-party satire, "Yatata, Yatata, Yatata." Despite the presence of several hits, none of the songs was on a level with the best of Rodgers and Hammerstein's earlier achievements. One of the reviewers, Richard Watts, Jr. (*NYP*), hearing Rodgers's old tune, "Mountain Greenery," played in the college prom scene, chided the composer for using this standard from his repertory. But Rodgers noted in his autobiography that he had been against using so obviously well known a selection of his own and had preferred to use something by Irving Berlin or George Gershwin, but had been talked into interpolating his own music. Agnes de Mille's choreography provided several of the balletic interludes (featuring dancer Kathryn Lee) for which she was renowned, and additional loveliness was offered in Mielziner's artful sets and Ballard's colorful costumes.

"ALMOST FAITHFUL" [Comedy/Blacks/Family/Marriage/Sex/Show Business] A/D: Harry Wagstaff Gribble; S: Richard Brown; L: George Lewis and Buster Hawkins; P/T: American Negro Theatre (OB); 6/4/48

Veteran Broadway writer-director Harry Wagstaff Gribble provided this light comedy (some thought it a farce)--whose title was written in quotation marks--for Harlem's chief black theatre company. The play was not specifically black in content and could have been acted by whites with few changes.

Frank Broderick (Dots Johnson) is a radio singer, married to Muriel Broderick (Alice Childress); he suffers a lapse from marital grace when he has an affair with a sexy, social-climbing pianist, Marlene Bruce (Yvonne Maedchen). The stage set shows both the apartment of the Broderick family in Harlem and that of the pianist on Riverside Drive. (The set was criticized for its excessive cramping of the action.) The long-suffering Mrs. Broderick uses her intelligence, patience, and self-reliance to quell the pianist's further designs on Frank.

The play showed promise, but was too complicated and overwrought to keep an audience continually interested. Brooks Atkinson (*NYT*) said that when the piece ended, "you are so exhausted from [Gribble's] infinite variations on a stereotyped theme that you feel you have seen three farces and two vaudeville units performing simultaneously in a psychopathic ward." "Lots of it is cliched," opined Herm. (*V*), "but the original moments are rewarding in their energetic humor."

Atkinson enjoyed the acting, but most others thought it "jangled and uncoordinated," as Thomas R. Dash (*WWD*) expressed it. Alice Childress received the warmest reviews. The cast included Inge Hardison, Frederick Carter, Hilda Haines, and Salvador Tomas.

ALONG FIFTH AVENUE [Revue] SK: Charles Sherman and Nat Hiken; M: Gordon Jenkins; LY: Tom Adair; ADD.M/LY: Richard Stutz, Milton Pascal, and Nat Hiken; D: Charles Friedman; CH: Robert Sidney; S: Oliver Smith; C: David Ffolkes; P: Arthur Lesser; T: Broadhurst Theatre; 1/13/49 (180)

The revue form--basically a somehow unified succession of songs, sketches, and dance routines--remained a frequent visitor to Broadway in the late forties, possibly because of the tourist trade's desire for light and undemanding entertainment. The 1948-1949 season offered several, the best being *Lend an Ear*. Several rungs down on the quality ladder from that show was *Along Fifth Avenue*, which failed to click despite such top entertainers as Jackie Gleason, Nancy Walker, Hank Ladd, and Carol Bruce to give it theatrical juice.

The theme tying this effort together was the street named in the title, and there were Fifth Avenue scenes set in places as diverse as Washington Square, Radio City, Harlem, and Lord and Taylor's department store, although one scene did digress to as far away as South America for what was becoming a standard ingredient in such shows, a rhumba number. Walker practically knocked herself silly to get a laugh in the scene. The lesser-known performers included eight-year-old black girl Judyth Burroughs, who, with Donald Richards, sang the delightful and much-noted "A Trip Doesn't Care at All."

The most noted moments included comedienne Walker's femme fatale torch song rendition of "Chant d'Amour" as sung to her "Irving." Bruce and Ladd were enjoyable together singing "Call It Applefritters," and there was a decent comedy song, "Mr. Rockefeller Builds His Dream House," presented by Ladd in the guise of John D. Rockefeller talking to a sightseeing group. "Skyscraper Blues," sung by Richards while ballet dancers Viola Essen, Zachary Solov, and others danced in the background, was fairly effective, as was "Challenge," danced by Essen and tap dancer Johnny Coy in a sort of competition between ballet and tap. Bruce, a critical favorite, included "Weep More" and "The Best Time of Day" among her better tunes. In one of the comedy numbers, set at Lord and Taylor's, a man was sprayed with a reputed aphrodisiac by the girl at the perfume counter (Walker), only to have a homosexual customer get turned on by him. Walker also garnered laughs in a sketch where her character downs poison, thinking it whiskey; while being interrogated by the police, she is told to keep moving to negate the effects of the poison, and her physical contortions sparked many guffaws. In another bit, three thirsty French foreign legionnaires entered, dying of thirst. Gleason then appeared, dressed immaculately in a legionnaire's uniform, with a skimpily dressed, gorgeous blond carrying his golf bags. He casually swept the other men aside, made a comically sweeping gesture with his arm, and, speaking in a high-toned voice, tore the house down with his line, "Do you mind if we play through?" In a cafeteria sketch, he received a custard pie in the face. Several critics commented on the normally overweight comic's newly svelte physique.

Despite enjoying a handful of routines, Brooks Atkinson (*NYT*) had the impression that the bulk of the program was mediocre and that the show lacked the air of freshness found in *Lend an Ear*. He complained as well of the show's wastefulness with regard to the talents of Walker and Gleason. In John Chapman's (*NYDN*) view, the show "is sprawling rather than compact, uncertain where it should be concise. Instead of being an extraordinarily pleasant revue, it is an ordinarily pleasant one." Howard Barnes (*NYHT*) judged the songs "uninspired and frequently vulgar" and Ladd's monologues "interminable." He added, "*Along Fifth Avenue* sprawls through some twenty-four scenes with a minimum of pace and almost no routining."

AMERICAN LEGEND [Revue] D: Mary Hunter; CH: Agnes de Mille; S: Joseph Anthony; C: John Pratt and Hugh Laing; P/T: American Actors Company (OB); 5/11/41

A Sunday-evening potpourri produced by a group of young Off-Broadway actors currently involved in a production of *Texas Town* by Horton Foote, one of its actors. Using their studio theatre at 108 West Sixteenth Street, they offered several one-acts, songs, and dances, the latter choreographed by Agnes de Mille, not yet recognized as a major dance arranger. Sets were by future director Joseph Anthony, who also danced in the program (he later served for a time as dance partner to de Mille).

Although E. P. Conkle's one-act, "Minnie Field," was among the unsuccessful elements, there were some pieces that were approved, including Paul Green's short folk play about farm life, "Saturday Night"; a musical satire called "Boston Singing School"; a musical piece by Andrew Rowan Summers called "Cherry Tree Carol," concerning the legend of Christ's birth; and the dance routines staged by de Mille, especially those with a decided country flavor to them. Brooks Atkinson (*NYT*) was disturbed by the actors' careless projection but concluded, "Despite several gestures toward art that are a pain at least in the neck . . . , there is enough fresh and joyous material in the bill to warrant an inquiring visit."

AND BE MY LOVE [Comedy/Family/Romance/Science/Sex/Theatre] A: Edward Caulfield; D: Arthur J. Beckhard; S: Raymond Sovey; P: Arthur J. Beckhard i/a/w Victor Hugo-Vidal; T: National Theatre; 2/21/45 (14)

There was much critical speculation as to why leading actor Walter Hampden would have wanted to waste his talent on this "meandering misdemeanor" (Robert Garland [*NYJA*]) that Rosamond Gilder (*TAM*) swore never rose "out of its pedestrian and amateur status." Lewis Nichols (*NYT*) said that the windy play was "another of those comedies which act like a pipe in the mouth of a cigarette smoker--all effort, no fun."

Hampden played John Hogarth, an aging matinee idol, famous for his charm, who seeks a respite from the pressures of his theatre life and acquaintances in the arms of some woman who does not know who he is and loves him for himself and not his reputation. He wanders by accident into a Lonely Hearts Get-Together and there, using the pseudonym of Henry Smith, meets such a woman, a pretty widow named Sarah Fenton (Lotus Robb, returning to the stage after a long retirement). They agree to take up residence in a "trial marriage" at her Riverhead, Connecticut, country home. Turning up there, however, are Sarah's daughter (Ruth Homond) and her meddling old-maid sister (Esther Dale). Not wanting to shock them, Sarah and Henry claim to be married. A pair of nosy neighbors (Edmonia Nolley and Sydney Grant) must also be mollified. When the truth about John and Sarah emerges, everyone is properly scandalized. Romantic complications also ensue between the daughter and a stupid sailor (Charles Colby). Things come to a head with the visit of John's leading lady, Ada Bennett (Violet Heming), who tries to lure the actor back to Broadway. It is now that everyone learns who "Henry" really is. John leaves for a week, but on the day that they had set for their wedding, he comes back to marry Sarah, who, to his surprise, turns out to be a famous research scientist. He will marry her, retire to the simple life, and take the job of Riverhead's water commissioner.

Many complained that the production was misdirected and that Hampden, never one to strike an audience's funny bone, had been sorely miscast as the actor, a role that required skillful self-parody. Jed Prouty, Viola Dean, and Graham Velsey were also in the cast.

AND SO THEY PERISH [Drama/Labor] A: Stacey Hill; D: Sara Harte; S/L: Karl Hueglin; C: John Collinsworth Wilkins; P: Footlight Players; T: Hudson Guild Theatre (OB); 4/17/50 (14)

A new Off-Broadway group presented this play in its basement theatre at 436 West Twenty-seventh Street. It told of the birth of a seamen's union, begun before World War I by Axel Thorson (Maury Hill), an able-bodied seaman disturbed by the cruel practices of shipping-trade management toward men of his ilk on the West Coast. Sailors are forced to sleep in foul conditions and eat rotten food. The politically balanced play depicts some of the malfeasance for which certain crooked union men are responsible.

"Although its theme is forbidding in relation to most of Broadway's productions," wrote Joe Pihodna (*NYHT*), "the play has a compelling topical appeal." Gros. (*V*) thought it "loaded with telescopic situations and forceless dialog."

ANDROCLES AND THE LION and **"POUND ON DEMAND"** S/C: Wolfgang Roth; P: American Repertory Theatre; T: International Theatre; 12/19/46 (40)
Androcles and the Lion [Dramatic Revival*] A: George Bernard Shaw; M: Marc Blitzstein; D: Margaret Webster; animal head: Remo Bufano; "Pound on Demand" [Comedy/Alcoholism/Irish] A: Sean O'Casey; D: Victor Jory

The fourth offering of the short-lived American Repertory Theatre was this double bill of Shaw's two-act comedy and O'Casey's one-act. The Shaw's most recent local productions had been in 1925 and 1938. O'Casey's work was being given its first New York showing. Among the actors in *Androcles* were John Becher (Lion), Ernest Truex (Androcles), Marion Evensen (Megaera), John Straub (Centurion), Richard Waring (Captain), June Duprez (Lavinia), Victor Jory (Ferrovius), Eli Wallach (Spintho), Efrem Zimbalist, Jr. (Secutor), William Windom (Retiarius), Raymond Greenleaf (Editor), and Philip Bourneuf (Caesar).

The play was very well received: its theme, once considered controversial because of a presumed spoofing of Christianity, was now understood as displaying great respect for Christian faith and humor. It was also considered timely as a demonstration of the principles for which men die. Brooks Atkinson (*NYT*) appreciated it because "it has the grace and inventiveness of a fairy story . . . , excellent and consistent characters and brilliant logic." George Jean Nathan (*TBY*) was surprised at how well its humor had held up. Rosamond Gilder (*TAM*) praised the beguiling production as "lively and diverting. It treads lightly on the grimmer aspects of its subject, insisting on Shaw the jester rather than Shaw the prophet."

Director Webster infused a healthy proportion of slapstick fun into the proceedings. John Mason Brown (*SR*), however, thought the "excessive buffoonery" a weakness because it partly smothered the play's true message. Truex was memorable in the leading part of the lovable, henpecked, quaking little man whose faith makes him big. There was outstanding work by Jory, Bourneuf, and Becher (dressed in a delightfully dignified lion mask). Duprez's Lavinia was a serious disappointment. (Nathan was almost alone in thinking all the performances "incompetent.") Also not liked was Marc Blitzstein's too-noisy score. Wolfgang Roth's highly original expressionistic settings were simple and witty, with white Roman motifs shown against a brightly colored background.

O'Casey's boisterous curtain raiser, the first work from his pen seen in New York since 1934, was on the lines of a low-comedy vaudeville sketch and concerned a couple of drunks (Truex and Bourneuf) in a Dublin post office where, seeking money for a drink, they attempt to draw a pound from one of their accounts. Others in the piece included Webster as a snooty customer mailing a package and Cavada Humphrey as the clerk. Considered dull and poorly acted, it did nothing to assist the evening, which could have done without it.

ANGEL IN THE WINGS [Revue] SK: Ted Luce, Hank Ladd, and Grace and Paul Hartman; M/LY: Bob Hilliard and Carl Sigman; D: John Kennedy; CH: Edward Noll; S/L: Donald Oenslager; C: Julia Sze; P: Marjorie and Sherman Ewing; T: Coronet Theatre; 12/11/47 (308)

A fairly popular, intimate revue starring nightclub dancer-comedians Paul and Grace Hartman, he of the comical hangdog expression, she of the pretty poker face and perky demeanor. Paul won the Tony for best actor in a musical and Grace for best actress in a musical. "They make much of little in a skimpy and uneven show," thought Howard Barnes (*NYHT*), in one of the few mildly unfavorable notices. George Jean Nathan (*TBY*) thought it better than most of its ilk, but was upset by its lack of novelty in using the same kinds of routines similar shows had worked to death. What Brooks Atkinson (*NYT*), on the other hand, described as an "extremely pleasant musical revue" employed an onstage company of nine and emphasized comedy. Robert Garland (*NYJA*) asserted, "Everybody in sight is gracious and gifted and just about what this all-too-serious-minded season needed."

Deadpan comic Hank Ladd acted as MC, offering dry, wisecracking monologues--filled with some hoary jokes--before various routines. Much of his humor was at the show's expense. One of his more risible comments was about the performer who was eliminated from the show because he wanted $300 a week and the Hartmans did not want to pay him a penny and they could not work out a compromise. Various numbers were parodistic, such as "Up Early with the Upjohns," a hilarious sketch that sent up radio breakfast shows hosted by married couples. "The Salina Select Garden Club" sketch featured the Hartmans as explorers in a travesty demonstration to a ladies' garden club of West Indian dancing; as the dance progressed, club member Mrs. Hokinson (Viola Roache) got caught up in it with rib-splitting results. Popular entertainer Hildegarde was spoofed in "The Glamorous Ingabord," whic allowed the Hartmans to portray country rubes whose naive behavior causes bedlam at a fancy nightclub. The Hartmans also did well in several of their trademark slapstick dances. Radio performer Elaine Stritch, in her Broadway debut, scored strongly as Ingabord (she parodied the singing of "The Last Time I Saw Paris") and also with her rendition of "Civilization," a hit song in conga rhythm. Other performers of note were eccentric tap dancer Johnny Barnes, whose chief number was "Tambourine." "If It Were Easy to Do" featured Nadine Gae and Peter Hamilton dancing an apache number. Among the titles of other numbers were "Breezy" and "Thousand Islands Song." In the company were Eileen Barton, Robert Stanton, and Bill McGraw. Before arriving on Broadway the show had played the summer theatre circuit under the title, *Heaven Help the Angels*.

(1) ANGEL STREET [Drama/British/Crime/Marriage/Mental Illness/Mystery/Period] A: Patrick Hamilton; D: Shepard Traube; S/C: Lemuel Ayers; L: A. H.

Feder; P: Shepard Traube i/a/w Alexander H. Cohen; T: John Golden Theatre; 12/5/41 (1,293)

One of the most successful shudder-inducing psychological melodramas ever produced on Broadway, *Angel Street* became a standard of amateur and professional groups for many years and was the source of the outstanding film, *Gaslight*, the play's original title when it was produced on the London stage in 1939. It came to New York after being seen in a summer-theatre version as well as in Los Angeles. Preopening gossip expected a flop, and the producers printed enough tickets for only a few performances. They were pleasantly shocked to learn that they had a hit.

This is a very tautly written suspense play closely observing the unities of time and place. Its time is the 1880s and its place a gloomily lit house on London's Angel Street. Its action involves the attempt by the apparently benign and exceedingly urbane Mr. Manningham (Vincent Price) to drive his young bride, Bella (Judith Evelyn), insane. Much of the fun comes from the audience's guessing which way madness lies. Manningham arranges things to appear as if the wife--whose mother died in an asylum--were responsible for various behavioral eccentricities, such as hiding things to annoy him. She seems unaware of these oddities until they are pointed out to her, which makes her begin to think that she has been doing them while suffering from mental lapses. Only the arrival of a good-natured, hearty Scotland Yard inspector (Leo G. Carroll) begins to make the innocent Bella believe that Manningham is a mad murderer who killed an old lady for her jewels in the same house fifteen years earlier and that she is his next victim. Manningham is still obsessed with finding his victim's expensive jewels, which is why he has returned to the scene of the crime. In fact, he married Bella solely to use her money to buy the house. With Bella's assistance, Inspector Rough proves his case beyond the shadow of a doubt. Manningham, aware that his desk has been rifled, begins to strangle Bella, but she is saved in the nick of time.

The critics appreciated the play's low-key, understated style, its looming sense of menace, its fully written characters, its carefully structured development, its lack of low-comedy relief, its deliberately and sometimes maddeningly slow pace, its reliance on psychological factors rather than physical ones to create suspense, and the author's ability to make the audience suspect that even the detective may be a maniac. There was concern by some, however, that despite the author's revisions during its pre-Broadway productions, the heroine's sudden hysteria in act three when she denounces Manningham seemed unprepared and out of place. Others thought this moment a dramatic highlight. Burns Mantle chose the play as one of the best of the year. Brooks Atkinson (*NYT*) believed that the author had told "an extremely slight tale of Victorian torture with perfect balance and suspense. He never raises his voice much higher than a shudder." Comparing it to an earlier hit play in the same vein by Hamilton, John Mason Brown (*NYWT*) commented, "If it is not quite so good as was its predecessor, it can still claim the high distinction of being the best, most uncompromising and most tingling thriller which has been presented hereabouts since *Rope's End** was first produced."

Aiding the play immeasurably were the memorable performances. "Vincent Price," said George Freedley (*NYMT*), "gives perhaps his best performance as the husband. His brutality, his silken villainy, his honest sensuality, his domination of his wife is perfectly portrayed. His presence is never absent from your mind whether he is on stage or not." Price's role had an enormous effect on his career, because he subsequently became famous for a wide gallery of villainous roles.

The then-unknown Judith Evelyn--this was her Broadway debut--provided a startlingly effective portrayal of the terror-stricken wife, which she had played in the Los Angeles production. Brown called her "an exceptional actress, possessed of magnificent intensity. Hers is no ordinary skill. Her vocal range is wide and her projection of the character complete."

Leo G. Carroll gave one of his most effective performances as the paternal Inspector Rough. In the only two other roles, those of Elizabeth, the faithful housekeeper, and Nancy, the seductive maid, Florence Edney and Elizabeth Eustis, respectively, gave expert performances.

One of the most memorable moments in the production came about by accident. Inspector Rough was supposed to hide when Manningham suddenly arrived home, but at one rehearsal, he forgot to take his hat with him. The cast gasped, "Oh, my God, the hat!" They then urged the director to keep the forgotten hat in, with the detective rushing out to retrieve it just in time. When the moment arrived in performance, audiences invariably would shout involuntarily, "The hat! The hat!"

(2) [Dramatic Revival] D: Richard Barr; S/L: Herbert Brodkin; C: Emeline Roche; P: New York City Center Company; T: City Center of Music and Drama; 1/22/48 (14)

One of a series of 1948 revivals initiated by José Ferrer at the City Center to provide popular-priced quality theatre with Broadway-level talents. Ferrer played the role of the murderous Mr. Manningham, Uta Hagen was his wife, Phyllis Hill played Nancy, Rough was acted by Richard Whorf, and Nan McFarland was Elizabeth.

To several, the production was "an electric and effective" (William Hawkins [*NYWT*]) one. Others thought the production irreparably hampered by being played in a cavernous playhouse; there were frequent complaints of inaudibility. Robert Garland (*NYJA*) was among those who thought the revival inadequate. A few felt that the material had been overexposed during the past few years (because of its frequent summer-theatre showings and the popular film version) and did not warrant a revival, especially by a company avowing artistic principles over commercial ones. Still, some, such as Brooks Atkinson (*NYT*), believed Hamilton's thriller to be as harrowing as ever.

The costumes and settings were approved, the direction was intelligent, and the unabashed acting was generally chill-inviting. Four string musicians performed in the pit, but the canopy that covered them effectively muffled their sounds and led to some critical swipes. Hagen, then married to Ferrer, made a good impression in the role of the intended victim. Judith Evelyn's performance in the original did not overshadow her the way Vincent Price's did Ferrer, who seemed needlessly histrionic at times. Whorf's Inspector Rough was well-balanced and acceptable.

ANGNA ENTERS (see *The Theatre of Angna Enters*)

ANIMAL KINGDOM, THE [Dramatic Revival*] A: Philip Barry; D: Harold Young; P: Equity Library Theatre; T: Hudson Park Branch of the New York Public Library (OB); 5/17/45

Barry's 1932 comedy was revived by the unpaid actors of the Equity Library Theatre in a modestly produced, middling production with inexperienced actors. The standout performance was Althea Murphy's as Daisy Sage. "She is attractive, with a voice which is made for comedy whether straight or with a catch in the throat," remarked George Freedley (*NYMT*). Elizabeth McCormick played Grace, Martin Greene was the pugilist-butler, Dorman Leonard was Tom Collier, and Mary Hayden was his wife.

ANNA CHRISTIE [Dramatic Revival*] A: Eugene O'Neill; D: Joseph Kramm; S: Harold Dessler; P: Equity Library Theatre; T: Guild for the Jewish Blind (OB): 12/47

By 1948 it was rare for the critics to attend productions of the Equity Library Theatre. Henry Hewes (*AC*) was the only one to see its presentation of *Anna Christie*, O'Neill's drama of a prostitute who returns to her seafaring father. Isabel Bonner played the title role well "enough to make the audience forget that she was physically miscast in the role. She gave the part a sort of Irene Dunne quality."

Joseph Kramm, who directed, played Chris, and Florence Dunlap played Marthy. The best performance was George Mathews's as Matt Burke. "Combining the build of a Notre Dame tackle and the innocent heart of a St. Bernard, he captured the affections of nearly everyone."

(1) ANNA LUCASTA [Drama/Alcoholism/Blacks/Family/Prostitution/Small Town] A: Philip Yordan; AD: Abram Hill and Harry Wagstaff Gribble; D: Harry

Wagstaff Gribble; S: Richard Bolton; P: American Negro Theatre; T: 135th Street Library Theatre (OB); 6/16/44 (19)

Although this was one of the biggest hits coming out of the black theatre of the 1940s, it was not originally written as a black play, nor was its playwright of that race. Philip Yordan's original intention had been to write about a Polish-American family living in Pennsylvania. Unable to find a Broadway producer for his drama, Yordan allowed agent Claire Leonard to show it to Abram Hill of Harlem's American Negro Theatre with the suggestion that the play might work if revised for black actors. During the year it took Hill to decide on the play's merits, director-playwright Harry Wagstaff Gribble became involved in the project; he helped in the rewrite and directed the play. It had three intensive months of evening rehearsals, the days being devoted by the actors to their bread-and-butter employment.

The play opened on a sweltering night in the airless library space usually em ployed by the company. The response was strong enough to encourage a Broadway production that became a hit, with the play chosen by Burns Mantle as one of the season's ten best. Still, not all of the reviews were warm. George Freedley (*NYMT*), for example, dubbed it "a mediocre drama indifferently acted but rapturously received by an audience which howled whenever there was the vaguest possibility of smiling." He also found the acting "indifferent . . . at best." Bron. (*V*) may have called the production "exciting melodrama done with vigor and force, exuding vitality through its performance," but he was sure that it would fail on Broadway, "the faults of plot and structure overbalancing its vivid characterization." But Robert Garland (*NYJA*) saw here "something new and vital in the showshop. Something to keep alive and encourage in every manner possible." (Actor Canada Lee, who was sitting next to Garland, whispered to him, "They've got something here, these enthusiasts." As it turned out, Lee would act in the Broadway version.) Louis Kronenberger (*PM*) caviled at its crudeness and improbabilities, yet marveled at its honesty and uniqueness in capturing a picture of real people and life. Burton Rascoe (*NYWT*) thought the occasion "one of the greatest thrills" of his theatregoing life, and the production worthy of the Moscow Art Theatre. Declaring, "You have never seen better acting in your life," he claimed that the play was "a movingly realistic tragi-comedy of middle-class Negro life, by a Negro [presumably a reference to Hill], and the first, I believe, of its kind."

After a prologue set in Noah's Bar in 1944, the play goes back to 1941 in a small Pennsylvania town. Anna Lucasta (Hilda Moses Simms) is a magnetically attractive trollop whose religious father, Joe (Alvin Childress), has caught her in bed with a man and has thrown her out of the house, while salving his sorrows in booze. Anna moves to Brooklyn, where she picks up men in a bar by the Gowanus Canal. The chance for her to redeem herself is presented in the person of a clean-cut youth named Rudolph (Earle Hyman), the son of an Alabama friend. Rudolph is coming north in search of a wife, and Anna plans to marry him as her ticket back to the family hearth. The boy has a packet of money that the family schemes in various ways to get their hands on. Their major hope lies in getting Anna to marry Rudolph. The family thinks more of the money than of Anna's soul. Rudolph marries Anna without being told of her past, although he prefers not to know. Once she is married, Anna's past comes back to haunt her, and her father threatens to tell her husband of it. Her husband is ready to take her back when he learns the truth, but Anna feels that she cannot always pretend to be respectable. Realizing that the marriage can never work, Anna leaves for Brooklyn in the company of her friend Blanche (Alice Childress), a colorful whore. Anna eventually kills herself. The play ends in an epilogue set in the Brooklyn bar.

Among the problems discerned by Wilella Waldorf (*NYP*) was the choice of having the educated and financially sound Rudolph come north from the deep South to get married, which seemed an unconvincing shift from what was probably the "old country" in the original version; and the vagueness of Anna's motivation in marrying Rudolph, which could have been either because of her true feelings or because of her greed.

Top reviews for acting went to Frederick O'Neal as Anna's pompous brother-in-law, Frank, Lionel Monagas as the barkeep Noah, and, especially, to the radiantly lovely Hilda Moses Simms (who later dropped the Moses) as Anna. Among other actors were Letitia Toole as Catherine, Alberta Perkins as Theresa, Betty Haynes as Stella, and Billy Cumberbatch in the small role of Danny, which later went to Canada Lee.

(2) [Dramatic Revival] (see the previous entry for additional production details) A: Philip Yordan (no adaptors credited); S: Frederick Fox; C: Paul du Pont; P: John Wildberg; T: Mansfield Theatre; 8/30/44 (957)

For Broadway the play was stripped down and revised once more, this time solely by its original author, although Gribble continued to direct. The action was considerably streamlined and shortened, and the originally tragic ending was changed to an improbably happy one. Comedy was much more in evidence than earlier. The prologue and epilogue--intended to bring in the war background--were removed, and the action remained in the prewar days.

These changes received mixed responses. Rascoe continued to believe this an event of major significance. He was particularly impressed by its failure to depict the black characters stereotypically and condescendingly. He claimed it to be "the first play of Negro life to recognize the fact that Negroes are individuals with pretty much the same problems, ways of living, speech and points of view as the whites." Waldorf commented that the play "has been greatly improved and slicked up. . . . In other respects it has been hoked up, rendered more obvious and revamped to conform more closely to the regulation Broadway groove." Like many others, she resented the "sappy ending" that had been added, in which, because of the prompting of the bartender, Anna goes back to Rudolph. Kronenberger had similar feelings: "It has been pared of certain crudities, and purified of its worst extravagances and melodrama; but gone, too, is an emotion--however blind, however blundering--that struck at the tragic sense of life, that suggested the loneliness and perversity that inhere in all humanity." The new version was shallower, more stagey, and more concerned with laughs, he said. Although a bad play, it was still theatrically fascinating enough, he believed, to be a hit, which it decidedly was. But Howard Barnes (*NYHT*) labeled it "a tedious charade."

Cast changes included moving Alvin Childress to the role of the bartender (he was too young for the father) and giving the father to George Randol; Georgia Burke taking the role of the mother, Theresa; Theodora Smith assuming Katie (changed from Catherine), the sympathetic sister-in-law; Rosetta LeNoire acting Stella; and Canada Lee playing Danny, the sailor, which role he accepted when the original joined the armed forces. Earle Hyman was making his Broadway debut in the production, as was Frederick O'Neal. The latter was deemed a major find.

(3) [Return Engagement] T: National Theatre; 9/22/47 (32)

A multicity tour by the play following its Broadway demise led producer Wildberg to venture a limited-run Broadway revival. George Freedley (*NYWT*) noted that the play's erotic elements had been coarsened over time and that "what was once said naturally has acquired a leer."

The acting was of a decent caliber, although the new actress playing Katie (Wesleen Foster) was amateurish. Isabel Cooley was Anna, Warren Coleman was Frank, Rosetta LeNoire resumed her role of Stella (Freedley said that she overplayed "embarrassingly" in some scenes), Frank Wilson played Joe, Laura Bowman was the mother, Slim Thompson was Noah, Duke Williams was Rudolph, Lance Taylor played Danny, and Sidney Poitier made his Broadway debut as Lester. He had joined the show as an understudy in 1946 and remained with it in its later touring phases until 1949.

ANNE OF ENGLAND [Drama/British/Historical-Biographical/Period/Politics/Women] A: Mary Cass Canfield and Ethel Borden; M: Alexander Haas; SC: Norman Ginsbury's play, *Viceroy Sarah*; D/P: Gilbert Miller; S/C: Mstislav Dobujinsky; T: St. James Theatre; 10/7/41 (7)

A "ponderous" (Brooks Atkinson [*NYT*]) costume drama set between 1704 and 1711 and revised for American audiences from a hit British play of six years earlier that had appeared under another title. The British version of the play had been done at a summer theatre in Harrison, Maine, with Margaret Webster and May Whitty sometime before *Anne of England* reached Broadway. Barbara Everest repeated her London role as Queen Anne and was supported by a troupe of top players, including Jessica Tandy as young Abigail Hill (later Mrs. Masham), Flora Robson as Sarah, duchess of Marlborough, H. H. Van Twardowski as the queen's consort, Frederic Worlock as the duke of Marlborough, and Leo G. Carroll as Secretary of State Harley.

The play was heavily decorated with gorgeous operalike settings reminiscent of the eighteenth-century designs of the Bibiennas and with resplendent costumes by the same man who did the sets, but apart from the fancy trappings, the play was lifeless and lacked any sense of the historical significance surrounding the characters, whose problems seemed boringly trifling. Despite several attractive characters, a few good scenes of conflict, and excellent acting, it remained moribund. "Neither the acting as a whole nor Mr. Miller's direction could supply the conflict and the commentary that the script lacked," argued Rosamond Gilder (*TAM*).

The work deals with the attempts of the powerful and ambitious duchess of Marlborough, stateswoman and wife of England's leading military figure, to obtain influence over the dowdy and pathetic Queen Anne by gaining a position for her young cousin, Abigail Hill, as an attendant upon the monarch. Abigail uses her new position, not to aid her cousin, but to enhance her own power, which she succeeds in doing to the consternation of the duchess, whose place she ends up supplanting. When the duchess is dismissed, the duke resigns, developments that lead eventually to a weakening of the British throne.

Jessica Tandy recollected the rehearsal of a scene when Flora Robson had to slap her face for having given brandy to the queen. Tandy stood there still holding the cup, and director Miller said, "I don't understand. Why do you just so quietly go and put that cup down? You would do something violent." Tandy responded that she could toss the contents in Robson's face. "Would you like that eight times a week over these very expensive costumes?" "Oh, no!" he replied, "I think maybe you'd better not. What you're doing is just fine" (quoted in Fred Fehl, *On Broadway*).

ANNE OF THE THOUSAND DAYS [Drama/Historical-Biographical/Marriage/Period/Politics/Religion/Sex/Trial/Verse] A: Maxwell Anderson; M: Lehman Engel; D: H. C. Potter; S/L: Jo Mielziner; C: Motley; P: Playwrights' Producing Company and Leland Hayward; T: Shubert Theatre; 12/8/48 (288)

This play had not fared well in its pre-Broadway tryout, and it took considerable energy to put it into proper shape. Maxwell Anderson later revealed that he had rarely undergone such a tortuous period of script revision. Director Bretaigne Windust was replaced by H. C. Potter, who oversaw the compression of the script from three acts into two.

Designer Mielziner originally had prepared a multiscened production using ten sets on a revolve, but the tryouts in Philadelphia were an agony of technical mishaps that revealed the unworkability of the conception. Mielziner had to abandon his sets for a simpler Elizabethan-style unit-set conception in dark green velvet, using a large central doorway and depending on lighting effects to create the uninterrupted scene shifts. Despite some complaints that the effect was monotonous, others thought that, as set off by Motley's vivid yet believable costumes, the set was highly appropriate. Follow spots, usually confined to musical comedy, were used to track the leading players around the stage and could be irised down to highlight just their heads.

The stress of all the changes on actor Rex Harrison, playing King Henry VIII, was so great, that he wrote in his autobiography, *Rex*, that "my digestive system collapsed. I went to a doctor and had X rays taken, which I understand are still being shown to medical students in Philadelphia as examples of what intestines can do under duress." When it eventually opened, after the necessary delays, *Anne* turned out to be a well-respected historical drama that employed a stylized poetic form not seen in Anderson's earlier Tudor plays, *Elizabeth the Queen** and *Mary, Queen of Scots**.

The drama, set in England between 1526 and 1536, hews rather closely--with some necessary dramatic license--to the historical facts concerning the lusty relationship between the politically crafty and personally charming Henry VIII and the self-willed, fiery-spirited Anne Boleyn (Joyce Redman), Henry's second wife and the mother of Elizabeth I. It is presented as flashback, a memory recalled on the night of Anne's death. At the beginning, Anne is in love with Percy, earl of Northumberland (Robert Duke), but Henry, married to Catherine of Aragon, and the lover of Anne's sister Mary (Louise Platt), falls for Anne and claims her for his own. He makes Anne pregnant and hopes that the offspring will be male, which leads Anne to demand his abandonment of Catherine and her own promotion to the throne. His decision to do just this leads him into conflict with the Church of Rome. He establishes in its place the Church of England as the official state religion. Anne gives birth to Elizabeth, made legitimate by her marriage to Henry, but he, disappointed in her inability to bear a male child, rejects her and turns elsewhere. He thinks that Jane Seymour (Monica Lang) might be the one to give him a boy. Anne is arrested on phony charges of adultery and tried. She refuses to accept a divorce and exile and goes to her death by beheading with a mixture of fear and pride.

Euphemia Van Rensselaer Wyatt (*CW*) was offended by some of the play's more suggestive dialogue (there are various sexual allusions), but otherwise considered that "*Anne* is one of the tensest and closely knit of Anderson's historical dramas with an impelling sense of doom from the first." In Brooks Atkinson's (*NYT*) eyes, the latter portion of the play dissipated the work's cumulative power by breaking the action up into too many small scenes, but still, he insisted, "the drama as a whole is a passionate chronicle of heroic people. . . . Mr. Anderson has the size to write about them in big strokes with ostentatious imagery. . . . No one else has the strength to write on this theatrical level and to use the stage with such abandon." But George Jean Nathan (*TBY*), while considering much of the drama appealing, felt that Anderson's ambition had overshot itself (John Mason Brown [*SR*] said much the same thing). He appreciated the unobtrusive blank verse, the lessened sense of "heavy striving" compared to previous Anderson efforts, the "fairly direct" story line, the occasional humor, and the "dramatic tang" to most of the soliloquies. Brown said that he had begun to suspect that what Anderson purveyed as poetic dialogue was not poetry after all, "but a sort of singsong in which very simple thoughts are ornately stated."

The acting of Harrison and Redman, both English, was of the finest quality, as was that of the fine supporting cast. George Freedley (*NYMT*) sang Redman's praises for "her fiery, tempestuous and imperious performance. . . . She combines beauty with tenderness, with humor and vigor. She fills the stage, a tiny virago." The part originally had been intended for Deborah Kerr, but MGM refused to release her from her Hollywood duties.

Harrison, made up to resemble a somewhat slimmer version of the famous Holbein portrait of Henry, was brilliant. To give him greater girth with foam rubber costume and makeup effects, plaster casts of his head and legs were taken. Harrison worked on lowering his voice and, wearing a foam rubber casing, rehearsed by walking with as lumbering a gait as he could manage. He not only looked the part but acted it with great conviction. He captured the king's physical and emotional changes over the decade during which the action transpires and made manifest the character's physical and mental vitality. He also spoke the lines with musical and intellectual understanding. For his efforts, he won that year's Tony as best actor. Making the award even sweeter was the fact that it was presented to Harrison by gossip columnist Hedda Hopper, with whom he had been feuding, and who had recently declared his career "dead as a mackerel."

In support were Percy Waram as Cardinal Wolsey, Wendell K. Phillips as Cromwell, John Williams as Norfolk, Harry Irvine as Bishop Fisher, Russell Gaige as Thomas More, Allan Stevenson as Henry Norris, Charles Francis as Anne's father, and John Merivale as Mark Smeaton. Understudying seven roles in the play was young Walter Matthau, in his first Broadway assignment. He got to play several roles during the run, but the one into which he put his greatest effort was that of a courier to the duke of Northumberland, which had one line. "I gave that part a lot of dedication," he later declared, with perhaps some exaggeration. "I used to do knee-bends in the wings to get short of breath and make my legs kind of rubbery. On the opening night in Philadelphia I was so keyed up to do a good job I did about a hundred knee-bends and rushed around the theatre to tire myself out. What an idiot! When I made my first entrance I fell flat on my face. I had to scream my line from down there and it didn't sound so good" (quoted in Allan Hunter, *Walter Matthau*).

ANNIE GET YOUR GUN [Musical/Historical-Biographical/Period/Romance/Show Business/Western] B: Herbert and Dorothy Fields; M/LY: Irving Berlin; D: Joshua Logan; CH: Helen Tamiris; S/L: Jo Mielziner; C: Lucinda Ballard; P: Richard Rodgers and Oscar Hammerstein II; T: Imperial Theatre; 5/16/46 (1,147)

Annie Get Your Gun, one of America's best loved and most successful musicals, was born of an idea--complete with Ethel Merman as the star--that came to book writer Dorothy Fields when she heard her husband describe a drunken soldier who had won a bunch of prizes at a Coney Island marksmanship booth. It opened to great acclaim after various unforeseen delays in getting it to Broadway. Its opening was pushed back three weeks because the stage was not structurally sound; during the hanging of the scenery a steel girder buckled and bricks began to fall. This occurrence led to the unfounded rumor that the show itself was in trouble.

It was originally supposed to have a score by Jerome Kern, but a reluctant Irving Berlin stepped in when Kern died in November 1945. The choice of Berlin meant that Fields would have to forgo writing the lyrics, which she would have written for Kern. Berlin represented a gamble, as the kind of integrated narrative musical for which Rodgers and Hammerstein, who were producing, were famous was not associated with Berlin's more conventional "hit song" approach. One major obstacle to Berlin accepting was that he would have to share the billing with other writers. Another was his fear that he might not achieve the standards represented by his producers. The resultant score--composed in a very brief period--was packed with hit tunes that became standards.

The show also benefitted from Merman, one of the most enthusiastic and dynamic performers of the day, in the leading role of Ohio-born sharpshooter Annie Oakley; the show was actually crafted to fit Merman's talents (although Mary Martin was very successful in the road show). It was the biggest hit in several years (a long London run ensued as well) and came along just when such a smash was needed. Unlike several other important musicals of the time, it was not meant as an advance in the musical comedy form but simply as a show aimed at being as entertaining as possible. Vernon Rice (*NYP*) spoke for many when he jotted, "*Annie Get Your Gun* on every count is an excellent musical comedy, and the way shows run these days it will probably run for a lifetime." However, the opening-night audience seemed unusually restrained during the first act, and the show's staff was worried that they were bombing. At intermission, director Logan asked Merman how she could cope with this house, and, according to Laurence Bergreen's *As Thousands Cheer*, she responded, "Easy. You may think I'm playing the part, but inside I'm saying, 'Screw you! You jerks! If you were as good as I am, you'd be up here!'" By act two the audience was with the show all the way.

Uneducated Ohio hillbilly Annie joins the Wild West Show of Buffalo Bill a.k.a. Colonel William F. Cody (William O'Neal) after defeating the show's crack shot, Frank Butler (Ray Middleton), in a match. She and Frank are attracted to one another, but she upsets Frank when she rockets to stardom with her new act of shooting out candles while riding on a motorcycle. He leaves Buffalo Bill to join Pawnee Bill's (George Lipton) Far East Show. Frank also resists her because he seeks a completely different type of bride than the homespun Annie. She takes consolation in her show-business profession and in being inducted into the Sioux tribe by Chief Sitting Bull (Harry Bellaver), who even agrees to invest in Buffalo Bill's show. The show tours Europe, and Annie meets many crowned heads. Still, economic misfortune faces the troupe on their return to America. Annie agrees to sell her valuable medals to help the troupe--combined now with Pawnee Bill's--survive. Standing between Annie and Frank is their rival marksmanship, so

Annie is convinced by Sitting Bull to let Frank win a shooting match against her. This turns the trick, Annie gives her medals to Frank in order to raise the needed funds, and Frank is willing to accept Annie's love. Along the way, they and/or the cast sing such tunes as "I Got the Sun in the Morning," "Doin' What Comes Natur'lly," "The Girl That I Marry," "You Can't Get a Man with a Gun," "Moonshine Lullaby," "I Got Lost in His Arms," "There's No Business like Show Business," "I'm an Indian, Too," "They Say That Falling in Love is Wonderful," "My Defenses Are Down," "I'm a Bad, Bad Man," and the show-stopping challenge song, "Anything You Can Do (I Can Do Better)," written in fifteen minutes.

No Broadway score ever had more hits. Berlin was at one point going to remove the now-classic "There's No Business like Show Business" because he thought that Rodgers and Hammerstein didn't like it. It was clear that his secretary had not liked it, however. When Berlin, entreated by the producers to put it back in the show, tried to find it, he could not. It was finally located under a phone book, where the secretary had carelessly filed it away.

The show profited by a fast-paced, lively, and often-amusing libretto (although some critics thought it flimsy) that rarely got in the way of the many songs and dances, all of which were closely connected to the book; a powerhouse staging with dazzling sets and costumes that allowed for multiple changes because of the globe-trotting plot; and sensational performances. Despite the long-lasting popularity of many of the songs, a few critics were not especially impressed by them on a first hearing. George Jean Nathan (*TBY*) was one such critic; he found that the lyrics "enjoy a measure of acceptable waggishness," but thought the music "below par." In between was Ward Morehouse (*NYS*), who argued, "Berlin's score is not a notable one, but his tunes are singable and pleasant and his lyrics are particularly good." Howard Barnes (*NYHT*), on the other hand, insisted that the score formed "a fascinating web of wit and melody for the action," and he was in the majority. There were few noticeable innovations in the show, although there was a choreographic reflection of contemporary trends in infusing ballet into musical comedy in several numbers.

Merman received some of the greatest raves of her career for this role. She was lauded for her singing, comic skills, and acting ability, largely because of the many opportunities given her by the show to reveal her multifaceted talents. "She can scream out the air of a song so that the building trembles; and she can be initiated into an Indian tribe in such a way that the event is singularly funny," wrote Lewis Nichols (*NYT*). "Her energy," noted John Mason Brown (*SR*), "is something the United Nations might well look into. . . . She breezes onto the stage as a threat. Yet, since all she threatens is the equilibrium, Miss Merman could serve the scientists as a model. From her they might learn that it is possible to devastate without destroying, and only by delighting." Always quick with a quip, Merman sometimes had to come up with one when mishaps occurred. For instance, when she shot her rifle into the flies, a stuffed bird was supposed to fall to the stage. One night, the gun failed to fire, but the bird fell regardless. Grinning, she lifted the prop and said, "I'll be goddamned. Apoplexy!"

Ray Middleton made a great impression too, although his acting took second place to his singing. Also in the show were Marty May, Daniel Nagrin, Lea Penman, Betty Anne Nyman, Alma Ross, Kenny Bowers, and many others.

ANNONCE FAITE A MARIE, L' (***The Tidings Brought to Mary***) [Dramatic Revival*/French Language] A: Paul Claudel; D/P: Ludmilla Pitoëff; S: Simon Lissim; C: Mme. Pierre Claudel; T: Barbizon-Plaza Theatre (OB); 5/20/41 (1)

Although most benefit performances have been excluded from this book, the present one is interesting enough to warrant its inclusion. It was staged, produced, and starred in by the Russian-born Ludmilla Pitoëff, who, with her husband Georges, had long been one of the most important figures in the Paris theatre. This was her sole American performance, the occasion being a fund-raiser for a French school in New York.

Claudel's 1912 allegorical drama, set in the Middle Ages, had been staged by the Theatre Guild in English in 1921. It was a later revision of the play that Pitoëff produced. In it the role of the leper, Pierre de Craon (Youl Bryner [Yul Brynner], in his New York debut), appeared only in the prologue.

Ludmilla Pitoëff played the saintly Violaine, and her daughter Varvara played Mara. "Interest in the play centered around these two actresses, whose performance was of impressive simplicity, beauty and dramatic richness," wrote C. L. H. (*NYT*). Brynner also played Jacques Hury, and Georges Pitoëff, Jr., played the apprentice.

ANOTHER LOVE STORY [Comedy/British/Family/Marriage/Romance/Sex] A/D: Frederick Lonsdale; S: Raymond Sovey; C: (ladies' dresses: Hattie Carnegie); P: Louis Lotito; T: Fulton Theatre; 10/12/43 (104)

Frederick Lonsdale, polished and epigrammatic British writer of drawing-room comedies, provided this lightweight but dull escapade about upper-class Americans in which the epigrams kept falling flat, the characters never added a third dimension to their fragile outlines (nor did they ever appear to be American and not British), and the triple love story sometimes got too tangled to unravel. As a vehicle for character actor Roland Young it was a decided disappointment.

"The play bristles with ineptitudes," decided Euphemia Van Rensselaer Wyatt (*CW*). Howard Barnes (*NYHT*) said that it was "more often a matter for yawns than laughter. [Lonsdale] has revived the husk of one of his brittle drawing room comedies, but he has not succeeded in keeping it from being desiccated and remote."

Young's role was that of George Wayne, who has gotten his job as a bank vice president by becoming engaged to Celia Hale (Fay Baker), the president's daughter. A philandering soul with eleven past mistresses to his credit, he really loves his secretary Maggie Sykes (Jayne Cotter, later known as Jayne Meadows) and dreads the prospect of marrying Celia. Running parallel with his story is that of Diana Flynn (Margaret Lindsay, a film actress in her Broadway debut), who was once the fiancée of Michael Foxx (Philip Ober), an adventurer who, after an argument, deserted her in Spain on the eve of their marriage. He is now engaged to Molly Asprey (Augusta Dabney), daughter of the wealthy Elsie Williams Browne (Doris Dalton) by her first husband, the wastrel artist John Asprey (Arthur Margetson). John has come to the Browne home at his former wife's invitation, hoping to bring his daughter's engagement to an end. Mrs. Browne--married to a pompous ass (Fred Irving Lewis)--falls in love with John again. Meeting Michael again at Mrs. Browne's home, Diana resolves to break up his engagement to Molly by inviting him to her bedroom and making it look as if they were having an affair. He catches on to her ruse and gives her a good spanking, but this only serves to make them realize that they are still in love with one another. Michael ends up with Diana, George with Maggie, and Mrs. Browne will divorce Mr. Browne and return to her first spouse.

Henry Mowbray played a butler named Mortimer, and Richard Barbee had another role.

ANOTHER PART OF THE FOREST [Drama/Blacks/Business/Family/Marriage/Mental Illness/Period/Prostitution/Religion/Romance/Sex/Southern] A/D: Lillian Hellman; M: Marc Blitzstein; S/L: Jo Mielziner; C: Lucinda Ballard; P: Kermit Bloomgarden; T: Fulton Theatre; 11/20/46 (182)

This is what might be called Lillian Hellman's "prequel" to her powerful melodrama, *The Little Foxes** (1939). It takes the same vulpine family, the Hubbards, and views them in 1880, twenty years prior to the action of the earlier play. The dramatist revealed in interviews that she had become so familiar with the inner workings of the rapacious Hubbards that when she saw audiences taking a morally superior attitude toward them--an attitude she considered hypocritical--she was jolted into writing another play in which she tried to uncover what had made them such monsters. A third play on the family was planned, but never completed. When the play began rehearsals, with playwright Hellman making her directing debut, it did not have a third act. It took a week for the actors to know how the play ended.

Making a striking Broadway debut in the role of the twenty-year-old Regina Hubbard (outstandingly played in 1939 by Tallulah Bankhead) was twenty-year-old Patricia Neal. She turned down the lead in *John Loves Mary*, which she had just been offered, to take the role. By coincidence, her roommate, Jean Hagen, was cast in the small role of Laurette Sincee. During the rehearsals, a rumor started that Hagen was going to be fired, and the news appeared in a gossip column. The idea that this would be publicly announced before a decision had been formally made so enraged Hellman that she determined to keep the actress and to get the best performance possible from her, which she did.

The dour play, although not achieving the commercial success of *The Little Foxes*, was well received and was selected by Burns Mantle as one of the season's ten best. The play's title derives from a common stage direction in Shakespeare's plays.

The patriarch of the Bowden, Alabama, Hubbards is Marcus (Percy Waram), a man born into poverty whose subsequent wealth derives from his post-Civil War days as a carpetbagging black marketeer of salt. A cultured man with tastes for classical literature and music, he is despised by the locals for his predatory ways. His oppressed, mentally unbalanced wife is Lavinia (Mildred Dunnock), who assuages her guilty conscience by attending a black church with Coralee (Beatrice Thompson), her black maid. There are two sons, Benjamin (Leo Genn) and Oscar (Scott McKay), both of whom are treated by Marcus as menials whom he pays but a pittance. He is, however, under the conniving control of his beautiful daughter, Regina, with whom his relationship borders on the incestuous. Regina longs to visit the fleshpots of Chicago. She is involved romantically with an aristocratic war veteran named John Bagtry (Bartlett Robinson), whom she hopes will take her to Chicago, but who eventually leaves her. John's genteel, flutteringly innocent sister Birdie (Margaret Phillips) attempts through Ben to borrow enough money from the Hubbards to save her plantation's cotton crop, but Regina obstructs the transaction when she discovers that Ben seeks to cheat Marcus and profit from it. The simpleton Oscar, who has been temporarily jailed for his activity with the Ku Klux Klan, wants to wed the town prostitute, Laurette Sincee, and expects to do so when his father gives him a thousand dollars. But when she gets drunk and makes demeaning remarks about her own superiority to the family, Marcus cuts off both his sons and expels them from the house. The lady departs on her own for New Orleans. Ben soon learns from a document hidden in his mother's Bible that his father was a traitor during the war and was responsible for the deaths of seventeen Confederate soldiers. He uses the proof, which would cause a lynching, to blackmail Marcus and take over the family business, assuming the tyrannical power of the crushed Marcus. Lavinia and her maid leave to found a Sunday school for black children, and Oscar is forced to wed Birdie. Regina is not permitted to go to Chicago and must marry a banker from Mobile. At the end, she subtly moves her chair from her father's side to that of Ben.

So much of the play represented a piling of one bilious incident and character on another that some critics thought it distasteful. It was also viewed as a coruscating attack on the evils of capitalism, as viewed through the behavior of people who fatten themselves at the expense of those less fortunate. Richard Watts, Jr. (*NYP*), was one of the most favorably impressed, observing that this was Hellman's "most fascinating play. . . . It is . . . a brilliant and distinguished work, of enormous power and impact." Most others had reservations. "Though Miss Hellman's characterizations are extreme to the point of caricature they are so infused with passion that they become horribly alive," acknowledged Rosamond Gilder (*TAM*), who went on to note the many standard but still effective melodramatic devices with which the play was filled. "The fun--the good, tingling, almost freak-show fun--of her melodrama," reported John Mason Brown (*SR*), "comes from the wholesale villainy of her characters." He also found that the social comment of *The Little Foxes* had been replaced by a purely local investigation of one family's villainies; this deprived it of its "abiding validity." It made for good theatre but had "little relationship to life." Respecting the sheer force and meticulous care of Hellman's dramaturgy, Brooks Atkinson (*NYT*) had to declare that "*Another Part of the Forest* is not so much a drama of people and ideas as a contrived theatre piece put together by sheer will power." Yet George Jean Nathan (*NYJA*) said of Hellman that she was "talent posturing as genius" and that her play was one "in which overwrought melodrama so supervises character that the whole thing occasionally edges uncomfortably close to travesty."

The actors were all admired, most notably Waram as the arrogant patriarch, although he sometimes let his cockney accent intrude in his role's Southern dialect (Genn's native Welsh also put in an occasional appearance, although he was otherwise quite good). Howard Barnes (*NYHT*) said of Neal that she "contributes an extraordinarily vital and memorable stage portrayal." She was awarded the very first Tony for the category actress, supporting or featured. When Tallulah Bankhead came backstage to visit Neal, she said to her, "Well, darling, you were wonderful, and if I told you you were half as good as I was, it would still be a hell of a compliment."

Also huzzaed was the way in which Mielziner's two interlocking settings of courtyard and interior mirrored the moral decay of the characters. Lucinda Ballard won the Tony for her costumes, although her award was in recognition for several shows, not just this one. The play was Kermit Bloomgarden's debut as a producer; he would have a distinguished career, during which he would produce all of Hellman's subsequent plays.

ANTIGONE [Drama/French/Politics/Romance] A: Jean Anouilh; AD: Lewis Galantière; SC: Sophocles' play of the same name; D: Guthrie McClintic; S: Raymond Sovey; C: (gowns) Valentina; P: Katharine Cornell i/a/w Gilbert Miller; T: Cort Theatre; 2/18/46 (64)

Anouilh's 1942 (produced 1944) revision and updating of Sophocles' Greek tragedy had been a major success in Paris, but its production as a vehicle for Katharine Cornell was widely considered an experiment; it met with sharply mixed reviews, with the emphasis on the negative. It was still running at Paris's Théâtre Atelier when it opened on Broadway in this English adaptation.

Sophocles' drama had been reinvented for a modern audience, with formal language blended with contemporary colloquialisms and anachronisms (such as references to automobiles), and with its ideas shaded to reflect--but very subtly so as not to offend the German censors--the political realities of France during the occupation. The infusion of modernisms in the dialogue made some feel that the tragic quality had been irretrievably abandoned. "*Antigone* is not a full-bodied evening at the theatre," believed Lewis Nichols (*NYT*). "Where it should be moving and strong it too often seems empty. Too much of its length drifts away in unrationalized talk by characters who are not quite living human beings." He suggested that the adaptation should have improved upon the restrictions placed on it by the circumstances of its original presentation and that its purposes could have been clearer for a New York audience. George Jean Nathan (*TBY*) disliked the play and thought it more sophomoric than Sophoclean. But Rosamond Gilder (*TAM*), who thought the language "adequate if undistinguished and occasionally violently out of key," demanded that the work be viewed in the context of its origins and argued that the play was an event of "heroic stature" that "lifts theatregoing from the realm of adolescent escapism to adult participation; it deals with the raw material of the tragic experience through which the world is living and deals with it in terms of exciting theatre."

The outline of the story, emphasizing the conflict between idealism and political autocracy, remained similar to that of Sophocles. Antigone (Cornell), daughter of Oedipus, refuses to obey the edict of the coldly rational King Creon (Cedric Hardwicke), her uncle, not to bury her brother Polynices, killed in rebellious battle against Thebes in a struggle that also saw the death of her brother Eteocles. Her sister Ismene (Ruth Matteson) tries to dissuade her by stressing the fate that lies in store for her, but is ignored. For her uncompromising intransigence, Antigone is hauled off to be executed. Her fiancé Haemon (Wesley Addy), Creon's son, argues for her unsuccessfully and, after she dies, kills himself, to be followed by the self-inflicted death of the queen, Eurydice (Merle Maddern, who had no lines). Creon, shown more sympathetically than in Sophocles, goes off to attend a cabinet meeting, ultimately to ponder the tragedy of his implacable logic and demands for law and order.

Among the changes wrought by Anouilh were the introduction of a nurse

(Bertha Belmore) for Antigone; a single, prose-speaking, cigarette-smoking Chorus (Horace Braham) who suggested a more appealing interlocutor than the traditional group of figures; a strong infusion of sentimentality, including a love scene with Haemon; a diminution of the Greek emphasis on religious values; a weakening of the character of Haemon; the portrayal of the guards as thuglike buffoons; the omission of Tiresias; the lack of remorse by the proud Creon; and so forth.

The hour-and-a-half intermissionless presentation suggested a blend of classical simplicity and modern minimalism by using a relatively bare stage with a semicircular three-stepped platform at the rear, backed by a grey curtain. Costumes were modern, Eurydice and Ismene in sleek robelike gowns, Antigone in a drab green negligee, the men in formal wear, including white tie and tails for Haemon and Creon. Nathan was displeased by the modern-dress approach, which he found "ridiculous," claiming that the effect was more Frederick Lonsdale than Greek tragedy.

For some, Cornell did not succeed in humanizing the stubborn Antigone, but others, such as Gilder, thought her performance brilliant. She wrote, "She gives a deeply moving performance. Her tragic mask was never more nobly worn. Her broad, low forehead, her wide-set eyes, her generous mouth, made for lamentation, the backward tilt of her head, challenging adversity, are part of a bold pattern that is at once modern and timeless."

Several chose to grant the acting honors to Hardwicke. "Creon frightened me more than any Nazi I have previously met on the stage or in reports or fiction," reported Euphemia Van Rensselaer Wyatt (*CW*). "Sir Cedric Hardwicke plays him with impeccable good form and inhumanity. His cold white face, his assurance, his ability, his penetration are calculated to shelve idealism in cold storage."

George Mathews and Michael Higgins played guards, and Oliver Cliff the messenger.

ANTON CHEKHOV SKETCHES [Dramatic Revivals/One-acts] A: Anton Chekhov; D: Michael Chekhov; S/C: Mstislav Dobujinsky; T: Barbizon-Plaza Concert Hall (OB); 9/26/42

"The Happy Ending" [Comedy/Romance/Solo]; "After the Theatre" [Drama/Romance]; "The Witch" [Drama/Marriage/Romance]; "I Forgot" [Dramatic Revival*]; "The Story of Miss N. N." [Drama/Solo]

A quintet of Chekhov pieces directed by the playwright's actor-director nephew, who also appeared in two of the pieces. (No producer was credited.) One of them, "I Forgot," about a comical fellow who cannot remember the title of a piece of music he has come to a music store to buy, had been seen in New York in 1935 in its original Russian. Chekhov now played this vaudeville sketch in English (his debut in the language) and, despite his thick accent, scored the evening's triumph, with George Shdanoff playing excellently opposite him as the music-store proprietor.

In "The Happy Ending" a railroad conductor (David Heilweil) finally brings himself to propose to a professional matchmaker (Deirdre Hurst). Puppy love is the subject of "After the Theatre," a one-person play with Penelope Sacks as the adolescent heroine.

Chekhov made his first appearance of the evening in the third piece, "The Witch," about a poverty-stricken old husband (Chekhov) and his much younger wife (Beatrice Straight), living in a filthy hovel, who allow a lost postman (Arthur Franz) into their abode during a snowstorm only for the husband to become dangerously jealous of the interloper, whom he eventually succeeds in driving away, to his wife's despair. Chekhov had appeared in this piece during his days with the Moscow Art Theatre. "I Forgot" followed, and the evening concluded with Straight in another solo piece, "The Story of Miss N. N.," about a noblewoman reminiscing about the unhappiness of the decade just past.

John Mason Brown (*NYWT*) declared of Michael Chekhov, "He is a player possessed of those virtues which distinguish Russian acting at its best. In him the Stanislavsky system blooms in native soil. To our tastes he may at times be overleisurely. He may occasionally pound comedy until it is shattered into broad and heavy farce. Yet he is a character actor of uncommon talents, and a comedian capable of astonishing depth no less than drollery."

Brooks Atkinson (*NYT*) took most of the rest of the company to task, however, for their inadequate acting of the two other pieces. He said of their work, "It is studious; it lacks spontaneity. They work their way through a sketch without joy, as if it were a challenge. Deliberate art strains the life out of it."

The company, founded by future star Straight, was made up of Chekhov's pupils. Straight pleased George Freedley (*NYMT*) very much in "The Story of Miss N. N." "Blessed with a beautiful face which displays real character and high resolve, endowed with a naturally lovely voice, Miss Straight made this soliloquy a memorable event."

ANTONY AND CLEOPATRA [Dramatic Revival*] A: William Shakespeare; M: Paul Nordoff; D: Guthrie McClintic; S: Leo Kerz; C: (women's) Valentina; (men's) John Boyt; P: Katharine Cornell; T: Martin Beck Theatre; 11/26/47 (126)

A nearly three-hour, two-act version of Shakespeare's sweeping Roman tragedy of the world well lost for love. It received responses ranging from the moderately approving to the vigorously enthusiastic and enjoyed a run unusual for this play, which hitherto always had failed in New York. Most people familiar with the work expected it to flop. When, before the opening, director McClintic ran into Jane Cowl, who had played Cleopatra in 1924, she interrupted his reply to her question about how the show was going by commiserating, "You don't have to say any more, Guthrie. Remember, I have done this play. And I have never felt sorrier for two people in my life than I do for you and Kit tonight." The revival, however, was considered physically beautiful, textually faithful (for the most part), and expertly acted.

As expected, the performance of radiant star Katharine Cornell as Cleopatra was itself deemed superlative, although not everyone thought so to the same degree. Brooks Atkinson (*NYT*), who faulted the production for its air of pedantry, was especially impressed by her death scene, played sitting upright on her throne, encased in a vast red mantle and with her exotic crown on her head. To this scene, said the critic, "she brings the style, authority and incandescence that become her best." He and several others felt that while Cornell excelled at the queen's majesty, she failed to snare the character's wantonness. He averred that she was "formal, good-mannered, a little fastidious." But John Mason Brown (*SR*) declared, "She has never given a more enchanting performance. . . . To be wanton and witty, lustful and regal, mischievous and sublime . . . is to ask for the impossible away from the printed page. Yet Miss Cornell succeeds in being all these things to an amazing degree." Cornell shared the Tony for best actress with Judith Anderson and Jessica Tandy.

Cornell was seconded by a convincingly authoritative, prideful, courageous, pleasure-loving, and excellently spoken Antony from sixty-three-year-old British actor Godfrey Tearle (his brother Conway had played the heroic role in the play's most recent Broadway mounting [1937]). For many, though, the standout performance was Kent Smith's as the play's conscience, Enobarbus. Wyatt thought him "the most human": "Square bearded veteran with grizzled hair, his comments on the passing scene are ripe with shrewd wit and his masculine appreciation of Cleopatra give a new pungency to the time honored description of the meeting of Antony and the Queen of Cydnus."

Other important roles were assumed by Ralph Clanton as Octavius Caesar, Ivan Simpson as Lepidus, Douglass Watson as Eros, and Maureen Stapleton as Iras. Charlton Heston made his Broadway debut in the minor character of Proculeius and Anthony (Tony) Randall his as Scarus, a messenger role in which the breathless character has half a dozen lines to describe the battle of Actium. Randall said in *Which Reminds Me* that even though he did not enter until ten o'clock, he was at the theatre at seven and, intent on doing well, spent three hours in preparation. "I banged my fists against the wall until they almost bled and shook the fire ladder backstage until it almost came off the wall, trying to experience the battle, trying to work myself into . . . a state of rage and frustration and despair" to help make the narration as vivid as possible. As he was about to enter one night, Cornell spoke to him: "Tony, some night why don't you try *not* preparing?" "So," wrote Randall, "the next night I went on without preparing and gave exactly the same performance."

To play Charmian, onetime great star Lenore Ulric was cast, although at age fifty-five (a year older than Cornell) she was mentally unstable and McClintic had to protect her from the slings of outrageous critics in Buffalo by telling her that her reviews were prompted by her costuming and then having new ones made for her. Others of note in the cast were Eli Wallach as Diomedes, Joseph Wiseman as Mardian, Joseph Holland as Pompey, and Charles Nolte as Sillus. One of the chief virtues of the cast, according to Brown, was its expertly musical and sparkling clear speaking of the difficult but exquisite verse.

The scenery, while gorgeous, was not overly detailed and employed smoothly shifted architectural units, such as Roman colonnades and Egyptian pillars, to swiftly transfer the action from one locale in the multiscened play to another. Brown thought the production the most visually striking of any Shakespearean revival in his time because it avoided being museumlike and evoked the audience's imagination in creating the ancient world. The costumes, too, were memorable, with Antony's forces in red, Pompey's in green, and Caesar's in blue, which was an invaluable aid in keeping the political alignments clear. This permitted a minimum of cuts in the text and an adherence to Shakespeare's scene order, with the scenes featuring Cleopatra properly placed amid the world events that encompass them. The principal cut was of the scene near the end when Cleopatra fails to seduce Octavius in the mausoleum.

ANY DAY NOW [Comedy/Business/Family/Gambling/Romance/Science] A: Philip Yordan; D: Robert Klein; S: Herbert Andrews; P: Erwin Piscator; T: Studio Theatre of the New School for Social Research (OB); 6/9/41

One of three pieces done in the season by professional actors mixed with amateurs studying with German émigré director Erwin Piscator at the New School. No one was paid for their services. It was staged (under Piscator's supervision, although the direction took many critical knocks) in the small New School theatre at 66 West Twelfth Street.

John Randolph (who took over at the last moment when Charles De Sheim passed away during rehearsals) had the leading role of Rudolf Dvoracek, a young South Side Chicago Polish-American blowhard, son of a hardworking, penurious family. The father (Robert H. Harris) is a barber, the mother (Dara Birse) a beautician; their shared shop is situated beneath their flat. In addition to Rudy, a gambler with a penchant for shady schemes, there is a brother who is a chauffeur (Ralph Bell) to a crooked judge, and another, the youngest (Gerald Kean), who is a studious but starving lawyer (the playwright's profession). When Ernst Muller (Walter Martin), the chemist head of the family of immigrant cousins living with them, comes up with a new chemical for giving a permanent wave, Rudy, always quick to think of get-rich-quick notions, tries to turn it into a fortune, his questionable methods almost ruining the family. The racketeer husband (Richard Odlin) of Irene (Pert Kelton), a friendly tramp who loves him, helps Rudy raise the needed cash, and the family barely escapes catastrophe with its bankbook intact, while Rudy ends up with Irene.

Randolph and Kelton were highly praised for their portrayals of the not-so-charming heel and trollop with a golden heart. While the play had clever lines and decent characterizations, it suffered from structural weaknesses. Sidney B. Whipple (*NYWT*) noted, "The play . . . is amateurish, extremely long and not always logical, but it demonstrates that Mr. Yordan has at least a modest gift for dialogue." This was the twenty-seven-year-old Chicago author's first play; his future credits would include the successful *Anna Lucasta*.

ANYBODY HOME [Drama/Law/Marriage/Romance/Sex] A: Robert Pyzel; D: Ralph Forbes; S: Louis Kennel; P: Phyllis Holden; T: John Golden Theatre; 2/25/49 (5)

Some critics looked askance at the fact that the star of this self-styled "romantic drama," Phyllis Holden, was also its producer. The suggestion was made that the actress, who had been seen in only two previous Broadway shows (one in 1932 and another in 1938), was offering a vanity production. The star's husband, a chemical engineer, wrote the play. After *Anybody Home* she never acted in New York again.

The piece is set among the horsey set of Westchester County, New York, all of the action taking place at the home of Kay (Holden) and John Howard (Donald Curtis). The stuffy John's law practice occupies more of his time than his neglected spouse. The couple have become gradually ever more estranged since the death of their child. A dashing young sportsman named Bill Gordon (Roger Clark) seeks to gain Kay's affections. When John returns home one day, he finds Kay in Bill's arms (although no serious offense has occurred), and accuses the pair of adultery. Bill turns to Kay's sexy sister Julia Henley (Katherine Anderson). Kay returns to John.

All the critics panned the piece for its laughable inadequacies. The lack of action and the incessant small talk among ineffectively dramatized characters bored the critics silly. "Rarely has an inept script been coupled with such maladroit acting," said Howard Barnes (*NYHT*). "This is the kind of play which yearns for a one-line notice. Like: *Anybody Home*. No," quipped Whitney Bolton (*NYMT*).

APOLOGY [Drama/Business/Family/Fantasy/Period/Religion/Romance/Small Town/War] A: Charles Schnee; D/P: Lee Strasberg; S/L: Samuel Leve; C: Paul Morrison; T: Mansfield Theatre; 3/22/43 (8)

This pretentious play provided an unusual opportunity for an experimental use of lighting, screens, and projections to create locales on a practically bare stage. Scene-setting furniture and props were rolled out as needed. The drama was enacted as if its plot was a slide lecture about the play's unsympathetic protagonist, with Elissa Landi presiding as the philosophical lecturer. As a scene appeared on a projection, the actors would take their places in a tableau and the projection would then seem to come to life. The lecturer, on stage throughout, was allowed to address the characters as well as the audience, to whom she explained their actions and motivations; she also pontificated tiresomely on various historical, religious, and cosmological issues. The theatrical technique did not work effectively, however, and "completely negated every theatre value without putting anything in its place," complained Rosamond Gilder (*TAM*).

Its story, moving from the turn of the century to 1942, was about Albert Warner (Theodore Newton), a selfish, mammon-worshipping businessman whose life story and search for life's purpose was enacted. A wealthy mill owner's (Clay Clement) son, he grows up playing with Florrie (Thelma Schnee, the playwright's sister), a lower-class girl, whom he loves, but upon graduating from Princeton, he decides to marry Betty (Erin O'Brien-Moore) when her father (Clay Clement, in the second of three roles) promises him a partnership in his successful New York department store. His greed thereupon leads him to evade being drafted for both world wars. He becomes a war profiteer while being puffed up for his war services; is asked for a divorce by his wife; pretends to have an affair; seeks comfort from his loneliness in the arms of his childhood nurse (Merle Maddern); and finds redemption and a better life for his previously neglected daughter (Peggy Allardyce) by going off to the war in Africa.

"Studiously artificial, awed by its own cosmic discursiveness, it is an ostentatious and hollow bore from beginning to end," yawned Wilella Waldorf (*NYP*). When the audience entered they were handed sheets bearing only the names of the actors and not their roles. A statement read, "Because of the character of this production, regular programs will not be distributed until the end of the play." The critics felt that this procedure served no purpose but to emphasize the management's belief that the play was a portentous one. Ben Smith, Lewis Charles, and James Todd were in the cast.

APPLE OF HIS EYE [Comedy/Romance/Rural] A: Kenyon Nicholson and Charles Robinson; D: Jed Harris; S: Raymond Sovey; P: Jed Harris i/a/w Walter Huston; T: Biltmore Theatre; 2/5/46 (118)

Walter Huston made his final Broadway appearance in this predictable May-December comedy in which he played a lonely, aging Indiana farmer named Sam Stover, a character drawn with a homespun kind of charm. The action takes place in

Highland Township, Montgomery County, Indiana, and employs an assortment of stock rural types to tell its tale of the Hoosier widower, whose son (Tom Ewell) and grasping daughter-in-law (Mary Wickes) hope to inherit his farm; their dreams become worrisome because of Sam's inordinate affection for Lily Tobin (Mary James), the much younger woman who comes to look after Sam's household when his elderly housekeeper goes to the hospital. The relationship brings out all the gossipers, who frown unstintingly on its propriety. Sam courts Lily by taking her to Chinese dinners and to a carnival, where he hurts his back in a wrestling match and realizes that he is too old for her. He decides to fire Lily but she announces that she likes him just the way he is and his mail-order wedding ring seals their fate.

The realistically staged play "has the lassitude of winter's age," groaned Lewis Nichols (*NYT*), "and the creaking muscles which are bad alike for those of late-middle years and the spoken drama." Howard Barnes (*NYHT*) commented, "Pungent dialogue and brilliant performances make *Apple of His Eye* well worth seeing, but the drama itself lacks the cumulative urgency which it is forever promising." But Burton Rascoe (*NYWT*) thought it "a delicate and endearing little item of rural Americana." Cast members included Roy Fant, Doro Merande, Arthur Hunnicutt, and Joseph Sweeney, among others.

ARE YOU WITH IT? [Musical/Barroom/Boarding House/Romance/Sex/Show Business] B: Sam Perrin and George Balzer; M: Harry Revel; LY: Arnold B. Horwitt; SC: George Malcolm-Smith's novel, *Slightly Perfect*; D: Edward Reveaux; CH: Jack Donohue; S/L: George Jenkins; C: Raoul Pène du Bois and Willa Kim; P: Richard Kollmar and James W. Gardiner; T: Century Theatre; 11/10/45 (266)

A somewhat dated book peppered with stale jokes and various suggestive lines and situations was compensated for by a bouncy, fast-paced production that was sufficiently energetic to help this piece become a minor hit in a season marked by few memorable musicals. The most amiable performance was turned in by comic Lew Parker as Goldie, a shady carnival barker who convinces a meek young actuarial whiz named Wilbur Haskins (Johnny Downs), fired by his Hartford insurance company for misplacing a decimal point, to join the colorful Acres of Fun Carnival. His girlfriend Vivian (Joan Roberts) follows. Wilbur is the kind of Milquetoast who orders milk in a barroom. His math abilities make him very helpful to the carny operators until he begins to show the customers how to beat the wheel of fortune. Eventually he uncovers a scam being played on the Nutmeg Insurance Company by the carnival's proprietor and gets his old job back.

Far from being a well-integrated musical, the show was more a succession of strung-together vaudevillelike numbers, including plenty of tap dancing, much of which featured Lou Wills, Jr., Duke McHale, and Bunny Briggs. Among the more memorable moments was the vision--seen in silhouette--of a Hartford boarding house as the attractive female residents awoke to the ringing of alarm clocks and arose, bathed, and donned their lingerie.

The cast was largely made up of unknowns, although Joan Roberts had been making a name for herself. Dolores Gray as sexy tent dancer Bunny Le Fleur was very well liked, especially for her comically innuendo-laden songs. June Richmond, an obese black singer, played the carnival's fat lady and sang "Poor Little Me." There was also a trio of singing and dancing midgets. Among the more appreciated songs were "Here I Go Again" and "This Is My Beloved."

Louis Kronenberger (*PM*) thought that the show got off to a good start, but his interest began to lag as the music wilted and the book fell apart. Rosamond Gilder (*TAM*) said that "it runs through the usual musical comedy gambit with little imagination and considerable bad taste." In between was Euphemia Van Rensselaer Wyatt (*CW*), who said, "It's fast, funny, teeming with color, dance and song but also . . . punctuated by bad taste." But Herrick Brown (*NYS*) called it "a fast-stepping and colorful show that has plenty to recommend it."

ARLENE [Comedy-Drama/Military/Romance/Sex/Youth] A: Henry Rose; D: James S. Elliott: P: Elliott Productions; T: Roerich Theatre (OB); 3/23/42 (4)

Seventeen-year-old James S. Elliott, then appearing in the hit comedy *Junior*

Miss, produced and directed this low-budget production at the small theatre on 103rd Street and Riverside Drive. It is set in a summer vacation cottage community and concerns the tragic outcome of a teenage girl's (Bette Grayson) confrontation with the vagaries of summer love. John Baragrey made his local debut as an American flyer in the RAF. The single review available, by Douglas Watt (*NYDN*), did not comment critically on the play, choosing merely to note that the most remarkable thing about the event was that it marked the debut of so youthful a producer.

ARMOR OF LIGHT [Drama/Bible/Period/Religion] A: Urban Nagle; D: Dennis Gurney; S: Greg Kayne; C: Irene Griffin; L: Joan Tyne; P: Blackfriars' Guild; T: Blackfriars' Playhouse (OB); 2/23/50

A semiprofessional production of Father Nagle's rather talky, highly episodic (twenty-five scenes) religious play about one of the apostles, offered during the Lenten season by a Catholic producing organization. The story is of Christ's arch enemy Saul of Tarsus (Stanley Phillips), a persecutor of Christians, who ultimately becomes a convert, changes his name to Paul, and champions fellow believers against the Pharisees, the Romans, and the worshippers of Zeus. For his troubles as a proselytizer he is stoned and scourged. Ultimately, he is beheaded by the Romans.

The play is concerned more with the events in Paul's life than with his character or those of the people around him; it also becomes so preoccupied with the latter that Paul himself is not given as total a concentration as his character requires. "Instead of selecting his material with a singleness of purpose to develop steadily mounting dramatic impact, [Nagle] has elected a scenario comprising numberless vignettes from the saint's career and peopled them with 50-odd players," complained Bob Francis (*BB*). "The result . . . repetitiously clutters-up and distorts the focus of a story which should deal primarily with inspiration rather than historical events." Richard Watts, Jr. (*NYP*), praised the "quietly restrained" work for being done "with intelligence and taste" and for telling its story "with a pleasant combination of directness and simplicity." Still, he found it less dramatic than earlier Nagle dramas because of its failure to fully explore the character of the saint, who came off as "a rather static figure in a pageant." Thomas R. Dash (*WWD*) believed that "there are a number of scenes that seem only to plod along. When interest sags, some dramatic scene comes along to give the production life and vitality."

Among those singled out by the critics were Paul H. A. Menard as Barnabas, Charles Gilbert as Luke, Hazen Gifford as Mark, Edward Joyce as the cripple made to walk again, and Tom O'Connor as the Lystrian captain. The hordes of actors crowding the tiny stage made many problems for the director, which he was not entirely able to overcome.

ARMS AND THE GIRL [Musical/Military/Period/Romance/War] B: Herbert and Dorothy Fields and Rouben Mamoulian; M: Morton Gould; LY: Dorothy Fields; SC: Lawrence Langner and Armina Marshall's play, *The Pursuit of Happiness**; D: Rouben Mamoulian; CH: Michael Kidd; S: Horace Armistead; C: Audré; P: Theatre Guild i/a/w Anthony Brady Farrell; T: Forty-sixth Street Theatre; 2/2/50 (134)

In 1933 Lawrence Langner and Armina Marshall, writing under the names Alan Child and Isabelle Loudon, provided Broadway with a successful comedy popularly called "the bundling play." Bundling was a colonial-period custom whereby young lovers could spend time together and save fuel on cold winter evenings by lying in bed separated by a sawtooth board. Their story was set in old Connecticut during the American Revolution and concerned the love affair of a fugitive Hessian soldier, deserting the British forces for the American, and the daughter of the farmer at whose house he takes refuge. This tale became the inspiration for this unsuccessful but occasionally effective musical--actually more like an operetta--in which some of the original characters' names were changed, and which starred Nanette Fabray and Frenchman Georges Guetary in the romantic leads. The bundling material was retained--in fact it was expanded to include two men--and offered Fabray some excellent laugh-provoking moments as she made wittily ribald comments about going to bed.

In most eyes, the adaptation of the book was "not conspicuous for originality, skill or beauty," as Brooks Atkinson (*NYT*) noted. "It is a mechanical and only moderately entertaining show," commented Hobe. (*V*). Howard Barnes (*NYHT*) labeled it "a beautiful, if somewhat ponderous entertainment," burdened with a book that was "wordy, repetitious and poorly paced." The several positive dissenters included Thomas R. Dash (*WWD*), who deemed this "a pleasantly beguiling and disarming show."

In this free version of the story, the heroine is named Jo Kirkland, and she is a patriot who considers herself a colonial Joan of Arc. She dresses in male military attire and carries a sword and a rifle. She is an active fighter for independence in the Connecticut countryside. In one scene, she blows up a bridge, and fish are tossed all over the stage. Enmeshed in the action is the story of her love affair with the Hessian, now called Franz. Jo suspects most people of being spies for the enemy, especially Colonel Mortimer Sherwood (John Conte). To her embarrassment, Sherwood turns out to be a trusted aide to General Washington. Finally, Jo's overzealous activities are halted in the interests of the Revolution, by the intercession of Washington (Arthur Vinton) himself, appearing at the end astride a large white charger.

There were a handful of highly approving critics, but to many, Gould's music was not of lasting quality; Kidd's choreography, while occasionally rousing, eventually paled; and Fields's lyrics were undistinguished. Pearl Bailey, playing a runaway slave named Connecticut, stole all her scenes--if not the show itself--and had two contagiously infectious numbers, "There Must Be Something Better Than Love" and "Nothin' for Nothin'," but neither song had much to do with the rest of the show. Richard Watts, Jr. (*NYP*), stated that Bailey "has never been more engagingly skillful, and her humorous brilliance made what I suspect are fairly ordinary songs seem witty and charming."

Guetary was considered an attractive embellishment to the Broadway scene and was commended for his acting, outstanding tenor voice, and considerable comic talents. His best songs were "I Like It Here," "A Cow and a Plough and a Frau," and "She's Exciting," while Fabray offered such tunes as "That's My Fella," "You Kissed Me," and "I'll Never Learn." The three stars stopped the show with their hilarious "Plantation in Philadelphia" number, which was also a dance highlight.

Important roles were played by Florenz Ames as a homespun officer and Eda Heinemann as his snippy spouse. Cliff Dunstan and Seth Arnold were also in the show, and the large dance ensemble included future choreographers Onna White and Peter Gennaro.

The big, white horse used in the show caused considerable apprehension among the cast members because such animals are unpredictable scene stealers. Although the horse behaved properly for a time, Bailey and Fabray harbored doubts about how long this would last. Eventually, he seemed to be getting a bit ornery, possibly from boredom, and the actors grew somewhat anxious. Finally, one night, as Fabray and Bailey (who told the story in *The Raw Pearl*) were standing nervously together onstage, the horse made his appearance "when plop, plop, plop, it fell. I heard Nanette say, 'Oops' and boy, the entire place went to pieces. It took the audience awhile to realize what had happened, but when they did, the band went to pieces, the audience was hysterical, the cast laid out on the stage, doors being flung open. Mr. Horse, with George aboard, took the biggest dump in history. I must give the actor credit; he sat tall in the saddle."

ARMY PLAY-BY-PLAY, THE [One-Acts/Military/War] S: Cirker and Robbins Studio; P: John Golden i/a/w the Special Service Branch Headquarters Second Service Command of the U.S. Army; T: Forty-sixth Street Theatre; 6/14/43 (1)
"Where E'er We Go" [Comedy] A: Private John B. O'Dea; D: Private Paul Tripp; "First Cousins" [Drama/Sea] A: Corporal Kurt Kasznar; D: Sergeant Gordon B. Thomson; "Button Your Lip" [Comedy] A: Private Irving Gaynor Neiman; D: Private Arthur O'Connell; "Mail Call" [Drama] A: Air Cadet Ralph Nelson; D: Joseph Ross Hertz; "Pack Up Your Troubles" [Comedy-Drama] A: Private Alfred Geto; D: Corporal Alan Wilson

The Soldiers and Sailors Club of New York was the beneficiary of the $100,000 in receipts taken in for a single performance of these 5 one-acts selected out of 115 as the winners of a servicemen's playwriting contest. The judges were Russel Crouse, Kenyon Nicholson, Elmer Rice, and John Golden, the latter contributing the prize money (which ranged from $100 to $40). Film beauty Myrna Loy played a bit part in one of the plays, giving the evening a cachet of glamour. Hers was the only female presence on the stage all evening, as all the plays dealt with men in wartime situations and all the players were soldiers.

The distinguished opening-night audience included, in addition to various military brass, the president's wife, the duke and duchess of Windsor, and the mayor. The latter four were all called up on stage by producer Golden and received tumultuous applause. In the intermissions there was music by an army band, and various soldiers entertained with specialty routines, among them Private Jules Munshin (later a popular comic actor), whose routine spoofed opera singing.

"Where E'er We Go" was set in a wooden barracks in Fort Lewis, Washington, and presented a cross-section of life in that locale, with poker-playing soldiers, a lothario bragging of his conquests, furloughs, and so on. A private (Sergeant Philip Kaplan) tries to raise the money from his mates to finance a trip to Los Angeles on his leave and, thinking that the company will be sent to the tropics, sells his warm coat for $10 to do so, but news arrives that leaves are canceled and that they are heading for what is rumored to be Alaska; the soldier who sold his coat collapses. It was a light comedy and was considered one of the better offerings. The company's actors hailed from Camp Wood. Private Paul Tripp, who also directed, was among them.

Next came "First Cousins," performed by the Special Service Branch Headquarters Second Command Service, New York City. It was set in the hull of a small German submarine. The serious tale was of a quartet of captured Americans on the sub, the commander of which (Corporal Kurt Kasznar, the author) is convinced by one of the captives, who is of German descent, that they are first cousins. The "cousin" kills the commander and the Yanks gain control of the sub. Kasznar, a Viennese refugee, already had begun to make an impression on the New York stage.

Third was "Button Your Lip," a comedy set in the barracks washroom at Camp Downey. It was a funny piece, reminiscent of a revue sketch. A brand-new rookie (Corporal Erving J. Engleman) keeps getting fouled up with camp regulations. The camp's rules about the dangers of loose talk provide the impetus for much of the action. The rookie brags that he knows Myrna Loy, and at the end of the piece Loy herself appears--she had a single line--to validate his boast. The actors were from Fort Monmouth. Among those who later made a name for themselves were Harold Gary and Arthur O'Connell, the latter also directing.

"Mail Call," a sentimental piece about courage under fire, takes place in the shelter of a nearly destroyed village behind the lines in Europe and has to do with a soldier who deserted and was shot. His buddies write a letter to one of his relatives, praising him for bravery. One of the soldiers, declaring that the dead man was a coward, refuses to sign. During a subsequent attack the dissenter proves cowardly, and the others force him to affix his name to the letter.

Last came "Pack Up Your Troubles," a comedy that used a company from Camp Upton. It was set in a warehouse at a receiving station and concerned a soldier trying to find out long distance about the sex of his newborn child; locating the right change and getting the right number are obstacles he comically encounters. He also manages to capture a pair of German saboteurs planning to blow up a troop train. Private Alfred Ryder and Private Jules Munshin were among the actors.

The critics deemed the overall program a delight and regretted that it was given only a single performance. Howard Barnes (*NYHT*) alleged that the program "has the exuberance and sincerity that makes the theater come alive and take an audience right into camp."

Because of the warm response and the request for more performances, the program was brought back on 8/2/43 at the Martin Beck Theatre (provided rent-free by Beck's widow). Two weeks of performances were scheduled, but the run was extended to 40 showings, the proceeds going to the Army Emergency Relief Fund. During the interim the pieces had been performed at President Roosevelt's residence in Hyde Park, and his wife, Eleanor, took the one-line part in "Button Your Lip" that had been played by Myrna Loy (the character's name was changed accordingly, of course). On opening night Mrs. Roosevelt appeared on stage to give a brief speech. The Myrna Loy role was taken by different female celebrities, such as Gertrude Lawrence and Glenda Farrell, at each performance during the run. The program was a great success with audiences (many among them being servicemen).

AROUND THE WORLD [Musical/Adventure/Gambling/Period/Sea] B/D: Orson Welles; M/LY: Cole Porter; SC: Jules Verne's novel, *The Tour of the World in Eighty Days*; CH: Nelson Barclift; S: Robert Davison; C: Alvin Colt; P: Mercury Productions; T: Adelphi Theatre; 5/31/46 (75)

After several years in Hollywood, Orson Welles returned to Broadway with this unsuccessful musical extravaganza based on one of his favorite childhood novels. He produced, directed, and adapted the work as well as acting the role of the villainous Inspector Dick Fix, who follows the hero around the globe in a series of disguises. He had taken on the role for a single performance during the out-of-town tryouts in order to show the actor playing it what he was after, but his performance was so effective that the actor quit, realizing that he could never duplicate it.

The $200,000 production was an elaborate one, designed to satisfy Welles's desires to place on stage the succession of spectacular locales required by the picaresque story. He dreamed up one unusual and extravagant scene and effect after another and spent so much money in production expenses that the cast, apart from himself, was limited to unknowns and little-knowns. Unfortunately, Cole Porter's hurriedly written score was second-rate and proved of great harm to the show's chances. By the time of the out-of-town tryout, the show was in bad shape, with a formless book, a weak score, and a warehouse of expensive sets and costumes lacking cohesion in their effort to tell of the round-the-world trip (made on a wager) of Phileas Fogg (Arthur Margetson).

There were thirty-four scenes in various London environments, at Charing Cross Railroad Station, Egypt, India, the Himalayas, a ship on the China Sea, a Hong Kong opium den, a circus in Yokohama, the movies, a California bordello, San Francisco, a Central Pacific railway car, the Rockies (where a train wreck was enacted), Medicine Bow, Bald Mountain, Liverpool, and so on. To produce so extravagant a show required large amounts of money, and the preproduction process was largely taken up with Welles scampering for financing and losing the investment of Michael Todd in the process when Todd refused to go along with one of Welles's more elaborate notions (Welles had wanted to have a well gush oil in one scene). Todd would one day make his own highly successful movie version of the story. One way Welles raised money was to do a number of guest appearances on the radio, earning as much as $5,000 to $10,000 a shot. He also committed himself to a number of film acting jobs in the future to get advances from Columbia Pictures (he called it "mortgaging my blood"). The show wiped out Welles's savings and--because of consequent tax problems--was a major reason for his subsequent long-time residence abroad. Welles's concoction turned out to be a lot of scenery without a show. The book was weak and the score (apart from "Should I Tell You I Love You?" and "Pipe Dreaming") was tepid.

The New York critics were mostly unimpressed, although a few, like John Chapman (*NYDN*) were highly favorable. Lewis Nichols (*NYT*) thought the show a disunified and stylistic hodgepodge; George Jean Nathan (*TBY*) complained that one minute he liked it and the next minute he did not, back and forth throughout the show.

Around the World, taking place in 1872, was set against a nineteenth-century-style proscenium to recapture the atmosphere of old-time melodrama and show business. The sets were largely composed of flying drops of gaslight-vintage appearance. The show had so many elements in it, including a circus act, miniaturized boats and trains, a mechanical papier-maché elephant, a flying eagle, film segments, and Welles himself doing a magic act, that it was accused by Robert Garland (*NYJA*) of having everything but the kitchen stove. (Fifty-five stagehands were employed to run it.) Welles reacted by making a curtain speech for which he pushed on stage a kitchen stove on wheels. Euphemia Van Rensselaer Wyatt (*CW*), kinder than most, described the work as "a devulgarized *Hellz-A-Poppin** [*sic*] with some sly wit and clever people; amusing pageantry; totem-pole Indians; real acrobats; magic and songs."

Because he was appearing on a Friday-night radio series at the time, there were no Friday-night performances. Welles tried to remedy the matter by giving the stage show as usual; suspending the action from ten o'clock to ten thirty so he could do his radio broadcast from the Adelphi's stage instead of the CBS studio (thereby providing the audience with two shows for the price of one); and then resuming the stage show. The unions rejected the proposal.

Welles was so upset by the critical attacks on the show that he used his radio broadcasts to rip the critics. Once he even threatened them with voodoo (critic Percy Hammond allegedly had died as a result of voodoo rituals performed by members of Welles's 1936 Caribbean version of *Macbeth**). The show was the second of the season inspired by Verne's book, the earlier one (also a flop) having been *Nellie Bly*. In the cast of Welles's mounting were Mary Healy, Larry Laurence, and Julie Warren.

ARSENIC AND OLD LACE [Comedy/Crime/Mental Illness/Old Age/Romance/Theatre] A: Joseph Kesselring; D: Bretaigne Windust; S: Raymond Sovey; P: Howard Lindsay and Russel Crouse; T: Fulton Theatre; 1/10/41 (1,444)

High up on the all-time list of long-run shows is this enormously successful farce-melodrama about murder by elderberry wine that has become a standby of amateur and professional theatres ever since. Written with Howard Lindsay's wife, Dorothy Stickney, in mind for one of the leads, it had been submitted to Lindsay and his partner Russel Crouse three years earlier under the title *Bodies in Our Cellar*. The producers bought it but, preoccupied with other projects, kept it on ice until it was finally revised and produced.

It was widely believed that a large amount of material was contributed by the successful playwright-producers, who shared in the royalties as coauthors without receiving authors' credit. (They themselves denied having made the improvements, but Cornelia Otis Skinner, in *Life with Lindsay and Crouse*, revealed that "they all but rewrote everything, changing many of the situations and introducing some new characters.") For every $500 invested, backers received $18,000. Lindsay and Crouse used to send the backers their checks with such salutations as "Dear Little Cherub," "You Lucky Stiff," or "You Money-Mad People."

Because Lindsay was appearing in *Life with Father* during the preparatory period of *Arsenic and Old Lace*, he did not get to see a performance of it until well after it had become a hit. The performance he viewed was given as a special one for the cadets at West Point. His comment was, "This seems to be a very funny play, something like a mixture of *The Bat* and *Charley's Aunt*. Maybe we ought to keep it open" (quoted in William G. B. Carson's *Dear Josephine*).

The idea for the play came to Kesselring when he tried to come up with a farcical story line about the thing that his own grandmother would be most unlikely to do. Murder was his answer, but since murder, at least one murder, did not seem funny, he decided to make his play about multiple murders, all within a preposterous situation that would remove the possibility of making the killings seem gruesome or cruel. The plot he conceived is about Aunt Abby Brewster (Josephine Hull) and Aunt Martha Brewster (Jean Adair), two old Brooklyn biddies who, on the surface, are the quintessential examples of kind, old, biscuit-baking, tea- and hot-soup-dispensing ladies. They charitably take into their spacious but decaying brownstone home a series of homeless, familyless old men, presumably to offer them room and board, but actually to solve their personal problems by poisoning them with arsenic-, strychnine-, and cyanide-spiked doses of elderberry wine. Teddy Brewster (John Alexander), their mad brother who thinks that he is Teddy Roosevelt digging the Panama Canal, and who is constantly rushing up the stairs shouting "Charge!" as if they were San Juan Hill, disposes of the corpses by burying them in the cellar, where appropriately solemn last rites are held. To him, the men are victims of yellow fever and the holes are canal locks. Twelve such persons have been buried when the play begins. Things begin to fall apart when a body is discovered in the window seat by nephew Mortimer (Allyn Joslyn), a theatre-hating theatre critic and the only sane Brewster. (A high point comes when he learns that he is a bastard and not heir to the strain of Brewster lunacy.) Learning of the previous murders, he bends his efforts to hushing up his aunts' homicidal hobby while seeing to it that they are safely ensconced in a suitable institution. They, for their part, can't see why he is making such a fuss over so trivial a matter. Complicating matters is the arrival of yet another Brewster, Jonathan, a convicted killer (also of twelve men) who has escaped from prison with a body of his own to dispose of. Accompanying him is his accomplice, Dr. Einstein (Edgar Stehli), a movie-mad plastic surgeon who is responsible for making him resemble horror-film actor Boris Karloff, who played the role in his Broadway debut. (The road version employed another Hollywood villain, Erich Von Stroheim, for whom the Karloff references in the dialogue were accordingly changed.) Jonathan would like very much to dispense homicidally with Mortimer. Other humorous infusions are provided by the local cop, Officer O'Hara (Anthony Ross), who has written a play that he will read at the slightest provocation, and by Elaine Harper (Helen Brooks), Mortimer's fiancée. At the end of the play, as the sisters are preparing to leave for the asylum, they suggest that the elderly head of the institution, Mr. Witherspoon (William Parke), will soon become their thirteenth victim, thereby topping Jonathan's total, which will give them competitive satisfaction. Mr. Witherspoon sips the brew, says, "Delicious!" and promptly passes on. The unusual curtain call included thirteen actors representing all the corpses supposedly buried in the cellar. (On opening night, after fifteen curtain calls, and with an audience willing to give more, the backstage crew refused to lift the cloth any more in hopes of driving the happy spectators out of the place.)

"Swift, dry, satirical and exciting, *Arsenic and Old Lace* kept the first-night audience roaring with laughter," reported Brooks Atkinson (*NYT*). "It is full of chuckles even when the scene is gruesome by nature. . . . The lines are bright. The story is mad and unhackneyed." Hobe. (*V*) called it "one of the most wildly hilarious Broadway shows in years. . . . It has a number of scalp-tingling moments, invariably turned into the dizziest kind of comedy and once more demonstrating the close relationship of terror and mirth." Richard Watts, Jr. (*NYHT*), averred, "While the thrills are surprisingly authentic and the comedy is genuinely uproarious, the abiding feature of the entertainment is that an incredible air of sweetness hangs about this farcical melodramatic insanity."

The evening was well served by outstanding direction, decor, and performance, with special brilliance provided by the two old aunts. As Rosamond Gilder (*TAM*) observed, "Both Miss Hull and Miss Adair succeed to perfection in conveying the really amiable quality of the elderly ladies, without overstressing or forcing their parts." Hull received an opening-night wire from Lindsay stating simply, "Tonight, Josephine."

The casting of Boris Karloff in the role of someone who resembled him was a delightful concept, although the actor was reluctant to undertake the part because, being shy, he had a fear of live audiences. He also insisted that there be at least three parts more important than his own, hoping that they would cover his inadequacies. Russel Crouse had to go to Hollywood to talk him into it. According to Skinner, he later told an interviewer, "I went to his house to sign him up with a pen in one hand and a contract in the other. But when he opened the door, I took one look at that face. I let out a scream that curdled milk for miles around and started running." Cynthia Lindsay said in *Dear Boris* that Crouse convinced Karloff to take the role by quoting one of the character's lines. When Jonathan is questioned about one of his killings, he answers, "I killed him because he said I looked like Boris Karloff." The good-humored actor loved the idea of mocking his own persona. During the run, the producers would tease the star about his $2,000-plus-a-week salary. They once paid him in nickels. Another time, they gave him a new contract, with his salary listed as $25 and whatever people threw on the stage. When Karloff humorously retaliated by threatening to quit unless given a salary increase to pay for makeup and powder, he received a large, elaborately decorated box that contained, wrote Skinner, "tooth powder, foot powder, baking powder, roach powder, gun powder, Seidlitz powders and powdered eggs."

During the run there was a benefit production of the play given at two special Sunday matinees beginning 12/12/43 with the young actors of the Professional Children's School. This was at the Hudson Theatre, to which the play had moved. The critics found it a charming and effective presentation.

ARTISTS AND MODELS [Revue] CN: Lou Walters; SK: Lou Walters, Don Ross, and Frank Luther; M/LY: Dan Shapiro, Milton Pascal, and Phil Charig; D: Lou Walters and John Kennedy; CH: Natalie Kamarova and Lauretta Jefferson; S: Watson Barratt; C: Kathryn Kuhn; P: Lou Walters and Don Ross i/a/w E. M. Loew and Michael Redstone; T: Broadway Theatre; 11/5/43 (28)

Singers Jane Froman and Frances Faye (who also played the piano) and come dian Jackie Gleason, each eventually a name to conjure with, were in this revue, which borrowed its title* from a series that appeared on Broadway from 1923 through 1930. The format was tired, the material was uninspired, and the show, for all its opulence, was a flop. George Jean Nathan (*TBY*) summarized it as "an elaborate 225,000 dollar [it actually cost $150,000] version of all the stale chorus numbers, cheap tunes, bad skits and old jokes that the worst of Earl Carroll's *Vanities**, along with *Viva O'Brien** and *Hairpin Harmony**, somehow overlooked." A bevy of fifteen beautiful showgirls was one of the show's main attractions (they opened the show with a "Parade of Models," each of them named after a perfume, such as My Sin, Midnight Madness, and Golden Day), but there were plenty of other contributions to keep one's eyes and ears, if not one's mind, attentive.

This was Jane Froman's first appearance since becoming disabled in a Clipper plane crash in Lisbon while on her way to entertain the boys in North Africa for the USO (a story told in the movie about her life, *With a Song in My Heart*). She had to perform sitting down, but no reference was made to her problem throughout the show. One of her numbers was as part of a minstrel show, when she sang "Swing Low, Sweet Harriet." Among her other songs were "You Are Romance" and "My Heart Is on a Binge Again." Froman's was deemed the most effective performance, possibly because of her pluckiness. As Euphemia Van Rensselaer Wyatt (*CW*) penned, "Jane Froman, beautiful and gallant, sings the best songs and puts enough verve in them to make you forget the cast hidden under the flounces of her costumes."

The show had an eclectic assortment of entertainers and entertainments, including circus tumblers, lavish production numbers, various singers, a ballet with Carol King, ballroom dancers such as Mary Raye and Naldi, a coyly decorous strip act with the stripper remaining fully dressed, and comedy routines featuring Gleason, Marty May, and Billy Newell, but most of them were unfunny. A sample of the comedy was the sketch called "Hollywood, or the Road to Manasooris," set on a tropical island and making sport of the virgin princess's chastity. One of Gleason's highlights was an impression of Jimmy Durante. A song within the sketch, "Sears-Roebuck," had a line about the use of the company's catalogue as toilet paper by rural citizens. "The revue formula needs imagination and flair," insisted Rosamond Gilder (*TAM*). "A succession of songs and skits will not of itself make a show when talent is lacking."

AS THE GIRLS GO [Musical/Family/Marriage/Politics/Sex/Women] B: William Roos; M: Jimmy McHugh; LY: Harold Adamson; D/S: Howard Bay; CH: Hermes Pan; C: Oleg Cassini; P: Michael Todd; T: Winter Garden; 11/13/48 (414)

When this musical, starring Bobby Clark and Irene Rich, opened in Boston for its tryout, it was given devastatingly negative reviews. Producer Michael Todd then set to work with his creative staff to completely rewrite the book, which had been intended as a political satire, in order to provide the kind of lavishly produced, low-comedy, girl-filled show for which he was famous. Clark, cast as the husband of the first woman president (Rich), had been playing what amounted to second banana in the original; now he was made top banana and allowed to wear his trademark painted spectacles and play with his standard cigar and cane. As the musical was reworked in New Haven, new sets, comic routines, and songs were added to show off

Clark's presence. Todd finally brought the show to Broadway, where he had to pay $340,000 to get it on. Despite the then-astronomical top ticket price of $7.20 he charged, the show remained in the red.

The production was in the rowdy style of a bygone Broadway, with a bevy of forty-two long-legged, skimpily dressed chorines (there were frequent comments on their relative nudity), considerable burlesque humor, and a decided absence of social commentary, serious music, or arty dance routines (although Bill Callahan and Kathryn Lee did have several balletic opportunities). The show also gained a big laugh by employing a huge screen to present the president's televised inaugural address.

The action is set several years down the line, in 1952, and concerns the election of the first woman president, Lucille Thompson Wellington (Irene Rich), and the feminist touches she brings to the job (such as Secret Service women). The brunt of the action falls, however, on the First Gentleman, as her ogling husband Waldo (Clark) is known, who takes advantage of his position to chase skirts and to intrude on his son Kenny's (Callahan) romance with Kathy Robinson (Betty Jane Watson). There is also a foiled attempt to spoil his wife's name by proving to the public that the goatish First Gentleman is an unfaithful womanizer.

His role gave Clark an opportunity to don numerous costumes and carry on with constant slapstick capers. In one funny scene he was dressed as a female mani curist (with hot towels stuffed into his chest to simulate a bosom); in another he insisted on giving the taciturn White House barber a shave and a haircut while practically talking the man to death.

There were only a few decidedly downbeat notices, among them George Freedley's (*NYMT*). Finding mediocrity in most of the show's creative departments, Freedley claimed that intrinsically promising subject matter was abandoned to create a vehicle for Clark. (A number of critics felt that Rich's role was underwritten so as not to detract from Clark's.) Howard Barnes (*NYHT*) thought the work little more than "a haphazard and laggard entertainment" notable mainly for Clark's raucously hilarious vaudevillian antics. But more common were the kudos of reviewers such as Brooks Atkinson (*NYT*), who called this "a bountiful and uproarious musical show." Kahn. (*V*) thought it "a tasteful, tuneful musical. . . . A beautiful show of beautiful people. It can't miss." Few critics respected the book, but what book there was served its purpose as a springboard for Clark.

There were a number of fine tunes with clever lyrics, among them, "You Say the Nicest Things, Baby," "There's No Getting Away from You," "Rock, Rock, Rock" (a foretaste of a coming musical style), "I've Got the President's Ear," "It Takes a Woman to Get a Man," and "Lucky in the Rain." The expert cast included Betty Lou Barto, Hobart Cavanaugh, and Dick Dana. Also coming in for much praise were the lovely sets of Howard Bay (who was making his Broadway directing bow) and the often-revealing costumes of fashion designer Oleg Cassini, in his first Broadway outing.

AS WE FORGIVE OUR DEBTORS [Comedy/Family/Legacy/Rural/Sex] A: Tillman Breiseth; D: José Ferrer; S/C: Carl Kent; L: Herbert Brodkin; P: Experimental Theatre; T: Princess Theatre; 3/9/47 (5)

The third offering of the Experimental Theatre's 1946-1947 season was this often lively three-act comedy said by George Freedley (*NYMT*) to have been inspired by Henri Becque's 1882 *Les Corbeaux* (*The Vultures*). The play had been waiting for a production for two decades, but most producers felt it too risky a venture. Even with several fairly positive reviews, no producer saw fit to offer it commercially. Freedley said that it suffered from excessive length and was desperately in need of cutting; José Ferrer was faulted for not having seen to this important directorial function, although most critics approved of his handling of the action.

Breiseth's work was set at a Minnesota farmhouse at which the nieces and nephews of affluent aunt Etta Sturkelson, who has died, gather for the funeral and reading of the will. What begins as sorrow for the dearly departed soon dwindles into an outpouring of rapacious and carnal behavior as the various family members bicker over their selfish claims to part of Aunt Etta's legacy (a farm, creamery shares, and $800 in cash). Expecting to be rewarded for what they perceive as their virtuous behavior, the family is astonished at the ironical attitude taken by the deceased in leaving her possessions to a promiscuous niece, Gonda (Dorothea McFarland), whose expectations are small, but whose good nature and honesty stand out against the background of familial hypocrisy. Not only does Gonda gain the creamery shares, she also runs off with her grasping sister's (Sylvia Stone) husband (Joel Ashley). The cash gets burned accidently, and the farm goes to a couple (Jennette Dowling and Somer Alberg) who maintained it in Aunt Etta's declining years.

To Brooks Atkinson (*NYT*), the comedy excelled at characterization and a style that was "droll and occasionally sardonic," but suffered from structural and thematic shapelessness. George Jean Nathan (*TBY*) noted the play's overextension of its theme, its faulty dramaturgy, and thinning comedy, but he praised its author's "good sense of character, . . . unorthodox dramatic mind, and . . . considerable gift for irreverent whimsicality." He also defended its "experimental" nature against those who claimed that its aims were too commercial. Good performances were turned in by Paul Ford (who excelled as a comic parson), Joyce Ross, Kenneth Tobey, Graham Velsey, and Will Lee, among others.

AS YOU DESIRE ME (***Come Tu Mi Vuoi***) [Dramatic Revival*] A: Luigi Pirandello; D: Ilia Motyleff; P: Equity Library Theatre; T: Hudson Park Branch of the New York Public Library (OB); 1/30/45

The young unknowns in this shoestring revival of the 1931 Italian drama were not ready for the play's subtleties despite the direction of the man who staged the original version in Italy with Marta Abba. "So difficult a play to act is this, so demanding of smoothness and professional ease on the parts of its actors, that it was scarcely a wise choice for the project," insisted George Freedley (*NYMT*), the sole critic attending. The role of the Unknown Lady fell to Mary Hayden, but she proved vocally monotonous and emotionally unconvincing. Betsy Staples and Michael Blair were also in the play.

(1) AS YOU LIKE IT [Dramatic Revival*] A: William Shakespeare; M: Henry Holt; D: Eugene S. Bryden; S/C: Lemuel Ayers; P: Ben A. Boyar and Eugene S. Bryden; T: Mansfield Theatre; 10/20/41 (8)

Alfred Drake, who would become a major star of musical comedy as well as one with a strong Shakespearean résumé, made his first venture into the world of the Bard with his performance as Orlando in this ill-fated revival. He was received cordially, especially by Brooks Atkinson (*NYT*): "He is intelligent and frank; and since he speaks his lines as though an ordinary person might conceivably understand their meaning, his Orlando is intelligible and engaging."

Others involved included Carol Stone (young daughter of famed comic actor Fred Stone) as Celia, Helen Craig as Rosalind, Harry Sheppard as Corin, Leonard Elliott as Touchstone, Arthur L. Sachs as Oliver, Philip Bourneuf as Jacques (Atkinson thought him the best Jacques he had ever seen), Paula Trueman as Phebe, and Kenneth Tobey in the tiny roles of William and Dennis. None were big stars, and the absence of "names" was considered a commercial drawback. The play had had a number of New York stagings since 1923, the last being in 1937.

The one-intermission production, which emphasized broad humor, was reasonably stylized. John Anderson (*NYJA*) described the set as "a large, circular mound, something like an igloo with fallen arches. Slender trees are stuck on it and the unit is mounted on a turntable. The actors are plainly uncomfortable on the slopes, so that the accessible playing area is virtually limited to a narrow apron of level territory between the mound and the footlight trough." Costumes were "timeless," being confined to no specific period and using elements from several. Rowland Field (*NEN*) commented, "Many of the men . . . seem attired in trapper outfits, suggesting the Daniel Boone era, while others include a Cossack with a balalaika and a comedy vicar with a red-and-white striped umbrella." There was nothing especially prepossessing about the design elements.

Reviews were noticeably mixed. Rosamond Gilder (*TAM*), while detecting certain faults, found that the production was high-spirited and charming, being "in the correct mood of fantasy and light-heartedness," although suffering now and then from "an archness, an over-enthusiasm, a surface playfulness that can become coy," and that often affects American productions of Shakespeare. Others found the staging lacking in lyricism and too dependent on obvious business. Louis Kronenberger (*PM*), convinced that the play itself was a tiresome bore, noted that the cast did what it could to liven up the proceedings, but went too far. "Everybody pranced and sported, and scampered and cavorted, and made merry and sang Ho! . . . Blame Shakespeare for some of the trouble, but Bryden's direction for more."

(2) D: Beverly Bush (based on an "original idea" of John Burgess's); S: Charles Elson; L: Stanley Jennings; P: Beverly Bush and John Burgess; T: President Theatre (OB); 7/3/45 (7)

This "modernized" adaptation of Shakespeare's vernal comedy was premiered at the University of Washington (from whence stemmed most of its company) and toured California before arriving on Broadway. The streamlined text had been reduced to seven scenes spread over three acts, with the concomitant elimination of a number of characters.

Director-producer Bush played Audrey, and coproducer Burgess (upon whose idea the production was based) played Orlando. Margretta Ramsey was Rosalind, Marian Hall was Celia, and George L. Headley was Jacques, but the only acceptable performance was Norman Budd's as Touchstone. Lewis Funke (*NYT*) found that despite the modern touches, including a cast dressed in gym shorts, "the pace is slow and tedious, and the over-all result a clumsy evisceration." George Jean Nathan (*TBY*) rejected the affair as insufferably amateurish.

(3) D: Donald Wolfit; S/C: Ernest Stern; P: Hall Shelton b/a/w Advance Players Association, Ltd., of London; T: Century Theatre; 2/20/47 (4)

One of five plays offered by England's Donald Wolfit Repertory Company (*King Lear**, *The Merchant of Venice**, *Hamlet**, and *Volpone** were the other plays). Wolfit played Touchstone, Alexander Gauge played the duke, David Dodimead played Frederick and Sir Oliver Martext, John Wynyard played Jacques, Geoffrey Wilkinson played Le Beau, Josef Shear played Charles and William, Kempster Barnes played Orlando, Eric Adeney played Adam, Malcolm Watson played Corin, Robert Algar played Hymen and Amiens, Rosalind Iden played Rosalind, Penelope Chandler played Celia, Ann Chalkley played Phebe, and Marion Marshall played Audrey.

Apart from Wolfit and Iden, this was a generally undistinguished troupe, and the reviews reflected critical disappointment in most of their ventures. George Jean Nathan (*TBY*), for one, noted that "The supporting company is of a distinctly provincial flavor and in the main grossly incompetent." Although the general opinion held that the production was an improvement over the company's disastrous *Lear*, it still seemed to most crude and poorly acted. The simple sets were composed of colorfully painted movable screens, which were not visually beguiling. Rosamond Gilder (*TAM*) claimed that the production lapsed "into banality and commonplace."

Wolfit's Touchstone, said George Freedley (*NYMT*), was, like the production, "all obvious, pretty, and heavy-handed." Brooks Atkinson (*NYT*) sniped that he was "a little too sophisticated for such humdrum virtues as intelligibility." But Richard Watts, Jr. (*NYP*), said that "he is pleasant and forthright, if understandably not hilarious." A bit better was the troupe's leading lady, Rosalind Iden, who was charming looking and managed to convey some appeal. "She is pretty to look at, and she plays with spirit and gaiety, and with no more archness than the part compels upon her," declared Louis Kronenberger (*PM*). Of Wynyard's Jacques, Atkinson gave one of the kinder comments in declaring that he "substitutes for the traditional melancholy a thinner and more sardonic spirit. Although the style is not fully resolved, he has caught hold of a good idea that is worth strengthening."

(4) M: Robert Irving; D: Michael Benthall; S/C: James Bailey; L: James Bailey and

Michael Benthall; P: Theatre Guild; T: Cort Theatre; 1/26/50 (145)

This sumptuously designed revival of Shakespeare's oft-produced bucolic comedy, achieved its record-breaking long run primarily because it starred outstanding stage and film actress Katharine Hepburn as Rosalind. It was her first Broadway appearance since *Without Love* in 1942. Hepburn's long legs, encased in tights, were pictured in numerous journalistic layouts and greatly enhanced the show's box-office possibilities. The reviews were mixed, however, and many dismissed the actress's classical acting powers.

Costarring with Hepburn were such excellent players as William Prince giving a solid performance as Orlando, Cloris Leachman as a decent but overshadowed Celia, Bill Owen as a human but not very funny Touchstone, and Ernest Thesiger as an aging but honest Jacques, reading his "seven ages" speech "in a low, restrained, almost confidential voice" (Robert Coleman [*NYDM*]). In their support were Burton Mallory as Adam, Aubrey Mather as the duke, Ernest Graves as Oliver, Michael Everett as Charles, Jay Robinson as Le Beau and Sir Oliver Martext, Dayton Lummis as Frederick, Frank Rogier as Amiens, Whitford Kane as Corin, Judy Parrish as Phebe, Patricia Englund as Audrey, and Robert Foster as Dennis and William. Most were considered fine to excellent, but the brunt of the notices went to Hepburn.

British director Benthall's first American production was praised for its beautifully idyllic sets and costumes, but division reigned concerning his staging. Richard Watts, Jr. (*NYP*), convinced (as were many others) that the play was mediocre Shakespeare, nevertheless was enthralled; he said that the production made "the lyric grace and sweetness of the text come alive, and the result is an evening of theatrical enchantment." "Benthall has made the flimsy story move, and even though at times it's over-paced and a little hectic, at least the play doesn't have the static quality of a Shakespearean comedy revival," wrote Bron. (*V*). But others, such as Brooks Atkinson (*NYT*), found it too busy and old-fashioned, with an excessive use of sound and stage effects.

To prepare her for her first Shakespearean role, Hepburn hired veteran actress Constance Collier as a coach. Still, there were a good many who felt that Hepburn lacked the proper charm for Rosalind, that she took too direct and forcible an approach to conveying boyishness, and that her individualistic qualities of personality and voice were intrusive. Most of the commentary mentioned not only her acting but her physical appeal. A serious detractor was Atkinson, who appreciated her looks but felt that she lacked the "romantic and disarming graces" to play the role. "She is not a helpless, bewitched, moonstruck maiden. . . . There is too much Yankee in Miss Hepburn for Shakespeare's glades and lyric fancies." He picked on her "tight" acting, her "hard and shallow" voice, and her twanging accent. Howard Barnes (*NYHT*) thought that Hepburn did have some scenes of poetic effectiveness, but, but by and large, she "reads her lines with a strident insistency that becomes uncomfortable." And Joseph T. Shipley (*NL*) averred, "Katharine Hepburn cannot make up her mind how to play Rosalind; her voice is at times matter-of-fact, but it ranges from such realism on up through the degrees of love to rapture until it seems a parody of itself. Her manners match her speaking." However, Whitney Bolton (*NYMT*), who thought the play itself "terrible, as any one knows," commented, "I think she was pure delight as Rosalind and . . . I also think that the very first professional good look at her legs revealed a pair as lissome and winning as any in sight." He asked, "Name me a Rosalind who could have drawn more genuine loveliness from the scenes with Orlando in the Forest of Arden, the major scene with Phebe in the Forest and the wedding scene at the end. Not only was she a joy to the eye, but she fell upon the ear with grace and sincerity." Bron. added, "Miss Hepburn, though slightly mannered and individualistic, gives a scintillating performance . . . , delivering the lines with fire and warmth. In femme garb she's a honey, and in the male attire . . . she's a leggy eyeful." Watts stated, "She plays with such spirit, tenderness, humor, grace and vitality and looks so beautiful, that her Rosalind becomes a characterization of sheer loveliness."

(1) ASCENT OF F-6, THE [Comedy/British/Family/Fantasy/Politics] A: W. H.

Auden and Christopher Isherwood; M: Robert Pennington and Haywood Morris; D: Robert Ramsey; P: On-Stage; T: National Arts Club (OB); 7/49

Auden and Isherwood's philosophical and satirical 1936 comedy, ranging in style from naturalism to symbolism, which had run for one thousand performances in London, was first staged here by a small Off-Broadway troupe, temporarily housed in a space at 15 Gramercy Park. The staging was arena-style, with the barest minimum of props and the sets depicted with skeleton-wire constructions. A chorus played an important role. The production was scarcely noticed by the critics, although one reviewer (name and source unidentified) did think it "a thoroughly moving and absorbing play."

F-6 is a virtually unclimbable and reportedly haunted mountain the scaling of which occupies most of the action. As the valiant climbers, led by Michael Forsythe Ransom (DeWitt Drury), attempt to reach the peak, their scenes are alternated with those of a staidly conventional lower-middle-class couple, Mr. and Mrs. A., who speak in singsong doggerel and listen to the reports of the expedition over the radio. The ascent is the masterwork of a group of greedy persons led by Forsythe's politician brother and a newspaper publisher (Thom Carney), both of them self-seeking; F-6, on the border, is believed to be vital to the British national interest. The climbers each view the expedition in light of some personal goal. These goals are viewed in the crystal ball possessed by the mute monks in an F-6 monastery, whose abbott (Frank Hammerton) warns Forsythe not to give in to the temptation to be his nation's savior. After each of his followers perishes, Forsythe alone reaches the peak and, after collapsing, experiences a fantasy in which he plays chess with his brother--transformed into a dragon--the pieces being Forsythe and his sibling's followers. Although Michael wins, he is blamed for the demise of his climbers. His mother appears to him as a young woman. When the lights change, he is dead. Although the chorus criticizes him for his egotistical goals, he is also praised by others as a hero.

(2) [Dramatic Revival] D: Morton Silk; P: We Present; T: Hudson Guild Theatre (OB); 9/6(?)/49

A practically unnoticed production of the play that followed the previous one by less than two months. It was staged in a basement theatre on West Twenty-seventh Street. Despite the novice players' imaginative attempts to come to grips with it, stated Joseph T. Shipley (*NL*), the play "remains a confused piece." Vernon Rice (*NYP*) added that like any good closet drama, it should have remained in the closet. "The satire on capital, on the will and society's strain toward nationalism and war, jingles along--both verse and thought--at an elementary level." The mother was played by Rica Martens, the mountain-climbing son by De Witt Drury, and the politician son by Alfred Garr.

ASK MY FRIEND SANDY [Comedy/Business/Literature/Marriage/Military/Romance] A: Stanley Young; D/P: Alfred de Liagre, Jr.; S: Watson Barratt; T: Biltmore Theatre; 2/4/43 (12)

Even delightful character actor Roland Young could not rescue this "sleepy and slow and not funny" (Lewis Nichols [*NYT*]) comedy from disaster, although he did his best to try. His role was that of Harold Jackson, a hard-drinking, successful, but bored publisher who meets a wacky young soldier, Sandy (Norman Lloyd). Harold, in his cups at the time, is convinced by the private, a disciple of Thoreau, that he will be a freer soul if he has no money to encumber him. Harold thereupon distributes all his hard-earned cash and begins to regret his foolhardiness when the bills come due, his heretofore frivolous wife (Mary Sargent) leaves him to become a riveter, his partner (Franklyn Fox) takes over the firm, and he has to seek work as a cabdriver. When a book he wrote eleven years earlier called *How to Live Better with Less Money* is published, he makes all his money back because of the publicity generated by his eccentric activities. He even gains back his wife.

Harold's decision to give away his fortune proved puzzling, and there was insufficient humor to sustain attention to the action. On the whole, said Burns Mantle (*NYDN*), it was "pretty silly, and, as entertainment, pretty flat." Anna P. Franklin and

Joseph Tso Shih were Young's servants, Kay Loring was his secretary, and Phyllis Avery was Sandy's jitterbugging girl friend.

ASSASSIN, THE [Drama/Crime/Military/Politics/Prison/Romance/War] A: Irwin Shaw; D: Martin Gabel; S: Boris Aronson; P: Carly Wharton and Martin Gabel i/a/w Alfred Bloomingdale; T: National Theatre; 10/17/45 (13)

A flawed and only sporadically effective melodrama suggested by the Christmas Eve 1942 assassination of French collaborationist Admiral Jean Darlan in Algiers by an idealistic French royalist. The motives behind the act had never been fully explained, and Shaw put his own spin on the case with this interpretation.

The Assassin involves a French monarchist general's (Clay Clement) convincing a young French royalist named Robert de Mauny (Swedish actor Frank Sundstrom, in his Broadway bow) incarcerated because of his Free French underground activities in a North African concentration camp to assassinate Admiral Vespery (Roger de Koven) with the promise that the royalist's friends will be released from confinement and that he, the royalist, will escape the firing squad by the substitution of someone else. Following the killing, the assassin discovers that the general is no longer in a position of authority and that he must die for his deed unless he reveals who put him up to it. He refuses to squeal and, following a prison-cell scene of farewell with his sweetheart, Helene Mariotte (Lesley Woods), goes to his martyrdom.

The play was talky and rhetorical, although considerably revised from the version which had debuted in London a season earlier. There was also skepticism about Shaw's inclusion of a stereotypical love interest. Louis Kronenberger (*PM*) had a "who cares?" attitude about the events depicted, as the subject was no longer timely. The result was melodrama that was "not as a whole exciting enough," with a hero who was more conventional than three-dimensional. His opinion was representative. However, several critics, such as Rosamond Gilder (*TAM*), while aware of its problems, thought that the play deserved better treatment. She wrote, "It was occasionally tedious, it fumbled its climaxes and lacked excitement and drive. . . . Yet . . . it provided an evening of intelligent interest as well as theatric pleasures in acting, writing and mise-en-scene."

The large cast included Carmen Mathews, Karl Malden, Guy Sorel, Richard Ober, and Harrison Dowd, among others.

AT WAR WITH THE ARMY [Comedy/Military/Romance/Sex/War] A: James B. Allardice; D: Ezra Stone; S: Donald Oenslager; P: Henry May and Jerome E. Rosenfeld i/a/w Charles Ray McCallum; T: Booth Theatre; 3/8/49 (151)

A training camp in Kentucky in 1944 was the background to this bullet-paced, often very funny comic strip of a play that starred Dean Martin and Jerry Lewis in the movie version. The play was enjoyed more as a series of humorous situations and gags than as a well-constructed farce, but it managed to keep audiences laughing for nearly half a season.

"The plot . . . is inconsequential, its message nil--the result is excellent slapstick fun, as harmless as it is ingratiating," wrote Rosamond Gilder (*TAM*). Brooks Atkinson (*NYT*) observed that while it went on too long for its own good and needed a change of pace, it had been rowdily directed, with "doors banging, clothes flying through the air into the face of the commanding officer and decorum getting a humorous shellacking." Thomas R. Dash (*WWD*) laughed loudly and often, but had to concede that the piece was better suited to campus revels than to Broadway. "It is somehow callow and amateurish and depends for its movement more on the slice of life type of humorous exposition than it does on its narrative content or any true wit." It had received its premiere a year earlier at the Yale Drama School, where the author was still a playwriting student of Marc Connelly's. (All three producers had just graduated from Yale, and the cast included three actors who were still attending--Mike Kellin, Tad Mosel, and William Lanteau.)

The piece--all of it taking place in the camp's orderly room--concerns the ways in which various wisecracking and goldbricking soldiers and citizens confront the problems of boot camp boredom; much of the humor revolves around a recalcitrant coke machine. There are run-ins with the local female inhabitants, red tape, and the military bureaucracy. What plot there is mostly concerns handsome First Sergeant Robert Johnson (Gary Merrill), who wants to join the effort overseas but mistakenly believes that he may accidentally have been responsible for the pregnancy of his former girlfriend, Millie (Maxine Stuart), a PX waitress. The captain (William Mendrek) orders him to uncover the man responsible, which leads to Johnson's earnest efforts to avoid being detected as the guilty party. From this premise a host of complications and misunderstandings arise until all is finally settled in a happy conclusion when Johnson learns that he has been wrong all along about his presumed guilt.

Of the three Yale actors, two become well known; one of these was gravel-voiced actor Mike Kellin, playing tough, whistle-blowing Staff Sergeant McVay. The other was Tad Mosel, later famous as a writer, playing a pathetic lost private trying to find his station, who drifted in and out until he inadvertently hit the coke-machine jackpot, releasing its flood of bottles and nickles.

Among the actors playing soldiers were Jerry Jarrett, Mitchell Agruss, and John Shellie. Director Stone's wife Sara Seegar played the gossipy wife of the captain, and another femme interest was provided by Sally Gracie as Helen Palmer.

AUTUMN HILL [Drama/Crime/Legacy/Religion/Romance/Rural] A: Norma Mitchell and John Harris; D: Ronald Hammond; S: Lemuel Ayers; L: A. H. Feder; P: Max Liebman; T: Booth Theatre; 4/13/42 (8)

A verbose, implausible drama set in the rural New England house in which the penny-pinching Mrs. Hatfield lived until her recent death. She has left behind her dour Yankee companion of twenty years, Gussie Rogers (Beth Merrill), whose pitiful life is made more so by the discovery that Mrs. Hatfield apparently never left a will. There arrives at the home Mrs. Hatfield's mobster nephew, Tony Seldon (Jack Effrat), leader of a gang of counterfeiters. With him is his redheaded girlfriend Julie (Elizabeth Sutherland), masquerading as his secretary. Tony needs a place to hide out from the feds. As next of kin, Tony also hopes to inherit his aunt's estate. A will, however, is found, but Gussie keeps it hidden while she tries to take Tony under her nurturing wing. Tony keeps busy in the basement making phony money, telling Gussie that he is a writer. But when a local minister (William Roerick) traces to the house a bad five-dollar bill placed by Julie in the collection plate, Tony murders him. When Gussie learns of the basement operation, she chases Julie away, her heart set on reforming Tony. The cops arrive to arrest Tony, but Gussie shoots the frightened crook to save him the agony of the electric chair.

Apart from Beth Merrill's believable performance, there was nothing here on which to spend one's money. As Robert Coleman (*NYDM*) put it, this was "a dull and undistinguished crime play. Your drama reporter found it tedious and taxing." The play, which was producer Max Liebman's first venture on Broadway, also employed James Gregory and Clyde Franklin.

B

BAL NEGRE [Revue/Blacks] D/CH: Katherine Dunham; P: Nelson L. Gross and Daniel Melnick; T: Belasco Theatre; 11/7/46 (52)

Top black choreographer and dancer Katherine Dunham and a company of fifty musicians and dancers offered this three-act show as a Broadway revue, but it was actually an evening of dance with little else for variety. Even the mostly "exotic" tropical folk dances lacked variety, thought Louis Kronenberger (*PM*), who appreciated the "spirit" and "picturesqueness" with which they were performed but considered the show "more *Kitsch* than art."

A good many of the pieces on the program were from earlier Dunham recitals. There were Brazilian numbers, Haitian ones, West Indian ones, American black ones, European ones, and even one in ragtime called "Nostalgia," played in a roaring twenties setting and demonstrating the bunny hug, the turkey trot, the Charleston, and other period ballroom dances. The latter proved to be more popular with audiences than the program's artier selections. Some of the other routines were the Latin-rhythmed "Motivos," the ritualistic "Shango," and "L'Ag'ya," a spectacular dance-drama by Dunham and set in Martinique.

"They are individually of a visual hypnosis," suggested George Jean Nathan (*TBY*), "but, when repeated over a two hour period . . . inclined to suffer from monotony." But Robert Coleman (*NYDM*) spoke up for those who enjoyed this "evening of torrid, high-spirited dancing and singing."

Top dancers in the show included Lenwood Morris, Lucille Ellis, Lawaune Ingram, Wilbert Bradley, and Vanoye Aikens. Singers in the show included Rosalie King, Jean Leon Destine, and future star Eartha Kitt.

BALLET BALLADS [Musical/One-Acts] B/LY: John Latouche; M: Jerome Moross; D: Mary Hunter; DS: Nat Karson; P: Experimental Theatre, Inc.; T: Maxine Elliott's Theatre; 5/9/48 (69)
"Susanna and the Elders" [Bible/Religion/Sex] CH: Katherine Litz; "Willie the Weeper" [Drugs/Fantasy] CH: Paul Godkin; "The Eccentricities of Davy Crockett" [Fantasy/Period/Rural] CH: Hanya Holm

The final offering of the Experimental Theatre's 1947-1948 season was this unusual three-part program consisting of dance-dramas accompanied by songs performed to a two-piano accompaniment by soloists and a large chorus under Hugh Ross's direction. A number of well-known dancers appeared, chief among them being Sono Osato, who played Cocaine Lil in "Willie the Weeper." After finishing its six subscription performances, which received only tepid notices, the show moved immediately to the Music Box Theatre for a commercial run.

"Susanna and the Elders" is set at a revival meeting where the apocryphal tale of the title characters is told in a sermon and enacted. Choreographer Litz danced the role of the virtuous Susanna herself, and Richard Harvey acquitted himself well as the parson.

In the blues fantasia, "Willie the Weeper," set in the unstable mind of the marijuana-addicted title character (sung by Robert Lenn, danced by Paul Godkin), there were seven dream episodes. Osato's sexy Cocaine Lil was a brilliant performance, and the musical background was a wonderful combination of blues and boogie-woogie, but the piece as a whole did not cohere.

The folklorish "Eccentricities of Davy Crockett," infused with tongue-in-cheek humor, was the evening's strongest work. It concerned tall tales--including the hooking of a mermaid (Betty Abbott)--associated with the American pioneer hero (Ted Lawrie) who died at the Alamo. It was the longest work on the program and depended less on choral accompaniment than movement to express its tale, which was to its advantage. It also had, in Holm's choreography, the most creative ideas, including a delightful bear hunt by six male dancers; the bear was well danced by William A. Myers.

Most critics were ecstatic. George Freedley (*NYMT*) considered this "the best show on Broadway." Robert Garland (*NYJA*) also was enthusiastic, especially about the Davy Crockett work, which he said had "freshness, excitement and Americanism that none of the others so overwhelmingly achieves." Hobe. (*V*) wrote, "The three pieces . . . are imaginative, entertaining and stimulating," although probably not a good bet for a commercial showing (he was right). But John Martin (*NYT*) was unimpressed: "The material itself is so essentially unchoreographic . . . that there is not much anybody could do with it."

BANJO EYES [Musical/Barroom/Fantasy/Gambling/Sports] B: Joe Quillan and Izzy Elinson; M: Vernon Duke; LY: John Latouche and Harold Adamson; SC: John Cecil Holms and George Abbott's comedy, *Three Men on a Horse**; D: Hassard Short and Albert Lewis; CH: Charles Walters; S: Harry Horner; C: Irene Sharaff; L: Hassard Short; P: Albert Lewis; T: Hollywood Theatre; 12/25/41 (126)

A likable musical remake of a hit 1935 comedy about Erwin Trowbridge (Eddie Cantor), a greeting-card salesman who, in this version, has a gift that allows him, in his dreams, to speak to race horses in their paddocks and learn--provided that he does not gamble--who the next day's winners will be. His particular friend among the horses is Banjo Eyes, a beast played by Mayo and Morton, a pair of Continental specialists in imitating the front and rear legs of horses. The horse costume they wore was specially built to allow considerable neck and eye movement, as well as to suggest with remarkable accuracy the capering movements of a horse's feet. Erwin and his wife Sally (June Clyde) are trying hard to save their money so they can have a baby. "We're Having a Baby," sung by Cantor and Clyde, was one of the better tunes in the show. As in the original, the salesman gets drunk at a bar, is kidnapped by three touts, Patsy (Lionel Stander), Frankie (Ray Mayer), and the tarty Mabel (Audrey Christie), and is held hostage while they try to get him to pick the winners for them, a frustrating arrangement since the horses refuse to reveal their secrets when money is being bet on them.

Blackface comic Cantor returned to Broadway for the show after many years of work in other media. As Brooks Atkinson (*NYT*) noted, "If memory serves, he is not quite so scrawny in the cheeks as he used to be. Any changes there may be in his personality are also for the better in the direction of softer amiability. Otherwise, he is the same briskly hopping singer of songs who prances rapidly from wing to wing and claps his hands with a kind of flutter to simulate excitement."

To most critics, the book and score were tepid. George Freedley (*NYMT*) "was bored to death" by what he deemed a pretentious, overdone show (it cost over $140,000). Burns Mantle (*NYDN*) declared that the libretto had manhandled the original: "Too much has been lost in the cutting to hold the story taut, and not enough has been added in the splicing to make up for the loss." "The pathos, the giddy insanity and convulsing desperation of the original are at present stated for the most part in the terms of a perfectly humdrum, often flat, and certainly uninspired song-and-dance show," complained John Mason Brown (*NYWT*). Without Cantor, the general opinion held, this show would not have stood a chance.

Cantor added further to the enjoyment of the audience by singing--in blackface--a medley of his favorite tunes, including "Ida," "Margie," "If You Knew Susie," and "Whoopee!" at the final curtain. Interestingly, some critics preferred the songs in the show to those Cantor already had made popular. The show did good business, but closed when Cantor, disliking New York's weather, decided to return to California's climes.

Among the entertaining contributors to the show were Sally and Tony De Marco, ballroom dancers (Sally, the eighth or ninth female partner in the act, was deemed by some not quite up to her immediate predecessor's level); gymnastic dancer Tommy Wonder; ballerina Gloria Gilbert; and the comical acrobatic dance trio, Lynn, Royce, and Vanya. Virginia Mayo, still an unknown, made her debut in the small role of Ginger.

BARBER HAD TWO SONS, THE [Drama/Art/Crime/Family/Politics/Romance/Sex/War] A: Thomas Duggan and James Hogan; D: Melville Burke; S: Phil Raiguel; P: Jess Smith; T: Playhouse; 2/1/43 (24)

Blanche Yurka returned to Broadway after four years in this grim melodrama (originally produced in Santa Barbara and San Francisco) in which she played to little effect the role of Mrs. Mathieson or "Ma," a widowed Norwegian barber with two sons, one loyal to his people and the other one a traitor. The play originally was a one-act and had been expanded with extraneous stuffing to make it three acts.

The action takes place in the village of Aalesund, where son Johann (Walter Brooke), an artist, is more interested in his sketches than in the Nazi invasion of Norway. He even thinks that he will be honored for his art in Berlin. He is engaged to marry the family boarder, schoolteacher Karen Barson (Tutta Rolf, a Norwegian refugee actress). His brother is the sea captain, Christian (Richard Powers), a patriot who also loves Karen and who collaborates with his friend Lars (Wolfgang Zilzer) to perform acts of bloody sabotage against the Germans occupying the town. Karen is a selfish wench who plays one brother off against the other in her own interests, although she prefers Johann, whom she convinces to flee Norway with her. She sleeps with a German to obtain passports and even robs money for her journey from Ma. When the latter learns what's up, she begs unavailingly for Johann to stay and fight for his country. She then leads the Nazis, who are searching for Christian, to Johann, knowing that they will execute him. Karen comes looking for her lover and, learning the truth, threatens to expose Ma to the enemy. Ma then puts a bullet through the pretty girl's chest.

The talented Yurka could not do much with her role, and a few accused her of overacting. There was some surprise at the brutality of a situation that forces a mother to have one of her own children shot and then kills the girl both her sons loved, and the stage action included several gory scenes of Nazi deaths. But the play itself was "labored and obvious" to Robert Coleman (*NYDM*), while Arthur Pollock (*BE*) announced that it "is one of the clumsiest of plays, having nothing to recommend it but the fact that there is a lot of boyish melodrama in it and it is the Germans who bite most of the dust." But a minority approved it, among them George Freedley (*NYMT*), for whom it was "a steadily interesting drama" that held everyone's attention until the final curtain.

BAREFOOT BOY WITH CHEEK [Musical/Politics/Romance/Sex/University/Youth] B: Max Shulman; M: Sidney Lippman; LY: Sylvia Dee; SC: Max Shulman's novel of the same name; D/P: George Abbott; CH: Richard Barstow; S/L: Jo Mielziner; C: Alvin Colt; T: Martin Beck Theatre; 4/3/47 (108)

George Abbott's penchant for doing lively shows about young people was evidenced in this passable college musical based on a popular novel. Gravel-voiced Nancy Walker, comedic young veteran of several earlier Abbott productions, played Yetta Samovar, an atheistic University of Minnesota coed whose political beliefs are a deep shade of red, who is bent on introducing Stalinism to the campus community, and who considers anyone less than pink a fascist or cossack. The sole adult character in the play is a shapelessly garbed sociology professor named Schultz (Philip Coolidge) who requires his students to read all of his works plus one by his son-in-law, and who comments sourly to the audience on the behavior of the students. The book focuses on an innocent freshman named Asa Hearthrug (Billy [William] Redfield), whose regular allowance makes him ripe for exploitation by the grasping officials (one of them played by Red Buttons) of the Alpha Cholera Fraternity. Yetta is one of three campus cuties with whom Asa becomes involved, the other two being a Junior Leaguer named Noblesse Oblige (Billie Lou Watt) and a studious type named Clothilde Pfefferkorn (Ellen Hanley). The latter eventually wins Asa's heart and his fraternity pin. Yetta and Noblesse agree to share all the other campus men. Asa also manages to overcome various other problems and to become the new campus idol and president of the student council, replacing handsome Van Varsity (Ben Murphy) in popular esteem. The situations inspired various collegiate production numbers, including a jazzed-up fraternity prom in which the then-popular bunny hug was the featured dance routine.

The less-than impressed George Jean Nathan (*TBY*) thought that the show presented "undergraduate life as a cross between imbecility and St. Vitus disease." Jane Corby (*BE*) commented, "The producers threw almost everything they had into the first act, with the result that it is top-heavy, and leaves only skimpy material for after the intermission. However, there's so much unrestrained good fun on top that it makes up for the deficiencies." A number of critics admired its bounce and verve, but admitted that the abundance of youthful energy displayed wore them out. The show's chief virtues were its production values, but it suffered from a mediocre score in which the closest things to standout tunes were "I Knew I'd Know," "Everything Leads to Love," "When You Are Eighteen," and "I'll Turn a Little Cog," the latter the inspiration for a big production number expressing Yetta's dream of a sovietized America.

Ellen Hanley, a Juilliard-trained performer, was deemed the biggest find of the show and Redfield came into his own as a leading juvenile, while Walker's comedy was good for constant laughs. "No one in her weight class," declared Brooks Atkinson (*NYT*), "knows more about crisp timing, the value of a quick gesture, the hilariousness of the dead-pan and the eloquence of a tough shrug of the shoulder." Other talents involved included Jack Williams, Patrick Kingdon, Tommy Farrell, Benjamin Miller, Shirley Van, Jerry Austen, and Solen Bury.

BARRETTS OF WIMPOLE STREET, THE [Dramatic Revival*] A: Rudolph Besier; D: Guthrie McClintic; S/C: Jo Mielziner; P: Katharine Cornell; T: Ethel Barrymore Theatre; 3/26/45 (87)

Katharine Cornell returned to Broadway in the play she had made famous in her 1931 production and in which she had toured all over the country in later years. It also played a brief time locally in 1935. The present revival came in the wake of a grueling six-month, 140-performance tour of the GI camps in Italy, France, and the Netherlands, where it had been an enormous success playing on impromptu stages.

Many wondered how such a romantic play could have so deeply affected soldiers near the battlefield, yet strange as the choice appeared, it proved a triumphant one. Besier's telling of the love story of Elizabeth Barrett and Robert Browning was still delightful entertainment, especially in the performance given the poetess's role by the great Cornell. Brian Aherne re-created his dashing Browning, Elizabeth's tyrannous father was played by McKay Morris, Brenda Forbes resumed her original role of Wilson, Emily Lawson took the part of Henrietta, Patricia Calvert assumed Arabel, Betty Brewer was Cousin Bella, Erik Martin stood out as Octavius, Roger Stearns played Henry Bevan, Chester Stratton was the captain, and Russell Gaige and Ivan Simpson were physicians. Flush the dog was played by Flush the dog, although in his present incarnation he was not a spaniel but a Skye terrier. Mielziner's outstanding 1931 setting was exhumed, as were his enchanting costumes.

Although a few thought that without Cornell the play would have descended into mushy melodrama, John Mason Brown (*SR*) was happy to learn that "it has withstood the ravages of time as few plays do which still ask to be accepted as contemporary." The production itself, noted several, seemed not yet to have adjusted from the need to play to huge soldier audiences in makeshift conditions to the requirements of acting in a Broadway house. Aherne, in particular, was accused of playing too broadly. "His timing made Browning more jumpy than vital," recounted Lewis Nichols (*NYT*), "his inflections made him more elocutionary than honest." Brown said, "He was all over the place, playing his love scene not as an individual but for all the soldiers outfront [*sic*]." And Morris's Moulton-Barrett was afflicted with what a number of reviewers thought a serious case of overacting.

Cornell remained Cornell, although she had abandoned the spaniel curls of her earlier production for a somewhat anachronistic head of flowing black hair (it was now flecked with silver). "It did not seem possible," reported E. C. Sherburne (*CSM*), "that the actress had ever given a finer performance, so rich was the texture of her expression, so individualized was her indication of the woman's inner turmoil and rapture. Miss Cornell attained an unflagging revelation of the sensitive, spirited woman she was acting, and won the just reward by cheers and a dozen curtain calls."

BAT, THE [Dramatic Revival*] A: Mary Roberts Rinehart and Avery Hopwood; P: On-Stage; T: 6 Fifth Avenue (OB); 9/1/48

This once very popular 1920 comedy-melodrama was revived by an Off-Broadway troupe at one of several performing spaces it occupied during its brief life. As usual, the production was scarcely attended by the critics. In this case only Richard Watts, Jr. (*NYP*), left to posterity an English-language review of the event (there was one in German).

The Bat closed a series of summer showings of old American plays by the company. It seemed dated and clichéd (the comic maid was particularly onerous) because it had been borrowed so many times by other works, and, said Watts, it was "ineptly" presented.

BATHSHEBA [Comedy-Drama/Bible/Military/Period/Sex/War] A: Jacques Deval; D: Coby Ruskin; DS: Stewart Chaney; P: Maximilian Becker and Lee K. Holland i/a/w Sylvia Friedlander; T: Ethel Barrymore Theatre; 3/26/47 (29)

This ungainly biblical drama, set in 1030 B.C., was the occasion for the inauspicious Broadway debut of British film star James Mason, who played King David. The story of David and Bathsheba was treated as "a would-be neo-Shavian social satire," reported the displeased Euphemia Van Rensselaer Wyatt (*CW*), who felt that the drama was disrespectful toward the Old Testament hero. Brooks Atkinson (*NYT*) called the play "long and diffuse" and filled with "tasteless and tedious leering" over the ancient tale.

Director Ruskin took over when Robert H. Gordon resigned during the tryout period. The original version of the play had been meant in a more serious vein, but Mason and Ruskin revised it to suggest an ironic comedy intention. During the out-of-town tryout in Philadelphia, the work was in such a mess that a spectator joined the cast on stage at the end to declare to the audience his pejorative judgment of it. George Jean Nathan (*TBY*) remarked that in its revision, "there is not only no quality whatever but little humor." But Howard Barnes (*NYHT*), while finding the work "less than compelling," nevertheless thought that it "progresses smoothly and avoids for the most part such pitfalls of costume drama as pompous manners and stilted speeches."

The story reveals David, a jaded and cynical monarch of Jerusalem, finding his interest in life revived by the sight from his balcony of his faithful, hero-worshipping captain Uriah's (Phil Arthur) gorgeous wife, Bathsheba (Pamela Kellino, Mason's actual wife), bathing in the nude. Bathsheba puts up no struggle when seduced by David and soon becomes pregnant. Uriah is told of her condition by David and decides to return only after being victorious in combat. David effectively rids himself of the chance of Uriah's return by sending him off to battle where there will be no chance of his survival. (This sorry episode in David's life is followed in the Bible--but not in the play--by that of David's sincere contrition and forgiveness by God following the high priest's telling him a story about the rich man who coveted his neighbor's ewe lamb.)

There were frequent critical negatives concerning Mason and Deval's depiction of the Lion of Judah as cynical and blasé, which seemed to jar with the traditional image of the heroic, spiritual, and poetic character of biblical legend. Atkinson thought that the bearded Mason looked "like a healthy [Frank] Sinatra." Stewart Chaney's lovely sets and costumes were for many the most expert contribution to the presentation.

The High Priest Nathan was Thomas Chalmers, the king's steward was Horace Braham, and a military leader, General Joab, was played by Rusty Lane. Blanche Zohar, Lenka Peterson, and Hildy Parks were in smaller roles.

BATTLE FOR HEAVEN [Drama/Historical-Biographical/Old Age/Religion] A: Michael O'Shaughnessy and Randolph Carter; D: Randolph Carter; P: Invitational Series of the Experimental Theatre, Inc.; T: Educational Alliance (OB); 5/17/48 (4)

One of five plays produced by the Experimental Theatre as part of its 1947-1948 Invitational Series, which awarded selected young American writers a simplified production given to an invited audience on a $150 budget at an Off-Broadway locale. This was an "inept" (Herm. [*V*]) attempt at a biographical drama about Christian Science leader Mary Baker Eddy (Hortense Alden), seen in the play at age eighty-six. "The yarn is a deadpan recital of the theory and history of Christian Science," wrote Herm., "all repetitiously done." Only Alden's efforts in the leading role were of value.

BE HAPPY [Musical/Yiddish Language] B/LY: William Siegel; M: Sholem Secunda; D: Abe Gross; CH: Lillian Shapero; S: Michael Saltzman; P: Menasha Skulnik; T: Second Avenue Theatre (OB); 10/11/42

A happy Menasha Skulnik vehicle that costarred Michal Michalesko and Miriam Kressyn. Infused with many jokes in English, the banal story was of the familiar triangle variety with a full dash of tear-jerking sentimentality.

Skulnik was Niftie Naftule, a waiter in an East Side nightclub, who falls in love with Liuba (Paula Lubelska), a refugee in Cuba, via her photo and goes there to marry her so she may enter this country. However, she is already in love with handsome Leon Moseloff (Michalesko), a married musician for whom she makes a play as soon as she arrives in New York. Leon's wife (Kressyn) takes umbrage at the budding affair and, after Leon must give blood to save his injured daughter (Malkele Bieler), wins back her erring spouse.

Miriam Kressyn was a standout, being considered by Kahn. (*V*) as the closest Yiddish theatre performer "to Broadway calibre. Her singing voice, charm, acting ability, chassis and ability to wear clothes are unparalleled in present-day Yiddish theatricals."

Burns Mantle (*NYDN*) concluded, "It is all done according to pattern, and . . . they told me the pattern is what guarantees success in Second Ave." The death of the Yiddish theatre seemed imminent in 1942, when this was the sole Yiddish show playing on Second Avenue, and its only competition was on Broadway in Molly Picon's *Oy, Is dus a Leben!*. The show featured Annie Thomashefsky, Yetta Zwerling, Seymour Rechtzeit, Fannie Lubritzky, and other familiar Yiddish entertainers.

BEAT THE BAND [Musical/Hotel/Nightclub/Romance/Show Business] B: George Marion, Jr., and George Abbott; M: Johnny Green; LY: George Marion, Jr.; D/P: George Abbott; CH: David Lichine; S: Samuel Leve; C: Freddy Wittop; T: Forty-sixth Street Theatre; 10/14/42 (68)

Book trouble plagued this jive-tempoed musical, although George Abbott provided as much swinging fun to the proceedings as was humanly possible under the circumstances. Even after the show opened, the perfectionist Abbott continued to make minor improvements, although he knew that the show was doomed.

The pamphlet-thin story tells of how Querida (Susan Miller, in her stage debut), accompanied by her bombshell of a maid (Juanita Juarez), comes north from the Caribbean to stay with her godfather. The godfather's penthouse, however, has been sublet to the screwy Hugo Dillingham (Jerry Lester). She finds herself being cared for by Hugo's bandleader brother, Damon (Jack Whiting), who impersonates the godfather at Hugo's behest. Damon's luscious girlfriend (Toni Gilman) has jilted him, but he discovers that the child he thought he was going to babysit for turns out to be a gorgeous and wealthy Latin eighteen-year-old, whose singing talents offer a plus to his band. Damon suffers from a prediliction tendency to sock the obnoxious hotel bosses who hire him, and his band gets demoted to playing in the furnace room of a fancy Washington, D.C., hotel, where, against the exposed pipes and *Walpurgisnacht*-like glow, the show's hottest number, "The Steam Is on the Beam," was performed. Damon manages to turn the furnace room into the town's most popular supper club. Meanwhile, Damon aids the pretty Querida to escape from detectives in the employ of her uncle, she keeps Damon's old girlfriend permanently out of the picture, and eternal love blooms before the curtain descends.

Few tunes proved memorable, the chuckles were too scattered, and the story line was flimsy, yet there was enough color, syncopation, and enthusiasm on tap to please many reviewers. Rosamond Gilder (*TAM*), for example, found the show "a constant bedazzlement." However, it was opinions such as John Anderson's (*NYJA*), who could not believe how Abbott "could have produced a show that is so stupendously uninteresting," that kept audiences at bay. Howard Barnes (*NYHT*), who found many incidentals to appreciate, commented, "What is badly wanting . . . is a comic twist to familiar situations and a compelling tempo to the action as a whole."

Tap dancer Eunice Healey played Hugo's sweetheart, Johnny Mack was the band's tap-dancing drummer, Leonard Sues offered some terrific trumpet solos, beautiful Joan Caulfield (in her Broadway debut) played a dizzy blond, ballet dancer Marc Platt displayed his talents in one or two numbers, and obese bandleader Romo Vincent was amusing as an agent.

In his autobiography, *"Mister Abbott"*, Abbott revealed that the show "was the poorest job of producing and directing that I ever did; I was guilty of mistake after mistake. The first mistake was in thinking that it was any good; the second was in the casting; and the third and biggest was in not abandoning it when it obviously was a failure."

BEAUTIFUL PEOPLE, THE [Drama/Family/Music/Religion/Youth] A/D/P: William Saroyan; S: Samuel Leve; T: Lyceum Theatre; 4/21/41 (120)

A controversial but generally liked Saroyan play (originally called *A Cup of Kindness* and *Pole Star and Pyramid*) that Burns Mantle pondered over strenuously before deciding not to include it as one of the ten best plays of the season. The chief reason deciding him against its inclusion was his opinion that, much as it was filled with charming atmosphere and eccentric character sketches, it did not conform to traditional standards of playmaking in its unconventional structure and lack of dramatic conflict and urgency. It was the kind of play, he believed, that required performance by sensitive actors to be appreciated, but that was seriously lacking when examined outside the context of the playhouse. The play reminded many of Saroyan's 1939 *My Heart's in the Highlands**.

The sentimental story, if such it may be called, concentrates on the family of Jonah Webster (Curtis Cooksey) of the Sunset Park section of San Francisco, where he preaches to the "beautiful people" in the street his love philosophy that "every life in the world is a miracle" and lives with his fifteen-year-old son Owen (ballet dancer Eugene Loring, in his Broadway debut) and his seventeen-year-old daughter Agnes (Betsy Blair, making her Broadway debut in a speaking role after being a chorus girl in *Panama Hattie*). For seven years Jonah has been supporting his family by forging the signature on the pension checks that keep arriving for the home's previous resident, now dead. The children have been raised to think that it is God who is their benefactor. Their rickety hillside home, with its porch, living room, and yard all exposed to the audience, is the only setting. Agnes, who forcibly expresses her aversion to boys until she falls in love with a shy youth, is so preoccupied with the thousand mice in her abode, revering them as God's creatures, that she is nicknamed "St. Agnes of the Mice." She is convinced that the mice spell out her name on the floor with flower blossoms. It is actually her uneducated sibling, who considers himself a poet and scientist, and who writes books of one word (such as "tree"), who does the deed. An older brother (Don Freeman, the well-known cartoonist of New York life), a cornet player, lives in New York and plans to return only after earning a million dollars, which he will then bring home to dispense freely. The family imagines that it can hear his music although he is across the continent. This music forms a leitmotif for the production. When he does return, he is more a hobo than a millionaire, but his return happily reunites the family. Although an insurance investigator (E. J. Ballantine) comes to check up on the pension, the family ends up continuing to receive its checks, only in larger amounts.

The average playgoer was confused by the whimsical style of this wordy but shorter-than-average play; it did, however, receive a number of warm comments. Saroyan's lyrical joy in life and his humanity, atmospherics, and good humor were greatly appreciated, although his dramaturgy came in for raps. Brooks Atkinson (*NYT*) asserted, "The four acts are hardly more than casual sketches, and there is about as much plot as you can crowd on to the head of a pin." Still, he thought that it was "a beguiling and tender little comedy with an ingratiating spirit of general good-will." Rosamond Gilder (*TAM*) thoughtfully explained that Saroyan's plays "are expressed in symbolic forms, visual as well as oral. They are in a sense dream-plays speaking directly to the unconscious through concepts relating to a lost and longed-for child-world of security and affection. His plays are not only shot through with music; they are themselves music, haunting, nostalgic, steeped in the pathos of half-forgotten things." The production itself, which Saroyan directed and produced, was lauded.

According to George Jean Nathan's *TBY* (1942-1943) Curtis Cooksey was cast in the role of Jonah when Saroyan saw him dressed at an audition with precisely the slovenly look the playwright was seeking for the role. Saroyan took pride during the rehearsals in having found so perfect an approximation of his character. However, on opening night, the actor, wishing to make the most of his opportunity, went out and "bought himself an elegant new wardrobe and, when he appeared on the stage, it was nigh impossible to distinguish between the bum that Saroyan had written and John Drew, or even William Faversham, in his fashionable prime."

BEES AND THE FLOWERS, THE [Comedy/Family/Marriage/Romance] A: Frederick Kohner and Albert Mannheimer; D: Albert Mannheimer; S/L: Edward Gilbert; C: Enid Gilbert; P: Mort H. Singer, Jr.; T: Cort Theatre; 9/26/46 (28)

Bron.'s (*V*) report on this contrivance declared, "Some of the lines are amusing, but more of them are flat and plain tiresome. The comedy is too flimsy to last." John Beaufort (*CSM*) called it "a rather callow, largely derivative, but sometimes amusing comedy." Others were even more disapproving. Its original title was *The Birds and the Bees*. Much was made of the fact that the play was sold to the movies for $50,000 (no film of it ever was produced).

Well-to-do divorcée Louise Morgan (Barbara Robbins), while on a holiday in Mexico, has remarried, her new spouse being Tack Cooper (Russell Hardie). When she returns to her New York penthouse, she wants to break the news gently to her three daughters (Rosemary Rice, Joyce Van Patten, and Sybil Stocking), who are crazy about their father and want Louise to remarry him. She installs Tack as a guest in the house, claiming that he is only a close friend, but this leads to the usual complications when the daughters seek to make him leave. Tack undergoes various obstacles in trying to win over the girls and eventually succeeds. There is also a subplot concerning a romance between the eldest daughter and a Columbia undergraduate (Michael Dreyfuss). Among the players was Sylvia Lane.

BEGGARS ARE COMING TO TOWN [Drama/Business/Crime/Nightclub/Romance] A: Theodore Reeves; D: Harold Clurman; S: Jo Mielziner; C: Ralph Alswang; P: Oscar Serlin; T: Coronet Theatre (formerly the Forrest Theatre); 10/27/45 (25)

A hoary plot lacking in novelty, a too-familiar nightclub setting, and a cast list packed with stereotypical gangster characters drawn straight from the Prohibition plays and movies of years earlier led to this play's being sent up the river. It presents the tale of Frankie Madison (Paul Kelly), sent to Sing Sing for fourteen years following an armed robbery committed with Noll Turner (Luther Adler) in which a man was killed. The suave Noll, meanwhile, through dubious if legal means, has amassed a fortune and turned legit, being the respectable proprietor of a fancy nightclub called the Avignon. When Frankie arrives expecting to be taken into partnership for his sacrifice, Noll prefers to buy him off to get rid of him. Frankie tries to start over with his old mob cronies, but when he discovers that they are now a "bunch of bums," that the old ways are defunct, and that a nightclub operates on sounder business practices than a speakeasy, he departs quietly with the sexy cigarette girl Florrie Dushaye (Dorothy Comingore), who has fallen for his hard-guy ways. The ending is ambivalent, making it unclear as to whether Frankie will take a route similar to Noll's or live off Florrie.

Beggars Are Coming to Town's title derives from a Mother Goose nursery rhyme, "Hark, hark, the dogs do bark; beggars are coming to town." A ponderous atmosphere afflicted its production, which seemed more concerned with issues of social significance concerning the resemblance of "reformed" gangsters to practicing ones than with melodramatic action. "The plot follows a devious and tedious course and arrives exactly nowhere," reported Howard Barnes (*NYHT*). Robert Garland (*NYJA*) said, "Things went slowly but surely from good to mediocre, from mediocre to bad, from bad to worse."

Clurman's direction was of little help in vivifying the exhibition. Herbert Berghof played the oily headwaiter, and among other actors were Alfred Linder, Julius Bing, E. G. Marshall, Adrienne Ames, Harry M. Cooke, Lou Gilbert, George Mathews, Tom Pedi, and Arthur Hunnicutt. This was the refurbished Coronet's first production under its new name. A successful 1948 movie starring Kirk Douglas and Burt Lancaster and called *I Walk Alone* was made from the story.

BEGGAR'S HOLIDAY [Musical/Blacks/Crime/Prison/Politics/Prostitution/Romance/Sex] B/LY: John Latouche; SC: John Gay's 1728 ballad opera, *The Beggar's Opera**; M: Duke Ellington; D: Nicholas Ray; CH: Valerie Bettis; S: Oliver Smith; C: Walter Florell; L: Peggy Clark; P: Perry Watkins and John R. Sheppard, Jr.; T: Broadway Theatre; 12/26/46 (108)

A raffish, Americanized adaptation of Gay's famous 1728 ballad opera, also known widely in its Bertolt Brecht-Kurt Weill version, *The Threepenny Opera**. The $325,000 show starred Alfred Drake as Macheath, depicted as a contemporary gangster, and featured Zero Mostel as Hamilton Peachum, Jet MacDonald as Polly Peachum, Denise Parks (replacing Libby Holman a week before the opening) as Jenny, Rollin Smith as Chief Lockit, Mildred Smith as Lucy Lockit, Avon Long as Careless Love, and Marie Bryant as the Cocoa Girl, while future director Herbert Ross and future dance star Marge Champion (still called Marjorie Bell) figured in several small dance roles.

Aside from the shift in period, the story remained similar to the original in most particulars. A then-unusual feature of the show was its multiethnic casting, freely mingling black and white actors to create a believable picture of a racially mixed city. Both the police chief and his daughter, for example, were played by blacks, which was significant in that there is a romantic relationship between Lucy and Macheath.

A florid assortment of thieves, pimps, and prostitutes was created against a colorful underworld background brilliantly designed by Oliver Smith. According to Rosamond Gilder (*TAM*), he flanked the proscenium opening with "fire-escapes that zigzag up on each side to a long iron-railed balcony running across the topmost reaches of the stage." This figured memorably when the vivid staging employed cops in red coats engaging in a colorful manhunt by running up and down the steps and across the balcony at the start and end of the show. All set changes, using two revolves, were performed *a vista*. For example, "A flat corrugated iron curtain--which might be the wall of an East River dock--rolls up to reveal the exterior of Jenny's bordello over which appear the soaring lines of Brooklyn Bridge."

Duke Ellington's score was widely enjoyed, one of its brightest spots being "I Wanna Be Bad," sung by Long as a would-be hoodlum. Other appreciated tunes were "Wrong Side of the Railroad Tracks" and "Tooth and Claw." Brooks Atkinson (*NYT*) liked what he saw, claiming that Ellington and Latouche "have constructed a musical play from the ground up with an eloquent score, brisk ballets and a cast of dancers and singers who are up to snuff." He also observed that the songs were so well integrated with the book that it would be difficult to extract any and turn them into hits. Unfortunately, the show refused to fuse cohesively for most and remained a disparate assortment of attractive features. "There is no dynamic centre to the production," sighed the otherwise pleased Gilder, who thought that the main problem might have been the too-amiable Drake's inability, for all his talent, to bring Macheath to convincing life as the dangerous rogue he is. George Jean Nathan (*NYJA*) called the show "a half-cooked exhibit with a few palatable items and with more that called for greater attention from the chef." He and not a few others found that Mostel's antics were decidedly unfunny in what should have been the major comic role, that of a dishonest political boss whose character was new to the story.

Director Nicholas Ray took over from John Houseman and himself had to call on the services of George Abbott for aid in getting the show, originally called *Twilight Alley*, on. Houseman and Abbott declined credit. It was Abbott, apparently, who fired Libby Holman, although she was then having an affair with Ray. According to Jon Bradshaw's *Dreams That Money Can Buy*, Ray had the job of giving the bad news to Holman. He told her as they were lying in bed after making love. Disgusted, she took a drink and said, "Everything I touch turns to shit." "Not me, old girl. You've still got me," Ray soothed her. "Not anymore, you son-of-a-bitch. You just fired me, and I don't mean sexually," she replied and ordered him to leave the room. Ray was officially axed the next day, but kept the formal directing credit.

Houseman, in *Front and Center*, recounted his experiences with the show, claiming that rehearsals were begun prematurely before the book and score were complete, and that the producers were "desperately short of money." Latouche was completely erratic with regard to finishing up the script, vanishing when needed and complaining about what Houseman and Ray (then the assistant director) had done to it. In the course of rehearsals, when additional music was needed, arranger Billy Strayhorn would dig up material from Ellington's drawers and find what would fit the scene. Numerous crises were faced when the bills for sets and costumes could not be paid until a wealthy alcoholic was found who was forcibly urged to provide the needed cash. The out-of-town opening in New Haven was calamitous, with the show's final twenty minutes practically improvised by the cast. Things were slightly improved for Boston, but Houseman decided to quit, and Abbott was brought in to doctor the show. "What might have been a triumphal theatrical novelty had been ruined by inadequate preparation and inept handling," wrote Houseman.

BELL FOR ADANO, A [Comedy-Drama/Military/Politics/Romance/War] A: Paul Osborn; SC: John Hersey's novel of the same name; D: H. C. Potter; S/C: Motley; L: William Richardson; P: Leland Hayward; T: Cort Theatre; 12/6/44 (296)

A Bell for Adano was generally recognized as one of the best plays dealing with World War II written and produced while the conflict was still raging. It was rumored to have been based on an actual incident reported to war correspondent John Hersey, upon whose Pulitzer Prize novel it was based, by novelist John Steinbeck. The rumor was denied by the responsible parties, but some refused to accept the denial. More a play about the meaning of democracy than one about the war per se, *A Bell for Adano* proved a strong-enough draw to hold the stage for close to a year and was selected for Burns Mantle's collection of the season's ten best. Agent Leland Hayward made a successful debut as a producer with the play.

It is 1943 and the war is still on, but the Allies have occupied much of Sicily, including the small fishing town of Adano, where the action is set. The thirty-five-year-old American major who has just taken command is a resourceful Italian-American from the Bronx named Victor Joppolo (Fredric March). He sets up his headquarters in the office of the former mayor (Rolfe Sedan), a corrupt supporter of the fascists. Joppolo determines to bring the town back to life, provide it with food, clean out its fascists, and, if possible, provide a substitute for the city-hall bell. The bell, melted down for rifle barrels, was a symbol of the town's lifeblood, and its absence has left an aching feeling in the inhabitants. One reason that food is a problem for the town is the hatred of the boss fisherman, Tomasino (Alexander

Granach), for all authority. Before he will have his fishermen return to their occupation, Tomasino must be convinced that the American major is decent and fair-minded. Brought together with Tomasino by the fisherman's pretty daughter, Tina (Margo), with whom the lonely but married major enjoys a platonic flirtation, Joppolo does demonstrate the ideals he stands for. In fact, he becomes a perfect representative of American ideals and justice and teaches the townspeople that a democratic government serves the people, not the reverse. Another obstacle is the order of an arrogant general (who is heard offstage but never seen) to prohibit from the town the mule-driven water and food carts that bring the people provisions. While passing through the town, the major had found the road blocked by such a cart and, claiming that the streets had to be cleared for the passage of the American army (even though the town was being bypassed by the invading forces), shot the mule and invoked his order. This brings extreme suffering to the people, who begin to suffer starvation, until the major decides to stick his neck out and revoke the order. An M.P. captain named Purvis (Bruce MacFarlane), afraid that he will get in trouble for the major's action, submits a critical report on the major's revocation. Although several lower-ranking soldiers try to prevent the report's being sent, it does eventually go out. Meanwhile, the major has befriended a naval lieutenant (Phil Arthur) and the navy eventually comes up with a bell from a ship named after an Italian-American hero. To the townspeople's delight, the bell proves a perfect replacement. However, news arrives that the major is being punished for having revoked the general's order. He is to be transferred to Algiers. Everyone is devastated, even Captain Purvis. As the major prepares to leave, the bell keeps ringing.

A few had quibbles with the play, but most rejoiced at its writing, ideas, and presentation. Howard Barnes (*NYHT*) thought it "eloquent, illuminating and altogether beautiful," with a central character of near-tragic dimensions who is brought down by the very principles for which he stands. He also claimed that March was giving "the finest performance of his career," a view with which many concurred. Wrote Rosamond Gilder (*TAM*), "Mr. March has created . . . the Major with subtlety and earnestness. He has brought that element of heart . . . to the task. Though his Joppolo may seem a little too polished for his background, Mr. March has caught the essential note--a candor, a directness, an honesty and a faith that are disarming and not a little moving." Wilella Waldorf (*NYP*) reported that Joppolo's experiences "are so illuminating, so inspiring, and at the same time so frightening, that the play sends its audience away . . . not only stirred but very thoughtful indeed." She did object, however, to the general's being kept offstage when seeing him would have strengthened the central conflict. (The character had been seen in an earlier draft.) Others, such as John Mason Brown (*SR*), approved his being kept offstage. On the other hand, George Freedley's (*NYMT*) criticism of the play centered on the thinness of its original story and the need to create an atmospheric stage production equivalent to the style effected by the novel. The result, he felt, was a loosely strung together sequence of episodes with an assortment of character types, the whole tenuously held together by the idea of replacing the town's bell. Freedley also took issue with what he deemed the incomplete characterization of the major, which he blamed both on the writing and on March's inadequate performance.

The expert cast included Everett Sloane as Sergeant Borth, Gilbert Mack as Giovanni Zito, Tito Vuolo as Giuseppe Ribaud, Leon Rothier as Father Pensovecchio, Miriam Goldina as Marguerita, Alma Ross as Carmelina, and Harold J. Stone as Gargano, among others.

BEST FOOT FORWARD [Musical/Films/Romance/School/Youth] B: John Cecil Holm; M/LY: Hugh Martin and Ralph Blane; D: George Abbott; CH: Gene Kelly; S/L: Jo Mielziner; C: Miles White; P: George Abbott and Richard Rodgers (uncredited); T: Ethel Barrymore Theatre; 10/1/41 (326)

George Abbott's first musical without a Rodgers and Hart score employed the services of two new songwriters, each of whom worked independently on his own music and lyrics, combining two sets of songs to produce one score. Rodgers agreed to coproduce but insisted that his name not be billed because he was fearful of the public suspecting a rift (which existed) between him and Lorenz Hart.

The show had no trouble casting its youthful male performers, since most were too young yet to be drafted. It abounded in new talent, such as June Allyson and Nancy Walker in their first major roles, although Allyson threatened to walk out at one point if additional verses were added to one of Walker's songs. With Gene Kelly choreographing his first Broadway show, *Best Foot Forward* proved a happy temporary antidote to the blues of a nation on the brink of war. It was blessed with an amusing and cohesive libretto (although it had its detractors), fast-paced direction, outstanding sets and costumes, a huge and extremely energetic company, superb dance routines, several excellent songs, and a host of young talents that critics felt would be peopling American entertainment media for years to come. Louis Kronenberger (*PM*) commented that the show, while no masterpiece, "is pleasing and lively and as fresh as milk in the pail."

The popular show was set on the campus of a prep school, the Winsocki School for Boys, where the prom is about to be held. Diminutive student Bud Hooper (Gil Stratton, Jr.), although the beau of Helen Schlesinger (Maureen Cannon), writes to gorgeous movie star Gale Joy (Rosemary Lane, a real movie star in her stage debut), asking her to be his prom date. He does it for fun, never expecting a response. Thinking it a good chance for publicity (her career needs a boost), her press agent, Jack Haggerty (Marty May), induces her to attend, although she at first has no intention of doing so. When the amazed Bud hears from Gale, he tells Helen that he is ill and won't be going to the prom. He also tells the movie star not to tell anyone who she is. At the ball, where she is immediately recognized, the kids, led by Helen, go wild and snatch off almost all her clothing trying to get her autograph. Bud's girlfriend nearly leaves him and he almost gets booted from the school, but a happy ending comes in time for the final curtain. Along the way, such songs as "That's How I Like the Blues," "The Three B's" (a show-stopping tune about barrelhouse, blues, and boogie-woogie), "Shady Lady Bird," "Everytime," "Just a Little Joint with a Juke Box," and "Buckle Down, Winsocki" (considered the best in the show and still occasionally heard) are performed.

Nancy Walker, as a wisecracking tough girl who shows up as a blind date at the prom, and June Allyson were among the many singled out for special praise. John Mason Brown (*NYWT*) picked Walker out: "Miss Walker is a superior comic. She knows her way around a song. She will not only go, but has gone, places as a performer because, in addition to her surety, she is blessed with an epidemic personality." John Beaufort (*CSM*) said of Allyson that she "is pretty and energetic and hearty-voiced enough not to be reminded that she does look amazingly like Betty Hutton, whom she once understudied." Other talented performers included chubby baritone Tommy Dix, dancer and clarinet expert Kenneth Bowers, tap dancer Betty Ann Nyman, and soprano Victoria Schools.

BEVERLY HILLS [Comedy/Films/Marriage/Sex] A: Lynn Starling and Howard J. Green; D: Otto Preminger; S: Donald Oenslager; P: Laurence Schwab and Otto Preminger; T: Fulton Theatre; 11/7/40 (28)

Brooks Atkinson (*NYT*) said that the authors of this opus--the director of which billed himself as Dr. Otto Ludwig Preminger--had "collected as many odious people as possible, scribbled malicious lines for them to speak, trapped them in some squalid situations and blamed the whole thing on Hollywood. Beautifully costumed, splendidly set, it is *The Women** in pants."

Beverly Hills, set in a beautiful home--replete with Oriental servants--in the famous film stars' neighborhood, presents a panoply of movie types from actors to agents and producers, all as nasty and scheming as can be. It focuses on the efforts of three predatory females to best one another for financial and sexual gain. Helen Claire played Lois Strickland, wife of a shy young scriptwriter named Leonard (Clinton Sundberg); she seeks to get him a job as writer for a new film, *Land of Cotton*, based on a best-seller, being financed by A. Trumbull Eastmore (William J. Kelly), the spouse of her friend May Flowers (Violet Heming), a onetime silent-film star. The man-hungry May sets her traps for the faithful Leonard, who really is not that interested in the *Land of Cotton* project to begin with. When he spends some time with May preparing speeches for her to give on a movement with which she is involved, a scandal rag spreads rumors of an affair. Advised by the catty Jean Harding (Ilka Chase), whose own husband is straying, to patch things up with Leonard, Lois does just that. A divorce between Eastmore and May likewise is avoided when May exercises her charms on the tycoon. With him back in her pocket, she shifts her attentions to a young actor. Leonard declares his artistic independence, accepting a job to do a new film produced by Darryl F. Zanuck.

A superb cast, including Enid Markey as a gossipy manicurist, Doro Merande as a children's nursemaid, and Robert Shayne as an actor's agent, could not bring the "shoddy little comedy" (John Anderson [*NYJA*]) to life. It wasn't funny enough and was too concerned with smirking double entendres. The play was one of three plays dealing with Hollywood life that opened within a two week period.

BIG KNIFE, THE [Drama/Alcoholism/Business/Crime/Films/Marriage/Sex] A: Clifford Odets; D: Lee Strasberg; S: Howard Bay; C: Lucille Little; P: Dwight Deere Wiman; T: National Theatre; 2/24/49 (108)

Once the golden boy of Broadway playwrights, Clifford Odets, after many years of writing screenplays, returned to the Great White Way with this uneven, inadequate, but sometimes excoriating picture of Hollywood. It starred another Hollywood émigré returning to New York, John Garfield, once associated with Odets during the time the two worked for the Group Theatre in the 1930s. Garfield had come back first, having appeared in the previous season's *Skipper Next to God*. During the pre-Broadway period, the play was extensively revised, including the omission of a couple of characters.

Garfield's role was that of Charlie Castle, idealistic movie superstar, whose artistic and personal ambitions (only vaguely expressed, noted the critics) make him long to rip off his contractual fetters and do his own thing. He finds it impossible, however, because there is a sin in his past. He is guilty of having killed a child while driving under the influence of alcohol with trollopy Dixie Evans (Joan McCracken) in his car. The malevolent studio boss, Marcus Hoff (J. Edward Bromberg), acting in cahoots with several others, including Charlie's agent (Reinhold Schunzel) and wife, covered up the crime by paying a loyal publicity man to take the rap and go to prison for ten months. Dixie gets a studio contract to keep mum about the incident. When Charlie gets uppity and refuses to sign a fourteen-year contract for $3,400,000, the boss threatens to reveal his guilt and have him sent to jail. Charlie is even more distressed when Dixie's drinking leads to her blabbing; this makes her a prime target for a planned murder by the studio powers. (She gets killed instead by a passing police car.) Charlie, meanwhile, is having marital difficulties with his wife Marion (Nancy Kelly), who has become disillusioned with him (among other things, he has slept with his best friend's wife) and says that she will leave if he signs the contract. When things get too tough to handle, and he sees no way to gain his liberty from the stranglehold of his success, Charlie takes a bath and slashes his wrists.

Plays about Hollywood were usually comedies with little serious to say about the film world, so Odets's drama was appreciated for its fiery indignation at Hollywood's venality and corruption, which he, to little avail, sought to relate to the nation as a whole. Odets told the *NYT* that the title of the play referred to "that force in modern life which is against people and their aspirations, which seeks to cut people off in their best flower. The play may be about the struggle of a gifted actor to retain his integrity against the combination of inner and outer corruptions which assail him, but this struggle can be found in the lives of countless people who are not on the wealthy level of a movie star."

The results, however, proved extremely talky, melodramatically overwrought, and clumsy, and apart from some striking characters and a few good lines (such as "A woman with six martinis can ruin a city"), was rejected by most of the critics. Some, like John Mason Brown (*SR*), were sure that the play was a thinly disguised dramatization of Odets's own disenchantment with the film business and that his failure to be more honest about the central character killed the play. Making Charlie a writer--someone who deals in ideas--rather than an actor, he felt, would have made the character's convictions that much more believable. Like others, he seriously questioned the supposed "integrity" with which Charlie is imbued. Ward Morehouse (*NYS*) called this "the worst play of [Odets's] career," describing it as "a plotty and weighty hodgepodge, a play that wallows in verbiage. A cumbersome and muddled drama [with] some of the most bewilderingly pretentious dialogue heard upon the New York stage in years." Brooks Atkinson (*NYT*) thought the dramatic structure ungainly and the weight of significance placed on the action more than the play could bear.

Garfield's performance was outstanding. John Beaufort (*CSM*) wrote, "Mr. Garfield's whole manner of playing, his restless energy, the outer vitality accompanied by the revelation of sapped inner strength, his sense of Charlie's defiant, bewildered desperation make a persuasive and appealing portrait of a man who has lost his way." Strasberg's direction also received accolades. Leona Powers played gossip columnist Patty Benedict, Paul McGrath played the boss's hatchet man Smiley Coy, and Frank Wilson, Theodore Newton, William Terry, and John McKee also figured in the performance.

BIG SHOT, THE [Musical/Yiddish Language] B: William Siegel; M: Abe Elistein; LY: Isidor Lillian and Jacob Jacobs; D/P: Menasha Skulnik; CH: Lillian Shapero; S: Michael Saltzman; T: Second Avenue Theatre (OB); 1/16/48 (67)

A formula musical comedy, mingling a good deal of English in with the Yiddish. It was directed by its star, Menasha Skulnik, who played Nifty Napkin, a waiter turned babysitter at a winter resort in Miami so that he can have a chance to sit down while working. Everyone calls him something else, from "Mr. Tablecloth" to "Mr. Knives and Forks." The plot centers on his agreeing to pose as the doctor-spouse of young Lillie (Lilly Lilliana) in order to temporarily trick her mother after Lillie has married badly.

The show included the usual blend of schmaltz and farce, a misunderstanding between Lillie and her true love David (Leon Liebgold) when he departs for Palestine to see his dying mother, a successful love pursuit of the reluctant Skulnik by the outrageously coiffed and dressed Yetta Zwerling, mistaken identity, and a scene of patriotic pageantry. Skulnik had a number of comical songs, such as "A Fellow Needs a Girl Like a Hole in the Head," presumably a spoof of "A Fellow Needs a Girl" in the recent Broadway show *Allegro*.

"There is one of the theatre's most finished comedians doing his stuff, surrounded by people who know theirs. There are colorful songs and dances, good settings . . . , funny situations, and some new jokes. . . . What more is needed for an evening of high entertainment [?]" queried Jeanette Wilken (*NYDN*). Jose. (*V*), however, lamented that Skulnik did not make his first entrance until an hour into the show, which required that he "work doubly hard to overcome the uninteresting and implausible proceedings." Cast members included Anna Teitelbaum, Jacob Susanoff, Sara Gingold, Willie Secunda, and Sam Gertler.

BIG TWO, THE [Comedy/Hotel/Jews/Journalism/Military/Mystery/Politics/Romance] A: Ladislaus Bus-Fekete and Mary Helen Fay; D: Robert Montgomery; S/L: Jo Mielziner; C: Bianca Stroock; P: Elliott Nugent and Robert Montgomery b/a/w David Bramson; T: Booth Theatre; 1/8/47 (21)

This "stuttering and trite" (Howard Barnes [*NYHT*]) mystery-melodrama was handsomely set in the lobby of the Waldhotel in Baden, within the Russian-occupied zone of Austria. It brought glamorous film star Claire Trevor to Broadway (from which she had been absent for fourteen years) in the role of Danielle Forbes, an American war correspondent, in Austria under false pretenses, trying to track down for her newspaper an American named Stone who had traitorously broadcast for the Nazis. Also seeking Stone is dashing, handsome Captain Nicholai Mosgovoy (Philip Dorn), an NKVD officer. A brief flirtation arises between these ideological rivals--who argue their respective political beliefs--before they truly fall in love, although an Austrian named Wirth (John Banner) is also in love with the reporter. Stone, using an alias, is discovered by Danielle (he is Meisl [Eduard Franz], the hotel proprietor). She protects herself from being expelled by the Russians by turning over her information, and all ends happily, in both political and emotional terms.

The much-revised play promised a topical political situation concerning entente between the Russians and Americans, but, as Louis Kronenberger (*PM*) declared, it emerged "a shoddy and straggly mixture of comedy, corn, melodrama, romance and political talk--a thrown-together affair that is constantly falling apart." Trevor received mixed notices, but movie actor Dorn, debuting on Broadway, stole the critics' hearts.

Felix Bressart was a black-market racketeer, Olga Fabian was a Jew searching for a sister deported to the concentration camps, and other roles were played by Robert Scott, Wauna Paul, E. A. Krummschmidt, and Martin Berline. Jack (Walter) Palance, in his Broadway debut, was a Russian soldier. A planned film version, for which $150,000 had been paid to secure the rights, was never realized.

In his memoir, *Events Leading up the Comedy*, producer Nugent revealed that he had lost faith in the play even before it opened in New York, and that he wanted to dissolve the partnership he and Robert Montgomery had made with plans to pro duce plays regularly in New York. Montgomery refused, but Nugent himself withdrew from the project, remaining its president in name only. When the play seemed to go well in its New Haven tryout, he began to feel as if he had made a foolish mistake, but the Baltimore critics confirmed his initial impression. This was followed, though, by positive responses in Philadelphia and Boston, only for the show to crash in New York. The producing company became increasingly inactive, and by the time it was dissolved, ninety percent of the initial capital had been lost.

BIG WHITE FOG [Drama/Blacks/Family/Jews/Politics/Prostitution/Race] A: Theodore Ward; D: Powell Lindsay; S/L: Perry Watkins; P: Negro Playwrights Company; T: Lincoln Theatre (OB); 10/22/40 (64)

A new black theatre company, located in Harlem at Lenox Avenue and 135th Street, began with a pro-Communist thesis play that, for all its drawbacks, was con sidered by some the finest work of its type yet to emerge from a black writer's pen. The play had been staged successfully in Chicago in 1938 under Federal Theatre Project auspices.

It is set in 1922 Chicago and focuses on Victor Mason (Canada Lee), an intellectual follower of black nationalist Marcus Garvey, the controversial leader who founded a back-to-Africa movement but was ultimately convicted of fraud. Seriously disturbed by the failure of his son Les (Kelsey Pharr) to receive a scholarship because of his skin color, Mason rejects the advice of his cynical friends and invests $1,500 in Garvey's movement, eventually loses it all, and by 1932 is suffering the poverty inflicted by the Depression. He believes that Garvey's conviction was a plot of white society. When, as part of an eviction strike in which both blacks and whites take part, he resists being thrown out of his home, he dies in a fusillade of police bullets. A subplot concerns the activities of his materialistic mulatto brother-in-law Dan (Edward Fraction), who chooses to be as exploitative as a white man by taking advantage of his own people, but comes to an equally disastrous conclusion when he is harmed by the Depression. Racial problems cause these men and their families to suffer various indignities, such as when Mason's daughter Wanda (Alma Forrest) commits prostitution with a white man in order to help the family keep its home, or when Les (who turns to communism under the influence of a Jewish friend [Jerry Grebanier]) is forced to drop out of college to help support the family.

The play is a bitter exploration of racial politics and prejudice, including the racial strife among blacks of different skin hues. The author's message, provoking the black man to unite with other oppressed minorities to fight against injustice, did not appeal to most reviewers, who agreed with Brooks Atkinson (*NYT*) that "communism is no longer a mystic dream, but Soviet Russia, which is a harsh, brutal, treacherous reality." Critical opinion held that the play was an example of good intentions unfulfilled. Richard Watts, Jr. (*NYHT*), for example, appreciated the social theme but thought the play "clumsy and defective" as well as "diffuse and inexpert." He added, "*Big White Fog* contains so many characters and is so filled with sub-plots that it is sometimes difficult to follow in its story maneuvers." John Mason Brown (*NYP*) noted, "The melodrama seems for all the world like an echo of every playwriting fault committed in the worst of the scripts presented down at the erstwhile Theatre Union."

Canada Lee got mixed reviews for his acting, but Louise Jackson as his irascible, light-skinned mother-in-law, Mother Brooks, was considered outstanding. Lionel Monagas was one of the better-known actors in the cast.

The Negro Playwrights Company included on its list of founders such names as Theodore Browne, Langston Hughes, and Owen Dodson; associate members included Paul Robeson and Richard Wright. They aimed to bring meaningful works about the black experience to New York in a noncommercial environment. A chief inspiration in their formation was the soon-to-be-defunct Group Theatre, whose collaborative approach they hoped to emulate. Unfortunately, they produced no work after *Big White Fog*. One reason was the company's failure to reach a large black audience, it having been estimated that the play was seen by 24,000 whites and only 1,500 blacks.

BIGGEST THIEF IN TOWN, THE [Comedy/Alcoholism/Death/Family/Journalism/Romance/Show Business/Small Town] A: Dalton Trumbo; D: Herman Shumlin; S/L: Leo Kerz; C: Eleanor Goldsmith; P: Lee Sabinson; T: Mansfield Theatre; 3/30/49 (13)

For many, such as Brooks Atkinson (*NYT*), who called it "as funny as a funeral," top screenwriter Dalton Trumbo's black comedy (his first play) may have dealt with a topic too ghoulish to laugh at. At any rate, it closed in two weeks despite the approving remarks of several, including Rosamond Gilder (*TAM*), for whom there "was much amusement, some acute satire of things which deserve it, [and] several moments of hilarity." More common were remarks like Hobe.'s (*V*): "Some of this seems pretty desperately manufactured and what should be funny is occasionally on the grisly side."

Its story is about what happens when John Troybalt (William J. Kelly), the wealthiest and crookedest man in Shale City, Colorado, kicks the bucket. After downing some rye while bemoaning the loss of this profitable corpse to a fancy Denver mortuary, the bibulous local undertaker, Bert Hutchins (Thomas Mitchell), and doctor, Jay Stewart (Walter Abel), contrive to snatch the late lamented in the hopes that they can arrange to have the man's family give them their burial business before the Denver firm is contacted. They manage to succeed in their wishes, and Bert dreams of how he will spend the undertaking profits to help his pretty daughter (Lois Nettleton, in her Broadway debut), who wants to be a dancer; his fantasy is disrupted when the deceased turns out not to be dead after all and revives on the embalming table. There follow various farcical attempts to deal with this development, including a scene in which a boozing evangelical druggist (Rhys Williams) prays that the corpse will die again. Finally, the old man dies for good, and all works out for the best.

Trumbo originally had intended the piece to be a socially significant study of a decent man who commits an immoral act in order to raise money for his daughter's education. Its first titles were *Aching Rivers* and *The Emerald Staircase*. During the out-of-town tryouts, he allowed the reaction of audiences to influence him to revise the play into a comedy bordering on farce, with the original theme discarded. For this, George Jean Nathan (*TBY*) severely reprimanded him, especially since the result was "a play that does not understandably fall to the ground simply because it tries to sit on two stools but that falls with a thud because it tries to sit on a stool that isn't there at all."

Trumbo was one of the "Hollywood Ten," a group of screenwriters jailed for failing to answer a congressional committee's questions regarding their possible Communist affiliations. Because of potential fallout from this political brouhaha, his name was eliminated from all preopening publicity for the play.

Thomas Mitchell gave an expert comic performance in this losing cause, and there were fine performances from the others, including Russ Brown as the town's newspaper editor, William J. Kelly, and Robert Readick as the daughter's boyfriend, a dancing soda jerk with whom she will go into show business as a team.

BILLION DOLLAR BABY [Musical/Crime/Nightclub/Period/Romance/Sex/

Show Business] B/LY: Betty Comden and Adolph Green; M: Morton Gould; D: George Abbott; CH: Jerome Robbins; S: Oliver Smith; C: Irene Sharaff; P: Paul Feigay and Oliver Smith; T: Alvin Theatre; 12/21/45 (220)

A fairly diverting musical that put the name of Joan McCracken, who had begun to gain attention in *Oklahoma!* and *Bloomer Girl*, into lights. Her vehicle, which seemed to George Jean Nathan (*TBY*) weakly derivative of the writings of Anita Loos (*Gentlemen Prefer Blondes*) and John O'Hara (*Pal Joey*), was moderately approved by other critics, who opined that it was sometimes fun but not consistently so. It is set in the "Terrific Twenties" and satirizes the legendary traits of that era, such as Prohibition gangsters, marathon dances, Atlantic City beauty contests, jazz music, bootleg booze, speakeasies, lavish *Ziegfeld Follies**-like revues (here called the "Jollities") and showgirls, and so on.

The plot is sprung by the character of Maribelle (McCracken), a Staten Island bathing beauty with a bitchy temperament, a yen for men, and the heart of a gold digger. She loses her bid for Miss America in Atlantic City and decides to abandon her humdrum existence for a life of excitement and money in the whirling world of the period. Engaged to a marathon dancer (Danny Daniels), she leaves him for a powerful mobster abnnd nightclub proprietor (David Burns), but falls for his bodyguard (William Tabbert). Rocky, the bodyguard, kills the mobster and is himself believed to have been riddled with bullets, leading to a fancy gangster funeral. Rocky turns up in Palm Beach, however, but Maribelle, who had temporarily gone back to her dancer, instead marries a sugar-daddy billionaire (Robert Chisholm) as Wall Street crashes on everyone.

A few lauded the work for its ambitious attempt at originality, but had to admit that it fell short of its purposes. Lewis Nichols (*NYT*) and others complained of a confusion of purposes in the book, which mingled a hard-boiled characterization of its heroine with soft-edged romance. Louis Kronenberger (*PM*) was worried by the work's failure to settle for burlesque of the twenties or to explore their melodramatic underpinnings. At any rate, he said, the show has "a hammer-and-tongs quality that never lets up, that begins as exhilarating, but winds up as wearing." Ward Morehouse (*NYS*) described it as "a raucous, spotty but generally satisfactory song-and-dance play." Morton Gould's score was also given generally down reviews, although Howard Barnes (*NYHT*) found it "rich and varied". Positive features were Jerome Robbins's often-scintillating dances and several funny numbers, such as one in which Maribelle behaves like a glamorous silent-film star, another parodying a 1920s-style production number ("A Lovely Girl is like a Bird") in which the showgirls were dressed as birds, and a comedy ballet called "Charleston."

Most agreed that Mitzi Green's incarnation of Texas Guinan (called Georgia Motley) was a performance highlight. There were some who quibbled about McCracken's performance, but most agreed with Rosamond Gilder (*TAM*), who described her as "small, expert, humorous and extraordinarily versatile. . . . Miss McCracken has an engaging, piquant personality and remarkable technique as a dancer." The company included Shirley Van, Eddie Hodge, and Althea Elder. Helen Gallagher was in the chorus and played several tiny roles.

BILLY THE KID [Dramatic Revival] A: Walter Woods; D: Eliza Downing; S: Robert Ramsey; C: Valerie Judd; P: On-Stage; T: 6 Fifth Avenue (OB); 8/4/48 (8)

A low-budget revival (it was done in the back parlor of an old brownstone) of a naively charming Western melodrama dating from 1890 and concerning the famous cowboy and killer of the title, with Darren McGavin making his New York debut in the role. Robert Garland (*NYJA*) said, "It's an enchanting adventure in off-Broadway playacting, amateur in the real meaning of the word." Of McGavin he declared that he "is exactly as he should be. If I were looking for a promising young player, I'd go to the bottom of the Avenue and look at Mr. McGavin." Richard Watts, Jr. (*NYP*), declared that the piece "is played with proper seriousness and no mockery, and the result is a joy to behold." McGavin, he added, "has real romantic style and suggests that he is a young actor worth the attention of the uptown managers."

The play idealizes the young killer, making him a loyal and upstanding lad who turns to bullets only after his mother and stepfather have been slain by a villain who tricked him into becoming a thief. He then engages in a series of noble escapades, often saving young damsels in distress. At the end he gets the villain, who happens to be his own dad (Scott Cooley).

Frank Cameron acquitted himself well in the role of Billy's Irish sidekick, Con Hanley.

BIRD CAGE, THE [Drama/Alcoholism/Business/Crime/Family/Marriage/Nightclub/Romance/Sex/Show Business] A: Arthur Laurents; M: Alec Wilder; D: Harold Clurman; S: Boris Aronson; C: Ben Edwards; P: Walter Fried and Lars Nordenson; T: Coronet Theatre; 2/22/50 (21)

Arthur Laurents's "hackneyed" (Brooks Atkinson [*NYT*]) flop about nightclub life was reportedly inspired by his own backstage experiences in such places. Essentially a melodrama about a ruthless jazz-club owner, the piece also attempted to project a message about how when little people gather together, they can find the guts to stand up to oppression. Bob Francis (*BB*) complained, however, that "Laurents has piled such incident upon incident in the creation of an amoral monster as to make a soap opera scripter blush." Howard Barnes (*NYHT*), who appreciated the drama's "showmanship," conceded that "much of the work is more hysterical than communicative." Thomas R. Dash (*WWD*) found it impossible to appreciate a play with a miserable louse as its hero. Despite its dramaturgic drawbacks, the play had a number of strong scenes, some racy dialogue, and flashy costumes and was well-enough staged and acted to provide a reasonably gripping evening in the theatre.

Melvyn Douglas played with sharp-etched accuracy the coproprietor of the Bird Cage, one Wally Williams, a fascistic, self-promoting, tuxedo-wearing wheeler-dealer who believes that might makes right, and that the means justify the ends, even if the means are blackmail and theft. When one of his entertainers, the beautiful India Grey (Eleanor Lynn), chooses the piano player (Laurence Hugo) as her romantic interest, Wally begins to get his dander up. More complications stem from the desire of Ferdy (Sanford Meisner), one of his partners, to sell his share of the business because he believes that his daughter's deaf and mute condition is a punishment for his sins in cheating the club's previous owner. Wally objects to the sell-out and is responsible for framing Ferdy, who loses his mind and kills his daughter. Wally also causes great anguish to his loving but alcoholic wife (Maureen Stapleton) by setting up India's attempted seduction by his seventeen-year-old son (Wright King) and also damages the hand of India's piano-playing boyfriend by slamming the keyboard cover down on it. Eventually, broke and unable to prevent the sale of his night spot, and abandoned by all his no-longer-cowed associates, the brutal and unrepentant Wally spitefully fires the place and dies in the blaze.

An interesting feature of the production was the three-level Aronson setting, showing the service bar, a dressing room, an office, and a much-used, winding staircase. Douglas, said Whitney Bolton (*NYMT*), was "believable, intense and on more than one occasion powerful." Stapleton (in her first major role) received equally commendable notices. The cast included Mike Kellin, John Shellie, Kate Harkin, Heywood Hale Broun, Jean Carson, and Rudy Bond.

Melvyn Douglas told in his autobiography (coauthored with Tom Arthur), *See You at the Movies*, that director Clurman, who could deliver brilliant lectures on various topics related to the play, seemed to lose interest in the mechanics of directing as rehearsals progressed. A day before the first dress rehearsal, Clurman still had not staged the Armageddon-like scene of the climactic fire, despite the need for complex blocking necessitated by the difficult set. Douglas said that he himself "began very tentatively working out the blocking with many a nervous glance at the director's chair. I needn't have worried--Harold was delighted somebody had taken over, and made not more than a few minor adjustments once I had finished." Subsequently, Douglas learned that Clurman frequently behaved like this when bored by the technical aspects of directing.

BIRD IN HAND [Dramatic Revival*] A: John Drinkwater; D: Ronald T. Hammond; S: Holak Studios; P: Ronald T. Hammond i/a/w Lee Shubert; T: Morosco Theatre; 10/19/42 (8)

A British comedy seen here in 1929, when it ran for 500 performances. It was revived with Frances Reid as Joan Greenleaf, Harry Irvine as her innkeeper father Thomas, Viola Roache as her mother, Herbert Patterson (a last-minute replacement when the original actor, Henry Barnard, fell ill) as Gerald Arnwood, the squire's son, J. W. Austin as the squire, and Harry Sothern, Romney Brent, and Nicholas Joy as the three guests asked to decide on whether Joan should be allowed to cross class lines and marry Gerald.

Rosamond Gilder (*TAM*) wondered why anyone bothered to revive this "ultra-English comedy which must have been sustained in its day by its acting and its local allusions, but which collapses of its own paper-thin weight on re-appraisal." Brooks Atkinson (*NYT*) was disturbed less by the play, which he (and several others) found still worthwhile, than by the performance, which he said was "loosely textured and indecisive. The comic scenes are done without finesse."

Many noted the poorly rehearsed staging and the frequently fluffed lines, making the presentation dolefully reminiscent of a barnstorming stock-company presentation. *Bird in Hand* was billed as the first in a series of revivals to be produced by Hammond, but it proved to be the last.

BLACKOUTS OF 1949 [Revue] CN/D: Ken Murray; M/LY: Charles Henderson and Royal Foster; S: Ben Tipton; P: David W. Siegel and Ken Murray; T: Ziegfeld Theatre; 9/6/49 (51)

This show, also known as *Ken Murray's Blackouts of 1949*, had been running successfully at Hollywood's El Capitan for eight years before packing its bags for the trip to Broadway. A New York television contract presumably was in the offing for Murray. *Blackouts* met with many bored responses from critics who found that its dull spots overpowered its shining ones. The show's less-than-hilarious humor was likely to run to such antique wheezes as "Marriage is a fine institution, but who wants to live in an institution?"

It was essentially a vaudeville show and included gorgeous showgirls (termed "glamourlovelies"), such as the voluptuous blond Pat Williams, and a bunch of aging blonds (called "elderlovelies"), along with standard acts. Cane- and cigar-wielding, brushtop comedian-producer Murray hosted the proceedings and was one of the few bright spots. Comedy sketches (often risqué), acrobatics, songs (mostly of the nostalgic variety, such as "Silver Threads among the Gold"), dances, animal acts, and a quick-change abbreviated version of *Oliver Twist*, featuring veteran vaudevillian Owen McGiveney in all the roles, composed the program. The show included a few modestly famous entertainers, such as one-legged tap dancer Peg Leg Bates (dressed as a pirate). Among those involved were D'Vaughn Pershing, a virtuoso pianist and clarinetist; singer Charles Nelson; black songwriter, singer, and pianist Shelton Brooks, singing his famous tunes, "Darktown Strutters' Ball" and "Some of These Days"; dance satirists Harris and Shore; Danny Alexander, who tap danced while jumping rope; Alphonse Berg, whose act was to drape gowns on living models at lightning speed; a delightful bird act trained by George Burton, Oscar winner for his short, "Bill and Coo"; and the French pair, Les Zoris, who offered a jungle fantasy dance.

Although many reviews were negative, a few critics enjoyed themselves. According to Brooks Atkinson (*NYT*), so much of the show's music was played at full blast that little of it could be appreciated until guitar-playing singer Nick Lucas appeared to perform some standards. He said, "*Blackouts* is a routine music hall show put on in an informal manner." "It's a pretty dismal show," offered Richard Watts, Jr. (*NYP*). But Robert Coleman (*NYDM*) greatly enjoyed the show's trip down memory lane. Thomas R. Dash (*WWD*) commented, "This fricassee of beautiful femininity and novelty vaudeville should prove entertaining to the paying customers."

BLIND ALLEY [Dramatic Revival*] A: James Warwick; D: J. B. Daniels; S: Frederick Fox; P: Marie Louise Elkins and Clarence Taylor; T: Windsor Theatre; 10/15/40 (63)

A popular-priced revival of the expert 1935 Freudian melodrama, starring Roy

Hargrave in his original role of Hal Wilson, the John Dillinger-like gangster who hides out from the law with his fellow fugitives at the home of a psychology professor (James Todd). The other members of the cast were new. Lila Lee now played the professor's wife. A program note certified that some stitching she did during the action was for Bundles for Britain. Bernadene Hayes played the gun moll.

"This tightly drawn drama of nerves kept the audience on the edge of their seats the whole evening. It's just as exciting in its cold-blooded way as it was five years ago," declared George Freedley (*NYMT*). Hobe. (*V*) dismissed the production as inferior, but most critics thought it, with the exception of James Todd's inadequate professor, tensely effective. All agreed that, as Richard Lockridge (*NYS*) expressed it, Hargrave was "searing, all tortured nerves and terrified bewilderment."

(1) BLITHE SPIRIT [Comedy/British/Death/Fantasy/Literature/Marriage/Sex/Spiritualism] A: Noël Coward; D/P: John C. Wilson; S: Stewart Chaney; C: (gowns) Mainbocher; T: Morosco Theatre; 11/5/41 (657)

Noël Coward's "improbable farce," as he called it, was chosen as one of the best plays of the year and has continued to be a favorite. In England its run was one of the longest of any play in London history. It also won the Drama Critics Circle Award for 1941-1942 as the best play by a foreign author. Coward decided to write this purely escapist entertainment when, upon returning to England from his travels, he discovered the gallant and even carefree attitude of the citizenry despite the pressures of a wartime existence.

It was an instant smash in London, the British provinces, and then in New York. "Nothing," said Rosamond Gilder (*TAM*), "could be more insubstantial than this playful excursion into psychical research, and nothing more amiably diverting. Mr. Coward has caught an absurd idea on the wing, whipped it into three acts of madly silly foolery and presented it with all the flourish of expert showmanship." Brooks Atkinson (*NYT*) called it "a completely insane farce that is also uproarious."

Coward's sophisticated ghost comedy, filled with brittle, frequently rapid-fire comic remarks and elegantly clothed characters, is set in the smartly fashioned country home of novelist Charles Condomine (Clifton Webb) and his acidulous second wife, Ruth (Peggy Wood), with whom his relationship is on the cool side. Seeking material for a story, Charles invites the wacky, bicycle-riding spiritualist Madame Arcati (Mildred Natwick) to conduct a séance. This results in the ectoplasmic materialization of the ghost of Charles's first wife, Elvira (England's Leonora Corbett, in her Broadway debut). Elvira, who bears a streak of malice, succeeds in annoying Charles by her spiteful treatment of Ruth, for whom she does not care. Unable to see Elvira, Ruth, thinking that Charles must be drunk, is upset when he responds to Elvira's questions. When Elvira's presence becomes real to her, Ruth turns jealous. Hoping to have Charles join her in the afterworld, Elvira schemes to have him killed in a car crash, but it is Ruth who takes the tampered-with car and leaves Charles a double widower. Madame Arcati, trying to get rid of Elvira, succeeds instead in bringing forth Ruth's ghost. Charles must contend with a house haunted by two spouses. Elvira is made to confess to her marital infidelities, but Charles has to admit that he was not so nice when he once hit Elvira with either a billiard ball or cue. Madame Arcati is called upon to help the ghosts depart once and for all, and Charles decides to travel to South America in the hope that ghosts can't travel over water.

Most critics found this a delightful piece, but some admitted that there were places where their interest lagged. Much of the fun was provided by special effects as trick props flew about or records went on just after they were turned off. The ghosts were depicted in gray (hair, gowns, and skin), with red lips and nails setting the grayness off.

The seven-member cast was excellent (the other roles were secondary), but Natwick practically stole the proceedings as the balmy medium (created in the London version by Margaret Rutherford) and provided the bulk of the evening's laughter. "This character," stated John Beaufort (*CSM*), "is played with athletic success by Mildred Natwick, who never falls into a dowager cliché to get her effects. Miss Natwick goes at the part with several sets of beads, an unforgettable Tam o'

Shanter, a gown of endless fringes and unmatchable style, and an energy which recalls one of the girls of the old brigade." Jacqueline Clark was an amusingly bustling maid, while the roles of Dr. and Mrs. Bradman were taken by Philip Tonge and Phyllis Joyce. In 1964 the show was musicalized as *High Spirits*.

(2) [Return Engagement] 9/6/43 (32)

Blithe Spirit closed in June 1943 for the summer. When it reopened at the same playhouse in September, it was in preparation for a touring engagement. The only cast change was the replacement of Leonora Corbett by Haila Stoddard, who was deemed excellent, but in some ways not yet up to the level of her predecessor.

BLOOD WEDDING (*Bodas de Sangre*) [Dramatic Revival*] A: Federico Garcàa Lorca; TR: Richard L. O'Connell and James Graham-Lujan; M: Jerome Moross; D: Boris Tumarin; CH: Hanya Holm; S/L: Ralph Alswang; C: Dorothy Croissant; P/T: New Stages (OB): 2/6/49 (35)

An ambitious Bleecker Street revival of Lorca's 1933 Spanish folk drama, seen here previously in 1935 under the title *Bitter Oleander*. A few critics appreciated the moody staging, Hanya Holm's dances, Jerome Moross's atmospheric music, and Ralph Alswang's sparely designed set (using only the most minimal props), but the play itself did not consistently keep their interest because its symbolism and atmosphere remained too Spanish and lacked universality. It appealed purely as a piece of experimental theatre for a select few.

"There is too much wailing and lamentation . . . for purposes of entertainment," thought Kelcey Allen (*WWD*), "and the tragedy, while gaunt and stark, does not yield that emotional catharsis that can compensate in part for the gloom." Despite fine direction and choreography, lamented Richard Watts, Jr. (*NYP*), "the final result does not make for a particularly impressive evening in the theatre." He placed a large part of the blame on the unevenness of the acting company, a view with which George Freedley (*NYMT*) agreed. But Ward Morehouse (*NYS*) advised that "the play has sufficient strength and delicacy to leave the impression of being a striking and unusual theater-piece that has been well done." Brooks Atkinson (*NYT*), apart from certain reservations concerning the "obtuse" translation and lack of "incandescence" in the playing, found this to be "a strangely beautiful theatre incantation."

The company included Sarah Cunningham as the mother, Louis Hollister as the bridegroom, Joan Tompkins as Leonardo's wife, Alexander Scourby as Leonardo (the only character with a name in this translation), Jay Barney as the bride's father, Peggy Allenby as a servant woman, Inge Adams as the bride, Sylvia Davis as death, and Peter Capell as the moon.

(1) BLOOMER GIRL [Musical/Blacks/Business/Family/Historical-Biographical/Period/Politics/Race/Romance/Small Town/Southern/War/Women] B: Sig Herzig and Fred Saidy; M: Harold Arlen; LY: E. Y. Harburg; SC: an unproduced play by Lilith and Dan James; D: E. Y. Harburg and William Schorr; CH: Agnes de Mille; S/L: Lemuel Ayers; C: Miles White; P: John C. Wilson i/a/w Nat Goldstone; T: Shubert Theatre; 10/5/44 (654)

This modest-sized hit was exceedingly colorful, with extravagant sets and costumes establishing a fanciful vision of life in small-town Cicero Falls, New York, during the Civil War days of 1861. Hoopskirt manufacturer Horatio Applegate (Matt Briggs), married to Serena Applegate (Mabel Taliaferro), wishes the youngest of his five daughters, Evelina (Celeste Holm, replaced later by Nanette Fabray), to marry a hoopskirt salesman. She, unlike her siblings, each of whom has married a salesman, rebels and teams up with her aunt, Dolly Bloomer (Margaret Douglass), in pursuit of women's rights. Dolly stands for the abolition of hoopskirts in favor of the pantalettes that eventually gained her name. Despite the harm this will do to the Applegate business, Evelina takes her side. Dolly, who is also an Abolitionist, sets up her headquarters in what once was the town's fancyhouse. Evelina participates in the abolition movement, too, and helps Pompey (Dooley Wilson), a runaway slave, escape via the Underground Railroad. She also falls in love with Jeff Calhoun

(David Brooks), a man who turns out to be a Kentucky slave owner searching for Pompey. When Jeff discovers that Dolly is shielding Pompey, a serious obstacle to romance is created. Soon the Civil War intrudes in such theatrical forms as a deeply moving ballet, a tabloid presentation of *Uncle Tom's Cabin** (with Joan McCracken as Topsy), and the attack on Fort Sumter. All ends happily as Jeff marries Evelina and frees Pompey.

The producers, wanting to take as few chances as possible, went to the hit show *Oklahoma!* for much of their talent, including designers Ayers and White, choreographer de Mille, and performers McCracken and Holm. Choosing a nostalgic story from the American past may have been yet another "borrowing." The show's many advantages were a listenable score with clever lyrics; several outstanding performances; thoughtful, if superficially handled, themes, concerned with freedom for slaves as well as for women; and de Mille's dances, which varied from the lighthearted and witty to the serious, especially in a powerful and moving Civil War ballet about women whose loved ones will never return to them from battle.

According to Edward Jablonski's *Harold Arlen*, the Civil War ballet caused ructions among the creative staff, lyricist-director Harburg exclaiming at one point, "Can't we get rid of this somber, dreadful ballet!" There was an artistic struggle with de Mille, who stubbornly resisted its removal, claiming that it revealed "women's emotions in war." She felt these emotions herself, as her own husband was overseas in the military. De Mille seemed eventually to give in and modified the number. Only a few, however, knew that she was continuing secretly to work on the unorthodox piece as she envisioned it. When the show was about to open in Philadelphia, where she planned to present the true version of the dance to see how the audience responded, it was decided to cut the entire number, even her watered-down version. Only a vigorous fight kept it in. The response was extremely favorable, and the number provided a degree of poignancy that was an important counterbalance to the show's lighter tendencies. Even Harburg admitted, "Goddamit! I've begun to like the dreary thing."

Howard Barnes (*NYHT*) determined that the piece was a "magical delight" that "blends songs, dancing, drama and spectacle into an enchanting and prodigal entertainment." Ward Morehouse (*NYS*) called it "a warm, melodious and beautiful song-and-dance show." Its disadvantages included a lack of unity stemming from too many things being crammed into its framework and a consequent inability to effect smooth transitions from one part to the other. In addition, remarked Rosamond Gilder (*TAM*), "Its songs and its movement do not flow inevitably from its story, which has a tendency to lose its way among the hoopskirts and high hats, the politics and prejudices and the more than usually inane love affairs of Cicero Falls." There was also the book, which most critics considered serviceable and unpretentious, if deficient in laughs; it was, however, "heavily overblown and dreary" to George Jean Nathan (*TBY*), who differed violently from most of his much more positive colleagues and tore almost everything about the show to pieces. Although not as severe, Wilella Waldorf (*NYP*) had to admit that the show was "a big, beautiful bore."

Of the performers, McCracken, in the role of Daisy the maid, stole the spotlight. Lewis Nichols (*NYT*) said that she "has become a comedienne of great charm and a raucous, spellbinding voice." Others approved her dancing and comic spirit, but vociferously rejected her singing. One of her highlights was an 1861 version of a striptease, "T'morra, T'morra."

Holm received encomiums for her charm and comic style but not for her looks or undistinguished singing voice. "For Heaven's sake, Miss Holm," shouted Waldorf, "go back to the drama where you belong. You're killing us." Vocally outstanding, however, was 300-pound black singer Richard Huey, who stopped the show with "I Got a Song." Huey's success with the song was remarkable, considering that in rehearsal he had had enormous difficulties learning its rhythms and had become so exasperated that he actually walked off stage without finishing it during a dress rehearsal. Arlen even wanted to write a replacement song that would be more singable. Songs the critics liked were "The Eagle and Me," a plea for racial tolerance sung by Dooley Wilson, "When the Boys Come Home," "Evelina," and "Right as the Rain," although none became standards.

(2) [Return Engagement] T: City Center of Music and Drama; 1/6/47 (48)

A national tour of the show concluded with a six-week, popular-priced ($2.40 top) revival at New York's City Center. The show seemed surprisingly fresh and alert to Lewis Funke (*NYT*) but some, such as George Jean Nathan (*TBY*) and Vernon Rice (*NYP*), thought it tired. The median view was that the show was a notch less effective than the original, but still highly enjoyable.

Cast changes were common, most newcomers being thought on a par with their predecessors. Best was Nanette Fabray as Evelina. "She has an infectious smile, a gay wit and her singing is easy to hear," recounted Funke. Dick Smart was the new Jeff Calhoun, and Joan McCracken had given over her role to Peggy Campbell, while Olive Reeves-Smith now played Dolly Bloomer, and Hubert Dilworth was a show-stopping Pompey.

BLOSSOM TIME (***Drei Mädel Haus***) [Musical Revival*] B/LY: Dorothy Donnelly; ADD. M: Sigmund Romberg and Heinrich Berte; D: J. J. Shubert; CH: Carthay; S: Watson Barratt; C: Stage Costumes, Inc.; P: Messrs. Shubert; T: Ambassador Theatre; 9/4/43 (47)

Ever since 1921, when this operetta based on the life and music of Franz Schubert premiered, it had been toured somewhere in the country and had had five Broadway revivals before the present one. In 1943 its book seemed duller and more dated than ever, especially in this uninspired, lackluster production. Particularly hard to take was the extreme obviousness of the humor, much of it mishandled by Doug Leavitt as Christian Kranz. The other principals were taken by Alexander Gray as Schubert, Barbara Scully as Mitzi, Roy Cropper as Baron Schober, and Robert Chisholm as Scharntoff. Also in the cast was Jacqueline Susann, the future best-selling novelist, playing the comic maid Greta.

The music remained irresistible for most, but the production values were skimpy and dull. Ward Morehouse (*NYS*) said, "It suggests a Poli or Baldwin-Melville stock producing company, having to bring along a new play every week. For its Broadway reappearance it should have been tricked up with better scenery and costumes. Also, a few more attractive people would have been helpful."

At the time of this show, Susann was having a dalliance with its producer-director, J. J. Shubert. According to Barbara Seaman's biography of Susann, *Lovely Me*, when the actress once came late to a rehearsal, Shubert screamed at her in front of the entire company, "Susann--you come in here late just one more time and you'll be walking the streets again."

BLOW BUGLE BLOW [Comedy/Business] A: Jack Schatz; D: Leonard Altobelli; P: Rochester Players; T: Provincetown Playhouse (OB); 12/11/40

A hapless farce produced by a semipro summer-theatre troupe from Rochester, New York, and purporting to satirize public-relations men. A timid suspenders maker (Alfred Hardy) hires a PR man (Leonard Altobelli) to make him famous as a celebrity and big-game hunter, which the PR man succeeds in doing until the client is nearly bankrupted. A happy conclusion straightens out all loose ends.

Most reviewers departed early, but Robert Sylvester (*NYDM*) remained and decided that "once *Blow Bugle Blow* untangled its awkward feet and learned to walk, it impressed some of us as being a potentially funny show," but one that needed a wise doctor to cure it of its ills.

BLUE COAL (see *Brother Cain*)

BLUE HOLIDAY [Revue] M/LY: Al Moritz; ADD.M/LY: Duke Ellington, E. Y. Harburg, and Earl Robinson; D/L: Moe Hack; CH: Katherine Dunham; S: Perry Watkins; C: Kasia; P: Irvin Shapiro and Doris Cole; T: Belasco Theatre; 5/21/45 (8)

A languid black variety show emceed by Willie Bryant and Timmie Rogers and starring Ethel Waters, with such noted performers in support as Josh White, Josephine Premice, Talley Beatty, the Hall Johnson Choir, and the Katherine Dunham

Dancers; still, it could not sustain life for more than a week. George Jean Nathan (*TBY*) explained that had the show's acts lived up to the true meaning of the word variety, it might have had a chance. Instead, the numbers were boringly familiar, with only a few routines of more than passing interest. Director Jed Harris had been brought in to slice thirty minutes from the show, but his ministrations proved fruitless, and the show still ran longer than audiences would have liked. Among the bits that created an atmosphere of lassitude in what should have been a spicy and variegated show were Waters doing two dramatic scenes from *Mamba's Daughters** and singing her famous hits with none of her wonted fire; the high-toned choreographic exercises of Dunham's troupe; and the spiritual singing of Johnson's chorus.

Lewis Nichols (*NYT*) lamented that a bunch of talented players had been "buried under a bushel measure of tedium." Highlights were folk singer and guitarist Josh White singing such songs as "The House I Live In" and "One Meat Ball"; boogie-woogie pianist Mary Lou Williams; the Hall Johnson Choir's rendition of "St. Louis Blues"; and Haitian dancer Josephine Premice rendering songs and dances from her native land.

One of Dunham's dancers was young Eartha Kitt, making her unnoticed Broadway debut. In her autobiography, *I'm Still Here*, Kitt recalled that she was dressed in a scanty hula costume in which, with a line of other girls, she was to wiggle her way across the stage, supposedly representing a beach. As they were rehearsing one day, a booming voice shouted from the house, "Get those naked bitches off my stage!" The shouter turned out to be Ethel Waters herself. After chasing the girls into the wings, Waters huddled with the show's creative team. The girls were then ordered to repeat their number, which they proceeded to do. Kitt continued, "Suddenly, without warning, a tap dancer (who turned out to be Ethel Waters' lover) entered . . . in front of us tapping on the beach in a routine from the Apollo Theatre. We all stood stunned, wondering how a tap dancer could tap on sand, but that was the way Ethel Waters wanted it and that was the way it stayed."

BORN YESTERDAY [Comedy/Business/Crime/Journalism/Law/Politics/Romance/Sex] A/D: Garson Kanin; S: Donald Oenslager; P: Max Gordon; T: Lyceum Theatre; 2/4/46 (1,642)

One of the biggest comedy hits of the 1940s and a work that has remained popular for many decades, *Born Yesterday* also propelled Judy Holliday (as Billie Dawn), Paul Douglas (as Harry Brock), and Gary Merrill (as Paul Verrall) into fame. Douglas, previously best known as a sports announcer, although he had done some acting, got his part after Kanin, looking for someone like Douglas, heard producer Jean Dalrymple ask why he did not get Douglas himself. By the time the show closed, it had earned $722,625.49 plus $360,000 from its share of the film sale.

Holliday, who became the most popular of them all, but whose career was cut short by a fatal illness, received her part only after its original star, Jean Arthur, had to be replaced when she fell ill during the tryout period. This was a blessing in disguise. According to producer Max Gordon in *"Max Gordon Presents,"* Arthur turned out to be a very difficult actress and was attempting to rewrite the play even before rehearsals began. Playwright-director Kanin stood behind the actress, rationalizing her behavior as stemming from shyness. She nearly drove Kanin crazy with her requests for revisions during the rehearsal process, although it was clear that she was simply trying to mask her fears at playing farce and at playing an obvious sex object. Arthur played the role in New Haven and then in Boston, but continued to plague the director and producer with her complaints, which now included problems with her health. (Many felt that this was a ruse to cover up the actress's insecurity.) Gordon was forced to replace her with her ill-prepared understudy, Mary Laslo (who also played a manicurist), in Boston, but very few people asked for their money back. June Havoc auditioned and seemed a likely replacement, but her commitment to S. N. Behrman's *Dunnigan's Daughter* precluded using her. A suggestion was then made to look at Holliday, a relative unknown who not long before had received outstanding reviews for the small role of a floozie in *Kiss Them for Me*.

Gordon said that the minute he met the actress he knew she was perfect for the part. When Arthur's health took a turn for the worse, Holliday was rehearsed in

Philadelphia, where she was hurriedly prepared in three days for the dress rehearsal. Considering the length and complexity of the role, this required herculean feats of stamina and memory for the actress. (According to Gary Carey's *Judy Holliday*, she later claimed to have consumed nothing but coffee and Dexedrine during the ordeal.) Not only were there many lines to learn, but also some tricky technical business such as the apparently spontaneous but actually minutely-worked out gin rummy game Billie plays with Brock.

The Philadelphia critics and audiences loved her, as would countless others in the years to come. But Douglas and Holliday both caused headaches to the producer, who said Douglas began to live his role offstage, drinking heavily and acting abusively, and Holliday started making demands for contract revisions and for the doubling of her salary. These demands were negotiated so that instead of the $1,000 a week she asked for, Holliday got $750 and a secondhand car, while also acceding to Gordon's request for a run-of-the-play contract. Gordon would have reason to be thankful for the latter, as Holliday's performance eventually became a major draw, and she stayed with the piece until May 1949, an unusually long time for a player to remain in the same role.

Harry Brock is a crude, English-mangling, middle-aged robber baron whose great wealth has sprouted from his junkyard business. His callous philosophy is that anything and anyone can be bought and that money means power. Rich enough to have at least one senator (Larry Oliver) in his pocket, he is staying in a garishly designed, $235-a-day room in a Washington, D.C., hotel with his diamond- and mink-adorned mistress, Billie Dawn, a vapid blond bimbo fresh out of the chorus line of *Anything Goes**. For tax purposes, Billie has been made president--on paper--of Brock's corporations, but he refuses the advice of his lawyer, Ed Devery (Otto Hulett) to marry her, thinking that he has more control over her in his present arrangement. Brock is seeking to gain legislation that will permit him to create an international cartel handling all of Europe's scrap iron. The uneducated Billie has a penchant for foolish remarks and malapropisms ("The country belongs to the people that inhibit it"), so Brock wants to have her educated to make her more suitable company for the wives of the politicians he seeks to woo. A bespectacled *New Republic* reporter named Paul Verrall--seeking an exposé of Brock--is hired to spruce up her mind, which leads to the discovery that Billy really has a brain under all those peroxided curls. She warms rapidly to the liberal ideas propounded by Paul and, from her delvings into Tom Paine and Sibelius, becomes increasingly socially and artistically aware. A Galatea molded by her new Pygmalion, she rejects the fascistic businessman (his maneuvers probably will send him to prison), falls in love with Paul, and goes off with him to live happily forever after.

Born Yesterday, Kanin's first Broadway play, was a quintessential wisecracking Broadway comedy, mingled with political satire, melodramatic plotting, romance, and touching sentiment. There were a few complaints about the play's occasional lags and its need for additional editing, but the reviews, on the whole, were red-hot. Ward Morehouse (*NYS*) said that it "offers some flip and fluent writing, some first-rate acting and an expert production, and it gives the Lyceum Theater a tremendously entertaining show." Robert Garland (*NYJA*) raved that it was "a funny play with unfunny implications; a touching, tender, terrifying showpiece with everything to recommend it to the theatregoer in search of entertainment, enlightenment or a swift kick in the great American complacences." Slightly less enthusiastic was George Jean Nathan (*TBY*), who reluctantly suggested that the play, which reminded him of "Shaw's *Pygmalion** rewritten by the Loos of *Gentlemen Prefer Blondes** in eccentric collaboration with the Pinero of *Iris*, becomes the stuff of a somewhat labored but ribaldly amusing comedy."

Oenslager's hilariously tasteless depiction of the hotel room was one of the show's strongest features. After describing how he designed it in *The Theatre of Donald Oenslager*, the designer noted, "The setting was conceived as subtle good-humored parody--a scenic satire. Many in the audience responded to this hotel suite . . . and thought it was very 'beautiful.' And that was the idea."

The comedy was granted performances of rapid pacing, split-second comic timing, colorful characterizations, and appropriate reality. "Miss Holliday," reported

Rosamond Gilder (*TAM*), "has in Billie a role that exactly fits her, giving her an opportunity to display . . . those qualities of physical, almost animal, appeal and of human tenderness and pathos that she managed to convey so vividly in her previous appearance [in *Kiss Them for Me*]." "Paul Douglas," noted Euphemia Van Rensselaer Wyatt (*CW*), "gives an astounding impersonation of a man who has less idealism than a Nazi but he also makes Harry Brock so ingenuous a big dog with a bone that it is possible to laugh at him." Carroll Ashburn, Mona Bruns, and Frank Otto were in the cast.

Garson Kanin, asked where he got the idea for the story, said that he combined two experiences of his to arrive at the final result. One was the period of his army service, when he was stationed in Washington. Another was his memory of a time in his youth when he had performed as a comedian in burlesque on Forty-second Street and had befriended an intellectual stripper named Belle. "One afternoon I found her reading *The Decline of the West*. She got me to read the works of Harold J. Laski. . . . My memory of her and my Washington experience were the two ideas that combined to become the play *Born Yesterday*" (quoted in Otis L. Guernsey, Jr., *Broadway Song and Story*).

BOUDOIR [Drama/Alcoholism/Crime/Marriage/Music/Period/Sex] A/D: Jacques Deval; S: Raymond Sovey; P: Jacques Chambrun; T: John Golden Theatre; 2/7/41 (11)

"Had it not been emphatically stated that Mr. Deval had written the play himself and written it in English, one might have thought that it was a somewhat stilted translation of a nineteenth-century drama which had become farce through the passage of time and the process of transposition," was Rosamond Gilder's (*TAM*) acidulous comment on this flop, which drew many unintended laughs. It was the French playwright's first work in English. Hobe. (*V*) said that it "may not be the season's absolute nadir, but it's bad enough. In fact, it's terrible."

Boudoir takes place in 1882 New York and traces the tale of Cora Ambershell (British actress Helen Twelvetrees, in her Broadway debut), a beautiful but grasping young adventuress with a lurid past, who is being kept by a wealthy old man, Edgar Massuber (Taylor Holmes). Gaylord (Staats Cotsworth), a butler with a penchant for wild piano playing, and his wife, Oriane (Else Argal, wife of the playwright, making her American debut), a maid, are hired by Cora, but Gaylord turns out to be Cora's ex-husband, divorced when he was sent to jail. The reformed Gaylord--whose musical career Cora killed--recognizes Enrico Palfieri (Henry Brandon), the rakish doctor who has been carrying on with Cora, as a fake; Enrico is actually a killer who strangles women for their jewels. Gaylord had met him while serving time in Leavenworth prison. Oriane thinks that Gaylord should inform Cora, but he decides to quit her employ instead. Cora manages, however, to get him drunk and forced out of the house. Oriane has Gaylord taken to an alcoholic clinic and then decides not to tell Cora the truth about Enrico, who, in the meantime, has been dallying with another woman (Jeraldine Dvorak). At the curtain, Oriane, disgusted with Cora for betraying Gaylord, keeps her mouth shut as Cora is about to have a fateful rendezvous with her homicidal lover.

BOURGEOIS GENTLEMAN, THE (see *The Would-Be Gentleman*)

BOY MEETS GIRL [Dramatic Revival*] A: Bella and Samuel Spewack; D: Rodney Hale; S: Cirker and Robbins; P: Lucia Victor's New York Stock Company; T: Windsor Theatre; 6/22/43 (15)

Lucia Victor's new, popular-price ($2.20 top on weekends, $1.65 other times) Broadway stock company offered its second presentation with *Boy Meets Girl*, the hit comedy of 1935, following a flop with *The Milky Way**. It was a better choice, but the quality of the production left much to be desired. Reported George Freedley (*NYMT*), "The play dragged, the cues were missed, the pace was snailish; a highly hilarious idea was booted into the ashcan by staging which would shame a high school in South Boston, Va."

When Freedley asked members of the company why their work was so mediocre, they responded that because of their noncommercial economic structure, they were only permitted a week's rehearsal by Actors Equity. This was deemed unfair when it was considered that the company guaranteed its actors two weeks of work, which is what regular commercial producers, who were allowed twenty-eight days of rehearsal, had to provide.

The roles of the screenwriters Robert Law and J. Carlyle Benson were played by Lewis Charles and Joey Faye, while Rosetti the agent was handled by Sanford Bickart, Larry Tom the cowboy star by Norman MacKay, movie executive C. F. by Gordon Nelson, Peggy the secretary by Catherine Linn, Susie the waitress by Sara Lee Harris (who gave the best performance), and Rodney Bevan by Marshall Reid. Few seemed to have a meaningful notion of their characters or the style demanded.

BOY WHO LIVED TWICE, A [Drama/Death/Family/Fantasy/Romance/Youth] A: Leslie Floyd Egbert and Gertrude Ogden Tubby; D: Paul Foley; S: John Root; P: Hall Shelton; T: Biltmore Theatre; 9/11/45 (15)

This heavy-handed play opened after seven years of preparation and closed in two weeks. It was rejected for being "some of the most confused and amateurish playwriting on record," according to George Jean Nathan (*TBY*), who pointed out numerous plays with similar themes to disprove the authors' contention that theirs was an original subject.

It deals with reincarnation as expressed in a story about a wealthy Long Island lad named Philip Hastings (John Heath), who dies in a horseback-riding accident. The mystical ministrations of his presumed sister Jeanne (Anne Sargent) bring him back to life, but he now has the soul of a dead midwestern army pilot, Lieutenant John Ralston, who was just killed in a plane crash. He seems completely at sea in his current environment; a psychiatrist (Vaughan Glaser) uses hypnotism to determine that there actually has been a transfer of souls. John's mother (Nellie Burt) arrives with the news that her dead son has been revived and insists that he is Philip. Philip falls in love with his sister, who, understanding that he is inhabited by another's soul, also falls for him. On the verge of incest, he contemplates suicide, but Jeanne saves him just as John kills himself, leaving Philip to feel that he has murdered John. The play concludes with the discovery that Philip is an identical Ralston twin stolen by Philip's presumed father Randall (Grandon Rhodes) when his wife lost a baby in childbirth, and that he is not Randall's son after all, which makes it okay for him to love Jeanne.

Heavily written and dully acted, the play was permanently interred and lived only once. Cast members included Claire Windsor, Stapleton Kent, and Strelsa Leeds.

BOYD'S DAUGHTER [Comedy/Business/Irish/Religion/Romance] A: St. John Ervine; D: Hiram Sherman; S/L: Johannes Larsen; P: W. Horace Schmidlapp, Joseph M. Gates, and Lee Shubert; T: Booth Theatre; 10/11/40 (3)

A commonplace, garrulous Irish comedy (originally titled *Boyd's Shop*) by one of the most noted literary figures of the day. Written in 1935, premiered in Liverpool in 1936, and making its transatlantic debut in 1940, the play is set in Northern Ireland's Ulster County and concerns the romantic dilemma of Agnes Boyd (Helen Trenholme), a village grocer's (Whitford Kane) daughter, who can't decide which young man to marry, the asinine clergyman, Reverend Ernest Dunwody (Hiram Sherman, who also directed), or the shopkeeper, John Haslett (William Post, Jr.) who has set up a business to rival her father's. Both men are new in town and disrespectful of their elders. The latter suffers the destruction of his store by fire and also gets a nasty bruise from a falling timber. He lucks out, however, in winning Agnes's affections away from the cleric. During a break between the scenes in act one, Sherman entertained the audience with an impromptu comic talk concerning such things as the problems in shifting the sets and the vicissitudes in bringing the play to production.

The play's principal interest lay in St. Ervine's scathing attitudes toward contemporary young people, but he expressed his feelings, said John Anderson (*NYJA*), "in dialogue that is badly over-written and in situations that are considerably overdrawn." "In addition to being a scrappily written play," scoffed Brooks Atkinson (*NYT*), "*Boyd's Daughter* is badly directed and poorly acted in the minor roles."

BOYS AND GIRLS TOGETHER [Revue] B: Ed Wynn and Pat C. Flick; CN/D/P: Ed Wynn; CH: Albertina Rasch M: Sammy Fain; LY: Jack Yellen and Irving Kahal; S: William Oden Waller; C: Irene Sharaff and Veronica; T: Broadhurst Theatre; 10/1/40 (191)

Lisping, fifty-four-year-old, master clown Ed Wynn was largely responsible for whatever success this Broadway revue mustered, but he did have a solid group of assistants, including near-operatic songstress Jane Pickens and ballroom dance team Reneée and Antonio (Tony) De Marco, as well as the gorgeous costumes of Irene Sharaff and the tunes of Sammy Fain. Wynn's unique style of comic foolery began when he made his appearance by popping out of a trunk piled atop a group of other trunks. He then proceeded to amble through the show in one wonderfully silly costume after another, often amiably butting into someone else's act. In one such bit, he intruded into an acrobatic turn (executed by the LaVarres) when he tried to unravel the performers' limbs, but soon found himself entangled in them himself. In another, Wynn appeared toward the end of a complex dance number set in a dance-practice studio with its "ballerinas, moderns, acrobatics, eccentrics and Wigman postulants" (Euphemia Van Rensselaer Wyatt [*CW*]). Wynn's bit had him dancing with a 200-pound contortionist named Dot Remy. Much laughter was aroused when, preparatory to its being used as a pathway for eight stunningly adorned beauties named after New York nightclubs, he laid down a stair carpet made of wool (it was 200 percent pure wool because sheep lead double lives). As he finished unrolling the carpet by the footlights, Wynn, flat on his belly, looked up at the audience and declared, "You won't catch Katharine Cornell doing this." Wynn's trademark comic props were also in the show, including a piano with a bicycle attached. Apart from such routines, the show suffered from a flimsy script and slow pacing.

Rosamond Gilder (*TAM*) declared, "Though his stock in trade is the oldest in the world, though his bag of tricks contains much the same assortment of idiotic oddments as the clowns of all ages have used, in Ed Wynn's hands they become fresh objects of delight and astonishment. With him the *vis comica* that informs Jolson takes on a childish abandon, a rustic, round-eyed zest. Eyebrows in air, mouth open, body angularly alert, Ed Wynn wanders startled, joyful, ingenuous, through a world of his own frenzied creation."

BRAVO! [Comedy-Drama/Mental Illness/Romance/Science/Theatre] A: Edna Ferber and George S. Kaufman; D: George S. Kaufman; S/L: Leo Kerz; C: Rose Bogdanoff (gowns: Castillo); P: Max Gordon; T: Lyceum Theatre; 11/11/48 (44)

Kaufman and Ferber, whose outstanding collaborations normally concerned theatre folk, returned to the fray with *Bravo!*, also about the theatre. It failed, but did bear traces of the authors' well-known talents. The opening came earlier than originally scheduled because Kaufman wished to avoid critical comparison with his ex-partner Moss Hart's *Light Up the Sky*, due to open at about the same time. Hobe. (*V*) thought it "a curiously lacklustre work. It is a transparently manufactured treatment of a hackneyed subject, with only occasional comedy to brighten the slow and obvious story-telling." "The hand of the plotter is heavy and the multitude of devices is wearisome and suspenseless," growled William Hawkins (*NYWT*), who could find nothing about the characters with which to connect emotionally. Almost a solo voice in the critical wilderness was George Jean Nathan (*TBY*); while expressing many reservations, he nevertheless believed this to be a play of "much incidental honest sympathetic charm," "droll observation of character," and "understanding humor."

The piece deals with a group of displaced European refugees, including Austrians, Germans, Poles, and Russians. All of them are living in New York and finding it difficult to adjust to their surroundings. At their heart is a romantic couple, a famous Ferenc Molnár-like Hungarian playwright, Zoltan Lazko (Oscar Homolka), and his mistress of two decades, a Hungarian star actress named Rosa Rucker (Lili Darvas, actual wife of Molnár). Their various refugee friends are given refuge in a West Side brownstone, where all the action is set. There is also a candy-making ex-judge (Edgar Stehli), reduced to wheeling clothes through the garment center; a female scientist (Elena Karem); a Russian archduchess (Zolya Talma) who is now a dressmaker; an Austrian prince (Oliver Cliff) working as a salesclerk; a Polish ballerina (Janet Fox); and the cabdriver-writer (Kevin McCarthy) with whom she is involved. A young actress named Lisa Kemper, a former prisoner of the concentration camps and a protégée of Zoltan, arrives and is cast in a play. She also has a romance with the literary cabbie. The playwright tries writing for Broadway in the American style and flops, while Rose can find only small roles to play. A friendly producer (Frank Conroy) is unable to sustain the losses of putting Zoltan's plays on, and the playwright and the young actress--ratted on by the jealous ballerina, who discovers that the actress has been a mental patient--are threatened with deportation. Their problems are solved, however, by philanthropist Bernard Baruch (not seen), whom Zoltan has met in the park. By the final curtain, Zoltan is planning a new play about America that will incorporate his grand romantic style. Among the most interesting characters is a gorgeous movie star named Jane Velvet (Jean Carson), who, despite her elegant appearance, speaks in the commonest manner. Another is a rich and selfish refugee (Fritzi Scheff).

There were many fine performances, but most critics selected Darvas as the darling of the production. Darvas had replaced European actress Rose Stradner in the role during the New Haven tryout.

BRIDGE TO THE SUN [Drama/Crime/Mental Illness/Mystery] A/P: Phyllis Carver and Burrell Smith; D: Phyllis Carver; T: Provincetown Playhouse (OB); 7/22/43

A vanity production, produced by and starring the authors, one of whomd also directed. It was a murder story about a wealthy but psychopathic young man (Smith) who strangles his wife (Carver) and confesses the crime to the police inspector (Thomas M. Heaphy). The play moves backwards in time to show events leading up to the crime. The murderer has a mental weakness that causes him to kill when he least expects it. Near the end he nearly throttles the maid, but is prevented just in time.

"Everything falls flat in this play," announced Burton Rascoe (*NYWT*). "It was badly rehearsed . . . and some of the acting was amateurish, but I don't believe even a well-rehearsed and well-chosen cast could make *Bridge to the Sun* interesting or exciting."

(1) BRIGADOON [Musical/Barroom/Fantasy/Romance] B/LY: Alan Jay Lerner; M: Frederick Loewe; D: Robert Lewis; CH: Agnes de Mille; S: Oliver Smith; C: David Ffolkes; L: Peggy Clark; P: Cheryl Crawford; T: Ziegfeld Theatre; 3/13/47 (581)

A landmark musical costing only about $160,000. Despite the absence of stars, it was the first big success for the team of Lerner and Loewe and was subsequently revived on many occasions. More a "musical play" than a musical comedy, this Scottish fantasy was considered a beautifully integrated show in which the staging, music, story, and dancing all were perfectly fused. It was selected as one of the season's ten best by Burns Mantle, being only the third time a musical had been so chosen. It also won the New York Drama Critics Circle award as best musical. Agnes de Mille shared the first Tony for choreography with *Finian's Rainbow*'s Michael Kidd, although no Tony was given to a play or musical during the award's first year.

Interestingly, Lerner and Loewe had been turned down by nearly every musical producer in town when they first wrote the show. The Theatre Guild might have been interested if the show's setting had been changed to America. Billy Rose decided to do it, but his terms were so dictatorial that Lerner and Loewe decided not to do the show at all rather than to accept them. According to Lerner's *The Musical Theatre*, Rose was so angry that he sent a telegram threatening legal action if any of the ideas he had suggested showed up in the work. When Lerner asked Rose by letter to list his ideas so that legal repercussions could be avoided, the pint-sized producer never replied. Finally, Cheryl Crawford, who had been out of town, returned and heard an audition that convinced her to do the show.

To raise funds for the modestly-priced production, Lerner and Loewe had to audition it fifty-eight times, and the show already was in rehearsal before their last audition was given. Ironically, the theatre in which it opened was one owned by Billy Rose. This reminded Lerner of the famous show business quip (which he attributed to George M. Cohan), "Throw that son of a bitch out of the theatre and I never want to see him again, unless I need him."

Brigadoon's charming, if saccharine, book concerns two young American men, Tommy Albright (David Brooks) and Jeff Douglas (George Keane), hunting in Scotland when they get lost on a mysterious brae and inadvertently come across an idyllic village whose name is the show's title. A fair is in progress, to be followed by the wedding later in the day of Jean MacLaren (Virginia Bosler) and Charlie Dalrymple (Lee Sullivan). Jean is getting married before her older sister Fiona (Marion Bell), who has not yet found her dearie. Tommy, unhappily engaged to a girl back home, seems likely to answer her desires, and an alliance also seems to be burgeoning between the comical pair of Jeff and the promiscuous Meg Brockie (Pamela Britton). Something about the delightful village seems awry; Fiona's birthdate, discovered in a family Bible, would make her over two hundred-years old, and the place itself is unusually anachronistic (they have never heard of telephones, for example). These mysteries are explained by the village schoolmaster, Mr. Lundie (William Hansen), who tells of the granting of the local minister's prayer in 1747 that the town appear only once every hundred years as a way of protecting it from disturbing outside influences. At the end of the day the place disappears once more into the mists. Only by someone leaving the place of his own free will can the spell be broken. When Harry Beaton (James Mitchell), spurned by Jean, decides to leave and break the spell, he is chased through the forest, only to be killed when accidentally tripped by Tommy. This so disturbs the latter that he leaves Fiona and returns to New York, but his fiancée's unpleasantness convinces him and Jeff to return to the Highlands hoping against hope to make Brigadoon reappear. Tommy's love is strong enough to effect the miracle, as it awakens Mr. Lundie, and the American once more joins his Scottish lassie.

Brigadoon is the show that introduced such familiar tunes as "Almost like Being in Love," "The Heather on the Hill," "Come to Me, Bend to Me," "Waitin' for My Dearie," and "I'll Go Home with Bonnie Jean," among others. The lilting score, much of it played by a combination of strings, with bagpipes in the background, provided perfect settings for the lovely dances of Agnes de Mille, which ranged from folk-dance-like routines to an intensely dramatic forest chase to a somber funeral number and a rousing sword dance, impressively danced by James Mitchell. With a sound book, an exceptional score, romantically stylized eighteenth-century settings, costumes of kilts and tartans, original and poetically fanciful choreography, and felicitously sensitive direction, the show pleased on multiple counts. John Mason Brown (*SR*) observed, "It has a book, literate, sensitive, and intelligent; . . . its music is charming. Its singing actors not only can but do both sing and act. Its dancers are unusually proficient. Its costumes are admirably conceived and contrasted; its settings, imaginative and colorful." Wrote Brooks Atkinson (*NYT*), "This excursion into an imagined Scottish village is an orchestration of the theatre's myriad arts, like a singing story-book for an idealized country fair long ago." "Simple, sweet and absolutely engaging, *Brigadoon*" seemed to George Freedley (*NYMT*), "the most rewarding musical of the season." The normally acidulous George Jean Nathan (*TBY*), who went expecting to hate the show, found that what he dreaded seeing had been treated "with so much taste, imagination, and humor that the result . . . is one of the most thoroughly engaging entertainments I have seen in a long time."

Among the show's drawbacks was its lack of effective comedy, the ponderousness of several songs, and an intrusive New York barroom scene in the last act. The director, choreographer, and designer were, at first, primarily concerned about the show's sentimental excesses. According to director Lewis's *Slings and Arrows*, when he first met with de Mille to discuss the show, the question before them was, "How do we set about killing Jeannette MacDonald?" referring to the star of so many schmaltzy film operettas. Designer Smith said that he had had to put the script down after reading the exchange between Tommy and the dominie. Tommy: "So you're all perfectly happy living here in this little town?" Dominie: "Of course, lad. After all, sunshine can peep through a small hole." Smith's reaction was, "If I had read any further I'd never have been able to design the show."

Lewis noted that the show's technical rehearsal in New Haven took so long that there never was an actual rehearsal. Tech rehearsal ended at 8:15 p.m. on opening night, so the assembled audience was allowed in to watch what was a combined world premiere and dress rehearsal. The Boston opening a week later was a nightmare. Early in the show, as several villagers passed in front of the downstage "tab" curtains while the forest scene upstage was being changed to the Scottish village, the curtains failed to open even though the orchestra was playing and the performers upstage of the curtain were presumably singing and dancing their "MacConnachy Square" number. The downstage actors finally fled into the wings instead of blending with the company that had not materialized; when the curtains ultimately did part--violently--the company was found in a variety of halfhearted and ridiculous positions. Just then, the MacConnachy Square backdrop flew up, revealing the theatre's bare back wall while, simultaneously, costume designer Ffolkes came running to the astonished Lewis, crying out, "Bunty Kelly's got the wrong socks on again!" "That, lads and lassies," wrote Lewis, "is specialization."

Nathan started a controversy by pointing out the striking similarities of the book to a nineteenth-century German story by Friedrich Wilhelm Gerstäcker called *Germelshausen* and noted the reluctance of Lerner to acknowledge this as his source. Lerner, for his part, claimed "unconscious coincidence" and also declared that Shakespeare borrowed his plots without harming his reputation. (The striking similarities in the stories are described in Abe Laufe's *Broadway's Greatest Musicals*.) But Lerner never acknowledged the debt and, years later, noted in *The Street Where I Live* that the real reason for Nathan's accusations of plagiarism stemmed from his jealousy over an actress in the show, who presumably preferred Lerner to Nathan himself.

(2) [Musical Revival] T: City Center of Music and Drama; 5/2/50 (24)

Cheryl Crawford again produced this outstanding show, now for a limited engagement at popular prices ($3 top). Although the cast was different, the creative staff was the same, and the show--just back from a major tour--was unchanged from the original version. It was in first-class condition and met with numerous superlatives. The new cast included Phil Hanna (star of the London version) as Tommy Albright, Peter Turgeon as Jeff Douglas, Virginia Oswald as Fiona, Susan Johnson as Meg, James Jamieson as Harry Beaton, Fred Stewart as Mr. Lundie, Ann Deasy as Jean McLaren, and Jeff Warren as Charlie Dalrymple.

John Chapman (*NYDN*) thought them "nice enough without being notable." Robert Garland (*NYJA*) recommended the production because it was "like a brand new show with captivating cast and superior surroundings." Herb. (*V*) concluded that de Mille's contribution remained the show's most durable ingredient. "The dance and musical numbers . . . have a fluidity and grace of motion that have seldom been equalled."

BRIGHT BOY [Comedy/Crime/Politics/Romance/School/Youth] A: John Boruff; D: Arthur J. Beckhard; S: Watson Barratt; P: Arthur J. Beckhard and David Merrick; T: Playhouse; 3/2/44 (16)

Lieutenant John Boruff, U.S.N.R., as this play's author billed himself, was also an actor. His first play had some interesting features and provoked some thought. It used a prep-school background to represent a microcosm of the world at large for a tale concerned with the problem of good and evil. The play could not sustain its intentions through three acts, however, and ended with a confused conclusion. Lewis Nichols (*NYT*) said, "It succeeds only in being somewhat sentimental in the wrong way, talky, anti-climactic and occasionally downright dull."

The protagonist is a boy named Allen Carpenter (Donald Buka), the extremely bright son of wealthy parents who have sent him to Brown Hall, an East Coast boy's school, where he encounters a number of youths who represent a cross-section of familiar types. The only adults are the headmaster (Ivan Simpson) and a kindly teacher (Liam Dunn). The sole girl is the headmaster's attractive daughter Margaret (Joyce Franklin), who provides the play with some youthful romantic interest. Allen and David Bennet (Charles Bowlby) are both newcomers to the senior class. Allen is a conniving heel who uses his superior intelligence to manipulate people in order to advance his own selfish interests. David is a decent boy of average intelligence. Soon after arriving, Allen is hazed by being thrown in the lake. Rather than squeal, he decides to take his revenge by more subtle means, using his reading of Machiavelli to gain power and respect. For example, he loans his classmates money that he himself has stolen from them. He and David engage in a rivalry for class president, which Allen wins, becoming even more of a hero when he dismisses the "loans" that he has made to his classmates. David finally manages to expose Allen and, because he has sensed the innate goodness in him, to make him reform his character, but Allen has a hard time convincing the others of his own guilt, so successful has he been at his mind games.

Bright Boy succeeded best in its depiction of life in a boy's school. What most riled the critics was the Hitlerian Allen's reformation. As George Jean Nathan (*TBY*) perceived, "Honestly developed, the character might have been a fascinating and prehensile figure, but the actor-author's presumption that you inevitably have to reform such a character if your play is to be a success operates not only toward cheap sophistication but turns the play into an irritating failure." Also annoying was the attempt to turn the work into an allegory about fascism and democracy.

As Allen, Donald Buka gave a performance that had many predicting stardom for him. Carleton Carpenter made his Broadway debut as a boy dubbed "Shakespeare."

BRIGHT LIGHTS OF 1944 [Revue] SK: Norman Anthony and Charles Sherman; M: Jerry Livingston; ADD.M: Norman Zeno; LY: Mack David; ADD. LY: Al Scofield; D: Dan Eckley; CH: Truly McGee; S/C: Perry Watkins; L: Al Alloy; P: Alexander H. Cohen i/a/w Martin Poll and Joseph Kipness; T: Forrest Theatre; 9/16/43 (4)

A mediocre show that was advertised as a revue but was little more than a glorified vaudeville show; a number of critics, feeling that they had been deceived by the billing description, panned it, but George Jean Nathan (*TBY*) claimed that, billing aside, the show was no worse than some current Broadway vaudevilles that had not called themselves revues and were not so brutally received.

The show was framed within a concept that began in Sardi's, the theatre restaurant (gorgeous hat-check girl Renee Carroll played herself), wherein the old-time vaudevillians Joe Smith and Charles Dale portrayed a pair of producers working as waiters and planning a vaudeville show. What they were planning then came to life as the show proper. Their patter introduced each act, a method that soon grew tiresome. The opening part of the frame device was decidedly unfunny, with lines like the following: One waiter says to the other, "Who's your backer?" The other responds, "The Angel Gabriel," to which the first retorts, "Oh, a trumpet player!" Smith and Dale did much better with their classic Dr. Kronkheit sketch, although it had some new, contemporary gags inserted. One, capitalizing on the current rationing practices, had the doctor saying to his patient, "If you don't keep quiet, I'll give you gas," to which the latter answered, "All right, I'll take six gallons."

Another headliner was James Barton, doing his familiar drunk sketch, "The Pest." John Kirby and his orchestra also gained some favor. Less popular were singer Frances Williams; a quartet called the Royal Guards, Caucasians who sang a black ditty as they gestured in the dark with phosphorescent gloves; Barton parodying *Tobacco Road**, in which he had played for years; crooner Buddy Clark; dancers Jere McMahon and Billie Worth; six-foot beauty Jayne Manners; and so on.

Arthur Pollock (*BE*) thought the show "almost as uninteresting as possible." Wilella Waldorf (*NYP*) said that "for the most part it is dismal" and wondered how anyone could have had the nerve to give it a title that suggested it might run into 1944.

BRIGHTEN THE CORNER [Comedy/Marriage/Sex] A: John Cecil Holm; D:

Arthur O'Connell; S: Willis Knighton; P: Jean Dalrymple; T: Lyceum Theatre; 12/12/45 (29)

This mistaken-identity farce vehicle for veteran deadpan comedian Charles Butterworth was set in an apartment on New York's Upper East Side. The star played a wealthy uncle, Jeffrey Q. Talbot, an inventor. He comes to visit his newlywed nephew Neil Carson (George Petrie) just after the departure of the bride, Jeri (Phyllis Avery), following a quarrel over her having washed his pipe in the sink to kill its awful smell. He wants to give his nephew a wedding present of $10,000 and an even larger sum when the couple has a child whom they will name after him. When young Dell Marshall (Lenore Lonergan), a newly married friend, shows up to pay the Carsons a visit, the gently tippling Uncle Jeffrey assumes that she is Mrs. Carson; she, realizing that her continuing the pretense can guarantee her friends the uncle's beneficence, goes along with his error for three acts. This leads to various naughty complications until he finally learns that she is not the person for whom he took her.

The plot and characters were deemed trite and worn out, the jokes and situations predictable. "A manufactured play," wrote Ward Morehouse (*NYS*), "it is crowded with familiar ingredients and as the evening progresses the author begins to run out of gags." "More clatter than play" was Lewis Nichols's (*NYT*) assessment.

Only Butterworth escaped relatively unscathed from the critical barrage. His part originally had been intended for Victor Moore, who preferred instead to do the musical *Nellie Bly*. When producer Dalrymple then decided on Frank Craven, she flew out to work with him in California, but found the veteran actor in the last stages of cancer. At comic journalist and critic Robert Benchley's suggestion, she turned to Butterworth, whose morale was at a low point because of his recent lack of work. Benchley promised the producer that the actor would be hilarious and even came to rehearsals to encourage Butterworth by his laughter. Unfortunately, Benchley died suddenly before the show opened out of town, which came as a terrific blow to Butterworth. Dalrymple said in her autobiography, *September Child*, that she never saw the show because she herself had been stricken, first with pneumonia and then with sulfa poisoning. Dulcie Cooper played a maid and Gene Blakely was Townsend Marshall, Dell's spouse.

BROKEN HEARTS OF BROADWAY [Drama/Business/Period/Romance] A/D: Ralph Matson; M: Pierre de Caillaux; P: Selected Artists, Inc., i/a/w Alan Corelli; T: New York Music Hall (OB); 6/12/44 (14)

A low-price ($1.20) travesty melodrama presented with beer and pretzels for the audience in a rooftop theatre atop the Central Opera House at 205 East Sixty-seventh Street. Such shows had become fairly common in the 1930s, and this was the first of the breed to pop up in the succeeding decade. As before, the audience--given paper hats and false mustaches and seated at tables--was invited to hiss the scowling villain and to sing along with the cast between the acts as familiar old-time tunes were played. On stage the actors overacted outrageously as they parodied what they took to be a nineteenth-century approach to playing melodrama.

George Jean Nathan (*TBY*) said that the management would have had to offer him seidels of free vodka, not beer, before he was tipsy enough to enjoy something like this. Moreover, despite some good actors, the acoustics in the 1,700-seat hall were so terrible that one spectator stood up to shout, "Will someone tell me what it's all about?" Many others screamed, "Louder!" The general response was summed up by Otis L. Guernsey, Jr. (*NYHT*): "After the first few twists of the whisker, the first narrow escape and the first hour of corny asides the whole thing becomes pretty tiresome."

Set in 1893 against the famous financial panic, the plot concerns angelic Prudence Faraday (Margaret Linskie); heroic leading man Peter Coverly (Derrick Lynn-Thomas); sinister, handlebar-mustachioed banker Osmund Blowhard (Steve Cochran, who went on to better things); the latter's beautiful but wicked daughter Daisy (Natalie Hammond Core); Prudence's sea-captain father Captain Faraday (George Spelvin, normally a phony name for a character who does not appear, but possibly meant here to suggest that one of the other actors was doubling in the part); and her gray-haired mother Mrs. Faraday (Louise Kelley). The captain's money has been entrusted to Blowhard, who cheats the old man of his gold, knocks him out with a paperweight, and casts Prudence and her mother into the street. Peter saves Prudence from the further machinations of the Wolf of Wall Street.

The between-the-acts entertainment featured blond beauty Bibi Osterwald, who received good reviews for her olio work as well as for her role as Sal in the melodrama. Otherwise, "the acting was at once atrociously exaggerated and invincibly wooden," sneered Louis Kronenberger (*PM*).

BROKEN JOURNEY [Drama/Broadcasting/Journalism/Romance/War] A: Andrew Rosenthal; D: Arthur Hopkins; S: Raymond Sovey; P: Martin Burton; T: Henry Miller's Theatre; 6/23/42 (23)

Dan Hardeen (Warner Anderson, in his Broadway debut) and Christina Landers (Edith Atwater) are foreign correspondents for NBC covering the horrendous events in Europe during the pre-Pearl Harbor years. They return to America for a lecture tour with the widowed Mrs. Landers's ten-year-old daughter, Trina (Joan McSweeney), in tow. They stop off at Dan's home town in Ohio, where he left behind his boyhood sweetheart, Rachel (Zita Johann). Dan's wanderlust suddenly dissipates, and he decides to settle down with Rachel and join the local newspaper with a half-partnership. Christina, who has been his mistress, is heartbroken and rejects the romantic advances of Rachel's brother, Hale (Tom Powers). Instead, in the wake of Pearl Harbor's bombing, she departs with Trina for Manila. Dan's wanderlust appears again when, on Christmas Day, he hears Christina on the airwaves, and he starts to contemplate a trip to the Philippines.

Aside from a few scattered lines and the promise of interesting material in a drama about radio correspondents, a relatively new breed of adventurers, the "somber, static and sour" (Herrick Brown [*NYS*]) play had little to offer. Predictable situations and overripe prose were among its problems. A cast of solid actors was at sea with the material and even the skilled Arthur Hopkins "was stymied by hackneyed writing and insufficient characterization," according to George Freedley (*NYMT*). Veteran Phyllis Povah was a scatterbrained neighbor, and Gordon Nelson played the newspaper owner.

BROOKLYN BIARRITZ [Comedy/Art/Crime/Family/Jews/Romance/Sex/Youth] A: Beatrice Alliot and Howard Newman; D: J. B. Daniels; S: Frederick Fox; P: Clarence Taylor and Marie Louise Elkins; T: Royale Theatre; 2/27/41 (4)

A fast closer that set its action on the beach in Brooklyn's Coney Island section. The real sand-filled stage, with an accurate depiction of the boardwalk, was the most interesting part of the event, which re-created with telling effect the activity and types who people the beach in summer.

The various plot strands and characters in the rambling play are brought into focus by the interest in them of the motherly Mrs. Berger (Clara Langsner), who is preoccupied with her son Milton's (Herbert Ratner) chances to get into medical school and with dispensing her Jewish recipes to characters like Mrs. Floherty (Guerita Donnelly), wife of the local Irish cop (Ralph W. Chambers). A married woman (Dorothy Libaire) kills herself when betrayed by her lover (Bertram Thorn). The husband (James Todd) kills the lover on the beach one night. Natalie (Ann Loring), a shop girl, loves a struggling but idealistic artist, Alec (Owen Lamont), but is herself loved by Milton. Finally, the artist, given the murdered man's cash by the cuckolded husband, is persuaded to earn a living by running hot-dog stands. Milton must bypass med school when his father's illness stands in his way.

Clara Langsner of the Yiddish theatre stole the acting honors in this *Street Scene**-like play of which Richard Lockridge (*NYS*) said, "It is all pretty uninteresting." Brooks Atkinson (*NYT*) labeled it "an amiable discursion . . . that never rouses itself into drama."

BROOKLYN, U.S.A. [Drama/Crime/Labor/Prison/Romance] A: John Bright and Asa Bordages; D: Lem Ward; S: Howard Bay; P: Bern Bernard and Lionel Stander; T: Forrest Theatre; 12/21/41 (57)

The activities of the notorious Brooklyn mob known as Murder, Incorporated, recently incarcerated because of the efforts of District Attorney William O'Dwyer, was the source for the action of this extremely hard-boiled crime melodrama written by a young journalist and a screenwriter. Much of the story derived from the official investigation into the gang's derelictions. The play even once had borne the title *Murder, Inc.* It was a nasty look at life among the mobsters of Brooklyn, dressed with excellent, graphically realistic, mood-establishing settings of a waterfront, a barbershop, a candy store, and Sing Sing. As authentic-sounding and -looking a group of actors as could be found was cast to play the gangsters. Their slang was considered an accurate and compelling aspect of the production.

"For brutality, obscenity and degradation it tops anything that Broadway has yet listed," complained Euphemia Van Rensselaer Wyatt (*CW*). She revealed that when one of the three murders in the plot was about to be carried out, that of a hoodlum taking a shave in a barber's chair, she fled the theatre. She later learned that a person seated near her had been "violently ill" when the murder was performed. However, for all the interest developed by the atmospherics, the play did not cohere, being too concerned with surface dramatics and lacking a central core to which its action could meaningfully cling. John Beaufort (*CSM*) was upset that the play did not take an editorial stand against the criminals it depicted, and others lamented the play's lack of insight into the evil behavior of the characters.

Smiley Mahone (Eddie Nugent) is a gunman with his eye on moving up his gang's corporate ladder. After he succeeds in demonstrating his ruthlessness, including his barbershop icepick murder of crusading longshoreman Nick Santo (Victor Christian), he is himself made the victim of a hit when it seems to the mob boss (Roger De Koven) that he is getting too big for his britches. Smiley outsmarts the gangsters who would rub him out but is captured instead by the DA's men, who have been using the services of mob informants. A scene--hated by the critics--in the death house pictures the criminals lamenting their eventual executions. A final scene is set in the candy store used by the gang as a hangout, with the proprietress (Adelaide Klein) planning to move to California to become a madam. A love interest is introduced between Nick Santo and manicurist Josephine (Irene Winston), but is short-circuited by Nick's murder. Josephine at the end is becoming enlightened about the way for workers to win progressive labor reforms.

Among the effective players of hoodlums were Byron McGrath, child actor Sidney Lumet, Robert H. Harris, Victor Wolfson, Henry Lascoe, and Tom Pedi.

BROTHER CAIN [Drama/Family/Labor/Law/Romance] A: Michael Kallesser and Richard Norcross; D: Charles Davenport; S: Louis Kennel; P: American Civic Theatre; T: John Golden Theatre; 9/12/41 (19)

"One of the slowest-moving, dullest dramas to have reached Broadway in a long time" was the widely shared verdict of Herb. (*V*) concerning this play coauthored under a nom de plume by Mt. Holyoke College drama teacher Lawrence B. Wallis. The laboriously told story is about Paul Kowalski (Frederic de Wilde), a young man from a Pennsylvania coal-mining family, whose three dullish brothers, Pete (William T. Terry), Hugo (Jack Lambert), and Joe (Royal Raymond) help pay for his law-school education only to resent him when, eager to be of assistance to the family, he returns home after graduating. When he reencounters the now fully developed Annie (Anita Lindsey), who was a mere slip of a girl when he went off to school, he only succeeds in making Hugo jealous, although Paul himself is not interested in her. Trying to overcome his siblings' resistance and to pay them back for their outlay, Paul abandons his legal aspirations to go to work in the unsafe coal mine, where his brother Joe is killed in an accident. When he seeks to make a claim against the mining company for the death of his brother, Paul ventures to take it to court under a New Deal compensation law, and victory seems imminent before the final curtain.

The work was condemned for poor acting, sets, writing, and direction. "People made faces as though they were performing for the deaf and dumb. People shouted at one another as though they were standing on opposite sides of the Hudson. People raced about the stage as though they were trying to win the Belmont Stakes," snarled Louis Kronenberger (*PM*). Only Polish-born actress Kasia Orzazewski's performance as the mother escaped censure.

During its run the play was revised and retitled as *Blue Coal*, but it was just as bad as when it opened. "It remains a badly written, poorly directed play," said Edgar Price (*BC*).

"BROWNING VERSION, THE" and "HARLEQUINADE" [British/One-Acts] A: Terence Rattigan; D: Peter Glenville; S/L: Frederick Stover; C: David Ffolkes; P: Maurice Evans i/a/w Stephen Mitchell; T: Coronet Theatre; 10/12/49 (69)
"The Browning Version" [Drama/Marriage/School/Sex/Youth]; "Harlequinade" [Comedy/ Marriage/Theatre]

Classical actor Maurice Evans made his first Broadway appearance in modern garb in this double bill of one-acts, one short and one long. The leading roles taken here by Evans and Edna Best were held in London (where the program was called *Playbill*) by Eric Portman and Mary Ellis; the director of the English production repeated his chores in New York.

Reviews ranged from very positive to disappointed, with the general opinion somewhere in between, but "The Browning Version" eventually became a frequently staged piece. George Jean Nathan (*TBY*) observed, "While neither of the items . . . amounts to anything critically and while both cover ground we have long been chummy with, they manage to provide a measure of mild diversion and, helped by fairly competent performances, serve to pass an evening for the not too demanding theatregoer."

"The Browning Version" opened the program. It constitutes a character study of a failed English public-school teacher of Greek named Andrew Crocker-Harris (Evans). After eighteen years at his job, Crocker-Harris is forced by illness to retire and take a lesser position elsewhere. He has descended from a promising scholar to a disliked pedant, unpopular with his students and despised by his slatternly wife, Millie (Edna Best), who has taken as her current lover Frank Hunter (Ron Randell), a younger schoolteacher. Crocker-Harris's world is crumbling, although he strives to remain coolly dignified through it all. The pompous headmaster (Louis Hector) informs him that he will not be entitled to his pension and that he must resign to a younger colleague his cherished spot at the farewell ceremonies. The teacher who is taking his post (Frederick Bradlee) and his wife (Patricia Wheel) arrive to examine his apartment, which they will inherit. The new man inadvertently informs Crocker-Harris that he is considered "the Himmler of the Lower Fifth," which hurts him because it means that he is feared as well as disliked. A young student (Peter Scott-Smith) appears with a farewell gift of Robert Browning's version of the *Agamemnon*, and this touch of human kindness so moves the crotchety teacher that his starched veneer cracks. Millie, however, shrivels him with her comment that the boy was only seeking a good grade. Frank is disgusted by this act of cruelty. When Frank tries to convince Crocker-Harris of the boy's sincerity, the older man shocks the younger by revealing that he has known of Frank and Millie's affair. He finally begins to stand up to his wife, who continues to demean him, and even insists to the headmaster that he be given his place at the farewell ceremonies.

Opinions on the play were divided, although the majority were favorable. Brooks Atkinson (*NYT*), marveling at the excellent performances, pondered whether the play itself was expertly written "or only superior hack-work." He decided for the latter, largely because Crocker-Harris was such a mediocre man. The play came off seeming "clever rather than genuine--Pinero watered down for modern taste." John Mason Brown (*SR*) wished that Rattigan had molded the materials into a full-length play because the necessary compressions had caused him to include harmful "artificialities." Still, he thought that the author had done "an expert and a moving job." But Howard Barnes (*NYHT*) was deeply impressed by what he viewed as "a new play of power and distinction. . . . A savage and moving tragedy of frustration and hatred." Arthur Pollock (*DC*) called it "sharp and sure, neatly articulated, a tight and constantly affecting drama."

Most critics considered Evans and Best masterly. Pollock wrote, "The Evans precision of speech, his natural eloquence, in this instance strictly subdued, his feeling, cut down in expression to a few significant little inflections and movements, makes his an electric performance."

"Harlequinade," Rattigan's self-styled "soufflé," designed to finish off the evening, was about a group of Shakespearean thespians, led by a vain and aging couple of Lunt and Fontanne-like hams, Arthur (Evans) and Edna Selby (Best), rehearsing *Romeo and Juliet**. Their mission is to bring culture to the masses, and they are preparing for a show in a town where Arthur once acted as a youth. The aging actor, playing young Romeo, learns that he is not only the father of a local girl (Eileen Page) but also a grandfather. The girl claims that her mother is Arthur's wife, which is true, since his divorce from the woman was never concluded by his solicitor, as he had been led to believe. This means that his marriage to Edna is bigamous. These and other such complications continue until all is satisfactorily resolved.

Part of the play's humor comes from its jabs at backstage life and its theatre in-jokes. Rosamond Gilder (*TAM*) called the piece "a slow and labored burlesque of [a] set of cardboard characters." The broad comic style seemed alien to Rattigan, thought Atkinson, and the actors were not qualified to give the piece the slapstick flavor it required. But Barnes, while dismissing the "slight and overwritten comedy," had warm words for the actors. Thomas R. Dash (*WWD*) considered the play "prankish and zestful," with "a rollicking performance" given by the company. According to Evans in *All This . . . and Evans Too!*, the double bill proved so confusing to one woman that she was heard to remark at its conclusion, "I can't understand why that dear old professor ever decided to go on the stage."

BRUNO AND SIDNEY [Comedy/Alcoholism/Romance/Science] A: Edward Caulfield; D: Philip Loeb; S/L: Robert Gundlach; P/T: New Stages (OB): 5/3/49 (6)

Bleecker Street's New Stages company, normally devoted to the experimental in drama, offered this feeble Saroyanesque farce in which Billy (William) Redfield had his first major role. It might have been hilarious, thought Howard Barnes (*NYHT*), but it "is more frequently diffuse and contrived than it is captivating." "The constant concentration on a single, not very momentous, subject palls," thought William Hawkins (*NYWT*). The bored Richard Watts, Jr. (*NYP*), regretted that "there isn't anything genuinely comic or charming or imaginative about the whole concoction." The play originally had been considered for a Broadway production by George Abbott, who eventually rejected it. George Jean Nathan (*TBY*) attacked the company for choosing such meretricious material over the more avant-garde possibilities it professed to favor.

Redfield played young history student Fred Goodrich, living in a remodeled Third Avenue tenement apartment. The previous tenants (June Prud'homme and Athena Lorde) have bequeathed to him the two eponymous pet mice. According to a crackpot doctor (Paul Mann), one of the mice, Bruno, who wears a jeweled collar, is allegedly seven years old, which would make him a very valuable commodity to a research center. Fred and his fiancée (Joan Tompkins) thereupon decide to insure the rodent. The fiancée's boss also shows a strong interest in procuring the animal. Other eccentric characters, including a neurotic girl (Edythe Wood) with a facial twitch, and three drunken neighbors (Jimmy Little, Lester Lonergan, Jr., and Salem Ludwig), join in the mouse safari, which constitutes most of the action. When he is caught, Bruno brings a disappointing price of only $375.

In the cast were Peggy Allenby, Kermit Murdock, Wendell Holmes, and George Cotton.

BUILDING 222 [Drama/Homosexuality/Mental Illness/Military/Religion/War] A: Edward Gilmore; M: David Perry; D: Gloria Monty; S: Paul Morrison; L: Ann MacKay; P: Abbe Practical Workshop; T: Master Institute Theatre (OB); 2/4/50 (3)

A highly interesting piece set in the building of the title, a barracks on a naval training base, where the psychologically troubled sailors are confined for observation. Danny Hoke (Bruce Hall), a confused hillbilly youth, is the primary concern of the drama, which suggests that he and the other disturbed men--amnesiacs, homosexuals, illiterates, epileptics, cowards, and so on--are the responsibility of society.

Danny wants to become a pilot but can not adjust to boot-camp regulations and, against his will, has been placed in Building 222. There he has been mistreated by the medical officer in charge, and his only faith is in a chaplain (Joseph Foley) who fails to understand Danny's need for individual attention. Unable to cope with this lack of understanding, Danny goes AWOL. The chaplain comes to his senses and realizes his error; he finds the distrustful Danny in the woods. While waiting for the chaplain to return with the doctor, Danny is killed by guards unaware of who he is.

Vernon Rice (*NYP*) commended the author for his sensitive and compassionate treatment of his characters. J. P. S. (*NYT*) asserted, "As a drama it had limitations, but the acting, direction, the lighting and the sets combined talent and diligent efforts with excellent results." He appreciated the dramatist's knowing depiction of mental disturbance exacerbated by the rigors of military life, but was unhappy with the lack of a central character for whom he could feel sympathy. He also noted that Gloria Monty "has struck a smashing blow for equal rights for women by her well-conceived staging."

BURLESQUE [Dramatic Revival*] A: George Manker Watters and Arthur Hopkins; D: Arthur Hopkins; CH: Billy Holbrook; S: Robert Rowe Paddock; C: Grace Houston; P: Jean Dalrymple; T: Belasco Theatre; 12/25/46 (439)

A surprisingly successful revival of the sentimental 1927 backstage drama. It outran the original by close to seventy performances. Most of its smash-hit status stemmed from the excellent performance of Bert Lahr in the role of the alcoholic burlesque performer, Skid, originally created by Hal Skelly. When he was off the stage, the play was in serious trouble. Lahr was playing his first serious dramatic role, a challenge he undertook to test his capabilities in a new direction. Because of his own burlesque background, he was in a unique position to bring new life to the script.

Even before it was scheduled for a Broadway revival, Lahr performed in two summer productions of the play, one in New Jersey in 1945 and one in Greenwich, Connecticut, in 1946. He himself made additions to the original play when he gave it in Greenwich. Hearing of the warm response to the production, Jean Dalrymple decided to produce it on Broadway, sight unseen, but its coauthor, Arthur Hopkins, was reluctant to allow the production because the play had been written for a dancer, not a clown. Only after Hopkins traveled to see Lahr in Greenwich was he convinced that the change was appropriate. When he agreed to the production, Dalrymple hired him--at his insistence--to direct. Dalrymple later regretted the decision, because, as reported in John Lahr's *Notes on a Cowardly Lion*, she felt that Hopkins tried to remove the hokiness from the show and to make Lahr less funny and more "legitimate." When she complained about the fact that the play was no longer funny, Hopkins replied, "It's not supposed to be funny." Hopkins was taken to task by various critics for the dullness of his work, yet Lahr admired him immensely and found his direction inspiring. Still, after the show opened, it tended to be looser and funnier whenever Hopkins was not present and more serious when he was. "Lahr used to whisper to the actors, 'Talk fast, talk fast,' hurrying through the dramaturgy to the burlesque entertainment," wrote John Lahr.

In the role of Skid's faithful and long-suffering wife, Bonny, which made a star of Barbara Stanwyck, was beauteous, flame-tressed movie actress Jean Parker. Her performance, while highly commendable, paled beside the brilliant contribution of Lahr. At one performance, the actress had a severe cold. When she had to sing "In the Gloaming," she went flat and broke character in order to tell the audience, "I gotta cold." This so enraged Lahr that he told her after the curtain fell, "You dumb son-of-a-bitch, don't ever do that again," to which she arrogantly replied, with a flounce of her short skirt, "All right, Pappy!" During the following act her cold made it impossible for her to hear the orchestra during her song "Peggy O'Neill." She then peered down at the musicians, saying "Where is everybody?" which broke up even Lahr.

The dated play, never very good to begin with, was even creakier and more stilted for the passage of time, although it had a strong nostalgia factor built into its appeal. Without Lahr to sustain it, it would have fallen apart easily, but his acting was memorable, and in the burlesque show fitted into the third act (staged by Lahr himself), his old-style rendition of "Is Everybody Happy?" and of a classic vaudeville sketch, "The Cop," in which he played a cop chasing a scantily clad girl (Irene Allery), revealed his unique theatrical powers. "The Cop" was revised to make the girl a stripteaser. As soon as the girl's bumps and grinds grew violent, Lahr would appear as a cop yelling, "Stop! In the name of the station house, stoooop!" The part allowed the actor to insert snippets from his own lengthy career as an entertainer; one outstanding example was "Ballin' the Jack" from the 1921 musical *Keep Smilin'*.

"Lahr's performance," wrote Lee Mortimer (*NYDM*), "is absolutely delightful; his drunk is restrained, believable and to be pitied; his comedy is as effervescent as himself." George Jean Nathan (*TBY*) was one of many convinced that all the major performances were superior to those of 1927. Ross Hertz, Joyce Mathews, Charles G. Martin, Jerri Blanchard, Bobby Barry, and Kay Buckley made valuable contributions to the show.

BURNING BUSH, THE [Drama/German/Jews/Law/Period/Religion/Trial] A: Heinz Herald and Geza Herczeg; AD: Noel Langley; D: Erwin Piscator; S: H. A. Condell; C: Donald Finlayson and Mike Chamberlain; L: Doris Einstein; P: Dramatic Workshop; T: Rooftop Theatre (OB); 12/16/49

A portentous, documentary courtroom drama based on the actual records of an 1882-1883 trial of Jews for ritual murder in Hungary. An earlier staging had been done in London. The trial was considered to be a precursor to the Dreyfus case in France and to the wave of anti-Semitism in Europe leading to Hitler's Reich. (Coauthor Herczeg had won an Academy Award for his screenplay, *The Life of Emile Zola*, in which the Dreyfus affair is presented.) Piscator's Off-Broadway production (on Second Avenue and East Houston Street) took full advantage of his spacious theatre, employing both the stage and auditorium for the action. Brooks Atkinson (*NYT*) believed that the play did not have commercial possibilities "because court procedure is diffuse and cumbersome, full of stock characters and routine by-play; and the narrative seems to have been written by the yard." The play, said Atkinson, profited greatly from a "stark and skeletonized" setting and a capable group of thirty-two actors in roles that were not deeply drawn. But S. G. (*WWD*) declared, "Despite some juggled lines and occasional overplaying. . . , the play successfully worked its stunning, thought-provoking message on the audience."

The trial is a clearly anti-Semitic one, based on an ancient superstition and prejudice concerning Jewish people. The judge (Robert H. Fuller) is a mean-spirited bigot. Six persons are put on trial for the alleged ritual killing in a synagogue of a young woman. To achieve the desired guilty verdict against the accused, a fourteen-year-old boy (Dalton Dearborn) is bribed to insist that he saw his own father among those committing the crime. The prosecuting attorney, a fair man, is forced by circumstances to resign. The defense attorney (Claude Traverse) fights an uphill battle in a case that has stacked the deck against him. A wealthy, Jew-hating baron (Paul Ransom) and member of parliament frequently reviles the defendants and their supporters. Eventually, the fact that the girl was actually a suicide is exposed, and the men are acquitted.

--BUT NOT GOODBYE [Comedy/Business/Death/Family/Fantasy/Period/Small Town] A: George Seaton; D/S: Richard Whorf; P: John Golden i/a/w Harry Joe Brown; T: Forty-eighth Street Theatre; 4/11/44 (23)

Plays in which the dead return to the living to clean up unfinished business were by no means new when this example of the genre was added to the list by movie writer George Seaton. Set in a small New England coast town in 1910, the play shows what happens when shipbuilder Sam Griggs (Harry Carey) suffers a heart attack, leaving his family in serious financial straits. He goes to the afterworld, where he meets his father (J. Pat O'Malley; the character is shown as a vigorous young Scotchman, while the son looks old enough to be the father). But he feels unable to remain there because his wife (Elizabeth Patterson) and two children (John Conway and Sylvia Field) need his presence back on earth to straighten out their finances. There the family learns that old Sam withdrew all his cash from the bank, but they are not aware that the money was then deposited in a real-estate investment partnered by Sam's friend Tom Carter (Frank Wilcox). Tom then decides to cheat Sam's widow out of her $5,000 earnings from the investment. He drops the check he owes her in her presence, and there is comic business as the ghosts of Sam and his father try to get her to find it. Although Sam is unable to do anything practical among the living, his dad manages to conjure up a thunder and lightning storm, and a bolt strikes Tom dead, foiling his villainy. (To signify his having been struck, Tom turned his back to the house and revealed his bare backside through a tear in his trousers.)

The play was pleasant enough, but for most lacked sufficient comedy and tended toward the saccharine and sentimental. An example of the humor was when one ghost said to the other, "I wouldn't be seen dead with you!" To Ward Morehouse (*NYS*) it was "a sparse and feeble comedy . . . amusing only occasionally, and containing homey reminders of the peach-jam era of the American drama." Nevertheless, the play received some mildly complimentary reviews ("human, easy-going, unusual," said Robert Garland [*NYJA*]) and was doing fairly well at the box office until Carey fell ill and had to leave the cast. One of the cast members was Wendell Corey in the role of the daughter's fiancé.

BY JUPITER [Musical/Marriage/Military/Period/Romance/Sex/War] B: Richard Rodgers and Lorenz Hart; M: Richard Rodgers; LY: Lorenz Hart; S: Julian Thompson's play, *The Warrior's Husband**; D: Joshua Logan; CH: Robert Alton; S/L: Jo Mielziner; C: Irene Sharaff; P: Dwight Deere Wiman and Richard Rodgers i/a/w Richard Kollmar; T: Shubert Theatre; 6/3/42 (427)

The last musical created by Rodgers and Hart was also their longest-running hit, the run cut short when star Ray Bolger left the show to entertain American servicemen abroad. It was based on a 1932 comedy that had starred Katharine Hepburn as Antiope. That comedy was itself the outgrowth of a 1924 one-act play. During the creation of the show, Lorenz Hart, who died not long after, was suffering the effects of severe alcoholism, and, at one point Richard Rodgers brought a piano into the hospital room where his partner was drying out so they could work on the songs together. When he was well enough, the witty Hart attended the rehearsals, at one of which musical director Johnny Green ran up on the stage, distressed by a song's rendering and shouting "No, no, no." Hart turned to director Logan and said, "Ahhhh, the Green is corn." In response to an affair between two cast members, each married to someone else, he wrote a parody of his own lyric that ran, "I've a terrible tongue and a pecker for two and Everything I've Got Belongs to You." But Hart was a trial to Rodgers because he was constantly disappearing for days at a time.

By Jupiter, called *All's Fair* during its out-of-town tryout period, when Richard Ainley played the role of Theseus (Ronald Graham), is set in Homeric Greece and follows the plot of the play with considerable faithfulness, only pausing now and then for the insertion of some new gag material or musical interpolation. As before, the chief humor derives from the sight of mincing men in a society dominated by butch female warriors. The Greeks order heroic Theseus, the timid Hercules (Ralph Dumke), and Homer (Berni Gould), the last presented as a "war correspondent," to Pontus to steal the fabled girdle of Diana, now in the possession of Queen Hippolyta (Benay Venuta); the girdle provides the queen with the strength to assure her power over the men in Pontus, all of whom are effeminate subordinates to the women. The chief male Pontian is the ringletted Sapiens (Bolger), coddled fiancé of Hippolyta and son of Pomposia (Bertha Belmore), who connives to have him wed the hard-boiled queen; his wife is too busy fighting the Greeks for him to be anything but a bridegroom in name only. He yearns for a honeymoon at the Nigerian Falls and is safeguarded from bawdy jokes about "traveling sales ladies." If the Greeks can steal the girdle, they can restore the Pontian men to power. Antiope (Constance Moore, in her Broadway debut) is Hippolyta's sister, who rebukes herself for never having raped any of her war victims, for which she was teased at military school. Theseus manages to tame Antiope with a kidnap and a kiss, and Sapiens, upon obtaining the girdle himself, learns to assert himself with Hippolyta and wear the pants in the family.

This was conceded to be slightly under par in the Rodgers and Hart canon, but was nevertheless a pleasant show with a number of outstanding moments. It was gorgeously conceived and produced (for $100,000) and starred several distinguished talents. One of the surprise standouts was the matronly, sixty-year-old Bertha Belmore, who stopped the show in a comic tap-dance routine shared with Bolger. Belmore was playing the same role she had played in the straight version of the story a decade earlier. Constance Moore, film and radio actress, was stunning to look at but not as stunning vocally. Her major solo was "Nobody's Heart Belongs to Me," and she duoed with Graham in "Careless Rhapsody" and "Here's a Hand." Theseus' several songs included "Wait Till You See Her." To shorten the show, and because it did not seem to fit comfortably anywhere, no matter how it was staged, it was removed from the score after the opening and reinserted toward the end of the run. Strangely enough, it proved to be one of the show's two most lasting contributions.

Among Bolger's numbers were "Life with Father" (which, as danced by Bolger with Belmore, turned out to be a surprising show-stopper), "No, Mother, No," "Everything I've Got" (the show's other eventual standard), "Now That I've Got My Strength," and a reprise of "Nobody's Heart." "Now That I've Got My Strength" was an ironically titled number written by Hart after he suffered a relapse and was visited in the hospital by Rodgers and the rehearsal pianist, who, needing a song to end act one, whistled the tune to inspire his lyrics. Rosamond Gilder's (*TAM*) was an apt description of the dancer-comedian: "From the top of his long face with its tragically pointing eyebrows, its great nose and hangdog contours . . . to the tips of his large, brightly clad feet, Ray Bolger is pure quicksilver poured into a comic mold. A remarkable dancer by any standard, he adds to the deft patter of his feet a sure and graceful use of every limb and muscle, an instinct for comic line and gesture, for perfect timing, for absurd counterpoint that amounts to genius."

Dancers Vera-Ellen, Robert and Lewis Hightower, and Flower Hujer provided expert dance sequences, and there were some physically striking showgirls cast as Amazons, chief among them being Jayne Manners. However, its central joke about reversal of the sex roles soon wore thin, there were dull stretches, and the obviousness of the outcome was clear early on. The score, too, was found wanting by a number of reviewers, although it also had its strong supporters. A few, like Wilella Waldorf (*NYP*), felt that "without Mr. Bolger's antics to give it zip . . . *By Jupiter* would prove fairly tame entertainment." Its success was attributed by some to the dearth of good new musicals in the wartime market. Others suggested that Hart's lyrics were too risqué for a radio play and would have to be revised for airwave consumption. In the cast was a distinguished British actress named Margaret Bannerman, who did not have very much to do.

According to Samuel Marx and Jan Clayton's *Rodgers and Hart*, Constance Moore was struck on opening night by a problem that Rodgers handled in his best bedside manner. She suddenly realized that after all the hassles of getting the show together, it was about to open and her stage career to be launched. She looked into the mirror to say to herself, "This is it," but discovered that she had no voice. She sent for Rodgers and croaked, "Find someone to take my place, Richard, . . . My voice is gone." But instead of becoming alarmed, Rodgers sat down calmly and said, "It's probably a little disease that's going around now. Ray Bolger has a touch of it, but it seems to have hit him in his legs which have turned to a combination of cement and rubber. Johnny Green was telling me that he thinks he has bursitis in his shoulder. I've even had it strike my fingers when I've had to play an audition. It always seems to hit us in our vulnerable spots. . . . Relax, love, you're going to be wonderful.'" Then, as he turned to leave, he added, "I wonder what happens to prostitutes."

During the run, Moore was replaced by Nanette Fabray. Before Fabray was cast, however, Rodgers conducted an extensive search for a suitable replacement. He noted in *Musical Stages* that he was stopped by an agent one day in Shubert Alley. "Understand you're auditioning for a new girl to take over Connie Moore's part." "That's right. Any suggestions?" "Sure have. Leila Ernst would be great in the part. Remember how good she was in *Too Many Girls** and *Pal Joey*?" "Leila's certainly a talented girl, . . . but she's too tall for the part." "Oh, I don't know," came back the industrious agent, "Have you seen her lately?"

C

CABALGATA [Revue] D/CH/C: Daniel Cordoba; P: Sol Hurok for Daniel Cordoba; T: Broadway Theatre; 7/7/49 (76)

A flamboyantly colorful Spanish revue of songs and dances, primarily the latter. *Cabalgata*, which means "cavalcade," proved to be "a fresh, vibrant evening's entertainment from the initial click of the inevitable castanets," reported Lewis Funke (*NYT*). The show, created in 1942, had been playing continuously in Spain and on tour in Latin America ever since. It came to New York from a West Coast engagement. Because it was essentially a dance show, non-Spanish-speaking audiences were able to enjoy it fully. The music had been selected from a study of 9,000 traditional pieces. A wide range of authentic Spanish dance styles was displayed by a company of sixty singers, dancers, and musicians.

Among the female dancers were the exquisite Carmen Vazquez, the critics' favorite, who showed her talent in the Asturias and Flamenco styles; Pilar Calvo, whose passionate nature was shown in the zambra; and lighthearted ballerinas Pepita Marco and Floriana Alba. Male dancers included José Toledano, Julio Toledo, and Fernandez Vargas. Solo dances were mingled with ensemble numbers, such as the electric "Rondalla Aragonesa" and "Jota." Drapes backed some numbers, and for others a colorfully painted backdrop was used.

A critical split decision greeted the show. Funke said that despite the all-Spanish nature of the program, it rarely descended into monotony and proved a richly diverting experience. But Richard Watts, Jr. (*NYP*), thought that it was indeed monotonous and was more for specialists than the average showgoer. The enthusiastic Robert Coleman (*NYDM*) felt that it "speaks through the feet, hands, figures of its graceful performers. There are no lulls. It moves with express-train speed and admirable precision." But Arthur Pollock (*DC*) decided that while it was "picturesque," "there is really nothing genuinely magnifico or terrifico or estupendo or prodigioso about it." He said that seen on a large Broadway stage, the company seemed "only average," none of its members being on the level of such famous Latin dancers as Carmen Amaya and Pilar Gomez.

During the run, the show changed its name to *A Night in Spain*.

CABIN IN THE SKY [Musical/Blacks/Death/Fantasy/Gambling/Marriage/Religion/Rural/Southern] B: Lynn Root; M: Vernon Duke; LY: John Latouche; D: George Balanchine and Albert Lewis; CH: George Balanchine; DS: Boris Aronson; P: Albert Lewis i/a/w Vinton Freedley; T: Martin Beck Theatre; 10/25/40 (156)

A popular musical folk-fantasy (originally titled *Little Joe*) about rural Southern blacks that had echoes of *The Green Pastures** and *Liliom**, that represented Vernon Duke's major Broadway effort, that provided George Balanchine with his first Broadway directorial job, and that allowed Ethel Waters to play her sole role in a Broadway book musical.

Brooks Atkinson (*NYT*) was one of many who raised their voices in praise of this production, calling it "original and joyous in an imaginative vein that suits the theatre's special genius." He later added, "It is the best Negro musical this column can recall and the peer of any musical in recent years." Arthur Pollock (*BE*) declared, "*Cabin in the Sky* has a quality, a fluent beauty and a vitality no other Negro song-play has had." Apart from minor reservations, the book (which some thought grew tiresome by the second act), score, decor, direction, and performances came in for numerous kudos. There were, however, a few mildly sour responses, such as that of Louis Kronenberger (*PM*), who recognized the show's appeal, but nevertheless found it forced and self-consciously cute: "It tries too hard to turn on the charm, which only leads to a certain amount of archness." Communist critic Ralph Warner (*DW*) took issue with the show's exploitative distortion of black life and culture, with stereotypical black characters who are cut from a white-man's low comedy conception--including their "plantation dialogue"-- and not from actual life.

Waters played Petunia Jackson, wife of the dying Little Joe (Dooley Wilson), a gambling, drinking, and womanizing scamp whose soul is eagerly anticipated by the red-costumed and horned Lucifer, Jr. (Rex Ingram). Petunia's earnest prayers on her spouse's behalf move the Lawd to grant the reprobate a six-month reprieve, which is bestowed by the Lawd's white-uniformed General (Todd Duncan). Little Joe will not remember his near-demise, but his future will be attended by the Lawd's General, who will remind him not to give in to temptation. Soon Little Joe is struggling between the powerful impulses represented by Lucifer, Jr., and the Lawd's General. One of the funniest scenes depicts Lucifer, Jr., in his air-conditioned office in hell, listening to his idea men on how to conquer Little Joe. When it appears that the General will win out, an Irish Sweepstakes victory engineered by Lucifer, Jr., puts Little Joe's soul in mortal danger. Little Joe goes on a binge that leads to a climactic dance-hall scene, where, in her efforts to save her husband from the sexy Georgia Brown (Katherine Dunham), the usually saintly Petunia throws caution to the wind and participates in a hot dance number. Even though she is shot by Little Joe, Petunia pleads for his soul so earnestly that he, along with her, is allowed to enter the pearly gates.

Ethel Waters gave a brilliant performance as Petunia (recaptured in the 1944 film version), a role she refused to undertake, noted Euphemia Van Rensselaer Wyatt (*CW*) "until the part of 'Little Joe' had been rewritten, for she said that, even on the stage, she couldn't ask God to save her husband unless he were given a soul." Waters noted in her *His Eye Is on the Sparrow* that she also objected to the role because Petunia, as first written, "was no more than a punching bag for Little Joe." Many of her lines and pieces of business were of Waters's own invention, she declared. "There is no one in our theater who has a more heroic quality than Miss Waters," observed Richard Watts, Jr. (*NYHT*), "and she can likewise be wonderfully gay and humorous when her scenes call for it." She was supported by equally memorable performances from the well-cast company.

The outstanding score was dotted with hits, including Waters's show-stopping number, "Takin' a Chance on Love" (Ted Fetter contributed to its lyrics), "Cabin in the Sky," "Love Turned the Light Out," "Do What You Wanna Do," "Dem Bones," and "Savannah." Singing some of this music was the splendid J. Rosamond Johnson and his choir.

Boris Aronson's designs were another major attraction, Rosamond Gilder (*TAM*) noting that "his settings are a combination of ingenuousness and ingenuity, lovely to look at, full of wit and meaning. His costumes are equally successful, as is his lighting and handling of almost all the many shifting scenes."

Balanchine's direction and choreography took full advantage of a splendid company, including Katherine Dunham (who played Georgia Brown, the femme fatale) and her dancers, among them Talley Beattey. Dunham's singing (especially of "There's Honey in the Honeycomb") and acting were surprisingly effective, but it was her dancing that was truly inspired, particularly an orgiastic boogie woogie that tore down the house in the last act. This was Dunham's first excursion from the concert stage into the arms of musical comedy.

The Russian-born Balanchine later admitted that his direction was principally visual and that someone else was hired to supervise the dialogue. "I did all this, the idea, how it looks and, you know, the whole thing. Only I did not do the conversation. Also, the sound, you know, blacks talk a certain way. How can anybody . . . ? They do themselves very well without me. No, I was just placing people and dressing them" (quoted in Fred Fehl, *On Broadway*).

CAESAR AND CLEOPATRA [Dramatic Revival*] A: George Bernard Shaw; M: Irma Jurist; D: Cedric Hardwicke; S/C: Rolf Gérard; L: Jean Rosenthal; P: Richard Aldrich and Richard Myers i/a/w Julius Fleischmann; T: National Theatre; 12/21/49 (149)

An "enchanting revival" (Howard Barnes [*NYHT*]) of the 1898 Shaw play set in ancient Egypt that originally had played here in 1906, was revived in 1925, and would return in 1951, two years later, in a splendid version starring Laurence Olivier and Vivien Leigh. In the present instance, Caesar was the redoubtable Cedric Hardwicke (who also directed and who had played the role twenty-five years earlier), suffering on opening night from laryngitis, and Cleopatra was the lovely and extremely able Continental actress Lilli Palmer. They were supported by a superb ensemble, including Robert Earl Jones as the Nubian slave and the porter, Bertha Belmore as Ftatateeta, Nicholas Joy as Pothinus, Ivan Simpson as Theodotus, Ralph Forbes as Rufio, Arthur Treacher (considered a brilliant stroke of casting) as the Englishman Britannus, Si (Simon) Oakland as Lucius Septimus, John Buckmaster as Apollodorus, Harry Irvine as the harpmaster and the priest, Mary Scott as Charmian, and Anthony (Tony) Randall as the major-domo.

The play remained not only a brilliant high-comic yet humanizing treatment of the relationship between the aging Roman dictator and the nubile Egyptian queen but a storehouse of intellectual sagacity on various issues, such as greatness of character and statesmanship. It was impressively staged and designed, as well as thoroughly well performed. The sets were considered simple but functional and imaginatively atmospheric. Richard Watts, Jr. (*NYP*), thought that "this playful, witty and immensely provocative variation on an historical theme emerges in all its brightness and splendor." But several critics, such as Robert Garland (*NYJA*) and Robert Coleman (*NYDM*), were disappointed and felt, as Coleman said, that the "production failed to put its best foot forward" and would undoubtedly improve when Hardwicke's voice returned.

Hardwicke's vocal problems were a serious drawback for Brooks Atkinson (*NYT*), who felt that his inability to speak his demanding part robbed the play of "lightness and sparkle." But Rowland Field (*NEN*) was among those who stood up for the actor, claiming that he dominated the production with his "impeccable and completely charming" portrayal, "combining dignity with disarming human traits and a keen sense of humor."

Atkinson was enthralled by Palmer's acting, which provided a "limpid, girlish, roguish Cleopatra" that would have delighted the playwright. He said that she "has caught all the innocence and capriciousness of the part and expressed the myriad aspects of it with lucidity and daintiness. She is all woman and also Shavian enough to be amusing." Nearly everyone agreed. John Chapman (*NYDN*), for instance, commented, "Lilli Palmer is the loveliest, most sexy Queen of the Nile since the original model. It also happens that she can act. Her performance . . . is vibrant with intelligence and humor."

During the run, Palmer fell ill and was forced to miss a performance. According to Hardwicke's *A Victorian in Orbit*, her understudy, Mary Scott (whom Hardwicke later married), was thrilled to replace her, especially because her mother was coming to visit. Meeting her mother at the station, Scott informed her of the good news that she'd be able to see her in that evening's performance. The older woman, however, was crestfallen: "You mean that I shan't get to see Lilli Palmer?"

CAFÉ CROWN [Comedy/Jews/Marriage/Romance/Theatre] A: H. S. Kraft; D: Elia Kazan; S: Boris Aronson; P: Carly Wharton and Martin Gabel; T: Cort Theatre; 1/23/42 (141)

Elia Kazan had his first major directing assignment with this mildly successful sentimental comedy based on the denizens of a popular Second Avenue Jewish restaurant, Café Royale, frequented by members of the Yiddish theatre and others of the Jewish intellectual community. The idea had been suggested to playwright Kraft by fellow screenwriter Nunnally Johnson, who was familiar with Kraft's nostalgic memories of Yiddish theatregoing. Kraft was reluctant, but after Johnson plied him with newspaper clippings about the Lower East Side and even offered to help him get started on the play, Kraft sat down to write.

His play starred Morris Carnovsky as David Cole (loosely based on Jacob Adler), flamboyant patriarch of a distinguished Yiddish acting family that has started to come apart because of the desire of daughter Norma (Mary Mason) to act on the English-speaking stage. David's extramarital affairs also have taken their toll on his relationship with his acting partner and wife, Anna (Margaret Waller). Norma is in love with Lester Freed (Sam Wanamaker, in his Broadway debut), a rising young American-born Jewish actor (based on Paul Muni) who is debating whether to accept a Hollywood contract or to take the lead in Cole's planned production at the Lipsky Theatre of a modernized, Yiddish version of *King Lear** set on Riverside Drive. Hymie (Sam Jaffe), the busboy at Café Crown on whom Cole normally depends for backing, has serious doubts about investing in Shakespeare, even when assured that Mme. Cole will appear in the specially written role of Mrs. Lear (a ploy to keep her from accepting an engagement with Mandelbaum in Brooklyn). After various developments, a shy young Australian man (Whitner Bissell) who has been hanging around turns out to be the Cole's long-lost son, born in Poland during a Cole tour, and he agrees to back *Lear* with his own funds. Lester is persuaded to leave for Hollywood on the night of the opening, and David goes on at a moment's notice in his place.

The play itself was deemed superficial and contrived, but reasonably acceptable as a vehicle for colorful performances and nostalgia for the waning Yiddish stage. It sought to capture with pungent authenticity the characters and ambience of the Second Avenue theatre scene and of a restaurant where the waiters cast scornful eyes on unfamiliar customers. For many, the results were flat. "Some of Mr. Kraft's incidental characters have a disturbing way of sounding like bad Odets or Saroyan," commented John Mason Brown (*NYWT*). "Much of his humor is no more than mechanical. But from time to time it has a ring which is sharp and incisive." Richard Watts, Jr. (*NYHT*), somewhat more affable, observed, "*Cafe Crown* is as pleasant, likable and warm-hearted as the characters it is affectionately contemplating. There is nothing stirring or exciting or of great dramatic import in the new play, but in its quiet, unostentatious way it manages to be modestly and agreeably refreshing."

George Freedley (*NYMT*), noting the excellence of the acting, said, "The producers can be proud of Elia Kazan's casting, as well as of his direction. He is not able to hide all the phoniness of the script, but he does wonders." On the other hand, Wilella Waldorf (*NYP*) declared, "The production in general is rather hit-or-miss under Elia Kazan's direction. There are plenty of ragged edges indicating the need of a few more rehearsals."

The cast included George Petrie as a Hollywood agent, Daniel Ocko as a vituperative critic writing his review before a show opens and reading it to the star, Jay Adler as an irritable waiter, Lou Polan as a stagehand, Mitzi Hajos as a minor actress, Paula Miller as the restaurant's proprietress, Robert Leonard as a hammy impresario, and Eduard Franz as a plagiarizing playwright engaged in rewriting *Rain** by placing it in the Catskills and making the Reverend Davidson a reformed rabbi.

Sam Jaffe's performance as the comical busboy drew the most laughs and practically stole the show. The real-life original for this character was a man named Herman Denzer, who watched over the activities in the Café Royale for forty years, earned tips by taking phone messages for restaurant regulars and cashing their checks, backed Yiddish theatre productions, and, while never relinquishing his busboy job, eventually became a wealthy man, with real-estate and stock-market holdings. Denzer was so pleased with Jaffe's performance of him that he carried the actor's reviews around with him. At a party given by Kraft at the restaurant shortly after the play opened, the playwright was cold-shouldered by several Yiddish theatre actors, presumably because he had stated in the play that the Yiddish theatre was in its twilight. When Kraft told the busboy of the chilly reception he had received,

Denzer took the writer by the arm and asked him if he had ever heard of "a Mr. Rosen." Kraft said no, to which Denzer responded, "He owned six, seven apartment houses in Brownsville, a fine man. He told me something once when I also needed advice. I never told this to anyone but I'm telling you, Mr. Hy, exactly what Mr. Rosen told me. Let them go fuck themselves."

In 1964 a musical version opened on Broadway under the play's original title.

CALICO WEDDING [Comedy/Business/Marriage/Sex] A/D: Sheridan Gibney; S: Frederick Fox; P: Lester Meyer and Richard Myers; T: National Theatre; 3/7/45 (5)

A "feeble and hopeless" (Ward Morehouse [*NYS*]) comedy first produced ten years earlier in summer stock and now updated and brought to Broadway. The material seemed as dated and clichéd as it had before being revised.

Its leading characters are George Gaylord (William Post) and his wife Mary (Grete Mosheim). The play begins with a prologue set in a radio listening post in Alaska, where Captain Gaylord recalls his marriage as he and another character talk about marital infidelity. The play proper then returns to 1937 when he and Mary are in the second year of their marriage, but George's preoccupation is with his advertising business, not his conjugal duties. When he forgets their calico anniversary, the frustrated Mary decides to teach him a lesson by making him jealous. She has a couple of drinks with an arctic explorer (Louis Jean Heydt, in the role he originated a decade earlier) just back from the pole. This leads to a trip to the boudoir, but as neither of them can remember what happened once they got there, the question is left open for the audience to decide. George himself decided that Mary was faithful, but no one in the audience cared a whit one way or the other.

Very little about the opus pleased anyone. The author, reported George Freedley (*NYMT*), "has treated his characters as puppets to be dangled at will without regard for probabilities." Star Mosheim, a German refugee actress, "acted for the entire evening in the manner of an Elisabeth Bergner giving an imitation of Billie Burke before the age of puberty," cracked George Jean Nathan (*TBY*). Eva Condon, Jane Hoffman, Forrest Orr, Mary Sargent, Jerome P. Thor, Barbara Joyce, and Joy Geffen were in the cast.

CALL ME MISTER [Revue] SK: Arnold Auerbach w/Arnold Horwitt; M/LY: Harold Rome; D: Robert H. Gordon; CH: John Wray; S: Lester Polakov; C: Grace Houston; P: Melvyn Douglas and Herman Levin; T: National Theatre; 4/18/46 (734)

The lighter postwar experiences of American men and women who served in World War II formed the springboard for this rousing musical revue in which almost every participant--from the creative team down to the players--was himself or herself a service veteran or had performed in the USO. All branches of the armed forces were represented. Coproducer Douglas, then a major in the army (later promoted to lieutenant colonel), had been staging shows for the troops in China, Burma, and India when he began to notice that the mimeographed copies sent to him of songs and skits written by Corporal Harold Rome and Sergeant Arnold Auerbach for the New York branch of the Special Services were clever and diverting. On leave in New York he looked the pair up and arranged to do a show with them when the war was over.

Headlining the show were singer-comedienne Betty Garrett (the only performer already recognized as a Broadway star), comic Jules Munshin, black baritone Lawrence Winters, and ballerina Maria Karnilova. Harry Clark and George Hall were funny comedians, dancers Betty Lou Holland and Bill Callahan were effective, Danny Scholl and Paula Bane were good young singers, and comic actor George S. Irving made his Broadway debut in the show.

The subject of the show was suggested by its title, which implied that military persons of rank were to be addressed as "mister" in civilian life. This advice was rendered in an opening number sung before a delightfully designed curtain on which the serviceman's discharge button was depicted in a comical distortion. The cast informed the audience that "dramatic critics have more power over us than Eisenhower." Some material was satirical, some was sentimental, and some was patriotic. Not all of it was on the same high level (such as the bit featuring Munshin showing how classical actor Maurice Evans would sound as a train announcer), but enough was to make the show a solid hit. As Euphemia Van Rensselaer Wyatt (*CW*) noted, "Some of the sketches are better than others and some are poorer but the average is superior." The overall tone was one of jubilation at the war's having ended. John Mason Brown (*SR*) said that the good-natured show was "a lively one, healthy and unsparing in its spoofing." Howard Barnes (*NYHT*) agreed, "*Call Me Mister* is a captivating show. It is fresh, vigorous and what was least to have been expected, it has great style."

Rome was highly praised for his excellent musical contributions and intelligent lyrics. "The Red Ball Express" was a lonely tune sung by Winters and dealing with a black truck driver traveling down the Normandy coast. Winters also sang the socially conscious but overly bromidic "The Face on the Dime" (a tribute to Franklin Delano Roosevelt) and the emotionally satisfying "Going Home Train," effectively set to the rhythms of a train bearing the doughboys (who served as chorus) homeward. "Off We Go" was a parody of the air force, seen through movie-influenced GI eyes as a world of snooty Noël Coward high life. One of Betty Garrett's best numbers was "Surplus Material," in which she was a canteen waitress whose sexual frustration had been exacerbated with the demobilization of her soldier customers to civilian life. An excellent comic sketch, "Welcome Home," concerned the homecoming of a soldier whose parents have been preparing to greet him by reading so much somber literature on the returning veteran that they expect him to be a psychological wreck. The mother, for example, thinks that she must convince her son that she has shared all his battlefield experiences. When she meets him at the door, she is dressed in a helmet and a gun belt with two revolvers and is more frightening than the nastiest top sergeant. Another funny sketch showed what Paul Revere would have encountered if he had had to cut through the modern army bureaucracy to get a horse to warn that the British were coming. Some material confronted the housing shortage, the problems of buying civilian clothes ("civvies"), the serviceman who returns to meet his newborn child, and so on. Among the few numbers that were not directly connected to the problems of the returning soldiers was one satirizing three Southern senators who are delighted to learn from a public-opinion survey that their popularity is only several points below that of athlete's foot. Another, "Yuletide, Park Avenue," showed a wealthy family singing the praises of various prominent New York department stores, all of which were named in the lyrics.

One of the best numbers came about in typical show-biz fashion. According to Melvyn Douglas and Tom Arthur's *See You at the Movies*, the show, when still in rehearsal, was in need of an up-tempo number just before the end of the second act. Composer Rome declared that he was out of ideas, but did have a nonsense song that he felt was not right for the show. "Play it," shouted his cocreators, "We'll find a way to use it!" The song, "South America, Take It Away," in which the eponymous land mass was advised to retrieve its congas, rhumbas, and sambas (ai, ai, ai), became the show's major hit tune.

(1) **CANDIDA** [Dramatic Revival*] A: George Bernard Shaw; D: Guthrie McClintic; S/C: Woodman Thompson (Katharine Cornell's clothes: Helene Pons Studios; Mildred Natwick's clothes: Johanna Klinge); P: American Theatre Wing War Service; T: Shubert Theatre; 4/27/42 (27)

This revival of *Candida*, a play in which Katharine Cornell first appeared in 1924 and which she revived in 1937, was mounted for the benefit of the army and navy relief associations. The work was intended for five special matinee performances only, but popular response was so strong that it remained alive for a month. It ended up bringing in $84,000 for the cause that had inspired it. The cast was composed of distinguished veterans, including Mildred Natwick as Prossy, Stanley Bell as Lexie, Raymond Massey as Morell, Dudley Digges as Burgess, and Burgess Meredith as Marchbanks.

Despite its having only one week's rehearsal, the production was brilliant enough for Brooks Atkinson (*NYT*) to call it "the foremost event of the theatre season," a sentiment with which almost all his colleagues agreed. Talking of director McClintic's contribution, Atkinson stated, "Although Guthrie McClintic's direction is not conspicuous, the entire performance is shot through with the sort of understanding of character that he brings to a play. He has gone instinctively to the heart of the problem and woven a shining performance out of human experience."

Because of familiarity with Cornell's earlier Candidas, the most notable performance for many was Meredith's Marchbanks, his first New York attempt at the role after playing it in half a dozen summer theatres. (Meredith was then a private in the army and had been given special leave to do this revival.) Richard Watts, Jr. (*NYHT*), called it "a masterpiece of American acting." Unlike his predecessors, who often turned the sulking poet into "a kind of hysterical minor monster," Meredith made it clear as to why Candida was attracted to him. "By the seemingly simple method of standing comparatively still and playing with a quiet, direct sort of masculine intensity, Mr. Meredith has given him dignity, force and intellectual honesty."

Of Massey, George Freedley (*NYMT*) wrote, "One of the most interesting and convincing Morell's [*sic*] I have ever seen is Raymond Massey. I feel quite sure that I have seen no greater humanity, understanding and humor (particularly humor) brought to the part by any other actor." A typical summation of Cornell's acting was John Mason Brown's (*NYWT*): "She is the Speicher portrait in the flesh, but granted a voice so rich and liquid that it lingers long in the ears after her final choice has been made. She is radiant, mysterious, compelling, all-mothering; sage with the sagacity of her sex as Shaw intended her to be; and yet simple as only a truly great artist can be."

One reason for the excellence of the Massey and Meredith interpretations probably stemmed from the freshness of McClintic's directorial approach, which was not content to rehash his earlier stagings of the work. According to Massey's *A Hundred Different Lives*, McClintic told the actors, "You are playing genuine human beings, not satirized freaks, as G. B. S. would have you believe." He then continued, "Don't worry about the comedy and the humour--all that will look after itself. There will be bigger and better laughs if you show Morell and Marchbanks to be real, credible people than if Morell is acted as a comic stuffed shirt and Marchbanks as an irresolute, shy genius. Remember this is still a play about a woman who must choose between two men and so selects the weaker because he needs her more. Now let's get on with it and try to make Candida's choice a difficult one."

(2) P: Katharine Cornell i/a/w Gilbert Miller; T: Cort Theatre; 4/3/46 (24)

Cornell revived the play yet again in 1946, but whereas Meredith's acting as Marchbanks was chief among the critics' many delights in the previous version, the up-and-coming Marlon Brando's Marchbanks divided the critics, with the predominant opinion being negative. Others in the company included Cedric Hardwicke as Mr. Burgess, Wesley Addy as Morell, Oliver Cliff as Lexie, and Mildred Natwick repeating her Prossy. The play was produced in a split-week tandem with Cornell's performance of *Antigone*, several of the actors appearing in both plays.

The production was considered less luminous than the 1942 one. Among Brando's detractors was George Jean Nathan (*TBY*), who announced that in his playing the "young poet's weakness becomes almost wholly a matter of weak acting," despite the actor's potential. He found Brando's speech monotonous and his sensitivity confined to a pale makeup and the quivering of his hand. Lewis Nichols (*NYT*) thought him unconvincing and no threat to Morell. John Mason Brown (*SR*), describing all the character's unattractive features, said that Brando captured these perfectly, but not his virtues. This led to his being "uncomfortable to watch, and even more distressing to listen to. He seems not so much an apostle of beauty as a stray delinquent." But Euphemia Van Rensselaer Wyatt (*CW*) thought his performance the closest in quality to that of Arnold Daly early in the century. She wrote: "That this is only his third appearance . . . makes Mr. Brando's performance the more remarkable; yet any uncertainty and shyness that may underly his intellectual assurance are part of Marchbanks' natural quality." She thought that he had "all the terrible precociousness of a boy Shelley and, what is more, looks like a poet as as well. . . . He is highly sensitive and intelligent and also seems to have a fine sense of comedy." John Chapman (*NYDN*) believed that Brando had "managed to make something different, something a little more understandable, out of the trying role."

The best of the other newcomers to the cast was generally thought to be Hardwicke, the worst, Addy. Hardwicke's comical bits included wearing a droopy mustache, speaking in a cockney dialect, sucking on a back tooth, and winking and squinting in a funny way; less appropriate was his frequent delivery of his lines directly to the audience. Addy was bland and colorless.

CANDLE IN THE WIND [Drama/Films/France/Journalism/Military/Prison/Romance/War] A: Maxwell Anderson; D: Alfred Lunt; S/L: Jo Mielziner; P: Theatre Guild and the Playwrights' Company; T: Shubert Theatre; 10/22/41 (95)

Candle in the Wind, one of Burns Mantle's ten best of the season, starred Helen Hayes in what aspired to be an uplifting anti-Nazi drama at a time of international crisis. It sought to reaffirm the value of love (the candle in the wind) and devotion to a righteous cause in the face of totalitarian horror. According to Hayes's *My Life in Three Acts*, Anderson had sought "to shake America out of its complacency and to build support for Britain and France." Moved by her patriotic fervor, Hayes accepted her role despite the warning of her husband, writer Charles MacArthur, not to do it. "No war has ever been won by a bad play," he declared. Written in prose, unlike Anderson's recent efforts, it proved MacArthur's contention, being a slow-moving disappointment that aimed higher than it flew.

The drama is set in German-occupied France. Hayes played Madeline Guest, a movie star whose French journalist lover, Raoul St. Cloud (Louis Borrell, who replaced Stianio Braggiotti in the rehearsal period), now a naval officer, is captured by the Germans. He has been saved from the French destroyer on which he was sailing when it was sunk at Dunkirk. Despised for his criticisms of Hitler, he has been imprisoned in a concentration camp outside of Paris. Madeline, who gradually comes to acknowledge the Nazi terror, has been making frequent unavailing visits to the camp to try to have the perversely humorous commandant, Colonel Erfurt (John Wengraf), release him. The German officer forbids her even to visit with her lover. Her hopes of freeing St. Cloud via bribes are dashed when the Gestapo double-crosses her. Through the assistance of Lieutenant Schoen (Tonio Selwart), a conscience-stricken, lower-ranking officer, who accepts as payment Madeline's expensive diamond ring, St. Cloud escapes and heads for England. This results in Madeline's being nastily interrogated, although she fails to give in. She condemns Nazi brutality and hatred and, her passport taken by the prison commandant, will probably be incarcerated for her troubles. Her biting curtain line is "In the history of the world there have been many wars between beasts and men, and the beasts have always lost and the men have always won."

The well-intentioned play seemed weak and talky, and even its depiction of Nazi atrocities looked pale compared with newspaper reports. The Nazi background was viewed as little more than an ominous milieu for melodramatic dramaturgy. Surface theatrics took the place of an in-depth consideration of the Nazi mentality. Brooks Atkinson (*NYT*) said that it "lacks dramatic fire." Louis Kronenberger (*PM*) broiled Anderson, calling the play "as ponderous and hollow a piece of high romantic rubbish as you would have found in a well stocked Victorian library." John Beaufort (*CSM*) argued that the play's use of a disenchanted Nazi to instigate St. Cloud's escape was unmotivated and dramatically false. Communist critic Ralph Warner (*DW*), however, approved the work's intentions, if not its realization, calling it "a forthright declaration of America's determination to face the Nazi danger, to fight it, and to end its threat to world freedom."

Helen Hayes offered a luminous performance that was considered superior to her vehicle, although she had a role that did not erupt emotionally until the scene of interrogation near the end. John Anderson (*NYJA*) observed, "Miss Hayes sustains the central part brilliantly, in spite of the fact that she has some of the most banal lines she has ever memorized. Her powerfully pitched performance often lends a tension to the scene that holds it together by sheer personal force and delicate persuasion."

The work also offered Alfred Lunt an opportunity for his first directing job on a play in which he did not appear with Lynn Fontanne. According to a letter written by Fontanne to Noël Coward (reprinted in Jared Brown's *The Fabulous Lunts*), the director thought that the play had definite possibilities but needed revisions that Anderson refused to make. "He seemed plunged into a sort of elephantine lethargy--nearly drove Alfred insane--and then finally did nothing at all. The minute Alfred's back was turned . . . [the producers] did some rearranging to his direction, took themselves into New York and had a terrible flop and served them damn well right."

Cast members included Evelyn Varden as Madeline's wisecracking couturière friend, Joseph Wiseman as a Nazi officer, and émigré actress Lotte Lenya (making a very strong impression in the small role of Cissie, a Viennese maid, which Anderson wrote expressly for her), among many others. Lenya once admitted that she did not like Helen Hayes and that she had played a practical joke on the star. According to a report in Donald Spoto's *Lenya*, "Miss Hayes had timed a speech so that after a certain number of steps she sat in a chair without looking. But one night, after they had disagreed about something in offstage conversation, Lenya moved the chair and Miss Hayes did a graceful fall. There was a naughty schoolgirl in Lenya, and she was proud of it."

CANTEEN SHOW, THE [Revue] M/LY/D: James Shelton; ADD.M: Alfred Simon and Langston Hughes; CH: Edward Sinclair; C: Lucinda Ballard; P: volunteer workers at the Stage Door Canteen (supervisor: Dwight Deere Wiman); T: Stage Door Canteen (OB); 9/8/42

The Stage Door Canteen was established on West Forty-fourth Street to provide a place for military men to enjoy a good meal served by people in the theatrical profession, with whom they could also dance. These volunteers--waiters, waitresses, busboys, kitchen help--decided to do more than serve coffee and doughnuts and put on this hour-long revue of original material with costumes borrowed from various sources and refitted for the occasion.

The cast was dominated by female performers. There were some amusingly topical songs as well as ballads, some cancan and tap dancing (the former to a lyric that referred to "the Stage Door can-can girls, sponsored by the can-canteen"), impersonations of performers like Nora Bayes, Sophie Tucker, and Marilyn Miller, and a few comic sketches thrown in for good measure. James Shelton (the composer) and Tom Rutherford were funny in a skit about a doctor, a machine, and a soldier. Rosetta LeNoire sang a song by Langston Hughes and Emerson Harper called "That Eagle." Intermittent performances were planned for the show as well as a possible tour of army camps. Members of the public wishing to see it had to pay a fee of $100.

CAREER [Comedy/Marriage/Music] A: Nan Kirby; D: John F. Grahame; S: Sally Nusbaum; P: Modern Play Productions, Inc.; T: Provincetown Playhouse (OB); 10/28/43 (7)

Very few critics remained to the end of this moribund comedy about a pair of young people, a soprano (Josephine Lombardo) and a baritone (Robert Feyti) who try to make a career in the world of grand opera. They have some opportunities to show off their voices in the piece, which recounts the hazards of breaking into this closed world. The young hopefuls make a deal with an aging and temperamental impresario (John Francis) who contracts to receive forty percent of their earnings for life once he establishes them in the business. He opposes marriage for the women he handles; if they are married, he is even more severe should they get divorced. The night that the soprano is to debut, he learns that she is secretly married.

"Skip this one with impunity," cautioned George Freedley (*NYMT*). "*Career* was almost bad enough to be shown uptown," sneered Lewis Nichols (*NYT*). Herrick Brown (*NYHT*) said that this "so-called play" was "singularly bad. *Career* has neither structure nor meaning."

(1) CAREER ANGEL [Comedy/Fantasy/Religion/Southern/Youth] A: Gerard M. Murray; D: Dennis Gurney; S: Avril Gentles; P: Blackfriars' Guild; T: Blackfriars Theatre (OB); 11/18/43

A promising but unfulfilled play by a priest affiliated with Our Lady of Mercy Church, Forest Hills. Produced originally by Cathedral High School in Brooklyn, it was revised for this Off-Broadway showing. Enough good words were said about it by the reviewers that its run was extended twice. The actors involved were all amateurs, although previous Blackfriars productions had used professional, but unpaid, actors. That arrangement so riled the theatrical unions that Equity was pressured into disallowing its members from performing for the troupe (and for five others placed on a blacklist).

The play is set in a Catholic orphanage in Georgia, the Bosco Institute, that is on the brink of bankruptcy. The careless administration of the orphanage by its founders, onetime actor Brother Seraphim (Angelo Benedetto) and former critic Brother Gregory (Liam Dunn), disturbs former businessman Brother Fidelis (Joseph Boley). Seeing the dilemma of Brother Seraphim, his wisecracking guardian angel (David Carman Jones) obtains heavenly permission to descend to earth and provide help to the brothers and the orphans. Because of his obvious ability to converse with the unseen angel, Brother Seraphim becomes the butt of people's unkind gossip. However, the angel aids Brother Seraphim in discovering that the orphanage is the long-lost "Hidden House," a historical location overlooked by General Sherman's razing campaign in 1864. Publicity about the orphanage's financial plight erupts, and money comes flooding in to save the place. A melodramatic episode in which Brother Seraphim tips off the FBI about a Nazi spy ring and saboteurs using the orphanage as a place to hide explosives is tacked on for good measure.

The critics found the play to be engrossing and occasionally poetic, the character of the angel to be amusingly slangy, and the reactions of the orphanage's residents to the supernatural among them delightful; however, the melodrama of the Nazis was considered intrusive and unconvincing and the author's apparent borrowings from other playwrights (Noël Coward's *Blithe Spirit* in particular) a weakness. Bert McCord (*NYHT*) called it "an agreeable evening's entertainment," but Wilella Waldorf (*NYP*) advised, "Some of *Career Angel* is downright childish, and most of it is reminiscent, but there is a quaintly novel touch about such a play going on in the cloistered surroundings of a religious institution."

(2) [Dramatic Revival] D: Don Appell; S: Carl Kent; L: Frederick Fox; P: Andrew Billings and Joseph Dicks i/a/w David Shay; T: National Theatre; 5/23/44 (22)

The interest generated in the play's original production was strong enough to stimulate a commercial Broadway production for it, with a professional director and cast. The latter included Donald Foster as Brother Gregory, Ronald Telfer as Brother Fidelis, Whitford Kane as Brother Seraphim, Glenn Anders as the angel, Mason Adams as another brother, and Carleton Carpenter as one of the boys.

The play had been extensively revised. Unfortunately, the revisions were of the wrong sort. George Freedley (*NYMT*) observed, "Sad to say, Father Murray cut many scenes . . . which were amusing or real and were related to the main theme. In their stead he or his advisers have substituted a few gags in bad taste, notably much talk about Mrs. Roosevelt's guardian angel." "Dramatic structure and a sustained mood are badly wanting," added Howard Barnes (*NYHT*). The direction did not come up to that of the original either, but there were good performances, particularly those by veterans Kane and Anders.

CARIB SONG [Musical/Blacks/Marriage/Sex/Tropics] B/LY: William Archibald; M: Baldwin Bergersen; D: Mary Hunter; CH: Katherine Dunham; S/L: Jo Mielziner; C: Motley; P: George Stanton; T: Adelphi Theatre; 9/27/45 (36)

Katherine Dunham and her dance troupe were the focus of this "long monotonous musical" (Euphemia Van Rensselaer Wyatt [*CW*]) set in a small West Indian village, its characters designated by such names as "The Singer" (Harriet Jackson), "The Fat Woman" (Mabel Sanford Lewis), "The Tall Woman" (Mercedes Gilbert),

"The Husband" (William Franklin), "The Fisherman" (Avon Long), "The Woman" (Dunham), "The Shango Priest" (La Rosa Estrada), and so on. Surprisingly, the show, spoken in pidgin English that some found hard to follow, lacked vitality and originality and closed in a month. It attempted to use the musical form to tell a tragic story, but did so with a lack of inventiveness.

Its action is instigated by the fisherman's love for a corn farmer's wife, which leads to the whispering of the other natives, the husband's jealousy, and his killing of his spouse. Rosamond Gilder (*TAM*) observed a "confusion of styles by the grafting of operatic techniques onto a series of folk scenes strung together loosely on the time-honored triangle plot."

Caribbean rhythms informed the music and dances, including a voodoo (called "shango") number and a dream ballet, and provided the show with its principal interest, but they could not dispel the "tropical lethargy" (Wilella Waldorf [*NYP*]) that enveloped the show. The music was competent but lacked variety.

For all her dancing skills, Dunham proved less than interesting as an actress and singer, and most of her choreographic work--largely based on Caribbean ritual motifs--was uninspired and repetitious. Lewis Nichols (*NYT*) said that it seemed more suited to a concert performance than a Broadway show. However, Dunham's shango number and a witty one in which she inveigled a pair of slippers from a peddler were memorable.

Mielziner's tropically lush sets and lighting and Motley's costumes were suitably colorful and spectacular, but were wasted. Avon Long, however, provided a show-stopping number in "Woman Is a Rascal," which allowed him to offer improvised dance material. One of the dancers in the show was the young Eartha Kitt.

CARIBBEAN CARNIVAL [Revue/Blacks] M/LY; Samuel L. Manning and Adolph Thenstead; D: Samuel L. Manning and John Hirshman; CH: Pearl Primus and Claude Marchant; C: Lou Eisele; P: Adolph Thenstead; T: International Theatre; 12/5/47 (11)

It was the "remarkably accomplished and original" (Brooks Atkinson [*NYT*]) dancing that stood out in this energetic but otherwise hapless revue--advertised as "the first Calypso musical ever presented" (although 1945's *Carib Song* would seem to qualify for that title)--set in the West Indies and employing a talented cast of black performers, many of whom hailed from the islands themselves. Before arriving on Broadway, it had been titled *Calypso* and then *Bongo*. With choreography and dance performances by Pearl Primus and Claude Marchant, including "Rookombay," a superlative voodoo ballet, it might have made a significant mark, but the sprawling show was poorly conceived and found itself wavering between being a conventional musical and a dance program. What continuity it had was provided by the presence of a blond *Life* magazine journalist (Pamela Ward) visiting the islands for a story and guided by a native policeman (Samuel L. Manning).

Marchant's memorable dances included "Canto de las Palmas" and "Enlorro"; in these, said Howard Barnes (*NYHT*), "he creates a pattern of movement . . . which makes his performance something more than a spot in a disorganized melange of night club turns." Ward Morehouse (*NYS*) regretted having to sit through what he called "shapeless and mirthless; there is a great sameness and monotony to it all."

Among the specialties offered were the perhaps too complexly worded ballads of the Duke of Iron, the exciting singing of Josephine Premice, the singing siblings called the Smith Kids, and the guitar-strumming Trio Cubana.

(1) CARMEN JONES [Musical/Blacks/Crime/Military/Romance/Sex/Southern/Sports/War] B/LY: Oscar Hammerstein II; M: Georges Bizet; SC: George Bizet's opera, *Carmen* (B/LY: Henri Meilhac and Ludovic Halévy), itself based on Prosper Mérimée's novel; D: Hassard Short and Charles Friedman; CH: Eugene Loring; S: Howard Bay; C: Raoul Pène du Bois; L: Hassard Short; P: Billy Rose; T: Broadway Theatre; 12/2/43 (502)

A smash-hit adapation of the famous Bizet opera *Carmen* that would have an extensive road tour following its run, be seen a couple of more times in New York before the decade ended, and enjoy two more revivals in the fifties. All the characters are now black and the time is the early 1940s, with Carmen Jones a worker in a World War II parachute factory in South Carolina. José (now called Joe) is a corporal in the army assigned to guard the factory as an M.P., Micaela becomes camp follower Cindy Lou (Carlotta Franzell alternating with Elton J. Warren), and the toreador Escamillo is changed to a boxer named Husky Miller (Glenn Bryant).

Oscar Hammerstein long had been concerned with the possibilities of presenting opera in a way that everyone could appreciate, not just aficionados. Thus, when the music was excellently rearranged by Robert Russell Bennett, it was not adapted to swing and retained its operatic values. This made it a chore to sing at eight weekly shows, so alternating casts were hired for the principal roles. Muriel Rahn alternated Carmen with Muriel Smith, and Luther Saxon took turns playing Joe with Napoleon Reed.

The libretto stuck pretty faithfully to the original, as did the sequence of most of the musical numbers. One of the few transpositions that did not work was that of making the smugglers' mountain camp into an elegant black country club near Chicago, to which city the action shifted for Husky's big fight. In the new telling, Carmen fights with another girl, is placed in Joe's custody, seduces him, gets him to go AWOL and flee with her to Chicago, takes up there with boxer Miller, deserts Joe, is stabbed by Joe outside the stadium as Husky defeats his antagonist in the ring inside, and is followed in death by Joe's suicide.

There was considerable appreciation of the fact that the integrity of the original had been so greatly respected in all its moods and variations. The new lyrics, set to titles such as "Dat's Love" ("Habañera"), "You Talk Just Like My Maw," "Dere's a Café on the Corner" ("Seguidilla," done as a jitterbug), "Whizzin' Away along de Track" (the smugglers' quintet), "Beat Out Dat Rhythm on a Drum," "Stan' Up and Fight" (the "Toreador Song"), "Dis Flower" (the "Flower Song"), and "My Joe," were approved as brilliant transpositions into the black idiom. The tight construction of the work did not permit any encores to disrupt the continuity.

Not only did this work profit from the great Bizet music, it also was exceptionally well produced in every department. There was generous praise for the dancing, lighting, costumes, sets, singing, acting, and direction. Some even thought the work an improvement over the original in its brilliant merger of music and theatricality. The lack of grand- opera posturing was one of the show's best features. Another was the variation in color from scene to scene, each having its own dominant hue. The rescoring was deemed a masterful one of great subtlety that did no violence to the original and at the same time seemed a natural outgrowth of the new libretto. All recitative passages were removed in favor of dialogue, which is actually how Bizet had conceived his work.

One of the most memorable scenes was the final one, set before the stadium in which the boxing match is going on. "The wooden walls," wrote Rosamond Gilder (*TAM*), "rise high and solid, curving forward, filling the background of the stage." Carmen and Joe remain on stage after the crowd has entered, and the sound of the crowd during the fight is heard. As a roar of triumph suddenly swells, Joe swiftly stabs Carmen, and the wall behind them becomes transparent, with Husky seen towering over his fallen opponent. The music of "Stan' Up and Fight" swells around the dying Carmen and the remorseful Joe, and the curtain falls.

This was a remarkably proficient work when one realizes how difficult it was to accomplish. No other Broadway musical adapted from an opera has ever been as successful. Howard Barnes (*NYHT*) thought the work "as wonderful and exciting as it is audacious. . . . *Carmen Jones* is something more than a major theatrical event. It opens infinite and challenging horizons for the fusion of two art forms." "Just call it wonderful, quite wonderful," enthused Lewis Nichols (*NYT*). Gilder felt that its adaptation had tended to diminish the tragic dimensions of the original by concentrating on the more colorful and colloquial aspects of the story, but agreed that once one accepted this reversal of values, the show became "a constant delight." Still, there were some opera lovers who claimed that the show did a disservice to Bizet's work, one of their several objections being to the frenetic drum routine performed by Cozy Cole in the cabaret scene at Billy Pastor's.

A great deal of the credit for the show went to John Hammond, Jr., who was assigned to scour the nation for excellent black performers, regardless of their professional fame. As George Jean Nathan (*TBY*) acknowledged, "He came away with such a new, fresh and exciting lot of musical play competences as has not been seen on a single stage in years." Many of these were making their Broadway debuts, having given up their non-show-business jobs to do so. Hammond took the job with out any remuneration, even paying for his own transportation expenses. Speaking of the talent Hammond found, producer Rose exclaimed, "Not one of 'em had ever been on a stage before [actually, Muriel Rahn was an exception to this claim]. Not one of 'em knew the difference between a spotlight and a footlight. But they knew how to sing up a storm, and as soon as I heard them in rehearsal, I said to myself, 'How sweet it is!'" (quoted in Polly Rose Gottlieb's, *The Nine Lives of Billy Rose*).

(2) [Return Engagement] T: City Center of Music and Drama; 5/2/45 (21)

This return engagement was prepared by Billy Rose as a warmup for a transcontinental tour. The production was somewhat pared down from its original to facilitate touring, and a few performers had been shuffled from one role to the other. Muriel Smith was now sharing Carmen with Inez Smith, while Napoleon Reed alternated with LaVern Hutcherson. In the supporting comic roles of Rum and Dink (originally played by Edward Lee Tyler and Dick Montgomery) were well-known entertainers Ford Buck and John Bubbles, known as Buck and Bubbles. "The show hasn't lost any of the spirit, color or excitement of the original Broadway production," noted Bron. (*V*).

(3) [Return Engagement] T: City Center of Music and Drama; 4/7/46 (32)

The show stopped in New York again during its constant touring obligations and seemed none the worse for wear. Said Lewis Nichols (*NYT*), "Its travels have not caused *Carmen Jones* to grow haggard, nor has repetition dulled the spirit of either itself or the players." At $2.40 top, the show was a terrific bargain. Many of the players from the previous production were back, including Muriel Smith, Napoleon Reed, and Buck and Bubbles.

(1) CAROUSEL [Musical/Crime/Death/Fantasy/Marriage/Period/Romance/Small Town] B: Benjamin F. Glazer; M: Richard Rodgers; LY: Oscar Hammerstein II; SC: Ferenc Molnàr's play, *Liliom**; D: Rouben Mamoulian; CH: Agnes de Mille; S: Jo Mielziner; C: Miles White; P: Theatre Guild; T: Majestic Theatre; 4/19/45 (890)

A now-classic musical that cemented the enormously successful partnership of Rodgers and Hammerstein that began with *Oklahoma!* That show for a long time continued to run directly across the street from this one. A good many of *Oklahoma!*'s creative lights--the director, choreographer, costume designer, and producers--were involved in *Carousel* as well.

As before, Rodgers and Hammerstein based their work on a play, in this case the Hungarian drama *Liliom*, which had had its American premiere in 1921, had been revived as recently as 1940, and previously had been considered for musicalization by both Puccini and Gershwin. Molnàr, however, was not interested in seeing it transformed, and only a viewing of *Oklahoma!* was able to convince him to allow the Theatre Guild to do the job with Rodgers and Hammerstein. The composer and lyricist had their doubts about the Hungarian background, however, and were not convinced that they could do the show until Rodgers came up with the idea of moving the story to a New England fishing village in 1873. The original character names were suitably revised. When Molnàr viewed a dress rehearsal, he, like many of the staff members watching, cried copiously; this led the Guild's Lawrence Langner (who recounted the story in *The Magic Curtain*) to worry for the $180,000 invested, as he thought that a Broadway audience might not relish so sad a show.

More worries were piled on during the out-of-town tryout when the show ran into second-act problems and had to undergo numerous revisions and repositioning of the numbers. With suggestions from Molnàr and the director, the show was greatly strengthened. According to Elliot Norton's "Broadway's Cutting Room Floor" (in George Oppenheimer's *The Passionate Playgoer*), one major change occurred when the Boston audiences would not accept a heaven--to which the lead male character goes on his death--depicted too literally as an austere New England parlor, with a stern Yankee character called He playing the harmonium, while his wife, called She, sat primly by. Rodgers, aware of the audience's unrest, told Hammerstein, "We've got to get God out of that parlor!" Asked where to put him, the composer said, "Put him on a ladder, for all I care, only get Him out of that parlor!" The librettist did just that, scrapping the parlor and rewriting the entire scene, with the deity presented as the starkeeper, standing on a backyard ladder and polishing the stars hanging on lines. When the show finally opened in New York, Rodgers had to watch it from the wings propped up on a stretcher because of an accident to his back.

The amusement-park carousel of the title is the one at which the loutish braggart Billy Bigelow (John Raitt, in his Broadway debut) works as a barker. In an opening ballet sequence Billy meets Julie Jordan (Jan Clayton, in her Broadway bow) and tries to date her, although the jealous Mrs. Mullin (Jean Casto), who loves Billy, looks on disapprovingly. Julie overcomes her hesitation, accepts, and soon after tells the news to her friend Carrie Pipperidge (Jean Darling), who is herself enamored of Mr. Snow (Eric Mattson). Billy turns out to be awkward and inarticulate when alone with Julie, whom he eventually marries (in *Liliom* they are lovers, not husband and wife). Julie becomes pregnant, to which thought Billy takes some getting accustomed. Having been fired by Mr. Mullin and needing money for his coming baby, the indigent Billy carries out a holdup with the rascally sailor, Jigger Craigin (Murvyn Vye); when capture is imminent, he commits suicide. Billy spends fifteen years in purgatory, where the starkeeper (Russell Collins) finally allows him to visit earth to perform a good deed and to visit his teenage daughter Louise (Bambi Linn), whom he discovers to be unhappy because of the shadow of his reputation. He offers her a star stolen from heaven, but when she refuses it, his rage erupts and he slaps her, although she feels no pain (a mirror of what had happened in life between Billy and Julie). He must then return to purgatory, although he does watch Louise graduate from school. Although she cannot hear him, he somehow inspires her with confidence by his singing "You'll Never Walk Alone."

Elevating the show into the musical stratosphere was the enormously rich and varied score, of which many songs became standards. Among them were "Carousel Waltz," "You're a Queer One, Julie Jordan," "When I Marry Mr. Snow," "If I Loved You," "June Is Bustin' Out All Over," "When the Children Are Asleep," "Soliloquy," "What's the Use of Wond'rin'," "Blow High, Blow Low," "You'll Never Walk Alone," "This Was a Real Nice Clambake" (dropped as "This Was a Real Nice Hayride" from *Oklahoma*!), and "The Highest Judge of All."

Carousel also benefited from exceptionally lovely sets and costumes, brilliant choreography, direction that individualized the chorus members and wove them into the action, and memorable performances from a cast with first-rate singing and acting abilities. None of the performers was a star, most of them being completely unknown. Several went on to filmic or theatrical success, but none became as popular as the handsome, powerfully built John Raitt, former University of Southern California athlete.

Raitt was reported to have been cast without an audition, but this was hyperbole, as he previously had gained the attention of the Theatre Guild when he successfully tried out as a replacement for the role of Curly in the touring version of *Oklahoma!* Despite their pointing to certain drawbacks, his reviews were generally very laudatory. Lewis Nichols (*NYT*) wrote, for example, "He has an excellent and powerful voice and is not afraid to use it. He is perhaps not as good an actor as singer; he lacks the easy swagger and arrogance which goes with the character." Others involved included Jay Velie, Franklyn Fox, Pearl Lang, Peter Birch, Annabelle Lyon, and Connie Baxter.

The libretto softened some of the play's hard angles and made the story more sentimental and the character of Billy more sympathetic, his rough behavior becoming acceptable as a cover for his own self-doubts. The blending of the book and the music was practically seamless and was thought an advance over the technique in *Oklahoma!* It even led John Mason Brown (*SR*) to ponder the work's genre: "The result is not a musical comedy, a light opera, or an operetta. Most simply stated, it is perhaps a play with music; a play which turns from dialogue to song, and from straight acting into dance, almost without one's becoming aware of it." *Carousel*'s bittersweet ending was unconventional and may have contributed to a shorter run than that of its predecessor. Still, most believed with Arthur Pollock (*BE*) that "all the ordinary hokum, artificiality and schmaltz so long characteristic of musical comedy is sifted out and what remains is pure, clear, simple beauty and sentiment." Hammerstein's lyrics received such approving comments as George Jean Nathan's (*TBY*) that they "are of a simple flavor in keeping with the tone of the book, avoiding any of the over-tricky and strained rhymes so close to the vanity of his . . . contemporaries." Cavils included the feeling that some of de Mille's dance numbers were overlong, that there was a need for more comedy, and that the pace needed quickening. The show was awarded the Drama Critics Circle Award for best musical of the season.

(2) [Return Engagement] T: City Center of Music and Drama; 1/25/49 (48)

After two years on tour, *Carousel* returned to Broadway with its latest cast, including Iva Withers as Julie Jordan, Stephen Douglass as Billy Bigelow, Christine Johnson (from the original cast) as Nettie Fowler, Eric Mattson (also from the original cast) as Enoch Snow, Margaret Moser as Carrie Pipperidge, Mario De Laval as Jigger Craigin, Jay Velie as Brother Joshua, Calvin Thomas as the starkeeper, and Diane Keith as Louise.

According to Brooks Atkinson (*NYT*), the cast was slightly below first-rate, playing more broadly than the original, but the show remained glorious and the songs perhaps even better appreciated now that they had become more familiar. William Hawkins (*NYWT*) noted, "After its long tour the show is still in great shape. Its tension is alive and its timing sure, and it has not suffered in any way from age or travel."

The popular-priced engagement charged only $3 top. It moved to the Majestic Theatre on 2/22/49 because of other commitments at the City Center.

CAT SCREAMS, THE [Drama/Crime/Death/Drugs/Literature/Mexico/Mystery/Romance/Sex] A: Basil Beyea; SC: Todd Downing's novel of the same name; D: Arthur Pierson; S: John Root; C: Mary Grant; P: Martha Hodge; T: Martin Beck Theatre; 6/16/42 (5)

A pension in La Jorta, Mexico, is the locale for the action of this murder mystery in which five killings transpire before the cause of the carnage is uncovered. The pension is inhabited by its proprietor, Madame (Lea Penman); a cynical, sadistic writer named Steven Tybalt (Lloyd Gough); the married woman (Doris Nolan) with whom he would like to rekindle a former relationship; her much older husband (Harry Sheppard); a poetry-loving, sex-starved spinster (Mildred Dunnock) who sees visions; a pretty Mexican girl (Cecilia Callejo); a pair of anthropology professors, father (Herbert Yost) and son (Gordon Oliver); and the pension staff. The superstitious old servant Micaela (Osceola Archer) possesses a Siamese cat named Mura that supposedly can discern the proximity of death. The cat shrieks, the servant faints, and Dr. Otero places the pension under quarantine. An epidemic of suicides in the village breaks out, followed by a succession of bizarre murders of the pension guests. The guilty party turns out to be Madame, who has been running an illegal drug-smuggling operation, but who is herself killed by drinking poisoned whisky.

The critics found the play "clumsy and foolish and childlike" (Richard Watts, Jr. [*NYHT*]), yet mildly entertaining fare for mystery buffs. Many in the audience could not restrain their titters at some of the more ludicrous goings on. Richard Lockridge (*NYS*) said that the play "begins by being laborious and ends by being preposterous."

CATHERINE WAS GREAT [Comedy/Military/Period/Politics/Sex/War] A: Mae West; D: Roy Hargrave; CH: Margaret Sande; S: Howard Bay; C: Mary Percy Schenck and Ernest Schrapps; P: Michael Todd; T: Shubert Theatre; 8/2/44 (191)

The critics trashed this opulent, one-joke, Mae West extravaganza in which the playwright-star assumed the role of Catherine the Great of Russia, but it had a successful New York run, as well as a profitable trip on the road. To be entitled to purchase tickets, audience members first had to buy war bonds, and this ploy actually raised $4 million in bond money. The lavishly produced piece (reportedly costing $150,000) gave the blond actress a chance to wear enormous headdresses and thirteen spectacular costumes emphasizing her fleshy contours; however, she wore such elevated shoes to add height to her diminutive frame that she seemed to be stomping rather than walking, according to Ibee. (*V*).

The play begins in a USO recreation room where a bunch of soldiers (among them Robert Strauss and Philip Huston) are discussing the amatory conquests of the great Catherine. The scene then shifts to 1762 Russia, and the soldiers' fantasies come to life as Catherine's public and private life is acted out with numerous changes of scene. Court intrigue and romantic affairs keep Catherine busy. Turkey, possessed of a new navy, is threatening Russia. An officer discovers that the ships are wooden, so he burns the entire fleet. Catherine confers with her ministers, issues manifestos, detects spies and enemies, considers freeing the serfs, and romances Ivan VI (Michael Bey), whose long incarceration has prevented him from ever seeing a woman before.

This was more a vehicle for the florid star than it was a serious exercise in Broadway dramaturgy. She even sang a bawdy song about wanting her men "strong, solid and sensational." On opening night, Gene Barry, in the romantic lead of Lieutenant Bunin, accidentally allowed his scabbard to get in the way of an embrace with the star. Her ad-libbed reaction was, "Lieutenant, is that your sword or are you just glad to see me?" Much of the monotonous action involved West parading around in her famous hip-swinging, honky-tonk manner, speaking in an amalgam of toney accents and her native Brooklynese, inviting various studs to come up and see her sometime, and occasionally tossing off a suggestive Westian crack (such as "I'll grant you a private audience and then we'll talk Turkey"), but the routine paled in the present context. Nor was it helped on opening night when the star kept blowing her lines. (There were many other first-night mishaps.)

In the extremely large cast there was only one other female speaking role, played by Elinor Counts. The other women were "ladies-in-waiting." The production was slow paced, tedious, and insufficiently amusing. It also veered on the ridiculous when West seemed to be taking her part seriously. "I never thought I'd live to call Mae West boring," sighed George Freedley (*NYMT*), "but apparently there is a time for everything. . . . General West may be a superb showman, but as a playwright she is an indifferent piccolo player." Wilella Waldorf (*NYP*) accused the piece of overkill and noted, "Basically it is uninspired historical drama of the cloak and sword school, neither good enough to challenge attention in its own field, nor bad enough to be as funny as Mr. Todd presumably thinks it is." Rosamond Gilder (*TAM*) concluded that this was "one of the most tasteless and extravagant displays ever to be presented as a play for adults."

West made a typical curtain speech on opening night, declaring to her die-hard fans, "Catherine had 300 lovers. I did the best I could in a couple of hours." Her cast included Ray Bourbon as a swishy hairdresser, Joel Ashley as Potemkin, and Don de Leo, Hubert Long, Mischa Tonken, and many others in assorted roles.

According to Art Cohn's *The Nine Lives of Michael Todd*, the show had undergone considerable revision before arriving on Broadway because Todd wanted the usual Mae West burlesque-style, caricature performance and the star wanted to play the role straight. Todd himself offered various suggestive rewrites (including the "Turkey" line quoted earlier). Another of his inventions was to have West inspect her courtiers, all of them dressed in tights, by sashaying along the line with her head down. When she had passed several men, she was to stop, pause, and then declare, "You're new here." In response to West's objections, Todd stated, "Let's face it, Miss West, this isn't a Helen Hayes vehicle," to which her stern reply was, "And who is Helen Hayes?"

CAUKEY [Comedy-Drama/Blacks/Family/Politics/Race/Romance] A: Thomas McGlynn; D: Dennis Gurney; S: Thomas Fabian; P: Blackfriars' Guild; T: Blackfriars' Theatre (OB); 2/17/44 (22)

The title of this propagandistic play of racial reversal--by a priest who was the son of actor Frank McGlynn--refers to "Caucasians," the downtrodden people who take the place in the action of American blacks. A caukey is the play's equivalent for a "nigger." In the society depicted, the black characters are the dominant race, being the landlords, gas-company owners, industrialists, shopkeepers, and so on. The whites are the slum-dwelling, frequently unemployed, and exploited minority for whom upward mobility is a near impossibility. The central caukey family shown is the Pringles. They live in a tenement whose landlord (John Tate) neglects to make basic repairs. They are visited by a gas inspector (William Johnson), a social worker (Claire R. Leyba), and a settlement worker (Geraldine Prillerman), all black. Ma Pringle (Ruth P. White) is a shiftless matriarch; Pa has run off. There are also a daughter, Lorraine (Cathy Parsons), and two sons. Henry (Robert Lancet) is black-hating and antisocial, George (Dennis McDonald) ambitious and upward-striving. George, the family's sole support, wants to get ahead and become a lawyer who will be of importance to his people. The majority society won't let him until the kindly lawyer, "Mister Ed" (Clarence Q. Foster), an idealist who wants to better the conditions of the white people, gets him a job as an office boy for a real- estate operator (Vernon Chambers) who is secretly planning to build a defense plant in the white ghetto, necessitating the destruction of the homes there. The Caucasians are advised not to vacate without a court order, and they put up a fight against eviction. In trying to defend his home, George is killed by the police. Meanwhile, Ed's romance with the daughter (Betty E. Haynes) of his boss is ruined because of his assistance to the white community.

Apart from its trick device of changing the characters' races, the play was unoriginal and its purpose, other than the "put yourself in another man's shoes" idea, seemed vague. Some felt that the problems depicted could have been those of poor whites as well as of poor blacks and that the issues that would have been specifically of relevance in terms of skin color were not really addressed. Robert Garland (*NYJA*) called it "fundamentally neither more nor less than the familiar melodrama about the cruel landlord and the tormented tenants." George Jean Nathan (*TBY*) said that honest as the play sought to be, it "takes on the fateful color of a stunt, and a stunt is hardly appropriate to the materials with which it seeks to deal, in this case solemnly." The acting of the semiprofessional cast--the blacks being members of the American Negro Theatre company--was too unimpressive to help the play where it needed it most.

CHAFF [Drama/Austrian/Crime/Marriage/Rural/Sex] A: Ferdinand Bruckner; TR: A. Zatz; D: Carl Heinz Roth; S: Lawrence Goldwasser; L: Doris Einstein; P: Dramatic Workshop of the New School for Social Research; T: President Theatre (OB); 3/17/48 (10)

This "cumbersome piece of Central European dramatic lumber, with some of the most awkward speeches of many a season" (George Freedley [*NYMT*]), was offered by Erwin Piscator's company, made up of students and faculty at his Dramatic Workshop. It was dully acted and directed and contained little that was believable. Two casts alternated, a Blue cast and a Red cast.

The action, staged on a revolve with selective realism, is set in the southeastern United States and deals with Storm (Keith Taylor), a currently impecunious farmer of upper-class breeding. In order to meet a wealthy widow in whom he is interested, he rides his horse into her car, killing the animal but gaining the woman's acquaintance. He has an ill wife (Ann Blackburn), who commits suicide when she learns that he has made Ellen (Anneliese Gellhorn), a vagrant, illiterate farm girl, pregnant. Ellen, as an act of self-preservation, claims that Storm killed his wife. The wealthy woman departs, and he is arrested, convicted, and sentenced to life imprisonment, but the conscience-stricken Ellen admits to perjury and--to critical surprise--has every reason to look forward to her and her baby being looked after when Storm is released and she has served her time in jail.

"The author and Mr. Piscator see in all this a gallant struggle for human rights, with considerable human significance," wrote Richard Watts, Jr. (*NYP*). "To me it seemed an inept, irrelevant and somewhat idiotic melodrama, with nothing in the way of ideas, emotion or theatrical effectiveness to justify it."

CHARLEY'S AUNT [Dramatic Revival*] A: Brandon Thomas; D: Joshua Logan; S/C: John Koenig; P: Day Tuttle and Richard Skinner; T: Cort Theatre; 10/17/40 (233)

Ever since its London debut in 1892, this farce has proved to be one of the most popular pieces on the modern stage. Fifteen years following its 1925 incarnation, which flopped, it was given its quintessential New York production. In the process, José Ferrer, in the role of Lord Fancourt Babberley, became a star. The hilarious hit production was the outgrowth of a trial presentation at the Westchester Country Playhouse in the summer of 1940. It proved, as John Mason Brown (*NYP*) commented, a welcome respite from the concerns of a world suffering from increasing fear of Adolph Hitler.

The critics were genuinely surprised to find that the old warhorse still had life in it. Referring to the direction, Brooks Atkinson (*NYT*) observed, "Without burlesquing the farce, Mr. Logan has caught a nice accent of knowing enjoyment which acknowledges the hokum of the plot." Euphemia Van Rensselaer Wyatt (*CW*) added, "Due credit must be given the director . . . for the fast and even tempo, the excellent stage business and the good humor and distinction of his cast." The production respected the original time frame of the play and carefully dressed its actors in costumes circa 1892. Many of the most hilarious moments were taken from a 1924 silent movie of the play made by Charles Chaplin's brother Sidney. To these Logan added many more of his own invention during a creative spree that found him in a state of "manic elation." As he wrote in *Josh*, "Ideas piled upon each other, gag on gag, routine on routine, the funniest scenes I had ever directed." He was helped greatly by the athletic Ferrer, who, said Logan, "at one point . . . ran across a crenellated ten-foot wall, jumped from that into a tree and climbed to the top, swinging to a concealed ladder in the flies, giving out a Tarzan yell." To get Lord Fancourt down from the tree and back into the old lady's dress he loathed wearing, Jack and Charley "tempted him down with a bottle of Scotch held at the neck of the dress. While they held the dress like a tunnel, Joe dived horizontally through the dress, his arms slipping into the sleeves and his hands grabbing the Scotch--all this without touching the floor."

After bestowing accolades on the rest of the cast, Rosamond Gilder (*TAM*) stated that it was José Ferrer "who carries off the laurels on this frivolous occasion. . . . Mr. Ferrer proves himself an outstanding comedian. The occasion calls mainly for horseplay of the cruder sort, but he manages to indulge in it with such raffish gaiety that its boisterousness becomes tolerable, its time-worn humors oddly engaging. Dressed as the fake aunt in grey curled wig and rustling black silk, he is always ludicrously masculine. His long, expressive face with its round laughing eyes, boldly theatric nose, and spacious mouth is alive with laughter, and though the play is as devoid of wit as it is of good sense, its antics become bearable in the contagious humor of his acting."

Abetting Ferrer were Thomas Speidel as Jack, J. Richard Jones as Charley, Mary Mason as Kitty, Phyllis Avery as Amy, Arthur Margetson as Colonel Chesney, Harold deBecker as Brassett, Reynolds Denniston (whose acting career began in South Africa when he played Charley) as Spettigue, Katherine Wiman, daughter of producer Dwight Deere Wiman, making her debut as Ela, and Nedda Harrigan as Donna Lucia, the real Charley's aunt. Harrigan, recently widowed, was opposed to taking the role, and Logan, who wanted someone very attractive for the part rather than a middle-aged character actress, worked assiduously to convince her to accept. Two days after rehearsals began, she quit and again had to be roped in by Logan's persuasiveness. During the production, Logan and Harrigan fell in love and, after Logan divorced his current wife, were married.

CHAUVE-SOURIS 1943 [Revue] CN: Leon Greanin; M: Gleb Yellin; LY: (English lyrics) Irving Florman; D: Michael Michon; CH: Vlacheslav Swoboda and Boris Romanoff; S/C: Serge Soudeikine; P: Leon Greanin b/a/w Mme. Nikita Balieff; T: Royale Theatre; 8/12/43 (12)

An attempt to revive interest in the intimate revue created by Russian expatriate Nikita Balieff in the post-Russian Revolution period and first seen in New York in 1922*. The last edition of the show had been seen locally in 1931. Part of its perennial charm had been the humor provided by the rotund and heavily accented Balieff in his role of MC or conférencier. A program made up of Russian songs, dances, and sketches was assembled for the present occasion, but the show died aborning. The late Balieff was sorely missed, his role being taken by producer Leon Greanin, who shared Balieff's broken English, but sorely lacked the charm needed to make the show as informally pleasant as had his predecessor.

Five of the numbers from the previous editions were revived, including "Katinka's Birthday" and "The Parade of the Wooden Soldiers." Each was somehow brought up to date, the latter, for instance, being given a contemporary addendum with Soviet soldiers singing a chauvinistic marching song. The sketches had contemporary overtones as well, such as one with a Russian sniper (Vera Pavlovska) and an American WAC (Georgianna Bannister). Among the best parts was the choral singing, in particular, a sequence called "Harvest Festival," with music by modern Russian composers. Some liked "The Gypsies," set in a villa of the turn of the century with an elegant mistress and master listening to the music of an invited band of gypsies. Singer Marusia Sava was the chief singer in this colorful number, with Georges Doubrovsky leading the gypsy chorus. Although most of the show was in Russian, there were some English pieces, such as "A Sailor in New York," with mimic Simeon Karavaeff, whose routine allowed him to give impressions of Ray Bolger and Al Jolson.

"The pity of it all," wrote Lewis Nichols (*NYT*), "is that between moments of cheerful music and dancing lie long stretches of material that is incomprehensible, or is more suitable for the broken hours of a night club, or, on numerous occasions, would be forgotten altogether."

CHERRY ORCHARD, THE (Vishnyovy Sad) [Dramatic Revival*] A: Anton Chekhov; TR: Irina Skariatina; D: Eva Le Gallienne and Margaret Webster; S/C: Motley; P: Carly Wharton and Margaret Webster; T: National Theatre; 1/25/44 (96)

The most recent revival of this Chekhov classic had been in 1933 when it was offered by Eva Le Gallienne's Civic Repertory Company in a version it had first revealed in 1928. Le Gallienne now shared the directorial duties with Margaret Webster and also assumed the role of Lyubov Andreyevna (Alla Nazimova had played it in the previous production, with Le Gallienne playing Varya). When Le Gallienne had to enter the hospital for an illness, Webster took over the role. On stage with Le Gallienne was Stefan Schnabel as Lopahin, Virginia Campbell as Dunyasha, Rex O'Malley as Epihodov, A. G. Andrews (a veteran who had first acted in 1862) as Firs, Lois Hall as Anya, Katherine Emery as Varya, Joseph Schildkraut as Gayev, Leona Roberts as Charlotta, Carl Benton Reid as Semyomov-Pistchik, and Eduard Franz as Trofimov.

The production and the play received mixed reviews (although the presentation earned a small profit). John Chapman (*NYDN*) called it "a lucid and affecting production which is quite splendidly performed." Burton Rascoe (*NYWT*) insisted that Webster "has not merely given [the play] a shot of adrenalin and stood it shakily on its feet: she has given it vibrant new life, vitality and spirit." Louis Kronenberger (*PM*) was one of several, though, who were not enthralled by the play itself or by the production. He found the writing static and the characters too childlike to be continually interesting. Kronenberger also faulted the production for failing to integrate the comedy and the pathos: "Too much of the comedy was pointed up; too many of the roles were turned into mere character parts. Some of the serious moments--notably Lopahin's when he exults over buying the property--struck the wrong note." Rosamond Gilder (*TAM*) regretted that the direction had not "succeeded in evoking the curious emotional climate in which this play is conceived. . . . Transplanted, translated, subjected to the quick-fire production methods economically inevitable in the present-day theatre, *The Cherry Orchard* suffers acutely and seems indeed to have lost much of its delicate aroma." George Jean Nathan (*TBY*) attacked the direction for its undue reliance on slapstick humor, turning the piece into a "jolly parlor comedy." "Almost every old vaudeville device save alone the idea of having Andreyevitch fall over the footlights and land on the bass drummer was introduced; the slap on . . . Dunyasha's backside, the stumbling over the furniture, the slapping of the forehead too forcibly and the resultant comical staggers."

There were differing opinions on the leads, Le Gallienne seeming to some to lack the character's childish temperament, her native intelligence being too evident for the feckless woman's character, and by others to have all the needed variety and color. Schnabel struck several reporters as physically right for the lumbering Lopahin but too prone to gesture extravagantly and not sufficiently enmeshed in the character's inner reality. Schildkraut was widely praised for playing his comic role with great restraint and for a carefully built-up portrayal of the eccentric brother, although he seemed to border on the humorously caricaturish at times.

Because his character had to enter in tears in the third act, Schildkraut, to Le Gallienne's exasperation, would not enter until he had the prop master spray his eyes with menthol to make him cry; the hypochondriacal actor only stopped when told that the concoction would harm his eyes for life. "From then on," wrote Le Gallienne in *With a Quiet Heart*, "the menthol-tears only appeared when someone very special was out front." The aged A. G. Andrews, despite the natural lines on his eighty-six-year-old face, appeared at the New Haven tryout with his face covered in makeup wrinkles to make him seem precisely Firs's eighty-seven.

CHEVALIER, MAURICE (see *Maurice Chevalier*)

CHICKEN EVERY SUNDAY [Comedy/Boarding House/Business/Family/Marriage/Period/Romance/Sex/Western] A: Julius J. and Philip G. Epstein; SC: the book of the same name by Rosemary Taylor; D: Lester Vail; S/L: Howard Bay; C: Rose Bogdanoff; P: Edward Gross; T: Henry Miller's Theatre; 4/5/44 (317)

The sibling scenarists who collaborated with Howard Koch on the classic movie *Casablanca* were responsible for this successful marital farce very freely based on a popular book of memoirs and set in a Tucson, Arizona, boarding house in 1916. The boarding house is run by Emily Blachman (Mary Philips), of Virginia's aristocratic Claiborne family. Despite her high-toned background, she takes pride in the reputation of her cooking and of her establishment. Her husband Jim (Rhys Williams) has many important titles, among them vice president of the bank, president of the streetcar company, and owner of the local laundry, and he is the loudmouthed type who loves to hear himself talk. He is mired in debt, however, and thanks his stars for the success of the boarding house, which keeps him, his wife, and their three youngsters, Oliver (Guy Stockwell), Ruthie (Carolyn Hummel), and Rosemary (Jean Gillespie) comfortable. Rosemary (the person on whose memoirs the original book was based) is enmeshed in a romantic relationship with a snobbish Bostonian (Wyrley Birch) whose ancestors were Pilgrims. (The romance fizzles when he is mistakenly thought to be a Nazi spy, and Rosemary ends up with a homely youth [Hugh Thomas] whose mother [Ethel Remey] wants him to be a poet and not a groceryman like his late father.) When Jim's business dealings put him in a position where he must sell certain of his holdings, he brings each prospective buyer home as a boarder. This leads to the house being filled with a cross-section of zany characters. There is the lecherous old prospector Uncle Jake (Roy Fant); the nymphomaniacal divorcée Rita Kirby (Ann Thomas); the bibulous ex-vaudevillian yodeler (Hope Emerson), who is Rita's mother; the nympho's husband (Frank M. Thomas), twice divorced from her, who wants to get rid of her mother because she always goes to him when their marriages end; Miss Gilley (Diana Rivers), the schoolmarm whose suitor, Mr. Robinson (Fleming Ward), keeps sneaking up the back stairs to visit her, even after they are wed; the tart-tongued black maid (Viola Dean); the vain widow, Mrs. Lynch (Katherine Squire), who hogs the sole bathtub; and so on. There are so many boarders that the Blachmans have to sleep in the living room. A financial windfall comes in time to relieve the family's finances before the final curtain.

Although the play--likened by many to *You Can't Take It with You** and *Life*

*Father**--caused considerable critical pleasure, it also was widely pointed out that it was almost plotless, being more a collection of situations, eccentric characters, and suggestive jokes than a conventional play. This riled Rosamond Gilder (*TAM*), who caviled that the playwrights and director "could not allow an engaging if eccentric family to untangle its affairs in peace but insisted on crowding the scenes with quaint characters, in rushing the principals up and down a long flight of stairs, in embroidering the whole affair with gags and gadgets." Robert Garland (*NYJA*) thought it "dull and undesirable." But George Jean Nathan (*TBY*), while noting the numerous risqué gags and situations and the pleasure taken by the authors on opening night whenever the audience laughed, confessed, "The worst of it is that I seem to have had almost as good a time as they did. . . . The indelicacies are for the most part so funny and so forthright and unmincing that they are irresistible." John Chapman (*NYDN*) called the piece "a human zoo which makes no more sense than a barrel of monkeys and is just as much fun."

CHILDREN'S HOUR, THE [Dramatic Revival*] A: Lillian Hellman; D: Anne Gerlette; P: Equity Library Theatre; T: Muhlenberg Branch of the New York Public Library (OB); 5/23/45

The very active new Equity Library Theatre (sometimes then referred to as the Library Equity Theatre) rarely drew reviewers, but George Freedley (*NYMT*), who attended more often than anyone else, and Robert Garland (*NYJA*) saw this revival of *The Children's Hour*, Hellman's controversial 1934 drama about lesbianism and mendacity. The actors offered "a sensitive and adult production," said Freedley, with Ruth Gregory and twenty-three-year-old future star Jo Van Fleet as the teachers. "They played with the highest possible professional skill." Mary Tilford, the evil child, was played by Lettie Stever at the performance viewed by Freedley and by Ivy Bethune at that seen by Garland. David Kerman was the young doctor. Garland said that the play remained "a sad and serious tragedy replete with half-hidden, half-unhidden, anti-social significance."

(1) CHOCOLATE SOLDIER, THE (*Der Tapfere Soldat*) [Musical Revival*] B: Rudolph Bernauer and Leopold Jacobson; AD: Stanislaus Stange; M: Oscar Straus; D: John Pierce and José Ruben; S: E. B. Dunkel Studios; C: Paul du Pont; P: Joseph S. Tushinsky and Hans Bartsch; T: Carnegie Hall (OB); 6/23/42 (24)

There were two revivals of this opera bouffe--first seen locally in 1909--in the 1920s, two in the 1930s, and two in the 1940s. The present one was part of a series initiated by producers Tushinsky and Bartsch (with the latter conducting the orchestra--to critical pans--for each revival) at Carnegie Hall, considered here as an Off-Broadway venue. The most noted performer in *The Chocolate Soldier* was Allan Jones, playing Lieutenant Bummerli, and he was supported by Frances Comstock as Aurelia, Helen Gleason as Nadina, Doris Patston as Mascha, A. Russell Slagle as Colonel Popoff, Michael Fitzgerald as Alexis, and fat comedian Detmar Poppen as Captain Massakroff, a role he had taken in the 1921 revival.

While not a particularly memorable production, it had its good points and sent the audience home relatively pleased. Jones was the chief draw. Observed Robert Bagar (*NYWT*), "He didn't disappoint the curious, for he made a rather dashing Lieutenant Bumerli [*sic*] and one who could sing the reachy vocal lines handily. Mr. Jones is completely at home on the stage. He moves about in an ingratiating manner, speaks his words with an assured air, and he even knows the trick of adding little convincers of facial expression to his impersonation."

One of the major innovations of the show was the interpolation of a *Lady in the Dark*-like ballet that appeared near the end of Nadina's rendering of "My Hero" (sung to a photo of Gary Cooper in *Sergeant York*). In it there were five Nadinas, four Bummerlis, a "modiste" and his two assistants, and a preacher, all of it to new music with an Oriental feeling by Karl Weber and Murray Rumsey. The interpolation--which was ineptly choreographed and lengthened the act unduly--was not appreciated.

The series was something of an event in the history of Carnegie Hall, usually restricted to straight and unadorned concerts. Tushinsky convinced the management to remove the pianos from the stage, install air conditioning for a summer program, and allow him to produce operettas on a stage not intended for theatrical presentations. These were the first legitimate theatricals on the theatre's stage.

(2) B(REV): Guy Bolton; LY(REV): Bernard Hanighen; D: Felix Brentano; CH: George Balanchine; S/L: Jo Mielziner; C: Lucinda Ballard; P: J. H. Del Bondio and Hans Bartsch for the Delvan Company; T: Century Theatre; 3/12/47 (70)

The second revival of the mildly dated show during the decade had book and lyric revisions (including the alteration of the spelling of certain names) and also added four Straus tunes from other works. Nadina was now played by Frances McCann, Bumerli by Keith Andes (in his Broadway debut), Mascha by Gloria Hamilton, Aurelia by Muriel O'Malley, Massakroff by Henry Calvin, Popoff by Billy Gilbert, and Alexius by Ernest McChesney.

McCann sang the outstanding number, "Come, Come, I Love You Only," with considerable élan and technique, and the rest of the company was extremely capable of handling the show's singing requirements. Andes was passable as Bumerli, but George Jean Nathan (*TBY*) found him "embarrassing to both song and story."

Of great importance were Mielziner's freshly realized Middle European settings and Ballard's exquisitely colored costumes. The direction was crisp and up-to-date, the choreography superb, and the comedy routines on the mark, although the critics differed about the contributions of obese comic Billy Gilbert. Brooks Atkinson (*NYT*) judged the evening "beautiful and likable," and Ward Morehouse (*NYS*) called it "an engaging and good-looking revival." But William Hawkins (*NYWT*) averred that only operetta fanatics would like the show, claiming that "this revival lacks refreshment and excitement."

CHRISTOPHER BLAKE [Drama/Family/Fantasy/Law/Marriage/Politics/Theatre/Trial/Youth] A/D: Moss Hart; S: Harry Horner; C: Bianca Stroock; L: Harry Horner and Leo Kerz; P: Joseph M. Hyman and Bernard Hart; T: Music Box Theatre; 11/30/46 (114)

Christopher Blake is about a twelve-year-old boy of that name (Richard Tyler) who is faced with the emotional trauma of seeing his beloved parents, Kenneth (Shepperd Strudwick) and Evie (Martha Sleeper), seek a divorce. The child's custody is in question and Christopher--at his parents' bidding, despite the judge's (Robert Harrison) warning to the contrary--must choose in the judge's chambers with which parent he will live. The parents each remind Christopher of how good they have been to him, which creates a psychological dilemma that affects the sensitive child enormously. He thus retreats into his imaginative fantasies as a way of confronting harsh realities. Four scenes depict his fantasies. In the first, which starts the play, he shoots himself on the White House grounds, where he is being celebrated as a national hero by President Truman (Irving Fisher); he dies in his parents' arms. In the next, he imagines himself a star actor who reduces his watching mother to tears by the pathos of his acting in a Christmas scene. Then comes one in a poorhouse in which his parents live. They send to Argentina for the rich Christopher, thinking him their lad, but on meeting them he denies that they are his parents, introducing another couple in their place. Finally, in the chambers, he is unable to make up his mind and breaks down. Now he imagines being humiliated in a courtroom scene under the rigorous questioning of a mean judge (Frank M. Thomas), while military schoolmates in the background ridicule him. Back in reality, the parents explain to the boy their reasons for their divorce, the father's explanation stemming from his having had an affair, although he would welcome a reconciliation. Evie's excuse is simply that she never loved her husband. Chris chooses in favor of his father.

Written at a time when the divorce rates were beginning to climb alarmingly, the play was of great value for demonstrating how painful the process of parental separation could be for sensitive youngsters. To many, it was a deeply touching work, made especially poignant by the acting of Richard Tyler, whose characterization was instantly appealing, and who was able to express a wide range of emotions undergone, including a scene of hysteria. The play's mingling of styles disturbed some reviewers, but others found it effective. Richard Watts, Jr. (*NYP*), exclaimed, "Despite several moving scenes and an eminently sensible ending, [the drama] seemed a curiously unsatisfying combination of fantasy and realism." Ward Morehouse (*NYS*) stated that Hart "has written some scenes . . . of heartbreaking poignancy, but a great deal of the play is overdone to the point of pretentiousness."

The production was a huge one, using a cast of forty-three as well as various extras, and with multiple changes of scenery shifted on five revolves. Several reviewers thought that the overly literal production swamped the play and allowed no room for the audience's imagination. Especially distressing was the fact that apart from the evocative dream sequence set in the imaginary courtroom, the other such sequences were made to look as solidly realistic as the reality-based ones. "Mr. Hart . . . conceived his characters with feeling and made the boy himself genuinely engaging, but he let his showman's instincts run away with his production," wrote Rosamond Gilder (*TAM*).

The actors included Francis de Sales, Peggy Van Fleet, Ronald Alexander, Kay Loring, and others. During the play's run Hart decided to revise it by replacing the original opening on the White House grounds with the one taking place in court.

"CHURCH STREET" (see *An Evening of Two Plays*)

CIRCLE OF CHALK, THE (***Der Kreidekreis***) [Dramatic Revival*] A: Klabund [Alfred Henschke]; TR: James Laver; D: James Light; M: Henry Zi and Jascha Horenstein; S: Cleon Throckmorton; C: Rose Bogdanoff; P: Erwin Piscator; T: Studio Theatre of the New School for Social Research (OB); 3/26/41

A highly tasteful revival of Klabund's 1924 adaptation of a thirteenth-century Chinese fantasy, *Hoei-Lan-Kin*, seen Off Broadway (as *The Chalk Circle**) in 1933 and later to be the inspiration for Bertolt Brecht's *The Caucasian Chalk Circle*. This was the second production of German émigré director Erwin Piscator's Dramatic Workshop, a group then made up of professional actors mingled with amateurs, the latter studying theatre at the New School. No one in the company was paid a salary, so Equity allowed only a few performances.

"Cleon Throckmorton's boldly colored settings, suggesting crude Chinese prints, evoked, with their ingenious use of Venetian blinds instead of curtains, a light-hearted Oriental atmosphere in keeping with a fairy-tale mood," stated Rosamond Gilder (*TAM*). Onstage property men were played straight and not for the then-usual comic effect in Western adaptations of Chinese theatre. Authentic onstage Chinese musicians provided the appropriate music, and German refugee actress Dolly Haas (who married famed *NYT* caricaturist Al Hirschfeld) played the lead, called Hai-Tang here, very effectively. "She is an exquisitely beautiful actress, with the limpid grace of a Chinese poem or print," rhapsodized Brooks Atkinson (*NYT*). "She speaks good English in a small and dainty voice and she can translate artifice into a poetic acting style."

Apart from Haas and several others, the acting was uneven. The others included Rose Quong, a Chinese actress who repeated her performance as Mrs. Ma from Basil Dean's London production, young Zachary Scott, who played Prince Po, and Anthony (Tony) Randall as Hai-Tang's brother. Both of the latter went on to become stars. Also involved were Richard Odlin as Chu-Chu and Ralph Morrison as Mr. Ma.

Several critics found the production overlong and too slow, but the delighted George Freedley (*NYMT*) offered the interesting observation that "the most important and interesting plays are frequently presented off Broadway."

CITY OF KINGS [Drama/Blacks/Medicine/Period/Race/Religion] A: Urban Nagle; D: Dennis Gurney; S: Floyd Allen; C: Irene Griffin; L: Joan Tyne; P: Blackfriars' Guild; T: Blackfriars' Theatre (OB); 2/19/49

Off-Broadway's Catholic theatre company offered this piece in which Father Nagle told the story of Blessed Martin, a Peruvian who had been beatified by the Roman Catholic church. The sizable, racially mixed company included several names later to be well known, including Anthony Franciosa and Vinie Burrows.

City of Kings--based on depositions of the period designed to further the central character's claims to sainthood--tells in seven scenes the story of Martin de Porres (Ellwood Smith), a mulatto born out of wedlock in 1580 Lima to black slave Ana Velasquez (Jacqueline Levy) and a Spanish grandee (Michael O'Hara). Martin's ambitious mother wishes him to be a doctor, and he does gain a license as an apothecary. But he enters the Dominican order under a vow of poverty and eventually becomes a lay brother devoted to helping the lame, the sick, and the abandoned. His ministrations at first annoy the other brothers, but he disarms them with his charm and his faith and is allowed to continue his good deeds. As the years go by, he becomes recognized as a healer and worker of miracles. By the end of his life orphanages are built at his insistence by the viceroy of Peru (Harold Anderson) and the archbishop of Mexico (Brett O'Hollewitt), and he is sought by powerful figures for his intercessions on their behalf.

Although somewhat on the lengthy side, the drama found much approval for its straightforward, nonproselytizing manner and for its humorously satirical touches. It was also seen as a blow on behalf of racial tolerance. Robert Coleman (*NYDM*) called it "a moving and absorbing study of a great soul. . . . You cannot see it and not be a better man or woman for the experience." And Richard Watts, Jr. (*NYP*), considered it "a warm, touching and entirely believable portrait of a saintly and selfless man." Ellwood Smith, a black singer, musician, and actor was very strongly commended for his memorable performance.

CLANDESTINE MARRIAGE, THE [Dramatic Revival] A: David Garrick; P: Modern Play Productions; T: Provincetown Playhouse (OB); 2/2/50

Only Whitney Bolton (*NYMT*) appears to have bothered reviewing this rare revival of Garrick's eighteenth-century comedy. He said that the company succeeded in the realms of textual editing, visually entertaining costumes, and technically feasible and attractive settings, but failed in its inability to bring the old piece to life. "As a production, *The Clandestine Marriage* was a gem. As a play, it was a good deal less," he concluded. Roy Pascal, Alan Crane, Alexander Maissel, Judy Diamond, Helaine Kopp, and Anita Gonzales were the names of some of the actors.

CLASH BY NIGHT [Drama/Crime/Marriage/Religion/Romance/Sex] A: Clifford Odets; D: Lee Strasberg; S: Boris Aronson; P: Billy Rose; T: Belasco Theatre; 12/27/41 (49)

Clifford Odets's drab *drame passionnel* was set on Staten Island in the rundown waterfront home of an uneducated, working-class couple, Jerry (Lee J. Cobb) and Mae Wilenski (Tallulah Bankhead). Polish-born Jerry's movie projectionist friend, Earl Pfeiffer (Joseph Schildkraut), with whom he became acquainted on a WPA project, rents a room in the Wilenski household. The cloddish Jerry is an adoring husband of no great intelligence and does not realize the danger of having his smooth, good-looking friend living in the same abode. Although reluctant to accept the arrangement at first, the discontented, frustrated Mae, who has an infant child, eventually accepts and is soon in love with Earl. When Mae plans to leave Jerry for Earl, Jerry gets tanked up on cheap booze and strangles Earl in his projection booth as Mae bangs futilely on the door. The play contains a secondary story concerning the dilemma of young, zealously religious Catholic schoolteacher Peggy Coffey (Katherine Locke) over whether or not to wed unemployed Joe W. Doyle (Robert Ryan, in his Broadway debut). Ultimately, after he lands a job, Joe convinces the still-reluctant Peggy to marry him on the grounds that, unlike Mae, she must face her responsibilities.

The play's strong suits were its vivid and living characters, its juicy vernacular language, its truthful-seeming ambience, and its engrossing first half; outweighing these factors were such weaknesses as an inability to inject originality into the developing crisis, an overly familiar triangular plot line, a failure to sustain in the second half the interest garnered in the first, and a "commonplace" (Brooks Atkinson [*NYT*]) theme. Burns Mantle (*NYDN*) thought it impossible to care for anything or anyone in the play. He also said that it was "handicapped in that it concerns unsympathetic, uninteresting subjects and is completely unrelieved in mood and tone." On the other hand, Rosamond Gilder (*TAM*), who was in the minority, found the play "a poignant picture of man's loneliness, of his yearnings and frustrations, of mischievous evil, of sorrow, ungainliness, love and death." She did think the second half "occasionally labored and repetitious," though.

The work was fortunate to have an excellent production with first-rate performances from a talent-laden company. Speaking of Bankhead, Gilder noted that her "performance . . . is a fascinating example of presenting the essence of character with very little regard to the external trappings. Like Odets' words, her performance expresses the thing itself. . . . Her Mae Wilenski is not only this particular restless, amorous, self-centered and self-indulgent woman; she is the incarnation of the type that exists everywhere."

Some, however, including the producer, the author, and the temperamental star herself, thought the high-born Bankhead miscast as a slattern. This made her very difficult during the rehearsal and tryout period. According to Polly Rose Gottlieb in *The Nine Lives of Billy Rose*, when Bankhead refused to read a new scene written for the Pittsburgh tryout, and Rose, Odets, Strasberg, and costar Cobb pressured her to do so, she reportedly fainted. One story said she even went to the hospital and nearly died from double pneumonia. Denying these tales later, she declared, "I don't faint. A Bankhead just draws a second breath and comes out fighting."

During the dress rehearsal in Baltimore, Rose sat in the auditorium, using a microphone to give the crew orders on lighting the show. Unnerved, Bankhead screamed, "Stop it! I can't stand it. How can you expect me to concentrate when you keep screaming through that microphone?" Rose apologized, explaining that it was his mistake, as he thought that she was just rehearsing for the lights and not the lines. "My mistake," she barked back, "was being in the play." To which Cobb chimed in, "No. Your mistake was not realizing that my part steals the show." Rose calmed everyone down temporarily, but when Bankhead saw that the billing read, "Billy Rose Presents Tallulah Bankhead in *Clash by Night*," the heat was on again, with the star insisting that according to her contract, her name must come first. Rose and she fought bitterly over this billing, but Bankhead got her wish. In fact, Rose removed his name from the Belasco Theatre's marquee entirely, but still managed to technically outsmart Bankhead by installing a ten-foot-high electric sign on the roof that glared, "Billy Rose Presents." She badmouthed the producer everywhere, calling him "that little bully." His reply on learning this was "How can you bully Niagara Falls?" Rose later admitted that he admired her toughness. "Tallulah cost me a lot of dough, and she made me bite chunks out of my orchestra seat, but I couldn't help admiring this Humphrey Bogart in lace panties."

Considerable respect was granted the work of Cobb and Schildkraut, among the others. A number of effective character touches were added by such actors as John F. Hamilton as Jerry's senile father, Seth Arnold as a grubby old fascist uncle, and Art Smith as a drunk.

(1) CLAUDIA [Comedy-Drama/Family/Illness/Marriage/Rural/Sex] A/D: Rose Franken; SC: a series of short stories by the author; S: Donald Oenslager; P: John Golden; T: Booth Theatre; 2/12/41 (722)

Despite some definite reservations from the critics, this expertly directed hit was chosen as one of the ten best plays of the season. Rose Franken, who had not been represented on Broadway since 1932's hit, *Another Language**, returned with a work concerning the title character (Dorothy McGuire). Claudia, a comically naive young woman, is torn between her feelings for David Naughton (Donald Cook), her architect husband of one year, and her mother, Mrs. Brown (Frances Starr), on whom she is uncomfortably dependent, although the play does not unduly emphasize their close relationship. The play, set in a lovely, remodeled Connecticut farmhouse, charts this amusingly unself-conscious child-bride's gradual maturation over a period of twenty-four hours. Claudia is immature enough to listen in on the party line, a habit that rebounds when she overhears her mother tell David that she--the mother--has a fatal illness. The developments that stem from this revelation, combined with Claudia's almost simultaneous discovery of her pregnancy, are what lead to her new awakening as a mature woman. A minor issue along the way is incited when, convinced that she has no sex appeal for her husband, Claudia innocently allows a rakish British neighbor, Jerry Seymour (John Williams), to kiss her; David, though, turns out to be quite understanding about it all. There is also a subplot concerning a married couple (Frank Tweddell and Adrienne Gessner) employed by the Naughtons as servants. David learns that the husband served time for forgery, although it turns out that the crime was actually committed by the man's son.

The role of Claudia was acknowledged as an excellent example of character drawing, but Franken's attempt to mingle sentimentality and pathos with comic buoyancy did not please everyone. Brooks Atkinson (*NYT*), among others, noted, "In spite of the many attractive qualities that skip lightly through the pattern of *Claudia*, the emotional sequences are a little hard to take." Wilella Waldorf (*NYP*) was really turned off: ""Mrs. Franken's play struck us as an artificial and strangely unmoving affair from beginning to end." More approving was Rosamond Gilder (*TAM*), who commented on how effectively the small cast, one-set, non-socially significant play provided human entertainment: "So deeply has Miss Franken cut into the hearts of these people that their personalities and the crucial events of their two days take on the importance and immediacy of things lived. They become part of experience." Richard Watts, Jr. (*NYHT*), approvingly stated, "There is a forthright emotional quality about . . . *Claudia* that is deeply touching, and it is deftly mixed with so much natural humor and such sanity of heart and mind that the narrative . . . becomes one of the fine things of this . . . dramatic season."

The play was Dorothy McGuire's--whose principal earlier role was as Martha Scott's successor as Emily in *Our Town**--ticket to stardom (she later played Claudia in the movies). "Her youth, her childlike, sensitive face with its upturned nose, and *bombé* forehead, her solid, young figure, are all assets," wrote Gilder. "As an actress she has a natural ability to convey the darting, discontinuous, illogically logical processes of Claudia's thought through the transparent mask of her face. She has also the gift of relaxation; she can be present on the stage without restlessness or fidgeting."

Among the other fine performances, that of veteran Frances Starr was considered one of the finest of her career. The colorful minor role of an opera singer who wants to buy the Naughton home was played by Olga Baclanova.

The production closed on 3/7/42, after 453 showings, took a ten-week vacation, and then reopened on 5/24/42. That run's 269 performances brought the total to 722.

(2) [Return Engagement] T: St. James Theatre; 5/24/42 (269)

Two and a half months after it closed and went on tour, *Claudia* made a return engagement with its original cast in place. Because the sets had not arrived yet from Boston, producer John Golden presented a speech to the packed house, using a flashlight that he said was necessary because of the "dimout." The production was offered at low prices ranging from $.25 (at matinees) to $1.65 ($3.30 was the average top at the time), and he got a big hand for declaring that the theatre would come back to life if others also produced their plays at low admission prices. Golden said that he didn't expect to make a profit from the engagement, but if he did he would donate it to a war charity.

CLOSING DOOR, THE [Drama/Family/Marriage/Mental Illness] A: Alexander Knox; D: Lee Strasberg; S: Paul Morrison; C: Robert Stevenson; P: Cheryl Crawford; T: Empire Theatre; 12/1/49 (22)

Actor Alexander Knox, who also played its leading role of Vail Trahern, was the author of this split-decision psychological thriller. Doris Nolan, his wife, costarred with him as his onstage wife, Nora. Because it deals with insanity, much of the play consists of clinical discussions of mental illness. According to Brooks Atkinson (*NYT*), this was a fault; another was that "the playwriting is meandering and wordy, as though the author did not know much about the theatre." Hobe. (*V*) thought that "the play has undeniably tense moments, but the suspense is not sustained and there is too much esoteric palaver." One of those who liked the piece, however, was Howard Barnes (*NYHT*), for whom it was "taut and terrifying." William Hawkins (*NYWT*) thought that it was "rife with suspense and tension." The play had undergone a lot of tinkering out of town, and when it opened on Broadway it still listed in the program a deleted character (and the actor, Alan Norman, who played him).

Trahern, a photographer, lives with his wife, young son David (Jack Dimond), and mother-in-law (Eva Condon) in a shabby loft apartment with an elevator that lets people off in the living room. Nora and Dr. Harriman (Richard Derr) believe that Trahern, who blames his father and brother for his woes, is going mad. Nora wants to get him into an institution where he can be treated. She fires a trollopy maid (Jo Van Fleet) who taunts her husband. Trahern outfoxes his wife's plans and, instead of going off to the asylum, returns to the house and nearly kills his son, whom he has confused with his brother. The boy's unconscious body is hidden in a closet, and a bloody towel is a clue to his whereabouts. Before the play ends, a glint of hope dawns for the confused Vail when he realizes who was the victim of his violence. Still, when the curtain falls, he has not yet been carted off to the asylum. The cast included Ronald Alexander, John Shellie, and Randolph Echols.

CLUTTERBUCK [Comedy/British/Hotel/Marriage/Sea/Sex/Tropics] A: Benn W. Levy; D: Norris Houghton; S: Samuel Leve; C: Alvin Colt; P: Irving L. Jacobs i/a/w David Merrick; T: Biltmore Theatre; 12/3/49 (218)

A fairly popular piece of British fluff, reminiscent of Noël Coward, first produced in London in 1946, and chosen as one of the season's ten best for the Burns Mantle collection. The unusually named title character (Charles Campbell), a tall, slender, and charming fellow, is briefly seen twice but--except for the final curtain--never heard (he communicates by writing notes). The action is set for two of its three acts aboard a luxury liner cruising the tropics; the middle act is at a tropical hotel. The characters include a pair of bored young wives. Jane (Ruth Matteson) is married to Julian Pugh (Tom Helmore), a cynical author, and Deborah (Ruth Ford) to Arthur Pomfret (Arthur Margetson), a fatuous rubber planter. When the women see the strange but charming Clutterbuck on deck, they remember their premarital affairs with him in Venice. Their spouses, who initially hate each other, become friendlier on recalling their own affairs with the sexy, featherheaded, baby-talking redhead named Melissa (Claire Carleton), who married the man. Clutterbuck and the ladies successfully revive their romantic past, and the husbands attempt--without success--to reacquaint themselves with Melissa's allure. The women find their friendship revived, but the husbands regard each other with renewed hostility. At the end, Clutterbuck speaks up, delivering some amusingly condescending remarks of congratulations to his fellow actors.

Not much happened in the play, and it survived mainly because of its "light and twinkling dialogue," according to Robert Garland (*NYJA*). Most critics thought the piece an easily digestible soufflé in which the author had gotten a good deal out of thin materials. Richard Watts, Jr. (*NYP*), defined the piece as "a good, old-fashioned sex farce." John Chapman (*NYDN*) called it "amiable, foolish and politely naughty."

This "glib, sparse and entertaining" comedy (Ward Morehouse [*NYS*]) was given superlative comic performances by Helmore and Margetson, especially the latter, while the women did not come off quite as well. Brooks Atkinson (*NYT*) thought that the direction had failed seriously to capture the light and stylized manner required by such material, depending too heavily on a realistic approach. Not all the critics liked the play, Hobe. (*V*) reporting that it "offers only moderate laughs and becomes progressively tedious." The role of a Chinese waiter was played amusingly by Tom Chung Yun.

COCK-A-DOODLE-DO [Drama/Fantasy/Romance/Rural/Sex] A: Iris Tree; M: Ned Rorem; D: Margaret Barker; CH: ("stylized movement") Felicia Sorel; S: Wolfgang Roth; C: Forrest Thayer; P: Invitational Series of the Experimental Theatre u/t/a/o the American National Theatre and Academy; T: Lenox Hill Playhouse (OB); 2/27/49 (6)

Iris Tree's allegorical play was little more than "an embarrassingly coy excursion into symbolism and obfuscation," reported Brooks Atkinson (*NYT*). Only Wolfgang Roth's low-budget set managed to escape critical scorn. The disaster included such promising newcomers as Charlton Heston (in his local debut), Darren McGavin, and Margaret Feury, as well as players like Eunice Anderson, Katherine Squire, Elizabeth Parrish, John Martone, and Dennis Harrison.

The tale was of a farm girl (Feury) who encounters a mystical fellow (Heston) named Az; he tells the sheltered lass that he is "from the land's end, the sea's end, where grass meets water." Their magical encounter leads to the girl's pregnancy, and the question of paternity soon occupies the minds of the other characters. When she reveals the truth, she defends her baby's father by saying, "He's gold and silver, fire and butterflies--he's LOVE!" "It's the sort of play," wrote Vernon Rice (*NYP*), "in which most of the actors are required to wear ballet slippers, look starry-eyed and recite pseudo-poetic lines, which they or no one else have any idea what they mean."

COCKTAIL PARTY, THE [Drama/British/Films/Marriage/Religion/Sex/Verse] A: T. S. Eliot; D: E. Martin Browne; DS: Raymond Sovey; P: Gilbert Miller b/a/w Sherek Players; T: Henry Miller's Theatre; 1/21/50 (409)

T. S. Eliot's *The Cocktail Party* was one of the most talked-about plays of the decade and was considered a significant event in the literary as well as the theatrical world. The published version enjoyed the rare distinction, for a play, of becoming a best-seller. A major reason for the critical fuss was the attempt by "the greatest of living poets" (Richard Watts, Jr. [*NYP*]) to write about contemporary characters and situations in verse. Both the notion of using verse to capture the unique flavor of modern speech and the relative quality of that verse became interesting bones of contention. Eliot wanted his verse to be unobtrusive and even was willing to allow his audience to accept his verse for prose in less intense scenes. "He wishes," noted John Mason Brown (*SR*), "by the rhythms of his casual speeches, rhythms perhaps unnoticed by playgoers, to prepare for those crises when his characters have been lifted into poetry by the intensity of their feelings."

Eliot's play had premiered at the Edinburgh Festival in August 1949, where it played for five days before being brought to Broadway with the same mostly English cast. Almost everyone involved with the work had expected it to run briefly. No one was more surprised to see it become a hit than Eliot himself, who also complained that critics were reading political and moral ideas into it that he had not intended. Eliot claimed that the play was based on Euripides' *Alcestis*, although Eliot scholarship declares the 1937 Charles Williams novel *Descent into Hell* to be a more immediate source. It had not previously been produced in London, but since the American-born Eliot was a British subject, it is here categorized as a British play. It was, in fact, awarded the Drama Critics Circle Award as best foreign play of the season.

Lavinia Chamberlayne (Eileen Peel) has just left her middle-aged London barrister husband, Edward Chamberlayne (Robert Flemyng). Although she arranged a cocktail party for a number of friends, Edward is forced to host the event single-handedly. One of the guests is Celia Copplestone (Irene Worth, the American actress, who worked mainly in England), with whom Edward has been having an affair. Others are Peter Quilpe (Grey Blake), a young film writer in love with Celia, but also a lover of Lavinia's; a nosy old gossip, Julia Shuttlethwaite (Cathleen Nesbitt); a traveler named Alexander MacColgie Gibbs (Ernest Clark); and an unusually self-assured, gin-drinking stranger (Alec Guinness), whose preternatural understanding pierces the shells of the spiritually depleted central characters, and who many assumed was a reflection of Eliot himself. Edward reveals to him that Lavinia has left him, and the man tells him that he will get her back but that Edward must not interrogate her. When Celia returns, she is disillusioned to learn that Edward is not anxious to marry her, but instead wants Lavinia back. A day later, the stranger informs Edward that Lavinia will be returning, figuratively speaking, from the dead. Telegrams sent to the other guests at the cocktail party summon them to Edward's home, and Lavinia also arrives. Alone together, the Chamberlaynes snipe at one another, he now being sorry for wanting her back. Unable to live with her, Edward moves to his club. The couple confront one another in the consulting room of the stranger, who is actually Sir Henry Harcourt-Reilly, a fashionable psychiatrist (Eliot's modern-day substitute for a father confessor). Edward and Lavinia's affairs with, respectively, Celia and Peter are exposed, and the psychiatrist gets the couple to accept and live with these revelations and with their mutual flaws; not being saints, they must learn to live with a bad job by making compromises. After they leave, Celia appears. To help her find atonement for a sense of sin that burdens her, Reilly advises her to seek a terribly difficult journey toward salvation. Two years later, the Chamberlaynes, having reconciled and managed to live in mutual tolerance, if not understanding, are to throw another cocktail party. Julia and Alex appear, both of them intended to be figures as mystical as Reilly. Alex has exotic tales of his experiences on some little-known island called Kinkanja. Peter, now a successful film writer, appears and is told by Alex that Celia, who joined a Christian nursing order and went off to treat diseased native peoples, was crucified near an anthill during a political upheaval in Kinkanja. Reilly explains that her horrible death was also her salvation and that by it she achieved a triumphant spiritual destiny. The cocktail party that is the result of the Chamberlaynes' life choice begins.

Reviews for the three-hour, relatively actionless play, which was one of the Burns Mantle ten best of the season, ranged from the ecstatic to the moderately approving to the dismissive, although nearly every review praised the actors to the heavens. A widespread interpretation held that Eliot had divided people into two categories, the average human beings, who must accept life's second best, and the saintly beings, those who find meaning in life through sacrifice and giving. Critics who delighted in it praised it for its unusual blend of high comedy and serious intellectual intentions. John Chapman (*NYDN*) called the work "a masterpiece of the modern stage" that was "absorbing, compassionate, inspiring and extremely witty." He stated that the language was "verse because it is held to a deliberately contrived pattern of statement, even though there are no rhymes and jingles in it. It is poetry because it is beautiful." Watts thought it "an authentic modern masterpiece, one of the two or three finest plays of the post-war English speaking stage." He felt that one of its greatest virtues was that each viewer would find a personal meaning in it according to his or her own "qualities of heart and mind." Somewhere in the middle was Hobe. (*V*), who described the piece as "a talky, self-conscious and confusing comedy. But it is also a provocative and generally entertaining work." Like a number of others, he found the circumstances related to Celia's fate obscure, noted that Eliot was not always clear as to when he was being realistic and when satiric, and, while considering the dialogue and ideas sometimes witty and stimulating, felt that they were also often "cryptic and . . . self-indulgent." Brooks Atkinson (*NYT*) described himself as "one theatregoer who does not understand Mr. Eliot's dogma but recognizes that it is genuine and worth understanding by means of the script, since it is too compact and too allusive to be assimilated from the stage." Even more convinced that the play was a closet drama rather than a piece of theatre was William Hawkins (*NYWT*), who claimed that it "was more suited to reading than hearing. I can see little reason why the American public should attempt to embrace it in this form." Hawkins described the language as "simple and elegant rather than soaring or vivid. [Eliot's] dramaturgy is so elementary, that whatever symbolism may be involved in mechanical repetition is lost in monotony." Brown, who took issue with much of the work, noted of the language, "Although on the printed page it looks like poetry, when spoken it seldom explains why it has been set as verse."

All of the actors came in for superlative notices. Watt said of Guinness, whom he had never seen before, "On the basis of this one brilliant performance, I think it is quite possible that he is the most accomplished actor extant."

COME BACK, LITTLE SHEBA [Drama/Alcoholism/Marriage/Sex/Youth] A: William Inge; D: Daniel Mann; S/L: Howard Bay: C: Lucille Little; P: Theatre Guild; T: Booth Theatre; 2/15/50 (190)

Broadway was introduced to St. Louis's William Inge, who would become a Main Stream mainstay, with this powerful, naturalistic domestic drama in which Shirley Booth and Sidney Blackmer gave the greatest performances of their distinguished careers, both of them receiving Tonys for their work. Its six-month run was more the result of a low operating cost than a widely praised drama because not only were the reviews mixed (despite its being one of the Burns Mantle ten best of the season), but business slackened considerably after the first few weeks. The play had tried out at the Westport Country Playhouse in Connecticut, operated by John C. Wilson and Theatre Guild leaders Lawrence Langner and Armina Marshall.

The action is set in an old house in a midwestern city inhabited by a middle-aged couple, the slovenly Lola (Booth) and her recovering alcoholic husband Doc (Blackmer), a usually gentle, but inwardly pained chiropractor with a meagre practice. Lola sadly ponders her past and its lost promises. She and Doc, who belongs to Alcoholics Anonymous, were married twenty years earlier when she became pregnant, but the marriage meant the end of his medical training. To worsen matters, the baby died. The play's title comes from a white puppy Lola once owned; ever since it vanished, she has been vainly hoping it will reappear. Her calls for it to come back are symbolic calls for her youth to return. A pretty college girl named Marie (Joan Lorring) rooms with Doc and Lola. She is a bit loose with her abundant affections, being engaged to a boy in Chicago (Robert Cunningham) but accepting Turk (Lonny Chapman), a college athlete, in her bed. When Doc, who admires Marie and dislikes Turk, realizes that they have been sleeping together, he is so disturbed that he falls off the wagon. Losing his temper in an alcoholic binge, he blames Lola for his slip, even threatening her with a hatchet. Ultimately, however, he returns to Lola's sympathetic bosom.

This closely observed study of frustrated souls was notable for its air of humdrum, everyday reality, which made the moments of searing emotional intensity, when they came, seem like volcanic explosions. However, while considered touching and perceptive, and even likened to the method of Chekhov, the dramaturgy was widely believed to be too thin for a full evening of theatre. Some reviewers, like William Hawkins (*NYWT*), found themselves enthralled, but tended to point to the brilliant acting, and not the writing, as the cause. Whitney Bolton (*NYMT*) wrote of "two of the best performances available to the eye . . . and a play which does not match up to them but has its own moments of power." Richard Watts, Jr. (*NYP*), judged the work "a slender and unfulfilled play," but added that "it has too much honesty and insight to be readily dismissed." To him the play seemed more like an outline than a complete work because, after a strong start, it grew dramatically sparse. But Arthur Pollock (*DC*), while admitting that the play was not as "striking or subtle" as other works done by the Theatre Guild in the past, thought that it was exceptional in the quality of its emotional depth. "Mr. Inge knows that there is nothing more touching than the little things, when they are on the level. So his play, a kind of pathetic comedy, is quiet and leisurely." The excellent company included Olga Fabian as the neighbor, Mrs. Coffman, Daniel Reed as a cynical old postman, John Randolph as a milkman, Wilson Brooks as Ed, and Paul Krauss as Elmo.

Watts wrote of Blackmer, "Sympathetic without being maudlin and scientifically accurate without being clinical, his picture of a man driven back to alcohol . . . is managed with rare skill and credibility. And he has a scene of emotional breakdown which, instead of being embarrassing, is genuinely moving." Booth's performance was especially noteworthy, as her major past successes had usually been in the roles of wisecracking second leads. Calling her "superb," Brooks Atkinson (*NYT*) observed, "She has the shuffle, the maddening garrulity and the rasping voice of the slattern, but withal she imparts to the role the warmth, generosity and valor of a loyal and affectionate woman." While the play was being tried out in Westport, its author and director were both dissatisfied with Booth. They wanted her fired and Joan Blondell hired because she had a "stock-company approach to rehearsals," according to Richard Maney in *Fanfare*. "She shuffled through the role and mumbled her lines, they complained. In a rare spasm of sanity the Guild hierarchy vetoed the proposal."

COME MARCHING HOME [Drama/Politics] A: Robert Anderson; D: Dennis Gurney; S: Avril Gentles; C: Valerie; L: Ray Colcord; P: Blackfriars' Guild; T: Blackfriars' Theatre (OB); 5/18/46 (23)

Robert Anderson was at the beginning of his distinguished playwriting career when he offered this promising drama at Off-Broadway's Blackfriars' Theatre. It won the first prize in the 1945 National Theatre Conference contest aimed at overseas servicemen. Anderson was a naval officer in the Pacific when he penned it. It fell short of being a fully realized work, but its sincerity and integrity were lauded.

The subject was the obstacles placed in the path of a returning serviceman who wishes to enter politics but whose idealistic goals are frustrated by the crooked machine in the Eastern city where he lives. John Bosworth (Clark Howat) is the veteran who is resistant to the idea of running for state senator against the incumbent machine candidate until his physical well-being is threatened should he accept the nomination. Standing up to the corrupt party in power, he rejects attempts to bribe him, avoids threats of blackmail, and loses various supporters who want a more pragmatic approach than his ideals permit. Finally, with defeat staring him in the face, he remains in the race in order to make his voice heard, with success suggested sometime in the future when his cry for clean politics will be heeded.

L. C. (*NYT*) thought that the play "is marked by occasional passages of good writing, [but] it somehow fails to attain the theatrical forcefulness that one might expect from its provocative theme." George Jean Nathan (*TBY*) thought that the play failed because of "its rabble-rouser writing and its author's inability to make its theme proceed naturally from his characters." Cast members included Inge Adams, Robert Fierman, and Thomas G. Monahan.

COMES THE REVELATION [Comedy/Period/Religion/Rural/Sex] A: Louis Vittes; D: Herman Rotsten; S: Ralph Alswang; P: John Morris Chanin and Richard Karlan; T: Jolson Theatre; 5/26/42 (2)

Two performances were all that this monotonous, popular-priced comedy set in 1827 Dorking, New York, could muster for a story described by its author as "a satire on the growth of a typical demagogue." It tells of a lazy farm boy named Joe Flanders (Wendell Corey), who, upon reading a book about the Indians being the lost tribes of Israel, declares that he has been called to preach his version of the gospel. Blessed with the gift of gab, this wenching charlatan convinces many of his neighbors of his vision, which includes polygamy (leading his wife to leave him), nonpayment of taxes, and land promotion. He induces his followers to invest in swampland properties that he recommends on the advice of a pair of con men. Trouble brews when these investments do not pan out. Joe's proclivity for extramarital sex also gets him in hot water, but he talks his way out of danger and leads his followers off to Ohio.

The play reminded some of an inferior *Tobacco Road**, partly because of the presence of Will Geer, who had played Jeeter Lester, in the role of Joe's drunken father, and partly because of its backwoods speech and ruttish humor. According to Louis Kronenberger (*PM*), "Mr. Vittes has no real sense of theater, no way of keeping a play within bounds, and only the most intermittent knack for dialogue." Corey gave an admirable performance, considering his ill-conceived role, and was ably assisted by a cast including Audra Lindley as the sister-in-law he seduces, Lesley Woods as his long-suffering wife, Grover Burgess, and others.

COMMAND DECISION [Drama/Aviation/Military/Politics/War] A: William Wister Haines; D: John O'Shaughnessy; S/L: Jo Mielziner; C: Julia Sze; P: Kermit Bloomgarden; T: Fulton Theatre; 10/1/47 (409)

A strongly dramatic hit play based on events of World War II experienced personally by the author. When Haines, already known as a novelist, submitted it to his publishers, they suggested that he novelize it, and the result was a best-seller. Meanwhile, he attempted to peddle the script to producers, several of whom took options but let them lapse, usually on the grounds that the public would not buy a war play so soon after the cessation of hostilities. But Kermit Bloomgarden decided to risk it. Before its New York showing, however, the play received the then-unusual benefit of a tryout production (with a different cast) at the Cleveland Playhouse in 1946, with the author attending the entire five weeks of rehearsal and revising as needed. The play was one of Burns Mantle's ten best of the season.

Its action is set entirely in a Nissen hut in England, in the office of Brigadier General K. C. Dennis (Paul Kelly), Headquarters of the 5th American Bombardment Division, Heavy. The time is before the invasion of Germany. Dennis must send his division on a series of three suicidal bombing missions deep into Germany where they will be unprotected by fighter planes, who will be out of range. The targets are just-discovered jet-plane manufacturing centers. When the death toll of American flyers rises dramatically, Washington's military upper echelons grow jittery. Dennis is even considered a murderer by visiting politician Arthur Malcolm (Paul Ford). Dennis's superior officer, Major General Kane (Jay Fassett), supports him, but quakes before the power of Washington's influence. Dennis agonizes over the loss of American lives and the need to prevent even further losses if the targeted jets ever get off the ground. He must act with ice-cold determination and ruthless logic if his goals are to be realized. But, under congressional pressure, Kane replaces Dennis with his friend, Brigadier General Garnett (Paul McGrath), who is not thrilled with the assignment. Dennis ends up being sent to China, but his replacement, thought to be more tractable, gives the order for the final mission against the factories.

The play was appreciated as a piece of solid theatre, melodramatically tense and psychologically engrossing, but far from being a work of art. It occasionally suffered from excessively long climactic speeches and contrived situations, but it also came to grips with potent ideas and expressed an individualistic point of view. Haines's close familiarity with the details of air-force procedures gave the work a sense of realism and integrity, and the presentation benefited from a razor-sharp cast that seemed completely authentic. George Jean Nathan (*TBY*) continued to prefer Harry Brown's *A Sound of Hunting* as the premiere World War II drama, but said that "here is three-fourths of an effective runner-up." His main argument was against the author's infusion of bothersome sentimentality into his drama. John Mason Brown (*SR*), though, said that *Command Decision* was "the most effective drama so far to have come out of this war." "As playwriting, it may have its jagged and routine moments; as produced, it is theatre of an exceptionally compelling kind." "Mr. Haines has succeeded in bringing this poignant issue with all its subsidiary implications into action on the stage through his sharp characterization of the personalities involved and the tension created by the conflict of opinion," observed Rosamond Gilder (*TAM*).

Kelly as the tortured Dennis gave "a superb performance," praised Brooks Atkinson (*NYT*), "hard, rational, driving." Kelly was one of three male actors receiving Tonys for their acting in 1948. Expert jobs in the all-male company also were contributed by Fassett, Ford, Lewis Martin as Major Lansing, John Randolph as Lieutenant Jake Goldberg, James Holden as Captain Lee, Stephen Elliott as Colonel Edward Martin, Arthur Franz as Captain Lucius Jenks, Edward Binns as Colonel Ernest Haley, Edmon Ryan as a war correspondent, and, in particular, James Whitmore (in his debut) as the cynical, wisecracking Sergeant Evans (the only enlisted man among the characters). Whitmore's role gave the usually grim play the necessary leaven of humor and was one of the most memorable things in the show.

COMMON GROUND [Drama/Jews/Journalism/Military/Politics/Show Business] A: Edward Chodorov; D: Edward Chodorov and Jerome Robbins; S/L: George Jenkins; P: Edward Choate; T: Fulton Theatre; 4/25/45 (69)

Choreographer Jerome Robbins's first job as a director of straight drama came with this play, on which he shared his duties with the author. Since the play involves a USO troupe that at one point does its act, Robbins's dance-oriented talents were likely to have come in especially handy in dealing with that material.

Common Ground was yet another war play, this one dealing with a troupe of American performers whose plane, touring to American camps in Italy, is forced down by the Nazis behind enemy lines shortly before the Allied capture of Naples. The troupe contains a wide range of ethnic types, representing the American melting pot, with Alan Spencer (Donald Murphy), a movie star of German ancestry; Buzz Bernard (Philip Loeb), the wisecracking Jewish comedian and MC; Nick (Joseph Vitale) and Kate DeRosa (Nancy Noland), a married vaudeville team, he being of Italian background and she of Irish; and Geegee (Mary Healy), a movie starlet of old American stock. The Gestapo, occupying the picturesquely bombed-out ruins of an Italian castle, intimidates them, and each reacts in his or her individual way, from the arrogance of the Italian to the casualness of the Jew and the cowardice of the nonethnic American. An anti-Semitic turncoat American journalist (Paul McGrath) also does what he can to bend his countrymen's minds. After they are forced to give a show, the company--apart from the Jew, who will be sent to a concentration camp--is offered immunity if its members use their talents on behalf of the Nazi cause; their alternative is to be shot. After some initial hesitation, the individual reasons for which consume some time, the entertainers accept death before compromise, although the hitherto spineless singer does not come around until the last minute. They walk off to their execution with a song on their lips.

Most critics found the material promising and the first act good, but the overall drama mediocre, preachy, and muddled. Lewis Nichols (*NYT*) contended that it "jumps from shrillness to extended wordiness, and midway through it changes its theme. Starting as an attack on the enemy, it ends by an account of how a group of Americans discovered they were Americans." The roles of an Italian captain (Luther Adler) and a German colonel (Peter Von Zerneck) were deemed caricaturish, the ending was hokey, and the dialogue often seemed to critics such as Euphemia Van Rensselaer Wyatt (*CW*) like a string of monologues. George Jean Nathan (*TBY*) accused the author of pasting together clichés from a dozen or more older plays, all of which were accompanied by "so many repetitious and dramaless speeches that one feels one is not in a theatre but at an indignation meeting at Carnegie Hall."

Philip Loeb's performance, ranging from amusing jocularity to brave acceptance of his fate, was most highly praised. Adler, however, was panned for an excessively theatrical performance, which he had to play in Italian. Lou Gilbert played an Italian soldier.

CONCERT VARIETIES [Revue] M: Morton Gould and others; CH: Jerome Robbins, Katherine Dunham, and others; DS: Carl Kent ("Interplay" ballet); P: Billy Rose; T: Ziegfeld Theatre; 6/1/45 (36)

Composer Deems Taylor was the dignified MC of this dance-oriented revue in which Billy Rose sought to create a concert-hall-type program with a Broadway touch. In it, youthful choreographic genius Jerome Robbins played an important part. Robbins danced with seven others, including John Kriza, Michael Kidd, and Janet Reed, in his ballet "Interplay," with music by Morton Gould (his "American Concertette"). The charming, if self-consciously cute, piece was based on dance games and demonstrated such interplay as that between "classical ballet and the contemporary spirit," as the program put it. Katherine Dunham led her dance troupe through three of her well-known, colorful Latin American routines, "Callate," "Rhumba," and "Tropics." Spanish and gypsy dance was represented by Rosario and Antonio, nightclub artistes. Popular comedienne Imogene Coca was on hand with William Archibald to deflate terpsichorean pretensions with their burlesque version of "Afternoon of a Faun."

The show was considered by Wilella Waldorf (*NYP*) to be too heavy on dance and not enough on comedy, although Zero Mostel did what he could to rectify the imbalance, especially with his parody of an Italian tenor, his mockery of a senatorial diatribe (already a tired part of his routine), and his imitation of a percolator. Another comic was Eddie Mayehoff, who did not satisfy the critics. Coca did some nondancing comedy, but was defeated by flat material. There was also the black boogie-woogie pianist and drummer team of Albert Ammons, Pete Johnson, and Sidney Catlett, and Latino tenor Nestor Chayres. Some thought that the most memorable part of the program was a marionette act called the Salici Puppets; one of its wooden performers startled spectators by lighting a cigarette and blowing smoke, and another did a remarkable job of playing a piano in perfect synchronization with an offstage performance. Their act concluded with the Salicis revealing themselves and their manipulation of the strings.

The show garnered mixed reviews, Robert Garland (*NYJA*) calling it "bright, brittle and vastly entertaining," while Burton Rascoe (*NYWT*) dismissed it as "on the sedate and cultural side."

CONCERTO FOR FUN [Miscellaneous/Solo] T: Mansfield Theatre; 5/9/49 (16)

A one-man show by a comedian and piano player named Henry L. Scott, whose gumption in assuming that he was worthy of a two-week engagement on Broadway had some critics scratching their heads. His routines included playing the keyboard with mittens, with his heels, with a grapefruit and orange, and with the cover shut, spoofing various playing styles, satirizing famous concert artists, and the like. Some of it was funny, but there was not enough to last for ninety minutes. His straight renditions included "Policinelle," "Second Hungarian Rhapsody," and the "Minute Waltz." As music critic Harold Schonberg (*NYS*) suggested, "It is night-club material, some of it amusing, some of it forced, none of it particularly inventive."

CONNECTICUT YANKEE, A [Musical Revival*] B: Herbert Fields; M/P: Richard Rodgers; LY: Lorenz Hart; D: John C. Wilson; CH: William Holbrook and Al White; DS: Nat Karson; T: Martin Beck Theatre; 11/17/43 (135)

A revival of the 1927 hit show based on Mark Twain's story, with Dick Foran taking the title role and Vivienne Segal portraying Queen Morgan La Fay. Vera-Ellen was Mistress Evelyn La Rondelle, Robert Chisholm was Arthur, Robert Byrn was Sir Kay, Julie Warren was the Demoiselle, John Cherry was Merlin, Katherine Anderson was Queen Guinevere, Stuart Casey was Sir Launcelot, Chester Stratton was Sir Galahad, and Jere McMahon was Sir Gawain.

A major reason for the revival was to occupy Lorenz Hart, who was then in the last stages of physical debilitation brought on by alcoholism. Revising the show did have a tonic effect, if only a temporary one, on the lyricist, who wrote half a dozen new songs to replace four of the originals. The best was the scintillatingly clever "To Keep My Love Alive," written for Segal and telling of how Morgan La Fay gets rid of unwanted spouses.

During this creative period, Hart remained on the wagon, but when his duties ended, he went on a binge that exacerbated his respiratory problems and landed him in the hospital. On the night of the opening he was very drunk and stood at the rear of the house. When Segal began singing "To Keep My Love Alive," he joined in with her, his voice growing so loud that people tried to shush him. He was then removed against his will to the lobby, where the audience, breaking just then for intermission, saw the embarrassing sight of him being ejected against his will by the theatre management. Soon he was dangerously ill and hospitalized. Five days after the opening, during a momentary air-raid- warning blackout, he died.

The revival was fairly faithful apart from the updating of the prologue, now set in 1943 and showing the predream characters as officers in the navy, WAVEs, and WACs. The score was given arrangements that reflected the swing rhythms of the day, and some of the older lyrics (as in "Thou Swell") were touched with 1943 ideas. In one newly written scene the locale was a munitions factory, which gave an excuse for a "Ye Lunchtime Follies" sequence parodying the "Lunchtime Follies" shows offered for munitions workers during the war. It featured a takeoff on Frank Sinatra by Chester Stratton. The show's most popular tune remained "My Heart Stood Still."

For some, there was a lassitude about the revival that not even its use of contemporary slang and lavish settings could dispel. Euphemia Van Rensselaer Wyatt (*CW*) complained, "Like some overstuffed furniture, this revival . . . suffers from the enervating sumptuousness of its own upholstery." Lewis Nichols (*NYT*) liked most of the show, but admitted that the book was sluggish in the first act and that "moments all through its length are not so funny as they would be in the best of all possible worlds." Yet Rosamond Gilder (*TAM*) approved, testifying that the show "has the color, the laughter, the richness and verve which make for good entertainment." The best reviews for performers went to Segal and dancer Vera-Ellen, although the latter's singing left something to be desired.

CONSUL, THE [Musical/Marriage/Politics] B/M/LY/D: Gian-Carlo Menotti; CH: John Butler; S: Horace Armistead; C: Grace Houston; L: Jean Rosenthal; P: Chandler Cowles and Efrem Zimbalist, Jr.; T: Ethel Barrymore Theatre; 3/15/50

(269)

Composer-librettist-director Gian-Carlo Menotti followed up the success of his 1947 operas for Broadway, "The Telephone" and *The Medium* with this "intensely dramatic and moving" (George Jean Nathan [*TBY*]) operatic success. The work was inspired both by a newspaper story about a woman who killed herself when unable to obtain a visa and by Menotti's own autobiographical experiences. It was successful enough to be awarded the best musical of the season award of the Drama Critics Circle.

Menotti created a true cold war opera in this serious work set in an unnamed police state beyond the Iron Curtain. John Sorel (Cornell MacNeil) is trying to flee the country for a freer land and has instructed his wife Magda (Patricia Neway) to obtain passports for herself, their child, and his mother (Marie Powers) so that they can meet up with him at the border. Both the baby and the mother die from the deprivations of poverty. Magda encounters the crushing bureaucracy of red tape involved in obtaining a passport from the consulate. The consul's coldly impersonal secretary (Gloria Lane) continually impedes her progress, as does a special agent (Leon Lishner) of the state, who always seems to be watching her. When she is finally allowed in to see the ever-occupied consul, she is shocked to discover that he is the very same agent who has been shadowing her. Totally frustrated in her attempts, she asks God for forgiveness and commits suicide by gassing herself.

The work was hailed for its individualistic musical achievement as well as its outstanding expression of a frightening human situation. Those who normally were averse to opera in English had to make an exception for *The Consul*. Menotti mingled realism, melodrama, satire, and surrealistic stylization, the latter in two nightmarish dream episodes used to heighten certain moments. In one, seen as the wife is dying, her husband, mother, and others whom the system has driven to their deaths appear in their coffin clothes.

Miles Kastendieck (*CSM*) was overwhelmed by the piece and referred to Menotti as "the great hope of modern opera. Not only has he created an important human document, but he has invested it with dramatic and musical intensity. Few moments on the stage of today are more heart-rending or more sincerely moving in the expression of anguish and despair." Howard Barnes (*NYHT*) believed that Menotti "has achieved scenes of high theatrical excitement and moments of genuine poignance. . . . The performances have the proper flourish, the settings and costumes are effective, and the musical accompaniment gives added eloquence to the writing."

The outstanding company included George Jongeyans (later Gaynes), Andrew McKinley, and the voice of Mabel Mercer. Patrica Neway walked off with the performance honors but, at two shows a week, her role was sung by Vera Bryner, herself the daughter of a former consul.

CONTRAST, THE [Dramatic Revival] A: Royall Tyler; D: Eliza Downing; S: Hubbell Pierce; P: On-Stage; T: 6 Fifth Avenue (OB); 7/22/48 (6)

During the summer of 1948, the Off-Broadway company called On-Stage performed a series of old American plays at a tiny space in the National Academy of Vocal Arts, a brownstone on lower Fifth Avenue. Among its offerings was patriot Royall Tyler's historically important social comedy *The Contrast*, written in 1787 and soon after premiered at New York's John Street Theatre.

The long-disused piece, acknowledged as America's first professionally produced comedy, still proved to have "a lot of charm and vitality and a good comic sense," wrote Richard Watts, Jr. (*NYP*). The production was not as good as the play, however. "If there is a general fault in the group," suggested William Hawkins (*NYWT*), "it is that the actors playing the lushes overdo their mannerisms until they fail to make their points."

The comedy of manners satirizes the colonialists' fondness for European fashions and ideas and comes out firmly for solid American virtues. It includes romance, satire, and patriotism and introduces the important character of the Yankee servant Jonathan (Scott Cooley), who would become a key character type in nineteenth-century American theatre.

(1) CORN IS GREEN, THE [Comedy-Drama/British/School/Sex/Youth] A: Emlyn Williams; D/P: Herman Shumlin; S: Howard Bay; C: Ernest Schrapps; T: National Theatre; 11/26/40 (477)

A season that thus far had found its only interest in comic material came face to face with a strong play in this highly successful autobiographical work by Welsh dramatist-actor Emlyn Williams, who had played the male lead in the original 1938 London version opposite Dame Sybil Thorndike. It closed in London because of the bombardment; Williams's desire to re-create his role on Broadway was abandoned when he joined the armed forces.

His moving play, set sometime in the 1890s, depicts the strenuous efforts of a heroically dedicated middle-aged spinster, Miss Moffat (Ethel Barrymore), to bring the light of education to the grimy youth of Glansarno, a poverty-stricken Welsh coal-mining village, where the boys go off to the mines at the age of twelve. Despite the objections of the pompous squire (Edmond Breon), she goes ahead with her plan to open a school in a nearby barn. Her principal inspiration is Morgan Evans (Richard Waring), a lad with unusual promise as a writer. She takes him under her wing and, over a two-year period, helps to lift him from the darkness in which his life would otherwise have been shrouded and to set him on the path of enlightenment. Several impediments to Morgan's progress arise. One occurs when Morgan threatens to return to the mines after his friends call him a sissy. Another stems from his seduction by Bessie Watty (Thelma Schnee), the sluttish teenage daughter of the housekeeper (Rosalind Ivan). Bessie's subsequent pregnancy and demand that Morgan marry her are introduced, but the threat is short-circuited by Miss Moffat's agreement to adopt the baby herself so that Morgan can go to Oxford. The suspenseful highlight comes when Morgan sits down to take the Oxford scholarship examination, which he passes. By the end of the play, Miss Moffat, too, has grown in stature as she moves from militant truculence to sincere warmheartedness.

The play was deemed uncommonly touching and human, its characters representative of a wide spectrum of closely observed individuals, from the stupid to the smart, from the fatuous to the farseeing. Although its slim story and various plot contrivances were noted, most critics were exceedingly taken by the drama. "Mr. Williams has written a play of devotion and wisdom," declared Brooks Atkinson (*NYT*), "and the people who have put it on the stage share his respect for the human truth it represents." Rosamond Gilder (*TAM*) noted, "The miracle of *The Corn Is Green* is not that it is a great or even an important play but that it is authentic and alive in its own right and that, concerning itself with things that matter, it makes those things seem of the utmost importance right there and then on stage." Burns Mantle chose it as one of the ten best of the year, and the New York Drama Critics Circle picked it as the best foreign play of the season.

The Corn Is Green was directed with uncommon skill and played with brilliance. As the feminist teacher, Ethel Barrymore, in her first hit in a dozen years, received many ovations. At first, she rejected the role in favor of *International Incident**, which added to her string of failures. The producer who had offered her the role, Victor Payne-Jennings, also had failed to cast the petite Helen Hayes in the part, because Hayes, despite having successfully acted the six-foot Mary of Scotland, thought herself too small for the part. When Payne-Jennings was unable to find a proper actress for Miss Moffat, he sold his rights in the play to Herman Shumlin, and this producer used his persuasive powers to talk Barrymore into doing it. It became the most successful role of her half-century career. John Mason Brown (*NYP*) stated that she "gives the finest, most thoughtful, and most concentrated performance she has given in many years. . . . Where in the past Miss Barrymore has often been content to be Miss Barrymore and nothing more . . . in *The Corn Is Green* she shows freshly found capacities as an actress. She listens vigilantly. Her mind is always upon what is happening. . . . All her latent nobility is mobilized, protected by the sheer sunshine of her humor, and given full advantage of her thinking and her charm." Producer Shumlin once told actor Tony Randall that on opening night Miss Moffatt was telling a secret to another woman when Barrymore suddenly went up on her lines. She told the other, "Don't move," walked offstage, got the line, returned, covered with, "It's all right, she's not around," and went on with her secret (reported in *Which Reminds Me*).

Richard Waring as the fifteen-year-old Morgan (the English-born Waring was actually twenty-eight) was also very warmly praised. Sidney B. Whipple (*NYWT*) pointed to "a performance that was vivid, compelling and as real to life as life itself." The expert cast included in its secondary roles such players as Mildred Dunnock as Miss Ronberry, a skittish spinster, and Rhys Williams as John Goronwy Jones."

(2) [Return Engagement] T: Martin Beck Theatre; 5/3/43 (56)

After it closed, the show went on a grueling, 23,000-mile, 383-performance transcontinental tour and then--two and a half years after its first Broadway showing--reopened at popular prices ($2.20 top). Barrymore and Waring remained in their former roles, but there were minor changes elsewhere in the cast. These included Perry Wilson as Bessy Watty; Tom E. Williams taking over from his brother Rhys as John Goronwy Jones; Eva Leonard-Boyne as Mrs. Watty; Esther Mitchell as Miss Ronbury; and Lewis L. Russell as the new squire. The corn still seemed green to the critics, who continued to shower the play with accolades, although there was some disagreement over the relative quality of the cast replacements.

(3) [Dramatic Revival] D: Herman Shumlin and Edward McHugh; S/L: Peter Wolf; C: Emeline Roche; P: New York City Theatre Company; T: City Center of Music and Drama; 1/11/50 (16)

Maurice Evans was the artistic director of the four-play series at the City Center of which this revival was the second production offered. The play, said Brooks Atkinson (*NYT*), had "lost none of its excitement and force." "It still has point, insight, acumen, human interest and drollery," asserted Thomas R. Dash (*WWD*). But Howard Barnes (*NYHT*) thought that "the revival misses much of the meaning and poignancy of the Williams work." William Hawkins (*NYWT*) felt that "the play seems to lack the distinction it originally appeared to have. Without any elevated writing, it remains a distinctly literate play, carefully put together, with a few urgent moments." George Jean Nathan (*TBY*) was at a loss to explain why *The Corn Is Green* had been selected for the City Center season, claiming, "The play is of no consequence."

The new Miss Moffat was Eva Le Gallienne, but Richard Waring (now thirty-eight) repeated his 1940 role of Morgan Evans. Le Gallienne had toured with the play the previous summer. Comparing Le Gallienne to Ethel Barrymore, Atkinson noted, "Miss Le Gallienne's swifter and more restless style is thoroughly persuasive, and she plays the part exceedingly well. What Miss Moffat . . . loses in imperiousness she makes up in drive, dedication and nervous energy." Arthur Pollock (*DC*) declared, "Miss Le Gallienne is a much perkier spinster. . . , vigorous and alert, sharpening up everything she does where Miss Barrymore got her effects with suavity." But Barnes believed that "Miss Le Gallienne is ill at ease throughout most of the proceedings." He faulted her for "failing to make her portrayal the combination of affection and wisdom that it should have been." Whitney Bolton (*NYMT*) regretted to say that "Miss Eva Le Gallienne is not at the top of her profession as the school teacher." In the very good supporting cast, Carmen Mathews played Miss Ronberry, Gwilym Williams played John Goronwy Jones, Robin Craven played the squire, Darthy Hinkley played Bessie Watty, and Eva Leonard-Boyne played Mrs. Watty.

COUNSELLOR-AT-LAW [Dramatic Revival*] A/D: Elmer Rice; S/L: Raymond Sovey; P: John Golden; T: Royale Theatre; 11/24/42 (258)

A hit revival of the successful 1931 drama, with Paul Muni repeating his role of attorney George Simon, bred the hard way on the Lower East Side, but having risen to power in the courts of criminal and divorce law. It was his performance in this role that led to his Hollywood stardom. A number of his original company's members returned for the occasion as well, and the resultant ensemble was considered one of the finest then playing. Most important was Jennie Moscowitz as George's mother, while smaller roles were repeated by Sam Bonnell, William Vaughan, and Elmer Brown. Among the principals, Jack Sheehan was the knavish

Charles McFadden; Olive Deering now played Regina Gordon, the secretary; Joan Wetmore was Cora Simon, George's bitter society wife; Clara Langsner offered a portrait of another Jewish matron as Sarah Becker; Joseph Pevney was the Communist Harry Becker (his once-ringing excoriation of capitalism now seemed comic and pathetic); and Ann Thomas acted Bessie Green, the Brooklyn-accented switchboard operator, and provided considerable comic relief.

According to Jerome Lawrence's *Actor*, when Muni asked Thomas how she achieved such an excellent Brooklyn accent, she replied, "By listening. . . . Brooklynites aren't as confused about their *R*'s as most people think. They don't say 'goil' for girl. They say, 'She's a very modrin gurrl'--like that." "In the modrin theater," said Muni to her, "you are my kind of gurrrl!"

Rice made some minor changes in the script, adding a few topical references (such as Joe DiMaggio for Babe Ruth, and a flight from La Guardia for a French Line sailing), placing its action in "spring 1939", and toning down its hero's leftist sympathies while making him seem more a grasping shyster than before. Rosamond Gilder (*TAM*) was one of many who felt that the play was still a solid piece of "theatre craftsmanship, a play built up of a hundred pieces of closely observed character and detailed business, all fitted together into a closely knit whole. If the speciousness of the plot is more striking today than when the play was first produced, the sharpness of character etching, the ingenuity of structure, the raciness of dialogue in Mr. Rice's play stand out as brilliantly as ever." In Richard Lockridge's (*NYS*) view, the play's edges had softened considerably, "but if it is not quite what it used to be, it is still an abundant and satisfying play."

Muni's performance was even richer than when he had first played the part and was a major reason for the revival's success. "With a soft voice and a loud roar," wrote Lewis Nichols (*NYT*), "with quietness, gentleness and fierceness in turn, he dominates the role as though he had started with it years before, as a child selling papers on the East Side, and had risen with it to the Fifth Avenue office of Simon and Tedesco. In the one role he is seven or eight Paul Munis, smooth and accurately setting forth as many phases as there are types crossing the threshold of the office."

During the post-Broadway tour, the play was presented in an un-air-conditioned Boston theatre, where the swish-swish of the audience's programs being used as fans was a sore distraction for the outraged star. Refusing to accept any explanations from the company manager, he decided to act so well that the audience would forget the heat and humidity. This seemed to work for a while, "But," said the manager later, "in the middle of Act Two, the audience wins. Muni picks up a sheaf of papers from George Simon's desk, walks to the apron rim, sits down with his feet dangling into the orchestra pit, fashions the papers into an improvised wind maker, and fans himself in tempo with the audience programs. The curtain has to come down, Muni's pulled offstage." The audience was given refunds, apologies were profferred all around, "and it never happened again" (quoted in Lawrence, *Actor*).

COUNT ME IN [Musical/Family/Military/War] B: Walter Kerr and Leo Brady; M/LY: Ann Ronell; D: Robert Ross (production "supervised" by Harry A. Kaufman); CH: Robert Alton; S: Howard Bay; C: Irene Sharaff and Freddy Wittop; P: Messrs. Shubert, Ole Olsen, and Chic Johnson i/a/w Richard W. Krakeur and W. Horace Schmidlapp; T: Ethel Barrymore Theatre; 10/8/42 (61)

Future drama critic Walter Kerr, then an instructor at Washington, D.C.,'s Catholic University, was a principal creator of this musical that came to Broadway after first being done as a campus show staged by the Reverend G. V. Hartke, O.P., with a cast of graduate students. Collaborator Leo Brady was also on the Catholic University faculty. It seemed so good in this version that a professional company was formed and the show brought to Boston, where it had a rousing response. On Broadway, however, *Count Me In* was counted out, largely because of "a lethargic and verbose libretto" (Abel. [*V*]). Lewis Nichols (*NYT*) yawned, "The writing is hackneyed; the lines are flat. Never was there a book that kept pushing the show off the stage so aggressively as this one." Kerr later confessed that he was too green to know what was happening as the show was inflated for Broadway standards. "What had been a sly, small, intimate show in Washington was blown up into a monster, and when you made it that big it wouldn't work anymore" (quoted in Fred Fehl, *On Broadway*).

The $65,000 show concerned a family's attempts to contribute to the war effort. Mama Brandywine (Luella Gear) is a sergeant in the WAAPS, daughter Sherry Brandywine (Mary Healy) is a Red Cross worker, son Alvin York Brandywine (Hal LeRoy) is an air-raid warden, and son Teddy B. Roosevelt Brandywine (Gower Champion) is in the air force. The harried, Milquetoastish Papa Brandywine (Charles Butterworth, returning to Broadway after a decade in Hollywood), desperate to assist as well (he meets constant rebuffs), is a mapmaker who tricks some Japanese spies in a Virginia internment camp by selling them a phony map he saw in a dream. When the Japanese navy suffers defeat because of his deception, the father is awarded a medal and gets to wear a uniform.

The undistinguished, derivative score (by the composer of the music for the famous Walt Disney cartoon, *The Big Bad Wolf*) was not abetted by effective lyrics or laughworthy comedy. Ronell was credited with being the first woman to write both music and lyrics for a Broadway musical. In the course of developing the show for Broadway, it had become loaded down with so many production elements that the original material simply could not support it. As Rosamond Gilder (*TAM*) observed, "The original book and Ann Ronell's music and lyrics as well are swamped in a welter of production numbers and specialties, some of them excellent, others tedious." Moreover, "There is not one moment of real human interest or even real sentiment in *Count Me In*," grumbled Euphemia Van Rensselaer Wyatt (*CW*).

Much of the show's humor satirized the distaff side's military involvement. Dance, as created by Robert Alton, was the musical's major contribution, especially as practiced by the lightning limbs of LeRoy, the outstanding talents of dance team Gower and Jeanne (Champion), tap dancer June Preisser, and eccentric dancer Alice Dudley, and in the show-stopping comic routine, "Who Is General Staff?" performed by a quartet of deceived Japanese (the Rhythmaires) led by Mr. Moto (Joe E. Marks). Also memorable were the exceptionally vivid red, white, and blue costumes of Irene Sharaff and the comic performances of Gear and Butterworth in underwritten roles.

COUNTERATTACK [Drama/Military/Politics/Russian/Sex/War] A: Janet and Philip Stevenson; SC: a play by Ilya Vershinin and Mikhail Ruderman; D: Margaret Webster; S: John Root; P: Lee Sabinson; T: Windsor Theatre; 2/3/43 (85)

Rather than being credited as adaptors of an earlier play, Janet and Philip Stevenson were billed as authors of a work originally written by a Soviet writing team. Their grim melodramatic war drama, excitingly staged by Margaret Webster, is set in a realistically depicted cellar in a small town somewhere on the Eastern Front in 1942 (the set and action were reminiscent of *Proof Thro' the Night*, another war play from earlier in the season). Eight unarmed Germans, seven men and a nurse (Barbara O'Neil, the play's only female), are trapped in the filthy cellar of a collapsing house, held prisoner there by two Red Army soldiers, the older Kulkov (Morris Carnovsky), and Kirichenko (Sam Wanamaker), the naive younger man who insists on shaving daily and who is later wounded by a German in an escape attempt. The job of the Reds is to interrogate the Nazis. A gripping battle of wits ensues as the jailers fight to keep the upper hand and prevent the wily prisoners, who try various tricks, from gaining their weapons and taking their lives. When the young Russian is wounded, the task of the other one becomes increasingly difficult. Things get more tense when, during a counterattack, an explosion closes all exits from the cellar and it is likely that all will die there of starvation. As time passes, the Communist and fascist points of view are held up and compared. The Communists display surprising humanity in their equal rationing of the available food and water. The attractive nurse is saved from being raped by her countrymen by the humane Soviets. A German miner (Martin Wolfson) is converted to the Marxist attitude and after three days, when things seem about to go the Germans' way, helps the Russians to regain control. All is saved when other Russians arrive to save their trapped comrades. A principle element of the suspense generated by the question of who will arrive as rescuers, the Germans or the Russians, is also thereby answered.

Some thought this an effectively tense melodrama, enlivened by an intriguing dose of political content and compellingly played. Others attacked it as obvious Soviet propaganda and could not believe the gentle treatment accorded their prisoners by the Red soldiers. Ward Morehouse (*NYS*) declared, "Much of it is taut, tricky, exciting stuff; some of it is static and tedious." Louis Kronenberger (*PM*) said, "It succeeds in being pretty good theater at the cost of being very bad drama, sacrificing too much that should appeal to your heart and mind for a straight assault on your blood pressure." A major point of confusion stemmed from the fact that neither side was supposed to understand the language of the other.

Rosamond Gilder (*TAM*) commended Morris Carnovsky for doing "a thoroughly convincing job with a part that provided material for his particular type of detailed and thoroughly explored performance. The last act, where after sleepless days and nights of fighting and watching he tries to keep awake while everything in him cries out for relief, was almost painfully realistic." Among the cast members were John Ireland (as an undercover Gestapo man), Karl Malden, Rudolph Anders, and Richard Basehart (in his Broadway debut).

Because the plot required that the only light in the blocked-off cellar was supposed to be coming from a single lantern, a clever arrangement of baby spots hidden among the props and furnishings was used to simulate the effect while giving sufficient light for the actors to be seen. According to her *Don't Put Your Daughter on the Stage*, director Webster wrote to her mother, Dame May Whitty, "The bitchery which goes on between seven entombed Nazis fighting for the baby spots would put to shame any star actresses of the limelight era." Webster's involvement with this Russian-originated play was one of several factors that ultimately got her into trouble with the State Department during the era of the McCarthy hearings beginning later in the decade.

"COX AND BOX" (see *The Pirates of Penzance* and *H.M.S. Pinafore*)

CRADLE WILL ROCK, THE [Musical Revival*] B/M/LY: Marc Blitzstein; D: Howard da Silva; T: City Center of Music and Drama; 11/24/47 (2)

Conductor Leonard Bernstein led a portion of the New York Symphony Orchestra (seated on one side of the stage) through a special two-performance revival of this 1937 left-wing morality musical *cum* opera. It was the first production using the posteresque, satirical show's full orchestral score, political circumstances (described in this series's previous volume) having led the original to settle for a single piano played by the composer-librettist himself. Bernstein, strongly under the influence of Marc Blitzstein, had staged a production of the play when he was a Harvard student in 1939 and had also played the piano in that version. Blitzstein had seen that production, and he became a close friend of the younger composer.

The work met with so enthusiastic a response that producer Michael Myerberg produced it commercially a month later (12/26/47) at the Mansfield Theatre, where it ran for a disappointing twenty-one performances. Virgil Thomson (*NYHT*) noted of the former showing, which was discussed primarily by music critics, "It has sweetness, a cutting wit, inexhaustible fancy and faith. One would have to be wholly untouched and untouchable (and who is?) by the humanity and the aspirations of union labor to resist it." Many other reviews of the November presentation were equally ecstatic, Olin Downes (*NYT*), for instance, saying that the work "has qualities of genius." Despite the naïveté of its ideas, it still packed an emotional wallop and electrified the theatre with its exuberance and passion. One or two, however, did file minority reports and declare the piece stale and dated.

On Broadway, it received both glowing and scornful notices, even the positive ones being peppered with comments on the datedness of the ideas. John Mason Brown (*SR*), for instance, noted, "Its very certainties at present seem quaint." Brooks Atkinson (*NYT*) agreed, but found the score so "eloquent," the lyrics so biting, and the production so graphically simple that the show's weaknesses were easily overlooked: "At the moment, it is impossible to recall another musical drama so candid, so original and so fresh in stage conception." Among the several detractors was George Jean Nathan (*TBY*), for whom the piece was "an only faintly passable stunt."

Like the production a decade earlier, it was offered by costumed actors on a practically bare stage using only several rows of chairs on which the actors sat in full view until they came forth--oratorio-style--to play their scenes. The company included Howard da Silva (who directed), repeating his role of Larry Foreman, and Will Geer, brilliantly repeating his as Mr. Mister. When it shifted to Broadway, Alfred Drake took over the role of Larry. At the City Center Shirley Booth (who received raves) was the simpering Mrs. Mister, but on Broadway Vivian Vance held the role; Robert Chisholm gave over his role of the sanctimonious Rev. Salvation to Harold Patrick when the show moved. There were a few other changes in smaller roles as well. In both showings Muriel Smith was Ella Hammer (and was deemed a standout), David Thomas was Harry Druggist, Jack Albertson was Yasha, and Estelle Loring was Moll. Conductor Bernstein--dressed in formal evening wear--narrated and took the small role of the clerk; he conducted the first three Broadway performances and then gave the reins over to Howard Shanet.

CRAIG'S WIFE [Dramatic Revival*] A/D: George Kelly; S: Stewart Chaney; P: Gant Gaither; T: Playhouse; 2/12/47 (69)

The Pulitzer Prize-winning *Craig's Wife*, originally produced in 1925, was one of the best American dramas of its period, renowned for its surgical examination of its neurotic title character, who is driven by the need for material security. The 1947 revival, its first in New York, revealed the work to be stageworthy but not thoroughly acceptable. Louis Kronenberger (*PM*) declared, "It still interests and at times even fascinates you," but he felt that it did not completely satisfy him because "the play does not go deep enough into the lady, or far enough out into life." He concluded that Kelly's drama was "not so much artificial as simply airless." Rosamond Gilder (*TAM*) decided that the lack of shading in the picture of Mrs. Craig made "the play more like an exercise in rhetoric than a mirror of human behavior." A few, such as Brooks Atkinson (*NYT*), believed the play dated, but others regarded it as still "a resolute and honest drama" (Ward Morehouse [*NYS*]).

In the role of the archetypically hateful Harriet Craig, who dominates her husband (Philip Ober) as a way of gaining her longed-for security, was Judith Evelyn. She was excellent despite her being forced by Kelly's much-criticized speeding-train direction to rattle off many of her lines at rapid speed. "Her Harriet Craig," wrote John Mason Brown (*SR*), "is more exotic than was Miss [Chrystal] Herne's. . . . She is sinister and slightly ghoulish, in addition to being hard. . . . Miss Evelyn plays . . . with such driving intensity, and so much resourcefulness, that she creates a memory of her own." Good work was also contributed by Kathleen Comegys as Craig's aunt, Miss Austin, Virginia Hammond as Mrs. Frazier, Dortha Duckworth as Mazie, Virginia Dwyer as Ethel Landreth, and Viola Roache as Mrs. Harold.

CRAZY WITH THE HEAT [Revue] SK: Sam E. Werris, Arthur Sheekman, Mack Davis, Max Liebman, and Don Herold; M/LY: Irvin Graham; ADD.M: Rudi Revil; D: Edward Clarke Lilley and Arthur Sheekman (sketches) and Kurt Kasznar; CH: Catherine Littlefield; S/L: Albert Johnson; C: Lester Polakov and Marie Humans; P: Kurt Kasznar; T: Forty-fourth Street Theatre; 1/14/41 (7)

The notices for this $165,000 revue of musical numbers and comedy sketches were so dismal that the show lasted only a week. It was emceed by comedienne and singer Luella Gear and starred Yiddish-dialect vaudevillian Willie Howard, who appeared in a series of pointless sketches that even his estimable talent could not wake from the dead. His biggest laugh came in one routine when, after having slain a relative, he blurted, "What have I done, murdered my own fish and blood?" Also helping to keep the sinking ship temporarily afloat was dancer-comedienne Betty Kean. "A plain girl, with perhaps a leaning toward adenoids, she can dance like a whizz and interpolate wry burlesques of show conventions as she rushes along," said Brooks Atkinson (*NYT*). Dancer-juggler Carl Randall and singers Gracie Barrie, Richard Kollmar, and Marie Nash were among the other talents stuck with this loser.

The show, which had begun as an intimate summertime revue at the Red Barn Theatre in Locust Valley, New York, had been changed almost completely in the interim, but the one number retained was the excellent "The Yacht Song," performed by Gear and telling of a young woman whose libido needs a yacht to set it free. Otherwise, Gear had little worthy to contribute. Howard's bits had him as a butcher boy trying to collect thirty cents from a nutty woman customer, becoming nutty himself in the process; a broken-down, spindle-shanked old Russian ballet master (Gear played his interpreter); a radio commentator giving marital advice to the double-talking Harold Gary; his impression of the eponymous hero of *Life with Father** in a lugubrious takeoff on that hit; and, among others, a gypsy waiter who "goes with the dinner" and insists on singing to the indignant patrons of a restaurant. Typical of the reviews was Richard Lockridge's (*NYS*), which began, "*Crazy with the Heat* is one of those rather frequently occurring revues which are smooth and iridescent on the surface as soap bubbles, but unfortunately also resemble soap bubbles in being hollow within."

(2) SK/D: Lew Brown (some sketches directed by Arthur Sheekman); M/LY: Irvin Graham; ADD.M: Rudi Revill; ADD.M/LY: Jack Lawrence; D: Catherine Littlefield with Carl Randall; S/L: Albert Johnson; C: Lester Polakov and Marie Humans; P: Kurt Kasznar and Ed Sullivan; T: Forty-fourth Street Theatre; 1/30/41 (92)

Immediately after closing, the show underwent a change of management, being taken over by columnist Ed Sullivan, under whose coproducership the show--which managed to open within the same month that the first edition closed--was deemed improved but still not hot enough to go crazy over. Several of the original headliners returned, including Howard, Kean, and Gear, now supplemented by such performers as Mary Raye and Naldi, ballroom dancers par excellence, fiery Puerto Rican singer-dancer Diosa Costello, operatic singer Carlos Ramirez (who scored with his rendition of "Figaro"), Danish piano-playing clown Victor Borge (unimpressive in his Broadway debut), and a trio of black tap dancers named Tip, Tap, and Toe. Some of the better pieces in the first edition were salvaged, and a few new things of value, including Jack Lawrence's popular song, "Yes, My Darling Daughter," were added. "The revue has its high spots," wrote George Freedley (*NYMT*), "but fails to add up to a show that can be recommended for your enjoyment."

CREAM IN THE WELL, THE [Drama/Alcoholism/Family/Romance/Rural/Sex/Western] A: Lynn Riggs; D: Martin Gabel; S: Jo Mielziner; C: Rose Bogdanoff; P: Carly Wharton and Martin Gabel; T: Booth Theatre; 1/20/41 (24)

Lynn Riggs, author of poetic plays about life in the great Southwest, was responsible for this lamentable psychological tragedy of doom and gloom set on a farm in Oklahoma just prior to its becoming a state. The morbid drama, directed with heavy-handed ponderousness, focuses on the evil Julie Sawters (Martha Sleeper), whose incestuous passion for her brother Clabe (Leif Erickson) has forced him off the farm despite their weakening father's (Ralph Theadore) need for his help. He leaves behind Opal (Perry Wilson), the girl he loves, who marries Gard Dunham (Myron McCormick) in revenge, although the latter loves Julie. Jealous of Clabe's affection for Opal, Julie drives the girl to kill herself in the nearby lake. Gard persuades Julie to marry him as his price for keeping her actions secret. Under Julie's influence, however, he becomes an alcoholic, and his farm goes to waste. Clabe returns from the sea, torn by his indecent feelings for his sister, and tries unsuccessfully to seduce her. The suffering Julie, aware of her feelings for her brother, ends her misery by drowning herself. A feeling of hope begins to invade the Sawter home.

Richard Watts, Jr. (*NYHT*), called this "a sadly ineffectual work," and George Freedley (*NYMT*) said that the "the play remains static and uninflected." Its point, according to Rosamond Gilder (*TAM*), was that "evil engenders evil." She added that this was blurred by the incest issue, which "is so complex and carries with it so many connotations that it distracts and repels instead of clarifying the issue." While disappointed, Gilder claimed that the play "still bears witness to the originality, poetic talent, warmth and vision of Mr. Riggs' writing." The cast included Mary Morris as the Sawter mother, Virginia Campbell as another Sawter sister, and Harry Bratsburg (Morgan) as an amusing lawyer.

CREDITORS (*Fordringsägare*) [Dramatic Revival*] A: August Strindberg; AD/D: Frank Corsaro; S/L: Robert Ramsey; P: On-Stage; T: Cherry Lane Theatre (OB); 11/21/49 (108)

On-Stage, a persistent Off-Broadway group, brought this creditable revival to fruition. The hour-and-a-half 1889 (1880, given in the 1920-1930 volume of this series, is a misprint) Swedish play had not been seen locally since Maurice Browne's 1922 version. The small cast included Beatrice Arthur as Tekla, DeWitt Drury as Adolph, and George Roy Hill (playing with an arm broken during rehearsal) as Gustav. Other Strindberg plays also were being revived in 1949 (*The Father** was being done both Off and on Broadway), largely because it was the centennial of his birth.

The play--a psychological examination of the battle between the sexes--still proved magnetic. "It is extremely skillful in its probing into motives and its dissection of human weakness and cruelty, and there is power in its storytelling," penned Richard Watts, Jr. (*NYP*), who greatly admired the "excellent" performances. Still, he thought its bitterness so extreme that the author's persuasiveness was blunted. Arthur Pollock (*DC*) was mesmerized by the intensity of the play. It "surprises at every turn, for the dramatist is digging constantly, boring in, uncovering the minds of his characters."

The then-little-known actors (Arthur would later be a star and Hill would become a major director) were considered better than those in the uptown *The Father*. "They speak the lines intelligently, letting them do their own work, meanwhile conducting themselves as reasonable and reasoning interpreters," noted Pollock. "They play with a most extraordinary spontaneity, particularly in the long expository sequences," insisted William Hawkins (*NYWT*). On 1/31/50 the troupe moved to larger quarters at 159 Bleecker Street, where it finished out the play's run, a record-breaking one for Strindberg in New York.

CRIME AND PUNISHMENT [Drama/Alcoholism/Boarding House/British/Crime/Family/Mental Illness/Period/Prostitution/Religion] A: Rodney Ackland; SC: Fyodor Dostoyevsky's novel of the same name; D: Theodore Komisarjevsky; S/L: Paul Sheriff; C: Lester Polakov; P: Robert Whitehead and Oliver Rea; T: National Theatre; 12/22/47 (64)

A strikingly dramatic, but artistically flawed, adaptation of the great Dostoyevsky novel, with leading British star John Gielgud as Raskolnikoff. There had been several earlier stage versions of the book under titles such as *Rodion the Student* and *The Humble**. The most recent New York adaptation had been given under the original title in 1935*. In 1931 there had been an Italian-language version, *Delitto e Castigo**. Moreover, 1939's *The Possessed** had borrowed material from the novel, along with other works by Dostoyevsky. The present version, first seen in London a year and a half before, was considered the cream of the crop.

Despite its having been a London hit, under the direction of Anthony Quayle, the New York director, Komisarjevsky, a onetime mentor of Gielgud's, made a number of revisions in the material; not all of them were to the satisfaction of the original adaptor. Among the additions was one designed to answer his question as to how the characters could go in and out of the set's boarding house without a key. To solve the problem, the character of a maid was introduced, and every time the doorbell (another addition) rang, she had to answer it, which only served to clutter an already-busy play.

The staging used a brilliant, multileveled, simultaneous setting that revealed in Breughelesque detail four separate flats, a hallway, and a staircase in Mme. Amalia's (Elisabeth Neumann) crumbling St. Petersburg boarding house, where Rodion Romanitch Raskolnikoff (John Gielgud) lives in 1860. It, together with the shabby period costumes, captured perfectly the appropriate atmosphere of doom and gloom. For some, like George Freedley (*NYMT*), Komisarjevsky's direction was considered a masterpiece of imagination and style, but others, like Howard Barnes (*NYHT*), thought that while there was "a great deal of first-rate theater," the pageantlike direction and massive backgrounds were responsible for "more extraneous confusion than definitive drama on more than one occasion." Rosamond Gilder (*TAM*) noted the "constant flow of movement, rising crescendos of gaiety or terror, sharp scenes of violence, madness, death, all crowding one upon the other" in the director's stylized presentation. Brooks Atkinson (*NYT*) reported that "it is a fascinating adventure into the centrifugal theatre, with temperamental people erupting all over the stage and some vivid individual scenes acted with color and skill."

A number of reviewers felt that for all the interest of the production, Ackland had failed to compress the novel into a successful play. One was Euphemia Van Rensselaer Wyatt (*CW*), who thought the production outstanding, but found that it failed to express adequately the background to Raskolnikoff's murder: "One knows virtually nothing about Rodion . . . except that he is a moody young student." This she blamed on Ackland's too-"diffused" treatment. John Mason Brown (*SR*) termed the play "a spoken synopsis of Dostoievsky's novel. It is that--and nothing more."

Gielgud's performance as the would-be superman ax murderer was an important achievement for this major British star, around whom the adaptation was focused. According to Gilder, "Mr. Gielgud has a role that gives full play to his extraordinary power of externalizing thought. Again and again . . . he manages to convey not only the over-all mood . . . , but also the movement of thought in the student's mind. Gielgud sustains . . . a continuity and growth that the text does not always supply in words." But George Jean Nathan (*TBY*) accused the star of indicating his inner torment by resorting to "the kind of grimaces associated with Willie Howard in the old vaudeville act when his brother Eugene took him to task for his unbecoming conduct with a nursemaid in the Park."

The company of over forty was exceptional, with memorable characterizations. Sonia, the girl who sells herself to aid her family, was luminously played by Dolly Haas; Katerina Ivanna, Sonia's half-mad stepmother, was poignantly etched by Lillian Gish, in a performance some thought the pinnacle of her art and a few considered the evening's stellar characterization; Petrovitch, the cunning police inspector, was in the hands of the widely praised Vladimir Sokoloff (although Brown panned him, finding him vastly inferior to Peter Ustinov's London original; Sokoloff was a replacement for Alexis Minotis); Marmeladoff, the drunken father, was beautifully played by Sanford Meisner; Razoumikhin the student friend of Raskolnikoff, was acted with imagination by Alexander Scourby; Marian Seldes played to great effect as Raskolnikoff's sister Dounia; and there were compelling contributions from Betty Lou Keim as Polya, Wauna Paul as Anyutka, Mary James as Lizavieta, Alice John as Alexandrovna, E. A. Krumschmidt as Looshinsky, and others.

Komisarvjevsky, a Russian émigré, was unpleasant to the Jewish and German actors auditioning for the play, turning his back on them. Gielgud often had to soften the director's attitude, going so far as to commit one of his famed gaffes by saying to one actress, "I'm sorry, dear. You're not blowzy enough." Komisarjevsky insisted on putting ten of his own acting students in the play, which only added to the chaos of rehearsals. When things began to fall apart because of the rancor building in the company, Gielgud himself took over certain scenes as Komisarjevsky sat by watching passively. Marian Seldes declared in *The Bright Lights* that the director's use of his students was against Equity rules and that not only were they banished from the production, but Komisarjevsky himself was asked not to come to the final rehearsals. She also noted that at one of the note sessions, the autocratic old director had ignored Lillian Gish, who was desperate to please him. When she asked him if anything were missing from her performance, his curt reply was, "Yes." Pause. "More rouge." After the opening, producer Whitehead convinced Gielgud to rerehearse the entire play; as he began to do so, the Russian director marched in and blasted the entire company, telling all those whom he disliked about how bad they were and then taking over the reins himself.

CRIMINALS, THE (***Die Verbrecher***) [Drama/Crime/German/Law/Politics/Romance/Sex/Trial] A: Ferdinand Bruckner; AD: Edwin Denby and Rita Mathias; D: Sanford Meisner; S: H. A. Condell; L: Hans Sondheimer; P: Erwin Piscator; T: Studio Theatre of the New School for Social Research (OB); 12/20/41 (15)

As usual in the productions staged by Erwin Piscator's New School workshop, there were some outstanding talents involved, most of them artists who had not yet become famous in the American theatre. In the present work, for example, the actors included European star Lily Darvas (in her American debut), Herbert Berghof, Warner Anderson (in his local debut), Paul Mann, Jack Bittner, and Martin Ritt. They participated with many others in a German play--originally done in 1928 by Max Reinhardt--purporting to explain the rise of Nazism. This version was moved up to 1931, during the waning days of the Weimar Republic, a time of confused liberalism, unemployment, and economic chaos, in order to emphasize its political relevance.

The play attempts to answer the question, who are the criminals responsible for what has happened to the Fatherland? Various potential suspects are depicted, with the burden of guilt going to the liberal ivory-tower intellectuals who allowed Germany to go down the drain as the strong-armed Nazis rushed to power. This stress did not sit well with certain reviewers who disagreed with it.

The main plot concerns a young man (Mann) whose noble family is impoverished and who becomes a leader of the Brown Shirts, inducing into the movement two brothers, an idealist (Chilton Ryan), who comes to regret his choice, and a pragmatist (Peter Lorca), who realizes how he can profit from his. The former brother participates in the slaying of an antifascist and learns too late that he has joined the wrong movement in his desire to better his native land. Supporting this plot is a secondary one about the love of a sentimental cook, Ernestine (Darvas), for a handsome, womanizing waiter, Tunichget (Anderson). Learning of his philanderings, Ernestine kills Tunichget's latest lover (Gertrude Gilpin) and plants evidence leading to Tunichget's arrest and conviction on murder charges. Another subplot deals with a young couple, Kummerer (Berghof), a poverty-stricken liberal philosophy student, and Olga (Emily McNair), his pregnant sweetheart. Ernestine at one point had offered to take the baby as a way of holding Tunichget, but when she is no longer able to, the starving Olga drowns the child. All the action concerns the inhabitants of the same Berlin apartment house. When the respective characters are arrested for murder, their days in court are shown in three simultaneous trial scenes. Despite the avowed innocence of the "murderers," each is convicted, the legal system being implicitly condemned as obtuse, inhumane, and inflexible.

The expressionistic work was criticized for not being an effective attack on Nazi ideology, for a clumsy adaptation that failed to capture the idiomatic differences of the various characters, for an overelaborate presentation with an excess of characters (thirty-three) and scenes on a stage too tiny to employ them well, and for a multiplicity of plots and subplots. The adaptation also softened much of the original's harshness, in particular by removing its various references to homosexuality. "If it is artistically a failure," decided Louis Kronenberger (*PM*), "it is interesting and provocative enough." Richard Lockridge (*NYS*) declared that the play suffered various inadequacies, most particularly its inability "to make characters, stories and ideas sharp and effective."

Director Meisner was praised for doing a good job under trying conditions. He made use of a Piscatorian epic-theatre device in having his actors occasionally address the audience directly on issues of importance or in straightforward soliloquies. Brooks Atkinson (*NYT*) said of Darvas, "She plays with charm and force, and also with remarkable exactitude. . . . It is honest, illuminating acting, that communicates the inner turmoil of an inarticulate character."

CRITIC, THE (see *Oedipus Rex*)

CRY OF THE PEACOCK (*Ardèle ou La Marguerite*) [Comedy/Family/French/Marriage/Mental Illness/Period/Romance/Sex] A: Jean Anouilh; AD: Cecil Robson; D: Martin Ritt; DS: Cecil Beaton; P: James Colligan and Donald Medford; T: Mansfield Theatre; 4/11/50 (2)

A dully adapted and presented version of Anouilh's bitter, philosophical comedy-drama *Ardèle* that gave no hint of the intelligence of the Gallic original. "This is as dreary and heavy-handed a play as I have witnessed all season," moaned John Chapman (*NYDN*). Howard Barnes (*NYHT*) thought it "a verbose and tasteless consideration of l'amour, with the accent on adultery. . . . It is a fantastic bore." Arthur Pollock (*DC*) rejected it for its grim, antiromantic theme, which he said reflected the author's belief that love was a cancer that infects everybody. Thomas R. Dash (*WWD*) defined the play as "an unpalatable mixture of frivolous, carnal, and sordid love superimposed upon one affair which is sanctified and pure by comparison." The play was also lambasted for its acting, which employed a mélange of foreign-accented players, paralytic directing (Ritt was a replacement for Leonora Corbett), and hurried decor.

It takes place in a château in 1912 where the members of a family have gathered to discuss the love of a middle-aged, hunchbacked sister, Ardèle (never seen), for a hunch-backed tutor (Richard A. Martin), whom they would like her to give up. The family members include a count (Oscar Karlweis), who is tolerant if sarcastic about his wife's (Marta Linden) dragging her lover (Philip Tonge) about with her. The count himself has brought his twenty-year-old mistress along and placed her in a nearby inn. The château belongs to the count's brother, the general (Raymond Lovell), married to an insane woman (Lili Darvas) ten years his junior, and whose voice (the cry of mating peacocks) can often be heard shrieking to him every few minutes from her offstage bedroom. The general himself, whose adulteries have driven his wife mad, is pursuing the kitchen maid (Lucille Patton). Also present is the countess's niece, Nathalie (Patricia Wheel), married to a son of the general now in Indo-China but in love with her husband's younger brother, Nicolas (Peter Brandon), who appears to bedevil her with his unfulfilled love. The family is scandalized by the romance of their hunchbacked sister, who is locked in her room and conducting a hunger strike. They want to get her to come out and discuss the situation rationally, but she forces them to talk to her through the door. Toward the end, the demented wife appears at the top of the stairs and announces that the hunchbacked lovers are together in the sister's room. The star-crossed hunchbacks then shoot each other. At the ironic close, two children appear, the countess's daughter (Mimi Strongin) and the general's boy (Clifford Sales), and they imitate grotesquely the behavior of their elders.

CUCKOOS ON THE HEARTH [Comedy/Crime/Literature/Mental Illness/Mystery/Rural/Science] A: Parker W. Fennelly; D: Antoinette Perry; S: John Root; P: Brock Pemberton; T: Morosco Theatre; 9/16/41 (129)

This moderately successful "shudder comedy" moved during its run from the Morosco to the Mansfield to the Ambassador, as it had to make room for previously booked plays. It had received a summer- theatre tryout at Bass Rocks Theatre, Gloucester, Massachusetts, under the title *Two-Story House*. The critics thought it something of a mishmash, with only Percy Kilbride's performance worthy of the admission price. To help boost sales, producer Pemberton borrowed a hint from the movies' practice of giving out free dishware; he had a country-store barrel placed in the lobby in which patrons could deposit their ticket stubs and their opinions concerning the dual solutions to the play's mystery. A drawing was held to distribute prizes.

Following a prologue in which general-store proprietor Amos Rodick (Walter O. Hill) tells the spectators what they are about to see, Donald Carlton (Carleton Young) departs from his Maine farm house for a bus trip to Washington, where government officials want to talk to him about his poison gas invention. He leaves his wife Charlotte (Margaret Callahan) alone with a sex-hungry, slow-witted Yankee cousin, Lulu Pung (Janet Fox), and the unwelcome and hard-of-hearing mystery writer, Zadoc Grimes (Howard Freeman; the character was patterned after critic Alexander Woollcott). Outside, it is a dark winter's night with the wind howling and the snow falling. Sheriff Preble (Kilbride) arrives to warn the occupants of the escape from a nearby asylum of a homicidal sex maniac. Despite being warned to the contrary, Charlotte soon admits to the house a trio of men (George Mathews, Frederic Tozere, and Howard St. John) bearing a man-sized wooden box. The men are Nazi spies trying to get a copy of the inventor's formula. One of them may be the murderous mental patient, who wants to kill Charlotte and Lulu. When the second act reaches its climactic curtain, with Charlotte screaming for her life, the rustic general-store proprietor, Amos, comes forth and informs the audience that what they have been watching was actually Grimes's writings brought to life. What really happened--and who the strangler really is--is then disclosed in act three, when Donald returns in time to save his darling wife.

The author's trick concept of mingling elements from *Our Town**, *The Man Who Came to Dinner**, *The Tavern**, and *Arsenic and Old Lace** proved confusing and ill conceived. Moreover, the double denouement was deemed unworthy and repetitious. The negative responses were typified by John Anderson's (*NYJA*) comment that "the total effect is a hodge-podge, much too overdone and wearisome in its details."

CUE FOR PASSION [Drama/Crime/Hotel/Journalism/Literature/Marriage/Mystery/Politics/Sex/Theatre] A: Edward Chodorov and H. S. Kraft; D: Otto Preminger; S: Herbert Andrews; P: Richard Aldrich and Richard Myers; T: Royale Theatre; 12/19/40 (12)

A technically maladroit mystery play that showed promise but was marred by a lack of real suspense. John Elliott (George Coulouris) and Frances Chapman (Gale Sondergaard), husband and wife, are prominent writers (some spectators suspected that they were based on real persons). The despicable John is involved in an affair with the seductive Vivienne Ames (Doris Nolan). He is preparing to make his debut as an actor, and his wife arrives for the opening. They quarrel furiously in his hotel suite, he accusing her of infidelity and threatening divorce. She fears for her reputation if a scandal about her should arise. In act two of this three-act melodrama, John is shot in his hotel bedroom. Frances, with the grudging approval of the district attorney (Douglas Gilmore), questions all the material witnesses, emphasizing as she does why the death had to have been accidental. Most of the characters turn out to be unpleasant. A young reporter accuses Frances of using fascistic methods (revealing this aspect of her character was one of the principal elements of the dramaturgy). His fiancé, Ann Bailey (Claire Niesen), is the daughter of a man who has been insulted in a book of John's. Before he died, John attempted to seduce Ann, and she was the last person known to have been with him. At the end, she reads a letter by John explaining the true facts of his death (a program note asked patrons not to divulge the outcome of the plot).

John Anderson (*NYJA*), describing the weakness of the drama, observed that "as a portrait of a woman it is caustically one-sided, and as a mystery play it doesn't quite achieve the tension of real thrillers." Among the actors receiving praise for their work in this erratic whodunit was Viennese refugee Oscar Karlweis (in his American debut), playing the author of the play in which John was to make his debut. Ralph Locke and Whitner Bissell also were involved.

CUP OF TREMBLING, THE [Drama/Alcoholism/Family/Journalism/Marriage/Mental Illness/Sex] A: Louis Paul; SC: Louis Paul's novel, *Breakdown*; D: Paul Czinner; S/L: Charles Elson; C: Natalie Barth Walker; P: Paul Czinner and C. P. Jaeger; T: Music Box Theatre; 4/20/48 (31)

This elaborately produced, long-winded, clinical saga was a vehicle for European star Elisabeth Bergner, who played the harrowing role of an alcoholic with extremely realistic attention to detail. The character was that of newspaper columnist Ellen Croy, contentedly married to lawyer John Croy (Millard Mitchell) and foster mother to young Ann (Iris Mann). The strains of her profession lead her to try to overcome a lingering neurosis by drowning it in drink, to which a bachelor friend, Walter Fowler (John Carradine), introduces her in a misguided attempt to be helpful. This eventuates in her increasing dissolution. Soon her family and friends are in despair over the outrageous behavior to which she is subject when soused, and her exasperated husband even gives her a beating when she recklessly demands a divorce. Over the course of the drama, various persons try to help her recover, including a Freudian psychiatrist (Martin Wolfson) who discovers her problem by interpreting one of her dreams. It turns out that Ellen's brutal father had abused her when she was four. His resentment of her for being a girl also marred her, and she subsequently attempted to disguise her femininity and even became a frigid and unresponsive wife. Ellen learns that her editor, William Lundemann (Anthony Ross), is himself a recovering drunk who has been getting help from Alcoholics Anonymous. With the assistance of Sheila Vane (Arlene Francis), an AA volunteer and herself a reformed dipsomaniac, Ellen finds God and begins the road to health.

Although admired for its earnestness and the importance of its subject, the clunkily episodic play was dismissed as dramatically incompetent. George Freedley (*NYMT*) observed, "This is a frequently interesting, mostly provocative, but occasionally dull and exasperating play." Brooks Atkinson (*NYT*), commenting on Bergner's vivid portrayal, wondered whether her minutely etched performance was "art or is it merely histrionic scholarship? Although it pictures everything vividly, it conveys no emotion."

Arlene Francis noted in her autobiography, *Arlene Francis*, that the play was so realistic that there were people outside of the play nightly who confused her with her role and wanted to know how she had conquered her drinking problem. Francis also remembered that the play's star, Bergner, was unusually well disciplined and theatre wise. At one rehearsal, Bergner was playing a scene in which Francis sat alone with her. "Lissen, sveet vun," said the star, "In dis scene you must go around from place to place, very nervous, in a continual movement, und *I* vill sit absolutely still in the center, lissening to you. All eyes vill be vatching YOU!" The naive Francis thought that Bergner was being generous until she realized that the audience would actually be focused on "the eye of the hurricane." Bergner seems to have taken more than a professional interest in the younger actress, for one day they were posing for a photograph and Francis called to Bergner's nearby husband, Paul Czinner, "Come on, Paul. Get in the picture! What good are two women without a man?" Bergner knocked Francis for a loop when she looked slyly at her and declared, "Darrrlink, you dun't know?"

Among the many well-known cast members were Phillip Tonge, Beverly Bayne, Louis Hector, and Hope Emerson.

CYRANO DE BERGERAC [Dramatic Revival*] A: Edmond Rostand; TR: Brian Hooker; M: Paul Bowles; D: Melchor G. (Mel) Ferrer; S/C: Lemuel Ayers; P: José Ferrer; T: Alvin Theatre; 10/8/46 (193)

A renowned revival of the 1897 Rostand play, last seen in 1936 in one of Walter Hampden's periodic revivals. The present version offered a scintillating performance of the long-nosed romantic hero by José Ferrer, with Roxane played by Frances Reid, Christian by Ernest Graves, Ragueneau by Hiram Sherman, de Guiche by Ralph Clanton, Le Bret by William Woodson, Jaloux by Francis Compton, Roxane's duenna by Paula Laurence, and Ralph Meeker, Nan McFarland, Howard Wierum, Leonard Cimino, and others in the large cast. The too-wordy text had been lightly trimmed, but the production ran until 11:30 P.M. and some critics thought that more cutting would not hurt.

Although a few, like Robert Coleman (*NYDN*), rated Ferrer's performance as not quite up to Hampden's, most considered him a virile, humorous, keen-witted, excellently spoken, passionate yet shy, sensitive, and poetic Cyrano. Some felt that his only drawback in comparison to the very tall Hampden was his lesser height. "He is easily the best Cyrano this generation has seen," reported Arthur Pollock (*BE*). "More limber and mercurial than Walter Hampden, quick and deft, sensitive and supple, he can, though not a big fellow, project the D'Artagnan character of the role and at the same time bleed it affectionately of all its poetry." John Mason Brown (*SR*), comparing Ferrer to Hampden, said that the former "is nimbler of body, which counts hugely in making the first act duel as exciting as it should be. Nimbler of mind, too; . . . His spirit is much younger; his blood more turbulent." But George Jean Nathan (*TBY*) thought that Ferrer lacked the requisite vocal powers for the part. "He begins well enough, but monotony of delivery gradually converts his performance from the theatrical heroic into the recitational." Ferrer's performance earned him the first Tony (shared with Fredric March) for a dramatic actor.

The production itself was fast-paced and colorful and had expert performances in all the important supporting roles. Brooks Atkinson (*NYT*) noted, for example, that Reid played "an enchanting Roxane with a skimming touch and daintiness of accent, as well as obvious enjoyment in the role." *Cyrano de Bergerac* still had the power to hold an audience enthralled by its swashbuckling panache. It provided abundantly colorful scenery, striking costumes, and vividly ferocious swordplay. The final scene, with Cyrano dying and Roxane becoming aware of his love for her, was considered deeply touching and beautifully staged. Atkinson dubbed the work "rattling good theatre in the cloak-and-doggerel vein."

During the run, Ferrer did the seemingly unprecedented when he allowed several scattered performances to be given with the understudies in principal roles. Woodson played Cyrano, Patricia Wheel played Roxane, Stewart Long played Christian, Charles Summers played Ragueneau, Wierum played Le Bret, and Robert Carroll played de Guiche. Although the production was sound, "There was an understandable tendency . . . for many of the people to give imitation performances of the actors they understudy, rather than enact those of their own creations," observed Vernon Rice (*NYP*). The stars themselves occupied the small roles normally played by the understudies, Ferrer, for example, being the surly poet and the hungry poet.

D

DAMASK CHEEK, THE [Comedy/Family/Period/Romance] A/D: John van Druten and Lloyd Morris; S/C: Raymond Sovey; P: Dwight Deere Wiman; T: Playhouse; 10/22/42 (93)

Coauthor John van Druten, hoping to write a comedy for British actress Flora Robson, hitherto identified in this country principally as the star of such serious dramas as *Ladies in Retirement**, was inspired to write this piece when he was struck one day by the atmosphere of the Hotel Ansonia on uptown Broadway. Something about its nostalgic and glamorous atmosphere of turn-of-the-century New York moved him as he investigated its lobbies. He called to mind a colorful aunt of his who had lived in New York then and had visited him in England from time to time during his childhood. Not having come to America until 1926, he relied on critic, cultural historian, and English professor Lloyd Morris to provide him with the appropriate background to make his play authentic. The play was written largely by correspondence, with Morris in New York and van Druten in California, followed by Robson's approval of the finished script. The play, a "pleasant-tempered excursion into polite comedy" (Brooks Atkinson [*NYT*]), was not quite a hit on Broadway, but it was admired well enough to make Burns Mantle's list of the ten best of the year. Its title comes from a line in *Twelfth Night**.

It is set in 1909 in the East Sixties living room of a wealthy and snobbish dowager, Mrs. Randall (Margaret Douglass), whose thirty-year-old son Jimmy (Myron McCormick) is secretly loved by Mrs. Randall's niece, a wealthy English spinster named Rhoda Meldrum (Robson), in New York to visit her aunt. Jimmy and Rhoda were brought up practically as brother and sister, so he ignores his second cousin's potential as a mate and even deprecates her virtues. His mother would like for Jimmy and Rhoda to become a pair, so she throws a dance in Rhoda's honor. Jimmy, though, uses it as an opportunity to announce his engagement to the beautiful young actress Calla Longstreth (Celeste Holm), of whom Mrs. Randall thinks very little. The starchy upper-class characters are shocked when the slightly soused Rhoda, in the course of the proceedings, leaves the party for a Central Park ride with Jimmy's womanizing friend Neil (Zachary Scott). Jimmy starts to realize that maybe Rhoda, not Calla, is the girl for him. Things look even brighter for Rhoda when Calla reveals to her that she is not so much in love with Jimmy as with the life of security he represents. The contents of Rhoda's pocketbook assuage Calla's fears, and all ends happily with Rhoda and Jimmy united. A secondary love interest is portrayed between Jimmy's young sister (Joan Tetzel) and Neil.

Entertaining as it was, the work was deemed lightweight and inconsequential. Burton Rascoe (*NYWT*), who loved its expert balance of humor and poignancy, opined, "The play is not great or significant in the stuffier sense; it is simply an enchanting study of human relationships, wherein the complications arise over the difference between inner emotions and the outward display of attitudes."

Robson gave a sparkling performance, but her role was considered not as challenging as her acting powers deserved, and she sometimes overpowered the writing by her presence and skill. Robson, a character actress whose appearance bordered on the plain, seemed surprising casting for a woman who steals a man away from Celeste Holm, but her characterization was so deft that she made the theft seem possible. One of her best scenes was a rough-house, hair-pulling fight with Holm that Howard Barnes (*NYHT*) called "a masterpiece of its kind."

The production had style and charm and offered appropriate escapist entertainment. To enhance the play's nostalgic quality, it employed various topical references, including one to the 1909 sensationalistic hit, *The Easiest Way**, and a slip was placed in the programs announcing that drama's performance at the Stuyvesant Theatre. There were fine performances by Peter Fernandez as Jimmy's adolescent brother and by Ruth Vivian in another supporting role.

DANCE ME A SONG [Revue] SK: Jimmy Kirkwood, Lee Goodman, George Oppenheimer, Vincente Minnelli, Marya Mannes, Robert Anderson, James Shelton, and Wally Cox; M/LY: James Shelton; ADD.M/LY: Herman Hupfeld, Albert Hague, Maurice Valency, and Bud Gregg; D: James Shelton; CH: Robert Sidney; S/L: Jo Mielziner; C: Irene Sharaff; P: Dwight Deere Wiman i/a/w Robert Ross; T: Royale Theatre; 1/20/50 (35)

Despite the heavy lineup of creative talents responsible for this "exceedingly uneven" (Howard Barnes [*NYHT*]) revue, it bottomed up in a month. Its major contribution was to introduce mild-mannered, bespectacled nightclub monologuist Wally Cox to Broadway. The show also featured talented newcomer Babe Hines, an amply proportioned black singer who was frequently encored. Future choreographer-director great Bob Fosse made his Broadway debut in the work, partnered by his then wife, dancer Mary Ann Niles. Also involved were actor Biff McGuire, who appeared in various skits; beautiful singer Hope Foye; and future choreographer Donald Saddler. Alan Ross and dancer-actress Joan McCracken (a later wife of Fosse's) appeared in a sketch called "The Lunts Are the Lunts," demonstrating how the Lunts might succeed as actors even by reading the phone book; comics Lee Goodman and Jimmy Kirkwood played in "Buck and Bobbie," a spoof of children's radio programs; flat-voiced comedienne Ann Thomas did a fairly amusing bit about a woman demonstrating self-defense techniques; a mirror device was used for a clever dance routine in "One Is a Lonely Number," sung by Heidi Krall; McCracken danced and sang "Strange New Look," accompanied by McGuire and dancer Bob Scheerer; ditzy comedienne Marion Lorne was an antique dealer who crashes a crumbling Charles Addams-like mansion haunted by ghouls and demons; and, in the evening's highlights, the deadpan Cox delivered a pair of hilarious monologues. In the first, called "Documentary," which parodied slum life as depicted in documentary films, he spoke about a gang of juvenile delinquents. In the second, his story concerned a dumb soda jerk named Dufo. "He garnered the only solid laughs of the evening with his small-talk, sudden comedy twists and throwaway lines," reported Robert Coleman (*NYDM*).

Brooks Atkinson (*NYT*) said that the show "looks like a carnival but sounds hackneyed and mechanical. . . . The sketches . . . are undistinguished, most of the music is dull and none of the performers is quite ingenious enough to make a silken evening of mediocre material." Rowland Field (*NEN*) submitted that "this is a melody show that is sorely in need of worthier sketch materials and tunes."

DANCE OF DEATH, THE (see *The Last Dance*)

DANCER, THE [Drama/Alcoholism/Art/Crime/Family/France/Homosexuality/Mental Illness/Prostitution/Show Business] A: Milton Lewis and Julian Funt; M: Paul Bowles; D: Everett Sloane; DS: Motley; P: George Abbott; T: Biltmore Theatre; 6/5/46 (5)

Producer George Abbott chose a lemon when he offered this clunky murder melodrama as a vehicle for dancer Anton Dolin's debut as a legitimate actor (Dolin took over during tryouts from dancer Leon Fokine). Lewis Nichols (*NYT*) declared that the producer lacked "a play that is gripping or makes quite enough sense."

George Freedley (*NYMT*) called it "a confused, carelessly written play which the best acting and direction in the world couldn't have saved."

Dolin played a once-famed Russian ballet star, Sergei Krainine, who has been mentally unbalanced for fifteen years and is being cared for in Paris by an English art connoisseur named Aubrey Stewart (Colin Keith-Johnston); the latter has spent his wealth in the effort to restore the dancer's sanity. Their relationship has homosexual implications. When the play begins, the body of a local prostitute--her back broken--has been found nearby. Aubrey suspects Sergei of the crime; so does a police inspector (Luis Van Rooten). Mingled with the mayhem is the subplot about Sergei's daughter, Madeline (Bethel Leslie), who wishes, before she marries, to determine if her father's madness is hereditary. Another subplot involves the attempts of Aubrey and the dancer's alcoholic wife, Catherine (Helen Flint), to discover the location of a safe-deposit box to which the wife has the key and in which a fortune is supposedly secreted. Before the play ends and he falls into the clutches of the law, Sergei has committed other murders, including those of his avaricious wife and his sophisticated caretaker.

DARK EYES [Comedy/Friendship/Romance/Theatre] A: Elena Miramova and Eugenie Leontovich; D/P: Jed Harris; S: Stewart Chaney; T: Belasco Theatre; 1/14/43 (230)

Two Russian émigrée actresses collaborated on this hit comedy about two Russian émigrée actresses and their erstwhile opera singer friend that was produced and directed by famed Russian-born Broadway impresario Jed Harris. It was reported that Harris and screenwriter Nunnally Johnson made revisions in the script that allowed for complimentary comments about the Red Army.

The play was blessed with an unusually attractive poster showing a beautiful Russian seductress, with the title emblazoned on the shako adorning her head. The few, brief words on the poster offered a minimum of information, omitting the names of the show's principal contributors. Some thought this unusually abbreviated text terrific advertising, but the reasons for it did not stem from a press agent's brainstorm. Instead, wrote that press agent (Richard Maney) in *Fanfare*, it came from Harris's distaste for the costars and coauthors. When the poster was first created, it bore their names in their dual functions, as it did his as producer-director, but he had grown so to dislike the women that he ordered their names removed, which decision also--under Dramatists Guild regulations--required the elimination of his own.

Natasha Rapakovitch (Leontovich) and Tonia Karpova (Miramova) have written a play but cannot find someone to finance its production. They are in dire financial straits and are even evicted from their apartment, having passed a bad check for $500 to the landlord to cover their back rent. They have a friend, Prince Nicolai Toradje (Geza Korvin), a fellow Russian, once in love with Natasha and now supposedly in love with Helen Field (Anne Burr), daughter of a wealthy industrialist, John Field (Jay Fassett). Prince Nicolai, finding them on a bench in Central Park, invites them to spend a weekend with him at the industrialist's Long Island home. The actresses and their singer friend Olga Shmilevskaya (Ludmilla Toretzka) move in, bag, baggage, balalaika, and samovar. There they endear themselves to Granny Field (Minnie Dupree) by celebrating her birthday with their charming Russian customs, including the donning of colorful native garments and the singing of Russian songs. They also engage in a hilarious argument among themselves over the relative talents of Peter Tchaikovsky. The widowed tycoon comes home from his dollar-a-year job in Washington, D.C., but instead of finding peace and quiet, he finds the three Russian thespians. They try to use their wiles on him to get him to back their play, but he sees through them, although he eventually falls under their spell. Love blossoms between him and Tonia (and is rekindled between Nicolai and Natasha), and he gives them a down payment of $500 (which they need to keep out of jail because of the check business) as an advance on financing their play.

Dark Eyes got off to a slow start but picked up speed soon enough to capture those whose attention might have begun to wander. It succeeded best by its good-humored poking of fun at Russian habits and characteristics. The Russians' accents proved amusing, and their seemingly artless performances were consistently delightful. Leontovich, wrote Rosamond Gilder (*TAM*), "is playful, rather than sharply comic, but there is a captivating buoyancy and verve about her kaleidoscopic changes of mood, her rushes of passion, of patriotism, of gallantry, of despair."

The play itself was considered trivial but entertaining and somewhat off the beaten path for a Broadway comedy; Harris's production was up to the mark in every way and may even have been better than the writing. John Anderson (*NYJA*) believed this to be "a gay, foolish, amiably absurd and somehow gallant and beguiling comedy." But Howard Barnes (*NYHT*), in the minority, complained that "nufortunately [the authors] have mixed the moods of their travesty in such an off hand manner that it has a tendency to sag badly when it should be hitting high spots of hilarity." Carl Gose played the Field son, and Oscar Polk was the genial butler.

DARK HAMMOCK [Drama/Crime/Legacy/Marriage/Period/Rural/Science/Southern] A: Mary Orr and Reginald Denham; D: Reginald Denham; S: Samuel Leve; C: Kermit Love; L: Jack Daniels; P: Meyer Davis and Sam H. Grisman; T: Forrest Theatre; 12/11/44 (2)

"A tepid melodrama which was neither well-written, well-acted nor well-directed," according to George Freedley (*NYMT*). Set in rural Florida in 1910, it tells of Cora (Mary Orr, the coauthor), an ambitious young Northern actress who has left the stage to marry an older man, a cattle raiser named Marvin Platt (Charles McClelland). Finding life with him dull, she wishes to kill him and cash in on the inheritance he has agreed on for her. She is further motivated by the attentions of young Carlos Antuna (James Ganon), who is attracted to her. Cora's method is to mix the liquified heads of sulphur matches in Marvin's nightly eggnogs. The inopportune arrival of a pair of spinster scientists, Dr. Florence McDavid (Elissa Landi) and her assistant Amelia Coop (Mary Wickes), seeking shelter from a storm, foils the plot when the ladies become suspicious. They find ploys to stick around until they have the proof that allows them to figure out the nature of the crime (they observe a jug of sulphur glowing in the dark) and ultimately to cause Cora's demise by the old glass-switching trick, in which the guilty party drinks the poison intended for another. The husband is cured with Epsom salts.

Stock situations and characters and repetitious dialogue were some of the play's faults. "Slow, wordy and unoriginal" was Rowland Field's (*NEN*) verdict. The company contained Arthur Hunnicutt, Scott Moore, and Mabel D. Bergen, who played an oversized black maid.

DARK OF THE MOON [Drama/Fantasy/Religion/Romance/Rural/Sex/Southern] A: Howard Richardson and William Berney; M: Walter Hendl; D: Robert E. Perry; CH: Esther Junger; S/L: George Jenkins; C: Peggy Clark and Ernest Schrapps; P: Messrs. Shubert; T: Forty-sixth Street Theatre; 3/14/45 (318)

Richardson and Berney's fantasy about the hill folk in the Smoky Mountains has remained a perennial favorite of university and small theatre groups, where the number of its performances rivals that of almost any other play. It was the Maxwell Anderson Prize winner for poetic drama at Stanford University in 1942 and was produced at the University of Iowa a year later. Another production at the Cambridge Summer Theatre inspired its production on Broadway, where it reemployed leads Richard Hart and Carol Stone.

Using backwoods dialect, it tells the tale of a witchboy named John (Hart) who convinces the skeptical conjur woman (Georgia Simmons) to transform him into a human so that he can love the human girl, Barbara Allen (Stone). Two witchgirls (Iris Whitney and Marjorie Belle) love him and do not wish to lose him. The conjur woman strikes a deal with John whereby he must return to being a witchboy if Barbara should prove unfaithful within the year. John descends to the town, where he wins Barbara Allen from her suitor Marvin Hudgens (John Gifford), having to resort to some superhuman feats to best his rival. But the local folk suspect who he is, and after Barbara gives birth, the midwives burn the baby for a witch. The townspeople thereupon hold a revival meeting at which the extremely reluctant Barbara is forced to submit sexually to Marvin. She dies, and John is forced to return to the mountains and the witchgirls. (The rape scene was deleted from the New York staging, although it was performed without incident when the play tried out in Philadelphia.)

Dark of the Moon is based on the old Scottish and English folk song "Barbara Allen," which Barbara at one point sings, and to which Howard Richardson supplied unfamiliar lyrics he discovered while researching American balladry for a thesis. The drama mixes backwoods characters and humor with spooky otherworldly doings and incorporates many familiar folk songs (adapted by Walter Hendl) in the action. It is a play of mood and atmosphere, with opportunities for special effects and homespun humor.

Although unique and laden with entertaining features, the play had various problems for reviewers. Euphemia Van Rensselaer Wyatt (*CW*) found the play's morality confused and its style a puzzling blend of "parody and poetry." The latter problem was clarified for her when she learned that the piece originally had been intended as a spoof of folk drama. Lewis Nichols (*NYT*) commented, "*Dark of the Moon* has a better idea than execution, it tries to do more than it has been able to accomplish." He found that the slim plot was too obviously padded by songs and talk. Rosamond Gilder (*TAM*) declared, "The treatment . . . is schematic and external, a succession of picturesque incidents rather than a play," with stock characters and without "dramatic life." Nevertheless, she had to admit, "the play is arresting and unusual." Many shared these mixed feelings, as, for example, Burton Rascoe (*NYWT*), who noted, "I found it an enriching and pleasurable experience, though I must add that I am not wild about it." But Wilella Waldorf (*NYP*) had few objections and insisted that the play "has gusto and vitality, lusty humor and a natural, easy-going way of introducing folk-songs that add up to an engaging evening."

George Jenkins provided an imaginative setting showing distant landscapes, with soaring mountains and rugged trees suggesting a world of magic and superstition. For interiors, only a suggestive scenic element or two was employed, such as a piece of roof or window. The set had to suggest both reality and fantasy, just as did the acting, but the latter was not always as successful in doing so as the former. One much-remarked-upon drawback was the revuelike costumes of the witchgirls, who wore spangled tights and chiffon and seemed violently out of place in the jagged landscape. John was much more effective: "His close fitting black garments, making him almost invisible . . . , his stylized movements with their suggestion of spreading wings, dark flights and unearthly wanderings, are excellent," decided Gilder. Among the members of the large cast were Ross Matthew as the conjur man, Frances Goforth as Miss Metcalf, Roy Fant as Uncle Smelique, Agnes Scott Yost as Mrs. Bergen, Conrad Janis (in his Broadway debut) as Floyd Allen, and Winfield Hoeny as Preacher Haggler.

DAVID'S CROWN [Dramatic Revival/Hebrew Language] A: Pedro Calderón de la Barca; TR: I. Lamdan; M: Shlomo Rosovsky; D: Alexei D. Dicky; S: M. Schmidt; P: Habimah Theatre u/t/a/o Theatre Incorporated and the American Fund for Palestinian Institutions; 5/9/48 (8)

Israel's highly reputed Habimah Theatre offered four productions in the Spring of 1948; the second was this Hebrew version of Calderón's Spanish biblical drama of incest, *David's Crown*. There were important roles for the three most gifted Habimah actors, Hanna Rovina, who played Tamar, Shimon Finkel, who played Amnon, and Aaron Meskin, who acted David. The piece was not especially well received, being called "a Sunday School lesson, lacking in drama" by George Currie (*BE*)

The drama concerns the latter years of King David's reign when his sons covet his throne. Daughter Tamar, commanded to keep son Amnon at bay, ends up seducing her brother, which dire deed leads son Absalom (Zvi Friedland) to kill Amnon and seize the crown himself. He is killed in turn by General Joab (Joshua Bertonov), and David, guilty of causing so much bloodshed, realizes that he will never be able to build the Temple. As the play concludes, sons Adoniyahu (Chaim Amitai) and Solomon (Raphael Klatzkin) struggle for the crown that David has rejected.

The play was presented on an extremely simplified but effective set composed of black velours, stylized props, and highly colorful decorative elements. The costumes were less appropriate and seemed "commonplace in design" to Brooks Atkinson (*NYT*). Most critics, unfamiliar with Hebrew and forced to depend on a synopsis, admired the vocally powerful, robust, and floridly theatrical acting (which included boldly stylized makeup), but had little valuable to say about the play. Richard Watts, Jr. (*NYP*), commented that this "gloomy and turbulent Biblical tragedy . . . represents the distinguished . . . visitors in one of their most vivid and arresting moods." He was particularly impressed by "the grim, savage incisiveness of the playing which completes the illusion that this is how those tempestuous old patriarchs . . . actually fought, loved, hated and died."

DAY BEFORE SPRING, THE [Musical/Literature/Marriage/Romance/University] B/LY: Alan Jay Lerner; M: Frederick Loewe; D: Edward Padula and John C. Wilson; CH: Anthony Tudor; S: Robert Davison; C: Miles White; P: John C. Wilson; T: National Theatre; 11/22/45 (165)

This early example of the soon-to-be-famous Lerner and Loewe partnership was "singularly flat," thought Rosamond Gilder (*TAM*) and several of her colleagues, although others, such as John Chapman (*NYDN*), considered it "urbane, humorous, [and] tuneful." Lewis Nichols (*NYT*) said of the show, "It trudges along without comedy, without literary sparkle or dance sparkle; it is, in short, heavy." But Burton Rascoe (*NYWT*) called it "a sweet and charming musical that has everything an operetta, American style, should possess." The pretentious and slow-moving libretto was a bit of a burden, and several reviewers regretted that various opportunities for satire and comedy had been overlooked.

A romantic triangle story, the play concerns the return to Harrison College for a reunion of Katherine (Irene Manning) and Peter Townsend (John Archer), wed for ten years. Katherine falls again for her old flame, Alex Maitland (Bill Johnson), a handsome novelist and man of the world, with whom an attempt at elopement had ended unsuccessfully when their car broke down and Peter arrived to win Katherine's heart. Alex's new best-seller *The Day before Spring* tells of the romantic life Katherine would have had had she married him. Again feeling Alex's allure, she ponders what she should do. The statues of Freud (Hermann Leopold), Plato (Ralph Glover), and Voltaire (Paul Best) come to life to advise her. She and Alex elope once more--she sends a copy of Alex's book to Peter--but meet with the same fate as a decade earlier when their car breaks down. Katherine decides to return to Peter, although she almost loses him to the uninhibited Christopher Randolph (Patricia Marshall).

The well-produced show had a number of potentially interesting touches, particularly a pair of ballets (danced mainly by Hugh Laing and Mary Ellen Moylan). In one the novel's events are danced as Peter reads; the other expresses the thoughts of Alex and his secretary-valet-handyman (Tom Helmore). These dances, however, proved in execution surprisingly uninspired and out of sync with the show's college-life atmosphere. The fashion for ballets in musicals, flourishing since *On Your Toes**, was beginning to pall.

Notable songs included "God's Green World," "My Love Is a Married Man," "You Haven't Changed at All," "I Love You This Morning," and "Friends to the End." Bert Freed was an important supporting player. Hollywood was interested enough in the show to pay $250,000 for the rights, but no film was ever made of it.

DAY OF JUDGMENT, THE [Drama/Jews/Music/Period/Romance/Yiddish Language/Youth] A: Jacob Sorsky; AD/D: Maurice Schwartz; SC: Sorsky's novel of the same name; M: Lazar Klutzman; S: Alexander Chertov; C: Suzanne Frisch; P/T: Yiddish Art Theatre; 10/6/41

A rambling, lugubrious, fifteen-scene play that seemingly took forever to reach its final curtain. The play seriously needed editing, its opening-night performance lasting three hours and twenty minutes.

Company doyen Maurice Schwartz adapted, produced, directed, and starred in this dramatization of the results stemming from a Jewish custom whereby two friends pledge their son and daughter to marriage even before they are born. The boy, born deformed, is so self-conscious of his appearance that he runs away at age thirteen. Rebecca (Miriam Rubini), the girl, although in love with Ilya (Anatol Winogradoff), wishes to keep her father's word and leaves for Vienna, both to be away from Ilya's wooing and to train her singing voice. She meets the famed hunch-backed composer, Professor Kramer (Schwartz), who is the boy she is engaged to marry. They wed, but the guilt-ridden Kramer, wishing to rid the girl of her burden, chooses martyrdom by falsely confessing to the killing of a czarist general (Jacob Ben-Ami) who has conducted pogroms against the Jews and who was actually slain by Kramer's sister (Berta Gersten). Kramer is executed, and Rebecca is free to marry Ilya.

Well-known company members in the play included Luba Kadison and Lazar Freed. Making her New York debut was singer and actress Miriam Rubini, recruited from Buenos Aires's Yiddish stage. The company occupied the temporarily renamed Jolson Theatre on Broadway for this production, of which B. I. (*NYWT*) declared, "It is difficult to believe that a showman of Mr. Schwartz's caliber could become involved in anything as tortuous and as empty-sounding as this bolt of fustian."

DAY WILL COME, THE [Drama/Fantasy/Jews/Mental Illness/Military/Politics/Religion/War] A: Leo Birinski; D: Lee Elmore; S: Frederick Fox; P: Harry Green; T: National Theatre; 9/7/44 (20)

Harry Green produced this well-meaning but jumbled drama and played the leading role of Abrum Dovid. The play itself was the only one of the war years to actually picture on stage the person of Adolf Hitler (Brandon Peters), displayed in monomaniacal and ranting colors. The white-bearded, aged, inordinately wise, and preternaturally prescient Abrum represents the Wandering Jew. He resides in a Russian village that lies in the path of Hitler's advance early in the war. The town is razed and the people flee to the swamps, but the patriarchal Abrum, who is believed to have supernatural powers, remains behind. Arriving in the town are several Prussian generals (Arthur Vinton, Stephen Roberts, Bernard Pate, and William Pringle), who resent Hitler's ascent and seek to use the Wandering Jew--who impresses them by an apparent memory of historical events he seems to have experienced--to convince the astrologically minded Fuehrer not to march on Moscow. (An original copy of Nostradamus in the Jew's house plays a role in this.) Hitler himself comes to the town and learns of the plot, condemns a general to death, and engages in a debate with Abrum. Hitler proclaims the need to foster the "master race" and stamp out Judaism and Christianity. Abrum tells Hitler that the latter will outlive the assault on Moscow to suffer great pain such as he himself has caused the Jews. The old man is killed by the Nazis, but returns as a spirit and drives Hitler to raving insanity.

The play was accused of meandering, implausibility, unevenness, predictability, artificiality, and an uncomfortable blend of realism and symbolism. Summing up, Wilella Waldorf (*NYP*) asserted, "*The Day Will Come* is a play that has some meat in it, but like so many dishes these days, is liberally padded with flat and flavorless filler. The meaty parts tickle the palate. The rest is just so much sawdust."

Although he resembled Hitler, Peters failed to do much more than caricature the German leader. Green, quipped George Jean Nathan (*TBY*), looked like "Monty Woolley even further disguised as Santa Claus."

DAYS OF OUR YOUTH, THE [Drama/Politics/Romance/Sex/Sports/University/Youth] A: Frank Gabrielson; D: James Light; S: Cleon Throckmorton; P: Erwin Piscator (Dramatic Workshop); T: Studio Theatre of the New School for Social Research (OB); 11/28/41

A warmly appreciated, although flawed, drama that Brooks Atkinson (*NYT*) called "a deeply human chronicle that communicates a good many aspects of the homely truth," and Arthur Pollock (*BE*) dubbed "probably the best play about American college life that has ever been done in New York." It suffered, however, from undue length and too episodic a structure (seventeen scenes) for the cramped stage used by this mixture of professionals and students studying under Erwin Piscator. Gabrielson's novelistic approach, said Kelcey Allen (*WWD*), "makes for a cumbersome and confused production." But for all its faults, there was a healthy amount of humor mingled with pathos, although the latter sometimes bordered on schmaltz. The "emotional scenes are embarrassingly sloppy and do not ring true," believed Louis Kronenberger (*PM*).

The play's subject is life on a college campus, where students of all backgrounds mingle in intellectual and emotional proximity. Instead of a close-knit plot, the play provides insights into the lives and problems of a select group of students. Central to the action are Charley Jones (Leon Janney), the extroverted big man on campus; Donald Bickley (Philip Brown), the introverted, suicidal poet and intellectual; Cynthia Wedge (Ruth Davis), the socialite beauty in love with socially inferior football star Francis Marakowski (Peter Hobbs), with whom neither marriage or sexual consummation are achieved; sexy Eleanor Burkman (Hannah Karol), embarrassed to be living over a butcher shop; Mary Sylvester (Sydna Scott), heiress to a fortune and guilty over it; Milton Liebman (Curt Conway), active in left-wing student politics; and many others. Each has his or her story, none taking precedence, and no central theme ties them all together. Few of them even know one another well. The play covers their four years from entering college to their commencement exercises. Each encounters varying fortunes, some of them meeting with sadness, others with success. Some find romance, others lose it. Through it all the author exposes various facets of college life, from the caste system of fraternities to the corruption behind subsidized sports. A theatrical device that proved tiresome was the loudspeaker-broadcast Voice of the Catalogue (Wyman Holmes), commenting periodically about things of interest to college students. In the cast were such performers as Clyde Franklin, Zamah Cunningham, Jack Bittner, Norman Tokar, and Teresa Hayden, who one day would be a well-known director and producer.

DEAR JUDAS [Drama/Bible/Period/Politics/Religion] A/D/P: Michael Myerberg; SC: a poem of the same title by Robinson Jeffers; M: Johann Sebastian Bach; CH: (and mime) Esther Junger; S/L: Albert Johnson; C: (and masks) Mary Percy Schenck; T: Mansfield Theatre; 10/5/47 (17)

In *Dear Judas*, Michael Myerberg adapted into dramatic form a poem by Robinson Jeffers dealing with the story of the Crucifixion. Myerberg attempted a poetic form of theatrical presentation to match the spirit of the material and incorporated mimes, the music of Bach (selected and arranged by Lehman Engel), choral singing, friezelike staging, modified modern dress (Jesus vaguely resembled a dude-ranch cowboy), arty sets and lighting, and masks (worn by the dancers--representing the dead--and Peter [Tony Charmoli], Simon [Richard Astor], and John [Betts Lee]). The pretentious result remained dully earthbound. It did not arrive without some controversy, its revisionist ideas about Judas and Christ having led the mayor and official censor of Boston to threaten its banning should it attempt to play there. A then-standing New York ordinance--which also worried the producers of *Journey to Jerusalem*--against presenting the divinity on stage was not invoked, and the play closed because of bad business, not censorship.

The piece is set in the Garden of Gethsemene and attempts to rationalize Judas's (Roy Hargrave) betrayal of Christ (Ferdi Hoffman), called here the carpenter, but its thought processes were convoluted and difficult to grasp. The gentle but high-strung Judas, who loves Jesus although he does not believe in his divinity, is frightened by the political and historical dangers of Jesus' revolution and because he thinks that Jesus will seriously damage his position among his followers. He therefore points his friend out to the centurions, thinking that this will end the danger; he has no idea that his betrayal will lead to Jesus' death. Jesus, a subsidiary character, is shown in an unfavorable light as a highly complex figure, power hungry and bearing a grudge against his mother (Margaret Wycherly).

Brooks Atkinson (*NYT*) considered the work an interesting failure, chiefly notable for its theatricalization and the laudatory performances, especially that of Wycherly. But George Jean Nathan (*TBY*), who faulted the acting and found the poetry monotonous, berated the production for its self-consciousness: "A script which can not stand up to its producer's faith in it has been further wobbled as theatre by the frequent imposition upon it of a misguided, declamatory and too sanctimonious staging and direction." The cast included Harry Irvine as Lazarus.

DEAR RUTH [Comedy/Family/Military/Politics/Romance/War/Youth] A: Norman Krasna; D: Moss Hart; S: Frederick Fox; P: Joseph M. Hyman and Bernard Hart; T: Henry Miller's Theatre; 12/13/44 (683)

One of the big hits of the war years was this slickly effective, fast-paced comedy by screenwriter Krasna that appealed because of tightly effective plotting, consistently funny lines and situations mingling human comedy and mechanical farce, an excellent blend of family and romantic complications, marvelous acting, and tip-top directing. Louis Kronenberger (*PM*) called it "popular entertainment that yields dividends in a good many directions," while holding reservations about the play's incessant going for gags and its lack of fully three-dimensional people. Most people agreed with Rowland Field (*NEN*) that this play, "written with keen skill and enthusiasm," was "a bright suburban family fable expressed in terms of rich humor mixed with wartime human interest." John Mason Brown (*SR*) could find no intellectual reason for praising the play other than to insist that it "IS funny. Very funny. Which should be ample reason for gratitude." *Dear Ruth* made Burns Mantle's list of the season's ten best.

A precocious adolescent girl named Miriam Wilkins (Lenore Lonergan) from Kew Gardens, Queens, engages in a correspondence with a flier, Lieutenant William Seawright (John Dall), fighting the war in Italy. She masks her own identity by writing under the name of her older sister, Ruth (Virginia Gilmore), a very pretty miss whose picture Miriam encloses and who has no idea of what is going on. Miriam is also politically inclined, considers her featherbrained mom (Phyllis Povah) and traffic-court-judge dad (Howard Smith) reactionary, and complains about them to Secretary of State Stimson. One day, Bill Seawright himself turns up at the Wilkins home, assumes that Ruth is the romantic pen pal who has written him sixty letters, and asks her to marry him. Ruth, however, who knows nothing about the letters, is engaged to a stuffed-shirt banker named Albert Kummer (Bartlett Robinson). Aware that the flier will be off for China in twenty-four hours, Ruth, hesitant about breaking his heart, agrees to marry him, assuming that once he has left, the romance will fizzle on its own. After a date, she finds him so appealing that she agrees to become engaged just before he is to depart. Various complications ensue when Bill's overseas orders are cancelled and he is assigned to Florida. He finally discovers who wrote the letters and that Ruth is engaged to Albert. After a subplot involving Bill's buddy, Sergeant Chuck Vincent (Richard McCracken), and his sister, Martha Seawright (Kay Coulter), concludes with Chuck and Martha being married by the judge, Bill takes his leave for Florida. Ruth realizes that she has fallen in love with the guy and begins to kick herself for letting him get away. Bill returns, however, having forgotten to leave Chuck's train tickets. Just before the curtain falls on a photo finish, the judge manages to tie his daughter to Bill in holy wedlock, but not before a sailor (Peter Dunn) sticks his head in looking for Miss Ruth Wilkins.

All the performances were delightful, but Howard Smith's judge, always ready with a quip, was the most successful. Young Lonergan, noted for her deadpan style and bullfrog vocal quality, scored highly, too. Dora, the comical black maid, was played by Pauline Myer.

DEATH OF A SALESMAN [Drama/Business/Family/Hotel/Marriage/Mental Illness/Sex] A: Arthur Miller; M: Alex North; D: Elia Kazan; S/L: Jo Mielziner; C: Julia Sze; P: Kermit Bloomgarden and Walter Fried; T: Morosco Theatre; 2/10/49 (742)

Arthur Miller's towering, Pulitzer Prize-winning play, which he called "Certain Private Conversations in Two Acts and a Requiem," and which originally was called *The Inside of His Head*, received thunderously approving notices. Whitney Bolton's (*NYMT*), for example, began: "The reason for which theater was created, and the exact reason why it never dies in spite of repeated onslaughts by more brash and upstart arts, is powerfully and majestically on view at the Morosco Theater. This is what theater is for. This is the theater at its highest high. This is Mr. Arthur Miller's superb and ravishing play, *Death of a Salesman*." The drama, which also won the Tony for best play and the Drama Critics Circle award for best American play and was one of the Burns Mantle ten best of the season, has remained one of the finest American plays ever written and continues frequently to be revived at home and abroad.

Producer Bloomgarden, who took the play after Cheryl Crawford turned it down (which caused her to cry more at its opening than the play itself), felt that the title should be changed, because "death" in a title seemed commercially unwise. He and his associate, Walter Fried (the two producers won Tonys for their contribution), wanted to call it by the more positive *Free and Clear*. Director Kazan said in *Elia Kazan* that he was adamant about keeping Miller's title. Bloomgarden and Fried got Kazan's approval to discuss the matter with the playwright, with Kazan not present. Kazan just had time to tell Miller that they wanted him to accede to a request to which Kazan was opposed. The title remained.

The play was conceived as a "tragedy of the little man," a work intended to strip away the veneer of the American middle-class dream of material success and reveal its shoddy foundation. Much discussion by subsequent criticism was preoccupied with whether, indeed, this was, or there could be a tragedy of so seemingly insignificant an individual.

Miller's socially oriented theme is expressed in a combination of realism and expressionism (deeply influenced by Tennessee Williams's *A Streetcar Named Desire*), as much of the action transpires in the fevered memory and imagination of the psychologically deteriorating, sixty-three-year-old, Babbitt-like protagonist, Willy Loman (Lee J. Cobb), whose name subsequently was deemed to be allegorically intended. In his autobiography, *Timebends*, Miller scoffed at the notion and revealed that the name (spelled Lohmann) that had lodged itself in his brain was that of the chief of the Paris Sûreté in an old Fritz Lang movie, *The Testament of Dr. Mabuse*. He himself did not become aware of the fact until seeing the movie a second time years afterward, when he heard the name called out by a frightened character and realized that its true significance "was a terror-stricken man calling into the void for help that will never come." The character of Willy, however, as opposed to his name, derived from an uncle of Miller's.

The story flashes back from the days in the present time just before Willy's death to various significant moments in the past that have led to his depression. Jo Mielziner designed a brilliant unit set suggesting in skeletal form Willy's two-level Brooklyn house, surrounded by overpowering apartment buildings painted on a scrim; it allowed for the plot to come to life in various sketchily indicated locales, including several rooms within the house, a restaurant, offices, and a yard. Mielziner was credited by Kazan with providing so brilliant a solution to the play's technical problems that it actually opened a key to the success of his own directing. This design (and several others created during the season) won Mielziner his first Tony. (The step-by-step evolution of this set and its 150-cue lighting plot is described in instructive detail by Mielziner in his *Designing for the Theatre*.) Given outstanding contributions in each of its artistic departments, *Death of a Salesman* was one of the most triumphant theatrical experiences of its time.

Willy Loman is a traveling salesman whose route takes him through New England; his sales figures are in serious decline and his mind keeps slipping into hallucinatory memories. He comes home to his wife Linda (Mildred Dunnock) in Brooklyn, having been unable to keep his car on the road. He and Linda are in a tighter financial bind than ever. His thirty-four-year-old son Biff (Arthur Kennedy, who won a Tony for a supporting performance), a former high-school football star, has just come home after an unavailing attempt to find himself in the Midwest and Southwest. Biff and his younger brother Happy (Cameron Mitchell), a woman-chaser of shallow values, think that the old man is losing his grip. Neither brother has been able to capitalize on life's opportunities, and both are desperately lacking in personal integrity. Willy remembers the boys when they were young and he tried to fill their heads with dreams of future greatness. He told them that to be well liked is the key to success, for that is how one will make money. Sell yourself, not your product, was his misbegotten message. He also remembers an affair with a woman (Winifred Cushing) in a Boston hotel room. Willy's friend and neighbor Charley (Howard Smith) wants to help him out with a job, but the prideful Willy resents the suggestion. He recalls his adventurous brother Ben (Thomas Chalmers), who made a fortune in South African diamonds. Linda breaks the news to her sons that Willy recently has tried to kill himself by attaching a rubber hose to the gas line in the basement. Biff and Happy promise to do what they can to help their father out. Biff decides to visit a businessman named Bill Oliver, who, when Biff was a local sports hero, offered to start him in business. Willy grows ecstatic at the idea and begins to dream of Biff's success. Willy, at Linda's insistence, asks his boss's son, Howard Wagner (Alan Hewitt), for a local route, but is fired instead and must borrow money from Charley (although he continues to turn down the offer of a job). Charley also has a son, Bernard (Don Keefer), a nerd when young, who, in contrast to Willy's boys, has become a successful attorney; Charley insists that he did nothing special in raising his son. Willy meets Biff and Happy at a restaurant, although they have--at Happy's insistence--picked up two girls (Constance Ford and Hope Cameron) before he arrives. Biff has gone to see Oliver, but was not remembered; he even stole Oliver's pen when he left. While the anguished Willy is in the men's room, the sons depart with the girls. More hallucinations come to Willy, who remembers when Biff, seeking his father's assistance upon being given a failing grade in school, came to Willy's Boston hotel, found him there with his mistress, and departed in sorrow and disgust. All of Willy's dreams have turned to ashes. His values have proved little more than dust. He himself is not "well liked." Hoping to regain his family's regard, and thinking himself--because of his insurance policy--more valuable to them dead than alive, Willy kills himself by crashing his car (the sound is heard from offstage). In the epilogue at his grave, his family and Charley gather. Linda, who always sacrificed everything for her husband and supported him when his sons turned against him, notes that the mortgage has been paid off and that they are finally free of encumbrances. Biff says, "He had the wrong dreams. All, all wrong."

The play had the power to make each viewer believe that it was about his or her life. Director Kazan thought it his favorite play because it hit so close to home in reviving memories of his own salesman father. "It is so simple in style and so inevitable in theme that it scarcely seems like a thing that has been written and acted," said the awed Brooks Atkinson (*NYT*). "A merciless and withering drama, it is packed with intensity and genuine theater," kudoed Ward Morehouse (*NYS*). "Virtually everything about *Death of a Salesman* seems perfect," observed Hobe. (*V*). "The play gives the impression that the events taking place . . . are actually happening and gives one the feeling of witnessing the terrifying collapse of a man's dreams and the destruction of his life." Not every review was positive, however. Joseph T. Shipley (*NL*) wrote an interesting explanation of why he thought that the play "essentially fails." He cited such things as thematic confusion, suggesting that Willy's problems stem not from the weakness of the American dream but because he is himself incompetent; that the picture of Biff was similarly confusing, Miller showing him repulsed by Willy's cheating but then himself acting just as dishonestly, and being more a misfit than a failure; and, among other things, that the play's complex time scheme made it very vague as to when various scenes were taking place.

Audiences were stunned by the power of the play, and it often took some moments before they applauded the final curtain. Men, especially, used to be seen sobbing at the end of the performance. At one performance Miller saw aging department-store tycoon Bernard Gimbel making his way up the aisle with an assistant, giving the man an order that henceforth employees were not to be fired for being too old.

Miller had very little rewriting to do during tryouts, the only major revisions coming in the restaurant scene when Biff tries to tell his father the story of what happened at Bill Oliver's. Because of the various levels of mendacity involved, the scene proved very difficult to act clearly. Miller took the scene home and simplified it, agreeing that the result was an improvement.

For most, Cobb's Willy was the stuff of which acting legends are made, although one or two critics thought that he overacted. William Hawkins (*NYWT*) provided a representative comment. "It is hard to imagine anyone more splendid than Lee J. Cobb as Willy. . . . The actor subtly moves from the first realizations of defeat, into a state of stubborn jauntiness alternating with child-like fear in a magnificent portrait of obsolescence." The hulking, large-sized Cobb was completely unlike the small man Miller--remembering his uncle--had felt that the part required. Cobb's brilliance soon convinced him that the actor was right when, during the casting process, he had insisted, "This is my part. Nobody else can play this part. I know this man" (quoted in *Timebends*).

Also monumental was the heartbreakingly touching Linda of Dunnock. A round-table discussion, published in Otis L. Guernsey, Jr.,'s *Broadway Song and Story*, revealed that Dunnock was the second choice after Anne Revere was unable to take the role. Kazan did not think Dunnock right for the part because her speech was too good for Linda and she lacked the proper earthiness. Dunnock said that she went home with the script, "cut out all the final consonants, told myself, 'Be earthy, be earthy,' put on a nondescript black dress and came out onto the stage of the Hudson Theater" to audition. Three weeks later, she was advised to pad herself because she looked too frail for the role. She did so, donned a wig and went back for another reading. "Suddenly a voice from the audience said, 'Take that stuff off.' I'd never been so humiliated." After being cast, she was frightened because she knew that under union rules, she could be fired if she did not prove herself within the first five days. "Kazan was directing with an old broomstick . . . . At the end of the fifth day, he came over to me and exclaimed, 'When I think I might have had somebody else!' This was the beginning of a very, very small love affair."

Just before the play was to open in Philadelphia, Kazan invited Cobb and Dunnock to hear a symphony at the Academy of Music. After the powerful performance ended, he told his actors that they should perform the play the same way. At the next rehearsal, using his stick, Kazan kept drilling Dunnock to speak louder and louder, until she broke down in tears and refused to do it that way. "Where are all the nuances?" she demanded. "We'll come to those in a couple of weeks," he replied.

Kazan provided one of the decade's most masterly jobs of direction and won a Tony for his work. "Here are all the force and skill of the characteristic Kazan performance," wrote John Beaufort (*CSM*), "together with perhaps a greater degree of compassion and tender concern with humanity than Mr. Kazan has heretofore achieved." Among the many memorable production elements, special tribute was paid to Alex North's haunting music, reminiscent of Debussy.

DEATH TAKES A HOLIDAY (*La Morte in Vacanze*) [Dramatic Revival*] A: Alberto Casella; AD: Walter Ferris; D/S: William Corington; P: Equity Library Theatre; T: Muhlenberg Branch of the New York Public Library (OB); 3/28/45 (4)

Free admission was provided for this showcase performance of Casella's 1929 fantasy that George Freedley (*NYMT*) deemed still worthy of being revived, its significance seeming even deeper in 1945 than earlier. The pace was slow, but the production was sensitively staged. Prince Sirki (Death) was played by Dorman Leonard, Katharine Bard was Grazia, George Zoritch was Corrado, former Metropolitan Opera singer Riccardo Martin was Baron Cesarea, and José Greco was Duke Lambert.

DECISION [Drama/Blacks/Crime/Journalism/Labor/Military/Politics/Race/Romance/Sex/Small Town/War] A/D: Edward Chodorov; S: Frederick Fox; P: Edward Choate; T: Belasco Theatre; 2/2/44 (158)

Edward Chodorov, best known for a lighter type of dramaturgy, wrote this intelligent and timely message melodrama while in Hollywood working on a screenplay. He could find no Broadway producer willing to take it on, so he invested his own money in it. The drama met with mixed reviews, but gradually became a reasonable success as good word of mouth about it spread. It was effective enough to be named one of Burns Mantle's ten best plays of the year.

Decision confronted the problem of a nation at war with fascism abroad while a similar threat to its civil liberties lurked at home. When it appeared, it was the only new American play of the season thus far to address directly a war-related problem. It echoed the thesis of a then-current best-seller about a like problem, John Roy Carlson's *Under Cover.*

A race riot in which there are a number of fatalities breaks out between the white and black workers of a small-town aircraft plant. Riggs (Raymond Greenleaf), the upright, humane school principal, quiets the unruly mob by claiming that the cause of the problem is a reactionary senator (not seen) who, backed by shadowy evil forces, stirred up trouble with the aid of Masters (Matt Crowley), the newspaper editor he manipulates. A committee is formed to investigate the accusation, with Riggs named as chairman. Affidavits against the politician are to be collected and turned in to the attorney-general. Supporting Riggs are blacks as well as whites, the unions, and various business leaders, big and small. Meanwhile, Riggs's son Tommy (Larry Hugo) has returned on a brief furlough from active duty, having been wounded in Sicily. He and a local math teacher, Harriet (Gwen Anderson), become engaged, and he finds heaven in the quiet familiarity of his home town. Riggs is being pressured to resign from the committee, but sticks to his guns. He is threatened by the editor and a slimy lawyer (Howard Smith), the latter accompanying a man (Lee Sanford) who claims that Riggs raped the man's sixteen-year-old girl (not seen). Riggs is jailed and found dead in his cell the next morning, his death being trumped up as suicide. The angry Tommy, to whom Riggs has fully explained the principles he stood for, decides to leave the town for good. He argues with his fiancée and others who try to get him to stay and help vindicate his father's name. Then the plant's workers ask permission for all 15,000 of them to attend Riggs's funeral as a show of solidarity. Tommy realizes where his duty lies and decides to remain and fight the local fascists.

An excess of melodrama, contrived plotting, too many set speeches that detracted from plausibility, too abrupt a conclusion, and a split focus on two protagonists, the son and his father, were among the play's acknowledged flaws. Otherwise, it was judged a vital and thoughtful contribution, extremely engrossing, and concerned with an issue of the greatest significance. Rosamond Gilder (*TAM*), for all her approval of the play's effect, found it difficult "to overlook the lack of distinction in the writing . . . and a tendency on the author's part to overstate not so much the political as the sentimental passages of his script." However, George Freedley (*NYMT*) reckoned it "a serious play of real distinction." Louis Kronenberger (*PM*) thought it a play of great moral responsibility that made "good theater," while Howard Barnes (*NYHT*) considered it "a challenging and sometimes moving work," despite its occasional use of "muddled and tedious soap-box harangues."

The play enjoyed an excellent ensemble performance, abetted by such players as Dickie Van Patten, Georgia Burke (outstanding as the former Riggs family cook, now a war worker), Grace Mills, Len D. Hollister, Jean Casto, Rusty Lane, Paul Huber, Merle Maddern, and Paul Ford (in his Broadway debut).

DEEP ARE THE ROOTS [Drama/Blacks/Crime/Family/Politics/Race/Romance/School/Small Town/Southern] A: Arnaud d'Usseau and James Gow; D: Elia Kazan; S: Howard Bay; C: Emeline Roche; P: Kermit Bloomgarden and George Heller; T: Fulton Theatre; 9/26/45 (477)

The most successful of a batch of contemporary dramas dealing with the problems--stemming from race or religion--of returning veterans. In this case, the story, written during the war by a pair of Hollywood screenwriters serving in the signal corps, concerns the plight of young Brett Charles (Gordon Heath), an officer and war hero, when he returns to the Southern mansion in which he was raised as the son of Bella (Evelyn Ellis), a trusted retainer. Having encountered little bias in Europe, he returns to his Jim Crow state seeking the same, but is confronted by the unreconstructed prejudice of the mansion's wealthy, aristocratic owner, retired Senator Ellsworth Langdon (Charles Waldron). The senator's eldest daughter is Alice (Carol Goodner), married to a Yankee (Lloyd Gough). The younger daughter is Genevra (called Ginny; Barbara Bel Geddes), Brett's childhood friend and the girl he loves. Brett turns down the scholarship to study in the North arranged for him by Alice and takes employment as the head of a school, where he hopes to work for the advancement of black people. He rouses local resentment when he enters the local library by the front door. When he is seen walking with a white girl, even more animosity is expressed, especially by the senator, who manages to frame Brett for the theft of his heirloom watch. Alice rejects her bigoted father's behavior until she learns that it was Ginny who was seen in public with Brett. A lynching is considered, but Brett is allowed to leave jail as long as he goes north. The rebellious Ginny stirs a hornet's nest by offering to go with him as his bride. Brett perceives the futility of her gesture, refuses to leave, and insists on remaining to work for the betterment of his race. An apologetic Alice agrees to aid him and Ginny departs alone for the North, but the senator remains unmoved.

The play's meaningful ideas and plea for understanding served it well in the eyes of many critics, but even more appreciated was its effectiveness as theatre, although its writing employed many familiar melodramatic contrivances. Lewis Nichols (*NYT*) acknowledged such flaws as the employment of the trumped-up theft, which detracted from the play's ideational flow. Also too obvious was the inclusion of the miscegenation theme. Moreover, said Nichols, the character of the senator was poorly drawn, his eventual nastiness not being prepared for in advance. Euphemia Van Rensselaer Wyatt (*CW*) noted that the authors had created "a thoughtful and thoroughly literate play, not so carefully balanced as their first [*Tomorrow the World*] but tense in interest from beginning to end." "The theme occasionally becomes turbid," declared Howard Barnes (*NYHT*). "The scenes are frequently overlong and ill-assorted. But it is a work of meaning, delicacy and emotional power." George Jean Nathan (*TBY*) pointed to some of the play's striking resemblances to Edward Sheldon's 1909 *The Nigger*.

Barbara Bel Geddes made an important advance in her distinguished career with her work as Ginny. Her honesty and sensitivity were highly lauded, and much of the play's success was attributed to her presence. Burton Rascoe (*NYWT*) racked his brain to come up with another actress in the past forty years "who had shown the exquisite resources of gesture, timing, voice modulations, facial expression and ability to get into her characterization that Miss Bel-Geddes [*sic*] showed last night." All the other performances were also considered outstanding as was Kazan's intelligent direction. The play was selected as one of the year's ten best.

DEEP MRS. SYKES, THE [Comedy-Drama/Alcoholism/Family/Marriage/Music] A/D: George Kelly; S: Eleanor Farrington; P: Stanley Gilkey and Barbara Payne; T: Booth Theatre; 3/19/45 (72)

Distinguished playwright George Kelly's first play of the forties was a deep disappointment, although it brought a measure of intelligence and thought to a Broadway sorely in need of dramatic weight. It was about a domineering woman who deserved to be placed in the pantheon of the theatre's bitches, already occupied by the eponymous heroine of Kelly's *Craig's Wife**.

Mrs. Sykes (Catherine Willard) is an egotistical middle-aged woman who has complete faith in her intuitive powers. She tyrannically rules the roost over her kindly husband (Neil Hamilton) and married son Ralph (Richard Martin). She is the leading figure in her equally unpleasant social circle. Mrs. Sykes is convinced that her husband, who obviously does not love her, is sending white lilacs to an attractive neighbor, a newlywed pianist named Mrs. Taylor (Katherine Anderson). Mrs. Sykes's gossip convinces one of her friends, the drunkenly voluble Mrs. Fentriss (Jean Dixon), that the flower sender is her own spouse. Mrs. Sykes's intuition strongly disagrees. Finally, Ralph admits to being the guilty party, but Mrs. Sykes's intuition does not allow her to believe him. Mr. Sykes then privately talks Ralph into returning to his wife (Gwen Anderson) and child.

The critics varied in the ferocity of their views, although all were negative. Most agreed that the play was so lugubriously paced and awkwardly staged by the author-director that its flaws seemed even more noticeable. George Freedley (*NYMT*) was embarrassed by how bad it was: "The play has no focus and no focal points. It meanders from one story to another and shifts its emphasis so often and so completely that it was hard to see that the author was getting anywhere except venting his spleen at women in general and mostly, apparently, at women he has known." "Neither as a philosopher nor as a playwright does George Kelly do aught but slide," sighed Joseph T. Shipley (*NL*). Still, George Jean Nathan (*TBY*), while agreeing that the play was imperfect, praised Kelly for psychological insights that "are uniformly honest, well-grounded and sound." Expert actors involved included Margaret Bannerman, Romney Brent, Tom McElhaney, and Ralph Glover, among others.

DEIRDRE OF THE SORROWS [Dramatic Revival] A: John Millington Synge; D: Richard Barr; S/L: Paul Morrison; P: Abbe Practical Workshop; T: Master Institute Theatre (OB); 12/14/49 (3)

A production of Synge's last play, written in 1910 (and still being worked on when he died at thirty-eight) and previously seen locally only in an unnoticed 1920 Off-Broadway presentation by amateurs. This first professional (actually, semiprofessional) New York production was sincere and simple, but its extreme Irishness was not geared toward attracting a large, general audience. The poetic play, replete with mythical and legendary Celtic underpinnings, was critically admired for its mood, its fanciful story, and its poetic diction. Richard Watts, Jr. (*NYP*), pointed to it as "among the glories of the world's dramatic literature, a beautiful, tender and moving lyric tragedy that is as lovely and haunting . . . as anything written in the English language since the days of Shakespeare." Brooks Atkinson (*NYT*) declared it "a masterpiece of romantic tragedy." But the dissenting Robert Garland (*NYJA*) thought, "This *Deidre* [*sic*] *of the Sorrows* sort of thing went out of style along with the suburban 'little theatre' in which it was the fashion."

The story is of the doomed romance of a boy, Naisi (Richard Venture), and a girl, Deirdre (June Bianca). She was raised to be King Conchubar's (David Orrick) queen, but when she meets the boy, she falls in love, and the pair get married by one of the boy's brothers. With the boy's two brothers accompanying them, they go to live on a remote island. Seven years pass and they become uneasy. A man (John O'Hagan) sent by the king of Ulster comes and convinces them to return. Their decision--despite their foreknowledge of what lies ahead--leads to tragic consequences for them and Ireland, and the three brothers meet their deaths.

"The actors . . . play it with all their honesty, going at it softly, caressingly," observed Arthur Pollock (*DC*). Unfortunately, they lacked the proper Irish rhythm of Synge's lines and were often unintelligible, making the already-obscure drama even foggier. Watts thought that the company grasped only "a small part of the spirit and quality of" the piece, but the enchanting writing nevertheless emerged to a fair degree. Paul Morrison's imaginatively sketchy sets were a major factor in the production, as was the insightful direction of Richard Barr. Professional Dorothy Patton, guest actress, played the nurse.

DELICATE STORY [Comedy/Hungarian/Marriage/Military/Romance/Sex/War] A: Ferenc Molnár; AD/D: Gilbert Miller; SC: a one-act play by Molnár, "The Patsy Baker's Wife"; S: Raymond Sovey; P: Gilbert Miller and Vinton Freedley; T: Henry Miller's Theatre; 12/4/40 (29)

Hungary's Ferenc Molnár was a refugee in America at the time this lighthearted play of his appeared on Broadway with British player Edna Best, absent in Hollywood for eight years, in the lead. The play--an expansion of a one-act--was all style but no substance, telling as it did of Mary Cristof, mother of three and coproprietor with her dullish husband Henry (Jay Fassett) of Cristof's Delicatessen Store in Switzerland. Mary, believing that it is her duty to mankind, has had half a dozen innocent flirtations with various young men fated to go to war. She is convinced that handsome men headed for near-certain death should enjoy the favors of sympathetic women. Young foreign reserve officer Oliver Odry (John Craven) patronizes the store daily for beer and sandwiches. Convinced that he loves her, and that she loves him back, Mary engages in a flirtation with him. The pair take a taxi ride and are involved in a minor accident, for which she receives a summons. This comes to the attention of her jealous spouse, who believed her to have been at her mother's when the scrape took place. A scene at the police captain's (Harry Gribbon) office regarding the incident becomes a comic highlight, more because of the eccentricities of the policeman than because of its dramatic relevance. Mary has a bigger setback, though, when she learns that her soldier is really in love with a stenographer who lives near the shop.

An expert production and a delightfully appealing performance by Best were the strongest features of the event, although there were expert turns put in by such actors as Harry Irvine and Arnold Korff. As for the play, Burns Mantle (*NYDN*) was fairly positive: "*Delicate Story* impresses me as being compounded of a collection of Molnar scenes that have been variously used in other comedies and with success. But there are also original twists and the story interest is tenuously but definitely sustained." More common was the opinion of John Mason Brown (*NYP*), who said that the comedy "has none of the smiling virtues one expects of a Molnar comedy. Out of nothing it makes less than nothing."

DELIVER US FROM EVIL [Drama/Crime/Death/Fantasy/Period/Religion/Romance] A: George Makaroff; SC: Nikolai Gogol's short story, "Viy"; S: Robert Lauren; P: William Boyman; T: Theatre Showcase (OB); 10/30/42

An Off-Broadway group organized as a showcase outlet for new theatre talent was responsible for this piece based on a Gogol story set in Russia during the 1840s. The play was better than the production, staged with lesser actors on a thimble-sized stage in a building once known as Unity Hall.

The sets, representing a farm kitchen and a family chapel, were used to back a tale imbued with mystical qualities and telling of Foma Brut, the young bell ringer and would-be priest. Foma, stopping at Sotnik's farm on his way to Kiev, becomes involved with Sotnik's ill-spirited wife, a witch who seeks to gain possession of him. He refuses her, being in love with farm girl Masha, and ends up accidentally slaying the wife after a struggle. He is forced by Sotnik to pray over the wife's corpse for two full nights in the chapel and succeeds by his religious faith (and the wiles of Masha) in overcoming her when she rises from the dead to kill him.

The sole review, by George Freedley (*NYMT*), omitted mention of the actors involved because of the low caliber of the performances. He felt that the play was not as good as the company's previous choice, Saroyan's "Across the Board on Tomorrow Morning," and suggested that the company next try an American play with a milieu in which it might feel more comfortable.

DEPUTY OF PARIS, THE [Drama/France/Historical-Biographical/Period/Politics] A: Edmund B. Hennefeld; D: Day Tuttle; S: Edward R. Mitchell; P: Associated Playwrights, Inc.; T: Henry Street Playhouse (OB); 3/21/47 (8)

A little-noticed but "sober and thoughtful play" (Brooks Atkinson [*NYT*]) by a practicing attorney and dealing with Jacques Dubois (Alexander Scourby), a French political figure of 1830. The semiprofessional production was competent, and Scourby, who became a highly respected actor, gave a solid performance.

His role was that of a scheming liberal politician who rises to power by his promises on behalf of the people but who actually fears the people and who turns out to be more a selfish demagogue than a hero. He seemed to reflect various contemporary leaders, including Adolf Hitler.

Joe Pihodna (*NYHT*) said that the work suffered from verbosity and excessive length, but was nevertheless absorbing. Atkinson thought the dramatic analysis of the leading character too subtle for stage purposes. "In the theatre a simple crook is more persuasive than a psychiatrical rogue."

DERRYOWEN [Comedy/Barroom/Gambling/Irish/Journalism/Politics/Romance/War] A: Michael O'Hara; D: Dennis Gurney; S: Avril Gentles; L: Rebecca Jennings; P: Blackfriars' Guild; T: Blackfriars' Theatre (OB); 10/28/46 (24)

An amateurishly acted and written comedy set in the tap room of Michael James O'Callaghan's (Seamus Maloney) small seaside inn on Ireland's west coast. It has a political theme related to Irish neutrality during World War II.

Ann Travis (Mabel McCallum) and Dan Kilcoyne (F. X. Donovan) are rival

American newspaper correspondents, formerly engaged to one another. They are seeking to investigate the presence of Axis spies in Eire. O'Callaghan and his pal Timothy Aloysius Keough (Gerald Buckley), a pair of rascally, comic types, conspire to stage a fake submarine landing by German spies as a ploy to win a five-pound bet. The result of their practical joke nearly puts them in the clink and inspires the romantic reunion of the bickering reporters, who have temporarily changed partners with an Irish couple, O'Callaghan's daughter Moira (Andrée Wallace) and Donagh, the RAF flyer (Dennis Harrison), who resigned his commission when he learned that the Allies were allowing the Soviets to acquire political sovereignty over Poland. The Irish couple also are reunited. The play's attempt to explain Irish neutrality amounts to little more than to blame it on Irish hatred of the British. "There is not an idea that is not commonplace, or a line of dialogue with any least life, or a situation that is not out of the old stage trunk," lamented George Jean Nathan (*TBY*).

DESERT SONG, THE [Musical Revival*] B/LY: Otto Harbach, Oscar Hammerstein II, and Frank Mandel; M: Sigmund Romberg; D: Sterling Holloway; CH: Aida Broadbent; S: Boris Aronson; P: Russell Lewis and Howard Young; T: City Center of Music and Drama; 1/8/46 (45)

This first New York revival of the once-popular 1926 operetta about romance and adventure in North Africa, with a dual-role hero, Pierre Birabeau (Walter Cassel), also known as the Red Shadow, was unusually weak. This was largely because the actors played the uninspired dialogue and lyrics "so as to bring out every bit of inherent foolishness. Not a little . . . is accented so as to suggest W. S. Gilbert had a hand in it somewhere," moaned Lewis Nichols (*NYT*).

The familiar songs ("orchestrated mayonnaise," said George Jean Nathan [*TBY*]), such as the title tune and "One Alone," were intact, but just barely, as the singers, especially the inadequate leads, Cassel and Dorothy Sandlin (as Margot Bonvalet), had to shout to make themselves heard over the blaring orchestra. Abetting the show's downfall were inferior sets from a superior designer, meagre choreography, and a second-rate supporting company.

DESIGN FOR A STAINED GLASS WINDOW [Drama/Historical-Biographical/Period/Religion] A: William Berney and Howard Richardson; D: Ella Gerber; DS: Stewart Chaney; P: Jack Segasture i/a/w OBS Productions; T: Mansfield Theatre; 1/23/50 (8)

Unlike their previous collaboration, the successful hillbilly fantasy, *Dark of the Moon*, Berney and Richardson's present play, about religious intolerance, was rooted solidly in reality. It was based on the actual story of Margaret Clitherow (Martha Scott), a martyred woman whose staunch faithfulness to her Catholic beliefs in anti-Catholic Elizabethan England ultimately led to her canonization.

The play is set in York, England, in 1571. When Margaret, baptized in the Catholic church, was ten, Queen Elizabeth rejected the papacy (for which she was excommunicated), and Margaret and her family became Protestants. Grown up, she marries the handsome butcher John Clitherow (Charlton Heston), content to avoid religious controversy and mind his worldly matters. Willam Clitherow (Charles Nolte), John's brother, and Margaret's friend Anne Tesh (Carroll McComas) are observant Baptists, but when the Catholic priest (John McKee) who baptized Margaret as a child is sought by the authorities, they hide him. When, as a result of his actions, William is caught and executed, Margaret reverts to her original faith, while a disgruntled former suitor, Robin Flemming (Ralph Clanton), converts to Protestantism. Margaret becomes more and more zealous in her secret defense of her beliefs, holding mass and providing opportunities for children to be taught Catholic dogma. Her oldest son (David Rosen) is shipped off to France so that he can be Catholic without fear. When Robin becomes a powerful earl, he discloses Margaret's activities. Rather than allow her husband and children to testify against her in a jury trial, she does not contest the charges and is sentenced as a traitor to die by torture.

The drama seemed academically stilted, its dialogue pallid, and its direction without a pulse. Because the authors lacked a poetic sense, wrote George Jean

Nathan (*TBY*), their effort was "little more than old-time costume melodrama, clumsily planned and written, in which the motif loses all dignity in a welter of . . . cobwebbed situations." "The play's chief fault," claimed William Hawkins (*NYWT*), "is a lack of characterization. The people . . . are there for one purpose apiece and they have no normal contradictions or facets."

Although Heston received mostly favorable notices, Nathan called him "a pretty fellow whom the moving pictures should exultantly capture without delay, if they have any respect for the dramatic stage." Others involved included Ralph Dobson and Neil Fitzgerald.

DESIGN FOR LAUGHTER [Revue] B/LY: William Mishkin and John Francis; M: Alexander Maissel; D: John F. Grahame; CH: Robert Feyti; S: Josephine Lombardo; C: Faylo; P: Modern Play Productions; T: Provincetown Playhouse (OB); 11/29/44

Modern Play Productions had produced a string of Off-Broadway offerings so dismal that critics dreaded going to their shows, and most deliberately stayed away. In the present case, the company produced a musical revue that proved to George Freedley (*NYMT*) that "this group is inept and amateurish in the worst possible sense of the word." Robert Garland (*NYJA*) trashed it as "pathetic." The show had a song titled "Where Romance Ends," sung by Liz Larsen; a quartet routine called "Pin-up Girls of 1898"; a bit called "High Spy" in which Madame X looked to Garland like "a lesbian in drag"; and so on.

DETECTIVE STORY [Drama/Crime/Journalism/Law/Marriage/Medicine/Romance] A/D: Sidney Kingsley; S/L: Boris Aronson; C: Millie Sutherland; P: Howard Lindsay and Russel Crouse; T: Hudson Theatre; 3/23/49 (581)

This virile melodrama of ideas added considerable spice to the 1948-1949 season with its nearly documentary picture of life in what *TAM*'s undesignated reviewer called an "astonishingly realistic New York detective squad room." It used a large company of actors to play the colorful squad-room types and was commended for its naturalistically etched acting and authentically detailed atmosphere. Kingsley, known for his naturalistic approach in plays like *Men in White** and *Dead End**, had spent considerable time in police stations and in the company of police officers preparing to write and direct this play. Throughout the run he refined and improved the piece, adding new lines and bits to make it ever more convincing. His well-made dramaturgical approach was familiar, but the effect was continually gripping.

"Although its ideas are neither new nor well phrased," thought *TAM*, "*Detective Story* is nonetheless compelling melodrama." Brooks Atkinson (*NYT*) believed Kingsley's style to be dated, but his play to be "powerful and straightforward." All it needed, he said, was inspiration. Kingsley's preoccupation with realistic detail made the projection of its basic ideas cumbersome. John Mason Brown (*SR*) agreed, citing the use of an unusually large cast and intricate plot devices to tell a story that could have been conveyed more simply. But, as Howard Barnes (*NYHT*) put it, "It is the wealth of acute observation, the explosive violence and moments of raucous humor which make it eminently entertaining." Whitney Bolton (*NYMT*) characterized the piece as "a skilled, restless, feverish and greatly absorbing piece of dramatic reporting accomplished with loving care." This drama was chosen as one of the ten best of the season.

The play transpires in the shabby squad room of the bustling (and fictional) 21st precinct, Manhattan. The shoplifters, mobsters, and other riffraff shown are each given their due in concisely written bits interwoven into the action. The chief character is the fanatically crime-hating plainclothesman, Detective McLeod (Ralph Bellamy), an idealist who professes to abide by the highest principles, but whose unforgiving judge-and-jury methods border on the sadistic and inhumane. A crook to him is a crook, no matter how he got that way, and deserves to be punished. His prime antagonist, whom he beats severely, is an abortionist, Dr. Schneider (Harry Worth), accused of killing two patients. When McLeod discovers that his own beloved wife Mary (Meg Mundy) not only had an affair before they were married, but even used the doctor's services, his principles come crashing down around him. ("It is Mr. Kingsley's thesis," advised Atkinson, "that no man should assume the Jovian prerogatives of making final judgments about other men.") The doctor fakes the seriousness of his injuries, pretending that they are fatal. McLeod realizes that he is as cruel a bully as his despised father before him. Try as he might, McLeod can not forgive his wife her transgression, and she walks out on him. A handcuffed crook (Joseph Wiseman)--a "four-time loser"--snatches a cop's gun, and McLeod, trying to get the weapon back, is shot to death. In an important subplot, a young veteran (Warren Stevens) has stolen from his boss to take his girl out in the style she requires, and the girl's sister (Joan Copeland) fights for the boy, whom she loves. McLeod, who treats the boy in his usual hangman style, reforms before he dies and lets the youth go.

A large number of expert characterizations were provided by the talented cast of thirty-four. Bellamy and Mundy were superb, especially the former. Like the author, he had done extensive preparatory research, including visiting New York squad rooms every night, all night, for six weeks. The most useful was the 30th Precinct, at Amsterdam Avenue and 151st Street, which also was used by director William Wyler in preparing the movie version of the story. Barnes said, "Bellamy carries the chief acting load with a remarkable range of restrained make-believe. His unswerving portrayal never fails the script."

In extremely capable support were Lee Grant, making her Broadway debut as a stupid young shoplifter; Horace McMahon as a police lieutenant; Robert Strauss as a detective; Michael Strong as a burglar; Alexander Scourby as a smooth gangster; Lou Gilbert as a police reporter (who functions as a sort of *raisonneur*); James Westerfield as a humane detective; and Les Tremayne as the abortion doctor's lawyer. There were also excellent bits by Jean Adair, Edward Binns, Patrick McVey, Earl Sydnor, Maureen Stapleton (as Miss Hatch), Michael Lewin, and others. So effective were the characterizations of these minor roles that Brown said that a major weakness of the play was that they were more true to life than the principals and their dialogue more honest "than the fancy and high-falutin' phraseology in which [Kingsley's] pivotal figures can indulge." Speaking of Grant, whose debut was exceptional, Bolton said that she gave the best female performance in the play. "She . . . is a young Fannie Brice. She is plain wonderful--and the thunder of applause she got at her exit certified it. . . . She never once dropped out of character or relaxed from the job assigned her."

In *When the Smoke Hit the Fan*, Bellamy told several amusing anecdotes about *Detective Story*. According to one, after the play had been running about a year, he and his fellow actors had to fight to concentrate so as not to fall into "the pattern that was formulated during the rehearsal period and followed from one performance to another." At one performance, McMahon and Bellamy were about to play a dramatic scene that began with McMahon in his T-shirt and his face lathered up for a shave. Bellamy suddenly noticed "a wild panic in [McMahon's] eyes" when the other actor went blank. "Then, as I stood there in terrible silence, Horace bellowed, apropos of nothing at all and at the top of his leather lungs, 'Keep your goddamned mouth shut!'"

Bellamy's difficulty in keeping himself focused was exacerbated by his acting concurrently in a hit TV series called *Man against Crime*. It was broadcast live on Friday nights, eight-thirty to nine, from studios at Grand Central Station. As soon as the broadcast ended, about two minutes before nine, the actor was rushed into an elevator and then into a squad car that, with sirens blaring, raced up Sixth Avenue to deposit him at the theatre, which held the curtain until his arrival. Only when the stage manager, waiting outside, saw him was the signal given to raise the curtain. "I would run to my dressing room upstairs and quickly change into my wardrobe for Jim McLeod . . . and just barely make my first entrance cue. Things aren't done that way today."

DEVIL'S DISCIPLE, THE [Dramatic Revival*] A: George Bernard Shaw; D: Margaret Webster; S: Peter Wolf; C: Emeline Roche; P: New York City Theatre Company; T: City Center of Music and Drama; 1/25/50 (127)

Margaret Webster's staging of Shaw's 1897 American revolutionary war comedy of ideas, last seen locally in a successful 1923 mounting, was offered for a limited engagement of sixteen showings under an arrangement with the unions that allowed for a low-budget presentation. The show was so well received, however, that Richard Aldrich, Richard Myers, and Julius Fleischmann decided to give it a commercial showing at Broadway's Royale Theatre (opening 2/21/50), but union regulations required that the show be completely refinanced and redesigned for that engagement. This cost the producers an estimated $40,000.

The star of the occasion was Webster's frequent collaborator, Maurice Evans (the "artistic supervisor" of the City Center company), essaying the role of Dick Dudgeon, with Dennis King opposite him as the show-stealing General Burgoyne. Hilda Vaughn was Mrs. Dudgeon, Betty Lou Holland was Essie, Logan Ramsey was Christie, Victor Jory was Anthony Anderson, Marsha Hunt was Judith Anderson, Louis Lytton was Lawyer Hawkins, Cavada Humphrey was Mrs. William, Gavin Gordon was Major Swindon, Ian Martin was the sergeant, and Robinson Stone was Titus Dudgeon. Despite only a two-week rehearsal period, the company was lauded for its overall excellence, although a few critics noted that various rough spots would be smoothed out as the run progressed.

The play and production were generally greeted with rapturous delight. Richard Watts, Jr. (*NYP*), claimed, "It is a completely beguiling melodramatic comedy and a thorough joy to behold." "Under the direction of Margaret Webster," wrote Thomas R. Dash (*WWD*), "the production is vivid and continuously engrossing." Arthur Pollock (*DC*) noted that Webster "has a gift for making lucid everything she does, for putting life in plays that will have a hard time dying so long as she is around."

Evans and King vied for honors in the leading roles. "It is Evans' lusty energy in the role of Dick that keys a riotous evening," applauded William Hawkins (*NYWT*). "He is run a close second in the shorter role of General Burgoyne by Dennis King, whose cynical elegance and rational sophistication make the British officer a complete delight."

A day after the opening, Evans became very ill with the flu and played the second night with a temperature of 103 and a doctor in attendance. By Wednesday, he was judged too ill to go on and had to forgo the remainder of the week's run, the first time in the actor's career that he had missed a performance. The understudy (James Daly, later a major actor) was too unprepared to go on, so the actor's personal assistant, Emmett Rogers, whose limited knowledge of the role derived from having attended all the rehearsals, agreed to act instead and managed to make it through the week. A large part of the inspiration he received, according to Evans's *All This . . . and Evans Too!*, was provided by director Webster, crouched in the Dudgeon family's capacious fireplace with a script and a flashlight and ready to prompt when required. Rogers received a standing ovation for his efforts.

DEVILS GALORE [Comedy/Death/Fantasy/Literature/Romance/Sex] A: Eugene Vale; D: Robert Perry; S: Howard Bay; C: Peggy Clark; P: William Cahn; T: Royale Theatre; 9/12/45 (5)

One of a string of Broadway flops early in the 1945-1946 season, this play was set on the thirty-fourth floor of a New York skyscraper, in the office of lubricious literary agent Cecil Brock (George Baxter). Brock, attempting to seduce a female novelist (Tony Eden) from the sticks, is accidentally killed by her when she cracks a lamp over his cranium. When one of Satan's henchmen (Ernest Cossart) arrives from hell (with suitable explosions) to retrieve his soul, Brock convinces the creature to allow him two more weeks on earth so that he can successfully accomplish his seduction and thereby send the devil back with two souls instead of one. The agent fails to accomplish his goal, so the devil goes after the lady himself, even falling for her in the process. She, however, ends up with the agent's office boy (Michael King), whom she loves. The agent--killed this time by Packy "the Flash" Gurney (Solen Burry)--travels downwards, and the devil's experiences teach him that hell has nothing on the devilish behavior of New Yorkers. He decides to change occupations and work for St. Peter in heaven.

Howard Barnes (*NYHT*) offered a typical response in declaring that the play "is as crumby as a piece of striesel cake. The acting is as labored as the script. The jests are as pointless as the pretentious appointments which grace the production. All in all, it is a piece of contrived balderdash." An example of the humor was a line like "Oh, the heaven with you." A number of special effects were used, such as smoke coming out of the telephone during a call from hell. The cast included Rex O'Malley as a hyperactive secondary devil.

DIAMOND LIL [Dramatic Revival*] A: Mae West; D: Charles K. Freeman; S: William de Forrest and Ben Edwards; C: Paul du Pont; P: Albert H. Rosen and Herbert J. Freezer; T: Coronet Theatre; 2/5/49 (181)

"Complete with ruffles, boas, plumes, cut glass, curves, undulating amble and nasal drawl" (Hobe. [*V*]), a somewhat slimmed-down Mae West returned to Broadway with a revival of her 1928 hit melodrama about sin and crime on the 1890s Bowery. She had just performed the piece for three months of twice-nightly performances in London, followed by a successful Montclair, New Jersey, stock-company showing, and then a pre-Broadway tour. In addition to featuring the blond bombshell in her original title role of the golden-hearted trollop, the play also had Louis Nussbaum and Jack Howard in their 1928 roles of Jacobson and Bill, respectively, and a large company of new acquisitions, including jazz singer Sylvia Syms making her acting debut as Flo, Steve Cochran as Juarez the bullfighter, Walter Petrie as the political boss, Charles G. Martin as his rival, Billy Van as a tap-dancing bouncer, Miriam Goldina (of the Habimah Theatre) as white slaver Russian Rita, and Richard Coogan as the handsome Salvation Army captain.

George Eells and Stanley Musgrove reported in *Mae West* that actors who audi tioned for the part of one of Lil's lovers had to come up behind West, reach around, and fondle her breasts before she would decide if they had what it took to perform with her. One unsuccessful applicant was told, in typical Westian style, "I think you better go out and live a little." When she met the actor several years later, he reminded her of his audition. "Yeah. I remember. Ya look like you've lived a little," she responded.

During the pre-Broadway performances, West and leading man Cochran engaged in a series of sexual liaisons in her dressing room. Once the pair arrived during a Baltimore rehearsal to find the assistant stage manager reading West's lines, and the star complimented the man on his effective reading. When he asked, "Why don't ya come down to my dressing room and see me sometime?" he broke up everyone else, but West thereupon decided to end the fling with Cochran. She soon, however, began an open and serious relationship with company pianist David Lapin, who was married and a father, and who came to wield a powerful influence over her.

On opening night, the gaudily garbed West was not completely up to her usual standards, as she recently had been ill, but was good enough to gain a standing ovation at the final curtain. She knocked off her famous innuendo-laden lines (such as "It's not the men in my life. It's the life in my men.") with her classical style of droll, sensual aplomb. A good portion of the third act was like an old Bowery beer-hall floor show, with West singing such tunes as "Frankie and Johnnie," "Some of These Days," and "Come Up and See Me Sometime."

"Although she impersonates a moll who can spur the carnal feelings there is poise, charm and humor in her delineation of the sinner," applauded Thomas R. Dash (*WWD*). Brooks Atkinson (*NYT*) noted how West managed to talk a good deal about sex while suggesting that it was better for a laugh than as something actually to be indulged in.

The ribald piece, a mix of melodramatic hokum and raunchy claptrap, was clearly dated, and its once-daring material seemed tame, if not actually quaint; however, the edge of burlesque given it by the performance made viewing it delightful. "Miss West's play is just as bad as it ever was and just as funny," laughed George Freedley (*NYMT*). "In fact, at least twice as funny now that she is an American National Institution."

Two weeks after the opening, West tripped and broke her ankle, causing the show to be shut down for months until she recuperated, but an insurance policy with Lloyd's of London allowed the idle performers to keep drawing their salaries. Still, the producers soon saw their economic status go from black to red as various costs had to be paid off despite the lack of income. West was finally able to perform again at the end of July 1949 and did so for a couple of weeks at a Central City, Colorado, festival, before the show was brought back to Broadway, this time at the Plymouth Theatre, where it reopened on 9/7/49.

DISTANT CITY, THE [Drama/Crime/Family/Prison/Prostitution/Religion/Romance/Sex] A: Edwin B. Self; D: Edward Byron; S: Samuel Leve; C: Helene Pons; P: John Tuerk; T: Longacre Theatre; 9/22/41 (2)

Many critics wondered how plays like this ever saw the light of Broadway, much less attracted actors of stature such as Gladys George, who played the leading role. George, normally cast as comic blonds, was here bewigged and shabbily dressed for the role of an atheistic septuagenarian mother, Mom Quigley, a former harlot who finds herself at the final curtain seeking religious truth. Mom has a slow-witted, forty-nine-year-old garbage collector son, Pete (Ben Smith), who hangs her up on the wall in her chair so she will be out of his way when he makes sponge cake. Mom tells him that he is a bastard after he discovers that the girl he loves, Edna (Gertrude Flynn), a maid in the minister's home, is pregnant by the minister's sadistic stepson (Leonard Penn). Mom convinces him to ask for the girl's hand in marriage, despite her condition. But Pete gets into trouble when the stepson, wishing to keep Edna's pregnancy secret, kills her and throws the blame on him. Pete is sent to prison, where Mom goes and prays for him with the chaplain (Morgan Farley). Mom finds God in the distant city of heaven, and Pete goes to the chair. Meanwhile, the minister arrives and turns out to be Pete's dad. Finally, Mom's prayers are answered. The minister's wife (Merle Maddern), aware of her son's crime, reveals the truth, and Pete's execution is called off.

"*The Distant City* is so incredible that it is impossible to be sure it actually occurred," gasped Wilella Waldorf (*NYP*). "Sometimes it was bad enough to be funny, but most of the time it was merely bad." In the doomed cast were such players as Robert Vivian, Lee Baker, and Len Doyle.

DR. HERZL [Drama/Historical-Biographical/Jews/Journalism/Politics/Religion/Yiddish Language] A: A. R. Lenz and G. Nilloff; M: Joseph Rumshinsky; D: Maurice Schwartz; S/L: H. A. Condell; P/T: Yiddish Art Theatre (OB); 12/20/45

An episodic telling of the life of Dr. Theodore Herzl (Maurice Schwartz), founder of modern Zionism, a story of particular pertinence when, in the wake of the Holocaust, Palestine (Israel) was the focus of intense efforts to open it as a homeland for the Jews. It was written by a pair of German refugees.

The play, deemed more suitable for its message than for its dramaturgy, covers the high points in Herzl's career, from his days as a journalist for Vienna's Neue Frei Presse at the time of the Dreyfus affair through his energetic, worldwide efforts--at the sacrifice of his personal and family life--on behalf of the establishment of a Jewish state, involving talks with the highest representatives of religion, business, and government. It concludes with his death in a sanatorium before his goal can be reached.

Schwartz, said L. C. (*NYT*), "brings a high degree of strength and magnetism to the role. . . . He played with the emotions of his audience with the skill of an accomplished artist." Herzl's wife Julia was excellently played by Muriel Gruber, and there were fine performances by Berta Gersten, Charlotte Goldstein, Luba Kadison, Menachem Rubin, and Isador Casher.

DOCTOR SOCIAL [Drama/Illness/Medicine/Romance/Science] A: Joseph L. Estry; D: Don Appell; S/L: Stewart Chaney; P: Harold Barnard; T: Booth Theatre; 2/11/48 (5)

Dean Jagger starred as Dr. Norman Farrar, a successful plastic surgeon who makes a healthy income from beautifying wealthy faces (he is nicknamed "Doctor Social" because of his high-class clientele). Dr. Farrar also engages in experiments to create a serum to promote rapid healing, prevent the formation of scar tissue, and stop the spread of cancer cells. An altruistic old teacher of his, Dr. Gordon (Al

Shean), wants Dr. Farrar to donate the serum to the American Cancer Society instead of profiting from it. Dr. Farrar is pressured into operating on a young woman; she has had two previous unsuccessful operations following her disfigurement in an explosion in a chemical lab belonging to the firm that seeks his formula. It is hoped that if he succeeds, a fortune can be made from marketing his methods. The patient, Lee Manning (Haila Stoddard), is discovered to be suffering from skin cancer. Dr. Farrar falls in love with the girl, who is also loved by young Dr. Morrisey (Ronald Alexander). With his serum, he saves her and, because of his love, decides to forgo the cash rewards and to donate his results to the good of mankind by turning his research over to the American Cancer Society and working in cancer research for $150 a week.

The piece was deemed an earnest but hopeless propaganda play. Robert Coleman (*NYDM*) called it "a short, talky, unconvincing script about a muddled genius." William Hawkins (*NYWT*) thought it "superficial and transparent."

Author Joseph L. Estry was reputed to be a pseudonym for plastic surgeon Maxwell Maltz (who wrote the book for the musical *A Lady Says Yes* under another nom de plume). The scientific details discussed in the play were based on actual research then being reported, as well as on advice proffered by the American Cancer Society. In the *Playbill* was a reprinted passage from a *Newsweek* article concerning the use of spleen extract to fight cancer. Donald Foster, Eda Heinemann, Drake Thornton, and Mae Questel had important roles, the latter offering comic relief as a woman seeking a nose job who fears that her unwanted proboscis will return on the faces of any children she may bear.

DOCTOR'S DILEMMA, THE [Dramatic Revival*] A: George Bernard Shaw; D: Guthrie McClintic; S: Donald Oenslager; C: Motley; P: Katharine Cornell; T: Shubert Theatre; 3/11/41 (121)

The first New York revival of Shaw's 1906 satire about doctors--in which art confronts philistinism--since its 1927 Theatre Guild presentation, this hit production starred Katharine Cornell as Jennifer Dubedat, Raymond Massey as Sir Colenso Ridgeon, and Bramwell Fletcher as Louis Dubedat, with Alice Belmore Cliffe as Emmy, Clarence Derwent as Dr. Schultzmacher, Whitford Kane as Sir Patrick Cullen, Cecil Humphreys as Sir Ralph Bloomfield Bonington, Ralph Forbes as Dr. Cutler Walpole, Colin Keith-Johnston as Dr. Blenkinsop, and Ralph Bell, in his Broadway debut, as Redpenny.

The acting gained kudos, as did Oenslager's expert 1906 period settings (which used some antique furniture borrowed from Cornell's own home), but to Brooks Atkinson (*NYT*), the still-witty play, despite a number of judicious cuts by the director, seemed much too verbose. Rosamond Gilder (*TAM*), however, wrote, "Thirty-five years have not dimmed its laughter; custom, far from staling its wisecracks, has turned them into happily recognized familiar quotations. As for [Shaw's] main thesis--the sins and skulduggeries of certain types of medical men--that also is timeless."

Cornell's role was a relatively small one, but her every appearance on stage was noteworthy and proof of her enormous talent. "Whenever she appears, this skittish and garrulous drama comes to attention for a moment," wrote Atkinson, "and communicates genuine emotion. There is something magnetically genuine about her; it pulls Mr. Shaw's capricious gabble together and rouses the interest of the audience." According to Gilder, "Her Jennifer is lovely, lambent--a Cornish princess out of a fairy tale. More than any actress on our stage, Miss Cornell traffics in the essence of theatre: glamour. She sweeps onto the stage and takes possession of it, master of an element which by instinct and through long experience she has made her own." The presence of Cornell meant that the production actually deemphasized the character of Dubedat in favor of his wife, a development that was further underlined by the only partly effective playing of Bramwell Fletcher as the husband.

Despite Cornell's overshadowing an outstanding company by her sheer presence, Raymond Massey demonstrated his mettle, too, in complementing her performance. George Freedley (*NYMT*) wrote, "Mr. Massey's awkward humanity redeems the doctor of smugness, the playing-at-being-God, which is the stumbling block of the actor who studies Sir Colenso Ridgeon. It is a pleasure to be reminded that he is an excellent comedian." This was the first of three productions in three years in which Massey would costar with Cornell, whom he referred to as "Miss Kitty."

At the time he was cast in this high-comedy role, Massey was afraid that the Broadway public would not accept him in any role that did not require a stovepipe hat, as he recently had been a tremendous success in *Abe Lincoln in Illinois**. Massey wrote in *A Hundred Different Lives* that Cornell told him "that one thing which confirmed her choice of me for Ridgeon was Shaw's description of him as wearing a high hat in the last act. She was tickled that there should be one vestigial remain of Mr. Lincoln even though I made it an Ascot grey topper." During the tryout in Cincinnati, Massey experienced the actor's nightmare when his mind went completely blank. It turned out that he had been suffering an amnesiac attack induced by a sulfa drug he had taken for a recent bout with the flu. When the attack hit at the start of his performance and he could not think of what to say to Cornell, he whispered, "I'm no use. I don't know what I'm doing. Just get the rag down as soon as you can." The brilliant actress did not blink an eye; she had played Jennifer only nine times before an audience, but, reports Massey, "without hesitation she gave a resumé of fourteen admittedly short speeches of Jennifer and Ridgeon, picked up the drawings and at the door delivered the curtain line which I should have given after her exit: 'Consultation free, cure guaranteed.'" When Massey had to leave during the run because of a film commitment, he was replaced by the young Gregory Peck, whose official Broadway debut would not be until 1942's *The Morning Star*.

DOCTORS DISAGREE [Comedy/Illness/Medicine/Romance/Sex/Women] A/D: Rose Franken; S: John Root; P: William Brown Meloney i/a/w Buford Armitage and Peter Davis; T: Bijou Theatre; 12/28/43 (23)

A "dated and artificial" (Rosamond Gilder [*TAM*]) tearjerker about the problems faced by women doctors with regard to the lack of respect for their abilities by their fellow physicians and the lack of interest men show in them because of their profession. Barbara O'Neil played an attractive surgeon named Dr. Margaret Ferris, and her physician boyfriend, Dr. William Lathrop, was played by Philip Ober.

The obtuse Dr. Lathrop wants his fiancée to chuck her career when she marries him. She refuses, but suggests that they live together unwed and continue their careers. He refuses. When a child falls ill, Dr. Lathrop advises her to operate, although her surgical procedure is a risky one in which other doctors have no faith. Telling off a male colleague (Judson Laire), she proceeds, the child recovers, its estranged parents (Dolly Haas and John Ireland) are reunited, and the betrothed physicians realize that married life for two doctors may not be so bad after all.

When the play, opened author Franken's *Outrageous Fortune* was still running, but it too was a failure. It was felt that *Doctors Disagree*, originally planned as a serial in a women's magazine, was overly sentimental, clichéd, and mechanical. Lewis Nichols (*NYT*) asserted that it was "too pat. The situations have all been told before, leaving no surprises." George Jean Nathan (*TBY*), referring to Franken's lack of originality in treating the theme of women's fight for professional recognition, said that she "not only contributes nothing new . . . but contributes so much that is theatrically and otherwise ham that her play takes on in sum the dramaturgical architecture of Cain's storehouse." Ann Thomas played a nurse, and Eda Heinemann and Ethel Intropidi played maids, all three being wisecrackers.

DOG BENEATH THE SKIN, THE; OR, WHERE IS FRANCIS? [Comedy/Adventure/British/Drugs/Fantasy/Hotel/Illness/Mental Illness/Politics/Prostitution/Romance/Verse/War] A: W. H. Auden and Christopher Isherwood; D: Alexis Solomos; S: Al Hurwitz; P: On-Stage; T: Cherry Lane Theatre (OB); 7/21/47 (27)

A group of aspiring young semiprofessional actors, most of whose work in the On-Stage company rarely drew press attention, managed to attract some uptown critics with its production of this 1936 British satirical allegory attacking Hitler's Germany and Britain's dullness. The troupe gave a fairly decent performance of the somewhat edited work, which Richard Watts, Jr. (*NYP*), noted was "not always the tidiest or most comprehensible playwriting imaginable." The piece ended after midnight, but few departed before then.

Of the actors, the best was Jean (Gene) Saks as the Vicar and Poet. Others of note were Louis Criss, Anna Berger, Irv Greenberg, Judith Malina (later famed for her Living Theatre company, which was founded the year of the present work) as Mildred Luce and the Ninevah girl, and Walter Mullen. Making her professional New York debut in a chorus role was Beatrice Arthur, who became Saks's wife. The Interplayers, using some of the same actors, offered another engagement (unreviewed) of the play at the Carnegie Recital Hall in December 1948; future star Kim Stanley lists her appearance in the play there as her New York debut.

The broadly comical work, which had so much "rowdy humor and hearty clowning" that Watts noted its resemblance to "a socially-conscious *Hellzapoppin'**," was no longer as topical as when it was written, so some of the material seemed dulled by time. Written in verse reminiscent of Gilbert and Sullivan and using a ten-scene structure (with seventy-six characters) similar to Brecht's epic-theatre style, it tells the story of young Allan Norman's departure from Pressan Ambo to search for Sir Francis Crewe, the missing heir of the late county squire. A new young man is sent on this mission annually, the prize for finding Sir Francis being the hand in matrimony of the squire's daughter. Allan and a cockeyed but fabulously smart dog companion set off with a pair of journalists and come to the mythical kingdom of Ostnia. Here Allan witnesses public executions conducted by the king, encounters extreme greed in the brothel quarters, finds a previous searcher now consumed by drugs, has a scary adventure in an insane asylum when the dog saves him from being murdered by the inmates, visits a hospital whose patients delight in their illnesses, finds another searcher who is killed on an operating table, falls in love with a dressmaker's dummy in the Ninevan Hotel, and then is nearly forced to commit suicide by the beautiful mannequin. Finally, he discovers that inside the dog's skin is the missing Sir Francis, whose observations of the cruelty and degradation of the world have made him hate it. They return home to find that the various branches of the establishment are bullying the local youth. Sir Francis refuses to have anything to do with this system and will fight only for what he believes in. He is slain by a crazed mother whose sons have died in the war, and Allan dazedly carries on. "The play . . . is overlong and sometimes obscure," wrote William Hawkins (*NYWT*), "but it is a rare and novel adventure in theater up to something more than simple entertainment."

DON'T, GEORGE [Comedy/Family/Marriage/Period/Romance] A: Katharine Laure; SC: Katharine Laure's short story, "Winner Takes Paul"; D: Dennis Gurney; S: Viola Kruener; P: Blackfriars' Guild; T: Blackfriars' Theatre (OB); 11/2/44 (22)

The first of four plays put on by this semiprofessional Catholic theatre group during the 1944-1945 season. The work did not greatly advance its reputation, nor did it set it back. "The characters are stock creations and there are few of the extra touches which go with high-royalty drama," asserted George Freedley (*NYMT*). Bert McCord (*NYHT*) faulted the play's construction but approved the author's "flair for dialogue," imagination, and ability to create varied moods. Burton Rascoe (*NYWT*), who criticized the play on several grounds, nevertheless found it more entertaining than "at least eight plays current on Broadway."

Covering the prewar years 1929 to 1941, the play examines a typical American family, the Aversons, living in an Eastern city. Mrs. Averson's (Carol Dunning) spinster sister Laura (Romola Robb) lives with the family, for whom she works like a dog. Her lover (Arthur Allen) has been gone for twelve years, since his dad went broke in the crash. He has only acknowledged her presence once in the entire period, when he sent her a postcard scrawled "Happy Christmas." After he becomes rich again, he returns to the faithful Laura, but the social-climbing Mrs. Averson tries to steal him so that he can marry her own screen-struck bobby-soxer (Eleanor Stafford). The fellow shies at the chance and, with the aid of Mr. Averson (Hal Hershey) and wisecracking young David Averson (Jack O'Neil), avoids the trap and settles for the sister, as he originally intended.

DON'T GO AWAY MAD [Comedy/Blacks/Death/Illness/Marriage] A: William Saroyan; D: Gloria Monty; S/L: Clay Watson; P: Robert O'Byrne and Gloria Monty for the Abbe Practical Workshop; T: Master Institute Theatre (OB); 5/9/49 (2)

William Saroyan, not represented on the New York stage for several years, was responsible for this barely reviewed, ill-received piece shown at an uptown Off-Broadway theatre to an invited audience. Brooks Atkinson (*NYT*), who left before the third act (partly because of the theatre's poor ventilation), called it "a weak and groping play." Richard Watts, Jr. (*NYP*), thought that it contained some good acting and some warmly sensitive writing, but that, on the whole, it was "unnecessarily long and garrulous, and much of it is merely tedious." The play's original title was *The Incurables*.

It takes place in the sunroom of Ward Three of the City Hospital of San Francisco, where various incurable male cancer patients are facing death and trying to lift each other's spirits to keep fighting for life. The chief character is an exuberantly talkative black man, Greedy Reed (P. J. Sidney). Much of the action is concerned with the expression of the patients' ideas. Another character is a bitter man (Jay Barney) who believes that if one hates enough, he can overcome the disease. At the end he kills a bartender who had stolen his wife and soured his son on him. Richard Venture was in the play.

DON'T LISTEN, LADIES [Comedy/Art/Business/French/Marriage/Sex/Women] A: Sacha Guitry; AD: Stephen Powys; SC: Giuseppe Verdi's operatic aria, "La Donna e Mobile"; D: Willard Stoker; S/L: Leon Davey; P: Lee Ephraim and Jack Buchanan; T: Booth Theatre; 12/28/48 (15)

A translation of a mildly indelicate, epigrammatic French marital farce done here by an English cast, with Jack Buchanan in the male lead. "It's an extremely thin and rather dated jest about the eternal battle of the sexes, but has some amusing moments and is adroitly played," was Hobe.'s (*V*) representative response. John Lardner (*TS*) added, "It's not so much that the playwright's situations are old--it's the old, hollow juiceless way he treats them that makes you wonder why . . . he bothered to write the play at all."

At the curtain's rise, Buchanan, playing M. Daniel Bachelet, cautioned the audience that the play to follow would concern women, and that they are the reason for all of man's problems. To avoid offense, he tells the women spectators not to listen. Daniel is a dapper, middle-aged dealer in antique furniture married to the considerably younger Madeleine (Moira Lister), the second Mme. Bachelet. His first wife was Valentine (Adele Dixon), who is still around as Daniel's business partner. Relations between Daniel and his present wife have become strained lately, he suspecting her of infidelity for failing to come home one night. Her excuse is that she was stuck at the top of the ferris wheel. Madeleine, striking back, uses an old love letter sent by Daniel to his first wife and accuses Daniel of fooling around. First wife Valentine, brought in to verify the truth of Daniel's defense, recognizes the rift in the marriage and seeks to sneak her way back into Daniel's affections. All is righted by yet a third woman, Julie (Ivy St. Heller), an old flame of Daniel's whom Toulouse-Lautrec once painted and who wants to sell the portrait to the antique dealer. A whiff of Madeleine's perfume brings the temporarily tottering husband back to his senses, although, when the curtain descends, he still has his doubts about Madeleine's faithfulness.

The cast included Hugh Miller, Austin Trevor, Ian Lubbock, Bartlett Mullins, and Joan Seton.

DOUBLE TROUBLE [Musical/Yiddish Language] B/LY: H. Hoffenberg; M: S. Solomon; ADD./M/LY: Lou Weissman; T: Clinton Theatre (OB); 10/21/49

Paul Burstein and Lillian Lux starred in this barely noticed Yiddish musical given at a former Yiddish vaudeville house. "There are some contradictory components in this opus, but the versatile thespers help bridge the lack of story line and overcome a familiar theme," noted Jose. (*V*).

Lux played two roles, Rae and Naomi Ehrlich, twin sisters. One is a convict serving time for prostitution, the other is an innocent. When the latter is on the brink of marrying Leon (Burstein), she is mistaken for her sibling and the romance is ended. Before the piece ends, the error is rectified and everyone lives happily ever after.

Gertrude Stein, Anna Appel, Esta Saltzman, Dave Lubritzky, and others were involved.

DOUGHGIRLS, THE [Comedy/Hotel/Military/Politics/Romance/Sex/War] A: Joseph Fields; S: Frederick Fox; D: George S. Kaufman; P: Max Gordon; T: Lyceum Theatre; 12/30/42 (671)

A delightfully broad, frequently off-color, wartime bedroom farce set in a Washington, D.C., hotel. It was inspired by Joseph Fields's experience in trying to get a hotel room in Washington; when one proved unavailable because of the war-related boom, he was forced to put up in Baltimore instead. In the crowded Capital Hotel are a madhouse assortment of amusing visitors, uniformed and not uniformed, all of them in search of a place to stay. The play's action, which covers six weeks, occurs in the same suite throughout and reveals the different occupants who seek solace there. Throughout the play, a host of such characters, major and minor, tramp through the place as the phone keeps jangling whenever a new catastrophe is ready to happen.

The central characters are a trio of lovely secretaries, Edna (Virginia Field), Vivian (Arleen Whelan, in her Broadway debut), and Nan (Doris Nolan), rooming together with their boyfriends, a pair of army officers (Reed Brown, Jr., and King Calder) and a civilian scientist (Vinton Hayworth). The gals' chief objective is to land wealthy husbands, namely a brigadier general (William J. Kelly), a philandering admiral (Thomas F. Tracey), and a rubber magnate (Edward H. Robins), all of them already married. The doughgirls are registered with the hotel as married to their respective lovers. Moving in with them is a Russian sniper (Arlene Francis) who has killed hundreds of Nazis (she is a caricature of Ludmilla Pavlichenko, a celebrated guerrilla fighter recently in the news). Barging in at odd times are the various straying tomcats; a flustered hotel manager (Sidney Grant); maids, bellhops, and so on; a little man (Harold Grau) who keeps coming in and out looking for somewhere to sleep; a female judge (Ethel Wilson) from Montana, whose judgeship really reflects her position as a referee at pie-baking contests; the general's wife (Natalie Schafer, a last-minute replacement), and others. Before the final curtain, wedding bells can practically be heard ringing for Nan, who must quickly marry her aviation lieutenant beau in order to be eligible to attend a White House luncheon in his honor. Wedding rings do not seem unlikely for her two companions in the near future.

Fields had two other hits running on Broadway when *The Doughgirls* opened, *Junior Miss* and *My Sister Eileen*. Because he had cowritten those comedies with Jerome Chodorov, he gave the Russian sniper in *The Doughgirls* the name Chodorov as an in-joke. With this thinly plotted but continually uproarious comedy satirizing Washington big- and littlewigs, especially those in the armed forces, he added "a bawdy, straight-shooting laugh getter" (George Freedley [*NYMT*]) to the season. "The comedy is gay and good-natured," noted Howard Barnes (*NYHT*), "as well as being a trenchant commentary on the Washington hurly-burly. The lines exploit every inflection of comedy that is inherent in them. . . . The situations form and dissolve in a fast-paced and persuasive continuity."

Fields was immeasurably aided by the brilliant comic inventions of Kaufman (who also did considerable rewriting of the script). Said Rosamond Gilder (*TAM*) of Kaufman, "The hand of the master can be discerned keeping the bright colored tiddledy-winks hopping about in agile parabolas, but always landing centre stage. Action, inventive business, wisecracks are of the true Kaufman brand." In rehearsal, Kaufman kept plaguing playwright Fields for bigger laughs on the exits, and Fields never seemed to satisfy the director's demands. Then, during a break in a rehearsal, a slovenly old cleaning woman slowly walked across the stage carrying her mop and pail before disappearing into the wings. "Jesus, George," said Fields, "she got off without a laugh." That ended, at least temporarily, Kaufman's comments about the exits.

Some critics booed the play's often-ribald humor, Wilella Waldorf (*NYP*), for example, chastising producer Gordon for wasting so much talent on a play "that is not only unfunny most of the time, but also in very bad taste." Gordon himself found some material in poor taste, particularly an exchange in which a mother of six complains that she had children at the drop of a hat and would be pregnant now if her spouse had not gone to Australia, to which another woman replies, "Yes, and he took the hat with him." However, his request to drop these or other lines was met with fierce resistance from writer Fields, who, under the powers granted him by the Dramatists Guild contract, put the cited lines back in after the play opened to raves.

The ribaldry of the play may have infected some of the cast members, for Francis told in *Arlene Francis* of some backstage japeries that involved herself and the three female leads. She was sharing a dressing room on an upper level with Doris Nolan, while the stage level dressing room was occupied by Virginia Field and Arleen Whelan. The upstairs actresses were annoyed that people coming backstage after performances often would stop at the lower room first and never get to theirs. They jokingly complained that visitors were being held in thrall by Whelan's flaming red hair. Francis and Nolan thereupon announced that there would be a Valentine's Day entertainment for the other women in the company. The pair went off to a hairdressing salon and had what they "privately called their public hair" bleached and shaved into the shape of a heart. On the day appointed, prior to a matinee, the women of the ensemble were gathered, and Nolan and Francis appeared draped in kimonos. After reciting a poem about Whelan and Fields, they whipped open their kimonos "and at the last line flashed our Valentines for a dynamite finish."

DOWN TO MIAMI [Comedy/Business/Family/Hotel/Military/Religion/Romance/Southern] A: Conrad Westervelt; D: J. B. Daniels; S: Stewart Chaney; P: Edgar J. MacGregor; T: Ambassador Theatre; 9/11/44 (8)

"A welter of witless clowning about racial problems" (Howard Barnes [*NYHT*]) that had the critics prizing it as the worst play thus far of the season. Reminiscent of *Abie's Irish Rose**, it managed to present both Jews and Gentiles in an unpleasant light as it told of two Springfield, Massachusetts, families vacationing at a big hotel in Miami, the banker Applegates and the department-store Mandels. One patriarch is Torrence Applegate (Herbert Heyes), the other Morris Mandel (Robert Leonard). Their long-suffering wives were played by Merle Maddern and Dora Weissman, respectively. The men are not on the friendliest terms because of business and cultural differences. Mandel banks with Applegate, but is not considered socially appropriate. They are on even worse terms when they learn that their children, Rufus Applegate (Charles Lang), a marine officer on furlough, and Gloria Mandel (Elaine Ellis), have fallen in love after she, with the connivance of an Irish cop (Brian O'Mara) has purposely placed herself in a situation where he could rescue her from the ocean. This despite the young folks being in Florida for the express purpose of being married off to others of their own faith. At any rate, love conquers all, as expected, and by the end, the biased parents become unbiased over a bottle of Scotch.

The play pounded out dozens of ethnic jokes about the Jews and Gentiles, with Leonard as the Jewish father playing in a dialect so broad it should have brought the B'nai B'rith down on him. "*Down to Miami*," expostulated Ward Morehouse (*NYS*), "is trite, long-winded, and terrible playwriting in its feeblest state." Robert Strauss, making his Broadway debut, had a small role in the proceedings.

DRAPER, RUTH (see *Ruth Draper*)

DREAM GIRL [Comedy/Barroom/Fantasy/Journalism/Literature/Mexico/Prostitution/Romance/Sex/Theatre/Trial] A/D: Elmer Rice; S/L: Jo Mielziner; C: (gowns) Mainbocher; P: Playwrights' Producing Company; T: Coronet Theatre; 12/14/45 (348)

Elmer Rice wrote and directed this hit fantasy-comedy (one of Burns Mantle's ten best plays of the season) starring his young wife Betty Field, who provided a remarkable tour de force performance in a role that required her onstage presence throughout almost the entire presentation, and that had her making numerous split-second costume changes. The length of her role was compared to that of Hamlet. So exhausting was it that the star came down with the flu after opening night and was temporarily replaced on night two by her understudy (Helen Marcy), whose excellence was much marked. However, as Rice noted in *Minority Report*, despite the publicity she achieved, "she never had the luck to follow up her sensational debut."

The highly inventive set by Mielziner, employing three small platforms riding silently on tracks, sideways, upstage, and downstage, allowed the multiscened play to move along swiftly without a pause. Mielziner's ingenious lighting played an active part in the transitions as well, all changes being done in full view of the audience. The production was deemed a perfect example of Broadway's technical virtuosity and polish. It was Rice's last success.

Dream Girl tells of a day and a half in the life of virginal twenty-three-year-old Georgina Allerton (Field), a persistent daydreamer and would-be novelist, who runs an unprofitable bookstore. The play recounts her various daydreams, beginning at 8 A.M. and ending at 4 P.M. the next day. Her dreams include a romance between her and her brother-in-law (Kevin O'Shea), who wants to divorce her sister (Sonya Stokowski) to marry her; a sinful alliance in Mexico with a guileful publisher (Edmon Ryan); a courtroom scene where she is on trial for having shot a no-nonsense book reviewer and would-be sports writer (Wendell Corey) who panned her novel; an episode in which she is a suicidal streetwalker; and a trip to the theatre with that same handsome journalist to see *The Merchant of Venice**. Before the curtain rises on Shakespeare's play, however, an announcement is made that the star, playing Portia, is ill and that refunds will be given to those who want them (which duplicated exactly what happened on the second night). Georgina goes on in the star's role, which she once played in high school. The work concludes with her eloping to Greenwich to marry the reporter, who has taught her to abandon her dreams for reality.

Lewis Nichols (*NYT*) and others suggested that the play needed cutting--especially in the early scenes--and that some of the author's targets were too easy, "But when he is traveling at the right speed, the scenes flow cheerfully along--some extremely funny, some warm, all developing the nice character the author and the distaff side of the house make of her." "It's all told skillfully and engagingly and represents a feat in stagecraft as well as one in playwriting," noted Ward Morehouse (*NYS*). It was "a very entertaining show" to Louis Kronenberger (*PM*). Among the small group who disliked the work were Wilella Waldorf (*NYP*), who dismissed the piece as "more like a set of revue skits than anything else." George Jean Nathan (*TBY*) called it "a poor play relieved at only widely spaced intervals by a little pointedly observed humor."

The critics loved Field. Her role, said Kronenberger, "calls . . . for a presiding knowledge of a bright but rather silly girl, but for immense versatility, too, and a very elastic comedy sense. Miss Field displays, with only rare lapses, all of these things. She is faithful to each of her roles, and funny in most of them. She is, in fact, about the most accomplished actress of her age now on Broadway."

Corey, whom Rice cast over many objections, received fine reviews as well and soon was in demand as a film actor. Also in the cast were Evelyn Varden, Will Lee, James Gregory, and many others; several played multiple roles.

In *Minority Report*, Rice disclosd that the play was originally intended to be a tragic one about "an inhibited little man who finds compensation for his frustrations in extravagant fantasies in which . . . he is the central figure." When he suddenly realized that it could be converted into a comedy about a young woman, "everything fell into place; when I sat down to write, it flowed along easily." He admitted that the work turned out to be "a love letter to Betty," although the actress was reluctant to undertake the role because of its great physical demands. The show was made into a musical called *Skyscraper* in 1965.

DREAM OF LOVE, A [Drama/Fantasy/Literature/Marriage/Medicine/Sex] A:

William Carlos Williams; D: Barbara J. Whiting; CH: Ted Dailbottom; S: Idell Carruth; P: We Present; T: Hudson Guild Theatre (OB); 7/26/49

Poet, novelist, and physician William Carlos Williams's first produced play was done by a new Off-Broadway group in a scarcely noticed staging in a West Twenty-seventh Street basement theatre. Richard Watts, Jr. (*NYP*), revealed that "it gives every evidence of being the work of a young, naive and inexperienced writer. Its excursions into both sex and dramaturgy are ponderous and terribly serious-minded. . . . [Williams's play is] pretentious, humorless and just a little silly." Arthur Pollock (*DC*), annoyed by Williams's use of vulgar language, observed, "As a dramatist, Mr. Williams is distressingly amateur."

A troubled wife (Gerien Kelsey) hides in a closet as a nosy milkman (Robert H. Fuller) tries to worm from a maid (Vinnette Carroll) the story of how the wife's husband (Lester Robin), a physician and poet, died in a hotel bedroom to which he had brought another woman. The milkman has read about the death in the papers and is interested sexually in the widow. After the milkman's departure, there is a flashback to the home life of the wife and husband, who ponders whether to continue in medicine or devote himself to poetry, some of which he reads to his wife. The other woman (Erica Feydn) pushes her way in, determined to get everything straightened out with the wife. An angry name-calling scene erupts. In another flashback, the other woman fights with her own spouse (DeWitt Drury) about the doctor. As the play progresses, the late husband appears to recall his youth and discovery of sex, his erotic memories being enacted by two dancers (Shirley Rhodes and Frank Aletter). The wife gets lost in her dreams, during which there are enigmatic appearances by both the milkman and the unfaithful husband. The piece "strives for imagination, psychological insight and lyric beauty," said Watts, "and achieves only ineptitude."

DREAM WITH MUSIC [Musical/Broadcasting/Fantasy/Journalism/Period/Romance/Sex] B: Sidney Sheldon, Dorothy Kilgallen, and Ben Roberts; M: Clay Warnick; LY: Edward Eager; D/P: Richard Kollmar; CH: George Balanchine (tap: Henry Le Tang); S: Stewart Chaney; C: Miles; T: Majestic Theatre; 5/18/44 (28)

Vera Zorina, famed Norwegian dancer usually known by only her last name, was given surprisingly little in the way of terpsichorean chores (although she did have a dream ballet) in this opulent (around $240,000) but boring musical in which she did have plenty to say and sing. Her performance was a major reason for attending the otherwise heavy-handed show. Composer Warnick adapted much of his music from artists like Saint-Saëns, Rimsky-Korsakov, Schubert, Beethoven, Grieg, Borodin, Dvorák, Haydn, and Tchaikovsky, although the music was so distorted in its new arrangements as to prove virtually unrecognizable. On opening night the show was rough, with flubbed lines, missed lighting cues, and the like, suggesting backstage technical incompetence. There was also some objection to the plugging of Lux soap in a scene during which Zorina supposedly took an onstage bath.

In the extremely weak book (vaguely reminiscent of *Lady in the Dark*), Zorina played Dinah, a radio soap-opera writer, who is romantically attached to the stuffy advertising executive, Robert (Robert Brink), her employer. There is also an attractive war correspondent named Michael (Ronald Graham). Dinah, worn out trying to figure out a conclusion to her show, falls asleep and dreams that she is Scheherazade of *The Arabian Nights*. She is wafted to Arabia on a magic carpet and encounters the people from her daily life transformed into fantasy figures. Robert is the sultan, to whom she must tell a new tale every night. Michael turns up as Aladdin. Her secretary Marian becomes a girl named Jasmin (Joy Hodges). Another principal character is Sinbad the sailor (Leonard Elliott), while his wife Mrs. Sinbad (Betty Allen) also figures prominently.

Herrick Brown (*NYS*) agreed with many others who felt that the production was "lavish and eye-filling and beautiful, but all too often ponderous." Arthur Pollock (*BE*) called it "one of the dullest musical comedies imaginable." Colibrettist Kilgallen, the famous columnist, was the wife of producer-director Kollmar.

When Zorina was flown on her magic carpet, she was supposed to step forth and float gracefully down to earth. She wrote in *Zorina* that one night, during a dance sequence involving the carpet, the wire supporting her slipped from her belt when she walked into space, and she came crashing to the floor. Dazed and somehow not yet feeling the pain, she continued to dance the rest of the number, becoming hysterical only after the curtain fell. A physician backstage noticed no broken bones, and she finished the performance. "The next night I had not one but two wires for safety. Talk about locking the barn door after the horse is stolen!"

DRUID CIRCLE, THE [Drama/Marriage/Period/Romance/Sex/University/Youth] A/D: John van Druten; S/L: Stewart Chaney; P: Alfred de Liagre, Jr.; T: Morosco Theatre; 10/22/47 (70)

In 1925 John van Druten pleased Broadway playgoers with *Young Woodley**, his romance set in an English public school called Mallowhurst. In *The Druid Circle* he told of life in a rural Welsh university during the same period and again placed a romantic affair at the heart of his story. The present play was literate and well crafted, but had limited appeal. Among the warmer critiques was Ward Morehouse's (*NYS*), who called it "a slight but penetrating and engrossing piece." Brooks Atkinson (*NYT*) thought that this was one of van Druten's best, "a mature piece of work--light in touch, but compassionate in attitude and critical of the inhumanity of old people toward the young." However, a slight majority sided with William Hawkins's (*NYWT*) opinion that "it seems to take place inside a delicate eggshell or under the thinnest sheet of ice. It never quite comes through its transparent caul to clutch or crash one's emotions." "It is . . . to be respected for its honesty and period skill," noted George Jean Nathan (*TBY*), "but in the end it does not satisfy." Shortly before the play opened on Broadway, its original period setting of 1912 was moved to the 1920s.

The partly autobiographical play's title alludes to an old term for English college professors. Chief among the characters is the crusty, narrow-minded, sexually frustrated, and tyrannical Professor White (Leo G. Carroll), turned sour by a lifetime in a stultifying environment; he holds a jealous grudge against the youth of his students. There is also a young teacher named Maddox (Boyd Crawford), who is married to Brenda (Neva Patterson), a lovely former actress expecting a child, a development that leads him to seek to leave the airless school, where he is beginning to feel trapped. The central action concerns Professor White's discovery of a love letter written by a student named Tom (Walter Starkey) to a girl named Megan (Susan Douglas), leading the old man to suspect terrible improprieties. In what was considered a deeply moving scene, he forces the hapless youth to read the letter aloud in the girl's presence, causing her to become hysterical and to vanish for several days. It is feared that she has killed herself. Various complications ensue, with Maddox championing the young people and he and his wife helping to restore the feelings of the young lovers once Megan does return. At the conclusion, the guilt-stricken old professor assumes some responsibility by resigning.

The acting was generally first-rate, especially that of Carroll and Ethel Griffies as White's sharp-tongued, invalid mother, who is aware of his shortcomings and gives him verbal hell for his behavior. Other performers included Merle Maddern, Noel Lesley, Aidan Turner, and Lillian Bronson.

DUCHESS MISBEHAVES, THE [Musical/Art/Fantasy/Period/Sex] B: Gladys Shelley and Joe Bigelow; M: Dr. Frank Black; LY: Gladys Shelley; D: Martin Manulis; CH: George Tapps; S: A. A. Ostrander; C: Willa Kim; L: Carlton Winckler; P: A. P. Waxman; T: Adelphi Theatre; 2/13/46 (5)

The tired convention of taking present-day characters back into time to live under the conditions of another period was employed once more in this unimaginative, $230,000 flop. It suffered from various malaises, not the least of which was comic repartee in which a maiden declares, "Oh, Señor, don't go, you bewitch me," and the object of her affections replies, "Aw, I'll be wit'choo later."

Joey Faye (a last-minute replacement) played a timid department-store handyman named Woonsocket who is conked on the head by thieves when they rob Goya's nude painting of the duchess of Alba from an art exhibition. He imagines that he is the lubricious Goya back in eighteenth-century Spain and that his dream girl, Crystal Shalimar (Audrey Christie), is the duchess. On his tail is the duchess's spouse (Philip Tonge), jealous of Goya's having painted her in the nude. The artist's goal is to find another woman with a similar mole on her thigh so that he can claim that she was the model, not the duchess. When the plot gets too hot, Woonsocket comes to himself again back in 1946.

The "overpoweringly dull" (Ward Morehouse [*NYS*]) show was excoriated for its poor book, lyrics, music, and performances. It also was damned for its persistently smutty tone. Faye's jokes fell one after the other like lead balloons. "A group of luckless players . . . find themselves completely defeated. It is odd to think that an entire company may be miscast, but it seems quite logical under the circumstances," thought Lewis Nichols (*NYT*). Company members included Paula Laurence, Penny Edwards, Larry Douglas, the Boyd Triplets, and George Tapps, whose dances were one of the few bright spots in the show. Songs included "Katie Did in Madrid" and "I Hate Myself in the Morning."

DUCHESS OF MALFI, THE [Dramatic Revival] A: John Webster; AD: W. H. Auden; M: Benjamin Britten; D: George Rylands; S: Harry Bennett; C: Miles White; P: Paul Czinner; T: Ethel Barrymore Theatre; 10/15/46 (38)

One of the more unusual revivals in the revival-laden 1946-1947 season was this one of Webster's then rarely produced Jacobean tragedy (written between 1612 and 1614). It was believed to be the first professional staging of the play in New York. The tale, placed in Renaissance Italy, is of the morganatic marriage of Giovanna, duchess of Malfi (Elisabeth Bergner), to her steward, Antonio Bologna (Whitfield Connor), with whom she has three children. Because they consider the children illegitimate, and because one bears incestuous feelings and the other pathologically possessive ones toward her, the duchess's brothers, the Cardinal (John Carradine) and Ferdinand (Donald Eccles), duke of Calabria, rebuke her; they seek to liquidate all five blots on the family escutcheon, the duchess, her presumed lover, and the three youngsters. With the aid of their cruel spy Bosola (Canada Lee), the revenge is accomplished, but the conspirators fall out and end up killing one another. In the course of the drama, the duchess, in her death scene, witnesses a series of frightening, fantastical tableaux intended to make her mind crack. She is shown the waxed figures of her deceased loved ones and an entourage of lunatics. These are followed by the entrance of her coffin-carrying murderers as a bell tolls.

Despite the play's very respectable position in English theatrical history, various reviewers questioned its selection for a Broadway revival; most said that it belonged in the library, not on the stage. George Jean Nathan (*TBY*) declared, "The writing is often merely turgid where it aspires to be rich crimson and purple, and the dramaturgy sketchy where it hopes to be elliptically driving." Its pace was lugubrious, its period scenery stodgy, and its effect undistinguished. George Freedley (*NYMT*) referred to its "fustian" and called it "bombastic." He said that the final scene of slaughter actually caused audience laughter by its excesses. Brooks Atkinson (*NYT*) reported that the scene of the duchess's death was completely devoid of scalp-tingling effects and was as interesting as having a tooth extracted.

The "baffling and embarrassing" (Howard Barnes [*NYHT*]) adaptation of the play was originally a project involving German playwright, Bertolt Brecht, then living in America. Brecht had begun the adaptation with a little-known poet called Hoffman R. Hays. After some progress had been made, Brecht decided to ask the better-known poet, Auden, to collaborate on the text, and Hays was abandoned. The project was put off for various reasons, but Bergner continued to prod the adaptors to finish their work, which underwent numerous revisions at her insistence. Brecht accepted most of her demands (such as interpolating material from other Webster plays and from one by John Ford), but Auden did not always agree. When a London version directed by George Rylands and starring Peggy Ashcroft and John Gielgud proved successful, Bergner's producer husband, Paul Czinner, hired Rylands to stage the present adaptation. Rylands, on learning of the changes in the text, refused to direct the work unless the revisions were removed. During the tempestuous out-of-town tryout period, most of his demands were met, and Brecht, wisely fearing a flop, removed his name from the credits.

Few of the performances were impressive. Although she brought a certain dignity to the role, Bergner's Teutonic accent made much of her dialogue, which required considerable grasp of its poetic rhythms, incomprehensible. Black actor Canada Lee, whose use of whiteface to play Bosola was much discussed, lacked conviction, although he had some mild supporters. His makeup also seemed obviously artificial and could not hide his native features.

DUET FOR TWO HANDS [Drama/British/Crime/Literature/Medicine/Period/Romance] A: Mary Hayley Bell; D: Reginald Denham; S: Charles Elson; C: Helene Pons; P: Robert Reud; T: Booth Theatre; 10/7/47 (7)

A dreary and absurd British horror play set in the windy Orkney Islands in 1904. Despite being a hit in 1945 London, it horrified no one in New York and was quickly tossed away. "Seldom has anything which purported to be drama been so blanketed with dullness," yawned Louis Kronenberger (*PM*). To Ward Morehouse (*NYS*) it was "melodramatic junk, diffuse and wavering."

There were able performers floundering in this tale of sensitive poet Stephen Cass (Hugh Marlowe), who lost his hands in a mountain-climbing accident and has the demented but brilliant surgeon, Dr. Edward Sarclet (Francis L. Sullivan), surgically attach to his wrists the hands of a dead man. (The program bore a note about the recently successful grafting of a thumb and a finger to someone's hand.) The new hands, however, belonged to a man hanged for a murder he did not commit. They somehow impart to their new owner aspects of the dead man's character and feelings. One such feeling is the love of the former owner for the doctor's daughter Abigail (Joyce Redman), whom Stephen has just met. For several scenes Stephen tries to figure out something else the white-gloved hands are telling him, which is to murder the surgeon, who was responsible for the killing that led to the hands' first owner's execution. Before murder is committed, though, the doctor dies of a heart attack.

The vivacious Redman and the obese Sullivan, British actors, and handsome American player Marlowe gave surprisingly deft performances despite the inanity of their material. Ruth Vivian and Wynne Clark rounded out the cast.

DUKE IN DARKNESS, THE [Drama/British/France/Mental Illness/Period/Politics/Prison] A: Patrick Hamilton; D: Robert Henderson; S/C: Stewart Chaney; P: Alexander H. Cohen and Joseph Kipness; P: Playhouse; 1/24/44 (24)

Successful British melodramatist Patrick Hamilton came a cropper with this all-male costume play (premiered two years earlier in London) set at the Château Lamorre in France in 1580. It concerned the good duke of Laterraine (Philip Merivale), a supporter of Henry of Navarre imprisoned for fifteen years in the château by his mortal enemy, the duke of Lamorre (Louis Hector). Incarcerated with him is his faithful secretary Gribaud (Edgar Stehli), whose mind is cracking. They occupy the time playing chess, fashioning escape plans, and bickering with one another. To gain more amenities from his captor, Laterraine has been feigning blindness for several years. Lamorre, afraid that if his prisoner escapes, the people will rise in his support, arrives to test Laterraine's eyes to see if he really is sightless. The effeminate Count d'Aublaye (Albert Carroll) holds a fiery poker to Laterraine's eyes, but he does not blink. An escape is planned for Laterraine by one of his followers, the handsome Captain Voulain (Raymond Burr, in his only Broadway appearance), who is incognito among Lamorre's château staff. To effect the breakout, it is necessary to get rid of the secretary, who has become a raving lunatic. He is tossed down to the courtyard after being poisoned. Laterraine's followers appear and help him to get out.

The swashbuckling melodrama--which could be seen as having a slight relation to contemporary world affairs--often fell into unconscious self-parody, was colorless, bombastic, and lacking in action, and employed two-dimensional characters. Louis Kronenberger (*PM*) said that it "lacks ingenuity, atmosphere, suspense," and was "without the slightest compensation in the way of character drawing or dialogue. It is simply old-fashioned melodrama with very little melodrama."

DUNHAM, KATHERINE (see *Katherine Dunham and Her Company*)

DUNNIGAN'S DAUGHTER [Comedy-Drama/Art/Business/Marriage/Mexico/Politics/Romance] A: S. N. Behrman; D: Elia Kazan; S: Stewart Chaney; C: (gowns) Mainbocher; P: Theatre Guild; T: John Golden Theatre; 12/26/45 (38)

A tiresomely rhetorical "high comedy," as its director called it, set in Mexico outside a small mining town and telling of Clay Rainier (Dennis King), a superficially charming but quite ruthless "gringo imperialist" and art collector, whose third wife is the beautiful young Ferne Rainier (June Havoc). Her father, a political boss named Dunnigan, killed himself in a Chicago prison. The household also includes Zelda (Jan Sterling), Rainier's daughter by a previous wife. Rainier mistreats Ferne as much as he does the local natives, whose water power he seeks to exploit for his own purposes. A sympathetic Diego Rivera-like Mexican muralist named Miguel Riachi (Luther Adler) offers her an opportunity to leave with him, but she opts instead for a childhood friend, Jim Baird (Richard Widmark). Jim is an idealistic junior secretary in the State Department who is wooing Zelda and is in Mexico to investigate Rainier's activities. Both men seek to inform Ferne of her spiritual enslavement to the tycoon. Baird's revelations include the fact that Rainier was responsible for Ferne's father's death, and it is this information that finally decides her to abandon Rainier's millions and depart with her stepdaughter's boyfriend for a considerably less luxurious lifestyle.

The talky, nearly actionless work, which underwent extensive revisions during its tryout period, including the shift of the locale to Mexico and the recasting of its major roles, was panned on several fronts. Lewis Nichols (*NYT*) thought it too literary and unfeeling for the stage, with an emphasis on form dominating that on substance. Nichols also argued that the character of Rainier was left too one-dimensional, his reasons for behaving as he does being vague and ill defined. George Jean Nathan (*TBY*) thought it Behrman's poorest play in years, which he attributed to the writer's increasing preoccupation with "economic, sociological, and political matters." Burton Rascoe (*NYWT*), comparing the play unfavorably to *A Doll's House**, commented, "There is no inevitability in the development of the theme, no firm establishment of character, and only a mild eyebrow-lifting surprise instead of a climax."

According to John F. Wharton's *Life among the Playwrights*, director Kazan refused to undertake the assignment unless it was produced by someone other than the Playwrights' Company, which the latter took as an insult. Behrman may have been behind this, as he was then seeking a way of disengaging himself from the company. The company tried various solutions, including a coproduction, but Behrman balked. Finally, the Theatre Guild produced the work and Behrman resigned from the Playwrights' Company.

Kazan did not benefit from the arrangement. In his autobiography, *Elia Kazan*, he decried the changes he was forced to make during the tryouts, which he said robbed the work of its meaning. He was so affected by the experience of kowtowing to the demands of the producers and the author's agent that he resolved henceforth never to stage a play that he did not himself produce.

(1) DYBBUK, THE (*Der Dibuk*) [Dramatic Revival*/Hebrew Language] A: S. Ansky; TR: Chaim Nachman Bialik; M: I. Engel; D: Eugene Vakhtangov; S: N. Altman; P: Habimah Theatre u/t/a/o Theatre Incorporated and the American Fund for Palestinian Institutions; T: Broadway Theatre; 5/2/48 (8)

The Habimah Theatre of Israel (then Palestine) visited New York with a repertory of four plays in 1948, its opening production being its famous version of *The Dybbuk*, staged many years earlier by Russian master Vakhtangov and shown in New York by the Habimah in 1926. It had been given over one thousand times in the company's thirty-year history. There had been a delay in the company's arrival because the Tel Aviv airport had been captured by the Arabs. The one other Jewish-controlled airport had no planes. The company fled to Cyprus by boat and then attempted to get to Athens, but had trouble gaining admission. Most of the company finally arrived at the theatre from the airport by midafternoon on opening day, but leading lady Hanna Rovina did not appear until 7 P.M. Consequently, the curtain went up late, but the actors seemed unfazed by the ordeal. The piece last had been seen locally in a visiting production by a Lithuanian group (1937).

The critics, struggling with a play in a language none understood, were not unduly impressed, and Howard Barnes (*NYHT*) referred to "a hop-scotch performance of a mumbo-jumbo play." Barnes went on to declare that the play's mystical story "is made the subject of such incantation, lamentation, cabalistic symbolism and odd entrances and exits . . . that it is generally more trying than engrossing." Yet he appreciated certain moments for their unusual power, especially when the beggars danced around the possessed Leah (Rovina) and she renounced her new fiancé. The beggars' dance was well integrated with the considerable amount of exotic-sounding music played during the drama. Makeup and costumes were touched by the grotesque, and the beggars were performed with neither arms nor eyes, their behavior "crippled and idiotic," according to William Hawkins (*NYWT*). Too much of the performance was slowly paced and deliberately acted, and it often grew tedious. But John S. Wilson (*PM*) appreciated the strength of the ensemble, the impressionistic sets, and the "calculated overstatement" of the acting, which he found helpful in capturing the appropriate atmosphere. The approving Brooks Atkinson (*NYT*) believed that "by comparison, the realistic theatre looks poverty-stricken and naturalistic acting seems hackneyed and sterile." Most audiences, though, had to make a special effort to appreciate the production. The company included Ari Warshower as Channon, the lover, David Vardi as the exorcizing rabbi, and Shimon Finkel as Leah's father Sender.

(2) D: Stephen van Gluck; CH: Kay Raphael; S: Richard H. Brown; P: Players Group; T: Grand Street Playhouse (OB); 4/13/50 (4)

This semiprofessional version of *The Dybbuk* came fitfully to life on the stage of the old Neighborhood Playhouse. The production was amateurish, for the actors were not able to fully project their earnestness across the footlights. Arthur Pollock (*DC*) said that they forgot "that what they do should project with sufficient clarity to make them always understandable." Philip Wolf played the messenger, Richard Edmund Williams played Channon, Abe West played Meyer, and Florence Marcus played Leah.

E

E = MC^2 [Drama/Science] A: Hallie Flanagan Davis with Sylvia Gassel and Day Tuttle; M: Arthur Kreutz; D: Monroe B. Hack; CH: Hanya Holm; C: Valerie Judd; L: Hans Sondheimer; P: Experimental Theatre of the American National Theatre and Academy i/a/w Columbia University's School of Dramatic Arts; T: Brander Matthews Hall (OB); 6/15/48 (3)

Hallie Flanagan Davis, who had headed the historically important Federal Theatre Project during its short life from 1935 to 1939, was the main writer of this "living newspaper," a form that had been one of the Federal Theatre Project's chief preoccupations. The subject was atomic energy, and the result was considered the best of the five offerings for which the Experimental Theatre was responsible in the 1948-1949 season. The piece had had an earlier showing in another version at Smith College the year before. To most, E = MC^2--originally titled *Dawn over Zero*--was informative, yet entertaining. John S. Wilson (*PM*) noted that it was "sharply written, amusing, brimming with vitality and, above all, a skillful and polished professional production." George Freedley (*NYMT*) disagreed and considered the staging maladroit, preferring the college production as "more effective," but acknowledged that the script itself had been improved. Yet Richard Watts, Jr. (*NYP*), had reservations about Davis's avoidance of too controversial a slant in her presentation because he thought that it robbed the piece of needed "dramatic forcefulness." He also thought a more poetic method was probably a better one to use in approaching so awesome a subject as "the hopes and fears of the atomic age."

Davis's script anthropomorphized the atom in the form of a peppy young woman (Billie Lou Watt) in tights who feels that she is misunderstood and wants to right the world's incorrect impression of her. With the aid of a supposed stage manager (E. G. Marshall), an assortment of theatrical devices, including brief sketches, slides, film clips, and discussions, are marshalled to explain the nature and potential--both for good and bad--of atomic energy. At the close there is a vision of the possibility of world destruction if the atom's powers are irresponsibly handled. A good deal of humor is incorporated to keep the didacticism lively. Actors involved included Geoffrey Lumb, Marian Winters, Ken Raymond, and Philip Sand.

EAGLE HAS TWO HEADS, THE (*L'Aigle á Deux Têtes*) [Drama/French/Literature/Period/Politics/Romance/Sex] A: Jean Cocteau; AD: Ronald Duncan; D/P: John C. Wilson; S: Donald Oenslager; C: Aline Bernstein; T: Plymouth Theatre; 3/19/47 (29)

This disappointingly dull import was an ornately composed, symbolic melodrama presumably inspired by the assassination of the Empress Elizabeth of Austria in 1898. In Paris and London, where it had been modestly produced, it was a hit; on Broadway, given a sumptuous staging, it flopped.

It starred Tallulah Bankhead as the unnamed queen of an unnamed Graustarkian nation. Her coat of arms is a two-headed eagle. On her wedding day ten years earlier, her groom was assassinated; now, longing for death herself, the veiled, lonely monarch celebrates her tenth year of widowhood and marriage by attempting to communicate with her husband's shade. Through her window, bent on killing her, comes the handsome anarchist Stanislas (film actor Helmut Dantine, in his Broadway debut), whom she knows under his pen name Azraël from the inflammatory poetry he publishes about her. He has been wounded in the knee by the police pursuing him, but the queen conceals him. Stanislas, who bears a striking resemblance to the queen's late husband, represents someone who can bring her death, but she falls in love with him and they become lovers. He believes that she will reform and become a benevolent ruler, but his idealistic wishes are dashed and he sees the impossibility of the affair. Thinking that she has betrayed him to the law, he poisons himself, although he does not die before being goaded into shooting his paramour, thus granting her her wish.

Critics wondered why Bankhead had squandered her talents on the talky, tedious script. There were unwanted laughs at the corny proceedings on opening night. "Seldom has so much emptyness [*sic*] been caught in so much plot," lamented Robert Coleman (*NYDM*). Rowland Field (*NEN*) called it "a long-winded elocutionary exercise without a redeeming feature." Rosamond Gilder (*TAM*) blamed the debacle on poor direction, a "heavy and pompous" translation, and inept casting. She noted the play's deeper, symbolical connotations and its subtle expression of the theme of illusion versus reality, none of which the production conveyed.

Bankhead--whose role was originally created for French star Edwige Feuillière--was stunning in her beautifully gowned role and suitably theatrical, but completely out of touch with the inner workings of the play. Apart from several expressive moments, said Gilder, Bankhead was monotonous and often unintelligible. (She had turned down the role of Blanche in *A Streetcar Named Desire* to appear in this turkey.) Nor was Dantine much better in the role written for Jean Marais. Others at sea included Clarence Derwent, Eleanor Wilson, and Kendall Clark.

Dantine was a replacement for Marlon Brando, who had played the role on the show's extended pre-Broadway tour. Clarence Derwent suggested in *The Derwent Story* that Brando's "youth was a handicap in his love scenes with Tallulah." Other reports claimed that Brando simply could not prevent himself from growing bored during a lengthy Bankhead monologue, would pick his nose and fix his fly to keep himself occupied, and overplayed his death scene, seeking a suitable place to die before allowing the play to continue. "The audience was in convulsions," wrote Richard Maney in *Fanfare*. "Spread-eagled on the stairway, head down, Miss Bankhead was having a few convulsions of her own. . . . Marlon had been mooning about for a full minute . . . when suddenly he collapsed as if spiked by an invisible ray. The curtain came down with the audience in hysterics." Brando's next vehicle was the *Streetcar* that Bankhead had let pass by. When Derwent later met playwright Cocteau and told him that he had had the pleasure of appearing in his play, the Frenchman replied, "You did not have the pleasure of appearing in the play *I* wrote."

EARLY TO BED [Musical/Prostitution/Romance/School/Sex/Sports/Tropics/Youth] B/LY: George Marion, Jr.; M: Thomas ("Fats") Waller; D/CH: Robert Alton; S: George Jenkins; C: Miles White; P: Richard Kollmar; T: Broadhurst Theatre; 6/17/43 (382)

A colorful and lively musical "fairy tale for grown-ups" (as it called itself) with plenty of pulchritude. It was, in fact, "generous in everything except plot which suffered from undernourishment and ended in collapse," according to Rosamond Gilder (*TAM*).

The plot to which she referred was set before the war in Martinique in the West Indies, in a bordello called "The Angry Pigeon," presided over by a former schoolteacher named Madame Rowena (Muriel Angelus). One of the regular visitors is the mayor (Ralph Bunkar). A penniless, broken-down matador known as El Magnifico (Richard Kollmar, the show's producer) arrives with his son Pablo (George Zoritch) and black major-domo (Bob Howard) and discovers that Madame Rowena is his former lover. She, to keep her present occupation secret, pretends that the place is actually a girls' finishing school, which leads to many complications. Soon, at El Magnifico's invitation, a California university's track team--on the island during a goodwill trip--comes to the brothel to use it as its training headquarters, providing even more confusion. Meanwhile, love blossoms for Pablo and Lois (Jane Deering), a young nightclub dancer he encounters when her car nearly runs him over.

"Fats" Waller's score was adequate if not especially notable, its chief contribution being "The Ladies Who Sing with a Band," which spoofs famous singers whose fame is attributable to their backup support. It was sung by Angelus, Deering, Mary Small, and Jane Kean. Other titles included "There's a Man in My Life," "Hi-de-Ho-High," "Slightly Less Than Wonderful," and "This Is So Nice." There was also "When the Nylons Bloom Again," sung by Howard and black singer Jeni Le Gon. The gorgeous chorines, the exciting choreography of Robert Alton, and the vivid, tropically colored sets and costumes were the chief things that stuck in people's minds when the final curtain fell.

"The performance is so much better than the basic material . . . that it is certain to catch on as a bit of escapist hot-cha," correctly predicted Howard Barnes (*NYHT*). One of the few to disagree was Burton Rascoe (*NYWT*), who thought the book "adult, ingenious and amusing."

Moralists were upset by the innuendo-laden show's setting in a brothel and by its off-color humor. When it tried out in Boston, the locale had to be changed to a gambling casino. Two dozen jokes also were allegedly excised during the Boston run because of smuttiness, but some thought this all a press agent's scheme to draw attention to the show.

EARTH JOURNEY [Comedy/China/Fantasy/Orientals/Religion/Romance] A: Sheldon Davis; D: Dennis Gurney; S: W. Emerton Heitland; C: Hildegart Brandes; L: Leo Herbert; P: Blackfriars' Guild; T: Blackfriars' Theatre (OB); 4/27/44 (16)

The conventions of classical Chinese theatre were attempted to tell this talky fantasy set in ancient China. However, the conventions were mostly spoofed for laughs. "Under this distortion," argued Otis L. Guernsey, Jr. (*NYHT*), "there is very little left to the script except a few laughs of a second-rate vaudeville flavor." The borrowed techniques were, in fact, ersatz, including as they did a large yellow disk to represent the sun and a bouquet of drooping flowers to suggest a garden. The play also failed to use music, which is an integral part of authentic Chinese theatre.

The story's unseen locales are described by a Chorus (Ian Maclaren), who also provides exposition when necessary. There is the ubiquitous property man (Alexander Cooper) of the Chinese stage, used here for laughs, dressed in black and placing props and furniture as needed. The plot concerns a temple idol (William Monsees) who, when a curse is put on him, comes to life with the mission of killing the cruel and all-powerful emperor (Robert Hayward) and his princess daughter, Tai Wan (Christina Soulias). Instead, he falls in love with the lovely princess and manages to reform the emperor. Having saved the princess from death, he is rewarded by the emperor by being made emperor for a day, during which he spreads the emperor's wealth among the nation's poor. This teaches the emperor benevolence. The idol-turned-man, refusing to carry out the wishes of the evil priest (Edward Steinmetz) who brought him to life, returns to being an idol once more, secure in the knowledge that the princess and her son will see him every day and that he has done well for the people. "*Earth Journey*," yawned Robert Garland (*NYJA*), "is merely a lacklustre imitation of *Yellow Jacket**, with none of it [*sic*] pseudo-Chinese appeal."

EAST LYNNE [Dramatic Revival*] A: Mrs. Henry Wood; D: Eliza Downing; P: On-Stage; T: 6 Fifth Avenue (OB); 8/28/48 (6)

This famous 1863 tear-jerking melodrama was given as part of a series of old American plays staged by a semiprofessional company during the summer of 1948. As with other plays in the series, *East Lynne* was not spoofed but played straight. In William Hawkins's (*NYWT*) view, this was a mistake, as the only way the clunky piece could still work was by satirizing it or playing it more broadly. But Richard Watts, Jr. (*NYP*), approved the approach: "Wisely and with remarkable restraint, the actors play it seriously and without roguishness, and there is no attempt to show how charmingly quaint everything is." Although Hawkins found the plotting easily predictable, he thought that the piece retained a definite interest and was not boring. But Watts hated the play, calling it "a dreadful thing to contemplate in the theatre."

EASTWARD IN EDEN [Drama/Literary-Biographical/Period/Religion/Romance] A: Dorothy Gardner; M: Andre Singer; D: Ellen Van Volkenburg; DS: Donald Oenslager; P: Nancy Stern; T: Royale Theatre; 11/18/47 (15)

Perhaps because not much is actually known about her mostly sequestered life, a number of dramas over the years (such as *Alison's House**, *Brittle Heaven**, and 1941's barely known *Escape Into Glory*) have taken as their subject the secret love life of nineteenth-century American poetess and spinster Emily Dickinson, played in the present effort by Beatrice Straight. Author Gardner based her drama on the interesting, if elusive, evidence--including hints supposedly scattered through Dickenson's obliquely styled poems--concerning the poetess's unrequited love for a Philadelphia minister, Dr. Charles Wadsworth (Onslow Stevens). Dickinson's words in this "philosophical and emotional conversation piece" (Otis L. Guernsey, Jr. [*NYHT*]) are paraphrases of her own poetry and correspondence. The result lasted only two weeks, but was selected by Burns Mantle as one of the ten best plays of the season.

Set in Amherst, Massachusetts, and Philadelphia, the play covers thirty years from the 1850s onwards, first showing Emily as an eager young lady awaiting an Adam to arrive in the Eden of her despotic father's (Edwin Jerome) house. The man turns out to be the minister she sees preaching during a trip to Philadelphia, but this intellectual paragon is married and has children. Their friendship slowly blossoms into love, and the minister subsequently makes several platonic calls on her in Amherst, one of these a product of the poetess's imagination. To break off the threatening relationship, he accepts a mission in California, and his final visit to the reclusive poetess comes after an absence of two decades.

A chief problem with the drama was its preoccupation with airy philosophical doodling--much of it about transcendentalism--and not with the stuff of dramatic confrontation; the emotional content was attenuated and insubstantial. A few critics, such as John Chapman (*NYDN*) and Brooks Atkinson (*NYT*), liked it moderately well. The majority agreed with Louis Kronenberger (*PM*), who pointed out, "Any stage piece about Emily Dickinson means dealing with the most inward of persons in the most outward of media." In the present case, the dramatist failed to make the story interesting: "Seldom has so intense and tingling a heroine become part of so sketchy and anemic a play." "At times the play bids fair to talk itself to death," commented Kahn. (*V*).

For some, Straight gave an insightful performance that went a long way to divert the audience's attention from an inert and repetitious script. Others felt that she did little to assist the evening and noted her weak vocal projection. An assortment of friends and relatives were played by actors such as Beatrice Manley, Kate Tomlinson, Barbara Ames, Ernest Graves, Mary Jackson, John O'Connor, and John D. Seymour.

EDGE OF THE SWORD, THE [Drama/Family/Marriage/Politics/Prostitution/Sex] A: George Bellak; D: Herbert V. Gellendre; S: Clay Watson; L: Ann MacKay; P: Abbe Practical Workshop; T: Master Institute Theatre; 11/10/49 (3)

The Abbe Practical Workshop was proving to be one of the better Off-Broadway groups in the late 1940s, as this first of their 1949-1950 offerings witnessed. As usual, the company was made up of semipros, supplemented by guest professionals; the latter in this case were Katherine Sergava (better known as a ballerina) and Kurt Richards. The timely drama was an interesting exposé of the survival of Nazism in postwar Germany, of the undisciplined behavior of the occupying forces, and of the latter's failure to imbue the conquered Germans with the spirit of democracy. The author's anger at the issues before him was considered a major flaw, as he was seriously in need of restraint in conveying his otherwise important ideas. Bellak had written "a caustic thoughtful play which minces no words in its forthright and honest challenge," according to Thomas R. Dash (*WWD*). J. P. S. (*NYT*) stated that it was "an engrossing and thought-compelling play." However, a *V* reviewer thought that Bellak had "resorted to stock characters and some tired dialog." Arthur Pollock (*DC*) claimed that the play "suffers from lack of pace and sharpness."

The story focuses on the response of a young family to the American occupation of its country. Corporal Ludwig Lorenz (Richards), a German veteran, returns home from a prison camp seeking peace, but discovers his fellow "patriots" brewing discord beneath the noses of the occupying authorities. His family plays along deceitfully while still supporting Hitler's ideas. His father (William Diamond) makes deals on the black market, his sister (June Bianca) is willing to prostitute herself for a chocolate bar, and his wife (Sergava) is a Nazi sympathizer. The latter's friends are led by a martinet (John O'Hagan) in the service of the American military government, doing what he can to make the American efforts on behalf of Germany seem phony. When the veteran sees a liberal friend (George Bandura) liquidated by these people, he turns against his wife and her colleagues in violent rage.

EDITH PIAF [Revue/French Language] D: Edward Lewis; P: Clifford C. Fischer; T: Playhouse; 10/30/47 (44)

Gaminesque Parisian chanteuse Edith Piaf made her first American appearance in this intimate revue in which she shared the stage with a number of Continental vaudeville acts. George André acted as *conférencier* or MC. Statuesque beauty Dorritt Merrill assisted him. André also did a delightful "Digital Dancing" number in which each of his fingers was dressed as a dancer. The first of two acts was taken up entirely with the supporting acts, including the show-stealing Les Compagnons de la Chanson, George and Tim Dorande (comic unicyclists), Les Canova (a group that impersonated statues), Lyda Alma and Vanni Fleury (a Greek dance team), and the Winter Sisters (Italian gymnasts). Of these, the first, a satirical singing group of nine homely Frenchmen dressed in white shirts and blue slacks, made the biggest impression. They sang (and pantomimed) with comic exactitude and Gallic flair such old songs as "Au Clair de la Lune," which tune they performed in the manner of an American jazz band, a cossack chorus, and a symphony orchestra.

The second half of the show was straight Piaf. She specialized in deeply emotional, often-pathetic tunes about working girls and girls in love, sung directly and without theatrical trappings. Her facial expressions were few and her gestures minimal but telling, revealing her mimic abilities. She sang of heartbreak and despair (her own life was a case study in pain), but always with an attitude of overcoming trouble with an unquenchable spirit. The diminutive, pale-faced, waiflike singer dressed down in her usual unglamorous way, wearing a simple, even severe, black dress. Her auburn hair was worn in shoulder-length ringlets, and her big, sad eyes filled the theatre with feeling. Among her songs, most of them long and dramatically rich, were "D'l'Autre Côte d'la Rue," "Y'Avait des Gars qui Marchaient," "Mariage," "Je n'en Connais pas la Fin," "L'Accordeoniste," and "Monsieur Saint-Pierre." She also offered a song in English, "All Dressed Up."

Her impact was not so much in the excellence of her voice, but in the depth and integrity of her delivery. At first, Brooks Atkinson (*NYT*) was unimpressed: "Her voice is loud with a metallic volume that would fill a street. She also sings off-key consistently." But the longer he listened, the more her sincerity grew on him. "She is a genuine artist in a particular tradition, making no concessions to a heedless metropolis abroad." "The power of Piaf," commented Euphemia Van Rensselaer Wyatt (*CW*), "lies in the tensile quality of her emotion as taut as a rubber band stretched to the snapping point."

EDWARD, MY SON [Drama/Alcoholism/British/Business/Crime/Family/Marriage/Period/Politics/Sex] A: Robert Morley and Noel Langley; SC: Noel Langley's novel of the same name; D: Peter Ashmore; DS: Raymond Sovey; P: Gilbert Miller and Henry Sherek; T: Martin Beck Theatre; 9/30/48 (260)

Corpulent British actor Robert Morley's first appearance on Broadway since his outstanding performance in the title role of *Oscar Wilde**, eleven years earlier, was in this hit play of his own coauthorship. One of Burns Mantle's ten best of the season, it was a still-running London hit when it opened on Broadway. Peggy Ashcroft, one of Britain's greatest actresses, costarred in her second New York performance. Both Morley and Ashcroft returned to England during the play's run. The play also served to introduce to Broadway English actress Leueen McGrath, who married American playwright-director George S. Kaufman during the run.

Edward, My Son was considered one of the best-acted plays of the season. Howard Barnes (*NYHT*) observed, "It has import and honesty; sardonic undercurrents and passages of moving beauty. Here is a drama of genuine stature." Most critics, however, were not as impressed by its literary qualities as by its capacity as a piece of dramatic writing into which good actors could sink their teeth. Each of the ten scenes was a minidrama with its own climax. "*Edward, My Son* is not a great play but it is great theater--an ugly story told with a keen knowledge of dramatic dimensions," said Euphemia Van Rensselaer Wyatt (*CW*). John Mason Brown (*SR*) claimed, "The story--as a story--is an interesting one." Despite excessive length and leisureliness, "the skill of its writing is undeniable. It has wit, dexterity, and, considering its basic unpleasantness, a kind of courage." Still, he declared, the piece confessed "itself in its every line and scene to be an actor's piece rather than a dramatist's play." The reason, he decided, was that "there is something hollow about its writing, something simulated and specious, which refuses to be hidden." George Jean Nathan (*TBY*) exercised his dissatisfaction concerning the play's clichéd dialogue, its mechanical methods, and its blatantly star-vehicle tactics.

It covers three decades, from 1919 to the late 1940s, and is concerned with the life of a successful but unscrupulous tycoon, Arnold Holt (Morley), who begins and ends the play by appearing before the curtain to introduce and conclude his story. When Arnold's son, Edward (never seen), needs a costly operation, Arnold successfully commits arson to raise the needed funds. This leads to ever-increasing economic acquisitions as Arnold employs a series of questionable methods to gain the money with which he can indulge his child, to whose nasty nature (he is referred to as "a stinker") the pampering father is blind. Arnold's ultimate pinnacle of power and wealth is built on a foundation of swindles, adultery, lies, and abortion; just as he spoils Edward, Arnold despoils others in his life. Arnold's wife Evelyn (Ashcroft) declines during the action from youthful romanticism to bitter, drunken despair and suicide. At the play's end, Edward's posthumous son is six years old, and, because of certain Labour party restrictions, Arnold has sold the family home and is planning to move with him to Palm Beach. Edward's widow, Phyllis (Dorothy Beattie), declines to go and wishes to remain in England with her son. The family physician, Doctor Parker (Ian Hunter), has suggested to her that Arnold will have the same pernicious influence on Edward, Jr., that he did on Edward. The furious Arnold leaves to go to Phyllis's house, planning to cut both the boy and his mother off if they do not follow his wishes. When he is gone, Phyllis, who has been hiding upstairs with the boy, is summoned forth by the doctor, who reassures her that Arnold will not return. Then Edward, Jr., is called, but only his balloon is seen emerging at the top of the stairs. In the brief epilogue, Arnold reappears and asks the audience members what they would have done.

Speaking of Morley, Rowland Field (*NEN*) reported, "The Morley performance . . . is truly something to admire and cherish in the theater. Here is acting that is emblazoned with artistry in its expression of changing moods in establishing a superbly etched character." Morley had a secret desire to experiment with the final scene, said Richard Maney in *Fanfare*. He would like to have had his own seven-year-old son Sheridan (later a respected critic and biographer), dressed precisely like Arnold in "black homburg, astrakhan-collared coat and walking stick," come down the steps instead of the balloon and inquire in his childish voice, "Which way did Grandpa go?"

Brown, noting the remarkable opportunities in Ashcroft's role to portray a woman over twenty-nine years, wrote, "Of each and every one of these opportunities Miss Ashcroft takes such admirable advantage that they give the impression of being golden rather than greasepaint." The role was considered a turning point in the actress's career, as she previously had been known primarily as an ingenue. Nevertheless, she had been very doubtful about accepting the part. According to Michael Billington's biography, *Peggy Ashcroft*, the highly self-critical actress feared that she "was out of her depth in a lavish boulevard piece where scenes were being rewritten on the wing (or in the wings) and lines altered and reshaped by the star and co-author." Memorable performances were contributed by McGrath as Holt's secretary and mistress, Torin Thatcher as a likable rogue, D. A. Clarke-Smith as a schoolmaster, and Patricia Hicks as a shopgirl.

EIGHT O'CLOCK TUESDAY [Drama/Crime/Mystery/Sex] A: Robert Wallsten and Mignon G. Eberhart; SC: Mignon G. Eberhart's novel, *Fair Warning*; D: Luther Greene; S: Lemuel Ayers; P: Luther Greene and James Struthers; T: Henry Miller's Theatre; 1/6/41 (16)

This murder mystery--based on a novel by a very popular detective story writer--attempted unsuccessfully to avoid the typical method of holding an onstage inquiry. It presented the questioning in the room where the murder was committed, with the past brought forward through flashbacks. "The experiment was interesting," noted Rosamond Gilder (*TAM*), "and often effective but proved over-laborious when the whole episode was re-created twice: first in the form of the lies everyone told to cover some aspect of inter-relationships and then as it really occurred."

The dramaturgic technique provided a platform for the idiosyncratic but memorable acting of Pauline Lord. John Anderson (*NYJA*) said, "She plays . . . with the usual nebulous mannerisms, half-sentences, odd pauses and jerky nervousness which can be so deeply affecting when she has a part charged with the necessary emotions, but which seem empty and overdone on the minor errands of such claptrap."

The despicable Ivan Godden (McKay Morris) has been murdered in his plush library, a paper knife through his ribs. Next door, at the Copleys, is a dinner party made up of a group of suspects, all of whom have a good reason for doing the deed. This group is gathered together for questioning by a sophisticated police detective (Bramwell Fletcher). Each begins to explain by stating where he or she was at eight o'clock Tuesday. Two prime suspects are the deceased's oppressed sister, Beatrice (Lord), and his cheating young wife, Marcia (Celeste Holm). As each recounts his or her last contact with the dead man, the scenes are acted out (which forced McKay Morris to keep scampering off and on the stage in the dark and occasioned a good laugh from the reviewers). At the conclusion, the murderer is discovered to have been a former flame of the victim's sister. As the character had not previously been introduced, it was felt that a major convention of good mystery writing had been ignored. Cast members included Cecil Humphreys, Margaret Douglass, Herbert Rudley, and Philip Tonge.

EMBEZZLED HEAVEN [Drama/Crime/Period/Religion] A: Ladislaus Bus-Fekete and Mary Helen Fay; SC: a novel by Franz Werfel; D: B. Iden Payne; S: Stewart Chaney; P: Theatre Guild; T: National Theatre; 10/31/44 (52)

Stewart Chaney's arresting settings, B. Iden Payne's thoughtful direction, and Ethel Barrymore's commanding presence were expended on a touching, dignified, and literate, but exceedingly slight, drama that, being adapted from a novel, suggested "a series of incidents rather than an integrated play," according to George Freedley (*NYMT*). Lewis Nichols (*NYT*) decried the lack of flesh-and-blood characters and the maudlin conclusion of the piece.

Barrymore played Aunt Teta, a wonderful Czech cook working for a noble family in a castle near Prague. The peasant woman is a devout Catholic and dreams of the day that her nephew Mojmir (as a child, Edward Fernandez; as an adult, Eduard Franz), whom she supports from birth for twenty-five years (from 1913 to 1938), will grow up to be a priest and gentleman who will pray for her soul. This, she believes, will guarantee her entry into paradise. She eventually discovers, to her great anguish, that the youth she thought had achieved her goals has been lying to her for years and is little more than a charlatan who works as a fortune-teller in a carnival. She takes up her abode with him and is befriended by a true priest (Martin Blaine), a young man of piety and kindness. A pilgrimage visit to the dying pope

(Albert Bassermann, the aged European star, in his American debut) in Rome restores her shattered faith in her salvation by teaching her that one gains heaven not by buying one's way in, but through the power of faith and love. Following her audience with the pontiff, she dies.

Barrymore was not really convincing as the peasant cook, being too sophisticated and attractive, but her colorful personality and theatrical genius made watching her performance a distinct pleasure. Indeed, Howard Barnes (*NYHT*) thought that she had "never been more magnificent. . . . For scene after scene she brings a laggard show to life and makes it glow with emotional and dramatic excitement." The role was a grueling tour de force in which the sixty-six-year-old actress was on stage almost continually from the first curtain to the last. Barrymore actually became ill with pneumonia shortly after the opening and had to take some time off to recuperate. The precarious state of her health was of such newsworthiness that at one point the electric news sign circling the Times Building in Times Square ran the headline, "GENERAL MAC ARTHUR LANDS AT LEYTE ETHEL BARRYMORE'S TEMPERATURE LOWER."

Bassermann made a distinct impression with an interpretation of great restraint and holiness. "He has the presence, the authority, the assured ease of a master," acknowledged Rosamond Gilder (*TAM*). "His voice is fitted to his stature, but his accent, though not inappropriate for the role, is sufficiently marked to be somewhat distracting." His wife, Else Bassermann, appeared in the small role of Mrs. Schultz. Also employed were Sanford Meisner as the gardener Bichler, Bettina Cerf as the countess for whom Teta cooks, Graham Velsey as a physician, and Wolfe Barzell as a nonagenarian.

EMPEROR JONES, THE [Dramatic Revival*] A: Eugene O'Neill; D: Jasper Deeter and Miriam Phillips; S: Mahlon Naill and Eleanor Plaisted Abbott; L: Mahlon Naill; P: Hedgerow Theatre; T: Cherry Lane Theatre (OB); 1/16/45

The Hedgerow Theatre of Moylan-Rose Valley, Pennsylvania, was already two decades old when it ventured to New York to play a month-long engagement of winter stock in Greenwich Village. Despite its long record of accomplishments as one of the nation's few regional theatres, it received barely any attention from the critics. Only two of its productions, this one and *Thunder on the Left** are given entries in this volume because of the paucity of reviews. Those who did go were not unduly impressed. Lewis Nichols (*NYT*) apparently was the sole critic to write of the present revival.

Company head Deeter, who had played Smithers, the cockney white trader, in the original 1921 production, revived his performance, but he was not specific enough in his characterization. "He doesn't make the trader much of anything--a mean character, taunting or sardonic," wrote Nichols. The production around him was mediocre. Arthur Rich played Brutus Jones, but was merely "workmanlike." The staging was on the simple, bare-stage side, which forced Rich to carry a burden he might otherwise have been able to share with atmospheric sets and lighting.

ENCHANTED, THE (***Intermezzo***) [Drama/Death/Fantasy/French/Politics/Romance/Youth] A: Jean Giraudoux; AD: Maurice Valency; M: Francis Poulenc; D: George S. Kaufman; CH: Jean Erdman; DS: Robert Edmond Jones; P: David Lowe and Richard Davidson; T: Lyceum Theatre; 1/18/50 (45)

Giraudoux's romantic fantasy, written in 1933 and also known in English by its French title, was an important part of French star Louis Jouvet's repertory. It was getting its New York premiere in this commercially unsuccessful version, which was nevertheless selected as one of the season's ten best.

The chief character is the lovely but emotionally restive, pedagogically unorthodox schoolteacher Isabel (Leueen McGrath), who meets in a forest outside a provincial town a handsome youth (John Baragrey). She believes that he is a ghost who killed his wife and her lover before taking his own life. Dissatisfied with reality, she feels that somehow, the dead can teach the living how to live because they are free from life's mundane worries. Isabel--the only one who can commune with the phantom--is relieved of her teaching position, but the ghost's good influence is felt by all the townspeople, who fall under his enchantment. The issue seriously disturbs the town's bureaucracy, including the mayor (Charles Halton), the fatuous inspector (Malcolm Keen), the knowing doctor (Russell Collins), and the supervisor of weights and measures (Wesley Addy), who loves Isabel. The inspector believes that Isabel's communing with the dead is a subversive act, dangerous to the well-being of the state. An attempt to exorcise the ghost leads to its shooting by two old men (Joe E. Marks and James O'Neill). The person killed is an escaped murderer, but the slain man himself now becomes a ghost. A verbal conflict arises in Isabel's room between the ghost and the supervisor, who wants Isabel to see that even the most everyday of lives can be very romantic. The living man is the victor and the ghost vanishes, but his disappearance sends Isabel into a deathlike trance. The doctor revives her by conducting a symphony of living voices and sounds.

The reviews were a blend of positive and negative comments, and most critics (Robert Coleman [*NYDM*] was one exception) remarked that they preferred the author's *The Madwoman of Chaillot* to *The Enchanted*. Some warmed to the play's blend of romantic conflict, satiric thrusts at bureaucracy, and thoughtful metaphysics. Others thought it intellectually muddled and not especially illuminating. It was also noted that the play was so filled with sagacious commentary that to divert one's attention for a moment was to risk losing a precious insight.

Kaufman's production was widely considered outstanding in the natural way his characters inhabited the play's fanciful world. William Hawkins (*NYWT*) wrote, "That the action is almost entirely intellectual is beautifully concealed by the production, and so brilliantly projected by the writing, that one could not be more absorbed by a blood and thunder melodrama." Arthur Pollock (*DC*), another strong supporter, jotted, "It is a beautiful comedy, sly, ironic, witty and beneficent, acted with great nicety, one of the plays that can persuade the theater to be proud of itself." A typically mixed notice was Rowland Fields's (*NEN*), which disclosed that the play, with its intellectual vagueness and many allusions, was often hard to follow, but was nevertheless "a stage work of fragile beauty and literary design." More direct dissenters included Joseph T. Shipley (*NL*), who said that Giraudoux had mounted his "bright idea on seven horses, which gallop off in every direction at once--leaving the audience breathless in the middle." Howard Barnes (*NYHT*) felt that "all that is wanting . . . is a coherent and unified dramatic pattern. . . . The love story . . . has passages of fine invention and emotional appeal, but it rarely soars into the realm of high fancy."

Excellent work was contributed by Una O'Connor as a deaf gossip, Frances Williams as her sister, and, Mimi Strongin as a schoolgirl. Although only a few faulted Kaufman's direction of the play, the adaptor, Valency, who originally was in favor of having Kaufman stage the play, gradually grew disillusioned with his work, which he believed missed the whimsical flavor of the piece, and, at one point in the out-of-town period, tried to get the producers to stop the production and hire another director to rework it. The play was the once nearly invincible Kaufman's eighth flop in a row.

ESCAPE INTO GLORY [Drama/Family/Literary-Biographical/Period/Romance] A: Hall Martin and David O. Woodbury; D: Barbara Bulgakov; P: Players' Company; T: Master Institute of the United Arts (OB); 3/28/41

Very few critics ventured up to the tiny playhouse on Riverside Drive and 103rd Street to see this play about Emily Dickinson by a struggling young non-Equity group hoping to set up a repertory season under the guidance of Leo and Barbara Bulgakov. Those who saw it were very impressed by the careful depiction of the Dickinson family, called here Austin, in its 1850 New England environment. The family is ruled by a dominating patriarch (Seth Arnold) who prevents his three daughters, older sister Hannah (Marguerite Lewis or Marcia Ward), middle sister Emily (Beatrice Kraft or Cecily Burke-Hennesy), and youngest sister Susan (Evelyne Kraft), from marrying. Albert (Alex Maruchness) is a brother with an even crueler temperament than the father. Through Hannah's influence, Emily ends a relationship with a married man (Dominick Paulsen), and Susan fulfills hers with her beau (Chilton Ryan).

Brooks Atkinson (*NYT*) found his teeth set on edge by the play's self-consciousness about its literary heroine and also took the actors to task for their amateurishness. Still, he appreciated the play's honesty and the "warmth, simplicity and beauty" of its latter two acts.

ESTER'KE [Drama/Jews/Period/Politics/Religion/Romance/Sex/Yiddish Language] A: Aaron Zeitlin; SC: Aaron Zeitlin's novel of the same name; D/P: Maurice Schwartz; M: Sholom Secunda; S: Alexander Chertov; C: Arthur Schick; T: Yiddish Art Theatre (Public Theatre) (OB); 10/17/40

The Yiddish Art Theatre returned to the Lower East Side (Second Avenue and East Fourth Street) after several years on Broadway with this large-cast, nine-scene, historical melodrama about religious persecution and romance, the first original work the company had staged in ten productions. The flamboyantly acted work, in which company doyen Maurice Schwartz played a faithful old peasant, opened the twenty-first consecutive season for the troupe.

Its setting was fourteenth-century Poland, ruled over by King Kasimierz (or Casimir) the Great (Samuel Goldenburg). The monarch loves Ester'ke (Miriam Riselle), a simple Jewish village girl, and makes her his mistress (he already has a queen [Luba Kadison]), but his love leads to serious problems because of their differing religions. A considerable emphasis is laid on the schemes of the king's villainous follower Matchko (Muni Serebrov), who blames the Jews and the ruler for the black plague afflicting the land. Several members of Ester'ke's family are even executed for their alleged crimes. Before the peasants become too unruly, the king, under the influence of Ester'ke, gains their love by his humane behavior on their behalf.

B. I. (*NYWT*) noted, "Mr. Schwartz, the extremist, has labored over the massive forms of art before, but seldom has he achieved the fluidity of design, savagery or tenderness of motion that are inherent in this" work. However, the play was "thinly threaded and runs an ever-weakening course." There was an outpouring of appreciation for Miriam Riselle's acting. B. I. said, "It will be a long time before the Yiddish Theater reveals another such fresh, disarming and at the same time vibrating young personality."

ETERNAL CAGE [Drama/Fantasy/Illness/Marriage/Medicine] A/D: Jules Denes; P: C. Sherman Hoyt; T: Barbizon-Plaza Theatre (OB); 3/21/45 (10)

This was, said George Jean Nathan (*TBY*), "a strictly amateur performance, and minus merit in any direction." Hungarian author-director Denes told of a married couple, Robert (Frank Gibney) and Marion Duncan (Sheila Bromley), the wife convinced that her physician spouse is a louse who keeps her trapped in an eternal cage of domesticity, barring her from a social life and even preventing her from smoking and drinking. An alcohol-induced dream allows her to leave him and flirt with other men. Back in reality, Dr. Duncan senses that he has lost control of his wife and gains her back when he takes up drinking and smoking himself, vices he disallowed her because of her bad heart. Marion realizes that he is better than she thought and the marriage is patched up.

The play was "dull and inept," declared Herrick Brown (*NYS*). Its small cast included Frances Dale, Johanna Douglas, and William Forrest.

EVE OF ST. MARK, THE [Drama/Family/Fantasy/Gambling/Illness/Military/Romance/Rural/Sex/Tropics/War] A: Maxwell Anderson; D: Lem Ward; S: Howard Bay; C: Toni Ward; L: Moe Hack; P: Playwrights' Theatre; T: Cort Theatre; 10/7/42 (306)

One of the most successful war dramas of the period, *The Eve of St. Mark*, like many of its competitors, provided loud offstage simulation of exploding bombs and artillery, but this one had the benefit of Maxwell Anderson's experienced dramaturgy and garnered not only critical but popular support despite a tendency of the contemporary public not to attend war plays. It was the first American play to deal directly with America's involvement in the war, most of the previous examples of the genre being concerned with European or English situations or merely showing the war itself merely shown as a background to native domestic concerns.

It came to Broadway after receiving some seventy-five productions around the country at little theatres participating in the National Theatre Conference, which sponsored its writing. In preparing the play, Anderson spent time at Fort Bragg to become acquainted with various soldiers. There he met Private Marion Hargrove, who became famous for his waggish army comedy (and who was the inspiration for the comic character, Private Francis Marion [James Monks], in the play). When Hargrove published some of his comic pieces in the best-selling *See Here, Private Hargrove*, Anderson wrote the foreword and then used some of the same material for comic dialogue in his drama. He dedicated the play to his nephew, Sergeant Lee Chambers, "One of the first to go, one of the first to die that we may keep this earth for free men."

The Eve of St. Mark is an episodic, twelve-scene work, using simplified set pieces on a turntable against a neutral background to allow for the swift progression of the action. It takes place on a farm, the barracks at Fort Grace, a restaurant, and the combat zone in the Philippines. The time covered is the period from April 1941 to June 1942. Its central character is Quizz West (William Prince), a sort of American everyman, a simple, honest, unsophisticated, and good-natured youth raised on a farm in upstate New York by loving parents (Aline MacMahon and Matt Crowley). When he is drafted, he leaves his folks and girlfriend (Mary Rolfe) behind. Quizz becomes one of the guys in the barracks, learning to gamble; strikes up a friendship with Francis Marion, eloquent and cynical descendent of Southern aristocrats; is tempted by a pretty tart (Joann Dolan) in an Amityville café when on leave; waits in fear as he and his fellows prepare to embark for overseas; contracts malaria in the Philippine swamp; engages in battle against the Japanese; and, after being made leader of a sick and fatigued band who have to choose whether to save themselves or risk their lives by staying at their guns in the face of certain death, chooses the latter and dies heroically. Meanwhile, as Quizz's life is presented, the effects of the war on his family, his girl, the soldiers, and others are effectively communicated.

Cavils pointed to the play's confusion of styles in its incorporation of a pair of blank-verse dream sequences (Quizz, in the midst of combat, first talks with his mother and then with his sweetheart) within an otherwise hard-hitting realism. Some reviewers spoke of wordiness and of a lack of form, others of excessive sentimentality. There was also a final scene with Quizz's family talking about building a new world that John Beaufort (*CSM*) said "develops into a tableau for a recruiting poster." George Jean Nathan (*TBY*), one of the more sourly disposed critics, thought the play nothing more than "hokum periodically deodorized with a humorous and feeling spray." Nevertheless, most were willing to forget its flaws and thank Anderson for having breathed significant life into Broadway. For example, it was accounted by Brooks Atkinson (*NYT*) "a profoundly moving play" that treated its subject with brutal honesty. "It is not only the most vivid play [Anderson] has written in years and the foremost play of the season, but it penetrates to the rockbottom truth of our men and women." "Here at last is a play to go to," praised Rosamond Gilder (*TAM*), "to look at, to listen to--something very simple and straightforward that has the courage to stand boldly by its convictions and dares to speak with humor and emotion about what so deeply concerns millions of Americans today." Howard Barnes (*NYHT*) saw here "a war drama of emotional tension, humor and poetic splendor. . . . It is touched with the eternal magnificence of great tragedy." Its first-act scenes of high spirits and raucous humor among the soldiers were deemed an invaluable contribution to the otherwise somber drama. Also noteworthy was--apart from the final scene--a lack of patriotic rhetoric. It benefited, moreover, from Anderson's close observation of contemporary soldiers in that their idiomatic speech seemed authentic and their characters true to life. Romantic attitudes toward war were replaced by an understated, cautiously realistic one, which mirrored that of the nation at large. Quizz's heroism thus became stronger and his death more poignant because it stemmed from necessity rather than vainglory.

Lem Ward's direction was highly applauded, as were all the performances, notably those of Prince and MacMahon. "The direction is swift, moving, stylized, but not over-mannered," contended George Freedley (*NYMT*). In the cast were George Mathews, Eddie O'Shea, Grover Burgess, and Carl Gose as Quizz's brother, who goes off to war at the end to take up where Quizz left off.

The play's title comes from a passage by poet John Keats: "On the Eve of St. Mark, if a virgin stand at the church door at dusk, she will see entering the church all those of the parish who are to die that year. If her lover should enter among the others, he will turn and look at her, may perhaps speak." These words inspired the two dream sequences that many found embarrassingly intrusive.

EVENING OF TWO PLAYS, AN [One-Acts] S: Robert Gundlach; C: Dorothy Croissant; L: David Herlwell; P: New Stages; T: New Stages Theatre (OB); 2/9/48 (40)
"Church Street" [Dramatic Revival*] A: Lennox Robinson; D: John O'Shaughnessy; "The Respectful Prostitute" ("La Putaine Respecteuse") [Drama/Blacks/French/Prostitution/Race/Sex/Southern] A: Jean-Paul Sartre; AD: Eve Wolas; D: Mary Hunter

A program of two one-acts given as its second production by a theatre company ensconced in a small converted movie house at 159 Bleecker Street in Greenwich Village. Many members of the company earned their living as radio actors. The longish "Church Street" had been seen locally in 1934 for a single showing on a two-play bill offered by Ireland's Abbey Theatre Players. It was one of the most popular pieces in little theatres nationwide. In it, character actress Florida Friebus (playing the spinster Sarah Pettigrew) received strong notices, but the general opinion was that the ensemble was ineffective. Among others in "Church Street" were Charme Allen, Edgar Stehli, Earl Hammond, Gertrude Corey, Dorothy Patten, and Ann Eliot. In a number of roles, alternate actors appeared at certain performances because some cast members had radio jobs. The second play, the evening's major presentation, did wonders for the tall, strikingly attractive Meg Mundy's young career. "Church Street" seemed a strange companion for the Frenchman's play, and Hobe. (*V*) called it "moderately entertaining but inconsequential" and "indifferently presented."

Sartre's two-scene drama (which critics were pleased to note contained little existentialist philosophizing) had caused a scandal in Paris because of its allegedly tasteless title and subject. About a racist America as seen through French eyes, its action transpires in an unnamed Southern town to which Northern prostitute Lizzie McKaye (Mundy) has recently come. On the train bringing her there, she witnessed the murder of a black man by one of the local bigwigs. To cover up the murder, important townsmen demand of Lizzie that she sign a document falsely accusing the dead man's (John Marriott) companion of having attempted to rape her, although the man has actually treated her respectably. After being bullied, threatened with jail, and bribed, she rejects the demand. A smooth-talking, ultrapatriotic senator (Wendell Holmes), whose white supremacist son Fred (Karl Weber) is her lover, gets her to change her mind. She changes it again, though, when she begins to feel deceived. The fugitive hides out in her place while someone else is lynched. Fred, his lust inflamed by the lynching, returns. When the black man attempts to escape, Fred shoots him. He then makes Lizzie an offer to keep her; after threatening him with a gun, she wearily gives in.

"The Respectful Prostitute" was deemed by most, such as Ward Morehouse (*NYS*), a "hard-hitting," often-profane, but always-gripping work. A few others, such as Robert Garland (*NYJA*), who called it "derivitive [*sic*] and disjointed," saw it as a fantasy of an unknown America that could only have been written by a non-American. Hobe. commented, "Despite minor exaggerations, 'Prostitute' is a penetratingly dramatic expose of a shocking and embarrassing situation, and it provides engrossing if uncomfortable theatre." Brooks Atkinson (*NYT*) wrote, "Let's dismiss the tastelessness and the impropriety, if they exist, and salute a tautly-written melodrama played sharply and brilliantly by a keenly directed cast." A strong minority opinion was registered, however, by John Mason Brown (*SR*), who thought the work overpraised, contrived, and melodramatically sensationalistic; he called it little "more than a cartoon luridly and effectively drawn with greasepaint." Some critics were thin-skinned about the language, Euphemia Van Rensselaer Wyatt (*CW*) even admitting to leaving the theatre in embarrassment.

Mundy's performance was hailed as a triumph. William Hawkins (*NYWT*) wrote, "The role demands shuttling between extremities of emotion, and Miss Mundy plays it with pitiless coarseness and snarling pliancy. That she, meanwhile, values its crass humor, and keeps the woman physically attractive is an extraordinary feat."

The success of the Sartre play led to its being brought to Broadway's Cort Theatre on 3/16/48; in a program that was known by its title, it sustained a robust run of 318 showings. Thornton Wilder's one-act, "The Happy Journey to Trenton and Camden" (D: Mary Hunter), a charmingly sentimental 1931 favorite of amateur theatres, replaced the Irish play. Seen earlier (1/23/45) in an Equity Library Theatre production (see "The Happy Journey"), it concerns a New Jersey family's trip in an old Chevrolet to visit a married daughter. The group reacts to various sights they pass along the road, the billboards, flowers, a gas station, poor directions, and so on. Much homey humor comes from the discomfort in the back seat of the little boy, Arthur (Clifford Sales). Like *Our Town**, it uses a stage manager (William Brower), who also becomes a character (the gas-station attendant). Its presentation employs a bare stage with four chairs suggesting the car. In the cast were Peggy Allenby as the cutely eccentric Ma Kirby, Mari Lynn as Caroline, Don MacLaughlin as Pa, and Jean Gillespie as Beulah.

Later in the run, Richard Harrity's one-act, "Hope Is the Thing with Feathers," became the curtain raiser. Harrity's piece previously had been seen in a program called *Six O'Clock Theatre* and then on a bill called *Hope's the Thing*.

EVERY MAN FOR HIMSELF [Comedy/Alcoholism/Films/Romance/Sex] A: Milton Lazarus; D: Arthur Ripley; S: Ernest Glover; P: Arthur Hutchinson and Arthur Ripley; T: Guild Theatre; 12/9/40 (3)

Broadway stalwart Lee Tracy returned to the stage after a five-year absence to give a suitably frenetic performance in the role of Hollywood screenwriter Wally Britt. His vehicle was the fourth--and worst--play of the season (all having opened within a month of one another) to deal with the tribulations of the Hollywood hoi polloi. (The play had received a tryout production two years earlier under the title *Once upon a Night*.)

Britt, a man given to occasional drunken sprees, and who usually can't remember the great story lines he thinks up when inebriated, has awakened from a four-day bender to discover that he had brought back to his Hollywood Hills home an attractive young woman named Helen (Margaret Tallichet), who pads about in his pajamas. He learns that he met and married her in Tia Juana the night previously. He is also harboring a homeless sound-effects man (Charlie Williams) and his pregnant spouse. Moreover, he has enlisted in the navy and promised York (John Gallaudet), a producer, to write a film based on a gangster named Rittenhoff (Wally Maher). He can not, however, recall a thing about this proposed vehicle for movie bad guy Humphrey Harrison (Grant Richards). His bride turns out to be both the producer's girlfriend and the gangster's ward and would-be sweetheart. The gangster and his brutish sidekick Grogan (Charles A. Hughes) propose to bump off the producer, which leads to the usual assortment of door slammings and hiding from danger associated with farce. The arrival of a police detective (Edgar Roland Murray) puts things to rights. The funniest parts of the action come from special sound effects, including that of an earthquake.

In Richard Lockridge's (*NYS*) view, "It is never much of a farce. It seems merely hurried where it should seem fast; scrambled foolishness instead of intricately meshed absurdity."

EVERYMAN (***Jedermann***) [Dramatic Revival*] A: Hugo von Hofmannsthal; TR: George Sterling; D: Walter Firner; P/T: Friendship House Church (OB); 5/8/41 (2)

A number of well-known players took part in this special revival of HofmanNsthal's Austrian version of the medieval morality play. The last local showing of this play was acted in von Hoffmansthal's German by Max Reinhardt's company in 1927. Among the mixed cast of Americans and Austrians were Stefan Schnabel as the Voice of the Lord God and Mammon, Richard Odlin as the Devil, Eda von Buelow as Everyman's Mother, and Maurice Burke as Everyman. The work was given in a church located at 1010 Park Avenue. Its refugee director was former director of the Österreichische Volksbühne of Vienna.

Brooks Atkinson (*NYT*) regretfully concluded: "What Mr. Firner has managed to do with lights, organ music, a beautiful chancel and a wide assortment of actors, may be amusingly naive, but it conveys none of the wondrous faith of the original play. The words of the text are fearfully cultivated. The acting is modern and superficial." Atkinson would have preferred less artful a production and more rough and primitive a text. "It must smack more of the church than of the theatre."

F

FAMILIAR PATTERN, THE [Drama/Jews/Law/Marriage/Sex] A: David S. Lifson; D: John F. Grahame; S: Sally NuSsbaum; P: Modern Play Productions, Inc.; T: Provincetown Playhouse (OB); 9/2/43

Set in the Bronx, this little naturalistic catastrophe concerns a neurotic Jewish law student named Sam Miller (Robert Feyti) who gets his empty-headed Bronx girlfriend Mildred Silver (Olga Novosel) pregnant and has to marry her. He thereupon must deal with her distressing family of philistines, especially his nasty new mother-in-law (Anne King), who cannot forgive her spineless daughter's traducer. He becomes so distressed by his mother-in-law's attacks that he abandons his law studies, his friends, and his ideals about using the law for the good of society. His attempt at rebellion fizzles, and he is forced to leave his wife.

"Not only was [Lifson's] story culled from the stage's morgue and his manner of writing from the *Young's Magazine* which flourished at the turn of the century," snarled George Jean Nathan (*TBY*), "but his imagination hewed steadfastly and undeviatingly to that of the trashier playwrights of the same period." Wilella Waldorf (*NYP*) commented interestingly that "the play might better be produced in Yiddish at one of the East Side theatres where they enjoy doing these things at the top of their lungs, with gestures." Lifson later wrote his Ph.D. thesis on the Yiddish theatre and published it as a book.

FAMILY, THE [Drama/Alcoholism/Boarding House/China/Family/Orientals/Politics/Romance/War] A: Victor Wolfson; SC: Nina Fedorova's novel of the same name; D: Bretaigne Windust; S: Boris Aronson; C: Carolyn Hancock; L: Moe Hack; P: Oscar Serlin; T: Windsor Theatre; 3/30/43 (7)

What seemed highly promising material for dramatization turned out to be extremely disappointing when realized in this large-cast, seemingly plotless, "meandering" (George Freedley [*NYMT*]) play. Set in 1937, it concerns a family of White Russians who fled their native land during the Kerensky revolution to take up abode in the British concession in Tientsin, China. They run a boarding house but continue to love their native land and to hope that someday they will return to it. The family, burdened by crushing poverty, consists of the old matriarch Granny (Lucile Watson), her daughter Tania (Marion Evensen), and her three grandchildren, Lida (Elisabeth Fraser), Dima (Alec Englander), and the handsome and bitter Peter (Nicholas [Richard] Conte). They take in as a boarder a tantrum-throwing, alcoholic Englishwoman, Mrs. Parrish (Carol Goodner), who develops a yen for the anguished Peter. There are also old Professor Chernov (Arnold Korff), whose predilection for sending angry letters to Mussolini, Hitler, and Roosevelt makes him seem mad to his wife (Katherine Squire), and, among others, a Chinese secret agent (Yung Ying Hsu), five Japanese boarders, a kindly German-Jewish doctor (Boris Tumarin) who has fled from Hitler, and a lady fortune-teller (Evelyn Varden). When the Japanese forces begin to bomb the city, a mass evacuation takes place.

Mrs. Parrish, who goes on the wagon, takes with her for safety the family's youngest grandson, while Peter escapes with Chinese beggars to Russia, it being suggested that he will join Mrs. Parrish in England when the fighting is over. The rest remain to await the Japanese.

John Anderson (*NYJA*) thought the early stages of the drama engrossing, but that it soon "went heavily to pieces, its drama static and cluttered, its emotions clogged with dialogue." Louis Kronenberger (*PM*) noted, "The whole play bogs down in incident and atmosphere; and a great deal of it moves all too slowly."

FAMILY AFFAIR, A [Comedy/Family/Sex/Theatre] A: Henry R. Misrock; D: Alexander Kirkland; S: Samuel Leve; P: Jesse Long and Edward S. Hart; T: Playhouse; 11/27/46 (6)

The author of this poorly acted play had an amusing premise and occasionally got off a clever line, but his play as a whole was a futile exercise. His idea was that Walter and Julia Wallace (John Williams and Ann Mason) have raised fraternal twins, the male (Joel Marston) of which has written a play about his own family, with his father depicted as a philanderer. When the parents come across the play and read it, they are disturbed by the portrayal. So are some of their friends, who reject the play as outrageous while behaving much as they have been shown in the writing. No one believes the son when he says that he did not write about them. The mother soon thinks that her husband is beginning an affair with his sexy young secretary (Jewel Curtis). Mom herself considers starting a fling with a psychiatrist (Anatole Winogradoff) who once wanted to marry her. When things thus start to go awry, the dramatist has to overcome major obstacles to restore the happy equilibrium that existed before he put pen to paper. The parents discover that they are better off without their peccadilloes--which never get far--and return to the comforts of the old moral order. A subplot concerns the twin daughter's (Margaret Garland) difficulty in choosing the right romantic partner.

"Mr. Misrock's antic rattles around . . . like a truck-load of bricks on a country road," moaned Brooks Atkinson (*NYT*). According to Louis Kronenberger (*PM*), "The plot thickens but the play refuses to jell; the characters are all live wires, but the juice has been turned off; the dialogue keeps ticking away but almost never remembers to chime." Emily Ross was a cast member.

FAMILY CARNOVSKY, THE [Drama/Crime/Family/Jews/Marriage/Medicine/Politics/Yiddish Language] A: I. J. Singer; SC: I. J. Singer's novel of the same name; M: Joseph Rumshinsky; D: Maurice Schwartz; S: H. A. Condell; P/T: Yiddish Art Theatre; 10/18/43

The twenty-fifth season of the Yiddish Art Theatre under Maurice Schwartz's leadership opened at Broadway's former Adelphi Theatre on West Fifty-fourth Street with this timely, seven-scene melodrama, which was the 125th presentation in the company's history. Adapted from a writer who had provided two earlier company successes, *The Brothers Ashkenazi** and *Yoshe Kalb**, the play depicts the struggles of a typical German-Jewish family during the twenties and thirties as Hitler came into power. It received warm praise and was recommended even for those who knew no Yiddish, so clear was its action (a detailed synopsis in English was also helpful).

The family of the title is headed by David Carnovsky (Isidore Casher), a Polish-born merchant and noted Hebrew scholar who settled in Berlin. The play opens there in November 1918 with the return from the war of his physician son Georg (Schwartz). Georg causes a split with his father when he decides to marry a Gentile girl (Muriel Gruber) rather than the rich Jewish daughter of his father's friend. Georg must then face his wife's bullying Nazi brother-in-law (Mario Gang), who is always saying "Heil Hitler!" Georg and his bride have a child, Jegor (Paul Levitt), who endures insults and torture in school because of his non-Aryan status. Feeling disgraced by his Jewish blood and professing belief in the Nazi line, he rebels against his father. Hitler's persecution of the Jews becomes unbearable, and Georg leaves Germany with his family to find refuge in New York. There the embittered Georg passes his state boards and reestablishes a secure family life. However, the clouds remain dark because of the psychological scars still born by Jegor from his treatment in Germany. Georg learns by chance that Jegor's sadistic Nazi teacher (Abraham Teitelbaum) has come to America and that he is the ringleader of a gang of saboteurs. Believing that the only solution to the problem is to slay the teacher ("an eye for an eye"), he degrades the man, kills him, and then surrenders to the law.

This work proved an excellent acting vehicle, if not a fully satisfying drama. George Freedley (*NYMT*) called it "a thrilling performance and one well worth seeing." Wilella Waldorf (*NYP*) described Schwartz's directing method: "He is a deliberate director, endlessly interested in small details. Although some of the playing and an occasional scene seemed overstressed and studied . . . Mr. Schwartz . . . does not hesitate to seat his players with their backs to the audience if it seems to him more natural that way, and conversation is carried on across a room from time to time with blithe disregard for the audience out front, just as if the actors were at home."

Most of the play's problems stemmed from a somewhat awkward transfer from the book to the stage. Still, Waldorf thought it "a serious, and often very moving, play." There was some concern that the ending was out of character for Georg, and that the scene diluted the value of what came before. Thomas R. Dash (*WWD*), for example, said, "It is spiritually unsound and causes a sudden wrenching of the spectator's feelings." Otherwise, he claimed, the "play is a turbulent, soul-stirring, starkly-realistic work, meaty and wise."

FAMILY REUNION, THE [Drama/Family/Mental Illness/Old Age/Religion/Verse] A: T. S. Eliot; D: Frank Corsaro; S: Michael Mear; L: H. Woodbridge; P: On-Stage; T: Cherry Lane Theatre (OB); 11/28/47

The New York premiere of Eliot's respected but obscure verse drama was in a little-noticed Off-Broadway showing by a new company on Commerce Street. It was so little-noticed that John Chapman, editor of the *Burns Mantle Best Plays of 1949-1950*, declared in his introduction to Eliot's *The Cocktail Party* that *The Family Reunion* "has not been viewed locally." Still, director Corsaro noted in *Maverick* that the piece ran for three months. Corsaro had directed a nonreviewed version of *No Exit* for the group in June 1947. The present play proved beyond the company's capabilities, but the actors' efforts were appreciated by the few critics who visited the play.

George Freedley (*NYMT*) announced that Corsaro "has directed . . . with sureness and with complete comprehension," the major hindrance to his success being his mostly young, semiprofessional cast's inappropriateness in the roles of older characters. The mystical 1939 play, concerning themes of sin and expiation, adapts elements of the *Oresteia* and *Hamlet** to a modern context, is composed according to the neoclassical unities of time and place, contains a ritualistic substructure, and incorporates a chorus, represented by the hero's uncles and aunts.

The piece is set in a North England country house and tells of the return of the long-absent Harry, Lord Monchensey (John Christie), on the occasion of a family reunion to celebrate his mother's (Olivia, known only by her first name) birthday. Believing that he has slain his wife, Harry is hounded by the Furies, although no one else sees them. At the request of his relatives, he is examined by a doctor (David F. Perkins) to determine his sanity. The physician uncovers the past deed that infects him, namely the desire his late father once had to murder his mother because of the father's love for an aunt, Agatha (Roberta Dixon), who prevented the crime. Harry decides to "follow the Furies," but his mother passes away of a heart attack when he departs. Agatha and Mary (Julia Meade), Harry's cousin, chant poetically as they circle the birthday cake.

"Although it is discursive," opined Thomas R. Dash (*WWD*), "it is shot through with sufficient melodramatic incident to keep it thoroughly interesting, even absorbing, for an intellectual audience." But Lewis Funke (*NYT*) declared, "It is practically impossible of understanding. . . . It is completely lacking in any dramatic structure or conflict. And its story is ordinary at that."

FATAL WEAKNESS, THE [Comedy/Family/Marriage/Sex] A/D: George Kelly; S: Donald Oenslager; C: Bianca Stroock; P: Theatre Guild; T: Royale Theatre;

11/19/46 (119)

An entertaining six-character, one-set comedy, excellently acted by Ina Claire (who returned to the stage after five years in retirement) and selected as one of the season's ten best by Burns Mantle. It pleased a fair proportion of the reviewers, who generally thought it uneven but still a refreshingly unsentimental and incisively comic view of an incurably sentimental middle-aged woman. Kelcey Allen (*WWD*) noted that it "is interesting from beginning to end. [Kelly's] dialogue is fluent, humorous and effective." "The play is one of Kelly's best," thought Ward Morehouse (*NYS*). "It reveals a playwright going about his job with perception and keen understanding of character." But John Mason Brown (*SR*) called it "a very minor, old-hat affair," while admitting, "It has its adroit touches which are as shrewd and knowing as only Mr. Kelly is capable of supplying." Less impressed was Arthur Pollock (*BE*), who found the subject and treatment "dated," the development static, and the pace languid, Kelly's chief contribution being the ability to make the dialogue sound natural. Louis Kronenberger (*PM*), acknowledging that the humor was sharp, argued that the work was too haphazardly composed and lacked organic unity. "Mr. Kelly is writing several kinds of comedy here, not all at a high level or with a fresh effect--but it *is* all comedy."

Claire played Ollie Espenshade, an exaggeratedly romantic woman, who discovers from a gossipy sister, Mrs. Wentz (Margaret Douglass), that Paul Espenshade (Howard St. John), her spouse of twenty-eight years, is having an extramarital affair. This fails to create the expected explosion, as Mrs. Espenshade no longer is in love with Paul. Once she gets satisfactory proof of the affair, she welcomes a divorce so she can travel freely with her divorced sister. A lover of weddings, where she can indulge her romantic daydreams, she even plans to attend Paul's, although her attitude shocks the Espenshades' obnoxious daughter Penny (Jennifer Howard), whose "advanced" ideas on the marital state have created various conflicts between her parents.

A large part of the play's popularity came from the radiant Claire's "darting performance--a humming-bird in full flight, incredibly swift, sure and bright-hued," according to Rosamond Gilder (*TAM*). "Her byplay with the telephone, with the inevitable handkerchief, with the general minutiae of living is deft and precise. She knows to a hair's breadth the exact amount of pause and hurry to make her point." The play was one of a few during the season that decided to move their curtains up to 8 P.M., although the practice did not catch on for years. In the cast were Mary Gildea as a maid and John Larson as Penny's husband.

(1) **FATHER, THE** (***Fadren***) [Dramatic Revival*] A: August Strindberg; D: John Stix; S: Eldon Elder; C: Robert Cowan; P: Studio-7; T: Provincetown Playhouse (OB); 7/20/49 (95)

Several figures who would later figure importantly in American theatre were involved with this relatively obscure mounting of Strindberg's 1887 naturalist classic, not seen locally since 1931. Set designer Elder, director Stix, and actor (later critic and director) Robert Brustein were seeing their names appear on a New York playbill for the first time. This was the second production by a new Off-Broadway group made up of recent Yale graduates, and it was considered a great improvement over their earlier work. Ward Costello played the captain, Ken Moxley was the pastor, Paul Rivet acted the orderly, Brustein was Nojd, Anne Shropshire played Laura, Ken Rockefeller was the doctor, Charlet Oberley interpreted the nurse, and Millicent Brower was Bertha.

The actors, said Arthur Pollock (*DC*), "dig right into it from the beginning, give it vigor and precision all the way through, make a better job of playing than most of the little off-Broadway summer groups are able to, get out of it very nearly everything Strindberg put there, tie it up tight." Joseph T. Shipley (*NL*) declared, "*The Father* is one of the most intense dramas of the past hundred years. In the unpretentious, understanding production of Studio 7, its power and its fierce beauty are richly conveyed."

The piece played to packed houses and was considered by some superior to the Broadway revival that opened later in the season. It was produced in honor of the

Strindberg centennial being celebrated in 1949. After the play's initial run, it was temporarily suspended, then revived again in October 1949.

(2) AD: Robert L. Joseph; D: Raymond Massey; S/L: Donald Oenslager; C: Eleanor Goldsmith; P: Richard W. Krakeur and Robert L. Joseph i/a/w Harry Brandt; T: Cort Theatre; 11/16/49 (69)

A highly distinguished company revived the drama on Broadway in this version, with Raymond Massey directing and playing the title role, Philip Huston as the pastor, Mady Christians as the captain's wife, John D. Seymour as the doctor, Mary Morris as the nurse, and, in her Broadway debut, beautiful Grace Kelly as Bertha, the daughter. She gave "a charming, pliable performance," thought Brooks Atkinson (*NYT*). George Jean Nathan (*TBY*) thought hers the only salvageable performance in the production.

Massey's recollection (in *A Hundred Different Lives*) that the "critical consensus seemed to be that it was a bad play with a bad reputation" is not entirely justified. Some, like John Beaufort (*CSM*), did consider the play "a dreary business, a piece of special pleading but not very admirable pleading which sheds little light and arouses little emotion." William Hawkins (*NYWT*) called it "dated," which view was strongly contested by Nathan. Many were on the side of Whitney Bolton (*NYMT*), who decided that this is "a play that holds taut, commands attention and is at moments piercingly touching."

Several reviewers thought that Massey had weakened his performance by also undertaking the direction. To Atkinson, Massey's performance was the major flaw in the revival, as it brought too much soft sensitivity to the role while lacking "the steel and force which the tragedy contains. Strindberg wrote the play like a fiend. Mr. Massey is an amiable actor who does not have much ferocity in his soul." Others were not so critical, but most sensed some drawbacks in the performance. Massey revealed in his autobiography that he suffered from claustrophobia every time he had to put on the straitjacket worn by the captain in the last scene. "I knew that my genuine fear did no good to my performance. It was just at the height of the 'Method-acting' vogue, a fad I had no use for, and I remember chiding myself for living my part. I still have the damn thing and it makes me sweat when I look at it!"

Christians's performance was more widely approved, but not universally so. "Miss Christians portrays the relentless wife, Laura, with a straight line of malevolence," wrote Beaufort, "broken only once or twice as the wife softens with reminiscence. She acts the woman monster with intellectual and emotional force." "When she comes on stage," noted Bolton, "you know that ferocity and murderous determination have entered the room." Still, Richard Watts, Jr. (*NYP*), preferred Anne Shropshire in the previous revival, and Arthur Pollock (*DC*) was one of several who found weaknesses in both the stars: "They blow up every detail, blurring the piece, cluttering it up, leaving it dripping with sweat."

(1) FAUST [Dramatic Revival] A: Johann Wolfgang von Goethe; AD/D: John Reich; S: Hans Sondheimer; L: Doris Einstein; P: Equity Library Theatre; T: George Bruce Branch of the New York Public Library (OB); 1/29/46 (4)

A slow-paced, showcase presentation of Goethe's immense German philosophical drama, shaved down somewhat, but not enough to make it thoroughly acceptable as stage fare. Its use of rhymed verse also proved disconcerting. George Freedley (*NYMT*), the sole reviewer present, noted, "Mr. Reichs [*sic*] version is smooth and plays easily for the most part, but rhymed verse rests uneasily on the ears of an American audience trained for prose or blank verse." Freedley griped that the first part of the performance, during the development of Faust's character, was static and could have been improved by "ruthless slashing." Even if some intellectual values were thus impaired, the dramatic impact might have been stronger, he said.

The best performance was Betty Buehler's as Margaret. "She is both beautiful to look at and to listen to. . . . She brings richness of texture, purity of reading, and sincerity of playing to a most exacting role," wrote Freedley. David McGregor Gibb was an adequate Faust, and Philip Sann played Mephisto "with the utmost in acrobatics and reverbatory [*sic*] sibilants."

(2) [German Language] A: Johann Wolfgang von Goethe; D: Leon Askin; P: Players from Abroad; T: Barbizon-Plaza Theatre (OB); 11/27/47

A group of German-speaking immigrant actors performed this tediously paced revival of the first part of *Faust*, with octogenarian Albert Bassermann as Mephistopheles, a role for which he was famous on the Continent. The vast and lengthy drama was squeezed uncomfortably onto the tiny Barbizon-Plaza Theatre's stage. The aged star's supporting cast was mostly second-rate, although graced by the performance of young Uta Hagen as Margarete.

Isra. (*V*) described Bassermann's performance by saying he played "with a mixture of painful acrobatics and sincere declamation that would be no less admirable, although possibly more convincing, in a younger player. He chooses to depict his devil as a sardonic devil in a rather comic costume, with a sword getting in his way more often than not." Brooks Atkinson (*NYT*) noted that he acted "with wonderful relish--as the evening wears on, getting more and more humor out of it." Leon Askin was a convincing and vigorous Faust.

Of Hagen, Atkinson said that she "plays beautifully in a soft, maiden-like style." Others included Else Bassermann as Marthe, Walter Engel as Raphael, and Stefan Schnabel as the Almighty.

FEATHERS IN A GALE [Comedy/Period/Romance] A: Pauline Jameson and Reginald Lawrence; D: Arthur Hopkins; S: Raymond Sovey; C: Aline Bernstein; P: Arthur Hopkins and Martin Burton; T: Music Box Theatre; 12/21/43 (7)

An inexpert and pedestrian comedy set in the Cape Cod town of Sesuit in 1804. It deals with an old New England custom of the "vendue" whereby an indigent widow is sold for a year to the highest bidder, usually to serve as a housekeeper or possibly as a concubine. The custom usually affected the widows of men lost at sea. In the play, there are three widows, and their ultimate purpose is matrimony. Peppered with supposedly quaint New Englandisms like "tarnation," "I swan!" and "glory be!" and riddled with clichéd lines, characters, and situations, the play was doomed from the start.

Pretty widow Annabelle Hallock (Peggy Conklin) is fast going broke because of her extravagances and her having kindly provided a home for a pair of sister widows, Matilda Phinney (Louise Lorimer) and Phoebe Fuller (Paula Trueman). When a clipper makes port nearby, the ambitious Annabelle sets her cap to no avail for the dashing captain, Seth Barnabas (Norman MacKay), pursuing him through the play and causing local tongues to furiously wag. Loving her is the young parson, Rev. David Thatcher (Harry Ellerbe), who cannot bring himself to intrude on her mourning period by asking for her hand. Ultimately, the women are sold at auction, and the house man (John Hamilton) purchases Matilda for $3, while Seth, unaware of Annabelle's plight till now, pays $1,000 to save her from another captain's clutches. The parson then discovers that the custom is illegal and ends it. Captain Seth turns Annabelle over to the parson, claiming the latter to be a more appropriate spouse for her.

"It is a pity that the play is so lacking in bounce, verve, suspense or comedy," moaned Burton Rascoe (*NYWT*). "The play as a whole lacked point or meaning," contributed Rosamond Gilder (*TAM*), "even such light meaning as rests in a good laugh." In the company were Zamah Cunningham, Stuart Brody, Aileen Poe, and others.

FIDDLER'S HOUSE, THE [Dramatic Revival] A: Padraic Colum; D: J. Augustus Keogh; P: Irish Repertory Theatre i/a/w Wendell Phillips Dodge and the Greenwich Village Stage Society and Opera Guild; T: Cherry Lane Theatre (OB); 3/27/41

Aged, blind actor Augustin Duncan proved still capable of garnering praise for his remarkable voice and presence when he appeared in this Irish folk-comedy as Conn Hourican, an itinerant musician. The piece--set in the midnineteenth century--had been titled *Broken Soil* when it first was produced in 1903 by Dublin's Irish Literary Theatre, forerunner of the Abbey Theatre.

The story it tells is of the restless, heavy-drinking, old widower Conn, who has retired to the family farm, where he lives with his two daughters, Maire (Margaret McCarthy) and Anne (Judith Magee). Conn, however, cannot resist the call of the road upon which for so many years he tramped from village to village with his music. The play's conflicts are between Conn and his older daughter, who does not comprehend his wanderlust, and with the neighbors, who suspect a man who does not share their passion for the land. Each daughter also has romantic problems, one loving the irresponsible Brian MacConnell (John Ireland, in his New York debut), the other loving James Moynihan (Gerald Buckley), whose father wants him to marry someone wealthier. Maire deeds the farm to her younger sister Anne, who thereupon weds James, while the older sister rejects her lover and goes forth with Conn to guide him on his farewell tour of Eire.

The once-respected work was now considered tame and undramatic, although its author's talent was clearly evident. The characters, said Richard Watts, Jr. (*NYHT*), "are never merely stock figures. There is a sort of practical reality about them and their talk, and for better or for worse, they are drawn from life, rather than from imagination." Otherwise, its chief interest was historical. A mediocre production did not make the old play any more agreeable.

FIFTH HORSEMAN, THE [Drama/Fantasy/Religion/Sex/War] A: Abraham L. Goldfein; D: Joseph Anthony; S/L: Robert Gundlach; P: Invitational Series of the Experimental Theatre; T: New Stages Theatre (OB); 6/13/49

A confusing message play, set on Cape Cod and dealing with the world's need to get on course morally before chaos descends. It concerns a bearded old wanderer (Henry Sharp) who claims to be God; a young woman (Julie Follensbee), unwed, who claims that her pregnancy is a result of immaculate conception; various acts of bigotry by the ignorant and prejudiced local populace; the claim that war is imminent; the frequent sound of overhead airplanes as well as that of the neighing steed ridden by the Fifth Horseman of the Apocalypse; and so on.

J. P. S. (*NYT*), referring to the impressive use of sound effects, called it "a tiresome amalgam of ponderous philosophy and disturbing technical devices that distract from rather than heighten the action." Herm. (*V*) rejected it as "an indigestible stew of mysticism, metaphor and mayhem."

FIFTY [Drama/Aviation/Military/Romance/War] A: Lyn Shubert; D: Leonard Altobelli; S/L: Clay Watson; P: Robert O'Byrne and Gloria Monty for the Abbe Practical Workshop; T: Master Institute Theatre (OB); 4/9/49 (3)

Movies might have been a better medium than theatre for the realization of this well-acted play, which concerns a group of fighter-squadron fliers in World War II, covering their experiences from their departure for Italy to the completion of their fifty missions. During the play, which examines their conflicts over a period of time and includes a love interest between a flier (Jim Conrad) and a Red Cross nurse (Gloria McGhee), the only female role, the novice fliers learn the various practical problems of combat flying. They reveal elements of heroism and cowardice. By the end of the play, only two are still alive.

Vernon Rice (*NYP*) appreciated the realism of the characters' behavior and dialogue, but saw nothing novel in what they had to say. But George Freedley (*NYMT*) thought it "an exciting and poignant play" with "some of the most interesting dialogue" he had heard all year. The semipro cast included William Kester, Ted Bauer, John Petrone, Al Daily, Tom Sharp, John Montell, and Richard Kleinman.

FINIAN'S RAINBOW [Musical/Blacks/Family/Fantasy/Labor/Politics/Race/Romance/Rural/Southern] B: E. Y. Harburg and Fred Saidy; M: Burton Lane; LY: E. Y. Harburg; D: Bretaigne Windust; CH: Michael Kidd; S/L: Jo Mielziner; C: Eleanor Goldsmith; P: Lee Sabinson and William R. Katzell; T: Forty-sixth Street Theatre; 1/10/47 (725)

One of several important musicals that made the season of 1946-1947 a memorable one. Some objected mildly to the fact that musicals like this one were moving the form more and more into matters of social significance and away from mindless pleasure for the tired businessman (it opened a night after Elmer Rice and Kurt Weill's *Street Scene*). However, despite the dangers of allowing socially provocative matters to intrude uncomfortably, the material never went too far in the direction of propaganda, and the songs were so consistently successful that even reactionaries were able to enjoy the show.

This "tuneful, colorful, dashing" (George Freedley [*NYMT*]) musical listed such things in its plus column as balletically lyrical as well as dazzlingly energetic choreography, an ingeniously contrived unit set, delightful costumes, superb direction, excellent performances, a topically relevant libretto, and a lusty score that included such perennials as "Look to the Rainbow," "Old Devil Moon," "Something Sort of Grandish," "How Are Things in Glocca Morra?" (the show's biggest hit), "If This Isn't Love," "When I'm Not Near the Girl I Love," and "Great Come-and-Get-It Day." Also gaining attention were "Necessity," "The Begat," and "When the Idle Poor Become the Idle Rich."

The show returned Scottish singer Ella Logan to Broadway fame after an absence of several years and catapulted David Wayne into the limelight. However, when Logan's insistence on star billing was rejected by the producers, who felt there that should be no stars in what was essentially an ensemble work, she left the show. A series of replacements failed to harm the quality of the show or its popularity with audiences.

Its story was inspired by two ideas E. Y. ("Yip") Harburg had for plays (neither with a musical in mind). One was to create a tale about a leprechaun and the three wishes permitted to the holder of his crock of gold. Another was to deal with a racist Southern senator somehow turned black and made a victim of the Jim Crow laws he supported. These two ideas were merged in *Finian's Rainbow*, whose musical form seemed more appropriate to the material than straight drama.

Simple-minded Irish immigrant Finian McLonergan (Albert Sharpe), having stolen the leprechauns' crock in Glocca Morra, Ireland, comes with it and his daughter Sharon (Logan) to Rainbow Valley ("where the bees make certified honey and spiders spin nylon webs") in the mountains of Missitucky, an imaginary Southern state. His fanciful dream is to grow rich by burying the crock where it will grow, just as America presumably grew rich by its deposits at Fort Knox. He is followed by Og (Wayne), a cunning, pointy-eared leprechaun seeking to get the crock back. Og, who, to his chagrin, finds himself becoming increasingly more human, falls in love with Sharon; she, however, goes for union organizer Woody Mahoney (Donald Richards). When the local sharecroppers hear rumors about gold in the soil, they begin to spend their hard-earned cash. Threaded through this romantic story is that of Senator Billboard Rawkins (Robert Pitkin), a bigot who seeks to illegally obtain the land from Finian and the sharecroppers. He is accidentally turned into a black evangelist when Sharon makes wish number one on the crock. The senator learns some valuable humanizing lessons from the switch, much of his time being spent as a member of a black singing quartet. Og has preserved enough of his leprechaun power to turn the bigot white again and to enable Susan Mahoney (Anita Alvarez), a wise mute who speaks through dance, to talk. Although the rumor about gold in the land is exposed as false, the sharecroppers happily learn that the soil is rich enough to grow enough tobacco to bring them wealth. Og accepts Susan as his love and Sharon fulfills her romance with Woody, and Finian's crock of gold is explained as merely a state of mind and not a physical reality.

Although there were occasional quibbles, the reviews were almost unanimously positive. Brooks Atkinson (*NYT*) advised that this was "a raree-show of enchantment, humor and beauty, to say nothing of enough social significance to hold the franchise." Among his "minor reservations" was the fear that "its stubborn shot-gun marriage of fairy-story and social significance is not altogether happy. The capriciousness of the invention does not last throughout the evening." Rosamond Gilder (*TAM*) classed it with *Oklahoma!* and *Carousel* because "it has an engaging story, a pleasing folk quality, a chorus made up of people and not merely of chorus girls and boys and a contagious lyricism, but it is entirely fresh and original." "Harburg and Saidy's play has wit, action, satire and tenderness with very amusing lyrics . . . and stirring music," added Euphemia Van Rensselaer Wyatt (*CW*). John Mason Brown

(*SR*) objected to the coarser humor and found some of the lyrics coy, but loved most of what he saw, noting that "this new musical does manage to advance gaily down a path at once charming and untrodden." George Jean Nathan (*TBY*) acknowledged that the book was more adept at dealing smartly with the social issues it confronted than did "the many plays boiled by our young radicals and other grousers." Yet Louis Kronenberger (*PM*), after listing all the show's virtues, had to observe, "*Finian* hasn't enough taste or sensibility or integrity; at the level it professes to work on, these deficiencies stick out like sore thumbs."

All the leads were widely hailed, including the enchanting dancer Anita Alvarez. Speaking of Wayne, John Chapman (*NYDN*) reported, "Never was a man-size spright more spritely. . . . He can cast a spell, or sing a song like 'Something Sort of Grandish,' or entertain children with gifts in a mail order catalogue, in a manner that is quite magical." Among the others involved were Dolores Martin, Eddie Bruce, Sonny Terry, Tom McElhaney, Augustus Smith, Jr., Jerry Laws, Lorenzo Fuller, and Louis Sharp.

FIREBRAND OF FLORENCE, THE [Musical/Art/Period/Romance/Sex] B: Edwin Justus Mayer; M: Kurt Weill; LY: Ira Gershwin; SC: Edwin Justus Mayer's play, *The Firebrand**; D: John Murray Anderson and John Haggott; CH: Catherine Littlefield; S/L: Jo Mielziner; C: Raoul Pène du Bois; P: Max Gordon; T: Alvin Theatre; 3/22/45 (43)

The Firebrand, a hit satirical romantic comedy of 1924 about the famous Florentine artist Benvenuto Cellini, was turned into this lavish ($250,000) but unsuccessful musical comedy that George Freedley (*NYMT*) called "a deadly costly, slowly paced bore." Lewis Nichols (*NYT*) said that it "lacks sparkle, drive, or just plain nervous energy; it is a little like an old-fashioned operetta, slowly paced and ambling." Despite being doctored out of town by George S. Kaufman, the work was scored for a lack of humor, uninventive dance routines, and an undistinguished score. Euphemia Van Rensselaer Wyatt (*CW*) felt that "in making the main theme a conventional romance, the satire [of the original] dissolves into somnolent and highly conventional intrigue." Earlier titles by which the show was known were *It Happened in Florence*, *Make Way for Love*, and *Much Ado about Love*.

Faithful to the original plot, the show tells about the artistic and romantic escapades of Cellini (Earl Wrightson); of his being threatened by the duke of Florence (Melville Cooper) with execution for killing an enemy; of the duchess's (Lotte Lenya, wife of the composer) being so fond of him that his life is spared; of his romance with a sexy model named Angela (Beverly Tyler), whom the duke also desires; and of various bedroom mixups, homicides, and so on. Finally, Cellini, deciding that Angela is a flirtatious interruption to his art, allows the duke to realize his passion for her, thus restoring himself to the ducal favor.

Weill's score was not highly recommended. Its tunes included "Sing Me Not a Ballad," "Come to Florence," "You Have to Do What You Do Do," "There'll Be Life, Love, and Laughter," "The Night Time Is No Time for Thinking," and "My Dear Benvenuto."

In writing the show, Weill was fulfilling a promise to Lenya to provide her with a role to boost her lagging career. However, lyricist Gershwin insisted that the role of the duchess go to Kitty Carlisle. Despite her performing a role created expressly for her, Lenya was widely thought to be miscast. Baritone Earl Wrightson, in his first lead role, impressed vocally but not as an actor. Only the colorful decor and Melville Cooper's comic performance redeemed the evening, although the actor (a replacement for Walter Slezak) was forced to read lines like the following, a response to a girl who said that she was a lady-in-waiting: "Well, you won't have to wait long." "The whole production," lamented Rosamond Gilder (*TAM*), "is a reversion to an earlier type rather than a step forward in the progress of American musical comedy." A previous attempt to turn *The Firebrand* into a musical was 1933's *The Dagger and the Rose*, with a book by Isabel Leighton, music by Eugene Berton, and lyrics by Edward Eliscu, but it flopped out of town.

FIRST CROCUS, THE [Comedy/Crime/Family/Romance/Small Town/Youth] A:

Arnold Sundgaard; D: Halsted Welles; S: Johannes Larsen; P: T. Edward Hambleton; T: Longacre Theatre; 1/2/42 (5)

Arnold Sundgaard's "sprawling and amorphous" (Brooks Atkinson [*NYT*]) play concerns a Norwegian family in the small town of Albion, Minnesota. The well-meaning but domineering matriarch is Inga Jorislund (Swedish-born Martha Hedman, returning to Broadway after nearly two decades), and her spouse of a quarter of a century is Ansgar (Herbert Nelson). Troubles with her children begin to darken the horizon. Oldest son Henrik (Edwin Philips), a struggling law student, wants to escape his mother's annoying remonstrances and get married to Violet (Jocelyn Brando, in her Broadway debut), his childhood sweetheart. Daughter Avis (Perry Wilson) suffers a broken romance and drops out of college because of her mother's meddling. Lars Hilleboe (Lewis Martin) falls in love with her, and wedding bells seem imminent. The central plot incident occurs when fifteen-year-old Milford (Eugene Schiel) is disgraced for cheating in a school contest to find the first crocus of spring; he was afraid of his mother's anger if he failed. When Milford needs a new coat, Inga pilfers money from the school funds, and Ansgar must then pay it back by selling his own favorite coat.

The Jorislunds and their neighbors were colorfully drawn and most were stageworthy creations, some providing refreshing interludes of comedy. However, sluggish direction, an undramatic, although fairly atmospheric, script, and the annoying personality of the loquacious mother damaged this "strange, muddled and uneven little drama," as John Mason Brown (*NYWT*) termed it.

FIRST MILLION, THE [Comedy/Crime/Family/Rural/Sex] A: Irving Elman; D: John Kennedy; S: Wolfgang Roth; P: Jimmy Elliott; T: Ritz Theatre; 4/28/43 (5)

Nineteen-year-old producer Jimmy Elliott, then acting in *Junior Miss*, offered his first Broadway production with this "quite bad" (Lewis Nichols [*NYT*]) farce set in a cabin in the Ozarks. The Boones are a hillbilly family of criminals, four sons dominated by Maw Boone (Dorrit Kelton), whose creed holds that before they can spend any of their ill-gotten gains, they must first have robbed $1 million. The family creed was bequeathed them by their deceased patriarch, Paw, whose words were, "The first million is the hardest." They have acquired $981,000, which is kept in a churn. The play concerns their efforts to obtain their final $19,000 through the crime of kidnapping the local banker (Harlan Briggs). All the forces of the law--including the dumb local sheriff (Russell Collins)--seem to be after them, and the radio reports their exploits on a round-the-clock basis. Mink Boone (Dort Clark) is a half-wit, Hoke Boone (Wendell Corey) a womanizer, and Sank Boone (George Cotton) a trigger-happy type. The fourth brother, Tom (Henry Bernard), is an honest fellow who wants to make rubber out of soybeans. He also provides the romantic angle with his love for an orphan girl (Lois Hall), whom Hoke at one point tries to seduce. Various complications crop up as the Boones manage to get the ransom money but lose it all when Sank decides to put fire to the entire stash.

A lack of good comic dialogue, completely implausible characters, a vague point of view, and confused performances were among this flop's most serious ailments. Most critics felt that the material had promise, but that, as Louis Kronenberger (*PM*) put it, the result was "a pointless muddled study in human wild life. It jumps the sense of probability, only to land in a ditch."

FIRST MRS. FRASER, THE [Dramatic Revival*] A: St. John Ervine; D: Harold Young; S/L: Charles Elson; C: Natalie Barth; P: Gant Gaither; T: Shubert Theatre; 11/5/47 (38)

An ill-advised revival, updated to 1947, of the English play, a 1929 hit on Broadway with Grace George as the eponymous Scottish heroine. The new star was the luminous Jane Cowl, who had played the piece on the straw-hat circuit in the preceding summer and was making her first local appearance in six years. Cowl was appropriately convincing in the role of the middle-aged divorcée whose ex-spouse (Henry Daniell) comes seeking sympathy after the nineteen-year-old Elsie (Frances Tannehill), for whom he has left her, discards him.

The theme of divorce was still pertinent, and there were several slick situations and lines that continued to interest a 1947 audience, but the drawing-room comedy was too thin and creaky to sustain attention. Richard Watts, Jr. (*NYT*), declared, "The one trouble is that the play is mild, commonplace and a little dull." Despite the play's frailties, noted Brooks Atkinson (*NYT*), it was a delight to observe "Miss Cowl's thoroughly professional, ingenious and animated performance. It has spirit, variety, and it has wit." Several others, though, considered her mannered and artificial. In supporting roles were Lex Richards as Ninian Fraser, Reginald Mason as Philip Logan, Emily Lawrence as Alice Fraser, Hazel Jones as Mabel, and Kendall Clark as Murdo Fraser. A sidebar on the show concerns its producer's boast that despite a generally approved scenic investiture revealing a lavish interior decor, the production budget did not exceed $12,500.

FIRST STOP TO HEAVEN [Drama/Boarding House/Literature/Marriage/Romance] A: Norman Rosten; D: Robert Henderson; S: Louis Kennel; P: Margaret Hewes; T: Windsor Theatre; 1/5/41 (8)

Poet Norman Rosten's first Broadway play employed several distinguished actors, but the play itself was easily forgettable. Eva Golden (Alison Skipworth), married to Carl Golden (Taylor Holmes), runs a Sixth Avenue boarding house in danger of being closed down by a building inspector (James Bell) because of code violations. Until the house is blown to smithereens to make room for a new subway's construction, Eva staves off the would-be dynamiters while ministering to a host of eccentric roomers. Among them is a young nurse (Elena Ryerson) whom Eva tries to fix up with a young pulp-magazine writer (Erik Walz), although the nurse is eyed affectionately by a hoodlum (William Challee). Eventually, Eva and Carl move to a chicken farm.

First Stop to Heaven seemed like a combination of third-rate Saroyan and third-rate Kaufman and Hart, in their *You Can't Take It with You** phase. Richard Watts, Jr. (*NYHT*), asserted that simply putting a bunch of offbeat types together in a house was no proof of dramatic ability. In this case, for instance, the characters turned out to be "dull and foolish and their dialogue . . . vapid, dismal and aimless." Burns Mantle (*NYDN*) called it "an aimless, plotless, witless affair." Joe E. Marks, Eduard Franz, and Douglas Rowland were among the guests at the house.

FIRST WIFE, THE [Drama/China/Family/Journalism/Marriage/Orientals/Politics/Youth] A: Pearl S. Buck; D: H. Lee Heagy and Wang Yung; S: Shun-hain Chang Chi; P: The Chinese Theatre; T: Barbizon-Plaza Theatre (OB); 11/27/45 (12)

A company of Chinese actors playing in English performed this new play by Pearl S. Buck, famed writer on Chinese and other subjects. Before the presentation, Buck herself appeared to deliver a brief lecture about the play and Chinese theatre. She stressed the importance of theatre in largely illiterate China, noted the chief differences between classical and modern genres, and observed the different expectations of American audiences from those in China. She declared that she wrote her play as a "transition" piece between the classical and modern styles at the request of the East and West Association because they "had no such play by a Chinese playwright readily available."

Its theme is the conflict between the old and new types of civilization in China as depicted in a tale about a young Chinese man (Allen Young) who returns to his rural village after seven years of study at Shanghai University. He has become modernized in dress and ideas. His family includes his mother, father (headman of the village), wife (Wang Yung, a well-known Chinese stage and film actress), and daughter (Marian Chang). Set on cutting all ties with ancient Chinese thought, behavior, and culture, which he considers backward, he plans to become a crusading journalist on an official newspaper in Chungking, to which he is formally summoned by the government, but because his old-fashioned, illiterate wife would prove an embarrassment, he wants to leave her behind. He rebukes his parents for insisting that he remain and father a grandson for them. His duty is not to them but to China, he insists, and he tells his wife that it is on China's behalf that he must leave her. The wife is further confused by his talk about China's need to build up its armaments. To her the problem is simply that he no longer loves her. She decides to leave the village, for her continued presence there without her spouse would be a disgrace to his parents, who would be shamed in the eyes of the villagers. Her own parents, however, are dead, so she has nowhere to go. After her husband departs, she thinks of suicide but rejects the notion. At the end, her fate is undecided.

Buck's theatre skills were no match for those she displayed as a novelist. L. C. (*NYT*) commented that her play "proves neither unusual nor exciting. Its dialogue is repetitious and its situations are unreal." "She has produced only a supine reading-room treatise," argued George Jean Nathan (*TBY*), "without either inner or superficial theatrical imagination."

FIVE ALARM WALTZ [Comedy/Films/Literature/Marriage/Theatre/Youth] A: Lucille S. Prumbs; D: Robert Lewis; S: Harry Horner; C: Helene Pons; P: Everett Wile; T: Playhouse; 3/13/41 (4)

Director Elia Kazan made his last Broadway appearance as an actor in this "noisy and tiresome" (Louis Kronenberger [*PM*]) four-performance flop for which some (not all) of his personal reviews were not much better than those for the play. He portrayed Adam Boguris, an off-the-wall, William Saroyan-like novelist (although the character is Bulgarian-American instead of Armenian-American) given to romping about his home in his underwear, no matter who is present. The novelist's supersmooth Clare Boothe Luce-like wife, Brooke March (Louise Platt), is a facile but successful playwright who dares her undisciplined, bellowing spouse into writing a play. He sets to the task, bringing all sorts of eccentrics into the house for him to study as character-types. Finally, his play is written and, while no one understands it, it becomes a hit. Brooke is wooed by a film director (Robert Shayne) who thinks she is unhappy with her lug of a husband, but she decides to stay with Adam after he comes home with a little Chinese boy (Harold Lui), saying that he adopted him.

Brooks Atkinson (*NYT*) had to note "that Robert Lewis's direction is bad, and that Elia Kazan's acting . . . is bad also. . . . Mr. Lewis's attempt to whip up *Five Alarm Waltz* into supernatural comedy results in robot acting in which most of the players are driven beyond their capacity and forced to throw their voices into overdrive gear. . . . As for Kazan, he is getting to be a self-conscious actor with purple patches and many little curlicues on the side." Curt Conway, Roman Bohnen, Helen Zelinskaya, Ann Thomas, and Howard Freeman were members of the cast.

FIVE'KE, THE SLAVE [Comedy-Drama/Yiddish Language] A: Samuel H. Cohn; M: Maurice Rauch; LY: Chaim Tauber; D: Judah Bleich; CH: Lillian Shapero; S: Michael Saltzman; T: Public Theatre (OB); 3/24/41

This was a lengthy comedy-drama with songs and dances focusing on two stepbrothers, the kindly Five'ke (Judah Bleich) and the dishonest, belligerent Morris (Morris Dorf), who come to America from Europe. En route, Morris betrays Five'ke, who is taken prisoner and returned home, where his wife (Dinah Halpern) dies from grief. The stepbrothers eventually set up a dress shop in New York, but Morris, again acting the traitor, has Five'ke kicked out of the business. Morris's physician son (Max Kletter) and Five'ke's daughter (Dinah Halpern, in a dual role) fall in love, but their parents oppose the match. Finally, all works out well and the evil stepbrother begs forgiveness from the good-natured Five'ke.

Max Wilner and Wolfe Barzell were among the company members, their troupe being from Brooklyn but trying to establish a place on the Yiddish Rialto of Second Avenue. Bernard R. Rachmel (*WWD*) called the play "an entertaining and pleasing concoction."

FLAG IS BORN, A [Drama/Fantasy/Jews/Old Age/Period/Politics/Religion] A: Ben Hecht; M: Kurt Weill; D: Luther Adler; CH: Zamira Gon; S: Robert Davison; C: John Boyt; P: American League for a Free Palestine; T: Alvin Theatre; 9/5/46 (120)

An unusual, hour-and-a-half, pageantlike Zionist play and production, created solely as a fund-raising and interest-generating inducement for the cause of a Jewish homeland (a free Palestine) in the period just prior to the 1948 establishment of the

State of Israel. After its curtain fell, director Luther Adler (who later took over the leading role when Paul Muni had to leave for a previous commitment) spoke to the audience: "At this very moment little boats are running the British blockade---will you give $250 to save the life of one Jewish man, woman or child? If your cheers mean anything, give now before you walk out of the lobby." The play was so successful that its planned limited engagement was extended. Many in the company donated their services free of charge. A total of $275,000 was raised, and with it, the Israeli navy bought an old ocean liner that it made into its flagship under the name S. S. *Hecht*.

The drama starred Muni, Celia Adler, Marlon Brando, and Quentin Reynolds. Muni played Tevya, a patriarchal Jew whose family and possessions have been stripped from him and who is setting out for the Promised Land with his wife Zelda (Adler). Fatigued, they stop to rest in a graveyard where they meet the embittered David (Brando), a youthful survivor of the Holocaust who has lost his faith in man and God. He is ashamed of the Jews for allowing themselves to be annihilated with out a fight. The orthodox older couple, however, still believe and, it being Friday night--the sabbath--they light their candles on a tombstone. This inspires Tevya's visions of Israel's historical and legendary glories, each narrated by a Speaker (Reynolds). These include a scene of choral singing in a synagogue, followed by visions of Israel's warrior kings, Saul (George David Baxter), David (William Allyn), and Solomon (Gregory Morton). Tevya follows Solomon's advice to address the United Nations, in a scene that shows Russia stomping out after refusing to acknowledge either anti-Semitism or Semitism. Despite the hypocritical England's attempts to silence Tevya (England was booed by the audience), the United States supports Tevya's claims to be heard, but the best he can achieve is to have the Jewish plight assigned to the organization's agenda. Then Tevya and Zelda lie down to die. When young David sneers at this solution, there appears a band of Israeli youth armed with machine guns and crying, "The bridge you seek is courage. Not to walk naked to a crematorium but to find manhood in struggle." David abandons his thought of suicide and proudly joins them as, to rousing martial music, a flag with the Star of David, made of Tevya's prayer shawl, is waved.

Most critics felt that the colossal cause was not served by an erratic script that failed to deliver the power inherent in the subject and got sidetracked in political details. Kahn. (*V*) wrote, "*Flag* is frequently engulfed in talk, and it is repetitious, but more frequently it depicts with vivid imagination . . . that here is a story that must be told not only to Jews but those of other creeds as well." Louis Kronenberger (*PM*) noted that it was written "with great sincerity, and it has vigorous and pathetic moments, but I could wish it had a great deal many more of them."

What saved the event for many were the inspired performances of Muni and Adler, especially the former. His portrayal, wrote John Chapman (*NYDN*), "is a work of admirable quality. It has strength and it has pathos; it has humility and it has humor. And I have never before heard Muni's fine voice used to such supreme advantage."

According to Jerome Lawrence's *Actor*, Muni, a demanding perfectionist, flagellated himself over the problems of his role and was especially concerned about achieving the proper makeup. He wanted director Adler to hire painters from Palestine to provide models from which he could copy. Adler recalled, "A Palestinian painter he wanted yet--to tell this great Master of Makeup how to be a Jew. My God, in his acting career, he'd played every kind of Jew that ever existed!" When Muni continually plagued Adler about a lengthy peroration his character had to deliver, complaining about his inability to concentrate or remember the words, Adler replied, "Muni, . . . I know you're speaking the truth. That's not a speech, it's a whole play, and if you want to blame Ben Hecht, all right--but I know where you come from and where *I* come from, so I'll say one word to you: *souffleur*. You want prompters? You can have as many as you like. You're at a lectern. We'll have a script there with letters the size of your hand; nobody's gonna walk out if you turn a page. But in addition: there'll be a prompter inside the lectern. Also one stage right. One stage left. One in your beard. And one in your *tochus*!"

The twenty-two-year-old Brando was so impressive that Adler recommended him to director Elia Kazan to play the lead in the movie *Gentleman's Agreement*, but Brando turned the chance down, preferring to stay with the play because he felt that the persecuted Jews needed his help. Hearing this, Hecht wired the actor: "DEAR MARLON. THE JEWS HAVE BEEN PERSECUTED FOR 3000 YEARS. THEY LIKE IT. TAKE THE JOB." (The role eventually went to Gregory Peck.)

After Muni's character died, Brando had to cover him completely with a flag, give a speech, and then march off. Muni asked him one day to cover only his body, so that his face, in death, would provide a striking image. But Brando forgot the note at the next performance and covered the actor's face. As he delivered his speech, he noticed out of the corner of his eye that Muni was very slowly pulling the flag away to reveal his face, inch by inch. "The old hambone couldn't stand not having his face in the final scene," recalled Brando. "I was afraid I'd break up, so I stopped in the middle of the speech, kneeled, pulled the flag away from his face and tucked it tenderly under his chin. His expression was beatific." Even though Muni was supposed to be dead, he was still in character. "If the curtain hadn't come down, he'd have acted out all the stages of *rigor mortis* setting in" (quoted in Fred Fehl, *On Broadway*).

FLAMINGO ROAD [Drama/Journalism/Politics/Prison/Prostitution/Romance/Sex/Southern] A: Robert Wilder and Sally Wilder; SC: Robert Wilder's novel of the same name; D: José Ruben; S: Watson Barratt; L: Leo Kerz; C: Emeline Roche; P: Rowland Stebbins; T: Belasco Theatre; 3/19/46 (7)

A hackneyed play whose "one and only contribution . . . to the historical record," noted George Jean Nathan (*TBY*), "is its articulation, for the first time on an American stage, of a certain four-letter word." "Dramatically, it is just plain poppycock," sniped Robert Garland (*NYJA*). "Even on its own terms it is not a very credible story. But what is worse," reported Louis Kronenberger (*PM*), "it lets what should be significant social drama dwindle into quite insignificant melodrama."

The story was about Titus Semple (Francis J. "Happy" Felton), an inordinately malignant, obese political boss in a Florida city. The action has him express his villainy toward a young woman named Lane Ballou (Judith Parrish), a stranded carnival cooch dancer. He has ordered her out of town because she has begun a relationship with one of his henchmen, Fielding Carlisle (Lauren Gilbert), whom Semple has been considering for a high political appointment when he himself is elected governor. When she refuses to depart, he gets her fired from various jobs and then has her arrested on charges of solicitation and sent to jail. She is released and becomes employed by a local whorehouse, but he continues to harrass her, even when she is accepted into a decent home by Semple's incorruptible rival (Philip Bourneuf). After the man protecting her is framed by the boss, Lane shoots the latter in the stomach. The local newspaper editor (Will Geer) lies that the shots came from a passing auto.

In the cast were Paul Ford, Bernard Randall, Tom Morrison, Marcella Markham, and others.

FLARE PATH [Comedy-Drama/Aviation/British/Hotel/Marriage/Military/Romance/Theatre/War] A: Terence Rattigan; D: Margaret Webster; S: Raymond Sovey; P: Gilbert Miller; T: Henry Miller's Theatre; 12/23/42 (14)

Director Margaret Webster took time off from Shakespeare to put on this British war play--currently a London hit--that brought Alec Guinness to America for the first time. Guinness was then in the British navy, his post being in Asbury Park, New Jersey, where he was involved in converting a hotel into a British naval barracks. Producer Miller, using the argument that this play had important propaganda value, obtained an eight-week leave for the actor. Every morning, when Guinness left the New York hotel at which he and other British naval personnel were billeted, he had to request permission to go ashore for rehearsal. He had heard that Miller liked actors who set a high value on their talents, although he had never previously earned more than thirty pounds a week. When Miller asked him how much he wanted, he replied, in the most casual tone he could muster, $500 a week. Miller gulped but did not argue and even paid the actor's taxes and union dues.

The play, which mingles laughter and sentiment, is really more about a romantic entanglement of the triangle variety than about the war, which seems simply a dramatic backdrop to the enactment of the characters' love problems. It takes place in a small provincial hotel near a flying field at Milchester, Lincolnshire, where the local RAF flyers and their wives go about their daily lives under the stress of bombing missions. Guinness played Flight Lieutenant Teddy Graham, married to stage star Patricia Graham (Nancy Kelly). She is visited by her former flame, aging movie star Peter Kyle (Arthur Margetson), who still wants her. Surrounding their love tribulations are a cockney gunner (Gerald Savory), a noble Polish aviator (Alexander Ivo), and their spouses (Helena Pickard and Doris Patston, respectively). Much of the tension in the play derives from the anxious waiting of the wives while their husbands are flying missions over Europe. Meanwhile, Peter tries to win Patricia back, and she vacillates until she decides that her duty is to remain with Teddy, a fine pilot but one wracked by fear and in great need of a loving wife's support. The movie star realizes his mistake and relents in his pursuit.

Author Rattigan was at the time a flight lieutenant in the RAF, and his familiarity with the temperaments and language of other RAF fliers in the wartime pressure cooker was a decided plus. A number of warm reviews welcomed the play, but it still could not draw audiences. Howard Barnes (*NYHT*) thought that it took too much time to become fully engrossing, but that when it did, it showed moments of power. George Freedley (*NYMT*) found it "convincing, tender and frequently quite touching." But John Anderson's (*NYJA*) view was that the play seemed more like fiction than real life, and Louis Kronenberger (*PM*) derided it as phony, clichéd, "tedious and tinny."

Of the three leads, said Rosamond Gilder (*TAM*), "Alec Guinness . . . gives the most arresting performance. . . . Though the role, like the play, is slight, he handles it with a delicate sure touch, with that flexibility and fire which is the essence of acting. Throughout the first part of the play he is casual and debonair, yet manages somehow to convey a sense of hidden stress. . . . Mr. Guinness has the ability of all good actors to project thought, to express the implicit as well as the explicit."

Guinness remembered in *Blessings in Disguise* that at the show's dress rehearsal in New Haven, the annoying sounds of what seemed to be a bird were heard in an auditorium ventilator shaft. Summoned to deal with the problem, the obese producer showed up dressed to the teeth in an expensive hunting outfit, including plus fours, with a double-barrelled shotgun under his arm. "Where's this goddamned bird?" he demanded. Told where the noise was coming from, he shoved his shotgun in the ventilator and pulled the trigger. The explosion caused the large chandelier over the auditorium to part from its mooring and come crashing down in splinters. After a silence, Miller declared, "That's the end of that lousy bird." That evening, after the painstaking process of cleaning the auditorium was over, and the curtain rose, "the wild gleeful squawks started all over again." "The only other sound was the mother of the leading lady (Nancy Kelly) remarking loudly on my personal appearance as I came on stage, 'My, he's got big ears.'"

FLEDGLING [Drama/Crime/Family/Illness/Literature/Mental Illness/Religion/Sex] A: Eleanor Carroll Chilton and Philip Lewis; SC: Eleanor Carroll Chilton's novel, *Follow the Furies*; D: Heinrich Schnitzler; S: Richard Whorf; P: Otis Chatfield-Taylor; T: Hudson Theatre; 11/27/40 (13)

A largely unconvincing problem play based on a popular novel by one of the coauthors; it was staged by the son of Viennese playwright Arthur Schnitzler, making his American directorial debut. Dealing with such weighty matters as mercy killing and the problems of religious belief, it tells the tale of a freethinking couple who are active proponents of atheism, although the wife, Grace Linton (Norman Chambers), originally was a Catholic. The husband, Hugh (Ralph Morgan), is a philandering novelist whose books express his ideas, ideas that have been instilled in the minds of their son and daughter. As the action progresses, Grace gradually succumbs to a horrible disease as a form of creeping paralysis slowly threatens her sanity. Secretly, Grace returns to the bosom of the church, which fact is revealed to the startled Hugh by Grace's Jesuit relative (Tom Powers). Daughter Barbara

(Sylvia Weld), unable to bear seeing her mother suffer so and accepting her father's teaching that each person is his or her own God, poisons her mother's prescription medicine with liquid nicotine. Some months later, a guilt-ridden, but still nonbelieving, Barbara appears at a party given by Hugh, learns that her father rejects her actions in following his own teachings, and poisons herself. Her dying words are, "Here's to light in the dark places and to God, if there is one."

The critics appreciated the authors' attempt to grapple with the problem of the nonbeliever's confrontation with the need for faith, but thought the premise marred by faulty playwriting. Richard Lockridge (*NYS*) noted how few of the characters were credible and declared, "The discussions are hackneyed, protracted and the cards are flagrantly stacked. The authors do not approve of euthanasia and they are stern against atheism." However, while he agreed with the general assessment that this was a talky and slow-moving work, John Mason Brown (*NYP*) thought it "a courageous play, adult in its dilemmas and in much of its thinking."

FLIES, THE (***Les Mouches***) [Drama/Crime/Family/French/Period/Religion] A: Jean-Paul Sartre; TR: Stuart Gilbert; D: Paul Ransom; CH: Trudl Dubsky-Zipper; S: Willis Knighton (projections and murals: John McGrew); C: Mathilda Ziegler; P: Dramatic Workshop of the New School for Social Research; T: President Theatre (OB); 4/17/47 (21)

The American premiere of Sartre's philosophical 1943 drama *The Flies* followed by several months that of his *No Exit*, although the former play failed to stir much critical interest and was ignored by many. This may have been owing partly to its production by a semiprofessional group of actors under the supervision of German émigré Erwin Piscator, who had trained them in his acting program. Company members Alfred Linder (as Aegisthus) and Frances Adler (as Clytemnestra) were professionals who taught at the New School. The play--one of a series of antiwar dramas produced by Piscator--was considered of experimental interest only. Piscator "supervised" the production, but someone else was credited with the direction. The Piscatorian method of "supervision," according to Maria Ley-Piscator in *The Piscator Experiment*, meant: "We work collectively, as a group, together, as a unit and as one person."

The Flies is a modern retelling in existentialist terms of the classical Greek myth of Orestes (Dan Matthews) and Electra (Carol Gustafson), told in various ancient plays beginning with *The Oresteia*. Written during the Nazi occupation of France, it managed to castigate collaborationists and to protest against tyranny without drawing down the fury of the Germans. Argos, where the play is set, is meant as a parallel to France under the Nazi occupiers, and Orestes suggests a resistance fighter (Sartre belonged to the French underground and had been a prisoner of the Germans). Electra is reduced to being a scullery maid for her mother, Clytemnestra, and the latter's paramour, Aegisthus, the murderers of Clytemnestra's husband and Electra's father, Agamemnon. The city is plagued by large, stinging flies representing the Furies, which circle about the large, blood-stained statue of Zeus in the square. Electra makes an offering of garbage to the statue and then meets Orestes, to whom she expresses her hatred for the reigning pair, although she does not yet recognize Orestes as her brother. Orestes has returned with his tutor (Nehemiah Persoff) from Corinth, where he has been raised in gentle ways. He soon views Clytemnestra, who revels in her guilty conscience, as do the local citizens. This is vividly revealed on "Dead Men's Day," when the people openly demonstrate their penitent natures in an orgy of guilt. Orestes now reveals himself to Electra. He finds the will to act, rejects submission to Zeus, and agrees to slay the king and queen. The deed throws the previously rebellious Electra into the throes of guilt when she sees the vengeful flies of remorse. Orestes, though, knows that he has done what had to be done and maintains his freedom from guilt, although the dictatorial god Zeus (Jack Burkhart) and the flies would have it otherwise. Zeus is repudiated and made impotent by Orestes' argument. Electra promises Zeus that she will atone, and the flies go from her to her brother. The people of Argos, set free by Orestes' actions, refuse to comprehend the freedom they have been given and drive their new king from the city. With him go the filthy flies, but their sting has been removed.

To establish the atmosphere surrounding the original Paris performances, the play was preceded by films of Hitler and the Nazi army goosestepping down the Champs-Elysées, and the theatre was decorated with reminders of the occupation period. Ley-Piscator remembered how much controversy was stirred up among cast and audience members by these scenes, which many felt were a violation of the play's "classical mold." Sartre heard about the notion and dispatched authoress Simone de Beauvoir to New York to look into it. To determine whether the films were appropriate, Piscator offered a pair of previews, in one of which the films were omitted and in the other of which they were shown. According to Ley-Piscator, without the films, the audience saw a good modern adaptation of a Greek play. With the films, the audience was aware of the powerful political parallels and was deeply moved. The films were used in the final production, and de Beauvoir approved of them, but, contrary to her intimations, most critics found them extraneous.

Some of the acting took place in the aisles, which a few found annoying. Most critics were very respectful, but there were occasional cavils. "The play has rewarding moments, for all its hysterical mannerisms," reported Howard Barnes (*NYHT*). He thought the "heavily academic" staging, however, detrimental to Sartre's work. Much more impressed was Richard Watts, Jr. (*NYP*), who was deeply moved by the writing, which revealed the author "as a dramatist of distinction and importance." He considered *The Flies* "a subtler, more thoughtful and more moving work" than *No Exit*, "and it has the added virtue of possessing several levels of provocative interest." Watts also praised the production highly, as did Robert Garland (*NYJA*), who thought it "amazingly proficient and professional," while expressing confusion about the play itself. Louis Kronenberger (*PM*) applauded Piscator's group for producing "a challenging and often absorbing play" and for doing it well. "*The Flies* . . . is one of the better philosophical dramas, or dialectical dramas, of our time," he observed. In the play was an actor named Bernie Schwartz as Nicias; Schwartz later became film star Tony Curtis.

FLIGHT TO THE WEST [Drama/Aviation/Family/Jews/Journalism/Marriage/Politics/War] A/D: Elmer Rice; S: Jo Mielziner; P: Playwrights' Company; T: Guild Theatre; 12/30/40 (136)

In a season dominated by musicals and comedies, Elmer Rice's attempt to add a tone of somber dramaturgy to Broadway's atmosphere was welcomed, especially as it confronted major issues of the day. The play had two runs, beginning with 72 performances under the Playwrights' Company banner and, after a brief hiatus, ending with 64 under a new management that played it at cut-rate prices. This was an intriguing, literate, but uneven work that nevertheless garnered a healthy share of bravos. The play was one of the ten best of the year.

Rice set his action aboard a transatlantic Clipper flight from Lisbon to New York (Jo Mielziner's illusionistic design of the interior was a major asset). On the flight are various refugees from Nazi oppression, representing a cross-section of significant types. Among them are Colonel Archibald Gage (James Seeley), a Texas oil-man with subconscious fascist tendencies who favors appeasement and praises Hitlerism; Louise Frayne (Constance McKay), an American journalist; Dr. Hermann Walther (Paul Henreid, then spelled Hernreid, in his American debut), a Nazi diplomat; Count Paul Vasilich Vronoff (Boris Marshalov), a suave Nazi spy passing himself off as a professor of Slavonic languages; a puzzled young Jewish liberal, Charles Nathan (Hugh Marlowe), and his pregnant young Gentile wife, Hope Talcott Nathan (Betty Field, who would marry Rice in 1942); Howard Ingraham (Arnold Moss), an older peace crusader and historian whose beliefs the Nathans advocate; Frau Clara Rosenthal (Eleanor Mendelssohn), an art dealer's Jewish wife whose family has scattered to the four winds and who sees nothing but doom for her people; and Marie Dickensen (Lydia St. Clair), a distraught Belgian woman accompanying her blinded American husband, Edmund (Don Nevins), as well as a daughter (Helen Renee) mutilated by a bomb and a baby born by a French roadside. The action is largely occupied by arguments concerning the conflicting views of the passengers, with the Nazi side given almost as fair a hearing as that favoring democracy. A number of dramatic situations arise, including the lady journalist's attempt to isolate the spy, which she succeeds in doing; he is captured and taken prisoner when the plane lands in Bermuda. The Belgian woman also gets dramatically involved when she tries to kill the spy, who is revealed as the officer responsible for the destruction of Louvain in World War I. Charles Nathan sacrifices himself and steps in the way of the bullet (he is wounded but not mortally), precipitating a fascinating debate between the Nazi and the liberal historian.

All the critics noted serious faults, but most were willing to overlook them in their desire to approve the well-meaning drama. Kelcey Allen (*WWD*) did not mind the play's discursiveness because "it is discourse that is intelligent and memorable." Richard Lockridge (*NYS*) was disturbed by the clumsiness of the plotting, which broke the action down into too many small stories and thus dissipated the sense of tension, but averred that this "is a moving, deeply intelligent play." He described its central theme: "That the conflict is one between rational madness and irrational sanity--between the inhuman juggernaut of logic and the feelings and faiths and uncalculated actions which make life human." After a thrilling first act, decided George Freedley (*NYMT*), "the remainder . . . bogs down in a morass of talk and melodrama." John Mason Brown (*NYP*) pointed out that the work was more like a debate than a drama. Louis Kronenberger (*PM*) commented on the lack of "unity of emotion" and on the play's verbosity. "It somehow--and this is why it really fails--tries to achieve the swift force and sure punch of a speech or an editorial while using the long-winded and discursive form of a symposium." The play was acted with memorable distinction, and included in its large cast Karl Malden, Paul Mann, and Kevin McCarthy in secondary roles.

Henreid wrote later in *Ladies Man* that when he was first asked to consider the role of the Nazi diplomat, the character was a brutish and uncouth man. His own experience of such people proved that Rice was wrong and that the man should be elegant and charming. Rice was interested in his ideas and allowed the actor to take the script home and work on the character. When Rice heard the actor's revisions, he liked them enough to rewrite the part accordingly.

FLOWERS OF VIRTUE, THE [Comedy/Crime/Illness/Labor/Literature/Mexico/Military/Politics/Religion/Romance] A/D: Marc Connelly; S: Donald Oenslager; C: Joe Fretwell III; P: Cheryl Crawford; T: Royale Theatre; 2/5/42 (4)

To a small town in Mexico (called in Spanish by the same name as the play's title) comes the wise and prescient American tycoon Grover Bemis (Frank Craven) to recuperate after a physical breakdown caused by stress and overwork following his struggle to warn America of the dangers of Nazism. Here, while living at the home of the humorously obtuse novelist-lecturer Carlotta Garcia (Isobel Elsom), he encounters conflict with the local Hitler, General Orijas (Vladimir Sokoloff), a Nazi agent who is trying to subjugate the local peasantry. Orijas has gained control of the village union and is robbing the workers of their already-small earnings. Trinidad Perez (S. Thomas Gomez), handyman and custodian of the electrical plant, wants to stop him by organizing a strike, but Orijas hopes to assassinate Perez and consolidate his power. When the mechanically capable Bemis cooperates with Perez to repair the local power station, and a statue of the town's patron saint, San Martin, is found outside the plant, the peasants believe that it was a miracle that fixed the station, of which notion they are not disabused. Stirred, the people overthrow the general and democracy is saved. Within this framework are minor subplots, such as one concerning the romantic affairs of Bemis's daughter (Virginia Lederer, formerly Virginia Welles, wife of Orson) with an archaeologist (Jess Barker).

Marc Connelly came nowhere near reaching the levels of skill he had demonstrated in such plays as *The Green Pastures** and *The Farmer's Daughter**. His comedy had plenty of local color, a good number of momentarily eye-catching minor characters, a splendidly sunlit setting, an optimistic theme, several fine performances, a fairly interesting third act, and little else. The characters were too overtly symbolic, the action was not compelling, its development seemed predictable, the dialogue was verbose, the conflicts were too feeble, and the direction was flat. "His comedy is simple, humorous and frequently charming," noted George Freedley

(*NYMT*), "but it fails to advance a single, sound, dramatic idea." In the large cast Leon Belasco and Kathryn Givney had significant roles.

FLYING GERARDOS, THE [Comedy/Circus/Family/Romance] A/D: Kenyon Nicholson and Charles Robinson; S: Horton O'Neill; C: Helene Pons; P: Edward Choate; T: Playhouse; 12/29/40 (24)

Cardboard characters, unimaginative plotting, and an uninspired production conspired to damage the chances of this otherwise promising comedy. It concerns a family of trapeze artists living in Brooklyn on the top floor of a home owned by a veterinarian (Harlan Briggs) who is associated with the circus.

Its story is about Donna (Lois Hall), the youngest member of the "Flying Gerardo" family, who falls in love with a Columbia University graduate-school whiz kid named William (Richard Mackay) and becomes fascinated with the world of books, museums, and lectures to which he introduces her. The well-built, acrobatic Donna and the puny William make an interesting pair, but her interest in matters of the mind threatens to ruin the family act. The flamboyant, redheaded Mama Gerardo (Florence Reed) tries to break up the affair, with the result that William--despite the ridicule of the others, including Donna--begins to build up his body in hopes of joining the troupe and being worthy of Donna's love. It all ends with William opting instead for the life of a clown, thereby becoming another member of the Gerardo clan.

George Freedley (*NYMT*) had only mild reservations and deemed the play "an amusing evening in the theatre," but more typical was the response of John Mason Brown (*NYP*), who admired the authors' esteem for their characters, but noted that "the comedy they have written is an inadequate expression of the respect they feel for them. . . . Such a play as does emerge is a silly, inept, and far-fetched little killjoy."

The play earned a footnote in New York theatre history by being the first Broadway play to open on a Sunday night. The playhouse it debuted in was owned by producer William A. Brady, long a campaigner for "Sunday legit," as it was called. Lyle Bettger was a cast member.

FOLLOW THE GIRLS [Musical/Military/Romance/Show Business/War] B: Guy Bolton, Eddie Davis, and Fred Thompson; M: Phil Charig; LY: Dan Shapiro and Milton Pascal; D: Harry Delmar; CH: Catherine Littlefield; S/L: Howard Bay; C: Lou Eisele; P: Dave Wolper i/a/w Albert Borde; T: New Century Theatre; 4/8/44 (882)

One of the great World War II hits, *Follow the Girls* could be better classed as burlesque than as legitimate musical comedy, although it did contain a libretto of sorts. The latter, basically a frame for specialty acts, concerned a burlesque stripper named Bubbles La Marr (Gertrude Niesen) who decides to contribute her talents to the war effort by putting her career on hold and entertaining the servicemen at the USO's Spotlight Canteen (based on the Stage Door Canteen). Her fat boyfriend, Goofy Gale (Jackie Gleason), classified as 4-F, is thus unable to see her because he has no military credentials. He steals a British sailor's uniform to gain entrance, but learns that Bubbles is now the object of a naval officer's (Lee Davis) affections. Goofy goes so far as to kidnap the officer and to try to make him feel seasick, only to succumb to his own suggestions himself. There is also a love complication involving canteen ballet dancer Anna Viskinova (Irina Baronova), who is suspected of espionage. The true German spy turns out to be a brunette named Phyllis Brent (Toni Gilman). As these characters work out their problems, the show keeps introducing songs, dances, sketches, and other acts. At one point Goofy fits his huge frame into a WAVE's uniform to gain access to his love, and an elderly officer makes a date with him. The story kept being forgotten in the welter of entertaining material constantly introduced.

A nightly highlight was sultry torch singer Niesen's singing of "I Wanna Get Married," a naughty number satirizing brides of varying types and temperaments, from the virginal to the alcoholic fifth-timer. It was accompanied by a parade of gorgeous chorines dressed as bridesmaids (almost all the showgirls in the show were blond). One encore after the other was sung, each more risqué than the one before it. Niesen, who surprised the critics by displaying a decided comic gift in addition to her well-known singing abilities, remained with the production throughout the long run, despite the defection of most of her supporting players.

Niesen's outstanding playing as the rough-edged burlesque queen (who did not, however, do a strip routine in the show) was balanced by the brilliant comic talent of Jackie Gleason, for whom stardom was predicted. Burton Rascoe (*NYWT*) wrote that Gleason was "a good-natured and likable pantaloon with some of that engagingly honest naivete which made Sonny Tufts such a pleasant addition to the ranks of movie players. Gleason does his stuff in an off-hand, apparently effortless manner, with none of that frantic, scenery-biting horseplay which some comedians indulge in." Much of Gleason's humor was ad-libbed, which made his costar so nervous that she wanted him fired after opening night. Niesen (quoted in James Bacon's *How Sweet It Is*) remarked, "When someone strays from the script, it's irritating to the other performers, but he got raves from the critics. When I read those, I learned to live with the ad-libs."

Famous ballerina Irina Baronova (of the Ballets Russe) also scored highly. In further supporting roles were tenor Frank Parker, comic dancers Buster West and Tim Herbert, ballroom dancers Jayne and Adam DiGatano, dancer Val Valentinoff, and dancer Dorothy Keller.

With a fast-paced and well-varied sequence of routines, a chorus of pretty girls doing nicely staged dance sequences, and colorful sets and costumes, the show took many people's minds off their troubles and ran for well over two years. It was especially popular with GIs on leave. Howard Barnes (*NYHT*) labeled it "a rowdy and engaging musical show." Wilella Waldorf (*NYP*) considered it "not only beautiful to look at. It is almost always pleasant to listen to. Above all, it never takes itself too seriously. There is a light-hearted, tongue-in-cheek, attractively goofy quality about the whole show." Rascoe described it as "a glorified and expanded night club floor show rather than a musical comedy and as such it is very good indeed--nothing to rave about, but fast-paced, clean, ingratiating, iridescent and entertaining." But Louis Kronenberger (*PM*) gagged on the book: "The book is cursed . . . by its general flatness and moldy humor. The first act is simply a compendium of fourth-rate gags."

The New Century was the former Jolson Theatre; it was thoroughly renovated for the opening, although the show eventually left it for the Forty-fourth Street Theatre to finish out its run.

FOOD FOR MIDAS [Drama/Business/Trial] A: Frederick Ford; D: Alfred Allegro; P: Players Repertory Theatre; T: Master Institute Theatre (Roerich Theatre) (OB); 1/30/42

A barely noticed semipro offering at the small theatre on Riverside Drive and 103rd Street. Its author was an unidentified banking expert writing under a nom de plume. He used the stage to communicate his notion that a bankers' combine was in control of the National Reserve Banks and thus was responsible for the world's economic dilemmas. This was expressed in a plot about a young man (Alfred Allegro, the director) who seeks to operate his factory on a profit-sharing plan with his workers, but who is ruined when the banks that have extended heavy loans to him recall the loans. He faces the bankers in court to defend his ideas, but the court cannot judge the merits of the case.

The writing was highly episodic and was tied together by a "Voice" that commented on the political ramifications of the action. B. B. (*NYT*) observed that the many scenes failed "to fit into any unified plot development," and that Allegro's direction was confusing and his use of recorded music too loud.

FOOLISH NOTION [Comedy-Drama/Fantasy/Marriage/Military/Romance/Theatre/War/Youth] A: Philip Barry; D: John C. Wilson; S/L: Jo Mielziner; C: (gowns) Mainbocher; P: Theatre Guild; T: Martin Beck Theatre; 3/13/45 (104)

The title of this comic blend of realism and fantasy was drawn from a poem by Robert Burns, "To a Louse--On Seeing One upon a Lady's Bonnet in Church." One of the few things most of those who saw it agreed upon was the amusement provided by Tallulah Bankhead acting at the top of her form; the play itself came in for a widely divergent assortment of opinions, most of them on the unfriendly side. It did, nevertheless, make the Burns Mantle collection of the season's ten best plays.

Jim Hapgood (Henry Hull) has been reported missing in action in the European conflict, he having joined a Scottish regiment in 1939. His wife, a famous actress named Sophie Wing (Bankhead), meanwhile has fallen in love with and is on the verge of marrying her costar, Gordon Roark (Donald Cook). After five years have passed, Jim is declared legally dead. Sophie has gotten over him, but still mourning for Jim and praying for his return are her eleven-year-old adopted daughter Happy (Joan Shepard), who does not like Gordon; Florence Denny (Barbara Kent), a young woman who loves Jim and has been caring for Happy; and Sophie's father (Aubrey Mather), a hammy retired professor of dramatic literature. News arrives via a cryptic phone call that Jim is alive and in New York. Thereupon, Gordon, the stepdaughter, the father, and Sophie imagine what Jim will look like and how the reunion will be handled. Each sees it in a different dramatic vein, so the scenes vary from wisecrack comedy to satire to melodrama to high comedy. Jim appears to Gordon in civilian garb, to the professor as a Scottish Highlander, to the daughter as an idealized marine, and to the self-dramatizing Sophie as ashes in an urn. But the actual scene of the return is like none of these, and Jim reveals that Sophie is free to wed her costar, for he himself has yearned all along for Florence.

The Enoch Arden-themed play was taken to task for being too talky and for a final scene that seemed contrived and less interesting than those that had preceded it (George Freedley [*NYMT*]); for being "brittle, adolescent and pretentious" (Howard Barnes [*NYHT*]); for being "more of a notion than a play" (Ward Morehouse [*NYS*]); for being "neither good comedy, good humor, nor good outstanding melodrama" (Robert Garland [*NYJA*]); and for using a device that, after "five repetitions of the same event, . . . proves tiresome in execution" (Rosamond Gilder [*TAM*]). Apart from Bankhead's presence, the chief ingredient approved by some critics was Barry's literate dialogue.

Of Bankhead, Barnes acknowledged, "Never has she been more assured, versatile and properly exhibitionistic." A few others were less kind. While the play was in its tryout phase, the temperamental actress's diatribes against author Philip Barry were reported to have caused him such angst that he burst a blood vessel and had to be hospitalized. Bankhead was supported by a cast including Mildred Dunnock and Maria Manton, the daughter of film star Marlene Dietrich, making her Broadway debut. She later changed her name to Maria Riva.

Jo Mielziner's set used a much-commented-on trick device by which a portrait of Jim was supposed to be hanging in the open proscenium space occupied by the missing fourth wall. Through special lighting and the use of a scrim, the picture, whenever it was supposed to be seen, could be viewed by the audience in a huge upstage mirror as if it were reflected there. This was Mielziner's first set since returning from active service in the armed forces.

FOR HEAVEN'S SAKE, MOTHER! [Comedy/Family/Jews/Marriage/Sex/Theatre] A/D: Julie Berns; S/L: Leo Kerz; P: David Kay; T: Belasco Theatre; 11/16/48 (7)

Ward Morehouse (*NYS*) began his notice by saying, "A weird little knicknack . . . which has, in some unaccountable fashion, achieved a Broadway production, pounded and clattered about the stage of the Belasco last night. It's awful." Rowland Field (*NEN*) considered it "a completely lost cause."

The meandering story deals with a still-glamorous and youthful-looking middle-aged stage star and Larchmont resident named Lucinda Lawrence (Nancy Carroll), mother of two grown sons (Alfred Garr and Robert White), who vainly wants to return to the theatre when an excellent new role comes along. Her wishes are sidetracked, however, when she becomes pregnant (much is made of her possibly having had an affair with a neighbor [Stiano Braggiotti]). Her comeback wishes are deferred in favor of her becoming not only a mother, but a grandmother of twins. This is perfectly suitable to Lucinda's stage-star spouse Edward (Herschel

Bentley).

Nancy Carroll's costar was the Yiddish theatre favorite, Molly Picon, playing the star's wardrobe mistress, Mrs. Rubin of the Lower East Side, whose son (Richy Shawn) is in the army with Lucinda's son, and who becomes involved in the Lawrence family's complications. Picon delighted everyone with a Jewish ballad sung in Yiddish and English, a dance, a somersault, and a comedic overseas phone call and stole what little there was to steal of the show. The significance of her role in the plot, however, was a mystery. The play was dismally written and even more poorly staged (author and director were the same person). The cast members included St. Clair Bayfield, Jacqueline Andre, and Margaret Draper, among others.

In *Molly!*, Picon revealed that the production started rehearsals with Harry Wagstaff Gribble as director, but that he and Nancy Carroll engaged in frequent and heated battles, with Carroll acting the high-handed and temperamental star and failing to learn her lines. Carroll behaved unprofessionally toward the rest of the company and also insisted on having her costumes custom-made; despite the play's being a comedy, she demanded that they be black. The disputes between Gribble and Carroll grew so bad that the director would frequently resolve his problems in drink, while the playwright would assume command, aided by Picon. Even the placid Picon blew up at her costar. After the Philadelphia opening, when the play was brutalized by the press, it almost closed. Gribble was released and the playwright took over (although Picon said that someone else--unnamed--was brought in). As the show was doing surprisingly good business, it went to Broadway, where it closed in a week. Reported Picon, "That had to be the most amateurish venture I've ever been in, and I vowed it would be a lesson to me forever after."

FOR KEEPS [Comedy/Family/Romance/Sex/Youth] A: F. Hugh Herbert; D/P: Gilbert Miller; S: Raymond Sovey; C: Kathryn Miller; T: Henry Miller's Theatre; 6/14/44 (29)

F. Hugh Herbert, author of the hit comedy *Kiss and Tell*, followed up that play's treatment of an adolescent character with yet another such approach, although of an entirely different girl and with entirely different critical and box-office results. The fundamentally serious subject was the psychological adjustments made by the neglected children of often-married parents.

Nancy Vanda (Patricia Kirkland, daughter of playwright Jack Kirkland and actress Nancy Carroll), is a fifteen-year-old who is too sophisticated for her own good. Brought up by her mother Norma (Joan Wetmore), she pays a visit to her four-times-wed father Paul (Frank Conroy), a self-centered commercial photographer, who is beginning his most recent honeymoon. Her smoking, drinking, and other obviously knowing ways lead the older (but still young) man Jimmy McCarey (Donald Murphy), her father's model, to woo her, thinking her at least nineteen. When he finds out, he backs off, although he agrees to wait for her to grow up. Dad, seeing what life with mom hath wrought, decides to take custody of the girl himself with his youthful present wife (Julie Warren), who has struck up a friendship with her husband's daughter.

The piece had stenciled situations and characters, and its development was easy to surmise. Arthur Pollock (*BE*) averred that Herbert "does not discover enough in his study of this unsettled young girl to give his play sufficient meat or marrow." Also, noted Lewis Nichols (*NYT*), "The first half . . . suffers from a talkativeness that makes it crawl at a snail's pace; and some of the last half, which could be touching, is unhappily sentimental." In the supporting cast were Grover Burgess, George Baxter, Zolya Talma, and Joseph R. Garry.

FOR LOVE OR MONEY [Comedy/Romance/Sex/Theatre] A: F. Hugh Herbert; D: Harry Ellerbe; S/L: Raymond Sovey; C: Anna Hill Johnstone; P: Barnard Straus; T: Henry Miller's Theatre; 11/4/47 (263)

This comedy provided an excellent Broadway debut vehicle for energetic, young, blond movie actress June Lockhart, daughter of character actors Gene and Kathleen Lockhart. Her vital presence was largely responsible for energizing the proceedings.

Another May-December love story, it tells of middle-aged, Broadway matinee idol Preston Mitchell (John Loder), who resides at Port Washington, Long Island. His invalid wife has just passed away and been buried. A thunderstorm is raging when drenched young dental assistant Janet Blake (Lockhart) bursts in, looking for a phone. She is escaping from a party at which everyone had too much to drink and her date tried to get fresh. Preston takes her in and makes her his secretary and good pal. The growing friendship raises eyebrows among the girl's prospective suitor (Mark O'Daniels), parents (Paula Trueman and Kirk Brown), and housekeepers (Grover Burgess and Maida Reade), as well as the leading lady, Nita Havemeyer (Vicki Cummings), who craves the actor for herself. Janet rescues Preston from Nita's clutches, and she and he realize that they are made for each other.

"It is synthetic, shallow and implausible, with single-dimensional characters, contrived situations and only intermittently amusing passages," grumbled Hobe. (*V*). Brooks Atkinson (*NYT*) believed, "No one would contrive quite so mirthless a basic situation and work at it quite so confidently without having apprenticed himself to a hokum factory."

Euphemia Van Rensselaer Wyatt (*CW*) reprimanded those responsible for the play's vulgar language, but found Lockhart "naturally and exuberantly young and delightful." "She is enchanting," wrote Atkinson, "and, except for a mechanical laugh, she acts with style."

FOR YOUR PLEASURE [Revue] CN/P: George M. Gatts; D: Frank Veloz; T: Mansfield Theatre; 2/5/43 (11)

A variety show (originally called *Dansation*) featuring a baker's dozen of ballroom dance routines, mostly with a Spanish flavor, by Veloz and Yolanda, as well as specialties by singer Susan Miller (whose repertoire included "Summertime" and "Brazil"), guitarist Vincente Gomez (strumming Spanish gypsy folk tunes), ballet tap dancer Billy Gary, accordianist Jerry Shelton, piano duets by Al and Lee Reiser (playing straight and boogie-woogie), and black spiritual chorus the Golden Gate Quartette (one of whose numbers, "Stalin Wasn't Stallin'," was an original tune celebrating Hitler's withdrawal from Russia).

Although the individual acts were praised, many thought that the show lacked comedy and pacing variety and did not belong on Broadway, but was better suited to a nightclub. Howard Barnes (*NYHT*) dismissed the effort as "remarkably tiresome. As a regular Broadway stage attraction, it made one long for noise, smoke and waiters knocking over glasses." Scho. (*V*) added, "Whole show is slow-moving, badly paced, badly lighted and poorly equipped with some ill-colored drops, a traveler and black cyc."

FORWARD THE HEART [Drama/Blacks/Family/Invalidism/Race/Romance/War] A: Bernard Reines; D: Peter Frye; S: Perry Watkins; P: Theatre Enterprises, Inc., and Leon J. Bronesky; T: Forty-eighth Street Theatre; 1/28/49 (19)

A well-meaning, four-character play of social significance, but of mediocre dramatic merit. William Prince played David Gibbs, a depressed young veteran who lost his sight in combat, and who returns to his Boston home after five years in a hospital. Deprived of the ability to tell people apart by race, he falls for his Boston mother's young black maid, Julie Evans (Mildred Joanne Smith), whose sympathetic attitude moves him deeply. He only learns of her race later and is so shocked that Julie is hurt by his response. He overcomes his initial reaction, however, and seeks to marry her. His mother, Mrs. Marian Gibbs (Natalie Schafer), is hysterically set against David's proposed nuptials with Julie, but neither this nor the sympathetic advice of his uncle George Whiting (Harry Bannister) can dissuade him. Ultimately, Julie herself refuses to marry David because she is aware of the pain that their relationship will cause them in an intolerant world. She suggests that perhaps in another twenty-five or fifty years, things may change.

The play's honesty and sincerity were praised, as was its great poignancy, but Brooks Atkinson (*NYT*) found the dramatic development cramped by the restriction to four characters and the excessive reliance on David and Julie to carry the plot. The limitation of the latter part of the play--once the suspense was lifted as to the revelation of Julie's blackness--to the simple question of whether or not they would marry also irked the critic. George Jean Nathan (*TBY*) argued that a blind hero is too painful for an audience to contemplate, that the treatment here was hackneyed, and that the play suffered from "writing repetitive and dramatically supine." Smith and Prince, especially the former, gave superlative performances in the play's only fully developed roles.

FOUR FLIGHTS UP [Drama/Crime/Mystery] A/D/P: Ken Parker; T: Provincetown Playhouse (OB); 1/7/48

This play was written when ice-skating star Ken Parker was sidelined from *Icetime of 1948* at the Center Theatre and took up writing to pass the time in the new fourth-floor apartment he had taken. He had learned from the landlady that a previous resident had committed a murder in the place, chopping up a male friend and then dumping the pieces in the river. The gruesome story inspired the novice dramatist to set it down as a play. The story was moved to Boston, and Parker him self was made a chief character under the name of Kim Taylor (Jerry Ellis).

After Kim and his pregnant wife Drucilla (Mary V. Malone) take a shabby apartment, her curiosity leads her to uncover the fact that dastardly doings have been done there. There is much ado about a killer who keeps the head of his slain companion in a handbag, and Drucilla--much like Mrs. North, the spirited heroine of Richard Lockridge's detective stories--gets into hot water before the mystery is solved. Robert Coleman (*NYDM*) called the results "an anemic little chiller-diller, played by talented though inexperienced young people, who have not been adequately drilled."

FOUR ONE-ACT COMEDIES [Dramatic Revivals/One-Acts] A: Anton Chekhov; S/L: Herbert Brodkin; C: Emeline Roche; P: New York City Center Theatre Company; T: City Center of Music and Drama; 2/5/48 (14)
"A Tragedian in Spite of Himself" ("Tragik Ponevole") D: José Ferrer; "The Bear" ("Medved") D: Richard Barr; "On the Harmfulness of Tobacco" ("O Vrede Tabaka") D: José Ferrer; "The Wedding" ("Svadba") D: José Ferrer

A program of four Chekhov one-acts (or "vaudevilles") given by José Ferrer's new company at the City Center. None appear to have been given professional performances in New York before. No translator was credited.

"A Tragedian in Spite of Himself," based on a Chekhov short story, was written in 1889. It is about Ivan Ivanovitch Topkachov (Richard Whorf), a civil servant burdened with packages, who is harried by his wife and neighbors to run errands for them when he commutes to the city every day from the country, and who then has to deal with more problems on returning home. He tells his troubles to a friend, Alex Alexeyevitch Murshkin (Robert Carroll), from whom he seeks a pistol with which to end his life. The latter, however, asks him to do him a favor in the country, which causes Ivan Ivanovitch to blow his top.

"The Bear," an 1888 piece, tells of a bullying, middle-aged creditor, Grigory Stephanovitch Smirov (Ferrer), who seeks money from Elena Ivanova Popova (Frances Reid), a young widow making more of her mourning period than she feels. Their confrontation leads to a challenge to resort to pistols. The man has fallen in love with the widow by now and asks for her hand; their embrace surprises the servant, Luka (Francis Letton), who arrives to kick him out.

"On the Harmfulness of Tobacco," a monologue first staged in 1887, takes place in a lecture hall and depicts the hen-pecked lecturer, Ivan Ivanovitch Nyukhin (Ferrer), husband of a boarding-school proprietress, delivering a talk suggested by the title but unable to resist chatting about his thirty-three years of marital difficulties and his desire to get away from it all.

"The Wedding," produced in 1889 and based on a short story, is set in a restaurant and presents the confusions and complications surrounding a wedding party as the vulgar guests and family members get into various farcical difficulties with one another. A major comic feature is the ancient, retired minor naval officer (Whorf) hired by the bride's snobbish mother (Paula Laurence)--who thought him a general--to give the reception a touch of class. He proceeds to deliver a boring nautical lecture that so enrages everyone--especially when they learn his true rank--that he gets tossed out. Its large cast featured John Carradine, Letton, Grace Coppin, Leonardo Cimino, Phyllis Hill, Victor Thorley, and Will Kuluva, the latter scoring as a Greek confectioner who attempts to deliver an important-sounding toast.

The general opinion held that this was a mildly diverting, but not very exciting evening of theatre, with various good performances and a number of weak ones. Brooks Atkinson (*NYT*) agreed with Chekhov's own condescending attitude toward these playlets, declaring them thin but amusing pieces revelatory of strains that would appear in the writer's later masterpieces. "On the whole they are not much more than apprentice work--formless, repetitious and verbose." He also did not much care for the broad and unpolished performances. Yet Howard Barnes (*NYHT*) approved the program: "They vary in mood, in form and in quality, but together they make for a rich and satisfying entertainment. . . . The venture is filled with true theatrical excitement." In between was Richard Watts, Jr. (*NYP*), who considered the plays "merely agreeable and rather impish little vaudevilles. . . . They seem gay improvizations [*sic*], tossed off in an antic moment, rather than carefully planned dramatic efforts."

4 SAINTS IN 3 ACTS [Musical Revival*] B: Gertrude Stein; M: Virgil Thomson; P: Louise Crane; T: Town Hall (OB); 5/27/41

An oratorio presentation of the avant-garde 1934 "opera" that had run for eight weeks on Broadway. It was shown now at a concert hall in the Broadway district and employed most of the original cast of black performers as well as the original conductor, Alexander Smallens.

Olin Downes (*NYT*), the music critic, said that "it was brilliantly successful," despite the sceneryless production. Visual appeal was provided by an onstage orchestra of twenty and by dressing the chorus in beige and tan robes, with Saint Therese I and II (Beatrice Robinson-Wayne and Bruce Howard) garbed in Spanish costumes, and with the Commere (Altonell Hines) and Compere (Abner Dorsey) wearing contemporary evening clothes. Downes noted that while he did not think the piece represented the direction modern opera would take, he found himself admiring it immensely on its own terms, despite its seemingly illogical text and unusual music. Thomson, he said, had taken Stein's nonsense prose and woven it into effective melodic patterns "with a felicity, a simplicity of harmonic vocabulary, a variety of rhythms, and a profound knowledge of prosody which are astonishing." O. G. (*NYP*), however, observed that the work "was the product and the expression of a quaintly sophisticated and exciting period that is no longer with us, and its precious, delicately handled absurdities now seem only pleasantly naive."

FOUR SHORT PLAYS [One-Acts] A: Helen Gholson Kittredge; P: Eugene Endrey; T: Provincetown Playhouse (OB); 12/3/40

"Time to Burn" [Drama/Prison] and "Reaper" [Drama/Death/Military/War] D: Eugene Endrey; "Man-Hunt" [Crime/Rural] and "Doing Nicely" [Comedy/Illness] D: Helen Gholson Kittredge

A dire evening of four one-acts, from which several critics rushed before they all were shown. "Time to Burn," as its title suggests, was about a young convict who, despite his efforts to convince the governor otherwise, is about to be executed in the electric chair for the crime of killing his brother. In "Reaper," set in a ravaged hut in Poland, a peasant girl talks a German storm trooper into killing her child because the father is a German. "Man-Hunt" followed the travails of a poetic criminal being hunted in the ranch country and contained an ample supply of gunshots. "Doing Nicely" was a farce set in a hospital and was the only piece that did not bring the Grand Guignol to mind. "It does seem as though Mr. Endrey could have done everybody a service with an ordinary ten-cent blue pencil," said Robert Sylvester (*NYDM*).

FOXHOLE IN THE PARLOR [Drama/Art/Friendship/Mental Illness/Music/Politics/Romance/Sex/War] A: Elsa Shelley; D: John Haggott; S: Lee Simonson; P:

Harry Bloomfield; T: Booth Theatre; 5/23/45 (45)

Montgomery Clift scored a personal triumph in this well-intentioned but preachy antiwar message play aimed at fostering world unity in accord with the ideals of the San Francisco Peace Conference. Unfortunately, the dramatist's message seemed muddled and uncertain, just as her title suggested a farce when it actually labeled a serious drama. It was the twelfth Broadway play of the season to be concerned with the plight of a returned serviceman.

Clift played pianist Dennis Patterson, whose war experiences have made him neurotically unstable. Although the doctors who have released him from an army hospital have pronounced him cured, he still suffers occasional mental setbacks. He lives in Greenwich Village, where his friends in the apartment across the courtyard, artist Tom (Russell Hardie) and Ann Austen (Flora Campbell), take a sincere interest in his condition and listen to the tales of the horror he experienced. Dennis talks of his soldier friend Henry (he even calls Tom by this name), a Jew who taught him the meaning of Passover before Henry and two other GI buddies were killed at his side in a foxhole. Dennis attempts to tell Ann's senator father (Raymond Greenleaf), on his way to the San Francisco conference, about the message of peace he should carry. Though vaguely expressed, these ideas convince the politician to bring Dennis along as part of his staff so that he may deliver his message himself. This deflects Dennis's harsh sister Kate (Grace Coppin), who, failing in her endeavors to get Dennis to come home with her to Oregon, tries unsuccessfully to have Dennis committed to an asylum.

Shelley's "languid and repetitious" (Lewis Nichols [*NYT*]) saga was unable to catch fire. "It seemed a rather artificially excitable essay that strives, with little actual skill, to discuss" the issues it confronts, thought Rowland Field (*NEN*). George Jean Nathan (*TBY*) rejected it as "a substantial mixture of feminine sentimentality and shallow thinking."

Clift was searingly convincing, but his role of the neurotic war victim was too similar to that he played in *The Searching Wind*, which put him in danger of being typecast. Herrick Brown (*NYS*) thought his performance "one of the best . . . at present to be found in town. He keeps an excellent rein on the role throughout and at the same time reveals vividly the lad's agony of spirit." The other cast members consisted of Reginald Beane, as a black servant of the Austens, and Anne Lincoln as a curvy model who falls for Dennis and offers herself to him. Lee Simonson's novel set pictured two apartments on either side of a courtyard; as the action shifted from one flat to the other, the set moved on tracks to put the one being used at center stage.

FRENCH TOUCH, THE [Comedy/France/Marriage/Politics/Theatre] A: Joseph Fields and Jerome Chodorov; D: René Clair; S/L: George Jenkins; P: Herbert H. Harris; T: Cort Theatre; 12/8/45 (33)

After several successes, the writing team responsible for this flop stumbled. "Instead of being easy," declared Lewis Nichols (*NYT*), "this one is forced; instead of being written in the warmth of an amiable spirit, it suggests two authors trimming a play with a cold chisel."

The too-complex plot centers on an egotistical French actor-manager-playwright of the Sacha Guitry type named Roublard (Brian Aherne). He lives with his third wife Giselle (Jacqueline Dalya) in his Paris theatre, darkened because of his refusal to cooperate with the occupying Germans. The Nazis persuade him to write a play that will demonstrate the happy relationship between France and Germany, but he conceives a play that will have two endings, one to satisfy the Germans, but another that will be revealed only on opening night when he will cry out patriotically, "Liberty, equality, fraternity" at the conclusion. Mingled with this main tale is material concerning Roublard's private affairs with his temperamental present and former spouses (Arlene Francis and Madeleine Le Beau), all three of whom the Nazis want to costar with Roublard for the effect the publicity will arouse.

The play was disliked, among other things, because of its lack of interesting characterizations, its theatrical in-jokes, its lack of focus in its split concern with the Nazi angle and Roublard's marital life, Aherne's unconvincing acting, and--despite the presence of leading French film director René Clair at the helm--a lack of believable French atmosphere. "It is no better than a theatrical zombie," regretted Howard Barnes (*NYHT*).

The best performance was that of John Wengraf as the Nazi minister of culture. Among others involved were John Regan, Ralph Simone, and Louise Kelley.

FROM MORN TO MIDNIGHT (***Von Morgens bis Mitternacht***) [Dramatic Revival*] A: Georg Kaiser; TR: Ashley Dukes; AD/D: John Buckwalter; M: Furlow Brown; CH: Sudie Bond; DS: Clay Watson; P: Edwin Child for Equity Library Theatre; T: Jewish Guild for the Blind (OB); 12/6/48

Only Brooks Atkinson (*NYT*) covered this Equity Library showcase presentation at 1880 Broadway, "supervised" by director Alan Schneider. The German expressionist play had last been seen locally in a Yiddish production in 1931. Of the many cast members in the present version, only Sudie Bond, who did the choreography as well as acting the role of the cashier's (John Glendenning) wife, became an important stage actress. Atkinson thought the piece dated, but well directed, designed, and acted, although his reservations pointed to the actors' need "to learn the difference between volume and shouting."

FRONT PAGE, THE [Dramatic Revival*] A: Ben Hecht and Charles MacArthur; D: Charles MacArthur; S: Nat Karson; C: Irene Aronson; P: Hunt Stromberg, Jr., and Thomas Spengler; T: Royale Theatre; 9/4/46 (79)

This revival of the 1928 hit farce-melodrama about hard-boiled Chicago newspapermen was unable to erase the memory of the brilliant original production and split the critics on its virtues. Hildy Johnson was played by Lew Parker, Walter Burns by Arnold Moss, Mollie Molloy by Olive Deering, Peggy Grant by Pat McClarney, Murphy by Bruce MacFarlane, McCue by Benny Baker, Schwartz by Ray Walston, Kruger by Pat Harrington, Bensinger by Rolly Beck, "Woodenshoes" Eichorn by Curtis Karpe, Diamond Louie by Joseph De Santis, Sheriff Hartman by William Lynn, Jennie by Blanche Lytell, Mrs. Grant by Cora Witherspoon, the mayor by Edward H. Robins, and Earl Williams by George Lyons.

The production respected the work's original period, and barely any changes were made to update the writing. It was appreciated for its universality, despite its atmosphere redolent of the roaring twenties. Vernon Rice (*NYP*), one of those who approved strongly, said that it was played "with rowdy reverence and jet-propelled speed." Brooks Atkinson (*NYT*) claimed that the play was still "exciting, impudent and funny." John Mason Brown (*SR*) insisted that the play "remains a far, far better play than most," but had serious reservations about the presentation. He called it "a dreary, inept affair; miscast, slouchily acted; and lacking, above all, in the fire and precision needed to do the script justice." George Jean Nathan (*NYJA*), also disliked the production; however, he argued that the play itself was a bit dated: "Though it is still far from unfunny, the play now misses much of the satirical drive that it had then." The weakest link for many was the performance of the usually excellent Arnold Moss, who seemed out of place in the role of Walter Burns. Several critics noted that the play's once-notorious profanity now sounded tame, but Euphemia Van Rensselaer Wyatt (*CW*) thought it "more annoyingly offensive" than before.

"FUMED OAK" and **"THE SHADOW OF THE GLEN"** [Dramatic Revivals*] S: Rob Price; P: Library Theatre Project; T: Hudson Park Branch of the New York Public Library (OB); 2/20/44
"Fumed Oak" A: Noël Coward; D: George Anderson; "The Shadow of the Glen" A: John Millington Synge; D: Robert Bell

Actors in the 1940s were constantly seeking venues that would allow them to perform gratis when they were not gainfully employed in the commercial theatre, but their efforts were rarely condoned by the actors' union, Equity. One plan to which Equity gave its grudging approval was the Experimental Theatre, which folded after several years. Stemming from that idea was another, much more long-lasting, and originally called the Library Theatre Project. This evolved into the their own relatively permanent theatre, but at first they were offered at various branches of the New York Public Library possessed of auditoriums. The first production under the plan was this double bill of one-acts by Coward and Synge, given at a library at 10 Seventh Avenue South.

The Synge piece had been seen locally in 1932 and 1934, when it had been given by the Abbey Theatre Players of Dublin. It now featured Harry Shepherd as Dan Burke, the jealous husband, Marguerite Morrissey as his wife, and Lester Fletcher as the lover. The direction, said George Freedley (*NYMT*), "was no more than routine."

In Coward's comedy, shown on Broadway in 1936 with Gertrude Lawrence and Coward as one of the pieces in *Tonight at Eight-Thirty*, the husband and wife were taken by Keith Barton and Louise Horton, while Lorraine Pressler played the bratty child and Rita Burwell acted the mother-in-law. In summing up, Freedley reported, "These two one-acts were reasonably well performed but if these actors want to progress they must strive for a higher excellence than this initial performance displayed."

FUNZAPOPPIN' [Revue] CN/M/LY: Ole Olsen, Chic Johnson, and Chuck Gould, Perry Martin; D/CH: Catherine and Carl Littlefield; S: Becker Brothers; P: Arthur M. Wirtz; T: Madison Square Garden; 6/30/49 (31)

Olsen and Johnson, zany madcaps who had been responsible for the sensational comedy revue *Hellzapoppin'* (1938), returned to New York with this large-scale show performed, not in a legitimate Broadway playhouse, but in the big sports arena, Madison Square Garden. Their brand of humor--much of it of the bathroom variety--involved considerable audience participation, and most of their wheezes were tried and true, not new. They mingled every crazy sort of laugh-provoking stunt in a kaleidoscope of high-energy comic madness. A large stage was set up at the west end of the arena, and the action went on practically everywhere, including the seating areas.

All sorts of munitions were fired left and right. A cannon was shot into the air, and a blizzard of feathers descended over all the spectators. A picture of a battleship was fired upon, only for the battleship to return fire and sink. Olsen, struggling to get out of handcuffs in five minutes, finally shot one arm off to free himself. When someone mentioned that cows do not fly, a bovine creature came plummeting to earth. Olsen and Johnson were barbers giving shaves in a railroad station that shook violently whenever a train rolled by. Comic Marty May did takeoffs on popular radio singers. There were numerous midgets scampering about as well as a vast array of chorus girls. A "gorilla" dashed madly about the auditorium, leaping over spectators as he proceeded from row to row. Every now and then a little man in a broad black hat and cloak ran across the stage, for no visible reason. Ladies in the audience had their hats snatched by clowns, chorines pulled men out of their seats to dance with them on stage, and so on.

"There is an incredible variety of detail, though the mood is always the same, and, though no particular talent is visible at any time, a terrific energy and goodwill are expended and immeasurable bedlam achieved," wrote Arthur Pollock (*DC*). Brooks Atkinson (*NYT*), who thought little of Olsen and Johnson's comic talents, called the show "a gargantuan honky-tonk presided over by two good-natured tent-show spielers who believe more in quantity than quality. The singing and chorus interludes are tasteless and untalented, and the unit set looks like a gigantic, neon-lighted funeral urn." Assisting Olsen and Johnson were Gloria Gilbert, the Clark Brothers, Gloria Short, William Hayes, the Choraleers, June Johnson (Chic Johnson's daughter), and J. C. Olesen (Ole Olsen's son).

G

G-II [Drama/Death/Fantasy/Illness/Science/War] A: Edmund B. Hennefield; D/S: Edward R. Mitchell; CH: Pearl Primus; C: Charles Quinan; P: Associated Playwrights; T: Henry Street Playhouse (OB); 5/27/48

"An exhaustingly bad play," growled George Freedley (*NYMT*). "Badly conceived, badly constructed, badly written, badly acted and badly directed," moaned Robert Garland (*NYJA*). Its potentially powerful subject was germ warfare. In the program was the description: "A fantasy projected in the near future, narrating the effects of a deadly plague sweeping the world as a result of the bombing of a German bacteriological warfare factory during World War II."

The virus (g-II) released is capable of attacking the mind and body and driving the infected person to kill himself. A young woman (Jeanette Clift) is married to a scientist (Henry Hart) who does experiments in the prolongation of human tissue, hoping to find a cure for the virus; while a prisoner of the Nazis, he may have been responsible for starting the epidemic. The wife contracts the disease, which causes her to confront death, represented as a Spaniard with a red garotte. This leads her to discover the other characters' true natures. She learns that her husband plans to use the cure selectively so as to foster a new master race and that he wants to create a race of slaves.

Pearl Primus and her troupe of dancers appeared in fantasy sequences accompanied by offstage drumbeats to perform rhythmic movements suggestive of the horrible effects of the virus. A number of other attempts at "experimental" staging techniques were included as well, and there were some flashy lighting effects.

GABRIELLE [Comedy/Illness/Literature/Marriage/Medicine/Music/Romance] A: Leonardo Bercovici; SC: Thomas Mann's short story, "Tristan"; M: Rudi Revil; D: Randolph Carter; S: Peggy Clark; C: Kenn Barr; P: Rowland Leigh; T: Maxine Elliott's Theatre; 3/25/41 (2)

An "extremely bad play" (Louis Kronenberger [*PM*]) based on a 1902 Thomas Mann short story that was developed into the novelist's *The Magic Mountain*. Kelcey Allen (*WWD*) opined, "There is so little action to the effort that it is difficult to tell why the acts end, why the play ends, or, getting down to cases, why it begins. It would be hard indeed to find a play with less action. Added to this, the dialogue is meaningless and dull. Any attempt to build up a character is completely missed."

The year is 1908. To a fashionable Swiss sanatorium in the Alps the blustering bourgeois businessman Anton Kloterjahn (Harold Vermilyea) brings his pretty wife, Gabrielle (Eleanor Lynn), a timid soul who has been seriously weakened from a difficult childbirth. Romance blooms in the heart of one of the invalids, eccentric minor novelist Detlev Spinell (John Cromwell), a vain idealist whose supposed passion for pure beauty leads him to drive Gabrielle, despite her condition, to climb mountains and to play the piano. It is the fatigue stemming from the latter that causes her to die, but in dying to preserve Detlev's vision of her unspoiled beauty.

Frederic Tozere played a doctor at the sanatorium, and others in the cast, most of them playing cynical patients, included Martin Wolfson, Byron McGrath, Frieda Altman, Wilton Graff, and Whitner Bissell.

GALILEO (***Leben des Galilei***) [Drama/Family/German/Historical-Biographical/Period/Politics/Religion/Science] A: Bertolt Brecht; TR: Charles Laughton; M: Hanns Eisler; LY: Albert Brush; D: Joseph Losey; CH: Lotte Goslar (executed by Joan McCracken); DS: Robert Davison; P: Experimental Theatre; T: Maxine Elliott's Theatre; 12/7/47 (6)

This production of Brecht's play, subsequently recognized as a modern classic, was given only a limited, noncommercial engagement for a subscription audience. A hoped-for extended run did not materialize because of the relative lack of critical interest. It received sharply mixed reviews, ranging from the ecstatic to the pejorative, and was gone in a week. Many found the material too literary, philosophical, undramatic, and loosely constructed to make good theatre. George Jean Nathan (*TBY*) called it "a dawdling biographical chronicle quite lacking in any distinction." Richard Watts, Jr. (*NYP*), considered it "interesting and worthy" as a treatment of the conflict between the demands of religion and science and between authority and truth, but concluded that "it is rarely more than mildly dramatic." Brooks Atkinson (*NYT*) found it "unnecessarily enigmatic" and guilty of putting form before content. Others appreciated its dramaturgic novelty, its mature subject matter, and its thematic pertinence to contemporary events (especially the development of the atom bomb). To Bron. (*V*) it was "adult, pertinent, dramatic and moving." Rowland Field (*NEN*) praised it as a "highly original and expressive German play that is presented . . . in a delightfully unconventional manner. And with a charming lack of formality." In Louis Kronenberger's (*PM*) view, it was "an exhilarating and often brilliant stage work, a grown-up experience in theater-going."

This is the story of the seventeenth-century Italian scientist who, when threatened by the Inquisition with death as a heretic, equivocated concerning his revolutionary discovery that the earth revolves around the sun. Galileo is shown as an intellectual of sensual nature, the contrast between his mind and body making him all the more human. The story begins with this Paduan scientist demonstrating to young Andrea Sarti (Michael Citro), son of his housekeeper (Hester Sondergaard), the earth's movement around the sun, thereby introducing the age of doubt to replace that of faith. To solve his economic needs, he does not stoop to claim as his own the invention of the telescope, actually created by a Dutchman, but his improvements of it help in his researches. He and his daughter (Joan McCracken) move to Florence rather than Venice because he will gain more money there, although he has to curry favor from the young prince (Larry Rosen). The court philosophers are shocked at his theories, but he manages to convince some important figures to accept them. The Church, however, refuses to allow him to publish his heretical ideas. He maintains his silence for eight years, but ultimately gives in to his burning desire to pursue the truth. This damages his daughter's marital opportunities, and he sees his ideas misunderstood. The Grand Inquisitor (John Carradine) is Galileo's chief opponent, persuading even the open-minded new pope (Donald Symington) to prevent Galileo's studies. Galileo is put on trial; his followers hope that he will not recant, but they are devastated when he does. He grows old and nearly blind under house arrest, living with his spinster daughter. The grown-up Andrea (Nehemiah Persoff) eventually learns that the great man has managed to save a copy of his *Discorsi* from the hands of the Inquisition, and Andrea is secretly given it to smuggle out of Italy. Galileo refuses to agree that he has been a hero after all and regrets not having resisted earlier and having allowed the powers that be to dominate his mind. He feels guilty for all the future generations he has betrayed.

The production was given on simple sets and with beautiful costuming. Atkinson, however, believed that the production "values showmanship above the drama." He and a number of others were disturbed by the device of having each scene introduced by three choirboys singing Eisler's music.

Laughton was making his first Broadway appearance in fifteen years, during which time he had become a Hollywood superstar. To some he was fascinating, to others he had not fully mastered the intricacies of the demanding role. Watts said that he brought a wealth of colorful details to the part, and that his "occasional mannered excess . . . does not conceal the fact that it is a characterization of force and insight. The most striking thing about it is its intelligence." Kronenberger appreciated the actor's ability to speak the dialogue "for all it is worth, with a full sense of its silkiness, its worldliness, its dawdled quickwittedness, and of the lazy heat and force that underlie it." Yet Atkinson accused him of throwing the part away: "He is casual and contemptuous; he is ponderous and condescending, and there is a great deal of old-fashioned fiddle-faddle in his" behavior.

Consistently good reviews were accorded McCracken and Carradine. Others involved in the large company included Fred Stewart, Dwight Marfield, Frank Campanella, Werner Klemperer, Wesley Addy, Don Hanmer, and Rusty Lane.

The production represented the second of three versions of the script, also known as *The Life of Galileo Galilei*. The first had been completed in Denmark in 1938-1939. The last would be finished in Germany and would be in rehearsal under the author's direction when he died (1956). Brecht had moved to California early in the war. From 1944 to 1946, he often visited the home of Laughton to work closely on revising and translating the drama, with the intention of Laughton's one day playing it. Although the actor was credited with its translation, he did not know a word of German. The work underwent a major evolution, especially in the matter of Galileo's recantation. In the 1938 version, the scientist's recantation was made as a practical means to allow him to reveal his new discoveries; in the later version, Galileo admits that his recantation was an inexcusable criminal act. Galileo also changed under Laughton's influence, originally being a selfless ascetic and later being more deeply humanized as a hedonistic egotist and fawning protégé of the Medicis.

Both Orson Welles and Michael Todd had wanted to produce the drama on Broadway, but their grandiose production ideas were anathema to Brecht and Laughton, who sought the kind of epic simplicity associated with Brechtian theatre. Brecht and Laughton broke off negotiations with Welles and Todd, who did not seem willing to allow for a truly collaborative production. Instead, they allowed it to be given under noncommercial auspices in June 1947 at Hollywood's Coronet Theatre. The rehearsals were marred by friction, including Brecht's so insulting choreographer Anna Sokolow that she resigned.

Galileo was being done at a time of increasing reactionary pressures from Washington against left-wing sympathizers, and many in the arts were undergoing questioning about their politics before the House Un-American Activities Committee. Laughton's attorney told the apolitical actor that he dare not make any potentially controversial public remarks because he too might find himself called up to testify. Director Losey himself was accused of Communist leanings and later had to go to Europe to continue his career. After the Hollywood version closed and the work was being readied for New York, Brecht appeared in Washington before the congressional committee, headed by J. Parnell Thomas. Brecht departed for Europe as soon as the inconclusive inquiry was completed. These circumstances made the timeliness of the play even more apparent.

Barrie Stavis's *Lamp at Midnight*, another important play about Galileo, opened Off Broadway the same season and created a controversy over which was the better play. See *Lamp at Midnight* for more on that controversy.

GARDEN OF TIME [Drama/Blacks/Fantasy/Period/Rural] A/D: Owen Dodson; SC: Euripides' *Medea*; M: Phil Moore; S/C: Charles Sebree; P: American Negro Theatre; T: 135th Street Library Theatre (OB); 3/7/45 (30)

Yale University, where author-director Dodson had gone to school, had seen this play before it was produced in Harlem. It was an interesting but failed experiment that tried to draw parallels between life in ancient Greece and that experienced by blacks in the American South of the late nineteenth century.

Acts one and two tell part of the legend of Jason (Dean Newman, one of the two whites in the production) and Medea (Sadie Browne) and the search for the golden fleece. The dark-skinned Medea falls in love with Jason and goes back to his land with him after they kill her brother (Gordon Heath), but she is ultimately rejected by him in favor of Creusa. Medea then strikes back at her spouse by causing the deaths of her children, pushing Jason to his death, and taking her own life. The third act then reenacts the same story within the context of a Georgia slave owner's (Newman) relationship with one of his black slaves, Miranda (Browne). Voodoo and jive talk are employed as parallels to mythology and poetic diction. A Haitian voodooist, Mama Leua (Elsie Benjamin), is the black equivalent of Hecate. All the Greek characters have equivalents that are acted by the same players.

Bron. (*V*) thought the idea intriguing but the execution uneven, sometimes confusing, and the transition from the Greek episodes to the American "too sudden and violent." He was also disturbed by the ambivalent theme, which veered from a message of hope for racial unity to one that said that such unity was impossible. George Freedley (*NYMT*) argued with the decision to move the play into the nineteenth century, finding the retelling of the Medea-Jason story sufficient unto itself. The latter part became "an intolerable bore," he declared. Louis Kronenberger (*PM*) took issue with the awkwardness and "lack of dramatic vigor" in the writing, as well as with its self-conscious poetic language.

The play employed a good deal of music and dance in its development. William Greaves, Austin Briggs-Hall, and Lawrence Pepper were among the cast members.

GAS [Dramatic Revival] A: Georg Kaiser; D: Irv Stiber; S: Robert Ramsey; CH: Bert Prensky; P: On-Stage; T: Cherry Lane Theatre (OB); 8/18/47

The first local showing of Kaiser's 1918 expressionist drama (the second of a trilogy) was offered by a group of ambitious young Greenwich Village actors as part of an ongoing series of experimental plays. The piece's prophetic ideas were one of its most interesting features, as were its frequent moments of heightened theatricality. The company was not well equipped to perform the difficult play, but the director made good use of his limited resources.

The characters all had capitalized allegorical names. Among the actors were Bert Prensky as the Gentleman in White, Anna Berger as the Mother, and Al Hurwitz as the First Gentleman in Black. In a minor role was Beatrice Arthur.

Gas is set in a gas factory whose workers enjoy a profit-sharing scheme and whose director, the Billionaire's Son (Marvin Silbersher), takes a salary equivalent to those of his workers. The unstable gas formula causes a massive explosion, but before long, the world's demands for the gas have everyone back at work. The Billionaire's Son refuses the workers' demand that he fire the Engineer (Jean [Gene] Saks), who is targeted as the scapegoat responsible for the explosion. When the Billionaire's Son's son-in-law, in military and financial disgrace, comes to seek assistance, he tries to convince the son-in-law to accept his responsibilities, but is confronted by five puppetlike tycoons who reject his profit-sharing methods. They want the Engineer fired and the factory reopened. The Billionaire's Son refuses to allow people to die in the interests of business; seeking a humanitarian solution to man's problems, he plans an agricultural settlement. The son-in-law, following an inhumane code of honor, kills himself. The workers meet to demand the firing of the Engineer and threaten to stop the gas if he remains. They are exhorted by the Billionaire's Son to be human and to abandon profit making. The Engineer, however, tells them to return to the factory, where they are rulers. The Billionaire's Son seeks protection from the violent workers. The factory is ordered to be reopened by the Government Commissioner (Jan Kindler), in spite of the warnings about the danger of another explosion. The Billionaire's Son is forced to give in, but his daughter promises to give birth to a man who will have self-understanding.

George Freedley (*NYMT*) thought that the company was in great need of being strengthened by more talented actors, but commended it for its valiant efforts in staging unusual works.

GAYDEN [Drama/Art/Crime/Family/Mental Illness/Romance/Sex] A: Mignon and Robert McLaughlin; D: Lex Richards; S/L: Willis Knighton; C: Emeline Roche; P: Gant Gaither; T: Plymouth Theatre; 5/10/49 (7)

Fay Bainter returned to Broadway as a sadist's mother in this "peculiarly unsatisfying play" (William Hawkins [*NYWT*]). She enacted Grace Sibley, a wealthy widow who despised her husband and whose spoiled, conscienceless, dilettante son Gayden (Jay Robinson) is diagnosed as being criminally cruel. This appraisal comes from Grace's physician brother Ned Whitaker (Clay Clement) following a series of deaths and other mishaps among Gayden's acquaintances. The deaths include the suicide by hanging of a cousin who was Gayden's roommate, the demise of a youth who fell off a roof during a game of follow the leader, an attempt at asphyxiation by a female friend, and the abandonment of her husband by a young woman (Gloria Stroock) who was subsequently rejected by Gayden. Gayden presently is preoccupied with the artistic education of a young lady named Emily Archer (Carol Wheeler), whom he presumably intends to destroy. Emily is accompanying Grace to the latter's wedding in South America. When Grace faces up to Gayden's psychopathic character, she lets Emily go, but, even after a serious confrontation, can do nothing about her loathsome son.

A lack of suspense and menace was a major drawback of this psychological melodrama, as was the playwright's constant reliance on rhythmically flat telegraphic dialogue in which barely any speeches were longer than a single line. Also annoying was the lack of a decent dramatic payoff. Howard Barnes (*NYHT*) thought the premise promising, but was disappointed at the authors' failure to develop the play's "thin thread of menace into a full-bodied and full-styled drama of suspence [*sic*]."

GENTLEMAN FROM ATHENS, THE [Comedy/Politics/Romance/Southern] A: Emmet Lavery; D: Sam Wanamaker; S/L: Ralph Alswang; P: Martin Gosch i/a/w Eunice Healey; T: Mansfield Theatre; 12/9/47 (7)

Anthony Quinn, already a movie star, made his Broadway debut in this predictable piece of hokum by Emmet Lavery, president of the Screen Actors Guild, who recently had been called before the House Un-American Activities Committee, where he had declared himself not to be a Communist. Quinn played a wealthy, ruthlessly aggressive Greek-American politician, Stephen Socrates Christopher, from the vineyard region of Athens, California, who has been elected to Congress. He has rented a historic Virginia mansion near Washington from Lee Kilpatrick (Edith Atwater), a blueblood who goes to work for him as his secretary. Following her advice, on the day he is sworn into office he makes a grandstand play by introducing a previously rejected bill for a United States of the World. He enrages other congressmen, one of whom he punches for calling him a Communist, and even gets barred from the floor. He uses his unscrupulous tactics--including threatened blackmail--to push his bill through. This leads to him being in danger of being ousted from office because of the disclosure that he bought his job. With his office on the line, he discovers incriminating evidence against the leader of the House, but is dissuaded from using it to save his position because the ends do not justify the means. He decides to return to California to win his seat back on truly Socratean terms.

Cardboard characters, broadly exaggerated plot complications, and a lack of wit were serious blemishes. "The story . . . has a high-minded purpose," stated William Hawkins (*NYWT*). "It misses because its execution is flimsily contrived." The blend of "farce, social significance and character study . . . mix like oil and water," lamented Robert Coleman (*NYDM*). The chief saving grace was the potent and robust presence of the convincingly rugged Quinn, but good work also was contributed by Lou Polan, Ethel Browning, Alan Hewitt, and Feodor Chaliapin (son of the great opera singer).

GENTLEMEN PREFER BLONDES [Musical/France/Hotel/Period/Romance/Sea] B: Joseph Fields and Anita Loos; M: Jule Styne; LY: Leo Robin; SC: Anita Loos's novel of the same name; D: John C. Wilson; CH: Agnes de Mille; S/L: Oliver Smith; C: Miles White; P: Herman Levin and Oliver Smith; T: Ziegfeld Theatre; 12/8/49 (740)

Twenty-eight-year-old, tall, blond, and huge-eyed Carol Channing, then considerably heavier than she was later in her career, was steadily stepping higher and higher on the ladder of Broadway stardom when she took a giant leap upwards with this popular musical. It was based on stories--first serialized in *Harper's Bazaar*--by Anita Loos, who (with John Emerson) was also responsible for a 1926 play by the same name* and with the same chief characters. Florenz Ziegfeld once had considered turning the material into a musical, but his idea was shelved when the play was written. Because Loos had never written a musical, she was given Joseph Fields as a collaborator, but she was not happy about the arrangement. She therefore allowed Fields to do most of the work, which was simply to take her 1926 script and edit it to make room for musical interpolations. When Billy Rose, in whose theatre the play was being produced, saw the libretto, he thought that it was terrible and immediately wrote a ten-page outline for a new book. Loos and Fields were impressed by it, although they were not told that it was by Rose (who wanted no credit). Loos then used the outline as the basis for a new script, but Fields's involvement so annoyed her that she convinced the producers to keep him away from the project and to allow her to write the script herself.

Like many other hits, the show had serious trouble raising the needed financing ($200,000 worth). After a fruitless series of backers' auditions, the producers suddenly struck it rich when they auditioned for Joshua Logan, Leland Hayward, Richard Rodgers, and Oscar Hammerstein II, the leading lights of *South Pacific*. When word got out (via the gossip columns) that each of these powerhouses had put up $5,000, the rest of the money was available within a few hours.

In this musical adaptation of the roaring twenties story, the towering Channing played the diminutive Lorelei Lee, the blond gold digger from Little Rock, while her brunette pal, Dorothy Shaw, was terrifically well played by Yvonne Adair, both of them looking as if they had stepped out of a John Held cartoon. (Twenty-five years later [1974], Channing would reappear in the show in a Broadway revival retitled *Gentlemen Still Prefer Blondes*--revised to make the action into a flashback--and again knock 'em dead with her unique personality and talent.) Both Adair and Channing had appeared in the recent *Lend an Ear*.

The search for a Lorelei had not been easy. Among the many talented stars considered had been Ethel Merman, but she rejected it, possibly because she could not see herself in a blond wig. Most of the other performers looked at were of the sexy blond type, and coproducer Levin later remembered, "We were looking at gorgeous blond seductresses when what we really wanted, though we didn't know it till we spotted it, was a girl who could make fun of a gorgeous blond seductress" (quoted in Gary Carey, *Anita Loos*). Loos and coproducer Smith then thought of Channing, whose *Lend an Ear* was still running, but director Wilson was interested in a performer then appearing in a show at the Westport Country Playhouse. Loos and Smith went to see her, and, by coincidence, Channing was sitting right behind them. They knew at once that the actress they had come to see was not in the same ballpark with the one behind them. Levin was induced to see Channing in her revue and agreed that she was perfect. The only question was about Channing's Junoesque size, Lorelei having been conceived as a more petite charmer. To Loos, however, this was not a disadvantage. "She can play Lorelei like a Great Dane under the delusion it's a Pekingese," she said, according to Carey.

The familiar story was enacted about Lorelei, who, engaged to button manufacturer Gus Esmond (Jack McCauley; the character's name was originally Eisman), embarks for France aboard the *Ile de France* with Dorothy and has rich men pursue her both on the ship and in France, where she stays at Paris's Ritz. Zipper king Josephus Gage (George S. Irving) presents one formidable rival to Mr. Esmond; the philandering Brit, Sir Francis Beekman (Rex Evans), presents another. Lorelei holds on to Gus, who is ready to drop her when he learns of her dalliances, and she creates a hit nightclub act to boot. Romance also blooms for Dorothy with handsome Philadelphian Henry Spofford (Eric Brotherson). The nostalgic but hilarious finale was staged in the style of the old *Follies** and *Scandals** revues of the twenties, with a company of gorgeous show girls strutting across the stage, heads adorned by waving plumes and arms held up to carry tassled props.

Structurally old-fashioned, but fast-paced, musically deft, and comically sparkling, *Gentlemen Prefer Blondes* hit the spot. It had undergone some significant surgery in Philadelphia, including the removal of a major dance routine, but the result was a considerable improvement. The dance number was based on an acrobatic apache number from the 1920s, in which a female dancer was tossed by two men about thirty feet across the stage, where she would be caught by a third. Agnes de Mille tried to duplicate the feat with her specially hired acrobatic dancers, but could only get the girl thrown about half the old distance. At one rehearsal, the girl crashed into an iron pipe and suffered a concussion. Whenever the number was repeated, people worried about the dancer covered their eyes. Just before the Philadelphia opening, the girl flew about fifteen feet before being missed by her catcher and landing in a dazed heap. When the curtain rose four hours later, the number was deleted.

Brooks Atkinson (*NYT*) tossed his hat in the air for this "vastly enjoyable song-and-dance antic put on with humorous perfection." Atkinson said that Channing "goes through the play like a dazed automaton--husky enough to kick in the teeth of any gentleman on the stage, but mincing coyly in high-heel shoes and looking out on a confused world through big, wide, starry eyes. There has never been anything like this before in human society." Channing, whose comic acting was hailed as loudly as her musical talents, had several songs that eventually became identified with her, such as "A Little Girl from Little Rock" and "Diamonds Are a Girl's Best Friend." (One of the show's biggest hits, however, "Bye, Bye, Baby," was sung by Gus.) John Mason Brown (*SR*), much of whose review was a paean to the young star, described her unforgettable voice, saying that it "bears only the slightest resemblance to any other voice. Although it can claim a sultry hoarseness, it is strangely thin. There is unexpected strength, however, in its thinness. It combines a wheedle with a treble, a squeak with a caress." When the show opened, she was not given star billing. Soon after the reviews came out, Channing was acknowledged as a bona fide star. The company included Alice Pearce, as a funny old lady in perpetual quest of champagne cocktails, and dancer Anita Alvarez, who helped make de Mille's sprightly dance routines come alive.

GEORGE WASHINGTON SLEPT HERE [Comedy/Family/Law/Legacy/Romance/Rural/Theatre/Youth] A: George S. Kaufman and Moss Hart; D: George S. Kaufman; S: John Root; P: Sam H. Harris; T: Lyceum Theatre; 10/18/40 (173)

This addition to the list of the best plays of the year was a mild hit, but one that most found not up to par when compared with other plays from the Kaufman and Hart collaboration; the farce, it should be noted, marked an end to that successful partnership. "Its theme is too meagre to carry it, and its whole tone, as a result, is forced," opined Louis Kronenberger (*PM*). John Mason Brown (*NYP*) called it "a good idea rather than a good play."

Based loosely on Kaufman and Hart's own experiences as country householders in Bucks County, Pennsylvania (the set actually resembled Hart's country house, Fair View Farm), the story follows the travails of a middle-aged New York couple, Newton (Ernest Truex) and Annabelle Fuller (Jean Dixon), and their nineteen-year-old daughter Madge (Peggy French) after Newton--without telling his wisecrackingly acidulous spouse--spends their last dime on a rundown colonial farmhouse in Bucks County. Not only does it lack the usual amenities, but the road leading to it and the well water, which is tapped only after considerable expense, turns out apparently to be on the property of the nasty next-door neighbor, Mr. Prentice (Richard Barbee). Moreover, Newton believed that the Father of Our Country had slept in the house, but belatedly discovers that the only famous revolutionary to have occupied it was Benedict Arnold. Nevertheless, the Fullers set forth to make it habitable, which leads to many comic plot developments. They succeed in prettifying the place, but the costs involved practically put the Fullers in the poorhouse. Various problems lead to foreclosure proceedings, with the Fullers expecting to borrow $5,000 from the presumably wealthy, but annoyingly self-centered Uncle Stanley (Dudley Digges, a late substitute for Berton Churchill, who died during the rehearsal period); Stanley has shown up as a weekend guest. He turns out to have been broke since 1929, but has enjoyed the fawning over him by the various relatives who have expected to inherit his fortune. In the farcical third act, as a good number of the characters drown their depression in a bottle of whisky each and then begin to wreck the house to return it to its original condition, it is learned from an old map found by another neighbor, Mrs. Douglas (Mabel Taliaferro), that the right of way and water actually are on the Fuller property. The frightened Prentice, a member of the foreclosing bank's board, who was set to buy the house and land himself, is duped by Uncle Stanley--who claims to have brought a check for $5,000--not only into abandoning legal proceedings, but into lending the family the needed money himself, and the property is saved.

The premise of city slickers trying to fit into country life, once established, was soon exhausted, and the authors were forced to include various artificial plot contrivances (especially the mortgage device) and eccentric characters, including a well-drawn perfect pest of a teenager named Raymond (Bobby Reddick); a greedy handyman (Percy Kilbride); a comic servant (Paula Trueman); and an actor (George Baxter) and actress (Ruth Weston) couple who are in the country to do summer theatre, and whose male half starts up an affair with the Fuller daughter. The latter, though, is quickly disillusioned and returns to her beau, Steve (Kendall Clark), in time for a happy ending.

Had there not been an assortment of risible gag lines, and had the third act not been hilarious, with its depiction of the downcast principal characters gathering in a circle and drinking a bottle of whisky each, the evening might have been a crashing bore. Also worth the price of admission were the many excellent performances. "Apart from the actors, who are off the top-shelf, *George Washington Slept Here* is a labored and empty enterprise," yawned Brooks Atkinson (*NYT*). Despite its so-so reception, the play has continued to be a favorite of summer and amateur theatre groups.

According to Malcolm Goldstein's *George S. Kaufman*, actress Jean Dixon, who had turned down a major role in Kaufman and Hart's *The American Way**, accepted her role in this comedy sight unseen, probably out of guilt. However, she was very unhappy during rehearsals, first because costar Ernest Truex stepped on her best lines and demanded center stage during their scenes, and second because she had a line, "I'm so sick of sucking up to Uncle Stanley," that she found offensive. When Kaufman, who had known her for two decades, asked since when she had become so genteel, she replied, "I always have been, only you never had the grace to recognize it," and stomped out, intending to quit the show. Kaufman had to eat humble pie and even changed "sucking up" to "buttering up" at the actress's suggestion. Eventually the entire line was cut. Another line, which had Dixon refer to the brattish Raymond as Huckleberry Hauptmann (a reference to Bruno Hauptmann, the convicted kidnapper of Charles Lindbergh's baby), was changed at her request so that she called the boy Huckleberry Capone.

The troubles with Truex, however, did not vanish so readily, and he continued to step on other actors' lines; Dixon would have walked out again if Kaufman had not insisted on her honoring her contract. At one out-of-town performance, when Truex leaped on a table in the third-act scene of mayhem and injured himself in a fall, one of the cast members whispered loud enough to be heard in the audience, "That's one line he won't step on again."

GET AWAY OLD MAN [Comedy/Films/Romance] A: William Saroyan; D/P: George Abbott; S: John Root; C: Miles White; T: Cort Theatre; 11/24/43 (13)

This play, reportedly composed in six days, was inspired by author Saroyan's experiences as a Hollywood movie writer under contract to Louis B. Mayer of Metro-Goldwyn-Mayer. Although Mayer was initially very high on the rising writer, the latter could not bear the pressures put on him and quit before three months were up. The role of the egomaniacal movie tycoon Patrick Hammer (Ed Begley) in the present play was based specifically on Mayer. When he had completed it, Saroyan had the audacity to announce that MGM could have it for a quarter of a million dollars if it acted by a deadline he established. According to *Saroyan* by Lawrence Lee and Barry Gifford, he wrote to MGM, "I sincerely recommend immediate purchase, sight unseen, as I believe this play is my greatest, perhaps one of the greatest ever to appear in this country, and in all probability my second play to win both the Pulitzer Prize and the Drama Critics Award." MGM refused, of course, and the play then went through various big Broadway producers, all of whom rejected it, until George Abbott decided that it was for him. It may have been, but it was not for the critics or the public.

The play was spotted with humor but lacked the typical quality of pathos familiar from other Saroyan works. It had some recognizable Saroyan touches, such as the character of the drunken cynic and a few other oddball types, but Saroyan's propensity for finding the good in everyone was altered with his vitriolic portrait of the hateful movie mogul, "the first full-length portrait of a heel that he has drawn," according to Rosamond Gilder (*TAM*). "The first act," said Lewis Nichols (*NYT*), "is slow and sounds like nothing so much as a parody of the old William Saroyan; the second act is reasonably funny in a brittle sort of fashion; the third act is long and spiritless." Noted Robert Garland (*NYJA*), "Where *Get Away Old Man* should be whimsical, it is labored; where *Get Away Old Man* should be tender, it is bathetic; where *Get Away Old Man* should be dyed-in-the-wool Saroyan, it is imitative."

Patrick Hammer, head of a major Hollywood studio, is a money-grubbing, overbearing, relentlessly womanizing, and otherwise despicable executive. To his film kingdom he has invited a rising young writer, Harry Bird (Richard Widmark), in whom he has discerned a marketable talent. Harry is depicted as ineffably wise and levelheaded as well as honest; he doesn't shy from calling Hammer a crook. (Saroyan offered a program note: "If any character in the play is based on any living person in the world, that person is myself.") Living with Harry is his usually soused, philosophically inclined companion, Sam (Glenn Anders). Hammer wants Harry to write a film script about mother love to be called *Ave Maria*. The idea rankles, but Harry is inspired to consider writing the story when he meets and falls for an extra named Martha (Beatrice Pearson), who will do anything to break into films. Hammer agrees to satisfy Harry's every whim if he will only write the story. These whims include an office with a pianola and a blackboard that the various characters use to set down their thoughts. Finally, unable to cope with Hollywood's demands, Harry departs for San Francisco, where he will marry Martha and be able to concentrate on his opus, should he choose to write it.

In the cast were Joyce Matthews as a fading screen star, Hilda Vaughn as a manicurist, William Adams as the mogul's yes-man, Sula Levitch as a piano player, Edwin Hodges as a *New York Times* reporter, and Mason Adams as a telegraph messenger. The best-received actor was Anders as the knowing lush.

GHOST FOR SALE [Comedy/British/Mystery/Romance] A: Ronald Jeans; D: Ilia Motyleff; S: Cleon Throckmorton; P: Daly's Theatre Stock Company and Alexander H. Cohen; T: Daly's Theatre (Sixty-third Street Theatre; OB); 9/29/41 (6)

A 1938 British comedy that seemed incredibly dated by 1941 when it was given its New York premiere at the new stock company established on West Sixty-third Street by twenty-one-year-old producer Alexander H. Cohen. The top price was only $1.65. The play had had mild success in London, but flopped dreadfully in New York. Hobe. (*V*) said, "It's a conglomeration of transparent, pointless, unexplained, illogical and tiresome whodunit contrivances, with unbelievable characters and impossible situations."

Sir Gilbert Tracey (Austin Fairman), wishing to buy his family's ancestral mansion in Hertfordshire, tricks his impecunious novelist brother, Martin (Evan Thomas), into selling it to him by making it appear to be haunted. Martin hopes to stave off the sale by writing a book about the manor and paying off his debts with the profits. Gilbert eventually succeeds in obtaining the place, only to discover that it may really have ghosts after all. One in particular is that of a Tracey forebear killed by an evil horse dealer who placed his body behind a secret panel in the library. Mixed in is a romance between Martin's practical-joking son, Geoffrey (Leon Janney), and a girl named Judy (Ruth Gilbert). Geoffrey, who has been responsible for fooling Gilbert into thinking the house haunted, ends up with the place, which should have been his to begin with.

The cast included Martin Balsam, making his local debut in a minor role. Ingenue Ruth Gilbert was lauded for her efforts.

GHOSTS [Dramatic Revival*] A: Henrik Ibsen; TR: Eva Le Gallienne; D: Margaret Webster; S: Watson Barratt; P: Louis J. Singer and the American Repertory Theatre; T: Cort Theatre; 2/16/48 (10)

This mediocre revival of the oft-revived Ibsen drama (last seen with Alla Nazimova in 1935) starred Eva Le Gallienne as Mrs. Alving, with Jean Hagen playing Regina, Robert Emhardt acting Engstrand, Herbert Berghof taking Pastor (here titled "Reverend Mr.") Manders, and Alfred Ryder cast as Oswald. The struggling American Repertory Theatre, making its third and final bid for acceptance, also played Ibsen's *Hedda Gabler** in its brief and dismal repertory season. There was a general conviction that *Ghosts* was dull, plodding, and tiresome. "In the wrong hands," wrote Louis Kronenberger (*PM*), "as the current production makes all too plain, *Ghosts* grows pretty ponderous, exhibiting its period weaknesses much more than its permanent strength." George Jean Nathan (*TBY*) argued that Le Gallienne's somewhat modernized adaptation only served to underline the datedness of the drama. Nathan, in a widely held view, considered the star's performance intelligent, but more like a dramatic reading than a stageworthy characterization. Berghof's overacted Manders came in for a barrage of scathing rebukes. Only Alfred Ryder was generally, but sometimes grudgingly, approved for his performance.

GIRL FROM NANTUCKET, THE [Musical/Art/Romance/Small Town] B: Paul Stamford, Harold Sherman, and Hi Cooper; M: Jacques Belasco; LY: Kay Twomey, Hughie Prince, and Rick Rogers; SC: a story by Fred Thomson and Berne Giler; D: Edward Clarke Lilley; CH: Val Raset and Van Grona; S/L: Albert Johnson; C: Lou Eisele; P: Henry Adrian; T: Adelphi Theatre; 11/8/45 (12)

Ward Morehouse (*NYS*) warned that this musical "is one of the very worst. This awkward and disconnected song-and-dance piece . . . offers routine music and lyrics, a dreadful book, and a general level of entertainment that makes the ill-fated *Mr. Strauss Goes to Boston* seem something to be pleasantly remembered." Representative of the humor was an exchange in which a female character said, "I appeal to you as a woman," and a male character replied, "You don't even appeal to me as a man." A song called "I Want to See More of You" was inspired by the hero's glimpsing a girl in a shower. A tune considered even smuttier was titled "Let's Do and Say We Didn't."

The haphazard story concerned a Nantucket house painter (Bob Kennedy) who uses binoculars to peep in on the dressing and undressing of the pretty miss (Adelaide Bishop) across the way from his job. He takes a job painting the sills of her bathroom window and is then mistakenly hired to paint a museum mural picturing the famous Nantucket fishing fleet. He accepts the commission so that he can be near the girl he has been ogling. Because of his lack of talent, the girl, an art student, ends up doing the job for him.

"There have been worse musicals," recoiled Euphemia Van Rensselaer Wyatt (*CW*), "but none so consistently inept." Most critics took pot shots at a pretentious first-act ballet concerning a fisherman's struggle with the sea and a whale. As it was being danced, a man standing on a rock spoke a pompous descriptive poem that was "a combination of Carl Sandburg, Joseph C. Lincoln and the March of Time," wrote John Chapman (*NYDN*). The cast included Jack Durant, Billy (William) Lynn, black tapsters Rapps and Tapps, Helen Raymond, and Jane Kean, who received the best reviews.

GLAMOUR PREFERRED [Comedy/Films/Marriage/Sex] A: Florence Ryerson and Colin Clements; D: Antoinette Perry; S: John Root; P: Brock Pemberton; T: Booth Theatre; 11/15/40 (11)

Originally called *Morality Clause*, this third play in a row (following *Beverly Hills* and *Quiet, Please*) about Hollywood dalliances was as mediocre as its predecessors; like them, it was written by screenwriters who wished to pour acid on film-colony life. It was considered tired goods, with laughless lines and stereotypical, unlikable characters. Richard Watts, Jr. (*NYHT*), thought it the worst of the lot, but Ibee. (*V*) thought it the best.

Its excuse for a story had to do with a matinee idol named Kerry Eldridge (Glen Langan), married to the long-suffering Lynn Eldridge (Flora Campbell), but an object of lust for former girlfriend Lady Bonita Towyn (Betty Lawford), a siren-like erstwhile nightclub dancer and present spouse of Sir Hubert Towyn (Robert Craven). Bonita--anxious not to have to settle in Australia with her husband--convinces Kerry to scrap his next film project in favor of costarring with her in *Night of Love*, to the disgust of Sam Goldwyn-like producer Bernard C. Goldwater (Louis Sorin). At the suggestion of Sir Hubert, Lynn threatens a Mexican divorce, which brings Kerry into line, and Goldwater decides to costar Kerry in *Night of Love*, not with Bonita, but with Lynn.

The best that Rosamond Gilder (*TAM*) could say for it was that it "had at least the virtue of being occasionally funny and moderately recognizable as to type," but John Mason Brown (*NYP*) pointed to "the debilitating confusion of the writing." Among the cast members were Elaine Perry, daughter of the director, Stefan Schnabel as a Russian director, and James Gregory as a cop.

GLASS MENAGERIE, THE [Drama/Family/Invalidism/Literature/Romance] A: Tennessee Williams; M: Paul Bowles; D: Eddie Dowling and Margo Jones; S/L: Jo Mielziner; P: Eddie Dowling and Louis J. Singer; T: Playhouse; 3/31/45 (561)

Tennessee Williams's first play to reach Broadway was given a landmark production that was a tribute to the perseverance of Eddie Dowling, its codirector, coproducer, and actor of the role of Tom. An idealistic theatre man who had had an up-and-down career and often had difficulty making ends meet because of his high standards, Dowling had a hard time in getting this lovely play to Broadway. Even though it was given a successful presentation in Chicago, the Theatre Guild's Theresa Helburn rejected it for her subscription offices because of its doubtful commercial possibilities in New York. In Chicago it had begun poorly, taking in only $3,300 during its first week there. It was on the verge of being closed for good, which the producer's staff advised, but Dowling's vociferous objections and pleas for an additional week's run won out. He received support from a number of important Chicago critics, and the box office began to improve until, in its fifth week, it began to show a profit. Still, the owner of New York's Playhouse, into which Dowling sought to book the work, hesitated because of his fear of financial failure. Only when rewarding terms insuring him against too great a loss were agreed upon would he let his theatre to the company. The play opened in New York to ecstatic reviews, won the New York Drama Critics Circle Award, was selected as one of Burns Mantle's ten best of the season, and has since become one of the best-loved and most often revived works of the modern theatre, here and abroad.

This is a memory play, mingling realism with expressionistic theatricalism, and with disguised but evident autobiographical resonances (Tennessee Williams's actual first name was Tom, like his hero's). An evocative musical score, suggestive lighting using scrims and special effects, and a narrator who is the hero looking back on the action and stepping into it were among the stylized touches for which it was lauded.

There are only four characters in the story, which is set in 1944 (the narrator's time) and 1935. The locale is the shabby St. Louis flat of the Wingfields: widowed mother Amanda (Laurette Taylor), whose telephone-lineman husband abandoned her when he fell in love with long distances; her mildly disabled, but inordinately shy daughter Laura (Julie Haydon); and her son Tom, a would-be writer working in a shoe warehouse, where he is nicknamed "Shakespeare," but biding his time before joining the merchant marine. A photo of Amanda's husband is prominently displayed and is even considered as another character in Tom's narrative, although he never appears. Tom, a merchant seaman in 1944, talks to the audience from the alleyway outside the house and introduces the characters and events. Amanda is a former Southern belle of refined background reduced to poverty and maintaining her household--her income comes from selling magazine subscriptions--despite her formidable setbacks. She persists in reminding her children of her glamorous youth in Blue Mountain. Laura, a potential old maid, has no men friends interested in dating her. She is supposedly a student at Rubicam's Business College, but has not been attending classes. Amanda, to her great dismay, discovers this. Instead of going to classes, where she could not control her nervousness, Laura has been going out to museums and flower galleries. Her only solace in life is her menagerie of glass animals, as fragile and in need of care as she is. The only boy she has ever admired is Jim O'Connor (Anthony Ross), who sang in the high-school operetta and called her "Blue Roses" because it sounded like pleurisy, the illness that kept Laura from school for a spell. Amanda rejects Laura's use of the word "crippled" to explain her condition and insists that Laura is magnifying it. Tom finds his solace from a boring job and confining home life by going to the movies, which precipitates a quarrel with Amanda, whom he calls a witch. He later apologizes and listens to his mother's request that he help find a beau for Laura. Tom then invites an acquaintance from work to dinner, precipitating a flurry of excitement on Amanda's part as she prepares to receive her daughter's "gentleman caller." Tom downplays the significance of the event, as the visitor does not know that he is expected to court Laura. Amanda dresses Laura as best she can in the fashion of a belle, but when Laura learns that the caller is Jim, the same boy she liked in school, she objects. On Jim's arrival she becomes ill, forcing Amanda to entertain him with her flow of nonstop conversation. Tom has paid his fees for the merchant marine with the money for the electric bill, and the lights dutifully go out after dinner, so candlelight must be employed. Jim and Laura are left alone for a lengthy duologue in which they reminisce and she gradually warms up to participate freely in the conversation. Jim is a man of charm and innate friendliness, a popular high-school athlete whose life after graduation has been a disappointment. He soon has the awkward girl dancing as the lights from the Paradise dance hall across the way play across the stage. He manages to break one of her glass animals, the unicorn, in the process, but is forgiven and even accepts the figure as a present. Although he kisses Laura, Jim has to back off because he is engaged and cannot even see her again. After he leaves, Amanda is outraged at learning of Jim's previous commitment and berates both Laura and Tom. A final scene shows Tom as narrator again, recalling his travels and the guilty persistence of his memories of Laura. It closes with his now famous lines: "I reach for a cigarette, I cross the street, I run into the movies or a bar, I buy a drink, I speak to the nearest stranger--anything that can blow your candles out! For nowadays the world is lit by lightning! Blow out your candles, Laura,--and so good-by. . . ."

A considerable amount of revision of Williams's original script, first called *The Gentleman Caller*, was undertaken before its Broadway opening. Among the things that were scrapped were Williams's use of projected titles for the scenes. The result, said George Jean Nathan (*TBY*) was "intrinsically less a play than a palette of sub-Chekhovian pastels brushed up into a charming semblance of one." In Howard Barnes's (*NYHT*) opinion, the play's "four characters, revealed by a top-notch cast in an extraordinarily sensitive script . . . , come together for passages of sheer theatrical brilliance." "Here is make-believe so real it tears your heart out," wrote Burton Rascoe (*NYWT*). John Chapman (*NYDN*) found himself hypnotized by the magic of the work. Ward Morehouse (*NYS*) declared that the play "is fragile and poignant. It is a vivid, eerie and curiously enchanting play." Critics noted their absorption (despite a lack of action); the depth of the character portrayals; the constant thread of truthful humor beneath the pathos; the unconventional dramatic form; the movingly poetic--sometimes excessively so--language; the evocative moods; the occasional profundity of the ideas expressed; the outstanding scenic and lighting contributions; the expressiveness of the musical accompaniment; and the unusual expertness of the acting ensemble.

Most notable of its performances was that of Laurette Taylor, once one of Broadway's most popular actresses, but for years the victim of alcoholism and a sorry wreck of her former self. She had made a temporary comeback with a brilliant performance in the 1938 revival of *Outward Bound**, but had not acted since. Seven years later, with her dipsomania presumably dismissed, she returned to create the role of Amanda Wingfield in a performance that became theatrical legend. Euphemia Van Rensselaer Wyatt (*CW*) observed that Taylor "has discovered the Duse method of making the most delicate delineation indelible. She seems to speak in whispers yet can be heard in the farthest seat in the balcony; her Southern accent is never accented and yet it colors not only her diction but her gestures; she appears too fluttery to be sure of her next line yet she dominates imperceptibly the whole action. Her gentleness may appear flabby but it is indestructible. . . . She is a presence, pathetic, comic and tragic that her son can never forget--nor her audience."

On opening night in Chicago, Taylor frightened everyone involved with the production when she could not be found before the performance. It was suspected that she might have reverted to her old drinking habits, although she had been a model of responsibility during the rehearsals. A search was instituted and the police were about to be called when designer Mielziner decided to check out the theatre's basement. There he heard running water and, checking further, discovered the star bending over a washtub, dressed in a filthy old dressing gown. She was dying Amanda's party frock herself, and her arms were dripping with lavender dye. The important costume, instead of being specially designed, had been bought ready-made to save money, but, at the dress parade, had not pleased the playwright. "So Laurette Taylor, on her own, had bought some dye and was trying to remedy matters," wrote Mielziner (in *Designing for the Theatre*).

GLASS SLIPPER, THE (*Az Üvegcipö*) [Dramatic Revival*] A: Ferenc Molnár; S: Charles Weber; C: Christine Thompson; P: Prevue Players; T: Barbizon-Plaza Theatre (OB); 10/18/40

A company of young semiprofessional actors flopped with this attempt at reviving Molnár's Hungarian Cinderella comedy, seen on Broadway in 1925. The "performance merely served to accentuate [the play's] faults," commented Herrick Brown (*NYS*), although he did admire the efforts of Ruth Ford in bringing to the principal role "a note of refreshing reality." Ford eventually became a respected actress.

GOD STRIKES BACK [Drama/Family/Invalidism/Military/Politics/War] A/P: Paul Nord; D: Betty Kashman; T: Concert Theatre; 2/26/43 (5)

The Concert Theatre on West Fifty-eighth Street (the former John Golden Theatre) was the scene of this "incoherent opus" (Wilella Waldorf [*NYP*]) about the Nazi invasion of Greece. Rose. (*V*) considered it "slow-moving and uninspiring, leading to a trite and hoary denouement."

Written by a Greek ex-journalist, the amateurishly staged and acted play tells of the tribulations suffered by the Greek people in the face of the Nazi hordes by setting its action in a home in an Athens suburb in which the Germans have set up their headquarters. The Nazis hold as hostages here a Greek artillery officer (David Kernan), who pretends to be retarded, and a brave guerrilla fighter's blind father (Thaddeus Suski) and sister (K. Yveli Aliki, a Greek actress in her American debut), whose house this is. The prisoners somehow managed to provide supplies for the resistance fighters, one of whom is captured and executed by the swinish Nazi major (Ralph Clanton). It evolves, however, that the dead man is the major's brother, that the blind man whose house has been commandeered is his father, and that he, the major, is not a true Aryan after all, but is half-Greek. Thus God has his revenge.

GOLDEN FALCON, THE [Drama/Adventure/Period/Politics/War] A: Daniel Rudsten; D/S: Edward R. Mitchell; CH: Ana Naila; C: George Higgens, Sylvia Farnham, Elizabeth Donnelly, and Grace de Leon; P: Associated Playwrights; T: Henry Street Playhouse (OB); 3/25/48

A third-rate, thirteen-scene swashbuckler set in seventeenth-century Russia and produced by a semipro group, one of whose actors was Neville Brand. The cramped theatre was the wrong venue for this type of material, but the play itself was "a stumbling effort," according to Joe Pihodna (*NYHT*). Hobe. (*V*) dismissed it as "inadequately produced, awkwardly staged and poorly played."

The story was about a Robin Hood-like cossack, Stephen Razin (Robert McGrane), who steals from the nobility and gentry and distributes his loot among the suffering serfs. Following a tribal custom, he must slay his Persian princess before leading his men into combat against the Russians, but he has lost his taste for war and is captured by the enemy.

GOLDEN LAND, THE [Musical/Yiddish Language] B: Julie Berns; M: Al Olshanetsky; LY: Jacob Jacobs; P: Judah Bleich; T: Second Avenue Theatre (OB); 10/17/43

A pleasantly flavorsome Yiddish musical with a story reminiscent of the life of songwriter Irving Berlin. It tells of a Jewish immigrant youth named Willie Singer (Leo Fuchs), who arrives here in 1908. He has such a talent for writing songs that he soon becomes a show-business celebrity, marries a fancy Hollywood actress (Dinah Halpern), and moves into a Park Avenue duplex, but continues to long for his "pumpernickel and lox" roots on the Lower East Side. The couple's irreconcilable differences--he wants her to settle down, she wants to continue her career--lead to a divorce. Willie, whose well of inspiration has run dry, fills it up again when he returns to Rivington Street and resumes his romance with his childhood sweetheart, Ruthie (Goldie Eisman). An amusing fillip to the proceedings was provided by a prompter (Wolf Barzell) who kept appearing between the scenes to make cracks about such things as the production, the Yiddish theatre, the audience, and so on.

Although most of the words were in Yiddish, there were occasional English interpolations. Bernard B. Rachmel (*WWD*) declared, "The book . . . hangs together more logically than less and does only slight violence to plausibility." A company of fifty included in principal roles Ludwig Satz as an old Jew who longs to return to the Holy Land, Jack Rechtzeit as a veteran tunesmith, and Aaron Lebedeff in a good comedy role. Tillie Rabinowitz and Fannie Lubritzky were also involved.

GOLDEN WINGS [Drama/Aviation/Military/Politics/Romance/Sex/War] A: William Jay (Lionel Aldous) and Guy Bolton; D/P: Robert Milton; S: Watson Barratt; T: Cort Theatre; 12/8/41 (6)

December 8, 1941, was the day the United States declared war on Japan; it was also the day on which this play about a love triangle in the RAF opened to an audience and critics too distracted by international events to give it much support. The play--earlier called *RAF*--was earnest and skillfully written, but seemed determinedly earthbound. One of its writers, the pseudonymous William Jay, then on active duty in the Middle East, was clearly familiar with the milieu depicted, that of RAF Spitfire flyers at the Chilgrove Service Club in England.

The chief character was the aristocratic Rex Gardiner (Lloyd Gough), a superb flight lieutenant, but a philandering cad. His girlfriend is the submissive Kay (Fay Wray), loved in turn by Norman (Gerald Savory). When Rex meets the sexy flyer Judith (Swedish actress Signe Hasso, in her American debut), he decides to make a play for her and throw over Kay. Judith, however, already has begun a relationship with another flyer, Tom, whose left-wing politics Rex despises. Rex goes after Judith anyway, and this precipitates a fight with Tom in which Rex, the superior officer, is struck. He promises to retaliate in the air. On their very next sortie, Tom's plane is shot down. Rex is brought up on charges of murder, but he insists that he had forgotten the quarrel in the heat of battle, and the play fails to clarify the issue of his responsibility.

The war was merely a colorful background to the mundane sexual intrigues of several of its participants in this unexceptional work. George Freedley (*NYMT*) described it as "indifferently contrived" and added that "in the face of a national crisis it seemed pettier and more futile than it would have last week when it was promised to us." The drama employed a cast largely made up of actors of British background. Among these were Valerie Cossart and J. W. Austin.

GOLDFISH BOWL, THE [Comedy/Family/Journalism/Politics] A: Vincent McConner; D: William Boyman; P/T: Theatre Showcase (OB); 6/15/42

Only Wilella Waldorf (*NYP*) appears to have covered this Off-Broadway presentation by a group dedicated to the showcasing of new theatre talent. Its home for the production was at 341 West Forty-seventh Street.

The Goldfish Bowl is a satire set in the White House and focuses on the president's wife, Martha Jefferson (Zita Rieth), a character modeled on Eleanor Roosevelt. Martha's busy lecture tours, her involvement in benefit balls, her daily column, her handling of family problems, including romantic entanglements, her ministering to various special interest groups, and so on are detailed within the framework of a story about what happens when a powerful Washington editor-publisher (Doris Daniels) seizes on a casual remark of the First Lady's about the tariff and decides to blow it up into an anti-Jefferson campaign issue.

Waldorf found the play "only mildly satirical" and "a little old fashioned." It had had an earlier presentation at the Woodstock Playhouse with Broadway star Luella Gear as Mrs. Jefferson. In the cast of the New York version, comic actor Joe Silver had a small role.

GOLEM, THE (***Der Golem***) [Dramatic Revival*/Hebrew Language] A: H. Levik; M: Moshe Milner; D: Boris I. Varshilov; S: J. Nievinsky; P: Habimah Theatre u/t/a/o Theatre Incorporated and the American Fund for Palestinian Institutions; T: Broadway Theatre; 5/16/48 (16)

A couple of days after the official birth of Israel, that nation's visiting Habimah Theatre offered this play of tragic dimensions, which it had shown here in 1927. The huge, clay, childlike monster of the title, brought to life by philosopher Maharal (Shimon Finkel) to protect the Jews, was portrayed by Aaron Meskin. Meskin managed to grip the audience in his compelling, highly pantomimic characterization and to convince it of his extraordinary power. His portrayal allowed for considerable humor when the golem is taught by Maharal how to behave. Other fine work was contributed by leading lady Hanna Rovina (disguising her femininity) as the Messiah (shared with Aaron Kutai), Zvi Ben-Haim as Tanchum, Zvi Friedland as Elijah, and Joshua Bertonov as Tadeush.

According to John S. Wilson (*PM*), the "production is stirring and studded with excellent performances." The company employed highly theatricalist means and succeeded very well in its creation of a baleful atmosphere. Several critics thought it the gem of the company's repertory; it was also the easiest to follow because of its considerable pantomimic action. A common complaint was the inscrutability of the synopses provided by the tour arrangers. On opening night an emotional ceremony followed the performance when actor Raymond Massey, speaking on behalf of Actors Equity and the American Fund for Palestinian Institutions, presented the troupe with American and Israeli flags, followed by the audience's singing of the "Hatikvah" and "The Star Spangled Banner."

(1) GONDOLIERS, THE, OR THE KING OF BARATARIA [Musical Revival*] B/LY: W. S. Gilbert; M: Arthur Sullivan; D: Charles Alan; CH: Felicia Sorel; S: Samuel Leve; P: Lyric Opera Company (Joseph S. Daltry and Herman Levin); T: Forty-fourth Street Theatre; 9/30/40 (24)

The opening performance in a series of Gilbert and Sullivan revivals by the young players of the Lyric Opera Company. The performances were deemed mediocre, Brooks Atkinson (*NYT*) opining that despite some good voices, the spirit of satire was sorely missing and the company was seriously overshadowed by the memory of the D'Oyly Carte Opera Company.

(2) D: R. H. Burnside; P: Boston Comic Opera Company and Messrs. Shubert; T: St. James Theatre; 3/3/42 (3)

Part of a repertory of Gilbert and Sullivan operettas. Helen Lanvin was the duchess of Plaza-Toro, Robert Pitkin was the Grand Inquisitor, Florenz Ames was the duke of Plaza-Toro, Morton Bowe was Marco Palmieri, Kathleen Roche was Gianetta, and her sister Mary was Tessa. The production was considered inferior to earlier pieces in the repertory.

(3) D: R. H. Burnside; P: R. H. Burnside i/a/w the Gilbert and Sullivan Opera Company; T: Ambassador Theatre; 2/21/44 (4)

Another unimpressive offering by the renamed Boston Comic Opera Company in its 1944 series. A number of actors were still with the troupe. The production was too slowly paced, the sets were on a high-school level, and, as Lewis Funke (*NYT*) commented, "The chorus is annoyingly stilted and some of the principals are too." Robert Pitkin in his 1942 role was one of the best in the show.

(4) D: Anna Bethell; S/C: Charles Ricketts; P: D'Oyly Carte Opera Company; T: Century Theatre; 1/26/48 (16)

The fourth revival of this comic opera during the decade was the handiwork of the great British preservers of the Gilbert and Sullivan tradition, visiting with a nine-piece repertory that totalled 136 performances. Martyn Green was the duke of Plaza-Toro, Leonard Osborn was Marco Palmieri, Charles Dorning was Giuseppe Palmieri, Gwyneth Cullimore was Gianetta, Denise Findlay was Tessa, Margaret Mitchell was Casilda, Ella Halman was the duchess of Plaza-Toro, Thomas Round was Luiz, and Richard Watson was Don Alhambra del Bolero.

The standout, as often in this company's work, was Green. "His precise singing style and his mock mincing manner capture the genius of Gilbert and Sullivan wonderfully," applauded Brooks Atkinson (*NYT*). He enjoyed the show considerably, declaring that the players "are singing it in the royal style, and even the orchestra, which was dragging its feet a month ago, is now singing with something that approaches Savoy rapture."

GOOD HOPE, THE (*Op Hoop von Zegen*) [Dramatic Revival*] A: Herman Heijermans; TR: Lillian Saunders and Caroline Heijermans-Houwink; D: Anita Grannis; P: Equity Library Theatre; T: Hudson Park Branch of the New York Public Library (OB); 12/4/45 (4)

A revival of the highly respected Dutch play whose last showing locally (in a return engagement) had been in 1930 under the auspices of the Civic Repertory Theatre, who first had done it in 1927. George Freedley (*NYMT*), as so often, was the only critic attending the workshop showings of the Equity Library Theatre. He found the play "deeply moving, extremely well acted and well worth producing." Nothing seemed dated about the work, and its point of view was still pertinent. The cast of unknowns included Nanom Kiam as the sailors' mother, Sarge Bensrick and Vance Gooden as the sailor brothers, Fiona O'Shiel as Jo, Angela Jacobs as Saart, Delmar Nuetzman as the bookkeeper, Ernest Rowan as the shipowner, and Josephine Glover as Truus.

GOOD MORNING, CORPORAL [Comedy/Marriage/Military/Sex/War] A: Milton Herbert Gropper and Joseph Shalleck; D/P: William B. Friedlander; S: Robert Barnhart; T: Playhouse; 8/8/44 (13)

John Chapman (*NYDN*) said that this comedy "is so inexpert, so unfunny, so mousy, that I can't think of much to say about it." Its featherheaded heroine, Dottie Carson (Charita Bauer), subscribes to a nutty patriotic streak that leads her to inveigle three different servicemen, an air-force corporal (Joel Marston), a sailor (Lionel Wilson), and a marine (Russell Hardie), to marry her while they are in their cups. They only learn what they have done after waking up with a hangover. As soon as the corporal, discovering that he is a married man, attempts to claim his marital rights, one of Dottie's other husbands, the marine, reported as missing in action, returns and demands to sleep with her. He is followed by the sailor husband, also thought MIA, who similarly requests his conjugal prerogatives. Finally, the corporal is pronounced the legitimate spouse of the moronic miss, and the play ends.

The situations were "calculated to leave patrons gasping with incredulity that the authors could so harass even the most gullible of audiences," howled Rose. (*V*). The play was larded with dirty jokes, often of a surprisingly single-entendre nature, and the heroine got the chance to run around in a series of negligees. One of the more indirect cracks had Dottie's pal (Frances Tannehill) say to the marine, "I wouldn't sleep with Dotty," to which he replied, "What's the use of two women sleeping with each other?"

GOOD NEIGHBOR [Comedy-Drama/Crime/Family/Invalidism/Jews/Marriage/Romance/Youth] A: Jack Levin; D: Sinclair Lewis; S: Frederick Fox; P: Sam Byrd;

T: Windsor Theatre; 10/21/41 (1)

The only thing notable about this event was that it was directed (and invested in to the tune of $25,000) by the famous novelist, Sinclair Lewis, whose own theatrical writings, apart from the Federal Theatre Project's offering of *It Can't Happen Here**, had never made much of a dent. His direction was slapdash and amateurish, and the play was not much better.

The well-intentioned but clumsy drama hoped to strike a blow for tolerance. It centered on Hannah Barron (Yiddish stage star, Anna Appel), Jewish matriarch, operator of a secondhand shop, and good neighbor to all, regardless of race or creed. When a half-witted German boy, Luther Kurtmann (Arthur Anderson), is falsely accused of murder, Hannah hides him while his father (Howard Fischer) seeks the real killer with the aid of private detectives. The Kurtmanns are anti-Nazi, but are considered to be Hitlerites by ignorant local people. Meanwhile, Hannah must take care of a bickering invalid husband (Gustav Shackt) and make good the $1,000 entrusted to her by her sailor son Dave (Sam Byrd, the producer), which she has given away in charitable chunks to the needy. Dave, however, needs the cash to get married now that he has returned from the sea. A band of hooded menaces calling themselves the Cavaliers and modeled on the Ku Klux Klan arrives to capture Luther, offering $1,000 for his person. Hannah defies them, is shot, and, via her life insurance, is able to provide for Dave the money he requires to marry his Hildie (Marcella Powers).

Brooks Atkinson (*NYT*) opined, "*Good Neighbor* is all thumbs as a play and is mixed up with more family crises and neighborhood complications than you can shake a blue pencil at."

GOOD NEWS [Musical/Yiddish Language] B/LY: Isidor Lillian; M: Joseph Rumshinsky; D/P: Menasha Skulnik; CH: Valentina Belova; S: Michael Saltzman; T: Second Avenue Theatre (OB); 9/27/44 (200)

Not a revival of the popular 1920s Broadway musical, but a schmaltzy Yiddish show with heavy doses of English and starring comedian Menasha Skulnik. It was chastised for being "ambiguous, repetitious, overlong" by Kahn. (*V*). Skulnik was supported by such lights as Miriam Kressyn and Max Kletter in a story that combined musical comedy with romantic drama.

It is about a woman (Kressyn) who has an affair with a naval officer (Kletter). The latter suffers amnesia when his ship is torpedoed, and he is sent to a military hospital, where a nurse wants his memory to remain in the dark so she can claim him for herself. His memory returns, however, and he goes back to the girl he left behind.

Esta Saltzman, Anna Thomashefsky, Dave Lubritzky, Willie Secunda, Anna Teitelbaum; Yetta Zwerling, Paula Klida, and Morris Tarlovsky were featured.

GOOD NIGHT LADIES [Dramatic Revival*] AD: Cyrus Wood; SC: Avery Hopwood and Charles Andrews's farce, *Ladies' Night*; D: Edward Clarke Lilley; S/L: Frederick Fox; C: Billy Livingston; P: Howard Lang and Al Rosen; T: Royale Thea tre; 1/17/45 (78)

One of those numbers that falls between being a new play and a revival. It was actually a revision, but is here classed as a revival because its changes were not overly extensive, being mostly in the way of updating. Its original had been a 1920 hit, and the revision had been a recent smash in Chicago, where, despite critical derision, it lasted for 100 weeks and 897 showings.

Broadway's version was deemed a cornball low comedy, but broadly funny enough to lure the out-of-town trade. Some called it burlesque without the music. A typical exchange was "I'm afraid I'm old fashioned," "Yes, one old fashioned after another," while another began, "Women are a closed book to me," followed by "All you need is a paper-cutter." It also had a bevy of beauties parading around in skimpy bathing suits, and one scene, aimed at the baldheaded men in row three, in which a striptease figured.

The fellow who has to hide out in the women's Turkish baths (called a "cosmetorium") was played by Skeets Gallagher, who was quite amusing, while James Ellison played the handsome young professor afraid of women, who, to his great embarrassment, also takes refuge in the baths. The situation gets especially irksome when his and his friend's wives show up there as well.

"Though freshly and expensively dressed," sighed Rosamond Gilder (*TAM*), "its humor, its structures and its general methods of presentation date back to the beyond." George Jean Nathan (*TBY*) adumbrated, "It has been vulgarized into the worst kind of drivel imaginable; it has no single moment of genuine humor; and its presented spectacle of semi-nude females comporting themselves like bootleg burlesque queens is less than edifying." Sex appeal was provided by good-lookers Sunnie O'Dea, Marlo Dwyer, Lisa Kirk, Rosemary Bertrand, Randee Sanford, and stripper Lana Holmes, while Kathryn Givney and Max Hoffman, Jr., were in supporting roles.

In February 1950 the play was adapted in abbreviated thirty-two-minute form under the title *Ladies Night in a Turkish Bath* and produced on a bill with a reissue of the movie *Jungle Jim* at the Selwyn Theatre on West Forty-second Street. Loy Nilson and Ty Perry directed. This was part of a series of such sensationalistic revivals offered by movie owner George Brandt, another being "The Respectful Prostitute." The main interest was in the undraped girls in the Turkish bath, where all the action now was placed. A striptease was performed by a well-rounded actress named Eve La Bouche. Still, said Hobe. (*V*), the production was "practically pure narcotic. Not even snicker-hungry patrons get more than an occasional kick out of it."

GOODBYE AGAIN [Dramatic Revival*] A: Allan Scott and George Haight; D: Marjorie Maynard; S: Tom Adrian Cracraft; P: Mary Elizabeth Sherwood; T: New Amsterdam Roof Theatre (OB); 11/9/43 (8)

The second production of Mary Elizabeth Sherwood's attempt to create a local stock company was this revival of a 1932 hit farce that had starred Osgood Perkins as Kenneth Bixby and first brought James Stewart to notice in a tiny part. The secretary, Anne Rogers, was now played by Barbara Coburn, Jim Boles played the Perkins role, Julia Wilson was taken by Camelia Campbell, her simpleton spouse was Gordon Nelson, and David Lewis was the lawyer.

The show, which was cast with unknown professionals and produced on a shoestring, was little more than a competent stock-company production; it missed the high-power talents of its original cast. Louis Kronenberger (*PM*) contended, "It is still a pleasant little comedy, but the band of actors that Miss Sherwood has gathered let it down badly. They go at it in a deliberate and often mechanical fashion; they fail to give the comedy the lift and dash of personality it needs to make it live entertainment." The stock company, which previously had produced *The Petrified Forest*, came to an end with this venture.

GOODBYE, MY FANCY [Comedy/Journalism/Politics/Romance/University/Youth] A: Fay Kanin; D: Sam Wanamaker; S/L: Donald Oenslager; C: Emeline Roche; P: Michael Kanin i/a/w Richard Aldrich and Richard Myers; T: Morosco Theatre; 11/17/48 (446)

This smash-hit comedy--one of the ten best plays of the season--was written by playwright-director Garson Kanin's sister-in-law and produced by his brother. The play--a comedy of political ideas--made good use of the services of such major talents as Madeleine Carroll (the English star, in her American debut), Shirley Booth, Sam Wanamaker, and Conrad Nagel.

Carroll played Agatha Reed, a liberal American congresswoman, who, despite having been expelled twenty years earlier from Good Hope College, Massachusetts, has agreed to accept, at the 1948 commencement exercises, an honorary degree from the institution, for which she bears a deep nostalgic fondness. She also still carries a torch for the college president, James Merrill (Nagel), her first love. Merrill, however, has become a platitudinous, faded liberal, and his kowtowing to the school's reactionary trustees reveals him to be without the courage of his convictions. Agatha's politics include her belief that the government should ratify the Sermon on the Mount as a means to survive in the harsh modern world. Romance blossoms and it looks like the pair will wed. Another liberal, Matt Cole (Wanamaker), a *Life* photographer in a shabby tweed jacket, is also on the scene. He was a one-night stand of Agatha's in Paris during the war (when she was a famous war correspondent) and tries to break into the relationship of the politician and the college president. Agatha has brought along a film about the horrors of war, but Merrill--fearful of upsetting the trustees, whose war-industry funds are necessary to the school's well-being--refuses to let the students see it. His spinelessness thus becomes as clear to Agatha as it has been to his own daughter (Bethel Leslie). Despite Merrill's belated decision to risk his job by showing the film, Agatha gives him up to marry the *Life* photographer.

Despite its dubious pretensions to being a thesis play, there was much here to enjoy on a nonintellectual level. "Mrs. Kanin is not stuffy about her thesis," reported Brooks Atkinson (*NYT*). "On the contrary, she is very droll and amusing." Robert Garland (*NYJA*) thought that Kanin had "written an ardent, adult play with laughter on the surface and, underneath, a fierce, almost frightening cry for common-sense." John Mason Brown (*SR*) conceded that "the issues in *Goodbye, My Fancy* have no other choice than to be diluted and to take the form of entertainment, amusing if synthetic, and cannily contrived with an eye to the box-office."

Carroll captured many critical hearts by her lovely appearance and charming performance, but Booth, as a wisecracking secretary, nearly stole the play from her. Also in the cast were Lillian Foster, Eda Heinemann, George Mitchell, Lulu Mae Hubbard, Tom Donovan, and Joseph Boland, among others.

GOOSE FOR THE GANDER, A [Comedy/Marriage/Sex] A: Harold J. Kennedy; D: Tommy Ward; S: Frederick Fox; C: (gowns) Valentina; P: Jules J. Leventhal and Frank McCoy; T: Playhouse; 1/23/45 (15)

Gloria Swanson, glamorous film star, made her Broadway debut in this "callow, sophomoric ineptitude" (Burton Rascoe [*NYWT*]). The play had been written at Swanson's request when, having worked in a touring production with Harold J. Kennedy, she made a deal with him. According to Kennedy's *No Pickle, No Performance*, she told him that if he locked himself in his hotel room to write from 11 A.M. to 6 P.M. every day, she would come by in the evenings and take him to any nightclub, restaurant, or theatre he desired. This was an offer he could not refuse.

She played Katherine Richardson, wife for ten years of David (Conrad Nagel). One day she returns from the milk farm to their Greenwich, Connecticut, home to discover her husband eating breakfast with the negligéed young Suzy (Maxine Stuart). Determined to teach her cheating mate a lesson, she invites three of her former swains, banker Jonathan (John Clubley), athlete Wally (David Tyrrell), and sophisticate Tony (Harold J. Kennedy, the author, who had the best lines) for a weekend get-together, with Suzy asked to hang around to help out. Things don't go quite as swimmingly as she planned, especially when, with all her clothes on, she has to rescue the athlete from drowning in the pool, but she and David are reconciled--he was never really unfaithful--by the end of act three.

Louis Kronenberger (*PM*) lamented that the stars had "been pitched into a comedy with an ancient plot and been left stranded among the author's desperate and unceasing witticisms." Swanson's stage technique left much to be desired, as she shifted moods distractingly, although she wore a succession of smashing outfits and looked terrific. Choo-Choo Johnson played a glamour-girl telegraph messenger.

Choo Choo Johnson was a statuesque blond showgirl who, wrote Kennedy, "had the most monumental frontal equipment I have ever seen. They used to come on stage like headlights seconds before she got there." Her role was inspired by the wartime unavailability of Western Union messengers. The character saw an ad for messengers and decided to use the service for her own purposes. Delivering messages only to rich men, she would arrive with the telegram tucked deep inside her cleavage. A huge laugh would be garnered when she announced, "I'm from Western Union," and Kennedy's character, looking her over in amazement, would respond, "What hath God wrought?" At one performance, however, Kennedy noticed a glazed look on her face that signalled a lapse of memory, even though she had only a few lines. He soon realized that what she had forgotten was her prop telegram, without which the play could not proceed, as Kennedy had to read the contents to Swanson in order to wrap up the play. Unable to do anything but hope for the best, he improvised, "You give me that telegram." "There's nothing there," she said, looking deep down between her breasts. This caused such a loud outburst of laughter that it gave the actress a chance to get back on track. As the laughter died down, she ad-libbed, "I forgot the telegram, but I remember what it said." She then recited the entire telegram from memory, "tied up all the loose ends of the play, brought the curtain down happily, and got the audience safely into the bars by eleven o'clock."

GRANDMA'S DIARY [Comedy/Broadcasting/Marriage/Military/Romance/Sex] A/D: Albert Wineman Barker; S/L: Raymond Sovey; P: American Theatre Group; T: Henry Miller's Theatre; 9/22/48 (6)

One of those plays about which critics argued as to whether it was the worst play they had ever seen. Howard Barnes (*NYHT*) termed it "a windy and witless contemplation of a postwar romantic imbroglio. Since the acting and direction are on a par with the writing, every one is even in this hapless enterprise." Thomas R. Dash (*WWD*) was outraged by "the most preposterous situations, the most wooden dialog and the most amateurish acting." The piece attempted to offer some satirical thrusts at radio along with its story of marital difficulties.

Army captain Peter (Herbert Evers) returns home from occupied Japan with his mistress Alice (Eileen Price), an army nurse, to learn that his wife Linda (Gertrude Rozan), a radio soap-opera writer, has been carrying on with a crooner (George Neise) appearing on her show. Linda's scripts are based on her reading of her grandma's diary. The action concerns the straightening out of these romantic entanglements, which end with the reconciliation of the husband and wife and the potential nuptials of the crooner and the nurse.

The cast included Augustus Smith, Leonard Elliott, and Robert E. Griffin.

GREAT BIG DOORSTEP, THE [Comedy/Family/Religion/Romance/Rural/Southern/Youth] A: Frances Goodrich and Albert Hackett; SC: the novel of the same name by E. P. O'Donnell; D/P: Herman Shumlin; S/L: Howard Bay; T: Morosco Theatre; 11/26/42 (28)

This comedy about a poor Louisiana Cajun family ran only a month, but it was greeted by many critics with heartfelt appreciation. George Freedley (*NYMT*) called it "the most engaging piece of Americana to drift into the theater in a dog's age," Wilella Waldorf (*NYP*) wrote that it "starts mildly, but becomes steadily funnier and more beguiling as it goes on," and Burton Rascoe (*NYWT*) strongly recommended it over the Lunt-Fontanne hit, *The Pirate*, that had opened a night earlier. Still, there were serious drawbacks, as Howard Barnes (*NYHT*) noted in pointing to the fact that "the plot gets in the way of the proceedings as often as it expedites them. The dialogue is frequently dull and characters disappear before you even become acquainted with them." John Anderson (*NYJA*) added that there was "not enough life in the comedy . . . to keep more than a few stray passages from anemic collapse." Still, there was considerable enjoyment of the flavorsome Cajun speech, the expert direction, the colorful characters, the picturesquely realistic set, and the generally convincing acting.

Commodore Crotchet (Louis Calhern) is a shiftless, bragging backwoodsman too lazy to succeed at anything, even his old WPA job. Mrs. Crotchet (Dorothy Gish) is a more stable individual, and there is a nice crop of Crotchet kids. One of them is an adolescent girl (Jeanne Perkins Smith) who, having lost her barber boyfriend (Ralph Bell), seeks a mate through the lovelorn columns of the newspapers. Another younger adolescent daughter (Joy Geffen) is similarly romantically inclined, although she has a strong vocation for becoming a nun. There are also a pair of adorable twin boys (Dickie Monahan and Gerald Matthews) and a teenage son (Jack Mann). The commodore's brother (Clay Clement), an inebriated river pilot, figures in the plot, as does a tightwad, rent-demanding landlord (Nat Burns). When the Mississippi floods, a beautiful marble doorstep comes floating down the river from someone's mansion and stops before the Crotchet's run-down shack. Crotchet is motivated to obtain a house to surround the doorstep, and the rest of the action details the efforts of himself and his kin to get their dream house (it is located next door and is being sold for taxes) without benefit of actual labor. At one point the pilot gives Crotchet a $100 check, which seems to solve all their problems, but the check bounces after the family has practically moved into a new house. The money is finally raised by the prayerful Mrs. Crotchet, whose penchant for raising lilies ultimately proves to be a profitable pastime.

As the Crotchet parents, Louis Calhern and Dorothy Gish, especially the latter, found highly suitable roles for their distinguished talents. Rascoe said that Gish was "a Kajun [*sic*] woman to the life, even to the Delta accent and way of talking . . . and she is appealing and naturalistic in every shade of feeling, from anger to solicitude, from inebriated joy to tragic disappointment."

GREAT CAMPAIGN, THE [Drama/Politics/Religion/Rural] A: Arnold Sundgaard; M: Alex North; D: Joseph Losey (w/Helen Tamiris); CH: Anna Sokolow; S: Robert Davison; C: Rose Bogdanoff; P: T. Edward Hambleton for the Experimental Theatre; T: Princess Theatre; 3/30/47 (5)

A fanciful political yarn produced with infusions of prairie-style music, square dancing, and choral singing. Although the stylized work began very promisingly, said Brooks Atkinson (*NYT*), with its affirmative view of the American people, its second act proved disappointing when it settled "down into a fairly literal narrative of a political swindle." "It is obvious in conception and clumsy in construction," declared the even less impressed George Freedley (*NYMT*). The "only intermittently interesting" (Richard Watts, Jr. [*NYP*]) piece mingled various theatrical conventions, from burlesque to satire to vaudeville with selective realism. Occasionally imaginative in its use of telescoped events and archetypal characters, it also fell into the trap of obviousness.

Sundgaard's satire is set in various midwestern locales, beginning in rural Minnesota, to which a group of religious crusaders have come seeking to participate in the end of the world. Returning home when the world survives, they learn a good deal about political campaigning. One of their number, the simpleminded Sam Trellis (Millard Mitchell), an Ohio farmer, decides to run for president as a people's candidate against the crooked machine candidate Wallie P. Hale (Robert P. Lieb). (Neither is nominated via a convention.) Sam's son Jeff (Thomas Coley) sides with Hale's campaign, and there follows a detailed depiction of how dirty politics manages to gain the election for Hale. Jeff steals his father's big speech, which Hale--standing hypocritically on his rival's platform--uses to sweep the election. By the time the play ends, the "people" have realized how their ideals have been stolen and they have been tricked, and they vow to change things in the future.

The large cast included Kay Loring, Frances Waller, John O'Shaughnessy, Ray Boyle, Paul Bain, Glen Tetley, and Erik Rhodes.

GREAT TO BE ALIVE! [Musical/Crime/Death/Fantasy/Mystery/Romance/Sex] B: Walter Bullock and Sylvia Regan; M: Abraham Ellstein; LY: Walter Bullock; D: Mary Hunter; CH: Helen Tamiris; DS: Stewart Chaney; P: Vinton Freedley i/a/w Anderson Lawler and Russell Markert; T: Winter Garden; 3/23/50 (52)

A haunted old Pennsylvania mansion was the beautifully designed setting for this ho-hum musical *cum* mystery-farce starring Vivienne Segal and Stuart Erwin. Erwin was retiring botanist Woodrow Twigg. Woodrow, a descendent of the original owners, lives in the mansion and is able to see and chat with its ghosts, which are visible only to virgins. Segal was Mrs. Leslie Butterfield, a wealthy New York divorcée to whom Woodrow sells the place. She, in turn, redoes the place in order to present it as a wedding gift to her niece Carol (Martha Wright), who is marrying Vince (Mark Dawson). The ghosts include a girl (Bambi Linn) whose fiancé (Rod Alexander) was killed at Gettysburg and a sophisticated matriarch (Valerie Bettis), who has various methods of chasing away living people. The ghosts do not want their home turned over to mortals and will do what they can to prevent it. Woodrow's sale of the mansion, however, will enable the spirits of the Civil War girl and her beau to finally get married--after eighty-seven years--by participating in the nuptials of Carol and Vince. In the course of the action, three people die and join the ghostly inhabitants. Woodrow is suspected of killing them, but the ghosts--promised that the house will be theirs alone and not the mortals'--help in uncovering the true killer, and Woodrow and Mrs. Butterfield fall in love. The mansion is left to the spirits, who, at the end, can no longer be seen by Woodrow.

Book and music problems were the major source of this old-fashioned show's failure, as it was beautifully produced, was excellently choreographed and danced (especially by Bettis, who also revealed acting talent), and had some entertainingly spooky numbers. "The book becomes attenuated and confusing, while Mary Hunter's staging of it is on the patchwork side," argued Howard Barnes (*NYHT*). "The humor is for the most part witless," thought Lewis Funke (*NYT*). "The music," responded Robert Coleman (*NYDM*), "is tuneful, undistinguished and reminiscent." In the company were Ken Carroll, David Nillo, Lulu Bates, Russel Nype, Don Kennedy, and, in the chorus, future acting star Janice Rule and Swen Swenson.

GREENER GRASS, THE [Drama/Blacks/Films/Race] A: Edward Davidson; D: Warren Coleman and Frank Wilson; S: Mannert Hubern; P/T: Actors Studio (OB); 4/4/50

The Actors Studio involved in this nearly overlooked production was not the famous workshop for Method actors, but a Harlem group doing plays on black themes. In this case, it offered a drama about a black movie actress who kills herself after it is discovered that she has been passing for white. *V* said that the "play . . . loses effectiveness through its tendency to lean a little too heavily on soap-box oratory."

Zaida Coles played the actress, but Claudia McNeill, still unknown, took top honors for her acting of the small role of a manicurist. William Hairston, Greg Hunter, and Kenneth Hibbert also were in the play.

GUEST IN THE HOUSE [Drama/Art/Family/Illness/Romance/Rural/Youth] A: Hagar Wilde and Dale Eunson; SC: Katherine Albert's novel of the same name; D: Reginald Denham; S: Raymond Sovey; P: Stephan and Paul Ames; T: Plymouth Theatre; 2/24/42 (153)

Into a cheerful Connecticut household, in which live the well-adjusted Proctors, Douglas (Leon Ames) and Ann (Louise Campbell), with their ten-year-old daughter Lee (Joan Spencer), comes a young woman relative named Evelyn Heath (Mary Anderson, in her Broadway debut). Motherless, sixteen-year-old Evelyn complains of heart trouble, and the sympathetic Proctors (he's an artist) agree to take her in while she recovers amid the natural surroundings of their country home. There resides in Evelyn a streak of extreme cruelty, and soon she conspires to set Douglas and his model, Miriam Blake (Pert Kelton), at odds with one another. In addition, she constantly rings a bell to demand attention from the harried maid, Hilda (Hildred Price); ceaselessly plays a recording of "Liebestraum"; drives Douglas to the bottle when he begins to lose contracts; causes a rift between the Proctors; leads Ann to grow morose and jealous and to border on a breakdown; influences young Lee to become a neurotic with symptoms like her own; and so on, until the truth about Evelyn begins to emerge. The death of her father, however, makes it difficult to evict her. Finally, Aunt Martha (Katherine Emmett), mother of the young man (William Prince) whom Evelyn is trapping into marriage, plays upon her fears of a bird presumably freed from its cage and induces her to have a heart attack.

Some critics playfully suggested that the mordant play reminded them of a cross between *The Children's Hour** and *The Man Who Came to Dinner**. Otherwise, they generally lauded the melodramatic work as being appropriately dire, but hardly pleasant entertainment. The character of Evelyn was considered one of the most hateful shown on a Broadway stage in years and one that the audience was glad to see receive her just rewards. Mary Anderson was highly praised for the malevolence of her characterization. A few thought the piece properly gripping, despite dramaturgic flaws, Brooks Atkinson (*NYT*), for example, declaring, "Shrewdly written, dextrously acted, it is likely to give you the horrors." Kelcey Allen (*WWD*) stated, "Although the story is at times hard to believe, it is packed with drama which holds your interest." Less favorable was Rosamond Gilder's (*TAM*) response: "*Guest in the*

House is theatrical as well as psychological buncombe, drawn crudely enough to attract novelty-seekers but without the justification of character analysis or the beguilements of humor." Louis Kronenberger (*PM*) agreed, calling it "essentially a lurid and overextended piece of trash." Frieda Altman and Richard Barbee were cast members.

GYPSY LADY [Musical/Period/Romance/Theatre] B: Henry Myers; M: Victor Herbert; LY: Herbert B. Smith (ADD.LY: Robert Wright and George Forrest); SC: Victor Herbert and Henry B. Smith's operettas, *The Fortune Teller* (1898) and *Serenade* (1897); D: Robert Wright and George Forrest w/Lew Kesler; CH: Aida Broadbent; S: Boris Aronson; C: Miles White; L: Adrian Awan; P: Edwin Lester; T: Century Theatre; 9/17/46 (79)

Two famous Herbert-Smith operettas were pillaged for their scores to support a new operetta libretto for which the tunes were reorchestrated by Arthur Kay to reflect contemporary musical tastes. The musical portions charmed audiences, but most found the rest of the show uninspired. *Gypsy Lady* premiered in San Francisco before trekking eastward.

Myers's new book was a derivative thing in the Ruritanian tradition. Alvarado (John Tyers) is a handsome actor who wants to wed the marquise of Ronce-Valle, Valerie (Doreen Wilson), but whose nonaristocratic heritage is frowned on by her father, the duke (Joseph Macaulay). Alvarado thereupon convinces the gypsy princess Musetta (Helena Bliss) to impersonate a royal princess and to marry the marquis, André (Gilbert Russell), Valerie's brother. Ballet master Fresco (Jack Goode) is persuaded to teach her the royal graces. Meanwhile, Musetta's gypsy chieftain father, Boris (Melville Cooper), also impersonating royalty, takes every opportunity to benefit from his new status. Ultimately, Alvarado falls for Musetta himself, but she rejects both him and André in order to marry her original gypsy lover, Sandor (George Britton).

The best liked of the old songs included "I Love You, I Adore You," "Romany Life," "Keepsakes," "Gypsy Love Song," and "Springtide." George Freedley (*NYMT*) dismissed the show as "an unqualified bore," and Brooks Atkinson (*NYT*) called it "nonsense" that had to be endured simply to hear some "pleasant melodies." But George Jean Nathan (*TBY*) celebrated the music for being "as charming as ever" and congratulated the performers, especially Bliss, for their singing. While rejecting the "facetious" new book, Nathan nonetheless believed that it "at least permits us for all its heavy winks pleasantly to recall a musical show era . . . in which heroines sang of fragrant romance instead, as nowadays, about doin' things that come natchu'lly or shooting a male in the tail [as in *Annie Get Your Gun*]." The extremely positive William Hawkins (*NYWT*) saluted the show for being "a lusty, vigorous musical. . . . It is funny and colorful and its music soars with gusto."

Clarence Derwent played a comical owner of a ballet school. Val Valentinoff was the chief male dancer, partnered by Patricia Sims. Kaye Connor and Suzette Meredith were among others involved.

H

(1) H.M.S. PINAFORE, OR THE LASS THAT LOVED A SAILOR and **"TRIAL BY JURY"** [Musical Revival*] B/LY: W. S. Gilbert; M: Arthur Sullivan; D: R. H. Burnside; P: Boston Comic Opera Company and the Messrs. Shubert; T: St. James Theatre; 1/21/42 (18)

Part of a series of Gilbert and Sullivan revivals. Paired with *Pinafore* was a ballet performed by the Joos Ballet Company. The Joos contribution on opening night was its well-known "The Green Table" ballet.

Pinafore was competently done, Brooks Atkinson (*NYT*) declaring, "It makes few pretenses, gives a compact performance of its job, omits the innumerable encores which are the curse of Gilbert and Sullivan and goes on its way." Florenz Ames was Sir Joseph Porter, Bertram Peacock was Captain Corcoran, Morton Bowe was Ralph Rackstraw, Robert Pitkin was Dick Deadeye, Kathleen Roche was Josephine, and Helen Lanvin was Buttercup.

On 2/28/42 "Trial by Jury" joined *Pinafore* as a curtain raiser and was given seven times. Florenz Ames was the judge, Mary Roche the plaintiff, Bertram Peacock the counsel for the plaintiff, Phillip Tully the defendant, Frederic Persson the foreman, and Robert Pitkin the usher.

(2) D: R. H. Burnside; P: R. H. Burnside i/a/w the Gilbert and Sullivan Opera Company; T: Ambassador Theatre; 2/14/44 (7)

A revival of the same bill by the renamed Boston Comic Opera Company, with a number of the same performers back in the roles they had played in 1942. It was a shabby presentation, with Catherine Judah a middling Buttercup and James Gerard equally poor in the role of Ralph Rackstraw. The production lacked spirit, and the sets and costumes were meagre looking. "The troupe did very badly indeed," announced Lewis Nichols (*NYT*).

In 1945 there were two new musicals adapted from *Pinafore*. See *Memphis Bound!* and *Hollywood Pinafore*.

(3) and **"COX AND BOX"** D: Anna Bethell; P: D'Oyly Carte Opera Company; T: Century Theatre; 1/19/48 (16)

H.M.S. Pinafore S: Joseph and Phil Harker; C: George Sheringham; "Cox and Box" B: F. C. Burnand and Madison Morton; M: Arthur Sullivan

This double bill was offered by England's famed Gilbert and Sullivan troupe as part of a nine-piece repertory season that totalled 136 showings. In the curtain raiser, Richard Dunn was Cox, Leonard Osborn was Box, and Richard Walker was Bouncer. *Pinafore* featured Martyn Green as Sir Joseph, Charles Dorning as Captain Corcoran, Thomas Round as Ralph Rackstraw, Darrell Fancourt as Dick Deadeye, Walker as Bill Bobstay, Radley Flynn was Bob Beckett, Helen Roberts as Josephine, Joan Gillingham as Hebe, and Ella Halman as Buttercup.

"No matter how many times [the company goes] through its merry course, they do it with the vigor of lusty followers of the brine," reported Lewis Funke (*NYT*).

(4) D: Dorothy Raedler; P: Masque and Lyric Light Opera Company; T: Jan Hus Playhouse (OB); 7/28/49

A group (either semiprofessional or amateur) from Elmhurst, Queens, made it across the East River to produce the work at the small theatre at 351 East Seventy-fourth Street. It was the first of a series of five nonreviewed revivals of Gilbert and Sullivan. L. C. (*NYT*) attended at least their *Pinafore* revival and contended that "they make it all appear rather easy. They sing intelligibly and with confidence." He praised them as well for their simplified and tastefully restrained direction. Singers selected for comment included Rue Knapp as Ralph Rackstraw, Wilma Robbins as Josephine, Marjorie Schloss as Buttercup, Michael Therry as Sir Joseph, and William O'Leary as Captain Corcoran.

(5) and **"TRIAL BY JURY"** D/P: S. M. Chartock; S/L: Ralph Alswang; C: Peggy Morrison; T: Mark Hellinger Theatre; 10/17/49 (8)

The last in a three-production series of Gilbert and Sullivan revivals offered by S. M. Chartock. It was considered a vast improvement over the company's earlier renderings of *The Mikado** and *The Pirates of Penzance**. The chief performers were Kathleen Roche as Josephine, Morton Bowe as Ralph, Ralph Riggs as Sir Joseph, Earle MacVeigh as Captain Corcoran, Jean Handzlik as Buttercup, and Joseph Macaulay as Dick Deadeye.

Brooks Atkinson (*NYT*) reported, "You may quibble a little over the thinness of satire in the performing. There is more grace and sweetness than asperity in this *Pinafore*."

In "Trial by Jury" Elaine Malbin sang the plaintiff, Riggs sang the judge, and Robert Eckles stood out as the usher.

HAIRPIN HARMONY [Musical/Broadcasting/Business/Music/Romance] B/M/LY/P: Harold Orlob; D: Dora Maugham; S: Donald Oenslager; C: Mahieu; L: Jeanette Hackett; T: National Theatre; 10/1/43 (3)

Harold Orlob wrote the book, music, and lyrics for this "witless, vulgar, inept and tasteless" (Lewis Nichols [*NYT*]) musical farce and also was its producer. That is one reason it was such an instant flop. It suffered many indignities during its tryout period, including a switch of directors (Carl Randall was replaced a week before the opening), and cost more money than its single set (borrowed from a flop show, *Pie in the Sky*, of two years earlier) might have suggested.

A young press agent named Bill Heller (Lennie Kent) is trying to get a sixteen-member, all-girl band and its vocalist (Maureen Cannon) onto the radio by selling them as a program for a baby-food manufacturer, Howard Swift (Carlyle Blackwell), to sponsor. The premise allowed for the female musicians to come on and off constantly to accompany the various songs and dances. There is a romance between the troupe's manager (Gil Johnson) and the vocalist. Heller tries to pass himself off to Swift as an infant in a carriage and blurts out some baby talk. This so impresses the manufacturer that he agrees to sponsor the band.

"This Harold Orlob offering is all of a piece and it is all awful," groaned Howard Barnes (*NYHT*). "The songs are neither felicitous nor corny. . . . The performing is as maladroit as the lines which the poor players are asked to mouth."

HALLAMS, THE [Drama/Broadcasting/Family/Illness/Marriage/Old Age] A/D: Rose Franken; S: Raymond Sovey; C: Bianca Strook; P: William Brown Meloney; T: Booth Theatre; 3/4/48 (12)

Although, strictly speaking, not a sequel to Rose Franken's 1932 hit, *Another Language**, this domestic drama concerns the same stuffy family. It came nowhere near the success of the first play, which ran for 348 performances.

Despite the occasional touches of sentiment and humor, said Howard Barnes (*NYHT*), "In no way do these compensate for the tedious stretches of an ill-conceived and random dramatic entertainment." Rowland Field (*NEN*) called it "more a series of character studies than a consistent, entertaining play." A few sided with

Richard Watts, Jr. (*NYP*), though, who said that the play was "a quiet, modest and almost steadily absorbing family chronicle, written, staged and acted with honesty and credibility." Most thought the author's direction mediocre.

In *The Hallams*, which did not require familiarity with the earlier work, the clannish eponymous family is examined in detail. The action displays the dominating and possessive behavior of old Mrs. Hallam (Ethel Griffies), the matriarch, who bullies the wives of her four coddled sons and who lives with her long-suffering spouse, Mr. Hallam (John McKee), ill with a weak heart. When Jerry (Dean Norton), Mrs. Hallam's tubercular grandson, returns from Saranac with his independently minded new radio writer-producer bride, Kendrick (Katharine Bard), the plot begins to thicken. Mrs. Hallam insists that the couple live with her; Kendrick insists that they live in her own apartment near the Fifty-ninth Street Bridge. The overly solicitous behavior toward Jerry of the old lady and of other relatives causes him to suffer a relapse and die. A further setback for the matriarch is the elopement of a granddaughter with a Jewish physician. Another son, Harry (Frank M. Thomas), is dying of cancer, and son Victor (Alan Baxter) plans to marry a widow. These blows are deflected by the staunch old lady, who will survive, come hell or high water.

The fine cast included Mildred Dunnock, Royal Beal, June Walker, Mildred Wall, and Matt Briggs, but everyone selected Ethel Griffies as their special favorite.

(1) **HAMLET** [Dramatic Revival*] A: William Shakespeare; D: Bernard Kay; P: Equity Library Theatre; T: Muhlenberg Branch of the New York Public Library (OB); 7/3/44

The first revival of *Hamlet* in the forties was only a partial one, being selected scenes staged by the showcase company sponsored by Equity. The entire action of the tragedy was encompassed by the use of a narrator filling in the gaps between the scenes presented. Excellent background music played over a speaker system accompanied the performance.

Director Kay took over the role of Hamlet at the last minute when the original player was unable to go on. "Frankly, he is not an ideal choice for Hamlet," acknowledged George Freedley (*NYMT*), the only critic to write about it, "but his reading of the part and ideas of staging and portrayal were extremely interesting."

Kay's company was drawn largely from the Paul Robeson production of *Othello**, in which Kay had a small role. Freedley was especially fond of the closet scene, in which an Oedipal conflict was explored between Hamlet and Gertrude (Vergel Cook), and which reminded the critic of the Arthur Hopkins-John Barrymore interpretation of the scene. Robert Sosman played Claudius, Graham Velsey was Polonius, William Weyse was Laertes, John Gerstad was Horatio, and Margaret Coates was Ophelia. "She was lovely and young and innocent . . . and managed to be modern in the best sense of the word," thought Freedley.

(2) M: Roger Adams; D: George Schaefer; S: Frederick Stover; C: Irene Sharaff; P: Michael Todd; T: Columbus Circle Theatre; 12/13/45 (131)

Maurice Evans, who had starred in a highly successful, uncut *Hamlet* under Margaret Webster's direction in 1938, returned to Broadway in a vigorous new production staged by George Schaefer and once more scored a hit. This eye-catching revival had first seen the light as a touring package shown to the American forces in the Pacific during World War II; it thus was known as the "GI *Hamlet*." The title was thought up by master showman Michael Todd, who, in putting the play on Broadway, stepped somewhat out of his usual line as a producer of brassy musicals featuring scantily clad showgirls. Actually, Evans--whose wartime duties had taken him away from Broadway for four years--was given complete authority as producer by the trusting Todd. Evans had feared that there would be a cold reception to his fourth New York *Hamlet* and was delighted to find himself warmly welcomed. The combined total of performances given by this new version in New York and on the road came to a hefty 425. As seen at the somewhat out-of-the-way Columbus Circle Theatre, it was "a swift-moving, cleanly blocked-out, palpably shortened version," according to Louis Kronenberger (*PM*).

The look was early nineteenth century, helping to bring the piece closer to a contemporary sensibility without its becoming too immediately realistic. This choice was fairly novel for Broadway, but similar approaches had been tried before elsewhere. Evans and his associates had chosen the specific period to make the story more comprehensible to GI audiences. A period in which men wore swords was essential, so the idea of Mittel-Europa in the early nineteenth century seemed appropriate. This also provided a world in which a decadent, military court would seem acceptable. References to the ghost's (Victor Thorley) armor were removed.

Evans's romantic, extroverted, unneurotic, virile, and soldierlike Hamlet suggested Lord Byron. He was a dominant figure in a landscape backed, aside from several exceptions, by lesser Shakespearean talents. He was appreciated for his charisma and his clarity of speech and intention, although some found him occasionally too superficially rhetorical and emotionally cool. Sarcasm, wit, and contemptuousness were more in view than emotional or intellectual depth. The interpretation emphasized Hamlet's complete sanity and revealed that his multifariously diverse reactions to the people surrounding him are "those of any normal and intelligent man placed in like positions" (George Jean Nathan [*TBY*]). John Mason Brown (*SR*) wrote that Evans's "voice is one of the finest musical instruments of our time. He does not so much read Shakespeare as release him. . . . He is that rarity among modern players, an actor who is able to act; who loves to do so; and who makes us rejoice in his acting."

Hungarian-accented Lili Darvas was not completely successful as Gertrude, nor was Frances Reid as Ophelia, while Thomas Chalmers's middle-aged, protocol-obsessed Polonius, Thomas Gomez's portly Claudius (looking like Edward VII), Emmett Rogers's Laertes, and Walter Coy's Horatio were adequate.

Responses to the costumes of Irene Sharaff, who garbed the women in evening gowns, and the sets of Frederick Stover, who allowed for the swift movement of the scenes, were mixed. Stover's set was described by Euphemia Van Rensselaer Wyatt (*CW*): "The solid architectural set is of the feudal hall with a glimpse of a Victorian drawing-room through folding doors; stone steps raise half the stage to a higher level, and cleverly contrived curtains, backdrops and lighting offer quick variety. One small corner of the stage lit up with an ivied French window creates a sitting-room for Ophelia. . . . For the Players and the duel, the hall is transformed with a backdrop into the Castle courtyard, showing the modernized wings of the palace." The Players themselves were dressed for their play within the play as the king, queen, and jack in a deck of cards.

Among the production's novel touches were the elimination of Ophelia's flowers during her mad scene, her prop being instead a children's alphabet book with illustrations that allowed her to point to the pictures of the flowers as she went from character to character. Instead of a single ghost, two were used, so that, with the aid of carefully timed lighting cues and perfectly aimed pinspots, the efforts to stop it on the battlements were baffled by the ghost's seeming to magically disappear and then appear again somewhere else in the blink of an eye. According to

Evans's *All This . . . and Evans Too!*, Alan Shayne, the actor playing the ghost's double (he also understudied Evans and played Fortinbras), was lit only from the neck up and wore for a costume just a cloak draped around his shoulders. One night, when the timing on the lights was off, the actor was revealed in his entirety, his cloak open down the front to show him standing there in his jockey shorts.

The cuts were heavy, among them the entire gravediggers' scene and that of Ophelia's death. The excisions sped the action along and gave the play a melodramatic quality. "The result," applauded Brown, "is a wonderfully exciting show, even if it is *Hamlet* with a large part of *Hamlet* left out." Evans has argued that the graveyard scene seems to fit very poorly into the play's dramatic structure because Horatio, inexplicably, never tells Hamlet beforehand of Ophelia's death, and also because, only a few lines after the scene, Hamlet is talking jauntily about his English adventure and giving Osric (Morton da Costa) a ribbing. In the company were Howard Morris as Rosencrantz, and Ray Walston (in his Broadway debut) as a courtier.

(3) [Return Engagement] T: City Center of Music and Drama; 6/3/46 (16)

A popular-priced, limited engagement showing of the Evans production, following its national tour. "As before," noted Robert Garland (*NYJA*), "it is a steaming, fiery, turbulent, electrifying, mettlesome, ebullient and obstreperous interpretation." However, Garland thought that the otherwise brilliant Evans had begun to lapse into the "elocutionary" in his readings, and that he was sometimes guilty of expressing sound before meaning. The major cast changes were Harry Sheppard's assumption of Polonius (played as a "conventional doddering clown," said Robert Coleman [*NYDM*]) and Whit Connor's of Horatio.

(4) M: Rosabel Watson; D: Donald Wolfit and Christopher Ede; S: Donald Wolfit and Eric Adeney; P: Hall Shelton b/a/w Advance Players Association, Ltd., of London; T: Century Theatre; 2/26/47 (2)

The last production in the five-play series (including *King Lear**, *As You Like It**, *The Merchant of Venice**, and *Volpone**) offered by the visiting Donald Wolfit Repertory Company of England, helmed by actor-manager Wolfit. Like its predecessors, it was found sorely wanting. "It is an exceptionally poor performance and production," lamented Kahn. (*V*).

One of the few positive features was a setting that allowed for rapid scene shifts and that incorporated a lengthy flight of stairs. Aesthetically, however, it consisted of backgrounds "of dull rudimentary design and substance, [with] no dignity nor pictorial value," according to Rowland Field (*NEN*).

Wolfit was at sea as Hamlet, being too mature for the role and far too physically bulky. His acting was overblown, bombastic, excessively external, and reminiscent of old-time stock actors. "He gives a strange performance of Hamlet," noted Ward Morehouse (*NYS*). "Certainly a tedious one. He hasn't the magnetism for the role. In moments he is over-deliberate and in others he is too hurried, getting wildly out of control. He is interesting in a few scenes, but too often is just hammy."

His leading lady, Rosalind Iden, was almost as disappointing as Ophelia, and even lesser work was offered by Alexander Gauge as Claudius, John Wynyard as Horatio, Eric Adeney as the ghost, Kempster Barnes as Laertes, Violet Farebrother as Gertrude, and Eric Maxon as Polonius. The latter was "an aged, infirm fellow who reminds one somewhat of a Hollywood cracker-barrel character," wrote Lewis Funke (*NYT*).

(5) D: Robert Eley; S: Janet Owen; C: Jimmy McElwain and Maxine Jaysen; P: New York Repertory Group; T: Cherry Lane Theatre (OB); 12/3/49

An effective shoestring production using a single stool, two tables, three chairs, and four projections. It was "a young and zestful reproduction," said Robert Garland (*NYJA*).

Bill Butler played Hamlet. George Freedley (*NYMT*) declared that his "performance is not yet a fully realized one. Frequently he hurries his lines inordinately, even beyond this concept of his, of a nervous, erratic prince. It is a tenable approach to the part and one which I found fascinating. Most of his soliloquies are relatively untouched, though lines here and there are as well read and as completely thought out as I have encountered in any other Hamlet." Brooks Atkinson (*NYT*) saw flashes of excellence in Butler, especially in the lines to the first player and in the scene in Gertrude's chamber, but felt what he did not bring his ability to the role in a consistent way.

Apart from Butler, there was very little acting to praise. Atkinson blamed the troupe for dull speaking. He said that they played the piece "as though it were a somber conversation," with the actors "swallowing their words, rushing their lines and behaving as though they were telling an interesting story to some intimate friends over a cocktail in a well-bred bar." He was especially distressed because so much of the staging and decor was exciting and effective.

The cast included Grace Holtby as Gertrude, Jack Burkhart as Claudius, Arthur Lewis as Polonius, James Winslow as Laertes, David F. Perkins as the ghost and first player, Enid Pulver as Ophelia, and, in what were among their earliest local appearances, William Hickey as Francisco and the player prologue and Anthony Franciosa as Horatio.

HAND IN GLOVE [Drama/Boarding House/Crime/Mental Illness/Mystery/Sex] A: Charles K. Freeman and Gerald Savory; SC: Gerald Savory's novel, *Hughie Roddis*; D: James Whale; S/L: Samuel Leve; C: Bob Davison; P: Arthur Edison; T: Playhouse; 12/4/44 (40)

A lurid, but "fairly routine" (Louis Kronenberger [*PM*]) psychological thriller set in Yorkshire, England, and dealing with a psychopathic killer named Charlie Ramskill (George Lloyd). It was not a true mystery play because the killer was known from early on (his first murder is shown in a prologue). What mystery there was lay in discovering how Ramskill would be caught.

Charlie Ramskill is a handsome shipyard worker who dons a trench coat and white suede gloves as he prowls the wharfs to kill and mutilate pretty young women, which he does as a neurotic response to his sexual impotence. The murderer takes up residence at Auntie B.'s (Isobel Elsom) boarding house. Auntie B. has a hapless young nephew, Hughie (Skelton Knaggs), a drooling half-wit who likes to wander at night. The sly killer decides to shift the blame for his misdeeds to the young moron. When it seems likely that the guilt will be placed on poor Hughie's head, a shrewd detective from Scotland (Aubrey Mather) arrives to figure things out and nab the true assassin.

Some critics felt uncomfortable in the presence of the too naturalistically depicted imbecile, whose portrayal as the scapegoat seemed in bad taste. Others thought that two mental cases in one play was more than they could bear. It was also noted that Ramskill's guilt was practically written on his face and that the inspector took too long to see it. At the same time, the play had a certain fascination in its grotesqueness and was better than others of its class that recently had seen the light. Lewis Nichols (*NYT*) could say, therefore, "The play . . . is not the greatest one ever written, being as full of holes as circumstantial evidence, but it does hold the interest." The cast included St. Clair Bayfield, Robert Craven, Jean Bellows, Islay Benson, Wallace Widdecombe, Victor Beecroft, and Viola Roache.

HAPPIEST YEARS, THE [Comedy/Family/Marriage/Science/Small Town/University/Youth] A: Thomas Coley and William Roerick; D: James Neilson; S/L: James Russell; P: Gertrude Macy; T: Lyceum Theatre; 4/25/49 (8)

This "painfully dull" (Lewis Funke [*NYT*]) vehicle for Peggy Wood was set in a small midwestern college town at the home of the Graves family. Whitney Bolton (*NYMT*) commented that it "suffers from molasses and glacier troubles. It tends to sweeten up at the wrong moment and to move with fairly tedious slowness. It starts slow, it ends slow and in between it has moments of the most casual do-nothingness available this waning season." Richard Watts, Jr. (*NYP*), called it "a comedy in which the central situation and the leading character are excessively tiresome and the minor incidents and lesser characters are fresh and agreeable."

Bertram Graves (Richard Bishop) is the college bursar. His daughter Martha (Judy Parrish) is married to Richard Johnson (Douglass Watson), a veteran studying for his chemistry degree on the GI Bill. There is a pretty science student named Joan (Louise Horton) who studies with Richard, and who is suspected by Bertram's foolishly suspicious, somewhat nitwitted wife Clara (Wood) of being a threat to her daughter's marriage. Her meddling leads to various complications, but Joan turns out to be a quite innocent scholar and the Johnsons patch up their misunderstanding.

The piece wasted several fine performances, such as those by Loring Smith and June Walker as Bertram's jocular traveling-salesman brother and his wife, and by old-timer Jessie Busley as a cheerful librarian who resides upstairs.

HAPPILY EVER AFTER [Comedy/Journalism/Marriage/Politics/Religion/Romance/Small Town] A: Donald Kirkley and Howard Burman; D: Crane Wilbur; S: Watson Barratt; P: Bernard Klawans and Victor Payne-Jennings; T: Biltmore Theatre; 3/15/45 (12)

Broadway's theatres were experiencing a shortage in the boom time of 1945, largely because of a glut of innocuous fluff like this. It starred Gene Lockhart as

Reverend Homer Whatcoat, a marrying parson of Elkton, Maryland, who is on the brink of tying the knot for his 10,000th couple, with all the attendant publicity to be generated by newsreel cameras and reporters. One of the reporters, Alec Dixon (Warren Douglas), learns that the parson is a phony with a medicine-show background and has never been ordained, leaving all 9,999 couples who have been processed through his marriage mill unmarried and their 40,000 to 50,000 children bastards. To expose the charlatan, Alec marries his coreporter, Rita Collins (Margaret Hayes), who wanted to wed him all along despite his reluctance. It turns out that the marriage is legal after all because of the discovery--to the parson's surprise as well as everyone else's--that many years earlier, while engaged as handyman and witness for another cleric, he was himself ordained a deacon in a sect of the Protestant church. The news unites the reporters in connubial bliss and also knocks a local crusader (Hans Robert), who wanted to exploit the story for his own political benefit, for a loop. At the end, the parson delivers a sentimental monologue on the virtues of married life, regardless of the ceremony that may or may not have been performed at the outset.

Lockhart's performance was satisfactorily cute and appealing, and his actual wife, Kathleen Lockhart, playing his dull-witted stage wife, also proved acceptable, as did Parker Fennelly as the reverend's professional witness. The "definitely lumbering" (Howard Barnes [*NYHT*]) play was sluggishly directed, lacked believable characters, and, on the whole, was just a "dreary little piece of theatrical shoddy," wrote Burton Rascoe (*NYWT*). In the cast were Barry Macollum, Herbert Heyes, Dulcie Cooper and George Calvert. Coauthor Kirkley was drama critic for the *Baltimore Sun*.

HAPPY AS LARRY [Musical/Crime/Fantasy/Marriage/Period/Romance/Sex] B/LY: Donagh MacDonagh; M: Mischa and Wesley Portnoff; D: Burgess Meredith; CH: Anna Sokolow; DS: Motley (mobiles: Alexander Calder); P: Leonard Sillman; T: Coronet Theatre; 1/6/50 (3)

Happy as Larry, one of the 1949-1950 season's fastest losers, was described by Bron. (*V*) as "a heavy-handed musical fantasy with obvious Irish inspiration [that] tries too hard to do too many things and so doesn't come off." The "furiously dull" (Brooks Atkinson [*NYT*]) show, concerned with woman's fickleness, had been seen previously in both London and Dublin and also had been given a showing at Amherst College in Massachusetts. It was originally a straight play, but Burgess Meredith was responsible for having it converted it to a musical, for which he was duly chastised.

Meredith played Larry, a tailor, who tells his seven fellow tailors of his grandfather, also a tailor and also called Larry (and also played by Meredith), who could not tell which of the two women he loved was good and which was bad. One of his wives (Barbara Perry) connived with her doctor-lover (Gene Barry) to poison him. The other (Marguerite Piazza) fans his grave because she had vowed not to remarry until the earth was dry. The Three Fates (Mara Kim, Diane Sinclair, and Royce Wallace) provide Larry and his friends with a device to travel back a half a century to the grandparents' youth in order to avenge the killing by getting rid of the doctor. To save his life by getting blood for a transfusion, the evil wife stabs the corpse of her late husband, but this resuscitates him, and the wife drops dead at the sight. The widow now attaches herself to the revived Larry.

The pseudopoetic dialogue, overly whimsical mood, and multifarious styles mixing fantasy and burlesque turned the critics off. Nevertheless, the show looked lovely, Meredith had done some effective staging, and he gave a good performance in his double role. "When he is off stage," thought Howard Barnes (*NYHT*), "the proceedings become unruly and frequently senseless." He said that the story "lacks substance, wit and sustained satire."

Several songs, such as "I Remember Her" and "October," were pleasant. Irwin Corey also provided some amusement as a nutty pharmacist, and Maurice Edwards, Frank Milton, Henry Calvin, Jack Warner, and Ralph Hertz were among others involved.

HAPPY BIRTHDAY [Comedy/Alcoholism/Barroom/Romance] A: Anita Loos; M: Robert Russell Bennett; ADD.M/LY: Richard Rodgers and Oscar Hammerstein II and James Livingston; D: Joshua Logan; S/L: Jo Mielziner; C: Lucinda Ballard; P: Richard Rodgers and Oscar Hammerstein II; T: Broadhurst Theatre; 10/31/46 (564)

Over the entrance to the Mecca Cocktail Bar in Newark, New Jersey, hangs the motto, "The Best People in Newark Pass through These Portals." Through these portals one rainy day passes the mousy little spinster librarian named Addie Bemis (Helen Hayes), dressed in mackintosh and galoshes, seeking one of its regular patrons, a bank cashier named Paul Bishop (Louis Jean Heydt), to warn him that her alcoholic father (Robert Burton) is after him. Paul is engaged in the clutches of a sexy blond (Lorraine Miller) in black satin, and Addie is brushed aside. Fortified by a succession of pink ladies and other concoctions, Addie decides to rescue him. The more she imbibes, the more the bar becomes a virtual paradise of color and light where anything can happen. Bottles are brilliantly illuminated, large dollar bills keep coming from her purse, her stool rises to twice its height, ordinary clothing becomes spectacular, and strangers become buddies. Soon Addie is dancing the tango, making a speech, and singing over the establishment's microphone a song composed by Rodgers and Hammerstein called "I Haven't Got a Worry in the World" as well as a mock operatic aria. Before the evening is over, she has struck her obnoxious dad over the pate with a bottle and won Paul away from the hussy.

Special hand and scenic props enhanced the fantastical effects. One was a bar stool that continued to grow higher and higher and swayed back and forth as Addie grew increasingly intoxicated.

Much of the joy in the "ingenious and charming comedy" (Ward Morehouse [*NYS*]) came from Helen Hayes's hilariously delightful cavortings. The thin play--originally titled *Blue Lounge*-- sagged here and there, but Hayes was always around to iron out its wrinkles. It was a change of pace from the more serious historical characters she had been playing and demonstrated her surprising versatility. "Like Ezechiel, Miss Hayes has clothed dry bones with flesh; also trivialities with tenderness," wrote Euphemia Van Rensselaer Wyatt (*CW*). "It is amazing to see not only how she creates drama in this absent play," exclaimed John Mason Brown (*SR*), "but how she manages to lend magic to all the clichés about the churchmouse-on-a-spree which are her assignment." Brooks Atkinson (*NYT*) said that she acted "with the sincerity and magic of an honest actress who enjoys the sentiment, warmth and showmanship of popular comedy, designed for nothing more than a little fun in the theatre." For her work, Hayes won the first Tony ever for an actress; it was shared with Ingrid Bergman, who won for *Joan of Lorraine*.

Hayes did not like the play at first and agreed to do it only on impulse when the playwright told her that if she were in it, Oscar Hammerstein would agree to produce it. After it went into rehearsals, it struck the star as "an amateur mess, and when we opened in Boston, it was a disaster," she recalled in *My Life in Three Acts*. She then found out that Loos had gotten Hammerstein to do the show because Hayes was in it, just as she had gotten Hayes by saying that Hammerstein was producing it. During the rehearsals, she appreciated director Logan's ability to make a point so succinctly that it would remain with her whenever she played a scene. In the scene where Addie does her torrid tango, she does a backbend during which she spots the bank clerk sitting with another woman. Addie waves meekly at him, which brought the house down when Hayes did it. She revealed that Logan, when staging the bit, had told her, "It's the first time Addie's ever seen Mr. Bishop upside down," and thereafter, whenever she did her backbend, she was able to keep the moment alive and funny.

Logan, in *Josh*, described the revisions that the play underwent after the Boston opening, the chief changes being the excision of all the bitchy lines spoken by Addie that, side by side with her more pleasant dialogue, seemed to give her a schizoid personality. This meant a grueling problem for Hayes, who had to revise her carefully worked-out character in a single day to accommodate the changes. At one point, Hayes absolutely refused to cut a sarcastic crack, spoken while drinking a pink lady. She argued that without the line her timing would be thrown off completely and that the sought-for laugh would not come. Finally, she agreed to try it Logan's way, insisting that the result would be failure. He then snippily told her to do it however she wanted. "Cut the lines, or don't cut them. This is your play much more than mine!" When, because of all the other cuts, the laughs at that evening's performance began to arrive early on and to keep building, Hayes realized that Logan was right and that she no longer needed the intrusive line because the audience's laughter completely changed her ideas about the timing. The next day, she was late for notes and rehearsals. When she finally showed up, she spoke very somberly to the company: "Please excuse me for being late, everyone. I was having a dreary breakfast of black coffee and humble pie."

Also in the show were Jean Bellows, Enid Markey, Grace Valentine, Jack Diamond, Ralph Theadore, Florence Sundstrom, Dort Clark, Philip Dakin, Harry Kingston, James Livingston, and others. For many years, Anita Loos tried to have a musical version of the play produced (score by Gerry Mulligan), but the closest a production ever got to Broadway was Birmingham, Alabama.

HAPPY DAYS, THE (*Les Jours Heureux*) [Comedy/Aviation/French/Romance/Sex/Youth] A: Claude-André Puget; AD: Zoe Akins; D: Arthur Ripley; S: Raymond Sovey; P: Raphael and Robert Hakim; T: Henry Miller's Theatre; 5/13/41 (23)

Zoe Akins was credited with being the author of this piece, although she was really its adaptor. Her work involved extensive alterations in the original (which was a hit in prewar Paris), including resetting it in Canada and making the characters French-Canadians. It brought the lovely Diana Barrymore back to Broadway for her second role of the season in which she had made her debut.

Barrymore played Marianne Gassin, a young lady spending time with her adolescent friends at her island home in the St. Lawrence River while her parents are away at a funeral in Quebec. She loves the arrogant Oliver Faber (Frederick Bradlee), who, although he loves her back, takes pleasure in making her uncomfortable. Pernette (Joan Tetzel), Oliver's sister, is affectionately eyed by the oafish Bernard (Peter Scott), but isn't sure of her own feelings. Marianne tries to make the cold Oliver jealous by inventing a story about her being in love with a flyer, with whom she has supposedly been corresponding. Just then, a young aviator, Michael Trent (Edward Ashley), forced down nearby, enters and immediately becomes the object of Pernette and Marianne's emotions. Moreover, Marianne's older sister Francine (Barbara Kent) also falls for Michael. The complications that ensue provide plenty of amusement until Oliver and Marianne realize how much they love one another, with the same going for Pernette and Bernard.

A number of critics, Brooks Atkinson (*NYT*) among them, were quite fond of the lightweight play and its actors, especially Barrymore and Tetzel, but others thought it mediocre. Burns Mantle's (*NYDN*) opinion was representative: "The young players are conscious of their youth, and try to capitalize on it; the author is conscious of the instability of her actors, and tries to protect them; the director is conscious of the comedy's juvenility and tries to overcome it. . . . Finally, the audience is conscious of the artificiality of the whole business and is unable to accept it as anything but obvious make-believe spotted with incidental scenes of fleeting appeal." Several critics faulted the play for its flimsy portrait of young people's concerns at a time when more serious issues should have been on their minds.

"HAPPY JOURNEY, THE" and **MERCHANT OF VENICE, THE** (a scene) P: Equity Library Theatre; T: Muhlenberg Branch of the New York Public Library (OB); 1/23/45 (3)

"The Happy Journey" [Comedy/Family/One-Act] A: Thornton Wilder; D: Enid Markey w/Sara Lee Harris; *The Merchant of Venice* [Dramatic Revival*] A: William Shakespeare; D: Frank Wilson

Wilder's long one-act play, later revised as "The Happy Journey from Trenton to Camden," was given its New York premiere in this program sponsored by Equity's showcase arm. A simple tale of a family taking an automobile trip from one New Jersey city to another, it employs the borrowed Chinese convention of a stage manager who sets the stage with the necessary props. He also reads the parts of several characters from a script. The play was the seed from which *Our Town** was developed. Its cast included Margaret Peters, Kenneth Dana, Geoffrey Warnick, Vance Gooden, and Vicki Thomas.

On the same bill was the prince of Morocco casket scene from *The Merchant of Venice*. Frank Wilson, the famous black actor, directed and played Morocco. Eve McVeagh played Portia, and Beatrice Manley was Nerissa.

A presentation of the Wilder play was added to the bill of "The Respectful Prostitute" in 1948. (See *An Evening of Two Plays*)

HAPPY TIME, THE [Comedy/Alcoholism/Family/Marriage/Old Age/Period/Romance/Sex/Youth] A: Samuel Taylor; SC: Robert Fontaine's novel of the same name; D: Robert Lewis; DS: Aline Bernstein; P: Richard Rodgers and Oscar Hammerstein II; T: Plymouth Theatre; 1/24/50 (614)

This hit comedy, musicalized under the same title in 1968, was only one of various attempts to dramatize a 1945 autobiographical novel by Robert Fontaine. Fontaine and his wife had done at least half a dozen scripts before producer Leland Hayward began to lose interest. Then Hayward asked the couple if Samuel Taylor could try a version of the play. Instead of rewriting one of the Fontaine scripts, Taylor did a completely new one based on the novel, and it was produced by Rodgers and Hammerstein. Hobe. (*V*) said of the result, which he called "a sort of French-Canadian combination of *Life With Father** and *You Can't Take It With You**," that it was "uneven and occasionally hokey," but nonetheless "a warm, tender, touching and enjoyable comedy." Many also included *I Remember Mama* in their comparisons.

Laughter and tears mingled in this nostalgic tale set in Ottawa in the 1920s. The play begins by familiarizing the audience with the various individualistic characters in the Bonnard household, among them Bibi (Johnny Stewart), a boy on the brink of puberty; Papa (Claude Dauphin), a tolerant, happy-go-lucky father who plays the violin at the local vaudeville house; Maman (Leora Dana), a prim but good-humored Scotch-Presbyterian mother disturbed by the behavior of her unconventional Gallic relatives; Grandpère (Edgar Stehli), a wise old reprobate; Uncle Desmonde (Richard Hart), a philandering collector of ladies' garters; the bibulous Uncle Louis (Kurt Kasznar), given to drinking wine from a water cooler he carries under his arm; and Mignonette (Eva Gabor, in her Broadway debut), a lovely blond maid who has taken the job after losing her vaudeville gig and who becomes the love object of Uncle Louis. Young Bibi's hormones are beginning to lead him to take an interest in sex, and he gets caught after stealing Mignonette's lingerie. He falls into more hot water by bringing a copy of a saucy French novel to school and also is accused by the braces-wearing brat next door (Marlene Cameron) of possessing a lewd drawing. For these crimes he is chastised by his sanctimonious headmaster (Oliver Cliff), but Papa and the two uncles briskly straighten out the educator. Papa finally sits down and explains to the eager youth the facts of life, skirting the physical elements while focusing on the spiritual.

Most saw it as a diverting assortment of character sketches lacking a consistent or well-constructed plot. The first act was the most serious culprit from a structural viewpoint. Brooks Atkinson (*NYT*) felt that one might have left at midpoint "under the impression that he was closing the door on some kollege komics." However, things rapidly improved in the second half, which was "tender, gallant and funny." According to Louis Sheaffer (*BE*), "It spreads at the same time an atmosphere of family affection, sunny tolerance and good-natured worldliness that takes much of the curse off its fabricated construction." George Jean Nathan (*TBY*) characterized it as "a good show but not a good play." The only mildly impressed Richard Watts, Jr. (*NYP*), advised that the play "has a certain warmth and charm which atone for much of its ramshackle quality. Its central story takes an unconscionable time to pass a given point, but there are individual scenes of fresh and rewarding humor." The cast, especially Dauphin and Dana, was considered exceptional and also included Gage Clark as a doctor, James O'Rear as a young suitor, and Mary Aurelius as an aunt.

Director Lewis had wanted his close friend Maureen Stapleton to play Maman, but Stapleton, for all her brilliance as an actress, had a deathly fear of auditions and refused to try out. Lewis convinced her that she had only to appear on the stage and be seen by the producers, who simply wanted to look her over. He told her to "just put on a pretty dress, comb your hair, be as beautiful as you are, get the part, and then we'll have loads of fun in rehearsal." By the time the actress worked up the nerve to audition, she was terrified. According to Lewis's *Slings and Arrows*, she looked "about half the height of the Maureen I knew" and "seemed to be sucking in her cheeks to the disappearing point." Lewis, aware that Stapleton had blown her chance, reassured producer Hammerstein that she was not ill, adding, "I think she's being pretty for you."

The actress who did get the part, Leora Dana, also had a strange audition. Dana had acted with Cloris Leachman in a summer-stock play seen by Lewis. Having confused the actresses in his own mind, he thought that producer Rodgers was referring to Leachman when he asked to see Dana. Believing Leachman completely wrong for the role, he gave in very reluctantly to Rodgers's demand to see Dana. When the actress he thought was Leachman stood before him, the following colloquy ensued: "You're not Leora Dana." "I'm not?" "No, you're Cloris Leachman." "I am?" Later, when the real Leachman's considerable talent was revealed in various roles, Lewis realized that she too could have played the part.

Lewis also told of the trouble he had trying to get Hungarian actress Eva Gabor to say "oui" instead of "vee," so she would sound believably French-Canadian. When all his efforts failed, Lewis had the line about her character's profession changed from "She is an acrobat" to "She's a Hungarian acrobat."

Another story concerns Kurt Kasznar, who, on opening night, had so severe a case of stage fright that he was sure he would faint when he entered. Lewis, summoned to Kasznar's dressing room, improvised by telling him that it was psychologically impossible to faint during a performance. "The adrenalin that's being pumped into your system when you're in front of an audience prevents the blood being drawn from your head. So you can't faint onstage. . . . Now, of course, as soon as you come off, you'll probably faint in the wings." Later, when the reassured actor appeared and began to get laughs, he had no trouble at all. He "even forgot to faint when he came offstage."

HARLEM CAVALCADE [Revue/Blacks] CN: Ed Sullivan; D: Ed Sullivan and Noble Sissle; CH: Leonard Harper; C: Veronica; P: Ed Sullivan; T: Ritz Theatre; 5/1/42 (49)

NYDN columnist Ed Sullivan conceived, codirected, and produced this black revue, but the result was considered a waste of fine talent. Euphemia Van Rensselaer Wyatt (*CW*) thought it merely "routine vaudeville with only a great deal of burnt cork to lend it shading. None of the singers taps the resources of drama and pathos in their race. The humor is so traditional that the best sketch is an adventure in a cemetery."

The show, which was offered twice a day, with three shows a day on Saturdays and Sundays, offered singing, dancing, and comedy, had nothing original to sustain it and got by (when it was getting by) on sheer talent, rhythm, and energy. Much of the material was familiar, such as Noble Sissle's old tune, "I'm Just Wild about Harry," done by the songwriter himself. Some of the humor had topical references, such as Flournoy Miller's routine of filling out a draft questionnaire. There was also the tried-and-true "His Honor, the Jedge" bit on hand. Singer Jimmie Daniels, comics Tim Moore and Joe Byrd, comedy dancers Poke and Moke, comedian Johnny Lee, dancer-drummers Red and Curley, oversized singers the Peters Sisters, dancers Wini and Bob Johnson, the sixteen-member chorus line called the Harlemaniacs, songstress Una Mae Carlisle, harmonic quartet the Delta Rhythm Boys, and others filled up the bill.

The general verdict was that the show, for all its enthusiasm, was overlong, monotonous, and lacking in freshness and originality in its sketch material. It was believed that the show was motivated by a couple of other vaudeville-type revues that had opened recently, *Keep 'Em Laughing* and *Priorities of 1942*.

(1) **HARRIET** [Comedy-Drama/Blacks/Family/Literary-Biographical/Marriage/Period/Politics/Romance/War] A: Florence Ryerson and Colin Clements; D: Elia Kazan; S: Lemuel Ayers; C: Aline Bernstein; P: Gilbert Miller; T: Henry Miller's Theatre; 3/3/43 (377)

New York welcomed with open arms this biographical drama about Harriet Beecher Stowe, the nineteenth-century novelist whose antislavery story, *Uncle Tom's Cabin*, was one of the most widely read and influential books of the period. The play was one of Burns Mantle's ten best of the year.

Its title role was another in a growing list of brilliant accomplishments for diminutive star actress Helen Hayes. Speaking of Hayes's performance, Rosamond Gilder (*TAM*) remarked, "She compasses the whole of it with that combination of precision and strength which is preeminently hers. She is both believable and winning as the rather plain little housewife, 'no bigger than a pinch of snuff.' . . . Miss Hayes brings into the picture a saving laughter, a disarming sparkle which are partly the original Harriet's and partly her own. Her quick gesture--outspread hand to face--the turn of her head, the bob of her cascading curls add their spice of warmth and conviction to her portrait. . . . Miss Hayes has a singular ability to convey . . . a sense of the latent power in the character she portrays. She does it by the device of reserve, by holding herself well within her potential striking force, so that there is always a further stretch, a further drive, a further impact possible."

Harriet is an episodic chronicle play covering sixty years in eight scenes; it begins in 1836, a week after Harriet Beecher's marriage to absentminded Professor Calvin Stowe (Rhys Williams) of Cincinnati. Soon a large number of Beecher relatives arrive and begin to argue about slavery, some of the family--most of whom later became avid Abolitionists--thinking that the problem should be solved by the South without outside interference. When the Kentucks begin crossing into Ohio to capture escaped black slaves, Harriet, Calvin, and their growing brood run from the slavery problem by moving to Brunswick, Maine. Most of the family have now switched to the Abolitionist cause, and many of them are expounding their views on lecture platforms and from pulpits (Harriet's father was the noted Congregational minister Dr. Lyman Beecher [Robert Harrison], and her brother was the charismatic preacher Henry Ward Beecher [Sydney Smith]). The problem, however, is not a crucial one for Harriet, who prefers to let others worry over it while she raises her children and keeps house. Although her family is opposed to her thoughts of becoming a professional writer, she does dabble in literary pursuits, turning out magazine stories and essays, but never dealing with slavery. Finally, as a result of her confrontation with the slave traffic on the Underground Railroad, Harriet becomes convinced of the seriousness of the issue. An elderly fugitive slave woman (Edna Thomas) is captured in her home. Both because of her conviction of the need to do something to help free the slaves and because she wishes to earn enough to buy a real silk dress, she begins to write *Uncle Tom's Cabin* as a serial story, culminating in its enormous reception by the public and its becoming a gigantic best-seller. Following the book's success, the Stowes move to Andover, Maine, where Harriet learns of and becomes distressed by the great controversy surrounding her story. A pacifist herself, she sees her work become one of the forces leading to the Civil War, in which her eldest son (Jack Manning) is wounded. She is elated, though, when President Lincoln holds a reception in her honor (he called her "the little woman who made a great war"), and she makes a speech on behalf of liberty and against those tyrants who would enslave mankind, the topical referencs being obvious to audiences experiencing World War II.

The play succeeded on several levels, but many liked it best for its scenes of family comedy, its picture of Harriet penning her immortal work while surrounded by a noisy household, and its various depictions of domestic complexities. Kelcey Allen (*WWD*) felt that it was "an unusually attractive drama for cultured audiences. Extremely well written, it is filled with human emotions, fine sentiment and humor and it has also force and dignity." John Anderson (*NYJA*) reported, "Miss Hayes, by the striking and vivid force of her performance, makes *Harriet* momentous and fascinating, one of the few plays in a poverty-stricken season to touch real value."

Other critics were somewhere in between, but a few shared the minority view of Louis Kronenberger (*PM*), who observed that Harriet Beecher Stowe "does not emerge as a very vibrant or compelling character; and her story, except for its one tremendous chapter, has little drive or drama." He and others noted that the authors had overlooked the crusader aspect of her character in favor of showing her as a humorously pleasant housewife perplexed by family crises.

The drama was given a superlative production, and Elia Kazan's direction was a major reason for the work's success. Kazan had replaced Gilbert Miller as director, although Miller was also the producer. Miller had been directing the piece for a week, but Hayes was distressed by his lackadaisical approach. Finally, she said in her sweetest manner, "Now, now, Gilbert, this simply won't do. We have got to have a *director*" (quoted in John F. Wharton, *Life among the Playwrights*). Kazan wrote in *Elia Kazan* that when he joined the company, he and Miller had the play read to them. During the reading, the portly Miller fell fast asleep, but Kazan soon energized the entire cast, which had been depressed by Miller's boredom. When Miller made a good suggestion, Kazan was quite surprised. "Do you think that will work?" asked Kazan. "Think!" replied Miller. "I know it will. I saw it work in Paris. . . . I am . . . the triumph of memory over a third-rate imagination."

Kazan was credited with having saved a lost cause and received a note from the authors on opening night: "Kazan, Kazan / The miracle man / Call him in / As soon as you can." He declared that his chief contribution to Hayes's performance was getting her to shed her typical sweetness-and-light methods for an approach that made her "a homespun, gritty zealot energizing her way out of the nineteenth century," but noted that Hayes found the task a formidable one because of its unfamiliarity in her bag of tricks. Once she got before an audience, however, she began to revert to "her repertory of adorable fandangos." Kazan's gentle reprimand puzzled the star, as her own approach had gotten her an ovation. Kazan had to acknowledge that it was just those aspects of her personality and style that he tried to eliminate that made her the enormously popular actress she was. "The less I liked her performance . . . the more enthusiastically the audience responded." He confessed that whatever miracles there were in his work were really attributable to her performance and that the work might have flopped without it.

Jane Seymour played Harriet's women's rights activist sister Catherine, William Woodson was Lowell Denton, suitor of the Stowe twins (Betty and Lenore Wade), Seth Arnold played Jerusha Pantry, and Joan Tetzel was one of Harriet's daughters. Others in the large cast included Guy Sorel, Carmen Mathews, Hugh Franklin, and Benedict McQuarrie.

(2) [Return Engagement] T: City Center of Music and Drama; 9/27/44 (11)

A limited engagement at popular prices ($2.40 top), used as a warm-up for a lengthy road tour. The play was deemed a workmanlike job made worth seeing, if not memorable, by Hayes's marvelous performance. Seven others of the original players returned. The chief cast replacements were Robert Emhardt for Rhys Williams in the role of Calvin Stowe and Richard Wilder for Sydney Smith as Henry Ward Beecher. Despite the large spaces of the City Center, the play got across, and the theatre's notorious acoustics seem to have been mastered in making the actors audible.

HARVEST OF YEARS [Drama/Alcoholism/Family/Marriage/Romance/Rural/Western] A: DeWitt Bodeen; D/P: Arthur J. Beckhard; S: Raymond Sovey; C: Peggy Morrison; T: Hudson Theatre; 1/12/48 (16)

In the California vineyard country of the San Joaquin Valley lives the hardy, Swedish-American Bromark family: the strong-willed matriarch Anna (Esther Dale), her four daughters, and assorted others. Alcoholic eldest daughter Margareta (Leona Maricle) loses her lover (Robert Crawley) to selfish youngest daughter Mellie (Emily Noble), who has tricked him into marriage. The three older daughters lead spinsterish lives of quiet desperation. Jenny Nelson (Lenka Peterson), a local girl, is engaged to Anna's farmer son Chris Bromark (Russell Hardie). Jenny leaves him for his one-armed war-veteran nephew Jules (Philip Abbott), who has just come home from France. Jules and Jenny are wed, but she dies in childbirth; Jules and Chris will raise the baby, and life in the farmhouse will go on.

The lethargically paced drama, ostensibly concerned with "the little things of life," was called "an aimless and tedious drama, a play of high intentions and failing utterly in dramatic impact," by Ward Morehouse (*NYS*). Howard Barnes (*NYHT*) saw some dimly convincing characters lacking "anything approaching dynamic situations" in which to come to life. The cast included Virginia Robinson and Philippa Bevans.

HARVEY [Comedy/Alcoholism/Family/Fantasy/Mental Illness] A: Mary Chase; D: Antoinette Perry; S: John Root; P: Brock Pemberton; T: Forty-eighth Street Theatre; 11/1/44 (1,775)

One of the all-time great comedy hits of the Broadway theatre, high up on the list of long-run shows, and still produced regularly in professional and amateur theatres around the world. Written by Denver newspaperwoman Mary Coyle Chase, this whimsical fantasy was first called *The Pooka*, but it had to go through eighteen rewrites before producer Pemberton, whose closest advisors were against the play, was satisfied with it.

Pemberton made just the right casting choices for the leads (although a series of actors--Jack Haley, Edward Everett Horton, Robert Benchley, and Harold Lloyd--had turned down the Elwood P. Dowd role). The casting as Elwood of onetime vaudevillian Frank Fay--on the basis of a brief conversation without an audition-- had a built-in fascination in that the actor had blown his personal fortune after succumbing to the bottle (his autobiography was called *How to Be Poor*); he was given a chance to demonstrate his recovery by his performance of this role, which put him back on top. Another smart decision eliminated the actor playing Harvey in a $600 rabbit suit with which the play had been equipped when it first opened out of town. The play only caught fire when the audience was allowed to use its imagination to "see" this nonspeaking character. It was selected as one of the season's ten best by Burns Mantle and also garnered the Pulitzer Prize for 1944-1945, beating out *The Glass Menagerie* in the process.

Elwood P. Dowd, a friendly tippler who likes to frequent Charlie's, and who usually has a buzz on, befriends Harvey, a six-feet, one-and-a-quarter-inches-tall rabbit, who is leaning against a lamppost when he first meets him. Harvey is technically a pooka, a creature from Celtic mythology. Elwood brings the wise and kindly rabbit home, becomes his inseparable companion, and even has a portrait painted of themselves together. Because only Elwood can see Harvey, a number of complications develop. Living with Elwood are his fluttery, widowed sister Veta (Josephine Hull) and her plain daughter Myrtle Mae (Jane Van Duser). Veta and Myrtle Mae find it discomfiting having to accommodate a rabbit whom they believe is imaginary, especially when a place must be set for him at table, or when Elwood introduces his friend to the ladies attending a reception given in the house by Veta. Fearing for her daughter's marital prospects, Veta brings Elwood to Chumley's Rest, a sanatorium managed by the famous psychiatrist Dr. William R. Chumley (Fred Irving Lewis). But when Veta explains Elwood's symptoms, the doctor's assistant (Tom Seidel) assumes that she is the afflicted one, and she is subjected to the treatment she had intended for her brother. Elwood charms Dr. Chumley into going out for the evening for a drink, and Harvey takes a fancy for the doctor, who, after some imbibing, sees the rabbit himself. The doctor is especially interested in Harvey's ability to stop clocks so that you can go anywhere and do anything and then return when the clock stopped without a minute having passed. Dr. Chumley suggests an injection of Shock Formula 977 for Elwood, and Elwood--after some hesitation, because it will mean giving up Harvey--consents, hoping to please Veta, who seeks power of attorney and the key to her brother's safety-deposit box. But a taxi driver's (Robert Gist) description of how nice people like Elwood become disagreeable grumps after being shocked changes Veta's mind. Her final decision is to leave Elwood as he is, and Veta, who herself has seen Harvey (he left when she said, "To hell with you"), accepts him as her brother's friend. Harvey's existence is never confirmed or denied by the playwright; the audience must make up its own mind, although the stage directions allow for mystical happenings, such as doors that open and close by themselves.

Chief among the objections was the slow pacing, especially in the first act. A few critics suggested the need for cutting. Beyond these minor shortcomings, however, the play was showered with encomiums. George Freedley (*NYMT*) called it "an enchanted and enchanting comedy for adults." Burton Rascoe (*NYWT*) could not recall ever having laughed so hard and continuously. George Jean Nathan (*TBY*), after noting earlier examples in burlesque and drama of the play's theme, commented, "Miss Chase has added so much of her own and has played over the whole a fantasy at once so paradoxically realistic and basically so in keeping with life that her exhibit, despite an overly long induction and a third act that suffers a bad twelve-minute let-down, amounts in sum to excellent entertainment." But Wilella Waldorf (*NYP*) took serious issue with Chase's treatment of her promising theme, maintaining that the play was a "crude farce" that tastelessly made sport of mental illness.

Fay and Hull were considered perfect in their roles, with her flurried manner but concrete perspective a perfect foil for his laid-back dreamer's ease. Fay, said Rosamond Gilder (*TAM*), "can make effective use of every asset at his command; his odd personality, dreamy, detached, gently-pathetic, his expert technique trained by years of exercise on the vaudeville stage, his actor qualities of impersonation and projection. None of our comedians, save Victor Moore, can so nicely combine wit and pathos. He is master of understatement; past master of the gentle art of evocation."

During the long run, various actors played Elwood, including James Stewart, Joe E. Brown, Bert Wheeler, Jack Buchanan, and producer Pemberton himself. Stewart, who took over on Broadway in 1947 while Fay went on a ten-week vacation, played the role in the movie and in the 1970 revival as well. His 1947 appearance was his first visit to Broadway since he left for Hollywood in 1935. It was believed by most critics that Fay was superior in the role. Others in the original cast included Jesse White as a sanatorium assistant, Frederica Going and Eloise Sheldon as local club women, Janet Tyler as a nurse, and John Kirk as a judge.

HASTY HEART, THE [Comedy-Drama/Death/Friendship/Illness/Military/Romance/Tropics/War] A: John Patrick; D: Bretaigne Windust; S: Raymond Sovey; P: Howard Lindsay and Russel Crouse; T: Hudson Theatre; 1/3/45 (204)

John Patrick scored with this touching yet humorous work set in the convalescent ward of a British general hospital on the Assam-Burma front during the war. The author wrote most of it on shipboard as he returned from the Burma front, where he had served with the American Field Service. It gave Richard Basehart his best role to date; his performance of a role requiring a convincing Scottish burr propelled him into the limelight. Fortunately, Basehart had been studying such an accent from a Scottish actor prior to acting the Earl of Bothwell in a stock company version of Maxwell Anderson's *Mary of Scotland**.

The play, "as often moving as it is funny" (Lewis Nichols [*NYT*]), pictures a diverse group of Allied soldiers recuperating in a hospital ward replete with mosquito-net-covered cots and bamboo-matting walls. There are guys from Australia, Britain, New Zealand, America, Africa, and so on. Lachlen (Basehart), a seemingly healthy, good-looking, but antisocial young Scot with only weeks to live because of a kidney ailment, joins the ward. He is ignorant of the gravity of his condition. The colonel (J. Colville Dunn) asks the nurse, Sister Margaret (Anne Burr), and the men to make the Scot's last days comfortable. Disgruntled and disheartened because of a rough life, and never having had a friend, he refuses any signs of kindness or friendship. But the others in the ward, especially the patient Yank (John Lund), refuse to leave him be and gradually win his acceptance. When he learns that they knew of his imminent death, he turns dour again, not wanting their pity. However, he comes around again when they prove otherwise, ignoring him or treating him with disdain, and, although given the chance to go home, he decides to remain in the hospital for his final days.

Sentimentality was difficult to eradicate from the play, and Patrick even gave in to the conventional dramatic device of creating a romance for the dying Scot with the nurse; the romance was especially unconvincing given the intractable nature of Lachlen's character. There was also a need for some cutting and elimination of repetitious actions. What succeeded was the heartfelt humanity of the characters and the sense that they were real people. The war itself was merely a backdrop to a drama of normal human beings coming into contact with one another under trying circumstances. "Although it may hit below the waistline supporting its kilt, the point is that it hits many times, and always with effect," applauded John Mason Brown (*SR*). "It's a play that arouses a genuine affection--it's so generous, so touching and withal so funny," laughed and cried Euphemia Van Rensselaer Wyatt (*CW*). But George Jean Nathan (*TBY*) was one of several who were sour: "Though his theme, while more or less familiar, is still functionable, he however so insistently strikes the same emotional chord, he so continuously grinds his heel into ground already furrowed, and he writes in so commonplace and unillumined a manner that it loses much of its pregnancy."

Speaking of the lead actor, John Chapman (*NYDN*) wrote, "Richard Basehart is exactly right. . . . His burr is thick but not overdone. The softening of his rigid aloofness into hungry loneliness, and then into an eagerness to live among fellow human beings, is a well-planned, well-played transition which inspires great sympathy and brings a rather lasting lump to the throat."

Douglas Chandler played the British Tommy, John Campbell was the Aussie named Digger, Victor Chapin acted the New Zealander called Kiwi, and Earl Jones (father of James Earl Jones, making his Broadway debut), played Blossom, the African.

The role of the nurse originally had been cast with Mercedes McCambridge, who would have made her Broadway debut in it. She wrote in *The Quality of Mercy* that "I never doubted for a minute that I was good in the part," but that the producers fired her on the ninth day of rehearsals because of her inexperience. She realized that they were right, but was puzzled by something director Windust said to her. "He said he had to let me go because I was 'pregnant with warmth,' and until I gave birth to that quality I was 'as ugly to watch onstage as a woman large with child.'" McCambridge thought that he was as full of air as his nickname, "Windy."

HATS OFF TO ICE [Revue/Ice] M/LY: James Littlefield and John Fortis; D: Catherine Littlefield and William H. Burke (skating numbers: May Judels); CH: Catherine and Dorothie Littlefield; S: Bruno Maine; C: Grace Houston; L: Eugene Braun; P: Sonja Henie and Arthur M. Wirtz; T: Center Theatre; 6/22/44 (890)

The huge Center Theatre in Rockefeller Center was once more host to a spectacular ice show produced by, but not starring, figure skater Sonja Henie, who confined her local performing to the shows she put on at Madison Square Garden (not covered here). Lavish sets and costumes, ice-skating ballets, chorus lines doing Rockette-like precision numbers on blades, comical skating routines, and new songs mingled with familiar ones were all part of a formula that began to take root in the late thirties and flourished in the forties. Tickets cost as low as $1.65, a bargain by any standards.

Outstanding skaters included Lucille Page, who stood out in "Sophisticated Lady" and "The Lazy Q," in which she was funny as a dude on a ranch; the Caley Sisters, Dorothy and Hazel; the Brandt Sisters, Helga and Inga; the Skating Rileys with their broad comic skills; tiny Paul Castle; Geoffe Stevens, Joe Shillen, and Jimmy Sisk as a comic trio of sailors (they were an attempt to replace the disbanded Four Bruises act); Gretle Uksila and Robert Uksila as Olive Oyl and Popeye; hurdle-jumping James Caesar; star comic skater Freddie Trenkler, whose dazzling acrobatic routines were hilarious, as when he swung out of a balcony box to chase his hat around the ice, or when he played a boisterous GI bugging his sergeant; attractive figure skaters Carol Lynne and Rudy Richards, the former highlighted as the goddess Diana and the latter praised for his "Boogie Woogie Bachelor"; and others. There were numbers titled "Pathway to the Stars," "Slavic Rhapsody," "Isle of the Midnight Rainbow," "A Persian Legend," and the like, to allow for a variety of musical rhythms to accompany the terpsichorean feats.

Although the public seemed not to tire of these shows, many critics found that they gradually grew tedious and repetitious. Most vociferous was George Jean Nathan (*TBY*), who saw little that was original here. The show, he said, "only induced the feeling that Ouspensky's theory of spiral time was something of an established theatrical fact and that one was viewing the same ice show back in the year 1940." The opening of the present opus lasted until nearly midnight, making it even more tiresome. Still, Howard Barnes (*NYHT*) found the opus "spectacular, swiftly paced and exceedingly tasteful."

HAVEN, THE [Drama/Crime/Literature/Marriage/Mystery] A: Dennis Hoey; SC: Anthony Gilbert's novel of the same name; D: Clarence Derwent; S: William Saulter; C: Noel Taylor; P: Violla Rubber i/a/w Johnnie Walker; T: Playhouse; 11/13/46 (5)

This "juvenile affair" (Robert Coleman [*NYDM*]) was a murder mystery that found no haven on Broadway. Rowland Field (*NEN*) commented, "This slow-moving mishap seemed talkily futile and completely lacking in originality and suspense."

It starred its author, Dennis Hoey, as Edmund Durward, a detective-story writer who resides in a reputedly haunted lodge at Cambridge, England. Edmund's latest mail-order bride, Agatha Forbes (Valerie Cossart) arrives, but is horrified to learn that the previous tenant drowned herself. A nosy landlady, Miss Martin (Viola Roache), who asks many questions, suspects Edmund of doing away with a former wife for her money while sailing in the Near East. Her curiosity leads to her being disposed of homicidally. Another victim is Grace Knowles (Eliza Sutherland), Agatha's knowing half-sister. Agatha, threatened with disaster, disappears for a while, too, and it is thought that she has become another victim of her bluebeard husband. When she reappears, the coroner (Ivan Simpson) interrogates both her and Durward on suspicion of the landlady's murder. Somehow, Durward is cleared of suspicion, but he accidentally poisons himself and the curtain falls.

Melville Cooper played a sly criminal lawyer in this dramaturgic "mediocrity" (Ibee. [*V*]). Queenie Leonard played the comedy maid.

(1) HE WHO GETS SLAPPED (***Tot, Kto Poluchaet Poshchochiny***) [Dramatic Revival*] A: Leonid Andreyev; D: Norman MacDonald; P: Library Theatre Project; T: Hudson Park Branch of the New York Public Library (OB); 4/22/44

One of the early productions of the company (later called the Equity Library Theatre) that had been formed by Actors Equity to allow theatre people to have a union-sponsored showcase for which they worked free of charge. *He Who Gets Slapped* had been introduced locally by the Theatre Guild in 1922. The present production was no match for the Guild's first-rate company, but the play was deemed still worthy of presentation. "Mystical and purposely obscure," noted George Freedley (*NYMT*), the only critic present, "it intrigues the mind and titillates curiosity." The offering was rough, having had insufficient rehearsal time. In the role of He, the clown, was Ralph Clanton.

(2) AD: Judith Guthrie; D: Tyrone Guthrie; DS: Motley; P: Theatre Guild; T: Booth Theatre; 3/20/46 (46)

A major revival of the play with Stella Adler as Zinaida, the lion tamer; Dennis King as He (here called "Funny"), the socialite-turned-clown; Tom Rutherford as Funny's false friend; Wolfe Barzell as Papa Briquet; Russell Collins as Jim Jackson; John Abbott as Count Mancini; Susan Douglas (a Czech émigré with flawless English, making her Broadway debut) as Consuela, the bareback rider; Jerome Thor as Bezano, the cool-hearted equestrian; and Reinhold Schunzel as the decadent Baron Regnard.

Apart from her renaming the title character, Judith Guthrie's simplified adapation--which played down the mystical elements--was deemed faithful to the original. On the debit side, George Jean Nathan (*TBY*) considered the drama a pretentious treatment of an easily penetrated theme despite its reputation for obscurity. He condemned Tyrone Guthrie's staging for being "so overswollen that the script frequently got lost in it." But most others found the play quite palatable and Guthrie's direction theatrically imaginative and appropriate. To Lewis Nichols (*NYT*), the drama was sometimes talky, but nevertheless impressed him as "touching . . . , sardonic . . . , humble." Euphemia Van Rensselaer Wyatt (*CW*) wrote that Andreyev "has lifted the curtain on a world of make-believe and leaves the philosophy to the audience; he has combined vision and imagination with the sure technique of a craftsman. He gives tenseness to the melodrama but not too much solemnity."

Guthrie's direction was especially applauded for its expert handling of large stage groupings. His bold work reminded Rosamond Gilder (*TAM*) of the timidity of most recent American theatre. She noted that Guthrie was assisted by an extraordinary Motley set, "one that . . . stretches to the roof of the theatre, opening wide backstage spaces and wings, evoking a total change of mood by the shifting of walls, screens, ladders, nets and mattresses." However, John Mason Brown (*SR*) pre ferred the 1922 Lee Simonson set, for the present one seemed too realistic to him, which only made the play's symbolic qualities that much murkier. Gilder noted one of Guthrie's most creative moments, depicting the conflict between the baron and Funny. The former, dressed in high hat and white gloves and carrying a cane, stood waiting for Consuela, while Funny, made up in a huge high hat, comical gloves, and stick, sat him out, as two shafts of light accented them "in stabbing lines of black and white."

HEADS OR TAILS [Comedy/Marriage/Politics/Romance] A: H. J. Lengsfelder and Ervin Drake; D: Edward F. Cline; S: Watson Barratt; C: Alice Gibson; L: Leo Kerz; P: Your Theatre, Inc. i/a/w "the theatre-going public"; T: Cort Theatre; 5/2/47 (35)

"A stupid mess" (George Freedley [*NYMT*]) that many considered the worst play of the season. Robert Garland's (*NYJA*) review simply said "No!" Otis L. Guernsey, Jr. (*NYHT*), called it "a tedious, inert farce salted with witless gags."

Diplomat Cornelius T. Sheldon (Les Tremayne) is having both career and marital problems. He plans to divorce his wife Helen (Audra Lindley) and marry someone else when he gets a new assignment through the offices of Senator Costamara (Frank de Kova). However, because Helen has misplaced Cornelius's diplomatic passport, thereby displeasing the State Department, the senator is unable to arrange for the new position. Insurance salesman Philip McGill (Jed Prouty) is interested in the same woman as is Cornelius, so he and the diplomat toss a coin for her, the loser to kill himself. Cornelius loses the wager, but since Philip's unwitting partner sells a large policy to Cornelius's mother, the company will lose a quarter of a million dollars if he commits suicide. However, the situation is happily resolved, the Sheldons are reunited, and no one dies.

The production represented a novel plan initiated by coauthor Lengsfelder to allow the public to share in the profits of a show. He raised the money for its presentation by accepting investments from 142 church and civic organizations and from over 3,000 private individuals. In the cast were Werner Klemperer in a featured role and Joe Silver in a minor one.

HEAR THAT TRUMPET [Drama/Alcoholism/Blacks/Crime/Marriage/Music/Race/Romance] A: Orin Jannings; D/P: Arthur Hopkins; S: Woodman Thompson; T: Playhouse; 10/7/46 (8)

Another homecoming drama, this one about a group of Chicago jazz musicians who, after the war, reform their group under the aegis of trumpeter Dinger Richardson (Bobby Sherwood). His piano-playing army pal Floyd Amery (Ray Mayer) joins him, but so does an older black clarinetist named Mumford (Sidney Bechet). The black man's presence prevents them from getting some bookings. A wealthy businessman named Alonzo Armonk (Frank Conroy) agrees to back the group and get them out of the nickel-and-dime dives in which they have been playing. His girlfriend, Erica Marlowe (Audra Lindley), captures Dinger's heart and then marries him. This drives the jealous businessman to seek revenge and prevents any progress from being made by the band until he is out of the way. He even sets the underworld on them and nearly breaks up the marriage. The obstacle is removed by his being poisoned by Erica, the evidence of her crime being covered by a fortunate car accident.

Hopkins's direction was deemed dully unimaginative, and the writing--presumably an attempt to capture in dramatic terms the form of a jazz improvisation--suffered from a meandering structure and ambiguity. The best parts stemmed from the alcoholic Floyd's caustic wit, expressed in "some very surprising billingsgate" (Brooks Atkinson [*NYT*]). There were other good scenes as well, but the play descended into too much self-consciously literary writing, replete with mystical symbols, and ultimately came unglued. "The author's failure lies in his attempt to project his theme, already muddled as it is, with elliptical dramaturgy which turns out to be so elliptical as to be inscrutable," groaned George Jean Nathan (*TBY*). Howard Barnes (*NYHT*) said that the work "spraddles through six scenes of increasing ineptitude."

A few decent performances were not enough to create an ensemble, and a number of players were histrionically inept. Most of the male actors were outstanding jazz musicians, some of them, like Sherwood and Bechet, of top-notch quality. Several jam sessions were injected into the proceedings. Marty Marsala was the drummer, Bart Edwards was the bass viol player, and Philip Layton was the trombonist. Lynne Carter played Floyd's girlfriend.

HEART OF A CITY [Drama/Alcoholism/Military/Romance/Theatre/War] A: Lesley Storm; D/P: Gilbert Miller; S: Harry Horner; T: Henry Miller's Theatre; 2/12/42 (28)

This sentimental wartime play was set largely at London's Windmill Theatre, near Piccadilly Circus, which was famed for having continued to perform its "Revudeville" shows throughout the blitz and upholding the old tradition that "the show must go on." The play, which gave work to thirty-one mostly British actors, provided a tingling blend of danger and frivolousness with its picture of the showgirls and theatre workers gallantly laughing in the face of death as they go about their business of providing entertainment despite the sounds of destruction whizzing by outside.

The story was thin and trivial, but its atmospheric picture of brave performers was touching and memorable. Author Storm had been a regular backstage visitor at the Windmill and wrote from her personal experience. Rosamond Gilder (*TAM*), who was moved, nevertheless observed, "As a play it is disjointed and at times surprisingly jejune, dropping to pieces at every exit and resuming its course with difficulty, offering material for a play in locale and external events rather than in the inner substance of drama."

Most of the episodic action is set backstage in the theatre's dressing room, where the scantily clad performers huddle for protection during the bombing or parade around while carrying out their duties. The old-hat plot concerns the romantic affection of the leading lady, Rosalind (Beverly Roberts), for Paul Lundy (Richard Ainley), an RAF pilot who fell for her while watching one of her shows. Unfortunately, the boozing songwriter Tommy (Lloyd Gough) also loves Rosalind, who has declined to marry him. A relationship between Tommy and soubrette performer Judy (English actress Gertrude Musgrove, in her American debut) develops, but the pair is killed during the blitz when he goes to the local pub and she follows after. In the course of the action, several British songs are sung, including a portion of "The Lambeth Walk."

In the cast were such players as Bertha Belmore, Margot Grahame, Dennis Hoey, and Frances Tannehill.

HEARTBREAK HOUSE [Dramatic Revival*] A: George Bernard Shaw; D: Frank Corsaro; S: Robert Ramsey; P: On-Stage; T: Bleecker Street Playhouse (OB); 3/21/50

One of Off-Broadway's most ardent bands of semipro thespians produced Shaw's "Fantasia in the Russian Manner on English Themes," as he called *Heartbreak House*, which last had seen local production in 1938 with Orson Welles as Captain Shotover. Milton Sells now handled the overwhelming role.

The critics loved the play and found its many ideas (such as its virtual prophecy of the atomic bomb) still stimulating, but had reservations about On-Stage's execution. Richard Watts, Jr. (*NYP*), noted that the play's "garrulousness . . . is almost as overwhelming as its wit, vitality and its wisdom." However, he conceded that "it is too much to expect inexperienced actors to get the proper variety into their handling of so much dialogue." Louis Sheaffer (*BE*) said that while it was certainly not up to the Welles version and often sagged, this three-hour marathon had its points, enough to make it worth the while of those who had never seen the play. "After a slow, rather shuffling start . . . the new production picks up meaning and bounce and turns into an evening of civilized fun. . . . There are occasional rough spots . . . and the players fall too often into a tendency to shout when the story becomes excited, but it's still a skilled, enjoyable performance."

Beatrice Arthur played Hesione Hushaby, Hariot Hart was Lady Ariadne, Barney Cates was the burglar, and George Roy Hill was Hector.

HEAVEN ON EARTH [Musical/Fantasy/Prison/Romance] B/LY: Barry Trivers; M: Jay Gorney; D: John Murray Anderson (production supervisor: Eddie Dowling); CH: Nick Castle; DS: Raoul Pène du Bois; P: Monte Proser i/a/w Ned C. Litwack; T: New Century Theatre; 9/16/49 (12)

There were some great musicals during the 1948-1949 season, but the opulently produced (about $300,000), dolefully whimsical, and "almost steadily unrewarding" (Richard Watts, Jr. [*NYP*]) *Heaven on Earth* was not among them. It starred Peter Lind Hayes as Irishman James Aloysius McCarthy, a philosophical Central Park horse-and-buggy driver with a do-gooder streak and a mute pixy secretary named Friday (Dorothy Jarnac, who danced her role) to aid him. (The echoes of *Finian's Rainbow* were noted by many.) The subjects of his Robin Hood tendencies in this story are a couple of young lovers, war vet John Bowers (Robert Dixon) and Mary Brooks (Barbara Nunn). John is homeless (a reference to the housing shortage) and lives in a park tree. With Friday's help, McCarthy houses the couple in a prefabricated exhibition dream house built in the park by H. H. Hutton (David Burns). Hutton is outraged and has the couple jailed, but the hack driver stages a protest rally and uses his imitations of various movie stars (a Hayes specialty) to frighten the builder into acquiescing so that a happy ending can ensue.

"It is more noisy than tuneful; more corny than comically inventive," thought Howard Barnes (*NYHT*). Ward Morehouse (*NYS*) pointed to "a shoddy book and a dreary score."

Hayes was considered okay for nightclubs but not a strong-enough performer to carry a Broadway show. During rehearsals, producer Proser informed critic Jack Gaver that the show would not resort to "the cliché of falling back on the night club or vaudeville routines of its leading player. Came the New York opening, and . . . there was Peter going through his floor show" (quoted from *Curtain Calls*).

The most refreshing performances came from songstress-comedienne Wynn Murray as Lieutenant Sullivan, Irwin Corey as the nutty, gibberish-spouting housing commissioner, Claude Stroud as Officer Clabber, dancers June Graham and Richard D'Arcy, and Dorothy Jarnac, whom Brooks Atkinson (*NYT*) thought deserved a show of her own. She had a show-stopping number with Hayes in which he used pantomime to deliver dictation to her and she danced her comprehension.

(1) **HEDDA GABLER** [Dramatic Revival*] A: Henrik Ibsen; AD: Mary Cass Canfield and Ethel Borden; D/P: Luther Greene; S: Paul Morrison; T: Longacre Theatre; 1/29/42 (12)

Hedda Gabler, which had been revived frequently over the years, was once more mounted on Broadway, this time with Greek star Katina Paxinou performing the title role. Supporting her were Margaret Wycherly as Juliana Tesman, Ralph Forbes as George Tesman, Karen Morley as Mrs. Elvsted, Cecil Humphreys as Judge Brack, and Henry Daniell as Eilert Lovborg.

Although she already had acted in London, the strikingly attractive Paxinou struggled unsuccessfully with the English language and with her inexperience of working with American actors. This created what Rosamond Gilder (*TAM*) viewed as a disharmony of effect stemming from the contrast of her personal style, involving considerable playing to the audience, with that of her company. "Her style," recounted Gilder, "which would take its normal place with her own company of players, stood out as something alien and separate, breaking the theatrical illusion and leaving both Madame Paxinou and her fellow players stranded." Euphemia Van Rensselaer Wyatt (*CW*) missed the character's humor and found the performance too heavily weighted toward malignancy, a view shared by others. Many also pointed to Paxinou's lack of subtlety. On the other hand, Brooks Atkinson (*NYT*) detected "the incandescence of a great actress" in the performance and praised her command of the character while condemning the unintelligibility of her English. Richard Lockridge (*NYS*) believed that the quality of the "bizarre" that the raven-haired Paxinou brought to the role with her studied mannerisms helped clarify both Hedda and the play more than previous interpretations had done. He said that it made her, with her foreign ways, seem a stranger to Ibsen's Norwegians, a visitor from some exotic and violent land.

The "pedestrian" (George Freedley [*NYMT*]) translation attempted to modernize the language, one example being the substitution for the stuffy "Fancy that, Hedda?" of "Can you imagine that, Hedda?" This weakened the character of George by making him seem less foolish than usual.

The acting of the company was generally approved, although no one other than the star stood out. Luther Greene's slowly paced direction was considered competent but unexceptional.

(2) TR/D: Eva Le Gallienne; P: Louis J. Singer and the American Repertory Theatre; T: Cort Theatre; 2/24/48 (15)

The second revival in a short-lived repertory season of Ibsen that attempted to revive the struggling American Repertory Theatre. It followed an unsuccessful version of *Ghosts**, also starring and translated by Eva Le Gallienne, although Margaret Webster, whose direction of *Ghosts* had not been approved, was credited with having "supervised" the production. Several critics, such as Lewis Funke (*NYT*), labeled the play dated and a museum piece that belonged in the museum or library.

Le Gallienne's first stab at Hedda since 1934 was not widely admired. Robert Coleman (*NYDM*) observed, "Her interpretation lacks vitality and authority. It is fumbling, spiritless and physically distracting. It lacks the classic line. It is trivial in stature." George Jean Nathan (*TBY*) was especially severe, faulting the actress for numerous limitations, including an inability to read Hedda with any depth of characterization, and for being unusually "frigid" of temperament. But a small minority admired her work, including Seymour Peck (*PM*), who rebuked the rest of the production and said, "Miss Le Gallienne has realized Hedda's personality most effectively, giving the part depth and understanding. It is a strong, yet disciplined characterization that only occasionally indulges in theatrical excesses."

A lack of inspiration marked the work of the supporting cast, which included Efrem Zimbalist, Jr., as Lovborg, Robert Emhardt as Tesman, Herbert Berghof as Brack, Marion G. Evensen as Miss Juliana Tesman, Merle Maddern as Berta, and Emily McNair as Mrs. Elvsted.

HEEPLE STEEPLE, THE [Drama/Circus/Romance/Sex] A: M. B. Zerwick and H. Peck; D: Carl Shain; P: Robert O'Byrne and Gloria Monty for the Abbe Practical Workshop; T: Master Institute Theatre (OB); 11/13/48 (2)

This first piece done by a group of semipros studying at the Abbe Practical Workshop was "not always a clear play nor one that at all times flows smoothly from scene to scene," thought Vernon Rice (*NYP*). "It does, however, have a consistent mood quality and some compelling interest." Thomas R. Dash (*WWD*) said that the play was not Broadway caliber but contained "a series of powerful scenes that mounted to dramatic crises."

The play is concerned with the shabby lives of a troupe of circus performers, including a lion tamer (Frank Scoblete), a strong man (John Montelle), his aging mistress (Lillian Little), a clown (Bill Golubock), his mercenary sword-swallower girlfriend (Jenna Fleet), the high-wire walker (John Petrone), his wife (Hope Cameron), an evangelist sandwich man (Victor Bartell), and so on. A chief story element tying these folk together is the love of the wife of the wire walker--who is obsessed with his work--for the strong man, who discards his mistress for her. The passions and jealousies incited by this situation lead to tragic results.

(1) HEIRESS, THE [Drama/Family/Legacy/Period/Romance] A: Ruth and Augustus Goetz; SC: Henry James's novel, *Washington Square*; D: Jed Harris; S/L: Raymond Sovey; C: Mary Percy Schenck; P: Fred F. Finklehoffe; T: Biltmore Theatre; 9/29/47 (410)

This hit of the 1947-1948 season was one of the ten best plays of the season and also garnered Tony awards for Basil Rathbone's acting and Mary Percy Schenck's costumes. The authors had had a previous play about a father-daughter relationship on Broadway, 1945's *One-Man Show*, also directed by Jed Harris. They assuaged their bad feelings about that failure by recalling that Henry James had been hooted at the opening of one of his plays, and they at least did not have to face that. Thoughts of James led to their rediscovery of his long-unread book *Washington Square*, similarly about a father and a daughter, and they soon wrote the present drama.

Although Harris was sent the script, the Goetzes were not very anxious to work with him again; when Wendy Hiller, whom he wanted for the lead, proved temporarily unavailable, they went elsewhere for a director and producer. This was not an easy task, as their adherence to the original's unhappy ending put many producers off. Oscar Serlin agreed to produce it, but he had the authors change the ending to a happy one in which the title character, instead of sending her deceitful but contrite lover away, calls him back. However, audiences in New Haven and Boston--where it was presented with the novel's title--reacted negatively to this artificial conclusion and the production closed out of town.

Harris now stepped in and insisted that he could fix the play and turn it into a success. He found a backer in producer Finklehoffe, who was gambling $35,000 on a play that already had flopped. Hiller was hired, other major casting changes (apart from Peter Cookson, who remained) were made, and, in addition to other textual revisions by Harris, the book's original ending was reinstated. Harris restored his badly slumping career to legendary heights by turning the play from a failure to a hit. In his account of the production, *Watchman, What of the Night?*, he took sole credit for the ending, but Martin Gottfried in *Jed Harris: The Curse of Genius* suggested that this was attributable to Harris's egocentricity, and that the revision was more likely a collaborative one. At any rate, Rathbone recalled in *In and Out of Character* that at the first rehearsal, the cast was gathered on stage, when Harris looked out into the house and said, "Those two people sitting out there are the authors. . . . If I catch any of you talking to those people out there you will be sacked immediately. Mr. and Mrs. Goetz know nothing about this play. I have completely rewritten it. Now let's get to work!"

The play begins in 1850, its locale the expensive home of widowed Dr. Austin Sloper (Basil Rathbone) in Washington Square, New York. It tells of the doctor's ugly-duckling daughter Catherine (Wendy Hiller), whose shyness is a major social disability. Dr. Sloper is a tyrant who holds a secret resentment of Catherine because her birth meant the death of Mrs. Sloper, whom he loved deeply and whose loveliness and charm Catherine sorely lacks. Despite her being the rightful heiress to her father's fortune, no beaus pay her court until the appearance of the handsome, well-bred, but poverty-stricken Morris Townsend (Cookson). Catherine is swept off her feet, but Dr. Sloper suspects Morris of being an adventurer and takes Catherine to Europe to get her away from him. Catherine retains her affection for Morris and arranges to elope with him when she returns. But Morris, discovering that she has been cut off from her father's money, jilts her on the night of the elopement. This kills all spark of feeling in Catherine, who inherits Dr. Sloper's money on his death. Morris, penitent, returns two years later and attempts to regain her good graces. When he comes to elope with her again, Catherine, having seen through his lies, refuses to let him in the house, which has become her old maid's tomb.

On opening night, wrote Gottfried, the eccentric director was drunk and paranoiac. He stood tensely at the rear of the theatre as the audience applauded during the curtain calls. As two critics moved up the aisle, he believed that he heard one of them carping about the play. Without warning, he began to beat the critic over the head with a rolled-up newspaper. When the other critic tried to protect his colleague, he received the same treatment before making his escape. Nevertheless, apart from some reservations on the part of the morning reviewers, the play received notices strong enough to turn the play into a hit.

The Heiress was brilliantly acted by all those already named, as well as by Patricia Collinge as Lavinia Penniman, Catherine's aunt, Betty Linley as Morris's widowed sister Mrs. Montgomery, and Augusta Roeland, Fiona O'Shiel, Katherine Raht, and Craig Kelly in smaller roles.

It seemed a somewhat static play, quiet and lacking in overt dramatics, but was nevertheless gripping because of its honest characterizations and lack of sentimentality. The play "maintains magnitude and merit," thought Robert Garland (*NYJA*). Thomas R. Dash (*WWD*) said that it was "distinguished for its simple but absorbingly developed story, the precision of its suave direction, and the capital quality of its performances." Brooks Atkinson (*NYT*) noted the difficulty of making a strong play about "a stupid woman," but otherwise found this a drama "of intelligence and good taste."

Atkinson was not convinced by Hiller's acting of what he thought an unactable part, but most of his colleagues thought her superb. "Miss Hiller has a sensitive touch," wrote Rosamond Gilder (*TAM*), "a retarded grace as though each action were thought out in advance but approached with a sort of spiritual reluctance. It is an admirable though perhaps unconscious transposition into acting terms of James' own stylistic manner."

Rathbone did the play because he was anxious to break the public's association of him with his successful Sherlock Holmes films. He found working with Jed Harris a fascinating experience, partly because Harris insisted that the actor wear the character's beard from the very beginning of rehearsals, and partly because the cast sat at a table and read for ten days before the blocking began. Not long after the opening, Rathbone fell while walking his dogs in Central Park and broke his arm badly. After the bones had been set by an idiosyncratic doctor friend of Harris's, the director instantly worked out a way for Rathbone to perform the play with his arm in a sling, doing all his business with his left arm only. This worked so well that many spectators actually thought that the sling and cast were intentional parts of the characterization.

(2) [Dramatic Revival] D: Basil Rathbone w/Jed Harris; S/L: Peter Wolf; C: Emeline Roche; P: New York City Theatre Company; T: City Center of Music and Drama; 2/8/50 (16)

The New York City Theatre Company was under Maurice Evans's "artistic supervision," but he did not act in all its productions. The last of the four plays put on under his aegis was this revival of *The Heiress*, starring Basil Rathbone in the role he first played in 1947; the original director assisted him in the direction. Betty Linley and Katherine Raht returned to their roles as well, but the others were newcomers, including the talented Margaret Phillips as Catherine, Edna Best as Lavinia, and John Dall as Morris.

There was nothing wrong with the revival (although a few critics thought that the large City Center dwarfed the play), and the new players were every bit as good as their predecessors, but there was some question as to why a repertory company whose goals were to emulate Britain's Old Vic should have chosen so recent a Broadway (and film) hit as part of its season. At any rate, the play was still compelling and worth viewing.

Phillips, who had played Catherine on a summer-theatre tour with Rathbone, was equal--even superior, in some eyes--to the performances of the original, Wendy Hiller, and Hiller's replacement, Beatrice Straight. She endowed the role, wrote Bron. (*V*), "with a fluttery, delicate aura that magically captures the mood of a discarded, distraught young maiden. Her rapid, bitter growth to maturity is also sharply etched, to make this quite a characterization." Rathbone's acting, said Brooks Atkinson (*NYT*), remained "unctuous in manner, but immaculately cruel, glib but monstrous, a perfectly designed piece of work." Dall, observed Whitney Bolton (*NYMT*), "is completely acceptable as the suitor. . . . One minute you believe him to be a nice boy with a sincere heart and the next you know him to be a low fellow out to snag the swag of an heiress."

HELEN GOES TO TROY [Musical/Fantasy/Period/Politics/Romance/Sex] B: Gottfried Reinhardt and John Meehan, Jr.; LY: Herbert Baker; M: Erich Wolfgang Korngold (adaptor); SC: Max Reinhardt's production of Jacques Offenbach's *La Belle Hélène*; D: Herbert Graf, Melville Cooper (dialogue), and Irving Landau (songs); CH: Leonide Massine; S/L: Robert Edmond Jones; C: Ladislas Czettel; P: Yolanda Mero-Irion for the New Opera Company; T: Alvin Theatre; 4/24/44 (96)

Austrian regisseur Max Reinhardt's version of Offenbach's operetta *La Belle Hélène*, seen years earlier in Berlin, was adapted for Broadway by his son and John Meehan, Jr., and by composer Erich Korngold. The latter adapted and cut considerably the original Offenbach score, added some of his own compositions, interpolated the well-known "Barcarolle" from *The Tales of Hoffman* (it was sung under the title "Love at Last"), as well as thirteen other Offenbach numbers, and also acted as conductor. The book was updated to sound topical and American; it had such new and dire gags as having Menelaus (Ernest Truex) respond to being called a louse by saying, "Yes, I am Menelouse." Some of the dialogue was considered blue, such as Menelaus' speech in which he remembers being drunk, falling into bed with his wife (who is there with Paris), and counting six feet sticking out of the covers. The adaptors, in a desperate grab for laughs, even lugged in a moment in which Menelaus sang a bit of Jerome Kern's "The Last Time I Saw Paris."

Lewis Nichols (*NYT*) suggested that the book lacked wit and required cutting, and George Freedley (*NYMT*) judged the book "heavy-handed, dull and tasteless." But there were also staunch advocates of the show, such as Howard Barnes (*NYHT*), who found it "good-looking, tuneful and great good fun."

This is the tale of the beauteous Helen of Troy (Jarmila Novotna, of the Metropolitan Opera House; Lillian Anderson at matinees), married to the mousy Menelaus and sexually accommodated by the handsome Paris (William Horne; Joseph Laderoute at matinees), brought to Sparta (in the operetta, but not in Homer) by Calchas to satisfy her needs. Helen and Paris eventually flee to Troy with Menelaus, his cohorts, and the wooden horse in pursuit.

What appeal the show had lay largely in its melodic score, adapted as it was, and in the unusual sumptuousness of the presentation. It was lauded for its exceptionally colorful and imaginative sets and costumes, an expert cast, and effective staging. There was some praise for a bacchanal created by Massine, but in general, his choreography was less than noteworthy.

Dumke and Truex were lauded, and many approved the operatic talents and looks of the Czechoslovakian-born Novotna, but George Jean Nathan (*TBY*) was seriously disturbed at how physically inappropriate she was for a woman whose face launched so many ships. Donald Buka played the rakish Orestes, Peggy Corday was Venus, Jesse White was Ajax I, Alfred Porter was Ajax II (the twin of the other Ajax and a new character), Gordon Dilworth was Agamemnon, and Hugh Johnson was Achilles.

(1) **"HELLO OUT THERE"** and **"MAGIC"** [One-Acts] D/P: Eddie Dowling; S: Watson Barratt; L: A. H. Feder; T: Belasco Theatre; 9/29/42 (47)
"Hello Out There" [Drama/Gambling/Prison/Romance/Sex/Small Town/Southern] A: William Saroyan; "Magic" [Dramatic Revival] A: G. K. Chesterton

Eddie Dowling and Julie Haydon, who had costarred in Saroyan's *The Time of Your Life** and would again hit the jackpot of theatrical immortality a couple of years later as Tom and Laura in *The Glass Menagerie*, costarred in this bill of two one-acters by Chesterton and Saroyan. The Saroyan piece showed how good his short plays could be when handled by the theatre's finest talents, as opposed to his own mishandling of a pair of his plays a month before.

Set in a jail in Matador, Texas, "Hello Out There" concentrates on Photo Finish (Dowling), a traveling young gambler who has been imprisoned for rape; he is the innocent victim of a vindictive married woman (Ann Driscoll) who seduced him and then disgusted him by asking for money. In his isolation, he keeps tapping on the floor with a spoon and calling out the words of the title. Ethel (Haydon), a frightened, equally lonely girl who works in the jail as a cook responds to his anguished pleas, and a romantic relationship immediately develops between them. He urges her to go to San Francisco, where she will have a chance to make a life for herself. When a lynch mob threatens to kill the gambler, she gives him a gun to protect himself. Nevertheless, he is shot by the husband (John Farrell) of the woman he allegedly attacked, and the anguished Ethel repeats the title phrase over his dead body. The body is then carried out to be hung from a tree.

Dowling and Haydon were, for many, luminous in their portrayals of the central roles. However, John Mason Brown (*NYWT*) thought Dowling too old for his role, the direction "amateurish," and the decor poorly realized.

The play was widely, but not universally, admired. "Although 'Hello Out There' is a small play, it is a perfect creation and the freshest episode in the theatre this season," wrote Brooks Atkinson (*NYT*). Howard Barnes (*NYHT*) said that the play "ranks with the finest pieces of its genre which have emerged on our stage." But Wilella Waldorf (*NYP*) thought that the piece seemed dated and too similar to the kind of earnest one-acts often seen at little theatres. Louis Kronenberger (*PM*) calculated that it was "not sustained; it lacks intensity. And it is not controlled; Saroyan wanders away, too often, into words." In general, it was viewed as a tragic depiction of a search for human compassion and for some meaning in life and was appreciated for its straightforward manner in contrast to some of Saroyan's more whimsical but artistically muddled efforts.

The piece first had been seen in the Lobero Theatre in Santa Barbara, California, where, with Dowling heading the cast, David O. Selznick produced it on a bill of one-acters. When it was dress rehearsing in New York, Saroyan brought a number of eccentric cronies to the theatre to watch. One was sidewalk chalk artist Bill Cody, who dressed like his cowboy namesake. Saroyan moseyed over to Cody after the rehearsal to ask his opinion of the play. With tears running down his cheeks, Cody replied, "Best goddamned show I ever saw." "Tell me, Bill, did you ever see a play before?" inquired Saroyan. "Nope--first show I ever saw," answered Cody (reported in Al Hirschfeld, *Show Business Is No Business*).

The main piece on the bill was a verbose 1913 allegorical English fantasy about the search for faith. It was first seen here in 1917 with Cathleen Nesbitt and O. P. Heggie in the roles now played by Haydon and Dowling. The story concerns an Irish lass named Patricia Carleon who believes in fairies until her faith in them is destroyed by a professional magician, who turns out to be the sprite she thought she saw in the duke's (Stanley Harrison) garden. There ensues a debate about illusion and reality, religion and science among the conjurer and several other interested parties, an agnostic physician (John McKee), a cleric with religious doubts (Bram Nossen), the humorous duke, who sees both sides of every question, and a gruff American oil tycoon (Jess Barker), the girl's brother. The conjurer performs a trick that may not be a trick but so confuses the American that he nearly loses his mind. To restore his sanity, the conjurer must reveal the nature of his illusion, although whether it was a trick or not remains for the audience to decide.

Some critics could not understand why Dowling chose to revive the play. Atkinson dismissed it as "a prolonged and somewhat tortured tergiversation in an outmoded style of writing." Edgar Price (*BC*) said that it was much too "talky and monotonous." Brown, however, appreciated it for its conversational brilliance, if not for the poor production he thought it received.

(2) "HELLO OUT THERE," THOSE ENDEARING YOUNG CHARMS (scenes), and **"THE SHY AND THE LONELY"** P: Equity Library Theatre; T: Muhlenberg Branch of the New York Public Library (OB); 11/8/44 (2)
"Hello Out There" [Dramatic Revival] D: Teresa Hayden; *Those Endearing Young Charms* [Dramatic Revival] A: Edward Chodorov; D: Aline MacMahon; "The Shy and the Lonely" [Drama/Military/One-Act/Romance/Sex] A: Irwin Shaw; D: Aline MacMahon

Equity's showcase theatre organization produced this revival of "Hello Out

There" (without the Chesterton play), and George Freedley (*NYMT*) thought it a better production than the much-heralded Dowling-Haydon original. Ramsay Williams played Photo Finish, Jeanne McNally was Ethel, John Arine was the revenge-seeking husband, and Geraldine Braun was the allegedly raped wife.

The bill also contained scenes from *Those Endearing Young Charms* (see that title for details) and a long one-acter by Irwin Shaw, "The Shy and the Lonely." Freedley called this "the hit of the day" and said that it was deserving of a Broadway move as it was. Mason Adams played the role of a virginal young soldier and was considered outstanding. The female romantic role was played by Joy Geffen.

HENRI CHRISTOPHE [Drama/Blacks/Period/Politics/Religion/Tropics] A: Dan Hammerman; D: Joe Hill; S/C: Charles Sebree; P: American Negro Theatre; T: 135th Street Library Theatre (OB); 6/6/45 (25)

A nineteenth-century king of Haiti was the subject of this "confused and static" (George Jean Nathan [*TBY*]) historical drama telling of the revolt by the islanders against the French colonialists and their crowning of Christophe (Frederick O'Neal). The same character was the subject of William Du Bois's *Haiti** (1938), staged by the Federal Theatre Project. Whereas that play had ended triumphantly with the expulsion of the French, the present one traces Christophe's rise from slavery to a position on Toussaint L'Ouverture's (Austin Briggs-Hall) staff and then to a career as a ruthless dictator whose behavior forces his people to rebel and his wife and the Church to turn their backs on him. Christophe's suicide ends the drama. The play included some voodoo dances in a vain attempt to stir up interest.

"Mr. Hammerman," wrote an unsigned *NYT* reviewer, "is . . . a talkative playwright rather than an inventive one; his drama lacks both excitement and internal energy." O'Neal's performance was unimpressive.

(1) HENRY IV (*Enrico IV*) [Dramatic Revival*] A: Luigi Pirandello; AD/D: John Reich; S: Warren Ream; C: Meg Wyllie; L: Cyril Simon; P: Lamont Johnson i/a/w Equity Library Theatre; T: Greenwich Mews Playhouse (OB); 5/47

A highly acceptable version of Pirandello's drama, first seen here in 1924 under the title *The Living Mask**. George Freedley (*NYMT*), the sole reviewer present, said that "it was a first-rate job of adapting into lucid and colloquial English the determinedly obscurist style of one of the modern theater's most subtle minds." Adaptor/director Reich helped make the play easily comprehensible by his effective staging.

In the title role of the man who pretends to be a medieval monarch, Herbert Berghof, said Freedley, gave "a striking and impressive performance." However, the performance lacked smoothness, ostensibly because Berghof was then preoccupied with rehearsals for a role in a Broadway play. Among others in the play were Mary Welch, Don Keefer, Robert McGrane, and Hugh Franklin.

(2) TR: Edward Storer; D: Alexis Solomos; P: On-Stage; T: Cherry Lane Theatre (OB); 12/10/47

This barely known revival by a group of valiant semipro troupers was "a routine-to-poor presentation" (George Freedley [*NYMT*]) because the cast and director could not communicate the play's meanings. The mumbling actors could not be understood, and none of them were up to the drama's demands, although Jean [Gene] Saks would have been far better if he had been able to project his intelligent characterization. Louis Criss was acceptable as Lolo.

HENRY IV, PART I [Dramatic Revival*] A: William Shakespeare; M: Herbert Menges; D: John Burrell; CH: (fights) Peter Copley; S: Gower Parks; C: Roger Furse; L: John Sullivan; P: Theatre Incorporated i/a/w the Old Vic Company; T: Century Theatre; 5/6/46 (14)

The first salvo in the memorable six-week, five-play repertory of London's visiting Old Vic Company, then headed by Laurence Olivier and Ralph Richardson, who played Hotspur and Falstaff, respectively. This was the Old Vic's first American tour as well as being the first postwar visit by any British company, so there was a built-in fascination for American audiences, who were thrilled to accept on their shores the intrepid Britons who had just endured such hell on theirs. Shakespeare's chronicle play had last been seen locally in 1939 in an excellent version, but the present one, cut only slightly, was even more brilliant because of the gallery of talent employed. Nicholas Hannen was Henry IV, Michael Warre was Prince Hal, Robin Lloyd was John of Lancaster, Peter Copley was Westmoreland, Cecil Winter was Blunt, Miles Malleson was Northumberland, David Kentish was Mortimer, Harry Andrews was Owen Glendower, William Monk was Douglas, Michael Raghan was Bardolph, Sidney Tafler was Poins, George Rose (in his American debut) was Peto, Ena Burrill was Mistress Quickly, Margaret Leighton (in her American debut) was Lady Percy, and Diana Maddox was Lady Mortimer.

In the opinion of many, the production brought the play to vivid life, with an expert, if not overwhelming, ensemble in support of brilliant turns by Olivier and Richardson. The latter, wearing a mountainous suit of heavy padding, conveyed the character's blustering humor and wit with great perception and was a figure of Rabelaisian amiability. John Mason Brown (*SR*) considered him "the most unsentimentalized and unflinchingly venal Sir John" he had ever seen. "He is a fellow deplorable yet lovable, delightful though conscienceless, greasy but grand, contemptible and superior, rowdy and aristocratic, all at one time." "He swaggers and staggers with magnificent aplomb," noted Howard Barnes (*NYHT*), "and bids for no mawkish sympathy, even in his more ignoble aspects." Richardson's tavern scene with Hal in which he played the king was unforgettable, as was his speech at Shrewsbury on honor.

He was well contrasted by Olivier's stammering Hotspur, rash, impetuous, and honorable to a fault. His energetic performance, lacking in the usual rant and stridency, was dynamic and compelling. His martial scenes were electric, and he proved quite touching with Lady Percy.

Lewis Nichols (*NYT*) praised the company for its unified conception and execution. "Its players, accustomed to one another, have thought out every move and every action in relation to each other and to the play itself. Their scenery is light and not scholastic; the accompanying music is simple and unobtrusive." Although the company's strength was widely praised, Brown thought the ensemble uninspired but "as a rule satisfactory." He and others felt that Michael Warre was the greatest disappointment in his failure to convey the royalty of Hal. Louis Kronenberger (*PM*) was one of several who argued that the verse was not as magnificently spoken as had been expected, and he too noted "a good deal of no more than adequate performing." He agreed with Brown about the merely competent values of the overall production. Brown noted its inability to make the outdoor scenes as effective as a film might have made them (a feeling exacerbated by his recent viewing of Olivier's movie of *Henry V*). George Jean Nathan (*TBY*) took serious issue with the "tediously conversational" direction, which he blamed for being unimaginative and plodding. What impressed Kronenberger, however, was "a fine sense of theater that never slips into mere theatricality, and an excellent sense of balance about the two sides of the play."

Work that stood out was provided by Leighton, Malleson, and Hannen. The play was given in tandem with the much less often seen *Henry IV, Part II*.

HENRY IV, PART II [Dramatic Revival] A: William Shakespeare; M: Herbert Menges; D: John Burrell; S: Gower Parks; C: Roger Furse; L: John Sullivan; P: Theatre Incorporated i/a/w the Old Vic Company; T: Century Theatre; 5/7/46 (6)

The last known local production of *Henry IV, Part II* had been in 1867, so its revival as part of the five-play repertory brought to New York by London's Old Vic on its first American tour was something of an occasion. As in the company's revival of *Henry IV, Part I**, with which it was played in tandem, it was memorable for the performances of its two leading players, Ralph Richardson and Laurence Olivier, the company's artistic directors. However, whereas Richardson continued to develop his brilliant Falstaff, who appears in both plays, Olivier displayed his remarkable versatility by representing the minor role of Justice Shallow. His performance had such humorous insight as to make it one of the most significant elements in the production. The contrast with his Hotspur in Part I was unusually striking, but the star would go on in other plays in the repertory to display yet further dimensions of his extraordinary range and chameleon-like ability to change his appearance.

Comparing Olivier's Hotspur to his Shallow, Euphemia Van Rensselaer Wyatt (*CW*) wrote, "Astoundingly enough, although Olivier as [Hotspur] appears to be a red-haired youth of rather stocky build, his Shallow's sparse white locks and long thin nose belong to a body which seems some thirty pounds lighter--the wraith of Sir John's [Falstaff's] student days at the Temple Inns of Court." Lewis Nichols (*NYT*) described this Shallow as "old and bent, with a squeaky, rasping voice and the manner of a male old-lady-in-the-shoe. The contrast between Shallow's niggardly affairs and Falstaff's grandiose ones makes the Olivier-Richardson scenes pure comedy on a towering level."

The production proved that the play was worth more frequent revival, although the script had been heavily edited, with healthy chunks excised to make it move swiftly and to keep the audience's interest high. The resulting version stressed the comic cavortings of Falstaff, Shallow, Mistress Quickly (Ena Burrill), and Doll Tearsheet (Joyce Redman) over the more somber historical events. This emphasis tended to make the banishment of Falstaff by Prince Hal (Michael Warre) that much more poignant.

John Chapman (*NYDN*) spoke for many in declaring that the play "is a glowing, vigorous work whose drama is relieved by superbly lusty, delightfully lewd comedy." Redman's luridly blowsy, inebriated Mistress Quickly--with its startlingly ample décolletage--was a comic gem, but Warre's prince was again deemed a drawback to the overall quality of the ensemble. Nicholas Hannen was Henry IV, Cecil Winter was the Chief Justice, George Relph doubled as Pistol, Miles Malleson was Justice Silence, Harry Andrews was Scroop, Margaret Leighton was Lady Percy, and George Rose quadrupled as Clarence, Bardolph, Peto, and Mouldy. Despite the praise for the production and its stars, there was still a feeling that the direction was not as imaginative as that provided in recent years by Margaret Webster's revivals.

HERSCHEL THE JESTER [Musical/Jews/Period/Religion/Romance/Yiddish Language] A/D: Maurice Schwartz; SC: Moshe Livshitz's story of the same name; M: Joseph Rumshinsky; CH: Selma Schneider; DS: Leon Poch; P/T: Yiddish Art Theatre (OB); 12/12/48

A musical folk-comedy adapted from material by Moshe Livshitz, who based his story on fact-based Jewish folklore. It is set in the Ukraine in the latter part of the eighteenth century and based on an actual jester.

Herschel Ostroloper (Maurice Schwartz) entertains the Rabbinical Court of the pious Hassidic rabbi Baruch (Boris Auerbach). In one hilarious scene, he cures the rabbi of a bone stuck in the latter's throat by causing him to laugh so loudly at two stuttering merchants that the bone comes flying out. This poor but rascally jester has idealistic tendencies and favors the oppressed over the rich. The main action stems from Herschel's opposition to his daughter Perele's (Sara Gingold) desire to marry Moyshe Nachum (Muni Serebrov), the foppish son (he speaks a tony Viennese brand of Yiddish) of the wealthy businessman Zalman (David Medoff). Herschel wants Perele to marry the orthodox student Michael (Anatole Winogradoff). Herschel also needs money to cover the debt he incurred when he borrowed to pay for his wife's (Anna Appel) burial, although she is very much alive. Various complications ensue, and Herschel escapes from several close calls by resorting to his canny wit, until the play ends with Perele getting the man of her choice and Zalman agreeing to spread his ill-gotten wealth around. Other plot ingredients concern a plot against the tsar.

"Mr. Schwartz clowns like an experienced buffoon, climbs all over the furniture when his wife comes after him with a rolling pin . . . , performs a jig deftly, kicks his leg high in the air, and sings a batch of characteristic Jewish songs," recounted Seymour Peck (*TS*). Schwartz's vehicle, however, was too long, had too much plot, and had too many similar songs and dances; on the other hand, it was filled with wonderful folk atmosphere, funny lines and situations, and excellent ensemble acting. Thomas R. Dash (*WWD*) called it "a racy, pungent, colorful folk opera that is played zestfully with broad humor."

HICKORY STICK [Drama/Romance/School/Youth] A: Frederick Stephani and Murray Burnett; D: J. B. Daniels; S: Frederick Fox; P: Marjorie Ewing and Marie Louise Elkins; T: Mansfield Theatre; 5/8/44 (8)

A well-intentioned, but amateurishly written drama about juvenile delinquents in New York City's blackboard jungle. Steve Cochran made an impressive Broadway debut in the role of James Kirkland, an idealistic war veteran who, after being wounded on Guadalcanal, returns from combat to take a job as a teacher in Truxton Vocational High School. This is a tough institution peopled by hard-core problem students and conducive to breeding more of the same. Kirkland wants to use progressive methods to give these kids a chance he believes they deserve. His experiences are focused on two students, the mentally twisted Steven Ames (Richard Basehart), a brilliant boy who reads Nietzsche and Schopenhauer, and Tony Pessolano (Vito Christi), a regular troublemaker. Tony becomes Kirkland's worshipper when the veteran reveals that he was the buddy of Tony's late brother, who was killed at Guadalcanal. Steven hates Kirkland and plans to turn Tony against him. When a gun is hidden at the school by Tony's gangster brother Joe (Dehl Berti), the sick Steven threatens Kirkland with it, but is killed by Tony defending his hero. Kirkland must now try to explain Tony's action to the authorities. Also of importance to the plot is the contrast between the liberal ideas of Kirkland and those of the cynical teacher Walsh (Lawrence Fletcher), who has no illusions about educating his charges and believes that the proper treatment for them lies in his strong fists. (The ironic outcome of this contrast was that the cynical teacher came off seeming the wiser.) There is, moreover, a romantic alliance of sorts between Tony's sister (Adrienne Bayan) and Steven, whom she cares for and supplies with books.

Loose ends in the plot, unpleasant characters, coarse language and jokes that seemed sensationalistic insertions, an unnecessary romantic interest, the failure to go beyond the obvious in solving the social problem stated, and an implausible melodramatic ending were among the reasons for the play's demise. "The play is contrived rather than felt, stagey rather than dramatic," observed Burton Rascoe (*NYWT*). It was very well acted, however. The cast included Frieda Altman, Farrell Pelly, Ray Fry, Lorraine Pressler, and others.

One of the authors, Murray Burnett, was the author of *Everybody Comes to Rick's*, the story that was made into the film *Casablanca*.

HIDDEN HORIZON [Drama/British/Crime/Mystery/Tropics] A: Agatha Christie; SC: Agatha Christie's novel, *Death on the Nile*; D: Albert de Courville; S: Charles Elson; C: Everett Staples; P: Messrs. Shubert i/a/w Albert de Courville; T: Plymouth Theatre; 9/19/46 (12)

This "talky and enervating" (Ibee. [*V*]) British murder-mystery import adapted by Agatha Christie from one of her own novels proved to be "dull in theme, dull in story, dull in the acting," according to Brooks Atkinson (*NYT*). It "had dialogue which made one hope for sudden deafness," griped Vernon Rice (*NYP*).

It was set on the paddle steamer *Lotus*, plying the Nile with a boatload of tourists. Kay (Barbara Joyce) is a wealthy young Englishwoman who marries Simon Mostyn (Blair Davies), a heel who jilts Jacqueline De Severac (Diana Barrymore) to marry the richer woman. The pistol-packing Jacqueline, who seems to follow Kay and Simon everywhere, shoots Simon in the leg and angrily threatens Kay's life. After Jacqueline imbibes several double brandies, her rival is shot dead in her cabin. While the passengers await the arrival on a launch of the police, the Archdeacon Pennyfeather (Halliwell Hobbes), the slain bride's uncle, engages in some persistent questioning, and Simon, too, does some detective work. During his sleuthing, the French maid (Edith Kingdon), who knows something, is shot by a hidden killer just as she is on the point of being bribed to name the murderer. The killer is uncovered by the clergyman from among the various passengers; these include a wealthy young Communist going under the assumed name of Smith (David Manners); Miss Fanny Ffoliot-Foulkes (Eva Leonard-Boyne); her niece (Joy Ann Page, stepdaughter of movie magnate Jack Warner); and a Hungarian doctor (Peter von

Zerneck). It turns out that Simon and Jacqueline have been in cahoots and that Kay has been killed in order to get hold of her fortune.

HIGH BUTTON SHOES [Musical/Business/Crime/Gambling/Period/Sports/University/Youth] B: George Abbott and Phil Silvers (uncredited); M: Jule Styne; LY: Sammy Cahn; SC: Stephen Longstreet's novel, *The Sisters Liked Them Handsome*; D: George Abbott; CH: Jerome Robbins; S: Oliver Smith; C: Miles White; L: Peggy Clark; P: Monte Proser and Joe Kipness; T: New Century Theatre; 10/9/47 (727)

Phil Silvers and Nanette Fabray were the star performers in this nostalgia-laden hit musical comedy based on a semiautobiographical book by Stephen Longstreet and benefiting from the first Broadway score by Styne and Cahn, who split up soon after. Silvers received strong notices, although there were cavils at some of his material. But Fabray stole the show. Robert Coleman (*NYDM*) wrote, "Nanette Fabray gives the best performance of her life, a performance of authority, skill, warmth and enchantment."

Actually, Fabray's role originally had been given to Vivienne Segal, who had a run-of-the-play contract. When composer Styne saw Fabray in *Meet the People*, he wanted to use her instead, but Segal's contract would not allow her to be replaced. According to Theodore Taylor's *Jule*, this led to a nasty trick played on Segal. She was invited to perform at a backer's audition, but then learned that the two prospective hit songs, "Papa, Won't You Dance with Me?" and "I Still Get Jealous," would not be played. When she inquired why, producer Kipness lied, "They're out. The boys are writing new material." "Then I'm out too," Segal replied. "The only reason I took the show was because of those numbers."

Fabray herself was originally reluctant to play the role because she was a young and vibrantly attractive performer, and the character was of a woman with an adolescent son. She did not feel that she was quite ready for mother roles, despite the promise of pretty costumes. But she finally accepted the assignment and was so good she won the Donaldson Award for the best musical comedy performance by an actress.

The show was conceived when Styne, a Beverly Hills neighbor of Longstreet's, one day came across an article about the latter's book, which immediately suggested a musical to him. The original libretto was by Longstreet himself, but when director Abbott, who took the job belatedly (he replaced Mary Hunter), read it a day before rehearsals were set to begin, he that realized he would have to rewrite it. Even before this, however, the script had undergone major revisions. Silvers had not been interested in the original text and only joined on when someone got the idea of shifting the show's focus to the then-minor role of huckster Harrison Floy. This focus remained after Abbott signed on. Longstreet now turned his back on the project (although he continued to receive handsome royalties), not even deigning to see the show until the closing night of the second Los Angeles company.

For a time, Silvers, as he wrote in *This Laugh Is on Me*, was dissatisfied, feeling that his own material was not funny enough and that Abbott was taking the wrong approach. Abbott, for his part, had difficulty appreciating Silvers's unique brand of physical humor. In one scene, where Floy was cornered by an angry group whom he had fleeced, Abbott gave him no dialogue to extricate himself from the crisis. Silvers decided at one rehearsal to grin widely at the threatening group and deliver an enthusiastically friendly "Glad to see ya!" It broke the company up, but Abbott was unmoved. "Phil, I don't want to restrict you, but--what's funny about that? It doesn't make sense?" he said and proceeded to cut the moment.

Finally, Silvers's contributions began to have telling effects during the Philadelphia tryouts. The word was out that the show was in trouble (Silvers himself had been suffering serious vocal problems), so he told Abbott that he would ad-lib his part, but always within the framework of the original story and period. This method clicked and earned him his coauthor's credit. During the Broadway run, he continually made improvements. By the fourth week he felt that he achieved the quality he would like to have presented at the opening.

Although none of Longstreet's lines were retained in the Broadway version, the author was nevertheless speaking to the press about who might play Silvers's role in a movie version (never made). This so infuriated Silvers that he wired Longstreet, "If I read any more press releases from you on who is going to do my role in the picture, I will play this show exactly as you wrote it."

After the show became a hit, its producers ran into legal difficulties when fired director Hunter sued and was awarded $1,500 plus three-quarters of one percent of the weekly gross. At first her claim for personal damages was overthrown, but an appeal earned her additional recompense. Another suit was brought by Mack Sennett because a major scene borrowed techniques used in his silent Keystone Kops movies. An out-of-court settlement took care of this claim.

The period is 1913, with its Model Ts and hobble skirts, the place is New Brunswick, New Jersey, and some of the characters are the Longstreet family themselves, including little Stevie (Johnny Stewart). Harrison Floy is a con man whose former neighbors, especially Sara (Fabray) and Henry Longstreet (Jack McCauley), think him a rising entrepreneur. Floy seems to Sara a likely mate for her sister Fran (Lois Lee), although Fran's heart is set on Rutgers football star Hubert Ogglethorpe (Mark Dawson), a native of Texas. Floy gets into trouble when, at a community picnic, he uses his pitchman skills to sell the neighbors some swampland owned by the Longstreets. When the ruse is discovered, a chase commences. The money is in Fran's hands, so Floy and his crony, Mr. Pontdue (Joey Faye), run off with her to Atlantic City, Floy proposing marriage to Fran as a way of getting his hands on the cash. Young Stevie overhears their plans, so the Longstreets follow in their Model T. On the beach at Atlantic City occurs the show's famous highlight, the brilliantly staged Mack Sennett Keystone Kops sequence devised by Jerome Robbins. "It's a masterpiece of fast fooling which begins on the beach and ends up with policemen, vamps, bathing beauties, crooks, plus a gorilla, losing themselves in and out of a long line of bathing houses with the audience gasping and in stitches," wrote Euphemia Van Rensselaer Wyatt (*CW*). Fran goes home to New Brunswick and Hubert. Pontdue robs the money from Floy and flees. When Floy catches up to him, there is little money left. Meanwhile, Fran and Hubert are back together in New Brunswick. Feeling guilty, Floy tries to recoup the money he has lost by betting against Rutgers in the football game with Princeton and even tries to fix the game by getting Rutgers to lose. Floy's ploy fails, and he begins to conjure up another scam, but the arrival of the police puts him on the lam again.

Robbins had a big success with his brilliant choreography, including a number with the Rutgers football team and their girls, a tango number featuring Helen Gallagher and Paul Godkin, and the picnic scene in which "Papa, Won't You Dance with Me?" was introduced and frequently encored. Among the better songs were "He Tried to Make a Dollar," "Next to Texas I Love You," "Bird Watcher's Song," "On a Sunday By the Sea," "Get Away for a Day in the Country," and "You're My Girl."

Despite the generally high level of approval for the show, some critics, such as George Jean Nathan (*TBY*), had to look hard for things to enjoy in what Nathan called an "inferior show." Several appreciated large portions of it but found too much simply a loosely strung sequence of burlesque or vaudeville routines. Especially distasteful to some was the homosexually oriented comedy song, "You're My Boy," sung by Silvers and Faye. More common were opinions like Brooks Atkinson's (*NYT*), which judged this "an immensely likable musical show in a vein that was equally funny but much less splendid on the old Columbia wheel," or that of Thomas R. Dash (*WWD*), who declared that it "proved fresh, bright and pleasantly diverting."

The Mack Sennet chase is probably the best remembered thing in the show and was recreated for *Jerome Robbins's Broadway* in 1989. During its dress rehearsal, however, an unforeseen problem arose when the opening and closing of the bathhouse doors added an unacceptable extra beat to the sequence. When the actor in the gorilla suit made a flub, the rehearsal was stopped and Robbins berated him. Silvers recalled that the actor was standing in his gorilla suit, "with only slits for eyes in its giant head. As Jerry shouted, the gorilla muttered to me: 'One more word out of him and I'll claw him to death.'"

Among the chorus dancers was future comic star Dolores (Dody) Goodman.

HIGH KICKERS [Musical/Hotel/Legacy/Romance/Show Business/Trial] B: George Jessel, Bert Kalmar, and Harry Ruby; M/LY: Bert Kalmar and Harry Ruby; SC: a "suggestion" by Sid Silvers; D: Edward Sobol; CH: Carl Randall; DS: Nat Karson; P: George Jessel and Alfred Bloomingdale; T: Broadhurst Theatre; 10/31/41 (171)

Legendary vaudeville songstress and "red hot Mamma" Sophie Tucker played herself in this lighthearted, nostalgic, and often off-color musical romp in which George Jessel played two characters, father and son, as well as cowriting the rather feeble book.

Still, Tucker dominated the entertainment, to which she gave mingled elements of burlesque, vaudeville, nightclub, and legitimate musical comedy. It tells a story that begins in 1910 when George M. Krause's (Jessel) show, *High Kickers*, is playing at an Eighth Avenue burlesque theatre. Krause collapses and hands on the troupe to his boy, George, Jr. (Dick Monahan as a child; Jessel as an adult). Thirty-one years go by and the dapper George, Jr., is trying out the latest version of the show in Chambersville, Ohio, with the uptight Mayor Wilberforce (Chick York) and his wife, Hortense (Rose King), watching from a box. The puritanical mayor stops the performance when Sophie, George, Jr.,'s foster mother, begins a striptease act. She has chosen to do it to protect ingenue Kitty McKay (Lois January), scheduled to do the act, from losing her true love, Jimmy Wilberforce (Lee Sullivan), the mayor's boy. (There was some controversy over the stout Tucker's routine, but she was dressed in tights, and some could not understand the commotion.) The company is arrested and a hilarious courtroom scene follows. In it, George, Jr., has to demonstrate his knowledge of show biz for the district attorney, which he does by presenting a slew of impressions of such figures as George M. Cohan and Eddie Cantor. Finally, the troupe's problems are resolved when Sophie recognizes in the mayor's wife a former burlesque queen.

There were some rude lyrics in Tucker's numbers, precipitating rebukes from several critics. Her best songs were "Didn't Your Mother Tell You Nothing," sung with gusto to a group of presumably innocent showgirls, and "I Got Something (I've Got My Man)," which contained a naughty line about a mattress. Brooks Atkinson (*NYT*) observed, "Miss Tucker is a singer in the grand manner. No matter what her material may be, she uses it with humor, deliberation and authority. The material this time is all in the key of the single entendre, written in a style that went out with mahjong, we hope. It is burlesque all right, but is it entertainment?"

Jessel endeared himself to the audience, frequently speaking directly to them and performing several funny and risqué routines, especially his classical bit in which, wearing a ridiculous mustache, he imitated a Teutonic lecturer giving a slide show. The supporting cast included show-stopping dancer-singer Betty Bruce, who was highly appreciated, especially for her "Cigarettes" number. There was also ex-vaudevillian Chaz Chase, swallower of flowers, lit cigars, and other objects.

Atkinson thought the show "malodorous and mediocre"; Ralph Warner (*DW*) warned, "For the modern generation of exacting musical comedy fans, it's pretty weak stuff"; and Louis Kronenberger (*PM*) commented, "You haven't seen such a ham show in years. Some of it was good ham, at which you laughed whether you wanted to or not; but most of it was bad. There was more vulgarity than there was humor to redeem it."

HIGHLAND FLING, A [Comedy/Alcoholism/Death/Fantasy/Gambling/Romance/Sex/Youth] A: Margaret Curtis; D/P: George Abbott; S: John Root; C: Motley; T: Plymouth Theatre; 4/28/44 (28)

Glasgow-born actress Margaret Curtis wrote herself a juicy role--the best thus far of her Broadway career--in this ghost fantasy set in a remote Scottish village, but the play was the sort that critics considered possessed of an interesting notion that had gone unrealized.

Charlie MacKenzie (Ralph Forbes), onetime laird of Cairn McGorum and fourth great-grandfather of the present laird, Sir Archibald MacKenzie (John Ireland), died a century and a half ago after being smashed on the head by a bottle in a pub brawl over a wench. His woman-hungry ghost still haunts his old village. It can be seen only by a balmy--or "dafty"--local woman called Silly (Curtis), who fancies herself the Lady of Shalott in love with the long-deceased laird of the castle, and by a precocious seven-year-old named Bessie MacGregor (Patti Brady). A devil of a fellow, the ghost enjoys scaring the pants off the local inhabitants. His mission is to guard the Stone of Scone, taken by the English under Edward I and supposedly resting in Westminster Abbey. That one is a fake, though, the real one being in the village castle. He is married to an angel named Jeannie (Frances Reid), who frowns on his naughtiness and wants him to join the heavenly fold. This is not possible until he breaks his earthly ties with the young dafty. He may, however, enter heaven--to which he is attracted by the promise of the willing lasses there--if he reforms one sinner as miscreant as he. He chooses the boozing village gambler and adulterer Rabbie MacGregor (Karl Swenson). Rabbie agrees to be reformed, but he intends his transformation to last for only a day and to return to his sinful ways as soon as the ghost has ascended to heaven. Rabbie has to fight considerable temptation in his path toward salvation. During a pub party celebrating both Rabbie's salvation and a visiting Scots-American's (Ivan Miller) retrieval of the Stone of Scone to Pittsburgh for safekeeping from the British, Rabbie lasciviously gooses a barmaid (Gloria Hallward). This brings the ghostly laird roaring back from heaven, which has not come up to his expectations, but he discovers that Silly has regained her wits and turned for love to his handsome descendent. The possessive Jeannie then comes along to take him back with her to the pearly gates.

There were several positive reviews, including George Freedley's (*NYMT*), who announced, "It does not completely come off, but it was well worth the try. There is humor, charm, fantasy and a salty robustness that makes Miss Curtis' play one of the most welcome comedies of the season." More common were opinions like Wilella Waldorf's (*NYP*) that the play was "a surprisingly tame little romp." Howard Barnes (*NYHT*) suggested that the author was herself aware of "the dramatic poverty of her material. Otherwise she would not have introduced a series of criss-cross themes which are never resolved in the play and only conjure up flurries of laughter."

George Abbott's production lurched too violently between farce and whimsical fantasy to establish a consistent style. George Jean Nathan (*TBY*) was so upset by the direction that he claimed that Abbott had ruined what had been "a refreshingly witty and winsome fantastic conceit." The cast included St. Clair Bayfield as a bibulous clergyman.

HILARITIES [Revue] SK: Sidney Zelinka, Howard Harris, and Morey Amsterdam; M/LY: Buddy Kaye, Stanley Arnold, and Carl Lampl; D: (supervisor) Mervyn Nelson; CH: George Tapps; S: Crayon; P: Ken Robey and Stan Zucker; T: Adelphi Theatre; 9/9/48 (14)

More a vaudeville or variety show than a revue, this "rickety" (Brooks Atkinson [*NYT*]) show was headlined and emceed by comic Morey Amsterdam and featured tap dancer George Tapps; pitchman comedian Sid Stone; the tap-dancing Holloway Sisters; double-talking monologuist Al Kelly; songstress Betty Jane Watson; adagio acrobats the Calgary Brothers, who nearly stole the show with their slow-motion drunk act; Egyptian magician Gali Gali; acrobatic trapeze clowns the Herzog Sisters; Cuban dancers Raul and Eva Reyes; beautiful black singer Enid Williams, with her deadpan style; dancers Harold and Lola, with Lola coiling herself around Harold as if she were a snake; Gil Maison's animal act, including a punch-drunk St. Bernard and a jitterbugging monkey; and various other acts. According to the reviewers, very little of the show merited the title *Hilarities*.

Howard Barnes (*NYHT*) said of Amsterdam, much of whose humor was decidedly blue, "He is not the most engaging of ring masters. Much of his comedy is forced; much of it is merely dull." William Hawkins (*NYWT*) wrote, "There are some first rate acts and some ordinary ones, but most definitely there are too many of them."

HIM [Dramatic Revival*] A: e. e. cummings; D: Irving Stieber; CH: ("Frankie and Johnny" sequence) Oliver Reed; S: Charlie Hyman and Bill Sherman; C: Maurice Beaton; L: Burt Drexler and Enzio Napoli; P: Interplayers; T: Provincetown Playhouse (OB); 7/26/48

This offbeat, stream-of-consciousness, expressionistic 1928 play was staged in "a gay and spirited revival" (Joseph T. Shipley [*NL*]) at the same theatre that had given it its first performance. Much of the satire on life seemed fresh and relatively accessible to Shipley, although he said that some of the material, such as the political references, could have stood updating. Robert Garland (*NYJA*) thought it "frequently profound, more frequently perverse and most frequently neither of the two. When it is neither of the two, it is a vaudeville show burlesquing a vaudeville show." Richard Watts, Jr. (*NYP*), enjoyed it more than in 1928, but noted that despite its "vigorous and imaginative writing . . . , as a whole it distinctly fails to come off." George Freedley (*NYMT*) observed that the pace was too slow, some of the play's meaning was missed by the actors, and the bawdy material was softened.

The title role was taken by John Denny, and me was played by Janet Shannon, but some thought that Gene Saks won the evening's honors as the doctor, drunk, plainclothesman, passenger, dictator (played like Groucho Marx), gentleman, and barker (one of the best scenes in the show). In the "Frankie and Johnny" sequence (featuring Oliver Reed and Della Lawrence), a new mute character, Fanny Fry, was introduced and played in drag by T. C. Jones, who made a career of such female impersonation. Harold (Harry) Guardino (in his New York debut) and Louis Criss were in the cast playing effeminate soldiers.

HIPPOLYTUS [Dramatic Revival] A: Euripides; AD: Leighton Rollins; M: Ned Rorem; D: John Reich; DS: John Blankenchip; CH: Ingeborg Torrup; P: John Reich for the Invitational Series of the Experimental Theatre u/t/a/o the American National Theatre and Academy; T: Lenox Hill Playhouse (OB); 11/21/48 (4)

An expert staging of the Greek classic, somewhat marred by occasionally static passages. A total budget of $500 did not prevent designer Blankenchip from providing imaginatively minimal sets and attractive costumes, and Rorem's musical accompaniment (with Rorem himself playing percussion) proved highly effective in capturing and sustaining the appropriate tragic mood. Brooks Atkinson (*NYT*) thought this "an effective theatre piece" and the well-staged production "simple and impassioned."

The cast was racially mixed, providing an early example of nontraditional casting. As Hippolytus, Donald Buka acquitted himself very well, and George Freedley (*NYMT*) and Atkinson were ecstatic about his work. Phaedra was played by black actress Muriel Smith. "Curiously enough," said Freedley, "she never reaches either the heights or depths of the role though she is always interesting and is extremely attractive to watch."

The chorus consisted of three women, Betty Buehler, Nancy Gordon, and Peggy Wagner, while black actress Osceola Archer played Phaedra's nurse. Marian Winters was Artemis, Horace Braham was Theseus, and Elizabeth Eustis was Aphrodite. Stuart Steve Brody was the messenger and attracted attention for his moving performance.

HOBOES IN HEAVEN (*Les Geux aux Paradis*) [Comedy/Alcoholism/Barroom/Death/Fantasy/Flemish/Religion] A: G. M. Martens and André Obey; M: Claude Arrieu; D: Dennis Gurney; S: David Reppa; P: Blackfriars' Guild; T: Blackfriars' Theatre (OB); 10/23/47 (26)

A Flemish farce-fantasy, given a two-year run in Paris in French, but here presented with lackluster, semiprofessional skill in an uncredited version. Robert Garland (*NYJA*) said that it was "badly acted . . . under . . . unsure direction . . . against murky backgrounds . . . with mediocre music. . . . Neither its humor, its significance, nor its raison d'etre is apparent."

It takes place in Flanders and begins with townspeople gathered for a Christmas Eve celebration at the Tavern of the Prolific. A pair of rascally, drunken celebrants, a fat innkeeper (Leo Herbert) and his bibulous pal (William Dunn), impersonating Christmas figures, are apparently killed by a car during a mission of bringing gifts to children; their bodies are brought into the tavern. A series of morally educational adventures follow in heaven and hell before they return to earth, where preparations are under way for their funerals. The events have been experienced while the men were in a coma. They give up the bottle and continue delivering their gifts.

The musical sequences were a narrative sung by a male quartet, "The Companions of the Road."

HOLD IT! [Musical/Films/Romance/University/Youth] B: Matt Brooks and Art Arthur; M: Gerald Marks; LY: Sam Lerner; D: Robert E. Perry; CH: Michael Kidd w/Irma Jurist; S/L: Edward Gilbert; C: Julia Sze; P: Sammy Lambert; T: National Theatre; 5/5/48 (46)

An "unmitigated bore" of a collegiate musical that was "imitative and derivate [*sic*] to the point that it sounds like a melange of every musical you ever saw," grum bled George Freedley (*NYMT*). Rowland Field (*NEN*) rejected it as "a discouragingly inferior melody show that is substandard in all ingredients." The source of these and similar views was a musical that contained the choreographic talents of Michael Kidd and the comic talents of Red Buttons as a Kampus Kutup, but was so dismally written and produced that it never had a chance.

Bobby Manville (Johnny Downs), an ex-GI student at Lincoln University, looked beautiful in drag when he played a female part in the varsity Mask and Pudding Club show (despite the school's being coeducational). Because Bobby lost $3,000 subscribed to by fellow students for trailers to house ex-GIs attending college, his photo is sent in to Mammoth Pictures, which is conducting a search for new beauties, with a $5,000 prize attached. Bobby wins and the complications thicken. Eventually, the truth outs, Bobby's gal Jessica (Jet MacDonald) gets the film contract instead, and the trailers can be paid for.

One of the better routines was a ballet representing the movie-struck dreams of Jessica. The cast included Bob Shawley as an effeminate student, Kenny Buffet, Ada Lynne, Larry Douglas, Douglas Gilbert, Patricia Wymore, and Pat (Patrick) McVey, in his Broadway debut. Songs included "You Took Possession of Me" and "Always You."

The money for this show was put up by Albany millionaire Anthony Brady Farrell, for whom it began a series of expensive theatrical dabblings, none of which was successful. Although not listed as such, he was virtually the coproducer of *Hold It!* because he took such an active interest in its realization. When the bad reviews appeared, Farrell pumped enough money into the production to keep it running (he lost about $300,000), but it had to close because its weekly gross was less than the limit established in the contract by the theatre's owners, the Shuberts. Nor could he move it to a non-Shubert theatre, because the Shubert contract required that he would first have to wait eight weeks to do so. Farrell thereupon decided to have a theatre of his own. He spent $1,500,000 to buy a movie house (then called the Warner Theatre) on Fifty-first Street and Broadway, renamed it the Mark Hellinger (after the Broadway columnist), and planned to reopen *Hold It!* there several months later. He even kept the over twenty members of the chorus on salary during the layover period, which cost him $1,000 a week. Renovation of the theatre cost another $250,000. Because of excessive financial demands by the authors of *Hold It!*, he decided not to rework that show, but to open with a revue called *All for Love*.

HOLD ON TO YOUR HATS [Musical/Broadcasting/Crime/Romance/Show Business/Western] B: Guy Bolton, Matt Brooks, and Eddie Davis; M: Burton Lane; LY: E. Y. Harburg; D: Edgar J. MacGregor; CH: Catherine Littlefield; S/C: Raoul Pène du Bois; L: A. H. Feder; P: Al Jolson and George Hale; T: Shubert Theatre; 9/11/40 (158)

All-around entertainer Al Jolson returned to Broadway after nearly a decade's absence and took up precisely where he had left off as one of the great stage personalities of the day. Jolson himself put up almost the entire $90,000 it cost to mount the production. His vehicle, said Brooks Atkinson (*NYT*), was "one of the funniest musicals that have stumbled on to Broadway for years." With a first-rate company, including Martha Raye, the irrepressible comedienne with the trenchlike mouth, and with a cleverly choreographed and unusually energetic chorus line, striking sets and costumes, and a rousing score, the show had plenty to recommend it, although its book was clearly just a corny excuse to have fun and show off the star's talents. "It is an expert revue, smartly paced, gawdy [*sic*], gorgeous, tuneful, outrageously funny," applauded George Freedley (*NYMT*).

On opening night an extra laugh was provided by what most took as Raye's verbal gaffe when she praised Jolson's character not for "saving the jewels," as the script put it, but for "saving the Jews." It later was confirmed that the gag had been rehearsed and was actually part of the script. Less seemingly improvisatory was the show-stopping number "Down on the Dude Ranch," hilariously rendered by Jolson, Raye, and big-eared low comedian Bert Gordon (popularly known as the "Mad Russian") in the role of a Yiddish-accented Indian named Concho.

Jolson's role was that of the Lone Rider, a radio singer whose popularity is predicated upon his being believed to be a daring, rough-and-ready cowboy ("Hi-yo, Goldie," he shouts). He is, of course, a sheer coward who turns white before anything resembling a gun or a horse. Thinking him the only answer to their problems, a posse of dude ranchers whose community has been besieged by the wicked Mexican desperado, Fernando (Arnold Moss), takes him out west against his will, and he soon finds himself in one colorful scrape after another. The plot contrivances allow him to dress up as a toreador, a Mexican miss in the Carmen Miranda mode, and a peon, not to mention the humorously dashing Lone Rider himself. Surrounding his troubles are various goings on, including a love affair between the juvenile played by Jack Whiting and the ingenue played by Eunice Healey.

Despite his excellent support, the evening was Jolson's. "Jolson walks on the stage . . . and takes possession of the audience," wrote Rosamond Gilder (*TAM*). "Footlights disappear, the orchestra pit is part of his playground, he pats the early arrivals on the head, welcomes the straggler, discourses on the amount of money each late-comer represents [and] tells each embarrassed late-comer how far the plot has gone and what he has missed." The old gag of needling the audience was "still good for a quarter-hour of uproarious fun," although it needed Jolson's "peculiar kind of exuberance, vitality and wit to give it point." When latecomers arrived, he might say, "My name's Jolson, the owner of the show. There are your seats. Now, are you comfortable?" One night, Jolson actually passed wind very noisily during the show. Instead of showing embarrassment, he remarked, "Jolie made a fartsola" and received an ovation for his frankness. Following the curtain calls, Jolson regaled his audience with a medley of his great hits, including "Mammy," "April Showers," "You Made Me Love You," and "Sonny Boy."

Martha Raye's contributions were nearly as important although some critics lacked enthusiasm for her unsubtle style; Burns Mantle (*NYDN*) decided, though, "Her clowning suggests a natural spontaneity, she is inventive and good fun."

The supporting company was highly praised, including rubbery dancer Gil Lamb, lovely showgirl Jinx Falkenburg, John Randolph, Joyce Matthews, and various specialty performers. The best-liked songs included "Walking Along, Minding My Business," "There's a Great Day Coming, Mañana," and "The World Is in My Arms."

When the show went into production, Jolson's then wife, Ruby Keeler, was in it, but their marriage was slowly crumbling and Jolson was carrying on with Jinx Falkenburg during the rehearsal and tryout period. During a scene in the show where Jolson's character did his broadcast routine, he even made ad-lib references to Keeler. Finally, Keeler decided to leave the show before it came to New York, although Jolson originally had wanted the show to bring them together again. Jolson at first refused to let her out of her run-of-the-play contract, but he eventually relented. Keeler remained for four more weeks, but the couple's relationship grew worse. Once, when she blew her lines, Jolson said to the audience, "You'll remember reading in the papers that I called someone stupid. Well, I'm not saying a word!" Eunice Healey, who replaced Falkenburg in the star's favors, took over Keeler's role.

The show went through various other trials out of town, including an incident during a Chicago performance when the star tripped, broke a small bone in his foot, and had to play the next day on crutches. Jolson had an entrance in which he had to appear with guns drawn in order to catch the bad guys. Since the Democratic National Convention was in progress in town at the time, he entered, turned to the house, said, "On the first ballot, it's Wallace 623, Bankhead 331 and McNutt 66," then turned back to the villains and barked, "All right, you guys, stick 'em up."

During the Broadway run, Jolson's health began to suffer, and he had to take a one-week break by recuperating in the hospital. Although he returned to the show, his ailments were serious enough for him to close the show for good. He never did another Broadway show.

HOLIDAY IN PARIS [Revue] SK/M/LY: Donald Heywood and Matty Mathews; D: Ted Eddy; CH: Mariane Christensen; C: Joanne Paula; P: Edward Gould and Kenneth Robinson, Jr.; T: Fourth Street Playhouse (OB); 12/26/49

The Fourth Street Playhouse (formerly the Second Avenue Theatre and Yiddish Art Theatre) was used for this downtown revue that had more wrong with it than right. Lights went on and off inappropriately, curtains rose when they should have fallen, stagehands were seen when they should not have been, the orchestra seemed unfamiliar with the score, and the cast, apart from headliners Smith and Dale, Lew Hearn, and Dick Buckley--all of them comics--was strictly bargain basement. Robert Sylvester (*NYDM*) dubbed the show "a big and completely confused variety shambles."

Old-time vaudevillians Joe Smith and Charley Dale re-created their famous and always-hilarious "Dr. Kronkheit" and shared "A Belt in the Back" with Hearn. Among the other performers were European singer Countess Carina Paves (dressed in a Dior gown), a clown act called the Three Irelands, the apache act the La Vernes, and dancer Bill Del Campo. The deadly lyrics included one verse that went, "I bow to no master, I'm Anna Lucasta."

Jose. (*V*) claimed, "Costumes, sets and sketches wouldn't even be good for a highschool production and the music was pedestrian. . . . It was the type show nobody would believe could happen."

HOLIDAY ON BROADWAY [Revue/Blacks] P: Al Wilde and Izzy Grove; T: Mansfield Theatre; 4/27/48 (6)

Black song stylist Billie Holiday was the draw at this very well received jazz entertainment in which she sang fourteen songs and was accompanied by the Bobby Tucker Quintet. The program also featured such top musicians as the Slam Stewart Trio, drummer Cozy Cole, and Bob Wyatt and Billy Taylor, players of the grand piano and Hammond organ. One of Cole's numbers was performed using the "black light" technique which made his drums purple and his drumsticks yellow, while only his teeth revealed his presence.

Holiday wore a scarlet dress adorned with white flowers at the waist. Similar flowers were in her hair. Her tunes, programmed as "Mood Tunes" and "Show Tunes," included "Easy to Love," "Driving Me Crazy," "I Cover the Waterfront," "Lovin' Man, Where Can You Be?" "Strange Fruit," and other similarly moody or bittersweet songs.

A few critics were disappointed at what they considered merely a nightclub act on Broadway. A small number were unimpressed by the star, but others agreed with Robert Coleman (*NYDM*), who wrote, "Miss Holiday is an amazing artist. She has a small voice that manages to reach vibrantly throughout a theatre. In the parlance of the two-a-day, she 'talks' a song. Her cadences and rhythms are peculiarly her own. Still, she does full justice to a composer's melody, while putting great feeling into an author's lyrics."

HOLLYWOOD PINAFORE, OR THE LAD WHO LOVED A SALARY [Musical/Films/Journalism/Romance] B/LY/D: George S. Kaufman; M: Arthur Sullivan; SC: W. S. Gilbert and Arthur Sullivan's operetta, *H.M.S. Pinafore**; CH: Douglas Couder (ballet: Anthony Tudor); S/L: Jo Mielziner; C: Kathryn Kuhn and Mary Percy Schenck; P: Max Gordon i/a/w Meyer Davis; T: Alvin Theatre; 5/31/45 (53)

A week after *Memphis Bound!*, a radical adaptation of *H. M. S. Pinafore* placed aboard a nineteenth-century steamboat, opened, it was followed by George S.

Kaufman's own revision. In his version, the material was reworked into a biting satire on Hollywood in a way that reminded many of the Kaufman and Moss Hart comedy, *Once in a Lifetime**. Like *Memphis Bound!*, however, the new show failed, even though it reteamed William Gaxton and Victor Moore, who had scored together in such hits as *Of Thee I Sing*.

The idea had come to Kaufman when, at a card game, he heard screenwriter Charles Lederer parody several lines from Gilbert and Sullivan's operetta. Lederer refused Kaufman's request to sell the parody lyric, but allowed the latter to buy Lederer's wife a gift. Kaufman thereupon decided to do an entire show parodying *Pinafore* and began to closely study the original by listening to records of it.

The words were new but the original Sullivan score was intact. In keeping with the filmdom conceit, Sir Joseph Porter became Joe Porter (Moore), head of "Pinafore Pictures"; Dick Deadeye became actors' and performing animals' agent Dick Live-Eye (Gaxton), with a patch over one eye; Ralph Rackstraw (Gilbert Russell) kept his name but became a screenwriter, dressed, as were his fellow authors, in prison stripes; and Little Miss Buttercup became Louhedda Hopsons (Shirley Booth), a gossip columnist based on Hedda Hopper and Louella Parsons. She was known as Miss Butter Up, and her famous song now contained sparkling references to contemporary Hollywood scandal, including the marriage of Orson Welles and Rita Hayworth and the animosity between Welles and William Randolph Hearst. Other examples of how Kaufman changed the old lyrics included Joe Porter's singing of how he was a man who could not say no and thus became the ruler of the stu-di-o, instead of how he got to be ruler of the King's na-vy. At the end of the piece, it turns out that Porter became studio head because of a mistake in Louhedda's column, and Ralph, who should have been named, abandons his $75-a-week salary for Porter's $50,000.

Unhappily, the material quickly grew obvious and ran out of comic steam. There were occasional moments of humor, as when the writers were tied and gagged when conducting a story conference for a movie based on Poe's "The Raven," with Porter downing graham crackers and milk. Such moments were too few. An extended ballet featuring Viola Essen was also memorable. It was titled "Success Story" and told of a small town girl who rejects love with her drugstore-clerk fellow, signs a movie contract, and becomes a famous, but lonely movie star. This ballet interpolated music from a variety of Gilbert and Sullivan sources. Jo Mielziner's single set represented the gigantic studio doors, outside of which stood a doorman (Dan De Paolo) announcing each entering person's salary, including the collie star, Silver Tassles, who earned $5,000 a week.

Lewis Nichols (*NYT*) had a commonly shared response: "*Hollywood Pinafore* shows zest only once in a while; it is one of those musicals which seem never to get fully under way. . . . The result is a little disappointing." John Mason Brown (*SR*) took detailed issue with the nature of the transplantation, which, despite its cleverness, he claimed was too violently yanked from its "native habitat. . . . In its new surroundings it shrivels, withers, and dies." George Jean Nathan (*TBY*) rejected it as "little more than an expensively staged minor and dated college show burlesque." Although the majority agreed with these opinions, there were a few who thought the show a success. Howard Barnes (*NYHT*) called it "varied and resplendent," and Burton Rascoe (*NYWT*) called it "a joyous thing--voluptuous and comical, sensuous and good-naturedly satirical, fast-paced, artistic and melodious."

The overall quality of the singing, dancing, and acting was admirable. The talented cast included Annamary Dickey as the film star Brenda Blossom, with whom Ralph is in love; George Rasely as a movie director; Mary Wickes as the studio secretary; and Russ Brown as a press agent.

HOME IS THE HERO [Drama/Marriage/War] A: Courtenay Savage; D: Dennis Gurney; P: Blackfriars' Guild; T: Blackfriars' Theatre (OB); 1/18/45 (23)

The frequently dramatized problem of the returning serviceman furnished the basis for this semiprofessional Off-Broadway play, but the subject was not treated with the skill so sensitive an issue demanded. It was, however, a more serious treatment than Rose Franken's recent *Soldier's Wife*.

At the heart of this play is the conflict between Jerry Merrill (Harold Heagy), who comes back from the war on a medical discharge to find that his wife Frances (Virginia Dwyer) has been involved in war work and wishes to continue, despite his desire that she stop. Her $65 is better than the meagre salary her husband earns. The situation is resolved by Jerry's announcing his departure, which prompts her to give up her job and be less greedy.

Lewis Funke (*NYT*) thought that the play failed to live up to its promise and that it was verbose and sluggish; Edba. (*V*) found that it remained consistently interesting despite its talkativeness; and George Jean Nathan (*TBY*) said that the author failed to dramatize his materials: "He simply reduces them to endless colloquies between the soldier and his mate, which leave his other characters in the position of supers idly standing around, without spears."

HOME IS THE HUNTER [Drama/Blacks/Business/Crime/Labor/Marriage/Politics/War] A: Samuel M. Kootz; D: Abram Hill; S: Irene Bresadola; P: American Negro Theatre; T: American Negro Theatre Playhouse (OB); 12/20/45 (18)

For its 1945-1946 season, the American Negro Theatre occupied a new and more commodious playhouse at 15 West 126th Street. This overacted four-character play concerned an issue that was to preoccupy a number of postwar playwrights, the problems faced by returning war veterans. As Lewis Funke (*NYT*) averred, however, in this case, "the author has handled his subject with little knowledge of the playwriting craft."

The melodramatically treated story was about Dawson Drake (Elwood Smith), who returns from the service convinced that the Nazis had the correct economic ideas and were equally valid in their notions about might being right. This fascist convert has inherited his father's (Evilio Grillo) large factory and immediately sets about crushing the union, which is seeking a thirty percent pay raise. He wrongly suspects his wife Ann (Clarice Taylor), whom he treats like a whore and who now despises him, of having an affair with the union leader (Maxwell Glanville), and kills them both. His father turns him in to the police at the end.

Louis Kronenberger (*PM*) claimed that the "author's seriousness and concern for right values have no chance to prevail against writing that is uniformly amateurish and preponderantly dull."

The play, although staged by a black company, lacked racial overtones and was appropriate for casts of any ethnic background. In 1945 four-character plays were still a relative novelty, and George Jean Nathan (*TBY*) even bothered to enumerate the few earlier examples of the genre in order to point out how difficult the feat of writing a successful one was.

HOME OF THE BRAVE [Drama/Jews/Mental Illness/Military/Religion/Tropics/War] A: Arthur Laurents; D: Michael Gordon; S/L: Ralph Alswang; P: Lee Sabinson i/a/w William R. Katzell; T: Belasco Theatre; 12/27/45 (69)

This first Broadway play by Arthur Laurents, then a successful young radio writer and army veteran, was a provocative war drama set on an island in the Pacific and dealing with the problem of nerve shock as experienced by a young Jewish soldier, Coney (Joseph Pevney), who has lost the ability to walk. (In the movie version, the character is black.) He is undergoing psychiatric evaluation at the hands of Captain Harold Bitterger (Eduard Franz) to determine the psychosomatic cause of his ailment. A new sleep-inducing drug is used in the analysis sessions to get the patient to relive his experiences. The play employs a sequence of flashbacks taking the action from the hospital room back to the hero's experiences on a mapping expedition in the jungle under Major Robinson's (Kendall Clark) command when, after the killing of his friend (Henry Barnard) by a Japanese sniper, he finds himself unable to walk. Coney suffers from delusions of persecution because of his Judaism. He believes that his late friend's disparaging remarks on his religion, spoken in sudden anger and followed by his own satisfaction at the friend's demise, led to guilt resulting in his paralysis. Having been subjected to anti-Semitism in his premilitary life, he has been further traumatized by his experience of it in the army. The psychiatrist helps to illuminate the deep-rooted reasons for the soldier's condition and, consequently, cures him. Coney is persuaded that all men are the same, that all fear is their own cowardice, and that this has nothing to do with one's faith.

Home of the Brave, selected as one of Burns Mantle's ten best of the season, was viewed as a serious study of a real problem, done with honesty and conviction, but not completely successful in terms of dramatic art. The seemingly forced discussions of religion weakened the play for Lewis Nichols (*NYT*), who liked the jungle island scenes for their terse, dramatic quality. He also felt that the play ran out of interest and had to tread water until the final curtain. Others felt that the dual themes of psychological trauma and religious persecution caused a lack of focus; various subordinate themes made the outlines even blurrier. Among the problems detected by George Jean Nathan (*TBY*) was the ending of the play proper with its second act cure and the employment of a "redundant" third act to fill out the evening. Rosamond Gilder (*TAM*) observed, "His writing is uneven; some of his soldier talk rings true, some of it goes off into magazine cliches that seem totally out of place. On the whole, however, Mr. Laurents succeeds admirably in handling an extremely difficult and important subject in theatre terms." An excellent revolving set allowed the action to shift locales with ease, although the offstage masking revealed stagehands eating their sandwiches while jungle warfare was waged several feet from their stations. Alan Baxter and Russell Hardie were the only other actors in the all-male company.

HOMECOMING [Drama/Family/Fantasy/Religion/Southern/War] A: Edward Peyton Harris; D: Edward Peyton Harris and Augustin Duncan; P: New Plays, Inc.; T: Provincetown Playhouse (OB); 11/16/42 (12)

"As bad as the drama gets," opined Richard Lockridge (*NYS*) of this work that sought to retell the story of Noah's flood in terms of a modern-day poor white trash family, the Eborns of Greenville, North Carolina. This parable was viewed by Joseph Pihodna (*NYHT*) as "long, tedious and boring." Most critics left early.

The action is set a few years in the future at the end of the war. As the Eborns prepare to celebrate the return from war of one of their three sons, carpenter Nate Eborn (Augustin Duncan), who has seen man's growing sinfulness during the war, begins to build an ark because he knows that there will be forty days of rain to wash away man's sins. He is married to a woman named Lot (Georgia Simmons), and each of his sons is engaged to be married. When the waters begin to rise, the clan boards the ark with plenty of supplies, as well as a pair of snakes, a pair of rabbits, and a pair of chickens. As time passes, various strains and stresses of close living arise, and the characters come to recognize and repent their sinfulness. When the rains cease, a rooster brings word that the waters are receding. The sinners revert to type and begin sinning again.

The Provincetown Playhouse was renovated for the production, replacing its old bench seating with regular seats (circa 1915).

HOPE FOR A HARVEST [Comedy-Drama/Race/Romance/Rural/Western] A: Sophie Treadwell; D: Lester Vail; S: Watson Barratt; P: Theatre Guild: T: Guild Theatre; 11/26/41 (38)

After a lengthy tour with this overlong, well-intentioned play, popular acting couple Fredric March and Florence Eldridge brought it to New York only to find that their out-of-town encomiums counted for little in the face of the theatre capital's critics. The latter's opinions held that the play was a worthy effort at a serious theme, but one that was not as theatrically effective as it might have been. In a season not dominated by important writing, Burns Mantle chose it as one of his ten best of the year. The play sought to come to grips with the future of American farming and the need, in the midst of plenty, to redeem native laziness with strenuous labor.

It tells of Carlotta Thatcher's (Eldridge) return to her family ranch in California after twenty years abroad. Instead of the healthy robustness she expected from the people back home, in contrast to what she saw in war-torn Europe, she finds that they are lethargic and lusterless. Moreover, the widowed Elliott Martin (March), who has always loved her, has shriveled from a sturdy peach grower into a soured, impecunious gas station manager with a bad attitude toward the hardworking Japanese and Italian immigrants buying up the land and making it flourish. The successful Italians are represented by Joe de Lucchi (Alan Reed, the radio actor who was the voice of Joe Palooka). Helping him is his daughter Antoinette (Judy Parrish). Carlotta optimistically rolls up her sleeves to get her ranch operative once more, calling for hard work and less emphasis on expensive mechanical gadgetry. Through her good offices, Elliott is regenerated, and his daughter's romantic entanglements (she loves one man [Arthur Franz] but is bearing the child of another) are straightened out. With marriage for Carlotta and Elliott a definite possibility, there is hope for a harvest in the future. Along the way, the play tries to come to grips with the issue of racial intolerance.

Louis Kronenberger (*PM*) insisted that the drama was "a deep disappointment, if not a downright failure," despite its intelligence and humanity. He accused the author of failing to develop her central theme, of being verbose, of repetition and triviality, of clumsy dramaturgy, and of an unconvincing happy ending. Brooks Atkinson (*NYT*) considered it "a loose and languid play." Rosamond Gilder (*TAM*) sided with the work, however, saying, "*Hope for a Harvest* is simple in structure, thoughtful, deeply felt. It is a play for those who see the theatre in other terms than fireworks, who can contemplate character, milieu and event and follow an idea with as much enthusiasm as they give to the disentangling of a murder clue."

For most, the performance of March was the most distinguished part of the production. Good work was contributed by the others, too, including Shelley Hull and Doro Merande.

HOPE FOR THE BEST [Comedy/Journalism/Politics/Romance/War] A: William McCleery; D: Marc Connelly; S: Motley; P: Jean Dalrymple and Marc Connelly; T: Fulton Theatre; 2/7/45 (117)

Jean Dalrymple, then a press agent, was being interviewed for an article by William McCleery, a Sunday supplement editor, when she mentioned that she was considering becoming a producer, but had not found the right property yet. The young man then announced that he would write a play for her and said that he already had had three plays produced at the University of Nebraska. The play he soon wrote owed its modest success largely to the fact that it brought Franchot Tone and Jane Wyatt back to Broadway from Hollywood for the first time in the decade.

As a piece of playwriting it was decidedly on the down side, but Dalrymple declared in *September Child* that it "always played to standing room only." She attributed its mediocre reviews to an opening-night disaster. "In the very first scene the character comedian [presumably Leo Bulgakov], who carried the bulk of McCleery's most amusing lines and comments, drew a complete blank. The entire first act virtually was improvised by poor Jane, Franchot and Doro Merande [as a garrulous housekeeper] who never once, I do believe, received a proper cue. No wonder some of the critics said it was 'talky.'"

A comedy with intellectual pretensions, it tells of Michael Jordan (Tone), a widely popular newspaper columnist with eleven million readers who writes homey, sentimental pieces. His fiancée, Margaret Harwood (Joan Wetmore), is a famous political columnist with a reactionary bent. When Michael, moved by the problems of a world at war, expresses his desire to move into political writing (with a liberal bent), his idea is scorned both by Margaret--who considers him intellectually second-rate--and his syndicate boss (Jack Hartley), although a Russian professor (Leo Bulgakov) thinks that he should do it. Michael's soldier brother, Sergeant Joe Jordan (Paul Potter), comes for a weekend to Michael's Connecticut home with his friend, Lucille Daly (Wyatt), a war worker who has read all of Michael's columns for three years. The worldly wise Lucille, who supports Michael's wishes, engages in a conflict of ideas with Margaret and winds up falling in love with Michael.

Despite their talent and fame, the stars, especially Tone, seemed to some not at ease in their ill-defined roles. Perhaps--apart from Dalrymple's excuse--this was because they were in an uninspired work of extreme verbosity, contrived dramaturgy, and inflated notions of self-importance. Tone's character seemed influenced more by his romantic urgings than any deep-seated political beliefs. The play appeared to John Chapman (*NYDN*) "more soap-box than stage, more debate than dramaturgy." Most agreed with him, including the reviewer for the author's own paper, but Rosamond Gilder (*TAM*) was one of a few who supported the play, if only with hesitation, as "three acts of entertaining dialogue and humorous situation." Still, she noted, "He has garnished his theme but has not quite achieved a play. His hero is engaging but static. There is no development of character nor does the play achieve force and drive or any sense of inevitable movement."

Jane Wyatt's role originally had been cast with Mercedes McCambridge, who played it during its early tryouts and received strong audience and critical approval. When the show moved to Washington, D.C., she was fired. In her *The Quality of Mercy*, she declared that she was told, "It was inconceivable that Franchot Tone would fall in love with someone who looks like you." Still, she had to play out her engagement while Wyatt watched and studied her nightly performances and then rehearsed with the cast during the day. To make the disheartened McCambridge feel better, she was given a solo curtain call on closing night in Washington, but the actress declined to take it, despite the audience's calling for her. She was crying her heart out in her dressing room because she had been replaced, not on account of her talent, but because she was not beautiful enough. "I thought I was gorgeous," she recalled. "Until then."

HOPE'S THE THING [One-Acts] A: Richard Harrity; S: (scenic supervision) Mordi Gassner; P: Eddie Dowling u/t/a/o the American National Theatre and Academy; T: Playhouse; 5/11/48 (7)
"Gone Tomorrow" [Death/Marriage/Religion] D: Eddie Dowling; "Home Life of a Buffalo" [Family/Show Business] D: Eddie Dowling; "Hope Is the Thing with Feathers" [Dramatic Revival] D: Joseph Kramm

A program of three one-acters. The third piece on the program, "Hope Is the Thing with Feathers," had been seen on 4/11/48 in a noncommercial presentation (called *Six O'Clock Theatre*) with two other one-acts at Maxine Elliott's Theatre. The same cast repeated their performances. The series was tied together by the narrative comments of actor Fred Stewart. All was done with an absolute minimum of scenery and props, reminiscent of *Our Town**.

The first play on the program was "Home Life of a Buffalo," a forty-minute piece about has-been vaudeville performers, Eddie (Eddie Dowling) and Josey McQuinn (Ray Dooley), and their son, Joey (Kevin Mathews), living on the West Side of Manhattan. Despite being down and out, the family sentimentally refuses to accept the demise of vaudeville. For fifteen years Eddie and Josie have kept their act in shape, ready for vaudeville's resurrection. When Eddie excitedly appears to announce that they have a booking, Josey deflates his bubble by observing that the contract is only for half of one week. A team of former show-business buddies, Otto (Vaughn Taylor) and Molly (Leona Powers), arrive. Using a Dutch dialect, Otto tells of how much better off he and Molly are since giving up their trained goat act and leaving the business, but this so infuriates Eddie that they are kicked out. The piece gave former comic star Dooley (Dowling's real-life wife) a chance to do her famous "squalling brat" routine and to sing her old standby, "Dirty Hands, Dirty Face."

"Gone Tomorrow" is a comic Irish-dialect sketch set in a poor flat in New York's Hell's Kitchen, where streetcar conductor Peter Muldoon (Ralph Cullinan) and his spouse (Peg Mayo) await the death of an atheistic old uncle in an upstairs room. They bicker over who is going to spring for the old man's funeral and begin to plan for a formal service in the Catholic church. A drunken funeral director (Barry Macollum) wangles for the rights to the burial, but a couple of ambulance drivers arrive to remove the body to a Protestant hospital, the old man having bequeathed his remains for scientific examination and ultimate cremation.

The program received mixed reviews. "Hope Is the Thing with Feathers" remained the best of the lot. Thomas R. Dash (*WWD*) decided that regardless of his subject, Harrity "writes with mature understanding of character, with a lambent flight of the imagination and with a keen sense of acrid humor. In addition he has a felicitous feel for language and expresses himself tersely with the right compactness and economy of words." Ward Morehouse (*NYS*) felt that the two new one-acts were not up to "Hope Is the Thing with Feathers," "but each reveals some vividness and originality." Richard Watts, Jr. (*NYP*), while observing a good deal of commendable material in "Gone Tomorrow" and "Home Life of a Buffalo," concluded, "There is something a trifle unsatisfactory, a bit incomplete, about them. They seem the original drafts of excellent comedies, rather than the completed project."

HORSE FEVER [Comedy/Family/Gambling/Hotel/Science/Sports] A: Eugene Conrad and Zac H. and Ruby C. Gabel; D: Milton Stiefel; S: Louis Kennel; P: Alex Yokel; T: Mansfield Theatre; 11/23/40 (25)

Alex Yokel, producer of the very popular *Three Men on a Horse** (1935), tried to duplicate his success with this inconsequential farce starring Ezra Stone as cocksure young inventor Orville Drum, whose family has inherited a thoroughbred named Trilby. Orville, inventor of such things as "heavenly hamburgers," made of meat and vodka, wants to use modern scientific methods to cure the horse of a neurotic condition that prevents it from breaking at the post. While the family is being hounded by creditors, he smuggles the horse into a hotel in a piano box and puts his psychiatric techniques to work on the poor nag, who is kept stabled in the bathroom. All the family's finances go into getting the horse in shape for the big race at Belmont. Finally, the big day arrives, but the day is rainy and Trilby isn't a mudder. She manages to break at the post, but comes in fourth. However, Uncle Joe (Millard Mitchell) saves the day by overlooking Trilby and betting the mortgage on the long-shot winner.

The play--concocted by three authors--was more a string of visual and verbal gags (some of them very funny) than a plausible, logically consistent comedy. "The farce never works up the lather you need for really first rate horseplay," averred John Anderson (*NYJA*). It was reminiscent of a cross between *Room Service** and *Three Men on a Horse*. Rosamond Gilder (*TAM*) berated it as "one of the season's silliest affairs." The cast included Lou Lubin as a tout.

HOTEL UNIVERSE [Dramatic Revival*] A: Philip Barry; D: Robert Hartung; T: Barbizon-Plaza Hotel (OB); 11/9/43

A showcase production of Barry's once-controversial philosophical drama of 1930, presented by a group of Yale Drama School graduates for an audience of theatre professionals and friends. It was a rare opportunity for New York theatregoers to see a play done in arena style, which was very unusual there at the time, although it was already in use at a small number of regional theatres. By the end of the decade, the idea would begin to catch on in New York.

Hotel Universe was a good choice for theatre in the round despite the tendency of newcomers to the style to wish for more elaborate settings. George Freedley (*NYMT*), the sole critic present, was happy to discover how much one's imagination could supply when a play like this was well directed. The production changed the locale from Toulon, France, to an island in Florida, and there were certain cuts in the text, such as the scene of the children's bickering over religion. Rather than have the butler enter periodically to announce the hours, a clock was employed. The entire production ran only one and a half hours. Pat Farley was played by the director, Ruth Miller was Ann, Jane Lloyd-Jones was Lily, and Robert Stone was the professor.

HOUSE IN PARIS, THE [Drama/Art/France/Period/Romance/Sex] A: Eric Mawby Green and Edward Allen Feilbert; SC: Elizabeth Bowen's novel of the same name; D: Clarence Derwent; S: Stewart Chaney; P: H. Clay Blaney; T: Fulton Theatre; 3/20/44 (16)

Ludmilla Pitoëff, a renowned European star who hitherto had appeared in New York only in a benefit production, made her full-scale Broadway debut as the predatory female lead in this "lumbering and inept" (Rosamond Gilder [*TAM*]) drama set in turn-of-the-century Paris. Pitoëff's acting did not fare much better than her vehicle, and it was suggested that, her reputation in France aside, she needed more seasoning on the American stage and with the English language before being foisted on the public.

Told in a lengthy prologue set in 1911, two flashback acts, and a third act again in 1911, the story concerns the middle-aged Madame Fisher (Pitoëff), a widow who drove her husband to an early grave, and who, in 1900, runs a pension in Paris for American and British girls studying art in Paris. Also living there is her daughter Naomi (Cavada Humphrey), whose life she makes miserable. The ruthlessly possessive madame ensnares the eccentric and weak-willed artist Max Ebhart (Michael Ingram), whom she loves, and makes him her puppet, hoping to have him become a banker who will secure her financial future. Max becomes engaged to Naomi, whom he does not love, while the British girl he does love, Karen Michaelis (Lorraine Clewes), is engaged to someone else whom her snobbish parents have selected. Before Karen leaves him for good to marry someone else, he impregnates her. Madame Fisher breaks Max's engagement to Naomi. Finding himself trapped in Madame Fisher's web, he kills himself. Max and Karen's child (Alastair Boyd Kyle) is raised by others and becomes a resident at Madame Fisher's. A decade later, Karen returns, seeking to reclaim him. The now elderly and ailing Madame Fisher undergoes a transformation of her character, gives the child back to his mother, and offers him useful advice.

"The novel is one of mood, suggestion, and overtones," explained George Jean Nathan (*TBY*). "The play that has been made from it is a very bad, exaggeratedly emotional melodrama that substitutes for the mood, suggestion and overtones facial contortions, silent spaces devoted to suggestion in the form of darksome stares at the audience, and overtones implied by a morbid wrinkling of brows." Pitoëff may have been panned, but so were most of her fellow actors.

An earlier version of the play had been staged in January 1944 in Toronto and Boston under the direction of William Harris, Jr., but the play was then shelved for revisions. The script was subsequently doctored, without credit, by Arthur Richman and Caroline Francke.

HOUSE OF BERNARDA ALBA, THE (*La Casa de Bernarda Alba*) [Drama/Family/Romance/Sex/Spanish/Women] A: Federico García Lorca; TR: James Graham-Lujan and R. L. O'Connell; D: Boris Tumarin; P: Studio Productions; T: Charles Weidman Studio (OB); 5/24/50 (3)

The New York premiere of Lorca's realistic folk tragedy, written in 1936 but first produced in 1945 in Buenos Aires, went practically unnoticed by local reviewers in its Off-Broadway studio-theatre production. The title role was played by Hilda Vaughn, then appearing on Broadway in *The Devil's Disciple*, from which she had received a brief leave of absence. The sole critic attending, Vernon Rice (*NYP*), observed, "*Bernarda Alba* escapes being a grand opera libretto of seething Spanish passions by the honesty and the truth found in its characters. . . . Mr. Tumarin instilled the rhythm of emotions slowly boiling into the excellent cast." The actresses in the all-female drama, not listed by role, included future star Kim Stanley, Marian Copp, Dorothy Patten, Betty Morrow, Sylvia Davis, Sarah Cunningham, Jacqueline Soans, Anne Boley, Isabel Bonner, and Zelda Benjamin.

The play--intended as a "documentary photograph"--is set entirely in the whitewashed Andalusian village home of the widow Bernarda and her five daughters, all of whom are single and in love with Pepe el Romano. Also living here are the feisty maidservant Poncia and Bernarda's aged and senile mother. The house becomes like a tomb for the girls after Bernarda buries her husband and vows that all shall mourn him for eight years. This leads to an increasing sense of unfulfilled sexual longing among the young women. The youngest daughter, Adela, becomes enraged on learning that the eldest, Angustia, who is the official heiress of the late father's estate, will be betrothed to Pepe. When Bernarda learns that Pepe may be seducing Adela, she stops ignoring the conflict among her daughters and tries to shoot the young man. She misses, but one of the sisters spitefully tells Adela that Pepe is dead, and the girl hangs herself. Bernarda overcomes any shame she may feel and, preserving her fierce brand of honor, proclaims that Adela died a virgin.

HOUSE POSSESSED, A [Drama/Family/Law/Mental Illness/Period/Romance]

A: Karlton and William Kelm; D/DS: Edward R. Mitchell; T: Henry Street Settlement Playhouse (OB); 11/21/47

The three Parsons sisters (Patricia Beaudry, Lucia Baker, and Iris March) are frustrated spinsters living in Massachusetts in 1921. They have a younger brother (Keene Curtis), who is an up-and-coming judge. The judge is in love with a young woman (Norma Sverd) married to a veteran of the war, but the husband is in a mental institution. Judge Parsons is trying to use his legal position to obtain an annulment of the woman's marriage so that he can marry her himself. The ultimately unsuccessful attempts of the three sisters to prevent the marriage of their brother constitute most of the action.

The play included a considerable amount of comedy to offset the more sober elements of the plot. A very funny performance was provided by Ruth Lillienthal as a maid who is blackmailed into providing one of the sisters, an alcoholic, with liquor. Another fine performance was given by Curtis, who one day would be a very active performer. Edba. (*V*), who left the sole notice of the production, said of him, "Keene Curtis gives an exacting and creditably restrained performance." The play itself, he said, was "for the most part well-written and splendidly acted."

HOW I WONDER [Comedy/Blacks/Family/Fantasy/Labor/Race/Science/University/War] A: Donald Ogden Stewart; D: Garson Kanin and George Greenberg; S/L: Donald Oenslager; C: Helene Pons; P: Ruth Gordon and Garson Kanin i/a/w Victor Samrock and William Fields; T: Hudson Theatre; 9/30/47 (63)

This well-intentioned piece about man's will to self-destruction was considered more a lecture than a play because it lacked dramatic credibility and life. Its central character was the confusedly liberal-minded astronomy professor Lemuel Stevenson (Raymond Massey). He is bedeviled by the philosophical issues current in a world potentially capable of blowing itself to dust and becoming just another star in the firmament. The threat of a third world war is being fostered by a reactionary tycoon named Henry Harkrider (Wyrley Birch). The professor spends most of his time on his comfortably disposed roof discussing his overwhelming problems with two fantasy figures, an impish creature representing his Mind (Everett Sloane) and Lisa (Meg Mundy), a beautiful dream woman from another planet, representing his feelings. He also has a wife (Carol Goodner) and romantic daughter (Bethel Leslie). Stevenson might become president of a college controlled by Harkrider, but his free conscience prompts him to stand up in support of an unjustly jailed black handyman, brother of his watchman (John Marriott). The man is actually a union organizer in a Harkrider factory, but Stevenson stands up to Harkrider. He also assures his position at the university when he discovers the planet--burned to a star by an atomic war--for which he has been searching the skies.

"None of this has really been dramatized," bewailed Louis Kronenberger (*PM*). "It is all text and no texture. And the feeling persists that even if all this makes excellent sense, it makes tedious theater." It went "through some garbled contortions that make a listener hang on for dear life to keep up with what is going on," complained William Hawkins (*NYWT*). Henry Jones and Byron McGrath were in the cast.

Raymond Massey recounted in *A Hundred Different Lives* how the first story conference for the play was run. Author Stewart's wife, Ella Winter, an imposing-looking woman of intellectual pretensions, spoke to Massey and producers Gordon and Kanin, who were hoping that the play would undergo some needed surgery, of her lofty ideas concerning the dramaturgy. After her initial eulogy, "Miss Winter then took over again, brushing our comments aside and renewing her praise of the existing script. She wound up, '. . . and of course, as we all say, the play's the thing, is it not?' 'Oh, shit!,' said Miss Gordon." On opening night, Massey received a telegram from his wife, "All work and no play. Love. Mrs. M."

HOW LONG TILL SUMMER [Drama/Alcoholism/Blacks/Crime/Fantasy/Law/Politics/Race/Youth] A: Sarett and Herbert Rudley; D: Herbert Rudley; S/L: Ralph Alswang; C: Enid Smiley; P: Leon J. Bronesky and Edward M. Gilbert; T: Playhouse; 12/27/49 (7)

A disastrously received drama about race relations, starring black folk singer

Josh White and his son, Josh White, Jr. Richard Watts, Jr. (*NYP*), said that the well-intentioned play was "so pathetically bogged down in confusion and ineptness that the result, despite the presence of some engaging actors, is a most dismal evening in the theatre." To Rowland Field (*NEN*) the opus was "an awkwardly tedious composition heavily burdened with social significance in slow motion."

Little Josh Jeffers (White, Jr.) is a black child who plays with white friends without any racial barriers perceived by any of them. His best pal is Johnny Burns (Charles Taylor), whose alcoholic lout of a father (Sam Gilman) one day interferes in the friendship, insults Josh by calling him racial epithets, and forbids Johnny to play with him. Josh is consequently haunted by race-related fears and nightmares. Josh's father (White), Mathew Jeffers, is a prominent lawyer but a morally weak man; his political campaign for Congress is backed by a white mobster who has exploited black people. Mathew believes that when he is elected, he will be an upright man of the people. The crook wants Mathew in power in order to cover up one of his (the crook's) misdeeds. (The story of Mathew's sellout in order to provide a good living for his family is told as a sort of realistic counterpoint to that of his son, shown in impressionistic dream scenes.) Mathew's wife (Ida James) and his doctor friend (Frank Wilson) beg him not to run. The gangster's armed henchman (Peter Capell) tries to bribe the doctor to lay off. Mathew realizes that there is no way he can shield little Josh from the pain of being black, and he bows out of the race.

Had the playwrights stayed with the child's problem and avoided that of the adults, the play might have been much better, suggested various critics. There was also displeasure about the tenuous connection between the play's conflicting styles. Fredi Washington, Leigh Whipper, Evelyn Davis, Arthur O'Connell, and Maxwell Glanville had roles in the play.

HOWDY, MR. ICE! [Revue/Ice] M/LY: Al Stillman and Alan Moran; D/CH: Catherine Littlefield (skating: May Judels); S/L: Bruno Maine; C: Billy Livingston and Katherine Kuhn; P: Sonja Henie and Arthur M. Wirtz; T: Center Theatre; 6/24/48 (406)

The sixth in the series of popular, family-oriented ice-skating revues that appeared regularly throughout the decade at the huge Center Theatre in Radio City (part of Rockefeller Center). Few critics thought the title attractive (Euphemia Van Rensselaer Wyatt [*CW*] called it "obnoxious"), but the production was spectacular and gorgeous and featured exceptional skating routines.

There were breathtaking moments, as when "Skippy" Baxter made his entrance as Mercury sliding downwards from an Olympian pinnacle. Equally startling was the pinwheel number formed of many skaters whirling about the stage. As the wheel spun, individual skaters joined on to it with remarkable precision timing. The show held few real surprises and stuck pretty much to formula ideas. Its music was based largely on popular tunes. There was a calypso number, a Christmas card number, a Thanksgiving number, an Easter number, a Sleeping Beauty number, a circus number, a jazz number, and on and on.

Headliners included comic acrobat Freddie Trenkler, blond and beautiful Eleanor Seigh of the 1948 U.S. Olympic skating team, Cissy Trenholm, Jinx Clark, Rudy Richards, Paul Castle, Buster Grace, the knockabout team of Eddie Berry and John Melendez, and clown "Sir" Frederick Werner, who skated in shoes.

The skating of individuals, teams, and chorus was so dance oriented that Wyatt had trouble finding an appropriate word to describe it. "Although everything is big and splendid," observed Brooks Atkinson (*NYT*), "nothing is especially original, and the few musical numbers written by Al Stillman and Alan Moran are vapid and hackneyed." Another much heard criticism was that the show packed in too many acts and that the effect began to weaken by the latter part of the presentation. Several commentators were upset by an animal act using a bear who was obviously unhappy and whose stool was yanked from under him so he would fall on the ice. "His feet evidently hurt him and he resents the muzzle so violently that in the middle of his tricks the bear scratches alternately at the offending leather," wrote the disgusted George Freedley (*NYMT*).

HOWDY, MR ICE OF 1950 [Revue/Ice] 5/26/49 (430)

This sequel to *Howdy, Mr. Ice!* was considered the finest yet in the seven-show series, although it actually was a revision of the previous show. Most of that show's cast was back, and the same team of creators was credited, but there was more interesting variety to the acts and a generally swifter tempo. Although most numbers from the previous production remained, there were several new additions as well.

Sid Krofft joined the show with his hilariously strutting puppets; the Preston adagio dancers--in which a female skater was swung so that her head practically hit the ice--were knockouts; a skating juggler named Trixie did some sensational stunts; a hauntingly ghost-like ballet sequence employed dancer-skaters wearing mirrored costumes; a patriotic procession made American hearts thump; the Bruises were hilariously acrobatic with a roughhouse hockey game among charwomen; and so on. On opening night there was one slight mishap when two women skaters lost control and went sailing into the orchestra pit; neither was hurt.

There had been 3,600 performances of the series as of opening night. Eight and a half million people had attended, and one record-breaking week brought in $69,000. The original ice-making machine installed in 1940 had produced fifty tons of ice a day, totalling 153,500 tons. One lover of the ice shows, a certain Mr. French, had attended 500 performances.

Howard Barnes (*NYHT*) attempted to define the form of these presentations: "It is part vaudeville, part circus, part musical and part sports event, a conglomeration that collects as many odd things as can be done on ice without any particular point of view or unifying artistic force. Some of it has humor, but there is no central satire; its story-telling is much less effective than that of ballet, and there is left only a certain admiration at what practise [*sic*] and coordination may accomplish." Some critics, like George Jean Nathan (*TBY*), continued to abominate these shows, but others, like Whitney Bolton (*NYMT*), could write, "I very much liked *Howdy, Mr. Ice of 1950* and enjoyed every brisk minute of it."

I

I GOTTA GET OUT [Comedy/Gambling/Romance/Sports] A: Joseph Fields and Ben Sher; D: Joseph Fields; S: Raymond Sovey; P: Herbert H. Harris and Lester Meyer; T: Cort Theatre; 9/25/47 (4)

A racily vernacular racetrack farce about bookmakers that was annoyingly maladroit in writing and production. It focused on Swifty (Reed Brown, Jr.), Bernie (David Burns), and Radtke (Hal Neiman), three bookies who operate out of a stable, from whence they keep a sharp eye out for the cops. Two of them have manicurist girlfriends (Peggy Maley and Eileen Larson). Involved with them is a college boy named Timmie (John Conway) who wants to earn enough to get married to Mary (Peggy Van Vleet), although she disapproves of his acquaintances. The lad, needing money for his nuptials, is too much in debt to the bookies to quit. The cops get wise to the operation, so the trio of bookies leave the stable. They set themselves up in the Long Island kitchen of Mrs. Clark (Edith Meiser), Mary's aunt. The aunt is supposed to be gone for the summer but returns before the phones are installed. The bookies use various ploys to talk her into renting them her place. Since she wants to raise funds for a charity, she is persuaded to visit Belmont Park with them to place some bets on her own behalf. The bookies themselves lose, but Mrs. Clark wins, although she is arrested as a front for the gamblers. However, all works out and Timmie and Mary get married.

"The authors seemed more concerned with pyramiding a number of gags and wisecracks than with evolving an interesting story," insisted Thomas R. Dash (*WWD*). "It is not sufficiently inventive to stand on its own four legs in the theater," cracked George Freedley (*NYMT*).

I KILLED THE COUNT [Comedy/British/Crime/Mystery] A: Alec Coppel; D: Frank Carrington and Agnes Morgan; P: Frank Carrington and Agnes Morgan i/a/w Messrs. Shubert; S: Emil Holak; T: Cort Theatre; 8/31/42 (29)

This murder-mystery comedy was first staged in London in 1937, had a hearing at New Jersey's Paper Mill Playhouse, and was well produced on Broadway, but the effort was considered wasted. Ibee. (*V*) attacked the play as "repetitious to a degree and quite incredible."

The body of a slain foreign nobleman, Count Victor Mattoni (Rafael Corio), is found in his London flat. Divisional inspector Davidson (Louis Hector) questions the three prime suspects (Robert Allen, Guy Spaull, and A. J. Herbert), one by one. Each confesses, and each confession is followed by a fadeout and the reenactment of the crime before the Scotland Yard detective and his assistant (Bertram Tanswell). The explanations are all plausible and supported by circumstantial evidence, which is corroborated by Samuel Diamond (Clarence Derwent), resident of a nearby flat. The grumpy Davidson's frustration grows greater when a woman (Louise Rogers) also confesses. All becomes clear upon the eventual revelation that the multiple confessions are part of a plot to get rid of the dastardly count by a conspiracy wherein no single individual can be identified as the murderer. Actually, it was the woman who did it, but neither she nor anyone else can be arrested because of a loophole in the law about charging more than one person for a crime known to have been perpetrated by a single person.

Pointing to the dramatis personae of conventional character types, Brooks Atkinson (*NYT*) asserted, "Mr. Coppel goes about the writing job as if he were making out a laundry list. The organization of the play is routine. The dialogue is commonplace. The plot would be suitable for a clever charade of bored week-end guests who have read all the crime fiction on their bedside tables."

In the cast were Le Roi Operti, Ethel Morrison, and Ruth Holden.

I KNOW MY LOVE [Comedy/Family/Marriage/Old Age/Period/Sex] A: S. N. Behrman; SC: Marcel Achard's French play, *Auprés de Ma Blonde*; D: Alfred Lunt; DS: Stewart Chaney; P: Theatre Guild and John C. Wilson; T: Shubert Theatre; 11/2/49 (246)

Broadway's reigning king and queen, Alfred Lunt and Lynn Fontanne, then in their sixties, regaled their faithful audiences with this adaptation of a French play whose action had been transposed to Boston. (In Paris the female lead had been played by Yvonne Printemps.) The comedy marked the twenty-fifth year of the Lunts' costarring career; its story was seen as symbolic of their relationship.

This is a "generation-jumping" play that begins in 1939, moves back to 1888, then forward to 1902, then ahead again to 1918, and finally ends in 1920. The respective years are projected onto a curtain for the audience's assistance. It offers its stars the opportunity to don various makeups to convey their aging through the years.

The Lunts began as an aged Back Bay couple, Thomas and Emily Chanler, celebrating their fiftieth anniversary, then became radiantly young to celebrate their engagement, and gradually reached middle age, when Thomas is having an affair with the best friend of his daughter. The Chanlers begin their relationship deeply in love, but their marriage must sustain many stresses, including Thomas's abandonment of a writing career for the textile business, his inadvertent responsibility for his brother's death, his service in World War I, and, finally, a bout of philandering that Emily cleverly handles in the thirtieth year of their marriage. The play seeks to demonstrate how the loving couple, mainly through the ministrations of the wise and perceptive wife, has remained loving through all the ups and downs of a half-century of marriage.

I Know My Love was a thespian holiday if not a dramatist's one. The play, griped Brooks Atkinson (*NYT*), "abuses the privilege of being light. It has nothing to say and very little to contribute to entertainment." He accused it of being clichéd, clumsily constructed, and lacking in wit. John Mason Brown (*SR*) concurred, but added, "What matters is not what the play is like as a play but what it becomes as a delectable theatrical experience because of the Lunts." He noted that despite their use of wigs and costuming to suggest age, they did not really rely on these "to do the real work for them. They are in complete command of all those subtleties and shadings in voice, expression, and physical bounce (or its recession) appropriate to their changing ages."

According to Maurice Zolotow's *Stagestruck*, one night during the run, Fontanne asked the stage manager to ask Lunt to come down the stairs "a little more quickly in the next scene than he did in the last, because he is holding up my lines and my timing is badly off." Lunt replied to the poor stage manager, "Tell Miss Fontanne that if she wants someone to come downstairs faster in the second act scene, she should have married a younger man."

In the cast were Esther Mitchell, William Le Massena, Geoffrey Kerr, Katharine Bard, Mary Fickett, Lily Kemble-Cooper, Henry Barnard, Hugh Franklin, Anne Sargent, Thomas Palmer, and many others.

After the show closed, the Lunts trouped around the country with it, encountering numerous mishaps, including a broken wrist for Fontanne that forced her to play through most of the tour with her arm in a sling.

I LIKE IT HERE [Comedy/Family/Politics/Romance/Small Town] A: A. B. Shiffrin; D: Charles K. Freeman; S: Ralph Alswang; P: William Cahn; T: John Golden Theatre; 3/22/46 (52)

A "long, tedious play" (Lewis Nichols [*NYT*]), stuffed with familiar jokes and situations, about a wise and caring Austrian refugee named Willie Kringle (Oscar Karlweis) who wangles a job as jack-of-all-trades for the family of henpecked New England English professor Sebastian Merriweather (Bert Lytell), his wife Matilda (Beverly Bayne), and daughter Laura (Mardi Bryant). Laura is in love with lawyer Brad Monroe (William Terry), but--through her ambitious mother's influence--is engaged to David Bellow (Donald Randolph), a town politician with his eye on the state senate. Willie, a domestic genius and emotional Mr. Fixit, convinces the upright Brad to run for office as an independent against the insincere David, who is backed by big business. Brad does, winning both the election and the girl, and Professor Merriweather, with the help of Willie and a bottle of booze, puts his wife in her place.

All that could be salvaged was Karlweis's excellent performance in a part and play that were unworthy of his efforts. Rosamond Gilder (*TAM*) noted that the play showed how far "the theatre . . . can fall into sheer inanity. . . . Mr. Karlweis is too good an actor to be driven to this sort of circus-in-a-vacuum."

I REMEMBER MAMA [Comedy/Family/Illness/Invalidism/Literature/Period/Youth] A/D: John van Druten; SC: Kathryn Forbes's autobiographical book, *Mama's Bank Account*; S/L: George Jenkins; C: Lucinda Ballard; P: Richard Rodgers and Oscar Hammerstein II; T: Music Box Theatre; 10/19/44 (714)

The 1944-1945 season saw a healthy number of hit productions, one of them being this nostalgic and amusingly sentimental piece based on Kathryn Forbes's recollections of growing up in a poor but honest Norwegian-American family on San Francisco's Steiner Street in 1910. Central to her memories was the influence of her warm and wonderful mother, acted in the play by Mady Christians.

Forbes's story came to dramatic life after being read by composer Richard Rodgers's daughter Mary, who so highly recommended it that before long not only had everyone in the family read it, but it was a hit with the family of Rodgers's lyricist partner Oscar Hammerstein as well. Rodgers and Hammerstein thereupon decided to branch out as entrepreneurs and produce the material as a play, their first endeavor in this vein. (They were to enjoy an extremely successful career as producers.) They interested John van Druten in the story enough for him to want to adapt it. It was van Druten's wish to cast the German-born Christians as Mama, but he was not certain that she would like the role because of her relative youth and inexperience in character parts. As it turned out, Christians already had written to Rodgers asking him to consider dramatizing the book and to think of her for Mama. The material became not only a popular movie starring Irene Dunne but a long-running television serial with Peggy Wood as Mama.

I Remember Mama is also remembered for introducing Broadway to Marlon Brando, who played Mama's fifteen-year-old son Nels. Brando was not new to the local stage, however, having acted in a series of student productions put on by Erwin Piscator's Dramatic Workshop at the New School for Social Research, where those who saw him considered him a comer. In 1979 Rodgers's unsuccessful musical version of the play, using the original title, was produced starring Liv Ullman.

As befits its literary origins, the play is an episodic string of some thirty scenes employing twenty-two players and mingling realism with stylization. It recounts five of the eight stories told by Forbes in her book. A tripartite setting showed the family kitchen *cum* living room raised two steps at center, with small turntables at the sides to wheel scenery into view for short scenes in various locales. The central area could be changed to a hospital hallway or a room in a farmhouse. By drawing a curtain across the central area a neutral forestage area could be used for yet other scenes.

The play begins with the grown-up Katrin (Joan Tetzel) shown writing the story that became her book. She then reads from it, commencing, "For as long as I could remember the house on Steiner Street had become home." She fills in the expository background about the Hansen family, Mama and Papa (Richard Bishop), a carpenter who quietly adores his spouse; her brother Nels; her sister Christine (Frances Heflin); and her youngest sister, the outspoken Dagmar (Carolyn Hummel). Also mentioned is the cultured English boarder, Mr. Hyde (Oswald Marshall), a former actor who reads to the family nightly. She concludes, "But most of all, I remember Mama," and as the lights change the action moves back to 1910 to depict the main actions of the play. When necessary, Katrin reads other passages of exposition to advance the play; she then steps into the action as her younger self. Katrin wants to be a writer; Nels a doctor; and Dagmar a veterinarian. Also brought on are three aunts, Aunt Trina (Adrienne Gessner), Aunt Sigrid (Ellen Mahar), and Aunt Jenny (Ruth Gates), the first-named a spinster, and the outwardly cantankerous, but inwardly kind Uncle Chris (Oscar Homolka), who keeps a woman (Louise Lorimer) and loves his flask. It turns out that this blustering peasant has a secret mission, to earn enough money to help disabled children walk without limping, he himself having a limp because his poor parents could not pay to have his problem corrected. But most of all, there is Mama, resourceful wife, cook, banker, housekeeper, friend, nurse, and guardian to keep everyone happy and secure in good times and bad. One story thread concerns Mama's bank account, which she tells the children is a robust one, but which they cannot draw from because she wants them to learn thrift. When Katrin graduates from school, Mama can get the money for a suitable gift--a celluloid dresser set--only by pawning her sole piece of jewelry, an heirloom brooch. Katrin returns the dresser set and redeems the brooch. Another sequence tells of Dagmar's being hospitalized for a mastoiditis operation and of Mama's disguising herself as a scrubwoman so that she can visit her daughter. Mama also is the lynchpin in the sequence about her getting a noted woman author (Josephine Brown) to pass judgment on Katrin's writing by paying the lady with a Norwegian recipe. Katrin's story brings the family $500 when it is published, a veritable fortune. Mama confesses that there never was a bank account. When asked what her story was about, Katrin reads from the manuscript, called "Mama and the Hospital," and repeats the first line, quoted earlier, and then a few others as the curtain falls.

It was widely appreciated that van Druten had respected the form of the original book. "His play is the theatre equivalent of a book of short stories, rather than the theatre equivalent of a novel," approved Rosamond Gilder (*TAM*). On occasion, dramatic interest lapsed or some cutting might have been employed but the overall play was warmly applauded. To Burton Rascoe (*NYWT*) it was "breathtakingly beautiful. . . . It is not a great drama . . . but it is superb theater." "The evening provides the sheerest, tenderest joy of the new season," exclaimed John Mason Brown (*SR*). But George Jean Nathan (*TBY*) objected to the narrator device, which he found shopworn and unnecessary, and to the excessive use of the side stages, which was too distractingly similar to movie flashbacks. He was impressed, however, by the author-director's simplicity and delicate restraint. "Episode after episode . . . is dramatically manipulated in its own artless terms and never once is there resort to an overemphasis which would play havoc with its simple internals."

Christians triumphed as Mama. "It just doesn't seem possible that anyone else could have done it so well. She is as shy and self-contained as she is wise; as practical as she is unselfish; as tender as she is reserved," declared Euphemia Van Rensselaer Wyatt (*CW*). Because of the large, excellently received cast, Brando's acting was not specifically described by most critics. George Freedley (*NYMT*) said that he "makes Nels good and slow and handsome and kind." E. C. Sherburne (*CSM*) declared him "likable."

ICEMAN COMETH, THE [Drama/Alcoholism/Barroom/Crime/Journalism/Mental Illness/Period/Politics/Prostitution] A: Eugene O'Neill; D: Eddie Dowling; DS: Robert Edmond Jones; P: Theatre Guild i/a/w Armina Marshall; T: Martin Beck Theatre; 10/9/46 (136)

Later generations were puzzled that no Pulitzer Prize winners were announced for drama during the 1946-1947 season, although plays like the present one and *All My Sons* would normally have been powerful contenders. *The Iceman Cometh*, often called an American *Lower Depths**, continues to loom as one of its author's greatest contributions, and--despite its verbosity and great length--is widely considered one of the best American plays ever. Although overlooked for the Pulitzer and the New York Drama Critics Circle Award (which went to *All My Sons*), it was critically acknowledged as a major contribution and was included as one of the season's ten best in Burns Mantle's collection. Although some believe that the production was not on a par with the writing and that the play did not get its definitive performance until it was revived in 1956, the reviews do not bear this out.

The four-act, four-hours-plus play, actually written in 1939, was the fifty-eight-year-old O'Neill's first offering on Broadway in a dozen years. Its production was delayed while O'Neill worked on a vast cycle of plays, most of which he ultimately destroyed. Other obstacles were the war, which seriously depressed O'Neill, and the playwright's health. It was the last of his plays he would live to see, although several important works were produced posthumously.

The play, based loosely on O'Neill's own experiences in his early years when he frequented a Hell's Kitchen waterfront joint called Jimmy the Priest's, is a mingling of naturalism and symbolism, with most of the characters inspired by actual onetime acquaintances of the writer. Its title, alluding to Jesus, is from the biblical phrase (Matthew 25: 6), "The bridegroom cometh." The iceman reference is to a gag associated with the central character, Theodore Hickman or Hickey (James Barton), who loves telling a story about leaving his wife in bed with the iceman. Harry Hope's saloon and flophouse on a hot summer day in 1912 is the setting. The denizens are fifteen hard-drinking bums living on their faded memories of past glories and their romantic dreams concerning themselves. Harry (Dudley Digges), the proprietor, an ex-Tammany Hall man, has not left the premises in twenty years. Among the others are a former dishonest cop (Al McGranary), a circus con artist (Morton L. Stevens), a pimping bartender (Tom Pedi), a graduate of Harvard Law School (E. G. Marshall), a former British infantry officer (Nicholas Joy), a black man (John Marriott), a one-time Boer War correspondent (Russell Collins), a former anarchist editor (Leo Chalzel), and Larry Slade (Carl Benton Reid), a philosophical alcoholic who once was a syndicalist-anarchist. He espouses a cynical philosophy that prefers the "pipe dream" to the truth as a way of making life bearable. He is made uncomfortable by the arrival of Dan Parritt (Paul Crabtree), who pours out his problems to Larry, once the lover of Dan's mother, and who has just been arrested with a gang of anarchists. After various others appear, including Pearl (Ruth Gilbert), Margie (Jeanne Cagney), and Cora (Marcella Markham), who think of themselves as "tarts" instead of "whores," and the day bartender Chuck Morello (Joe Marr), the popular and long-awaited Hickey arrives. Hickey, however, is no longer the happy-go-lucky, boozing hardware salesman he used to be, but a reformed alcoholic with a message. He wants the startled derelicts to follow his path, give up the bottle, cast aside their whiskey-induced pipe dreams, and face the truth, as he has. He works on them one by one to get them to act on the illusions that have so long sustained them. As a party is being prepared, the pressures brought by Hickey's proselytizing begin to cause fissures in the formerly content group. When the angry bums force him to declare what has caused his conversion, he reveals that his wife, whom they suspect must have been having an affair with the iceman, is dead. Soon the men are arguing and fighting with each other as a result of Hickey's reforms, with Larry understanding that the iceman in Hickey's home was death. Under Hickey's influence, former ward heeler Harry leaves to renew his old political ties, and the correspondent goes out seeking a reporter's job, while others also attempt to get their lives back on track. Hickey expects that they will all return, their delusions erased and with only truth to confront them. Gradually, the disillusioned men do return, and Hickey, his self-confidence slowly fading, now tells Larry that his wife was murdered. Later, Hickey explains in a lengthy monologue how he himself killed his wife, who constantly forgave him his philandering and other sins, and whose angelic nature and faith in him led him to despise her. He rationalizes his behavior by claiming to have been insane and is led off by the police. But he has managed merely to give the derelicts back the illusions they temporarily had abandoned. Only Parritt, who betrayed his mother, and Slade cannot take up where they left off. Parritt follows Larry's advice and kills himself; as the others become reabsorbed in alcohol, Larry painfully confronts life without illusions.

There was a surprising split in critical opinions. Brooks Atkinson (*NYT*) hailed the production for the excellence of its deeply introspective, somber dramaturgy shot through with comic vitality and said that it was "preeminently actable." He dubbed the performance "a masterpiece of tones, rhythms and illumination." There was too much talk for his taste, but at least it was "good talk--racy, angry, comic drumbeats on the lid of doom." "It is a far from perfect play, but it has the standards and elements of greatness which is more likely to produce division of opinion than slick perfection or downright tawdriness," noted George Freedley (*NYMT*). George Jean Nathan (*NYJA*) huzzaed the play's arrival, which he said made most of the past twelve years' American plays "look like so much wet tissue paper." While wishing it were shorter and less repetitious, he nevertheless counted it one of O'Neill's finest works for its comprehension of human nature and its expression of compassion for mankind's painful existence. "Out of the whole emerge in no small degree the profound essences of authentic tragedy." Yet John Beaufort (*CSM*), while admiring much of what he saw, felt that the sum total of O'Neill's drama left much to be desired "as a comment on life or about the characters as people. Out of the depths, out of cynicism, irony, and sensitive pessimism, Mr. O'Neill seems to be crying a hollow cry." It was "never truly tragic," he lamented. Beaufort, too, believed that a great improvement might have been made by shortening the play. Several others shared his view, among them Robert Garland (*NYJA*).

John Mason Brown (*SR*), who also railed against the play's length, considered the production "one of the most satisfying and masterly presentations our stage has yielded. Eddie Dowling . . . has faced a problem of staggering proportions, and somehow managed to solve it." He said that the treatment of the often silent characters was more than convincing. Dowling's "groupings are fluid; his modulations of pace admirable; and his eye for the pictorial unflagging." The effect of life transmuted into art through the combination of directing and scenery was remarkable. The stage pictures, Brown declared, reminded one of artists George Bellows and Grant Wood.

The finest acting, by most accounts, was Digges's as the irascible but kindly Harry. James Barton, too, was considered brilliant by some, especially for his delivery of the fifteen-minute monologue in the last act. Beaufort observed, for example, that he "conveys magnificently the slick salesmanship, the likableness, loneliness, and strangeness of Hickey." But a number of critics (including Brown and Nathan) opined that the actor was not up to the role's demands and that it would have been better played by Dowling himself.

ICETIME [Revue/Ice] M/LY: James Littlefield and John Fortis; D: Arthur Wirtz and William H. Burke; CH: Catherine and Dorothie Littlefield (skating: May Judels); S: Edward Gilbert; C: Lou Eisele and Billy Livingston; L: Eugene Braun; P: Sonja Henie and Arthur Wirtz; T: Center Theatre; 6/20/46 (405)

The same producers who were responsible for various "icetravaganzas" of the period, including a regular series at Madison Square Garden, returned to the huge Center Theatre with this spectacular version featuring twenty-four numbers. The old formula was in place and there were few surprises.

Returning to the postwar fold were the low-comical Bruises, reduced to three (Monty Stott, Geoffe Stevens, and Sid Spalding) from four and reprising their routine as dowdy charwomen. Comedy was also the specialty of tiny Paul Castle and the virtuosic Freddie Trenkler; the chief figure skater was pretty Joan Hyldoft. Other acts included barrel jumper James Caesar (who also leaped blindfolded through a hoop of knives); trick double skaters Helga Brandt and Inge Brandt; and acrobatic Jack Reese, who did a complete somersault on skates. There were numbers for young children, such as "Mary, Mary, Quite Contrary" and "Old King Cole." There were cossack dances, high-speed routines, and considerable acrobatics. A minstrel show concluded act one, with such old standards as "Mandy" and "Shine On, Harvest Moon." There were also the familiar production numbers with colorfully lavish backgrounds, such as "The Nutcracker Suite," "The Garden of Versailles," "Sherwood Forest," and "The Dream Waltz," with its white and yellow hussars.

Most critics were deadly tired of such presentations, most especially George Jean Nathan (*TBY*), who announced, "Totally lacking in imagination, it repeats everything in the antecedent exhibits in even less attractive costumes and even less slightly scenic cut-outs." And Otis L. Guernsey, Jr. (*NYHT*), described it as "a gorgeous monotony which seems to get showier and emptier as the evening passes."

ICETIME OF 1948 [Revue/Ice] M/LY: James Littlefield, John Fortis, Al Stillman, and Paul McGrane; D: Catherine Littlefield; CH: Catherine and Dorothie Littlefield (skating: May Judels); S: Bruno Maine and Edward Gilbert; C: Lou Eisele, Billy Livingston, and Kathryn Kuhn; L: Eugene Braun; P: Sonart Productions; T: Center Theatre; 5/28/47 (422)

The follow-up to the successful *Icetime* had the date of the following year attached to its title. It opened a month after the previous work closed. Less a new show than an improved version of its predecessor, it retained much earlier material, which it combined with a considerable amount taken from other Sonja Henie-produced works, such as those seen at Madison Square Garden.

The extravagant offering included over fifty chorus members, some of whom fell on opening night, one girl sliding into the orchestra pit. The comic star was the inimitable Freddie Trenkler, but the Bruises were back again and as funny as ever. New to the show was nonskater Joe Jackson, Jr., son of a famed vaudevillian, doing the tramp on a break-away bicycle routine perfected by his late father. Handsome figure skater Lloyd "Skippy" Baxter was a headliner once more, and several of his numbers were shared with flawless figure skater Joan Hyldoft. Expert adagio dances were offered by Claire Dalton and Fred Griffith. The Brandt sisters returned, as did James Caesar and many others. Such production specials as "The Dream Waltz," "The Nutcracker Suite," the minstrel act, and others were again on the twenty-four scene bill.

"From a purely theatrical standpoint it leaves much to be desired, but it has such come-ons as speed, accidental and deliberate tumbles and chopped ice to keep it a perennial favorite with hot-weather amusement seekers," wrote Howard Barnes (*NYHT*). But Ward Morehouse (*NYS*) said that his "principal complaint is the almost unending sameness to the proceedings, number after number."

IF IN THE GREENWOOD [Drama/Journalism/Politics/Sex/Verse] A: Victoria Kuhn; D: Dennis Gurney; S: Avril Gentles; P: Blackfriars' Guild; T: Blackfriars' Theatre (OB); 1/16/47 (28)

A decided lack of enthusiasm marked the critical response to this semiprofessional offering by a young Washingtonian. Her confused play, written in free verse, is set in a mythical country that, at a time of international crisis, wants to recall its idealistic ex-leader (Ray Colcord) to assist it in joining the United Nations in search of world unity. The leader sees this as a chance to put into practice his ideas on world peace, but his unctuous, materialistic rival wants to use the UN for evil purposes. The latter uncovers proof of an affair between the idealist's wife (Katherine Hamilton) and his chief advisor. If the idealist does not withdraw, the other will bring the affair to public attention. Then the illicit lovers jump off a cliff into the sea. Not yet broken, the widowed husband rallies and sets out to defeat his enemies. The talky play concludes that one must put one's own house in order before undertaking to help solve the problems of the world.

The press agreed with George Freedley (*NYMT*) that "Miss Kuhn's play is hopelessly inadequate for any theater and certainly wasn't ready for professional reviewing."

IF THE SHOE FITS [Musical/Fantasy/Period/Romance] B: June Carroll and Robert Duke; M: David Raksin; LY: June Carroll; SC: the *Cinderella* fairy tale; D: Eugene Bryden; CH: Charles Weidman (tap: Don Liberto); S: Edward Gilbert; C: Kathryn Kuhn; P: Leonard Sillman; T: Century Theatre; 12/5/46 (21)

George Jean Nathan (*NYJA*) wrote of this $300,000-plus musical comedy, "Not only isn't there . . . one good tune but there isn't anything that resembles music of any kind." As for humor, he declared, "the producer . . . thought that he had a load of it in a fat comedian [Joe Besser] who puts his hand to his hip and minces around the stage . . . pronouncing Ecce Homo." John Chapman (*NYDN*) spiked the show as "a witless and offensive affair which has the effrontery to dirty up the fairy story about Cinderella."

As Chapman reported, the story was based on the familiar fairy tale, with Cinderella played by Leila Ernst, the fairy godmother, called Lady Eve, by British low comedienne Florence Desmond, and Prince Charming by Edward Dew. Set in the fanciful kingdom of Nicely, it was graced with a lovely and mechanically ingenious collapsible setting designed to turn like the pages of a children's pop-up book, with the sets springing up when brought into view. The critics rejected the book writers' smutty treatment of the story (for example, jokes about Cinderella's virginity or the sexy undulations of the fairy godmother when she tries to get Prince Charming for herself), the lack of good music, and the lethargic writing and staging. One of the few amusing moments came when Desmond did her out-of-context impressions of three famous movie personalities. Players of note were Adrienne, Barbara Perry, Jody Gilbert, Eleanor Jones, Eddie Lambert, and Jack Williams.

"ILE", "IN THE ZONE," and **THE MAN WHO CAME TO DINNER** [Dramatic Revivals*] D: Terry (Teresa) Hayden; P: Library Theatre Project; T: Theatre Workshop (OB); 2/20/44
"Ile" A: Eugene O'Neill; "In the Zone" A: Eugene O'Neill; *The Man Who Came to Dinner* A: George S. Kaufman and Moss Hart

An odd bill of two 1917 O'Neill one-acters and a greatly abbreviated version of Kaufman and Hart's 1939 hit comedy by the showcase arm of Equity later known as the Equity Library Theatre. The "experimental" production "had everything go wrong with it that is possible to happen in the theater," lamented George Freedley (*NYMT*).

Bill Marceau and Camille Staneska as the whaler captain and Mrs. Keeney were the standout performers in "Ile." Director Hayden had to take over the male role of Davis in "In the Zone" when an accident prevented the original player from performing. "Her performance was astonishingly good," revealed Freedley. Bill Marceau was a good support as Driscoll.

The Kaufman and Hart piece was so heavily cut that someone in the audience said that it should have been called "The Man Who Dropped In for a Sandwich." Morton Da Costa played Sheridan Whiteside "reasonably well," according to Freedley. Supporting him were Sydna Scott as Maggie and Camille Staneska as Miss Preen.

I'LL TAKE THE HIGH ROAD [Comedy-Drama/Business/Family/Films/Politics/Romance/Small Town/War] A: Lucille Prumbs; D: Sanford Meisner; S: Paul Morrison; P: Clifford Hayman and Milton Berle; T: Ritz Theatre; 11/9/43 (7)

Comedian Milton Berle was one of the producers responsible for this "downright moronic" (Burton Rascoe [*NYWT*]) play that had the critics complaining that Broadway had taken a backward step with its presentation. Lewis Nichols (*NYT*) dubbed it "a faintly incredible stencil copy of movie classics of the grade below C."

Film star James Cagney's sister Jeanne (in her Broadway debut) was the briefly employed star of this opus, playing the role of Judy Budd, a telephone operator at a factory turning out airplanes for the war effort. The head of the company (not seen) is a man whose record for war production and liberal employment practices makes him the subject of an inspirational film to be premiered in the factory's town of Mansondale, Long Island. The star of the film is a handsome young actor (Michael Strong, making an impression in his first major role), who is to escort Judy to the premiere because she has won the factory's contest as "Miss Average Girl." Judy suspects that her supposedly benevolent boss is in cahoots with a dangerous American fascist wanted by the FBI, she having eavesdropped on a conversation between the two. She completely ruins the premiere by denouncing the boss from the stage. He is arrested by the FBI, while the plant falls under government control. Judy drops her local boyfriend in favor of the movie star, who has also fallen for her, and promises to wait for him until he returns from the war. Much of the play concerns Judy's family, including her parents (Wanda Lyon and John McGovern), her kid brother (Allan Rich), and an eccentric uncle (Len Doyle).

Leo Chalzel played a movie director. Also involved were Ethel Remey and Lester Lonergan.

I'M IN LOVE [Musical/Yiddish Language] B: William Siegel; M: Abe Ellstein; LY: Isidor Lillian and Jacob Jacobs; D/P: Menasha Skulnik; CH: Lillian Shapero; S: William Gordon; T: Second Avenue Theatre (OB); 11/20/46

A "sprightly entertainment" (Jose. [*V*]), whose charms stemmed largely from the almost continual onstage presence of Menasha Skulnik. Its book, however, was second-rate, and the production was on the niggardly side. Skulnik played Yoina Pletzel, a former cop who must marry the niece of a recently deceased person in order to inherit that person's fortune. The marriage does not pan out, and Yoina returns to a former girlfriend.

Jose. noted that by producing, directing, and starring, Skulnik had spread himself too thin and could not attend to all the many details that make a show a total unity. Only his own performance was fully realized. Others in the cast included Yetta Zwerling, Leon Liebgold, Anne Winters, Lilly Lilliana, Jacob Susanoff, Max Rosenblatt, Moses Feder, Annie Thomashevsky, and Anna Teitelbaum.

(1) **IMPORTANCE OF BEING EARNEST, THE** [Dramatic Revival*] A: Oscar Wilde; D: George Benard; S: Delos; L: Warren B. Shannon; P: Philip Drury for Equity Library Theatre; T: Hudson Park Branch of the New York Public Library (OB); 11/11/45 (4)

A showcase revival of Wilde's great comedy, with Philip Drury as Algernon, William Dorn as Jack Worthing, Gertrude Kinnell as Lady Bracknell, Margretta Ramsey as Gwendolyn, Marjorie Tas as Cecily, Ivy Foster as Miss Prism, and George Benard as Reverend Chasuble. Ramsey and Kinnell were said by George Freedley (*NYMT*), the only critic there, to have given the best performances.

Of the production, Freedley reported, "The Wildean lines are extremely funny and I found myself laughing uproariously at a great many scenes. This is one of the liveliest and most amusing of the Equity productions." He opined that "Benard has directed the piece so shrewdly and with such elaborate emphasis upon formality that he has caught the artificiality of the play without making it either dull or ridiculous." The comedy's most recent revival had been in 1939.

(2) [Dramatic Revival*] M: Leslie Bridgewater; D: John Gielgud; S/C: Motley; L: William Conway; P: Theatre Guild and John C. Wilson; T: Royale Theatre; 3/3/47 (81)

A near-perfect rendition of the often-produced 1895 comedy. Another Wilde comedy, *Lady Windermere's Fan**, was still running in a successful revival when the present production opened. Director Gielgud, who had been performing the piece in England on and off since 1930, now showed his stuff to New York, with a brilliant British company that included himself in his usual role of Jack, Robert Flemyng as Algernon, Margaret Rutherford as Lady Bracknell, Pamela Brown as Gwendolyn, Jane Baxter as Cecily, Jean Cadell as Miss Prism, John Kidd as Reverend Chasuble, and Richard Wordsworth as Lane.

With so many fine repertory-trained actors, the result was not a concatenation of disparate performances, but a beautifully welded ensemble. In their mouths, Wilde's epigrammatic dialogue sparkled as if freshly minted. Rosamond Gilder (*TAM*) rhapsodized, "There is a gusto about their performance, a kind of joy in the game that carries the audience irresistibly into the mood of absurdity and fun. Wilde's paradoxes are batted to and fro with the agility of championship tennis. The neat balance of players, the superbly absurd counterpoint of the whole procedure is carried out in the details of Mr. Gielgud's direction and the buoyant precision of his company's performance." Euphemia Van Rensselaer Wyatt (*CW*) thought that the key to the revival's success was "not only because the Gielgud company plays with the quintessence of wit but because they treat the play *not* as moderns farcing caricatures of Victorians but as solid Victorians poking fun at themselves." Several critics marveled at how amusing the play was when its characters were made human instead of period caricatures and the lines were not read as jokes. The dialogue was spoken almost with disdain, in a dry and casual fashion, instead of being pounced on as obvious laugh getters.

Perhaps the two most memorable performances in this amiable company were those of Gielgud and Rutherford. Gielgud displayed a virtuosic sense of comic timing, carefully measured but organic movement and gestures, and articulation for which he was famous. Through his deadpan solemnity, he succeeded not only in conveying the humor of the character, but managed to conjure up a sense of sympathy for him.

Rutherford, said Brooks Atkinson (*NYT*), "is tremendously skillful--the speaking, the walking and the wearing of costumes all gathered up into one impression of insufferability." Those who had seen Edith Evans's portrayal in Gielgud's wartime London version, however, admitted to a preference for her. Most vocal of such was John Mason Brown (*SR*), who said that the portly Rutherford "fills the eye, even if she does not fill the bill. She sails in--begloved and boa'd, a parasol in her hand, her lorgnette poised, with an aviary as a hat--a great brown mass of matronliness." Yet he felt that she did not do enough with her lines. "She parrots Wilde without adding to him in terms of her own craft."

Gielgud and company also appeared during the season in *Love for Love*.

IN BED WE CRY [Comedy-Drama/Business/Marriage/Romance/Science/Sex/War] A: Ilka Chase; SC: Ilka Chase's novel of the same name; D/P: John C. Wilson; S: Joseph B. Platt; C: (gowns) Adrian; T: Belasco Theatre; 11/14/44 (47)

Ilka Chase starred in this play of her own authorship based on her best-selling novel. Her presumably sophisticated drawing-room drama was "teddibly, teddibly smart but dramatically as corny as a Nebraska silo," rasped John Chapman (*NYDN*). The play's chief saving grace was its occasionally successful acid-dipped wisecracks, usually spoken by the playwright-star, well known for her ability in the quip-delivering department.

Chase--who wore a different Adrian gown in each of the seven scenes--played Devon Elliott Wainwright, successful head of a great cosmetics firm, whose husband Tim (Francis DeSales) is the company's chief chemist. Bored with a life of creating makeups and scents and with a position that puts him on his wife's payroll, the proud Tim leaves Devon for a role in the army medical corps. The sexually frustrated beauty queen turns for solace to the suave but insincere European refugee Kurt Fabri (Frederic Tozere). After divorcing Tim, she is about to marry Kurt when she discovers that he is having an affair with her refugee shop manager, Maria Sellner (Elena Karam). Confronting him, she receives a sock in the kisser for her troubles. That ends the affair with Kurt. Tim, meanwhile, is killed in the war. Thank goodness, however, for her business manager, Jasper Doolittle (Paul McGrath), has been waiting for her in the wings all along.

"For the most part," thought Robert Coleman (*NYDM*), "it is forced and peopled with characters just this side of stained glass window figures." To George Jean Nathan (*TBY*), the play gave "the nasal impression . . . of a lot of very wet, soiled underclothes pinned up on a line to dry. The perfume is hardly edifying." The cast included Ruth Matteson, Virginia Kaye, and Eleanor Audley, among others.

IN TIME TO COME [Drama/France/Historical-Biographical/Period/Politics/War] A: Howard Koch and John Huston; D/P: Otto Preminger; S: Harry Horner; C: John Koenig; T: Mansfield Theatre; 12/28/41 (40)

In Time to Come, one of Burns Mantle's ten best of the year, was originally a play by Howard Koch titled *Woodrow Wilson*, but when John Huston joined him on the project, the title was changed. Despite appreciative reviews, the audience for the play did not exist in large-enough numbers to sustain it.

This was a carefully composed, dignified biographical drama about President Wilson, creator of the League of Nations, and the signing of the Treaty of Versailles. (A play on the same subject had been planned by Sidney Howard.) It was set between 1917 and 1921, with scenes in the White House, on the deck of the S. S. *George Washington* approaching Brest Harbor, in the president's house near Parc Monceau, and in a conference room at Quai Dorsay. The work seemed especially pertinent because of current world events and Wilson's prediction that war would once more terrorize the world unless a peace based, not on economic gain, but on human principles could be established among the nations of the world working together for their mutual benefit. Parallels with World War I and II were striking. The play's timeliness was even more marked when, three weeks after Pearl Harbor, it opened with a prologue showing Wilson (Richard Gaines) addressing Congress to ask for a declaration of war against Germany and her allies.

One drawback facing the playwrights was that Wilson was an especially uncharismatic leader, yet had to sustain a full-length drama about him. For some this problem was never overcome, as witness Euphemia Van Rensselaer Wyatt's (*CW*) remarks. Noting the authors' success as screenwriters, she said, "Their viewpoint is tolerant; their use of available material intelligent; they have chosen a great subject and they have evolved--another screenplay. The most obvious weakness of the drama is that the authors have taken an idea for their hero. Their enthusiasm is centered on the League and not on its creator," a character she felt remained "inscrutable" and was never more than just an outer shell. But for most, their efforts worked, and many agreed with Rosamond Gilder (*TAM*) that "coming at this time in world events, *In Time to Come* is an absorbing and vital presentation," to which might be added George Freedley's (*NYMT*) praise, "Despite the weaknesses inherent in episodic work this drama has a vitality and an integrity which infuses it to the exclusion of every other consideration."

Following the prologue, the play reveals Wilson's frustrating experiences as political opposition blocks his far-reaching goals; part of the opposition stems from Wilson's high-minded attitude, which prevents him from cooperating or consulting with important power figures, such as Senator Lodge (House Jameson). In Paris he confronts and is unable to contend with the duplicity of the cynical Allies. Very effective is his conclave with the other members of the Big Four, Clemenceau (Guy Sorel), Lloyd George (Harold Young), and Sonnino (Rene Roberti). Prior to setting out on an important speaking tour of America, he argues with Lodge and comes off the weaker of the two. Ill and broken, his dream of an effective League of Nations destroyed by concessions he has been forced to make, he spends his last day in the White House contemplating his fondness for the nation and his wish to aid it, if possible.

Nedda Harrigan played the president's wife, Edith Bolling Wilson, and there were competent performances from William Harrigan, Russell Collins, James Gregory, Alexander Clark, John M. Kline, Harold J. Kennedy, and Arnold Korff, and others. Richard Gaines split the critics about his performance as Wilson, some thinking him a perfect likeness, others finding him wooden.

INFERNAL MACHINE, THE (*La Machine Infernale*) [Dramatic Revival*] A: Jean Cocteau; TR: Carl Wildman; D: Alexis Solomos; S/L: Steve Brodie, Charles Hyman, and Bill Sherman; C: Maurice Beaton; P: Interplayers; T: Provincetown Playhouse (OB); 6/16/48

Cocteau's modern and somewhat esoteric French parody of Sophocles' *Oedipus Rex**--in which the events cover seventeen years--had been seen in a previous Off-Broadway version in 1937. It was now being offered by a new Off-Broadway group as its opening production.

Both the play and its imaginatively conceived production were greeted warmly by most, although there were reservations. John S. Wilson (*PM*) appreciated Cocteau's ability to blend comedy and tragedy and his capturing of the human dimension of Sophocles' grand characters. Herm. (*V*) declared, "This group rates high praise, not only for attempting the play but in carrying it off with finesse and verve." William Hawkins (*NYWT*), though, thought that "the company is . . . out of its depths."

Oedipus--shown as a callow and big-headed nineteen-year- old--was played by Louis Criss, the sphinx by Nancy Jane Stiber, the flighty, age-conscious Jocasta by

Trescott Ripley, Tiresias by Fred Porcelli, the phantom of Laius by Eddie Frost, the Theban matron by Anna Berger, Anubis by Oliver Reed, the soldier by John Denny, the statue by Henry Colman, the young soldier by Michael Michelas, and the chief by Harold (Harry) Guardino (in his New York bow).

INJURY SUSTAINED [Drama/Family/Medicine/Politics] A/D/P: Ben Levinson; T: Provincetown Playhouse (OB); 10/23/40

It was the critics who felt that they had sustained injuries after sitting through this dreary vanity production in which the author-director-producer also played a leading role. Most admitted to having left in the middle. Not only was the story "crowded with incongruous or impossible situations," wrote Sidney B. Whipple (*NYWT*), it was "promptly snuffed out the moment it reached the stage by some of the most murderous acting it has ever been my privilege to witness."

Bearing a faint resemblance to Ibsen's *An Enemy of the People**, the play concerns political corruption and medical malpractice in a story about a politician (Mel Davis) who tries to capitalize economically on a job-related injury to his son (Edward Hussey). The son, seeking to help his father gain funds for his campaign, connives with a sleazy doctor to make his injuries seem life-threatening. The politician's mostly corrupt family is contrasted with the idealistic policies of a noble physician, Dr. Newman (Ben Levinson), who seeks to provide clean politics and improved sanitation for the town. When the son's injuries turn out to be truly serious, Dr. Newman saves him, although the son suffers paralysis. The ill-natured son's resentment at not being able to collect the insurance money he was seeking so disturbs Dr. Newman that he leaves for greener pastures.

INNOCENT VOYAGE, THE [Comedy-Drama/Adventure/Crime/Mental Illness/Period/Sea/Sex/Youth] A/D: Paul Osborn; SC: Richard Hughes's novel, *A High Wind in Jamaica*; S: Stewart Chaney; C: Aline Bernstein; P: Theatre Guild; T: Belasco Theatre; 11/15/43 (40)

This drama did not last long but was selected as one of the ten best of the year by Burns Mantle. It was judged an unsuccessful adaptation of the popular and well-respected novel from which it was drawn, yet, in a year not overwhelmed by fine specimens of dramatic writing, it served its purpose reasonably well. Osborn had done the adaptation after Clare Boothe Luce tried and failed to come up with anything satisfactory.

Euphemia Van Rensselaer Wyatt (*CW*) called it "a play full of action and color but without any point whatsoever." George Jean Nathan (*TBY*), acknowledging Osborn's dramaturgic lapses in being unable to capture Hughes's incisive probing of the children characters' minds and in making the story too pretty, nevertheless argued that "his play manages to project what he has selected from the tale with considerable charm, tenderness and humor." He did take serious issue, though, with the direction, the acting of the children, and the incorporation of the "dully superfluous" prologue.

Mr. and Mrs. Thornton (Guy Spaull and Norah Howard) of Jamaica send their five young children off to England on the *Clorinda* in 1860. An aunt is scheduled to meet them when they stop in Cuba, but otherwise they are unchaperoned. En route the ship is overtaken by pirates. The pirates soon learn that they have not only acquired a hefty pile of loot but also have mistakenly brought the Thornton children aboard their ship, the *John Dodson*. The ship becomes for the boys and girls--outwardly well behaved but hellions at heart--the scene of a great adventure. When they become a pain in the neck to the pirates (who like them despite themselves), the gruff Captain Jonsen (Oscar Homolka) wants to get them out of his hair; the kinder first mate (Herbert Berghof), however, will hear nothing of it. The plot contrives to have one of the children, eleven-year-old Emily (Abby Bonime), kill in self-defense a Swedish captain (Arvid Paulsen) whom the pirates have imprisoned upon commandeering his ship for its provisions. When a British gunboat, *Royal William*, captures the *John Dodson*, the captain and his mate must eventually face trial for the crime, despite Emily's confession, which no one will accept. The task of deciding on their guilt rests with a naval judge (Clarence Derwent) who wants to hang them.

Finally, the action shifts to the *Royal William* for the delayed trip to England.

Lewis Nichols (*NYT*) was concerned that Osborn had not been able to establish a consistent tone for the play, veering from comedy to melodrama and back. Ward Morehouse (*NYS*) thought that the play, while engrossing, was "undisciplined . . . jumbled, lacking in cohesion." Several were disturbed by the presence in the action of a mulatto girl, Margaret (Lois Wheeler), also kidnapped, who becomes a whore for the pirates and goes crazy after witnessing the killing. One of the finest things about the production was its scenic design, for which Stewart Chaney contrived the contours of three different ships set against backgrounds of considerable variety.

Of the adult actors, Homolka and Berghof were excellent. Rosamond Gilder (*TAM*) wrote, "Herbert Berghof as the mercurial Otto is an excellent foil for Homolka. He gives the role a certain gay naivete; his Otto is smart, blustering and disarming." Among the children were brothers Guy and Dean Stockwell (children of Harry Stockwell, an actor then playing Curly in the touring version of *Oklahoma!*). Other Thornton youngsters were Carolyn Hummel and Mary Ellen Glass. Also involved was Boris Marshalov.

INNOCENTS, THE [Drama/Death/Fantasy/Mystery/Youth] A: William Archibald; M: Alex North; SC: Henry James's novel, *The Turn of the Screw*; M: Alex North; D: Peter Glenville; S/L: Jo Mielziner; C: Motley; P: Peter Cookson; T: Playhouse; 2/1/50 (141)

William Archibald, a native of the British West Indies, successfully transposed for the theatre James's chilling short novel. He had begun his four-character (plus two non-speaking roles) adaptation as a film scenario and made eight revisions before the piece was finished as a play. Unlike critic Edmund Wilson, who argued that the governess in the story never saw real ghosts because she was insane, Archibald believed that the ghosts were real and that they took possession of the children. He wrote in *TAM*, "The children were my method of creating supports for this play of suspension. I used them to charm the audience and veil the direction; but, as though making them their own enemies, I also used them (more than Henry James did) to create their own destruction--or, more correctly, to allow it. . . . This transference of tragedy from the governess to the children is . . . the greatest difference between the book and the play."

Archibald's intellectual ghost thriller is set in a large British country house in 1880. Miss Giddens (Beatrice Straight), a young governess, has been hired by a strange man in London to look after his orphaned nephew and niece at the house. Shortly after Miss Giddens arrives at the lonely mansion, she learns that her two young charges, Flora (nine-year-old Iris Mann) and Miles (thirteen-year-old David Coles), are in the viselike grip of the phantoms of a dead steward, Peter Quint (Andrew Duggan), and maid, Miss Jessup (Ella Playwin), who died violently. The only other living character is the housekeeper (Isobel Elsom). A previous governess killed herself. The ghosts become so powerful a presence that even Miss Giddens sometimes sees their outlines. Miss Giddens patiently tries to free the children's minds of the phantasmal influences and has some success with the more tractable Flora, but the boy is soiled by evil beyond repair. Miss Giddens struggles to free him from his chains and finally succeeds in her endeavors, but the moment that Peter Quint is exorcised from Miles's soul, the boy's heart gives way and he dies in her arms.

The play, chosen as one of the ten best of the season, was deemed an unrelentingly suspenseful drama, although not one of any particular substance. Joseph T. Shipley (*NL*) was one of the many impressed critics: "For sheer power of eerie mood of evil, no play of recent seasons has surpassed . . . *The Innocents*." Arthur Pollock (*DC*) agreed, noting, "*The Innocents* is a taut, close-knit, smooth little thriller, mild-mannered but constantly exciting." And Hobe. (*V*), who commented that the play was "the spookiest play of the season," expressed some annoyance that it was also "perhaps the most mystifying mystery in memory. Instead of resolving the manifold puzzle, the final curtain leaves practically every question unanswered."

A handful of critics thought that without the brilliant acting it received the play would not have succeeded. The children were especially remarkable, in a season noted for a series of brilliant child performances. Wrote Shipley, "It is amazing to see the insinuations of evil, the sly trickery with the adults, the fear that gathers to genuine terror, so subtly and surely caught by these child players."

Straight's luminous acting inspired Thomas R. Dash (*WWD*) to declare that she "contributes one of the most adroit and memorable studies anywhere on Broadway today. She is both poignant and pulsatile. . . . In the final scene with the lad . . . Miss Straight charges the play with fierce emotional power. It is an electric portrayal, tremulous and vibrant throughout."

Elsom also was outstanding, as were the direction, the foreboding decor, and Alex North's strange, unearthly woodwind music. The play was the second recent adaptation of a James story to do well on Broadway; the first, *The Heiress*, was given a brief revival shortly after *The Innocents* opened.

INSECT COMEDY, THE (*Ze Zivota Hmyzu*) [Dramatic Revival*] A: Josef and Karel Capek; AD: Owen Davis; D: José Ferrer; CH: Hanya Holm; S/L: Herbert Brodkin; C: Emeline Roche; P: New York City Center Theatre Company; T: City Center of Music and Drama; 6/3/48 (14)

A revival of the Czech fantasy that first had played here in 1922 as *The World We Live In* (but in the same Davis adaptation) and that is also known as *From the Life of Insects*. It was given by the short-lived company headed by José Ferrer at City Center. Ferrer played the poet-butterfly Felix, and his company included George Coulouris as the vagrant, and Robinson Stone as the professor, with butterflies played by Phyllis Hill, Tom Poston, and Rita Gam; marauders by Mildred Joanne Smith, Paula Laurence, Robert Carroll, Annabelle Lyon, and Ray Walston; and ants by Leonardo Cimino, Alexander Scourby, Robert Carroll, Tom Poston, Ray Walston, and Ferrer (as the yellow commander). In the epilogue, Nan McFarland was the woman.

Once considered a fascinating satirical parable of human life, the play now seemed to several reviewers quaint and only mildly diverting. "The world again is trying to recover its balance and its values," wrote Lewis Funke (*NYT*), "but *The Insect Comedy* now seems no more than a tract, lacking in flesh and blood, and its ideas fail to move or stir no matter how much truth they contain." Some critics, though, thought the piece pertinent and worth reviving. "Still timely, provocative and intriguing," said Bron. (*V*).

Ferrer's production was a mostly acceptable one, although Ferrer did not fare too well as an actor in some eyes. The various insect characters were given choreographic movements, and there was one especially effective scene, the march of the warrior ants and their battle for the right to a path between two blades of grass. Vernon Rice (*NYP*) was surprised that so effectively stylized a performance was possible with the mere two weeks the stock company had for rehearsals. Because of budget limitations, the costuming eschewed trying to provide representative insect costuming and adopted a more flexibly imaginative style that suggested insect qualities while retaining human parallels.

INSIDE STORY [Comedy/Family/Journalism/Military/Romance/Theatre/War/Youth] A: Peter Sheehan; D: Dennis Gurney; P: Blackfriars' Guild; T: Blackfriars' Theatre (OB); 10/29/42

The Blackfriars' Guild, an Off-Broadway showcase theatre in which--in its early days--professional actors worked without pay in hopes of being spotted, began its 1942-1943 season with this "agonizingly amateur" (Arthur Pollock [*BE*]) satirical farce about Irish-American Jane Carroll (Elsbeth Hoffman), feminist editor of a crusading little political magazine called *Inside Story*, which has lost its office space because of lack of income. She moves with her file cabinets and typewriter into her loudmouthed, ex-fire chief father's (Robert Hayward) home and tries to edit the magazine from there, despite the intrusions of various Irish neighbors, a would-be thespian sister (June Meer), and a brat kid sister (Patsy O'Shea) on roller skates who writes poems about the "lousy Japs." One of her chief concerns is to do an inside story about India, of which she knows next to nothing. A phony Indian (Albert Carroll) provides her with the information she thinks will make a good story. A major element in the action is her confusion about whether or not she loves Paul Moore (Douglas Keaton), her assistant. When Paul is in uniform and ready to go off to war, she realizes that she loves him after all. Finally, her magazine is saved and she and Paul are united.

George Freedley (*NYMT*) considered most of it "crude and inept," yet some, like Robert Coleman (*NYDM*), thought the playwright worth encouraging. J. Augustus Keogh, formerly of the Abbey Theatre, gave a fine performance as Swivelhead Duffy, a garrulous old neighbor.

INSIDE U.S.A. [Revue] SK: Arnold Auerbach, Moss Hart, and Arnold B. Horwitt; M: Arthur Schwartz; LY: Howard Dietz; SC: John Gunther's book of the same name; D: Robert H. Gordon; CH: Helen Tamiris; S/L: Lemuel Ayers; C: Eleanor Goldsmith and (gowns) Castillo; P: Arthur Schwartz; T: New Century Theatre; 4/30/48 (339)

A passel of talent got together to produce and perform this successful intimate revue, with comic stars Beatrice Lillie and Jack Haley leading the charge. The states-hopping material--inspired, but not directly based, on Gunther's book about his travels around the country--did not live up to the expectations aroused by its distinguished contributors, but the performances, staging, and decorative features compensated sufficiently to make the piece a year-long hit. "As musical shows go, it is a thoroughbred that represents the best brains in our showshop," declared Brooks Atkinson (*NYT*). Euphemia Van Rensselaer Wyatt (*CW*) called it "the acme of the American made revue." John Mason Brown (*SR*) was disappointed that the material was not actually derived from Gunther's book and that the potential satire was therefore greatly weakened. But he liked it for what it did accomplish, calling it "glossy in its feel [and] professional in its touch."

Lillie's standout characters, played in her brilliantly witty burlesque manner, included a famous star's (Jane Lawrence) superstitious maid foreseeing a flop on opening night; the priggish leader of a choral society leading them in a rendition of "Come, Oh Come to Pittsburgh" (pronounced "Peetsburgh"); a Chillicothe movie fan who thinks herself a glamorous Viennese creature who inspires romantic musical compositions; a Plymouth Rock mermaid singing of herself as "A Seacow Named Desire"; and a Mardi Gras queen. Brown regretted that there were times when Lillie could not be on stage because of her human need to rest. "With one lifted finger or one raised eyebrow she can do more damage than a policeman with his nightstick. She fights dignity with its own weapons and routs it. . . . She is a perfect caricature come to life. . . . Miss Lillie is the best; the undisputed, the matchless best, and the deftest of female zanies."

Haley captured laughs with his tired guest in a Florida hotel room trying to sleep, but getting little help from the room's many allegedly slumber-inducing gadgets; his master waiter at the New York School for Waiters teaching apprentices how best to annoy customers; his singing "Rhode Island Is Famous for You" with Estelle Loring; and, in a scene with Lillie playing a squaw, "We Won't Take It Back!" his New Mexican Indian telling white men why his fellows refuse to take the country back.

Other well-liked contributors included dancer Valerie Bettis (especially in "Haunted Heart," the show's most lasting tune, danced under the Golden Gate Bridge; and dances at the Kentucky Derby, the Wisconsin State Fair, and Chicago, where she was a moll in "Tiger Lily"); Hoosier comedian Herb Shriner, with his hick mannerisms reminiscent of Will Rogers; dancers Rod Alexander and Eric Victor; baritone John Tyers; supporting players Joan Mann, Thelma Carpenter, William Le Massena; and, making their local debuts, comedians Carl Reiner and Lewis Nye.

INSPECTOR CALLS, AN [Drama/British/Crime/Family/Mystery/Period/Romance/Sex] A: J. B. Priestley; D: Cedric Hardwicke; DS: Stewart Chaney; P: Courtney Burr and Lassor H. Grosberg; T: Booth Theatre; 10/21/47 (95)

Priestley's unusual mystery drama with an "Am I my brother's keeper?" theme is set in Brumley, an industrial city in the English North Midlands, in 1912. All the action transpires in a large, suburban home owned by the smugly self-satisfied Birling family. They are Arthur (Melville Cooper), the prosperous middle-aged father; Sybil (Doris Lloyd), his wife; Eric (John Merivale), his son; and Sheila (Rene Ray), his pretty daughter. Eric and Sheila are in their twenties. Dressed formally, they are at dinner with Gerald Croft (John Buckmaster), the aristocratic young man who plans to marry Sheila, when Inspector Goole (Thomas Mitchell) calls, inquiring about the background of Miss Smith, a girl who has just killed herself. He shows each person a picture of the deceased, drawing from each their personal guilt in the circumstances that led to her death. Arthur dismissed the girl because she took part in a strike. Sheila had her fired from her job in a shop. Both Eric and Gerald had had affairs with and abandoned her. Sybil refused the unwed mother (pregnant by Eric) assistance. After Inspector Goole leaves, the parents' prime concern is to save themselves from scandal, but Sheila and Eric are racked about their mutual guilt. They go over their various confessions and decide that the whole thing is a hoax, that the girl never existed, and that the inspector, whom the police claim not to know, was an imposter. After they resume their former selfish behavior, they receive a phone call informing them that a Miss Smith has committed suicide and that they will shortly be visited by an inspector. (The debt to Gogol's *The Inspector General** was clear.)

Various reviewers thought this mystery *cum* morality play confusing, too literary, and only intermittently dramatic. "The play is not entirely satisfactory," complained William Hawkins (*NYWT*), "perhaps because it is bald fantasy told in terms of physical reality. Explanations of coincidences, and the inspector's motives and identity are left to the listener." Brooks Atkinson (*NYT*) admired the play's thesis, but felt "swindled" by the trickiness of the dramatic treatment. Representing an opposing viewpoint was Euphemia Van Rensselaer Wyatt (*CW*), who thought it "an absorbing play, easily Priestley's masterpiece; a play with such deep undercurrents that it can't easily be forgotten." John Chapman (*NYDN*) called it "a tidy, quietly humorous, excellently played exercise in holding an audience with a seeming minimum of effort." Opinions on the acting varied as well, the most approval going to Cooper and the least to Mitchell.

(1) IOLANTHE, OR THE PEER AND THE PERI [Musical Revival*] B/LY: W. S. Gilbert; M: Arthur Sullivan; D: R. H. Burnside; P: Boston Comic Opera Company and Messrs. Shubert; T: St. James Theatre; 2/23/42 (5)

Part of a Gilbert and Sullivan repertory. Florenz Ames was the Lord Chancellor, Robert Pitkin was the Earl of Mountararat, Morton Bowe was Lord Tolloller, Helen Lanvin was Queen of the Fairies, Kathleen Roche was Phyllis, and Margaret Roy was Iolanthe. It was thought to be one of the more effective of the pieces produced, with memorable turns by Roche and Ames, the latter being the best Lord Chancellor that Brooks Atkinson (*NYT*) had ever seen.

The small orchestra failed to capture the satire in the music, and some of the staging and performances also left something to be desired. The weakest element was the comedy.

(2) D: R. H. Burnside; P: R. H. Burnside i/a/w the Gilbert and Sullivan Opera Company; T: Ambassador Theatre; 2/22/44 (6)

The renamed Boston Comic Opera Company still employed the services of some of the performers who had appeared here in 1942 when it offered this production as part of a 1944 series. In general, it was better than some of the company's previous offerings, most of which were received with distaste. The scenery, however, looked as if it were on its last legs to Lewis Nichols (*NYT*), and "the unfortunate fairies in their silver turbans," reported Euphemia Van Rensselaer Wyatt (*CW*), "looked like a bevy from a stage sultan's seraglio or strays from a burlesque."

(3) D: Anna Bethell; C: Norman Wilkinson; P: D'Oyly Carte Opera Company; T: Century Theatre; 1/12/48 (16)

Among the 136 performances totalled by England's visiting Savoyards in their nine-piece visiting repertory was this revival of *Iolanthe*. It featured Martyn Green as the Lord Chancellor, Richard Dunn (taking over for the under-the-weather

Darrell Fancourt) as the Earl of Mountararat, Richard Walker as Private Willis, Charles Dorning as Strephon, Ella Halman as Queen of the Fairies, and Denise Findlay as Iolanthe.

"Their rendition . . . is full of zest, gaiety and good will," concluded Lewis Funke (*NYT*). Green's Lord Chancellor, said the reviewer, was "everything you know it should be. It is properly perplexed, spiced with the right amount of spoofing."

IPHIGENIA IN TAURIS (***Iphigenia auf Tauris***) [Dramatic Revival/German Language] A: Johann Wolfgang von Goethe; D: Victor Barnowski; P: Players from Abroad; T: Barbizon-Plaza Theatre (OB); 4/8/49

Continental star Elisabeth Bergner had an opportunity to perform in her native German in this "tasteful and competent" (Richard Watts, Jr. [*NYP*]) small-scale revival of Goethe's classic. She was costarred with Herbert Berghof as Orestes, while Luther Rewalt was Thoas, Ulrich Haupt was Pylades, and Theo Goetz was Arkas.

Watts was happy to announce that Bergner's recent proclivity for mannered and fussy performances, which had marred her outstanding reputation, was forgotten when she was acting in her native tongue. In place of the coy and arch methods she lately had been guilty of "was a quiet and credible sweetness. . . . This was a performance of genuine beauty and demonstrated clearly that Miss Bergner is an exceptional actress when she sets her mind to it." Berghof, reported Watts, was "sometimes theatrically impressive and sometimes merely theatrical."

(1) IT HAPPENS ON ICE [Revue/Ice] CN/D: Leon Leonidoff; M: Vernon Duke, Fred E. Ahlert, Peter De Rose, and Will Hudson; LY: Al Stillman, Mitchell Parish; ADD.M/LY: Morton Gould, Raymond Scott; CH: Catherine Littlefield with Robert Linden; DS: Norman Bel Geddes; P: Sonja Henie and Arthur M. Wirtz; T: Center Theatre; 10/10/40 (180)

The large stage of the Center Theatre in Rockefeller Center was remodeled to accommodate this spectacular "musical icetravaganza," coproduced by figure skating champion Sonja Henie and headlining ice stars Hedi Stenuf (a Viennese skater trained in ballet) and Lloyd "Skippy" Baxter and low comedian Joe Cook. Norman Bel Geddes designed every element of the beautiful production, which required the removal of three hundred orchestra seats to provide room for the stage, which was covered with fifty tons of ice and occupied thirteen thousand square feet. Up to now, such shows were the province of arenas such as Madison Square Garden, but *It Happens on Ice* made the Center America's first ice theatre. The production cost between $225,000 and $250,000. A series of shows under the same management would keep the Center busy throughout the decade.

There were several exceptional skating numbers staged by Catherine Littlefield and employing an attractive cohort of talented performers, but the program attempted a touch of variety in the antics of the nonskating Cook, who was accompanied by a host of his eccentric trademark gadgets. For most, Cook's humor--which included juggling bits--could not quite fill the capacious space (many thought that the English comic ice team, the Four Bruises, was much funnier in a sketch about four oversized charwomen). Most of the original songs employed failed to make more than a temporary impression (although "The Moon Fell in the River" by Parish and De Rose was lauded as a potential hit). Two competent singers, Felix Knight and Joan Edwards, handled most of the musical infusions. Cook did his routines on ice, aided by a self-designed baby walker. His seven-man Boulder Dam symphony, reminiscent of a Rube Goldberg cartoon, was his most hilarious routine.

Standout numbers included an adaptation of *Swan Lake*, "The Legend of the Lake," with Stenuf as the princess. A jitterbug number called "Don't Blow That Horn, Gabriel," played to a tune by Vernon Duke and featuring the one-named Le Verne, was another highlight, as was the waltz number in black and white, "R.S.V.P." Fourteen-year-old Mary Jane Yeo did a charming routine on ice as Curleylocks, accompanied by three skaters dressed as bears, and comic skater Dr. A. Douglas Nelles tickled many funny bones.

Rosamond Gilder (*TAM*) declared that the show was "grandiose and breathtaking, on occasion--in individual and group movement--startlingly beautiful, but often . . . curiously unexciting." A complaint about such shows, heard periodically over the years, was that they palled before the concluding number because ice skating, no matter how brilliant, is not sufficiently entertaining to keep one's interest for a full evening in the theatre. Noted Richard Lockridge (*NYS*), "There seems to be something about skates that makes even a pretty girl vanish coldly into the abstract."

(2) [Second Edition] CN: Leon Leonidoff; D: Gene Snyder; M: Vernon Duke, Peter De Rose, Fred E. Ahlert, Dorival Cayammi; LY: Mitchell Parish, Al Stillman; S/L: Norman Bel Geddes; C: Norman Bel Geddes and Willa Van; P: Sonja Henie and Arthur M. Wirtz; T: Center Theatre; 4/4/41 (96)

A second edition of the popular ice revue opened after three weeks on the road, during which it was shaped into a production widely considered superior to the original. Joe Cook was no longer in the cast, but the comedy was nevertheless one of the strongest elements on view. Especially successful in getting laughs among the new cast members was comic skater Freddie Trenkler, who loved to burlesque the figure skaters, while the Four Bruises from the first edition returned to contribute their guaranteed quota of hilarity. As before, they made their mark with a routine in which they skated as four huge charwomen, using their pails and mops for an unforgettably funny hockey game. Ruby Mercer and Richard Craig (with help from Jack Kilty, who was also in the original) replaced Joan Edwards and Felix Knight in the singing department, and there was a host of new skating acts, among them Betty Atkinson, doing a striking drum-majorette routine while turning somersaults, and Fritz Dietl, who specialized in trick skating on stilts. A number of the original performers returned, including lead skaters Hedi Stenuf and "Skippy" Baxter, and various big production numbers remained in the show from the first edition. Scho. (*V*) asserted, "This revised edition now plays more like a revue than the confused music-spectacle routining it had heretofore, with the result that the show reels off at a fast pace."

The first and second editions totaled 276 performances. After a four-week layoff, the show reopened on 7/15/41 in a slightly revised version that added another 386 performances to the total, bringing it to 662. The main addition was a chair-jumping act by Swiss barrel-jumping champion Georg von Birgelen. One of the chief points of interest was the performance of Baxter, who only a week earlier had been in a car crash, and whose career was generally thought endangered. Baxter, however, suffered only mild contusions and his graceful, acrobatic skating seemed unimpaired.

IT TAKES TWO [Comedy/Marriage/Sex] A: Virginia Faulkner and Dana Suesse; D: George Abbott; S: John Root; P: George Abbott and Richard Aldrich; T: Biltmore Theatre; 2/3/47 (8)

Hugh Marlowe and Martha Scott were the players at the heart of this disastrous marital farce (earlier called *Apartment K-17*) about a bickering young couple, the boorish Todd and the unreasonable Connie Frazier, who settle into a New York apartment after years of constant billet switching during the war. Their marriage flounders when she learns that Todd wants to go off on an engineering project in Louisiana for two years with his buddy Monk (Anthony Ross). Connie threatens divorce, and they seek to sublease their apartment so they will not have to give it up during the housing shortage. Meanwhile, they share the place by occupying separate rooms. Various characters wander into their apartment under the guise of being would-be tenants. A crucial one is a statuesque blond named Comfort Gibson (Temple Texas) with a penchant for straight gin and for removing her shoes. Monk has his eye on her, and she remains for the night while Connie is away with Monk's wife Bee (Vivian Vance). When Connie returns, she mistakenly thinks that Comfort has been with Todd. Todd also misunderstands Connie's offstage conversation with a handsome neighbor, Bill Renault (John Forsythe), who ends up punching Todd in the eye. When things are cleared up, Todd and Connie are reconciled.

Apart from their amusing depiction of Bill, said Brooks Atkinson (*NYT*), "the authors have written nothing that would upset the gravity of a club of sedate bookkeepers." The dramatists, wrote Richard Watts, Jr. (*NYP*), "have devised a comedy that makes its dull people important to the plot and the enlivening ones of incidental value, with results that are not encouraging to report." The play seemed contrived, had little fresh to offer, and put people off by its constant marital squabbling. The best acting reviews were for the relatively unknown John Forsythe.

IT'S A GIFT [Comedy/Family/Legacy/Period/Religion/Romance/School/Sex/Small Town/Youth] A: Curt Goetz and Dorian Otvos; D: Robert Henderson; S: Samuel Leve; C: Rose Bogdanoff; P: Goval Corporation; T: Playhouse; 3/12/45 (47)

This "thoroughly dirty little play," as George Freedley (*NYMT*) dubbed it, earned its footnote in theatre history by providing Julie Harris with a role for her Broadway debut. She played Atlanta, the seventeen-year-old daughter of prolific parents who also have eleven younger kids (the youngest is four), each of whom figures in the action.

The play begins in the Hazelton, Pennsylvania, home of Professor Theodore W. Hermann (Curt Goetz, the author, a Swiss playwright and actor of some repute in Europe) and his wife Matilda (Valerie Van Martens, Goetz's offstage wife) in 1911. The large family receives notice that the professor's sister, cast out years before for bearing an illegitimate child and subsequently having moved to Montevideo, Uruguay, has died and left a $750,000 legacy for Atlanta. The professor sails to South America with Atlanta and the family preacher, Reverend Endicott (Whitford Kane); they are secretly followed by Atlanta's boyfriend Herbert (Michael Strong). In Montevideo the highly moral professor learns that the sister became a famous singer and used her earnings to set up schools for needy girls. This leads to a scene in which a girls' school is mistaken for a brothel. At any rate, the plot hinges upon the will's revenge-inspired stipulation that someone in the family must have a bastard before the money can be obtained. If no baby is forthcoming by a specified date, the money goes to the girls' schools. The professor, who desperately wants the money, finds himself between a mercenary rock and a moral hard place and tries to capitalize on the erroneous idea that Atlanta might be pregnant by Herbert. The day is saved, however, when the professor discovers that his own marriage was not legal because the ceremony was performed on a vessel too small to be recognized by the law, and that all his children are bastards.

Critics objected to the play's confusion of genres, being at times a farce, a comedy, and a melodrama, and to its sexual innuendoes, but there were some who found a good deal of it genuinely funny. "It's neither more nor less than a double entendre talk-fest," scoffed Robert Garland (*NYJA*), but Bron. (*V*) observed, "It has some rich humor and poor taste, some excellent portrayals and some very dull moments, and quite a few laughs."

Harris was greeted by praise for her attractiveness and pleasant performance. Supporting actors included Morton Da Costa, Suzanne Caubaye, G. Swayne Gordon, and others.

IT'S ABOUT TIME [Revue] SK: Peter Barry, Arnold Horwitt, Arthur Elmer, Sam Locke, David Greggory, and Reuben Shipp; M: Will Lorin and Al Moss; ADD.M: Genevieve Pitot; LY: David Greggory; D: David Greggory; CH: Helen Tamiris; S: William Martin and Walter Ketchum; C: Stephanie Klein; P: Martin Blaine; T: Barbizon-Plaza Concert Hall (OB); 3/30/42 (4)

An unsuccessful intimate revue of which Brooks Atkinson (*NYT*) concluded that it was "colorless mimicry of stuff that is done with originality and skill on Broadway." Rowland Field (*NEN*) thought it "consistently amateurish in materials and performance." The work had started life as a summer show called *Talk Out Loud* presented at Unity House, a labor-union resort in Forest Park, Pennsylvania.

It was the usual assortment of songs, dances, and sketches, there being twenty-four pieces on the program. The show was framed within a lecture by Prof. X-427 to a group of honor students in the year 5042 A.D., and the numbers that followed were examples of life in the twentieth century. An example of the sketch material was

"Art of the Ballet," in which Leonard Elliott offered a burlesque lecture with off-color humor. "Blue" comedy underlined various offerings, such as the song "It's Better with a Sweater." Elliott also did a bit called "A Night at Town Hall," which poked fun at international singing styles. Another routine lampooned radio soap operas.

Despite the negative press it received, the show did offer a platform for such talents as Mimi Benzelle, Jane Hoffman (who did fairly well as the teacher of a women's swimming class), Paul Mann, and Helen Tamiris, the modern dancer who was then also appearing at the Rainbow Room. Tamiris's numbers included one about circus performers and another about a waterfront murder.

IT'S UP TO YOU [Miscellaneous] A: Arthur Arent; M: Earl Robinson; LY: Alfred Hayes, Lewis Allan, Hy Zaret, Woody Guthrie; D: Elia Kazan (film: Henwar Radakiewicz); CH: Helen Tamiris; S: Howard Bay; C: Peggy Clark; L: Moe Hack; P: U.S. Department of Agriculture; T: Academy of Music (OB); 3/30/43 (1)

A branch of the U.S. government (aided by the Skouras Theatres, the American Theatre Wing, and several food-industry associations) sponsored this hour-and-a-quarter wartime propaganda effort concerning the nation's need to ration food during the crisis; despite its educational purpose, the work was considered an excellent piece of theatre. As Mark Schubart (*PM*) wrote, "Most of it is entertaining and engrossing. For *It's Up to You*, over and above its message, is a lively production."

Written by one of the chief "living newspaper" writers of the 1930s, it used similar techniques to provide an episodic, twenty-seven-scene production, with live action mingled with film and slide projections on a basically sceneryless stage. It was staged in the cavernous space of a huge, 3,500-seat movie theatre on East Fourteenth Street. Duplicate versions of it were to be made available for presentation in 2,100 theatres nationwide within the next six months, and an abbreviated version of the present show was scheduled for showing, free of charge, in the weeks to come.

It began with a film showing America's fertile farms being plowed, followed by the cessation of labor because the farmers claimed to have no market for their goods. Hungry women from different nations appeared on stage crying out for food in their native tongues, after which appeared a hungry American soldier from Bataan. The farmer, now realizing that he had a market, got to work, but not before pointing to the audience and saying, "From now on, it's up to you." The ensuing scenes were backed by large projections taking the action into such places as a farmer's home, a meat market, and Guadalcanal; in the latter, two marines were shown as lost and starving. A scene of black market meat selling was shown, and when a greedy patron (Hilda Vaughn) expressed her fear that she was about to faint without her daily steak, dancer Helen Tamiris, portraying a cow, appeared (and stopped the show) with her satirical number, "Porterhouse Lucy, the Black Market Steak." Some of Alfred Hayes's lyrics went:

Now she drives up to the butcher's in a limousine;
It was ten feet long and painted Kelly Green.
Her chauffer was a tough guy from the slaughter yards;
He went around ripping up ration cards.

Cast members included Percy Helton, Louise Larabee, Dorrit Kelton, Lester Lonergan, Jr., Edward Nannery, Ralph Bell, Woody Guthrie, George Spaulding, Richard C. Hart, Guy Spaull, Wendell Corey, and John McKee, among others.

IVY GREEN, THE [Drama/Family/Literary-Biographical/Marriage/Period/Romance/Sex] A: Mervyn Nelson; D: Roy Hargrave and Richard Barr; DS: Stewart Chaney; P: Hall Shelton; T: Lyceum Theatre; 4/5/49 (7)

A cast of first-rate players performed this "well-intentioned but tedious" (Hobe. [*V*]) dramatization of Charles Dickens's (Irish actor Daniel O'Herlihy in his first and only Broadway role) life and loves over a thirty-four-year period, with an accent on the latter. In the end the great novelist, depicted as something of a pompous boor, is shown declining into senility. George Jean Nathan (*TBY*) cared little for how factual the account was and assailed the playwright for a characterization that made Dickens seem a "complete and entire . . . ass." The play, announced Howard Barnes (*NYHT*), "is neither illuminating nor theatrically effective."

The eight-scened action, all of it set in the excellently re-created Tavistock House, Dickens's London home, was tied together by a loudspeaker narration delivered by Judith Evelyn, who played Dickens's wife. As she spoke, the new scene would come into view behind an ivy-framed scrim. Dickens marries Catherine Hogarth, a Scotswoman, in 1836. She turns out to be a dull and simple hausfrau who supplies him almost yearly with a new child (ten altogether) and is responsible for him seeking solace in the arms of other women. After a brief relationship with Catherine's sister Mary (Joy Reese), a long-term relationship with another sister, the selfish Georgina (Carmen Mathews) develops. Then, in old age, Dickens turns to a silly young actress, Ellen Ternan (June Dayton). In 1870 he dies and the faithful Catherine finally asserts herself. Instead of following his wish to be cremated, she has his vainly dyed red hair made white again and commands that his body rest in state at Westminster Abbey.

Hurd Hatfield played Dickens's publisher; Ernest Cossart was the bibulous father of the writer, John Dickens; Oliver Cliff was Daniel Maclise; Ruth White was Martha Tripham; Neva Patterson was the Baroness Angela Burdette-Coutts; and Barnard Hughes acted Martin. Judith Evelyn's was the most widely approved performance. This was the second biographical drama of the decade about Dickens, the first having been *Romantic Mr. Dickens*.

J

JACKPOT [Musical/Gambling/Military/Romance/War] B: Guy Bolton, Sidney Sheldon, and Ben Roberts; M: Vernon Duke; LY: Howard Dietz; D: Roy Hargrave; CH: Lauretta Jefferson (ballet: Charles Weidman); S: Raymond Sovey and Robert Edmond Jones; C: Kiviette; P: Vinton Freedley; T: Alvin Theatre; 1/13/44 (69)

This fairly expensive show ($170,000) did not hit the jackpot because of a deficient book that completely defeated its talented principals. The story tells of pretty defense worker Sally Madison (Nanette Fabray), who is first prize in a war bond lottery. The three marines who win her--and $50,000--are Jerry Finch (Jerry Lester), Winkle Cotter (Benny Baker), both comic types, and Hank Trimble (Allan Jones), a good-looking guy with a great voice. All three vie for Sally's hand in marriage, but handsome Hank predictably wins the jackpot. The other fellows link up with a couple of military femmes played by Mary Wickes and Betty Garrett.

The comic players struggled valiantly to turn their tired material into something funny, and there was a moderately amusing takeoff on the balletic Broadway choreography of Agnes de Mille called "Grist for de Mille," with satirical digs at *Oklahoma!* and *One Touch of Venus*, but otherwise the show remained tiresomely earthbound. A few critics were miffed by the numerous double entendres. "Somehow the show is routine and uneventful," responded Ward Morehouse (*NYS*). "The book isn't very good and comes to a dead halt at intervals throughout the evening."

Dancers Althea Elder, Billie Worth, Peter Hamilton, Florence Lessing, and Flower Hujer were among those singled out for praise. Of the principals the standout was Betty Garrett, who livened up the show whenever she appeared. Some of the songs were "Sugarfoot," "One Track Mind," and "I Kissed My Girl Goodbye."

JACOBOWSKY AND THE COLONEL (***Jacobowsky und der Oberst***) [Comedy-Drama/German/Jews/Military/Politics/Romance/War] A: Franz Werfel; AD: S. N. Behrman; M: Paul Bowles; D: Elia Kazan; S: Stewart Chaney; P: Theatre Guild i/a/w John H. Skirball; T: Martin Beck Theatre; 3/14/44 (415)

This hit play had an unusual genesis, recounted by playwright Behrman in *People in a Diary*. At a dinner party hosted by Austrian refugee director Max Reinhardt, Behrman met German refugee writer Franz Werfel. Werfel told the fascinating, yet highly amusing, story of how he had escaped from France. An engrossing thread concerned a Polish-Jewish businessman named Samuel S. Jacobowsky, who escaped in the company of an anti-Semitic Polish colonel. Behrman thought that it contained the seed of a play. "Two men in an ambivalent relationship, two men from the opposite ends of the earth though they are countrymen--opposites physically, spiritually, mentally, held together during flight by a common enemy and a vehicle--they hate each other--they part--they find they miss each other." Behrman told Werfel that the latter must turn the anecdote into a play, but Werfel thought that Behrman should do it, and that the director might be Reinhardt.

After Behrman began to write, he learned that Werfel had betrayed him by beginning to work closely on his own version in collaboration with Clifford Odets. Behrman never found out what had cooled the German author toward his own work. About a year later, the Werfel-Odets script was going into production by the Theatre Guild when Behrman was asked by them to rewrite it from scratch because it was proving unworkable. Behrman rewrote every line in the play, which already had been cast and was called *Jacobowsky and the Colonel.* The title, however, bothered everybody involved, as it seemed unpronounceable. After the show opened, actor Louis Calhern said that before one Saturday matinee he had seen two bearded Jewish men staring at the marquee and overheard one say to the other, "Jacobowsky and the *what?*"

While the play was still in its Boston tryout phase, Werfel began to demand that Behrman's name be removed from the billing, which seemed unreasonable to the playwright, who had written all of the new dialogue. For whatever reason, Behrman concluded, he and Werfel were now enemies. "I never heard a word from him although he was not averse to collecting the major part of the royalties."

The action covers five days from June 13 to June 18, 1940, as the Germans are on the verge of conquering France and occupying Paris. In six loosely strung-together scenes, the story is told of the attempt of a small group to escape the Germans. The chief persons in the party are Colonel Stjerbinsky (Calhern), a haughty, aristocratic, anti-Semitic Polish officer; his orderly Szabuniewicz (J. Edward Bromberg); his passionately patriotic French mistress Marianne (movie actress Annabella, in her Broadway bow); and the humble Polish-Jewish refugee S. L. Jacobowsky (Oscar Karlweis). Jacobowsky and the colonel meet in the laundry of a small Parisian Left Bank hotel used as an air-raid shelter. The adaptive Jew, who speaks eight languages fluently and is a master at the art of escaping from one nation to another (he has been chased from Warsaw, Berlin, Vienna, Prague, and now Paris), has purchased a car, but cannot drive it. He talks the reluctant colonel into driving it for him and thus saving both their lives. At the start of their journey they must drive north--despite the presence of the Germans--to rescue Marianne from the invaders. In trying to cross France to meet up with the English corvette on the coast at Hendaye, where the colonel must transmit secret papers to the Polish government-in-exile in England, they run into numerous obstacles. It is always the improvisatory cleverness of Jacobowsky that saves them, despite the colonel's initial disinclination to accept aid from so distasteful a source. At one point the Jew not only saves the colonel (whom Jacobowsky describes as having "one of the finest minds of the fifteenth century") from being executed by the Germans, but also manages to convince the latter to fill the car's tank with gasoline. Marianne falls in love with Jacobowsky while remaining in love with the colonel. This nearly precipitates a duel between the men. Despite the colonel's unmitigated prejudices, he, too, comes not only to respect Jacobowsky but to love him. For his part, the Jew acknowledges his own improved feelings for the colonel. At Hendaye, only two in the party can cross to England and continue there to fight for France's freedom. The colonel is the obvious choice; Jacobowsky, for whom he once had only contempt, is selected to go with him, and Marianne must remain behind.

More a character comedy than one of plot, the piece offered humor mingled with mild sentiment and with a good dash of uplift thrown in. The occasional criticism of the Jew offered the right balance to what might have been his glorification. George Freedley's (*NYMT*) major criticism was of the overblown political messages stuffed into the dialogue. Louis Kronenberger (*PM*) argued that the promising play descended into hokum melodrama. George Jean Nathan (*TBY*) carped about "a periodic dramaturgic choppiness and an occasionally too gusty dialogic wind," but otherwise approved the work because of "what was in the main intelligent observation embroidered with intelligent wit and humor." Euphemia Van Rensselaer Wyatt (*CW*) felt "that *Jacobowsky and the Colonel* is the most brilliant, amusing and distinguished play of the season."

The production gave further evidence of Elia Kazan's growing directorial power (Howard Barnes [*NYHT*] said that Kazan was "rapidly becoming a great director"), but he could not infuse the cast with the required quality of Frenchness. Many of the French words and names were mispronounced consistently, which jarred with the authentic French accent and manner of Annabella. In fact, the multiple accents, real and feigned, annoyed a number of critics. Still, Viennese actor Oscar Karlweis had a brilliant success as Jacobowsky. "He has pathos, passion and humor at his fingertips," wrote Rosamond Gilder (*TAM*), "he has the supreme actor's gift of identification and he has a keen sense of style. His Jacobowsky can, therefore, be both . . . lovable, absurd and rather touching." (Karlweis had a heart attack after the play later opened in Chicago and died soon after.)

Calhern's tall and dashing colonel was a perfect foil for the small, common-looking Karlweis, swaggering as he did with the proper panache, bluster, and superiority the role demanded until circumstances taught him to see more deeply than had been his wont. Expert comedy was offered by Bromberg's overweight, Sancho Panza-like orderly.

Annabella gave beauty to the proceedings, although her acting was uneven, and Burton Rascoe (*NYWT*) even wrote that she made him ill. (The actress sent him a bottle of castor oil in reply.) Expert performances were rendered by Donald Cameron in two roles, Herbert Yost as the tragic gentleman, and Harold Vermilyea as a Gestapo official. Also in the large company were Jane Marbury, Philip Coolidge, Burton Tripp, Hilda Vaughn, Peter Kass, and E. G. Marshall, among others.

A German-language opera was made of the play by Giselher Klebe in 1965, using the original title. *The Grand Tour*, a musical comedy version, came to Broadway in 1979.

JANIE [Comedy/Family/Journalism/Military/Romance/Small Town/War/Youth] A: Josephine Bentham and Herschel Williams; SC: Josephine Bentham's novel of the same name; D: Antoinette Perry; S: John Root; P: Brock Pemberton; T: Henry Miller's Theatre; 9/10/42 (642)

With *Junior Miss* a big hit, it stood to reason that others would attempt to cash in on audience interest in life among the bobby-sox set. *Janie* happened to be one of the few that clicked, despite the many comparisons it provoked with the earlier comedy, and despite some tepid reviews.

The play is set in the small town of Hortonville, near Camp Longstreet. Its heroine, sixteen-year-old Janie Colburn (Gwen Anderson), daughter of a newspaper publisher (Maurice Manson) and his wife (Nancy Cushman), has a high-school sweetheart named Scooper Nolan (Frank Amy). She also has a precocious and predatory six-year-old sister, Elsbeth (Clare Foley), who figures frequently and amusingly in the action whenever she demands a nickel to get lost. Janie, who wants to do her share for the war effort, finds her romantic attentions diverted by nineteen-year-old Private Dick Lawrence (Herbert Evers), a recruit from Yale whose widowed mother, Thelma Lawrence (Linda Watkins), is Janie's mother's feather-brained visiting friend. Thelma herself is emotionally involved with the foolish John Van Brunt (Howard St. John), Mr. Colburn's managing editor. Janie's fondness for Scooper seems like merest puppy love when she is with Dick. At Dick's suggestion, Janie and her two friends (Margaret Wallace and Betty Breckenridge) throw a party for a few of Dick's fellow servicemen from camp while her parents are at a country-club dance. Little Elsbeth is disposed of by Dick at her grandmother's house. Two hundred soldiers and one redheaded sailor (Kenneth Tobey) show up for the shindig. The party gets out of hand, the house becomes a mess, and the liquor supply--served by the black butler (John Marriott), who gets drunk himself--is depleted by the time the Colburns return. Dad is enraged and even gets arrested when he punches the chief of police, so Janie has a lot of explaining to do before the night is out. But father's feathers are unruffled soon enough, especially when a government priorities man (W. O. McWatters) enters and sees to it that he gets a new printing press for his paper.

Brooks Atkinson (*NYT*) had a fairly good time, especially because of the antics of young Elsbeth, whom he considered the play's "most original item." To Kelcey Allen (*WWD*), the play was "genuinely entertaining . . . , with smart dialog, an abundance of hearty laughs, and . . . a youthful fresh quality." Howard Barnes (*NYHT*), while cautioning against throwing one's hat in the air, advised that "*Janie* is disarming, amusing and down to earth in its contemplation of the American scene."

But not a few critics had serious reservations. Burns Mantle (*NYDN*) found that "the young people are obviously straining to be amusingly naive and the adults are consciously trying to be funny and still keep reasonably clear of caricature."

JANUARY THAW [Comedy/Family/Legacy/Rural/Sex] A: William Roos; SC: Bellamy Partridge's novel of the same name; D: Ezra Stone; S: Watson Barratt; P: Michael Todd; T: John Golden Theatre; 2/4/46 (48)

The fact that super showman Michael Todd produced this "thin little comedy" (Lewis Funke [*NYT*]) came as a surprise to the critical community. Reminiscent of *George Washington Slept Here*, the play is set in a recently restored colonial farmhouse in rural Connecticut into which moves the New York family of Mr. and Mrs. Herbert Gage (Robert Keith and Lulu Mae Hubbard). It is soon discovered that the bill of sale allows the Rockwoods (Charles Middleton and Helen Carew), who used to own it, to reside there for the rest of their natural lives. The Rockwoods, an eccentric farm couple presumed dead, are actually very much alive and descend upon the place to take advantage of their rights. After many squabbles caused by living under bucolic circumstances, with the city slickers getting the raw end of the stick, the families are reconciled when the hicks turn out to be helpfully adept at dealing with problems that perplex their urban opposites. Harmony between the two factions comes to the farmhouse at the end.

Barely competent acting and less-than-adequate directing served only to emphasize the shortcomings of the occasionally earthy, but mostly moribund, script, based on a best-seller. Laughs were sought from jokes about political parties, plumbing (a chamber pot figured prominently), and sexual double entendres. "Since the comments are both obvious and witless, there is very little . . . that can pass for entertainment," noted Otis L. Guernsey, Jr. (*NYHT*). The cast included Lorna Lynn, Charles Nevil, Natalie Thompson, John McGovern, Charles Burrows, and Henry Jones, among others.

JASON [Drama/Marriage/Sex/Theatre] A/D: Samson Raphaelson; S: John Root; P: George Abbott; T: Guild Theatre; 1/21/42 (125)

A drawing-room comedy (originally tried out in Stockbridge, Massachusetts, as *In My Opinion*) set in the luxuriously comfortable apartment of Jason Otis (Alexander Knox), a fastidious and priggish New York theatre critic (he was likened to George Jean Nathan), who lives there with his lovely but pretentious young bride Lisa (Helen Walker). Crashing into the well-insulated serenity of this household in the guise of a Western Union messenger is the handsome, eccentric, and euphorically self-centered playwright, Mike Ambler (Nicholas [Richard] Conte), whose main purpose is to have Jason read his new play and comment on it. Subsequently, the Saroyanesque playwright induces the critic to bring in various members of the masses from the streets, thereby exposing him to the pain and sorrow in the world as well as to its joys. Mike also proceeds to woo the lovely Lisa, whom he reveals to be poor white trash instead of the Southern aristocrat she pretends to be. When Jason must review the playwright's first produced play, he writes approvingly of it, although he has seen Mike and his wife kissing. But Jason catches Mike trying to run off with Lisa, which makes him change his review to a pan of both Mike and his play. This helps to regain Lisa's affection. After he kicks Mike out and accepts Lisa's apology, he decides to write yet another review, an approving one, admitting that people like Mike can be distasteful yet can also reveal the good in mankind to persons like himself.

"The main theme is the rediscovery by the critic of certain vital forces both within and without, against which he had built barriers of indifference or denial," wrote Rosamond Gilder (*TAM*). She further noted that despite some effective moments, Raphaelson "has made the mistake of handling real people unrealistically, of slipping up on the simple technical details of a drama critic's job, but chiefly in not making the issues he presents seem in any way important or interesting in themselves." Euphemia Van Rensselaer Wyatt (*CW*) commented that it was a shame that Raphaelson also directed his play, "as he has brought out nothing clearly but his own aptitude for good phrases. For all the brilliance of the writing, no one on the stage ever seems completely honest." *Jason* was one of the year's ten best.

The best performance was Conte's as the flamboyant playwright. Tom Tully, Edna West, and E. G. Marshall (a comic standout as a bored second-class seaman) were cast members.

JEB [Drama/Blacks/Race/Southern] A: Robert Ardrey; D/P: Herman Shumlin; DS: Jo Mielziner; T: Martin Beck Theatre; 2/21/46 (9)

A well-meaning, but dramaturgically flawed, recounting of a returning black war vet's travails when confronted by the ignorance of racism in his Southern home town. (That season's *Deep Are the Roots** dealt with a similar theme.) The play had several powerful scenes, but as drama it was too discursive and lacking in a theatrical sensibility that might have raised it to more appealing heights. Vernon Rice (*NYP*) surmised that it would have been more effective if written by a black, as white writers could not as successfully "get really deep into the Negroes' souls" to express their tragic plight. However, Rosamond Gilder (*TAM*) considered it thematically "gripping," if theatrically unsuccessful.

Jeb Turner (Ossie Davis, in his Broadway debut) is a decorated, one-legged war hero who used to work in the Louisiana sugar fields. In the armed forces he has learned to operate an adding machine, and he now seeks a white-collar job using his skills in the local sugar mill. Jeb is rejected by the relatively tolerant mill manager (Santos Ortega), who at first backs him, but who is put under pressure because the job is traditionally considered a white man's, this despite the present holder's being a "white trash" drunk. The disillusioned vet, wishing to test his ability on the mill's adding machine, breaks into the timekeeper's shack one night as his terrified girlfriend (Ruby Dee, in her first significant role) watches. He is spotted and falsely accused of having a white girl with him, for which he is beaten and driven from town. His girlfriend, faithful up to now, deserts him. He flees to the North, where he is robbed by other blacks, and then decides to return to Louisiana and fight with liberal whites for civil rights.

Davis made a very strong impression as Jeb. Also in the cast were Laura Bowman, Wardell Saunders, G. Harry Bolden, Frank M. Thomas, Grover Burgess, and others.

JENNY KISSED ME [Comedy/Religion/Romance/Youth] A: Jean Kerr; D: James Russo; S/L: Ralph Alswang; C: Eleanor Goldsmith; P: James Russo, Michael Ellis, and Alexander H. Cohen i/a/w Clarence M. Shapiro; T: Hudson Theatre; 12/23/48 (20)

Leo G. Carroll turned in a polished performance as a Catholic priest, Father Moynihan, in this "predictable and inconsequential" (Hobe. [*V*]) comedy. The play is about the good father's efforts on behalf of Jenny (Pamela Rivers), the eighteen-year-old orphaned niece of his housekeeper, Mrs. Deazy (Frances Baviar), when the girl's presence in his household threatens to become longer lasting than he bargained for. He would like her to find a nice fellow and get married. The girl's plain-Jane appearance seems a hindrance, so he expends himself in efforts to spruce her up, researching the proper methods in the columns of women's magazines. The efforts prove successful, but Jenny marries the boy of her choice, schoolteacher Michael Saunders (Alan Baxter), not Father Moynihan's (Brennan Moore).

This was a formula comedy, mechanically written and directed. James Russo took on the directorial chores from John O'Shaughnessy, who quit during the tryout period. Euphemia Van Rensselaer Wyatt (*CW*) thought it "irksome that . . . Jean Kerr hasn't bothered to give her very funny dialogue a better story." She assumed from the title that the play was mainly about Jenny, but discovered that it was really about the priest, which made "the plot foundation . . . flimsier than ever." George Jean Nathan (*TBY*) considered it a "pale, amateur" copy of J. Hartley Manners's once-popular *Peg o' My Heart**.

The play originally had been staged at Catholic University (where Kerr and her husband Walter were then teachers), and one of the actors from that production, Brennan Moore, came with it to Broadway. Among others in the cast were Will Lee, Sara Taft, Bonnie Alden, and Ruth Saville.

JOAN OF LORRAINE [Drama/Historical-Biographical/Period/Politics/Prison/Religion/Theatre/Trial] A: Maxwell Anderson; D: Margo Jones w/Sam Wanamaker; DS: Lee Simonson; P: Playwrights' Company; T: Alvin Theatre; 11/18/46 (199)

Since enormously popular film star Ingrid Bergman was the leading player in this interesting but seriously flawed play (originally called *Warrior's Return*), the crush of opening-night bobby-soxers crowding the entrance to the Alvin made access to the playhouse "like being put through a meat grinder," according to Louis Kronenberger (*PM*). The Swedish actress delighted the critics as well as her fans. "She *is* radiant and enchanting," offered Kronenberger, "perhaps not as an actress, but simply as a human being. She has a childlike gawkiness which is better than grace, and a beauty that has very little to do with being beautiful; and in a 'spiritual' role like her present one these things are seen at their best."

The role was Bergman's first on Broadway since her 1940 debut in a revival of *Liliom**. It had been offered to her by Maxwell Anderson when he completed the play in 1944, and her interest in it was piqued at once, as she had long wanted to play Joan of Lorraine. However, other commitments, including a European tour of GI camps, delayed the project's realization, although, as preparation for the production, she read parts of the play to the soldiers.

Actually, Bergman's role was a double one, comprising that of Mary Grey, an actress, and Jeanne d'Arc, the character played by Mary in the play-within-the-play. During the play's preparatory period, she continued to pester the director and playwright to deemphasize the Mary Grey character and build up Joan's part even more, with as many of the maid's actual words incorporated as possible. This led to some conflicts, as director Jones was committed to protecting the dramatist's work.

The dramatic framework depicts the rehearsal process--on a bare stage with scanty props and bits and pieces of period costumes gradually being added throughout--for a play about the historical character and shows Mary's debates with Jimmy Masters (Wanamaker), the director (who also doubles as the grand inquisitor), over the playwright's (not seen) changes to his script. Mary feels that the playwright has desecrated the idealistic character of Joan by making her a compromiser who will cooperate with evil men. She argues that Joan would never have crowned the dauphin (Romney Brent) if she had known that he was a "crook." There is a chance that Mary will leave the show. Jimmy, aware of the compromises he himself is forced to make in his job, argues that the dramatist's point of view is honest and realistic. This leads to a post-lunch-break discussion with Jimmy and the entire cast about the meaning of faith, during which he explains his own faith, which is in democracy and which he believes is best demonstrated in the theatre. Joan struggles with the issue of faith during her trial scene and after her later recantation. She then hears her voices (audible to the audience, too) during her prison scene and recaptures her faith in words that strike home with Mary, who comes to see that Joan's minor compromises are insignificant in the face of her unswerving beliefs. Mary now feels comfortable in playing the role, regardless of the author's revisions, for Joan's message will come through despite any attempt to filter it. She then acts with conviction the final scene of Joan's going to the stake. (The play-within-the-play follows the familiar events in Joan's life, with scenes at Domremy, Orléans, Reims, and Rouen. In the trial scene, some of the historical Joan's words are incorporated.)

The artificial device of framing the play about Joan within a rehearsal (a device eliminated from the movie version, also starring Bergman), was widely viewed as a gimmick, interesting in itself because of its depiction of the production process, but not conducive to distinguished playmaking. Some had problems accepting the idea of so high-minded a confrontation between a moralistic star and a philosophical director. There were also difficulties in following Anderson's fuzzily presented thematic issues of faith, compromise, and idealism. The general response was to greet the event as an entertaining evening in the theatre and the play as a less-than-adequate and somewhat pretentious work of dramatic literature. One who thought the dramaturgic device a worthwhile one, however, was Rosamond Gilder (*TAM*). Anderson's "approach gives freshness to his theme and enables him to dot his i's and cross his t's so that even those who run the fastest from any exercise of the mind may read." However, more were unimpressed. "Mr. Anderson is not successful in drawing a parallel between a Broadway actress and Joan," announced T. R. (*CSM*). "The play gives him an opportunity to express lofty thoughts about the function of the theater, about democracy and the need for faith today, but his conclusions are vague and undefined." Many also felt that Anderson's play was no match for George Bernard Shaw's *St. Joan**.

Before arriving in New York, the play was to be shown in Washington, D.C., at the Lisner Auditorium on the campus of George Washington University, but that theatre and Washington's National Theatre both had Jim Crow laws that offended the star. Bergman publicly disputed these policies and vowed never to return to Washington until such laws were abolished. Opening night at the Lisner was greeted with picketing by the Committee for Racial Democracy. Bergman was branded a "nigger lover" by bigots at the stage door. The actress was also distressed by various technical problems involved in playing in the large auditorium, especially the difficulty of being heard. When director Jones was unable to calm her nerves or provide answers to her projection problems, Bergman lost confidence in her and turned to costar Sam Wanamaker--also her director in the play-within-the-play--for aid. Playwright Anderson, fretting about these developments, therefore fired Margo Jones during the tryout period and hired Wanamaker (who was given shared billing as director). The playwright's stage-manager son, Alan Anderson, was hired as Wanamaker's codirector, but did not get billing.

Wanamaker was excellent in his acted roles. Ironically, although he replaced Jones as director, the twenty-seven-year-old actor had needed her to fight Anderson to have him cast because he did not seem to the sixty-year-old playwright to have the proper weight to play two roles requiring great presence and authority. To convince Anderson of his maturity, Wanamaker grew a mustache for the role.

Jefson/Georges de Tremoille was played by Roger De Koven, Kipner/Regnault de Chartres by Harry Irvine, Long/Dunois by Kevin McCarthy, Miss Sadler/St. Margaret by Joanna Roos, Champlain/Father Massieu by Joseph Wiseman, Noble/La Hire by Martin Rudy, Sheppard/Alain Chartier by Berry Kroeger, Dollner/Pierre d'Arc by Kenneth Tobey, Abbey/Jacques d'Arc/Cauchon by Lewis Martin, and Charles Elling/Durand Laxart by Charles Ellis.

JOHN BROWN [Drama/Family/Historical-Biographical/Period/Race] A: Theodore Ward; M: Elmer Bernstein; D: Gene Frankel w/Dave Nevel; DS: Fred Wunch; P/T: People's Drama (OB); 5/3/50

This play appears to have been the first commercial presentation of arena staging in New York. (There previously had been a few noncommercial attempts.) It was produced in a converted garage at 212 Eldridge Street on the Lower East Side. "The hall lends itself splendidly to [arena staging] from the point of view of acoustics and sight lines," thought William Hawkins (*NYWT*).

The then-unusual staging arrangement was the production's strongest attraction, as the play and performance were ruthlessly panned. The play tells of the events leading up to the raid on Harper's Ferry in which Abolitionist John Brown (Irving Pakewitz) was killed. The focus is on the conflict between Brown and his sons (one of them played by the young Rod Steiger) and their wives; although they support his antislavery views, they are oppressed by this gaunt and flint-eyed man's personal brand of messianic fanaticism. Five periods in Brown's life are presented, beginning in 1856 in Kansas and ending on a farm near the Harper's Ferry arsenal.

The company had neither the script nor the skills to make good use of their novel theatre. Most thought the arena staging idea very promising because of the added intimacy it afforded. The acting took place on a small platform surrounded on four sides by bleachers; entrances were made down aisles at the corners.

Hawkins said that the story is "told in a straight line and monotonous manner. The conflict neither deviates nor progresses. The characters are not particularly person alized." He also was depressed by the considerable overacting of the cast and the ponderously paced direction. Director Frankel--eventually an important theatre figure--was selected as the debacle's chief culprit.

Within a month, a more notable demonstration of the arena format arrived with the revival of *The Show-Off** (5/31/50) at the Edison Hotel.

JOHN BULL'S OTHER ISLAND [Dramatic Revival] A: George Bernard Shaw; D: Hilton Edwards; S: Molly McEwan; P: Dublin Gate Theatre u/t/a/o Richard Aldrich and Richard Myers i/a/w Brian Doherty; T: Mansfield Theatre; 2/10/48 (8)

This first revival since its 1905 New York debut (following its London premiere) of Shaw's political comedy satirizing English and Irish types marked the opening of a three-play repertory by Dublin's visiting Gate Theatre, founded in 1927. The play's four acts had been reduced to three.

It tells of a visit to anglicized Larry Doyle's (Micheal MacLiammoir) home town of Rosscullen, Ireland, from which he has been gone for eighteen years, in the company of his fatuous British realty business partner, Thomas Broadbent (Edwards), their plan being to make the town a garden city. The locals want Larry to run for Parliament, but his political ideas on a wide range of subjects, including home rule and free trade, shock them. More to their tastes is the wealthy, popularly conventional, and sentimental Broadbent, who wins both the nomination and the heart of Larry's former sweetheart, Norah (Meriel Moore).

The company did not fare well with this loquacious, dated, only historically interesting selection, which neither its acting or directing could do much to enliven. "The play is very long, quite repetitious and affords too few laughs," went Ibee.'s (*V*) majority opinion. As for the Gate players, Louis Kronenberger (*PM*) averred that apart from several acceptable actors, "there is nothing very exceptional about it as a troupe, and nothing very exciting." The visionary ex-priest Keegan was played by Edward Golden, and other important parts were taken by Denis Brennan, Norman Barrs, Roy Irving, Bryan Herbert, and Liam Gannon.

JOHN GABRIEL BORKMAN [Dramatic Revival*] A: Henrik Ibsen; TR/D: Eva Le Gallienne; M: Lehman Engel; DS: Paul Morrison; P: American Repertory Theatre; T: International Theatre; 11/12/46 (21)

The ambitious but short-lived American Repertory Theatre offered a revival of Ibsen's antiromantic 1896 drama, not seen locally since Eva Le Gallienne's version in 1926. Le Gallienne again directed while resuming the role of Ella Rentheim, and her supporting cast included Margaret Webster as Mrs. Borkman, Marion Evensen as Malene, William Windom as Erhart Borkman, Mary Alice Moore as Mrs. Fanny Wilton, Victor Jory as the title character, Anne Jackson as Frida Foldal, and Ernest Truex as Vilhelm Foldal.

The intermissionless production, staged in five continuous scenes, with sets moved swiftly on a revolving stage, sharply divided the critics. Some thought the dour play too symbol-laden and lugubrious, Howard Barnes (*NYHT*), for instance, declaring that the production scarcely sufficed "for a sustained or illuminating theatrical experience." John Chapman (*NYDN*) declared it to be "theatrical claptrap of astonishingly cheap quality." But Brooks Atkinson (*NYT*) thought tha the work still held up and considered the production "a masterpiece."

Whereas Atkinson and several others were highly laudatory of the acting, a few critics, such as Barnes and George Jean Nathan (*TBY*), were less than complimentary. Most agreed that Margaret Webster was excellent as the hateful Mrs. Borkman. "She is handsome and authoritative at the same moment that she is being abominably possessive," thought George Freedley (*NYMT*). Le Gallienne was a fine foil as Mrs. Borkman's worn-out, dying, but still-feisty twin sister. Whereas Webster was bold and intensely dramatic, Le Gallienne was restrained and tightly controlled. "Her wraithlike Ella is a completed characterization," noted John Mason Brown (*SR*), "knowledgeably drawn and projected."

There was more divisiveness concerning Jory, "dark, pompous and convincing" to Rosamond Gilder (*TAM*), but "neither touching nor arresting" to Barnes. Truex, however, enjoyed one of his career highlights in the small role of the tragic little clerk with dreams of being a poet.

Webster, who passionately hated the restrictions placed on production by the unions, remembered in *Don't Put Your Daughter on the Stage* that during a scene change in Boston a lamp had to be taken off and that an extra property man had to be hired to do this simple task. The lamp was a beautiful, expensive, and irreplaceable one, and she pleaded with the stagehand, "For God's sake be careful of that lamp--make sure you have a clear exit," to which he nodded. When the scene change came, the man ran onto the stage, grabbed the lamp, and ran off straight into a ladder, totally destroying the lamp. "I felt a surge of such murderous rage that I really and truly could have killed him."

JOHN LOVES MARY [Comedy/Friendship/Hotel/Marriage/Military/Politics/Romance] A: Norman Krasna; D: Joshua Logan; S/L: Frederick Fox; C: Lucinda Ballard; P: Richard Rodgers and Oscar Hammerstein II i/a/w Joshua Logan; T: Booth Theatre; 2/4/47 (423)

The action of this "farce comedy," as it was called by various critics, is set in the apartment of pompous Senator James McKinley (Loring Smith) and his wife Phyllis (Ann Mason) at New York's St. Regis Hotel. Sergeant John Lawrence (William Prince) returns from the war to his fiancée, Mary McKinley (Nina Foch, in her Broadway debut), daughter of the senator. Mary is delighted to have him back safe in her arms, and the parents plan for a wedding in three days. The kicker is that John has married Lily (Pamela Gordon, Gertrude Lawrence's daughter), a British music-hall dancer who loves his combat pal Fred Taylor (Tom Ewell), but who could not gain entry to the United States unless she did so as a war bride. The pal, who saved John's life, is already married, however, having thought Lily lost; his wife is pregnant, to boot. John, who does not tell Mary the truth, must discreetly obtain a Nevada divorce--which will take six weeks--from Lily in order to marry the girl he really loves. It is the complications arising from his attempts to delay the wedding that occupy the play's remainder. John finally explains the dilemma to Mary, who is as understanding as she would have been had John told her the truth in the first act.

Many thought the play enjoyable, but more for its acting and direction than for its dramaturgy, which was deemed slick and contrived and not altogether plausible. Most widely shared was the view of Richard Watts, Jr. (*NYP*), who said that the piece was "manufactured rather than written," but with the right production was "bright, expert and entertaining." Brooks Atkinson (*NYT*) found the whole thing too complexly plotted and "heavy-footed."

Tom Ewell became a star via his hilarious performance as the comedy lead. Rosamond Gilder (*TAM*) described him: "Mr. Ewell has a wonderful comic mask, short and broad, incredibly flexible and capable of expressing bafflement, perplexity and innocent good humor with the greatest ease." Just as much credit for the show's success went to Ewell as to director Logan, whose inventive staging compensated for "the weakness of a thin plot," as Rose. (*V*) put it. "Logan has extracted everything possible from the characterizations, each bit of stage business is used to a nicety, and no one portrayal is so exaggerated as to become either a buffoon or unbelievable." Logan himself felt that he had gotten undue credit that belonged to the playwright, and his guilt even led him to begin drinking too heavily.

In *Josh*, Logan remembered a time in the tryout period when he, Krasna, and Rodgers and Hammerstein tried to fix the ending to the second act. "Sample suggestions: the boy goes out, the boy comes back, the father and the mother get furious, they don't get furious, there's a violent argument, there is no argument at all." As they debated the possible solutions, their tempers grew hotter. Then Logan had a brainstorm. "I know what should happen! The father and mother see the boy out and go to bed, and the boy comes back in the room, kisses the girl and takes her off into the bedroom." With his face purple from rage, Hammerstein spluttered, "Anyone who would make a suggestion like *that* is a cad!"

Good performances were contributed by Ralph Chambers, Lyle Bettger, Harry Bannister, and Max Showalter. Future star Cloris Leachman was Nina Foch's understudy.

(1) JOHNNY BELINDA [Drama/Crime/Invalidism/Medicine/Romance/Rural/Sex/Trial] A: Elmer Harris; D/P: Harry Wagstaff Gribble; S: Frederick Fox: L: A. H. Feder; T: Belasco Theatre; 9/18/40 (321)

The play from which the famous tearjerker movie starring Jane Wyman was made was itself a hit, its title role in the capable hands of Helen Craig. This was a melodrama packed with so many plot contrivances that Brooks Atkinson (*NYT*) wondered what would be left for the plays left to open that season: "There has seldom been such a complete play on any stage."

Belinda McDonald, who lives on Prince Edward Island, off the coast of Nova Scotia, has been deaf and mute since early childhood. She endures a grim existence as the daughter of a local widower, Black McDonald (Louis Hector), who calls her "Dummy" and treats her as little more than a domestic animal, forcing her to haul heavy sacks for his mill. Life begins to dawn for her through the gentle help of the newly arrived Dr. Jack Davidson (Horace McNally), who teaches her sign language as well as how to read. Belinda is cruelly seduced by bully Locky McCormick (Willard Parker) and has his baby. Belinda is driven to emotional distraction by the scorn of her neighbors, who reject her for her "sin." Black dies after being struck by lightning, and the doctor goes to Montreal to raise funds to aid the hapless girl. Meanwhile, McCormick, who has married another, comes to take the child for himself. Belinda shoots him and then must stand trial for murder. A courtroom scene in which she must explain her action in sign language leads to her acquittal; life with the sympathetic doctor looms on the horizon. As with the climactic moment in William Gibson's later drama, *The Miracle Worker*, in which Helen Keller's achievement in saying "water" released the audience's floodgates of emotion, this play has a moment in which the handicapped heroine similarly taps the audience's tears as, at the final curtain, she rushes to her child and manages to say "Johnny" as she embraces him.

The play's success stemmed more from its unusual subject matter and its touching central performance than from its quality as drama. "Hampered by the essential trickiness of its subject matter," wrote Rosamond Gilder (*TAM*), "the play never succeeded in getting really under way. It remained a stunt, a tour-de-force to the end." Sidney B. Whipple (*NYWT*) believed the author's intentions to be noble, but that he had tangled them "up by an eagerness to crowd the stage with quaint and needless characters, by an overdose of melodrama, and by a host of amateurish and artificial devices to keep the main story alive."

The contribution of the star, whose entire role was limited to gestures and one word, was lauded widely, as when Euphemia Van Rensselaer Wyatt (*CW*) commented that the author "is deeply in the debt of Miss Helen Craig who imbues each melodramatic situation . . . with such poetry of feeling and expression that the action becomes a frame for the beauty of her Belinda." Jane Bancroft, Jules Epailly, and Ralph Cullinan were among others in the cast.

(2) [Dramatic Revival/Yiddish Language] TR: Isidore Lash; D: Jean Platt; S: Saltzman Brothers; P: Nathan Goldberg and Jacob Jacobs; T: Public Theatre (OB); 3/43

A Yiddish-language adaptation of the play that came to Second Avenue after touring to various cities, including Brooklyn, where it played in December 1942. The adaptation, in keeping with the interests of Yiddish theatre audiences, interpolated several songs and dances, but otherwise the play was faithfully followed. "These [additions] have not in one wit [*sic*] detracted from the absorbing hold that the play has on its audience, but have, in fact, tended to relieve the tenseness between scenes of heart stirring situations," opined the unnamed *WWD* reviewer.

Jean Platt, the director, played the title role, David Popper played Locky, Nathan Goldberg played Black, and Gustave Berger played Dr. Davidson. Platt, who knew no Yiddish, had taken over the role on Broadway (her sister Lucille had played it just before her) and had acted it on the road.

JOHNNY DOODLE [Musical/Fantasy/Period/Politics/War] B: Jane McCleod and Alfred Saxe; M: Lan Adomian; D: Alfred Saxe; CH: Felicia Sorel; S/L: Clay Yurdin; C: Bonnie Fegere; P/T: Popular Theatre (OB); 3/18/42 (6)

An amateurish "musical play" produced in a small theatre at 320 West Fifty-seventh Street. According to Brooks Atkinson (*NYT*) and several others, however, in its use of songs and legends to tell a coherent story, it offered a promising premise for dramatic writing. Atkinson liked the lyrical qualities that such an approach might create as an alternative to narrowly realistic dramaturgy, and despite this work's failure, he saw in it "an underhum of life."

Johnny Doodle tells the story of America's struggle for freedom from 1776 to 1942, using well-known folk songs as a medium to communicate the tale. As a Hudson River ferryboat, captained by a homespun old skipper (Art Smith), sails through history (the action is his fantasy), such familiar events as the Boston Tea Party, the American Revolution, the War of 1812, the building of the Erie Canal, the creation of the steamboat and railroads, the Lincoln period, the development of agriculture in the West, and so on are depicted in such songs as "Hey Betty Martin," "A Mule Named Sal," "The Wreck of the 97," "The Tarriers' Song," "The Farmer Is the Man," and so on, with dances sometimes accompanying the music. A rousing Virginia reel square dance to "The Farmer Is the Man" was one of the highlights. Scenery was minimal, being little more than a few boxes moved around as needed, and costumes were changed onstage by the addition of simple but appropriate elements, such as a hat or long skirt, or by the use of a prop, such as a musket or bag of grain. The cast played multiple roles in the eleven scenes.

The work was considered less a play than a compilation of old songs; the newly written interludes were a distraction from the charm of the music and singing. Most agreed with Louis Kronenberger (*PM*) that despite the show's promise, its creators "somehow haven't been able to give their pageant any of the warmth and freshness and democratic glow it was meant to have." The cast of nearly twenty included Tom Pedi and John O'Shaughnessy.

JOHNNY JOHNSON [Dramatic Revival*] A: Paul Green; D: Alfred Saxe; S: Fritz Lanz; C: Helene Smith; P: Popular Theatre; T: Provincetown Playhouse (OB); 5/3/41

A semiprofessional Off-Broadway revival of Green's 1936 unusual antiwar satire with music. The present version, with Peter Heywood as the title character, chose to cut all the music and turn the event into a straight play. Director Alfred Saxe made various other amendments to the script, including a revision of the indecisive final scene, so that Johnny now participated in a series of battle scenes during which he pleaded with both sides to stop the slaughter.

An anonymous critic (*NYP*) pointed out that this was a superior version to the one created by the Group Theatre, which had "cluttered up the true simplicity of the play," but this production, too, was not deemed worthy of the work. "Although the Popular Theatre players are giving *Johnny Johnson* a certain extravagance of comedy that is somewhat gratuitous to the work, their enthusiasm and effort to please more than make up for their lack of polish," declared L. C. (*NYT*). All agreed that the play, especially with its antiwar theme strengthened, was much more pertinent in 1941 than five years earlier.

JOHNNY ON A SPOT [Comedy/Alcoholism/Crime/Journalism/Politics/Prostitution/Romance/Sex/Southern] A/D: Charles MacArthur; SC: a play by Parke Levy and Alan Lipscott that was itself based on a story by George A. Hendon, Jr., and David Peltz; S/C: Frederick Fox; P: John Shubert; T: Plymouth Theatre; 1/8/42 (4)

A sizable company, including Keenan Wynn in his first starring role, went quickly down to defeat in this door-slamming political farce set in the office of a corrupt Southern governor. The booze-loving, demagogic governor, a candidate for the United States Senate, never appears in the play, he having died in a brothel while on an alcoholic binge, which is reported at the end of the first act. The votes are still being counted, so his underlings set about keeping the news of his demise secret for the next twenty-four hours; meanwhile, under the guidance of the governor's energetic public-relations man from the North, Nicky Allen (Wynn), they try to straighten out his crooked affairs and arrange for his passing to take place in more respectable quarters. This involves considerable law-bending manipulation in order to keep the press and the police (in the service of the opposing party) at bay. Also, the body gets misplaced midway. Consequently, the action introduces a large assortment of eccentric characters, including Pearl La Monte (Dennie Moore), the governor's colorful whore;

Julie Glynn, a secretary (Edith Atwater) in love with Nicky; Barbara Webster (Florence Sundstrom), who also loves Nicky and stands in Julie's way; Doc Blossom (Will Geer), a funny quack doctor and bird fancier; a screwball judge (Joseph Sweeney); and so on.

The critics held that there was much that was funny in the piece (called *Off the Record* during its tryouts), but that the laughs were too sporadic and the writing "mechanical and spiritless" (Richard Lockridge [*NYS*]). Wilella Waldorf (*NYP*) commented that the play not only failed to amuse her, it even left her "slightly nauseated."

Brooks Atkinson (*NYT*) discerned Wynn's abilities, saying that he played his part like the "champion of a six-day bicycle race. He is the most accomplished young comedian in our theatre. When a good script falls into his hands he is going to make Broadway sit up and take notice." Also in the large cast were Tito Vuolo, William Foran, and Paul Huber.

JOHNNY 2 X 4 [Drama/Crime/Music/Nightclub/Prostitution/Show Business] A/P: Rowland Brown; D: Anthony Brown; S: Howard Bay; T: Longacre Theatre; 3/16/42 (65)

Seventy-five actors were in this soppy melodrama set in a Greenwich Village speakeasy between 1926 and 1936. The club's name is "Johnny 2 X 4," after that of its proprietor (Jack Arthur), known for his skill on a portable two by four foot piano. In the course of the play, several jazzy songs were sung (including two by Eleanor Wyckoff and Marie Austin), a few dances were performed, there was an appearance by the Yacht Club Boys, who were big in the twenties, and Leonard Sues provided a standout trumpet solo of "Blues Prelude." There was even a complete house band from radio station WNEW onstage under Leonard Pitt's direction. The play was disappointing, having nothing new to say about the era it depicted. Its gangsters, crooked cops, struggling entertainers, bartenders, hangers-on, and floozies were all familiar types and its action the stuff of countless bootleg plays and B-movies. Hobe. (*V*) called it "a tawdry and rather dated bit of hokum melodrama." Ralph Warner (*DW*), referring to its numerous nightclub acts, said that it had "everything but a plot." Howard Bay's exceptional set, however, was widely hailed.

Johnny is a decent guy whose buddy is a slick young bootlegger named Coaly Lewis (Barry Sullivan). The latter is after a young singer (Wyckoff), who eludes him and goes on to a Hollywood career. Coaly eventually dies when another hoodlum shoots him in retaliation for Coaly's shooting of his rival's younger brother. Johnny grows weary of the whole shebang and turns his place over to the barkeep. At the final curtain, the body of Coaly's killer falls out of a phone booth.

Actors of note involved included Isabel Jewel as a hooker, Harry Bellaver and Bert Frohman as punks, and, in her Broadway debut, Betty (Lauren) Bacall as one of the many bit-part players. For her walk-on role, which had no lines but did give her a chance to jitterbug, she earned $15 a week but had to provide her own clothes.

JOURNEY OF SIMON McKEEVER, THE and **"I'VE GOT THE TUNE"** P: National Council of the Arts, Sciences, and Professions; T: Carnegie Hall (OB); 6/21/49 (1) *The Journey of Simon McKeever* [Drama/Invalidism/Medicine/Old Age] A: Arthur Laurents; SC: Albert Maltz's novel of the same name; D: J. Edward Bromberg; "I've Got the Tune" [Musical Revival*] B/M/LY: Marc Blitzstein; D: David Pressman

Writer Albert Maltz had been one of the blacklisted "Hollywood Ten" who had refused to cooperate with the House Un-American Activities Committee investigations into communism in the film business. As a result, Twentieth-Century Fox, which had paid $35,000 for the rights to his novel, decided to cancel its filming. To protest this political interference in the arts, Arthur Laurents created a forty-five-minute stage version of the book, and it was produced for a single performance (following one given on the West Coast) as a means of raising funds to subsidize Maltz and others who were being denied the right to practice their craft. The event proved a sell-out. It demonstrated that Maltz's work had nothing at all subversive in it and that the suppression of his rights was outrageous.

The production was costumed but had no sets. Its episodic action was linked together by a narrative delivered by Frederick O'Neill, standing at one side of the stage. Herb. (*V*) said that the work came off as "an intensely human and moving composite of laughs, tragedy, despair and hope."

Simon McKeever (Elliot Sullivan) is a seventy-three-year-old arthritic who lives in a Glendale, California, home for the aged. News of a woman doctor, Amelia Balzer (Hester Sondergaard), who has developed a miraculous cure, inspires him to hitchhike to her office, 378 miles away in Stockton. With barely any money, he begins the arduous trip, although he can hardly walk. Along the way he encounters people good and bad, helpful and not, but fulfills his goal. It turns out, however, that his form of ailment is incurable. Instead of being depressed, he is elated that his experiences in learning about his fellow men have given him the desire to write a book, and he begins the return trip with a new lease on life.

Actors involved included Virginia Downing, Salem Ludwig, Curt Conway, Madeleine Lee, and Steven Hill.

Blitzstein's short musical play, "I've Got the Tune," first seen in 1938, was the evening's curtain raiser. Its cast included Richard Boone, Kenneth Remo, Madeleine Lee, Adelaide Klein, Hope Foy, and others. "The half-hour of music and story proved highly disappointing in both departments," thought Herb., who added, "The idea and its execution are pedestrian, labored and obvious."

JOURNEY TO JERUSALEM [Drama/Bible/Period/Politics/Religion] A: Maxwell Anderson; D: Elmer Rice; S/L: Jo Mielziner; C: Millia Davenport; P: Playwrights' Company; T: National Theatre; 10/5/40 (17)

Young Sidney Lumet, whose acting experience had been largely on the Yiddish stage, and who one day would become a major film director, joined the cast at short notice to play the role of the gentle twelve-year-old Jesus (here called Jeshua) in this exquisitely designed but "curiously unmoving" (George Freedley [*NYMT*]) episodic biblical drama. Inspired by an episode in the Gospel of St. Luke, the play tells of when Jesus is taken by his parents, Mary (Arlene Francis), called Miriam here, and Joseph (Horace Braham) to Jerusalem to celebrate Passover. Before departing from Nazareth, they hear the citizenry bewail the failure of the Messiah to come and alleviate the conditions under which the Romans, led by the Hitlerian Herod Antipas (Frederic Tozere), force them to live throughout the land. En route to Jerusalem, Jeshua's family is set upon by robbers but rescued by the prophet Ishmael (Arnold Moss). He had been among the unsuccessful rebels who were crushed when, led by Judah, they tried to overthrow the Romans. He sees in Jeshua the Messiah and manages--in the most dramatic scene--to get Jeshua into Jerusalem past the census taker, who is seeking boys of Jeshua's age because of Herod's fear of the Messiah's coming. In the city, Jeshua's display of logic and wisdom at the temple alerts one among the wise men there that he is indeed the Messiah, but dread of the ruler forces the man to keep silent. Soon after, Ishmael reveals the boy's anguished destiny to him, and Jeshua, filled with disappointment at his nonheroic mission but also with pride, thereupon tells it to his parents. Ishmael dies, but Jeshua inspires the oppressed people to have hope.

Anderson's noble attempt to dramatize Jesus' spiritual awakening was timely, coming as it did when the world was threatened by yet another repressive force and hoping for a Messiah; however, "He has written in monotone and all his eloquence is muted," wrote Richard Lockridge (*NYS*). It was widely viewed that Anderson's writing was unequal to his subject. Burns Mantle (*NYDN*) avowed that it was "a static drama punctuated by fragmentary bits of holding beauty."

The best acting was that of Moss and Francis. Moss had left the cast of the recently opened hit Al Jolson show, *Hold On to Your Hats*, to do this play. The fine cast also included Charles De Sheim as Shadrach, Alice Reinheart as Mira, Joseph Wiseman as the Beggar and the 2nd Money Changer, James Gregory as Festus, Joseph Kramm as Malachi, and Karl Malden as the Centurion.

According to John F. Wharton in *Life among the Playwrights*, a then-standing statute forbade the representation of "the Deity" on stage, and the company was unsure about whether its use of the boy Jesus was legally acceptable. "The matter was discussed at several company meetings; Max [Anderson] finally decided that his own name, backed by the Company's prestige, would carry him through; there was a feeling of standing together. I thought of those meetings in 1971 when I attended *Godspell* and *Jesus Christ Superstar* (the above-mentioned law had been repealed). Such productions would have left Broadway aghast in 1940."

JOY FOREVER, A [Comedy/Alcoholism/Art/Business/Romance/Sex] A: Vincent McConnor; D: Reginald Denham; S: Stewart Chaney; P: Blevins Davis and Archie Thomson; T: Biltmore Theatre; 1/7/46 (16)

An amateurishly written and produced one-set play by a first-time author. Its title came from a poem by John Keats.

Guy Kibbee returned from Hollywood to star as Benjamin Vinnicum, a forgotten Hudson River School artist living in a barn-studio at Fort Tryon Park in upper Manhattan. He has long since retired from active involvement in the art scene. He earns his living as an advertising sandwich man for a Chinese restaurant and takes comfort with his bottle and a former model, Tina (Dorothy Sands), who serves as his housekeeper *cum* mistress. In his studio, piled high with his old paintings, the old codger is visited by various cronies. An art critic named Archer Barrington (Nicholas Joy) discovers the long-lost artist, and the latter's paintings are soon being valued at $1 million. There is such interest in their purchase that the harried artist decides to give them away, first come first served. He returns to his painting (given up thirty years earlier) and plans to marry Tina. The play includes a subplot in which the artist advises a young female artist (Ottilie Kruger) to abandon her creative aspirations in order to marry the fellow she loves and to "create life" instead of art.

Robert Garland (*NYJA*) opined that *A Joy Forever* "is no thing of beauty." A somewhat kinder Rosamond Gilder (*TAM*) decided that the work was "an amiable excursion into whimsicality" that "did not have enough comic vigor or originality to weather the rigors of New York's theatrical climate." In the cast were Loring Smith, Natalie Schafer, Seth Arnold, William Nunn, Lois Bolton, and others.

JOY TO THE WORLD [Comedy-Drama/Business/Films/Labor/Romance/Sex] A: Allan Scott; D: Jules Dassin; S: Harry Horner; C: Beverly Woodner; L: Jean Rosenthal; P: John Houseman and William R. Katzell; T: Plymouth Theatre; 3/18/48 (124)

Mixed reviews were the fate of this thematically weighty, rapidly played satire on Hollywood. It had strong topical interest because of the current blacklisting going on in Hollywood under the reactionary pressures of the House Un-American Activities Committee. Director Dassin was at the time having his own problems with the committee because of his alleged left-wing stances.

Its presumed concern with the issue of movie censorship, said Brooks Atkinson (*NYT*), led to confusing results. "Since so much is at stake in the ethical topics Mr. Scott raises, the mediocrity of his writing and the meretriciousness of his comedy gags are embarrassing." (This scathing review led to a lengthy rebuttal letter sent by producer Houseman to the *NYT*). But Ward Morehouse (*NYS*), despite reservations, believed that Scott had "written enough amusing scenes to make his comedy more than passable." Howard Barnes (*NYHT*) thought it "warm and moving."

Houseman recalled in *Front and Center* that the playwright kept promising to cut the script but never actually did so. "Before and after rehearsals he remained neurotically obdurate in his refusal to edit." When begged to do so by Houseman and Dassin, he would reply, "I'll cut, fellows . . . I swear I'll cut! But let me hear it just once with an audience!" When he did finally hear it in performance (in the New Haven tryout), the effect, said Houseman, was so depressing that none of his ultimate revisions could "entirely obliterate that first unhappy impression." In Boston, the play ran into censorship problems because it was reputed to be subversive; had numerous expletives and expressions such as "God!" "bitch," and "whore"; had a female character who looked too provocative as she sized up the leading man; and used references to men and women sleeping together.

Young producer Alexander Soren (Alfred Drake) works for Atlas-Continental Pictures, where he is a shrewd businessman with no high ideals; his biggest hits have been movies with lots of sex. Using a ghostwritten radio speech at which he barely has glanced, he has made a call for freedom from censorship. This has caused a filmdom furore, and he calls in the speech writer to be dressed down, but the writer turns out to be Ann Wood (film actress Marsha Hunt, in her Broadway debut), a lovely young Ph.D. of liberal persuasions working in the research department. Soren invites her out to dinner and the pair become lovers. Her ideas invigorate and reform him, and his decision to produce a movie about labor leader Samuel Gompers gets him embroiled in controversy with his superiors and loses him his job. He signs on with another studio run by his old boss, Sam Blumenfeld (Morris Carnovsky), whose son's death in the war has moved him in an idealistic direction concerning the purpose of movies. He also offers to make Soren his heir. Soren then goes off to marry Ann.

Drake and Marsha Hunt made a strong impression. The actress would become a victim of the Hollywood witch-hunts. Myron McCormick played J. Newton McKeon, the type of cynical, boozing publicity man he specialized in. Good performances were turned in also by Mary Welch, Hugh Rennie, Bert Freed, Peggy Maley, Leslie Litomy, Clay Clement, Theodore Newton, and Kurt Kasznar.

JUNIOR MISS [Comedy/Family/Romance/Sex/Youth] A: Jerome Chodorov and Joseph Fields; SC: a series of stories in the *New Yorker* by Sally Benson; D: Moss Hart; S: Frederick Fox; P: Max Gordon; P: Lyceum Theatre; 11/18/41 (710)

One of the blockbuster comedy hits of wartime Broadway, it followed the path earlier taken by its authors (who wrote the then-still-running hit, *My Sister Eileen*) in successfully adapting to the stage stories originally published in the *New Yorker*.

It brought to the fore a sixteen-year-old actress named Patricia Peardon in the leading role, she having been discovered while sitting in the anteroom of producer Max Gordon's office waiting for a young actor friend seeking a part. A stage manager, seeing her, asked her if she was an actress, to which she replied in the affirmative, having done some acting in the past, although this was not her objective at the moment. This daughter of a naval commander was asked to return later in the day, prompting her to rush home and make herself look more mature for her audition. Director Moss Hart had her read for the part of Lois, the older sister, but her reading was not successful and she was about to be dismissed. Hart then surmised that perhaps she was not quite as old as she had made herself up to appear, and he had her read in her real persona. Peardon landed the part and temporary Broadway stardom. A typical review of her was Richard Watts, Jr.'s (*NYHT*): "It was a stroke of fortune when young Miss Peardon was hit upon for the part. A thoroughly delightful young actress, just gawky enough, just blooming enough and just pretty enough, she is completely darling in the part, and in her last scene, looking freshly lovely in her first evening dress, she is a heroine of which any play should be proud." Although Peardon remained in the theatre, her starring days ended with this play.

The title of the play refers to giddy bobby-soxer Judy Graves, age about thirteen, who lives in an uptown Manhattan apartment with her mother, Grace (Barbara Robbins); her father, Harry (Philip Ober), a struggling lawyer; and her older sister, Lois (Joan Newton), age about sixteen. Judy is the wild-eyed, overly imaginative adolescent with a Miss Fix-It penchant, Lois the blossoming young would-be debutante concerned with dates, dances, and clothes and holding a righteous disdain for silly thirteen-year-olds. Judy, whose mind is crammed with the trivia of Hollywood movies, lets her imagination go to work when, seeing her dad give an innocent kiss to Ellen Curtis (Francesca Bruning), daughter of his employer, J. B. Curtis (Matt Briggs), she convinces herself and her equally enthusiastic "bosom friend," the squeaky-voiced Fuffy Adams (Lenore Lonergan), that Mr. Graves is having a fling with the young woman. Judy has an uncle named Willis (Alexander Kirkland), a lawyer who was nearly disbarred and has been away a long time. Not knowing the truth about him, Judy dreams up the idea when he returns after ten years that he is an ex-con who committed a horrid crime, but is really a good man who simply needs the right woman to straighten him out. She and Fuffy then scheme to pair Ellen and Willis, which leads to their falling in love and getting wed. But the boss fires Mr. Graves when he finds out about it. The family is definitely in hot water now, but Judy, sure enough, comes through and puts things back the way they ought to be.

There was structural weaknesses in the play, but its admittedly slim story, engaging characters, and delicious comic dialogue were effective enough to cover over all such flaws. Staged with memorable élan and inventive business and acted with intelligence and comic spirit by a cast of nineteen, *Junior Miss* had all the ingredients to please a wartime audience seeking escapist fun. Rowland Field (*NEN*) noted, "Here is one of the season's most genuine delights, a play that is keenly observant and brimful of human qualities in achieving its comic purpose." Brooks Atkinson (*NYT*) called it "a harum-scarum antic and a darlin' play." Kelcey Allen (*WWD*) said, "It breathes the spirit of youth and is replete with wit, sentiment, charm, amusing situations and clever dialog." Yet Wilella Waldorf (*NYP*) was of the opposite opinion, claiming, "*Junior Miss* is a surprisingly poor piece of play writing, decidedly below par as Broadway standards go, and . . . Moss Hart . . . has sometimes rendered this distressing fact more obvious by his frantic attempts to cover it up."

In addition to previously mentioned actors, there were outstanding performances by Jack Manning, Billy (William) Redfield, and Peter Scott as variously gauche young men interested in Judy and Lois and by Paula Laurence as a nonchalant comic maid.

JUPITER LAUGHS [Drama/British/Medicine/Religion/Romance/Science/Sex] A: Dr. A. J. Cronin; D: Reginald Denham; S: Raymond Sovey; P: Warner Brothers i/a/w Bernard Klawans; T: Biltmore Theatre; 9/9/40 (24)

British novelist A. J. Cronin, author of *The Citadel*, could not translate his literary skills into those required by dramaturgy. His weakly directed first play prompted Brooks Atkinson (*NYT*) to comment, "Taken literally as a narrative, the story is maudlin and the characters are cut out of colored cardboard. . . . *Jupiter Laughs* looks like a play and sounds like a play, but never achieves dramatic existence." "Written in many scenes and with many pauses, the play seemed more a novel than a stage piece," intoned Rosamond Gilder (*TAM*). The play's premiere was in New York because the war had caused its London production to be canceled.

The action is set in the common room of a British "Nerve Sanatorium" for nervous disorders where Dr. Paul Venner (Alexander Knox), a bitter, agnostic medical scientist who is having an affair with a colleague's (Philip Tonge) wife (Nancy Sheridan) is on the verge of a major medical discovery. He alienates everyone around him, including the scheming matron, Fanny Leeming (Edith Meiser). Dr. Venner falls in love with a beautiful, idealistic young physician, Dr. Mary Murray (Jessica Tandy), whose heart is set on going to China as a missionary. Their various emotional conflicts stem from their difference of opinion concerning the existence of God. After various plot contrivances, Dr. Murray dies in a valiant attempt to save Dr. Venner's scientific papers, threatened by a fire set by the discarded mistress, whose deed has been prompted by the matron. Dr. Venner, hoping to find the faith that guided Mary, goes off to China in her stead, her prayer book in his pocket.

There were several excellent performances, including those of Knox, Tandy, and Meiser.

JUST MY LUCK [Musical/Yiddish Language] B: William Siegel; M: Abe Ellstein; LY: Isidor Lillian and Jacob Jacobs; D/P: Menasha Skulnik; CH: Lillian Shapero; S: Michael Saltzman; T: Second Avenue Theatre (OB); 9/27/47

A Yiddish "operetta" starring Menasha Skulnik. Ample chances were also afforded costar Yetta Zwerling, who had appeared with Skulnik for years, usually as a man-crazy character. "Whether one understands the Yiddish language or not, one never fails to interpret the projections of the pasty-faced, languid Skulnik, who quite conceivably is the top comedian in the Yiddish idiom today," wrote Kahn. (*V*).

Skulnik was Pinie, a delicatessen worker, who travels to Europe to marry his sister-in-law Mania (Lily Lilliana) so she can enter America. Her husband, Pinie's brother (Leon Liebgold), is missing in action with the U.S. Army. Complications stemming from mistaken identy ensue, but the brother appears, although blinded. Before the end, his sight is miraculously cured and he is reunited with his bride. Pinie ends up with Perl (Zwerling), his near-sighted cousin who has been after him throughout.

Skulnik's routines involved him singing "Pinie the Sailor Man" dressed in navy whites and "The Scotchman from Orchard Street," in which he dressed in kilts. He also did a medley of popular tunes with Zwerling.

K

KATHERINE DUNHAM AND HER COMPANY [Revue/Blacks] D/CH: Katherine Dunham; DS: John Pratt; P: S. Hurok; T: Broadway Theatre; 4/19/50 (37)

A dance revue created by influential black choreographer Katherine Dunham. Some of the material was from her traditional repertory, but because it had undergone continual revision and polishing, even the familiar routines were still exciting and fresh. The critics, as usual, differed on what numbers they preferred. Most of the dances were African, West Indian, or South American in flavor. Some had a decidedly ethnologic flavor, and torrid, pelvic gyrating sexuality was present almost throughout, although several commentators felt that Dunham's work had been more primitive and unabashed in the past.

There were two editions to the show, the second one opening on 5/9/50 with three additions to the program. Dances seen during the series included a Bahian dance, "Batacuda," in which Dunham coiled and uncoiled a rope about her waist; the Florida dance shimmy called "Barrelhouse," which was a challenge piece with two dancers trying to outdo each other; "Flaming Youth," a takeoff on the roaring twenties, which showed off Lucille Ellis's talents; "Afrique," featuring Dunham as an Afro-Egyptian monarch; "Veracuzana," in which she was an unfaithful wife; the somewhat too-arty "Jazz in Five Movements"; "L'Ag'ya," a narrative dance--including zombies--based on a triangular romantic tale in eighteenth-century Martinique; the undulatingly erotic "Ritual of Fertility"; and others.

The three dances that joined the show on 5/9/50 were "Tropics," with Dunham in one of her most popular characters, smoking a cigar and carrying a bird cage on her head; "Rites de Passage," a puberty ritual for a boy; and "Shango," about a boy possessed by a snake and freed by a ritual from this danger.

Dance critic John Martin (*NYT*), referring to former Dunham presentations, attested that "there is not one of them that is not performed with incomparably more skill and theatrical effectiveness than in the old days." Robert Coleman (*NYDM*) observed that Dunham "is a handsome, exotic and arresting artist. It is fascinating to watch her changes of mood from comedy to satire, from blues to drama. She dominates the stage whenever she is on it."

The company included Vanoye Aikens, Lenwood Morris, Jon Lei, and, among others, Wilbert Bradley. "It is really a first-rate company all around," noted Martin, "spirited, beautifully rehearsed and exciting to watch in action." Not all others felt similarly, Robert Garland (*NYJA*), for one, being surprised to discover that this was "a mild, monotonous and muddled show."

KATHLEEN [Comedy/Family/Irish/Medicine/Religion/Romance/Sex/Youth] A: Michael Sayers; D: Coby Ruskin; S: Charles Elson; C: Rose Bogdanoff; P: Bea Lawrence; T: Mansfield Theatre; 2/3/48 (2)

An amateurish, farcical Irish import set in a village near Dublin and spoken in brogueish accents. The title character is an eccentric nineteen-year-old girl (Andree

Wallace), daughter of history professor Jasper Fogarty (Jack Sheehan) and madly in love with love. She wants a man who will love her as she is, without strings attached. (She is intended as a symbol of Ireland [Kathleen ni Houlihan], and the other characters are equally symbolic.) Things get rolling when--as a test of faith--she falsely declares that she is pregnant, thereby exciting her father, her doctor-uncle (Frank Merlin), and her priest-uncle (Whitford Kane). The mystery is who the father might be, there being three suspects, all suitors: the rich man's son, Seamus MacGonigal (Henry Jones), the poor man's son, Christy Hanafey (James McCallion), and the army engineer, Lieutenant Aengus MacOgue (Whitfield Connor). Kathleen declares that she will go to whoever will claim both her and the child. Her story is that she got "kissed" at a party in Dublin but, because of the darkness, is not sure who it was. The doctor has his doubts about his niece's veracity. Seamus, pressured by his father and the priest, offers to marry Kathleen, followed by Christy, and then the lieutenant. She chooses the latter, but it turns out that though they will marry, there will not be a baby after all, at least not right away.

The play seemed "merely noisy and silly and a little tasteless and more than a little dull," decided Louis Kronenberger (*PM*). Despite a press release that explained the play's allegorical significance, the critics accepted the commentary with a grain of salt.

KEEP 'EM LAUGHING [Revue] CN/D: Clifford C. Fischer; SK: Arthur Pierson and Eddie Davis; P: Clifford C. Fischer b/a/w the Messrs. Shubert; T: Forty-fourth Street Theatre; 4/24/42 (77)

One of several vaudeville-type shows to appear on Broadway in the 1941-1942 season. It played twice a day and three times on Saturdays and Sundays. Conceiver-director Clifford C. Fischer was responsible for an earlier show, also well recived, *Priorities of 1942*, that was still running. Although well liked, *Keep 'Em Laughing* was generally considered inferior to its predecessor. The new show possessed a powerhouse of talent, including Zero Mostel (in his Broadway debut following his success on radio and in night clubs), William Gaxton, Hildegarde, Victor Moore, Paul and Grace Hartman, and Jack Cole.

Although overlong, much of it was hilarious and none of it was dull, thought Brooks Atkinson (*NYT*). George Freedley (*NYMT*) called it "brassy, bright, tuneful and funny." Others felt that it could have been funnier and were surprised that the most laugh-provoking thing in it was a dog act. This show-stealing act was the Bricklayers, one of whose routines had the canines, dressed snappily in sweaters and overalls, running up and down ladders, carrying bricks and lumber, and building a house; then an accident occurred to one of the workers, whose concerned wife (played by a little child on a scooter) raced on to assist him, accompanied by a dog ambulance. The Hartmans proved effective with their intelligently conceived satirical dance routines, especially one that mocked the Arthur Murray type of ballroom dancing. Veteran comic Victor Moore did not score his usual success because the critics were unimpressed by his old "Change Your Act or Back to the Woods" sketch, with which he had made his first hit as a vaudeville performer years before, and which by now had become stale. William Gaxton, Moore's frequent costar, who also served as MC, did better with "Authoritis," his sketch about a movie writer, and with his medley of hit tunes, including "You Do Something to Me." Several critics observed that Gaxton had put on weight since his last Broadway outing. Moore reappeared late in the show to share with Gaxton a sketch in which he tried to buy a white handkerchief from the latter and ended up with a pearl-handled revolver. Jack Cole and the three women in his troupe were popular with their rhythmic Eastern dances based on Hindu rituals, and the good-looking nightclub star Hildegarde made a hit with her personable and intimate style of singing (which she did while accompanying herself on the piano), but not with her mediocre songs. In one song, "Something About a Soldier," she made effective use of some soldiers in the audience. There was also a spectacularly acrobatic dancer named Miriam La Velle very amusing material from comic xylophonist Fred Sanborn. Mostel did several bits, including his imitations of Jimmy Durante, Charles Boyer, Hitler, and a Roseland jitterbug. Atkinson described him as "a roly-poly zany with a voice that rattles in the cellar, eyes that cross and a face that gets foolishly distorted when he is making a political speech. For a first appearance in a large theatre he is doing remarkably well." This production was succeeded by a similar one titled *The Top-Notchers* (see that entry) that simply changed the acts but kept the run going.

KEN MURRAY'S BLACKOUTS OF 1949 (see *Blackouts of 1949*)

KIND LADY [Dramatic Revival*] A: Edward Chodorov and George Haight; D: Felix Jacoves; S: Watson Barratt; P: William A. Brady; T: Playhouse; 9/3/40 (107)

A fine revival of the psychological chiller about a kind old lady who becomes a prisoner in her own home at the mercy of a band of art thieves. It had chilled Broadway in 1935, but its run was interrupted by the illness of its star, Grace George.

George was once more in the role of Mary Herries, which she had continued to act in various summer-theatre engagements; her growth in the role was noted by various critics, who strongly recommended the play on the basis of her performance. Rosamond Gilder (*TAM*) declared, "Hers is the technical proficiency of a certain period in the American theatre, a period when theatre craftsmanship was essential, when the requirements of repertory gave actors both training and experience. . . . Lovely, with a dainty, porcelain beauty for which ruffles, lace and flowers are proper accompaniment, Miss George is never the sweet old lady such trappings suggest. She draws a sharp line between sentiment and sentimentality, keeping the outline of her performance firm, her movements crisp, her voice vital and alert."

The tightly knit play was deemed to have been improved by the elimination of its prologue. Its slick villain, Henry Abbott, was acceptably acted by Stiano Braggiotti, but he lacked the smoothly sinister quality of the original actor, Henry Daniell. Clarence Derwent, Ivy Troutman, and Oscar Stirling were among those offering first-class support, and young Dorothy McGuire was very convincing as Ada, an epileptic. Marie Paxton as the maid, Rose, and Elfrida Derwent as Mrs. Edwards reprised their 1935 roles. Felix Jacoves's direction was found somewhat lacking in crucial scenes requiring a mood of menace.

The play, said George Freedley (*NYMT*), "has stood the test of time better than most thrillers," and Richard Lockridge (*NYS*) thought it "one of the small masterpieces of its kind."

KING HENRY VIII [Dramatic Revival] A: William Shakespeare; M: Lehman Engel; D: Margaret Webster; CH: Felicia Sorel; DS: David Ffolkes; P: American Repertory Theatre; T: International Theatre; 11/6/46 (40)

The failure of the promising but short-lived American Repertory Theatre founded by Margaret Webster and Eva Le Gallienne often has been attributed to its somewhat esoteric choice of plays during its one and only season. A good example would be its first production, this excellent revival of the rarely seen *King Henry VIII*, a minor Shakespearean work (written in collaboration with John Fletcher, with some parts possibly by Philip Massinger) not seen locally since 1916.

Briefly, it concerns Henry's rejection of Katherine as queen for Anne Boleyn (Bullen in the play), Henry's stripping of Cardinal Wolsey's powers, and Katherine's death. Despite a sometimes stunning visual presentation, the work was not exciting enough to fire general interest, and the troupe's subsequent offerings followed much the same pattern.

The cast in the present work had some very solid actors, including Philip Bourneuf as Prologue and first chronicler, Eugene Stuckmann as second chronicler and Capucius, Richard Waring as Buckingham, Raymond Greenleaf as Norfolk, Walter Hampden as Wolsey (the leading role), Eli Wallach (in his Broadway debut) as Cromwell, William Windom as sergeant of the guard and Surrey, Victor Jory as Henry VIII, Efrem Zimbalist, Jr. (in his Broadway debut), as Suffolk, Eva Le Gallienne as Katherine of Aragon, Ernest Truex as the lord chamberlain, Angus Cairns as surveyor and Garter King of Arms, John Becher as Lord Sands, June Duprez as Anne Bullen, Margaret Webster as an old lady, and Mary Alice Moore as duchess of Norfolk, among others.

The encouraging general opinion was that the rambling play itself was not remarkable but that the production was a sumptuously designed one further distinguished by fine acting and direction. John Mason Brown (*SR*) concluded that the play itself "is a tedious work, unresolved, spotty, and meager even in its poetry." "With David Ffolkes . . . Miss Webster has opened up a picture book of history which can only be compared to Olivier's *Henry V* (the picture) in rich color and beauty," wrote Euphemia Van Rensselaer Wyatt (*CW*). Brooks Atkinson (*NYT*) noted, "Out of an indifferent play the American Repertory Theatre has fashioned a memorable performance and a notable production." He said that the play itself was little "more than a procession of woes and reports of court political knavery."

The principal parts of Katherine of Aragon and Wolsey were in the very capable hands of two experienced players, both of whom, according to most (but not all) critics, were up to the task. Rosamond Gilder (*TAM*) offered the moderate opinion that Le Gallienne and Hampden "acquitted themselves with earnestness and nobility. That no major chord was struck by either is due to a certain dryness in the text as well as in the performance. Shakespeare and his collaborator or collaborators have not succeeded in bringing either alive; they are figures in a tapestry." Their chief support came from the actors of Henry VIII, made up like the Holbein portrait, and Buckingham; Waring in the latter gave what many thought the evening's most powerful portrayal.

The cast in general was lauded for its clear and expressive speaking of the verse, and Webster was praised for her lucid and often visually striking staging, despite a script that tended to longeurs. She made a good many alterations in the text, chopping out parts she believed were not by Shakespeare, most notably the Cranmer plot, and adding narrator-characters (the chroniclers), reading from Holinshed, to clarify for the audience the more arcane aspects of British history. (Some thought that the chroniclers were overused and took up too much time.) The original five acts and sixteen scenes were reduced to two acts and thirteen scenes. Of considerable import was the score by Lehman Engel, which offered musical background to a sizable portion of the proceedings and was nearly enough to provide "a dramatic concert," as Atkinson observed.

(1) KING LEAR [Dramatic Revival*] A: William Shakespeare; M: Henry Cowell; D: Erwin Piscator; CH: Lotte Goslar; S: Antonin Heytheum; L: A. H. Feder; P: Erwin Piscator; T: Studio Theatre of the New School for Social Research (OB); 12/15/40

Refugee director Erwin Piscator, one of the giants of the German stage, had been resident in America for two years before directing a production here. *King Lear*, his first effort, was at the Off-Broadway Studio Theatre he ran in conjunction with his theatre classes at the New School on West Twelfth Street. It starred Sam Jaffe as Lear, with Rachael Adams as Goneril, Margaret Curtis as Regan, Lysbeth Lynn as Cordelia, Herbert Ranson as Kent, Ross Matthew as Gloucester, Erford Gage as Edgar, Roger De Koven as Edmund, and Herbert Berghof as the Fool. The latter was accompanied by a group of mummers, played by Lotte Goslar and her dancers. It "turned out," said Hobe. (*V*), "to be a director's debauch, an actor's purgatory, and a playgoer's nightmare."

As expected, this was no conventional *Lear*. It abandoned realistic scenic backgrounds in favor of a curtainless, symbolic arrangement of strikingly lit, irregular, semi-circular platforms placed on four ascending levels--the image of a pyramid was invoked for some, a wedding cake for others--on a revolving stage set before a neutrally colored fish-net cyclorama. (The noise of the actors' feet on the hollow platforms and the slow turning of the revolve were serious detriments.) Actors appeared and exited through poorly masked portals at the sides or through the auditorium. Set changes were accompanied by a stagehand entering holding a screenlike banner on which was painted the name of the new locale. Unusual sound effects were provided by Harold Burris-Meyer, but these--particularly of Lear's ranting during the raucous storm scene--proved distracting and unpleasant to listen to.

Piscator's approach was to make Lear--depicted as a doddering, half-senile old man--a fascistic dictator, a theme stressed by the inclusion as an epilogue of a speech from *Troilus and Cressida* predicting the self-consumption of all-consuming power. "This would seem to be as remote from Shakespeare's actual intent," griped

John Anderson (*NYJA*), "as it is from *Peter Pan** and as sensible as trying to prove that *Winnie the Pooh* is really a technological discussion of State ownership of bird baths."

Despite the powerful visual aspects of the presentation, the work stumbled in matters of acting and directorial interpretation. Jaffe proved quite inept at acting Shakespeare, having none of the appropriate vocal skills. The critics noted that he was a beardless Lear, although the published photos of him in the role show a hirsute makeup. Berghof's thick Teutonic accent seriously marred his fool, played, said Anderson, as "a sort of *echt Deutsche* black tights-jester [*sic*] via Werner Krauss-cum-Caligari." Few of the others were more than passable, none of them being equal to the poetry of the author. Brooks Atkinson (*NYT*) said that Piscator showed little aptitude for the play: "The performance is loose and flabby and the emotion is exterior."

(2) M: Rosabel Watson; D: Donald Wolfit and Christopher Ede; S/C: Ernest Stern; P: Hall Shelton b/a/w Advance Players Association, Ltd., of London; T: Century Theatre; 2/18/47 (8)

Following a Canadian tour, the Donald Wolfit Repertory Company of England visited New York with *King Lear* and four other plays (*As You Like It**, *Hamlet**, *The Merchant of Venice**, and *Volpone**). For the most part, the critics rejected the company as provincial, hammy, and ill equipped to represent the British tradition in the staging and acting of the classics. It got off on the wrong foot with its almost unanimously dismissed version of *Lear*, with Wolfit in the title role, his leading lady Rosalind Iden as Cordelia, Alexander Gauge as Kent, Eric Maxon as Gloucester, Kempster Barnes as Edgar, Frederick Horrey as Edmund, Geoffrey Wilkinson as the fool, Violet Farebrother as Goneril, and Ann Chalkley as Regan.

The play was performed at breakneck speed in two hours and forty minutes; its scenery and costumes were defiantly unattractive, and its performances were bellowing and unpoetic. Directorial weaknesses were evident everywhere. Brooks Atkinson (*NYT*) said that only the choice of play was acceptable. "That is the only unhackneyed element in this carnival of bombast and attitudinizing." Rosamond Gilder (*TAM*) said that because the company "made no attempt to understand the text or grasp or convey the meaning of the words spoken, there was no play at all--only some painted canvas, some crudely costumed and made-up performers and a vast emptiness of spirit." John Mason Brown (*SR*) described the company as "a band of players, all lungs and reverberations, who envelop the tragedy in a fog of incomprehension."

Wolfit played Lear as if he, the actor, were appearing in a nineteenth-century revival instead of a twentieth-century one, with chalk-white makeup and scraggly beard and wig. Nevertheless, most critics admitted that the star was occasionally impressive, if far from brilliant, that his voice was strong and tireless, that his diction clear, and that he could be a decent Lear if well directed. But he tended to externalize too much, to speak in a declamatory fashion, and to melodramatize the role without sufficient intellectual grasp of the character's thoughts.

(1) KING RICHARD III [Dramatic Revival*] A: William Shakespeare; M: George Hirst; D: George Coulouris; S/C: Motley; L: Jean Rosenthal; P: Theatre Productions; T: Forrest Theatre; 3/24/43 (11)

The last performance of this popular Shakespearean history play had been in 1934, starring Walter Hampden. The present mediocre rendition was directed by and starred Greek-born actor George Coulouris. The critics were rather reserved, seemingly finding whatever praise they could because it was the only Shakespeare revival of the season, and some Shakespeare, they reasoned, was better than none at all.

The most notable things about the performance were the imaginative Motley costumes and permanent multileveled setting, the rapid pace of the staging, and the colloquially humorous, consistently Machiavellian characterization of the title role (which, however, was unsuccessfully realized). Otherwise, said Ward Morehouse (*NYS*), it "lacks stature as a production; it is routine and undistinguished."

There were adequate-to-fine performances by Philip Bourneuf (generally considered the best of the lot) as Buckingham, Mildred Dunnock as Queen Margaret, Norma Chambers as Queen Elizabeth, Helen Waren as Lady Anne, Harold Young as Clarence, Anthony Kemble-Cooper as Hastings, Tom Rutherford as Edward IV, Harry Irvine as the Lord Mayor, Ralph Clanton as Catesby, and John Ireland as Richmond.

Coulouris, argued George Freedley (*NYMT*) lacked the "fire and the brittleness of steel" the critic sought. Morehouse said that his villainy seemed transparent and, while "interesting" at moments, his was "never a soaring or electric" interpretation. Howard Barnes (*NYHT*) observed, "While trying to make his offering simple and Elizabethan, [Coulouris] has merely succeeded in making it a bit turgid." Hobe. (*V*) took Coulouris to task by noting, "He doesn't reveal either the acting range to realize the full possibilities of the part, or the personal magnetism to carry the play." Louis Kronenberger (*PM*) reported of Coulouris's acting, "It has nothing wooden about it; it is often dynamic and sometimes individual. But it misses the real intellectual forces in Richard, and the sardonic contemplation of his own villainies. It seems to miss, too, the joy Richard took in dissembling. . . . Mr. Coulouris' Richard is almost always impatient, with a rapid and jerky manner of speech, a sinister look and a feverish air." On the other hand, Coulouris was praised by Burton Rascoe (*NYWT*) for eschewing the usual declamatory fustian of the part and making Richard seem conversationally natural and realistic. "By, in a way, underplaying the part he not only brings out unsuspected values in it, but lets the other parts take on unsuspected values also." Thus, said Rascoe, the other roles became more human and less artificial.

The text employed was a considerably pared-down First Folio (removed, for example, were the ghosts, the bishop of Ely, and the duchess of York), with some scenes rearranged to enhance the dramatic flow. The additions of Colley Cibber were eliminated. The set resembled an Elizabethan stage in some particulars. Rosamond Gilder (*TAM*) described it: "The whole stage frame is used--the curtain rising to the top of the proscenium arch to disclose a structure of aspiring forms and broken arches that can suggest the Tower of London, a street, castle, or a vague terrain. . . . In the centre, on the principle of the Elizabethan inner stage, is a low arch that follows the lines of the Traitor's Gate. The platform above this with the stairs that lead to it on either side make a variety of acting levels and permit the action to flow continuously from scene to scene."

(2) D: Richard Barr; DS: Richard Whorf; P: Herman Levin; T: Booth Theatre; 2/8/49 (23)

Versatile theatre man Richard Whorf played the lead in this revival, as well as designing the entire show. The duke of Clarence was played by Will Kuluva, Hastings by Robert H. Harris, Anne by Frances Reid, Elizabeth by Polly Rowles, her sons Grey and Dorset by David Clive and Douglass Watson, Stanley by Orrin Redfield, the Lord Mayor by Walter F. Appler, Richmond by Michael Sivy, Buckingham (the role he played in the previous revival) by Philip Bourneuf, Ratcliff by Ray Walston, Margaret by Grace Coppin, and Tyrell by Nehemiah Persoff. There was--apart from one or two minority opinions--considerable approbation for this company, whose members spoke well and provided sharply etched characterizations. Most outstanding was the performance of Bourneuf.

Other striking ingredients in the revival included Whorf's low-budget unit setting, which was dominated by a pair of Roman arches suggestive of the Tower of London; the pit was incorporated into the design and arranged so that entrances and exits could be made from it. Careful editing clarified the play's dramatic line.

Whorf's performance was decidedly melodramatic and occasionally used a red spotlight to illumine Richard's features. Brooks Atkinson (*NYT*) thought the attempt worthwhile if not especially "distinguished." "His Richard is lean, fanatical, nervous, quickminded and cold-blooded. He is a cripple with a bad leg and a crooked back, scheming to get by treachery the sweets that nature has withheld from him." However, said Atkinson, there was too much emphasis on the use of rapid pacing to avoid boredom, and Whorf was accused of a lack of variety in the expression of Richard's cunning. A similar complaint came from several others, such as Howard Barnes (*NYHT*), who commented, "The revival remains in one strident key, with scarcely an interlude of emotional clarity or eloquence." George Jean Nathan (*TBY*) took issue with the simplification of the drama to a "cops-and-robbers" melodrama, the inconsistency of Whorf's interpretation, and the inferiority of the company. "The evening sums up to no more than a profile of the classic for Class-B little theatres." But there were also strong supporters, such as Ward Morehouse (*NYS*), who found this production "fast-moving; it has life and spirit, and Richard Whorf turns in a first-rate performance. . . . His Duke is a sly and cunning monster . . . , and toward the end, just before he is slain . . . , is a figure of agony and terror." Richard Watts, Jr. (*NYP*), reported that the production "has pace, color and a mounting violence that never ceases to be engrossing." Whorf's Richard, he declared, "is alive with ferocity, mercilessness, guile, hatred of all mankind and contempt for all the world. It has its own kind of humor, too. . . . Whorf also has the great virtue of knowing how to speak Shakespearean verse in a manner that sacrifices neither its tremendous vitality nor its moving eloquence."

KISS AND TELL [Comedy/Family/Medicine/Military/Romance/Sex/War/Youth] A: F. Hugh Herbert; SC: the radio series, *Meet Corliss Archer*; D/P: George Abbott; S: John Root; T: Biltmore Theatre; 3/17/43 (962)

This "fresh, funny and completely beguiling" (John Anderson [*NYJA*]) blockbuster hit was inspired by the then-popular radio series, *Meet Corliss Archer* (which grew out of a magazine serial in *Good Housekeeping Magazine*), for which F. Hugh Herbert was a scriptwriter. It was another addition to the growing heap of Broadway comedies raking in the cash with stories of adolescent female love (see also *Junior Miss* and *Janie*).

In this minor variation of *Romeo and Juliet**, set entirely on the back porch of the Archer family home, the chief culprit is fifteen-year-old Corliss Archer (Joan Caulfield, in her first important role), who has a soldier brother named Lenny (Richard Widmark, then a radio actor, in the role that first brought him to attention; his replacement was the equally unknown Kirk Douglas). Home on a seventy-two hour leave, Lenny secretly marries Mildred Pringle (Judith [Judy] Parrish) before he goes overseas. (Mildred also has a brother, the chubby Raymond [Tommy Lewis], whose dryly philosophical remarks are funny enough to practically steal the show.) The marriage is secret because of enmity between the Pringle and Archer families, and only Corliss, who has sworn in blood not to tell, knows about it. Mildred is pregnant, and Corliss goes with her to the doctor. When Mrs. Archer (Jessie Royce Landis) sees her daughter leaving the obstetrician's office and questions her, Corliss, covering for Mildred, says that she went there because she is pregnant. There is a neighbor's seventeen-year-old boy, Dexter Franklin (Robert White), who is enamored of Corliss and who is given to exclaiming "Holy cow!" on numerous occasions. Corliss names this adolescent as the expectant papa, which leads to humorous dissension among the respective families. Raymond runs back and forth as a spy between the warring families, offering hilarious words of wisdom. When news of Lenny's heroism in downing three Nazi planes is received, Mildred finally reveals the truth, and a happy ending arrives for all.

Audiences loved the likable characters, the amusing situations, and the mingling of poignant scenes--such as when Lenny tells his bride that he must go off to combat--amid those of sheer farce. The play was selected by Burns Mantle as one of the ten best of the year. Commented Rosamond Gilder (*TAM*), "F. Hugh Herbert . . . knows his youngsters well. Aside from the essential vulgarity of the main joke, his dialogue is well observed and often hilarious." Arthur Pollock (*BE*) reported, "It has good, sound belly laughs, . . . and chuckles and rumbles, cluckings and grins. Its laughter is of the most comfortable sort, arrived at humanly and without too much artificial stimulation."

The actors all received strong approbation. Lewis Nichols (*NYT*) wrote of Caulfield, "She is going to be a fine actress, for . . . she gives a most exact portrait of the combination of childishness and dignity which form that happy season of age." Frances Bavier played a funny cook, Robert Keith was terrific as the distressed Mr. Archer, and Dexter's parents were taken by Paula Trueman and Calvin Thomas. All was made to work perfectly by the genius of George Abbott's direction.

KISS FOR CINDERELLA, A [Dramatic Revival] A: James M. Barrie; D: Lee Strasberg; CH: Catherine Littlefield; S: Harry Horner; C: Paul du Pont; P: Cheryl

Crawford and Richard Krakeur i/a/w John Wildberg and Horace Schmidlapp; T: Music Box Theatre; 3/10/42 (48)

A revival of the whimsical British comedy that first appeared on Broadway in 1916 with Maude Adams as Miss Thing, a penniless cockney drudge who, in wartime London, takes pity on four starving refugee orphans by building makeshift sleeping quarters for them and sharing with them her boiled potatoes and tea. She is investigated by a curious and handsome policeman (Ralph Forbes), who thinks that she may be a spy. She tells the orphans that she is going to Cinderella's ball, but falls asleep in her doorway, and, while nearly freezing to death in a snowstorm, dreams that she is Cinderella at the ball (which offers a chance for some amusingly fantastical staging and dancing) and that the kindly policeman is Prince Charming.

The starring role was now undertaken by two-time Academy Award winner and famed European actress Luise Rainer, in her Broadway debut. She had recently been divorced from playwright Clifford Odets, with whom director Strasberg had worked closely in Group Theatre days. Although Rainer had played the role in a 1941 summertime engagement in New Jersey, the choice of a vehicle for her debut was deemed a weak one because she, with her heavy German accent, was miscast as a London slavey. The sentimental comedy itself, set during World War I, was found by many to be dated when compared with what was then happening in bomber-plagued London. Its fanciful qualities seemed seriously out of place in 1942, even though the script had been larded with several references to bring it up to date.

Louis Kronenberger (*PM*) derided the play's gooey emotionality: "When he wrote this tale, Barrie assuredly sold out to the confectioners; he displayed a positively unerring eye for everything sentimental and saccharine and cute." Rosamond Gilder (*TAM*) remained convinced of the quality of the writing, but felt that the production lacked the proper "nostalgic charm."

Speaking of Rainer, whom she felt to be the biggest drawback, Gilder wrote, "Her gaunt frame, her dark, drawn face suggest that this Cinderella is herself a refugee from a starving Europe rather than an imaginative little London slavey doing a bit of rescuing on her own." The most outstanding acting came from British actors Ralph Forbes and Cecil Humphreys (as Mr. Bodie, the artist for whom Miss Thing works). Also in the cast were Edith King and Le Roi Operti.

KISS ME, KATE [Musical/Crime/Gambling/Marriage/Period/Theatre] B: Bella and Samuel Spewack; M/LY: Cole Porter; SC: William Shakespeare's play, *The Taming of the Shrew**; D: John C. Wilson; CH: Hanya Holm; DS: Lemuel Ayers; P: Arnold Saint-Subber and Lemuel Ayers; T: New Century Theatre; 12/30/48 (1,077)

Kiss Me, Kate was one of the great musicals of the 1940s. It succeeded in almost every department, including score, lyrics, book, performers, direction, choreography, and design. Comedy and sentiment mingled exhilaratingly with now-classic songs to keep audiences enthralled throughout. It represented a triumphant return to his former brilliance of painfully crippled composer-lyricist Cole Porter, whose score some thought the best of his life. "It's solidly enjoyable," wrote Hobe. (*V*), "with one hummable tune after another, many of them with slyly amusing lyrics." These memorable numbers included "Another Opening, Another Show," "We Open in Venice," "Bianca," "Why Can't You Behave?" "So in Love with You Am I," "I Hate Men," "Too Darn Hot," "Where Is the Life That Late I Led?" "Brush Up Your Shakespeare," "Wunderbar" (conceived as a satire on Viennese waltzes but appreciated instead for its lilting melody), "Always True to You (In My Fashion)," "I've Come to Wive It Wealthily in Padua," and "Were Thine That Special Face." Some of the lyrics were lifted directly from the Bard of Avon, and nearly every song had a tight relationship to the development of the action. Brooks Atkinson (*NYT*) observed, "Porter has written a remarkable melodious score with an occasional suggestion of Puccini, who was a good composer, too. . . . All his lyrics are literate, and as usual some of them would shock the editorial staff of *The Police Gazette*."

One of the songs that was usually encored was "I Hate Men," soloed by Patricia Morison. The encore had special lyrics written for it. One performance was given for an audience made up largely of benefit subscribers, normally considered a deadly group to play for; on this occasion they were especially unresponsive and showed little sign of life after this song was sung. The nettled musical director thereupon turned to the spectators and spoke: "Well, you're going to get an encore whether you want it or not," and get it they did (quoted in Jack Gaver, *Curtain Calls*).

The idea of taking a cue from Shakespeare to create a musical comedy was still relatively novel, having been begun only a dozen years earlier with *The Boys from Syracuse**. Here, the idea was given a novel twist by framing the plot of *The Taming of the Shrew* within a story of a battling pair of divorced but still-in-love stars, the egomaniacal actor-director Fred Graham (Alfred Drake) and the tempestuous Lilli Vanessi (Patricia Morison), who are engaged in a tryout of Shakespeare's farce in Ford's Theatre, Baltimore. All the action occurs between 5 P.M. and midnight, from the moments after a run-through to the period after the first performance. A great deal is made of the parallels between Kate and Petruchio and Fred and Lilli in what follows. Lilli turns jealous when she learns that flowers she thought Fred intended for her were meant for Lois Lane (Lisa Kirk), the actress playing Bianca. During their performance of Shakespeare's play, Lilli, professing that she is a realistic actress, gives Fred's ribs the brunt of her elbow, whereupon Fred whacks Lilli's behind with enormous vigor, which only makes Lilli respond with slaphappy results. Mixed in to all this is the subplot about the love affair of Lois Lane and actor Bill Calhoun (Harold Lang), cast as Lucentio in Shakespeare's farce, and whose gambling debts lead a pair of dopey thugs (Harry Clark and Jack Diamond) to seek collection of the $10,000 owed. (Their soft-shoe "Brush Up Your Shakespeare" was a show-stopper.) A further complication stems from Bill's having signed Fred's name to the IOU. By the end of the musical, the IOU has become meaningless because the hoodlums' boss has been killed, and Fred and Lilli--like Petruchio and Kate, whose story dovetails with their own--have reached a romantic truce, she having abandoned her engagement to wealthy Washingtonian Harrison Howell (Denis Green).

The conception for the show (called *Shrew* during its preparatory stages) had come from producer Saint-Subber's experiences working backstage during the Lunts' *Taming of the Shrew* for the Theatre Guild in 1935, when he observed them bickering offstage as well as on. Saint-Subber years later suggested the idea to Samuel Spewack, who agreed to do a show on the topic if Porter would do the music and lyrics. The musical comedy inexperience of the Spewacks, the mediocre Porter track record the last few times out, the failure of Alfred Drake to find a hit since *Oklahoma!*, and the decade-long absence from Broadway of Patricia Morison (cast only after bigger stars, such as Mary Martin, turned the show down), made financing the show a major obstacle. Twenty-four auditions over a year's time were required to raise the $180,000 nut, and it took seventy backers to compile the sum. In what may have been record time, the investment was paid off in sixteen weeks.

Drake moved even higher on the ladder as Broadway's leading musical comedy actor, and Morison, lately of Hollywood, made a striking impression in her first major Broadway role. "Alfred Drake . . . is sheer perfection," wrote Rowland Field (*NEN*), "both as an extraordinarily likeable light comedian and in his many and varied singing tasks. . . . He is especially suited to the Shakespearean background of the production, for he is an actor of poise and grace in addition to his flair for nimble wit." As the second leads, Kirk and Lang were also extremely impressive, Lang making waves with his exceptional dancing (especially in "Too Darn Hot," shared with Eddie Sledge and Fred Davis).

Thomas R. Dash (*WWD*) declared the show to be "one of the merriest, wittiest, most frolicsome and most talented musical carnivals that" he had seen in many months. Richard Watts, Jr. (*NYP*), reported that this "smash hit of epic proportions" was "beautiful, tuneful, witty, gay, high-spirited and delightfully sung, acted and danced."

Hanya Holm's imaginative, eclectic choreography embraced such diverse styles as "classic ballet, modern dance, jitterbugging, soft-shoe, acrobatics, court, and folk dance," according to Walter Sorell's *Hanya Holm*. Holm, a believer in Labanotation, a system for recording dance routines in writing, had her choreography preserved in this fashion and registered under a copyright. This was the first Broadway musical to employ this practice. Sorell declared that the practice has served several vital purposes: "It has given the choreographer the possibility to be recognized as the owner of his own work, and it has established a choreographic composition as an entity apart from any specific performance of it."

KISS THEM FOR ME [Comedy/Aviation/Business/Hotel/Medicine/Military/Romance/Sex/War] A: Luther Davis; SC: Frederic Wakeman's novel, *Shore Leave*; D: Herman Shumlin; S: Frederick Fox; P: John Moses and Mark Hanna; T: Belasco Theatre; 3/20/45 (110)

Comedienne Judy Holliday made a striking debut in this "sparse and straggling" (Ward Morehouse [*NYS*]) comedy--previously called *Uncle Sugar* and *The Lonely Leave*--about three navy pilots on leave in San Francisco. The neurotic Crewson (Richard Widmark), married but indifferent to a girl back in Great Neck and father of an illegitimate child, the quiet, happily married Mac (Richard Davis), and the chubby, confused Southerner, Mississip (Dennis King, Jr.) are the navy fliers who, after three years on a carrier in the South Pacific, have four days of shore leave. They anticipate a wild time of booze, babes, and boogie-woogie in their fancy Nob Hill hotel suite. Their method of recruiting girls is to hand out cards saying, "Nylons for Sale in Room 000." This brings into their midst a goofy young war worker named Alice (Holliday), who patriotically obliges servicemen with no strings attached and soon sets her sights on Mac, although she ends up with Mississip. Shortly after the boys settle in, their time is invaded by a ship manufacturer (Robert Allen), who wants to exploit them as speech-making heroes to deter absenteeism among his workers. When they give the shipbuilder the brush-off, he angrily arranges for them to be summoned to a military hospital for a physical exam. Mississip is classified as ready for discharge because of an enlarged spleen and Crewson for noncombat duty because of fatigue. They also discover that there is a hitch in the legality of their leave papers. The red tape of the "paper navy" entangles them so unhappily that the resourceful Crewson contrives for them to escape the boredom of civilian life by stowing away on a flight to the Pacific so that they may return to flying missions against the enemy.

The play seemed to some clumsily structured, unevenly comical, and having some of its characters poorly drawn. There was a mismatch between its occasional straining for farce and its more thoughtful and realistic treatment of the difficult psychological adjustments required by men returning from combat. Wilella Waldorf (*NYP*) junked it as "confused, rambling and disjointed." It did have several favorable responses, though. Rowland Field (*NEN*), for example, maintained that it was "a very human, amusing and often poignant story." Lewis Nichols (*NYT*) liked the first two acts, but thought that the third brought down "the whole play like a pack of cards."

Holliday, before landing her part, was seriously thinking of giving up performing and becoming a writer. She scored a smashing success in her debut. "Miss Holliday, in appearance a Renoir come to life, manages to convey, even through the inanity of her lines and the squeaky nasal tones of her voice, a warmth of feeling, an animal sweetness and tenderness that is surprisingly touching," said Rosamond Gilder (*TAM*). Holliday won the Clarence Derwent Award for best supporting performance of the year.

Other parts were taken by Jayne Cotter (as a society girl with whom Crewson falls in love; the actress later became Jayne Meadows), George Mathews, Daniel Petrie, Paul Ford, Virginia Kaye, Sonya Stokowski, Edward Crandell, and John McGovern.

KORB'N [Drama/Family/Jews/Labor/Politics/Religion/Romance] A: David Blum; D: John F. Grahame; P: Modern Play Productions; T: Provincetown Playhouse (OB); 9/20/44 (24)

A semiprofessional staging of a melodrama (its title means "sacrifice" in Hebrew) set in 1935 and concerned with a Jewish papa named Abraham Cohen (John Francis) who is upset because his son Sammy (Robert Feyti) is preoccupied with left-wing union politics when he should be getting married in the temple. Similarly distraught is his fiancée Sally (Josephine Lombardo), who wants him to pay more attention to her and less to his agitational duties. But he goes his own way regardless. When a scab is killed, Sammy is arrested and charged with murder.

"The writing is at once intense, like jungle fever," argued George Jean Nathan (*TBY*), "and unrelievedly amateurish."

L

LADY, BEHAVE! [Comedy/Mental Illness/Romance/Sex/Theatre] A/D: Alfred L. Golden; S: Frederick Fox; P: Hugh Bennett; T: Cort Theatre; 11/16/43 (23)

George Jean Nathan (*TBY*) rejected this sex farce as "an amateurish succession of dialogues" deserving of "garbage-can honors." "To say that it is bad is to state the clinical details as gingerly as possible, and with the kindest of bedside manners," chimed in Lewis Nichols (*NYT*).

What was considered a tasteless plot tastelessly told concerned a mild-mannered man named George Morton (Jack Sheehan), whose ex-wife Louise (Pert Kelton) wants to fire him with ambition. She persuades him to rent the apartment of a psychiatrist who was chased out of town by a patient's irate spouse; despite his lack of professional qualifications--apart from having read a bit on the psychology of sex--he begins to receive patients, with Louise working as his secretary. His clients are all mentally unbalanced, among them an oversexed woman (Madge Skelly) who keeps snipping off pieces of men's clothing with scissors; an iceman (Thomas Hume) who is too cowardly to throw the bomb he carries around in a shoe box; a man-starved socialite (Carol Stone) who ends up marrying the iceman; and a repressed tragedienne (Lois Dow) who really wants to strip in burlesque. George uses hypnosis in order to get his clients to throw off their armor and free their libidos. He succeeds well enough to make him believe in his own powers. There is some plot flummery about the actress's husband (Karl Weber) running after Louise, and it is resolved with George retrieving her and establishing a prosperous business.

LADY COMES ACROSS, THE [Musical/Adventure/Fantasy/Hotel/Romance] B: Fred Thompson and Dawn Powell; M: Vernon Duke; LY: John Latouche; D: Romney Brent; CH: George Balanchine; S/C: Stewart Chaney; P: George Hale i/a/w Charles R. Rogers and Nelson Seabra; T: Forty-fourth Street Theatre; 1/9/42 (3)

This futile exercise was a completely revamped version of a show called *She Had to Say Yes*, starring Dennis King, that had closed out of town a year earlier. One of the few things remaining from it was Stewart Chaney's scenery, which the new version was careful to retain. Despite a host of creative talents, the show just lay there and refused to budge.

It tells of a young woman named Jill Charters (Evelyn Wyckoff, replacing English performer Jessie Matthews at the last moment when the latter became ill) who dreams that she is a European counterspy. This allows her to work with the handsome FBI agent Tony Patterson (Ronald Graham) in her search for the papers held by Nazi agent Alberto Zorel (Stiano Braggiotti). She goes to work for Zorel in his dress shop, which is a front for his espionage activities. At the estate of the wealthy and man-hungry dowager, Mrs. Riverdale (Ruth Weston), Jill manages to get the papers (which are hidden in Mrs. Riverdale's girdle), to escape from danger in the nick of time, and to marry the G-man.

"*The Lady Comes Across,*" wrote Richard Lockridge (*NYS*), "gives the impression of having been tossed together by a good many people, working in separate and probably sound proof rooms, each ignorant of the activities of the others."

Among those in the debacle were comic dancers and singers the Martins; dance team Gower and Jeanne (he was Gower Champion), who played kiss-and-make-up lovers; solo dancer Marc Plant; comedienne Wynn Murray, who had put on weight after losing it; Mischa Auer, surprisingly unfunny in a role requiring him at one point to dress in drag as a baroness; and, receiving the best reviews, nightclub star Joe E. Lewis, who sang several songs from his own repertoire, "February," "The H. V. Kaltenborn Blues," and "You Can't Get the Merchandise."

LADY IN DANGER [Comedy-Drama/Australian/Crime/Journalism/Literature/Mystery/Politics] A: Max Afford and Alexander Kirkland; D: Clarence Derwent; S: Harry Gordon Bennett; P: Pat Allen and Dan Fisher; T: Broadhurst Theatre; 3/29/45 (12)

A "clumsy and slow-going" (Ward Morehouse [*NYS*]) murder mystery that in its original version was by Max Afford alone and was set in London with the villains depicted as Nazi spies. In the revision by Afford and Kirkland, the action was moved to Melbourne, Australia, and the enemy was the Japanese, although their presence was represented by Nazi agents with Japanese flags. This was presumably more suitable, since Afford was an Australian radio writer and the play was originally staged in that country.

It is about the poisoning by a cat with curare-dipped claws of an Australia-Firster and his chauffeur (the latter's body is discovered when it falls out of a closet). The suspect is mystery novelist Monica Sefton (Helen Claire), born in Japan, knowledgeable about poisons, and married to an American war correspondent (James Gannon) whose job was endangered by the dead man's complaints. The slaying is investigated by the writer's husband and friends, and by the amusingly slow-thinking Chief Inspector Burke (Clarence Derwent, the director). The case is solved in the nick of time before the suspect is herself done to death by a lethal injection from the real murderer, a Nazi agent *cum* German psychiatrist (Kirkland, the coauthor) in the flat next door.

To George Jean Nathan (*TBY*) it was "largely the conventional mystery number, if much worse and much duller than usual." George Freedley (*NYMT*) called it "a languid play . . . dragged across the stage by a willing but slightly embarrassed cast." The company included Elfrida Derwent, Vicki Cummings, and Ronald Alexander, among others.

LADY IN THE DARK [Musical/Fantasy/Journalism/Mental Illness/Romance/Sex] B: Moss Hart; LY: Ira Gershwin; M: Kurt Weill; D: Hassard Short and Moss Hart; CH: Albertina Rasch; S: Harry Horner; C: Irene Sharaff and Hattie Carnegie; L: Hassard Short; P: Sam H. Harris; T: Alvin Theatre; 1/23/41 (162; 305; total: 467)

A revolutionary musical comedy telling the story of Liza Elliott, a fashion-magazine editor undergoing psychoanalysis to cure her of insecurity. Book writer Hart's personal experiences on the analyst's couch inspired him to write this highly successful show (originally called *I Am Listening*) that starred Gertrude Lawrence and made Danny Kaye a star in his first Broadway role. Also debuting on Broadway were Macdonald Carey and movie hunk Victor Mature. Lyricist Ira Gershwin provided lyrics for his first show since the death of brother George.

The work was originally planned as a straight play starring Katharine Cornell, but the possibilities of its dream scenes convinced Hart to turn it into a musical. In fact, apart from "My Ship," it was only during the psychoanalytic dream sequences that the songs were sung. Lawrence had to be convinced to temporarily abandon her aspirations for dramatic acting and return to musical comedy. Only when she learned that Irene Dunne was being asked to take the role did Lawrence decide to do it. Its opening had to be delayed for a week when Lawrence came down with the grippe, but after it opened, it became one of the major successes of her brilliant career. The show was taken off for eleven summer weeks because Lawrence had so stipulated in her contract, and when it resumed in September with a number of cast changes, it piled up an additional 305 performances.

This was a surprisingly literate work of considerable length and $130,000 worth of lavish spectacle and technical complexity, running almost three hours and making use of four turntables for its scenic effects. It tells of Liza Elliott's travails when she realizes that midway in her career, unable to concentrate on her work and bothered by annoying dreams, she is on the verge of a breakdown. She thinks that she is happy in her relationship with married publisher Kendall Nesbitt (Bert Lytell), who founded her magazine, but, as her reason for not marrying him, uses the excuse that his wife will not divorce him. Soon she is on the couch of Dr. Brooks (Donald Randolph), where her subconscious thoughts come to life in effectively staged and lit sequences, making abundant use of ballet and music. The work moves between the four dream sequences in which she explores her neuroses and her nerve-wracking behavior at the office, where the staff must walk on eggs and where she and Charley Johnson (Carey), the no-nonsense ad manager, are at odds. She also becomes involved with a shallow movie star, Randy Curtis (Mature). In the memorable "Circus Dream" sequence, she is put on trial for indecisiveness, with the ring master (Kaye, who also played Randall Paxton, an overtly lavender fashion photographer in Liza's waking life) as judge, Charley as the prosecutor, and Randy as defense attorney. In this sequence, Kaye sang "Tschaikowsky," a show-stopping, rapid-fire, tongue-twisting patter song made up of the names of great composers. During the same sequence Lawrence marvelously rendered the delightfully naughty, jazzily sexy, hip-swingingly raucous "The Saga of Jenny," about a miss who couldn't make up her mind. Another important fantasy sequence, "Childhood Dream," touchingly explains Liza's problems by flashing back to when Liza was a child and revealing how she was psychologically damaged by her parents telling her that she was ugly. Her inferiority complex drove her to become an aggressive career executive. Liza finally comes to the realization that many of her troubles stem from her sexual frustration in having denied her real love for Charley.

Kaye's "Tschaikowsky" number helped make him famous. Land. (*V*) commented, "On style and class . . . he ties 'em up tight. Everything is halted for the tumult. This demonstration puts Kaye in the select company of those performers who pass by the name, pillars of strength. He has the manner, the range, the quickness of a deluxe trouper." Michael Freedland wrote in *The Secret Life of Danny Kaye* that Kaye was afraid that the success of his "Tschaikowsky" (spelled "Tchaikovsky" by Freedland) would not be welcomed by Lawrence. He gradually noticed that during the run the song was not going over as well as it was supposed to. Deciding to find out why, he turned upstage during the number one night to notice that Lawrence, supposed to be harmlessly swaying there on a swing, was distracting the audience by flicking her scarf. Determined to get even, he took the swing seat for her "Jenny" number, which he dampened by raising an eyebrow and twitching his nose. Thereafter, the story goes, neither stole the other's big number. Lawrence's husband and biographer, Richard Aldrich, declared in *Gertrude Lawrence as Mrs. A* that Lawrence, angry over the upstart's success, was advised that the best way for a true star to compete with such an interloper was to top him; she thereupon revised her rehearsed, more sedate approach to "Jenny" and improvised the jazzed-up rendition that took the show back from Kaye and made the song a sensation.

Lady in the Dark arrived in a season notable for the advances being made in the musical form, vying as it did with such forward-looking works as *Cabin in the Sky*, *Pal Joey*, and *No for an Answer*, Marc Blitzstein's experimental work. The critics raved about the wonderful performances, the elaborate and opulent sets with their *a vista* turntable changes, the colorful and stylish costumes, the tuneful score, the clever lyrics, the imaginative choreography, and the entire conception, although there were certain reservations about the book. Brooks Atkinson (*NYT*), however, noted few drawbacks, saying, "The splendours of the production rise spontaneously out of the heart of the drama, evoking rather than embellishing the main theme." However, John Anderson (*NYJA*) believed that the work was dragged earthward every time the action returned to the clinical world of the doctor's office, and that it soared every time it left. "Mr. Hart's framework is his heroine's frame of mind. But somehow the Freudian implications of her trouble seem to cast shadows across a rainbow amusement." In John Mason Brown's (*NYP*) opinion, the play's stature as drama was miniscule, but as stagecraft gigantic. He found the script predictable and sluggish, but the presentation "little short of miraculous." Sidney B. Whipple (*NYWT*) had to admit that the story "becomes repetitious and dull." For all the quibbles, the script was chosen as one of the ten best plays of the year. Much honor was paid to Weill's score. Rosamond Gilder (*TAM*), for example, noted, "It builds and sustains the peculiar moods of the dream-sequences and makes possible the swift shifts in emotional color so characteristic of the dream world."

Lawrence's tour de force role, requiring her to be onstage almost throughout, was a grueling one. Brown said that it was practically a one-woman show. "And she has never given a more fascinating, disciplined, or compelling performance. . . . Miss Lawrence sings. She dances. She is all sunshine. She is troubled. She is a high school girl. She is a distressed victim of indecision. In fact, she is asked to run almost the full gamut of dramatic emotions not only from A to Z but from Z to A. . . . It is a joy . . . to note the unsparing intensity of her playing which keeps her, at her quieter moments, perched upon her high heels far off the ground." There were also fine jobs done by Margaret Dale as a sarcastic editorial assistant and Natalie Schafer in the role of fashionplate Alison Du Bois.

When the show reopened in September 1941 Eric Brotherson replaced Danny Kaye, Willard Parker replaced Victor Mature, Walter Coy replaced Macdonald Carey, and Paul McGrath replaced Bert Lytell. The show went on tour after it closed. It had a return engagement at popular prices on 2/27/43 for an additional 83 performances. New cast members included Hugh Marlowe as Charley Johnson and Richard Hale in the role of the doctor. The show was as good as ever, said all the critics.

LADY OF FATIMA [Drama/Fantasy/Period/Religion/Youth] A: Urban Nagle; D: Dennis Gurney; S/L: David Reppa; C: Irene Griffin; P: Blackfriars' Guild; T: Blackfriars' Playhouse (OB); 2/12/48 (41)

The semiprofessional actors at the Catholic theatre organization called the Blackfriars produced this pious Lenten drama--written by a priest--about the miraculous 1917 appearance of the Lady of the Rosary to a group of children in Fatima, Portugal. The keen interest of religiously oriented theatregoers was evidenced by the selling out in advance of its six-week run.

Reminiscent of *The Song of Bernadette*, the play concerns the vision of the Lady of the Rosary to two girls, Jacinta (Naomi Mitty) and Lucia (Anna Stubits), and a boy, Francisco (Edward Villella, the future ballet star), while minding their sheep. They then face the disbelief of parents, villagers, clergy, and the anticlerical government. The children undergo frightening inquisitions, are put in jail, and are even threatened with being boiled in oil. Proof that they are not lying comes when the vision reappears in a cavern. After two of the children die in an epidemic, as foretold by the Lady, Lucia, who survives, becomes a nun devoted to effecting world peace through spreading the idea of devotion to the rosary.

Certain narrative bridge scenes were staged in the heart of the auditorium, making it necessary for the four actors involved to get to and from their places quickly in the dark, but leading to a good deal of awkward stumbling about in the process. These sequences eventually were dropped and replaced by a single commentator who offered occasional remarks.

Robert Coleman (*NYDM*) thought that the play "tells an inspiring story dramatically," but George Freedley (*NYMT*) argued that "Father Nagle has not been very successful in dramatizing his true religious story because it doesn't lend itself to the theater satisfactorily." He did, however, think that the children were "the perfect child actors." A different trio shared the roles on alternate nights.

LADY SAYS YES, A [Musical/China/Fantasy/Military/Period/Sex] B: Clayton Ashley (Dr. Maxwell Maltz); M: Arthur Gershwin and Fred Spielman; LY: Stanley Adams; D: J. J. Shubert; CH: Boots McKenna (ballets: Natalie Kamarova); S: Watson Barratt; C: Lou Eisele; L: William Thomas; P: J. J. Shubert i/a/w Clayton Ashley; T: Broadhurst Theatre; 1/10/45 (87)

George Gershwin's brother Arthur wrote part of the score of this lavishly produced but "dull and commonplace" (Robert Coleman [*NYDM*]) musical that starred gorgeous blond film star Carole Landis in her stage debut. The critics set up a chorus of "nos" to its story about Lieutenant Anthony Caufield (Arthur Maxwell), a young naval officer, who enters a hospital for nasal plastic surgery (the librettist was a plastic surgeon) and falls for the woman receptionist, Ghisella (Landis). However, his virility comes into question because of an alleged Florentine superstition that a man whose nose is repaired surgically will suffer in his lovemaking capabilities. As he goes under the ether, he dreams of being in Florence with Ghisella in 1545 and then in the garden of the emperor of China. The people from the hospital scene reappear in the dream as parallel characters, with Ghisella turning up as a Venetian courtesan. In his dream he proves his masculine powers, and when he returns to reality, he wins Ghisella's love.

A lethargic production, few instances of humor, a pedestrian score, and a flimsy book pulled this show--originally titled *A Lady of ?*--down. An example of its wit was when one character was asked about his taste for Kipling and replied, "I don't know. I've never kippled." "It is an exhibit handicapped by a burdensome book and a dearth of humor and up-to-date material. For the most part it is strictly routine stuff and lacking in both pace and invention," was Rowland Fields's [*NEN*]) opinion.

Landis sang fairly well in a husky voice and looked terrific in a variety of period costumes, but her performance was not distinguished by anything special. The show-stopping number was called "Brooklyn, U.S.A.," and was an interpolation by Will Morrissey sung by Sue Ryan, the comic female lead. The comic male lead was Bobby Morris, who had a funny scene in which he boxed with a hirsute prizefighter. The show took pride in its advertised "thirty lovely ladies of fashion and passion," the two most important being eye-opening dancer-model Christine Ayres, wearing precious little, and striking-looking Jacqueline Susann. According to Susann's biographer Barbara Seaman in *Lovely Me*, the bisexual Susann and Landis had a lesbian love affair that was mirrored in several books by Susann, including the best-selling *Valley of the Dolls*. Jack Albertson and Martha King were also in the show.

LADY WHO CAME TO STAY, THE [Drama/Death/Family/Fantasy/Mental Illness/Mystery/Romance/Sex/Youth] A: Kenneth White; SC: R. E. Spencer's novel of the same name; D/P: Guthrie McClintic; S: Donald Oenslager; T: Maxine Elliott's Theatre; 1/2/41 (4)

The first Broadway play of 1941 was this unsuccessful chiller based on an old ghost story. Despite several excellent performances, particularly those of Mildred Natwick and Mady Christians, and a fine production, this morbid exercise in insanity and the supernatural was just "a silly, maudlin piece of willful adolescence that seems especially mal à propos in the modern world," thought Brooks Atkinson (*NYT*).

Three eccentric old sisters live in a spooky old Victorian mansion with Katherine (Beth Merrill), their late brother's penurious young wife. The eldest sister, Phoebe (Evelyn Varden), is mad and witchlike, the middle sister, Emma (Christians), is cruel and sadistic, and the youngest, kindest sister, Millie (Natwick), is a man-starved old maid. The older sisters, who share an incestuous love for their late sibling, vent their hatred and resentment on Katherine and her daughter, Ann (Augusta Dabney). Katherine dies, and her piano-playing ghost arrives to haunt Phoebe. The evil Phoebe angrily attacks the spook but is killed for her troubles. Phoebe and Katherine proceed to haunt the house as if they were rival ghosts. Millie sees to it that Ann leaves the house to marry her young man (Horton Heath). Emma has Katherine's young son Roger (Dickie Van Patten), who lives elsewhere, brought to the house so she can vent her hatred on him by whipping him until he is nearly dead. Then Millie dies, but not before sending young Roger away to his sister's side. Her spirit, too, returns. Emma, the one remaining sister, besieged by the three ghosts and fearing for her sanity, sets the house on fire to wipe out all the evil, herself included, thereby giving the technicians a chance to create a spectacular stage blaze.

LADY WINDERMERE'S FAN [Dramatic Revival*] A: Oscar Wilde; M: Leslie Bridgewater; D: Jack Minster; DS: Cecil Beaton; P: Homer Curran i/a/w Russell Lewis and Howard Young; T: Cort Theatre; 10/14/46 (228)

The only previous local showing of this epigrammatic 1892 Wilde comedy-drama since its 1914 production with Margaret Anglin had been a brief series of matinees in 1932. In contrast to that shoddy revival, the present one--which originated on the West Coast following a London success--was a lavish, stylishly stylized one offered with Penelope Ward in the title role, Cornelia Otis Skinner as Mrs. Erlynne, Rex Evans as Lord Augustus, Evan Thomas as Mr. Dumby, John Buckmaster as Lord Darlington, Estelle Winwood as the duchess of Berwick, Henry Daniell as Lord Windermere, and Stanley Bell as Mr. Hopper. The direction was based by Jack Minster on the notes of John Gielgud, who had staged the work successfully in London.

Cecil Beaton's extravagantly chichi sets and gorgeously colored costumes (reproduced from the London production) were a revelation and were almost worth the price of admission themselves. As Rosamond Gilder (*TAM*) observed, "Cecil Beaton has let loose on the stage a cascade of satins and laces, tiaras and waving plumes, oversized artificial flowers and upholstered furniture." Beaton also appeared in the role of the acidulously witty Cecil Graham, the first time he had acted professionally.

In general, the critics thought that the play was worth reviving and its brittle repartee still amusing, especially when it could be done as expertly as in the present case. Brooks Atkinson (*NYT*), who had several cavils about Wilde's dramaturgy, felt that the members of the company "come as close as anyone can to persuading you that there is a dance or two in the old girl yet." But John Mason Brown (*SR*) thought that the play's melodramatic contrivances were no longer capable of being taken seriously and, indeed, were conducive to laughter. The characters' behavior he found to be "patently absurd," while agreeing that their dialogue remained "wonderfully witty."

Many considered Skinner's performance one of the finest of the season. "Cornelia Otis Skinner," wrote George Freedley (*NYMT*), "has wrought a tour de force in her beautifully emotional playing . . . , topped with surface wit and brilliance. She is extraordinarily beautiful in the role, particularly in her last act costume." But Gilder felt that the actress lacked "a third dimension." Ward was even more widely praised. Euphemia Van Rensselaer Wyatt (*CW*) said that she "seems the essence of good breeding. Her Lady Windermere has a delicate rarity which makes Darlington's exit and Mrs. Erlynne's sacrifice not too high a price for salvaging her sensibilities."

LAFFING ROOM ONLY [Revue] B: Ole Olsen, Chic Johnson, and Eugene Conrad; M/LY: Burton Lane; ADD.LY: Al Dubin; D: John Murray Anderson and Edward Cline; CH: Robert Alton; S: Stewart Chaney; C: Billy Livington; P: Messrs. Shubert w/Ole Olsen and Chic Johnson; T: Winter Garden; 12/23/44 (233)

Some thought that this Olsen and Johnson madcap opus was not ready to open on Broadway and needed more tryout time (opening night suffered from numerous mishaps), but it still managed a healthy run, although nowhere near that achieved by the pair's earlier revues, *Hellzapoppin'** and *Sons o'Fun*. Like those exhibitions, it was a frenzied assortment of rough-and-tumble zany bits, songs, and dances, a good deal of it taking place in the audience, with an emphasis on broad humor, but it either was not as good as its predecessors or the formula was beginning to wear thin.

The favorite song was "Stop That Dancing," sung by pert Betty Garrett and expertly danced by William Archibald, but the number that eventually became a long-popular tune was the satirical hillbilly tune, "Feudin' and Fussin'." There were questionably tasteful political sketches spoofing Eleanor Roosevelt (the performer wore an ugly mask of the First Lady), the president, and Governor Thomas Dewey; a soldier and sailor racing around the auditorium dressed in bras and girdles; a bunch of chorus boys dressed as choir boys ending their rendition of "O Holy Night" in a stage box by shooting off blank cartridges; a man who kept popping up in the auditorium holding several squirming bunnies by their ears and shouting "Harvey!";

a midget dressed as a baby and thrown into a spectator's lap before being smacked on the head with a paper club; a man in a box shouting in the dark that he was going to shoot the rat who invaded his home and then holding up a stuffed rat when the lights came on; a man made up like a statue to resemble Rodin's *Thinker,* seen first in this guise and then on a toilet; three Russian soldiers whose rifle barrels went limp when they tried to shoot a spy, but stiffened when a scantily clad woman stepped between the spy and his executioners; and so on and on.

Dancers of note included Frances Henderson, Lou Wills, Jr., Kathryn Lee, and Kenny Buffett, as well as eccentric dance team Mata and Hari. In one of the latter's better numbers, they interpreted an entire Olympic team in all their events, including horse racing. Among the vaudeville performers in the show were Frank Libuse and the team of Willie West and McGinty.

Howard Barnes (*NYHT*) wrote that the show "sprawls across the Winter Garden stage with a singular lack of fun or taste." Robert Garland (*NYJA*) called it "a tactless, tasteless and tiresome burlesque show."

LAMP AT MIDNIGHT [Drama/Historical-Biographical/Period/Politics/Religion/Science] A: Barrie Stavis; M: André Singer; D: Boris Tumarin; S: Robert Gundlach; C: Dorothy Croissant; L: David Heilwell; P/T: New Stages (OB); 12/21/47 (51)

Barrie Stavis's Off-Broadway drama about Galileo Galilei, the controversial Renaissance scientist, opened only a couple of weeks after Brecht's *Galileo*, starring Charles Laughton. Stavis's treatment was originally planned for production by the Experimental Theatre, which then rejected it in favor of Brecht's work.

George Jean Nathan (*TBY*), while aware of its significant flaws, especially its reliance on "protracted argumentation," considered it "by far the better of the two." Euphemia Van Rensselaer Wyatt (*CW*) insisted, "Emphatically *Lamp at Midnight* is much the better play." Brooks Atkinson (*NYT*) agreed, reporting that it was "a deeply moving play with a passionate theme and a resolute point of view." Others, though, deemed it inferior. Robert Garland (*NYJA*) believed that Brecht's was "the better play" and that this was a talky and unwieldy work. George Freedley (*NYMT*), while approving certain scenes, claimed, "It is mostly a pedestrian and confused drama of greater weightiness than dramatic effect." Richard Watts, Jr. (*NYP*), straddled the fence, finding problems with both works: "The Brecht play . . . possessed a more striking intellectual content, but the Stavis work has greater emotional forcefulness."

The character of Galileo (Peter Capell) in this version is far less the sensual glutton made of him by Brecht (and Laughton) and far more the pious Catholic, whose rejection by the Church is thus made more poignant and the Church's policies and methods (the Inquisition) more reprehensible. Galileo's struggle to reconcile his scientific interests (particularly his confirmation of the Copernican system) with his religious devotion occupy much of the action. A central scene is the one between Cardinal Bellarmine (Paul Mann) and Galileo in which the cleric informs the scientist that the result of telling men of the real center of the universe would be to create new heresies. Galileo ultimately submits to the Inquistion's pressures. He does so not out of physical fear but because he believes that he will be damned if he is responsible for fostering a schism of faith. The story is told in many scenes with many characters. A revolve--which proved noisy and awkward--was used to shift the scenes.

The cast included Ralph Camargo as Sagredo Niccolini, Florentine ambassador to the Vatican, Kermit Murdock as Cardinal Barberini, Paul Mann as Firenzuola, Kathryn Eames as Galileo's daughter Polissema, and Dorothy Patten as the mother superior. Others in the large company included Martin Balsam, Willard Swire, Jay Barney, Joe Silver, Michael Howard, and Leon Janney.

Just as there was disagreement over the relative value of Brecht's and Stavis's dramas, so was there critical difference over who made the better Galileo, Laughton or Capell. Similarly, some thought the production outstanding, and others said that it was inferior.

LAND IS BRIGHT, THE [Drama/Business/Crime/Family/Military/Old Age/

Period/Politics/Romance/War/Youth] A: George S. Kaufman and Edna Ferber; D: George S. Kaufman; S/L: Jo Mielziner; C: Irene Sharaff; P: Max Gordon; T: Music Box Theatre; 10/28/41 (79)

Thirty actors were in the cast of this superficially impressive chronicle play whose creative team was one of the best of the time. The work--earlier called *Three Acts*--was crammed with action covering three generations in the family dynasty founded by Lacy Kincaid (Ralph Theadore), nineteenth-century industrial tycoon, who built the $5-million Fifth Avenue mansion in which the entire play transpires.

"It is a play of events and pasteboard people," sighed Rosamond Gilder (*TAM*). "Every one of the incidents and even the characters might easily be found recorded in the memoirs and memories of America's first families, yet all this possible authenticity does not make *The Land Is Bright* seem real. . . . Its intent is presumably to present the *mores* of typical American millionaires, but the net result is an ingenious, swift-moving melodrama which derives its precedents not from life but from the stage." "Generous in eye appeal, it is emotionally meager, bitterly satiric and below the entertainment standard of previous work by the authors," concluded Flin. (*V*). And Louis Kronenberger (*PM*), who admitted that it was engrossing, claimed, "Not a thing in the play is real; not a thing is even life-sized. The interpretation is not merely hackneyed and hand-me-down; but even what truth might reside in the triteness is lost in a flood of extravagance and exaggeration."

The patriotic play, which takes its title from a poem by Arthur Clough, quoted by Winston Churchill in a memorable speech of hope in April 1941, tells of the degeneration of a wealthy family and of its ultimate regeneration in the face of World War II (which, the play intimated, the United States should enter). Through the play many of the characters grow older, requiring several changes of makeup.

It begins in the 1890s in the tastelessly elaborate expanses of the mansion Kincaid has built for his wife and children with the money he earned as a Western robber baron involved with the ruthless acquisition of railroads, copper, and the like. He spends his millions on such follies as buying a middle-aged Polish count (Arnold Moss) for his eighteen-year-old daughter, Tana (Martha Sleeper), to marry, because his onetime waitress and now social-climbing wife (Phyllis Povah) thinks it the thing to do. Son Grant (Leon Ames) rejects the society girl his folks had picked for him in favor of a chorus girl (Muriel Hutchison). Soon after, Lacy is shot by his old mining partner (G. Albert Smith), from whom he has stolen securities. Twenty years pass, and the now-anti-American Tana is preparing for her fourth Continental marriage. It is the age of Prohibition, and her brother Grant, now the successful head of the clan, is father to three flaming youths who frequent speakeasies. His reckless daughter Linda (Diana Barrymore) is not only involved with a gangster but accessory to a murder. One son, Wayne (Hugh Marlowe), is a hedonist, and another, Theodore (William Roerick), is a spoiled mama's boy who gets kicked out of Harvard. The play then moves to 1941 on the occasion of Grant's seventieth birthday, when the aged Tana has decided to return home from Europe to live in America, which she belatedly has come to appreciate. Her son (Arnold Moss) by the count is now in a Nazi concentration camp, and she is going to ransom him. Theodore has died (Linda's gangster friend shot him); Wayne is working as a dollar-a-year man in Washington; and Linda, whom Grant holds responsible for Theodore's death, returns from the West with her hard-working rancher husband (Robert Shayne); despite having redeemed herself, she is ignored by her bitter father. Grant offers Wayne control of his business interests, but Wayne turns him down and Grant begins to understand that the Kincaid way is not the best way, and that it is time to give and not to take so that a new moral order may be established for the future of society. Grant concedes that something must be done to wipe out Hitler. His air-cadet grandson (John Draper) replies with the patriotic tag line, "We'll fix that."

Dickie Van Patten, Grover Burgess, Flora Campbell, and Louise Larabee were among the actors involved in what was recognized as an outstandingly acted, directed, and designed piece of theatre.

LAND OF FAME [Drama/Military/Politics/Romance/War] A: Albert and Mary Bein; SC: an original story by Charles Paver and Albert Bein; M: Joseph Wood; D:

Albert Bein; S: Frederick Fox; C: Grace Houston; P: Albert Bein and Frederick Fox; T: Belasco Theatre; 9/21/43 (6)

A flop play about Greek resistance fighters that afforded radio actor Ed Begley a chance to make his Broadway debut. His role was that of a bullying German general named von Obermann.

Occupied Greece in the summer of 1942 is the drama's setting. Its central characters are a band of guerrillas, mostly peasants, fighting in the hills to bring democracy back to their country. The action shifts between the Nazis' general headquarters in the town of Talom and the various hideouts of the guerrillas in the hills. The leader of the guerrillas is Peter Melinas (Norman Rose), a former officer in the Greek army. He leads his band on sabotage raids under cover of darkness, seriously upsetting the occupying forces. Trying to determine Peter's whereabouts, the Nazis torture people, including a shepherd boy (Kenneth Le Roy) and Peter's fiancée Angela (Beatrice Straight). The Nazis hold the people of Talom hostage and promise to kill them if Peter does not give himself up. A Byron-quoting Gestapo man, Lieutenant Werner (Stefan Schnabel), has grown disgusted with his side and decides to betray it. He sacrifices his life for the guerrilla cause, and his death is a signal to Peter and his men to rush in and overcome the Nazis, which they do in a shoot-'em-up finale, although Peter dies in the battle.

The play lacked cohesion, being too loosely structured, failed to clearly distinguish among the minor characters, became artificially melodramatic and self-consciously theatrical, and, despite some name actors, was uninspiringly performed. For example, Beatrice Straight, ultimately an Academy Award winner, "hung up a record for amateurishness in acting, which I think will be hard to beat this season," according to Burton Rascoe (*NYWT*). However, Begley got some good reviews, Kelcey Allen (*WWD*) reporting, "His study of the shrewd and vicious commanding officers is admirable in substance and detail. Mr. Begley is a middle-aged actor and why New York was never given a chance to see him until the arrival of this play is one of the many mysteries of the theatre."

The material was also getting to seem old-hat on Broadway, which recently had had several similarly themed plays, most notably *The Moon Is Down*. "The Beins simply haven't written a play brilliant enough to rise above the general monotony of the routine anti-Nazi plays that have gone before," declared Wilella Waldorf (*NYP*). The cast included Whitford Kane as an old wagon maker turned guerrilla, Richard Basehart as a Nazi, and Royal Dana Tracy, Karl Weber, and Jack Bittner as Greeks.

LAND'S END [Drama/Friendship/Hotel/Romance/Sex] A: Thomas Job; SC: Mary Ellen Chase's novel, *Dawn in Lyonesse*; M: Paul Bowles; D: Robert Lewis; DS: Donald Oenslager; P: Paul Feigay i/a/w George Somnes; T: Playhouse; 12/11/46 (5)

The action of this uninvolving work was set in the gloomy Cornwall locations of St. Ives and Tintagel and was a modern retelling of the medieval legend of Tristan and Iseult, associated with the region. Donald Oenslager provided five sets heavy with brooding symbolism, and Paul Bowles added heavily portentous music. "Unfortunately," reported Rosamond Gilder (*TAM*), "neither the script nor the actors could support the required mood, nor was Robert Lewis' direction sufficiently fluent or inventive to enrich a thin narrative." "Where it aims to be poetic it is merely verbose. Where it strives to be tragic it is only heavily lugubrious," wrote Richard Watts, Jr. (*NYP*).

Ellen Pascoe (Helen Craig) is a fish chopper engaged to Derek Tregonny (Walter Coy), a fisherman. He is also loved by Ellen's best friend, Susan Pengilly (Shirley Booth), another fish chopper. During a stint serving well-to-do guests at the small but fashionable Tower Hotel, a young American professor (Theodore Newton) gives her to read the legend of Tristan and Iseult, and she starts to imagine her romance with Derek in terms of the famous story. When Susan reveals to her that she is in love with an engaged man, Ellen, not realizing that the man is Derek, encourages her friend to pursue her happiness at all costs. Thus Derek betrays Ellen with Susan, but eventually his split loyalties prompt him to jump off a cliff at Land's End. At his dismal funeral, the two women decide that they need each other's friendship.

Frieda Altman, Fred Stewart, Merle Maddern, Jay Barney, and Minnie Dupree were in the cast.

LAST DANCE, THE (***Dödsdansen***) [Dramatic Revival*] A: August Strindberg; AD: Peter Goldbaum and Robin Short; SC: August Strindberg's drama, *The Dance of Death* (*Dödsdansen*); D: John O'Shaughnessy; DS: Ralph Alswang; P: James Russo and Michael Ellis i/a/w Theatre Associates, Inc.; T: Belasco Theatre; 1/27/48 (7)

A free adaptation of Strindberg's 1901 drama (produced in 1905) of a love-hate marital relationship, with the action shifted from Sweden to a colonial outpost on a semitropical island in 1910. There also were a number of other radical revisions. The piece had a strong company, with Oscar Homolka as Edgar, the overbearing major; Jessie Royce Landis as Alice, his wife of two decades, who despises him; Philip Bourneuf as Curtis, the doctor she loves; Anne Jackson as Judith, Edgar and Alice's daughter; and Richard Hylton as Curtis's son Alan.

This was the play's first New York staging in English, a more faithful German version having been seen in 1923. It was "so incredibly dull," reported Howard Barnes (*NYHT*), that even these actors "are stopped dead in their tracks." George Jean Nathan (*TBY*), acknowledging the relative faithfulness of the plot's externals to the original, castigated the adaptors for having "executed on the innards of the play [what] amounts to a gall-bladder operation performed with a sherbet spoon." However, it received warmer reviews from several others, such as Thomas R. Dash (*WWD*), who thought it "a fitfully intriguing play which builds up cumulatively after a fearfully slow start." He thought that it let down at spots, but possessed "characterizations that are eminently true and convincing." Like others, though, he accused it of being static and uninterestingly verbose.

The main action concerns the quarreling, drunken major, manipulative military governor of the island, and his unhappy wife, each blaming the other for their misery, although the cruel husband is chiefly to blame. He interferes in his best friend Curtis's life, being responsible for the breakup of Curtis's marriage. Curtis attempts to place the island hospital under a civil administration, but Edgar obstructs this plan and establishes a military rule for the institution. He meddles as well in the romance of Judith and Alan, trying to substitute an aging officer for the latter in his daughter's affections. These and other irritating things lead Alice to long for the major's death. Her wishes are finally satisfied when, after an argument with Judith, he dies of a stroke. Although he is dead, he continues to hold his wife in his grip, for, as John Chapman (*NYDN*) observed, "Her hatred and fear of him are all that is left her to live by."

The performances of Landis, Jackson, and Bourneuf were admired, but Homolka walked off with the honors as the verminous, surly major.

LAST GENERATION, THE [Drama/Family/Politics/War] A: David Millman; D: Sibyl Ward; S: Patricia Reynolds; P: Max Malin and David Millman; T: Malin Studio (OB); 12/15/42 (2)

The Malin Studio on West Forty-fourth Street was converted to a theatre for several productions, although it originally was used as a rehearsal hall. *The Last Generation* was a self-styled "timely melodrama about an invasion of England," but the result was what Rose. (*V*) called "a meaningless, undramatic play." Acted by a third-rate company, it was set in 1940 and concerned the capture by an English farm family of a pair of Nazi spies and the successful prevention of a Nazi invasion from Europe.

The only latent talent shown was by Robert Kibbee, son of character actor Guy Kibbee. "The direction and acting are so incredibly bad," announced George Freedley (*NYMT*), that he refused to mention any names.

LAST STOP [Comedy-Drama/Business/Crime/Old Age] A: Irving Kaye Davis; D: Erwin Piscator; S: Samuel Leve; C: Rose Bogdanoff; P: Victor Hugo-Vidal; T: Forrest Theatre; 9/5/44 (23)

Erwin Piscator, famed European director then living in New York, had not convinced local critics of his expertise in previous outings, nor did his reputation make any advances with this "silly and soporific" (Howard Barnes [*NYHT*]) mélange of comedy and maudlin melodrama. Only the performances of the leading players prevented the evening from being a total loss.

The arrogant socialite Catherine Chandler (Catherine Doucet) has obtained possession of an old ladies' home through questionable means and runs it to squeeze as much profit from it as possible, to the detriment of its pathetic aged residents. A newcomer to the home is a senior citizen named Mrs. Anna Haines (Minnie Dupree), who discovers that the home belonged to her father and was foreclosed by the present proprietor under suspicious circumstances. Mrs. Chandler wants to sell the place for a sizable sum to a nightclub owner and move the old ladies to a rickety but profitable firetrap. This prompts Mrs. Haines to lead the senior citizens on a hunger strike. To stop her, Mrs. Chandler frames the old lady on a charge of arson, but, with the aid of an old gardener (Seth Arnold), Mrs. Haines proves that her nemesis stole the house. Then, after telling off her own avaricious family (Raymond Bailey, Mavis Freeman, and Effie Afton), she takes it over herself to be run the proper way.

"The satire is but half cooked, the melodrama late in developing, the drama calculated to give one the jitters and the comedy macabre," shivered Robert Coleman (*NYDM*). The play lacked a clear story line and effective dramatic conflict, said George Freedley (*NYMT*). He noted that Piscator "has handled a number of his group scenes effectively but has laid on his melodrama much too heavily and has failed to articulate even the inadequate story which the author provided."

One of the production's major problems was the practically inaudible performance of Doucet, whom the critics took to task. The cast included Enid Markey, Frederica Going, Mary Gildea, Nell Harrison, Daisy Belmore, Grace Valentine, and Eda Heinemann, among others.

LATE CHRISTOPHER BEAN, THE [Dramatic Revival*] A: Sidney Howard; D: Justina Wayne; P: Equity Library Theatre; T: Hudson Park Branch of the New York Public Library (OB); 5/1/45 (2)

One of thirty-seven productions staged in the 1944-1945 season by the young Equity Library Theatre project, most of them ignored by reviewers. In the case of *The Late Christopher Bean*, "the rather slipshod revival . . . proved nothing so much as that the play is still practically indestructible," noted the sole critic attending, George Freedley (*NYMT*). Director Wayne acted the role of Abby very well, Robert Ober was Dr. Haggett, David Bell was Warren Cramer, and Ralph Wallace was the art critic.

LATE GEORGE APLEY, THE [Comedy/Family/Period/Romance/Youth] A: John P. Marquand and George S. Kaufman; SC: John P. Marquand's novel of the same name; D: George S. Kaufman; S/C: Stewart Chaney; P: Max Gordon; T: Lyceum Theatre; 11/21/44 (384)

A Pulitzer Prize novel of 1938 was the source for this hit play (one of the season's ten best) satirizing the upper-class Brahmins of Boston. When it tried out in that city, it was pleasantly received, apart from technical objections to several factual comments in the dialogue, and was deemed an accurate observation of the previous generation of Bostonians. Kaufman subsequently defended some of the historical liberties he and Marquand had taken, such as placing Felix Frankfurter on the Harvard faculty a full two years before he actually taught there, and a reference to the Copley Plaza Hotel, not yet built in the year of the play's action. The play was an expert collaboration by a writer, Marquand, who claimed to know nothing of dramaturgy, and one, Kaufman, who knew nothing of Boston. Kaufman's masterfully restrained and ungagged direction (unlike his usual style) was a major reason for the play's acceptance.

A big difference between the play and the novel is the latter's concern with the entire life of George Apley, while the play focuses only on eight days in 1912, with a brief epilogue set thirty years later. A considerable number of internal differences between the play and the novel exist, but the play captures the spirit of the book, if not its specific plot details.

Leisurely action was balanced by an abundance of laughter in this nostalgic comedy dealing with the wealthy George Apley (Leo G. Carroll), a well-born, highly respectable Bostonian, married to Catherine (Janet Beecher) and father of two, Eleanor (Joan Chandler) and John (David McKay). They and most of their class-conscious Beacon Hill relatives regard Boston as the center of the universe and consider those from elsewhere as nothing short of foreigners. George epitomizes Beacon Hill insularity. The rebellious John Apley falls in love with a Worcester girl whose father is a manufacturer in the dyeing business; this knocks the stuffy George for a loop. He struggles to maintain his dignity and poise while being pressured by a more realistic relative, cousin Roger (Percy Waram), to accede. Finally, he decides in favor of the match. "Worcester isn't Boston," he announces, "but it is in Massachusetts." However, the girl's blunt father (Howard St. John) prevents the marriage on the grounds that certain types of people simply do not mix. More trouble stems from daughter Eleanor, who is enamored of a Yale man (John Conway) who hails from Greenwich Village and gives lectures at Harvard that actually poke fun at the poetry of Ralph Waldo Emerson. This relationship succeeds. In the epilogue, which takes place in 1942 after the death of George (thus the title), John, who has made a socially correct marriage to cousin Agnes (Margaret Phillips), shows signs of turning into a man very much like his late dad. Throughout the play are scenes and lines satirical of Boston smugness and rigidity.

The critics noted that not much happened in the work, but that it had excellent dialogue and character depictions. There was disagreement over whether it was as effective as the novel, and some took issue with a few Broadway wisecracks that Kaufman apparently had injected into the otherwise appropriate dialogue. However, the overall reception was highly positive. Wilella Waldorf (*NYP*) said that the play "is genuinely comic in the best theatrical sense." Howard Barnes (*NYHT*) considered it "a brilliant comedy of manners," replete with "substance, humor and a pervasive period atmosphere." Ward Morehouse (*NYS*) praised it as "an urbane, literate and completely charming play." But Louis Kronenberger (*PM*) claimed it to be inferior to its source and to be "a little thin, a little too mixed up in its tone, and more than a little repetitious in its humor." Rosamond Gilder (*TAM*) maintained, "When the emphasis of the play veers toward the young people's tenuous love affairs, its sentimentality increases while its laughter dies away."

Leo G. Carroll had one of his finest roles as George Apley and was commended highly for his excellent performance. In preparing for it, he was taken by Marquand to the latter's Boston club to soak up the proper Brahmin atmosphere. The value of the excursion hit home when Marquand attempted to register the actor at the door and the old man there, learning that Carroll was a New Yorker, gave him a separate guest book to sign, the one reserved for non-Bostonians or "aliens." Wrote Burton Rascoe (*NYWT*), "Leo G. Carroll turns in a masterpiece of a performance as George Apley, blending his comical characterization of a lamentable stuff-shirt with just enough touches of dignity and pathos to make the portrait seem warmly human and not a caricature." Others in the outstanding cast included Mrs. Priestly Morrison, Byron Russell, Margaret Dale, Reynolds Evans, Catherine Proctor, Ivy Troutman, and Sayre Crawley.

LAUGH TIME [Revue] P: Paul Small and Fred Finklehoffe, Jr.; T: Shubert Theatre; 9/8/43 (126)

Paul Small and Fred Finklehoffe were among the producers attempting to revive vaudeville in the early forties by mounting such shows in legitimate theatres. Like their *Show Time* and *Big Time* (the latter did not come to New York), it originated on the West Coast. The producers placed a note in the program: "We have never conceded the corpus delicti. We have disbanded the pallbearers, halted the requiem, on the laudable suspicion that *Laugh Time* will demonstrate that the burial of vaudeville, circa 1932, was premature." The result, said Scho. (*V*), was "an outstanding click in the pure vaudeville metier." It offered twelve shows a week, including five matinees and a show on Sunday.

The show's best-known performers were Ethel Waters, comics Bert Wheeler and Frank Fay, tap dancers Buck and Bubbles (who also went in for some piano playing [Bubbles] and singing [Buck]), and the popular dog act, the Bricklayers. Ballroom dancers Jane and Adam Di Gatano, apache dancers Lucienne and Ashour, and trampoline acrobats Adriana and Charly were among others on the bill.

Fay won plaudits for his expert comic telling of shaggy-dog stories and for his handling of MC duties. Euphemia Van Rensselaer Wyatt (*CW*) said that he "is able to raise laughs without any apparent effort and to be funny without being coarse. His own restraint increases as the audience grows more boisterous but he can tell the pulse of their humor like an old practitioner and he has the gift of making his dry sallies sound spontaneous." One of his most appreciated gags concerned an actor who earlier had been so good a salesman that he sold a widow who was burying her husband a suit with an extra pair of pants.

High-hatted and impish Bert Wheeler was also good, doing his standard act of eating (usually an apple, but this time a sandwich) while talking to the audience about his troubles, especially those with the producers. His stories included one about how he was talking to his girl in a phone booth when one of the producers commandeered the phone, ordering both Wheeler and the girl out of the booth. Fay and Wheeler appeared often in tandem, with Wheeler being Fay's straight man.

The great singer Ethel Waters began her performance singing a series of numbers in a dignified concert style while standing beside a piano, her numbers including "Taking a Chance on Love," "Happiness Is a Thing Called Joe," "Heat Wave," "Cabin in the Sky," and "Stormy Weather." Rosamond Gilder (*TAM*) found that this manner of presentation did not suit her neariy so well as when she sang her songs within the context of a dramatic structure with a characterization to give life to the music.

An apology was made to the first-night audience that the scenery had been lost en route from the coast, but the critics said that no scenery was needed and that the allegedly substitute velours used to back the show were sufficient for all purposes.

LAUGH, TOWN, LAUGH [Revue] P: Ed Wynn; T: Alvin Theatre; 6/22/42 (65)

A straight vaudeville show starring Ed Wynn and appreciated for its expert blend of comedy, music, and various specialty numbers. The company, notable for its international flavor, included lovely singer Jane Froman, whose throaty, if overacted, vocalizations included "Tea for Two," "Sleepy Lagoon," "I'm Breathless," "One Dozen Roses," "Three Little Sisters," and "Don't Sit under the Apple Tree." George Jean Nathan (*TBY*) compared her to "blues singers so vain of their vocal gifts that they render Broadway juke-box songs as if they were operas by Wagner." Also on the program were badminton champions Ken Davidson and Hugh Forgie; priceless comic duo Smith and Dale with their inimitable "Dr. Kronkheit" sketch; fiery flamenco artist Carmen Amaya, backed by a large number of musical relatives; the Herzogs, an Australian trapeze act consisting of a quintet of young women; a dog act, Hector and Pals; the Russian choral group, the Volga Singers; a singing, dancing, and acrobatic act from Argentina called the Hermanos Williams Trio; and the hilarious Portuguese juggler-ventriloquist, Señor Wences, who drew humor from his conversation with a dummy he drew on the side of his hand and with another that was just a head in a box. Lewis Nichols (*NYT*) said, "He can smoke, sneeze and box the compass verbally all at once."

Ed Wynn was his Perfect Fool self, with his funny hats, silly jokes, and crazy gadgets, some new, some old; he tied the many acts together with his constant comings and goings. Wynn performed with a broken hand, the result of a rehearsal accident with a mule and a breakaway cart. Not only did it fail to hinder him, he made comic sport out of it, using his cast as one more weapon in his arsenal of humor. Wynn made his entrance from a huge hot dog, punning about stepping out of his roll in the show. During the intermission he rambled through the house, asking the orchestra at one point on opening night to play "The Sidewalks of New York" in honor of former governor Al Smith.

The vaudeville shows of the early forties posed as revues by being given specific titles. Barely any scenery was used and there were no original sketches. Herrick Brown (*NYS*) commented, "We haven't run across any better cure for the blues in some time than Mr. Wynn's new show. If most bills had been half as good as that concocted by the self-styled Perfect Fool, vaudeville would never have died out in the first place."

LAURA [Drama/Crime/Mystery/Romance/Sex] A: Vera Caspary and George Sklar; SC: Vera Caspary's novel of the same name; D: Clarence Derwent; S: Stewart Chaney; C: Robert Lanza; P: H. Clay Blaney i/a/w S. P. and Roy P. Steckler b/s/a/w Hunt Stromberg, Jr.; T: Cort Theatre; 6/26/47 (44)

Several plays of the 1940s were based on material that already had been successful as films. One example was *Rebecca*; another was *Laura*, which used the same story as the 1944 movie of the same name, famous for its haunting theme song. As was true of *Rebecca*, the play was second-rate in comparison with the movie. A few critics mildly appreciated it, such as Euphemia Van Rensselaer Wyatt (*CW*), who placed it "in the upper register of melodramas. True it never acquires the eerie atmosphere nor continuous thrills of *Angel Street* but its characters come to life and dominate the action." But Brooks Atkinson (*NYT*) felt that none of the unappetizing characters "seems worth a whole evening in the theatre, despite the ingenious plot." George Jean Nathan (*TBY*) thought that more talented hands it could have been handled more effectively, "but in these it has become simply another garrulous and stenciled failure." A crucial problem in transferring the story to the stage was the need to offer important exposition in dialogue that the movie was able to handle in flashbacks.

The tale is sparked by the discovery of a murdered woman found in the apartment of Laura Hunt (K. T. Stevens, daughter of movie director Sam Wood), an advertising writer. It is believed that the beautiful Laura is the victim, although it is impossible to verify because the face has been shot away with a sawed-off shotgun. Laura's fiancé Shelby Carpenter (Tom Rutherford) is a suspect. After the funeral, Laura herself turns up, still alive, having spent the weekend in the country. The victim turns out to be a friend who had been using the apartment. Before he meets the living Laura, handsome, literate Detective Mark McPherson (Hugh Marlowe) falls in love with her from her portrait. After he gets to know her, he marries her. The clues implicate Laura herself, but Detective McPherson refuses to believe her guilty. The perpetrator turns out to be the witty, middle-aged, hedonistic writer Waldo Lydecker (Otto Kruger), in love with Laura, but impotently unable to physically express his feelings.

Kruger (who replaced John Loder during the tryout period) received several strong reviews for his unctuously superior manner, but Stevens was not widely approved. When the play had failed out of town the previous season, Miriam Hopkins had held the leading role.

LEADING LADY, THE [Comedy-Drama/Marriage/Period/Romance/Theatre] A: Ruth Gordon; D: Garson Kanin; S/L: Donald Oenslager; C: Mainbocher; P: Victor Samrock and William Fields; T: National Theatre; 10/18/48 (8)

Ruth Gordon wrote and starred in this turkey, and it was directed by her husband. Neither could bring it to life, although Gordon's acting was considered better than her writing.

The nostalgia-laden play is set in the years from 1899 to 1902 and has a theatrical theme. It concerns a glamorous husband-and-wife starring team, Gerald (Ian Keith) and Gay Marriott (Gordon). Gerald is a self-centered, socially conscious, and bullyingly abusive husband. The devoted Gay, once a chambermaid, forgives him his faults. Gerald makes a comeback after an illness, but a critic (John Carradine) so incenses him by his regard for Gay that he throws a tantrum and dies. The devoted Gay is unable to escape his grip over her and to get her life or career back on track. She soon is plagued by debt. Two years of failure lead to her retirement, but the faith shown in her by Harry (Wesley Addy), a romantically interested playwright, restores her faith in herself, and she prepares herself for a successful return to the footlights.

Gay's character, thought Brooks Atkinson (*NYT*), was ineffectively dramatized and less interesting than the lesser characters who surround her, causing the play to seem "curiously elusive and fitfully eventful." Gordon's "nervous brilliance, several expert supporting portrayals, and an ornamental production," wrote Howard Barnes (*NYHT*), "do very little to hide a want of invention, wit and genuine feeling."

Good work was put in by Ethel Griffies as an old character actress, William J. Kelly as another stage veteran, Mildred Dunnock as Gay's maid, Douglass Watson as a stage manager, Margot Stevenson as a character based on Maude Adams, James MacColl as a character based on Clyde Fitch, and Brooke Byron as a young actress. Among others in the play were Margaret Barker, Sonia Sorel, Ossie Davis, and Guy Spaull.

LEAF AND BOUGH [Drama/Alcoholism/Family/Romance/Rural/Sex/Small Town] A: Joseph Hayes; D: Rouben Mamoulian; S/L: Carl Kent; P: Charles P. Heidt; T: Cort Theatre; 1/21/49 (3)

Joseph Hayes's first play showed glints of promise, but was far from suitable Broadway fare. It sought to explore the differences between two midwestern families, one living on a farm and one in the local small town. The action shifted from one Indiana household to the other in alternating scenes.

The Warrens are the respectable farm family, riddled with various psychological misfits. The Campbells are the town family, a decadent and mean-spirited brood, including an alcoholic father (Anthony Ross), a neurotically discontented mother (Alice Reinhart), and bibulous, lecherous brother Glenn (Charlton Heston). Farm girl Nan Warren (Coleen Gray) and music-loving bank clerk Mark Campbell (Richard Hart) fall in love. The families object and interfere, and Nan's father makes her leave home. Glenn, unable to bear the loss of Mark, begs the father to steal Mark's savings and temporarily convinces Mark of Nan's unfaithfulness. Mark then rapes Nan on a hilltop. Love sputters and nearly dies, but, following the death of Nan's wise old grandfather (William Jeffrey), is rekindled at the end when Mark asks for and receives forgiveness.

Hayes's writing had poetic touches that reminded some of Tennessee Williams (*Summer and Smoke* seemed a likely influence), but it was ultimately doomed by murky ideas and mannerisms. It also was not helped by too ambitious a production, including excessively detailed settings, and directorial pretentiousness that swamped the play's simplicity. George Jean Nathan (*TBY*) said that the author wrote "consistently in purple ink, platitude, and theatrical stencils," and that his characters were "as lifeless as senescent rubber." Richard Watts, Jr. (*NYP*), noted some powerful moments, but decided that Hayes had, on the whole, "set down some very maudlin scenes and some extremely tedious and unpersuasive characters." Tom McElhaney (as an alcoholic doctor), Jared Reed, David White, Dorothy Elder, Louise Buckley, and Mary Linn Beller were in the play.

The play had had its first staging at Margo Jones's Dallas theatre. Hayes, who would gain fame as the author of the novel and play *The Desperate Hours* several years later, was disgusted with the experience, feeling that he had been betrayed. He said that he was so anxious to get the production on that he revised the play as requested by the producer and director until the result was a distortion of the original. He came to the realization that neither man really knew what he was talking about and tried in vain to have the play closed out of town. "By the time I realized what had happened, not only had the script lost all resemblance to what I had been trying to do, but the play had been miscast in some cases and the sets had been built as realistic and detailed as a Hollywood set--all against the grain and mood of the play as conceived" (quoted in Jack Gaver, *Curtain Calls*).

LEAVE IT TO CHARLEY [Musical/Yiddish Language] B: Louis Freiman and Isador Friedman; M: Abe Ellstein; LY: Isidor Lillian and Jacob Jacobs; D: Menasha Skulnik and Isador Goldstein; CH: Lillian Shapero; S: Michael Saltzman; P: Menasha Skulnik; T: Second Avenue Theatre (OB); 2/13/49

Yiddish clown Menasha Skulnik entertained in Yiddish with large dollops of English thrown in in this musical comedy, which was much like his other vehicles. Although it was fast-paced and pleasantly engaging as a show, the real cause for delight lay in Skulnik's performance. As Richard Watts, Jr. (*NYP*), declared, "It has the virtue of being lively and passably tuneful, and the chorus is properly willing and industrious. But it is not being unfair to say that everything else is just a stage wait for its star."

Skulnik was a shy little milkman named Charley Cucumber who is sent by his best friend, composer Victor (Leon Liebgold), to tell the composer's fiancée Evelyn (Lilly Lilliana) that he--the composer--can not keep his date because he has to go to Denver, where his mother has just died. This leads to much confusion when Charley errs in his mission; Charley winds up taking Evelyn to a cabaret, getting drunk, and marrying her. Meanwhile, he is being pursued by two other women (Yetta Zwerling and Anna Teitelbaum). But before the nuptials can be consummated, Victor returns and the plot entanglements get untangled.

Skulnik sang a number of very funny songs, such as "I Can't Describe It But I Know What I Want," "Charley Knows His History," and, with the audience joining in, "I'm Not in a Hurry, I Got Plenty Time." A highlight was his medley with costar Zwerling, in which they parodied popular song hits as she indefatigably wooed him and he held her at bay.

Skulnik, with "his usual deadpan antics, his facetious gait and the little aftermath hop" (Thomas R. Dash [*WWD*]) was a big success. Top support was offered by Jacob Susanoff and Anne Winters.

LEND AN EAR [Revue] SK/M/LY: Charles Gaynor; ADD. SK: Joseph Stein and Will Glickman; D: Hal Gerson and Gower Champion; CH: Gower Champion; DS: Raoul Pène du Bois; P: William R. Katzell, Franklin Gilbert, and William Eythe; T: National Theatre; 12/16/48 (460)

Carol Channing blazed into stardom via her appearance in this delightful intimate revue in which she was just one of a number of barely known, but unusually talented young performers. The piece had been written seven years earlier and premiered at Carnegie Tech in Pittsburgh, where William Eythe was then a theatre student. This production was followed by another at Cohasset, Massachusetts, in a summer-stock theatre. Eythe tried to interest Broadway in it, but his efforts were interrupted by the war and his own burgeoning career as a stage and screen leading man. In 1948 he became involved in producing at the tiny Las Palmas Theatre in Los Angeles, and offered *Lend an Ear* as one of his presentations. Broadway now lent an ear to the show, which had cost $30,000 in Los Angeles and would need over three times that sum in New York. The show, by now, had evolved from the original Pittsburgh version and included a lot of new material and revisions of the old songs and sketches. Eythe, a straight leading man in the movies, demonstrated surprising musical comedy abilities in the show.

Brooks Atkinson (*NYT*) judged that the offering was "a model of skill and taste in this style of fooling." "There is not a dull number in the carload," bravoed Thomas R. Dash (*WWD*), "and some of the skits are brilliant in their lampooning." Gower Champion's athletic choreography came in for wide approval.

The show began by introducing the company as though its members were at a rehearsal for the material to follow. That material provided a mostly very funny bag of satirical sketches and musical routines. Perhaps the outstanding sequence was a musical comedy parody purporting to reveal a touring version of a fictional old show called *The Gladiola Girl*. Eythe was its leading man and Yvonne Adair was the Charleston-dancing heroine. Carol Channing also figured prominently in the routine. The premise was that the 1948 audience was getting a chance to see an authentic 1920s show that had been lost in the boondocks since 1925. Renee Anderson and Eythe were excellent in "Neurotic You and Psychopathic Me," a laughworthy sketch about an analyst and his patient. Anderson's most loved bit was her folk song or "Ballade" sung to a strange stringed instrument she called a "twang." A piece of charming choreography was about the agonies of dance school; it featured Dorothy Babbs and Bob Scheerer as diminutive waltzers falling in love and was called "Friday Dancing Class." Also effective was "Santo Domingo," a satirical Latin American number set in a modern village in the West Indies. When originally done in Pittsburgh, this number was played straight, But by 1948 similar Latin dance routines had become so commonplace that it was decided to do the number as a spoof. In "Three Little Queens of the Silver Screen," fun was made of silent movie stars of the Mary Pickford, Theda Bara, and Perils of Pauline varieties. A risible sketch featured husband-and-wife moviegoers Channing and Eythe giving their impressions of three films they had seen, one a Laurence Olivier movie that inspired them to speak with Shakespearean tones, one a Mayfair drawing-room comedy that brought out their best British accents, and one a French love story that excited their amorous proclivities. Channing was a hilarious partner to George Hall in the show's finale, "Words without Song," which was a grand opera performed--because of some mishap--without the music; it beautifully highlighted opera's gloriously hammy acting style.

There were several effective songs in the revue, including "I'm Not in Love," sung by Adair, and "When Someone You Love Loves You," vocalized by Robert Dixon and Gloria Hamilton as future dancing star Gene Nelson and Antoinette Guhlke danced in the foreground. Du Bois's mostly blue-shaded sets, composed of tall venetian blinds that could be varied by lighting and set pieces, were matched by equally sophisticated and often-amusing costumes.

William Hawkins (*NYWT*) rhapsodized about Channing, calling her "a remarkable personality . . . who with her timing and range is for our money one of the funniest people extant. A buxom blonde with enormous eyes, she can be ecstatically idiotic of [*sic*] viciously sophisticated in a twinkling."

LET FREEDOM SING [Revue] SK: Sam Locke; M/LY: Harold Rome; ADD. M/LY: Marc Blitzstein, Earl Robinson, Lou Cooper, Walter Kent, Lewis Allen, Jack Gerald, David Greggory, John Latouche, Hy Zaret, and Roslyn Harvey; D: Joseph Pevney and Robert H. Gordon; CH: Dan Eckley and Ken Whelan; S/L: Herbert Andrews; C: Paul du Pont; P: American Youth Theatre; T: Longacre Theatre; 10/5/42 (8)

A mediocre intimate revue, patriotically related in subject matter to the war, offered at popular prices ($2.75 top), and created by a group of youthful players who began it in Brooklyn and saw it go through numerous changes before it got to Broadway. The same group had offered the previous season's *Of V We Sing*. It was the kind of show that critics lauded for the enthusiasm of its performers more than for the quality of its achievement.

The best-known player was Mitzi Green, most of whose material was inferior, but who did well with "Private Jones" (a rehash of Harold Rome's "Franklin D. Roosevelt Jones" from *Pins and Needles**) and "Grandpa Guerrilla" (a "Russian killer-diller Pancho Villa"). One of her lesser numbers was "The Lady Is a WAAC," a patriotic version of "The Lady Is a Tramp," which Green had sung on Broadway in *Babes in Arms**. She also sang "I Did It for Defence," in which she told of giving her most priceless possession to a young recruit, the possession teasingly referred to turning out to be a tin-foil collection.

Singer-comedienne Betty Garrett was also coming into her own at this time and was considered effective with her rendition of Rome's "History Eight to the Bar" tune, set in a schoolhouse, with Garrett the teacher using boogie-woogie to teach about the American past. She was also in the *What Price Glory?** parody, "Women in Uniform," shared with Green, in which the pair played WAACs arguing over the first man that comes along.

The top men performers were comedians Phil Leeds and Berni Gould, who left the hit *By Jupiter* for this flop. A sketch called "Tactics," in which they were street-corner civilians arguing over war strategy, was mildly successful. Leeds's comic song, "Flowers in Bloom," was generally appreciated, too. Baritone Lee Sullivan was the lead male singer (one of his high spots was "The Little Things We Like," shared with Green), while Mordecai Bauman offered Earl Robinson and Lewis Allen's The House I Live In," a patriotic tune that is still occasionally heard in its Frank Sinatra rendition. One sketch attacked Hitler, Mussolini, and Hirohito; another noted the problems of finding a place to sleep in wartime Washington, D.C.; and so on.

The show was produced on a low budget and used minimal sets and minimal, but colorful, costumes. A drawback was the overloud amplification system. *Let Freedom Sing* was likened to *Pins and Needles* in its style, but was considered vastly inferior to that long-running show. Most critics were patronizing, George Freedley (*NYMT*) calling it "slightly pretentious, friendly, well-meaning." Rowland Field (*NEN*) called the sketches "deplorably amateurish," the general opinion being that the songs were superior to the comedy.

LET'S FACE IT [Musical/Marriage/Military/Romance/Sex/War] B: Herbert and Dorothy Fields; M/LY: Cole Porter; ADD.M/LY: Sylvia Fine and Max Liebman; SC: Russell Medcraft and Norma Mitchell's play, *The Cradle Snatchers**; D: Edgar J. MacGregor; CH: Charles Walters; S: Harry Horner; C: John Harkrider; P: Vinton Freedley; T: Imperial Theatre; 10/29/41 (547)

Danny Kaye, who had been a major discovery in a supporting role in the *Lady in the Dark* the previous season, continued his startling ascent to stardom in this show's leading role. Seconding him in the female lead was Eve Arden (later replaced by Carol Goodner), in her breakthrough assignment. Milton Berle and Martha Raye had turned these roles down before they were given to Kaye and Arden. Rosamond Gilder (*TAM*) described Kaye as "a khaki playboy with an immortal comic mask, infinitely malleable, wide-mouthed, large-eyed, broad in the ear, with hands as eloquent and precise as his torrential speech."

Let's Face It--which opened five weeks before Pearl Harbor--was inspired by a newspaper story read by Vinton Freedley concerning certain female patriots who felt it a duty to entertain new draftees (the contemporary word was "selectees") at their homes in order to boost the soldiers' morale. The idea was combined with the plot of a popular 1925 comedy to create a musical about three jealous Southampton, Long Island, matrons, Maggie Watson (Arden), Nancy Collister (Vivian Vance), and Cornelia Pigeon (Edith Meiser), who, when their husbands go away on a suspicious fishing trip, decide to invite a trio of recruits from nearby Camp Roosevelt to a house party. The young soldiers are Jerry Walker (Kaye), Eddie Hilliard (Jack Williams), and Frankie Burns (Benny Baker). Each already has a girl friend, Jerry's being Winnie Potter (Mary Jane Walsh), Eddie's being Jean Blanchard (Nanette Fabray, having recently changed her name from Fabares), and Frankie's being Muriel McGillicuddy (Sunnie O'Dea). Various complications occur when Jerry is suspected of hanky-panky by Winnie, and when the husbands finally come home, but everything works out neatly, and the situations are happily resolved.

Broadway had a new hit to contend with in *Let's Face It*, which was praised for its choreography, direction, sets, costumes, book, score, and performances. To John Mason Brown (*NYWT*) the show was "a smooth-running, uproarious and delectable affair with almost everything to recommend it." Abel. (*V*) commented on the book, saying that it was "bright, saucy, meaty and timely." John Anderson (*NYJA*) thought that the show "looks deliriously like a masterpiece."

This was the first show inspired by the war to set some of its action in a military training camp, although such settings had already begun to appear on the screen. Kaye was a major contributor, stopping the show with several numbers, including two excellent rapid-fire patter-song interpolations by his wife, Sylvia Fine, and Max Liebman. (Both had been introduced previously in Kaye's nightclub act at the Martinique.) They were "A Modern Fairy Tale" and "Melody in Four-F," the latter being an especially clever double-talk number about the tribulations of a draftee's induction into the army. Nearly every reviewer noted "Melody in Four-F" as the most memorable number in the show.

Porter's score did not have any songs that became standards, but they were admired for their literate lyrics if not for their tunes. Among them were "Farming," "You Irritate Me So," "Jerry, My Soldier Boy," "I Hate You, Darling," "Ace in the Hole," "A Little Rumba Numba," "Let's Not Talk about Love," and "A Lady Needs a Rest."

There was a considerable amount of dancing in the show, with dance highlights being performed by Fabray and Williams, O'Dea, and the new team of Mary Parker and Billy Daniel, most of them backed by an excellently drilled chorus line. The show's relentless pace and energy pleased many, Brooks Atkinson (*NYT*) commenting, "Everything about *Let's Face It* is bright and brisk and continuously enjoyable." However, the breathless Euphemia Van Rensselaer Wyatt (*CW*) averred, "*Let's*

Face It covers its crudities--there are not many nudities--by sustaining such a breakneck pace that it is difficult to remember particular scenes--they merge into one bright colored blur! Everyone speaks or sings as fast as possible and no one in the huge hard-working company relaxes."

José Ferrer replaced Kaye in February 1943 but, for all his talent, could not keep the show running, and it closed within a month.

As with any Broadway hit, famous stars often came to see the show, and the cast would get excited whenever someone special was spotted in the house. Tallulah Bankhead showed up one night, with a black wig, diamond tiara, and harlequin glasses that she hoped would keep her presence a secret from the actors. With her was a gentleman in formal attire and a wide, red ribbon across his chest. Eve Arden noticed Bankhead and knew that she was up to some sort of practical joke. She warned Kaye and asked him to keep a straight face no matter what happened. In one scene, as Arden proposed a toast, the man's ribbon lit up with the words "Call for Philip Morris," Bankhead's radio sponsor. Arden did not break, but completed the toast, and no one on stage laughed, dampening the trick. Later, Bankhead complained, "How in the world did you recognize me, dahling?" "Somehow," recalled Arden in *Three Phases of Eve*, "Tallulah was Tallulah, even if disguised as Shirley Temple."

LETTERS TO LUCERNE [Drama/Friendship/Romance/School/War/Youth] A: Fritz Rotter and Allen Vincent; D: John Baird; S: Raymond Sovey; P: Dwight Deere Wiman; T: Cort Theatre; 12/23/41 (23)

Although it ran only for three weeks, this war-inspired play was selected by Burns Mantle as one of the ten best of the year. It originally had been written by a Viennese composer, Fritz Rotter, who submitted it to Hollywood agent Rosalie Stewart. Stewart thereupon provided Allen Vincent to spruce up its English and other features, and producer Wiman, in California on a talent hunt, picked up the play for Broadway. He then cast it with the daughters of various celebrities, such as conductor Leopold Stokowski's daughter Sonya, actors Richard Barthelmess and Mary Hay's daughter Mary, actor-director Clive Brooks's daughter Faith, writer Stephen Morehouse Avery's daughter Phyllis, and his own daughter Nancy. Most of them proved too inexperienced to make much of an impression. The cast was led by an outstanding German refugee player, Grete Mosheim, in her first important American part. She was much admired and scored a personal hit.

Mantle chose the play because he favored it, but admitted that many of his colleagues did not. Rosamond Gilder (*TAM*), who was generally favorable, observed that the play, "while in no sense an important or very adept script, has a human quality in its quiet plea for tolerance which will bring it to the attention of groups looking for intelligent material to perform." George Freedley (*NYMT*) thought that it lacked variety but managed to provide effective scenes of comedy mingled with deeply moving ones.

A finishing school for wealthy young women in Lucerne, Switzerland, in the late summer of 1939 is the setting for the play. It is run by the gracious headmistress, Mrs. Hunter (Katherine Alexander). Six senior students of different nationalities (English, German, Polish, French, and two Americans) are shown to be close and loving friends, oblivious of the storm clouds of war bordering on their idyllic location. Nightly in their dormitory they share with one another their letters from home, and each is thus conversant and concerned with the personal backgrounds of everyone else. The divisive sword of war enters their lives, and the girls take sides. The Polish girl, Olga (Stokowski), in love with Hans (Carl Gose), Erna's brother, declares her loyalty to the decent German girl, Erna (Mosheim), and the American Bingo (Wiman) also continues her friendship for Erna. The others, however, become Erna's enemies. Things become dramatic when a letter arrives informing Olga that the Germans have killed her parents in Warsaw, Hans being one of those responsible. Everyone turns against Erna until she, too, gets a letter, which reveals that her parents hate the Nazis and that Hans had deliberately crashed his plane and killed himself rather than bomb the Polish city.

For Richard Lockridge (*NYS*), the plot proved too predictable and thus lacked the poignancy it needed. John Anderson (*NYS*) concluded that the authors failed to convey the girls' grief upon their learning from their letters how the world outside was going to hell. The play, he said, was an "emotional vacuum." He and others also found the focus on personal emotions in the face of the European tragedy too trivial for concern. John Mason Brown (*NYWT*) complained that the idea of using letters to develop the plot turned "out to be not only a stuntish but a static device." The cast included Lilia Skala, Beatrice de Neergaard, and Alfred A. Hesse, among others.

LEYENDA DEL BESSO, LA (***The Legend of the Kiss***) [Musical/Romance/Spanish/Spanish Language] B: Enrique Reoyo, Antonio Paso, Jr., and Silva Aramburu; M: Soutullo and Vert; P: Evaristo Corredor and Hernando Silva; T: Cosmopolitan Opera House; 11/19/42

This first of a planned series of Spanish musicals (zarzuelas) was reminiscent of a Viennese operetta in its book and style, while its music reminded some of the Italians Mascagni and Puccini. It came to New York after an extensive South American tour and was said to be the first professionally produced zarzuela ever seen locally. Paul Bowles (*NYHT*) observed, "The general impression . . . was that an Italian company was giving a show in Spanish, and there was an Italian approach to all the singing as well as to the use of popular Spanish music." N. S. (*NYT*) called it "leaden, dull and drab, with interminable dialogues between the solos and musical ensembles that lengthened the acts out of all proportion to the conventional story that they had to tell."

The story concerns a handsome nobleman (Fausto Alvarez) who falls for a pretty gypsy girl (Maria Robles), learns that any nongypsy who kisses her will be cursed, tries to dodge the disaster and kisses her, but is broken hearted when she moves on with the gypsies.

LIAR, THE [Musical/Period/Romance/Sex] B: Edward Eager and Alfred Drake; M: John Mundy; LY: Edward Eager; SC: Carlo Goldoni's eighteenth-century play of the same name (*Il Bugiardo*); D: Alfred Drake; CH: Hanya Holm; S/L: Donald Oenslager; C: Motley; P: Dorothy Willard and Thomas Hammond; T: Broadhurst Theatre; 5/18/50 (12)

Alfred Drake, then at the top of his form as Broadway's leading male musical comedy star, coauthored and directed this "pedestrian and dull musical" (Robert Coleman [*NYDM*]). Drake, on a leave of absence from *Kiss Me, Kate*, took over the direction from Norris Houghton during the out-of-town tryouts. The show might have closed after a mere four performances, so severe were the critical attacks, but complimentary remarks written by a Broadway columnist led the producers to try to come up with the cash to eke out a longer run. All they could manage, though, were an extra week's performances.

The Liar was based on a commedia dell'arte-inspired comedy by Italy's Carlo Goldoni, but the promising idea remained earthbound. Although it was brightly cos tumed and--with its revolving set--scenically clever, the writing and conception lacked the necessary imagination. According to which critic one read, the performers either failed to capture the required style and buoyancy or used their unending exuberance and flair to cover up script deficiencies. Howard Barnes (*NYHT*) maintained, "In it the flourish is used instead of wit and musical machinery substituted for melody. Performed with an overwhelming vivacity, *The Liar* drowns out some of the worst spots in a minor satire and manages to let a few bright spots come through the hullabaloo." John Chapman (*NYDN*) alleged that "there are some awfully long stretches of unexciting plot and the net effect is squashy rather than bouncy."

Sixteenth-century Venice is the background for the action, which transpires in a single day. The plot is more an excuse for comic japeries than a well-knit narrative. Most of the leading characters are stock commedia types, including Arlecchino (Joshua Shelley), Pantalone (Melville Cooper), Brighella (Russell Collins), Colombina (Paula Laurence), and Dr. Balanzoni (Philip Coolidge). The title refers to the jaunty, rascally, but romantic knave, Pantalone's son, called Lelio (William Eythe, who took over the role shortly before the opening). He is a youthful poseur who returns to his home town, from which he long has been gone, and soon finds himself enmeshed in a web of lies. His study of plays keeps numerous plots available in his mind. He has abandoned a widow (Barbara Ashley) in Rome and is now in pursuit of two sisters (Barbara Moser and Karen Lindgren), the daughters of the doctor. All sorts of confusions ensue from his lying ways (he boasts of being the king of Sicily) until, at the conclusion, the widow catches up with Lelio and, in order to tame him, shames him before the others.

Playing minor roles in the show were Martin Balsam and Leonardo Cimino as servingmen and Walter Matthau as a guard.

LIBERTY JONES [Drama/Fantasy/Illness/Military/Politics/Romance] A: Philip Barry; M: Paul Bowles; D: John Houseman; CH: Lew Christensen; S/C: Raoul Pène du Bois; P: Theatre Guild; T: Shubert Theatre; 2/5/41 (22)

Philip Barry, master of American high comedy, surprised theatregoers with this "stilted and uninspiring" (Rosamond Gilder [*TAM*]) attempt at a patriotic political allegory done in an abstract theatricalist style.

In the luxurious apartment of the amiable capitalist Uncle Sam (William Lynn) and Aunt Glory (Martha Hodge) overlooking Rock Creek Park, Washington, D.C., lies Miss Liberty Jones (Nancy Coleman). She is near death from neglect and is ministered to by the venial Nurse Cotton (Katherine Squire) and a quartet of doctors of Education, Divinity, Letters, and Law (Norman Lloyd, Murray O'Neill, Allan Frank, and William Mende), who cannot find a cure for her ailment. The Three Shirts (Victor Thorley, Louis Polan, and Richard Sanders), representing the totalitarian powers (they wore shirts of black, brown, and red, respectively), haunt Liberty's dreams and conspire with the nurse to poison her. There arrive on the scene naval aviator and representative liberal Tom Smith (John Beal) and his alter ego Dick Brown (Tom Ewell). Also helpful is Liberty's old commonsensical Irish nurse, Maggie (Ivy Scott). Tom, who is reluctant at first to give up his freedom, revives the expiring Liberty, and they fall in love. To rid her of the three political gangsters, Tom appeases them; given a finger, they soon demand an arm. Tom weds Liberty, and when the Three Shirts appear to demand her, Tom buckles on his sword and slays them. Tom and Liberty then soar off to cross the mythical tin bridge over dark and troubled times, with Liberty returning sans her spouse.

The play's prose dialogue was occasionally varied by rhyming couplets as well as songs and dances, with a considerable amount of expressive music provided by Paul Bowles. Raoul Pène du Bois contributed exquisitely imaginative settings and costumes. In *Run-Through*, director Houseman said that the work, originally written as a straight play, had evolved by the time he began production into more of a musical than a play. He also noted that the allegorical elements were not in the original version of the work, which it was titled *The Wild Harps Playing*.

Most critics praised the colorful production (although several compared it to a high school pageant) and the author's intentions, but panned the writing, rapping its heavy-handed and sometimes obscure symbolism and viewpoint. "While its spirit is fine and unafraid," commented Richard Watts, Jr. (*NYHT*), "its manner of expressing it is frequently lacking in eloquence and almost invariably without dramatic forcefulness." Euphemia Van Rensselaer Wyatt (*CW*) declared, however, "Mr. Barry has made an original and imaginative contribution to the American theater, full of shrewd political comment."

LIFE OF REILLY, THE [Comedy/Crime/Gambling/Hotel/Sports] A: William Roos; D: Roy Hargrave; S: Samuel Leve; P: Day Tuttle and Harald Bromley; T: Broadhurst Theatre; 4/29/42 (5)

This ill-fated farce, which had been kicking about Broadway offices for nearly half a decade under the title *Triple Play*, had nothing to do with the similarly titled TV sitcom of the 1950s (which spelled the name "Riley"). Set in a Brooklyn hotel, it focuses on a dim-witted Brooklyn Dodgers lefty pitcher named Rocket Reilly (Peter Hobbs), whose mentally slow team is in a nine-game losing streak. A gambler (Loring Smith) and his wife (Glenda Farrell), thinking that the suspended pitcher will not be hurling in the next day's game against the Giants, bet against the Dodgers. They are wrong, however, as Reilly is scheduled to pitch. However, the superstitious pitcher has been convinced by the fortune teller to whom he is addicted that he is going to murder someone before midnight. This leads the nervous gambler to find a way of making Reilly think that he has actually killed someone; his plot--employing blank cartridges--leads him to become Reilly's supposed victim. The distraught ballplayer turns himself in to the cops, but they, knowing how valuable his arm is to the upcoming game, refuse to buy his story, even giving him the third degree to establish his innocence. Eventually the truth is revealed, and Reilly not only goes to the mound, but resolves his mixed-up romance with his girlfriend (Charita Bauer).

The play's best gag came when a friend was trying to talk Reilly out of giving himself up and asked, "You don't want to die, do you?" "I would be dying for something I believe in," Reilly replied. When asked, "What's that?" he said "Capital punishment." The farce ran out of gas early on, lacked imaginative acting and direction, and could not be helped even by the infusion of some humor provided by a St. Bernard (Mona). It also lacked plausibility, as the Dodgers were then a very hot team, having won the National League pennant in 1940. Richard Watts, Jr. (*NYHT*), claimed that the play had a funny third act, but otherwise was "as feeble-minded as its central character." George Mathews and John Call played other brainless Dodgers, and Guerita Donnelly, Len Hollister, Norman Tokar, and Polly Walters were also in the company.

LIFE SENTENCE [Drama/Family/Friendship/Homosexuality/Romance/Sex] A: Philip Van Dyke; D: Marjorie Hildreth; S: Willis Knighton; P: On-Stage; T: Cherry Lane Theatre (OB); 10/7/47

A foggy, self-important, expressionistic play given by an adventurous Off-Broadway company. It is about David (Charles Mason), a young intellectual going through various crises at a turning point in his life because he wishes to break free of his complex web of relationships with his mother (Anne Farrell), the girl he is contemplating marrying (Margaret Gillespie), his gay friend (Bill Kenevan), a woman (Olivia)--called a "prostitute" by the others--with whom he has sex, and so on. The title refers to his having been sentenced to a life with these people and his difficulty at finding independence.

The piece was produced as if it were a rehearsal, and various characters came forward periodically to address the audience about the action. George Freedley (*NYMT*) thought that the expressionistic style muddied the story line, which made the piece difficult to follow. Richard Watts, Jr. (*NYP*), said that it was "a sadly dreary" experience.

LIFE WITH MOTHER [Comedy/Business/Family/Marriage/Period/Romance/Youth] A: Howard Lindsay and Russel Crouse; SC: *Life with Mother*, a collection of vignettes by Clarence Day, Jr.; D: Guthrie McClintic; S: Stewart Chaney and Donald Oenslager; C: Donald Oenslager; P: Oscar Serlin; T: Empire Theatre; 10/20/48 (265)

Life with Father (1939), with its seven-year tenure, had been one of the longest-running plays in Broadway history. Lindsay and Crouse therefore created this sequel to it that opened at the same theatre where the earlier play had been produced. Despite good reviews and a decent run, the show still wound up losing $40,000. Whereas *Life with Father* had cost about $23,000 to produce, rising production costs brought the sequel in for about $90,000. Because they felt that the public's familiarity with *Life with Father* was enormous, the new venture's simple advertisement in the New York papers ran:

Mr. and Mrs. Clarence Day
At Home
On Wednesday evening, October twentieth
from eight until eleven o'clock
at Fourteen hundred and thirty Broadway
Entertainment

Lindsay resumed his old role of Father Clare Day, and his real-life wife, Dorothy Stickney, again played his onstage spouse, Mother Vinnie Day. Also returning from the earlier play were Dorothy Bernard as Margaret, the cook; Ruth

Hammond as Cousin Cora; A. H. Van Buren as the family doctor; and John Drew Devereux as Clarence, Jr., the eldest of the carrot-topped Day brood, now a Yale undergraduate. Father Day remained the blustery stuffed shirt with a short fuse, while Mother Day remained the scatterbrained matriarch who somehow rules the roost and knows what is best for herself and her family.

"Miss Stickney . . . is the same charming combination of gentleness, guile and obstinacy and Mr. Lindsay is Clare incarnate," wrote Euphemia Van Rensselaer Wyatt (*CW*). The critics loved having the lovable--and, by 1948, nearly iconographic--Days back on Broadway, with their humorous eccentricities and 1880s period charm. Their everyday triumphs and foibles reflected a nostalgic and somehow universal image of American family life, and the delicious contrast between the choleric Father and the vacuous but determined Mother made a perfect stage relationship. The play they were in, however, amusing as it was (it was one of the season's ten best), was considered just a tad beneath the quality of *Life with Father*.

"It is more laboriously contrived. It is thinner, and there are moments when it barely hangs together as a drama," noted Brooks Atkinson (*NYT*). "The comedy is neither as hilarious nor as nostalgic as its eminent predecessor, but it is a pleasant elongation of a drama which became very much a part of American life." John Mason Brown (*SR*) argued that "it gives every indication of having triumphed over the jinx of sequels, as surely as Mr. Roosevelt overrode the popular prejudice against a third term. . . . It may be a little broader in mood and manner, but certainly in intention and effect it is identical with [the] earlier play."

The central premise stems from the celebration by the Days of their twenty-second anniversary. Mother demands that Father give her the engagement ring that he never bought her before they were wed. Things warm up when she accidentally learns that Bessie Skinner (Gladys Hurlbut), to whom he had been previously affianced, did receive such a ring and has never taken it off. Bessie, still flirtatious, but now fat and middle-aged, once again confronts Father Day, but Mother manages to get the upper hand and to gain the sought-for jewelry. The action also concerns the engagement of Clarence, Jr.; the propensity of young Harlan Day (Robert Wade) for reciting memorized poems, although no one wants to hear them; the surprise weekend visit of Cora and her new husband, Clyde Miller (Robert Emhardt), the midwestern "Hay, Grain, and Feed" man; the locking of horns between know-it-all Clyde and know-it-all Father Day; and so on. Stock-market crises, familial finances, maids who come and go, problems with the children's allowances, and other matters also take up a good portion of stage time.

The play was briskly directed (almost like vaudeville, thought Atkinson), yet was filled with warmth and good feeling. There was not a weak performance in the production, and Lindsay and Stickney once again achieved the heights of light comic acting. The action is set in the country (at Harrison, New York) and New York City (on Madison Avenue), so the original city set by Stewart Chaney was resuscitated, while a new country-house drawing room with bright pink wallpaper was created by Donald Oenslager.

Dorothy Stickney suggested that one reason the play may not have run longer was its title. In *Openings and Closings*, she wrote, "People must have been subconsciously thinking that it would be *Life with Father* all over again, which they had already seen. We should have called it *The Engagement Ring*, which was what it was about."

LIFELINE [Drama/British/Sea/War] A: Norman Armstrong (Norman Lee and Barbara Toy); S: Lemuel Ayers; D: Dudley Digges; P: Gilbert Miller; T: Belasco Theatre; 11/30/42 (8)

A "pedestrian" (Howard Barnes [*NYHT*]), all-male, British war play--then still running in London--that focused on the heroism of the merchant marine, who daily faced the danger of bombs and torpedoes by sailing across the ocean in rusty ships with failing engines to bring supplies to the Allied powers. Part of the problem stemmed from the attempt to suggest, within the theatre's limited resources, the many threats to a ship at sea. As Lewis Nichols (*NYT*) suggested, the story required a movie to do it pictorial justice.

The play had a full complement of colorful but stenciled character types. Urban Nagle (*CW*) believed that the otherwise promising play's problem lay in its emphasis on a group hero and not on a single individual to whose problems the audience could relate. But George Jean Nathan (*TBY*) said that the play "was so sketchily amateurish that the essentially heroic theme was reduced to the proportions of some such melodramatic comic strip as *Vic Jordan*."

The action occurs in the saloon of the 5,000-ton tramp steamer *Clydesdale*, setting out for Liverpool from Nova Scotia with a cargo of gasoline. Sailing in convoy, it falls behind because of engine problems and is attacked by a submarine, which it sinks. It catches up to the convoy but is soon victimized by bomber planes, and an explosion sets fire to one of the holds. The order to abandon ship is given by the surly captain (Rhys Williams), and the men take to the boats. Several days later, one group of men come across the steamer, which has not sunk, and they reboard her, extinguish the still-burning fires, restart her engines, and manage to make port with her despite barely any crew and an inoperable rudder.

Director Dudley Digges played the ship's steward, Colin Keith-Johnston played the cynical first officer who becomes a martinet when the original skipper dies, Whitford Kane was the engineer, George Keane and Everett Ripley were officers, and Bob White was a teenage apprentice. Their ensemble was a strong one, but not strong enough to overcome the play's drawbacks.

LIGHT UP THE SKY [Comedy/Hotel/Marriage/Theatre] A/D: Moss Hart; S/L: Frederick Fox; C: Kiviette; P: Joseph M. Hyman and Bernard Hart; T: Royale Theatre; 11/18/48 (214)

This was a popular *drame à clef* about the theatre, and those in the know could detect the originals upon whom some of the theatrefolk involved presumably were based. (Playwright Hart dutifully denied that any of the characters were modeled on real people.)

During its tryout period, the play had the air of a serious comedy intending to make some important statements about the theatre. The out-of-town audiences liked the funny parts and rejected the serious ones, so the play underwent major revisions to make it a comedy, pure and simple. The fact that the show's troubles in Boston were reflected in its own plot was sheer coincidence. Hart's numerous revisions turned the piece into a hit, and critics who saw it both in Boston and New York were delighted by his clever improvements, although the Boston revisions were made while the playwright was sick with a temperature of 101.

The play's title, according to the program, comes from a line in an old play called *The Idle Jest* that reads: "Mad, sire? Ah, yes--mad indeed, but observe how they do light up the sky." There was no such old play, however, the program note being Hart's practical joke, and he took malicious pleasure in the efforts of the critics to track down the imaginary piece.

The single set is a lavish hotel room at Boston's Ritz-Carlton, where the egotistical, Gertrude Lawrence/Tallulah Bankhead-like star, Irene Livingston (Virginia Field), is staying with her gin rummy-playing mother, Stella Livingston (Phyllis Povah). It is 5:30 P.M. and Irene is opening that night in a play by a young new playwright, the shy, idealistic, and theatrically innocent Peter Sloan (Barry Nelson). The new play has something to with the falling of an atomic bomb in Radio City. Important to the action are the art-collecting, Billy Rose-like producer, Sidney Black (Sam Levene), and his sharp-tongued, Eleanor Holm-like wife, Frances (Audrey Christie); the flamboyant and effeminate Guthrie McClintic-like director, Carleton Fitzgerald (Glenn Anders); a sarcastic but knowing veteran playwright, Owen Turner (Philip Ober); a theatrically naive typist, Miss Lovell (Jane Middleton); a drunken Shriner from down the hall (John D. Seymour); and a plainclothes detective (Ronald Alexander). The main characters appear to be full of undying love for one another before the play opens. At 12:30 P.M., following the performance, during which the audience--made up mostly of a Shriners' convention--walked out, they are a pack of nasty vipers going for one another's throats. The disgusted young playwright plans to quit the theatre for good. But at 3:30 A.M., when the reviews turn out to be raves, camaraderie reemerges and they are all once more part of the brotherhood of man.

Playwright Sloan, who has learned some valuable lessons, is coaxed back into the fold and thereupon prepares to undertake the revisions needed to bring the play to Broadway.

The play--one of the seaon's ten best--was deemed a viable blend of door-slamming farce and caustic satire on the commercial theatre, but although most of the reviews were quite favorable, it was not considered flawless. Howard Barnes (*NYHT*) observed, "In the wryest passages . . . there is an agreeable good nature about the writing which makes much of the piece vastly entertaining. What is wanting is dramatic construction of more consequence." He found the characters colorful, but their strings "too often discernible." Even less impressed was John Lardner (*TS*), who accused the play of seeming "to be covered with scaffolding. The fact is, it's a mechanical, put-up job of playwriting in essence." The very enthusiastic John Mason Brown (*SR*) opined, however, "The fascination of seeing 'plain' a group of such supercharged and extraordinary personalities is a major source of the very real fun the evening provides." He thought that Hart had succeeded in revealing "what is at once zestful, incredible, entertaining, and ridiculous in the theatrical temperament in general." William Hawkins (*NYWT*) declared this "an extremely funny, high riding comedy that is pitiless in its comment on the theater while brazenly in love with it."

Hart directed the piece at breakneck speed. According to Brooks Atkinson (*NYT*), "The performance races around the stage like a volcanic circus, everybody shouting, everybody making exits and entrances and slamming doors."

The rumors that the show was about famous celebrities, especially Billy Rose and Eleanor Holm, provided delicious fodder for the gossip columnists and good preopening publicity for the show. Hart assured whoever asked that the characters were composites and even mollified the suspicious Rose by having dinner with him and his wife before the premiere. At the opening performance, Rose was seen laughing loudly. Rose soon after wrote in relatively complimentary terms about the show--he called it "funny"--in his *NYHT* column. He agreed that the characters were essentially composites and suggested that Hart himself was a crucial part of the Sidney Black character, as well as of the younger and older playwright characters. Each revealed a part of Hart that he considered inherent in his own personality, but would never reveal except to his psychiatrist (Hart was widely known to have been analyzed). In a later column, Rose apologized for having called the play funny and observed that a second viewing revealed it as not so funny after all, its opening night laughter stemming from the recognition of its in-jokes by the "hep" Broadway crowd attending. Rose later told Jack Gaver (in *Curtain Calls*) that he was upset with Hart, not for lampooning him, but for never showing him the script, although Hart had promised to do so, and that he found distasteful all the publicity tidbits published before the opening regarding the possible connection between the characters and people Hart had known for years.

LILY OF THE VALLEY [Drama/Crime/Death/Fantasy/Prostitution/Religion] A/D: Ben Hecht; S/L: Harry Horner; P: Gilbert Miller; T: Windsor Theatre; 1/26/42 (8)

The New York City morgue was the unusual locale for this "heavy-footed and soporific" (Kelcey Allen [*WWD*]) allegorical drama about the ghostly materialization of the day's unclaimed dead as they are talked about and photographed by a police lieutenant (Clay Clement) and a photographer (Joseph Pevney). Among the six shabby corpses is a hooker in her sixties (Alison Skipworth), a longshoreman and union organizer (Myron McCormick), an old scrubwoman (Minnie Dupree) who jumped from a window, and a young girl (Katharine Bard) who was killed accidentally when she inhaled the gas fumes from someone else's suicide. Unseen by the morgue workers, they are, however, miraculously visible to the itinerant visionary preacher, Reverend Swen Houseman (Siegfried Rumann), who temporarily sets up his revival meetings there when his nearby Bowery mission is burned down. He, representing God, communicates with the raffish spirits and shares their often mawkish stories. The longshoreman, for instance, would like to organize his fellow dead. One of the ghosts is a miser (John Philliber) who tells the Norwegian cleric where he has hidden $40,000, which Swen then finds and brings back. Seeing it, a crazy body washer (Will Lee) kills the preacher and robs him, but the crime is solved soon after, and Houseman himself appears as a ghost.

Brooks Atkinson (*NYT*) admitted that the play was "strange, original and imaginative," but added that he--like many other critics--had no idea of what the author was getting at. "With recurrent reminders of mortuary detail, with no central story and very long monologues, it was a stiff ordeal for the audience to visit with the wretched bedraggled dead people for three acts," commented Euphemia Van Rensselaer Wyatt (*CW*). The play's weak critical response led the author to fulminate against the press in a nasty letter to the *NYT*.

LINDEN TREE, THE [Drama/British/Business/Family/Marriage/Medicine/Music/Old Age/Religion/Science/University/Youth] A: J. B. Priestley; D: George Schaefer; S: Peter Wolf; C: Frank Thompson; P: Maurice Evans; T: Music Box Theatre; 3/2/48 (7)

Earlier in the season, Priestley's *An Inspector Calls* had divided the critics, but managed to hold on for several months. His *The Linden Tree*, however, was gone within a week, although it was a London hit. Most found it verbose, dull, seemingly written in a hurry, and too English in its ideas. The drama was intended to express the author's concerns for the present and future state of England. "To extend his slender treatise into a full-length play, he has spun endless words around a static situation which has no dramatic excitement," declared William Hawkins (*NYWT*). "It's not very interesting," conceded Louis Kronenberger (*PM*), "and not the least bit dramatic or alive."

Boris Karloff played Professor Linden, a sixty-five-year-old professor at an English college in the provincial town of Brumanley, where he lives with wife (Barbara Everest) and his adolescent daughter (Marilyn Erskine), who wants to be a musician. For his birthday he is visited by his two grown daughters and son (Halliwell Hobbes, Jr.). One of the older daughters (Cathleen Cordell), wed to a French Catholic, finds salvation in religion. The other (Viola Keats) is a doctor whose faith is in medical research, while the cynical son, stripped of any faith by the war, is a greedy trader. Only the youngest daughter takes pleasure in life. Professor Linden refuses to accept the recommendation of his family and the Regents Board that he retire. He believes that it is his duty, as it is everyone else's in a country seemingly without hope, to abandon defeatism and to persevere with one's work, regardless of any desire for personal happiness. He must also contend with his wife's urgent wish to move to London and escape from the town's dull provincialism. He decides to stay in Brumanley with his youngest daughter and his housekeeper (Una O'Connor). Although stripped of most of his teaching duties, he plans, in the hopes of promoting world peace, to inform the younger generation of the wonders of history.

When Priestley heard that Karloff was being cast in the play, he told producer Evans, "Good Lord *no!* Not Karloff! Put that man's name on a marquee and people will think my play's about an axe murderer. I'll take your word for the fact he could play it, but I can't risk it." To this, Karloff cabled a reply: "Dear Mr. Priestley. I am sorely disappointed that you do not wish me to do your play. It is a beautiful play, and I promise you I wouldn't have eaten the baby in the last act." Priestley thereupon gave in and cabled Evans, "Let him do it" (quoted in Cynthia Lindsay, *Dear Boris*).

LISTEN, PROFESSOR! (***Mashenka***) [Comedy/Family/Romance/Russian/Youth] A: Alexander Afinegenov; TR: J. J. Robbins; AD: Peggy Phillips; D: Sanford Meisner; S: Howard Bay; C: Lucinda Ballard; P: Milton Baron i/a/w Jean Muir and Toni Ward; T: Forrest Theatre; 12/22/43 (29)

A disappointing adaptation--with an even more disappointing English title--by Broadway press agent Peggy Phillips of a Soviet domestic comedy-drama seen in Moscow in 1939 but set in 1936. Its author was killed in a Nazi air raid during the siege of Moscow. It was weakened by stereotypical characters and a lack of action, among other things.

Dudley Digges was the star, playing the role of grumpy old Professor Okayemov, a specialist in seventh-century history whose fifteen-year-old granddaughter

Masha (Susan Robinson) comes to live with him when his widowed daughter-in-law Nina (Viola Frayne), with whom his relations are strained, decides to remarry. A clash of the generations ensues when the professor finds it impossible to take his head out of the ancient world and put it into the present day. Much of his confusion arises when Masha brings home her friends from the school collective, all of them filled with optimism concerning the future. A subplot concerns Masha's falling for a young engineer acquaintance (Martin Blaine) of her grandfather who is himself in love with a neighbor who is a singing teacher (Frances Reid). Masha eventually realizes that the engineer is too mature for her. Gradually, as the professor guides her hesitatingly through the shoals of growing up, and he becomes interested in the lives of her and her friends, the curmudgeon comes to see the light in Masha's modern ways and in those of the USSR. When Masha's mother, whose new marriage has failed, comes for her, the girl refuses to abandon her grandfather, whom she has come to love. The professor resolves the dilemma by inviting the mother to come and live with him and Masha.

Digges gave one of his finer performances, and Howard Bay provided a distinctively realistic set of the professor's study, but Sanford Meisner's direction failed to capture the appropriate moods suggested by the action. There were a small number of positive reviews, such as that of Burton Rascoe (*NYWT*), who called it "utterly delightful, pulse-quickening and richly humorous." But the majority agreed with Ward Morehouse (*NYS*), who wrote that *Listen, Professor!* "wanders indecisively through three acts and fails pretty steadily as a play." The play's title was laughed at by various critics, although an earlier English title, *New Horizons*, might have been thought more fitting. Peter Fernandez played one of Masha's friends, as did Michael Dreyfuss, Peggy Allardice, and others.

LITTLE A [Drama/Marriage/Music/Sex/Small Town] A: Hugh White; D: Melville Burke; S: Watson Barratt; C: Ernest Schrapps; L: Leo Kerz; P: Sam Nasser i/a/w Henry Lambert; T: Henry Miller's Theatre; 1/15/47 (21)

Although George Freedley (*NYMT*) called this "the most exciting melodrama since *Ladies in Retirement**," and several others thought it generally worthwhile, if flawed, it flopped and was quickly withdrawn. In the middle was Rosamond Gilder (*TAM*), who saw in it a melodramatic handling of material similar to that in *Craig's Wife** (revived a couple of weeks after this play opened) and felt that it had an excellently conceived first act, but admitted that it eventually succumbed to improbabilities. On the very negative side, Brooks Atkinson (*NYT*) observed, "Mr. White's nickelodeon ideas of dramatic writing make *Little A* progressively unbearable."

It takes place in a large house in a small northern California town and concerns Aaron Storm (Otto Kruger), a wealthy man known even to his face as "Little A" and who always has been in the shadow of his late father, "Big A." He has been married for nineteen years to Lucinda (Jessie Royce Landis), an unpleasantly dominating woman, whom he was practically forced to wed. Their visiting college-age child is Donald (Robert Wiley), who hates Aaron. The latter has long held suspicions about the youth's parentage. He is unhappy at his canning factory, too, where he is despised by his colleagues. The brightest light in his life is the musically talented orphan girl, Mary Howard (Ottilie Kruger, real-life daughter of the star), who lives with the Storms and works for the family as a semiservant. A local physician, Dr. Duncan Brown (Wallis Clark), with whom he plays chess, is his only other solace. When Aaron reprimands Donald for attempting to rape Mary, he learns from Donald that his son is not only a bastard, but is the child of Big A. It also develops that Lucinda's miserable treatment of Aaron's mother caused her to go crazy and die. Aaron, toying with the idea of shooting Lucinda, allows her to take possession of his gun, and when Lucinda attempts to shoot him, she kills her son instead, thus ridding Aaron of his dual nemeses.

There were very strong performances by Otto Kruger and Jessie Royce Landis, and good jobs were submitted by Frances Bavier and Harry Mehaffey.

LITTLE BROWN JUG [Drama/Crime/Family/Mystery] A: Marie Baumer; D: Gerald Savory; P: Courtney Burr; S/L: Frederick Fox; T: Martin Beck Theatre;

3/6/46 (5)

Marie Baumer's attempt at a psychological thriller misfired, but not as seriously as its quick closing might imply. The play reminded George Jean Nathan (*TBY*) of numerous similar ones, only he found it more feeble than most. Others thought its plot lacking in credibility and its characters in plausibility. Louis Kronenberger (*PM*) said, "It lacks sound psychology and is very lean on thrills." Yet Howard Barnes (*NYHT*) considered it "a singularly disarming and diverting show." Especially worthwhile was Percy Kilbride's excellent performance in the leading role.

Kilbride played Ira, a handyman and gardener who witnesses the accidental death by defenestration of the drunken Henry Barlow (Ronald Alexander) during a quarrel among Henry, his wife Carol (Marjorie Lord), and her mother, Irene Haskell (Katherine Alexander). The homeless Ira uses his lunatic's guile to blackmail the women into taking him into their Connecticut home, threatening to report the death as murder (Irene had slapped Henry before he fell) if they do not. He gradually dominates the pair and has them scared witless until the women, joined by Henry's worldly brother Norman (Arthur Margetson), manage to defeat his plans and force him to confess.

Arthur Franz and Frieda Altman were in the small cast.

LITTLE DARK HORSE (***Pamplemousse***) [Comedy/Blacks/Family/French/Illness/Race/Sex/Youth] A: André Birabeau; AD: Theresa Helburn; D: Melville Burke; S: John Koenig; C: Frank Spencer; P: Donald Blackwell and Raymond Curtis; T: John Golden Theatre; 11/16/41 (9)

A "dull and humorless" (Richard Watts, Jr. [*NYHT*]) 1937 French comedy set in a provincial village. Its tryout had been the previous summer in Westport, Connecticut. It recounts the scandalous reaction of his family when François Monfavet (Grant Mills) falls ill and they discover that he has been paying tuition at a military school for an illegitimate child who is actually a mulatto (R. V. Whitaker). The boy had been fathered while François--already married and the father of three--was engaged as an engineer in the Belgian Congo. François's sympathetic children agree to accept the boy into the bosom of the family. To protect the family's reputation, it is made public that the child is the son of François's bachelor brother Emil (Walter Slezak).

The production lacked the appropriate French flavor and was considered only sporadically effective. Its unenlightened treatment of miscegenation was considered tasteless, as were its many jokes about color. As John Anderson (*NYJA*) pointed out, "Somehow the spectacle of a little black boy being used as a comedy gag in what for him was a tragical situation appeared considerably less than convulsing." The fact that the chief characters are unable to relate to the black child as a human, but must hush up his relationship to them, was deemed foolish and insensitive.

Ann Mason, Katherine Givney, Leona Powers, Rolfe Sedan, and, most importantly, Cecilia Loftus as François's mother were in the cast.

LITTLE DARLING [Comedy/Family/Literature/Romance/Sex/Theatre] A: Eric Hatch; D: Alfred de Liagre, Jr.; S: Watson Barratt; L: William Richardson; P: Tom Weatherly; T: Biltmore Theatre; 10/27/42 (23)

For Brooks Atkinson (*NYT*), the most memorable aspect of this stenciled comedy was the presence of its ingenue star. "Since her plump debut in *Out of the Frying Pan* two seasons ago Miss [Barbara] Bel Geddes has become an enchanting creature of less rotundity and greater charm. She has an uncommonly pleasant voice. In addition to that, she is an actress."

Otherwise, this first play by screenwriter Eric Hatch (*My Man Godfrey*) was "more a succession of situations, a few of them amusing, than a continuously flowing story," wrote Hobe. (*V*). "Its characters are inconsistent and not particularly attractive." George Jean Nathan (*TBY*), noting the familiarity of its theme, called the treatment "for the most part commonplace, obvious, and cheap."

Leon Ames played Kenneth Brown, a successful but stuffy writer of slick magazine stories for women, separated from his wife and adored by his lovely secretary (Karen Morley), whom, for some reason, he ignores. He has a Chinese houseboy (Peter Goo Chong) given to such caricaturish expostulations as "Hello, bossy," "Hello, missy," and "Oh, hell." When Kenneth's wife dies, his twenty-three-year-old daughter Cynthia (Bel Geddes) comes to live with him, but she, having been indoctrinated by her mother, finds him stiff and unpleasant. Wishing to gain her affection, he shifts gears from humdrum papa to dashing playboy and begins to take her blond friend and former school roommate, Alice "Bushy" Bushfelter (Phyllis Avery), out on the town, going with her to all the local hot spots. She interests him enough for him to read his secret sex play, *Old Lech*, to her, and the pair then run off for two months, during which time he becomes a hit dramatist. Cynthia is furiously jealous of "Bushy" now and tries without success to get her own boyfriend, Teddy Graves (Arthur Franz), to help her break up the relationship. Then she brings Bushy's boyfriend from Milwaukee (Erik Martin) onto the scene to drive a wedge between Bushy and her dad, and by the final curtain Kenneth finally comes around to realizing that he actually loves his secretary, while the other lovebirds look forward to happy futures.

(1) LITTLE WOMEN [Dramatic Revival*] A: Marian de Forest; D: Jessie Royce Landis w/Gus Schirmer, Jr.; P: Eddie Dowling; T: City Center of Music and Drama; 12/12/44 (23)

A limited-engagement, holiday-season revival of the 1912 adaptation of Louisa May Alcott's classic story of the March family. It had been seen locally in 1931 and 1932 with the present director in the role of Jo. For most, the sentimental play continued to provide engaging family entertainment. It was given a sincere and worthwhile revival, and there was no attempt to make the material any more cloying than it already was. Judicious cutting removed any longeurs.

Mary Welch made her Broadway bow as Jo and reminded some of Katharine Hepburn, who played the role in the movies; Margot Stevenson was Meg; Frances Reid was Beth; and Susanna Garnett was Amy. Professor Baher was taken by Herbert Berghof, while the March parents were played by Velma Royton and David Lewis. The cast also included Harrison Dowd, Grace Mills, Clark Williams, and John Ruth.

According to George Jean Nathan (*TBY*), the revival was so proficient that "the venerable minor American classic took on a surprising freshness and a measure of unaccustomed life and provided an amiable theatrical evening." One of the few sour notes was provided by Louis Kronenberger (*PM*), who thought, "The play creaks even as a period piece. Too often, among other things, you can call off the lines before they are uttered."

(2) [Dramatic Revival] D/P: Frank McCoy; T: City Center of Music and Drama; 12/23/45 (16)

In this new production, again offered for Christmas audiences, Jo was played by Margaret Hayes, Meg by Gloria Stroock, Amy by Billie Lou Watt, and Beth by Dortha Duckworth, and the March parents were once more played by Velma Royton and David Lewis, while Jack Lorenz was Professer Baher. Others involved included Georgia Harvey, Clark Williams, Richard Camp, Grace Mills, and Harrison Dowd. The production was "slipshod" and "uninvitingly inferior," growled George Jean Nathan (*TBY*), who was disturbed by the mismanagement of a playhouse originally intended to offer New Yorkers the best of theatre, music, and dance.

LIVE AND LAUGH [Musical/Yiddish Language] B: H. Kalmanowitch; M: Ilya Trilling; LY: Isidor Lillian; D/P: Herman Yablokoff; CH: Moe Zaar w/Norma Phillips; S: Michael Saltzman; T: Second Avenue Theatre (OB); 10/7/41

Like many other Yiddish theatre productions, this one mingled sentimental drama with musical comedy, throwing in a couple of ballets and an operatic sketch for good measure. It proved entertaining, although it occasionally strained credulity.

It concerns the efforts of watch manufacturer Samuel (Muni Serebrov), his family, and his partner Nathan (Menasha Skulnik) to live and laugh despite the various travails placed in their way. The action involves the remarried manufacturer's vengeful first wife (Charlotte Goldstein) and a villain (David Popper) from the past of Miriam (Bella Mysell), the second wife. The villain is slain by Miriam to protect her honor. The manufacturer takes the rap and goes to prison for fifteen years. Beatrice (Harriet Shelly), Samuel's daughter by his first wife, grows up with the burden of a convict father and a drunken tramp mother, but everything is ironed out in time for a joyous conclusion.

The plot meant little, but the performances were strong and worth viewing. The popular Skulnik, claimed the unnamed *WWD* reviewer, "again puts to good advantage his gifts as the 'deadpan' comedian of the Yiddish stage. Once more he demonstrates his undoubted ability to hold his audience as he sings his patter or clowns his dance routine or puts across his 'straight' part."

LIVE LIFE AGAIN [Drama/Death/Family/Fantasy/Period/Romance/Rural/Small Town/Verse] A: Dan Totheroh; D: Sawyer Falk; S: Albert Johnson; C: Grace Houston; P: S. S. Krellberg; T: Belasco Theatre; 9/29/45 (2)

Dan Totheroh, once a highly promising dramatist, returned to the stage after many years in Hollywood with this critically blasted, pretentious verse play attempting to tell a *Hamlet**-like story within the context of a Nebraska prairie village. It was "a dreary evening from beginning to end," sighed Ward Morehouse (*NYS*). Louis Kronenberger (*PM*) dubbed it "a completely earnest play that is also a hopelessly bad one." Critics found the Freudian play completely lacking in tragic dimension and its dialogue self-consciously literary and out of place in the rural setting.

The starkly depicted locale is Bison Run, Nebraska, at the turn of the century. Morose farm boy Mark Orme (Donald Buka) suffers from a pathological fixation for his late mother, who died under what he suspects were suspicious circumstances while he was away at school. Mark communes with his mother, whose voice comes to him in the sound of a train whistle in the cornfield or while he embraces his girlfriend (Mary Rolfe). He becomes convinced of his father's (Thomas Chalmers) culpability in the death when the latter marries his gentle Swedish maid, Hilda Paulson (Beatrice de Neergaard). He thereupon shoots his father. As the father lies dying, Mark learns that he is innocent, and there follows a bathetic outpouring of previously repressed feelings of love between son and parent. Throughout, a choral function is played by a group of gossiping townswomen.

Director Falk was dean of the theatre department at Syracuse University, where the play was first produced. In the cast were such players as Parker Fennelly, Lester Lonergan, Jr., Mary Boylan, and Grace Mills.

LOCO [Comedy/Business/Family/Illness/Marriage/Sex] A: Dale Eunson and Katherine Albert; SC: a magazine story by Dale Eunson; D/P: Jed Harris; S: Donald Oenslager; C: Emeline Roche; T: Biltmore Theatre; 10/16/46 (37)

Waldo Brewster (Jay Fassett) is a wealthy but dull Wall Streeter. His wife (Beverly Bayne) fails to understand him, and he cuts off his daughter (Elaine Stritch) when she weds a dancer (Si Varlo) whom Waldo mistakes for a gigolo. While out one evening with a business acquaintance (Morgan Wallace) and his girlfriend (Marlo Dwyer), he meets the latter's friend, a beautiful but gabby Conover model named Loco Dempsey (movie actress Jean Parker, in her Broadway debut). His libido is stirred, and he invites Loco to spend a winter weekend at his snowbound Maine hunting lodge. Before they make it to bed, however, Loco contracts the measles, and Waldo must nurse her through her illness, an experience through which he becomes wiser and resolves to turn over a new leaf with his family. Waldo returns to town to find his daughter home from Japan and pregnant. Her spouse flies home to join her. Waldo is subsequently frightened by the news that Loco is going to blackmail him, but the rumor proves to be unfounded, as the model is really a peach of a girl. Waldo, influenced by Loco's rectitude, is reconciled with both his daughter and his wife, but before the final curtain falls is scratching himself behind the ears.

There were some scattered laugh lines that showed a modicum of wit, and the Conover model suggested a pale version of Judy Holliday's quintessential bimbo in *Born Yesterday*. Arthur Pollock (*BE*) commented of the authors, "Their dialogue is often quite fetching. But they are faint, a little hazy. Their play lacks definition. It sprawls and is thin." And Brooks Atkinson (*NYT*) offered, "Incompetently written, large sections of it seem like a prolonged non sequitur." Parker Fennelly and Barry Kelley were actors in the cast.

LONG WAY FROM HOME, A [Drama/Alcoholism/Blacks/Crime/Gambling/Marriage/Religion/Sex/Southern] A: Randolph Goodman and Walter Carroll; SC: Maxim Gorky's play, *The Lower Depths**; D: Alan Schneider; S/L: Leo Kerz; C: Rose Bogdanoff; P: Nat Karson for the Experimental Theatre, Inc., u/t/a/o the American National Theatre and Academy; T: Maxine Elliott's Theatre; 2/8/48 (6)

Russian-born Alan Schneider made his New York directing debut with this ambitious but unsuccessful transformation of Gorky's Russian drama, *The Lower Depths*, into a play set in an American black milieu (the playwrights were white). Schneider replaced Sanford Meisner, with whom coauthor Goodman had not been happy. The process of convincing the producers to allow the unknown director to take over was an arduous one, recounted in Schneider's *Entrances*. After agreeing to remove Meisner, producer Karson himself decided to do the job (although he had no directing experience), with Schneider--who had been hoping to direct--asked to be the assistant director. Schneider's resistance paid off when he was finally asked to direct (for a total fee of $200). Karson, disgruntled about losing the directorial nod, turned out to be one of the most useless producers with whom Schneider ever was to work and spent most of his time at the racetrack, rather than at the theatre. When he finally came to a run-through, Karson acted as if he were disgusted and announced that he was taking over. The threat, however, seemed to pass, but on the day of the opening, it reemerged, and Schneider was told that he was to be barred from the afternoon rehearsal he had called before the evening's performance. But when Karson attempted to take over the rehearsal himself, the entire cast walked out, complaining of feeling too ill to rehearse. A bit later, a note arrived from Karson at the drugstore where everyone had gathered. "Dear Alan, we're waiting for you. It's going to be a terrific show." The crisis had passed.

The majority of critics saw little to praise aside from the fine performances and direction. Robert Garland (*NYJA*) could not accept the transformation. He argued that he was almost deceived for a while, but eventually began to see that the characters were "merely unhappy and long-suffering Moscovites reproduced in blackface." And William Hawkins (*NYWT*) declared, "There is a basic lack of authenticity . . . which results from the superimposing basically Russian philosphizing [*sic*] on a North Carolina slum." Ward Morehouse (*NYS*) thought it "curiously unmoving." "Slavic introspection and defeatism are not well served by the instinctive exuberance of Negro acting," advised Howard Barnes (*NYHT*).

The setting is a basement residence under a pool hall somewhere near Durham, North Carolina. Here reside, in squalid conditions, a number of black people representing a cross-section of character types, most of them riffraff and misfits. The action is much the same as in the Russian original, with mood and atmosphere taking precedence over plot. The people include the philosophical Preacher (Alonzo Bosan), who appears among the quarreling, gambling, and drink-sodden folk to overturn their despair and bring them hope. The residents include Duke (Henry Scott), Bessie (Edna Mae Harris), Dee (Harry Bolden), Four-Eyes (Catherine Ayers, whose performance won the Clarence Derwent Award, but who never acted again), Silky (Maurice Ellis), Sad-Act (William Marshall), Lily (Mildred Smith), Joebuck (Josh White), Grady Horn (Augustus Smith), Celine (Fredi Washington), Cotton (Earl Sydnor), and Marcy (Ruby Dee). The chief dramatic incident is when Celine, wife of the place's owner, Grady, scalds her sister Marcy's legs because Celine has lost her lover, Joebuck, to Marcy. Joebuck then kills Grady and will be executed for the crime.

Schneider gave a detailed account of his rehearsals of the show in *Entrances*. He told, among many other things, of how a piece of business in which he had the actors check for food in the set's garbage cans disturbed the scenic designer, Leo Kerz, who felt that his design was being disturbed and had to be reassured that the can tops would be properly replaced. Kerz also created a fuss when Schneider asked him to move a heavily laden clothesline to another angle so as to prevent the actors from strangling themselves on it when they crossed the stage. But the thing that most infuriated Kerz was when he saw a character lying in a bunk using a pencil stub to fill in the crossword on a newspaper meant to represent wall insulation. To him, this meant that Schneider was behind a plot to deface the set. To satisfy the designer, a compromise had to be reached wherein only a few squares a day could be filled in. "I was appalled at the extent of this talented scene designer's inability to understand the relationship between his setting and what took place within it," wrote Schneider.

LONGITUDE 49 [Drama/Blacks/Crime/Sea] A/D: Herb Tank; M: William Moore, Jr.; S: Ed Walsh and Idell Carruth; P: Freedom Players; T: Czechoslovak Hall (OB); 5/50

A space at 347 East Seventy-second Street was used for the production of this socially conscious play. It was by an ex-merchant marine who used his experiences to describe problems of racial discrimination aboard a merchant ship docked in Iran.

A black crew member (Sidney Poitier) is chosen by the mostly white crew to correct the oppressive conditions aboard ship. The bigoted first mate (Vic Winton) opposes this, as does the captain (Al Nadler), who, however, is more moderate. The crew's delegate ends up being killed by the first mate. The men must then decide what action to take against the villain.

The play was considered saltily written, with authentic detail and honest character depictions. The role of an Irish sailor was played in whiteface by black actor Frank Silvera, who did a highly creditable job. Gros. (*V*) thought the work "a solid all-around construction job, with acting, production and scripting fine." "It's a sturdy play, well and sturdily acted," wrote Arthur Pollock (*DC*), "except for the fact that in their eagerness to be real and true the actors sometimes forget to get on with the story."

LOOK MA, I'M DANCIN' [Musical/Legacy/Romance/Show Business] CN: Jerome Robbins; B: Jerome Lawrence and Robert E. Lee; M/LY: Hugh Martin; D/CH: George Abbott and Jerome Robbins; S: Oliver Smith; C: John Pratt; P: George Abbott; T: Adelphi Theatre; 1/29/48 (188)

Nancy Walker again proved herself one of Broadway's brightest zanies in the starring role of this show, which was admired also for its rocket-fast staging, its clever choreography, and the dancing of classically trained Harold Lang as arrogant choreographer Eddie Winkler; still, the show was "steadily disappointing" (Richard Watts, Jr. [*NYP*]) because of its average book, music, and lyrics. Howard Barnes (*NYHT*) said that "the book . . . is less of a satire than a series of gags fed to the leading comedians between tunes."

Walker was Lilly Malloy, a would-be ballet dancer and ugly-duckling brewery heiress. In order to get a chance to further her artistic aspirations, she backs the Russo-American ballet company run by one F. Plancek (Robert Harris). (Her memorable first entrance was arranged to have her walk down a ramp at Pennsylvania Station to the ballet company car, draped in furs and leading a Russian wolfhound.) She tours the country with the troupe, dancing in its chorus and getting involved in various tribulations. Eddie wants to revise the classic choreography and add a modern touch to it. Eventually, dressed in a tutu, Lily does his side-splitting version of "Swan Lake," and its hilarity propels her from chorus line to stardom; she even winds up owning the troupe. Meanwhile, a love affair balloons, is deflated, and is then inflated again between the egotistical Eddie and one of the dancers (Janet Reed). Eddie learns the value of humility.

The show's background allowed it to make ample fun of ballet dancers and dancing. One of the funniest numbers, "The Pajama Dance," came in the second act and concerned a group of insomniacs pretending to be sleepwalkers in the narrow aisle of a Pullman car. Less successful was the Mack Sennett-inspired "Mademoiselle Marie," reminiscent of a similarly inspired number in *High Button Shoes*. Well-liked songs were "I'm Tired of Texas," "I'm Not So Bright," "The Little Boy Blues," and, most popular, "Shauny O'Shay."

Walker's homely looks and ebullient personality rolled the critics in the aisles. "Miss Walker is a comedian with an intuitive sense of timing and inflection whose humor never betrays her genial good nature," noted Euphemia Van Rensselaer Wyatt (*CW*). "Big Bertha is about as near as she comes to subtlety," laughed John Mason Brown (*SR*). "A headline is her notion of innuendo; a chimney her idea of an exclamation point. Still, she does win and deserve her laughs at doing all the expected things either with the lines . . . or in burlesqueing the tarlataned realms of Degas." During the run, Walker kept losing her voice and had to take a number of leaves, sometimes for weeks at a time. She was understudied by her sister, who resembled her but lacked her unique talent. George Abbott wrote in *"Mister Abbott"* that the show might have been a major hit if Walker had not been ill so frequently.

Lang's success was also great, especially with his opening number, "I Gotta Dance," performed in answer to the veteran dancers' question as to what dances he can do. It showed his abilities in a wide-ranging assortment of styles.

Top dancers joining Lang in the show were Tommy Rall, Katharine Sergava, and a number of other highly respected dancers. Funny-looking and -sounding comedienne Alice Pearce also contributed to the good times, while singers Don Liberto, Loren Welch, and Virginia Gorski were no slouches either.

According to Abbott, the wolfhound with which Walker made her memorable entrance caused a serious backstage dilemma at one performance. A stagehand had given him a bone to gnaw on, and when it was time for his entrance, the dog refused to give up the prize, snarling viciously at anyone who tried to take it. However, the man Abbott had put in charge of the dog (he was also playing a redcap) was adept with animals, "and he was able to drag the beast onstage just at the last minute, though the audience may have wondered why the dog was looking so longingly offstage right."

LOST IN THE STARS [Musical/Blacks/Crime/Politics/Prison/Race/Religion/Sex/Trial] B/LY: Maxwell Anderson; M: Kurt Weill; SC: Alan Paton's novel, *Cry, the Beloved Country*; D: Rouben Mamoulian; S: George Jenkins; C: Anna Hill Johnstone; P: Playwrights' Company; T: Music Box Theatre; 10/30/49 (281)

A "musical tragedy" about the racial problems in South Africa, based on a well-known novel by a white South African writer. It was admired for its singing, its music, and its social and artistic aspirations, but a small number, influenced by their memory of the novel, considered it not wholly effective in theatricalizing its material. Joseph T. Shipley (*NL*), who found the dramatic structure too episodic and unable to make convincing the coincidences of the plot, declared, "This story . . . builds through some scenes touching in themselves, but without the development that in a novel confers reality and depth of feeling." But Whitney Bolton (*NYMT*) wholeheartedly approved the transplantation, although there were several scenes that fell flat. Overall, however, "A needed, important, beautiful [*sic*] contrived job has been done and . . . its occasional falters do not prevent the full flower of emotion which the play produces." Hobe. (*V*) thought it "a tender and moving musical drama," not especially commercial in its subject matter, but "so tastefully and skillfully done that it rates as a probable boxoffice success." Howard Barnes (*NYHT*) believed that the work had "excitement, flavor, heart and a stern authority." It was selected as one of the season's ten best works.

The expert way in which the music--which makes considerable use of choral singing--and story were integrated was remarked on widely. Top songs included the title number, "Thousands of Miles," "Train to Johannesburg," "The Little Grey House," "Who'll Buy?" "Trouble Man," "Stay Well," and "Big Mole." Weill's haunting score evoked the black musical styles while being original to himself. "It has the religious fervor of the chant and the plaintive quality befitting the pathos of the story," wrote Kelcey Allen (*WWD*).

Set in a hill village and in Johannesburg, this is the tale of a saintly Zulu preacher of Natal, Stephen Kumalo (Todd Duncan), who leaves his village for the city to find his son, who has not written in months. There he discovers that the errant boy, Absalom (Julian Mayfield), has, during a robbery attempt, accidentally killed a white youth named Edward Jarvis (Judson Rees). Edward was an important friend to the oppressed blacks; his wealthy, white supremacist father, James (Leslie Banks), is a neighbor back in the village. Absalom, now in prison, is tried for and convicted of murder; he is sentenced to be hung. James, confused and miserable, discovers a shared grief with Stephen and becomes his friend. The piece ends on a note of reconciliation and mutual understanding between the two fathers. The work powerfully conveys the system of apartheid, with all its racist evils; the economic discrimination practiced against blacks; and the political demagoguery of the white leaders.

Mamoulian's staging was highly effective, especially in its use of group movement and its ability to convey the atmosphere of the locale and people. Duncan's performance, both his singing and acting, were superb. In the large and gifted cast were Warren Coleman as a shopkeeper, Frank Roane as a choral leader, William Greaves as the thief who involves Absalom in the murder, Inez Matthews as Absalom's live-in lover and the mother of his child, Sheila Guyse as a honky-tonk performer, and, in other roles, Laverne French, John Morley, William Marshall, Georgette Harvey, and Guy Spaull.

When the show opened to good reviews, both Weill and Anderson, said John F. Wharton in *Life among the Playwrights*, acted smugly superior, as if, despite major tryout problems, the play had been foreordained a hit. But when business slackened, they panicked and even ordered the show's press agent and business manager to guarantee sold-out houses, as if that were possible. "Max became more and more irascible and Kurt more and more excitable. Bill [Fields, the press agent] said to me, 'I'm scared that Kurt is going to have a heart attack.' He died from just such an attack on April 3, 1950."

LOUISIANA LADY [Musical/Period/Prostitution/Romance/Sex/Southern] B: Isaac Green, Jr., and Eugene Berton; LY/M: Monte Carlo and Alma Sanders; SC: Samuel Shipman and Kenneth Perkins's play, *Creoles**; D: Edgar J. MacGregor; CH: Felicia Sorel; S: Watson Barratt; C: Frank Thompson; L: Leo Kerz; P: Hal Shelton; T: Century Theatre; 6/2/47 (4)

A 1927 play was the origin of this scrawny turkey that kicked off the new season. It is set in 1830 New Orleans, where a "high-class" brothel is run by Madame Corday (Monica Moore, replacing Olga Baclanova), who has been forced into this business by a pile of debts. Arriving to visit her during Mardi Gras time is her convent-bred daughter, Marie-Louise (Edith Fellows), on leave from a finishing school. Madame Corday and her employees go out of their way to disguise the true purpose of their occupation from the innocent lass. There is a dastardly slave-trading villain (George Baxter) who is a threat to the madame and her daughter, whom he desires, and a romantic pirate named El Gato (Ray Jacquemont), who saves the slavery-bound cargo, sets them free in Haiti, and wins Marie-Louise.

A complete lack of imagination and wit pervaded the humorless book, and the derivative nine-tune score did not lag far behind. "It plods along through its two acts without ever becoming even adequate entertainment," moaned Herm. (*V*). "There may have been more objectionable shows," groaned William Hawkins (*NYWT*), "but there can seldom have been any duller."

The show's sets and costumes were salvaged from a show that closed during tryouts, *In Gay New Orleans*. The company included singer Victoria Cordova, comic actor Charles Judels, and acrobatic dancer Lou Wills, Jr.

LOVE FOR LOVE [Dramatic Revival*] A: William Congreve; D: John Gielgud; S: Rex Whistler; C: Jeannetta Cochrans; L: William Conway; P: Theatre Guild, John C. Wilson, and H. M. Tennent, Ltd.; T: Royale Theatre; 5/26/47 (48)

A streamlined revival of Congreve's 1695 Restoration comedy, seen locally in 1925 and 1940. The current offering was helmed by John Gielgud, who also portrayed Valentine. Gielgud had pruned the play considerably, toning down its more vulgar expressions and removing its sailor's hornpipe sequence. Richard Wordsworth was Jeremy, George Hayes was Scandal, Cyril Ritchard was Tattle, Adrianne Allen was Mrs. Frail, John Kidd was Foresight, Pamela Brown was Angelica, Malcolm Keen was Sir Sampson Legend, Marian Spencer was Mrs. Foresight, Jessie

Evans was Miss Prue, Robert Flemyng was Ben, and Sebastian Cabot was Buckram. Various members of this visiting company were also engaged during the season in a successful revival of Wilde's *The Importance of Being Earnest*, also staged by and starring Gielgud.

The play was received with mixed opinions. Brooks Atkinson (*NYT*) much preferred the company's production of Wilde to that of Congreve. Although he found many of the actors polished and appropriately comic, he wrote that "the performance as a whole lacks the brittle, lacquered uniformity of the previous work" and said that the play often seemed tedious and tiresome. A kinder opinion was Euphemia Van Rensselaer Wyatt's (*CW*), who wrote, "Mr. Gielgud and his company have given all their art and their grace to Congreve; gaiety and elegance are the keynotes of the production." Warmer still--at least about the production--was John Mason Brown (*SR*), who thought it unlikely that a better version of the play could be offered. In his view, the English company played the work as if to the manner born, and he liked its avoidance of the artificial fripperies and mincing manner so often affected by Americans in playing Restoration comedy. "Among all their graces their chief distinction is . . . that they act the many dazzling passages of high comedy at their disposal so that the mind of Congreve speaks through his artifices." However, he had to admit that the play itself "seems as much of a bore as a delight." Brown's most prominent difficulties were with the overly literary and "bloodless" scenes of high comedy, which required too much concentration to follow word for word, and with the excessively complex plot.

Gielgud's Valentine was played straight as a high-minded lover instead of for high comic style and was consequently judged insipid and dull by various writers. Atkinson said that the character came off "as a pleasant, well-mannered young man without much strength of personality--more at home in a library than at Will's coffee house." But Brown considered his acting "a technical triumph; admirably spoken, gracefully postured, unflaggingly thought. He is a man who, in his scenes of feigned madness, is a prose sketch of Hamlet."

LOVE GOES TO PRESS [Comedy/Journalism/Military/Romance/Sex/Show Business/War/Women] A: Martha Gellhorn and Virginia Cowles; D: Wallace Douglas; S: Raymond Sovey; C: Emeline Roche; P: Warren P. Munsell and Herman Bernstein; T: Biltmore Theatre; 1/1/47 (5)

This disappointing, American-created farcical satire on war correspondents previously had played in London with some success; six members of its original cast came to Broadway with it. Coauthor Gellhorn formerly had been wed to novelist Ernest Hemingway.

The play is set at the Allied press camp, Poggibonsi, Italy, in 1944, during the war. The two chief characters are sophisticated female war correspondents (the same profession previously followed by the playwrights). One is Jane Mason (Joyce Heron) of the *New York Bulletin*, the other Annabelle Jones (Jane Middleton) of the *San Francisco World*. Annabelle comes across her ex-husband, Joe Rogers (William Post, Jr.), from whom she parted because he, a reporter for a rival paper, used to steal her material for his own purposes. Joe, rumored to be engaged to Daphne Rutherford (Georgina Cookson), a daffy English actress entertaining the soldiers, begins to steal Annabelle's stories for his own byline again, which once more cools off Annabelle. Her pal Jane falls for officious Major Philip Brooke-Jervaux (Ralph Michael), a British public relations officer, previously disdainful of women correspondents. Daphne, meanwhile, has made a name for herself by accidentally getting into combat and ends up with a Hollywood contract. Although love has gone to press, the women check out of their affairs in order to follow assignments to Burma.

"Love and the press have rarely seemed sillier," sighed Arthur Pollock (*BE*). "It is all quite elaborately dull and synthetic," disapproved Rowland Field (*NEN*).

LOVE IS NO HEAVEN [Drama/Crime/Marriage/Sex/Show Business/Small Town/War] A/D/P: Paul Burton-Mercur; S: Dick Corbin; T: Malin Theatre (OB); 3/15/43

At 135 West Forty-fourth Street stood a primitively equipped small theatre (previously a rehearsal hall) with a minute stage and creaking seats known as the Malin Studio or the Malin Theatre, the latter being its name when it produced this "inept and amateurish and generally painful" (John Anderson [*NYJA*]) vanity affair about a pair of sisters named Claire Trent (Doris Deane) and Esther Powers (Anita Carroll). The blond and statuesque Claire wants to forget her burlesque queen past--although she has been offered a Hollywood contract--and become a respectable matron, for which purpose she has wed Dr. Robert Trent (Joseph Hoar). But Dr. Trent is not the answer, for he seduces and betrays Claire's sister. Pregnant by the physician, she rejects the man she loves (Dick Corbin), but is unable to tell him why. He leaves to fight the Japanese. Esther then shoots the doctor (the gun almost failed to go off on opening night) and hides the gun in a vase of flowers. Roland Fuller (Lew Talkov), the local prosecutor (who loves Claire), is baffled by the slaying and cannot find the murder weapon. (None of the critics remained to find out if the murderess or the gun were ever discovered.)

The actors, said Wilella Waldorf (*NYP*) "managed to keep their faces straight although the audience found some of the most serious lines uncommonly amusing." She added that the play "is written almost entirely in cliches, and the verbiage often becomes so elaborate that it is difficult to keep from falling into the same style in reviewing it."

LOVE LIFE [Musical/Business/Family/Fantasy/Marriage/Period/Politics/Show Business/Trial/Women/Youth] B/LY: Alan Jay Lerner; M: Kurt Weill; D: Elia Kazan; CH: Michael Kidd; S: Boris Aronson; C: Lucinda Ballard; P: Cheryl Crawford; T: Forty-sixth Street Theatre; 10/7/48 (252)

Elia Kazan took one of his rare digressions into musical comedy direction with this mildly successful, frequently novel, but ultimately inadequate "vaudeville" starring Nanette Fabray and Ray Middleton; Fabray won the 1949-1949 Tony for an actress in a musical. The show's fantastical concept was to tell its satirically bitter story of American marriage as seen through the experiences of a single couple, Susan and Sam Cooper (Fabray and Middleton), over the years from 1791 to 1948, allowing their marital ups and downs (mostly the latter) to be seen in relation to the nation's economic and industrial progress. An overarching idea--questioned by various critics--is that life was better in preindustrial times. The show presents the eternally youthful Susan and Sam journeying through the years within a vaudeville-show framework. Actually, the show employs several genres. Lyricist Lerner is was quoted in Gene Lees's *Inventing Champagne*: "We tried to employ practically every form of dramatic storytelling. For example, one scene is written in the American ballad style; another is like a little musical play; another is in sketch form; another is in musical comedy form, and still another is straight dramatic form."

It opens with a magician (Jay Marshall) causing Sam to levitate and using Susan as a body to saw in half. When the magician suddenly departs, leaving the couple in this awkward situation, Susan and Sam must ponder how she has become half housewife and half provider, while Sam is simply up in the air. In 1791 the bloomingly happy young couple and their two kids (Cheryl Archer and Johnny Stewart) move to Mayville, and Sam earns his living as a carpenter. America's economic transitions bring gradual dissension into the Cooper home. A vaudeville routine helps to make the transition for Sam from carpentry to factory work in 1821; by 1890 Susan is a suffragette leader, her shaky position represented by a children's trapeze act. The Coopers' marital problems come to a head in 1920 with Susan, newly liberated by women's suffrage, becoming distracted by the jazz age and Sam getting wrapped up in business maneuvers. The entire second part of the show is set in 1948, when the whole family wears glasses. Sam and Susan, preoccupied with their careers, split up and he moves out. A Punch-and-Judy divorce court ballet follows, and Susan is offered, by a minstrel show finale, her choice among astrology, cynicism, or romance. By the show's end, the couple are walking a tightrope back toward each other.

The critics carped over Lerner's excessively negative ideas on the marital state; the vaudeville concept also wore thin for many, as it seemed too loosely connected to the thematic substance. Euphemia Van Rensselaer Wyatt (*CW*) loved the score and the performances, but had trouble with the writing: "*Love Life* is a tortuous approach to idealism, a mixture of good and excessively bad taste." The disappointed Brooks Atkinson (*NYT*) confessed that "it is cute, complex and joyless--a general gripe masquerading as entertainment." "*Love Life* switches moods so rapidly and often, that it sometimes seems ashamed of them," lamented William Hawkins (*NYWT*). "Some sequences are pointed, clear and witty. Others are so querulously introverted that they suggest a person taking out his innards for a morbid and puzzled look at them." But there were strong supporters, too, such as George Freedley (*NYMT*), who raved about its unconventionality: "*Love Life* is the most intelligent and adult musical yet offered on the American stage."

Songs selected by various critics to laud included "Here I'll Stay with You" (the show's biggest hit), "Green-up Time," "Progress," "Economics" (sung by a black quartet), "Love Song" (beautifully sung by Johnny Thompson as a hobo), "I Remember It Well," "This Is the Life," and "Mr. Right."

LOVE ME LONG [Comedy/Romance/Sex] A: Doris Frankel; D: Margaret Perry and Brock Pemberton; S: John Root; C: Margaret Pemberton; P: Brock Pemberton; T: Forty-eighth Street Theatre; 11/7/49 (16)

Later in the season Shirley Booth would score the greatest success of her career in *Come Back, Little Sheba*; looked at with hindsight, therefore, the failure of the present effort was providential. Its plot, very reminiscent of Noël Coward's *Private Lives**, concerned two engaged couples, Abby Quinn (Booth) and Jim Kennedy (Russell Hardie) and Ike Skinner (George Keane) and Margaret Anderson (Anne Jackson). Using the postwar housing shortage for its impetus, the story concerns the attempts of the two couples to move into the same apartment. It turns out that Abby and Ike had been twice married and twice divorced and that Jim and Margaret once were interested in each other. The cynical Ike and Abby grow restless with their uninteresting companions and run off to a hotel room together. By the time they guiltily return the next day, Jim and Margaret have fallen in love.

The play was charged with the crimes of allowing its presumably charming characters to be ineffably boring, of having a plot that could be predicted within the first few minutes, and of lacking more than half a dozen modest laughs. This was, avowed Richard Watts, Jr. (*NYP*), "a dull, familiar and lugubrious comedy which still hopes wistfully that it is possible to get a laugh by mentioning the Dodgers." "The situation creaks, and the dialogue is as forced and labored as the singing of a prima donna with a bad voice coach," scoffed Robert Coleman (*NYDM*).

The cast included Harry Bannister as a harassed landlord, Heywood Hale Broun as a telephone man, Daniel Reed as Margaret's game inventor father, and Jennifer Howard as an interior decorator.

LOVE ON LEAVE [Comedy/Family/Hotel/Military/Romance/Sex/Youth] A: A. B. Shiffrin; D: Eugene S. Bryden; S: Paul Morrison; P: Charles Stewart and Martin Goodman; T: Hudson Theatre; 6/20/44 (7)

Many spectators departed in midperformance from this fitful sex comedy about a young girl's sexual curiosity. It tells of Lucy Wilson (Rosemary Rice), the fifteen-year-old daughter of a famous specialist in child psychology, Sam Wilson (Millard Mitchell). Intrigued by the conduct of a trampy local girl (Joann Dolan) and wishing to taste life so she can become an actress, Lucy sneaks out of her house in Astoria, Queens, dressed as whorishly as she can, to follow the tart to Times Square. There she ends up in a seedy hotel room with a saintly young sailor named Nick Hardy (John Conway), whom she attempts vigorously to bed. The sailor, unlike those then typical on the stage, is a fine, upstanding fellow with a mind as clean as soap. Recognizing that Lucy is lying about her age and experience, and thinking of his own sister at home, he returns her to her family, but she tries to shift the blame from herself to the boy, claiming that he got her drunk and seduced her. The police (Roderick Maybee and John Farrell) are dragged in, but the family doctor (Ross Matthew) settles matters satisfactorily, and Nick ends up with Lucy's sister (June Wilson).

The general line taken by the critics was that to handle the subject of juvenile delinquency as farce was socially irresponsible. Besides, said Herrick Brown (*NYS*), it was "a crude and badly written charade from any angle." "It would be hard to say whether *Love on Leave* is most lacking in taste, skill or sense," scoffed Louis Kronenberger (*PM*). "It lurches from comedy to farce, it alternates chatter with shrieks, half its characters are burlesques and the other half bores."

Mary Sargent, James Dobson, Stanley Bell, Bert Freed, Ramsay Williams, and Eleanor Gordon were in the play.

LOVELY ME [Comedy/Family/Hotel/Romance/Show Business/Youth] A: Jacqueline Susann and Beatrice Cole; M: Arthur Siegel and Jeff Bailey; D: Jessie Royce Landis; S: Donald Oenslager; C: Eleanor Goldsmith; P: David Lowe; T: Adelphi Theatre; 12/25/46 (37)

Jacqueline Susann, soon to be famous as a novelist of popular pulp fiction and other writings, had acted on Broadway before coauthoring this dismal comedy in which Luba Malina gave a colorful, if not unanimously approved, performance. It is set in the expensive hotel-apartment of frequently married ex-film star and would-be nightclub chanteuse Natasha Smith (Malina) on Central Park South. The heavily accented Russian performer has taken the name Smith to avoid being typed as a foreigner. Natasha's threatening financial situation and the possibility of eviction prompt her to seek one more wealthy spouse, her fifth. The Russian-born lady is supporting a sponging aunt (Barbara Bulgakov) and her own precocious daughter (June Dayton), in love with a dog raiser (Paul Marlin). Natasha must also ensure the cash to send the girl to Harvard. Seemingly permanently ensconced in a corner is a wordless young composer (Arthur Siegel), working on his unfinished symphony. Scrambled into Natasha's efforts to land a bumbling suitor, Thomas Van Stokes (Reynolds Evans), are two ex-husbands, Stanislaus Stanislavsky (Mischa Auer), a former flagpole sitter, and Mike Shane (Millard Mitchell), a theatrical press agent. During the play the star gets to sing two new but not highly thought-of songs.

The much-doctored play--inspired by someone named Lya Lys, a former neighbor of Susann's--originally had been called *The Temporary Mrs. Smith* and, with Francine Larrimore in the lead, had been given two separate tryout tours under the producership of Vinton Freedley before he abandoned it. The original director was Billy Gilbert, who was replaced by Thomas Mitchell, who was replaced by Gilbert, who was finally replaced by Jessie Royce Landis. The play's final title arrived when the very pregnant Susann looked into a mirror and asked, "How could this happen to lovely me?" which also was the inspiration for one of the songs Malina sang.

George Freedley (*NYMT*) called the play "a sad affair." Brooks Atkinson (*NYT*), while noting its several amusing passages, concluded, "Its humor is transitory and more often than not just plain hackneyed." George Jean Nathan (*TBY*) said, "The humor is sub-vaudeville; the acting of the leading roles was of a bad musical comedy brand; and the direction loud if not funny."

Because the Adelphi was booked for another show, *Lovely Me* was moved to the Coronet after two weeks, but there, too, another show had been booked previously, so that when no third theatre became available, the show had to close. According to Susann's biographer, Barbara Seaman, whose book bears the same title as the play, *Lovely Me* had become popular through word of mouth and was selling out when it folded.

LOVERS AND FRIENDS [British/Family/Marriage/Military/Romance/Theatre] A: Dodie Smith; D: Guthrie McClintic; S/C: Motley; P: Katharine Cornell and John C. Wilson; T: Plymouth Theatre; 11/29/43 (168)

After appearing in a series of distinguished revivals for several years, Katharine Cornell selected this romantic but banal new British "woman's play" in which to appear. Her costar was Raymond Massey, who recently had played opposite her in *The Doctor's Dilemma*. The small-cast drama was set in London with a prologue occurring in Regent's Park in 1918, three acts in a drawing room in 1930, and an epilogue in Regent's Park in 1942. As usual, the production evinced all the signs of talent and good taste associated with plays starring and produced by the great leading lady, which was fortunate in that the play itself would otherwise have proved "an insufferable bore," according to Lewis Nichols (*NYT*).

Rodney Boswell (Massey), a young British officer in World War I, and Stella (Cornell) meet on a blind date in Regent's Park when Stella, an actress, is sent by her friend, Lennie Lorimer (Carol Goodner), another actress, who must break her date with Rodney. Rodney forgets his love for the absent actress and falls instead for Stella, whom he marries. By 1930 they have two sons and he has become a successful barrister. However, he grows bored with Stella and gets involved with a scheming young secretary named Martha Jones (Anne Burr). He desires a divorce from Stella so he may marry the secretary. Stella, meanwhile, returns to the stage and begins a flirtation with Edmund Alexander (Henry Daniell), a famous and witty novelist-playwright with whom she plans to leave for America. Events, however, soon open Rodney's eyes to the fact that Martha is a pathological liar, and he and Stella reconcile. Years later, in 1942, Stella and Rodney are in Regent's Park. Lennie, Stella's actress friend, has married Edmund. Stella and Rodney are grandparents. They find amusement in recalling the folly of their youth.

This was a classic example of the polite drawing-room drama associated with the modern English stage. The characters were all reserved and articulate, and the action of the play made very little progress from beginning to end. However, as Rosamond Gilder (*TAM*) argued, "At no point is the listener caught up in the events on the stage or in the sufferings of Stella and Rodney." Despite the universality of the problems exposed, "Miss Dodie Smith's style does not tend to transcend her material," continued Gilder. "She cannot lift the particular into the general." George Jean Nathan (*TBY*) characterized it as "a smear of childish, sentimental greasepaint which is less a play than a vehicle, like a baby carriage." Katherine Hynes played a maid.

In *A Hundred Different Lives*, Massey recalled that one of the lines spoken by Carol Goodner, "Do you ever take your youth out and play with it?" used to stop rehearsals because it broke up the actors, especially Goodner. Director McClintic, being mischievous, refused to cut the line, but eventually had to when the actress was unable to "stop the tears caused by repressed giggling."

LOWER NORTH [Comedy-Drama/Barroom/Marriage/Military/School/Sex/War] A: Martin Bidwell; D: David Burton; S: Raymond Sovey; P: Max J. Jelin; T: Belasco Theatre; 8/25/44 (11)

This "aimless and inexpert" (Ward Morehouse [*NYS*]) first play by a film writer (then in the navy) is about a group of California boot-camp buddies in training for the navy's quartermaster rating. It shows them preparing for exams, nursing their grievances at being in the navy, cavorting at the local saloon, and dealing with various aspects, joyful and tragic, of barracks life. The title comes from the part of the ship where the soldiers' bunks are located.

A wide variety of familiar types from different parts of the country is represented, such as the Texan (Dean King, formerly Dennis King, Jr.) with a gargantuan appetite; the orphan (Robert Myers) who worked at a CCC camp; the rangy cowboy (Arthur Hunnicutt) who longs for his horse; the tough lover-boy sailor (Dort Clark) whose sweetheart marries a draft reject; the sixteen-year-old kid (Douglas Jones) who admires--with possibly homosexual feelings--the Lothario because he reminds him of his brother in the air force; the tough but soft-hearted chief petty officer (Rusty Lane) who must make a unified company out of this mixed bunch; and so on. Among important nonnaval characters are a marine veteran of Guadalcanal (John Conway), drinking to forget what he has lived through; a bartender (John Farrell) at the Rendezvous Bar; and a couple of bimbos (Blanche Faye and Blanche Gladstone) searching for sailor love. Paul Ford played a minor role.

The principal action in the essentially plotless play follows Jim (Kim Spalding), who wants to go and remain AWOL to be with his pregnant wife Mary (Sara Anderson), but who is convinced by his pals to return to camp, where they have covered up his absence (a sign of their growing unity). When he does, he not only finds understanding from the petty officer, but becomes his section's honor man and realizes that the nation's cause is bigger than his personal concerns.

Otis L. Guernsey, Jr. (*NYHT*), saw no reason to be concerned with the play's pasteboard figures, none of whom were stageworthy, and all of whom were enmeshed in a script filled with movie clichés. "There are isolated scenes which hold the audience's interest," alleged George Freedley (*NYMT*), but the playwright "lacked the skill to put them together as a coherent whole." On opening night the curtain was delayed when the third-act set, suspended in the flies, came crashing to the stage before the play began.

LUCKY DAYS [Musical/Yiddish Language] B: William Siegel; M: Sholem Secunda; LY: Isidor Lillian; D/P: Menasha Skulnik; CH: Valentina Belova; S: Michael Saltzman; T: Second Avenue Theatre (OB); 10/15/43

Menasha Skulnik, Miriam Kressyn, and Michal Michalesko were the stars of this formula Yiddish operetta. Yetta Zwerling was sterling in comic support. A highlight was the diminutive Skulnik's appearance in a zoot suit and his singing in Yiddish with Zwerling of "Pistol Packin' Mama." Such routines were seen as part of a Yiddish theatre trend--designed to bolster sagging ticket sales--by appealing to non-Yiddish-speaking audiences.

With the invasion of Poland by the Nazis, a Polish family has suffered many hardships. The husband (Michalesko), now a famous eye specialist in America, believes that his wife (Kressyn) and child were killed in air raids on his home town. He has married a woman who wants all his love and does not want to share it with his memories of his late wife. He cannot get his Polish wife and child out of his mind, though. A blind woman comes from Poland seeking eye treatment from this doctor. She turns out to be the supposedly deceased wife. The seemingly insurmountable plot complications are eventually ironed out, and the doctor is reunited with his wife and child.

The critics viewed the work as sentimental but entertaining rubbish that gave audiences a few good songs and dances, a thorough immersion in bathos, and funny routines by popular comedians. Especially good was Skulnik playing his typical "nebbish" role, described by Thomas R. Dash (*WWD*) as "the jilted one, the one who always gets the dirty end of it and in turn makes fun of himself and then boasts swaggeringly. . . . His clowning is vastly amusing and his dead-pan expression helps his style of comedy. He is either wisecracking in his droll fashion, singing racy lyrics . . . or clowning." The cast included David Lubritzky, Annie Thomashefsky, Anna Teitelbaum, and many others.

LUTE SONG [Musical/China/Family/Marriage/Orientals/Period] B: Sidney Howard and Will Irwin; M: Raymond Scott; LY: Bernard Hanighen; SC: the Chinese play *Pi-Pa-Ji* by Gao Ming (sometimes known as *Pi-Pa-Ki* and attributed to Kao-Tong-Kia or Tse-Ching); D: John Houseman; CH: Yeichi Nimura; DS: Robert Edmond Jones (gowns: Valentina); P: Michael Myerberg; T: Plymouth Theatre; 2/6/46 (142)

An entirely non-Asian cast (apart from the doubtful strain of Oriental blood claimed by Yul Brynner) performed this unusual "Oriental drama with music," based on a classic of the Chinese stage, written toward the end of the Yüan era (1279-1368). Colibrettist Irwin had been fascinated with Chinese theatre ever since his San Francisco youth in the 1890s. Over the years he had worked on many revisions of the play for the American stage and, in 1928 when a French translation appeared at the University of Maryland, began to work on a version with Sidney Howard, although they were not thinking of a musical. It had a well-liked summer-stock tryout at the Berkshire Playhouse in 1930, but was not optioned for Broadway. Other presentations followed outside of New York, most effectively in a University of Hawaii showing using actors of Chinese ancestry. In 1944 movie producer John Byram suggested to theatre producer Michael Myerberg the idea of doing it as a musical vehicle for Mary Martin, which would not have been so unusual given the fact that the fourteenth-century original was performed with musical accompaniment, as is all classical Chinese theatre. The adaptation was successful enough to be selected as one of Burns Mantle's ten best of the season.

This is the tale of a young scholar named Tsai-Yong (Brynner) who chooses not to take the path to personal advancement represented by undergoing the nation's civil-service examinations, but to remain home with his loving bride Tchao-ou-Niang (Martin). Recognizing the importance of the exams, Tchao-ou-Niang and his parents (Augustin Duncan and Mildred Dunnock) prevail upon him to take them, but she vows to care for his parents and to wait faithfully for his return. Tsai-Yong's having read 6,000 books leads to his appointment as chief magistrate, but also to his forced marriage to Prince Nieou's (McKay Morris) daughter Princess Nieou-Chi (Helen Craig). The arrangement prevents him from informing his wife and family of what has transpired. His parents starve to death during a famine, and his wife, who buries them, has to sell her beautiful hair and become a beggar to survive. An arduous journey, bearing her husband's lute, brings her to his home in the capital, where her identity is recognized by the kindly princess, who reunites husband and wife. Seeing their mutual affection, Prince Nieou annuls his daughter's marriage.

In the original, the women share Tsai-Yong, but Mary Martin and her real-life husband insisted on a bowdlerized ending, believing that a character played by a star of her stature should not have to share a man with anyone else. This was done over director Houseman's objections, and he said in *Front and Center* that he "never ceased to regret" allowing Martin to have her way. He also recounted several other difficulties he had with the actress.

Robert Edmond Jones's exceptionally beautiful, gorgeously colored designs (the last of his career) were not enough to turn the show into a financial success, but were viewed as an outstanding contribution to the specialness of the event. "The settings . . . are both simple and extravagant," wrote Euphemia Van Rensselaer Wyatt (*CW*), "but their extravagance is always within the limits of a noble design. The lighting is magic and the celestial vision and the Buddhist Temple make everyone draw their breath faster." But John Mason Brown (*SR*) felt that the simple story was swamped by decor.

The musical was considered too offbeat for general consumption, and its intentions were more honored than its realization. For most critics, its pace was too leisurely and its score uninvolving. But George Jean Nathan (*TBY*) rebuked such critics, insisting that "it is . . . charming and affecting and, for all its undeniable intermittent lags and lapses, something like the sound of a mandolin in the prevailing din of trombones."

Except for a few promising moments at the start, employing a narrating stage manager (Clarence Derwent) and a property man (Albert Vecchio), authentic Chinese staging conventions were omitted in favor of an ersatz chinoiserie of movement and acting styles. Derwent declared in *The Derwent Story* that producer Myerberg gave him and fellow actor McKay Morris permission to build their parts up as they saw fit in order to add humor to the show. Derwent researched the writings of Confucius and Mencius and stole many of their aphorisms, as well as adding some made-up ones of his own. These, he claimed, added "distinction" to the show.

Lewis Nichols (*NYT*) complained of a stylistic disjunction among the music, designs, and story and thought the overall effect one of "jumpiness." Rosamond Gilder (*TAM*) surmised that "there has been not enough time, thought or sustained experimentation expended in the production to give it unity in its new idiom."

Martin, who sang most of the songs, was generally fine--if too American--but even she could not save the work. Gilder described her as she appeared on her first entrance: "The grace of her line as she stands on the step above [her husband], the attentive, submissive angle of her head, the porcelain quality of her heart-shaped face strike exactly the right note. Her silhouette, the movements of her body, her use of hands and arms have the requisite style but the range of her speaking voice is limited." Her best song was "Mountain High, Valley Low."

Brynner, who was either twenty-five or thirty-one at the time, depending on which sources one accepts, got mildly approving reviews, but nevertheless was thought highly enough of to be given the Donaldson Award as most promising newcomer of the season. Rex O'Malley was one of the actors in the large cast, and Nancy Davis (later Mrs. Ronald Reagan) made her debut in the role of Si-Tchun, a lady in waiting at the court. Houseman in *Front and Center* remembered her as "a pink-cheeked, attractive but awkward and amateurish virgin." The daughter of the prominent orthopedic surgeon who cared for Mary Martin's chronic back problems, she was hired at Martin's urging, although Houseman wanted to fire her during the show's tryout period.

LYSISTRATA [Dramatic Revival*/Blacks] A: Aristophanes; AD: Gilbert Seldes; M: Henry Brant; D: James Light; CH: Felicia Sorel; S/L: Ralph Alswang; C: Rose Bogdanoff; P: James Light and Max J. Jelin; T: Belasco Theatre; 10/17/46 (4)

An ambitious but ponderously "dull and stumbling" (Howard Barnes [*NYHT*]) revival of the Seldes version of Aristophanes' "make sex, not war" comedy, last seen locally in 1930. Seldes's adaptation, however, appears to have been coarsened to make it more sexually provocative.

In the present showing, the very large company was black and included Etta Moten as Lysistrata, Fredi Washington as Kolonika, Mildred Smith as Myrrhina, Mercedes Gilbert as Lampito, Leigh Whipper as the leader of the Old Men's Chorus, Pearl Gaines as the leader of the Old Women's Chorus, Rex Ingram as the president of the senate, Emmett "Babe" Wallace as Kinesias, and, in his Broadway debut, Sidney Poitier in the small role of Polydorus.

In his autobiography, *This Life*, Poitier revealed that he had a powerful case of stage fright at the opening. Unable to remember his first line, he said whatever lines he could recall as the actor opposite him tried to help him by giving him the appropriate cues. The confusion that developed caused hilarity in the audience, which he knew was not caused by the play, as his was not a comical part. After continuing to get all his lines mixed up, he walked off, but the audience applauded. The actors backstage, instead of reprimanding him, told him that the audience loved him, but he did not believe them, changed into his street clothes, and left before the curtain calls. When a couple of critics pointed to his scene in their reviews, he realized that he had not killed the play, but neither could he, at the final three performances, repeat what he had done, as by now he was sure of his lines and could only play them straight. The opening-night performance, however, was seen by producer John Wildberg, who gave Poitier a role in the touring version of *Anna Lucasta*, which kept him working for three years.

Rosamond Gilder (*TAM*) thought that the idea of a black production was perfect for this bawdy, energetic play. She implied that it fell apart whenever it took itself too seriously, but she was delighted when it too infrequently let its hair down. A major problem was in getting the modern actors to embody the ancient play's manner. "There was a general awkwardness of gesture and stiffness of carriage and speech that denoted bodies and minds wrapped up in unfamiliar togas. And the play seemed unnecessarily long and padded." George Freedley (*NYMT*) thought the production an affront to the black race and "a degradation of a magnificent comedy." Brooks Atkinson (*NYT*) appreciated the cast's exuberance, but thought that more restraint could have been shown in depicting the "Minskyized" bawdy scenes, especially when Myrrhina did a striptease to entice her husband. Much as he liked the production in general, he, like several others, noted that the play tended to drag.

M

(1) **MACBETH** [Dramatic Revival*] A: William Shakespeare; M: Lehman Engel; D: Margaret Webster; S: Samuel Leve; C: Lemuel Ayers; P: Maurice Evans i/a/w John Haggott; T: National Theatre; 11/11/41 (131)

Margaret Webster and Maurice Evans continued their unparalleled series of successful Shakespeare revivals with this distinguished production of the Bard's Scottish play. There had been seven productions of it locally in the 1930s, the last one being the 1937 version by the visiting Barter Theatre of Abingdon, Virginia. The present offering starred Evans as the Thane and Judith Anderson as his wife (a role she already had played in London opposite Laurence Olivier), with Harry Irvine as Duncan and the Doctor, William Nichols as Malcolm, Ernest Graves as Donalbain, Erford Gage as Lennox, John Ireland as the sergeant and first murderer, Staats Cotsworth as Banquo, Herbert Rudley as Macduff, and Viola Keats as Lady Macduff.

The production was deemed the finest presentation of the play most of the reviewers had ever seen. Although outwardly conventional in most respects, it was lauded for the tremendous tension and excitement it evoked and for its successfully haunting creation of the mood of supernatural and mortal skulduggery. Rosamond Gilder (*TAM*) thought it "well paced and absorbing throughout," and Richard Watts, Jr. (*NYHT*), found it remarkable in being able to combine "the melodramatic violence with the brooding eloquence of the play." One of the few critics to turn thumbs down was John Anderson (*NYJA*), for whom the work was "dull and listless and wholly lacking in the force needed to drive its lunging melodrama across the stage." (In *Don't Put Your Daughter on the Stage*, however, Webster expressed her belief that for all its good qualities, the production lacked mystery and that the scenic investiture was "too heavy and too literal.")

Its setting--an indeterminate Scottish historical period--used a forestage and a unit setting that could be varied with the addition of inset pieces. Samuel Leve's designs, however, were not entirely successful, being rather austere, muted, and, in some eyes, cluttered. Webster's direction was particularly brilliant in capturing all the drama of the murder of Duncan and the subsequent alarums surrounding it. Lehman Engels's driving score--played by a live pit orchestra and supplemented by offstage effects--was a major contributant, as were Lemuel Ayers's costumes, woven from cotton but made to look more substantial through a clever trick of weaving.

Because of the production's extremely complex technical requirements, its stage manager referred to it, wrote Webster, as "a whistling bitch." At the New Haven tryout, the stage manager was struck by stage fright, and only the last-minute arrival of another stage manager prevented a disaster. As with most productions of this supposedly haunted play, there were various mishaps. One involved the smokepots that Evans had suggested using to help make the witches vanish during their scene on the heath. The flash of light--created by a flashbulb in the smokepot powder--was a substitute for a mechanical disappearing device that had failed to work. Evans's idea had its revenge when, during a New York performance, a flash-pot spark set his tartan cloak on fire and an audience member had to shout out a warning to him. He immediately flung the garment into the wings. (In 1980, at a luncheon honoring news broadcaster Walter Cronkite, the audience member who had sounded the alarm introduced herself to Evans.) The greatest proof of the show's susceptibility to catastrophe was the bombing of Pearl Harbor, which came less than a month after the opening, and the selection for the draft of the forty-year-old Evans.

Evans, not a physically impressive actor, had to work to overcome his lack of stature, but his intelligence and sensitivity were memorable enough to outweigh his relatively slight appearance. He said in *All This . . . and Evans Too!* that he based his interpretation on Lord Acton's aphorism, "Power corrupts and absolute power corrupts absolutely." It was his intention for the audience to extrapolate from Macbeth a statement about the dictators then tearing Europe apart. He wore a black wig and short beard and bore no resemblance to any of his previous Shakespeare parts. Also in his corner was the extreme clarity with which he spoke his lines and the many imaginative details with which he patterned his characterization of Macbeth as a psychologically anguished, intellectually acute killer. Such, for example, was the baffled way in which he listened to the witches on the heath, the caution with which he conversed with his wife upon their first meeting, the horror he expressed when the impact of his deed dawned on him, and the militant attitude he took at the conclusion. Some, however, thought him not quite as effective in the role as he had been in others. Richard Lockridge (*NYS*), for example, found his readings a bit too cerebral and lacking in the proper fire and passion, while Wilella Waldorf (*NYP*) cautioned the actor about a habit he was getting into of mouthing his words and overstressing his consonants.

Anderson's Lady Macbeth, considered the revival's pièce de résistance, was statuesque and brimming with tragic strength, but also deeply imbued with a smoldering sensuality that she wisely used to handle her hesitant spouse, for whom she presumably had a great passion. Gilder commented, "Her anguish of fatigue after the banquet; her broken, shattered gestures, her uncertain walk, her white face and outstretched hands--palms down, long fingers outspread and curved back--in the sleep-walking scene are well observed and admirably projected." Gilder's sole reservation was that in her first scene Anderson appeared too much the "ambitious modern matron" and was insufficiently the "ruthless . . . daughter of violence." In John Mason Brown's (*NYWT*) view, Anderson projected the role "with a sulphurous villainy and an imagination unequaled by any of the Lady Macbeths of our time."

Anderson, a perfectionist, was so concerned about getting the physical details of her sleepwalking scene down correctly that she arranged through a doctor friend to observe an actual sleepwalker, who was induced while under hypnosis to display her somnambulist behavior. Anderson even had the doctor ask the adolescent subject to wash (imaginary) blood from her hands, and the girl's actions were then borrowed and theatricalized by the great actress. Anderson would also like to have had a scene of herself in bed with Macbeth, but the director had to dissuade her from this illogical conception.

The witches' scenes were problematical because Webster chose to use a loudspeaker for sound effects that, in their mechanical obviousness, jarred with the Shakespearean mood. However, the direction of these scenes was vivid, especially the second one, which was interpreted as a projection of Macbeth's feverish imagination after the banquet. One of the three witches was played by a man (William Hansen).

The Hecate scenes, probably a later interpolation, were cut, as was Macbeth's fight with young Siward. The ghost of Banquo was not acted, but was represented by a flickering light. Also, instead of having Macduff enter at the end with Macbeth's head, the preceding fight was concluded by Macbeth's being forced over the battlement walls to fall to the moat below. There were expert performances from the supporting cast, especially Cotsworth's Banquo, but Evans and Anderson were what brought in the crowds.

(2) M: Alan Bush; D: Norris Houghton; DS: Paul Sheriff; P: Theatre Incorporated i/a/w Brian Doherty; T: National Theatre; 3/31/48 (29)

British stars Michael Redgrave and Flora Robson brought their interpretations of the Macbeths to Broadway in this version staged by American Norris Houghton; the production had been seen in London (135 performances) and on tour in Canada before coming here, where a number of the roles were taken over by American actors. The British Robson, however, was a replacement for another English actress, Ena Burrill. The mixed British and American cast included Stephen Courtleigh as Duncan, Geoffrey Toone as Banquo, Whitfield Connor as Macduff (and an armed head), John Cromwell as Lennox, Hector MacGregor as Ross, Elliott Reid as Mal colm, John McQuade as Siward, Arthur Keegan as Young Siward, Beatrice Straight as Lady Macduff, and Russell Collins as the porter. Among the small-part actors were Paul Mann as Menteith and the older murderer, Julie Harris as one of the witches, and Martin Balsam as one of the Three (a trio of male witches added to the three weird sisters).

Although Brooks Atkinson (*NYT*) liked it well enough to predict a long run, the reviews were mixed and the revival closed in a month. Atkinson said that the production "brings Shakespeare's great murder play to the stage intact in a vibrant performance that transmutes a classical ritual into a stunning and reverberant work of art. No one else in the contemporary theatre has drawn so much horror and ferocity out of it." Dissenters included Howard Barnes (*NYHT*), who claimed that it was "a striking, but generally unsatisfactory revival."

The approach was to suggest a non-specific barbaric period, with somberly moody skies and pre-Gothic towers and costumes that dressed the military in well-used, roughhewn garments. It was hoped that the performance would create a world of gritty realism. Some thought the results admirable, others were doubtful. One of the more negative attitudes toward the costumes was expressed by John Mason Brown (*SR*), who rejected them as "scraggly and nondescript," succeeding only "in being mainly of that baggy-wrap-around and burlap-boot variety which is the curse of Shakespearean supernumeraries."

Houghton's staging eschewed academic overtones for melodramatically swift and vigorous action, especially in the vivid battle scenes. The fight between Macduff and Macbeth--using broadswords and small shields--was a rampaging, brutal, athletic affair that covered the entire set and had the audience on the edge of its seats, especially when it seemed that Macbeth was on the verge of killing his enemy.

Redgrave, wearing an untrimmed, manelike wig and beard, was greeted with both hosannas and jeers. For some he was a powerful, lusty, but very human Macbeth, whose increasing involvement in bloodshed gradually overwhelms him. Few disputed that he had the physical size, rugged appearance, and booming voice required. "Redgrave is the greatest Macbeth I have seen," wrote Euphemia Van Rensselaer Wyatt (*CW*). "A commanding figure--despite the wiggiest of wigs--who contrives to keep some sympathy alive for the tortured creature he creates." She was not pleased with his occasional inaudibility during his soliloquies, such as "Tomorrow and tomorrow," but added that "his horror over the King and Banquo is really moving." She noted this Macbeth's passionate affection for his spouse and his ultimate inability to feel sorrow for her--or anything else--by the time of her death. Brown thought Redgrave an outstanding blend of warrior and poet, villain and hero, thinker and doer. But he believed the portrayal inconsistent, noting, for instance, "It becomes weak, soft and fuzzy after the murder of Duncan at the very moment when Macbeth has gained sufficiently in strength to turn murderer without the promptings of Lady Macbeth." Unlike Wyatt, Brown considered Redgrave's portrayal of affection for his wife doubtful. "He takes his orders from her because he is her husband, not because he is her lover." Those rejecting Redgrave's performance were led by George Jean Nathan (*TBY*): "He not only spends most of the evening downstage giving the audience the cute rolling eye and with dimpled smirk reciting his speeches but, when forced by the more violent action upstage, presents an excellent impersonation of a circus sideshow wild man conniving to become boss of the lot."

Most were disappointed by Robson. Brown commented, "She lacks the vocal placement, the granite strength, the fearful drive" of the role.

With the help of the often-haunting musical score, the weird sisters (played by diminutive, clawed and bearded actresses) were woven into the fabric of the play in such a way as to make their presence integral. Houghton and Redgrave were "determined that the opening moments should create awe and unease in the spectators, not self-conscious, amused disbelief in the reality of three hags stirring a pot of haggis. . . . 'Out, out, damned pot!', we cried," recalled Houghton in *Entrances and Exits*. Houghton therefore interpolated the Three, a trio of masked, nine-foot-tall, monolithic, male figures, who spoke the opening lines; when Macbeth and Banquo appeared, the withered, cauldronless witches emerged to confront them from the folds of the Three's robes as the latter faded into the mist. In the apparition scene, when Macbeth commands the witches to call their masters, they turned upstage and pointed to the now visible Three, and as Houghton noted, Macbeth would "become aware at last that he was defying unearthly forces." The hags then vanished and the Three summoned the apparitions themselves. During various scenes of violence, one of these monolithic figures would appear, including being a third murderer joining the standard two prior to Banquo's killing. Banquo's presence as a ghost at the banquet was also effectively handled, the method being to have him appear in the flesh at the table, turning around on his stool to reveal a slit throat and the blood running down his bare chest.

(3) D: John V. Graham; S: Sally Nussbaum; L: Martha Dreyfus; P: Modern Play Productions; T: Provincetown Playhouse (OB); 2/14/50

Hardly any members of the reviewing corps attended this Off-Broadway revival by a troupe of unknowns. One who did, Whitney Bolton (*NYMT*), thought the experience a harrowing one because of the tension and suspense the actors capably conveyed. "In place of howls and posturing, we saw the tense fitful movements of terrified people, and heard their desperate, unhappy words."

Macbeth was played by John Francis and Lady Macbeth by Mimi Randolph. "The sense of real persons, trapped in a web of their own making, could not have been better presented than by these two," wrote Bolton. Roy Pascal's Macduff and Alexander Maissel's Banquo were equally fine. The production was excellently handled, despite the tiny stage, and the costumes and lighting contributed greatly to the effect.

MADAME IS SERVED [Comedy/Legacy/Marriage/Sex] A: Joe Grenzeback; SC: Guy de Maupassant's short story, "L'Héritage"; D: Fred Stewart; DS: Henry Martin; P: Richard Beckhard for the Six O'Clock Theatre u/t/a/o the Equity Library Theatre; T: Charles Weidman Studio (OB); 2/14/49 (4)

Although described as an arena staging, this production was actually in the three-quarters round. It was of a play based on a Maupassant story that is primarly concerned with character depiction rather than plot.

A group of middle-class persons are attempting to gain possession of an inheritance. The central concern is with a woman (Philippa Bevans) who must have a child if she is to earn the money from her late aunt. Her husband (James Karen) being incapable of fathering a baby, the feat is accomplished by his best friend (William Robertson); the legacy is obtained.

Brooks Atkinson (*NYT*) thought that a capable dramatist might have made something of this material, but that Grenzeback was not the man for the job. "After an amusing first act he has nothing to give it that a fairly alert playgoer cannot foresee. In this decadent age the reticence of his characters seems prudish." Atkinson bemoaned the fact that for all the intimacy of the space, the actors were barely intelligible. But Vernon Rice (*NYP*) was very excited about the project and urged theatregoers to see it. "The intimacy of the small auditorium, the frailty of the play and the confidential, stylized acting make seeing the comedy a happy experience."

MADE IN HEAVEN! [Comedy/Hotel/Marriage/Sex] A: Hagar Wilde; SC: a short story by Hagar Wilde; D: Martin Manulis; S: Lawrence Goldwasser; P: John Golden; T: Henry Miller's Theatre; 10/24/46 (92)

A sophisticated suburban couple, Zachary (Donald Cook) and the somewhat younger Elsa Meredith (Carmen Mathews), married ten years, have just concluded a cocktail party at their home one Sunday evening at 11:30 P.M. The fatigued Zachary, an ad executive, prefers to hit the sack, while Elsa has things to talk over with him. A major argument evolves, and Zachary departs for a New York hotel. He pines for his wife and she for him, although her friends try to prevent the couple from reconciling. To make Zachary jealous, she befriends Laszlo Verties (Louis Borel), a handsome young European, but their relationship is harmless, he being a faithful husband. Escorted by Laszlo, Elsa dashes off to the hotel to make up with her spouse, only to find a beautiful blond (Ann Thomas) in his room (nothing untoward has occurred, though). Elsa prepares to go to Reno, but Zachary returns and the pair are reunited. A subplot concerns efforts to get Elsa's sister (Katharine Bard) married. The cynical girl is in love with Philip Dunlap (Tony Bickley), but is afraid of the conjugal state because of what it does to those who enter it.

Audiences seemed to laugh uproariously at lines that sounded very lifelike, but apart from one or two exceptions, such as Arthur Pollock (*BE*), the critics were dismissive. George Jean Nathan (*TBY*) scalpeled the slick comedy for its stereotypical ingredients and noted, "The writing is the kind that hopefully fishes in the depths of character with wisecracks, and that mistakes mere vulgarity for robust humor." Brooks Atkinson (*NYT*) thought it "mechanical and humorless." The play had had a summer-theatre tryout in Westport, Connecticut, under the name *It's a Man's World!* Cast members included Lawrence Fletcher, Marrian Walters, Sarah Burton, and Jane Middleton.

MADWOMAN OF CHAILLOT, THE (***La Folle de Chaillot***) [Comedy/Business/Fantasy/French/Mental Illness/Politics/Trial] A: Jean Giraudoux; AD: Maurice Valency; M: Alfred Hague; D/P: Alfred de Liagre, Jr.; S/C: Christian Bérard; L: Samuel Leve; T: Belasco Theatre; 12/27/48 (368)

Giraudoux's posthumous play--ultimately acknowledged as a modern classic--sharply divided the reviewers into yes- and no-sayers and became a highly controversial entry into the season's sweepstakes. It started off very tentatively at the box office, but developed into a substantial hit and was selected not only as one of the ten best of the season, but also as the Drama Critics Circle choice for best foreign play.

Its original, highly acclaimed staging had been under the baton of Louis Jouvet in Paris in 1945. The breathtaking sets for that production were re-created for the Broadway incarnation, which was in an adaptation that took considerable liberties with the very talky original. In 1969 the piece was musicalized on Broadway as *Dear World*.

Paris in the spring of next year is the setting for this unusual piece, inspired by a real Paris madwoman known as "Bijou." The Prospector (Vladimir Sokoloff), the President (Clarence Derwent), and the Baron (Le Roi Operti) are three financiers who think that there is oil beneath the streets of the city and, at the Chez Francis, a Chaillot café, are making plans to wreck Paris in order to obtain the resource. Around them swirl various eccentric characters, among them Countess Aurelia (England's Martita Hunt, in her American debut), the madwoman of Chaillot, who happily lives in her illusions and is treated with enormous respect by the others (partly because she owns the café). The red-haired countess's bizarre costume, redolent of the 1880s, includes a lace parasol, beaded mantilla, flowered toque, lorgnette, and police whistle. Her annoying presence seriously disturbs the evil financiers. Pierre (Alan Shayne), a young agent of theirs, choosing to jump into the Seine rather than detonate an explosion on their behalf, is brought on by a policeman (Ralph Roberts) and falls for the pretty young waitress (Leora Dana, in her Broadway debut) when he comes to. The madwoman attempts to encourage the young agent with her tales about the joys of life, although her references are all to the long-gone past. Gradually, the madwoman learns of the evil plans of the financiers and how modern men such as they have destroyed the world's happiness. A chief informant is the philosophical ragpicker (John Carradine), who, with the others, convinces her that only the mad and such as they are still free. The madwoman hatches a plan to rid the world of the financiers by spreading a story that there is oil beneath her house. Three other similarly bizarre Parisian madwomen, Mme. Constance (Estelle Winwood), Mlle. Gabrielle (Nydia Westman), and Mme. Josephine (Doris Rich), arrive at her invitation to confer with her at a mad tea party. Mme. Constance, "the madwoman of Passy," has a pet dog that is not there. A mock trial, with the ragpicker acting as defense attorney, is held to try the financiers in absentia for their crimes against mankind. The financiers and various others who have heard of the madwoman's supposed oil arrive, are led down a staircase leading to the Paris sewers, and then are trapped there by the madwoman. An atmosphere of peace and beauty suffuses the place, the young agent and the waitress kiss, and the madwoman returns to her offbeat ways.

Many critics likened the fanciful and decent-hearted play to the writing of William Saroyan and to Lewis Carroll's *Alice in Wonderland*. Euphemia Van Rensselaer Wyatt (*CW*) described the play as "a fable of the power of goodness and simplicity over greedy power in an entrancing mingling of wisdom and folly." She congratulated the producer on providing "a work of art so unusual in its conception, so mellow in its charity, so superbly full of wit and yet so deeply cutting in all its warning." Brooks Atkinson (*NYT*) despaired of the "sluggish" second act, but felt that it was "a small price to pay for the wit and whimsical loveliness of a wise fantasy."

Atkinson was one of several critics who loved the play but thought that the production, for all its fine qualities, was not really up to the writing. Another such critic--he thought this "one of the most interesting and rewarding plays to have been written in the last twenty years"-- was John Mason Brown (*SR*). Brown felt the lack of true Parisian atmosphere and the need for more cutting, but he shouted bravos for Hunt's and Winwood's acting. Of the former, he wrote, "She is as haunting as Toulouse-Lautrec's Madame Lender, whom she so closely resembles. She is a harridan, chalk-pale of face and crowned with mounds of dyed red hair. . . . Yet she is a queen, too. Her manner is both imperious and gracious." Hunt won that year's Tony as best actress.

There were, of course, critics who thought the piece less than excellent. One was Robert Coleman (*NYDM*), who noted, "Too much of its humor and satire fail to come across the footlights for a successful and satisfactory evening of theatre." The severely disappointed Richard Watts, Jr. (*NYP*), thought that "there is a curious, creeping dullness that begins early . . . and grows increasingly overpowering as it goes along." Several such critics--most vocally, George Jean Nathan (*TBY*)--suspected that the blame lay more with Valency's adaptation than with Giraudoux's original, although Nathan had many unkind things to say about the production as well.

MAEDCHEN IN UNIFORM (***Gestern und Heute***) [Dramatic Revival*] A: Christa Winslow; D: Frank Gregory; S: Jayn Fortner; C: Helen Coule; P: Equity Library Theatre; T: Muhlenberg Branch of the New York Public Library (OB); 2/28/45

An excellent revival of the 1931 German play that had been shown locally in 1932 under the title *Girls in Uniform* at the same time as the film version, spelled *Madchen in Uniform*, was being shown. Frank Gregory, the 1932 director, resumed that task, revising the episodic play to make it more compact and suitable to the tiny library theatre where this showcase production was mounted.

The overbearing lesbian headmistress was played by Edit Angold, Frau Polachek the dancing teacher by Lotta Palfi, the French teacher by Helen Cule, the English teacher by Virginia Birch, the seamstress by Charlotte Knight, the kindly Fraulein von Bernberg by Ellen Andrews, the portress by Mary Boylan, Manuela by Mary James, and other schoolgirls by Jayn Fortner (the set designer), Constance Kistner, and Elizabeth Wilson; the latter, who played Edelgard, eventually became a leading character actress.

George Freedley (*NYMT*) thought the production outstanding and the play worthy of a Broadway revival because of its insight into "Prussian character and German ideals." He was backed by the few other critics who saw it, it even being urged that the City Center of Music and Drama produce the play as one its revival series. Burton Rascoe (*NYWT*) commended the set designer for a highly imaginative, yet very simple, scenic arrangement. In it, she "ingeniously contrived to have two depths to the stage by using a platform before the stage proper for the drill and reception room scenes and the stage itself for the more intimate or confined scenes."

MAGDALENA [Musical/Labor/Military/Period/Politics/Religion/Romance] B: Frederick Hazlitt Brennan and Homer Curran; M: Heitor Villa-Lobos; LY: Robert Wright and George Forrest; D: Jules Dassin; CH: Jack Cole; S/L: Howard Bay; C: Irene Sharaff; P: Homer Curran and Edwin Lester; T: Ziegfeld Theatre; 9/20/48 (88)

John Raitt's first appearance on Broadway following his big success in *Carousel* was as the anticlerical Pedro in this lavishly produced ($350,000) but "profoundly dull" (Brooks Atkinson [*NYT*]) "musical adventure" (actually more of an operetta) that had been successful in Los Angeles and San Francisco. Although it failed in New York, many respected theatre professionals thought it a major work, ahead of its time, and deserving of eventual resuscitation. It was even believed by those close to the show that a major reason for its being panned was the very warm response it received in California, the implication being that New York's critics preferred to demonstrate their independence of provincial critical responses.

The show employs the music of Brazil's distinguished and prolific composer, Heitor Villa-Lobos, and (apart from a brief scene in a Paris bistro) is set in Colombia, in the jungle country near the Magdalena River, in 1912. Robert Wright and George Forrest were familiar with all 1,170 compositions of Villa-Lobos, and when he arrived in New York, they worked with him to adapt the score from his earlier work; they even added their own pastiches in his style when a serious illness prevented him from developing certain moments himself. As Wright noted, "If he controlled the copyright to a piece, he'd deliver that and rewrite it. If he didn't . . . , we'd say, 'You need so many bars of music that do such and such. And we'd make that and show it to him. That's how 'The Broken Pianolita' [the best-known dance number in the show] was done" (quoted in Glenn Loney, *Unsung Genius*, which offers a detailed account of *Magdalena*'s development).

Although the music, the gorgeous production values, and Jack Cole's exotic and erotic dances were extremely pleasurable, the book was "awkward and ponderous," said Ward Morehouse (*NYS*). George Freedley (*NYMT*) thought it "complicated and completely uninteresting." Howard Barnes (*NYHT*) concluded, "*Magdalena* is a big, tuneful operetta extravaganza in which a South American jungle background does little to relieve a general tedium." Among the small number of those who favored the show was the influential George Jean Nathan (*TBY*), who agreed that the book was musty, but dismissed the importance of a musical libretto in a show that was primarily valuable for its musical quality, as he said this one was. He also noted the exceptional choreography, the brilliantly colored sets and costumes, and the excellence of the company. Louis Biancolli (*NYWT*) said that the composer had revealed two new facets of his talent: "a flair for sustained comic writing [and] a marked gift for long melodic breath through extended dramatic sequences."

The heavily plotted libretto sets the feelings of Colombia's Muzo Indians, who mine emeralds for General Carabana (Hugo Haas), a dictatorial type who has seized the tribal mines, and those of the general's associates. The chief of the newly converted Muzo workers is the beautiful Maria (Dorothy Sarnoff), whose demands lead to a workers' strike that brings General Carabana back from his Paris revelries. Maria loves Pedro, the lusty bus driver, who is the mestizo leader of the pagan Indians, but he despises her Christianity and plans a revolution against the general. Pedro steals a statue of the Madonna as part of his plot. Because of certain plot twists, Maria promises to wed Carabana, but the general's French mistress (Irra Petina), a great cook, kills him by overfeeding him delicious prepared food and drink as she sings "Food for Thought." Finally, after Pedro's bus falls over a cliff and he realizes that the Madonna has been spared from damage, he accepts Maria's faith and is converted to Christianity.

Choreographer Cole was an indefatigable perfectionist and was not happy with one very complex waltz number. According to Loney, he continued to develop it even after the production opened, but it took four weeks to complete because of union regulations about the number of hours the dancers could rehearse. Finally, the completed number was to be shown at a matinee, but as Wright and Forrest walked uptown to the theatre, Cole, furious, came racing past them in the opposite direction. Stopped and asked what was the matter, Cole exploded in a stream of expletives and said that he was finished with the show. "I went to the door, and they said, 'Who are *you?*' I said, 'I'm Jack Cole,' and they told me to get a pass!" Cole took off that evening for California and never returned to see the show.

MAGIC TOUCH, THE [Comedy/Literature/Marriage] A: Charles Raddock and Charles Sherman; D: Herman Rotsten; S: Louis Kennell; P: John Morris Chanin; T: International Theatre; 9/3/47 (12)

This show nearly did not open (the curtain was delayed) because the theatre's leaseholder insisted on being paid money owed him by the producer. Considering the critical attack, it might have been better off if it had not opened. Howard Barnes (*NYHT*) asserted that it was "as bumbling a bit of make-believe as has ever ushered in a new season. Whatever dramatic sorcery it inspires is contrived with a baseball bat rather than a wand." Ward Morehouse (*NYS*) designated it "a hapless and hopeless little transient, a dull and childish concoction."

The central characters are a young, married New York couple, Jeff (William Terry) and Cathy Turner (Sara Anderson), struggling to survive on his small weekly salary of $28.50. Jeff's publisher boss, J. L. Thompson (Howard Smith), suspects that a charming book, telling how one can devise a budget to live on such a frugal income, can be wrought from their hardships. Jeff wants a raise, but the boss will not give it to him because that would spoil the idea behind the book. Jeff does not rest until the work is between covers, but the book fails and the couple separate. They are reunited, though, when the book begins to take off after a trick ad clicks with the public. Along the way, a variety of supposedly comical characters, including a trio of Cathy's former boyfriends from Dayton, Ohio, get involved, but to no artistic avail.

In the cast were Frances Comstock, Le Roi Operti, Norman Tokar, Carleton Carpenter, and Hope Emerson, among others.

MAGNIFICENT YANKEE, THE [Comedy-Drama/Historical-Biographical/Law/Marriage/Old Age/Period/Politics] A: Emmet Lavery; D/P: Arthur Hopkins; S/C: Woodman Thompson; T: Royale Theatre; 1/22/46 (160)

An episodically structured biographical drama about Oliver Wendell Holmes (1841-1935), associate justice of the Supreme Court (1902-1932), with Louis Calhern generally considered superb in the role. Emmet Lavery's leisurely dramatization covered the life of Boston's "great dissenter" from the year of his appointment to the court at age sixty-one to that of his retirement at age ninety-one. The man himself, famed for his liberal views and championship of human over property rights, was outlined, as was the world that formed a background to his actions. The chief sources of research were onetime Holmes secretary Francis Biddle's biography (*Mr. Justice Holmes*) and that of Catherine Bowen (*Yankee from Olympus*). The author also received help from Supreme Court Justice Felix Frankfurter and John Palfrey, friend and legal aid to Holmes.

The drama begins slowly and builds its effects by a cumulative method of adding pertinent details, all of its action being set in the library of Mr. Justice Holmes. Scenes from Holmes's private life with his dryly witty wife, Fanny Dixwell Holmes (Dorothy Gish), are mingled with important moments in his public affairs. Holmes is first shown examining his new house in Washington following his appointment to the bench by Theodore Roosevelt, and subsequent scenes are set in 1911, 1916, 1921, 1929, and 1933, when the retired judge is called on by the newly inaugurated Franklin Delano Roosevelt (who is in the wings ready to enter when the curtain falls). Into the action are inserted such historically interesting figures as Henry Adams (Fleming Ward), Owen Wister (Sherling Oliver), and Louis Brandeis (Edgar Barrier). The events conspire to depict the justice as a man of warm and deeply human qualities, a lover of sherry and Rabelais, and a wrestler with philosophical problems. Each of his yearly Harvard Law School-selected secretaries ("Holmes's Annuals") is treated like a son by him, and, in a richly sentimental scene, all of them gather on his eightieth birthday to sing to him.

One of Burns Mantle's ten best of the season, *The Magnificent Yankee* was not deemed a major dramatic creation, but was appreciated instead as a work of somewhat superficial but nonetheless engaging stage biography, supported enormously by the inherent interest in the life of the man portrayed. The performances of Calhern and Gish were of great value, too, especially the former, whose career reached a high point with his authentic portrait. Both he and Gish had to make various makeup changes to suggest their advancing age.

In favor of the play was Howard Barnes (*NYHT*), who wrote, "The theater has composed a portrait of great breadth, dignity and feeling in *The Magnificent Yankee*." And John Mason Brown (*SR*) claimed that the play was "warm, uncommon and welcome." Acknowledging its lack of conventional dramaturgy, he applauded its exhibition of two truly virtuous human beings, its "compelling and moving" depiction of happiness, and its quiet patriotism. "What it lacks in the routine stuffs of drama is precisely what makes it touching, endearing, even ennobling." But Lewis Nichols (*NYT*) decided that the drama was not equal to its subject, primarily because the emphasis was more on Holmes's *Life with Father**-like sentimental domestic experiences than on his legal or philosophical opinions. (The frequent comparisons of the play to *Life with Father* probably were exacerbated by the fact that both Gish and Calhern had played the leads in that play.) George Jean Nathan (*TBY*) bemoaned the lack of conflict and action, and a picture of Holmes lacking "the mind, wit, force, and quality associated with the man." The cast included Mason Curry, Nicholas Saunders, William Roerick, Philip Truex, Robert Healy, Edwin Whitner, and Bruce Bradford, among others.

MAGNOLIA ALLEY [Comedy/Boarding House/Marriage/Prostitution/Religion/Sex/Southern/Sports] A: George Batson; D: Carl Shain; S/L: Edward Gilbert; C: Guy Kent; P: Lester Cutler; T: Mansfield Theatre; 4/18/49 (8)

There were a sizable number of interesting actors in this ribald turkey stuffed with clichéd situations and stereotypical characters. It is set in a small Southern town where, between mint juleps and recollections of past amours, the raffish Laura Beaumont (Jessie Royce Landis) runs a racy rooming house in Magnolia Alley filled with nonpaying guests. Most crucial are Andy Hamil (Jackie Cooper, former child movie star in his Broadway debut), an ex-pugilist thrown out of commission by World War II and separated from Laura's nasty daughter Nita (Anne Jackson), who has deserted him for a wrestler. The pretty young Joadie (Hildy Parks), Laura's adopted daughter, is in love with him, and there is also the religiously fanatical servant girl, Angel Tuttle (Julie Harris), daughter of a preacher. Another interesting lady is the prostitute Maybelle (Bibi Osterwald). These and other characters engage in multiple plot complications, most important being those that ensue when Nita returns to the boarding house for a brief visit and leaves with $500, Maybelle's life savings. The money is recouped when Colonel Stacey (Fred Stewart), a neighbor who turns out to be a former military chaplain, offers to provide it in return for Angel's hand. A handsome new boarder (Douglas Rutherford) with a taste for juleps joins the ménage shortly before the final curtain.

Many critics flayed the wisecracking play, Hobe. (*V*), for example, calling it "a witless and tasteless comedy." "It's a comedy that doesn't play; it just ambles and rambles," moaned Ward Morehouse (*NYS*). The cast included Frances Bavier, Brad Dexter, Robert White, and Don Kennedy.

MAID IN THE OZARKS [Comedy/Art/Romance/Rural/Sex/Southern] A: Claire Parrish; P: Jules Pfeiffer; T: Belasco Theatre; 7/15/46 (103)

A highly controversial comedy, reputed to be pornographic, and basically a takeoff on hillbilly radio programs and plays like *Tobacco Road**. Originally called *Blue Mountain*, it had made a lot of money during an eighty-six-week Los Angeles run and a sixty-two-week Chicago engagement. During one week in Milwaukee it pulled in the very comforting figure of $15,000. After five years of traveling through the hinterlands, it arrived in New York, where its producer predicted that it would be "the worst play that has ever hit Broadway." Despite its come-on advertising showing a striptease, the play bored most critics, such as George Freedley (*NYMT*), who thought that it would put visiting censors to sleep. The striptease itself was mild, and the performer never took off more than a modicum of clothing. William Hawkins (*NYWT*) called the exhibit "crude, distasteful, amateurish and boring."

The comedy is set in the Arkansas mountains in the kitchen of the primitive Calhoun home. There are two sisters, Lydia (Johnee Williams) and Frances Tolliver (Gloria Humphries), waitresses from Hot Springs. A moonshine maker named Temple Calhoun (Jon Dawson) falls in love with Lydia--who previously has committed bigamy--and returns to his country home with her and her sister. Lydia, seeking to earn some cash, agrees to pose nude for a local artist, but the area women tar and feather her for her breach of decorum. She runs off with the artist, and Temple marries Frances, although he has wavered throughout the play regarding which sister he really wants. Mingled into the plot are an assortment of eccentric mountain types. The jokes are about such things as the human anatomy, plumbing (or what passes for it in the Ozarks), bedbugs, body odor, bodily functions, dirty feet, and the uses to which mail-order catalogues are put in the backwoods.

MAKE MINE MANHATTAN [Revue] SK/LY: Arnold B. Horwitt; M: Richard Lewine; D: Hassard Short and Max Liebman; CH: Lee Sherman; S: Frederick Fox; C: Morton Haack; L: Hassard Short; P: Joseph M. Hyman; T: Broadhurst Theatre; 1/15/48 (429)

Hilarious comedian Sid Caesar made his Broadway debut in this hit revue that included the comic talents of Joshua Shelley and David Burns. Also in the cast were Biff McGuire, Sheila Bond, Nelle Fisher, Eleanor Bagley, Danny Daniels, Max Showalter, Perry Bruskin, Ray Harrison, Hal Loman, Jack Kilty, and Kyle MacDonell. The show alternated sketches and well-staged and choreographed musical numbers, all of them somehow related to life in Manhattan. Robert Garland (*NYJA*) thought it "young, fresh and brashly entertaining," and Rowland Field (*NEN*) believed that the show was "fashioned with keenly observant intelligence and winning skill." Less impressed was Howard Barnes (*NYHT*), who wrote, "For most of the time the work is frenetic and pointless."

Caesar received very warm notices for his versatile clowning, Brooks Atkinson (*NYT*) noting that "he can mimic anything from a subway vending machine to a dial telephone or taxi driver, and rush through it with tremendous speed. Mr. Caesar is imaginative and clever, working in a rich medium." In the vending machine routine--written by Caesar himself--he was a gumball machine that got pounded around for not giving more than one gumball per penny. Deciding that honesty is not the best policity, the machine then keeps both the pennies and the gumballs. The owner of the machine beams at this, says, "Hey, this kid has talent," and promotes it to a glitzy slot machine at a quarter a pop. Caesar scored highly in "Hollywood Heads East," playing a bereted and jodhpured film director with an affected British accent who comes to New York to make a movie. But a retired garment worker, Mr. Rappoport (Burns), refuses to move from the bench where the film is going to be made. To humor him, the director gets into a discussion with him about garment making and eventually becomes so steamed that he drops his fancy accent and betrays his real origins by shouting, with a Yiddish accent, "When it comes to a garment, I already forgot what you ever knew." Mayor O'Dwyer (played by Showalter) was a character in the sketch. Caesar was at the heart of "A Night Out," which he based on his own experiences. While he could go on a date to dinner and the theatre in 1938 for five dollars, he could barely pay the cab fare for that sum in 1948.

According to his autobiography, *Where Have I Been?*, when Caesar joined the show, he was booked to do only two numbers. By the time it opened he was in twelve of the revue's twenty-one numbers. Having been hired for only $250 a week with the option to leave after giving two weeks notice, he had become so important to the revue that he was able to ask for and receive a new contract giving him $1,500 a week and five percent of the weekly gross. When he left the show, he was replaced by Bert Lahr.

Burns was outstanding in a number called "Any Resemblance," where he was a fur-collared drama critic who is passing on the reins to a younger critic who has the appropriate qualifications for the job: this new man is deaf and blind, hates the theatre, and promises to pan every show he sees. In "Full Fathom Five," Burns was a Milquetoast trying to buy a fountain pen. He was pushed into a tank of water and, despite nearly drowning, discovered that the "atomic pen" could write under water. In "Welcome to First Avenue" he played a man welcoming delegates to the soon-to-be-built United Nations Building. A few critics thought Burns the best thing in the show.

Shelley stood out in "Subway Song," in which he was a boy from 242d Street in the Bronx whose girlfriend lives at the other end of the subway line, Brooklyn's New Lots Avenue. He was also a scream in "Traftz," a spoof of the Schrafft's Restaurants, where they serve dishes such as poached eggs with marshmallow sauce.

Eleanor Bagley had a show-stopping number in "Movie House in Manhattan," about a Park Avenue movie theatre so grandiose that "nobody cares if the picture stinks." Another popular number spoofed the current Rodgers and Hammerstein show, *Allegro*. The song considered the show's catchiest was called "Saturday Night in Central Park."

MAKE WAY FOR LUCIA [Comedy/Period/Women] A/D: John van Druten; SC: the "Lucia" novels of E. F. Benson; DS: Lucinda Ballard; P: Theatre Guild; T: Cort Theatre; 12/22/48 (29)

The stodgy English village of Tilling in 1912 is the locale of this arch drawing-room comedy of manners in which British players Isabel Jeans and Cyril Ritchard appeared. Jeans played the beautiful widow, Mrs. Emmeline Lucas, a poseur who, because of her pretended knowledge of Italian, prefers to be called Lucia (with the Italian pronunciation). She takes a summer rental in Tilling from the local social pillar, Mrs. Mapp (Catherine Willard), and immediately presumes to establish herself as a social and cultural leader; the nosy, domineering Mrs. Mapp, however, wishes to be so perceived herself. A rivalry that constitutes the bulk of the action ensues. The genteelly bitchy pair resort to every wile and subterfuge at their com mand to gain an edge in matters relating to the community and eligible bachelors. Lucia is aided and abetted by the epicene Georgie Pilsen (Ritchard). Another important male figure in the women's lives is the snobby bluestocking Major Benjamin Flint (Philip Tonge). In the end, it is the disarming Lucia who is the victor.

The play was exquisitely designed in comically stylish fashion and acted in the properly affected British manner, but it was too precious and coy for an American audience. Although "there is much that is bright, playful and quietly amusing in" the piece, thought Richard Watts, Jr. (*NYP*), "it all makes for slender and intermittent entertainment." Herrick Brown (*NYS*) believed that van Druten's play, "while amusing enough at moments, gets lost far too often in sheer talk, and not too brilliant talk at that. And his plot is definitely tenuous when stretched over a whole evening." Viola Roache, Ivan Simpson, Essex Dane, Guy Spaull, and Kurt Kasznar (as an Italian composer) were among those involved.

MAKE YOURSELF AT HOME [Comedy/Romance/Theatre] A: Vera Mathews; D: Johnnie Walker; S: William Noel Saulter; C: Janice Walker; P: Albert Chaperau and Johnnie Walker; T: Ethel Barrymore Theatre; 9/13/45 (4)

This comedy, written, acted, directed, produced, and designed by Broadway unknowns (the writer and producers were better known in Hollywood), was the fourth straight flop of the young 1945-1946 season. It satirized the current housing shortage in a story about brassy, fading movie star Mona Gilbert (Bernadene Hayes, replacing Sally Eilers, who quit after the Philadelphia tryout). She returns to New York to revive her career in a Broadway play. Mona attempts to regain possession of her apartment from sexy Southern lass Honeybelle Collins (Bonnie Nolan), to whom it was sublet and who resides there with her older lover (Donald McClel land). The girl is happy to make room, but not so her Popsie. Mona's play is a one-night flop and she considers retiring, but word arrives of box-office business following her brother's (Donald White) giving critic George Jean Norris a black eye.

The play contains several lines that brought the house down, not because of their intrinsic humor but because they unintentionally mocked the play itself. One was the reply to a question, "Do actresses and actors always celebrate after a first night?" The answer: "Not after this one." Audience members trooped out in droves before the final curtain. "Not even punching a critic could preserve this one," concluded Lewis Nichols (*NYT*). Among the actors were Suzanne Jackson and Philip Huston.

MAN, THE [Drama/Crime/Mental Illness] A: Mel Dinelli; D: Martin Ritt; S/L: Jo Mielziner; C: Julia Sze; P: Kermit Bloomgarden; T: Fulton Theatre; 1/19/50 (92)

A rather chilling psychological melodrama about a psychopathic murderer who terrorizes a frail and trusting widow. The latter is Mrs. Gillis (Dorothy Gish), who hires the well-spoken Howard Wilton (Don Hanmer) as a handyman to work around her Victorian-style rooming house. Howard at first appears to be a pitiful soul with an inferiority complex who is in need of love and affection. He soon, however, reveals various persecution complexes and a tendency to lapse into homicidal and sadistic behavior, although he can not recall his bad deeds after he has done them. He kills the widow's dog, locks the widow in the house, and grows increasingly disturbed the more she tries to contact the outside world. Finally, in a surprise ending, after trying desperately to control his murderous impulses, he kills the kind Mrs. Gillis.

Brooks Atkinson (*NYT*) appreciated the harrowing time he had in the theatre, but expressed a preference for truly evil villains and not those so obviously in the thrall of a mental disturbance. Howard Barnes (*NYHT*) claimed that the play was "loaded with suspense and fine acting. . . . The central idea may be thin and somewhat fraudulent, but it has emerged as an engrossing piece of theater." But William Hawkins (*NYWT*) alleged, "Despite expert performances . . . it simply is not as absorbing as you wish it were."

Young movie actress Peggy Ann Garner, in her stage debut, was a silly bobbysoxer, and other roles were played by Richard Boone, Robert Emhardt, Frank McNellis, and folk singer Josh White, Jr.

(1) MAN AND SUPERMAN [Dramatic Revival*] A: George Bernard Shaw; D: Maurice Evans and George Schaefer; S: Frederick Stover; C: David Ffolkes; L: George Schaefer; P: Maurice Evans; T: Alvin Theatre; 10/8/47 (294)

Shaw's once-shocking, antiromantic, philosophical modern comedy about the life force and the superman, inspired by the Don Juan story, was written in 1903 and first seen locally in 1905. It did not premiere in London until 1911 and had not been revived in New York since 1912. It enjoyed a hit production in the hands of producer-codirector Maurice Evans, who also played the leading role of John Tanner. As is often the case, the present revival of the very long, four-act play did not include the "Don Juan in Hell" scene. To offset criticism at the omission, a printed slip was placed in all programs asking the audience if they would be interested in attending a special matinee at which the scene would be performed. There was a strong response, but the matinee was never given. Even without the scene, however, the work scored a major success.

Richard Watts, Jr. (*NYHT*) reported that with Evans "in top form, the wry Shavian commentary on the life-force is a delight and a joy, so witty and wise, so brilliant and so fresh that it emerges as one of the Master's most enduring works." Ward Morehouse (*NYS*) agreed that this was "a gay and enormously entertaining evening." There were critical comments on the play's considerable verbosity, but most observers were delighted with the talk because of its high level of comic literacy. The ideas--concerning topics such as conventional morality, sex, the idea of the superman, women, and love--no longer seemed alarming, but the wit and wisdom with which they were expressed were as delightful as ever. Various writers commented on how up-to-date Shaw's themes seemed.

The company included Malcolm Keen as Roebuck Ramsden, Chester Stratton as Octavius, Frances Rowe as Ann Whitefield, Josephine Brown as Mrs. Whitefield, Phoebe Mackay as Miss Ramsden, Carmen Mathews as Violet Robinson, Jack Manning as Henry Straker, Tony Bickley as Hector Malone, Jr., and Victor Sutherland as Malone, Sr. Evans was greeted with raves. Thomas R. Dash (*WWD*) proclaimed, "Maurice Evans is spirited and eloquent and delightfully articulate. If there is a slight tendency to declamation, it is inherent in the nature of John Tanner . . . to make fiery and shattering speeches."

This is the story of confirmed bachelor, misogynist, and social radical John Tanner's strugle to resist the manifold temptations of Ann Whitefield. A self-proclaimed superman claiming invulnerability to womanly wiles, he loudly insists that no woman will ever lure him into the hateful state of marriage, but Ann, representing the life force, sets her cap on beating down his defenses. Warned by the cockney chauffer, Henry Straker, of Ann's intentions, Tanner flees to Spain, but Ann pursues him there and enslaves him.

Evans directed the play with a slight touch of stylization and artificiality, sometimes infecting it with the mood of Oscar Wilde. Of the superb supporting cast, the one receiving the strongest approval was British actress Rowe, making her New York debut.

(2) [Return Engagement] T: City Center of Music and Drama; 5/16/49 (16)

Following the close of business, Evans took his dandy revival on a 15,000-mile tour of America that concluded in Milwaukee. He then produced this two-week run at the City Center. According to some, the production remained in first-class condition, but others felt that the sheen was gone. William Hawkins (*NYWT*) observed, "Much of the literate subtlety and sophistication of the original company's playing has gone by the board for broad effects." Brooks Atkinson (*NYT*) spoke for several critics in saying that Frances Rowe was especially guilty of this flaw. Not in the original cast were Nan McFarland as Violet, Dorothy Eaton as the maid, Morton Da Costa as Henry Straker, and James Daly as Hector Malone, Jr.

MAN WHO HAD ALL THE LUCK, THE [Comedy-Drama/Business/Family/Romance/Small Town/Sports] A: Arthur Miller; D: Joseph Fields; S: Frederick Fox; P: Herbert H. Harris; T: Forrest Theatre; 11/23/44 (4)

Future playwriting giant Arthur Miller did not have all the luck when, at twenty-nine, he made his Broadway debut with this almost instant flop. The play was a pared-down version of an already-published script that had been included by Edward Seaver in his anthology, *Cross-Section*. George Freedley (*NYMT*) thought the published version "formless and ambling," but its characters interesting. The need to cut the lengthy play for Broadway consumption, he believed, had "robbed it of most of its values." Freedley recognized in the unformed Miller "a mind and writing talent which some day may learn how to focus his plot and his characters so that a clear dramatic image will be created." He also advised the fledgling dramatist to provide his plays with stronger story lines than that offered here. Others also detected a fresh talent, despite the play's drawbacks. John Chapman (*NYDN*), for example, said, "He has a sense of theatre and a real if undeveloped way of making stage characters talk and act human."

Everything young David Beves (Karl Swenson), an uneducated auto mechanic in a small midwestern town, touches seems to turn to gold. Whenever disaster threatens, something fortunate always seems to be the outcome. David has trouble repairing a Marmon 8, but a knowledgeable, freedom-loving, Viennese refugee mechanic named Gustave Eberson (Herbert Berghof) happens by and does the job for him, after which the two become partners. His girlfriend Hester's (Eugenia Rawls) father objects to their match but is run over by the Marmon when he sets out to kill David, thereby clearing the road to marriage. Later, when the pregnant Hester falls, David fears for the health of the baby. The child, though, turns out not only healthy but a boy, which is precisely what David wanted. After David buys a filling station, the state builds a highway past it. He invests his profits in a mink farm and succeeds, despite a possibility that his mink may have been poisoned. On the other hand, his none-too-bright brother Amos (Dudley Sadler) has, with the aid of their ambitious father (Jack Sheehan), been training in the cellar since he was ten to be a major-league pitcher. Amos, however, learns from a Detroit Tigers' scout (Lawrence Fletcher) that despite his great fastball, he has not been trained properly to use his intelligence on the mound and so will not be a pro ballplayer. This causes Amos to have a serious psychological setback. The unhappy father, once a sailor, decides to go back to sea. David is so successful at everything that he begins to fear some sort of retribution for his good luck. He finally learns, through the medium of his Viennese partner, that his success is not so much a matter of luck as it is of sheer hard work, and that the divinity that shapes our ends is in our own hands. That is the American way, says Eberson, who rejects David's fatalism as irrelevant European folderol.

Many critics thought the play a muddled piece of philosophical dramaturgy with a confusing point of view. Why, for example, asked Lewis Nichols (*NYT*), should Amos have failed, since he too applied the principle of hard work to attaining his goal? George Jean Nathan (*TBY*), one of the play's severest critics, wondered how the playwright's theme was congruent with a plot in which so many of the developments in David's life result from sheer accident and have no relation to some special work ethic. A typical response was Howard Barnes's (*NYHT*), who called the play "incredibly turbid . . . and stuttering in execution. . . . The play writhes through an unpleasant, unexciting and downright mystifying maze." Arthur Pollock (*BE*) considered it "a labored but very earnest little play." "It is an ambling piece," thought Ward Morehouse (*NYS*), "strangely confused at times and rather tiresome for a considerable portion of the evening."

Not all the critics were negative. Burton Rascoe (*NYWT*) thought that Miller had managed to take a profound idea and put it into down-to-earth terms. "There is nothing pretentious, arty or preachy about his play, and . . . he put over his argument in a faultlessly convincing manner." This was "a work meriting attention and support," offered Rowland Field (*NEN*). The cast included Grover Burgess, Forrest Orr, Agnes Scott Yost, Sydney Grant, and James MacDonald.

In *Timebends*, Miller revealed that the work originated in two actual incidents. One he heard of from an acquaintance whose husband, a gas-station owner with a streak of paranoia, had hanged himself. The other concerned the drowning of his cousin's husband, a handsome, successful businessman. These incidents coalesced into a story that confronted "the unanswerable--the question of the justice of fate, how it was that one man failed and another, no more or less capable, achieved some glory in life." He also viewed the piece as somehow related to "the paralysis of will in the democracies as Hitler moved . . . to the nations of Europe." He wrote the story first as a novel, but, unable to find a publisher, converted it into a play. The story underwent many revisions as it neared its final form, and Miller said that the experience helped him find himself as a playwright.

MAN WITH BLOND HAIR, THE [Drama/Crime/Jews/Politics/War] A/D: Norman Krasna; DS: Howard Bay; P: Frank Ross; T: Belasco Theatre; 11/4/41 (7)

A moderately entertaining but extremely unconvincing melodrama set on New York's Lower East Side where a pair of Nazi flyers, Rudolph (Rex Williams) and Sturner (Bernard Lenrow), have been captured and jailed by the police after escaping from a Canadian prison camp. A gang of local youths, led by a Jewish rookie cop (Curt Conway), plan to spring the Germans and give them a good hiding. Sturner flees, but Rudolph is taken to a rooftop and told to jump after his tormentors have left. However, the cop's girlfriend (Eleanor Lynn), also Jewish, not wanting the fellows to get in trouble, tells Rudolph to climb down the fire escape (an earlier title was *Fire Escape*), and she hides him out in her mother's (Dora Weissman) tenement flat. Catered to with kindness and momma's good Jewish cooking, the Nazi's faith in his inhumane creed crumbles and another convert to democracy is born. Meanwhile, one of the local boys is killed by a G-man while trying himself to shoot the other Nazi.

A major objection was to the approving picture of the protofascist neighborhood youths. The characters lacked reality, the situations were contrived, the premise was unbelievable, and only occasional scenes came to dramatic or comic life. Louis Kronenberger (*PM*) called the play "a farrago of incompetence, tastelessness and absurdity, lacking even the excitement that crude melodrama can very often provide." In the cast were Alfred Ryder, James Gregory, and Coby Ruskin, among others.

MANDRAGOLA [Dramatic Revival] A: Niccolo Machiavelli; TR: Ashley Dukes; D: Carl Shain; S: Nancy Starrels; L: Doris Einstein; P: Michael Tobin for Equity Library Theatre; T: George Bruce Branch of the New York Public Library (OB); 4/8/46 (4)

One of the more interesting choices for a showcase presentation in the young Equity Library Theatre's schedule, this is the early sixteenth-century Italian comedy about a young man named Callimaco (Earl Hammond) who wants to bed the beauteous Lucrezia (Mary Best). He conspires with various persons, including a priest and the girl's mother Sostrata (Helen Stevens), to convince the woman's husband Nicia (Leo Fainberg) that if he wants his thus-far-barren wife to become pregnant, she must partake of a concoction made of the mandrake root (mandragola), but that the first man to sleep with her after she drinks it will die. Callimaco arranges to be that first man, fathers Nicia's child, and becomes Lucrezia's lover.

The production, staged with an attempt at commedia dell'arte style, enjoyed a fine performance by Gene Fuller as the comic servant Siro. "His voice, facial expressions and tripping walk, in all its wicked innocence made [the] audience laugh long and hard," wrote George Freedley (*NYMT*). "There is a quaintly bawdy amusement about the whole thing which was brought to the fore by an unusually good cast and some very expert direction," applauded Freedley. Vernon Rice (*NYP*) stated, "All the players were in good form and sustained the light, airy mood so necessary for a production of this kind."

MANHATTAN NOCTURNE [Drama/Literature/Marriage/Mental Illness/Prostitution/Sex/Trial] A: Roy Walling; D: Stella Adler; S: Perry Watkins; P: Walter Drey and George W. Brandt; T: Forrest Theatre; 10/26/43 (23)

This windy play starring Eddie Dowling was "pretty much on the confused side," grieved Lewis Nichols (*NYT*), "even during those moments when it is not downright tedious." Dowling played Peter Wade, a novelist of slipping talents whose marriage is on the rocks. He takes a room in a brothel in order to give his wife (Lorraine MacMartin) grounds for divorce. The prostitute he hires to act as corespondent is a hard-on-the-surface, soft- underneath girl named Ann Stevens (Terry Holmes) who is suffering from emotional confusion stemming from amnesia caused when her lover deserted her for someone else. Peter and Ann find comfort in one another's presence and plan on starting over together on a farm upstate, but she gets arrested for soliciting. Peter stands up for her before the judge (Howard Smith) and manages to get her released and also to jog her memory into working order again. Both the hooker and the writer are regenerated by the experience; he begins a new novel, she is inspired by its first fifty pages, and they begin a new life together.

Although the critics lambasted the play, they were ecstatic about new actress Terry Holmes. Dowling, too, gave a sterling performance. After George Jean Nathan (*TBY*) enumerated the play's many melodramatic clichés, he concluded, "The highly proficient performances of Mr. Dowling and Miss Holmes . . . succeeded occasionally in rubbing a bit of the makeup off the script, but the foundation cream stuck." Holmes never acted on Broadway again. Wendell Corey had a minor role in the play.

MAN'S HOUSE, A [Drama/Bible/British/Family/Invalidism/Jews/Period/Religion/Romance] A: John Drinkwater; D: Dennis Gurney; S: "George Spelvin"; L: "G. E. Mazda"; P: Blackfriars' Guild; T: Blackfriars' Theatre (OB); 4/1/43 (16)

The first New York showing of a Drinkwater play originally presented at Great Britain's Malvern Festival in 1934 and soon after in London. Its only American production had been several years earlier in Great Neck, Long Island. Produced during the Lenten season, it was a tasteful, if undramatic, religious drama set in Jerusalem at the time of the Crucifixion. It tells of the effects of Jesus' death on the family of a wealthy Jewish merchant, Salathiel (Augustin Duncan), who holds a scoffing attitude toward Jesus (not seen) and his disciples. Salathiel has two daughters, the blind and cynical Esther (Cavada Humphrey) and Rachel (Ruth Homond).

His son Mathias (Frank Gibney) is a ruthless, calculating philistine who seeks to have Jesus arrested as a rabble rouser. Esther's blindness is cured by Jesus' touch, and Rachel, the favorite, leaves home with her lover, David (Dan Gallare), to become one of the Nazarene's followers. Brother Nathan (Graham Velsey), another convert, follows them into exile. Following the resurrection, Esther marries the Roman officer (Sam Banham) who ended Christ's suffering on the cross. Salathiel and Mathias are left alone, the son unregenerate, the father too cowed by his son to follow in the footsteps of his vanished children.

"The construction is frequently awkward," opined George Freedley (*NYMT*), "and it is not helped by the pontifical direction given it by Dennis Gurney. The company was unsure in its lines, which also slowed up the evening and frequently left the business high and dry and the situation's meaning anything but clear." Otis L. Guernsey, Jr. (*NYHT*), declared that the play "succeeds only in telling its theories in static speeches rather than focusing them on the audience by dramatic action." Royal Dana Tracy and Albert Carroll were in the cast.

MANY HAPPY RETURNS [Comedy/Family/Marriage/Sex] A: Clare Kummer; D: Peter Berneis; S: Stewart Chaney; P: Harry Bloomfield; T: Playhouse; 1/5/45 (3)

This play earned its footnote in theatre history by the fact that film star Mary Astor made her Broadway debut in it. The critics, for the most part, liked her, which is more than can be said for their response to the play. Author Kummer was so upset by what she alleged were the unwarranted revisions made by the management that when she failed to stop the show from opening, she lodged a protest with the Dramatists' Guild; her plea in court to be awarded $5,000 was as unsuccessful as her play. George Jean Nathan (*TBY*) ventured the opinion that whatever the form of the original, it had to have been better than what was produced. "Even as offered, a comedy not without some sly remaining wit and intrinsic charm was to be detected through the thick, wet cloud of wholly unsuitable casting, dismal acting, miserable stage direction, and rankly gratuitous manuscript revisions." Lewis Nichols (*NYT*) said that the play "sent the drama rocking as far back on its heels as the drama can go without falling."

A middle-aged banker named Henry Burton (Neil Hamilton), learning that his banker son (Don Gibson) is leaving his wife (Nell O'Day) for divorcée Cynthia Laceby (Astor), looks Cynthia up and tries to pay her off to leave his son alone. He finds himself falling for her himself, however, as does his banking partner (Rex O'Malley). Cynthia loves Henry, too, and only made a play for the son to land Henry. Henry, however, returns to his own wife, and the partner gets the divorcée.

Cast members included Nan Butler, Michael Dreyfuss, and Jayne Cotter, later known as Jayne Meadows.

MARINKA [Musical/Period/Politics/Romance] B: George Marion, Jr., and Karl Farkas; M: Emmerich Kalman; LY: George Marion, Jr.; D: Hassard Short, George Marion, Jr., and Karl Farkas; CH: Albertina Rasch; S: Howard Bay; C: Mary Grant; L: Hassard Short; P: Jules J. Leventhal and Harry Howard; T: Winter Garden; 7/18/45 (165)

An old-fashioned "romantic musical" that was well cast and sumptuously produced--although lacking in *alt Wien* atmosphere--but that was tiresomely dated and of little interest to a 1945 audience. The pleasant, if derivative and uninspired, music by Viennese refugee Kalman had echoes of his Middle European background, but also included numbers intended to sound distinctly American. One, "Cab Song," was clearly reminiscent of *Oklahoma!*'s "Surrey with the Fringe on Top," while "Old Man Danube" self-consciously mirrored "Old Man River" from *Show Boat**. Most approved of the songs was the show-stopping "When I Auditioned for the Harem of the Shah," sung by Luba Malina, who stole the show as a promiscuous countess.

The pedestrian book was based on the notorious 1889 Mayerling affair (previously treated on the stage in Ernst Vajda's 1927 *The Crown Prince** and in Maxwell Anderson's 1937 *The Masque of Kings**) in which Crown Prince Rudolph (Harry Stockwell) of Austria-Hungary and Maria Vetsera or "Marinka" (Joan Roberts) were mysteriously slain (or was it suicide?) in a hunting lodge at Mayerling. The tale is framed by scenes in a Connecticut drive-in movie theatre where some young moviegoers, having watched the 1937 film dramatization of the incident, agree that the ending is too sad. Among them is the son of Rudolph's coachman, who tells what really happened, which provides a story expressed in would-be comic terms with a happy ending in which Rudolph and Marinka, having been banished by the benevolent Emperor Franz Josef (Reinhold Schunzel), flee to America, where they take up life as farmers.

Burton Rascoe (*NYWT*) thought the idea of romanticizing the life of the womanizing crown prince was "a little repulsive." A typical response was Ward Morehouse's (*NYS*): "Its comedy is labored and its book both familiar and cumbersome, but it's always good to look upon and it is agreeable to the ear." Several critics, such as George Jean Nathan (*TBY*) had a field day ridiculing the libretto's historical license.

The romantic leads, both of whom had played the leads in *Oklahoma!*, were considered seriously miscast because of their blatantly American characteristics. Among the featured performers were dancer Ronnie Cunningham, Taylor Holmes as Count Lobkowitz, Ethel Levey as Madame Sacher, Leonard Elliott as Francis, and obese clown Romo Vincent as the comic Bratfisch.

MARRIAGE IS FOR SINGLE PEOPLE [Comedy/Family/Films/Nightclub/Romance/Theatre] A: Stanley Richards; D: Stanley Logan; S: Frederick Fox; P: Ruth Holden and Virginia Kronberg; T: Cort Theatre; 11/21/45 (6)

A reworking of a familiar plot idea lay behind this tired, dully performed comedy. Its action is set in a New York penthouse to which Lottie Disenhower (Gertrude Beach), an artless miss from the vineyards of Fresno, California, comes when her comedy playwright fiancé, Reginald Hecuba (Nicholas Saunders), leaves for naval duty. She travels eastward to meet his sophisticated family, who are in the midst of trying to close a deal with a Hollywood producer. Although her boyfriend's intentions were never completely aboveboard, she manages in New York to win over all his highfalutin friends and family and to end up winning a glamour contest run by a nightclub, as well as the hearts of a movie actor (Robert Sully) and producer (Frank Otto). Finally, she marries the dramatist's younger brother (Joel Marston) after the playwright returns with a dusky South Seas native (Vivian Mallah) on his arm.

Otis L. Guernsey, Jr. (*NYHT*), claimed that "all of the . . . characters are uncontrolled burlesques of the types they are supposed to represent. Their witless conversation tears the fabric of the comedy to shreds." Louis Kronenberger (*PM*) announced, "Dreadful as the play is, it has almost found a cast and director to match it." In that cast were Nana Bryant as the writer's mother, Anne Francine as a Hollywood gossip columnist, and Florence Sundstrom as the producer's wife.

MARY OF MAGDALA [Drama/Bible/Period/Religion/Romance] A: Ernest Milton; D: Dennis Gurney; S: Avril Gentles; C: Valerie and Virginia Todahl; P: Blackfriars' Guild; T: Blackfriars' Theatre (OB); 3/25/46 (25)

A sincere telling of the biblical story of the title character, but one that was, like many of its ilk, insufficiently dramatic to consistently hold the stage. "*Mary of Magdala*," sighed Lewis Funke (*NYT*), "is not clearly drawn and lacks the necessary dramatic quality to make it an important experience." George Jean Nathan (*TBY*) found the results "affected and inert." But Euphemia Van Rensselaer Wyatt (*CW*) professed to find "style in its writing and philosophy as well as wit in its lines."

The plot covers the familiar ground, with Mary (Helen Horton) a figure of loose morals whose sophisticated acquaintances are the high and mighty of the time. Her lover is the Roman officer, Quintus Superbus (Ray Colcord). Mary is beginning to suffer pangs of conscience from her dissolute life. She is especially interested to learn that Jesus has brought back Lazarus from the dead. She decides to follow the teachings of the Nazarene and fetches spices for the burial following his Crucifixion. Her disillusion following the burial is shattered by the Resurrection, and several doubters, but not the pagan officer, accept Christ.

Robert Carroll played Othmar and Douglas Gordon was Bodmin.

MARY ROSE [Dramatic Revival*] A: James M. Barrie; D: Harrison Dowd; P: Equity Library Theatre; T: Hudson Park Branch of the New York Public Library (OB); 11/28/44 (2)

A showcase revival of the 1920 British fantasy. The title role was played by Leah Elaine Easton, who acted "with charm, belief and understanding," according to George Freedley (*NYMT*). Cameron was played by Michael Blair, Harry by William Weyse, and Simon by Robert Gallagher.

The play was still intriguing to Freedley but Robert Garland (*NYJA*) did not think much of it, saying, "Tonight's revival certainly is the most uncalled for, the most phony, the most out-dated, the most nauseating."

MASTER BUILDER SOLNESS (***Bygmester Solness***) [Dramatic Revival*] A: Henrik Ibsen; AD: Marie Donnet; D: Miranda d'Ancona and Audrey Hilliard; DS: Eugene Walter; P: Repertory Theatre, Inc.; T: Cherry Lane Theatre (OB); 5/25/50

One of the many Off-Broadway companies springing up in the late forties was responsible for this revival of the 1892 Norwegian play better known in English as *The Master Builder*. Its most recent revival had been in 1931 by the Civic Repertory Company.

L. C. (*NYT*) was impressed by the production and said that the actors performed "it intelligently and with an understanding of the author's penetrating character study." But Arthur Pollock (*DC*) thought that "often . . . it looks as if the play had been put on because it has roles the actors have been dying to play sometime and not because they were capable of playing them."

The simple background was composed mainly of a large window against which branches were framed. Donnet's new version removed many of the Victorian expressions of the old William Archer translation to make the dialogue sound more modern. Halvard Solness was played by John Scanlan, his wife by Donnet, and Hilda by Miranda d'Ancona (who wore slacks for the part), with Winton Sedgwick, Henry Waldon, Audrey Hilliard, and James Arenton in other roles.

(1) MAURICE CHEVALIER [Revue/Solo] P: Arthur Lesser; T: Henry Miller's Theatre; 3/10/47 (46)

Popular French singer and raconteur Maurice Chevalier, who had not performed on an American stage since 1934, regaled Broadway with his specialty songs and impressions in this essentially one-man revue. He was accompanied on the piano by Irving Actman. Despite the simplicity of the presentation, opening nighters shelled out up to $9.60 a seat (the price was halved for subsequent showings).

The none-too-long program included "Bonsoir Messieurs Dames," "Ah! Qu'elle Est Belle!," "La Leçon de Piano," "Vingt Ans," "A Barcélone," "Weeping Willie," "Quai de Bercy," "Mandarinades," "Place Pigalle," "La Symphonie des Smelles de Bois," and such favorites as "Valentina," "Louise," "You Brought a New Kind of Love to Me," and "Hello, Beautiful."

Chevalier was once again his jaunty, dashing, ultracharming self, with his bowed legs and dazzlingly toothy smile, the lower lip thrust forward. He wore three different hats, usually at a typically rakish angle. He also wore a mandarin jacket in one number. The dashing boulevardier's hair had grayed and his red cheeks were more mottled than before. "He still sings infectiously on about five notes like one whose traveler's tales are set to music," reported Brooks Atkinson (*NYT*).

His songs were mostly in French, as the titles suggest, and they dealt with the familiar themes of love, colorful locales, youth, and so on. His introductions to the songs were in his trademark accented English, which was so much a part of his appeal. "A finished clown, he clowns more than he used to," declared Arthur Pollock (*BE*), "talks more between songs. In fact, . . . his songs almost seemed negligible after his explanations of them." Well liked among his new songs were "La Symphonie des Smelles de Bois," a song about the war and the sound of wooden-soled shoes--which all had to wear in Paris--on the street, which he accompanied with a tap dance; and "Quai de Bercy," about the pleasure taken in the smell of wine on the quai by those too poor to drink it. On opening night the star greeted various celebrities in the house, even asking Claudette Colbert if he was pronouncing "psychoanalyst" correctly.

(2) [Return Engagement] T: John Golden Theatre; 2/29/48 (33)

Chevalier returned to Broadway for a limited engagement under the same management with a program considerably like his previous one, including several of the earlier show's songs among the eleven he performed. Irving Actman again accompanied him on the piano. The new numbers were "J'ai du Ciel dans Mon Chapeau," "It's Good to Fall in Love," "George Bernard Shaw" (a spoken monologue in English), and "Fox à Poil Dur." More familiar were his renditions of "Mimi," "Louise," "Valentina," and other favorites associated with him.

Richard Watts, Jr. (*NYP*), provided an honest assessment: "Clearly he is one of the great performers in amusement history. His songs are pleasant but not remarkable. His voice is engaging but hardly notable. His program has grace and brightness, but it certainly lacks impressiveness. Yet Mr. Chevalier can take charge of an audience with such assurance and authority that his control virtually amounts to a dictatorship." Brooks Atkinson (*NYT*) thought that the evening was on the thin side, that many of the numbers were not worth the effort expended on them, that Chevalier's performance lacked subtlety, and that a Broadway stage was not the place for this type of presentation.

MAYOR OF ZALAMEA, THE (***El Alcalde de Zalamea***) [Dramatic Revival] A: Pedro Calderón de la Barca; TR: Edward Fitzgerald; D: James Light; P: Readers Theatre; T: Majestic Theatre; 1/27/46 (2)

Despite crushing reviews for its first effort, *Oedipus Rex**, the Readers Theatre company forged ahead with yet another effort to provide New York audiences with staged readings of classical works. It used professional actors holding unmemorized scripts in their hands while playing without costumes on a bare stage. Like its predecessor, this presentation was rejected as inherently untheatrical and unworthy of attention apart from its purpose of giving voice to a little-produced work.

A production method that varied from *Oedipus Rex* was that whereas that drama had kept all the actors on stage seated in chairs throughout, the present offering allowed the actors to make their exits and entrances from the wings. The play in question was Calderón's seventeenth-century drama about politics, crime, and justice in connection with a captain's (Jack Manning) attempt to seduce a wealthy farmer's (Herbert Berghof) daughter (Ellen Andrews) after the military man is quartered at the fearless farmer's home.

"Subject to no more than a reading," concluded Lewis Nichols (*NYT*), "it loses its action . . . and neither the story nor the language rises to any great tragic heights." George Jean Nathan (*TBY*) thought the failure to cast top-notch actors a major drawback; he also thought that good direction was lacking. The background narration was provided by Eugene O'Neill, Jr. Among the actors were Leonardo Cimino, Frederick Downs, Amelia Romano, Will Davis, and Gregory Morton.

ME AND HARRY [Drama/Crime/Mental Illness/Romance/Sports] A: Charles Mergendahl; D/P: Robert Henderson; L: Betty Burch; T: Humphrey-Weidman Studio Theatre (OB); 4/2/42

The most interesting thing that happened to this play on opening night was that its producer-director was arrested for selling seventeen seats to an unlicensed production. Those who had paid for their tickets were told at the first intermission that they would receive a refund.

The "exasperating play" (George Freedley [*NYMT*]) itself is set in a Boston photographer's (Bruce Adams) studio frequented by an odd assortment of characters who speak in stream-of-consciousness style, saying whatever pops into their heads. One of the characters is a blond receptionist (Mary Heath) with a psychopathic attraction for abusive men; she ignores the nice young boxer (James Morley) who loves her. Also seeking her affections are a flashy salesman (Harald Bromley) and a childlike young man from Vermont named Jamie (Norman Budd), who, knowing of her taste in dangerous men, boasts of how he killed "Harry" back home. When it gradually becomes clear that Jamie is a mental defective, an attempt is made to have him committed to an asylum, but he dies in trying to escape.

Budd gave an effective portrayal of the insane youth, but the play, which several critics likened to the work of William Saroyan, was panned. "It is a gloomily unsettling affair and looking back on it after a few minutes in the every-day world, I find myself loath to believe it ever happened," griped Richard Lockridge (*NYS*).

ME AND MOLLY [Comedy/Business/Family/Jews/Marriage/Music/Religion/Romance/School/Youth] A: Gertrude Berg; M: Lehman Engel; D: Ezra Stone; S: Harry Horner; C: Rose Bogdanoff; L: Leo Kerz; P: Oliver Smith, Paul Feigay, and Herbert Kenwith i/a/w David Cummings; T: Belasco Theatre; 2/26/48 (158)

This sentimental genre comedy--selected as one of the ten best plays of the season--was inspired by the enormously popular radio show "The Goldbergs," which had been on the air since 1929 and would soon become a major television series. The Goldberg family was the creation of Gertrude Berg, who also immortalized the role of the plump Jewish matriarch Molly Goldberg. In *Me and Molly* she was making her stage debut. Many of those in the show would be part of the TV series. In 1973 Kaye Ballard starred in the title role of *Molly*, which was based on this 1948 script.

The play, dotted with homely details of Jewish family life, is set in the Goldberg's three-room Bronx apartment in 1919 and begins with the family moving in, having progressed from its Lower East Side neighborhood. The thinly plotted action concerns the efforts of Molly's ill-tempered husband Jake (Philip Loeb) to own his own dress business and his distaste for working in someone else's employ. His ambitions are thwarted by an inability to raise the necessary capital. Along the way, various homely details of life among the Goldbergs intrude, such as buying a piano, daughter Rosie's (Joan Lazer) music lessons, match making, son Sammy's (Lester Carr) coming bar mitzvah, Molly's night-school efforts to learn to read and write English, and so on. Ultimately, Molly makes Jake successful with her idea of selling half-size dresses "so that a woman can go out of a store without being altered."

Most critics agreed with Euphemia Van Rensselaer Wyatt (*CW*): "There is no literary value to *Me and Molly* and not too much drama--its unassuming simplicity is its passport." The play was on the long side and had a rambling structure, but the characters were so warmly drawn and their problems so down to earth that many found it easy to forgive the author for her dramaturgic flaws. Brooks Atkinson (*NYT*) called the play "a leisurely, intimate, cheerful portrait of interesting people, and the humor is kind-hearted." Less well disposed was Otis L. Guernsey, Jr. (*NYHT*), who noted, "No doubt Miss Berg's pen was motivated by great sympathy and tenderness, but not much of her feeling comes across the footlights in this play."

The large cast included Eli Mintz as Uncle David; David Opatoshu as the bachelor Mr. Mendel, who falls in love with piano teacher Vera (Margaret Feury); Louis Sorin as the wealthy Cousin Simon, who refuses to invest money unless what he is investing in is a proven success; and many others.

ME, THE SLEEPER [Drama/Family/Marriage/Mental Illness] A: Jack Balch; D: Joseph Kramm; L: Ralph Alswang; P: Invitational Series of the Experimental Theatre u/t/a/o the American National Theatre and Academy; T: Master Institute Theatre (OB); 5/14/49 (4)

A surrealistic, pseudopoetic piece about a psychologically disturbed war veteran and his descent into madness. Its theme was the compromises made by people in the search for truth. The play had premiered in 1946 at the St. Louis Community Playhouse, and its author had been a drama editor for the St. Louis *Post-Dispatch*.

At the start, Luddy (Robert Pastene) is having a vision of a beautiful girl (Margaret Draper), but it turns out that he is being interrogated by the police, who are looking for a murderer. The girl is imaginary, as is another character who represents Luddy's more distasteful side. Later scenes in his imagination involve Luddy's wife (Isabel Bonner), his past life with his mother and father, the latter lamenting that he cannot have a family of musicians, and so on.

Many audience members felt that the play's effect was to make the title apply to them. Brooks Atkinson (*NYT*) observed that "the play strains and bursts in its attempts to be different. The precious formula for successful dramaturgy certainly does not contain any element of the hackneyed. But neither does it call for the obscure; nor for the fanciful when there is a mundane issue to be resolved."

(1) MEDEA [Dramatic Revival] A: Euripides; AD: Robinson Jeffers; M: Tibor Serly; D: John Gielgud; S: Ben Edwards; C: Castillo; L: Peggy Clark; P: Robert Whitehead and Oliver Rea; T: National Theatre; 10/20/47 (214)

John Gielgud directed this striking revival of the Greek revenge classic and (for a brief period until replaced by Dennis King) played Jason to the overpowering Medea of Judith Anderson, who won the Tony for her acting. Among others in the cast were Florence Reed as the nurse, Don McHenry as the tutor, Grace Mills as the first woman of Corinth, Kathryn Grill as the second, Leone Wilson as the third, Albert Hecht as Creon, Hugh Franklin as Aegeus, Richard Hylton as Jason's slave, Marian Seldes (her Broadway debut) as one of Medea's attendants, and Richard Boone (his Broadway debut) as a soldier.

The last revival of the play had been in 1918, starring Margaret Anglin. The present one was freely adapted by poet Robinson Jeffers, with many long speeches shortened and the chorus reduced to three women of Corinth, who were closely integrated into the dramatic structure. The original's messenger speech was reassigned to the character of the nurse, who by this time had become a familiar character to the audience. Instead of using Euripides' dragon chariot at the end, Medea barricaded her home against her unfaithful spouse while displaying to him from within the corpses of her slain children. The language was poetic but accessible and lacked the convoluted syntax of earlier versions. John Mason Brown (*SR*) noted that Jeffers "has employed his poet's skill to streamline the text, to bring it closer to the contemporary stage. . . . Mr. Jeffers's language, though not always satisfactory, has about it--at its best--a driving iron quality that Gilbert Murray's more liquid version cannot claim. What it loses as poetry it gains as theatre."

Medea was one of Anderson's greatest triumphs. "Judith Anderson," wrote Euphemia Van Rensselaer Wyatt (*CW*), "plays Medea with an emotional sweep, a variety of gesture and inflection which makes it a transcendent performance. . . . It is such an appalling part and must make such an emotional demand upon the actress that one wonders how Miss Anderson can endure the strain of it." Brooks Atkinson (*NYT*) claimed this to be "a landmark in the theatre." The actress released "a torrent of acting incomparable for passion and scope. . . . She is barbaric by inheritance, but she has heroic strength and vibrant perceptions. Animal-like in her physical reactions, she plots the doom of her enemies with the intelligence of a priestess of black magic--at once obscene and inspired. Between those two poles she fills the evening with fire, horror, rage and character."

Florence Reed was outstanding as the nurse. She had been a midrehearsal re placement for Aline MacMahon, who was fired. The latter sent a magnanimous opening night telegram to the cast: "CONFIDENT YOU WILL MAKE HISTORY TONIGHT. MACMAHON." Some critics were unhappy with Gielgud's Jason (George Jean Nathan [*TBY*] said that he gave "the effect of a tenor Siegfried cast as a bass Hagen"), but Brown found him to be "as effective as any man could hope to be in Medea's presence. Helmeted and hidden behind a borrowed beard as he was, I must confess I would never have recognized him." Brown, unlike most of his approving colleagues, took issue with Gielgud's "stodgy" direction, however, finding it adequate but uninspired. He especially disliked the handling of the choral group. For a setting Ben Edwards created a sweep of steps and a pair of great doors leading to Creon's palace.

Harold J. Kennedy described in *No Pickle, No Performance* about how Anderson prepared for her fiery acting in *Medea*. Medea's first words on entering were "Death! Death!" requiring her to be at an emotional peak from the very start. To reach this peak she would work her feelings up to a state of frenzy, using any means she could. One night, a half hour before the curtain, Anderson called the stage manager into her dressing room and told him to inform that "old bitch," Florence

Reed, not to dare and move a muscle during Anderson's soliloquy. The stage manager thereupon visited the flamboyant old character actress and delivered the message verbatim, to which Reed nonchalantly replied, "Tell Judith to go fuck herself." The stage manager did not report this to the star. When the curtain rose, Reed was in place on stage and Anderson was pacing backstage before her entrance. Passing the stage manager's desk, she asked if her message had been delivered. "Yes, Miss Anderson. You're on." "What did she say?" "You're on, Miss Anderson." "Tell me what she said," the increasingly excited star hissed. "She said, Miss Anderson, that you should go fuck yourself." "DEATH!" Anderson screamed, "DEATH!" as she burst onto the stage.

(2) [Return Engagement] D/P: Guthrie McClintic; T: City Center of Music and Drama; 5/2/49 (16)

A gruelling eight-month tour had preceded this limited return engagement of the previous production, which had closed because of a dispute between the star and her producers. The work had been restaged by Guthrie McClintic. William Hawkins's (*NYWT*) assessment was that the direction had been improved, McClintic having "vastly increased the fluid motion of a play which could easily seem verbose."

Judith Anderson's opening-night performance was her 501st in the title role. Many, including Atkinson, thought her even better than before because of the added emotional variety she brought to the character. Newcomers included Henry Brandon as Jason, Mary Servoss as the first woman of Corinth, Marian Seldes (who had a smaller role in the original) as the second, Martha Downes as the third, Frederic Worlock as Creon, Hilda Vaughn as the nurse, and Bruce Gordon as Aegeus. Don McHenry was still the tutor.

(1) MEDIUM, THE and **"THE TELEPHONE"** [Musicals] B/M/LY/D: Gian-Carlo Menotti; S/C: Horace Armistead; L: Jean Rosenthal; P: Chandler Cowles and Efrem Zimbalist, Jr., i/a/w Edith Luytens; T: Ethel Barrymore Theatre; 5/1/47 (212)

"The Telephone" [One-Act/Romance]; *The Medium* [Crime/Death/Family/Mental Illness/Romance/Spiritualism]

An interesting pair of musical works that their composer called "lyrical comedy and drama," but that many others categorized as either operas or musical plays. They were successful enough to warrant several later New York revivals as well as frequent production elsewhere. After premiering at Columbia University's Brander Matthews Theatre (OB), they had been given at the uptown Heckscher Theatre (OB; 2/47), but only the music critics reviewed the event. The extremely warm critical response, however, encouraged the producers to move the works to Broadway's commercial arena.

The evening began with the one-act curtain raiser, "The Telephone," which was a satirically comic two-character piece about a young man named Ben (Frank Rogier) trying to talk to Lucy (Marilyn Cotlow), his ladylove, to propose to her before he leaves town for a new job. Lucy, however, almost never gets off the phone, so he cannot get his two cents in until he leaves for the station and calls her on a pay phone.

Although some thought this the lesser of the two pieces, it had its fair share of critical admirers. One was Arthur Pollock (*BE*), who called it "a little story, quick and amusing." Among its detractors was John Mason Brown (*SR*), for whom it was "about as depressing as a fat woman in slacks." He thought the plot old-hat and too thin to fill a half hour's entertainment; he also thought it ridiculous for a character to have to sing a line like, "Let me go and get a handkerchief."

More impressive was the two-act *The Medium*. It is a melodramatically powerful, Grand Guignolesque piece (termed a "tragedy" by its creator) concerning a phony, red-haired, bibulous medium named Madame Flora (Marie Powers), who offers rigged séances with the help of her daughter Monica (Evelyn Keller) and a strange, mute gypsy boy named Toby (Leo Coleman), who loves the daughter. During a séance with a pair of elderly parents (Beverly Dame and Frank Rogier) seeking to contact their late children, Madame Flora's guilty conscience is exacerbated by her belief that she is being strangled by a spirit. Made even more fearful by drink, she goes into a closet to kill her evil self, but from it tumbles the mute, who was hiding within.

Rowland Field (*NEN*), who dubbed it "a sombre work set to striking music," said that it was "exceptionally sung," especially by the contralto star, Powers, an opinion with which most concurred. Her acting was as appreciated as her vocal talents. Brown was deeply taken by *The Medium*, finding its marriage of music and drama quite compatible, the fusion producing "arresting results." He was amazed at how effectively it had been staged and designed when compared with what he deemed the "amateurish" presentation of "The Telephone." Less impressed was Brooks Atkinson (*NYT*), who, comparing it to another progressive musical theatre work of the season, *Street Scene*, said that the difference between the two lay in the fact that "in *Street Scene* the music illustrates the drama. In *The Medium* the drama is the music." He also disputed Menotti's use of "tragedy" to label the work, calling it instead "hardly more than a superficial narrative."

George Freedley (*NYMT*) thought that the works might have been improved by more imaginative and professional staging. Like some others, he also held that there was too much musical dialogue that would have been more effective if spoken. Still, while not highly impressed by "The Telephone," he considered *The Medium* "genuinely thrilling." More positive was Otis L. Guernsey, Jr. (*NYHT*), who thought that the theatre's disparate arts had been combined with "consummate artistry and great distinction. Regardless of the tag which one chooses to put upon them . . . these works . . . have imagination, emotional force and showmanship." Horace Armistead's scenery for *The Medium* won that year's Tony.

(2) [Return Engagement] P: New York City Center b/a/w Chandler Cowles, Efrem Zimbalist, Jr., and Edith Luytens; T: City Center of Music and Drama; 12/7/48 (40)

This return engagement was basically the same production described above, although many new singers were involved. In "The Telephone" the two characters were played by Maria D'Attili and Paul King. Marie Powers and Leo Coleman reprised their *Medium* parts, but Monica was now alternated by Evelyn Keller (of the original) and Derna De Lys, while the parents were Paul King and, in alternation, Derna de Lys and Maria D'Attili.

Atkinson, who was hesitant about the pieces the first time he heard them, now had changed his mind and said that he liked "them very much indeed. For without being overwhelming they are theatre that is thoroughly awakened. The music, which is humorous for the first play and fiendish for the second, is like a theatrical incantation." Seymour Peck (*TS*) asserted that "it is . . . a rare accomplishment to make opera exciting, lifelike and touching all at once." He also thought the production of *The Medium* "swifter and more poignant" than the former presentation.

MEET A BODY [Comedy/Crime/Death/Journalism/Mystery/Romance] A: Jane Hinton; D: William Castle; S: Willis Knighton; P: H. Clay Blaney; T: Forrest Theatre; 10/16/44 (24)

All three acts of this comic murder mystery were set in a mortuary living room on the Lower East Side. Into this dreary place, operated by the Scottish John MacGregor (Whitford Kane) and his wife Margaret (Ruth McDevitt), comes a somewhat unbalanced criminologist-newspaper publisher (Le Roi Operti), who gives the funeral director and Manny Siegelman (Al Shean), his Jewish crony from acrossed the street, an envelope containing $10,000 to pay for his own funeral, with detailed instructions (including no embalming) on carrying it out. He expects to be slain, he explains, because there are four people looking to do him in. Shortly thereafter, his corpse turns up outside the door. Subsequently killed--two of them via a rare Oriental poison--at the undertaker's are the publisher's mistress (Helene Ambrose), his secretary (John McQuade), and his lawyer (Forrest Orr), each with something to gain from the dead man's unlamented departure. A stupid cop (Harry Gribbon) arrives to figure out the killings, but cannot think of a motive. There turn out to be two murderers. One is an escaped convict called "the Dancer" (Stephen Morrow), who has it in for the Scottish undertaker because the latter refused to back the killer's alibi, thereby sending him up the river. A policeman (John Boyd) ends up being strangled by him. (When pursued, the fugitive leaped into the audience and was followed by an agent of the law before returning to the stage.) The other is the publisher himself, who ingeniously arranged things to get revenge on his enemies. During all this, a romance blossoms between the undertaker's soldier son (Paul Potter) and the daughter (Nan Butler) of the dead mistress.

Critical response attacked the play on many grounds, chief of them the fact that the events were worked out so confusingly that few could make sense of the action. The comedy was uncomic, the thrills were unthrilling, and the suspense was unsuspenseful. The play never managed "to be anything better than elementary," sneered Arthur Pollock (*BE*). Rowland Field (*NEN*) said that after a fairly amusing first act, the piece ran out of ideas and became "a routine comedy who-dunnit that misses the mark by a wide margin."

MEET THE PEOPLE [Revue] SK: Ben and Sol Barzman, Mortimer Offner, Edward Eliscu, Danny Dare, Henry Blankfort, Bert Lawrence, Sid Kuller, Ray Golden, Milt Gross, Mike Quin, and Arthur Ross; M: Jay Gorney and George Bassman; LY: Henry Myers; D: Mortimer Offner and Danny Dare; S: Frederick Stover; C: Gerda Vanderneers and Kate Lawson; L: Ray Holmes; P: Hollywood Theatre Alliance; T: Mansfield Theatre; 12/25/40 (160)

After successful runs in Hollywood, San Francisco, and Chicago, this socially conscious intimate revue--which was created by a group of frustrated performers having a hard time breaking into movies--made a strong impression on Broadway, although it had to compete for opening-night audiences with *Pal Joey*. It was a fine assortment of thirty songs, comedy, and dances, reminiscent of the left-wing revue, *Pins and Needles**, performed by an excellent--but then largely unknown--young twenty-eight member company, including Jack Gilford, Nanette Fabray (billed as Nanette Fabares and making her Broadway debut), Jack Albertson, and Doodles Weaver. Less well known to future generations but scoring highly were tap dancer Jack Williams, impressionist and comic dancer Elizabeth Talbot-Martin (she took off on Aimee Semple McPherson, Katharine Hepburn, Greta Garbo, and Eleanor Roosevelt), and comic singer Marion Colby. During the run Shelley Winters (then spelled Winter) joined the company prior to the national tour. It was her Broadway debut.

Numerous topical targets were excoriated, poked fun at, or simply used as inspiration, among them the movie colony, Okie migrants, the United States Senate, the president and his wife, trade unionism, the Bill of Rights, and so on. Surprisingly, none of the material took issue with fascism or war. Weaver had a funny routine in which he told a story of a thousand rabbits. Albertson and Eddie Johnson did an old-time vaudeville-like routine, straw hats included, in which they mocked "The Same Old South" as a place of lynchings, racial injustice, and child labor. Gilford was a hit as a movie fan in a sketch in which he lectured on how movies are made, playing both the audience and all the characters in standard gangster, hospital, and mystery films. Fabray was well liked in "Hurdy Gurdy Verdi," a hilarious routine that had her trying to sing a Giuseppe Verdi aria interspersed with dance segments. Weaver stood out in a bit in which he was a radio announcer re-creating a race on the Indiana speedway. "Let's Steal a Tune from Offenbach" had a group of late, great composers urge a modern composer to steal a tune from Offenbach, not them.

Some critics thought that a few numbers were mediocre, but they approved the show as a whole. More enthusiastic was Scho. (*V*): "One thing *Meet the People* proves definitely--the living theatre can never die so long as new talent like these kids can be found. Plus, naturally, the sparkling sketch and song material provided them; plus also the swifty [*sic*] paced direction, expressive scenery and costuming. It's a little show that ranks in brilliance with the first *Little Show** and first *Americana**."

Shelley Winters recalled in *Shelley* how thrilled she was when she joined the show, despite her lack of dancing expertise. She worked assiduously to learn the dance numbers. On the fifth day of rehearsals, by which time the union required that she be notified if she was going to be fired, she was told by choreographer Dare that despite her other talents, she could not dance. Instead of accepting this as news of her firing, she showed up at rehearsals on the sixth day and worked away for the assistant choreographer. When two potential replacements showed up, they were told they were in the wrong theatre by the doorman, whom Winters had plied with rye and strudel. Upon Dare's arrival, Winters was reminded of what he had told her the day before, but, since she was still working on the sixth day, he could not fire her. She worked so hard at mastering her material that by day seven he gave in and told the stage manager, "Get Shelley fitted for her costumes." During the show, she had trouble keeping in time with the other dancers in a mini strip tease number, but her lagging behind proved so amusing to the audience that Dare let her keep the business in.

MEMBER OF THE WEDDING, THE [Drama/Blacks/Family/Rural/Southern/Youth] A: Carson McCullers; SC: Carson McCullers's novel of the same name; D: Harold Clurman; DS: Lester Polakov; P: Robert Whitehead, Oliver Rea, and Stanley Martineau; T: Empire Theatre; 1/5/50 (501)

One of the most poignant and beautifully played dramas of the decade, this touching piece about the pain of growing up lit the skyrocket that emblazoned Julie Harris's name as a star in the firmament, elevated Ethel Waters to renewed grandeur as a superb dramatic actress, and launched the career of seven-and-a-half-year-old Brandon De Wilde, who would become a star but die tragically young. Before it arrived in New York, the show's chances looked slim because the material seemed too tenuous for Broadway's tastes, and because its form--adapted from a respected novel--was not what conventional attitudes held to be appropriate for a play.

McCullers, disturbed by someone else's attempt to dramatize her story, had taken Tennessee Williams's advice and undertaken the task herself. The play was written in 1946 in Williams's Nantucket cottage as he wrote *A Streetcar Named Desire* across the table from her. (He may have provided valuable assistance in her writing, as well.) She wrote in *TAM* that the play was unconventional because it deals with inward action, not outward. "The antagonist is not personified, but is a human condition of life; the sense of moral isolation." McCullers likened the play's nature to that of classical drama and pointed out that it also "is concerned with the weight of time, the hazard of human existence, bolts of chance. The reactions of the characters to these abstract phenomena projects the movement of the play." Not perceiving this, but moved by the play's human insights, critic Brooks Atkinson (*NYT*) wrote, "If the drama were nothing but character sketches and acting, *The Member of the Wedding* . . . would be a masterpiece." He blamed the fact that "the play has no beginning, middle or end and never acquires dramatic momentum" on its genesis in a novel. Yet, he concluded, it "may not be a play, but it is art."

Director Clurman, whose work was considered one of the finest staging jobs in recent seasons, responded to the claims that the play had no action by noting (in *Lies like Truth*) that no play can be well acted if it has no action. The action may seem obscure, but it is there. "The action springs from . . . Frankie Addams' desire to get out of herself, to *become connected* or identified with a world larger than that which confines her to" the kitchen and her stultifying environment. "The play is the lyric expression of its strong central action; the direction consists in finding a physical or visual equivalent for every emotion that is the concomitant of the action."

Whatever it is, Broadway audiences reveled in the play's virtues for a season and a half, and the piece remained a frequently performed work for decades to come. Most compelling of its fascinations is the character of Frankie Addams, a twelve-year-old tomboy played by the then twenty-five-year-old Harris with closely cropped boyish hair in a tour de force display of versatility and imagination. Frankie is a lonely child with a desperate need to be a member of something. Her brother Jarvis (James Holden) is getting married, and the fantasy-bedevilled Frankie conspires to join the bride and groom on their honeymoon and to live glamorously with them forever after ("We is me," she says). Although there are a number of others in the play, the chief characters include, in addition to Frankie, the family's four-times-married black cook with a blue glass eye, Berenice Sadie Brown (Waters), and Frankie's amusing, bespectacled, seven-year-old cousin, John Henry West (De

Wilde); both are Frankie's closest companions, Berenice treating the motherless Frankie with exceptional understanding. The action takes place in a ramshackle kitchen and yard in a rural Southern community. Frankie suffers great anguish when her brother and his bride depart without her. She even runs away with her father's pistol, but comes home at four in the morning. Soon, she is deprived of John Henry's presence when he dies of meningitis. Berenice's reefer-smoking foster brother, Honey Brown (Henry Scott), gets into trouble for slashing a man with a razor and has to make his escape. Some months later, he dies. Frankie, though, has a boy named Barney (Jimmy Dutton) interested in her, is moving into a new house, and shows signs of ripening into maturity. Berenice, however, will not be going with the Addams family. Despite Frankie's promise to visit her, Berenice knows that she will not come. It is Berenice who is lonely at the end.

Many thought that the chief attraction was the acting, not the play. One representative of this view was Howard Barnes (*NYHT*), who affirmed that the drama "moves at a snail's pace through two acts in which the literary origin is all too apparent to a final burst of hysterics and melodrama." More approving was Rowland Field (*NEN*), who testified that this "pathetic, wryly comic account of a very young girl's mental stress. . . is fascinatingly poignant and real." Despite the mixed notices, the play was selected as the Drama Critics Circle Award (best American play) winner for 1949-1950

Each of the three leads received glowing notices. William Hawkins (*NYWT*) observed, "Julie Harris has great resource, both imaginative and physical, in her portrayal. . . . She must be fractious, fantastic, and ugly, heroic in her own mind, antagonistic and presumptive, utterly unreasonable, and with all of that, always touching. Miss Harris does it with extraordinary success, with lightning changes and inner consistency."

John Chapman (*NYDN*) noted of Waters, "Miss Waters is giving her best performance in the theatre--a piece of acting that is loving and lovable and profoundly expert. . . . Whenever the author fails to take command of the stage, Miss Waters takes command, and it is a great pleasure to fall under her quiet authority." Waters originally had turned the role down because the character as first written was "sordid and ugly," as she wrote in *His Eye Is on the Sparrow*. She continued to resist it even when she had serious financial problems and truly needed the job. A major objection was Berenice's lack of religious faith, which made her a character too distasteful for the pious actress to play. A meeting with Carson McCullers, however, led to Waters being permitted to create her own interpretation, and a contract was signed. At one point in the play, Waters got to sing, with deep feeling, the religious hymn, "His Eye Is on the Sparrow."

Barnes said of De Wilde that he played "with exceptional skill. His timing is always perfect and he reads his lines like a veteran." Director Clurman later recalled (in Fred Fehl's *On Broadway*) that De Wilde had never acted before but had an astonishing ability to remember whatever he was asked to do. As an example, Clurman said that the child was not used to hearing any audible reaction to his lines at rehearsal. One day Clurman brought about fifteen people in to watch a session, and De Wilde, surprised by their laughter, turned to look at them. Clurman warned him that when more people came, there would be even more laughter, and that he was never to look at the audience and to wait until they stopped laughing before continuing. When he got the chance to put this advice to work, De Wilde waited too long, until the last bit of laughter had ended, but he did not turn to look out. So Clurman praised him for what he did right, but told him not to wait until all the laughter stopped. "You must wait until you feel the laughter subsiding and then speak so there won't be a break." From then on De Wilde was perfect and, while observing the technical requirements, maintained his spontaneity. "Children, when they're good and not spoiled and have some ability, are always spontaneous. It's only when they get too professional that it's very difficult for them to be real." This was true of De Wilde, who ultimately had to take acting lessons to recapture the honesty of his earliest work.

Others in the fine company included William Hansen as Frankie's father, Janet De Gore as Janice, Margaret Barker as Mrs. West, and Harry Bolden as T. T. Williams. A musical version failed in 1971 under the title, *F. Jasmine Addams*, which is the name by which the fantasizing Frankie would like to be known.

MEMPHIS BOUND! [Musical/Blacks/Romance/Show Business/Trial] B: Albert Barker and Sally Benson; M: Don Walker; LY: Clay Warnick; SC: W. S. Gilbert and Arthur Sullivan's operetta, *H.M.S. Pinafore**; D: Robert Ross w/Eva Jessye; CH: Al White, Jr.; S/L: George Jenkins; C: Lucinda Ballard; P: John Wildberg; T: Broadway Theatre; 5/24/45 (36)

By one of those occasional theatrical coincidences, two shows inspired by *H.M.S. Pinafore*, but placing their stories in completely different backgrounds, opened within a week of one another. The first was the present show, the second was *Hollywood Pinafore*. Both were failures. The latter used the conceit of Hollywood's movie world for its background, the present one--originally called *Send Me a Sailor*--set its action in the deep South, with the characters a troupe of black entertainers hoping to sail down the Mississippi for Memphis on the showboat *Calliboga Queen*. The vessel has been grounded on a sandbar in Calliboga, Tennessee, for years because of a steering mishap for which Pilot Meriwether (sixty-seven-year-old star Bill "Bojangles" Robinson) was responsible. Meriwether resides in the local jail to keep from having to marry Aunt Mel (Edith Wilson), owner of the ship. Trying to get the money needed to refloat the ship, Aunt Mel seeks to put on a production of *Pinafore*, but the company wants to do it in a swing version, to which she objects. They nonetheless manage to put their abridged production on, with Meriwether agreeing to play the admiral, although Aunt Mel ultimately rings down the curtain on it. Moreover, lack of a license sends everyone to jail, but they are eventually tried and freed. A dream scene allows for an abridged version of "Trial by Jury,"* which, as someone announced, is usually on the bill with *Pinafore*.

Unlike *Hollywood Pinafore*, this show was not really a faithful adaptation of the original into another period and place but was instead a framework that allowed for extensive excerpts from Gilbert and Sullivan's show, as adapted to the changed circumstances with new lyrics and a jazz and boogie-woogie beat. Some new tunes by Don Walker also were included.

The expensive show itself caused few tremors, most of it seeming lame and uncreative, but the production was sporadically entertaining. Especially noteworthy was the appearance as Pilot Meriwether (the parallel to Sir Joseph Porter) of the great "Bojangles" Robinson. As ever, he did his famous up-and-down-the-stairs dancing without missing a step or a beat and seemed ageless in his undimmed vitality and charm. His rendition of the tune known in Gilbert and Sullivan's version as "Never Mind the Why and Wherefore" (here dubbed "Ring the Merry Belles") at the end almost redeemed the rest of the show.

Another top dancer, Avon Long, figured importantly in the role of Windy Carter (the parallel to Captain Corcoran), a rival of Roy Baggott (Billy Daniels in the Ralph Rackstraw parallel role) for the hands of the trio of Andrews Sisters-like singers--Lily Valentine (Sheila Guyse), Penny Paradise (Ida James), and Henny Paradise (Thelma Carpenter)--subsituting for Josephine. Others in the fine cast included Ada Brown (as the Buttercup parallel, Mrs. Paradise), Frank Wilson, and Oscar Plante.

Many found the first act, when *Pinafore* was swung, to be acceptable, but the second act seemed a mistake. Howard Barnes (*NYHT*) thought the swing concept "neither novel nor arresting" and the result reminiscent of "an uneven cafe floor show." Wilella Waldorf (*NYP*) complained that "no uniform pattern seems to have been set for the travesty, which wavers between a Tennessee Negro troupe's conception of how to perform *Pinafore* and a sophisticated Broadway exercise in modern rhythms." Burton Rascoe (*NYWT*) professed the thing to be "curiously lacking in zip and zingo." There was likewise confusion about why the characters wore nineteenth-century plantation-days garb when the time was listed as the present. Still, a couple approved the show, Herrick Brown (*NYS*), for example, finding it "a gay and eye-filling evening for the summer trade," and Arthur Pollock (*BE*) deciding that "its humor is amiable if never brilliant, its dialogue pleasantly colloquial, its settings and costumes sightly."

MEN IN SHADOW [Drama/Aviation/British/Military/War] A: Mary Hayley Bell; D: Roy Hargrave; S/L: Frederick Fox; P: Max Gordon; T: Morosco Theatre; 3/10/43 (21)

A farfetched but occasionally exciting English war melodrama (still playing in London at the time) set in the loft of a disused mill near a French farmhouse owned by a family sympathetic to the Allies. (Frederick Fox's set--"a lofty, shadowed attic with huge wooden wheels and mysterious cogs and braces," according to Rosamond Gilder [*TAM*]--was one of the best things about the production.) Here are hidden three downed American fliers-turned-saboteurs, Kenny (Everett Sloane), Polly (Francis De Sales), and Lew (Roy Hargrave, the director). From the loft they collaborate with the French underground and send signals to raiding American and RAF bombers, but the Germans suspect that something is up. The downed pilots care for Wally Mordan (Dean Harens), another downed American who broke both legs in his parachute drop. The buxom old farm woman Cherie (Michelette Burani), the play's only female, sets the fractures crudely with splints and no anesthetic as Mordan is persuaded to sing vulgar limericks. Another downed pilot, Enshaw (Ernest Graves), this one with an exaggerated British accent, is also taken in and seems on the up-and-up, but is eventually recognized as a German spy by Wally, who saw him several years earlier at the German legation in Shanghai. Lew, despite an aversion to violence, engages the spy physically and, using jiujitsu, breaks his neck (there was an audible sound effect). He then stabs to death a pair of invading Germans. (These scenes were reported to have caused women spectators in Boston to faint.) The mill is taken over by a Nazi company as a billet, and Lew must contrive a way to get the injured Wally to safety with the rest. He and the others manage to get him out through a trap door high up in the slanting roof, and everyone escapes, although no explanation is offered as to how the four are going to evade the Nazi regiment surrounding the mill.

The play--doctored for American audiences by Joseph Fields--had touches of authenticity in its use of French and German dialogue when necessary, and Hargrave gave an energetic if one-level performance of the hero, showing fluency in French as well as considerable athletic ability during the scenes of physical heroics. The big fight scene was especially exciting. "If it doesn't put Ernest Graves, who gets the worst of it, in the hospital before the run of the play ends I'll be surprised," declared Burns Mantle (*NYDN*).

Some, like Mantle, were willing to overlook the play's faults because of its skillful staging and melodramatics, but others were less kind. "Much of it is lurid to the point of absurdity," said Louis Kronenberger (*PM*). "Some of it is never very clearly explained. Almost all of it is contrived on the formula of the Marines turning up in the nick of time. . . . None of it . . . will survive the merest critical glance. But it is all of a piece--melodrama unencumbered by 'meaning' and blood-and-thunder unrelated to blood and tears."

MEN IN WHITE [Dramatic Revival*/Yiddish Language] A: Sidney Kingsley; TR: Meyer Schwartz; M: Ilya Trilling; D: Robert H. Harris; S: Michael Saltzman; P: Herman Yablokoff; T: Second Avenue Theatre (OB); 12/25/40

Producer Herman Yablokoff presented this 1933 Pulitzer Prize-winning play in Yiddish because he wanted the Yiddish theatre to begin dealing not only with Jewish subjects, but with those that concerned American society as a whole. B. R. R. (*WWD*) rated the experiment highly, claiming that "the presentation loses none of the power or effectiveness of the original."

The role of Dr. Hochberg, chief surgeon, was taken by director Harris, who had once played the role in English. Bernard Kisner played Dr. Ferguson, the young intern.

MEN TO THE SEA [Drama/Blacks/Boarding House/Marriage/Mental Illness/Military/Religion/Sea/Sex/War] A: Herbert Kubly; D: Eddie Dowling; S/L: Howard Bay; C: Grace Houston; P: Dave Wolper; T: National Theatre; 10/3/44 (23)

New York Herald Tribune reporter Kubly's first play was an attempt at a serious and sympathetic examination of the problems faced by those who wait, that is, the wives of servicemen whose mates are off at war. In the present case, the servicemen are navy men and their wives are residents of Madame Mosh's (Grace Mills) shabby boarding house near the Brooklyn Navy Yard.

Five lonely wives are looked at. One is Christabel (Toni Gilman), whose spiritually inclined gun-captain husband Duckworth (Randolph Echols) reads François Villon and the Bible to his crew. Of the five, only she and a black woman named Hyacinth (Mildred Smith), married to Reuben (Maurice Ellis), remain faithful to their husbands. The two-timers are Julie (Joyce Mathews); the sluttish Hazel (Maggie Gould), who gets pregnant by another sailor; and the sixteen-year-old Bonnie (Susana Garnett), whose husband went off to combat before their vows could be consummated. As the women celebrate Christmas at a raucous party at the boarding house, the men at sea huddle on the gun deck discussing God. Duckworth is killed in an air raid, and his wife, who has borne his child, sees a candle flame go out at the same moment. Upon learning of his death, she loses her mind, seeking him in every sailor she meets in the street and bringing them back home with her. She only comes to her senses and finds solace in religion when Duckworth's buddies return without him. The cuckolded husbands, influenced by the saintly Duckworth, forgive their wives when they learn of their infidelities.

Moralizing sentiments mingled uneasily with tawdry episodes, and realism with symbolism, in this earnest but uneven and depressing drama. The reviews varied from outright pans (which predominated) to praise with reservations to outright kudos. Lewis Nichols (*NYT*) dismissed it as "a highly pretentious play, full of sound and fury, and not signifying very much in the history of the drama." In Rosamond Gilder's (*TAM*) view, the playwright lacked discipline: "He labors his points and embroiders them with quotations that seem forced. But he has imagination and gusto, an ear for the vernacular, a kind of abundance and verve" that deserved encouragement. Burton Rascoe (*NYWT*) was powerfully impressed and raved about "the first war play we have had so far that is not either hackneyed or obvious or spurious in theme but one of the few plays in recent years which has a challenging idea, designed to shake up our complaisances."

Michael Strong played the husband of Hazel, Joe Verdi was an organ grinder, James Alexander was a British sailor, and Richard Camp, Tom Noonan, James Elliott, and Paul Crabtree had other roles.

Before coming into New York, the play had run into censorship trouble in Boston and New Haven, but--to the regret of critics like Euphemia Van Rensselaer Wyatt (*CW*)--the cuts made there were restored for Broadway. Among the objections to the play that the management had to fend off--with documented evidence in the way of published accounts--were those denying the validity of the work's assertion that many wives were finding it impossible to remain pure while their husbands were away at war. Other objections were to the discussion of sex in front of a statue of the Virgin Mary (Christ was substituted without protest), to a bedroom scene, and to the singing of a jazzed-up version of "Silent Night." Although he quarreled with the play on artistic grounds, George Jean Nathan (*TBY*) staunchly defended its morality. Kubly's "play, muddled and amateurish though it be, is . . . a lot cleaner than any number of plays with similar themes which have been welcomed by church and lay authorities."

MEN WE MARRY, THE [Comedy/Literature/Marriage/Romance/Rural] A: Elisabeth Cobb and Herschel Williams; D: Martin Manulis; S/L: Donald Oenslager; C: Helene Pons; P: Edgar Luckenbach; T: Mansfield Theatre; 1/16/48 (3)

Shirley Booth took a flop in this "little insomnia cure" (Richard Watts, Jr. [*NYP*]) in which she played Maggie Welch, a writer of second-rate fiction living in a fashionable Maryland country home where she is visited for a weekend house party by two man- and money-crazy friends from her school days, Leda Mallard (Doris Dalton) and Julie (Marta Linden). Each has her hooks into a different wealthy man (John Williams, Neil Hamilton, and Joseph Allen, Jr.) at the party. Maggie's daughter Mary (Anne Sargent), a war widow, is in love with Peter (John Hudson), a poor medical student, but the three older women disapprove of him, seeking a richer prospect in his stead. Their meddling nearly wrecks the love affair and almost destroys their own romantic interests as well. As the three women lament the sour turn of events, they are overheard by Mary, who saunters forth and regains Peter, while the hysterical women manage to bring back their own prospects as well, although Leda abandons hers to return to her politician spouse.

Robert Coleman (*NYDM*) declared that the piece began with a decent idea but was "smothered . . . to death beneath masses of boring, sleep-provoking dialogue." An acceptably comic performance was turned in by Margaret Hamilton as a maid.

MERCHANT OF VENICE, THE [Dramatic Revival*] A: William Shakespeare; M: Rosabel Watson; D: Donald Wolfit and Christopher Ede; C: Sheila Jackson; P: Hall Shelton b/a/w Advance Players Association, Ltd., of London; T: Century Theatre; 2/22/47 (6)

One of the items in the five-play repertory offered by England's visiting Donald Wolfit Repertory Company (the others were *King Lear**, *As You Like It**, *Hamlet**, and *Volpone**). This was their third offering; coming after the widely panned *Lear* and *As You Like It*, it showed signs that the company was not quite as bad as the earlier showings had led most critics to believe.

Howard Barnes (*NYHT*) declared that it was "scarcely an inspired production, but it is competent and colorful." It had clear diction, effective pacing, decent characterizations, and a decrease in shouted lines. The scenery was restricted to only the simplest effects, being essentially varying arrangements of draperies.

Wolfit was Shylock, Rosalind Iden was Portia, Alexander Gauge was Antonio, Geoffrey Wilkinson was Launcelot Gobbo, Marion Marshall was Nerissa, John Wynyard was Bassanio, and Zillah Tomlin appeared as Jessica when Penelope Chandler was prevented by illness from doing so on opening night.

Wolfit made up as Shylock in the melodramatically villainous manner used by nineteenth-century star Edmund Kean. The interpretation abandoned any idea of playing the character for sympathy. Wolfit also seemed less elocutionary than he had in his Lear or Touchstone. Wrote George Freedley (*NYMT*), "It was a well sustained performance, though he was given perhaps too much to hurling himself physically upon the floor with a thud that could be distinctly heard in Row M. He plays Shylock uncompromisingly enough to satisfy the most ardent anti-sentimentalist." Robert Garland (*NYJA*) believed it "the best Shylock I have ever seen." But Louis Kronenberger (*PM*) thought the performance too interested in "surefire" theatrical effects and not enough in deeper significance. Bron. (*V*) thought the portrait offensive to Jews at a time of increasing attempts to improve relations between interdenominational groups. The Shubert family of producers had indeed asked Wolfit not to put this play on as part of his repertory.

Iden's Portia was perhaps the actress's best portrayal of the repertory season. "Her Casket Scenes have grace and charm and she is very alive in the court of justice, reading the Quality of Mercy speech impulsively, informally and very dramatically," observed Ward Morehouse (*NYS*). Almost everyone else, with the possible exception of Gauge, ranged from mediocre to execrable, a condition that plagued almost every one of the company's revivals.

(See also "The Happy Journey.")

MERMAIDS SINGING, THE [Comedy/Barroom/Family/Hotel/Military/Romance/Sex/Theatre] A/D: John van Druten; S: Raymond Sovey; P: Alfred de Liagre, Jr.; T: Empire Theatre; 11/28/45 (53)

John van Druten had two hit plays (*The Voice of the Turtle* and *I Remember Mama*) running on Broadway when this less successful work--its title drawn from T. S. Eliot's poem, "The Love Song of J. Alfred Prufrock"--opened. Its reviews were mixed, a few thinking it a minor gem, others being less enthusiastic. John Mason Brown (*SR*) thought it frequently charming and wise but excessively talky. Ward Morehouse (*NYS*) reported that it was entertaining and provided with "some perceptive writing, some bold and bright dialogue," and a fine production, but its characters lacked credibility and the play was ultimately too "sprawling" and "listless" for complete appreciation. He and others noted the weak third act. Lewis Nichols

(*NYT*) thought the plot "thin and wispy" and the work as a whole "forced and tedious." However, George Jean Nathan (*TBY*), while noting the hoariness of the subject matter, found van Druten's treatment of it "a most engaging evening in the theatre" because of the writer's "intelligence, experience, and literary and emotional grace."

The tale is of an impulsive, dewy-eyed twenty-year-old, Dee Matthews (Beatrice Pearson), who meets famous and attractive playwright Clement Waterlow (Walter Abel) during the out-of-town tryout of his new play and falls in love with him, even though he is married, the father of two, and twice her age. Her persistent attentions--despite the protests of her mother (Frieda Inescort) and various other acquaintances--restore his sagging self-image, but before their relationship destroys his family, his conscience wins out, and he decides to break off with her and return her to the young naval officer (Walter Starkey) to whom she is engaged.

The company included Lois Wilson, Jane Hoffman, Jack Manning, Arthur Griffin, Harry Irvine, and Dina Merrill in her Broadway debut as "a girl."

MERRY DUCHESS, THE (***Der Lustige Krieg***) [Musical Revival] B/LY: uncredited; M: Johann Strauss; D: John Hand; P: New York Light Opera Guild; T: Barbizon-Plaza Theatre (OB); 6/23/43 (2)

A revival of an old Johann Strauss operetta (a more accurate translation of the title is *The Merry War*), done in English by a semipro group of light opera singers. It concerns a war between the gentlemen warriors of Genoa and the amazon soldiers of Malaspina, who are commanded by the regent princess (Helen Stanton) and her sister Violetta, the countess of Lomellini (Brenda Miller). There is a romance between Violetta and the Genoese general Spinola (Calvin Thomas). The uncredited adaptation included several updated references, such as one about selling shoes without ration cards and another to the MACs (Malaspina Auxiliary Corps).

Wilella Waldorf (*NYP*) stated that "the aims are lofty but the acting, and much of the singing, weak."

(1) MERRY WIDOW, THE (***Die Lustige Witwe***) [Musical Revival*] B: Victor Leon and Leo Stein; M: Franz Lehár; LY: Adrian Ross; D: John Pierce and Felix Brentano; P: Joseph S. Tushinsky and Hans Bartsch; T: Carnegie Hall (OB); 7/15/42 (39)

The last time this 1905 Viennese operetta had played locally had been in 1931. As then, it was now produced as part of a series of popular-priced operetta revivals, these under the general producership of conductor Joseph S. Tushinsky and Hans Bartsch.

The production, said George Freedley (*NYMT*), referring to the haste with which it was mounted, was "slapdash." He complained that it suffered chiefly from Tushinsky's faulty arrangements, which incorporated "jazz, swing, and even the samba, or something vaguely resembling it." Wilella Waldorf (*NYP*) attacked the production itself: "Some of the staging seems almost to have been designed as a burlesque of the old-style opulent operetta." But others felt that despite its creakily romantic plot and embarrassing attempts at humor (Mark Schubart [*PM*] called the work "a halting, tedious relic"), the show's music was so outstanding that the revival was worth a visit.

The title role was played by Helen Gleason, who was encored for her "Vilia" rendition, but her lack of dancing ability meant a diminution of the show's famous "Merry Widow Waltz." Prince Danilo was played by Wilbur Evans, and he and Gleason were considered by George Jean Nathan (*TBY*) an improvement over earlier pairings in these roles. Nish was played by John Cherry, Natalie by Elizabeth Houston, and Camille le Jolidon by Felix Knight. In the role of Baron Popoff, comedian Eddie Garr was allowed to improvise considerably, including the use of such phrases as "My momma done tol' me," "It's the nuts," and "That's all, brother!" which many found off-putting within the tone and context of the show. The effect, thought Nathan, "was akin to placing one's nose on a window and then whimsically slamming down the window."

(2) B: Sidney Sheldon and Ben Roberts; LY: Adrian Ross and Robert Gilbert; D:

Felix Brentano; CH: George Balanchine; S: Howard Bay; C: Walter Florell; P: Yolanda Mero-Irion for the New Opera Company; T: Majestic Theatre; 8/4/43 (322)

The first of a series of Broadway-quality operetta revivals by the New Opera Company, which a season earlier had gained some attention in musical but not theatrical circles for its opera stagings, although its participation in *Rosalinda* was applauded by the theatre critics. *The Merry Widow* was a big success, its cast including Polish tenor Jan Kiepura as Prince Danilo, Hungarian soprano Marta Eggerth as Sonia Sadoya, the merry widow, David Wayne as Nish, Ruth Matteson as Natalie, Robert Field as Jolidon, Melville Cooper as Popoff, Gene Barry as Novakovich, and Ralph Dumke as General Bardini.

The leads (husband and wife in real life) were deservedly famous singers but second-rate actors who not only tended to employ the flamboyant style of grand opera but whose English was sometimes unintelligible. Still, the lush sets and costumes, the conducting of Robert Stolz (conductor of the 1905 premiere in Vienna), the vivid and imaginative waltz and cancan choreography (with show-stopping dancers Milada Mladova and Lubov Roudenko), the deadpan comedy of Melville Cooper, and the general taste of the entire revival were attractive enough to garner critical and popular support.

Some revisions had been made to the libretto by Sheldon and Roberts, although they were careful to avoid the trend toward inserting topical jokes. Their revisions were especially helpful for Cooper's performance, he being "one of those rare comedians," wrote Euphemia Van Rensselaer Wyatt (*CW*), "who can infuse a gesture with wit and make the routine continental type of comedy sparkle." There also was some interpolated Viennese dance music and a Polish song for Kiepura.

Lewis Nichols (*NYT*) said that this was "a diverting and colorful revival of one of the catchiest of operetta classics." On opening night there were so many reprises and encores that the show did not close till after midnight.

(3) [Return Engagement] T: City Center of Music and Drama; 10/7/44 (32)

A limited-engagement resuscitation of the previous production, with Kiepura and Eggerth repeating their roles, but with changes in other members of the cast. These included Karl Farkas as Popoff, Nils Landin as Jolidon, Gordon Dilworth as General Bardini, Alan Vaughan as Novakovich, and Norman Budd as Nish, with premieres danseuses Babs Heath and Nina Popova matched by premier dancer Jack Gansert.

Eggerth had improved greatly, being much easier to understand, but Kiepura had gotten much worse. "Due allowance can be made because of a good voice," lamented Lewis Nichols (*NYT*), "but . . . Mr. Kiepura . . . struts and poses, and the Prince is far from a creature of Moravian charm." In other ways as well, the show was not as good as it had been. Commenting on the book, Louis Kronenberger (*PM*) remarked, "With its skittish airs and faded humor, it stood exposed for what it was without Melville Cooper and others in last year's cast to brighten it up."

MESSAGE FOR MARGARET [Drama/British/Marriage/Sex] A: James Parish; D: Elliott Nugent; S: Donald Oenslager; C: (gowns) Valentina; P: Stanley Gilkey and Barbara Payne i/a/w Henry Sherek, Ltd.; T: Plymouth Theatre; 4/16/47 (5)

One of a number of 1946-1947 plays that could not eke out even a week of performances. This import (still running at the time in London) had a small cast of five led by such strong players as Mady Christians and Miriam Hopkins. The drama, however, a variation on the timeless wife-versus-mistress conflict, proved ineffectual, and the performances were not sufficiently interesting to distract from the tired writing. For New York the play had an additional character, a maid (Janice Mars), added to the dramatis personae, and the locale was switched to a local habitat (Gramercy Park) from its English one.

"It moves slowly and some of the dialog and incidents are hard to believe," acknowledged Kelcey Allen (*WWD*). Rowland Field (*NEN*) added that it "turned out to be an unreasonably artificial drawing room drama with much ridiculous dialogue stressing some biological situations of debatable taste."

Its title and plot derive from the last words of the dying publisher, David Hayden, killed in a car crash, to his business partner (Roger Pryor): "Give my love to Margaret and bless her for all she has done for me." The trouble is that Margaret is not only the name of David's adoring but childless wife (Christians) of fifteen years, but is also the one by which David called Adeline Chalcot (Hopkins), his brazen mistress, who used it as a pen name. The action of the play is based on attempts by the women to determine for whom David's last words were intended. The mistress tells the wife that they will forever have a unique love-hate relationship based on their mutual intimacy with David. Before the play concludes, the wife has attempted the murder of the ruthless hussy, who, to further complicate matters, is pregnant by the deceased husband. Moreover, Robert Chalcot (Peter Cookson), Adeline's discarded spouse, who has agreed to pretend that Adeline's child is his, dies accidentally by falling from a defective balcony. The play never makes it entirely clear whom David meant by his dying words.

METROPOLE [Comedy/Business/Journalism/Romance] A: William Walden; D: George S. Kaufman; S: Edward Gilbert; C: Bianca Stroock; P: Max Gordon; T: Lyceum Theatre; 12/6/49 (2)

Metropole is the name of a *New Yorker*-like weekly magazine; its fiery editor, Frederick M. Hill (Lee Tracy), is based on the *New Yorker*'s famed editor, Harold Ross, whose methods the play attempted unsuccessfully to satirize. Author Walden had himself worked for the real-life magazine.

Metropole is focused on the tribulations of the tempestuous, absentminded, disheveled editor, former husband of four wives, who rails at everyone who works for him and reigns over a manic establishment, yet who manages to produce a weekly magazine that is the best in its class. The central premise concerns the founding by a publishing magnate of a rival magazine, *The Gothamite*, which pilfers the best staff members from under Hill's nose. The rival editor is one of Hill's ex-wives, the still ardent Miss Harrington (Edith Atwater). In spite of his many demands on behalf of his staff, he gets no help from his business office. The new magazine is published on the very day that Hill's contract expires. The temporarily jobless editor is cheered up by various pals and girlfriends. One of the latter, an actress named Carolyn Hopewell (Arlene Francis), tries to use her connections to buy out the *Metropole*. The day is saved, however, when the public writes in in such protesting numbers that Hill is restored to his position.

Neither the play nor the farce-oriented production pleased the critics, despite the presence of some outstanding actors. Brooks Atkinson (*NYT*) declared it to be "played on the level of a prolonged bellow that is at first deafening and eventually stupefying. Perhaps they play it noisily to conceal the limitations of a contrived and static script." Louis Sheaffer (*BE*) charged that it was "a mild to-do, labored in its attempts to be funny rather than spontaneous about it, good for only one or two genuine laughs, no more." The respectable cast included Jane Seymour, Frances Waller, Jean Carson, Reynolds Evans, Henry Jones, Gavin Gordon, Reed Brown, Jr., Royal Dano, and John Glendenning.

MEXICAN HAYRIDE [Musical/Crime/Gambling/Hotel/Mexico/Romance/Sports] B: Herbert and Dorothy Fields; M/LY: Cole Porter; D: Hassard Short with John Kennedy; CH: Paul Haakon; S: George Jenkins; C: Mary Grant; L: Hassard Short; P: Michael Todd; T: Winter Garden; 1/28/44 (481)

A quarter of a million dollar price tag was reportedly attached to this opulent musical (which charged a $5.50 top) starring the irrepressible Bobby Clark, who appeared replete with his trademark cigar and painted spectacles and was backed by a 115-member cast. The show had been conceived for Victor Moore and William Gaxton, but their demand to work for sixteen percent of the gross instead of a straight salary lost them the job. To advertise the show, a huge, $10,000 sign, painted by pinup artist Alberto Varga and displaying a beautiful girl in a reclining position (her legs were seventy-one feet long), was placed over Broadway and took ten days to get into place. Although the show had a long run, it had had many portents of disaster before arriving on Broadway. During the Boston tryout period, a pit musician died in producer Todd's arms during a rehearsal. There were postponements of the Boston opening because of the late arrival of sets and costumes. When the costumes arrived, the $700-apiece lace hoopskirts used in a big number were ruined and nearly impossible to replace because of wartime shortages. But the indefatigable Todd had them replaced nonetheless.

The hackneyed book was merely a lavish vehicle for Clark's hilarious antics, featuring him as Joe Bascom (alias Humphrey Fish), a numbers racketeer on the lam in Mexico from the FBI and from a shrewish wife (Marjory Leach). When female American bullfighter Montana (June Havoc) throws the ear of a bull she has killed to the embassy attaché (Wilbur Evans) she loves, it lands in Joe's lap, leading to his selection as the American representative during Mexico-America Good Fellowship Week. Urged on by promoter Lobos Campos (George Givot), he sets up an illegal lottery after cheating Montana of her money. The Mexican authorities pursue him, and he eludes them by a series of wacky disguises, including the use of a false nose to impersonate a flute player in a mariachi band and false buck teeth to portray an Indian woman selling tortillas in Taxco. (On her back the squaw bore a papoose that had a cigar in its mouth and Clark's painted glasses on its face.) As he runs from the law, the show leaps all around Mexico for spectacular scenic delights, including bullrings, hotels, Ciro's, a palace at Chepultepec, bistros, and the like.

It was not one of Cole Porter's banner shows, the biggest hit being "I Love You." According to Art Cohn's *The Nine Lives of Michael Todd*, Porter wrote the song when Todd, trying to inspire the depressed composer, bet him that he could take the most clichéd words, "I love you," and, using only one note for each word, create a hit song. Kudos also went to "What a Crazy Way to Spend Sunday," "Count Your Blessings," and "Carlotta," none of the latter of lasting importance.

Choreographer Paul Haakon also danced in the show and was a standout with his dance as a bullfighter. The show also found room for dancers Paul and Eva Reyes, Spanish singer and guitarist Corinna Mura, Edith Meiser in a brief comedy role, and Luba Malina as a sexy Russian. The show's first half was considered beautiful but boring, but its second half outstanding because of the comical opportunities it gave to Clark. Reviews ranged from the reserved one of Howard Barnes (*NYHT*), who called it "a big, brash and generally undistinguished extravaganza," to the sheer rave of Robert Garland (*NYJA*), who declared it "so funny, so tuneful, so beautiful, that you could hardly believe your eyes and ears."

The fact that June Havoc, who received tremendous approbation, was the sister of stripper Gypsy Rose Lee was mentioned by several reviewers who said that her role made good use of family traits. John Chapman (*NYDN*) described her thusly: "This lady has a facade which is nothing like a Greek temple, but noble all the same; a pair of legs Mistinguett could have envied, and the most remarkable observation platform since Henry Dreyfuss designed the Twentieth Century Limited."

Although there is no space to recount it here, readers should be alerted to the delightful story "Minnie and Mr. Clark" (in George Oppenheimer's *The Passionate Playgoer*), about a theatre cat who one night stole one of Bobby Clark's best scenes.

MEXICAN MURAL [Drama/Fantasy/Invalidism/Mexico/Politics/Religion/Prostitution/Romance/Sex] A: Ramon Naya; D/P: Robert Lewis; S: Herbert Andrews; L: Wil Washcoe; T: Chanin Auditorium (OB); 4/26/42 (4)

A sprawling, symbol-laden, colorful, and sometimes imaginative play in four intertwined "panels" offering a multifaceted and highly critical view of Mexican religious and secular life. Singer Libby Holman backed the show because she felt that she had dramatic talent and wanted a role in which to demonstrate it. It was staged in the postage-stamp-sized quarters of an auditorium on the fifty-second floor of East Forty-second Street's Chanin Building. The titles of its four "panels" were "Vera Cruz Interior," "Miracle Painting," "Moonlight Scene," and "Patio with Flamingo." *Mexican Mural* had been written in 1939, won a contest sponsored by the Group Theatre, and garnered the author a Rockefeller Playwriting Fellowship Award. It possessed a number of very talented players, among whom Montgomery Clift and Holman provided memorable performances.

The uneven presentation was marred by cloudy and undisciplined writing, but some thought it gifted with vitality and gut-wrenching emotion as well. George Freedley (*NYMT*) claimed, "It seemed to me that this was one of the most powerful pieces of dramatic writing I had encountered in some years. This is not really a finished piece of writing in the accepted sense of the word." More typical was Richard Watts, Jr.'s (*NYHT*), comment: "There is much intensity of emotion but little dramatic force or clarity. . . . The work is so vague and muddy and overwrought in its symbolism . . . that it becomes laboriously dull."

Vera Cruz is the locale of the action, which occurs on Ash Wednesday, a day after carnival. Revealed is a poverty-stricken society oppressed by bandits, despotic politicians, perverse religiosity, and corrupt moral values. The purpose of the work is ostensibly to get the people to cast off their religious superstitions and political oppressors and return to a simpler, more human way of life. Its episodes treat the story of an ill-fated love between a neurotic mother's (Kathryn Grill) repressed daughter (Perry Wilson) and a crippled boy (Clift) who attempts to kill himself, but who gains in stature when his doctor father (Spencer James) is killed by the local dictator, the Red Head (Kenneth Tobey); of a peasant woman (Holman), mother of ten, who witnesses the death of her infant when she cannot afford to feed it, while the doctor refuses her the pennies she could use, but spends them on a prostitute; of the Madonna's (Norma Chambers) coming to life, but failing to help the baby; of the brutality of the Red Head, whose Goldshirts shoot down his enemies, including the doctor's son, at the carnival; and the decision of the fascist dictator's disillusioned daughter (Norma Chambers) to leave for Guatemala in order to ponder the problems of the people.

Robert Lewis's direction was notably detailed in its no-holds-barred depiction of the seamiest aspects of the dramatic world. His cast included David Opatoshu as a male prostitute, Kevin McCarthy as a rowdy sailor, and many others, most of them nonunion actors.

(1) **MIKADO, THE** [Musical Revival*] B/LY: W. S. Gilbert; M: Arthur Sullivan; D: R. H. Burnside; P: Boston Comic Opera Company and Messrs. Shubert; T: St. James Theatre; 2/3/42 (19)

Part of a series of Gilbert and Sullivan revivals by the Boston Comic Opera Company. This one had the longest run of the lot. It shared the stage with two ballets by the Joos Ballet Company, "The Big City" and "A Ball in Old Vienna". Robert Pitkin played the mikado, Morton Bowe was Nanki-Poo, Florenz Ames was Ko-Ko, Bertram Peacock was Poo-Bah, Frederic Persson was Pish-Tush, Kathleen Roche was Yum-Yum, Mary Roche was Pitti-Sing, Margaret Roy was Peep-Bo, and Helen Lanvin was Katisha.

Topical references were added to remind the audience of the war with Japan, including having a character sing in the first chorus, "We are gangsters of Japan." Unhappily, the revival, said Brooks Atkinson (*NYT*), was "mediocre," only Florenz Ames's Ko-Ko being worth the ticket. A program note sought to allay any patriotic displeasure with the choice of this show in post-Pearl Harbor audiences by stating, "Almost three score years have passed since William S. Gilbert wrote *The Mikado*, depicting the Japanese in the light that history now records--sly, witty and deceitful, unconscionably corrupt, and treacherous. Greatest humorous librettist in the annals of the stage, Gilbert satirized their rulers and their customs with shafts of wit that made the opera the unparalleled success of more than half a century. Recognized as inveterate imitators, the fact that they have chosen the world's worst as a model (thereby sustaining Gilbert's opinion) does not and should not alter the libretto's comic status or the melodic delight's of Sullivan's supreme score."

(2) D: R. H. Burnside; P: R. H. Burnside i/a/w the Gilbert and Sullivan Opera Company; T: Ambassador Theatre; 2/11/44 (6)

Veteran musical theatre director R. H. Burnside was responsible for a series of Gilbert and Sullivan offerings early in 1944. Although its name was changed and there were cast changes, this was essentially the same troupe as described in the previous entry. In *The Mikado* Robert Pitkin, Florenz Ames, and Kathleen Roche repeated their roles, while Bertram Peacock now moved to Pish-Tush and Robert

Eckles took on Pooh-Bah. James Gerard alternated with Allen Stewart as Nanki-Poo, Kathryn Reece was Pitti-Sing, Marie Valdez was Peep-Bo, and Catherine Judah was Katisha.

The revival was second-rate. "It is a stock version which disgraces no one, nor will bring anyone fame," decided Lewis Nichols (*NYT*). A chief fault was its lack of the right comic feeling. The staging and performances were wooden and uninspired. Microphones were used for amplification. The company retained the line, "We are gangsters of Japan" from the last revival.

George Jean Nathan (*TBY*), discussing the series, declared, "Stage settings and costumes had the appearance of being the offspring of parents born in the beer garden operetta atmosphere of the 1890's."

(3) D: Anna Bethell; DS: Charles Ricketts; P: D'Oyly Carte Opera Company; T: Century Theatre; 12/29/47 (40)

England's famed Savoyards, the D'Oyly Carte Opera Company, last seen in New York in 1939, returned with a nine show repertory totalling 136 performances. *The Mikado* featured Darrell Fancourt as the mikado, Thomas Round as Nanki-Poo, Martyn Green as Ko-Ko, Richard Watson as Pooh-Bah, Charles Dorning as Pish-Tush, Peter Pratt as Go-To, Margaret Mitchell as Yum-Yum, Denise Findlay as Pitti-Sing, Joan Gillingham as Peep-Bo, and Ella Halman as Katisha.

To some, the revival was deemed less than sparkling, although Green and Fancourt, especially the latter, did their best to lighten up the occasion. It was well sung, but somehow lacked "crackle," thought Brooks Atkinson (*NYT*). Euphemia Van Rensselaer Wyatt (*CW*), however, found it "pure delight." George Jean Nathan (*TBY*) appreciated the voices, but despaired of the woeful sets and costumes and the unimaginative direction.

(4) D/P: S. M. Chartock; S/L: Ralph Alswang; C: Peggy Morrison; T:Mark Hellinger Theatre; 10/4/49 (8)

The first in a three-show series that lasted a week each. The mediocre company was appreciated for its enthusiasm and panned for its lack of "style and polish," as Brooks Atkinson (*NYT*) put it. It also lacked, in Ralph Riggs, an effective Ko-Ko. Among the other players were Morton Bowe as Nanki-Poo, Robert Eckles as Pooh-Bah, Earle MacVeigh as Pish-Tush, Kathleen Roche as Yum-Yum, Jean Handzlik as Katisha, and Joseph Macaulay as the mikado.

George Jean Nathan (*TBY*) took the troupe to task: "Not only was the company in the main ill-suited to G. and S., but the direction was even more so. The performances, where they should have been quicksilver, were leaden."

MILKY WAY, THE [Dramatic Revival*] A: Lynn Root and Harry Clork; D: Rodney Hale; S: Cirker and Robbins; P: Lucia Victor's New York Stock Company; T: Windsor Theatre; 6/9/43 (16)

A noisy revival of the 1934 comedy that already had been made into one movie under its original title and would be remade in 1946 as *The Kid from Brooklyn*. The present version was offered by a new group attempting to set up a Broadway stock company at popular prices ($1.65 top). The idea of a summer-stock company in New York was inspired by the current gas shortage, which prevented people from attending summer stock in the countryside. But the result was "a ragged production of a straggling farce," in Howard Barnes's (*NYHT*) opinion. "The play was far from incandescent when it was first shown here. . . . Today it is a cold turkey." "Rodney Hale's direction is so slow that the whole audience longed to yell for pace and be quick about it," advised George Freedley (*NYMT*).

The milkman who turns champion pugilist was played by Joey Faye, Lewis Charles was Gabby, Max Leavitt was Spider, Helen Gillette was Mae, Lila Lee played the role of the wisecracking Anne (originally taken by Gladys George), and Stanley Phillips was Speed McFarland. None were up to their predecessors. John Anderson (*NYJA*) believed that Faye, then emerging from burlesque into legitimate comedy, was seriously miscast. "His comic method is raucous, aggressive, and unrestrained. He is at his best when he goes into a sort of noisily insane double talk. His most plaintive manner would never lead me to believe that he was ever a gentle milkman."

(1) **MILLIONAIRESS, THE** [Comedy/British/Business/Medicine/Romance] A: George Bernard Shaw; P: Dramatic Workshop; T: President Theatre (OB); 4/6/49 (13)

One of the few late 1940s offerings by the semiprofessionals at Erwin Piscator's Dramatic Workshop to get more than just a passing critical notice, if that, was this revival of Shaw's 1936 farce, never shown before in New York. Richard Watts, Jr. (*NYP*), acknowledged that it was third-rate Shaw but noted that third-rate Shaw is an improvement over most of what one gets to see. J. P. S. (*NYT*) declared that the piece had a few charms, "but the major ingredients produce ennui." The production was on the mediocre side, lacking polish, but the piece still kept one's interest.

The story is meant to demonstrate a thesis about how those with talent and ability will rise to the top and that those with domineering traits should dominate. Epifania is a domineering millionairess married to the athletic Alastair (Myron Rubin), who is seeking a separation. To marry her, he had to build £150 into £50,000 within six months. He succeeded by kiting checks. He keeps himself from boredom with a girlfriend. His wife, on the other hand, would like to kill herself for having made a bad match. Epifania dines at an inn with her "Sunday husband" Adrian (Woodrow Parfrey) and kicks him down the stairs when he dismisses money. The refusal to be impressed by her of an Egyptian doctor (Claude Traverse) who treats her for the convulsions she fakes makes her want to marry him. He puts her to a family test by making her earn her living for half a year. Beginning with a menial job, she works herself up to becoming owner of a fancy inn. Threats of suit and countersuit emerge between Adrian and Epifania. She then works her wiles on the reluctant Egyptian and convinces him to marry her.

(2) D: Boris Marshalov; S: Bob O'Herne; C: Robert MacIntosh; P: Equity Library Theatre; T: Neighborhood Playhouse (OB); 6/4/49 (3)

Only William Hawkins (*NYWT*) covered this revival, which included such actors as Charlton Heston, Anthony (Tony) Randall, and Teresa Hayden. Hawkins said that it "was all acted pleasantly if without any great penetration or style, by a company which keeps the play racing vocally."

MINNIE AND MR. WILLIAMS [Dramatic Revival*] A: Richard Hughes; D: Eddie Dowling; DS: Mordi Gassner; P: John Gassner and David Dietz; T: Morosco Theatre; 10/27/48 (5)

New York's first Broadway showing of a 1924 English satire originally called *A Comedy of Good and Evil* and seen in a 1938 Off-Broadway mounting. In the present version the Welsh clergyman was played by Eddie Dowling, his one-legged wife Minnie by Josephine Hull, who stole the show, and Gladys, the devilish one, by Elizabeth Ross. The company also included such stalwarts as Clarence Derwent, Grace Mills, and Geoffrey Lumb. In Brooks Atkinson's (*NYT*) opinion, the play was "tenuous and untheatrical--too slight for a full evening in the theatre." Howard Barnes (*NYHT*) noted that "it is lost, somewhere behind the playwright's vision, in a confusion of philosophies, sight gags, gaping peasantry and a consistent refusal to come to the point."

John Gassner, one of the producers, was an eminent critic and theatre scholar, but his taste in commercial comedy was not well represented by this effort. The production was fraught with problems from the start. Red paint was accidentally spilled over Josephine Hull's coat at a rehearsal. The plastic prop used for the leg, operated with a button-and-spring mechanism, created difficulties when required to perform. Hull had a serious conflict with her director when--sure of getting a laugh--he asked her to make the leg behave foolishly as she played hymns on an organ. To the pious actress, such behavior would be sacrilegious. Her tears convinced Dowling to forgo the bit, whereupon Hull decided that the laughs were too good to dismiss and agreed to do his bidding. "After all, I think God has a sense of humor," she suggested (quoted in William G. B. Carson, *Dear Josephine*).

MINSTREL BOY, THE [Drama/Literary-Biographical/Old Age/Period/Politics/Romance/War] A: W. A. S. Douglas; D: Dennis Gurney; S/L: David Reppa; C: Irene Griffin; P: Blackfriars' Guild; T: Blackfriars' Theatre (OB); 10/14/48

The semiprofessional Blackfriars' troupe offered this "sensitive and moving" (Robert Coleman [*NYDM*]) biographical play about eighteenth-century Irish poet and balladeer Tom Moore. To suggest his aging, three actors played Moore: as a child, Victor Vraz; as a young man, Tom Donahue; and as an old man, Charles Dolan.

The piece covers the poet's life from childhood to his last years and is interspersed with Moore's songs, which played an important role in Irish history. These included such famous numbers as "Minstrel Boy," "Endearing Young Charms," and "Wearin' of the Green." Moore, the son of a Celt grocer, was an intellectual and musical child prodigy, a friend of Richard Brinsley Sheridan and Robert Emmet (Robert Emmet, an actor with the same name as his role), with whom he attended Trinity College. In the play, he and Emmet join the hotheaded undercover army of Napper Tandy (Michael Garrett). On the night of the disastrous Vinegar Hill uprising of 1798, Emmet is caught and hung, but the interference of Moore's mother (Charlott Knight) and priest, Father O'Halloran (Brian Doyle), prevent him from being captured and executed. Convinced by Father O'Halloran to turn his considerable talents to balladry, Moore leaves for London to use his songs in a campaign to earn royal favor for the cause of the Irish people. In the end, he is an old codger living on the bounty of a tavern keeper. The play also includes his romantic attachment to Kitty Devlin (as child, Patricia White; as a young woman, Virginia Romley).

Some critics considered this one of the best pieces yet done by the Blackfriars and recommended it to theatregoers. Richard Watts, Jr. (*NYP*), described it as "frankly romantic, sometimes rather touching, and, to its credit, simple and informal. Not surprisingly, it is at its best when it sings." However, Watts felt that Moore was not really the best subject for a play, having lived a not especially dramatic life and having occupied most of his time in comfortable English surroundings rather than in the thick of the kind of turmoil that would have made him a true hero. George Freedley (*NYMT*) thought that it would be pleasing mainly for "Irish-American audiences which are indulgent enough to overlook a poor play and some pretty indifferent acting."

Tenor Tom Donahue was excellent as Moore, both in the singing and the acting of the role. Also commendable were the imaginative yet simple settings of David Reppa.

MIRACLE IN THE MOUNTAINS [Drama/Crime/Fantasy/Period/Politics/Religion/Sex/Trial] A/D: Ferenc Molnár; DS: Robert Davison; P: Archer King and Harrison Woodhull; T: Playhouse; 4/25/47 (3)

Onetime king of the Hungarian playwrights, Molnár, now resident in America, provided this turkey of major dimensions. It was severely scorned for "mawkish and maudlin" (Brooks Atkinson [*NYT*]) writing, clumsy acting, and inept directing. George Freedley (*NYMT*), suggesting that it read better than it played, declared, it "turned out to be almost completely unconvincing and so outrageously acted under the author's direction that a first night audience was embarrassed." (The word "unconvincing" appeared in several reviews.)

Termed "a legend" by the playwright, the work is set one hundred years earlier in a small mining town somewhere in the Carpathian mountains. Haydon played Cicely, a servant girl who has a child by the mayor (Frederic Tozere). When the child's death becomes known, she is accused of murder because of animosity stemming from her affair with the schoolmaster (Pitt Herbert). She seeks sanctuary at a monastery, where she encounters a mysterious Christ-like attorney named the Prior (Victor Kilian), who takes up her cause. He fails to pry a confession from the powerful mayor. A courtroom scene shows him trying to establish the servant girl's innocence. He leads the judge to a mountain top where the little victim is resurrected and then bears Cicely off to heaven as everyone stands by in astonishment. The child's death is attributed not to the sinning girl but to the mayor.

The large cast included Salem Ludwig, E. A. Krummschmidt, Katherine Anderson, Manart Kippen, and others.

MIRACLE OF A GHETTO, THE [Drama/Yiddish Language] A: H. Leivick; M: Sholem Secunda; D: Jacob Ben-Ami; CH: Benjamin Zemach; S: H. A. Condell; P: Joseph Green; T: New Jewish Folk Theatre (OB); 10/10/44

A sprawling but gripping attempt to capture on stage the resistance of the Warsaw ghetto to the Nazis in April 1943. The highly charged play, dealing with material that would one day reach Broadway in Millard Lampell's dramatic version of John Hersey's novel *The Wall*, tells of a small congregation of Chassidic Jews hidden in their temple's cellar on Passover Eve. The occupants are busy preparing the seder while also arming themselves and hiding guns under the floor. The frightened flock is encouraged by Isaac the Sage (Menachem Rubin) telling them, "In the name of God, do not despair." Only Israel (Jacob Ben-Ami, the director) feels that armed resistance is not the Jewish way. Isaac comes out on top in a moral debate, and the people leave to fight or die. Numerous casualties result but barely any assistance comes from the Warsaw underground, which offers only a handful of ammunition. When a girl named Rachel (Muriel Gruber) risks and loses her life to obtain the arms, the reluctant Israel is incited to get the arms himself. His return three days later is on the Sabbath morning, and the Jews are praying in the bombed-out temple courtyard. He hands over his pitiful cache, but the futility of his efforts is shown by the imminent arrival of the enemy. The frightened Jews now heed the voice of the newly militant Israel, who fires them up to do battle, "not only for the Name of God, Kiddush Ha-Shem, but also for the dignity of man and the dignity of his people." They will fight to the death, and those who survive will join the partisans outside the city in the countryside.

This was "a timely, absorbing drama . . . fashioned from the headlines," approved Kahn. (*V*). E. C. Sherburne (*CSM*) claimed, "Jacob Ben-Ami staged the play with sure feeling for the indication of tension, in even the most colloquial scenes. He acts with tragic power and fire." Yet George Jean Nathan (*TBY*) categorized it as "an overemotionalized melodrama adorned with rituals of the Hebrew faith."

It had been accorded an expensive production, with a cast of over fifty, many from the Yiddish Art Theatre, whose activities had been temporarily suspended. The company included Berta Gersten, Isadore Casher, Dora Weissman, Mark Topel, Goldie Lubritzky, Abraham Teitelbaum, and Dinah Halpern.

MISER, THE (*L'Avare*) [Dramatic Revival*] A: Molière; M: Julian Seaman; D: Dan Levin; S: Richard Burns; C: B. J. Harris and James Doll; P: Theatre Classics; T: Walt Whitman School (OB); 3/26/50

The first revival of this classic comedy in New York during the century. In Lewis Funke's (*NYT*) view, it turned out to be "a thoroughly enjoyable" production, but in Vernon Rice's (*NYP*), it was "a spiritless and straggling production." One of the few other reviewers present, Thomas R. Dash (*WWD*), was on Funke's side, terming the show "a merry romp," played tongue in cheek. "Their robust style of acting plus the basically funny situations in Moliere's work add up to an enjoyable evening." It was the second offering by a new Off-Broadway troupe (the first was an apparently unreviewed version of *The Cenci* by Percy Bysshe Shelley). Entrances were through the less-than-one-hundred-seat auditorium and exits behind a partition. The Walt Whitman School was at 25 East Seventy-eighth Street.

Simply stated, the old story is that of an obsessive gold hoarder named Harpagon (William Jackson). He woos a young woman who also happens to be his son Cleante's (Henry Waldron) beloved. Only the son's gaining control of the old man's money convinces the latter to give up the girl to get back the cash. A subplot concerns the desire of the miser's daughter, Elise (Dorothy Steele), to marry the man of her choice (Larry Blyden, a future star).

A show-stealing job was provided by Donald Somers as Master Jacques, the coachman and cook. "He has a vinegary voice, a good sense of timing for a comic line and experienced presence on the stage," said Funke. Louise Larabee, Rice's favorite, was the seductive Frosine, Ellen Humphrey was Mariane, and Charles S.

Purcell was La Fleche.

MISS LIBERTY [Musical/Art/France/Hotel/Journalism/Period/Romance/Sea] B: Robert E. Sherwood; M/LY: Irving Berlin; D: Moss Hart; CH: Jerome Robbins; S/L: Oliver Smith; C: Motley; P: Irving Berlin, Robert E. Sherwood, and Moss Hart; T: Imperial Theatre; 7/15/49 (308)

This promising musical did not fulfill its promises, although a large advance sale allowed it to run an entire season. The first promise it broke was that of opening on July 4; circumstances pushed the curtain back almost two weeks. Despite a lineup of tremendous creative and performing talents, the show--much revised in a month-long Philadelphia tryout--never clicked and had barely any lastingly popular songs, apart from "Let's Take an Old-Fashioned Walk."

The subject concerned romantic developments in the 1880s stemming from events encircling the erection of the Frédéric Auguste Bartholdi-designed Statue of Liberty, which was given as a gift by France to America. When young photographer Horace Miller (Eddie Albert) takes the wrong pictures at a ceremony honoring publisher Joseph Pulitzer's (Philip Bourneuf) donation to pay for the statue's base, he loses his job. Pulitzer, meanwhile, is in a fierce circulation war with rival publisher James Gordon Bennett (Charles Dingle). At the behest of his *Police Gazette*-reporter girlfriend Maisie Dell (Mary McCarty), who feels that he can get his job back thusly, Horace goes to France to seek out the model used by Bartholdi (Herbert Berghof). Meeting Monique DuPont (Allyn McClerie), he mistakenly assumes that she is the model and arranges to return to the United States with her. Unbeknownst to the faithful Maisie back home, Horace is falling in love with Monique. Maisie talks Bennett into sponsoring a U.S. tour for Monique, but when the girl arrives, she learns for the first time that she is the victim of mistaken identity. She achieves national popularity, despite the deception. The truth emerges, and Bennett has Horace thrown in jail for fraud. Pulitzer, however, bails him out and hires him. Horace chooses Monique over Maisie. The statue is dedicated and the words of Emma Lazarus's poem, "Give Me Your Tired, Your Poor," set to music, conclude the saga.

The opulently designed show seemed disappointingly old-hat, formulaic, pedestrian, and unoriginal. Its lack of comedy was especially deplorable. Howard Barnes (*NYHT*) called the libretto "aimless and witless." According to *TAM*'s unnamed reviewer, "Sherwood's book is plot-heavy and barren of humor; Berlin's score is embarrassingly reminiscent; the principals are only so-so." "It looks as if Mr. Sherwood, a thoughtful man, set out to write a musical comedy with a purpose," suggested John Beaufort (*CSM*). "The purpose was apparently abandoned in Philadelphia."

Among the finer tunes were the comical "Homework," sung by McCarty, and the amusingly cynical blow at tourists, "Only for Americans," sung by an under-the-bridge Parisian madwoman called the Countess (Monique's mother), played by elderly Ethel Griffies, who practically stole the show. Jerome Robbins's choreography, as often, was memorable, including his Parisian masquerade and a hilarious "Follow the Leader" jig at a policemen's ball. Dancer Tommy Rall was outstanding in these numbers. One of the chorus girls was future comic actress Dolores (Dody) Goodman. Also in the company were Maria Karnilova and Gloria Patrice.

A thorough account of the evolution and demise of the show is in Laurence Bergreen's *As Thousands Cheer*. He told of how the idea for the show had come from Sherwood, who had wanted the story to be about Pulitzer's campaign to raise funds for the statue's assembling after it was delivered to America and lay in pieces on the dock. The tale was to be expanded by the story of Bennett's sending a reporter to Paris and bringing back the statue's model, a prostitute, who is lionized as a symbol of liberty. But Berlin's own research disclosed that the model was actually the sculptor's mother, which forced Sherwood to rethink his approach.

Sherwood and Berlin, wanting no suggestions from outsiders, produced the play themselves, but the two were not able to develop a fruitful collaborative relationship. This hindered their ability to create a truly integrated show in the highly reputed Rodgers and Hammerstein vein. Sherwood, who infrequently attended rehearsals, was reluctant until quite late in the process to allow anyone to tamper with his bookish script. At one point director Hart threatened to quit unless changes were made.

To save money, no major stars were hired, and young Allyn McClerie, who was unhappy with the proceedings, did not have the breadth to cope with her underwritten role. When she asked Hart if, to lighten things up, she could smile at times, he said she could. "But where?" she asked. "I don't know," he replied. "You'll find a way." She admitted to having been completely at sea in the part.

Berlin's ego got in the way, and he was sure that his songs would all be hits, especially the one with Emma Lazarus's words. When he beamingly played the song for composer Gordon Jenkins and bragged about being the first to write a song to those words, Jenkins told him that he himself had composed and recorded such a song several years earlier. This so infuriated Berlin that he screamed profanities at Jenkins and told him to "Get the fuck out." The song remained in, and Berlin was so convinced of its ultimate success that he planned to create a foundation that would shunt all the song's profits to charity. One of the most promising songs, "Mr. Monotony," was cut at the suggestion of Rodgers and Hammerstein. When none of the songs became big hits, Berlin was crushed.

MR. ADAM [Comedy/Marriage/Military/Politics/Science/Sex] A/D/P: Jack Kirkland; SC: Pat Frank's novel of the same name; DS: Phil Raiguel; T: Royale Theatre; 5/25/49 (5)

The atomic explosion that figures in the premise of this smutty bedroom farce was nothing like the bombs the critics detonated in their reviews. Many agreed with Brooks Atkinson (*NYT*) that it "takes all awards for the worst play of the season."

Set outside Tarrytown, New York, it declares that a nuclear fission lab's explosion has rendered all the world's males sterile except for Homer Adam (James Dobson), although the women are still able to conceive. Because of his importance to the procreation of the human race, Mr. Adam's well-being becomes the preoccupation of the government and the military. Women attempt to storm the barriers to lie with him. The government would like him to remain on platonic terms with his wife Mary Ellen (Elisabeth Fraser) while devoting himself to the project of repopulating the earth. After he and his wife ponder their dilemma, Mr. Adam agrees to go along with the wishes of the establishment if national boundaries, tyrants, armies, and wars are forever eliminated. But as this will threaten the positions of those now in power, the idea is resisted. Finally, the plot wangles its way to a conclusion by the discovery that the initial premise is not true after all.

Mr. Adam had been soundly thrashed during its ten-week pre-Broadway tour (it was banned in several cities), but no improvements were discernible. The premise, said Atkinson, was treated by the author "with consistent squalor, tastelessness and stupidity." Rosamond Gilder (*TAM*) denounced it as "a tawdry and pathetically unprofessional play" acted with "grotesquely exaggerated performances." Two of the few decent acting jobs were turned in by Howard Freeman as an army colonel and Frank Albertson as a journalist.

MR. AND MRS. NORTH [Comedy-Drama/Crime/Marriage/Mystery] A: Owen Davis; SC: a series of *New Yorker* magazine stories and a novel, *The Norths Meet Murder*, by Frances and Richard Lockridge; D/P: Alfred de Liagre, Jr.; S: Jo Mielziner; T: Belasco Theatre; 1/12/41 (163)

This lighthearted comedy-melodrama mingling laughter with screams was based on stories by the Lockridges, the male half of that team being the drama critic for the *NYS*. Herrick Brown of that paper assumed Lockridge's duties to report on the play. He noted that it was "entertaining and breezy." The work was the source of what became a movie as well as a highly successful radio and TV series. It also was chosen as one of the ten best plays of the year. This was the third play of the season to be based on stories in the *New Yorker* (the others were *My Sister Eileen* and *Pal Joey*).

Pam (Peggy Conklin) and Jerry North (Albert Hackett) are a charming, well-bred young Greenwich Village couple. Returning home after a night away, the Norths open the liquor closet to discover the corpse of the rather unpleasant attorney spouse of someone (Barbara Wooddell) the Norths know. Lieutenant Weigand (Philip Ober), a handsome, young, Columbia University-educated detective, is assigned to solve the case, with the hilariously flighty Pam and the harried Jerry being the prime suspects. Accompanying Weigand is his dryly laconic, comically rough-edged sidekick, Detective Mullins (Millard Mitchell). Another murder transpires in the kitchen, this one being of the old mailman (Frank Wilcox) who witnessed the killer on the stairs, and the Norths are threatened with arrest. The list of suspects soon is enlarged to involve a number of eccentric North acquaintances (one of them played by Owen Davis, Jr.). As the cops are on the verge of arresting Jerry, it is the scatterbrained but obviously intelligent Pam who finally solves the case. The killer turns out to be one Clinton Edwards (Lewis Martin), an embezzler who killed to save his secret.

Much of the play's humor derived from the social aplomb displayed by the Norths in the midst of a murder investigation being conducted in their apartment on Greenwich Place. Pam, for instance, practically treats the case as a parlor game. Most critics were not as impressed by the plot as they were with the delightful character depictions, especially those of the Norths. Brooks Atkinson (*NYT*) confessed that for him, "*Mr. and Mrs. North* never quite acquired the momentum of a going play." George Freedley (*NYMT*) noted, "As a mystery drama, the play is loosely constructed and hardly up to par. Its virtues lie in its characters and its ability to capture some of the delights of living in New York." Burns Mantle (*NYDN*) asserted, however, "I like it. These are real folk caught in a web of plausible and amusing situations. There is laughter in it and a touch of sentiment, a craftily sustained suspense and not more than a dash of the old murder play hokum." The acting was highly praised, and the cast included Tito Vuolo and Lex Lindsay.

MR. BARRY'S ETCHINGS [Comedy/Art/Crime/Hotel/Journalism/Politics/Romance] A: Walter Bullock and Daniel Archer; D: Brock Pemberton and Margaret Perry; S: John Root; C: Margaret Pemberton; P: Brock Pemberton; T: Forty-eighth Street Theatre; 1/31/50 (31)

One of two flops shown during the 1949-1950 season in which veteran Lee Tracy starred. Tracy was his usual amiable and nimble self in the role of Judson Barry, a master copper-plate engraver who exercises his considerable skills by etching $50 bills purely for his own amusement. Although he does not intend to use the money for selfish purposes, this casual screwball can not turn down the requests for cash of various needy charities (a hospital, a polio fund, a historical society, and so on) and of a mayoral campaign hopeful of ousting the greedy mortician who wants to control the town. Thus bundles of phony cash amounting to $207,000 are sent off as needed. Word of Judson's talents finds its way to a gang of professional counterfeiters, led by the gun moll "Fifty" Ferris (Vicki Cummings); their regular etcher is in jail. Also interested in Mr. Barry's etchings is the Treasury Department, which sends agent Tom Crosby (Scott McKay) to investigate. Both the gangsters and the T-man arrive claiming to be journalists working for the same national magazine. The crooks are foiled and Barry is himself arrested, but his popularity with the public, publicized in print and on the air, leads to his release and a Hollywood offer for his life story. A romance between the T-man and Barry's niece (Gaye Jordan) also blossoms.

This was "a slow-moving affair with almost no tension and very few lines worth guffawing at," responded Brooks Atkinson (*NYT*). "It is the kind of play that can be counted on to delight the kind of people who never go to the theatre," scoffed Arthur Pollock (*DC*). The cast included Frank Tweddell, Dort Clark, Amy Douglass, Gene Blakely, Tom Reynolds, and, as Barry's worried sister, Ruth Hammond.

MR. BIG [Comedy/Crime/Mystery/Politics/Romance/Theatre] A: Arthur Sheekman and Margaret Shane; D/P: George S. Kaufman; S: Donald Oenslager; T: Lyceum Theatre; 9/30/41 (7)

Writer-director George S. Kaufman made his debut as a producer with this "elaborately labored and commonplace" (Brooks Atkinson [*NYT*]) mystery-farce, originally called *Premiere*. He had had to engage in a legal squabble with Lee

Shubert over the rights to the piece before he emerged victorious. Both Kaufman and Shubert had seen the play when it was given a trial showing at Columbia University, with the authors--both of them screenwriters--using the pseudonym Grant Woodford. Kaufman offered to buy the rights immediately. Even though one of the authors already had made an informal agreement with Shubert, Kaufman proved a more attractive target, and they agreed to let him have the piece. To satisfy Shubert, he was given a seventeen-and-a-half percent share of the show. Nobody profited, however, because the production proved to be a dud.

It takes place in the theatre itself and begins with the actors of a play taking their curtain calls when the star (George Baxter) suddenly drops dead, having been murdered by a poisoned dart. In attendance in the audience are District Attorney Harley L. Miller (Hume Cronyn), a candidate for the governorship, and Police Commissioner Oscar Cullen (Harry Gribbon), another ambitious politician. They promptly begin an inept investigation, in the course of which Miller occasionally delivers a few words on behalf of his candidacy. Police fill the theatre, preventing anyone from leaving while the crime is being investigated. (During one intermission bingo was played and during the other sandwiches were served.) The action goes in for twist after twist, with the cast and crew of the play-within-the-play getting involved, as well as a physician (Richard Barbee), a crooked lawyer, and an assortment of others. Among the disclosures is the fact that Paula Loring (Fay Wray), the leading lady, was the fiancée of the late actor and that another actress (Betty Furness) was his mistress. He was also the love object of a rich contractor's (Jack Leslie) wife (Eleanor Phelps)--the rich man being Miller's principal backer--and was the subject of professional jealousy among other actors. Finally, the least likely suspect is charged with the crime.

There were a few uproarious moments, but the piece as whole was dull and lifeless, and few of its characters were believable. With its constant use of the aisles and spectators, it reminded some of the popular revue, *Hellzapoppin'**, but it did not hold a candle to that zany show in the laugh department. "The whole thing gets nowhere because all the stunts seem forced, most of the script is impossible, and *Mr. Big* is a bore," growled Louis Kronenberger (*PM*). In the cast were black comedian Oscar Polk, Barry Sullivan, Judson Laire, Florenz Ames, Le Roi Operti, E. J. Ballantine, and Mitzi Hajos in a tiny role as a street vendor.

MR. PEEBLES AND MR. HOOKER [Comedy/Blacks/Labor/Race/Religion/Rural/Sex/Small Town/Southern] A: Edward E. Paramore, Jr.; SC: Charles G. Givens's novel of the same name; D: Martin Ritt; S: Frederick Fox; C: Eleanor Goldsmith; P: Joseph M. Hyman; T: Music Box Theatre; 10/10/46 (4)

A folksy modern morality play set in a rural Tennessee Valley community, with a prologue taking place a few years after the war and the action proper occurring in 1939, before the community's flooding by the Tennessee Valley Authority. Its premise is to pit God against Satan in the form of mortal men named, respectively, Mr. Peebles and Mr. Hooker.

Fundamentalist preacher Brother Alf Leland (Paul Huber), a crusty old anti-New Dealer, lives in a cabin with his grandson Brother Wally (Tom Coley), a would-be preacher waiting for the call. Alf's black servant Hattie (Juanita Hall) tells him of the town's labor problems, involving union organizers. Moreover, according to the new minimum-wage law, she should be earning more than she is being paid. Alf dismisses her comments, saying that the laws don't apply to servants of the Lord. Brother Wally, engaged to Ellen Sorrel (Dorothy Gilchrist), is unhappily involved with Mrs. Craine (Randee Sanford), the nymphomaniacal wife of the man whose church's ministry he hopes to assume. Mr. Peebles (Howard Smith), looking like a hod carrier, arrives with Mr. Hooker (Rhys Williams), dressed like a country vestryman. It soon is clear that they are the Old Testament's wrathful Jehovah and the Devil and that they are engaged in a struggle for the souls of humankind. Peebles wants to inspire Wally's sermons, but Hooker sees the relationship of Wally to Mrs. Craine as an opportunity for a broken commandment. The local town is encountering not only labor difficulties (Preacher Craine [Neil Skinner] dynamites a union picnic and riots ensue), but racial tensions (resulting in lynchings) as well. Mr.

Peeble's gentle son, a carpenter called the Stranger (Jeff Morrow)--obviously Christ--appears, but he cannot set things aright, and he is even arrested by the sheriff (Ralph Stantley) as a rabble-rouser. Things get too irritating for Mr. Peebles to bear, and Christian forgiveness seems futile. He saves Wally from death (a gunshot from the rejected Mrs. Craine) and sends him and Ellen away before using a Stillson wrench to flood the sinful village.

Many considered the play's first act superlative, especially because of its humorous charm and crackling hillbilly dialogue, but added that the play took a nosedive in acts two and three. To Howard Barnes (*NYHT*) it was "a remarkably tasteless and tedious charade." Richard Watts, Jr. (*NYP*), said that the author had selected "hopeless" material for dramatization and was unable to decide how much of it to treat comically and how much seriously. Arthur Hunnicutt and Grover Burgess were in the cast.

MISTER ROBERTS [Comedy-Drama/Military/Sea/War] A: Thomas Heggen and Joshua Logan; SC: Thomas Heggen's novel of the same name; D: Joshua Logan; DS: Jo Mielziner; P: Leland Hayward; T: Alvin Theatre; 2/18/48 (1,157)

This play--one of the season's ten best--was barrelling along on the road of long-run success when, for unknown reasons, twenty-nine-year-old coauthor Thomas Heggen killed himself (coauthor Joshua Logan was convinced, however, that Heggen's death was accidental). Heggen and Logan had created a World War II comedy-drama that had all the right ingredients for Broadway's audiences, from the brilliant lead performance by Henry Fonda, returning to the stage after eleven years in Hollywood, and its blend of hilarious and bawdy navy men's humor, salty language, and moving wartime sentiment, to a superbly directed production remarkably faithful to the details of daily life on board a navy vessel. Jo Mielziner's brilliantly realistic cargo ship had some old sea dogs feeling as if they were back on board their old ships.

Mister Roberts came to New York so highly touted that it was a hit before it opened. Heggen had based the story on his own naval experiences during the war, while Logan had served in Air Forces Combat Intelligence. Logan won that year's director's Tony and shared the playwriting Tony with Heggen, and the play itself won another Tony. Fonda was a Tony winner for his performance, but the award was shared with two actors in other plays.

The play is set in the South Pacific on a rusty old cargo ship, the *AK 601* (also called *The Reluctant*), plying the waters, as the script declares, between Tedium and Apathy, making an occasional side trip to Monotony and Ennui. In other words, the ship is in the Pacific's backwaters, far from where the fighting is, and the men are desperately bored with their seemingly useless contribution to the war effort. The time is the closing months of the war, the action ranging from before V-E Day to several weeks before V-J Day. The bullying captain (William Harrigan), whose command stems from his merchant marine background, runs the ship with a tyrant's mailed fist and treats the crew almost as if they are slaves helping to get him a longed-for promotion. Because he finds the idealistic Lieutenant (jg) Doug Roberts (Fonda) useful to him, and because of his jealousy of this well-loved, well-educated first officer, he refuses to accept Roberts's frequent requests for a transfer to combat duty. Roberts's requests also look bad on the ambitious captain's record. A good deal of the frustration of Mr. Roberts and the crew centers around the captain's well-tended palm tree, which symbolizes his selfish rule. Ultimately Mr. Roberts tosses the damn thing overboard. The captain is aware of the culprit but can not prove it. Mr. Roberts and his superior strike a secret bargain that will provide the crew with a much needed, and hugely enjoyed liberty, but it means that Mr. Roberts must forgo his desires for a transfer and he must also treat the captain with respect. The crew misunderstands his behavior and begins to lose faith in him. When the truth is learned, they connive, via forged papers, to gain him his transfer and celebrate by giving him a medal ("The Order of the Palm") made in the machine shop and toasting him with "jungle juice" served from a fire extinguisher. A letter from Mr. Roberts later arrives in which he commends the men on the ship for their contribution to the war effort. In the same mail comes the news that Roberts has been killed in battle with the Japanese.

Many reviewers considered this the best war play since *What Price Glory?** George Freedley (*NYMT*) felt that the play began slowly, but from three-quarters of the first act until the end, "it is a swell show that has the audience clamoring for more, laughing and crying almost at the same time." Richard Watts, Jr. (*NYP*), commended it for being "such warm, full-blooded, hilarious and moving entertainment, in addition to its impressive qualities as honest and forthright dramatic entertainment." John Mason Brown (*SR*) provided a detailed comparison of the original novel and the dramatization to show how well the adaptation had been made. "In spite of all the canniness of its planning," he suggested, "the dramatization retains a superb unstudied, almost improvised, quality."

On opening night the audience was unable to stop clapping, it was so enthused by the experience, and one curtain call followed the other, ad infinitum. Henry Fonda finally stepped forth and said, "That's all Josh Logan wrote for us, but if you really want us to, we'll do it all over again" (quoted in Peter Hay, *Broadway Anecdotes*).

The excellent large supporting cast included Robert Keith as Doc, Mr. Roberts's cynically philosophical medical pal; David Wayne as the comical braggart Ensign Pulver; Rusty Lane as Chief Johnson; Joe Marr as Dowdy; Harvey Lembeck as Insigna; Ralph Meeker as Mannion; Karl Lukas as Lindstrom; Steven Hill as Stefanowski; Marshall Jamison as a military patrolman; and John Jordan and Murray Hamilton as shore patrolmen. The sole female role was taken by Jocelyn Brando (Marlon's sister), playing a WAC nurse whose onshore bathroom is spied on with binoculars by the men, and whose visit to the ship leads to one of the show's funniest scenes.

Because the men in the cast had to look suntanned, the producers chose not to use makeup for the effect and, instead, placed a battery of sunlamps in the theatre's basement. Every day the actors went there for their daily tanning session.

Harrigan's bitter, envious captain was a memorable performance, praised for its complete believability. As the handsome, modest, and kindly Mr. Roberts, Fonda had one of his greatest roles. "He is lanky and unheroic," reported Brooks Atkinson (*NYT*), "relaxed and genuine; he neatly skirts the maudlin when the play grows sentimental, and he skillfully underplays the bombastic scenes."

In *Josh*, Logan told in detail the story of the show's evolution. He revealed that when Heggen's own dramatic adaption proved ineffective, Logan undertook to cooperate in rewriting it. His many crucial contributions included responsibility for the central conflict concerning the captain's forbidding the men to go ashore and Roberts's striking the secret deal so that they could go. But after the first of the play's two acts was completed, Heggen wanted all the writer's credit as well as all the writer's royalties. Logan reminded Heggen that he, Logan, had written much of act one, which Heggen acknowledged and appreciated. Logan then told him that he could have all these contributions for nothing. When Heggen asked for an explanation, Logan calmly responded, "You can have the first act free, *if* you are able to accept it as yours and still look people in the eye. And then you can goddamned fucking well write the second act by yourself, Buster." When Logan began to walk away, Heggen called him back. "I can't write this son of a bitching play alone. You know that." But Logan declared he would not cooperate if the marquee were to read "By Thomas Heggen." Heggen thereupon agreed to share the writing credit, but would only allow Logan one-third of the royalties.

Because the play ends unhappily, with its hero dead (as in the original novel), Logan received flack from those who felt that he should provide a more upbeat conclusion. Logan absolutely refused to give in to such suggestions, which he rightfully felt would kill the integrity of the work.

The casting of the title character was originally to go to either Fonda or Wayne. Both attended a reading of the piece to gauge their reactions. Fonda had a film commitment, but he was so impressed that he was willing to do whatever he could to break it so he could act in the play. Wayne was also very impressed and decided on his own that Fonda was better for Roberts and that he himself should play Pulver. The part of the captain went to the brother of Logan's wife, Nedda

Harrigan. She was reluctant, however, to have her brother in the show because their relationship was on the cool side. An appointment was made for William Harrigan to audition one afternoon. The audition went flawlessly, almost as if the actor had been born to play the part. Logan looked out into the auditorium and saw his wife. "Wasn't he good?" she asked. "Nedda, he was marvelous, brilliant. How on earth could he get those readings so perfectly?" "I gave them to him," she said. "I've been working like a dog all morning." "I thought you didn't get along." "We did today."

Before it opened, Logan noticed that the play was fifteen minutes too long. Actor-playwright Emlyn Williams, noted for this kind of thing, was asked to come in and do some snipping. Overnight, Williams completed the job, cutting "nearly every adjective, adverb and needless dependent clause. He cut any repeat of the same idea." For his troubles, he received a pair of gold scissors engraved with Logan's, Heggen's, and producer Hayward's names.

One laugh line that Williams did not cut, but that eventually had to go, was removed because it was considered so offensive that it was feared that the police would close the show. The line, which always brought the house down, was spoken by Pulver, who is planning to use fulminate of mercury to make a firecracker. When Doc asks where Pulver would get such a hard-to-find ingredient, Roberts says, "I don't know. He's pretty resourceful. Where did he get the clap last year?" Fonda hated to see the remark go, but he was allowed to reinsert it when James Stewart came to see the show during the run. Thereafter, it was sneaked in at occasional performances until a female spectator's complaint forced it to be removed for good.

MR. STRAUSS GOES TO BOSTON [Musical/Hotel/Marriage/Music/Period/Politics/Romance] B: Leonard L. Levinson; M: Johann Strauss, Jr., and Robert Stolz; LY: Robert Sour; SC: a story by Alfred Grünewald and Geza Herczeg; D/P: Felix Brentano; CH: George Balanchine; S: Stewart Chaney; C: Walter Florell; T: Century Theatre; 9/6/45 (12)

A stale musical based on the actual visit of Viennese waltz king Johann Strauss, Jr. (George Rigaud), to Boston in 1872, where he conducted the World Peace Jubilee with an orchestra of 1,000, a chorus of 20,000, and 150 featured soloists. The book focuses not on these elements, which might have been ripe for satire, but on the energetic pursuit of the handsome composer by the wealthy Brook Whitney (Virginia MacWatters), who believes the publicity declaring him a bachelor (a ploy designed to arouse feminine interest in him). Overwhelmed by the romantic attention created by his presence, he wires his wife Hetty (Ruth Matteson) to come and save him. She arrives on a fast ship and, with the assistance of President Grant (Norman Roland), regains her husband's attentions.

"The authors of the book have forgotten nothing they ever learned about old-fashioned operetta," yawned Lewis Nichols (*NYT*), "and they have put everything they learned into this one." "*Mr. Strauss* is a period piece without any period atmosphere," believed Euphemia Van Rensselaer Wyatt (*CW*). George Jean Nathan (*TBY*) derided shows such as this with their stereotypical plots about the love lives of famed composers. The truth, he said, is that most such individuals "have been as appealingly romantic as a severe case of Parkinson's disease." The humor was in the vein of one character saying, "I'm homesick," and another responding, "I wish she were home, sick."

Apart from the original Strauss contributions, the score by refugee Viennese composer Stolz was undistinguished. Nor were there distinctive performances by the leads or by Ralph Dumke as Strauss's tour manager. The show was visually uninspired, and Balanchine's dances were unmemorable, although well done by principal dancer Harold Lang. Arlene Dahl, in the small role of Mrs. Taylor, made her Broadway debut in the show, while Helen Gallagher was a member of the corps de ballet.

MR. SYCAMORE [Comedy/Fantasy/Literature/Marriage/Religion/Small Town] A: Ketti Frings; SC: a short story by Robert Ayre; D: Lester Vail; S: Samuel Leve; P: Theatre Guild; T: Guild Theatre; 11/13/42 (19)

An oddball attempt at a comic fantasy about John Gwilt (movie actor Stuart

Erwin, in his Broadway debut), postman of the small town of Smeed, who dislikes his job of twenty years and has become upset by people's greed, belligerence, and thoughtlessness. He frequents the local library, where he reads books on philosophy and mythology. Having read the story of Philemon and Baucis, and inspired by a suggestion of the poetess-librarian, Estelle Benlow (Enid Markey), he decides to become a tree. He digs a hole, removes his socks, plants himself, and wills himself to take root, despite the remonstrances of his wife Jane (Lillian Gish), whom he tries to convince to be a tree as well. Although she leaves him, she soon comes back to make him as comfortable as she can, feeding him and applying a mustard plaster at the sign of a cold. Pretty soon, Gwilt sprouts leaves and roots and is transformed into a stately sycamore tree. The town goes wild, Gwilt is ridiculed, the local parson (Russell Collins) brands him a sinner, and people pay fifty cents a shot to view him. After a while, everyone takes the miracle for granted, and even a bird bath planned in Gwilt's honor is forgotten. However, Jane and other townsfolk find comfort in sit ting in the backyard beneath the postman's bosky branches.

This play's premise proved more than most could accept, although a number of critics appreciated some of its charm. Louis Kronenberger (*PM*) decided that the work was better than its subject might have led one to expect because it downplayed the whimsical element, but that it was "too flimsy a play, too undramatic a fantasy, too protracted a treatment of a single idea, to be fun for any length of time." He and others also felt that the lack of pungent satire and laughs was a major drawback. Brooks Atkinson (*NYT*) pointed out, for instance, that "Mrs. Frings does not seem to be able to develop her idea with either the satire or the spiritual passion that would transmute it into a vibrant work of art." George Jean Nathan (*TBY*) thought that it would have been a good idea to bring a small dog that figured in the action on just before the final curtain and to have had it "lift its leg moistly against the tree. Not only would the business provide a welcome laugh against the antecedent dullness but it would also provide a valid criticism of both the play and the sappy philosophy inherent in its arboreal theme."

There were wasted performances by Leona Powers, John Philliber, Harry Bellaver, Franklyn Fox, Harry Townes, Harry Sheppard, and Otto Hulett, among many others. Erwin, noted Rosamond Gilder (*TAM*), "gave a remarkably touching and dignified performance. His simple attack, his quiet, forthright honesty lent full value to what there was of poetry and honest imagination in the play." She also said that "Lillian Gish . . . was appropriately tearful and devoted, displaying once again that peculiar quality of pathos and eternal youth which is so markedly her own."

MRS. GIBBONS' BOYS [Comedy/Crime/Family/Politics] A: Will Glickman and Joseph Stein; D/P: George Abbott; S: John Root; C: John Robert Lloyd; T: Music Box Theatre; 5/4/49 (5)

A "damp whiz-bang" (Brooks Atkinson [*NYT*]) of a farce that was one of director-producer George Abbott's worst setbacks. Unfortunately, much was made of the fact that the similarly sorry *Bruno and Sidney*, which he had turned down, opened Off Broadway a night earlier and was just as loudly condemned.

Mrs. Gibbons' Boys starred Lois Bolton as the scatterbrained widow, Mrs. Gibbons, mother of three sons (Richard Carlyle, Ray Walston, and Tom Lewis), two of whom are escaped convicts; the third is on parole but heading for trouble. Mrs. Gibbons blindly refuses to face the facts about her boys, believing them to be fine citizens who are the poor, mistreated victims of the law. She will not, however, allow the parolee to talk to his brothers because parolees must not associate with habitual crooks. A gas-company employee's (Francis Compton) proposal to Mrs. Gibbons sets the plot in motion. The boys plot the robbery of the suitor, whom they ultimately mug and loot, and also give a crooked politician (Edward Andrews) his comeuppance before they go back to the penitentiary, thereby allowing Mrs. Gibbons to get married.

Howard Barnes (*NYHT*) thought it "a dismal dissertation . . . that should have died aborning." It also was "tasteless and devastatingly dull." The cast included Royal Dano, who practically stole what there was of the show as a stupid fugitive named Horse, Glenda Farrell as a wisecracking neighbor, William David as an officer of the law upon whom Mrs. Gibbons uses jiujitsu, and Richard Taber.

MRS. JANUARY AND MR. X [Comedy/Family/Politics/Romance/Small Town] A: Zoe Akins; D: Elliott Nugent and Arthur Sircom; S: Paul Morrison; C: Adrian; P: Richard Myers; T: Belasco Theatre; 3/31/44 (43)

The character of the titular Mrs. January was played by charming comedienne Billie Burke, but her choice of a vehicle was unfortunate. The aging Burke looked so good that time seemed to have stood still. "Her step, her figure, her smile are young--so young that she can even wear a tailored suit with slacks and look smarter in them than most of the present generation," according to Euphemia Van Rensselaer Wyatt (*CW*). Her costar, playing the role of Mr. Ex (for ex-president), was Frank Craven. (Some sources give his titular name as Mr. X and others as Mr. Ex.) The play originally had been titled *Plans for Tomorrow*.

The very wealthy, featherbrained Mrs. January has been wed thrice and has offspring of different nationalities from her marriages. Concerned about the coming "revolution," she has adopted left-wing beliefs and raised her children with similar ideas. To be ready for the social upheaval, she rents, for $40 a month, one-half of a two-family house in a small New England town and puts up her domestic staff of butler, cook, chauffeur, and so on in a fancy mansion. Her landlord is the Coolidge-like, taciturn ex-president, Martin Luther Cooper, with whom she soon has a romantic relationship culminating in marriage, with Cooper planning to run again for president on the Republican ticket. Mrs. January's brother (Nicholas Joy), who dislikes the politician, tries to put a crimp in his plans, but his plans are foiled and it seems likely that Cooper will succeed at the polls.

Burke and Craven carried this vehicle for all it was worth, with Burke occasionally tearing down the house with lines such as, "After all, communism is only Christianity with the Christianity left out." Setting off Burke's breathless, fluttering, and elfin style was the dryly restrained, underplaying Craven.

As for the play, it was considered too tangled in plot, especially with the material built up around Mrs. January's children, and excessively windy in the dialogue department. George Jean Nathan (*TBY*) was one of the few to admire it, albeit with reservations, noting, "Slight and at times strainful though the exhibit may be, it is nevertheless a generally amusing and often drolly conceived little play." More common were opinions like that of George Freedley (*NYMT*), who dismissed the play as "slender and talky."

Among Mrs. January's children was one named Wilhelmina, played by future star Barbara Bel Geddes. Other cast members included Henry Barnard, Helen Carew, Phil Sheridan, Edward F. Nannary, and Bobby Perez.

Elliott Nugent was still starring in *The Voice of the Turtle* when he undertook to direct this project. During its out-of-town tryout period in Wilmington and Philadelphia, he would commute from New York, which was a tremendous drain. Because he could not do the same for Boston, Sircom was hired to help out there and so became codirector.

MRS. KIMBALL PRESENTS [Comedy/Crime/Romance/Theatre] A/D: Alonzo Price; S: Cirker and Robbins; P: Ted Gerken and Joe Chandler; T: Forty-eighth Street Theatre; 2/29/44 (7)

A tawdry, tedious farce that George Jean Nathan (*TBY*) dubbed "twaddle." Louis Kronenberger (*PM*) declared, "It is all very deplorable, and rather hard on the cast, which is not a very gifted one to begin with."

Two indigent actors, the handsome juvenile named Dick Hastings (Michael Ames) and his homelier friend Harold J. Burton (Arthur Margetson), are in need of funds to pay off a bad check passed by Harold. A federal officer (Jesse White) is apparently after Harold. Hoping to pull off a con job, they rent a fashionable Sutton Place apartment, and Harold pretends to be Dick's butler. They persuade lovely producer Connie Kimball (Vicki Cummings), who has cast them in a play, to give them a long term contract and a bonus. Harold thinks that she has designs on Dick, who is secretly engaged to Cynthia Lane (Elizabeth Inglise). Dick must therefore play up to the producer until his finances are in order. The officer turns out actually to be a movie scout seeking to sign Harold to a seven-year contract at $500 a week. Mrs. Kimball finds that Harold is more to her liking than Dick, and the latter gets the movie contract and can safely marry his sweetheart.

Bruce Evans, Joan Cory, and Hall Shelton were in the cast.

MISTRESS OF THE HOUSE (*Fröken Julie*) [Dramatic Revival] A: August Strindberg; AD/D: William de Lys; CH: Betty Jane Keith; DS: Adolph Aldrich; P: Portable Theatre Productions; T: Carnegie Recital Hall (OB); 1/30/50 (4)

This was a barely noticed adaptation of Strindberg's naturalistic classic, *Miss Julie*, first produced in 1889 and never shown in New York before. The locale was switched to the American South of New Orleans at Mardi Gras time, and the relationship of the leading characters, here called Miss Julia (Paddye Whittington) and John (Carl Holmes), was altered to that of a plantation owner and her black servant.

The basic story, set in the large kitchen of an estate, is that of an aristocratic, neurotic young woman who, during a night of celebration (Midsummer's Night in the original), is seduced by a serving man. Upon realizing the lowliness of the man to whom she has given herself, she commits suicide. The action from beginning to end of the long one-acter is continuous, although interrupted by a celebratory dance. As the action transpires, Miss Julia and the servant slowly reveal the hereditary and environmental factors that have shaped their characters.

"Play is confusing, slow-moving, and is weak in its commentaries on the plight of the Negroes," wrote the unnamed *V* reviewer. Joe Pihodna (*NYHT*) believed that Strindberg would have approved the adaptation because it corroborated his thesis about "the degeneracy of the aristocracy and the rise of a lowly but more stable class." However, he found the production incompetently acted and directed. Alfreda Digges played Christine, the cook.

MOLEHILLS [Drama/Family/Marriage/Sex] A: Muriel Roy Bolton; D: Anne West; P: Dean Goodman; T: Provincetown Playhouse (OB); 7/10/46

A "repetitious, dull and sometimes just downright annoying" (Robert Coleman [*NYDM*]) Off-Broadway play that was one of several produced by Dean Goodman at the Provincetown in the summer of 1946; the critics generally stayed home.

The "often irritatingly insipid" (Jane Corby [*BE*]) play's premise was to suggest the various ways in which the mood of the moment can determine the actions taken by individuals. It deals with the Drake family, consisting of a philandering father (Mark Wood); a gadabout mother (Fran Malis) who discovers lipstick on her husband's shirt; a daughter (Lou Prentis) seeing an aging roué; and a son (Edwin Spangler) seeking to borrow money to renovate a rundown cabin. The principle action concerns how Mrs. Drake responds to her husband's presumed unfaithfulness, her moods varying from one act to another.

MOMENT MUSICAL [Comedy/Marriage/Military/Romance/Sex/War] A: Charles Angoff; D: Dennis Gurney; P: Blackfriars' Guild; T: Blackfriars' Theatre (OB); 5/31/43 (10)

The Blackfriars' Guild had for several seasons been in the vanguard of experimental New York theatres, producing plays with salaryless casts as a way of exposing new writers and performers to the public. Actors Equity, the actors' union, had grudgingly permitted such ventures, but now, as on numerous future occasions, it decided that enough was enough and that it would no longer condone the use of Equity actors in such workshop productions. Unfortunately, the critics could not make a strong stand on behalf of the theatre with regard to the present "dull and windy" offering (Howard Barnes [*NYHT*]) written by a former editor of *American Mercury* magazine currently serving in the army. George Freedley (*NYMT*) was forced to condemn it as "one of the worst pieces of literary tripe that was ever shown on any stage."

Thelma (Eileen Heckart), an advertising executive living in New York, is visited after a decade by a pair of married friends from her home town of Norman, Oklahoma. A pair of Thelma's friends, Henry (Dayton Lummis) and Philip (Jack Woods), take Evelyn (Catherine Bradford) and Dorothy (Joan Croyden) out for a good time, and Dorothy and Henry, a soldier, fall in love. Dorothy does not desert her family, though, and forces herself to return to a loveless life with her spouse and two kids, while Henry prepares to be sent off to war. (The Blackfriars' Guild, a Catholic organization, approved of this ending in its program because it conformed to Catholic teaching regarding the proper solution to a problem of extramarital temptation.)

The most notable performer was young Eileen Heckart, of whom Burton Rascoe (*NYWT*) declared that she, "unconsciously perhaps, displayed great possibilities as a highly personable comedienne."

MONTSERRAT [Drama/Art/French/Military/Period/Politics/Sex/Theatre/Youth] A: Emmanuel Roblès; AD/D: Lillian Hellman; S/L: Howard Bay; C: Irene Sharaff; P: Kermit Bloomgarden and Gilbert Miller; T: Fulton Theatre; 10/29/49 (65)

An uncreative adaptation of a French drama set in Spanish-occupied Venezuela in 1812. Montserrat (William Redfield) is a young Spanish officer who has gone over to the side of the revolutionary leader and patriot Simon Bolivar. The latter is at large and being sought by the Spanish authorities. Montserrat is aware of Bolivar's hiding place. To get the secret of the rebel's whereabouts from him, he is sub jected to psychological torture. Six innocent citizens--four men and two women--are dragged in and used by Izquierdo (Emlyn Williams), the sardonic colonel, to convince Montserrat to tell what he knows. One man is a merchant (Reinhold Schunzel), who offers his wife to the colonel in exchange for his life; another is a Creole wood sculptor (William Hansen); another is an actor (John Abbott) who sees no reason to be involved in politics; and there is a defiant Indian boy, Ricardo (George Bartenieff). One of the women is a mother (Vivian Nathan), the other an Indian girl named Felisa (Julie Harris) whose bold conviction, like Ricardo's, concerning Bolivar's importance is responsible for keeping Montserrat--who is ready to submit--silent. These victims, each of whose lives is somehow investigated during the play, are to be killed after an hour if Montserrat does not talk. Finally, they are taken out and shot, one by one. Bolivar is reported safe, Montserrat's silence having bought him the necessary time. Finally, the officer himself is put to death.

The drama's pertinence to the contemporary world was clear, but it was argued by some that beyond its intellectual virtues, it was somehow unable to touch their feelings deeply. For those inclined to overlook the play's message about a man's willingness to die for the cause of freedom, said Arthur Pollock (*DC*), this would be a "dull or 'talky' play, even uneventful," because the plot structure was so simple and straightforward. To him, though, it was "a thrilling play, with little speeches here and there that cut like knives and reach the bone." Thomas R. Dash (*WWD*) thought it "a soul-searing adaptation . . . packed with trenchant and remorseless power." But more critics sided with John Mason Brown (*SR*), who described the play as "so repetitious and static a bore that one can hardly wait to have its victims shot." Richard Watts, Jr. (*NYP*), found that "it is oddly less powerful in its emotional impact than its deeply tragic theme would have suggested, and its strength is curiously hampered by a monotony that has crept into it." Brooks Atkinson (*NYT*) argued that the play never made the ideals of the revolution important enough to warrant the deaths of the six characters.

It was widely agreed that Williams was superb as Izquierdo, some thinking his portrayal so fascinating as to make the others, especially Redfield, pale by comparison. "Mr. Williams gives a perfect performance of frigid fury, contempt and decision. Suiting his style to the drama, he scrupulously underplays the part of a monster--his manners impeccable and his nerves almost, though not quite, under inhuman control," wrote Atkinson. The cast included Kurt Kasznar, Richard Malek, Nehemiah Persoff, Stefan Gierasch, Gregory Morton, Francis Compton, and others.

Hellman found that she was ineffective as a director because she was intimidated by Emlyn Williams, but she had other directorial problems as well. According to William Wright's *Lillian Hellman*, when the show was trying out in Boston, she was having trouble getting the right results from an actor. Producer Bloomgarden told her that the man was a Method actor and needed time to grow into his role.

"What the hell is method acting anyway?" she wanted to know. Bloomgarden said, "I studied with Lee [Strasberg] for a while. He had us acting an orange." "An orange, eh?" replied Hellman. The actor was fired the next day.

(1) MOON IN THE YELLOW RIVER, THE [Dramatic Revival*] A: Denis Johnston; D: Helen Harvey; S: Richard Corbin; P: Equity Library Theatre; T: Muhlenberg Branch of the New York Public Library (OB); 5/7/45

"An extremely creditable revival" (George Freedley [*NYMT*]) of Johnston's poetic Irish drama, which had played locally in 1932 under Theatre Guild auspices. Although it remained verbose, the play was nicely directed for mood and character in this free performance by the showcase arm of Actors Equity. John Newland played Darrell Blake, Robert O'Brien played Willie, Guy Spaull played Dobelle, Robin Craven played Captain Potts, Charles Thompson played George, and Hy Amity played Tausch.

(2) D: Morton Silk; P: On-Stage; T: National Arts Club (OB); 7/28/48

This Off-Broadway resuscitation was "a reasonably good production," thought George Freedley (*NYMT*), who reserved much of his griping for the sweltering, un-air-conditioned circumstances in which he had to view the play. Richard Watts, Jr. (*NYP*), opined that the play was one of the finest in the modern repertoire, being "a strange and difficult work . . . because of its subtle preoccupation with the dark backwaters of character and emotion."

Although the arena-style acting area was too cramped for the actors, and the director had not mastered arena staging, the piece was honestly, if uninspiringly, conveyed by the semipro actors. Watts concluded that "the presentation seems more a thoughtful and appreciative reading of the play than the finished production." Edwin Strome played Tausch, Robert Latta played Willy, and John Krchniak played Dobelle.

On-Stage employed two spaces in the summer of 1948, this arena theatre in Gramercy Park and a large room in a brownstone at 6 Fifth Avenue.

MOON IS DOWN, THE [Drama/Military/Politics/Sex/War] A: John Steinbeck; SC: John Steinbeck's novel of the same name; D: Chester Erskin; S: Howard Bay; P: Oscar Serlin; T: Martin Beck Theatre; 4/7/42 (71)

John Steinbeck adapted his own highly respected and very recently published best-seller to the stage in a faithful version that did not share the same ecstatic reception as its progenitor. A debate developed between the book's supporters and the play's detractors concerning Steinbeck's propagandistic purposes, but the public stayed away in any case. Much of the debate focused on Steinbeck's decision to show the play's Nazis not as inhuman beasts, but in what some thought a sentimentalized way as civilized people victimized by their ideology. Some even claimed that the sympathetic, democracy-respecting chief Nazi became the actual hero of the play. There was also the strong feeling that the author should have been exhorting the public to go out and fight its damnedest to beat its enemies and not merely to suggest that the fight would one day be won anyway because a free nation cannot be conquered.

The Moon Is Down, one of Burns Mantle's ten best of the year, is a timely work concerning the fight for survival of the citizens in a neutral country when invaded by a tyrannous force. According to many critics, it had a strong optimistic viewpoint and was written with considerable sincerity in its depiction of the conflict between fascism and democracy, but remained too cerebral in its orientation and failed to provide the emotional force needed for successful drama. Hobe. (*V*) felt that it lacked any single character for the audience to rally around, leading to a removed and impersonal effect. "In the reading," wrote Louis Kronenberger (*PM*), "the drama was enkindled by the rhetoric; in the theater, the rhetoric . . . often seems stilted and formal." Yet there were a few who felt, like Rosamond Gilder (*TAM*), that "the power and the poignancy of Steinbeck's play lie in its immediacy, its ability to express world issues with the terrible nearness of little things, its affirmation of the dignity and nobility of man. . . . There is no doubt that he has succeeded in expressing in pure theatric terms an eloquent plea for democracy, a stirring call-to-arms to all free fighting spirits."

A mining village in an unnamed country (presumably Norway) has been overrun by the Nazis, aided by Correll (E. J. Ballantine), the local power-hungry quisling. They have come here for the town's precious coal resources and not to harm the residents, although some of them, such as Captain Loft (Alan Hewitt), are the typical bloodthirsty type. The gentlemanly Colonel Lanser (Otto Kruger) establishes his headquarters at the home of Mayor Orden (Ralph Morgan), and it is here that all the action transpires. Colonel Lanser, who excuses himself as simply someone carrying out orders, apologetically asks the mayor to have his townsfolk mine the coal for the invaders. The gentle and bewildered old mayor resists, declaring that his people prefer to act and think for themselves. He must do what the people want, not the other way around. As the days go by, the Nazis brutalize the town, one of them even trying to rape a local widow (Maria Palmer). Various acts of violent resistance by the people--including sniping and sabotage--against the Nazis transpire until the Germans decide to starve the inhabitants in retaliation. When this fails, the mayor is taken hostage. Still, the resistance continues until the town is bombed by British flyers, alerted by a pair of townsmen who escaped to England. Colonel Lanser, in revenge for his slaughtered troops, sends the mayor to the firing squad, which he faces unflinchingly with the words of Socrates on his lips. The message: A free people cannot be defeated but will continue to fight for their freedom.

Many believed that the understated acting and heavy-handed direction were a fault in a play needing vivid theatrics to hold attention. Then again, there were those who strongly defended the performances. Russell Collins, Leona Powers, Joseph Sweeney, William Eythe, Carl Gose, Whitford Kane, and Jane Seymour were among those in the play.

MOON VINE, THE [Comedy/Crime/Period/Religion/Romance/Small Town/ Southern/Theatre/Youth] A: Patricia Coleman; D: John Cromwell; S/C: Lucinda Ballard; P: Jack Kirkland; T: Morosco Theatre; 2/11/43 (20)

George Jean Nathan (*TBY*) said of this artificial concoction about life in the deep South that it "is . . . written in such a mixture of moods--farcical, straight comedy, dramatic, melodramatic, and tragic--that it is next to impossible to figure out its author's dramaturgical intention, although it is easy to figure out that she knows nothing of dramatic construction." Set in 1905 Louisiana, the play has a flighty belle of an eighteen-year-old heroine named Mariah Meade (Haila Stoddard, wife of the producer), who is affianced to but not in love with a missionary off converting the heathens in the Australian bush country. A young thespian (a trade seriously frowned upon by the local religious zealots) named Danny Hatfield (Arthur Franz), originally from the town, is stranded nearby while touring in *Ten Nights in a Barroom**, and the stagestruck Mariah falls for him at once. She has her friend Ellen (Mary Lou Taylor), Danny's sister, write a letter in which it is announced that the missionary has died of the plague. Mariah uses the chance to act her grief to the hilt, imitating the famous tragediennes of the day. Danny, for his part, is in trouble because an important politician was killed in a New Orleans brothel while Danny was acting a scene from *Romeo and Juliet** there with a well-read prostitute. He is wanted in court to testify as a witness. Danny, overwhelmed by Mariah's mourning, decides to go to the revival meeting, confess his sins, and become a missionary so he can marry her. This is too much for Mariah, and although she almost takes too much time in offering her forgiveness, she and Danny elope to join a stock company in Cincinnati.

Some enjoyed the play's Southern atmosphere and period touches, and there was a pleasant dance number or two performed by Stoddard and Franz. However, most agreed with Hobe. (*V*) that "the play has only isolated humor and no real comic gusto. In addition, it is overloaded with needless incidental characters and irrelevant incidents."

Philip Bourneuf was a young lawyer in love with Maria, John McKee was Danny's father, A. Winfield Hoey was a hypocritical Bible-thumping preacher, Will Geer was was a Southern gent, a black comic actor named Drop Dead played a role of that name, Vera Allen played Mariah's mother, and Grace Coppin played a grandmother, while a pair of maiden aunts were taken by Kate McComb and Agnes Scott Yost. Yul Brynner (then spelled Youl Bryner) was cast in the small role of a Southern gentleman named Andre. His Southern accent, said Ward Morehouse (*NYS*), was "as believable as hominy served to an Eskimo."

MORE THE MERRIER, THE [Comedy/Crime/Politics/Romance] A: Frank Gabrielson and Irvin Pincus; D: Otto Preminger; P: Otto Preminger and Norman Pincus; T: Cort Theatre; 9/15/41 (16)

Most critics dismissed this well-cast comedy (first called *The Great Whitewash*) as a tasteless job, especially for its principal laugh-getting grotesquerie, a corpse on roller skates. Howard Barnes (*NYHT*) dubbed it "a dull and witless burlesque." Robert Coleman (*NYDM*) said that the authors "have written a number of funny episodes, but they've strung them on a thin and incredible plot." Otto Preminger's direction was panned for being cluttered and too insistently fast-paced.

It transpires in a spectacular castle in the Colorado Rockies owned by gubernatorial candidate Harvey Royal (Louis Hector), who leaves it under the management of young Daniel Finch (Frank Albertson), his replacement public-relations man, while he attends to the dedication of one of his philanthropic projects in Denver. While he is gone, a band of stranded tourists in a snowstorm take occupancy, thinking the castle a hotel, with Finch and Royal biographer Joe Dolma (Keenan Wynn) allowing them entry because they want to raise cash for their own trip to Denver. Royal, unable to fly, returns to find the crowd in his home. A pair of ex-gangsters (Millard Mitchell and Teddy Hart), attempting to rob one of their fellow passengers (Jack Riano), accidentally kill him, leading Finch, Dalmo, and Dalmo's girl friend, Bugs Saunders (Grace McDonald), to try and hide the corpse, at one point putting him on roller skates to deflect suspicion from the guests. When the furious Royal finds the corpse, he tosses it over a livng room balcony railing and then believes that he is responsible for the death. The investigating prosecutor, Forrest Lockhart (Will Geer), Royal's political rival, won't buy the story that the man was dead before the fall, but it eventually turns out that the corpse was a wanted felon, and Royal accepts the credit for his demise.

The large company included Doro Merande, J. C. Nugent, Arnold Saint Subber (the future producer), and G. Albert Smith.

MORNING STAR, THE [Drama/British/Literature/Marriage/Medicine/Sex/War] A: Emlyn Williams; D/P: Guthrie McClintic; S: Stewart Chaney; T: Morosco Theatre; 9/14/42 (24)

Gregory Peck acted his first principal role in this "tangled and meretricious" (Brooks Atkinson [*NYT*]) English war play (then in the tenth month of its London run) about the blitz (with all the sound effects that then were becoming standard Broadway devices). He played Cliff Parrilow (acted by author Williams in the English original), a brilliant young doctor, fresh out of medical school, who has invented a vitally important surgical procedure for correcting cardiac bomb shock by restoring the victim's heart rhythm. He is the son of Mrs. Parrilow (Gladys Cooper), in whose middle-class Chelsea home the action occurs. Living here in August 1940 are Cliff; his wife Alison (Jill Esmond); his pilot brother (away at war); an older physician, Dr. Datcher (Cecil Humphreys), who pays rent; his servant (Rhys Williams); and the char lady (Brenda Forbes). Much of the action revolves around Cliff. Because his fellows at the hospital do not accept his medical breakthrough, and because he has been given routine hospital work to do, he turns to writing novels and plans to go to Hollywood until his former teacher, Dr. Datcher, seriously criticizes his book. He also is distracted from his good wife by the sexy gold digger, Wanda Baring (Wendy Barrie, in her Broadway debut). Ultimately, enlightened by the death of his brother, he abandons Wanda and returns to his wife, hoping to aid the people of London in their need. Denied the right to experiment on a dying man with his surgical method, he does get a chance to show its effects when an air-raid warden is mortally wounded, but the man, after briefly reviving, expires. Before the play ends, Cliff learns that he is to become a father.

Despite some effective characterizations (owing primarily to the excellent performances of the largely English cast) and many telling touches suggesting that the author had actually experienced the blitz, the play seemed talky and artificial, its episodic plot hackneyed and overstuffed with familiar contrivances, and its ideas unoriginal. The play's ultimate purpose seemed to be to demonstrate the indomitability of the human spirit in the face of tragedy. However, to Rosamond Gilder (*TAM*), "The battle of London is overshadowed by the petty issues of a purely personal conflict among synthetic characters." George Jean Nathan (*TBY*) remarked of Williams, "His characters are mainly out of a theatrical warehouse; his dialogue is largely sugar-cured; and the majority of his situations have hitherto enjoyed service in other plays."

Peck made a very effective showing. "After a nervous first act," wrote George Freedley (*NYMT*), "Gregory Peck settled down to prove himself the most likely leading-man material we have seen on the stage recently. Looking rather like Gary Cooper, he has a pleasing manner, a good voice and an inner clarity which made the surgeon believable even when the author was straining credulity to the utmost." Burton Rascoe (*NYWT*) announced, "Especial praise must go to Gregory Peck, a remarkable young actor . . . sensitive, intelligent, expert and an uncommon type . . . who by the playing of the war-shocked and regenerate doctor promises to go far."

This play should not be confused with the 1940 work of the same title* (apart from the absence of the definite article) starring Molly Picon.

MUM'S THE WORD [Miscellaneous/Solo] CN/P: Jimmy Savo; D: Al Webster; T: Belmont Theatre (OB); 12/5/40 (12)

A largely unsuccessful effort at a (practically) one-man show conceived by and starring veteran comic pantomimist Jimmy Savo. The diminutive, derby-hatted, sad-eyed Savo's talent was deemed by many more suitable for a vaudeville act or for inclusion in a musical comedy than for a full two hours with no assistance other than the between-the-scenes "verbal annotations" of Hiram Sherman and the piano accompaniment of Herbert Kingsley.

Savo employed a few old routines, but most of the ten-scene show was fresh. A pair of scenes, one in which--dressed as a weary dock worker--he sang "Old Man River" and another about a Bowery bum hungrily eyeing a chestnut vendor's roasting wares, verged on pathos, while the rest were in a humorous vein. His comic bits included "The Emergency Call," in which he played a hospital porter who gets to perform emergency surgery, and "Washerwoman in Love," in which he played a lovelorn scrubwoman dancing with a suit of long underwear. There was the fairly enjoyable one about a lovesick Swedish girl picking flowers on her way to church, the one in which he played Eve--wearing baggy long johns with a fig leaf attached--in the Garden of Eden, and the one featuring M. Jourdain from Molière's *Le Bourgeois Gentilhomme**, which Savo once had starred in at Westport, Connecticut. But the best pieces on the program were his epilogue renditions of two songs he had made popular in vaudeville, "Did You Ever See a Dream Walking?" and "River, Stay Away from My Door," both accompanied by his unique physical expressiveness.

The evening grew monotonous, complained John Anderson (*NYJA*), because Savo's style was "in a minor key," rendering the evening "pretty pallid and tedious. His sketches have a good deal of variety but they are not often sustained or very inventive." One of the few who liked the show was Brooks Atkinson (*NYT*), for whom this was "a rare and lovable evening in the theatre."

MURDER WITHOUT CRIME [Drama/British/Crime/Marriage/Mystery/Sex] A: J. Lee Thompson; D: Bretaigne Windust; S: Raymond Sovey; P: John Howell Del Bondio, Tom Weatherly, and Bretaigne Windust; T: Cort Theatre; 8/18/43 (37)

Bretaigne Windust coproduced, directed, and starred (as a last-minute replacement for Michael Dyne) in this four-character, "machine-made" (Rosamond Gilder [*TAM*]) British murder mystery, produced in London as *To Fit the Crime*. Reminiscent of Patrick Hamilton's infinitely superior psychological thriller *Rope's End**, it deals with a neurotic philanderer named Stephen (Windust). When he learns that his estranged wife (Viola Keats) is returning to him, he gets into a quarrel with his mistress Grena (Frances Tannehill), of whom he wishes to rid himself, and accidentally stabs her with a dagger. Thinking her dead, he hides the corpse in a long ottoman before the fire. He then becomes the psychological victim of his malicious, Freudian-oriented landlord, Matthew (Henry Daniell), who envies his prowess with the opposite sex and suspects foul play in the Mayfair flat. Stephen erupts in an emotional outburst and departs. Matthew then examines the place and discovers that Grena is still alive, having merely been wounded and knocked unconscious. He gets Grena out without telling Stephen and, when the latter returns, baits him so sadistically that Stephen plans to murder him in order to cover up the original non-murder. The twist comes when Matthew, thinking to poison Stephen, accidentally drinks the poison himself, with Stephen bound to suffer the consequences for having killed him.

The characters were all contemptible and shallow, the plot was filled with stencils, and the play had no relief from its unmitigated gloom and verbosity. "It was," concluded Ward Morehouse (*NYS*), "a talky, rambling, and only occasionally effective melodrama." Still, a few critics found the play a suitable exercise in the genre, John Chapman (*NYDN*), for instance, judging it "a very pleasantly tense psychological melodrama." Henry Daniell was widely approved for his fascinating portrayal of the vicious landlord.

MUSIC IN MY HEART [Musical/Military/Music/Musical-Biographical/Period/Romance] B: Patsy Ruth Miller; M: Peter Tchaikovsky; LY: Forman Brown; D/L: Hassard Short; CH: Ruth Page; S/C: Alvin Colt; P: Henry Duffy; T: Adelphi Theatre; 10/2/47 (125)

Following a tradition of creating Broadway musicals out of the lives of famous European composers (such as Franz Schubert, Frederic Chopin, and Edvard Grieg), *Music in My Heart* chose Russian master Peter Ilych Tchaikovsky (Robert Carroll) for its biographical subject. All the music was adapted (by Franz Steininger) from Tchaikovsky's own melodies.

The action is set in the nineteenth-century Russia of Alexander II and concentrates on the composer's love affair with the exquisite French prima donna Desirée Artot (Martha Wright, in her Broadway debut). After demonstrating her love for Tchaikovsky, she abandons him for the affections of his good friend, Captain Gregorovitch (Charles Fredericks) of the Imperial Russian Guard. Left alone in the empty opera house, the heartbroken composer plays his "Song without Words."

The cast included comedian Jan Murray (in his Broadway debut) as the comical leader of an opera claque and Vivienne Segal as a humorous ballet mistress (the work included several ballets). The chief dancers were Olga Suarez and Nicholas Margallanes. Uninspired lyrics had been added to the composer's music.

The critics lambasted the pretentious show. "I should like to call a halt on biographies of composers until such time as they can be made truly biographical," groused John Chapman (*NYDN*), "and not flimsy excuses for getting good tunes for free." Louis Kronenberger (*PM*) noted, "The doings at the Adelphi Theater . . . were too sheerly idiotic to be regarded as obscene, but they made it impossible for Broadway to cast a single stone at Hollywood for any cinematic sacrilege whatever, or to refer to a soap opera except in terms of the highest respect."

Carroll did all his own piano playing, but John Chapman did not realize this and made a serious contretemps in his notice by claiming that the piano business was faked and that a professional was in the wings providing the real performance. This misstatement was printed in the *NYDN*'s early edition and had to be revised for the later editions, where it was accompanied by the critic's apology to Carroll, "who not only plays Tschaikowsky [*sic*] but also plays the piano."

MY DEAR PUBLIC [Musical/Business/Romance/Theatre] B: Irving Caesar and Chuno (Charles) Gottesfeld; M/LY: Irving Caesar, Sam Lerner, and Gerald Marks; D: Edgar J. MacGregor; CH: Felicia Sorel, Lauretta Jefferson, and Henry Le Tang; S: Albert Johnson; C: Lucinda Ballard; P: Irving Caesar; T: Forty-sixth Street Theatre; 9/9/43 (44)

This show was a cross between a musical comedy and a revue and was, in fact, labeled a "revusical story" by its producer. The revue aspect, for its part, was in reality a vaudeville show, vaudeville--considered dead since 1932--undergoing a brief wartime revival with Broadway producers putting on such shows as if they were "legitimate." The show had been tried out on the road in 1942 and then was closed down for revisions. The revisions, including a new cast and new songs, were insufficient to stir approbation. Wrote Hobe. (*V*), "The book is labored and tedious, its score is commonplace, the comedy is stubbornly unfunny, production and staging are inadequate and the cast is light on stars, either for entertainment or boxoffice draw."

It starred wild-haired dialect comedian Willie Howard as zipper manufacturer Barney Short, who finances a Broadway musical for a temperamental genius named Byron Burns (Eric Brotherson). Barney is in love with a soubrette (Nanette Fabray) and urged to produce the show by his ex-actress wife, Daphne Drew (Ethel Shutta), who wants to star in it. This situation is used as a frame--one that was almost immediately forgotten--for the display of various acts, none of which had anything to do with one another. The unexciting material deadened even the talents of Howard, Fabray, double-talking Al Kelly, character actor Jesse White, tap dancer and singer Georgie Tapps, comic David Burns, and others. A highlight came with the appearance of black singer Rose Brown, who stopped the show singing "Color Line," but was hindered by poor direction.

Howard offered many of his old routines, some with variations. For example, his famous bit about a Yiddish-speaking orator giving a soapbox lecture about communism ("Comes the revolution and you will eat strawberries!") was revised for a Scotch burr. He roused laughter in his duologues with Al Kelly as his stooge, and his song "If You Want to Deal with Russia" struck some as funny. However, the show was a dud, and on opening night, people kept walking out during its performance.

MY FAIR LADIES [Comedy/Business/Romance/War] A: Arthur L. Jarrett and Marcel Klauber; D: Albert Lewis; S: Watson Barratt; C: Mabel Johnston; P: Albert Lewis and Max Siegel; T: Hudson Theatre; 3/23/41 (32)

Celeste Holm and Betty Furness (the movie actress, in her Broadway debut) costarred as Lady Keith-Odlyn and Lady Palfrey-Stuart in this "innocuous" (Brooks Atkinson [*NYT*]) farce that had no relation to the similarly titled musical of later years. The ladies in question are American chorus girls impersonating English noblewomen, having arrived here on false passports issued to them by a friendly foreign-service officer when they were stranded in war-torn London. They pass themselves off as foreign refugees, widowed and pregnant. When they arrive in a clipper, they are taken by Helen Gage (Mary Sargent), a socially minded suburban matron, to her home in Mt. Kisco, New York, where the local social leader (Ethel Morrison) fawns over them. A pair of eligible young men (Russell Hardie and Alfred Etcheverry) woo them and remain faithful even when--to Mrs. Gage's chagrin--their ruse is revealed by a drunken playboy (Otto Hulett) who saw their picture in the papers. Meanwhile, the girls help a young couple to elope (Toni Gilman and Thomas Coley), reform the playboy, and help Mr. Gage (Herbert Yost) out of his business difficulties. It turns out that the chorines have served the British cause well by bearing the titles of two women engaged on the Continent as British spies.

"There is nothing believable in its exposition," grumbled Burns Mantle (*NYDN*). "The characters are dummies speaking set and labored lines. The story is a flimsy fiction. The situations are directly out of the stock drawer." In the company were future novelist Jacqueline Susann, Lionel Ince, and Vincent Donehue, among others.

MY FRIEND YOSSEL [Musical/Yiddish Language] B: Isidor Friedman and William Siegel; M: Sholem Secunda; LY: Isidor Lillian; D: Mike Wilensky; CH: Valentina Belova; S: Michael Saltzman; C: Gropper; P: Menasha Skulnik; T: Second Avenue Theatre (OB); 3/3/44

A Yiddish musical that, for all its downplaying of the genre's usual bathos, nevertheless was clogged with a complex melodramatic plot about Melech (Jacob

Zanger), a restaurant owner who, seeking to swindle Sam Brazin (Michal Michalesko) in a matter concerning a stolen car, betroths his daughter to him. About to be arrested, Sam takes off for Canada, and his buddy Yossel (Menasha Skulnik), who is the heart interest of Sheine Chaye (Yetta Zwerling), takes the rap instead. Sam declines into alcoholism, but is saved by the cabaret singer Manya (Miriam Kressyn) and forgives those who nearly wrecked his life.

"The result is a pleasant and entertaining musical more nearly approaching the better Broadway standards than the average Yiddish musical of this type," wrote Thomas R. Dash (*WWD*).

MY NAME IS AQUILON (***Empereur de Chine***) [Comedy/Crime/French/Romance] A: Jean-Pierre Aumont; AD: Philip Barry; D: Robert B. Sinclair; S/L: Stewart Chaney; C: Lilli Palmer's gowns: Valentina; Arlene Francis's gowns: Castillo; P: Theatre Guild; T: Lyceum Theatre; 2/9/49 (31)

Viennese actress Lilli Palmer and Parisian actor Jean-Pierre Aumont--both of them already film stars--made their American stage debuts in this innocuous play, the original of which (a Paris hit) was from Aumont's pen. Nothing they or anyone else--including Stewart Chaney, who provided an elegant setting--did could keep this "pointless" (Brooks Atkinson [*NYT*]) comedy alive. The play's title during tryouts had been *Figure of a Girl*.

Aumont later declared in *Sun and Shadow* that he was appalled at Barry's adaptation, but could not get him to change it. Barry would answer his protestations with the comment, "You are a charming boy, but you don't know the American public." Aumont also said of the final title, "I do not know to this day what that was supposed to mean." After the New Haven opening, which Aumont's wife told the shocked Barry was "shit," the adaptor continued to make revisions, but these only worsened matters.

Pierre (Aumont) is a persistent but charming liar who lives in a world of self-dramatization and takes the phony name of Aquilon. Having learned to live by his wits as an underground fighter during the war, he has been succeeding in the high-risk endeavor of smuggling banknotes and gold. His romantic panache appeals to all the play's women, especially Christine (Palmer), the daughter of his employer, Victor Benoit-Benoit (Lawrence Fletcher), and his employer's wife--Christine's stepmother--Madeleine (Arlene Francis), who suffers a letdown when she learns of his lying and illegal proclivities. He, for his part, is uncomfortable with the thought of going straight. As he and Christine grow closer together, he cuts down on his lying and the hitherto militantly honest Christine increasingly fails to tell the truth.

The play was watered down somewhat from its original version. In the latter, Aumont's character has an affair with Madeleine, who is depicted as Christine's birth mother. For Broadway, she became the girl's stepmother, and the affair was dropped in favor of a sexual suggestion made to her. "Through five tedious scenes, it takes all the cunning of smart performers to keep one vaguely interested in the denouement," announced Howard Barnes (*NYHT*). "When it occurs, it has all the pat conventionalities of a cinematic climax."

Atkinson described Palmer as "playing with quiet charm and modest sincerity. She is a slight, alert young lady with fluid gestures and a sunny smile. . . . Miss Palmer is the finest thing that has happened to the Gotham stage for quite a long time." Aumont, then a major film star, was less impressive. George Jean Nathan (*TBY*)--who raved about Palmer--described him as "a chunky young man with mayonnaise hair and feet several sizes too large for his body."

Aumont wrote that he was astonished on opening night to discover that Palmer "softened her performance to three pitches below mine, in a register, tempo, and style which had nothing to do with our six weeks of rehearsal and our four weeks of previews." Thinking she must be ill, he worked harder to salvage the show, but later realized, "I was only undermining myself. The harder I tried to create some movement, the more restrained Lilli appeared to be." Afterwards, he learned that Palmer, disturbed by lukewarm out-of-town reviews, had hired a German acting coach (Elsa Schreiber) to help revise her performance. In *Change Lobsters and Dance*, Palmer admitted that the help she received from Schreiber saved her performance, but said nothing about Aumont's reaction.

The cast also included former model Doe Avedon, Donald Hanmer, and Phyllis Kirk.

MY ROMANCE [Musical/Music/Period/Religion/Romance] B/LY/D: Rowland Leigh; M: Sigmund Romberg; SC: Edward Sheldon's play, *Romance**; CH: Frederick N. Kelly; S: Watson Barratt; C: Lou Eisele; P: Messrs. Shubert; T: Shubert Theatre; 10/19/48 (95)

Edward Sheldon's 1913 mushily romantic drama *Romance*, which had made a great star out of his wife, Doris Keane, and which she had last played locally in 1921, was the inspiration for this hackneyed and old-fashioned operetta that Brooks Atkinson (*NYT*) called "pretentious fiddle-faddle." As before, the work begins with a prologue in which Bishop Armstrong (Lawrence Brooks) cautions his grandson against marrying an actress, which warning is followed by a flashback of his own unhappy love affair with the great Italian diva, Mme. Cavallini (Anne Jeffreys). The prologue (and epilogue) were set in 1948, and the flashback returned to 1898.

George Freedley (*NYMT*) called the adaptation "excruciating" and Rowland Leigh's "lyrics . . . as horrible as his book." "It has not improved with age," decided Howard Barnes (*NYHT*), "nor the clumsy melodic translation which it has been accorded. Leigh has settled for stilted dialogue and witless lyrics in his share of a dismal enterprise." Some of Sigmund Romberg's music was salvageable, although most of it was reminiscent of his past endeavors. Best of the lot was "In Love with Romance."

Romberg was a replacement for another composer whose score was abandoned during the out-of-town tryouts. The only worthwhile comedy in the piece came from one or two funny lines delivered by Luella Gear as Octavia Fotheringham. The beautiful Jeffreys was not universally admired for her acting skill, but her singing pleased some reviewers. The large company included Hazel Dawn, Jr., Rex Evans, Doris Patson, Allegra Varron, Nat Burns, and Melville Ruick, among others.

MY SISTER EILEEN [Comedy/Art/Family/Journalism/Literature/Military/Prostitution/Romance/Sex/Sports/Theatre] A: Joseph A. Fields and Jerome Chodorov; SC: a series of *New Yorker* stories by Ruth McKenney; D: George S. Kaufman; CH: Paul Seymour; S: Donald Oenslager; P: Max Gordon; T: Biltmore Theatre; 12/26/40 (866)

A smash-hit comedy based on the autobiographical stories of Ruth McKenney about a pair of sisters from Columbus, Ohio, who take up residence in a Greenwich Village basement apartment. The opening-night curtain almost did not go up as scheduled because the real-life Eileen of the play's title had been killed with her husband, writer Nathanael West, in a California car crash a week before. However, it was decided that the best thing for the depressed company was for the show to open on time, which proved a wise decision and helped to lift everyone's spirits.

The play had come to be written by Fields and Chodorov after they had read the collected stories in book form and had learned that Ruth McKenney already had written a play based on the material in collaboration with Leslie Reade. As McKenney had had no luck getting her script produced, she allowed Fields and Chodorov to try their luck with a dramatization. The result--which derived from only two stories in the collection--so pleased writer-director Moss Hart that he contacted the proper parties and led the way to its production. The comedy was selected as one of the ten best plays of 1940-1941. It was adapted into two films, became the basis of the hit musical comedy *Wonderful Town*, and served as the inspiration of a TV series.

My Sister Eileen, which takes various liberties with its autobiographical background and which is more a string of incidents than a carefully plotted play, calls its heroines Ruth (Shirley Booth) and Eileen Sherwood (Jo Ann Sayers, in her Broadway bow). The plump and red-headed Ruth is a hopeful writer, the beautiful blond Eileen an aspiring actress whom men can not keep from ogling. On their first day in New York, they rent a grubby basement apartment in Greenwich Village from a rascally Greek landlord, Mr. Appopolous (Morris Carnovsky), a flamboyant would-be painter who charges them $45 a month. (The original for this apartment was on Christopher Street.) A subway is being blasted underground, and loud explosions punctuate much of the action. At the rear, a large, arched window reveals the colorful life passing by on the street outside, although passersby can be seen only from the waist down. Ruth strives to get her stories published, and Eileen hopes to get an acting job, but the money runs low as they meet up with numerous complications. Lonigan (Tom Dillon), the local cop, suspects the girls of hanky-panky because the apartment was formerly occupied by a hooker, Violet Shelton (Effie Afton). A man (Charles Martin) stops by, thinking that the place is still being used as a brothel, and Violet herself makes several appearances, even trying to get the gorgeous Eileen work as a stripper or a nude volleyball player on a naturists' ranch. A gin-swigging pro football player named the Wreck (Gordon Jones), living in sin upstairs with the pregnant Helen Wade (Joan Tompkins) and constantly singing his Georgia Tech song, befriends the sisters. At one point he is forced to camp out in the tiny flat when Helen's prudish mother (Helen Ray), unaware of her daughter's relationship to him, pays a visit. A tabloid reporter named Chic Clark (Bruce MacFarlane) has the hots for Eileen and contrives to get her alone by pretending that his editor will give Ruth a chance if she covers a story about a shipload of coffee millionaires just arrived from Brazil. Also angling for Eileen is the young drugstore clerk, Frank Lippencott (Richard Quine). The good-looking assistant editor of *Manhatter* magazine, Robert Baker (William Post, Jr.), falls for Ruth and encourages her, losing his job in the process. Ruth likes him but learns that Eileen also finds him appealing. Ruth, off on the phony assignment, winds up bringing home a half-dozen immaculately white-uniformed Brazilian naval cadets, who speak only Portuguese and mistake the girls for women of easy virtue. When one of them puts on a conga record, they all form a line to dance, with Eileen leading the line in an attempt to lure them out of the place. (Their scene was one of the brightest moments of the season.) The Sherwood dad (Donald Foster) arrives to retrieve his daughters, but the girls refuse to leave. Ruth actually lands a job with Chic's newspaper, and Eileen receives an apology and a commendation from the Brazilian consul (Joseph Kallini). Eileen chooses Frank so that Ruth may have Robert, and the Sherwoods decide to renew their lease when Appopolous promises that the blasting is over, their rent will be reduced, and renovations will be made. No sooner have they signed than a powerful noise shakes the place. The blasting is over but the drilling has begun.

A major reason for the play's success was the accuracy with which it limned the travails of those who come to New York with little in their bank accounts and try to find a decent residence while making a life for themselves amid the thrills and heartache of the big city. Its glimpse of the bohemian life of Greenwich Village was also a strong attraction. Brooks Atkinson (*NYT*) and others believed that the contribution of director Kaufman to the fun was as significant as that of its credited writers: "Until Mr. Kaufman's stiff demurrer arrives tomorrow morning, this column will go on believing that he has done as much for a merry antic as any of the authors." "*My Sister Eileen* is heart-warming and uproarious," cheered Rosamond Gilder (*TAM*). "It needs neither explanation nor apology." John Mason Brown (*NYP*) described it as "side-splitting," "convulsing," and a "brilliantly integrated comedy." "It is Miss McKenney's ability to laugh at herself and her troubles which grow more and more outrageous that make it all funny instead of tragic, which her story in real life might easily have been," advised George Freedley (*NYMT*).

The cast was lovingly applauded, with top honors going to Shirley Booth. Brown wrote, "Shirley Booth once again demonstrates her superlative skill. She is warm, human, resilient, hopeful. There is no other actress on our stage . . . who can excel her when it comes to the precise firing of a Kaufman line." Eda Heinemann as a prospective tenant contributed in a minor role.

The scene in the play in which the two sisters discover that each has feelings for the same man was apparently too sentimental to stomach for the hard-boiled director, who was uncomfortable about staging it. According to Malcolm Goldstein's *George S. Kaufman*, when he came to the scene in rehearsal, he put down his script, turned to the authors, and said, "All right. You two wrote it. Now you can direct it."

MY WEDDING NIGHT [Musical/Yiddish Language] B: Isidor Friedman; M: Abe Ellstein; LY: Isidor Lillian and Jacob Jacobs; D/P: Menasha Skulnik; CH: Valentina Belova; S: Henry Delecoleri; C: Gropper; T: Second Avenue Theatre (OB); 1/19/46

Menasha Skulnik, clown prince of Second Avenue in the 1940s, appeared in one vehicle after the other tailored to his unique characterization of a nebbishlike poor soul; his characters' names differed, but their shy, doltish manner always remained. He was called Motel in *My Wedding Night*, a musical in which, as usual, everyone on stage practically faded into the scenery when he was onstage, cracking up the audience. The other actors accepted this as they were part of a continuing company and usually played similar roles in other Skulnik vehicles. Ben Rosenberg (*NYP*) said of the present one, "It's a typical Skulnik show, devoid of Broadway pretentiousness perhaps, but packed to the hilt with belly laughs, lively tunes and occasional sprightly dancing by a group of well-trained girls."

The story tells of how schoolteacher Reizele (Miriam Kressyn) tells her Auntie Bessie (Anna Teitelbaum) that she loves Leon (Muni Serebrov), a handsome nightclub singer she met on vacation in Mexico. Bessie herself loves Isaac (Isidor Friedman), a Catskills farmer, and she is soon seen in his Fallsburgh home, where she meets his foolish son Motel. To put Motel on his own, he is sent to Bessie's brother Hirsh (Moses Feder) for a job. As luck would have it, both he and Leon, Reizele's boyfriend, arrive at the same time. Reizele, seeking parental permission to marry her boyfriend, pretends to be pregnant, but, by mistake, Motel is hurriedly married to Reizele instead. Fortunately, Leon and Motel are old friends, and Motel later divorces Reizele and marries her man-hungry sister Sheindel (Yetta Zwerling), while Reizele and Leon tie the knot.

Robert Garland (*NYJA*) considered this a Broadway-level show, saying that it had "a fine, fresh, unpretentious quality not always to be found in its more studied and cut-to-Broadway counterparts." Part of the fun came when Skulnik sang one of several comic numbers, such as "Motel, the Cowboy." The actors included Annie Thomashefsky and Dave Lubritzky.

N

NAKED GENIUS, THE [Comedy/Crime/Literature/Romance/Sex/Show Business] A: Gypsy Rose Lee; D: George S. Kaufman; S: Frederick Fox; C: Billy Livingston; P: Michael Todd; T: Plymouth Theatre; 10/21/43 (36)

Gypsy Rose Lee, the intellectual stripper, penned this comedy (with valiant infusions by director Kaufman), but it proved a boring "yawn from curtain to curtain," according to George Freedley (*NYMT*). Its first titles had been *Seven-Year Cycle* and *The Ghost in the Woodpile*. Lee had hoped to play the lead, but, to her disappointment, producer Todd preferred to cast movie star Joan Blondell, whom he was to wed in 1946. When the play kept bombing during its out-of-town tryouts, Kaufman begged producer Todd to close it, and Lee agreed, but Todd refused to listen to them, preferring to continue doctoring the script. The super showman advertised his show with the slogan, "GUARANTEED NOT TO WIN THE PULITZER PRIZE. IT AIN'T SHAKESPEARE BUT IT'S LAFFS."

Despite its bad press, Todd's exploitative methods--including a title he dreamed up with the word "naked" in it--managed to turn the show into a sellout that was playing to standing room only and grossing over $17,000 a week. When asked how the show could have succeeded, he pointed to the ignorance of the pleasure-seeking wartime crowds, many with money from high-paying defense jobs. Still, Todd closed the show after only a month of performances. According to Art Cohn's *The Nine Lives of Michael Todd*, the producer explained: "In show business you can't please everyone, but I believe pleasing less than half is not a good percentage, therefore in my eagerness to please the public I am closing the show despite the fact that it is earning a substantial profit. I believe the money I might be losing as a result is not as important as the good will of the people who might not like the show." A truer reason for his altruism was that he already had sold the play's film rights to Twentieth-Century Fox for a substantial sum and, under the Dramatists Guild contract, had to have it run on Broadway for three weeks to guarantee the sale. Otherwise, he would have closed it out of town. (The movie, with Carmen Miranda, was called *Doll Face*.)

The play was a semiautobiographical piece about Honey Bee Carroll (Blondell), a stripper with intellectual pretensions, who spends her money faster than she earns it. Her best-selling autobiography (with the same title as the play) actually has been written by a ghost-writing gangster named Sam Hinkle (Lewis Charles). She is loved by her manager, Stuart Tracy (Millard Mitchell), but she wishes to move into higher social echelons by marrying Charles Goodwin (Donald Randolph), the son of her publisher. The wedding is to be a major affair held at her country home with tickets sold and the profits given to the Ladies' Aid Society. The marriage to the upper-crust fellow does not come off because he gets cold feet when he learns that her book was ghosted, and she ends up marrying the manager instead. Subplots concern some stolen underwear sold by a ladies' room matron (Doro Merande) and "fenced" by Honey Bee's unscrupulous mother Pansy (Phyllis Povah), and an attempt by the ghostwriter to blackmail the stripper.

The Naked Genius was judged unfunny, dirty, and tiresome. Howard Barnes (*NYHT*) dubbed it "a dull whimsy, full of stale gags and inept performing." Yet the minority voice of Robert Garland (*NYJA*), while noting all the play's drawbacks, had to admit that "there are other times when it is slapstick farce at its most slapstick and farcical."

Joan Blondell, back on Broadway after a dozen years in movies, looked right but seemed ill at ease in a poorly scripted role. The cast included Frieda Altman, stripper Georgia Sothern as a rival stripteaser named Alibassi, Rex O'Malley as an effeminate ladies' clothing designer, Bertha Belmore as a G-string maker, and others, among them animal trainer Gil Maison, whose trained animals offered some fun in the wedding scene.

(1) NATHAN THE WISE (***Nathan der Weise***) [Dramatic Revival] A: Gotthold Ephraim Lessing; AD: Ferdinand Bruckner; M: Joel Spector; D: James Light; S: H. A. Condell; C: Rose Bogdanoff; L: Hans Sondheimer; P: Erwin Piscator; T: Studio Theatre of the New School for Social Research (OB); 3/11/42 (11) [Broadway production: P: Erwin Piscator i/a/w the Messrs. Shubert; T: Belasco Theatre; 4/3/42 (28)]

German author Ferdinand Bruckner's free adaptation in verse of his countryman's 1779 philosophical drama calling for religious toleration--it was banned by the Nazis in 1933--was so well received in its Off-Broadway presentation that it moved to Broadway. There, however, it fared less well and remained less than a month. This was said to be the play's first professional production in English.

Bruckner's colloquial verse and his pared down script seemed to many a significant aid in making the play accessible to a modern audience, although John Mason Brown (*NYP*) averred that "One only wishes Mr Bruckner's verse were better and that he had condensed individual speeches as fearlessly as he has pruned the plot."

The play is set in Jerusalem at the time of the Third Crusade, a period of virulent religious bigotry. A Knight Templar (Alfred Ryder) who is a prisoner of the Saracens has saved the life of Rahel (Olive Deering), the daughter of the benevolent Jewish trader Nathan (Herbert Berghof). When he discovers that Rahel, whom he loves, was raised a Jew although she is actually a Christian, he insists on Nathan's being executed, and the case is brought before the Mohammedan Sultan Saladin (Bram Nossen). Rahel, a respecter of all three faiths, fiercely defends her father from wrongdoing, and the knight comes to understand the need for religious tolerance. The final tableau symbolizes the mutual respect for one another of the representatives of the three religions.

Lessing's enlightened message was timely fare for 1942. Bruckner's adaptation removed many of the incidental romantic developments surrounding the love story in the original in order to concentrate on the author's plea for understanding. One of the highlights was the scene in which Nathan, seeking to explain that Christianity, Judaism, and Mohammedanism are equally true religions, tells the Sultan the parable of the three rings. But the general critical opinion was well summed up by Richard Watts, Jr. (*NYHT*), who observed that the play "remains a garrulous and undramatic work, with the nobility of its spirit atoning for its essential tediousness, but, as competently presented . . . it is unexpectedly interesting in its rather literary fashion."

Several critics thought Berghof outstanding. Brooks Atkinson (*NYT*), for example, declared that he "is giving one of the most radiant performances of the season. He manages to be compassionate and humble without losing his self-respect as a person and without wallowing in sentimentality."

After it moved to Broadway from Greenwich Village, Burns Mantle (*NYDN*) had this to say: "It is still effective drama, staged with skill and acted with frequent touches of moving eloquence. But now it becomes just another theatre attraction for the crowd and loses something of its appeal as a pilgrimage for the few."

(2) T: Studio Theatre of the New School for Social Research (OB); 2/21/44

Two years after its original staging, the play was revived at its original theatre with its original director, designers, and star, and several of its original supporting players. Berghof as Nathan and Gregory Morton as the patriarch repeated their roles. Doris Winston now played Daja, and Elizabeth Lynn played Rahel. Ryder was replaced by the more effective Derrick Lynn-Thomas. Jack Bittner moved up from a minor role as a monk to the more important lay brother, while Jay Williams played the Sultan Saladin.

George Jean Nathan (*TBY*) proclaimed the production to be little changed from that of 1942 and noted that the play seemed less theatrical and more literary than ever, proving "something of a resounding opiate." To Robert Garland (*NYJA*), however, it was the play's "quality of quietude, of composure and control, that gives the work its undeniable effectiveness." Wilella Waldorf (*NYP*) believed that, compared to the first showing, "the pace is brisker, and the attack more pithy."

Waldorf observed of Berghof that he "has gained in poise and assurance . . . , and his portrayal also benefits from the fact that he now speaks English with far more clarity and ease."

(1) **NATIVE SON** [Drama/Blacks/Crime/Family/Journalism/Law/Politics/Prison/Race/ Romance/Trial] A: Paul Green and Richard Wright; SC: Richard Wright's novel of the same name; D: Orson Welles; S: James Morcom; L: Jean Rosenthal; P: Orson Welles and John Houseman i/a/w Bern Bernard; T: St. James Theatre; 3/24/41 (114)

A powerful drama based on Richard Wright's outstanding novel about the social forces that drive Bigger Thomas (Canada Lee), a black man, to murder a white girl and cover up the crime. It was staged in ten intermissionless scenes in a production of tremendously increasing tension under the brilliant, if overly melodramatic, command of Orson Welles. Wright's work was intended to demonstrate how white oppression breeds resentment, ignorance, and violence among blacks. To keep them totally focused on the stage action, patrons were given slips of paper informing them that they would get their programs at the end of the performance.

The play begins with a prosecutor's comments, then flashes back to Bigger's poverty-stricken family, living in a rat-infested slum. Bigger, carrying a huge chip on his shoulder, and has a propensity for violence, takes a job as chauffeur to the wealthy Dalton family and, against his will, finds himself one night in young Mary Dalton's (Anne Burr) bedroom when she comes home drunk. She is a thoughtless girl who keeps company with a well-meaning Communist agitator named Jan (Joseph Pevney). To keep her from revealing his presence--her blind mother (Nell Harrison) is in the room--he puts a pillow over her mouth, but her struggle forces him accidentally to suffocate her. The body is burned in the basement furnace, but a reporter (Paul Stewart) detects the evidence that points to Bigger's guilt. Bigger flees but is captured (in an exciting scene involving Bigger firing into the audience and the police, hiding there, firing back), imprisoned, and put on trial. His defense is handled by the radical lawyer, Paul Max (Ray Collins; the character's radicalism was softened), a friend to the oppressed who pleads for Bigger on the basis of the man's deprived upbringing and racial suffering. Bigger is found guilty and condemned to the electric chair. In the death-house, Bigger and his attorney try to find a common ground as members of the human race.

Several critics noted that the events depicted in the novel were treated from the subjective viewpoint as Bigger reacted to and thought about them, but that on stage the story was played out in objective terms that robbed the original of much of its great impact. Complaints were also registered against the work's excessive violence and its tendency toward verbosity. Rosamond Gilder (*TAM*) thought that those who had not read the book would be confused by the omission of some of its important scenes. Yet, she said, "the play in the hands of so inventive and bold a director as Orson Welles proves violently exciting, absorbing, not a little lurid, as might well be expected." Richard Watts, Jr. (*NYHT*), opined that the work was "less impressive than" the novel and not always capable of communicating its theme, but acknowledged that "it is a taut and almost constantly arresting drama."

Gilder noted that the episodic work was unified by the use of "a shifting proscenium and side-walls of brownish brick. . . . The successive scenes are ingeniously devised for variety in size and shape and even in stage level, occasionally opening out to take in the whole fore-stage, apron, orchestra pit and auditorium, as in the trial scene." Speed, unusual sound and lighting effects (especially when Bigger is cornered in a warehouse), and various melodramatic techniques made for a compelling production, although the methods employed sometimes drew too much attention to themselves.

Some were offended by the hard-hitting dynamics of the work, Euphemia Van Rensselaer Wyatt (*CW*), for example, departing early because "the producers have no regard to niceties--the realism is vicious, the blasphemy continuous, the brutality of compound increase." There were those who, like George Freedley (*NYMT*), thought that for all the pyrotechnical effects, nothing could be done to prevent the play "from dragging endlessly upon the stage in an inconclusive fashion."

Canada Lee rose to stardom as Bigger. "Certainly no one could ask for a more satisfactory physical or vocal representation of all that is tortured, harried, and understandably resentful in [Bigger Thomas] than Canada Lee supplies," wrote John Mason Brown (*NYP*). "Mr. Lee is a fine actor who so far as words, gestures, looks, and spirit go is finely able to communicate the complex emotions which must boil within the anguished heart of Bigger. In every objective way Mr. Lee realizes the stifled goodness, the justifiable ferocity, the cornered desperation, and the final poignant sense which must invade Bigger that he has just begun to live in the hours after he has been doomed to die."

In addition to Lee, there were memorable performances by Evelyn Ellis as his mother, Erskine Sanford as Mr. Dalton, and Rena Mitchell as Bigger's girlfriend Clara (Bessie in the novel), whom Bigger eventually kills. Also in the cast were Philip Bourneuf, Everett Sloane, and Frances Bavier.

Paul Green was unhappy with Welles's treatment of his adaptation. In addition to cutting some black spiritual singing and other dramatic moments, Welles chose to eliminate a good deal of Green's poetic tone and to convey as much as possible of the gut-level emotion that he detected in the original. Green also felt that the theme of the individual's moral responsibility for his own acts was being softened in favor of too great a left-wing slant in which society was blamed for Bigger's crime. Welles's effect of having Bigger assume a Christ-like posture in his cell near the end was especially distasteful to Green, because he felt that the analogy was false. Green, Houseman, and Welles could not come to an agreement about the ending, and the former reportedly stormed out of a rehearsal in disgust.

(2) [Dramatic Revival] D: Orson Welles; S: James Morcom; P: Louis and George M. Brandt; T: Majestic Theatre; 10/23/42 (84)

Following its original run, the play was bought by the Brandts (owners of a moviehouse chain who had been introducing legitimate plays into some of their local theatres) and produced for popular prices in Brooklyn, the Bronx, and elsewhere. This "tour" had not been continuous and had occasionally taken time off for several of the actors to do other work. Thus this low-priced ($1.65 top) presentation was not so much a true revival as a somewhat modified and continued version of the original production. It retained, however, only a few of the original cast members, among them Canada Lee and Anne Burr, and added John Ireland as the reporter and Alexander Clark as the prosecuting attorney.

The script was somewhat revised to include references to World War II and the problems of Jim Crowism in the military, an intermission had been added, and the scenic effects had been pared down for reasons of economy. George Freedley (*NYMT*) questioned if Orson Welles had approved of the changes, despite his name being given as the director.

The pace was not as dynamic, the lighting was inferior, and the scene shifts took too long. Still, "It is as much worth seeing as ever," avowed Louis Kronenberger (*PM*). He claimed that Lee's performance was better than before--"more imaginative, more varied, more complete. As acting, it shows a surer knowledge of voice and stance and gesture, while as interpretation it conveys Bigger's tangled and inchoate emotions with greater clarity." "Canada Lee," claimed Rosamond Gilder (*TAM*), "has added a figure of heroic dimensions and tremendous implication to the theatre's gallery of great portraits."

NATURAL MAN [Drama/Blacks/Crime/Fantasy/Gambling/Labor/Period/Prison/Race/Religion/Southern] A: Theodore Browne; M: (adapted by) Vereda Pearson; D: Benjamin Zemach; S: Sanford Engel; P: American Negro Theatre; T: 135th Street Library Theatre (OB); 5/7/41

This play, produced in a tiny Harlem theatre located in the library at 102 West 135th Street, the home of the Schomberg Negro Collection, was a socially conscious dramatization with music of the legend of John Henry (Stanley Greene). Its premiere had been with the Federal Theatre Project in Seattle (1937), and the play won its author a Rockefeller Playwriting Fellowship, making him the first black to be so awarded. The play was the second done by the American Negro Theatre and the first to be reviewed by the daily press.

John Henry's epic tale--signifying the proud black man's will to survive at all costs--is told in nine scenes, most of them a series of dream sequences. It begins with his agreeing to compete against a steel-driving machine in West Virginia's Big Ben Tunnel, a sunrise-to-sunset competition on which his fellow workers wager heavily. John Henry must compete because his white boss (Alvin Childress) knows that he killed a Georgia chain-gang guard. If he loses, he will be turned over to white justice. The dream sequences now commence, starting with a scene on the chain gang where the men dream of freedom; John Henry kills the sadistic guard because the latter whips a convict who has died of exhaustion. Fleeing, John Henry seeks the help of a preacher (Frederick O'Neal) at a camp meeting, but is turned down out of fear of the white man's vengeance. His plea for help among the underworld figures of Beale Street in Memphis is likewise rejected. He becomes a hobo, then is accused by white workers of "scabbing" for a Northern factory for which he goes to work. He gets in a fight and is arrested, then brutally taunted by the white prisoners. Finally, the action returns to the present and John Henry, overcome with fatigue, dies, but the "mechanical man" goes on. The unequal contest is over.

The primitive conditions of the performance were thought by Brooks Atkinson (*NYT*) to have seriously hindered its success, since the episodic play requires the creation of multiple locales. But George Freedley (*NYMT*), referring to a play titled *John Henry**, said, "With all its faults, this play seemed much superior to the scenically splendid version of the same folk material written by Roark Bradford and presented last season on Broadway." Freedley's major objection was the work's failure, once it had presented its thesis of the historical oppression of blacks, to arrive at any appropriate solution to the state of affairs. Communist critic Ralph Warner (*DW*) faulted the play's black nationalism, as he saw it, and would have preferred a theme pointing to black and white harmony. John Anderson (*NYJA*) thought some of it clumsy but much of it "both vivid and vigorous."

The production, staged by a member of Israel's Habimah Theatre, was theatrically exciting, using songs and dances and a black gospel choir (the Pearson Choir), although there was an odd disjunction of Russian-Jewish theatricality and black folk atmosphere. The cast included Alice Childress, of considerable importance in later black theatre activity.

NAUGHTY NAUGHT ('00) [Musical Revival*] B: John Van Antwerp (Gerald Krimsky); M: Richard Lewine; LY/D: Ted Fetter; CH: Ray Harrison; S/L: Kermit Love; C: Robert Moore; P: Paul Killiam i/a/w Oliver Rea; T: Old Knickerbocker Music Hall (OB); 10/19/46 (17)

An unsuccessful revival of a moderately effective 1937 musical burlesque on old-time melodramas, with the audience allowed to cheer the virtuous hero and hiss the sneering villain. Its production was in a renovated and renamed former movie theatre (the Clifton) on Second Avenue between East Fifty-fourth and East Fifty-fifth streets.

It received some pleasant comments, such as that by George Freedley (*NYMT*), who wrote, "It is lively; it is amusing in a broad way; it meets the needs of those who feel honor-bound to hiss the villain; it provides a definitely un-mental way to spend the evening." But several critics were aghast. William Hawkins (*NYWT*), for instance, declared, "The result comes out as a pretty loose knit amateurish affair."

Audiences sat at cocktail tables and were able to purchase drinks while watching the show. Various variety routines were performed between the acts, followed by sing-alongs of sentimental old tunes, with dancing and a floor show following the final curtain. One of the olio acts featured a trapeze performer, Ullaine Malloy, who performed over the heads of the spectators.

In the show proper, villain P. de Quincy Devereaux was played by John Cromwell, Spunky by Teddy Hart, Frank Plover by Leonard Hicks, Jack Granville by Kenneth Forbes, Cathleen by Virginia Barbour, and Claire Granville by Ottilie Kruger. The acting was in the exaggerated tradition common to such spoofs.

NELLIE BLY [Musical/Adventure/Barroom/Journalism/Period/Romance] B: Joseph Quillan; M: James Van Heusen; LY: Johnny Burke; SC: a story by Jack Emmanuel; D: Edgar J. MacGregor; CH: Edward Caton and Lee Sherman; DS: Nat Karson; P: Nat Karson and Eddie Cantor; T: Adelphi Theatre; 1/21/46 (16)

Apart from one or two strongly positive reviews, the majority of the critics strongly condemned as second-rate this lavishly produced musical comedy starring William Gaxton and Victor Moore. Inspired by an actual event, it concerns an 1889 female journalist named Nellie Bly (Joy Hodges), whose publisher, Joseph Pulitzer (Walter Armin), decides to promote his newspaper, the *New York World* by having Nellie try to beat the *Around the World in Eighty Days* record of Jules Verne's fictional hero, Phileas T. Fogg. Frank Jordan (Gaxton), the managing editor of a rival newspaper, the *New York Herald*, decides to keep up his readership by employing the Milquetoastish ferryboat attendant Phineas T. Fogarty (Moore) to race Nellie. Jordan accompanies Fogarty on his travels and falls in love with Nellie. Much of the comedy stems from the hero's mishaps, such as getting seasick, being forced to make a balloon ascension, being disguised as a female in a sultan's harem, and so on.

An enormous amount of pre-Broadway fixing was wasted on this $300,000 loser. Its original book writers, Morrie Ryskind and Sig Herzig, quit during the process. Louis Kronenberger (*PM*) judged that the show "proves hollow as a drum--one of those melancholy contraptions that just never come to life. The book is forever around, and forever in trouble." "All that is wanted," sighed Howard Barnes (*NYHT*), "is a bit of fresh comic invention or a tune to whistle." An example of the humor was a line about Phineas's being so ill that the rigor was waiting for the mortis to set in.

Neither Gaxton nor Moore were comfortable with their roles. Some life was infused into the moribund show by Benay Venuta as Battle Annie, a tough saloon keeper, and there were occasional dance highlights provided by Lubov Roudenko, Jack Whitney, and an all-male group called the Debonairs. In the large cast were Robert Strauss, Drucilla Strain, and Harold Murray.

NEW FACES OF 1943 [Revue] SK/LY: John Lund; ADD.SK/LY: June Carroll and J. B. Rosenberg; M: Lee Wainer; ADD.M: Will Irwin; D: Laurence Hurdle; CH: Charles Weidman and John Wray; S/C: Edward Gilbert; L: Carlton Winkler; P: Leonard Sillman; T: Ritz Theatre; 12/22/42 (94)

The third in Leonard Sillman's *New Faces** series of revues, although Burns Mantle counted *Fools Rush In** of 1934 (Mantle mistakenly gave 1938) as part of the series. The thirty-scene show offered an abundance of new faces, but George Jean Nathan (*TBY*) could not find any that also represented novel talents. "They merchanted much the same old routine thing, and not one-hundredth so well as the old, established faces."

The show consisted of a troupe of young nightclub entertainers doing songs, dances, and sketches, some with topical pertinence. Orson Welles was satirized in "Welles of Loneliness," another scene concerned a tour through Radio City, and another dealt with an employment agency where a hard-to-get cook (because of wartime shortages) gives her employer, the First Lady, the once-over. Among the moments various critics pointed out, if not with excessive enthusiasm, were impersonator Tony Farrar as "The Nearsighted Bullfighter" or pretending to be Fannie Brice impersonating dancer Paul Draper; toothy black songstress Ann Robinson singing "Shoes" and doing her improvisatory ("riff") singing; the torch song "Love, Are You Raising Your Head?" sung by Laura Deane Dutton; clown Irwin Corey with his too-long lecture on *Hamlet**; a song-sketch spoofing Broadway agents and called "The Ten-Percenters"; one on Thornton Wilder and William Saroyan called "Skin of Your Life" in which sketch writer and lyricist Lund played a flaming homosexual in a barber's chair; eccentric comedienne Alice Pearce; and dancers Hie Thompson and Diane Davis.

Only Pearce and Corey became show-business names to conjure with. Lewis Nichols (*NYT*) deplored the lack of good comic sketches, and John Beaufort (*CSM*) called the show "nearly always second and sometimes third rate."

NEW LIFE, A [Drama/Aviation/Business/Family/Marriage/Medicine/Politics/Show Business/War] A/D: Elmer Rice; S: Howard Bay; C: Rose Bogdanoff; P: Playwrights' Company; T: Royale Theatre; 9/15/43 (70)

A play of ideas and deep feeling that had powerful and meaningful scenes but was dramaturgically flawed in various ways. Set entirely in the maternity ward of an East Side hospital in Manhattan, it tells the tale of Captain Robert Cleghorne (George Lambert), an aviator, and his wife, radio singer Edith Charles Cleghorne (Betty Field [Mrs. Elmer Rice]). She is due to deliver a baby, but he is supposedly lost somewhere in the Pacific. She has her son in a scene that partly depicts the delivery, and then learns of her husband's safe return. Robert is the son of wealthy Arizonans (Walter N. Greaza and Merle Maddern), who opposed the marriage. These reactionary steel magnates wish to raise the child in their own social circles to give him the advantages of wealth and class in the postwar years. Robert, who does not have much backbone, thinks that they have a good argument, but Edith, born of a humble background, refuses to agree, insisting that she will raise the boy to be a person of substance and "independent spirit." Robert spends an evening discussing various issues raised by the play with Edith's liberal-minded merchant seaman friend (John Ireland) and this leads him to concede that she is right. The baby's future is made to suggest the future of America.

Betty Field turned in a wonderful performance that did much to make the play appealing despite its innate problems. Some of the latter were enumerated by Lewis Nichols (*NYT*), who said that Rice's "latest play is a little stereotyped, its characters are a bit too pat; the craftsman is there to direct the lines, but an evening in the theatre with a craftsman only leaves a dismal feeling that something is lacking." Some of the characters, as several noted, were almost allegorical in their attitudes, the grandfather, for example, representing Big Business and Edith and her friends Liberalism. There was also the opinion that Rice had hinted at many problems but had failed to answer or shed light on them satisfactorily. "He has written a play on a subject concerning which he really has no ideas he wants to put forth," wrote Arthur Pollock (*BE*). And George Jean Nathan (*TBY*) took Rice to task for his obsession with infusing crusading ideas into his plays.

One of the controversial features of the play was the childbirth scene, in which only Edith's head was shown (through a hole cut in a black curtain) as she spoke in a monologue. Some people found the scene realistically harrowing, although it was done with restraint. Interestingly, actress Field was actually pregnant with her and Rice's second child during the run. Two months after the show closed, she gave birth.

Good jobs were contributed by Ann Thomas as Edith's wisecracking actress friend and by Blaine Cordner as the hospital's staff doctor. Joan Wetmore, Fredericka Going, Kenneth Tobey, and Ann Driscoll were also in the play.

(1) NEW MOON, THE [Musical Revival*] B: Oscar Hammerstein II, Frank Mandel, and Laurence Schwab; M: Sigmund Romberg; LY: Oscar Hammerstein II; D: John Pierce; P: Joseph S. Tushinsky; T: Carnegie Hall (OB); 8/18/42 (24)

A series of operettas produced by Joseph Tushinsky, who also conducted, included this 1928 standby. George Jean Nathan (*TBY*) took issue not merely with the shoddy revival but with the original work, which he said was as dull, corny, and musically derivative in 1928 as it seemed in 1942. He thereupon took issue with those critics who looked on *The New Moon* through nostalgia-filled eyes as a slightly faded version of a once-wonderful piece of work.

This is the show that offered such perennials as "Lover, Come Back to Me," "Softly, As in a Morning Sunrise," "Wanting You," "One Kiss," and "Stout-hearted Men," among others. The cast included Ruby Mercer as Marianne Beaunoir, Wilbur Evans as Robert Misson, Teddy Hart as Alexander, Gene Barry as Captain Duval, Everett West as Philippe, Doris Patston as Julie, and Hope Emerson as Clotilde. Baritone

Evans got the lion's share of the notices among the singing principals, but Hart did very well with the comic relief and was inadvertently funny when his wig fell off at one point and at others when he had to ad-lib while waiting for actors who had missed their entrances.

In general, the revival was considered as ill prepared as its predecessors in the series, *The Chocolate Soldier** and *The Merry Widow**. In Edgar Price's (*BC*) words, "Poorly rehearsed, the cast staggered through its lines and on several occasions noticeably missed cues that left them whispering for their proper words."

(2) D: José Ruben; CH: Charles Weidman; S: Oliver Smith; P: Perry Frank for the Belmont Operetta Company; T: City Center of Music and Drama; 5/17/44 (45)

This popular-price revival (the cheapest seats were $.75) was the opening show in a projected summer season of operetta revivals (called the Festival of Famous Operettas) at the City Center. The critics continued to pan the book as tiresome and seriously dated.

There was some disagreement over the quality of the production. Lewis Nichols (*NYT*) and Louis Kronenberger (*PM*), for example, found it inadequately directed and choreographed. The latter wrote, "It is . . . a thoroughly dull production, listlessly paced, indifferently staged, heavily acted and execrably danced." Most others agreed, but George Freedley (*NYMT*), who called it "bright and colorful," was one of several who approved the presentation. One of the few reasons to attend was to hear opera singer Dorothy Kirsten in the role of Marianne. Another fine singer, Earl Wrightson, was cast as Robert, while Johnny Morgan played the comic role of Alexander, Harold Gordon was Ribaud, Elizabeth Houston was Julie, Dorothy Ramsey was Clotilde, and John Hamill was Philippe. The principal dancers employed were Peter Hamilton and Zoya Leporsky.

NEW PRIORITIES OF 1943 [Revue] M/LY: Lester Lee and Jerry Seelen; D: Jean Le Seyeux; CH: Truly McGee; P: Clifford C. Fischer i/a/w Messrs. Shubert; T: Forty-sixth Street Theatre; 9/15/42 (54)

Another in a series of vaudevillelike revues produced by Clifford C. Fischer, this one following in the wake of *Priorities of 1942*. It had some name performers, including Henny Youngman, Bert Wheeler, Harry Richman, Carol Bruce, and the dog act called the Bricklayers that had been so popular in the earlier show. "The acts that wander onto [Fischer's] stage built nothing but a vague sense of boredom, even the famous dog number having lost its old magic," reported Rosamond Gilder (*TAM*). Louis Kronenberger (*PM*) announced that the show "fumbled and floundered for very long stretches, and only caught its stride for very short ones."

Wheeler (with deadpan stooge Hank Ladd) and Youngman (who was the program's MC) were the featured comics. Brooks Atkinson (*NYT*) described the latter as "the Broadway version of 'A Slow Train Through Arkansas'--a joke-book that can be purchased in old-fashioned railroad newsstands. The jokes run on at about thirty-five miles an hour, one leading directly to the next with a minimum of switching onto branch lines." Youngman stood at the mike with a slight grin and simply rattled off his gags. "If he doesn't slay you with the first, second or third joke, he will probably lay you out with the fourth or fifth," reported Atkinson. The comic also brought out his trademark violin between jokes. Slick and debonair Harry Richman was a faded and off-key version of himself in trying to put over "I Love a Parade" and other ditties, and Carol Bruce was another singing disappointment, even though she warbled "St. Louis Woman," "The Man I Love," and "Louisiana Purchase," which she had introduced on Broadway. Also on hand were the Acromaniacs, a comic tumbling team; dancers Harrison and Fisher, with a comically sexy travesty number called "Amphitryon 39"; burlesque terpsichorean Sally Keith, who dazzled with her twirling tassels; and others.

Some numbers were considered in poor taste, such as one in which a chorine's costume was auctioned off piece by piece by Richman to raise war-bond money. On opening night, toy manufacturer Louis Marx paid $25,000 to remove the final bit of the model's garment, a muff held over her "nadir," according to the appalled George Freedley (*NYHT*).

NEW WAY TO PAY OLD DEBTS, A [Dramatic Revival] A: Philip Massinger; D: Charles Pollachek; P: Equity Library Theatre; T: Hudson Park Branch of the New York Public Library (OB); 12/25/45 (4)

A showcase revival of the famous Jacobean melodrama, once an extremely popular piece in the repertoire of such colorful leading actors as Edmund Kean, but not seen locally for at least sixty years. The present low-budget showing with unknown players worked effectively in an arena arrangement, making the action as intimate as possible. The star role is the flamboyant Sir Giles Overreach, played here by Bernard Hoffman. George Freedley (*NYMT*), the only reviewer to show up, said that he "is a bigger man physically than I would contemplate (always remembering the great Edmund Kean) as Sir Giles. He has, however, considerable variety as an actor and is extremely acceptable in the part." Others involved included Paul Andor, Louise Lunden, Charles Pollachek, Muriel Gallick, and Rita Fredericks.

NEW YORK IDEA, THE [Dramatic Revival] A: Langdon Mitchell; D: Eliza Downing; S/L: Elizabeth Lehrman; C: Valerie Judd; P: On-Stage; T: 6 Fifth Avenue (OB); 8/17/48

On-Stage, a troupe of Off-Broadway semipros, was busy in the summer of 1948 with a series of revivals of famous old American plays, among them this 1906 semi-classic drawing-room comedy of manners (which originally had starred Minnie Maddern Fiske) about the increasing popularity of divorce among upper-class New Yorkers. The few critics in attendance differed in their assessments. Despite a humdrum revival, said Brooks Atkinson (*NYT*), the piece was enjoyable because "it is still pertinent, it is notably well constructed and more substantial than many of its witty successors." But Robert Garland (*NYJA*) argued that it "is neither a good play nor a good example of the playwriting of its period. . . . It is as dated as a dolman."

The rather wordy dialogue was a bit of a hassle for a company that had produced the piece with only four days of rehearsal. The company included Laurie Amidon as Grace Phillimore, Penny Chapman as Cynthia Karslake (the Fiske role), Tom Halli as Philip Phillimore, Marie Ryburn as Mrs. Phillimore, Scott Griffin as Matthew Phillimore, Frank Cameron as Jack Karslake, Lynn Biro as Vida Phillimore, and James Harwood as Sir Wilfred Cates-Darby.

The story is that of the recently divorced Cynthia's preparations to marry a judge, Philip Phillimore; of the judge's divorced wife's attraction to Cynthia's ex, John; of the delay in the wedding when Cynthia has cold feet; of her happiness in discovering that the judge's wife will not marry John, as she feared, but will wed an English gentleman, Sir Wilfred; and of the discovery that Cynthia and John are still in love and technically still married.

NEXT HALF HOUR, THE [Drama/Death/Family/Fantasy/Period/Sex/Youth] A: Mary Chase; D: George S. Kaufman; S: Edward Gilbert; C: Mary Percy Schenck; P: Max Gordon; T: Empire Theatre; 10/29/45 (8)

Mary Chase's first play after her smash hit *Harvey* was a big letdown. sighed Louis Kronenberger (*PM*) noted, "She has . . . written a play whose good things are infrequent and incidental, and whose weaknesses are ultimately crushing." More serious than her whimsical first play, it nevertheless was concerned with fanciful occurrences.

Fay Bainter was Margaret Brennan, a native Irishwoman living in the United States in 1913 and imbued with superstitious belief in her indigenous folklore. She believes that she has the power to foretell catastrophe, which is signalled by the shrieking of a banshee prior to someone's death; however, only she can hear it. She suspects that her nineteen-year-old son Pat (Jack Ruth) is heading for disaster because of his dalliance with a married woman (Thelma Schnee) and tries to head off trouble by blurting the story out to the woman's railroad-worker spouse (not seen), thinking that he will forgive Pat for his youth. When Margaret's bachelor brother (Art Smith) dies soon after, she thinks that it was his demise that triggered the banshee's wails. She sends her beloved younger son Barney (Conrad Janis) on an errand to prevent Pat from meeting with the woman, but the husband, thinking the boy to be Pat, murders him. Margaret learns that "the next half hour belongs to God" and not to human meddling with fate.

Not even George S. Kaufman's astute direction could provide the too sentimental and verbose play with the right mood of mysticism, suspense, or interesting action. It was "a long and tedious piece of business, relieved only intermittently by bursts of good acting," revealed Lewis Nichols (*NYT*). Kaufman had other concerns to sadden him at this time, because his wife Beatrice passed away during the rehearsal period.

Francis Compton, Pamela Rivers, Jean Adair, and Larry Oliver were among those back looking for work within a week.

NIGHT BEFORE CHRISTMAS, THE [Comedy/Business/Crime/Romance] A: Laura West and S. J. Perelman; D: Romney Brent; S: Boris Aronson; P: Courtney Burr; T: Morosco Theatre; 4/10/41 (22)

Mr. and Mrs. S. J. Perelman, the authors of this screwball trifle, could not provide it with the proper levity of tone or consistency of construction to guarantee it as an audience pleaser. It tells of a pair of comical safecrackers, Otis J. Faunce (Forrest Orr) and Ruby (George Mathews), who rent a luggage store on Sixth Avenue with the sole intent of having access to a basement wall adjoining a bank; their intent is to drill through the wall into the financial institution's coffers during the Christmas vacation. Meanwhile, their efforts are impeded by customers interested in the luggage they ostensibly sell; by the arrival of escaped convict Leo (Harry Bratsburg [Morgan]), who masterminded the scheme up at Sing Sing; and by a romance that is blossoming between Leo's gorgeous ex-girlfriend, Denny Costello (Phyllis Brooks, who quit the hit *Panama Hattie* to appear in this flop), and Byron (Herbert Nelson), the pharmacist down the block. At the end, the crooks blast through the wall only to find that they have opened the way to a delicatessen's storage room, demonstrated by their appearance covered in sausage links and potato salad. They luck out, though, when the bank president (William David) offers them $10,000 for their lease.

Louis Kronenberger (*PM*) opined, "Somehow *The Night Before Christmas* rambles and repeats itself without ever becoming funny." Ruth Weston and Louis Sorin were featured in supporting roles, and Shelley Winters (then spelled Winter) had the small role of Flora.

NIGHT OF LOVE [Musical/Music/Romance/Sex] B/LY: Rowland Leigh; M: Robert Stolz; SC: Lily Hatvany's play, *Tonight or Never**, as adapted by Fredric and Fanny Hatton; D: Barrie O'Daniels; S: Watson Barratt; C: Ernest Schrapps; P: J. J. Shubert; T: Hudson Theatre; 1/7/41 (7)

The original Hungarian play on which this operetta dud was based had--despite critical ennui--a healthy Broadway run in 1930; its musical adaptation lasted but a week. Brooks Atkinson (*NYT*) derided its formula mannerisms, Richard Lockridge (*NYS*) attacked the "vapidity" of the adaptation, and Richard Watts, Jr. (*NYHT*), said that it "sets new standards for dullness and ineptitude." The music, the book, the performances, and the decor were all given their share of the blame.

As in the source play, the plot concerns an opera singer (Helen Gleason) who needs to find someone to love before she can bring the proper ardor to her technically sound but emotionally arid singing. Assuming that the remedy is a certain handsome fellow (John Lodge) she assumes is a lothario, she spends a night of love with him, only to discover that he is a scout for the Metropolitan Opera. He signs her, they contemplate a future of beautiful music together, and she gets rid of her noble suitor (Robert Chisholm), who has never done much to stoke her fires.

Martha Errolle and Marguerite Namara were members of the company.

NIGHT WATCH IN SYRIA [Drama/Bible/Period/Religion] A/D: Alexander King; P: The Script Clinic; T: Malin Studio (OB); 1/4/43 (7)

Author-director Alexander King appeared before his play began to deliver an introductory talk and to hand out cough drops in hopes of averting distracting hacking noises from a potentially bronchial audience. His talk informed the audience of his dislike of biblical plays, costume dramas, and experimental theatre, all three of which were represented by his offering.

It was set in the time of Jesus, but the actors wore modern dress--the clothes seemed like the actors' own street dress--and spoke contemporary colloquial English. The setting was bare except for several tables and chairs, the lighting was makeshift, and the presentation was poorly rehearsed, as was made evident by the muffed dialogue.

King's subject was the effect of the Crucifixion on various persons in Jerusalem, such as the Roman soldiers, Mary Magdalene (Regina Moor), Lazarus (William Sanders), beggars, Peter (Harron Gordon), miscellaneous sailors, and Jesus' brothers (Bruce Marcus and Melvin Davis). Based closely on the Synoptic Gospels of the New Testament, the drama covers the events on the night of the Crucifixion. Mary Magdalene is the catalyst whose conversion to faith in Jesus' message and divinity leads unbelievers and skeptics to discover Jesus for themselves.

There was some discomfort in hearing the biblical tale expressed through such slang expressions as "knocking his block off" or referring to the driving of the moneylenders from the temple as "double crossing the poultry dealers." John Anderson (*NYJA*) concluded, moreover, that King "has taken a bold and even provocative idea and let it drift idly, almost aimlessly, through nine scenes."

NIGHTS OF WRATH (*Les Nuits de la Colère*) [Drama/French/Politics/War] A: Armand Salacrou; TR: Maria Piscator and John McGrew; M: Herbert Hertzfeld; D: Maria Piscator; S: Willis Knighton (projections: Fred Wunch); L: Doris Einstein; P: Dramatic Workshop of the New School for Social Research; T: President Theatre (OB); 11/30/47 (26)

The first New York staging of a play by leading modern French dramatist Salacrou was a semiprofessional version of a work concerning the French resistance originally done in France by Jean-Louis Barrault a year earlier. The credits said that the piece was "produced and directed under the supervision of Erwin Piscator," although his wife was billed as having "staged" it.

A lengthy piece of considerable interest, it was given an inventive staging and decor using Piscator's usual revolving stage. The stained-glass projections, however, disturbed George Freedley (*NYMT*) as being inappropriate. The actors were not fully up to the difficult play's demands, but the work was considered worthy. Edba. (*V*) observed that this was "intensely gripping drama, well directed and adequately presented by the semipro cast." It grew tedious in its second act, thought Brooks Atkinson (*NYT*), but Salacrou's "topic is real, his characters vigorous and his attitude valid; and the improvised form of his story is absorbing and illuminating." The piece takes particular issue with those who, in 1944, during the Nazi occupation of France, remained neutral, being neither for the resistance or collaborationists. In such times, goes Salacrou's thesis, those not with you must be assumed to be against you. In the course of the play various non-realistic devices are employed, including the appearance of three dead men, an *attentiste* or neutral, a collaborationist, and a resistance fighter, who explain their political positions during the conflict.

The focal character is Bernard Bazire (Scott Hale), whose long-time friend has been wounded during a resistance act of destroying a German supply train. Bazire is a middle-of-the-roader, not wishing to get involved nor to endanger his family; he has his wife seek a doctor. The man she returns with is a collaborationist; instead of being helped, the wounded man is tortured by the Gestapo and killed, as are other resistance fighters.

NINE GIRLS [Drama/Crime/Medicine/Politics/Sports/Theatre/University/Western/Women/Youth] A: Wilfred H. Pettitt; D: Reginald Denham; S: John Root; P: A. H. Woods; T: Longacre Theatre; 1/13/43 (5)

A cast made up of nine young actresses, all of them supposed to be sorority sisters at West Lake University, floundered in this "singularly obvious and unexciting" (Howard Barnes [*NYHT*]) two-act murder melodrama set during a weekend party in the girls' clubhouse high in the Sierra Nevadas. One of the girls, Mary (Adele Longmire), is a killer from a working-class background who has murdered a friend because of social and romantic jealousy. (The murder is reported over the radio.) She uses prussic acid to poison the sweet and trusting Alice (Barbara Bel Geddes), who knows of the first murder from a letter she receives, and tries to make the death look like a suicide. Mary is foiled in a third cover-up attempt, this one on the life of her best friend Eve (K. T. Stevens), who has launched an investigation of the slayings and figured them out. She and Mary have a rough-and-tumble fight, but Mary kills herself with some leftover prussic acid.

Verbosity, lack of suspense, and a poorly conceived murderess who acts more from maliciousness than from growing fear of being found out contributed to the play's demise. Louis Kronenberger (*PM*) moaned, "Despite a few interesting moments, *Nine Girls* is confused and unconvincing in the crucial matter of characterization, is inexpert in its stagecraft, and utterly commonplace in its writing."

There were promising performances, however, from Irene Dailey as the comically athletic Shot Put, Maxine Stuart as a medical student (who has poison in her bag), Kayo Copeland and Marilyn Erskine as chattering pledges, Ruth K. Hill as a political radical, and Mary McCormack as a would-be actress named Glamor Pants whose recitation of Lady Macbeth's sleepwalking scene almost unnerves the murderess enough to give herself away. The play's title before reaching New York was *This Little Hand*.

NINE MONTH MIDNIGHT [Drama] A: Phil Bard; D: Lucia Victor; DS: David Berman; P: Robert O'Byrne and Gloria Monty for the Abbe Practical Workshop; T: Master Institute Theatre (OB); 2/17/49 (2)

A cloudily symbolic drama about a blind war veteran (William Kester) who lost his vision in the invasion of Italy. He is now trying to confront his situation as he contemplates suicide in the predawn hours. The piece, about which little more is known, was given a relatively acceptable production by this group of semipros. The company included Richard Venture in the role of a wandering poet.

"Much of the drama . . . was painfully pretentious," reported J. P. S. (*NYT*), who referred to "large quantities of symbolism in an inconclusive plot."

NINETEENTH HOLE OF EUROPE, THE [Comedy-Drama/Irish/Literature/Politics/Prostitution/Religion/Romance/Sex/War] A: Vivian Connell; M: George Bassman; D: Bill Ross; S: Lester Polakov; C: Forrest Thayer; P: Invitational Series of the Experimental Theatre, Inc., u/t/a/o the American National Theatre and Academy; T: Lenox Hill Playhouse (OB); 3/27/49 (4)

This experimental antiwar play by a respected Irish author had been around for some time, and various people (including critic Brooks Atkinson [*NYT*]) had shown considerable interest in it, but the work as produced proved seriously inadequate. "A wordy, repetitious and static drama that fails to develop its provocative theme or hold up as theatre," was Hobe.'s (*V*) negative assessment. Richard Watts, Jr. (*NYP*), thought that apart from the high mindedness of the theme and a glint of good writing here and there, the play was "muddled, verbose, pretentious and curiously dull and pointless." Most believed that the $500 production was on as depressing a level as the writing.

The play is set in the future following a war that has destroyed Europe and turned it into a plague-infested disaster area placed by the rest of the world under quarantine. Rats are constant enemies, and the few people still alive drink moonshine liquor to keep their spirits up. Some of these people, huddled together at a desolate waterfront, include a cross-section of aristocrats and commoners, ranging from a former king (Oswald Marshall) and queen (Nina Varela) to a whore (Martha Hodge). Another important role is that of Jude, a sad old royal nurse (Margaret Wycherly). Through a considerable amount of rhetoric, the play exposes the demagoguery of leaders in politics and religion. Among the characters is a pacifist poet named Mark (Alexander March), who proclaims the thesis that reason, not war, must prevail. Circumstances, however, drive even him to violence--he kills a wicked moonshiner (Bern Hoffman)--in the interests of justice. He and an innocent girl, Nada (Barbara Ames), decide to put their idealism to the test in helping to create a new world together.

Kurt Kasznar played a priest, and Lee Marvin played a soldier (receiving good reviews in his second New York role). Although generally panned, the play did receive a warm notice from George Freedley (*NYMT*), who deemed it "a great theatrical experience." Atkinson, who thought highly of the play's ideas, despite its gabbiness, was vastly disappointed with much of the acting.

(1) NO EXIT (***Huis Clos***) [Drama/Death/Fantasy/French/Homosexuality/Hotel/Journalism/Politics/Romance/Sex] A: Jean-Paul Sartre; AD: Paul Bowles; D: John Huston; S/L: Frederick Kiesler; P: Herman Levin and Oliver Smith; T: Biltmore Theatre; 11/26/46 (31)

Sartre's "philosophical melodrama," which subsequently became an international classic of the postwar period. The author was then the most talked-about thinker in France because of his espousal of the new philosophy of existentialism, which was incorporated in this drama. Although it received some approving reviews and was chosen as the best new foreign drama by the Drama Critics Circle, the production was unsuccessful, despite direction by John Huston and a cast consisting of French star Claude Dauphin (in his Broadway debut) as Cradeau (generally known in other versions as Joseph Garcin), Peter Kass as the bellboy, Annabella as Inez, and Ruth Ford as Estelle. The play is a long one-act first published as *Les Autres* (*The Others*) and also known in English by other titles, such as *In Camera* and *Vicious Circle*. Before being shown here, it had been seen in various European countries, and was still running in Paris.

The hour-and-a-half play's setting is hell, represented unconventionally as a shabbily ugly hotel room with red and green plush sofas and a bricked-up window to which entrance is made via doors operated by a seedy bellboy. The three characters--strangers in life--consigned to spend eternity here must do so without the usual amenities of doors, windows, mirrors, bells, toothbrushes, and the like. Even sleep has been banished. As the action progresses, the characters learn that they are doomed to forever judge one another and themselves and that "hell is other people." In life, Cradeau was a pacifist reporter who was also a collaborationist, Inez was a sadistically inclined, lesbian postal worker, and Estelle was an attractive, vain, and nymphomaniacal American socialite. An occasional glimpse is permitted them of earth, where they were each guilty of serious emotional and physical crimes. They are also locked in an insoluble erotic triangle wherein Inez longs for Estelle and Estelle for Cradeau, while Cradeau, despite his wish to satisfy Estelle's cravings, is impotent because of self-doubt. Most of their time is spent in arguing with one another or in remembering their guilty deeds, such as when Cradeau sadistically forced his wife to serve coffee to him and his mistress in bed; or when Inez drove her cousin to his death because of her love for the cousin's wife, and of the women's deaths when the wife killed them by turning on the gas; or when Estelle committed adultery, killed her bastard baby, and was responsible for her lover's suicide. Cradeau's pacifist idealism is brought into question, and it is revealed that he was executed for trying to escape fighting in the war. He needs Estelle's faith in his heroism, but Estelle's positive attitude is not genuine, stemming from her erotic desire for him. Cradeau cannot satisfy her because he needs to resolve his doubts about his courage. Cradeau now must get Inez to believe in his heroic ideals. He tries to argue that he could not demonstrate his ideals because he died too soon, but Inez rebuts his argument. When Estelle again attempts to seduce Cradeau, as retaliation against Inez, Cradeau once more is impotent because of Inez's reminders of his cowardice. The three finally realize that they have an eternity of mutual suffering before them.

Brooks Atkinson (*NYT*) called *No Exit* "a fascinating and macabre play . . . played with horrible logic and pitiless skill." He and many others felt, however, that it could have been ten or fifteen minutes shorter. Also like others, he appreciated Bowles's version of the original, although John Mason Brown (*SR*) argued that the "intermittent colloquialisms" annoyed him. Atkinson believed that Sartre's point was that "man is alone in this world; he is responsible to his own will and decisions; no one can save him from himself." Rosamond Gilder (*TAM*) wrote that in this play, "we glimpse a state of mind, a stage of being, different from anything exhibited on our own stage--a kind of ruthless intellectual passion, a clarity, an intensity that is extraordinarily arresting." Brown, who was impressed by Kiesler's nightmarish setting, which suggested "a padded cell . . . as constricting as a straitjacket," acknowledged some of the play's drawbacks, but found it much better theatre than most of the plays then current. "At least it abandons the familiar stencils and grapples with an unusual idea. A mind is at work in it; a mind, alert, audacious and original, which has been touched by the agony of the modern world." But George Jean Nathan (*NYJA*) decided that the work was "largely bosh, since its platitudinous thesis that the individual is a unit in this world and is responsible for his salvation to himself alone is dramatized in characters who are such arbitrary, open-and-shut setups that the argument becomes one-sided almost to the point of caricature." Nathan also pointed to some of the philosophical contradictions he depicted in Sartre's ideation. Still, he thought Sartre's dramaturgy "interesting enough."

(2) [Dramatic Revival] D: Frank Corsaro; P: On-Stage; T: Cherry Lane Theatre (OB); 6/9/47 (38)

An unheralded, practically unreviewed revival of the play by a group of Off-Broadway semiprofessionals who offered a busy season of productions on Commerce Street. The bellboy was Glen Alvey, Garcin was Alexis Solomos, Estelle was Sally Sigler, and Inez was Brenda Ericson.

Nathan (*TBY*) took the occasion to belittle Sartre's alleged profundity, calling the play's various philosophical snippets "platitudes" and reminding readers that the theme, "Hell is other people," was used by Nikolai Gogol, who declared, "Hell is not oneself but others." Of the production he said not a word. For some reason, director Corsaro (in *Maverick*) remembered Nathan having given the production a "glowing notice (my first)." Corsaro also recalled that actor Solomos--"a sawed-off Charles Boyer from Greece"--had a strange phobia and was always relieved when Corsaro was in the theatre, "for he could be reassured I would run backstage to tell him if his trousers had fallen down around his ankles unexpectedly."

(3) D: Robert T. Eley; P: New York Repertory Group; T: Cherry Lane Theatre (OB); 7/6/48

The Cherry Lane was again the home for a revival of the play, but this time under another group that found in *No Exit* a promising piece to produce on a low budget. In the view of the sole critic attending, Thomas R. Dash (*WWD*), "*No Exit* . . . , despite its frenzy of passions, . . . tends to monotony and is interesting primarily for the author's macabre ideas and his scourging style of writing." He castigated the production for its reliance on shouting and encouraged "modulation" to create "greater subtlety, poignancy, and effectiveness."

Jack Burkhart played Garcin, Beatrice Arthur was Estelle, and Eleanor Fitzpatrick ("the best of the group," wrote Dash) was Inez. Arthur was cautioned that she could improve "if she did not sneer so insistently."

NO FOR AN ANSWER [Musical/Alcoholism/Labor/Politics/Romance] B/M/LY: Marc Blitzstein; D: William E. Watts; DS: Howard Bay; T: Mecca Temple; 1/5/41 (3)

Three Sunday evening performances at the future City Center were given of this interesting experimental opera that was critiqued by the daily drama critics. Brooks Atkinson (*NYT*) assured his readers that this was really more of a "music drama" than an opera; many members of the cast were well-known "straight" actors.

Because of a lack of funds, the work was staged without sets against a background of dark curtains and within a framework of exposed lights that kept varying the mood. A few highly selective props assisted in defining locales. The musical accompaniment, reminiscent of Blitzstein's *The Cradle Will Rock**, was confined to the composer himself playing the piano in the pit. The simplicity of the event, said Atkinson, underlined its "sincerity. It is infinitely more dramatic than a full stage setting could be."

Like *The Cradle Will Rock*, this was a left-wing-slanted, prolabor effort concerning the efforts to organize a union by a group of summer resort workers in the postsummer season when the workers are left stranded. (On opening night some reactionary types in the balcony tried to disrupt the performance and not only stirred others to shout, "Throw 'em out!" but caused some of the actors to muff their lines.) The workers are aided by a Greek-American lunch-counter proprietor (Martin Wolfson) whose son (Robert Simon) is a union organizer. The son is also romantically involved with a girl (Norma Green). They also are assisted by a wealthy but alcoholic young man (Lloyd Gough) married to the district congressman's sister (Olive Deering), who gradually becomes a staunch supporter of the workers. The conflict is with the resort managements who conspire with the police to have the organizers arrested for the unlicensed selling of alcohol. Even worse, the leading organizer is slain and the Diogenes Social Club, the workers' meeting place, is torched. But the congressman's sister vows to fight tooth and nail for the workers' cause.

The dramaturgic materials were deemed to be thin, but Blitzstein's powerful score made the event memorable and the characters' problems emotionally vivid. Especially potent were the rousing choral numbers featuring the workers at the social club. There was considerable dimensionality to the various characters, although they remained symbolic figures designed to illustrate Blitzstein's thesis. Blitzstein also succeeded in writing songs that stemmed naturally from the circumstances and dialogue. "Mr. Blitzstein achieved in this production . . . a kind of beauty and excitement which the theatre too often lacks," avowed Rosamond Gilder (*TAM*). "Like a sketch or cartoon, it achieved strength by the use of simple lines and the elimination of detail. Like a car toon, also, it avoided subtlety, driving its message home with sledge hammer blows, 'insisting' that America remember its ideals." George Freedley (*NYMT*) found the piece "a curious combination of hard-boiled language and thinking and the sheerest kind of sentimentality," but he admired most of it.

Cast members included Alfred Ryder, Curt Conway, Eda Reiss, Martin Ritt, and Carol Channing in her New York debut. Channing, playing a night club singer, got a special notice from John Mason Brown (*NYP*), who said that she "shared with the composer a round of applause for her singing of 'I'm Simply Fraught With You,' a burlesque of a sophisticated popular song."

The Dramatists Guild and Actors Equity, together with such well-known sponsors as Lillian Hellman, Herman Shumlin, and Arthur Kober, permitted the show as an "experiment" to see if the presentation could lead to a fuller production.

NO MORE LADIES [Dramatic Revival*] A: A. E. Thomas; D: Norman MacDonald; P: Equity Library Theatre; T: Hudson Park Branch of the New York Public Library (OB); 2/7/45

In 1934 this had been a successful comedy starring Melvyn Douglas and Ruth Weston. It was now revived by the showcase branch of Actors Equity as one of thirty-seven free offerings in 1944-1945. The play had been updated, one of the characters was dropped, and the time was moved to the present. A poor production could not hide the play's innate delights. Especially distressing was the awkward direction, with actors clumped in groups and often masking one another.

Booth Colman, a great-grandson of actor Edwin Booth, played Lord Moulton and was the best thing in the show. The play had opened earlier at the George Bruce Branch of the New York Public Library in Harlem before moving to the Hudson Park Branch.

NO WAY OUT [Drama/Business/Crime/Gambling/Marriage/Medicine] A: Owen Davis; D: Robert Keith and Owen Davis; S: Edward Gilbert; C: Ernest Schrapps; P: Robert Keith; T: Cort Theatre; 10/30/44 (8)

Another opus from the fecund pen of Owen Davis, this one set in the Old Trent Mansion in a large city in upstate New York. "The truth is," said Howard Barnes (*NYHT*), "the new offering is unpleasant, plot-heavy and completely unresolved." George Jean Nathan (*TBY*) thought it "utterly worthless." It offered Robert Keith a juicy role, so he produced and codirected it.

The play deals superficially with the issue of medical ethics in its story of the secretly sinister but outwardly charming Dr. Niles Hilliard (Keith), who withheld treatment from his wife's late husband so the man would die and he could marry the wealthy widow, Cora (Viola Frayne). After he has blown her fortune in stock-market speculation (a fact of which she is ignorant), he seeks to gain another fortune from his wife's heiress daughter, Barbara Trent (Nancy Marquand), who is suffering from a strange glandular ailment called Addison's disease. He withholds her medicine through a deliberate misdiagnosis of the disease so that she will die and he can gain control of her riches. (His life is being threatened for a large sum he owes.) Since Cora trusts Dr. Hilliard completely, it looks as if he will get his way. The only ones to distrust him are the honorable black butler, Napoleon (John Marriott), and another physician, Dr. Enid Karley (film actress Irene Hervey, in her Broadway debut), a guest who is the sister of Barbara's fiancé Bob (Jerome P. Thor). Having secretly diagnosed the girl's condition, she suspects what Dr. Hilliard is up to but thinks that her belief in the Hippocratic Oath prevents her from exposing another doctor's questionable methods. Finally, she realizes where lies her duty and manages to expose the doctor, and the plot rumbles to an end.

Davis had not truly explored the implications of his theme, having opted instead for a typical melodramatic treatment. The play was considered glib, facile, and clichéd. Louis Kronenberger (*PM*) said that it "smacks theatrically of the Dark Ages, or at least the gaslight era. . . . The plot is fabricated, the characters are cut from whole cloth, and the dialogue is so stilted that far better actors . . . would have trouble getting it said." The players included Viola Roache, Jean Casto, and Donald Foster.

NOT IN OUR STARS [Comedy/Business/Family/Politics/Romance] A: George H. Corey; P: Experimental Theatre, Inc.; T: Biltmore Theatre; 4/25/41 (1)

Because the Experimental Theatre was organized to produce plays primarily as a showcase for writing and performance talent, with none of the artists paid for their services, Actors Equity restricted its productions to a single matinee performance (albeit at a Broadway playhouse). To some, this production of George H. Corey's comedy about an Irish-American family in New York City was deemed sufficient excuse for the Experimental Theatre to be given a new lease on life, following its unsuccessful efforts with *The Trojan Women* and *Steps Leading Up*.

Reminiscent of Sean O'Casey's *Juno and the Paycock**, the play was mildly entertaining, despite a clumsily expository first act and the need for a considerable amount of tightening throughout. The latter two acts had such comic energy for Brooks Atkinson (*NYT*) that he could not help appreciating such ingredients as its "racy characters, inventive story, pungent dialogue." Others were less impressed, Richard Lockridge (*NYS*) noting that even with doctoring he saw no chance of the play going beyond "dull competence." Despite an alleged interest in it by several important producers and even by a film company, the play never had a subsequent life on stage or celluloid.

The piece was performed in the appropriately seedy basement apartment setting of the hit comedy, *My Sister Eileen*, then playing at the Biltmore. The Hoolihan family is having a hard time making ends meet, their chief income deriving from their work as janitors and rent collectors in a bank-owned building. The son (Walter Burke), really a decent fellow, has just been paroled from reform school, but his parole is contingent on a family member holding down a steady job until the boy can get a position of his own. The pretty daughter (Frances Reid), engaged to a would-be policeman (Leo Needham), works part-time as a waitress; the fiancé's chances for a cop's job will be enhanced if the family drums up enough votes for the local alderman (Loring Smith). The braggart father (Harold Vermilyea) is a garrulous, get-rich-quick schemer, and the mother (Ruth Thane McDevitt) is the family anchor. The major crisis is resolved when a wealthy uncle, the undertaker Cousin Willie (Hallam Bosworth), is finally convinced to provide the funds with which the family can open a sand and gravel business.

John Ireland was in the cast.

NOW I LAY ME DOWN TO SLEEP [Comedy/Romance/Sea/Sex/War] A: Elaine Ryan; SC: Ludwig Bemelmans's novel of the same name; D: Hume Cronyn; P: Nancy Stern III and George Nichols; S: Wolfgang Roth; C: John Derro; L: Richard Bernstein; T: Broadhurst Theatre; 3/2/50 (44)

A fifty-some-odd-character, thirteen-scene, picaresque comedy set in Biarritz, on board a Greek freighter, and in Ecuador. It starred the married team of Fredric

March and Florence Eldridge and introduced Charles Chaplin, Jr., to Broadway. Opinions on March's acting were divided, but most believed that Eldridge was superior. The critics felt that adapting a play from a novel by Bemelmans was loaded with difficulties because of that author's idiosyncratic style. Many said, therefore, that the Marches' vehicle, which employed scenery resembling Bemelmans's drawings, while occasionally quite interesting, was too loose-limbed and diffuse and its characters too sketchily drawn for popular consumption. William Hawkins (*NYWT*) thought the material "pretty weird, and despite its nature, not too clinical. On the other hand, it is monotonous and not very funny." Richard Watts, Jr. (*NYP*), remarked, "The proper lightness of touch was almost altogether missing, and the fun was but rarely forthcoming." The result was "a curiously pointless play." On the minority plus side was Howard Barnes (*NYHT*), who rejoiced that the adaptation was "gay, lusty and full of strange meaning. . . . The general tenor of the proceedings is enchanting."

The offbeat piece concerns a vain, swaggering, fabulously rich, food-loving, skirt-chasing, epileptic Ecuadorian called His Excellency, General Leonidas Erosa (March), who dresses in elaborate military and other garb and keeps a vast entourage. Most important of the latter is Miss Leonora Graves (Eldridge), a prim and prudish, very British governess whom he rescued twenty years earlier from a suicide attempt in the Thames. She has been in love with him all this while, although he always looks elsewhere for his sexual dalliances. With the outbreak of war imminent, the life-loving general departs by ship with his entourage for his native Ecuador, but the death-loving governess insists on taking along a coffin. In Ecuador, the general is buried by an earthquake in an underground cavern, where he has a subterranean swimming pool. With him are his chef (Henry Lascoe) and Polish refugee valet (Milton Parsons); a rescue mission tries to dig them out. Nearly a month later, as they are reached, the general has an epileptic fit and dies by drowning in his swimming pool. Miss Graves is left with the illegitimate baby of a semiretarded Indian girl, Chimene (Irene Moore), who had been impregnated by the general, but who was killed in the postquake panic.

The company included Stefan Schnabel, Helen Seamon, Rick Jason, Booth Colman, Lili Valenty, Gregory Morton, Jacqueline Dalya, Roy Poole, and many others, most in multiple roles.

O

O MISTRESS MINE [Comedy/British/Family/Politics/Romance/Sex/Youth] A: Terence Rattigan; D: Alfred Lunt; S: Robert Davison; C: (gowns) Molyneux; P: Theatre Guild and John C. Wilson; T: Empire Theatre; 1/23/46 (452)

Terence Rattigan's lightweight domestic comedy--chosen as one of the ten best plays of the season--had been produced during the V-2 bombing in wartime London as *Love in Idleness*, with Alfred Lunt and Lynn Fontanne in the leads. It was meant to divert theatregoers' minds from the destruction going on about them. The piece was then performed for the GIs in their European camps following the Allied victory. When it arrived on Broadway, the stars were the same but the title different. It rang up a robust number of performances before embarking on a lengthy national tour.

The Lunts turned the piece into a delightful romp for their own delicious talents. The run epitomized the Lunts' extraordinarily disciplined approach to keeping a popular production fresh and exciting. According to Lawrence Langner's *The Magic Curtain*, just before the play was about to close, Lunt said to juvenile actor Dick (formerly Dickie) Van Patten, "I have a new idea for this scene. I think it will improve it. We have one more chance to try it before we close the play."

Lunt played Sir John Fletcher, a wealthy British cabinet minister, married to a worthless and unfaithful woman (Ann Lee) who refuses to divorce him, and living stylishly in 1944 with the charming widow Olivia Brown (Fontanne) in a Westminster house. The widow's seventeen-year-old son Michael (Dick Van Patten), a disciple of socialist Harold Laski, returns from Canada, where he was sent for safety's sake when considerably younger. He forces a rift between his mother and the minister because of his holier-than-thou moral and political ideas; he is offended not only by the immoral liaison but by the minister's conservative ideas. Olivia and Michael move into a simple flat in Baron's Court, but when the son matures over the period of several months and falls in love himself, his manner toward his mother's alliance greatly softens. Sir John arrives to offer his hand in legal marriage to Olivia, announcing that he will divorce Lady Fletcher regardless of the consequences to his position.

The play's many weaknesses and flaws were especially evident when the Lunts were not present, which, fortunately, was infrequent. Rosamond Gilder (*TAM*) judged the piece "a smooth, gay, highly polished vehicle for their very special high jinks. The Great Lovers of the American theatre have never been in better form, never more beguiling and deft." John Mason Brown (*SR*) rejected the opinions of those, such as George Jean Nathan (*TBY*), who dismissed the play as beneath the Lunts. (Nathan said that the play was "minus invention and wit.") He, instead, approved it because "its unimportance is the point of Mr. Rattigan's play, and one of the sources of its pleasures." He preferred to think of it in terms of the opportunities it afforded the stars and the laughter it stimulated among the spectators. According to Lewis Nichols (*NYT*), "They build up to jokes, snap their fingers, and the jokes seem hilarious. They take part of *O Mistress Mine* as high comedy, part as farce, and they are not too high above burlesque to use that on occasion."

The play was really more Fontanne's than Lunt's (it had been created with Gertrude Lawrence in mind); he had what was basically a supporting role, but he did not care, he said. Maurice Zolotow quoted him in *Stagestruck*: "Sometimes Lynn has the play, and sometimes it's my play." Lunt, however, was preoccupied as the director, and he did an enormous amount of work to get the script into shape and to build up his role. According to B. A. Young's *The Rattigan Version*, the actor would chip away at the play in terms of what would work for an audience and what would not. Rattigan remembered Lunt's method: "Sir John Fletcher, the minister, that was Alfred's part, well, isn't he a little brutal here? And my, but he was a dreadful reactionary, and in this passage here he was such a disagreeable Tory, and 'they won't like that, you know.' And he'd lose the audience in this scene here." Ultimately, the script was transformed into a vehicle for the stars, and Lunt's role was as much a star turn as Fontanne's. Even after opening in New York, the Lunts continued to make revisions.

The Broadway run was suspended for a six-week period at one point when Lunt had to have a kidney-stone operation. This cost the production $100,000. It was his continuing weakness that brought the run to an end, not a diminution of audience interest. Still, the Lunts took the play on tour and their combined time with it in London, New York, and on the road made it the longest run of their careers. As Jared Brown noted in *The Fabulous Lunts*, Lunt would later declare, "*O Mistress Mine* was the biggest money-maker we were ever in. We never played to an empty seat, and we never got a good notice on it, either." The stars were ably supported by such actors as Esther Mitchell, Marie Paxton, and Margery Maude.

OBSESSION (***Monsieur Lambertier*; *Jealousy***) [Dramatic Revival*] A: Louis Verneuil; AD: Jane Hinton; D: Reginald Denham; S/L: Stewart Chaney; C: (gowns) Adrian; P: Homer Curran i/a/w Russell Lewis and Howard Young; T: Plymouth Theatre; 10/1/46 (31)

A new adaptation of a French boulevard drama that had been seen on Broadway in a 1928 Eugene Walter version called *Jealousy*. The play's most unusual feature was its reliance on only two characters, originally played by Fay Bainter (as Valerie) and John Halliday (as Maurice) and now interpreted by Eugenie Leontovich and Basil Rathbone. The principal revision, said some, was that the French heroine had been made a Russian, renamed Nadya. Brooks Atkinson (*NYT*) felt that the new version treated the subject more seriously than its predecessor. Otherwise, the story--about a jealous bridegroom who murders his bride's former lover on the night they arrive home from their wedding--remained much as it had been eighteen years previously.

Rathbone and Leontovich provided what most (George Jean Nathan [*TBY*] was among the exceptions) considered dignified performances, although the actress's heavy accent was not much helped by a serious cold on opening night. Apart from its two-character stunt value, few critics saw much to salute in the production, which had begun on the West Coast and had toured the country as it made its way to Broadway. "In the act of being ingenious," reported Louis Kronenberger (*PM*), "the author forgets to be anything much else." Several questioned its premise of a man who does not express his jealousy until after he has married, although he already he has lived with his bride for a long period, and, said Bron. (*V*), "Its talkiness and many dreary stretches militate against its success."

O'DANIEL [Drama/Journalism/Military/Politics/Romance/War] A: John Savacool and Glendon Swarthout; M: Alex North; D: Paul Crabtree; S/L: Herbert Brodkin; P: Experimental Theatre, Inc., i/a/w the Theatre Guild; T: Princess Theatre; 2/23/47 (5)

The Experimental Theatre, Inc., was active in 1946-1947 with a series of five-performance showings of new plays, most of which were not critically approved. One example was *O'Daniel*, set over a time period ranging from 1943 to 1952 and dealing with the rise to the presidency of an unscrupulously ambitious former GI. The person in question is named Dan (Walter Coy), who, from 1943 to 1945, served in Italy, where he opportunistically obtained self-serving jobs. Following his stint, he becomes the publisher of a reactionary GI pulp magazine designed to stir up its disillusioned postwar readers against the government. He is so successful that in 1948 he has organized 15 million veterans into a powerful fascistic voting bloc destined to gain political control. The oratorically gifted demagogue is propelled into power as the Republican nominee in 1952 and seems destined to become a dictatorial chief executive in 1953. Set against him through this fable as a sort of moral mirror is the wealthy but extremely decent girl, Alex (Anne Burr), he loves and marries.

Some critics thought that the playwrights showed promise for the future, although the present "experimental" work was inadequate by Broadway standards. It was written in an episodic style that reminded George Jean Nathan (*TBY*) of the living newspapers. However, Nathan argued that the writers "have simply thrown their theme in pieces at an audience instead of dramatizing it as a whole." *O'Daniel* had a scarifying theme and some powerful scenes, contended Brooks Atkinson (*NYT*), but the work was weakened by a failure to come to firm grips with the complex central role, a much-echoed sentiment. "The character analysis of Dan is not wholly clear in either idea or form. Certainly it is garrulous."

Performers involved included Jack Manning, Royal Raymond, William Munroe, Billy M. Greene, Rudi Bond, Norman Budd, Keene Crockett, and Robert P. Lieb.

ODDS ON MRS. OAKLEY, THE [Comedy/Gambling/Journalism/Marriage/Sex/Sports] A: Harry Segall; D: Arthur Sircom; S: Frederick Fox; P: Robert Reud; T: Cort Theatre; 10/2/44 (24)

"A silly and incompetent farce" (Ward Morehouse [*NYS*]) about newspaperman Oliver Oakley (John Archer, in his Broadway bow) and his ex-wife Susan (Joy Hodges), whose divorce agreement--they were married but a year--allows for each to take possession in turn for three months at a time of Fanny, a racehorse they won in a raffle. As Susan's racetrack bum of a father (Morton L. Stevens) soon discovers, Fanny (who never appears) wins purses for Susan but either finishes last or does not run for Oliver. Susan is not pleased with this because she would like to get back with Oliver, not widen the breach. A gambling syndicate soon capitalizes on the months of Susan's ownership and does what it can to keep the couple apart. The gamblers suspect that Fanny's winning has something to do with keeping Susan celibate. But Susan decides to lose her chastity so that the horse will lose and she can win back Oliver. She bets another racehorse owner (Bruce MacFarlane) that if Fanny loses she will sleep with him. Fanny loses, but the other man chooses to be sportsmanlike about claiming the spoils, and Susan and Oliver get together again.

"An unusually dismal farce," rasped Wilella Waldorf (*NYP*). "One of those ponderous little jokes," frowned Rosamond Gilder (*TAM*). "Talky, cumbersome, silly and dull," yawned Lewis Nichols (*NYT*). Hildegarde Halliday and Allen Kearns were trapped in this piece that earlier had held such titles as *It Runs in the Family*, *Fanny*, and *Our Fanny*.

(1) OEDIPUS REX (*Oidipous Tyrannos*) [Dramatic Revival*] A: Sophocles; TR: William Butler Yeats; D: James Light; P: Readers Theatre; T: Majestic Theatre; 12/16/45 (2)

James Light, Joel Schenker, and Henry G. Alsberg, calling themselves the Readers Theatre, were the founders of a group formed to promote the simplified presentation of seldom-produced classical dramas through a technique that would gain in popularity in the postwar years, although mainly on college campuses. When it was used professionally, it was more often than not in the form of what came to be called staged readings, usually as a means of inexpensively trying out new scripts. For its production of *Oedipus Rex* the group used no sets or costumes, the lines were read from scripts in the actors' hands, and the movement was minimal. The lack of costuming robbed the event of the illusion that a radio performance might have conjured up.

There was a wide disparity in acting styles among Blanche Yurka's Jocasta, Frederic Tozere's Oedipus, William Adams's Creon, Harry Irvine's Tiresias, Art Smith's herdsman, Robert Harris's first messenger, Martin Wolfson's priest, and Frederic Downs's second messenger. A single actor, William Hughes, was the chorus, and Bram Nossen was the Chorus Leader.

The presentation was preceded by an explanation provided by Eugene O'Neill, Jr. "As an experiment," wrote Lewis Nichols (*NYT*), "the performances . . . could be called interesting, although as an hour or two in the theatre it seemed somewhat less than satisfactory." George Jean Nathan (*TBY*) concurred: "The plan put into motion here is a mongrel one, and will not serve."

(2) [OEDIPUS] and **THE CRITIC** L: John Sullivan; P: Theatre, Inc. i/a/w the Old Vic Company; T: Century Theatre; 5/20/46 (8)
Oedipus TR: William Butler Yeats; M: Anthony Hopkins; D: Michel Saint-Denis; S: John Piper; C: Marie-Hélène Dasté; *The Critic* [Dramatic Revival*] A: Richard Brinsley Sheridan; D: Miles Malleson; CH: (fight) John Copley; S/C: Tanya Moiseiwitsch

The Old Vic Company, in its first American tour, had pleased New York with its opening productions of the two parts of *Henry IV**, principally because of the acting of artistic directors Laurence Olivier and Ralph Richardson. It was less successful with its *Uncle Vanya**, but achieved its crowning glory with this unusual presentation of *Oedipus* on the same bill with Sheridan's 1778 satirical burlesque about the theatre. Olivier's remarkable versatility in playing the title role in the tragedy and the hilarious Mr. Puff in the comedy helped build the legend surrounding this giant of the contemporary stage. The feat came to be referred to as "Oedipuff." Most critics raved about the jointly presented plays, but George Jean Nathan (*TBY*) was less impressed. He noted that "without Olivier to spark them they would have been largely run-of-the-mill."

Oedipus, given its first local regular production since its one-performance showing by the Abbey Theatre in 1933 (in the same translation), starred Harry Andrews as Creon, Richardson as Tiresias, Ena Burrill as Jocasta, Miles Malleson as the first messenger, Michael Warre as the second messenger, George Relph as the herdsman, and Nicholas Hannen as the chorus leader. George Rose was one of the chanting, fourteen-member chorus of Theban elders, and Jocasta's attendants were played by Margaret Leighton, Joyce Redman, and Nicolette Bernard. Among the crowd of walk-ons was Julie Harris. Director Saint-Denis had taken on his job after a disagreement between Olivier and the original director, Tyrone Guthrie.

The staging employed a simple Grecian set consisting of a pair of towering pillars set apart by a step and platform. Primitive statues of Apollo and Athena made it clear that its period was, appropriately, archaic rather than fifth century B.C.

Into the tense atmosphere established by the opening supplication came Olivier's cocksure Oedipus, a youthful figure made up to look like a handsome Greek god. He brought to the role the necessary impetuosity, arrogance, insolence, and pathos. John Mason Brown (*SR*) had to admit that Olivier was a "great" actor. His Oedipus, he said, "is one of those performances in which blood and electricity are somehow mixed. . . . It is as awesome, dwarfing, and appalling as one of nature's angriest displays. Though thrilling, it never loses its majesty." Brown noted that when Oedipus finally realized his guilt, he "releases two cries which no one who has heard them can hope to forget. They are the dreadful, hoarse groans of a wounded animal. . . . They are sounds which speak, as no words could, for a soul torn by horror. . . . Yet . . . they serve only to magnify the stature of Oedipus's kingly woe." To conjure up these startling sounds, Olivier remembered how ermine are trapped by arctic hunters. The animals are lured to salt spread on the ice, and when they try to lick it, their tongues stick to the ice. Olivier shared the agony of the ermine in delivering his unforgettable screams.

The Yeats version of the play was approved for its sinewy strength, power, and clarity. Michel Saint-Denis demonstrated his outstanding directorial skills, which outshadowed those of John Burrell, the company's chief director.

In contrast to the dark and stately manner of *Oedipus*, *The Critic*, last seen locally in 1925, was played broadly with exaggerated makeups, gestures, and vocal patterns. Olivier, playing Mr. Puff, the eighteenth-century equivalent of a gossip columnist whose play is being mangled by an acting troupe, appeared in hilariously foppish period costume of tights and lace, a tiny cocked hat fastened to his powdered wig with a long hatpin, and a Hogarthian button of flesh added to the tip of his nose. Olivier turned the character, wrote Brown, "into a fellow all energy and unction, laughter and lightness, who scampered and skittered around the stage, blowing the dust off Sheridan's old prosody." In the finale, commented Euphemia Van Rensselaer Wyatt (*CW*), he was "borne aloft to the proscenium on some waves, and reappears jauntily on a cloud and swings down on the curtain cord."

This feat of acrobatic derring-do had met with near disaster in London when a rope he grasped to effect the shift from cloud to cord came loose, forcing him to grab a piano wire and hang thirty feet over the stage until gently--and embarrassingly--eased down by the stagehands. Something similar occurred in New York when a rope-ladder he employed broke free and sent him hurtling to the floor in pain. Olivier subsequently had a series of nightmares about falling from the flies or from the sky in an airplane disaster. He was supported by amusing performances from Relph as Mr. Dangle, Leighton as Mrs. Dangle, director Malleson as Sir Fretful Plagiary, Rose as Sir Christopher Hatten, Michael Warre as Sir Walter Raleigh, Hannen as governor of Tilbury, Redman as the confidant, and Richardson as the wordless Lord Burleigh. The fast-paced production's highlight was the rehearsal of a play within the play, which afforded opportunities for *Hellzapoppin'**-like farcical zaniness when everything likely to go wrong on such occasions did. However, for some, the rapidity of the dialogue led to occasional unintelligibility, which was especially true of Leighton.

(3) [OEDIPUS REX] [Hebrew Language] TR: Saul Chernikhovsky; D: Tyrone Guthrie; S: Sebba; P: Habimah Theatre u/t/a/o Theatre Incorporated and the American Fund for Palestinian Institutions; T: Broadway Theatre; 5/22/48 (8)

The Habimah Theatre of Israel was playing here at the moment its nation was officially born, the company having made its way out of the country during violent fighting between Jews and Arabs. Its repertory in New York included this revival as staged by leading English director Guthrie. Some thought it the jewel in the company's crown. Others, like Brooks Atkinson (*NYT*), averred, "Viewed through the barrier of the language, it is competent without being original or inspired." Shimon Finkel was Oedipus, Hanna Rovina was Jocasta, Aaron Meskin was Kreon, Chaim Amitai was Tiresias, Nachum Buchman was a man from Corinth, Ari Kutai was the messenger, Joshua Bertonov was the old shepherd, and David Vardi was the chorus leader, there being seven others in the chorus.

Many considered the treatment of the chorus the production's strongest feature because of its cohesiveness and the integrity of its ensemble work. Each member stood out sharply and intelligently when called upon, yet was able to subdue his personality when group effects were called for. Guthrie kept varying their physical positions to create an ever-changing and fluid group, yet maintained definite rhythmic patterns of movement and speech. "By moving the chorus about in almost ballet-like fashion and treating many of their lines as those of a group of old gossips who hang around the palace steps, he has succeeded in making them a vitally integral part of the flow of the play," raved John S. Wilson (*PM*).

Much of the play's power for an American audience was lost because of the use of Hebrew. William Hawkins (*NYWT*) blamed Guthrie for failing to invest the staging with more interesting pictorial qualities illustrative of the dramatic action's development. Because of the strain required to concentrate, the first half of the production was especially somnambulistic.

Opinions on Finkel's Oedipus generally were divided. He seemed to Bert McCord (*NYHT*) mechanical and lacking in dynamism, and his lines were delivered monotonously. Yet Wilson thought the performance "a brilliantly sustained effort in which he achieves some electrifying moments." No one, however, considered him a match for Olivier.

Very moving was Rovina's wild-eyed and even frantic Jocasta, and a standout job was Meskin's exciting presentation of the messenger. The scenery was simple and serviceable, consisting of a circle of four or five columns and several steps or levels across the width of the stage.

OF V WE SING [Revue] SK: Al Geto, Sam D. Locke, and Mel Tolkin; M: Alex North, George Kleinsinger, Ned Lehack, Beau Bergersen, Lou Cooper, and Toby Sacher; LY: Alfred Hayes, Lewis Allen, Roslyn Harvey, Mike Stratton, Bea Goldsmith, Joe Barian, and Arthur Zipser; D: Perry Bruskin; CH: Susanne Remos; P: American Youth Theatre i/a/w Alexander H. Cohen; T: Concert Theatre; 2/11/42 (76)

A semiprofessional company that had showed this work on weekends at the tiny Malin Studio Theatre and the equally small Barbizon-Plaza Theatre under the title *V for Victory* now saw its work picked up by producer Alexander H. Cohen for Broadway consumption at what once was the John Golden Theatre on West Fifty-eighth Street and most recently had served as the Filmarte, a movie theatre. Shelley Winters said that she was in one of the earlier manifestations.

Billed as a "topical revue," it was an intimate, mildly left-wing show in the *Pins and Needles** format, to which it was unkindly compared, offering the usual assortment of songs, dances, jokes, impersonations, and the like, and brought a comic named Phil Leeds to critical attention. "He has the true gift of absurd improvisation, of clever timing, of pause and rush, of invention and abandon," raved Rosamond Gilder (*TAM*). Betty Garrett and Curt Conway were the others in the cast who went on to develop strong theatrical careers.

The assortment of numbers included a takeoff on broadcasting, "NBC Goes to Broadcast"; "Ivan the Terrible," about a radio transmission of a Hitler speech; "You've Got to Appease with a Strip-Tease," in which Lee Barrie and Adele Jerome did a comedy strip with references to the war (this had been Winters's routine); a satire on Brooklyn Dodger fans called "Brooklyn Cantata"; "Mother Love," which spoofed schmaltzy George Jessel and Al Jolson vaudeville acts; "Juke Box," a parody of jitterbug fans; "Don't Sing Solo," a standout song as performed by Garrett; "Freedom Road," in which black singer John Flemming sang about the need for racial tolerance; "One Way Passage," which threw darts at reactionary Southern senator Martin Dies; "Gertie the Stool Pigeon's Daughter," with Lettie Stever as the girl who lives under the shadow of having a father who doesn't believe in unions; and so on.

The music was performed with two pianos, and the sets consisted of little but draperies. Prices ranged from only $.55 to $1.65, so the critics, for all their reservations, advised patrons that their money would not be wasted on the low-budget show. It was an enthusiastically performed but not very funny or brilliantly conceived revue and had mainly the youth and appeal of its cast to recommend it. As Richard Watts, Jr. (*NYHT*), phrased it, it was "filled with fine intentions, but scant achievement."

OH, BROTHER! [Comedy/Art/Crime/Legacy/Romance] A: Jacques Deval; D: Bretaigne Windust; S: Samuel Leve; P: Maximilian Becker and Peter Warren; T: Royale Theatre; 6/19/45 (23)

Eccentric comic actor Hugh Herbert--known for his iterations of "woo woo"--returned to Broadway after eighteen years in this "pretty damned silly play" (Lewis Nichols [*NYT*]). He played Charles Craddock, a chess player who is also a burglar. In the course of looting a wealthy home in Daytona Beach, Florida, he and two accomplices, a waif (Susana Garnett) and an artist (Don Gordon), discover that the family they are robbing has a long-lost son who is a missing heir. Because of his great love of chess and desire to enter a tournament requiring a $1,000 entrance fee, Charles induces the young artist to impersonate the missing heir. The gorgeous girl (Arleen Whelan) who is sister to the missing heir--and who gets to parade around in two different bathing suits--falls in love with the artist and he with her, adding further complications to the plot before love solves all problems.

The piece was an irregular blend of farce and sentiment and lacked enough funny lines and situations to keep audiences engrossed. It "has neither the wit nor the pace to keep itself clicking," thought Otis Guernsey, Jr. (*NYHT*). In the cast were Catherine Doucet, Forrest Orr, Lyle Bettger, and Eva Condon.

OH, MR. MEADOWBROOK! [Comedy/Marriage/Romance/Sex/Theatre] A: Ronald

Telfer and Pauline Jameson; D: Harry Ellerbe; S: Wolfgang Roth; C: Lucille Little; P: John Yorke; T: John Golden Theatre; 12/26/48 (64)

Ernest Truex played one of his trademark Milquetoast characters in this confused comedy loaded with double entendres that George Currie (*BE*) put in the running for "the worst play of recent times." Truex's role was that of shy, middle-aged, English taxidermist-bachelor Japhet Meadowbrook, whose psychiatrist suggests that he visit America to learn about the birds and bees. He stays at the Connecticut home of playwright Harland Vye (Harry Ellerbe, who also directed) and his attractive wife Constance (Grace McTarnahan), where he becomes the prey of three women, Grace, a hard-boiled female dramatist named Nesta Madrigale (Vicki Cummings), and the Scottish housemaid, Sophie McDonald (Sylvia Field). At the conclusion, he returns to England in the company of the latter.

Truex was his usual estimable self, but there was little he could do for this "losing cause," as Robert Coleman (*NYDM*) put it. "A labored concoction enlivened only occasionally by some amusing performances," decided Bron. (*V*). Morton L. Stevens played a theatrical producer.

OKLAHOMA! [Musical/Romance/Rural/Sex/Western] B/LY: Oscar Hammerstein II; M: Richard Rodgers; SC: Lynn Riggs's play, *Green Grow the Lilacs**; D: Rouben Mamoulian; CH: Agnes de Mille; S: Lemuel Ayers; C: Miles White; P: Theatre Guild; T: St. James Theatre; 3/31/43 (2,248)

One of the most popular and influential musicals of all time, *Oklahoma!* marked the beginning of the brilliant musical theatre partnership of Rodgers and Hammerstein, formed when Rodgers broke up his previous partnership with Lorenz Hart (who would die later the same year). The show came at a time when the venerable Theatre Guild was nearly broke (it had only $30,000 in its coffers) after having produced too few hits in its last several seasons. Guild leader Theresa Helburn conceived the notion of turning Lynn Riggs's 1931 folk play into a musical and the idea appealed to Rodgers, who was given permission by the ailing Hart to seek another collaborator. Hammerstein, who was selected, had himself been interested for some time in making a musical out of Riggs's play (with Jerome Kern) and even brought his idea to Helburn only to learn that she had already spoken about such a work with Rodgers. Alfred Drake was cast as Curly and Joan Roberts as Laurey, and they participated in the fund-raising efforts for the show, but this was an arduous process because few people thought the show a sound investment.

Oklahoma! was a milestone work, advancing the technique established by such earlier shows as the Princess Theatre musicals and *Show Boat** of integrating all its effects and tying the music, songs, and dances to a distinctive and adult story told intelligently, with consistency, and with fully developed characters. Extremely important was the psychological nature of the fundamental conflict. Nothing was allowed to detract from the overall harmony of effect or to hinder the progress of the action. It was selected as one of Burns Mantle's ten best plays of the year.

The show opened in New Haven, Connecticut, in March 1943, under the title *Away We Go!* and was subsequently called *Swing Your Lady*, *Cherokee Strip*, and *Yes-sirree* before *Oklahoma!* was settled on. Some who saw it out of town felt that it was a certain flop. An informant of columnist Walter Winchell wired him the following: "NO GIRLS, NO LEGS, NO JOKES, NO CHANCE" (quoted in Peter Hay, *Broadway Anecdotes*). Broadway jokesters referred to it as "Helburn's Folly." When it opened in New York, though, many reviewers were aware that they were viewing a masterpiece, although a few took some convincing. The show ran for over five years, and its national company was on the road for ten and a half. It was produced internationally, its London version snaring the all-time record at Drury Lane with a run of 1,548 performances. The Guild's finances were restored to robust health, and the show's individual investors were richly rewarded. A decade after the show opened, the Guild had earned more than $5 million on an $83,000 gamble. Investors putting $10,000 in the show earned back $250,000 within five years. Its long run made it the champion in this category for fifteen years. Each of the original players was succeeded by a string of others.

The story, which closely follows that of the source play, is set in Indian Territory early in the century. Curly is a handsome young ranch hand in love with Laurey, who lives with Aunt Eller (Betty Garde) on the latter's farm. He wants to take her to the box social, although he has to admit he doesn't own a surrey with the fringe on top. Will Parker (Lee Dixon; the character is not in the original play) arrives from an exciting trip to Kansas City. The fifty dollars he has won in a steer-roping contest will allow him to marry Ado Annie (Celeste Holm). Annie, however, is torn between her attraction to Will and to the Persian peddler Ali Hakim (Joseph Buloff), whose invitation to go to a hotel with him she has mistaken for a proposal of marriage. Curly learns that among his rivals for Laurey is the unpleasant farm hand Jud Fry (Howard da Silva; the character was Jeeter in the original play), whom Laurey has agreed to have drive her to the box social. Curly decides to take the attractive Gertie Cummings (Jane Lawrence) to the party instead, which upsets Laurey. Annie's shotgun toting father (Ralph Riggs) scares Ali into proposing for real. The jealous Curly goes to Jud's smokehouse, which is adorned with pictures of naked women, to tell him to stay clear of Laurey. When Jud breaks through Curly's roundabout way of offering him advice, he grows angry. After Laurey's friends express surprise at her seeming preference for Jud, she lapses into a dream that is enacted as a ballet (with Marc Platt as Curly and Katharine Sergava as Laurey). (Agnes de Mille's dream ballet, reminiscent of her popular ballet of six months earlier, *Rodeo*, was considered one of the major contributions to the show in its infusion of a brilliant example of this type of dance into the mainstream of musical comedy.) The dream, in which Jud bests Curly in a fight and carries her off, makes her realize that Jud is not for her. Soon the box social is given, with Jud and Curly bidding to buy Laurey's box supper, Curly having to sell his gun and horse to win the bidding. Ado and Will have meanwhile agreed to marry and have set the date. Jud makes advances to Laurey, but her rejection angers him. Shortly after Curly and Laurey agree to wed, Jud returns and a fight breaks out between the two men; Jud dies on the blade of his own knife. Curly is acquitted by a judge who is present and Curly and Laurey depart in a surrey with the fringe on top.

Beautifully interwoven with the story are such now-familiar songs as "Oh, What a Beautiful Mornin'," "The Surrey with the Fringe on Top," "Kansas City," "I Cain't Say No," "Many a New Day," "People Will Say We're in Love," "Pore Jud Is Daid," "Out of My Dreams," "The Farmer and the Cowman," "All Er Nuthin!" and "Oklahoma." Lewis Nichols (*NYT*) dubbed the work a "folk operetta" and suggested that Oklahoma grab the title tune for its state anthem; it eventually did just that.

The critics praised the variety and excellence of the songs, the expert integration of music, comedy, and drama, the cleverness and emotional depth of de Mille's choreography, the intelligence of book and lyrics (although Louis Kronenberger [*PM*] referred to the book as "just one of those things"), the excellence of the combined realism and stylization of the sets, the colors and concepts of the costumes, and the superiority of the players and direction. Speaking of de Mille's work, Rosamond Gilder (*TAM*) noted how she demonstrated that "a dance can be comic, gaily satiric as well as lyric and robust. Miss de Mille's dances do not interrupt the action with an arbitrary restatement of a lyric theme in terms of movement, but on the contrary they move the plot forward, enlarging its scope." The show's now-famous dream sequence Gilder described as follows: "Its bevies of awkward farm girls and long-limbed horsemen astride imaginary broncos sweep the stage with gusts of merriment; they are the essence, the embodied spirit of the hearty girls and boys whose vigorous measures enliven the other scenes of the play."

George Jean Nathan (*TBY*) found it difficult to say more about the show than that it "constitutes agreeable entertainment," but most critics were lavish with their superlatives. "*Oklahoma* is the most beguiling, the most enchanting musical piece in many a long day," crowed George Freedley (*NYMT*). "One song after another picks you up and carries you along with it. We'll still be singing them a dozen years from now." "*Oklahoma* is fresh, lively, colorful and enormously pleasing," commented Burton Rascoe (*NYWT*).

There was abundant praise for all the principal performers, several of whom became major stars on the basis of their work in *Oklahoma!* Alfred Drake, said Freedley, "has the makings of a new star. He has acting ability far above the average, looks, personality and a beautiful and flexible voice. His acting and singing of the cowboy lover goes a long way towards making the play a success." Rascoe was bowled over by Holm, who "simply tucked the show under her arm and just let the others touch it. This is an astounding young woman, Miss Holm. . . . When you see and hear her sing the rather naughty song, 'I Can't [*sic*] Say No,' you are in for a tickling thrill. And you just wait for her next number. . . . Miss Holm, with her fresh beauty, has too much talent to be quite credible." Also making memorable impressions were Buloff, Garde, and da Silva.

OLD ACQUAINTANCE [Comedy/Friendship/Literature/Romance/Sex] A: John van Druten; D: Auriol Lee; S: Richard Whorf; P: Dwight Deere Wiman; T: Morosco Theatre; 12/23/40 (170)

Two of Broadway's most gracious actresses, Peggy Wood and Jane Cowl, led the cast of this charming, excellently acted "woman's play" about love and license among literary New Yorkers. Playgoers tasted a light soufflé of a play, a bit short on substance, but guaranteed to leave a pleasant taste in the mouth.

Cowl played Katherine Markham, the passionate, intellectual novelist whose works sell only to the cognoscenti, while Wood was Mildred Watson Drake, a prolific authoress who has become wealthy from the best-sellers she has penned. The two are old acquaintances from a Harrisburg, Pennsylvania, childhood whose friendship--de spite occasional squalls--has withstood the pressures of competing careers and varying fortunes. Katherine, whose love life has been colorful, is now involved with Rudd Kendall (Kent Smith), a much younger man. Mildred is divorced and has a pretty, but too-sophisticated, eighteen-year-old daughter, Deirdre (Adele Longmire). While Katherine is making up her mind as to whether she will marry Rudd, a major complication is introduced when he falls in love with Deirdre. Although the situation leads to a bitter quarrel between the writers, they soon make up, and the young lovers end up happily together.

The dramatis personae were very well written, their weaknesses and strengths clearly demonstrated, and their humanity well conveyed. "The two novelists," wrote Rosamond Gilder (*TAM*), "with their divergent natures, their rivalries and love affairs, their recriminations and reconciliations, are vividly sensed and tolerantly drawn." Less dense was the story they took part in, set in a Washington Square apartment and one on Park Avenue. Richard Whorf's sets skillfully captured the different personalities of their supposed residents. Typifying the responses of most critics, Richard Watts, Jr. (*NYHT*), commented that the play "is not a drama of deep emotions or high excitement, but in its quiet and restrained fashion it manages to be human, likable and almost consistently interesting in a manner which makes up in intelligence and warmth for what it may conceivably lack in depth."

Universally admired was the direction, for its civilized demeanor, and the acting, especially that of the leading ladies. Brooks Atkinson (*NYT*) believed that Wood was "giving the best performance of her career--honest, aware and lucidly projected." Gilder said of Cowl, "Her comedy technique, with its skilful use of pause, its hesitations, its sudden rush of words; her gestures underlining a point or elaborating an unspoken comment, are all admirably suited to the qualities of mind and heart the character demands."

OLD FOOLISHNESS, THE [Comedy/Family/Irish/Politics/Religion/Romance] A: Paul Vincent Carroll; D: Rachel Crothers; S: Donald Oenslager; P: John Golden; T: Windsor Theatre; 12/20/40 (3)

This Irish import concerns a pretty colleen named Maeve McHugh (Sally O'Neil) who leaves her live-in lover, Francis Sheeran (Sean Dillon), a fiery political revolutionary, in Dublin and goes off to his family farmhouse in County Down to ask them to assist their fugitive son. Here Francis's two brothers, the sturdy but cloddish farmer Peter (Roy Roberts) and the poetical scholar Mike (Vincent J. Donehue) fall in love with her. Francis himself soon arrives, and Maeve is torn among the three, finally--for some reason few of the critics could fathom--ending the standoff by going off on her own to think things over.

The relatively simple plot--inspired by the story of Pelleas and Melisande--was overlaid with an air of mysticism, especially as represented by the pixielike hedonist Dan Dorian (Walter Burke), and there were suggestions concerning the symbolic meanings of Maeve (Ireland) and the three brothers (conflicting aspects of Ireland--the soldier, the scholar, and the man of the land), but the latter elements were insufficiently absorbing or clear, and the play was thought a failure. Richard Watts, Jr. (*NYHT*), commented sadly, "It is so muddy, confused and unpersuasive in its narrative and its ideas that it must be set down as an additional misfortune of the week." Making the situation worse was an inadequately staged and acted production, with a m?lange of Irish accents.

OLD LADY SAYS "NO!," THE [Drama/Fantasy/Historical-Biographical/Irish/Period/Politics/Theatre] A: Denis Johnston; D: Hilton Edwards; S: Micheal MacLiammoir and Molly MacEwen; C: Micheal MacLiammoir; P: Dublin Gate Theatre u/t/a/o Richard Aldrich and Richard Myers i/a/w Brian Doherty; T: Mansfield Theatre; 2/17/48 (8)

Dublin's visiting Gate Theatre company offered this controversial 1929 expressionist play, intended as a scathing satire on modern Ireland, as part of its visiting repertory. Originally called *Shadowdance*, the "romantic drama" combines music, poetry, and choral interludes. The play's final title was suggested to the author when the work was rejected by Lady Augusta Gregory of the Abbey Theatre, who wrote a big "No!" across the first page.

It tells of a Speaker (or actor: Micheal MacLiammoir) playing Irish heroic patriot Robert Emmet on the stage of the Dublin Theatre in flamboyantly hammy nineteenth-century melodramatic style when he is arrested while in the act of saying farewell to his sweetheart, Sarah Curran (Meriel Moore). In the process, he suffers a head injury, and a doctor sends another actor to seek a rug to keep him warm. Meanwhile, the actor's feverish imagination (evoked by throbbing drum beats and a pulsing light) propels him through a series of rapidly evolving scenes set in 1803 as he seeks "the heroic heart of modern Ireland," in Euphemia Van Rensselaer Wyatt's (*CW*) phrase. The actor, thinking himself the real Emmet, confronts the difference between the idealist's Ireland and the actual, depressing truth. Before he passes out at the end, he delivers a combination of Emmet's final speech and the eulogy for O'Donovan Rossa delivered by Patrick Henry Pearse. The scene was played against huge shadows of great Irishmen, from Jonathan Swift to George Bernard Shaw. The doctor returns, covers the actor with a rug, and brings down the curtain.

New York's critics thought the material fresh and often fascinating but too Irish and obscure for general appreciation. Declared Wyatt, "The play loses immeasurably when given before an audience immune to local allusions, for the allegory is too localized for universality." Brooks Atkinson (*NYT*), who commended the playwright's poetic gifts and theatrical inventiveness, nevertheless admitted--in a review echoing many others--that "too much of it is too close to gibberish," that it was "loose and sprawling," and that it was too long to sustain continued interest. MacLiammoir was outstanding in the leading role, and his company supported him very well.

ON STRIVERS ROW [Dramatic Revival] A/D: Abram Hill; S: Charles Sebree; P/T: American Negro Theatre (OB); 2/28/46 (27)

This play had had several earlier amateur performances before being given the present revival. The Rose McClendon Players had done it in 1939, a 1940 version was seen at the American Negro Theatre in 1940, and a musical version was shown at Harlem's Apollo Theatre in 1941. Most saw no pressing reason for the revival, George Jean Nathan (*TBY*) declaring, "It lacks any suggestion of wit and is further deadened by verbosity." L. C. (*NYT*) thought that a good idea had been "wasted by a general lack of cohesiveness in the plot" and a lack of "sharp-cutting wit."

The play, a satire on social climbing in the Harlem community, is set in a house on West 139th Street, a place called Strivers Row because of the residences there of well-to-do black families. It concerns the socially prominent Van Striven family, whose Radcliffe-educated daughter Cobina (Javotte Sutton) is preparing to make her debut. A party is being planned from which black neighbors who do not conform to the Van Strivens' concept of appropriate (white-influenced) behavior are excluded. Their own snobbish attitudes, however, are held up to scorn. One of the guests is sweepstakes winner Ruby Jackson (Jacqueline Andre), a lower-class cook invited by Oscar Van Striven (Stanley Greene), who wants to sell her some worthless property in Queens so she can build her dream house there. Ruby, her garish friend Beulah (Sally Alexander), and Beulah's zoot-suited beau Joe (Fred Carter) attend the party and provide a cartoonish example of lower-class attitudes. A fight engineered by Joe, who has been paid to do so, breaks out, and the party ends in catastrophe. In the aftermath, Ruby tells Mrs. Van Striven (Dorothy Carter) and her mother, Mrs. Pace (Hattie King-Reavis), that they are snobs and does not accept their rationalization. After various other actions, Ruby is accepted as a friend by the Van Strivens in a feeble but happy ending.

ON THE SEVENTH DAY [Drama/Broadcasting/Family/Fantasy/Journalism/Mental Illness/War] A: Urban Nagle; D: Dennis Gurney; S: Blackfriars' Studio under the direction of Leo Herbert; L: Rebecca Jennings; P: Blackfriars' Guild; T: Blackfriars' Theatre (OB); 3/6/47 (25)

A semiprofessional offering attended by only a handful of critics, this was a "modern morality play" written by a Catholic priest. Like many other plays of the day, it had a fantasy background, its principal locale being a heaven wherein various principalities and archangels consider the problems of human relations.

Lieutenant Oriel (Doug Randall), a cynical archangel, fed up with humanity, is turning over his post to Lieutenant Raphael (Joseph Lane). He returns to earth to bring back his successor and to introduce him to the problems of men. He focuses on the Smith family, whose son Jack (Mel York) was in the armed forces throughout the war and lost his mental balance following the atom bombing of Hiroshima. The response of the archangels is enhanced via a series of radio talks on mankind's problems in which the media are personified in the persons of Mike (Mike Garrett), Cam (Pauline O'-Hare), and Mr. Press (Jack Delmonte). Coming under attack are the war, the media, the educational system, communism, the atom bomb, commercialism, the lack of spiritual values, and so on. "About the only item Father Nagle forgot to include is bad plays like *On the Seventh Day*," wrote George Jean Nathan (*TBY*).

ON THE TOWN [Musical/Military/Romance] B: Betty Comden and Adolph Green; M: Leonard Bernstein; LY: Betty Comden, Adolph Green, and Leonard Bernstein; SC: the Jerome Robbins and Leonard Bernstein ballet, "Fancy Free"; D: George Abbott; CH: Jerome Robbins; S: Oliver Smith; C: Alvin Colt; L: Peggy Clark; P: Oliver Smith and Paul Feigay; T: Adelphi Theatre; 12/28/44 (462)

On the Town joined the 1944-1945 parade of hits and introduced to Broadway the vibrant talents of librettist-lyricists Comden and Green and composer Bernstein (who also shared lyric credits for one song). Their musical contributions included such tunes as "New York, New York," "Come Up to My Place," "Carried Away," "Lonely Town," "I Can Cook, Too," "Lucky to Be Me," and "Some Other Time." Comden and Green also proved their worth as performers, with the attractive female half of the team playing Claire de Loon while Green took the role of one of the three central sailor figures, Ozzie. The pair were brought in to the project by Bernstein to replace John Latouche, who was originally slated to be the lyricist.

When the show was being written, Bernstein needed an operation on a deviated septum and Green one on his tonsils, so the two artists, to save time, had their operations at the same time and shared the same hospital room, where they worked while they were recovering. Wrote Joan Peyser in *Bernstein*: "It was quite a scene in that hospital room--rather like a Marx Brothers movie. Radios blared. Arguments accelerated over card games. Pieces of *On the Town* were sung full voice. But they did a lot of work." Comden and Green were initially opposed both to the show's title and to its three-sailor theme, thinking that the result would be too much like a grade-B movie.

Although ostensibly based on "Fancy Free," a well-known 1944 ballet about three gobs on leave and trying to pick up girls in New York, the show used none of Bernstein's music or Robbins's choreography from that piece, and Bernstein insisted that the two works were quite different, the only similarity being the use of three sailors. The plot fol lows three similar sailors, Gaby (John Battles, who replaced Kirk Douglas because the latter could not sing), Ozzie, and Chip (Cris Alexander) on their twenty-four hour furlough in the Big Apple. The action is precipitated by their spotting a picture in the subway of "Miss Turnstiles," a girl named Ivy Smith (Sono Osato) who is a student of music and art, and by their decision to find her. Their expedition takes them to famous landmarks, such as the Museum of Natural History, Central Park, Times Square, various nighteries, and Coney Island. There are romantic interludes with Chip and taxi driver Hildy (Nancy Walker) and Ozzie and anthropology student Claire. With his pals thus occupied, Gaby manages to find Ivy on his own. She turns out to be a Coney Island belly dancer, and the facts about her on the "Miss Turnstiles" picture are all fabrications.

The book was not greeted as a work of great significance, but few denied that it was extremely clever and workable within the framework of the show's premise. Howard Barnes (*NYHT*) thought it "a feeble frame," but John Mason Brown (*SR*) said that it "makes fair sense, and fairer nonsense." Much pleasure was gained from its frequent satirical sallies at aspects of New York life and culture. Lewis Nichols (*NYT*) celebrated the show's arrival by noting, "Everything about it is right. It is fast and it is gay, it takes neither itself nor the world too seriously, it has wit. Its dances are well paced, its players are a pleasure to see, and its music and backgrounds are both fitting and excellent." Brown revelled in what he regarded as a masterpiece of innovation, a show that was to the urban landscape what *Oklahoma!* was to the rural.

As originally written, the script called for the scenes to be tied together by a prologue in night court, a locale to which the action would periodically return. The writers loved the concept, but Abbott hated it and early on told them that while he loved everything else in the show, the prologue and flashbacks had to go. Green was enraged and attempted with Comden to convince the director to keep the material in. Abbott's answer was, according to Peyser, "OK. I'll tell you what. You can have either me or the prologue." Abbott stayed, the prologue did not. Abbott proceeded to make many other cuts and revisions before the script was completed.

Especially noteworthy was how effectively Robbins had brought the art of ballet to Broadway dance (this was his premiere as a musical comedy choreographer). His choreography, said Rosamond Gilder (*TAM*), proved him "adept in the art of translating ordinary, insignificant events and gestures into the poetic idiom of the dance." One of his most effective creations, Gilder declared, was the scene in the subway, with the movements of the throng of workers and gum-chewing secretaries gradually blending into dance. "The rhythm of the moving train, picked up by the music, is accentuated little by little in one swaying figure, then another, and finally bursts into a pattern of movement that embraces the whole stage, bursting the confines of realism and becoming an expression of all the weariness, hurry and passion for escape with which every clattering subway train is laden." Robbins later noted, "One of the important things in the show that was not noted was the mixed chorus. It was predominantly white, but there were four black dancers--and for the first time, they danced with the whites, not separately, in social dancing. We had some trouble with that in some of the cities we went to" (quoted in Otis L. Guernsey, Jr., *Broadway Song and Story*).

Bernstein's music was not universally approved, but most critics would have agreed with E. C. Sherburne (*CSM*): "The varieties of his rhythms, his satirical tonal embroideries, and the surprises offered by his vaulting rhythms leave the listener startled with the realization that he made it, like the man on the flying trapeze."

Every principal cast member came in for accolades, but most highly acclaimed was dancer Osato. "She manages," wrote Brown, "to combine the cool beauty of Sorine's 'Pavlova' with a sense of humor subtler than Fannie Brice's, but Brice-like in its contagious qualities. Miss Osato is a genuine addition to our musical comedy stage. She is a young person, arresting and brilliantly endowed, who is already a personage." She was also an interesting early example of nontraditional casting, being a Japanese-American cast in the role of a Caucasian during a time when this country was at war with Japan. Although most critics lauded her dancing ability, a few had reservations about her singing and acting. Other cast members included

Florence MacMichael, Remo Bufano, Susan Steel, Alice Pearce, Robert Chisholm, Jeanne Gordon, and Ray Harrison.

ON WHITMAN AVENUE [Drama/Blacks/Family/Race] A: Maxine Wood; M: Paul Bowles; D: Margo Jones; S/L: Donald Oenslager; P: Canada Lee and Mark Marvin i/a/w George McClain; T: Cort Theatre; 5/8/46 (150)

Margo Jones made her solo Broadway directorial debut with this predictable, amateurishly written drama whose theme was a harbinger of Lorraine Hansberry's *A Raisin in the Sun* of thirteen years later. It is set in Lawndale, an upscale midwestern suburban development, and concerns what happens when liberal-minded Toni Tilden (Perry Wilson), a young idealist, rents an apartment in her parents' two-family home to the family of black veteran David Bennett (Canada Lee) during her parents' absence on a trip. The neighbors are incensed at the presence of a black family in their white enclave and hold a meeting to express their anger. A bitter confrontation with the Bennetts provides the black family with a month's respite. Several days later some young white hooligans incite David's young brother (Richard Williams) to draw a knife. When Toni tries to disarm him she accidentally is slashed. Her apparently liberal but actually bigoted mother (Ernestine Barrier), now returned, takes the side of the prejudiced neighbors in trying to oust the family. The real estate company pressures Toni's unbiased father (Will Geer) into forcing David's family to move (it threatens not to renew the lease on Tilden's store), David's grandfather (Augustus Smith) suffers a near-fatal heart attack when the Bennetts are evicted, and Toni leaves home.

The play was condoned for its meaningful theme but not for its unpracticed dramaturgy. "The fact remains," sighed Lewis Nichols (*NYT*), "that it is just not good theatre." The playwright relied too heavily on literary allusions (many from Walt Whitman) rather than ordinary speech, she allowed for a cluttered sequence of actions that stood in need of editing, and the white characters were too consistently drawn in unflattering colors. George Jean Nathan (*TBY*) pointed to the many stencils in situation and dialogue, and declared that the cards were stacked in favor of the black viewpoint by casting superior actors to play the black roles. In the company were Hilda Vaughn, Martin Miller, Abbie Mitchell, and Robert Simon, among others. The play managed to survive as long as it did because of cut-rate prices.

ONCE OVER LIGHTLY [Musical Revival] B: Laszlo Halasz; M: Gioacchino Rossini; LY: Louis Garden and Robert Forshaw; SC: Rossini's opera version of Pierre-Augustin Caron de Beaumarchais's play, *The Barber of Seville*; D: Robert H. Gordon; CH: George Mead; S: Richard Rychtarik; P: Saul Colin i/a/w Henry Leiser; T: Alvin Theatre; 11/19/42 (6)

A reportedly "Americanized" adaptation of *The Barber of Seville*. The music was advertised as being untouched, while the Sterbini libretto was supposedly replaced by one more faithful to Beaumarchais's original play, with a dose of contemporary humor added. Thus Figaro (Igor Gorin) announced on entering, "I'm the well-known barber of Seville, who gets in everybody's hair." Other slangy expressions included, "What's cookin'?" "I'll say it's a racket," and "It is my motto, never be blotto." But there was considerable disappointment at the extent of the adaptation. Music critic Robert Lawrence (*NYHT*) reported that the program "would have you believe that the authors have gone back to the original comedy of Beaumarchais for their material. . . . But, truth to tell, this is the same old *Barber of Seville* in doubtful English, with only the harpsichord recitatives left out and streamlined dialogue put in."

The theatre critics said that the show should not have been presented as theatre when it was really just thinly disguised opera. "It seems to me idiotic to try to sell Rossini, with false whiskers and an assumed name, to musical comedy devotees--the group who are most likely to find it tame if not downright tiresome," reasoned Louis Kronenberger (*PM*). Grace Panvini was Rosina, Carlos Alexander was Don Basilio, Felix Knight was Almaviva, Adele Warner was Bertha, Richard Wentworth was Dr. Bartolo, and Myron Szandrowsky was Florella. A small chorus replaced the grandiose one usually accompanying more conventional revivals of the work.

ONE TOUCH OF VENUS [Musical/Art/Boarding House/Crime/Fantasy/Hotel/Prison/Romance/Sex] B: S. J. Perelman and Ogden Nash; M: Kurt Weill; LY: Ogden Nash; SC: an 1885 novella by F. Anstey, *The Tinted Venus*; D: Elia Kazan; CH: Agnes de Mille; S: Howard Bay; C: Paul du Pont, Kermit Love, and Mainbocher; P: Cheryl Crawford i/a/w John Wildberg; T: Imperial Theatre; 10/7/43 (567)

Audiences were wise to the fact that this show had all the ingredients that spelled hit and were willing to shell out an unusual $100,000 in advance sales before it even opened. The idea for the show had been designer Aline Bernstein's, who gave a copy of Anstey's *The Tinted Venus* to composer Weill with the suggestion that it might make a good musical. Producer Crawford (according to her *One Naked Individual*) took on the project because its subject promised a work that would allow a split vision of reality as seen by mortals and immortals, allowing the contrast to make a socially meaningful point. It was decided to cast Marlene Dietrich as the goddess Venus. Dietrich kept delaying her agreement to do the show, which was taking shape in a libretto by Bella Spewack called *One Man's Venus*. Dietrich went so far as to make frequent musuem trips to study pictures and statues of Venus and to practice draping herself in different arrangements of chiffon, and Crawford finally got the star to sign a contract. After rereading Spewack's libretto, however, Crawford decided that she did not care for it, as it failed to make the social points in which she was interested. When Spewack was told that her script was being scuttled and another writer was being sought, she fainted. She never spoke to Crawford again. A new script was written by Perelman and Nash, but Dietrich turned it down, telling the dumbfounded Kurt Weill that it was "too sexy and profane" for her. A search for a new star was undertaken. Gertrude Lawrence, Leonora Corbett, and Vera Zorina were among those approached, but all refused, the latter because her ex-husband, choreographer George Balanchine, told her not to do a show choreographed by Agnes de Mille. Finally, the role went to Mary Martin, for whom it would be her first leading role on Broadway.

Martin was no Dietrich, but she was a young star on the rise who was returning to Broadway after several years in Hollywood. She was a bit reluctant to take the part because she had doubts about her appearance and could not see herself in the role of the beauteous Venus. Her husband, Richard Halliday, thereupon took her to the museum and showed her all the statues of Venus, not one of them resembling any of the others. As quoted in Crawford, Martin stated, "He finally convinced me that I didn't have to be Venus de Milo or Marlene Dietrich." Making the decision easier were the ideas of fashion designer Mainbocher, now doing his first theatrical costumes. It was Martin herself who persuaded the designer to design her costumes by singing the score's "That's Him" in such a way that Mainbocher asserted, "If you will sing the song exactly like that in the show, I'll do the costumes."

Also returning to Broadway was John Boles, who had last played there in 1926, had subsequently gone into films, and then had retired. Playing opposite Martin in the leading romantic role was radio singer Kenny Baker, whose one and only Broadway role this would be.

The standard out-of-town troubles besieged the show, especially in the design area. Howard Bay had created gray velveteen draperies that served as a sky and as a proscenium decoration. When first seen, they reminded Perelman, according to one version, of the inside of a coffin, and in another version, an enlarged prostate gland. Others had equally dismal descriptions. Mainbocher made a suggestion about replacing them with a more delicate decor adorned with doves. When Bay expressed a lack of familiarity with doves, Mainbocher pointed out a window to some nearby pigeons. "Something like those," he said, and Bay then created a lovely effect to replace the velveteen. By the time all the important changes in costumes and sets had been made, $25,000 had been added to the budget.

Martin created obstacles of her own, such as when, just before the tryout opening, she objected to one of her lines as being too vulgar. The line was, "Love is not the moaning of distant violins; it's the triumphant twang of a bedspring." She was persuaded to keep it in temporarily until a new one could be substituted, but, as so often is the case, when she heard the great laugh it provoked, she decided to keep it in.

Mixed responses greeted the Pygmalion and Galatea-like fantasy, but it survived to become a big hit. Because of certain superficial stylistic resemblances the show was likened to *Oklahoma!*, but there was little similarity between the two apart from their dream ballets and sense of integration of story and score.

Boles played Whitelaw Savory, a sophisticated New York art dealer who imports a priceless, 3,000-year-old statue of Venus. Baker was Rodney Hatch, Savory's barber, who sees the statue at the art dealer's museum, the Whitelaw Savory Foundation of Modern Art, where he has gone to exercise his tonsorial talents on Savory. Rodney is engaged to the bitchy Gloria Kramer (Ruth Bond); thinking to see whose finger is more slender, the statue's or his Gloria's, Rodney slips Gloria's installment-paid engagement band on the former and after the heavens provide some special effects, the flimsily gowned Venus comes to life. She explains that she has been under a spell that the ring has broken and that she loves Rodney for having rescued her. Rodney tries to shake her, but she pursues him to his boarding house, puzzled by her failure to seduce him. After he complains about her scanty garb, she goes to Radio City and steals a dress from a store-window mannequin (she glides magically through the plate glass), putting it on as a curious crowd gathers to watch. Savory, who loves her, saves her from being arrested. Venus intervenes in a scene at the bus terminal where Rodney awaits Gloria and her overbearing mother (Helen Raymond). Rodney and Gloria argue, and he becomes annoyed with the goddess. At the barber shop, Venus makes Gloria disappear, which results in Rodney's being accused of killing her, arrested, and sent to the Tombs. Venus uses her powers to free him and the pair spend a night together in a hotel. At his urging, Venus brings Gloria back but the latter, entering from a closet, comments nastily about Rodney and Venus and leaves after ending the engagement. Ultimately, Venus decides that she and Rodney could never be happy in his suburb of Ozone Heights, and after a clap of thunder and a momentary blackout, she returns to stone so that she may go back as a statue to the land from which she came. Rodney is rewarded, however, when a simple Ozone Heights girl (also played by Martin) who is Venus's spitting image walks into the museum as an art student, inspiring hopes of future bliss.

The show made Mary Martin a solid Broadway star, with her singing, dancing, and acting talents on display in a succession of dazzling Mainbocher creations that were one of the chief draws of the production. Robert Garland (*NYJA*) proclaimed, "Miss Martin has grown into a performer of the first magnitude. . . . Not only is she lovely, but . . . she can dance, sing and project a serious scene . . . with the best of them." Some, however, had certain reservations, Wilella Waldorf (*NYP*), for example, not thinking much of Martin as a singer, but respecting her ability to talk a song and otherwise put one over.

There were outstanding performances by all the principals, as well as by Teddy Hart as a cabdriver and Paula Laurence as Savory's acidulous secretary. Sono Osato, Peter Birch, Robert Pageant, and Lou Wills, Jr., provided terpsichorean delights, with ballerina Osato outstanding in "Ozone Heights" (a dream ballet in which Venus ponders life with Rodney) and "Forty Minutes for Lunch." Abel. (*V*) said that she "makes a terrific impact. She almost steals the show." The score's only subsequent standard was "Speak Low," a duet for Rodney and Venus, although the critics liked "That's Him," sung by Martin while sitting on a straight-backed chair, and "The Trouble with Women" (a funny barbershop quartet), among other tunes.

One Touch of Venus was approved for its adult wit, its lavish production elements, Weill's offbeat and subtle melodies (for which he did his own arrangements), de Mille's choreography, and the various performances. Waldorf was pleased "to attend a new musical comedy that is adult, professional, often comic and genuinely musical." Not approved were those passages where Nash's very clever lyrics proved too difficult to catch, the lack of sufficient humor (especially for the talented Teddy Hart), an occasional sense of overkill from one or another of the creative staff, and a too-slow-to-start first act, possibly stemming from Kazan's inexperience as a musical director. Representative of the many who found both good and bad in the show was Euphemia Van Rensselaer Wyatt (*CW*), who that believed the book barely scratched the surface of the source novel's possibilities and also was baffled by what made Venus chase the unprepossessing Rodney. "Compared to the average musical," she noted, "*One Touch of Venus* rates high, but as a fantasy it lacks the charm of *I Married an Angel**. It is too self-conscious to be wholeheartedly gay and lacks the simple jollity of Ethel Merman. Its point of view is cynical, its wit inclined to innuendo but grace it has in Mary Martin."

The show won a number of Donaldson Awards (this was the first season in which they were given). Among them was second place for best supporting performance (female), which went to Laurence. According to Cheryl Crawford's *One Naked Individual*, Laurence went up in her lines for the only time in her career one night after the show had been running for some time. There was a scene when she had to stand at the side watching the lengthy dance finale to act one. Her cue to speak finally came when Martin said to Boles, "Cheer up, darling, don't look so glum. This is our wedding day." Laurence would then comment, "Well, cupid, you certainly loused that one up!" On the fateful day in question, Martin accidentally changed her words to "Clean up, darling, it's the wedding . . . ." Laurence was so confused that, using an expletive she had never said aloud in her life, she spouted, "Well, cupid, you certainly fucked that one up!" Martin and Boles looked stunned, the actors backstage were in hysterics, and the orchestra played cowbells and cymbals.

ONE-MAN SHOW [Drama/Art/Business/Family/Romance/Sex] A: Ruth Goodman and Augustus Goetz; D/P: Jed Harris; S: Stewart Chaney; T: Ethel Barrymore Theatre; 2/8/45 (36)

Jed Harris chose this interesting variant of the silver-cord idea to produce after a fourteen-month layoff from Broadway, but despite considerable commendation, the piece lasted only a month. It was considered by many a penetrating treatment of a psychologically incestuous relationship between a man and his twenty-six-year-old daughter.

The Gardner Gallery on Fifty-seventh Street in New York is run by Lucian Gardner (Frank Conroy) and his daughter Racine (Constance Cummings). Racine's mother died when the girl was young. From the time she turned sixteen, her father has been training her as an art dealer. As a team they have succeeded in the discovery and selling of new artists, although the quality of the expensive work they exhibit is aimed more at vanity buyers than true aesthetes. The art-gallery background gives the play considerable opportunity to discuss art and the art world. Under the prodding of her father, Racine uses her considerable charms to woo the potential buyers. Various men have wooed the attractive Racine, but she has turned them all down because she holds too close an attachment to her father. The brilliant Lucian is also guilty of deviously restricting his loving daughter--who owes all her opinions to him--from a natural development of her womanly feelings. When James Dockerel (Hugh Franklin), a struggling young artist, threatens to gain Racine's lasting affection, Lucian's machinations short-circuit the relationship. Then there is a wealthy lawyer and art patron, Emory Jeliffe (James Rennie), who offers to take Racine as his mistress and is willing to finance a coveted art museum for Lucian as the price. Again, Racine's attachment to Lucian interferes. Finally, a firm-minded young State Department official named Francis Kearny (John Archer) manages to explode Racine's Freudian fixation to win the girl for himself (although the millionaire by now has proposed marriage) and to take her with him to Costa Rica, leaving papa behind as a "one-man show."

Several critics thought this a compelling and honest treatmeant of an adult theme, others thought it overobvious and artificial, while yet others fell somewhere in between. Howard Barnes (*NYHT*) opined that "the show is pretentious rather than profound; blunt where it might have been keen-edged." Lewis Nichols (*NYT*) was disappointed in what seemed a promising play because "the evening remains simply one of ingredients; the good qualities are not merged together." He pointed to the arbitrary shifts from comedy to serious drama and the lack of convincing character motivations. But the majority agreed with Burton Rascoe (*NYWT*), who insisted that it was "a brilliant and distinctive contribution to modern drama, subtle, psychologically incisive and deeply moving."

There was some disagreement over the lead performances, especially that of

Cummings. "Miss Constance Cummings should be nominated for one of the finest performances of the season as the beautiful and hapless victim of an obsession," wrote George Freedley (*NYMT*) in one of the most positive critiques. "She commands the stage, is warm, loving and yielding, in turn. Her voice is exciting and her facial expression a joy to watch." There were fine jobs done by Conroy, Archer, Kasia Orzazewski as a cook, and Elizabeth Brew as a gallery visitor.

ONE-WOMAN THEATRE [Miscellaneous/Solo] C: Stewart Chaney; T: Town Hall; 2/28/42

A one-woman performance of dramatic material by French diseuse Marianne Lorraine, a striking redhead who formerly had appeared in a similar bill at a local nightclub under the name Marianne Oswald. Wearing a blue-gray gown without jewelry and standing against a simple setting of black screens, she performed songs and poems in both English and French, her selections including Alfred Hayes's "When I Dance with My Bill," several poems by Archibald MacLeish and Carl Sandburg, a poem by an anonymous child, "Little Boy Will Not," and García Lorca's "Lament," among other pieces. Some of the material was accompanied by piano and accordian music.

Her work was not strongly received by the critics, although the audience was very enthusiastic. She seemed more natural and appealing in the French portions of the show, her English readings being "theatrical rather than dramatic," according to Vernon Rice (*NYP*). George Freedley (*NYMT*) commented, "What had a certain, cerebral charm in a bistro is lost in the width of the Forty-third Street music hall. She has a bold hoarse voice and large, vigorous gestures, but they failed to fill a theater auditorium."

(1) **ONLY THE HEART** [Drama/Blacks/Business/Family/Marriage/Sex/Small Town] A: Horton Foote; D: Mary Hunter; P: American Actors Company; T: Provincetown Playhouse (OB); 12/5/42

This company's fifth season opened with another of Horton Foote's investigations into the provincialism of small-town Texas life, it being considered by many the best of the lot. Several reviewers even thought that it would make satisfactory fare for Broadway (where it later was produced). Its title was from a poem by Heinrich Heine ("They flourish and flourish from year to year, and only the heart is withered and sere").

George Freedley (*NYMT*) called it "a tense, well-articulated drama," needing only a bit of editing and revision to make it truly first-rate. Richard Lockridge (*NYS*) had reservations, but still could declare, "It is an interesting play; it is done expertly and with feeling; it belongs in the theater." However, Wilella Waldorf (*NYP*), while finding Foote's work promising, said that the "dialogue is over-written and his play drags. His characters seem to be saying the same thing over again, not once, but several times." Arthur Pollock (*BE*) was upset by the playwright's failure to make any larger points in his too objective survey of his characters' suffering.

Set in Richmond, Texas, beginning in 1935, and covering about a year and a half, the somber play, unrelieved by humor, centers on the bitter, ruthless, and shrewd Mamie Borden (Hilda Vaughn), who determines to use her business abilities to make a fortune for her brood. Mamie is a control freak who manipulates the lives of those around her. She has destroyed her school-teacher-sister India's (Jeanne Tufts) love life, leading India to become a spinster. The man she would have wed has become the town drunk. Mamie is so preoccupied with her business interests that she neglects her daughter, Julia (Constance Dowling), who hardly knows her. Her husband Tom (Freeman Hammond), who for some time has been having an affair with a black woman (Jacqueline Andre), tolerates Mamie's attitude because he is afraid that she will tell Julia of his dalliance. When Mamie, however, connives to have Julia break up with the penniless man she loves and marry the boring but rich Albert Price (Richard Hart), Tom decides to leave her. Albert is employed in managing Mamie's affairs. Julia's marriage eventually founders when Albert--who also takes a mistress from the wrong side of the tracks--becomes just like Mamie. Julia runs off with the fellow she would have married. Albert, too, abandons Mamie, but she is partially placated for her various setbacks by the success of her oil investments, which will make her the richest person in town; she will, however, have no one with whom to share her money.

(2) [Dramatic Revival*] S/C: Frederick Fox; P: American Actors Theatre (formerly American Actors Company); T: Bijou Theatre; 4/4/44 (47)

Foote revised his play for Broadway's intimate Bijou Theatre in this production, with the cast reduced to only five characters, all of them with new actors. Mamie was now played by June Walker, India by Mildred Dunnock, Julia by Eleanor Anton, Albert by Will Hare, and Tom by Maurice Wells. The character of the black mistress was now changed to an immigrant Bohemian, although she was not shown. The period was moved back from 1935 to 1921. Mary Hunter resumed her directing chores.

Walker proved disconcerting as the bitchy matriarch, her casting possibly an attempt to go against type so as to soften the harsh features of the role. Moreover, reported Rosamond Gilder (*TAM*), Foote's revisions, which tended to smooth over the less pleasant facets of the characters and situations, "weakened the impact of a play that needed amplification and deepening rather than prettifying." George Jean Nathan (*TBY*), who cared little for the original, now described the work as "a monotonous and painfully dull rehash of the theme of the domineering mother who brings unhappiness and worse to her family through her uncompromising selfishness." George Freedley (*NYMT*), who liked much of the original, was disappointed, believing that Foote had managed to seriously enfeeble his play through his revisions. Howard Barnes (*NYHT*) commented, "The theme is far from exciting, the dramatic structure is faltering, and the venon has been almost wholly extracted."

OPEN HOUSE [Comedy/Prostitution/Romance/Sex] A: Harry Young; D: Coby Ruskin; DS: Leo Kerz; P: Rex Carlton; T: Cort Theatre; 6/3/47 (7)

This example of "unbelievably boring witlessness" (Richard Watts, Jr. [*NYP*]), inspired by the housing shortage, brought aging comedienne Mary Boland back to Broadway to play one of her stereotypically nitwitted eccentrics. She was a widow named Mrs. Bartlett who decides to open her large heart and house--situated in a tony neighborhood--to people seeking lodgings. Her new tenants are a pair of ex-GIs (John Harvey and Don Gibson) and the sister of one, a voluptuous girl (Joyce Mathews) with plenty of boyfriends. When a nasty female neighbor (Ann Dere), who wants to gain possession of the house for herself, complains about Mrs. Bartlett's violation of the zoning laws, the house gets raided as a brothel and the neighbor gets arrested in the process. Happy endings ensue for everyone. Mrs. Bartlett marries the indigent uncle (Curtis Cooksey) of the young couple, and the complaining neighbor's pretty daughter (Augusta Roeland) weds one of the tenants.

Howard Barnes (*NYHT*) commented that the playwright had "achieved the dubious distinction of writing a first act which promises nothing but boredom and carrying through the project to a grimly chaotic and tedious conclusion." In the cast were Harold Grau, Dave Tyrell, Del Hughes, Ben Loughlin, Will Kuluva, and others.

(1) OTHELLO [Dramatic Revival*] A: William Shakespeare; M: Tom Bennett; D: Margaret Webster; DS: Robert Edmond Jones; P: Theatre Guild i/a/w John Haggott; T: Shubert Theatre; 10/19/43 (295)

The first revival of *Othello* in New York during the twentieth century was in 1914. There were subsequently a number of additional ones, including three in the 1930s, but the total number of performances for all of these did not come close to that achieved by this landmark presentation, which remains (in 1992) the longest-running Shakespeare revival ever offered on the Broadway stage. It was directed by Margaret Webster, the most commercially successful director of Shakespeare in American history, caused tremendous controversy by its casting of forty-five-year-old black actor Paul Robeson in the title role (conventionally played by white actors in dark makeup), and had a brilliant performance of Iago by José Ferrer and a memorable one of Desdemona by Uta Hagen, Ferrer's then wife. Backing them up were Webster herself as Emilia, Jack Manning as Roderigo, Averell Harris as Brabantio,

James Monks as Cassio, Philip Huston as Lodovico, Henry Barnard as a messenger, William Woodson as Montano, Edith King as Bianca, Robert E. Perry as both the doge and Gratiano, and Jack DeShay and Graham Velsey as senators.

The choice of a black actor for Othello, today more common than the casting of a white man, was provocative in 1943, even though blacks had played the role before, most notably Ira Aldridge in the nineteenth century. (Aldridge, however, had to emigrate to Europe to establish his distinguished career.) Robeson himself had played the part in London in 1930 opposite Peggy Ashcroft and in 1942 had given it a trial (under Webster's direction) in Cambridge, Massachusetts, Princeton, New Jersey, and Philadelphia. The tour was necessitated by the difficulty of finding a commercial management willing to risk a play having a black actor make love to and kill a white woman. When it was clear that audiences were excited by the project, various managements expressed an interest, but it was fourteen months before the production came to New York because of Robeson's prior commitments. However, just before the show was to go back into rehearsal, a controversy erupted within the company when the Theatre Guild, for several reasons but largely because of their contract demands, decided to replace Ferrer and Hagen with Stefan Schnabel and Virginia Gilmore. Robeson and Webster backed the Ferrers' demands, but the Guild refused to listen until Robeson put his foot down. Webster by this time was content with Schnabel and was upset about Robeson's power play. While placating all concerned parties, she seethed inwardly and wrote her mother, Dame May Whitty, that she behaved "as if I loved them and didn't want to pitch them off the balcony into 52nd Street" in order to "get a show out of that big, black jelly-fish and those two conceited little asses and make us all happy and bursting with harmony and enthusiasm" (quoted in Martin Duberman, *Paul Robeson*).

Despite the many academic arguments pro and con on the racial suitability of the casting, the question came down to one point, noted George Jean Nathan (*TBY*): Can the actor act the role? Nathan decided that he could not, but others differed, some vociferously. In Nathan's opinion, the very tall and athletically robust Robeson certainly looked right as the Moor (although, he argued, nobody else in the cast looked right as Venetians), but lacked the inner qualities required for it. Nathan described Robeson's performance as suggesting "mainly a Walter Hampden in blackface, overly rhetorical, monotonous, rigid, and given to a barely concealed consciousness of its vocal organ tones." A number of critics who otherwise raved over the performance commented unfavorably on the actor's self-conscious use of his famous vocal chords, which sometimes gave the effect of intoning or even singing the lines. Webster herself was never happy with his performance and felt that he was unable to convey the inner fire and anger of the role. In general, Robeson was given ecstatic reviews, modified here and there with minor reservations. For example, Euphemia Van Rensselaer Wyatt (*CW*) wrote, "Paul Robeson . . . invests the Moor with grandeur. The grandeur of a brave and simple nature. His tenderness toward Desdemona is as touching as his despair over his lost illusion. . . . His voice, with its organ tones, swells to the poetry." This critic's only quibble was over Robeson's reading of the lines about the handkerchief's magic properties, from which she could not tell if he was sincere or merely trying to frighten Desdemona; this was important, said Wyatt, who believed that much of Othello's character is bound up with his belief in witchcraft. Lewis Nichols (*NYT*) was impressed by Robeson's great stature, his striking vocal power, and his ability to go from being the roaring soldier to the tender husband. "He can be alike a commanding figure, accustomed to lead, a lover willing to be led and the insane victim of his own ill judgment." Wilella Waldorf (*NYP*), who had seen Robeson's London Othello and thought it mediocre, was forced now to change her mind, for this was "a tremendously impressive embodiment of the Moor. . . . His tortured reaction to Iago's scheming is immeasurably more affecting now than it was . . . thirteen years ago, when he did much more sweating and groaning." She found that the actor's blackness was a definite asset in explaining why Othello so readily falls into Iago's trap: "He was different from the men around him. He could never quite convince himself that [Desdemona] had ever actually fallen in love with him." Opening-night enthusiasm for the portrayal was overwhelming, with at least ten curtain calls and numerous shouts of "Bravo!" Director Webster spoke several words of thanks, declaring how much she and Robeson had longed for such a reception, never believing that it would actually occur. She then turned to the star and said, "Paul, we are all very proud of you tonight," which set off cheers throughout the house. However, she was later to write with disappointment of his acting (see *Don't Put Your Daughter on the Stage*) and of his widely varying performances.

The widest acceptance was of the slightly built Ferrer, whose Iago was completely unlike that of most previous actors, who broadcast their villainy the moment they appeared and could never have fooled even a dim-witted Othello. Instead, Iago was the perfect con man, completely believable in all his machinations. No specific hints as to the causes of Iago's behavior were offered, Ferrer choosing simply to establish the character as a man of basic evil who behaves as he does because that is the nature of the man. "The actor has a light walk," said Nichols, "and a light touch, and his Iago is a sort of half dancing, half strutting Mephistopheles, who does what he does probably in good part because there is pleasure in it." "His playing is forthright and honest; his villainy is cut from the same cloth," stated George Freedley (*NYMT*). "Colloquial and modern in his reading . . . , he gives the part an immediacy which does much to hasten the progress of the plot and facilitate the pace."

In what some thought a thankless role, Uta Hagen offered physical beauty and emotional sensitivity. "Miss Uta Hagen plays with pathos and charm, the traditional gentle misused lady of melodrama," recounted Wyatt. John Chapman (*NYDN*) observed, "Her slight, husky voice, which seems but a whisper, is uncannily clear and a tonal match for Robeson's sonorous outgivings. She seems the true, unworldly wife that Shakespeare wrote--feminine, submissive, puzzled and, finally, more resigned to her violent end than terrified of it." Most critics commented favorably on the great poignancy of her final scene.

Overall, the production, edited to two acts and eight scenes, was outstanding, being beautifully integrated, well paced, expertly designed, and excellently spoken. Howard Barnes (*NYHT*) commented that despite his belief that the play was not up there with the best of Shakespeare's tragedies, "it is so illuminated and held in a taut and thrilling pattern at the Shubert, that it becomes, in many respects, something new and wonderful in the theater."

(2) [Return Engagement] T: City Center of Music and Drama; 5/22/45 (24)

Following its lengthy run and a further trip on the road, the production reappeared in New York as part of the series of revivals at the City Center. Everything about the original was intact, including most of the cast, and the performances, especially Ferrer's, had grown richer and more fluent. However, some critics still faulted Robeson for declaiming rather than acting his role. One of the few changes in the cast was Edith King for Margaret Webster as Emilia, a change that had been made before the original run ended. At the Center's low prices (from $.90 to $2.40), it was considered a bargain well worth seeing, although the theatre's terrible acoustics remained a major drawback.

(1) OUR LAN' [Drama/Blacks/Period/Politics/Race/Romance/Rural/Southern] A: Theodore Ward; M: Joshua Lee; D/S: Edward R. Mitchell; P: Associated Playwrights; T: Henry Street Playhouse (OB); 4/19/47 (12)

The first of the works done by the new Associated Playwrights group to gain some strong critical approval was this black drama about white betrayal set in Georgia during the post-Civil War era. It was given an excellent performance; some thought that while it needed revisions, it was better than most plays then being done in the commercial theatre. Particularly valuable were the performances of William Veasey and Muriel Smith, who, said Richard Watts, Jr. (*NYP*), "are currently giving two of the finest and most stirring portrayals of the season." They were praised not only for their acting but for their excellent singing. Other actors in the large company involved included Valerie Black, Chauncey Reynolds, Edmund Cambridge, Luther Henderson, and Clarence Williams.

During the Civil War, General Sherman advised a group of former black slaves to assume control of an island off the coast for agricultural purposes and for their own self-respect and well-being. Following the war, things begin to sour for them as the Union troops fall gradually under the influence of the white plantation owners, who seek to regain the island, and the Andrew Johnson government in Washington decides to take the land back. The blacks decide to fight for their precious land and find themselves bloodied but unbowed in the pitched battles that follow against their former liberators. Into the fabric of the political plot is woven a love story between Joshua Tain (Veasey), the noble black leader, and a girl named Delphine (Smith). Spirituals sung with great skill and poignancy by the company were an integral part of the production and helped to make the experience deeply moving.

This high-minded drama--on which Ward had worked since 1941--was a valuable exploration of a long-hidden aspect of the Reconstruction period, often idealized from a favorably white perspective. The highly favorable Watts suggested that the play, seeking to avoid overly emotional expression, was sometimes too subdued. He and others were also uncomfortable with the romantic subplot. Several critics were in favor of moving the play to Broadway, which wish was fulfilled, but without commercial success (see next entry). One of them, Herm. (*V*), termed it "an honest, sensitively-wrought folk drama . . . with a contemporary relevance." But Louis Kronenberger (*PM*), while lauding the subject matter, believed that the play's treatment "is just not cohesive and intense enough."

(2) D: Eddie Dowling and Edward R. Mitchell; DS: Ralph Alswang; P: Eddie Dowling and Louis J. Singer; T: Royale Theatre; 9/27/47 (41)

This Broadway incarnation of *Our Lan'* failed to make the trip uptown without harmful effects. During the move, said Brooks Atkinson (*NYT*), it had "acquired theatrical dimensions but lost simplicity." The piece's various weaknesses seemed greatly magnified on the large Royale stage.

John Mason Brown (*SR*) reasoned that Eddie Dowling's production was overproduced. He noted, "Whatever drama there was stayed stubbornly on the far side of the footlights. It was contained in the theme rather than ignited by its handling. It got lost in a setting . . . in which the good earth never ceased to be painted canvas and the nearby ocean seemed miles away." The professional polish brought to the staging tended to underline the naïveté of the writing. There were also complaints that the work's reliance on spirituals to fill in emotional gaps was monotonous and excessive, although George Jean Nathan (*TBY*), one of the play's several faithful defenders, supported what he called the playwright's honest use of them "to hearten and forward his dramatic action and to color his theme interiorly." Among the new actors involved was Julie Haydon, playing a white teacher from the North.

OUR TOWN [Dramatic Revival*] A: Thornton Wilder; D/P: Jed Harris; T: City Center of Music and Drama; 1/10/44 (24)

A popular-price ($1.65 top) revival of the very popular and influential Pulitzer Prize-winning 1938 play, with Jed Harris resuming his directorial and producing duties, and with Martha Scott returning from Hollywood to again play Emily. Frank Craven was scheduled to take over the role of the stage manager but was prevented from doing so because of a Hollywood commitment, so playwright Marc Connelly assumed the part. Evelyn Varden in the role of Mrs. Gibbs and Doro Merande as Mrs. Soames were back, but the rest of the cast was new. These included Curtis Cooksey as Mr. Gibbs, Donald Keyes as Howie Newsom, Ethel Remey as Mrs. Webb, Montgomery Clift as George, Carolyn Hummel as Rebecca, Parker Fennelly as Mr. Webb, Arthur Allen as Professor Willard, and William Swetland as Simon Stimson. One of the walk-ons playing a townsperson was Eileen Heckart.

The production was in most respects a carbon copy of the original. Instead of exposing the bare walls of the stage, as in the 1938 version, this one enclosed the acting space with black velour curtains. Connelly's Broadway debut as the stage manager was effective, although he seemed a bit nervous and had to be urged by some balcony sitters to speak up, which he did. As George, Clift gave "a sensitive, understanding performance," thought Rosamond Gilder (*TAM*).

The critics appreciated the chance to see the lovely play again. Noted Burton Rascoe (*NYWT*), "The play is at once a document and a thing of classic and compelling tenderness."

OUT OF MY HOUSE [Drama/Alcoholism/Blacks/Family/Legacy/Religion/Small Town/Western] A: Horton Foote; D: Mary Hunter, Horton Foote, and Jane Rose; S: Joseph Anthony; P: American Actors Company; T: Theatre of the American Scene (Charles Weidman Studio) (OB); 1/7/42

Horton Foote, who had gained attention with his *Texas Town* the previous season, followed it up with another examination of small-town Texas life in this work. Brooks Atkinson (*NYT*), while finding the first three "parts" of the work somewhat "loosely-contrived," discovered that the play concluded with "a vibrant and glowing last act that is compact and bitterly realistic and also remarkably well played." George Freedley (*NYMT*) agreed, finding that, apart from the last act, the work was "confused, broken, poorly knit, overlong, [and] pitched so high as to be almost hysterical." Other critics, while finding much to fault in both writing and production, tried to be encouraging to the young playwright.

The play looks critically at four loosely connected aspects of life in a Texas cotton town, where class distinctions sharply separate the population. The first scene is set in an eatery called Tell's All-Nite Restaurant at one in the morning and introduces various levels of the bored local society. A Bohemian-American girl (Jane Rose) has left her farm and is pining for the return of her truck-driver spouse. Some slumming young members of the Mavis family, the town's boozing aristocracy, make fun of her and are attacked by Jack Weems (William Hare), a youthful, drunken idler, for their comments. Part two is set in the cabin of Red Mavis (Nancy Milroy), a girl with reactionary ideas, who goads her brother into a drinking bout that kills him. Part three is a farcical treatment of religious evangelism and treats of Nora and Sue Anthony (Gertrude Corey and Mary Hunter), a pair of old-maid sisters living on the hope that their aunt will die and leave them her fortune. Things go awry when they introduce their religious zealot of a new sister-in-law to the aunt. The fourth scene returns to the idler of the first, who loses his house to his social-climbing, bank-clerk brother (Casey Walters), with whom he argues about whether one must behave servilely toward the powers that be in order to get ahead or whether even poverty is better than to be so shamed. The argument is presented that only the unity of one man with another and not their separation by social class can provide hope for America. The play also finds room to treat the problems of black Americans with understanding. Each scene is briefly linked by a return to the all-night restaurant.

The Theatre of the American Scene was the new name taken by the Charles Weidman Studio (also known as the Humphrey-Weidman Studio) at 108 West Sixteenth Street, which had been the home of this company for several productions. This was a very intimate space, with eight or ten steeply banked rows of seats facing an acting space that was the studio floor itself, there being no stage proper. Lighting marked the beginning and end of acts, as there was no curtain.

OUT OF THE FRYING PAN [Comedy/Marriage/Politics/Theatre] A: Francis Swann; D: Alexander Kirkland; S: Cirker and Robbins; P: William Rogers Deering and Alexander Kirkland; T: Windsor Theatre; 2/11/41 (104)

Six starving young actors--three men and three women--come to New York and share--platonically, for the most part--a brownstone apartment over that of Mr. Kenny (Reynolds Evans), a Broadway producer with a hit mystery melodrama currently running. The monthly allowance of one of them, the very naive Dottie Coburn (Barbara Bel Geddes, in her Broadway debut), pays the rent. A pair of actors, Tony and Marge (Sellwyn Myers and Louise Snyder), it will develop, are secretly married and expecting a baby. The fledgling actors spy on Mr. Kenny through chinks in the floor and try to figure out a way to lure him into their apartment so they can show him their own performance of his hit show. Complications arise when Dottie's father (Henry Antrim), a Boston politician and theatrical censor, arrives, learns of his daughter's unconventional living arrangements, and threatens to withdraw her allowance. The group keeps failing to capture Mr. Kenny's attention because he is preoccupied with winning a prize as an amateur cook for a shrimp dish he is preparing. When, late one night, he is unable to complete the recipe without some flour borrowed from his upstairs neighbors, the price for his request is an instant audition. The trying conditions--including the harried landlady's (Mabel Paige) continued interruptions--under which they present the performance are good for many belly laughs.

The semiautobiographical screwball comedy was gussied up with many in-jokes about the acting profession, which accounted for much of the humor it provided. One such joke was when a character asked, "What's wrong with the Group Theatre?" and was told, "Nothing that George Abbott couldn't cure," referring to Abbott's reputation as a play doctor. The character of producer Kenny was said to be modeled on gourmet chef and producer Crosby Gaige. The play got its start in a summer theatre in Ellicott City, Maryland. Arthur Hopkins is said to have aided in the direction, although he was uncredited for it.

It was considered suitably entertaining, if not a laugh-a-minute barrel of fun. Rosamond Gilder (*TAM*) declared, "As a picture of the fringes of Broadway the farce is perhaps more accurate than encouraging. It lacks the drive and romantic bite of *Stage Door**, the rough-and-tumble gaiety of *What a Life**, but it provides some moments of light-hearted entertainment and much harmless merriment." Ralph Warner (*DW*) called it "a fresh, breezy, fluffy and enjoyable show." Brooks Atkinson (*NYT*), though, thought it overdone and illogical.

A note in the program stated, "The characters and events in this play are purely imaginary and anyone claiming resemblance or similarity ought to be ashamed to admit it." The best performances belonged to Alfred Drake as Norman Reese, Stanislavsky disciple and leader of the thespian band, and Florence McMichael (in her Broadway bow) as a dizzy friend who drops by and is enlisted to play the corpse in the ersatz melodrama. George Mathews was also in the play.

Herb. (*V*), commenting on eighteen-year-old Barbara Bel Geddes's performance, noted that she was the daughter of stage designer Norman Bel Geddes and pointed out that "it's virtually impossible to tell where life leaves off and acting begins, which makes her more than passable for the role." Atkinson, however, noted that "Norman Bel Geddes's plump and blonde daughter is still in the apprentice stage of histrionics." Several commented on the baby-talk quality of her speech.

OUT OF THE PICTURE [Drama/Art/British/Politics/Romance/War] A: Louis MacNeice; M: William B. Goldberg; D: Irving Stiber; CH: Ellen R. Albertini; S: David Berman; P: Interplayers; T: Interplayers Theatre (OB); 6/30/49

The Interplayers, ensconced in their small theatre in the Carnegie Building, began their second summer season with this foggy British satire first produced in London in 1937. The "experimental" piece was considered out of focus and of limited appeal. Thomas R. Dash (*WWD*) described its style as a "curious mixture of sardonic satire, songs, ballet and recitative asides by individuals and choral groups." Among the play's multiple themes was an attack on man's homicidal drives that lead him to war. It was too opaque for many to grasp, and the author's ideas did not blend clearly with his story. "The writing, while frequently brilliant and imaginative, is completely esoteric," decided Dash. "Perhaps because he has not a great deal to say, the author has proved [*sic*] his play on the stage like a jigsaw puzzle fresh from the box in an effort to demand attention by distraction," concluded William Hawkins (*NYWT*).

A struggling and frustrated artist (John Denny) has managed to complete only one work, "The Rising Venus," which is taken from him to pay for his many debts. The model (Nancy Stiber) used in the painting promises to get it back for him if he will fulfill her wishes, but, to the model's chagrin, he falls for the narcissistic movie star (Virginia Baker) who has bought his picture at an auction house. Then, on the eve of the declaration of war, he kills the peace minister who has resigned his post, but is himself poisoned by the model. The world is then destroyed.

The actors did as well as they could with the difficult material, although Richard Watts, Jr. (*NYP*), said that they were "trapped in Mr. MacNeice's heavy-handed humor and tedious pretentiousness." Gene Dow was a psychiatrist who treats the actress, and Henri Beckman was an auctioneer who sells art like a revival meeting evangelist. Also in the cast were Anna Berger, Louis Criss, and Fred Porcelli.

OUTRAGEOUS FORTUNE [Drama/Family/Homosexuality/Jews/Medicine/Music/Race/Romance/Sex] A/D: Rose Franken; S: Raymond Sovey; C: (gown) Valentina; P: William Brown Meloney; T: Forty-eighth Street Theatre; 11/3/43 (77)

After this play's adverse reception in Boston, Gilbert Miller pulled out of his producer duties, and author Rose Franken's husband, William Brown Meloney, assumed the role of producer. With its themes of homosexuality and anti-Semitism, it caused considerable controversy among the reviewers, but it suffered from too many dramaturgic flaws and failed to last long enough to turn a profit. This was one of the few plays of the 1940s with an outspokenly homosexual character. A chief asset was the performance of greatly admired character actress Elsie Ferguson, back on Broadway after fourteen years of retirement (she was a country neighbor of the Meloneys).

The heavily plotted play takes place in a New Jersey beach house inhabited by an upper-middle-class Jewish family. The family is headed by Bert (Frederic Tozere) and Madeleine Harris (Margalo Gillmore). They live together with Bert's foreign-born mother, Mrs. Harris (Maria Ouspenskaya), the glue that holds the family together. Bert, a banker, is a good husband and father and a man of principle, proud of his religion and sensitive to the slings and arrows to which it is subject. Madeleine is restless and has fallen for Barry Hamilton (Dean Norton, a former prizefighter and baseball player, cast against type), a young Gentile violinist of ambivalent sexuality, whom she has invited for the weekend, and who is her teenage daughter's music teacher. Bert's younger brother Julian (Brent Sargent), engaged to neighbor Kitty Fields (Adele Longmire), is a homosexual. When he breaks his engagement to her, Kitty tries suicide. Julian also lies that Barry made a sexual pass at him. There is also a Jewish family physician, Dr. Edward Goldsmith (Eduard Franz), married to an Irish woman (Margaret Hamilton), and unable to land a coveted hospital position because of his religion. The lives of all these persons are affected and rehabilitated by the arrival with Barry (her current lover and Greenwich Village neighbor) of a glamorous and mysterious outsider (the reasons for her celebrity are never explained) with a notorious past named Crystal Grainger (Ferguson). This wise and caring harlot is responsible for bringing love back into the insular Bert's life, for deflecting the ambivalent Barry--who subsequently takes an interest in Kitty--from becoming homosexual, and for getting the uptight Bert to accept his brother Julian's sexual orientation. (Her explanation of a man's homosexuality is to say that he has "too many F-cells" in his makeup.) She eventually dies bravely of the heart disease with which she is afflicted.

There were too many threads left lying about by the play to make a closely knit fabric. It had scattered scenes of great impact, but lacked cohesiveness. This was a shame because, said Robert Garland (*NYJA*), the play contained "a deal of wisdom, observation, tolerance, and wry and ofttimes bitter humor." "Miss Franken," observed Lewis Nichols (*NYT*), "has darted around among her various ideas like a drummer in a jazz orchestra, pounding first one and then the other and settling nothing." Yet George Jean Nathan (*TBY*) acknowledged, "Out of the tangled web there emerges nonetheless what amounts to a drama, albeit fitful, that touches with liberal understanding and with high dignity upon the complex facets of the life and loves of the characters it deals with. Nor is sound and searching humor lacking." Many critics likened the character of Crystal to the central role in the old play, *The Passing of the Third Floor Back*. Despite its mixed reviews, the play was selected as one of the ten best of the season by Burns Mantle.

Franken responded to the criticism that her play was confusing by insisting that an audience was more likely to be intrigued by a play when it left them something to chew over, rather than having everything predigested for them. Her play was based on a novel about three women involved with homosexual men, *Twice Born*, that she had published in 1935, but that was withdrawn from circulation soon after because of its then unmentionable homosexual subject matter. When Kaier Curtin (author of *We Can Always Call Them Bulgarians*) spoke to Franken in 1980 to ask whether she had intended to write a plea for tolerance of gay men, she adamantly denied the implication and insisted that she never had any sympathy with homosexuals, except for those who sincerely wished to change. Homosexuals, she averred, "are sick and their liberation movement, like the women's, almost makes me sick. I never needed to be liberated by anyone! Neither do the homosexuals--they just need to change their ways."

Margaret Williams, playing a comic black maid, was in the cast. The performances were all distinguished, but the most lauded was Ferguson's. Rosamond Gilder (*TAM*) wrote: "Still beautiful in the grand, histrionic manner; she has style and poise and an immense gusto. Her entrance in a tight-fitting suit with an improbable hat slammed at an angle over one eye; her reappearance later coming down the stairs in a white Valentina gown . . . are in the best tradition of the theatre theatrical. She has warmth and glow, a buoyancy that carries her across the stage in strong, clean sweeps, an unfailing sense of the interplay of word and gesture."

OUTSIDE THE DOOR [Drama/Death/Fantasy/German/Military/War] A: Wolfgang Borchert; TR: Erwin Piscator and Zoe Lund-Schiller; M: Arthur Kreutz; D: Erwin Piscator; S: H. A. Condell; L: Hans Sondheimer; P: Dramatic Workshop of the New School for Social Research; T: President Theatre (OB); 3/1/49

The German author of this play died of tuberculosis in 1946, aged twenty-six. His postwar expressionist play received only one review, Brooks Atkinson's (*NYT*), which cited the repetitiveness of the ideas, but declared that it strongly denounced the conditions that lead to war. "Herr Borchert's theme transcends nationality and ideology. It holds that the common men, selfish and complacent, is [*sic*] responsible for the horrors that accompany and follow world conflict." Atkinson acknowledged that it was not "great drama," but that it was an intensely written work by one who had known the pain of war.

Its central character is the insane ex-soldier Beckman (Martin Baum), who is "outside the door" and is symbolic of all similar outsiders. At the beginning he stands at the edge of the Elbe. He then jumps in. But he is rejected by death, and the river, unwilling to accept him, returns him to the world. He encounters the Other One, a symbolic figure who represents himself and others he has met before. Assured by the Other One that there is a tomorrow, Beckman disagrees, unwilling to accept that good exists in the evil world. He rebuffs the Other One as someone who has made false promises, who did not account for his postwar alienation. But Beckman is made by the Other One to confront life, and he goes through various experiences, learning from an old officer to play music on an xylophone made of human bones, meeting an assortment of women, young and old, and whispering in search of fathers, husbands, sons, brothers, and bridegrooms. He asks his colonel to assume responsibility for the dead soldiers but is turned away. At a cabaret he behaves like a clown and sings about those "outside the door," but this chills the customers, and he is snubbed once more. Returning in desperation to his mother, he finds only strangers in his home, his family being dead. The Other One tells him that life goes on and he should live. But it is too late for Beckman, for he is already dead in a world of the living dead.

Erwin Piscator used his trademark turntable to provide an excellent staging. Elsa Rolland, Jane Moultrie, Gene Saks, and Vinette Carroll were in the cast.

OVER 21 [Comedy/Aviation/Films/Journalism/Literature/Marriage/Military/War] A: Ruth Gordon; D: George S. Kaufman; S: Raymond Sovey; P: Max Gordon; T: Music Box Theatre; 1/3/44 (221)

Actress Ruth Gordon had a hit with her first play, in which she starred as novelist Paula ("Polly") Wharton, a quip-tongued sophisticate modeled on Dorothy Parker. The title refers to the fact that people over twenty-one are reputedly unable to absorb new information, a pseudoscientific observation that the action of the play refutes. Forty-five-year-old Gordon wrote her comedy when her recently married husband, twenty-nine-year-old author-director Garson Kanin, joined the armed forces and she left the stage to keep house for him in Washington, D.C., while he attended to his duties. With unwonted time on her hands, she used the opportunity to pen the piece. Her experience with the service personnel she met through Kanin served her well, and she gave herself a wisecracking, Dorothy Parker-like part perfectly suited to her stage personality. Various characters were based on real-life friends of Gordon. Burns Mantle liked it well enough to select it as one of the ten best of the season.

The one-set, relatively small-cast piece takes place entirely in 26D Palmetto Court, Miami, Florida, a small bungalow in a colony occupied by the families of men engaged at the Army Air Force Training Command across the road. The fashionable Polly and her groom, Max Wharton (Harvey Stephens), the famous newspaper editor (based on Thornton Wilder and Ralph Ingersoll), arrive to take possession of the shabby place from Roy (Tom Seidel) and Jan Lupton (Beatrice Pearson), who are leaving now that Roy has graduated from Officer Candidate School and has been assigned to Crocker Field in the boondocks of Arkansas. Because of that place's inconveniences for officers' wives, Jan will not be going there, to the couple's dismay. Max has left his newspaper career to attend OCS, although he is nearly forty. His New York publisher, Robert Drexel Gow (Loring Smith; the role was based on Herbert Bayard Swope), is violently opposed to losing his great editor to the war effort and will do whatever he can to lure him back. Polly has come to Miami from Hollywood, where she was working on a screen version of her best-selling novel, *Fellow Americans*. Their bungalow, explains Jan, has a number of decided plumbing and lighting inconveniences. Before the Whartons can make themselves comfortable, the Luptons return because of a delay in their train schedule, and Polly--alone after Max returns to the field--takes the couch while the Luptons are accorded the bedroom. This leads to comic complications when business with the location of the living-room light switch forces Polly to be locked out of the house in her nightgown. The Luptons finally leave, and the play attends to Max's fear that he will wash out and be unable to learn enough to pass the officers' examination, and to the efforts of Gow, who arrives three weeks later to convince Max to give up and return to the paper. A visit from Colonel Foley (Carroll Ashburn), his wife (Dennie Moore), and his mother-in-law (Jessie Busley) occupies much of act two, with the Foley family gaga over the presence of celebrity Polly and filled with innocuous questions about Hollywood personalities she knows. Gow does what he can to sour Foley on Max, but he is shut up by the Whartons. Polly worries where Max will be assigned when he graduates, but that is a secret until the last minute, says Foley. When the Foleys leave, Max berates Gow for his selfish attitude, and Gow, claiming that Max will never pass OCS, departs. Three weeks later, Max has graduated 271st out of a class of 353. The Foleys arrive to present Max with a gift. Because of a misunderstood remark of Polly's, they believe that Max wants to be assigned to Crocker Field. Thus Foley pulled strings to have him sent there. After the Foleys leave, the Whartons argue over Polly's insistence that she follow Max to Arkansas. Gow reappears, having been accepted back into the service in the rank of major. He has decided to sell the paper, which upsets Max and Polly. David O. Selznick-like Hollywood producer Joel I. Nixon (Philip Loeb) arrives with his secretary (Kay Aldridge), needing Polly's help with the *Fellow Americans* script. Talking over the script's problems inspires Polly with the idea of assuming the editorship of the paper, thus making it unnecessary for Gow to sell. Gow buys the idea, Max leaves for Arkansas, and Polly plans to follow and to take on the newspaper after Max's six-week flight-training period.

The reviews were varied. As a vehicle for Gordon's eccentric talent, the play provoked many laughs, especially as vivified by the ingenious farce direction of George S. Kaufman. Noted Euphemia Van Rensselaer Wyatt (*CW*), "Miss Gordon's sense of the humorous in the lines and Mr. George S. Kaufman's sense for stage business is a highly risible combination and the honest devotion of the two celebrities who take army life so seriously gives a solid foundation to the comedy." Rosamond Gilder (*TAM*) was an advocate of sorts. She said that the play "has enough cracks directed at current foibles, enough horseplay and G.I. jokes, to keep a wartime audience in gales of laughter. It has no distinction either in writing or performance, but all Miss Gordon's mannerisms of gesture and voice, her self-conscious gurgles and forays, her tricks of speech, are entertaining ornaments for a frivolous occasion." Some thought the first act hilarious, the second moderately amusing, and the third lagging far behind both in humor and in human interest; George Freedley (*NYMT*) thought that Gordon should have had Max fail the exam and decide that he could better serve his cause by editing the paper. One of the severest pans came from George Jean Nathan (*TBY*), who took issue with the role Gordon had created for herself, a character who gets the best witticisms, who dresses in the most elegant frocks despite the shabbiness of her surroundings, and who benefits from many other self-serving attributes. He also did not think much of many of her wisecracks nor of her attempts to effect a tone of "bitter irony" that came out instead sounding like "shallow meanness."

Producer Gordon was recuperating from an operation when he first read the script, and he was so delighted with it he nearly burst his bandages from laughing. However, when he showed it to Kaufman, the latter, according to Gordon's *"Max Gordon Presents"*, was unimpressed, saying, "It's not a play. . . . There's hardly a plot, and it depends almost entirely on lines." When Gordon strongly disagreed, frequent Kaufman collaborator Moss Hart was asked for his opinion, and he felt as did Kaufman, but also thought that the piece could be rewritten into shape. Kaufman thereupon agreed to direct it and made a significant contribution to the shape of the final script. Hart also came to some rehearsals and added good suggestions. For all the work's success, Kaufman never did think much of it.

Gordon was so happy with the play's possibilities he was ready to spend whatever was necessary on it. Ruth Gordon wrote in *My Side* that when she insisted that the high-priced Mainbocher design her clothes, she warned the producer of the designer's astronomical fees. "Don't tell me about the cost of buttons when I got an Act Two like *I* got!" he insisted. But when the bill arrived, Gordon called his star, "Ruthie, I'm not going to pay any lousy dressmaker thirty-seven hundred dollars!" When the actress reminded him of her warning, he replied, "Ruthie, I don't care *what* you told me. I never paid it and I won't. The whole wardrobe for *My Sister Eileen* didn't cost *half* that!" The producer, however, eventually gave in.

The role that Beatrice Pearson eventually played originally had been assigned to producer Dwight Deere Wiman's beautiful but inexperienced daughter, Tottie Wiman. The poor girl, however, could not pronounce Arkansas, calling it Ar*kan*sas. "Arkansaw," shouted Kaufman. "Oh? Give me a pencil. My part says Ar*kan*sas." It was decided to fire her, and Kaufman chose to send her a telegram instead of telling her personally. He wrote, "Dear Miss Wiman, we are sorry we feel we must replace you. We need a more experienced actress. I am sure we can use you in some other play someday. Please return your part." He then signed it, "Best wishes, Max Gordon."

OVERTONS, THE [Comedy/Gambling/Marriage/Sex/Theatre] A: Vincent Lawrence; D: Elisabeth Bergner; S: Edward Gilbert; C: Hattie Carnegie; P: Paul Czinner; T: Booth Theatre; 2/6/45 (175)

Once-promising playwright Lawrence, gone from Broadway for fourteen years while busy in Hollywood, returned with this commercially successful yet artistically deficient comedy about marital infidelity. Refugee actress Elisabeth Bergner made her debut as a director (her husband produced), but did not impress too many by her often-interesting but erratic staging. The talented cast came in for few commendations.

The tony suburban Overtons, Cora (Arlene Francis) and Jack (Jack Whiting), have been happily wed for eight and a half years. Their friends consider them eccentric and outmoded in their happy connubial state and even believe them to be secretly disgusted with one another. One such friend is the seductive Judith Bancroft (Glenda Farrell), a predatory actress with her painted talons out for Jack. Judith is courted by Bill Minot (Charles Lang), ex-all-American athlete, and kept by wealthy financier James Lawson (Walter N. Greaza); the latter's interest in the irreproachable Cora leads him to wager Judith that she cannot steal Jack away. Much of the action centers on Cora's suspicion--abetted by the suggestions of Bill and James--of an affair between Jack and Judith after she sees her spouse entering the actress's bedroom just as she was undressing. Cora leaves Jack, and he, his pride wounded, not only adamantly refuses to explain his actions but announces that if she goes he will not take her back. Cora, learning the truth (Judith had been changing clothes to accompany Jack on a mission to borrow $80,000), eventually does return to his arms, while James, touched by the Overtons' unflinching faithfulness, helps them out of a financial jam.

Talkativeness, pretentious dialogue, predictable comedy, and a mixture of styles were a few of the black marks against this effort. "The dialogue outlining this temporary domestic misfortune runs from philosophy to an attempt at light drawing room comedy," moaned Howard Barnes (*NYHT*), "but in either mood it is underlined with nonsense." Louis Kronenberger (*PM*) called it "a play it is just not possible to say anything pleasant about." A rare supporter was Burton Rascoe (*NYWT*), who regarded the play as "a bright and honest, credible, fast-moving, suspenseful and amusing domestic farce-comedy."

OWL AND THE PUSSYCAT, THE [Comedy/Period/Politics/Prostitution/Show Business] A: Stanley Bortner; D: Robert T. Eley; S: Mallory; P: New York Repertory Group; T: Cherry Lane Theatre (OB); 7/31/48

John S. Wilson (*PM*) could not think of a good reason the New York Repertory Group chose to stage this period comedy set in 1903. The author "has filled it with such a lack of imagination, in such a shallow, one-dimensional fashion, that every twist and turn is not only obvious but tritely and trashily obvious."

A quartet has been invited to sing "The Owl and the Pussycat" at the White House for Teddy Roosevelt, so they try to rehearse it. For three acts they try to rehearse it, but a quarrel erupts between the female accompanist and a singer; a singer's wife goes into labor; a Sunday-school teacher tries to shut down a brothel; and the danger arises that the group leader, the local chief of police, may be fired because the mayor hates President Roosevelt.

The cast included future star Beatrice Arthur, Jimmy McElwain, Christine McKeown, Jack Burkhart, and Florence Stanley, among others.

OY, IS DUS A LEBEN! (***Oh, What a Life!***) [Musical/Historical-Biographical/Jews/Theatre/Yiddish Language] B/D: Jacob Kalich; M: Joseph Rumshinsky; LY: Molly Picon; CH: David Lubritzky and Lillian Shapero; S: Harry Gordon Bennett; P: Edwin A. Relkin; T: Molly Picon Theatre; 10/12/42 (139)

Audiences visiting this "musical cavalcade" of petite, forty-four-year-old Yiddish theatre star Molly Picon's career (written and directed by her husband) were given a brief English synopsis because the entire production--apart from snatches in English--was in Yiddish. Before arriving in New York, the piece was shown in eleven Canadian and American cities, and the star was delighted to find so many spectators who still understood enough Yiddish to follow the dialogue. The show (at the former Jolson Theatre) covered many years, beginning with a prologue introducing some of the great names of the Yiddish theatre's past, such as David Kessler (Isadore Casher), Jacob Adler (Boris Auerbach), Sigmund Mogilesco (Sam Kasten), and Boris Thomashefsky (Michael Welinsky). It then moved on to Picon's childhood (she was born in Philadelphia in 1898), when she made her debut at the Arch Street Theatre in 1910 for fifty cents a performance. It followed with such highlights as her experiences in Yiddish companies in Boston; her meeting with Kalich (played by himself), the immigrant actor who would be her spouse and mentor; his marriage proposal; her success in a play (*Molly Dolly*) written by him for her; her trip to Europe to better her Yiddish and polish her technique; her performance in Bucharest when an anti-Semitic student fired a gun, missed her, and killed an old man, followed by her waving the American flag and giving a rousing lecture on freedom; her visit to Poland to meet Kalich's family; her return to the Second Avenue stage in triumph; and so on through the years as she became the most popular player on the Yiddish stage.

The show allowed the versatile gamine to sing, dance, tell funny stories, do imitations of Fannie Brice, Charlie Chaplin, and Eddie Cantor, and act with sentiment. Most of her numbers were those she already had made famous. Most successful was her rendition of "I Don't Want to Be a Man," sung in English.

"She is a talented person," wrote Burns Mantle (*NYDN*). "Her voice is warm, her manner friendly, her sense of comedy is sure and her feeling for character, both in comedy and drama, wins a response that is as definite as the rhythm of the songs Joseph Rumshinsky has been for writing for her these many years." Speaking of the show, Wilella Waldorf (*NYP*) reported, "Sometimes confusing, often a little childish, its better parts are strangely arresting." In supporting roles were Yiddish theatre stalwarts

Anna Appel, Dora Weissman, and Tillie Rabinowitz.

P

PAL JOEY [Musical/Nightclub/Romance/Sex/Show Business] B: John O'Hara; M: Richard Rodgers; LY: Lorenz Hart; SC: John O'Hara's *New Yorker* stories; D/P: George Abbott; CH: Robert Alton; S/L: Jo Mielziner; C: John Koenig; T: Ethel Barrymore Theatre; 12/25/40 (374)

Because this musical had as its hero a realistically depicted, cynical gigolo, it was considered a milestone in the development of American musical theatre. *Pal Joey* was based on a series of salty epistolary stories by John O'Hara appearing in the *New Yorker*, with O'Hara--who had suggested the project--himself doing the libretto, although his failure to attend the rehearsals and production meetings seriously annoyed his coworkers and even provoked Rodgers to send him a telegram, "SPEAK TO ME JOHN SPEAK TO ME." The show was rather controversial, its subject of a kept man being thought distasteful by several critics, especially Brooks Atkinson (*NYT*), whose comment, "Although *Pal Joey* is excellently done, can you draw sweet water from a foul well?" rankled the creators. Fortunately, it had a brilliant score by Rodgers and Hart and all the genius that its outstanding director, choreographer, and designers could muster, plus brilliant performances by Gene Kelly--in the role that made him a star--and Vivienne Segal.

Richard Rodgers wrote in *Musical Stages* that before it opened, director-producer Abbott demonstrated a lack of faith in the show that irked the creative staff. When designer Mielziner was told by Abbott to keep his costs as low as possible and choreographer Alton was not allowed to hire two extra chorus girls, Rodgers went to Abbott and asked him to give up the show on the grounds that he was not the ideal person to produce it. But Abbott, for all his doubts, was not ready to hand *Pal Joey* over to anyone else, and his attitude thereafter improved.

The show effectively captured the atmosphere of the second-rate niteries it depicted. Richard Watts, Jr. (*NYHT*), called it "a brilliant, sardonic and strikingly original musical comedy," unusual in its consistently hard-boiled, unsentimental atmosphere. Hart's hard-hitting lyrics blended perfectly with the rough-edged quality of O'Hara's bitter prose. Richard Lockridge (*NYS*) enjoyed the show's rich humor, especially that of the central character, but thought that it occasionally "stops rolling and stumbles into routine. . . . But it is always lively and almost always funny." Sidney B. Whipple (*NYWT*) considered it "a bright, novel, gay and tuneful work, made interesting by the rich characterizations of its book." John Mason Brown (*NYP*) praised the first act's originality and imagination but found that act two grew gradually tiresome as intrusively melodramatic plot elements began to interfere with his enjoyment.

Joey Evans (Kelly) is a handsome, boastful nightclub dancer and MC in a Chicago dive who drops the sweet Linda English (Leila Ernst) to bed down Vera Simpson (Segal), a wealthy and sexually available society matron, in order to get the funds to open his own glitzy joint, Chez Joey. (An excellent dream ballet was built around the nightclub's opening.) Vera also sets Joey up in his own posh apartment.

There Linda tells Vera that someone is planning to blackmail her over her affair with Joey. Linda convinces Vera that her motives in telling of the scheme do not stem from jealousy, as she has come to realize how worthless Joey is. Vera drops Joey, leaving him to search for another "mouse" to give him what he needs.

Atkinson said of Kelly that he acted Joey "with remarkable accuracy. His cheap and flamboyant unction, his nervous cunning, his trickiness are qualities that Mr. Kelly catches without forgetting the fright and gaudiness of a petty fakir. Mr. Kelly is also a brilliant tap dancer . . . and his performance on both scores is triumphant." It was widely believed that Kelly's natural charm went a long way toward making the despicable Joey palatable. He himself had serious doubts about whether the audience might not find the cynical character too offensive. He therefore tried to evoke a characterization that would show that Joey was not a scheming villain but simply had no clear concept of right and wrong. "For example," explained Kelly (quoted in Clive Hirschhorn's *Gene Kelly*), "he would accept his promiscuity as a matter of course, completely unaware of the hurt he was causing, and just when he was being especially offensive, I'd look at the audience, smile at them, and go into a song and dance, turning the character around, almost." He said that the key to the character came when he expressed his fears that the audience would dislike him to John O'Hara, and the latter replied, "No, they're going to hate Joey, but they're going to like *you*."

"I Could Write a Book" was one of Kelly's standout singing numbers. Segal scored highly with her acting and singing, especially with the great song, "Bewitched, Bothered, and Bewildered," which Abel. (*V*) thought too risqué for radio or the kiddies. Hart had not written any special encore lyrics for the song, and despite a cool reception to the song in Philadelphia, Broadway's opening night audience demanded them. Luckily, Segal remembered a lyric that Hart had written but thrown away. When director Abbott later asked her how she ever remembered it, she "told him I was so damn mad Larry [Hart] didn't write any encores for me, I had to remember something." (Quoted in Samuel Marx and Jan Clayton, *Rodgers and Hart*.) She also got to sing such tunes as "Take Him" (with Leila Ernst) and "Love Is My Friend." And June Havoc as Gladys Bumps, a sexy nightclub performer, was a hit with her rambunctious comedy performance and her singing of songs such as "That Terrific Rainbow" and "Plant You Now, Dig You Later." Havoc began rehearsals with a small part and gradually demonstrated so much talent that her part was considerably expanded. Jack Durant as the hoodlum Ludlow Lowell was excellent with his acrobatic dancing and singing of "Do It the Hard Way." There was also the amusing strip number, "Zip," satirizing the intellectual pretensions of Gypsy Rose Lee, performed by Jean Casto. A week before the opening, Casto had suffered severe burns to her hands during the Philadelphia tryouts, but insisted on remaining with the show and wore mittens in her number on opening night. In the chorus and playing the small role of Victor was Van Johnson, who would succeed Kelly as Joey and go on to a successful film career. He was picked out by Abel. for managing "to project himself quite vividly." Also holding small roles were future film directors Stanley Donen and Robert Mulligan.

PANAMA HATTIE [Musical/Military/Politics/Prostitution/Romance/Sex/Tropics/Youth] B: Herbert Fields and B. G. De Sylva; M/LY: Cole Porter; D: Edgar J. MacGregor; CH: Robert Alton; S/C: Raoul Pène du Bois; P: B. G. DeSylva; T: Forty-sixth Street Theatre; 10/30/40 (501)

The season of 1940-1941 got off to a rousing start with a series of smash-hit musicals, among them this colorful Cole Porter show starring Ethel Merman, with a backup cast including such stellar performers as Betty Hutton (June Allyson was her understudy), Arthur Treacher, and James Dunn. There were also Rags Ragland, Frank Hyers, and Pat Harrington, constituting a trio of dame-hungry American gobs played in bawdy, low-comedy-burlesque style. Opined Richard Watts, Jr. (*NYHT*), "Here is Broadway girl-and-music saturnalia at its peak, humorous, tuneful, hard-boiled, sentimental, rapidly paced and handsome, filled with good low comedians and beautiful girls and starring the wonderful Miss Ethel Merman in the leading role. You really shouldn't ask for much more." *Panama Hattie* proved popular enough to become the first musical since 1928's *New Moon** to run for at least 500 performances.

Talking of Merman's rise to stardom, Abel. (*V*) observed, "Long an outstander in her own right as a song interpreter, Miss Merman has become punchier, sockier, more mellifluous. The shade of scat-sing stridency that remained as a heritage from her early . . . vocal schooling is now entirely nonexistent, and she emerges the No. 1 musical comedy femme interpreter of lyrics." Merman's big numbers included "Let's Be Buddies," the biggest hit of the show, sung with young Joan Carroll; "I've Still Got My Health"; "Make It Another Old-Fashioned, Please"; and "Who Would Have Dreamed." She also stopped the show in "You Said It," shared with Treacher, Ragland, Hyers, and Harrington. Hutton scored with "All I've Got to Get Now Is My Man" and "Fresh as a Daisy."

The critics found the book thin but serviceable, the score excellent if not vintage Porter, and the comic elements, production values, and performances worth recommending strongly. Producer B. G. De Sylva was at the top of his form at the moment, presiding at the same time over the concurrent hits *Louisana Purchase** and *Du Barry Was a Lady**, the latter of which Merman left in order to take on the title role in the present show.

Set in Panama City, which permitted a musical score infused with Latin tempos, *Panama Hattie* provided a book with topical overtones as it told the story of reformed but flamboyant heart-of-gold Canal Zone hooker Hattie Maloney, who falls for Nick Bullett (James Dunn), a Panama Canal employee and scion of a fine Philadelphia family, who patronizes the bar Hattie frequents. Before she will marry Nick, Hattie wants to meet his eight-year-old daughter Geraldine (Joan Carroll, a Shirley Temple-like eight-year-old who received rave reviews), whom he has not seen since his divorce seven years earlier. Nick worries about how he and the kid will get along and how the latter will relate to Hattie. Geraldine arrives in the company of an English butler, Vivian Budd (Arthur Treacher), and bursts into laughter at her first sight of the gaudily dressed Hattie, whom, after some initial discomfort, she becomes fond of and teaches to dress like a lady. This occurred during the show-stopping "Let's Be Buddies" number. (In *Merman*, the star later recalled, "At the beginning of the number my hat had a bird on it and there were bows, bows, bows all over my dress and shoes. During the song Joan, who had converted to my side, appeared to be snipping the trick bows with scissors so that as we finished singing she had turned my outfit into a simple orchid-covered dress.") Part of the plot involves the schemes of Leila Tree (Phyllis Brooks) to steal Nick from Hattie. The climax of the story comes when the canal is endangered by a bomb planted by fifth columnists (Geraldine is made the unwitting carrier of the bomb, which is hidden in a candy box), and Hattie races along a treadmill to save both the canal and Nick.

In addition to the work of the stars, there were outstanding specialty performances by dancers Carmen D'Antonio, Nadine Gae, Harry Rogue, and others. The only sour note concerning the performances was the fairly widespread opinion that Hutton was giving an overenergetic performance that was greatly in need of toning down. Euphemia Van Rensselaer Wyatt (*CW*) called her "an annoyingly irrepressible acrobatic comedienne."

PAPA IS ALL [Comedy/Family/Marriage/Religion/Romance/Rural] A: Patterson Greene; D: Frank Carrington and Agnes Morgan; S/C: Emeline Roche; P: Theatre Guild; T: Guild Theatre; 1/6/42 (63)

New York turned this play down, but it had been an enormous favorite on the road before opening on Broadway. Its original staging had been at New Jersey's Paper Mill Playhouse. The play's humorous picture of a Pennsylvania Dutch Mennonite family continued to appeal to high-school and community theatre groups for many years. Given an authentic-looking farmhouse kitchen decor and Mennonite costumes, and employing charmingly twisted folk patois in the dialogue for comic effect, the play was reminiscent of Synge's *The Playboy of the Western World** with its story of a son who takes out his resentment of his brutal father by physical means.

The play's title, in the local idiom, means "Papa is dead." Papa (Carl Benton Reid) is the clubfooted, tyrannical patriarch of the Aukamp family of Lancaster, Pennsylvania, thinking himself the voice of God for his family and standing in the way of nearly every mortal pleasure his wife and children desire. He is stingy, bigoted, sadistic, and zealously religious. Because they are not given legitimacy by the Bible, no phones or electricity are allowed. He keeps his rein on the family with the occasional use of a horsewhip. His sweet, patient wife (Jessie Royce Landis) is completely under his domination. He seeks to shoot a youth merely for taking his daughter (Celeste Holm) to a movie. When he forces his son Jake (Emmett Rogers) to drive him to the boy's home, Jake comes home without papa, declaring that he is "all" after having been killed in a railroad-crossing accident. Now that he is gone, his family begins to enjoy life, a phone and electricity are installed, and pleasure in his demise is shared by the neighbors as well. But, as in *Playboy*, papa returns, having been merely knocked out by the monkey wrench blow given him by his son. Fortunately, a state trooper (Royal Beal) arrives to arrest papa for his attempt at murdering his daughter's suitor, although papa had attacked the wrong man.

Louis Kronenberger (*PM*) thought the characters phony and the play hokum. "It takes the line of half exploiting melodrama and half kidding it; or you might say that it carries the plot to the point where it goes all to pieces, and then proceeds to throw the pieces around for laughs." And John Anderson (*NYJA*) noted, "It isn't good enough of a play to be satisfying and not bad enough to make much difference." Despite the negative responses of most important critics, several had fairly warm words, Rosamond Gilder (*TAM*) declaring that it was all "skilfully whipped together with sufficient invention to hold attention," and Brooks Atkinson (*NYT*) opining that the play was "completely entertaining." No one argued about the quality of the acting, everyone holding his or her own and Landis, Reid, and Rogers proving outstanding. Dorothy Sands was also excellent as a comically loquacious neighbor.

PARK AVENUE [Musical/Family/Marriage/Romance] B: Nunnally Johnson and George S. Kaufman; M: Arthur Schwartz; LY: Ira Gershwin; D: George S. Kaufman; CH: Helen Tamiris; S/L: Donald Oenslager; C: Tina Leser (Leonora Corbett's gowns: Mainbocher); P: Max Gordon; T: Shubert Theatre; 11/4/46 (72)

Lyricist Ira Gershwin's last Broadway show before departing for other pastures was this opulently produced, but "singularly unimposing" (Brooks Atkinson [*NYT*]), opus satirizing the much-married socialites of the street named in the title; although the action takes place at a fancy Long Island home, it is presumed that the residents also have homes on Park Avenue. It sought to be a sophisticated, chichi musical but only succeeded in being a one-joke show whose wit was sadly intermittent. "The constant hitting of the single divorce note makes for ultimate torpor," yawned George Jean Nathan (*TBY*). Although most critics turned thumbs down, a few ap proved the show, including Richard Watts, Jr. (*NYP*), who called it "bright and amusing" and thought the admittedly "slender" book "frequently witty."

Its "strikingly underwritten" (Arthur Pollock [*BE*]) book followed the tribulations of the four-times-wed and none-too-bright snob, Mrs. Sybil Bennett (Leonora Corbett), whose daughter Madge (Martha Stewart) is affianced to Ned Scott (Ray McDonald), a charming Southern boy from Charleston, South Carolina; their big wedding is in the works. Mrs. Bennett invites her three exes (Robert Chisholm, Raymond Walburn, and Charles Purcell) with their current wives (respectively, Martha Errolle, Mary Wickes, and Ruth Matteson), although keeping track of them proves confusing to her. She is even planning to drop her present spouse (Arthur Margetson) in favor of another, and the other couples also begin to move from partner to partner. When Ned sees the world of marriage and divorce into which he is leaping--he compares the family to that in *Tobacco Road**--he tries to run away. All is resolved when one of the exes chooses a bride who turns out to be his daughter by a former marriage, which brings all to their senses for the moment. They return to the spouses with whom they began the evening, and Ned and Madge are joined.

The idea of the potential incest of a man with his daughter disgusted producer

Gordon, who also felt that the audience was upset by it. He wanted Kaufman to change it somehow, but the director refused until after the show already had opened. Finally, realizing that perhaps the situation was proving distasteful to the audience, Kaufman and the playwright revised it so that the man discovers, not that the girl is his daughter, but that she is only eighteen and therefore too old for him.

The score was generally undistinguished and hard to hear over the loud orchestrations. Among its better-liked titles were "Don't Be a Woman If You Can" and the calypso-rhythmed "Land of Opportunity."

After she was cast, Leonora Corbett demanded the star's prerogative of refusing any of the songs written for her. When the music was played for her at her apartment, there was a handsome man there who was not introduced. As the guests were leaving, producer Gordon asked the actress who the man was. "He's in cotton," she answered. "And," cracked Kaufman, "dem dat plants it is soon forgotten" (quoted in Malcolm Goldstein's *George S. Kaufman*).

One of the best performances was by David Wayne as a divorce lawyer. Wayne was cast only after a succession of others had been fired, including Jed Prouty, Ralph Riggs, and J. Pat O'Malley.

PARLOR STORY [Comedy/Journalism/Marriage/Politics/Sex/University/Youth] A: William McCleery; D: Bretaigne Windust; S: Raymond Sovey; C: Bianca Stroock; P: Paul Streger; T: Biltmore Theatre; 3/4/47 (23)

William McCleery's "amiable but dull" (Howard Barnes [*NYHT*]) comedy followed the classical precepts of the unities closely, being set in a single place (a professor's home in a midwestern university town) and taking place in a single evening when the lame-duck governor's (Paul Huber) decision on the new university president is impending. Professor Charles Burnett (Walter Abel), a former crusading journalist, is the popular choice. Governor Bright wants to make the correct decision because it will mean votes in the election. Burnett eventually is chosen, but only after various complex developments including the conspiring of his reactionary former editor, Mel Granite (Royal Beal), to trick him into leaving the university and returning to journalism, and the counterconspiring on her husband's behalf of Mrs. Burnett with the governor. Within the far from classically simple action is a romance of one of the Burnetts' daughters (Carole Wheeler) and young Eddie West (Richard Noyes), a college reporter who has written a controversial editorial on marriage that leads to his being accused of left-wing leanings. The climax comes with the decision of Burnett as to whether he will expel his prospective son-in-law or reach a compromise with his old boss and the governor in order to be named president. Obviously, compromise is a word he does not know. All the twists of the plot are designed to elicit talk on diverse issues, such as academic freedom, marriage and divorce, adolescent views of sex, political dishonesty, freedom of the press, and so on.

The nicely acted play drew mixed notices, Euphemia Van Rensselaer Wyatt (*CW*) representing the plus side in commenting, "*Parlor Story* is a comedy with humor, insight, charm and pleasant people." On the more heavily represented minus side was Brooks Atkinson (*NYT*), who, while thinking the dialogue "beguiling" and the scenes with the young people "not only light and humorous but occasionally touching," described the work as a whole as "a rather dreary problem play." George Jean Nathan (*TBY*) thought the plotting mechanical and predictable; he believed as well that the writing was a trivialization of the various important topics discussed. Officers of the law were played by Dennis King, Jr., and Frank Wilcox.

PARTITION [Drama/Orientals/Politics] A: C. Hart Schaaf; D: John F. Grahame; S: Sally Nussbaum; P: Modern Play Productions; T: Provincetown Playhouse (OB); 10/28/48

This unimportant play by a Cornell University professor who once had held an international relief post received only one notice. Its subject was the futile attempts of a United Nations commission to establish peaceful conditions in the fictional Indian province of Silapur, where Moslems and Hindus are at each other's throats. It displayed the obfuscation and political infighting that goes on in UN committees, as represented by the thick-wittedness of the participants.

The "play does not contain the elements of powerful drama which might have been realized" given the situation being dramatized, wrote J. P. S. (*NYT*). The best acting was by John Francis as the sly and witty Soviet representative who admits that his negative vote on Silapur's partition is dictated by the Kremlin and does not come from his own heart.

(1) **PATIENCE, OR BUNTHORNE'S BRIDE** [Musical Revival*] B/LY: W. S. Gilbert; M: Arthur Sullivan; D: R. H. Burnside; P: R. H. Burnside i/a/w the Gilbert and Sullivan Opera Company; T: Ambassador Theatre; 2/25/44 (4)

The sixth in a series of revivals by the renamed Boston Comic Opera Company, which had not included this work in its 1942 season. Robert Pitkin played Colonel Calverley, Bertram Peacock was Major Murgatroyd, Roland Partridge was Lieutenant the Duke of Dunstable, Florenz Ames was Reginald Bunthorne, Frank Murray was the solicitor, Allen Stewart was Archibald Grosvenor, Kathryn Reece was Lady Angela, Marie Valdez was Lady Saphir, Mary Lundon was Lady Ella, Catherine Judah was Lady Jane, and Kathleen Roche was Patience.

It was a modestly effective presentation, with nothing exceptional to recommend it and such drawbacks as shoddy scenery to hamper its effectiveness. Ames's Bunthorne was the best performance. "In fine tradition he minced and sang the part broadly and merrily, as it should be," claimed L. C. (*NYT*).

(2) D: Anna Bethell; S: George Sheringham; C: George Sheringham and Hugo Rumbold; P: D'Oyly Carte Opera Company; T: Century Theatre; 2/9/48 (16)

The final presentation in the nine work repertory brought here by England's famous Gilbert and Sullivan troupe, which totalled 136 performances during its visit. Martyn Green was Bunthorne, Ella Halman was Lady Jane, Joan Gillingham was Lady Angela, Gwyneth Cullimore was Lady Saphir, Muriel Harding was Lady Ella, Margaret Mitchell was Patience, Richard Walker was Colonel Calverly, Leonard Osborn was the duke of Dunstable, C. William Morgan was Major Murgatroyd, and Charles Dorning was Archibald. "Outfitted in gay new costumes . . . the players as usual are a pleasure to behold and hear," noted Lewis Funke (*NYT*).

(1) **PATRIOTS, THE** [Drama/Historical-Biographical/Period/Politics/Sex] A: Sidney Kingsley; D: Shepard Traube; S: Howard Bay; C: Rose Bogdanoff and Toni Ward; L: Moe Hack; P: Playwrights' Company and Rowland Stebbins; T: National Theatre; 1/29/43 (172)

Sidney Kingsley had worked on this play for two years before putting it aside to join the army in the rank of sergeant. He said later that he wrote it "at a time when it looked as though this nation, this democracy, might very well be destroyed. Hitler was marching. Nothing was stopping him. Mussolini had thrown in with him. And then the Soviet Union signed a pact with him. I thought to myself, 'I am just going into the army. What is this country which I might be called upon to die for? What is its essential nature?'" (quoted in Otis L. Guernsey, Jr., *Broadway Song and Story*). As he researched the problem, he realized that his answer would be found in the story of this country's founding (the original title was *Thomas Jefferson*). The drama also bore a contemporary parallel in the conflict between the liberal President Roosevelt and the nation's reactionary elements.

While stationed at Governor's Island, New York, Kingsley took up the work again and used his wiles to find an appropriate writing space. The barracks attic he found, however, turned out also to be a rifle range. Finally, after two more years, the play was produced and proved a notable contribution, being chosen as one of Burns Mantle's ten best of the year and also garnering the Drama Critics Circle Award for 1942-1943. Its importance to the world of 1943 was great enough for the Playwrights' Company to produce it as its first play not by one of the dramatists belonging to its immediate circle.

Produced in the year of the bicentennial celebration of Thomas Jefferson's birth, the play seeks to uphold the ideals of democracy propounded by the author of the Declaration of Independence. It is set in the last decade of the nineteenth century and, following a prologue, begins with Jefferson's (Raymond Edward Johnson, a radio actor in his Broadway debut) return from France, where he was ambassador. His wish to retire as a farmer to Monticello is put aside in favor of his reluctantly accepting the position of secretary of state under President Washington (Cecil Humphreys). Much of the following action is then taken up with his bitter quarrels over the future of the nation with his political antagonist, Secretary of the Treasury Alexander Hamilton (House Jameson). Jefferson, a firm Constitutionalist, stands for the rights of the common man--equal opportunity for all--and for states' rights, while Hamilton, a Federalist, distrusts and despises the "masses" (he calls democracy "our disease"), is skeptical of the Constitution's strength to hold the union together, and prefers a highly centralized and autocratic, even aristocratic, form of government, as well as an aggressively capitalist economy. To Jefferson, Hamilton represents a dangerous threat to the Bill of Rights and the Constitution. Their differences suggest the beginnings of America's two-party system. During the decade covered by the drama, Hamilton has an affair with a married woman, which gets him into a conflict with her husband, and is implicated in scandals involving blackmail and embezzlement. He believes Jefferson to be secretly responsible for his embarrassments and responds by writing smears in which Jefferson is depicted as a lecher and an otherwise disreputable person. Jefferson ultimately proves victorious when he is elected to the presidency in 1800 (Hamilton aided in his enemy's election rather than see the vote go to Aaron Burr) and delivers his famous inaugural address as the play's finale.

The drama was applauded for its contemporary significance, for its relative faithfulness to history (many authentic passages were interpolated into the dialogue), for its ability to take dramatic liberties in turning dry history into sound dramatic material, and for the overall excellence of its painstaking production, particularly the brilliance of Howard Bay's multiple sets. Those who complained that Hamilton was unflatteringly depicted as a villain were reminded that the play considered him as much a patriot as Jefferson, if perhaps a misguided and overbearing one. There was a problem as well with the sometimes too-zealous attempt to duplicate Jefferson's literary style in his speech, so that he often sounded too stiff and bookish and not sufficiently down-to-earth. Still, said Rosamond Gilder (*TAM*), "There emerges a full-length portrait of Jefferson, supported by sound sketches of Hamilton and Washington, with a crowded background of lesser figures." George Jean Nathan (*TBY*) listed a number of dramaturgic lapses that irked him, but he still contended that "so honest is it at bottom, so unostentatious in its deeper dramatic current, so intelligently handled in general, and so genuinely stirring in its overtones and after-image that it amounts in sum not only to the most critically acceptable full-length offering of the season but to one of the most skillful historical-biographical plays our American theatre has disclosed."

Johnson's portrait of Jefferson was considered by Lewis Nichols (*NYT*) to be on a par with Raymond Massey's of Lincoln several years earlier, although others felt him somewhat lacking in dynamism. The roles of James Madison and James Monroe were played, respectively, by Ross Matthew and Judson Laire. Kingsley's wife, Madge Evans, took the role of Patsy, Jefferson's daughter. Hope Lange made her Broadway bow as Anne Randolph, and the cast also included Frances Reid as Martha Jefferson, Francis Compton, Juano Hernandez, and Leslie Bingham.

Cecil Humphreys, who was giving a superlative portrayal of Washington, and looked very much the part, was hurt in a street accident a week after the play opened and was replaced within twenty-four hours by the slightly less effective Edwin Jerome. A more serious catastrophe occurred during the rehearsals of the play when highly promising young director Lem Ward died of a combination of pneumonia and a heart attack and had to be replaced by Shepard Traube.

(2) [Return Engagement] S: William Kellam; T: City Center of Music and Drama; 12/20/43 (8)

During the show's road tour, it stopped in New York for a limited return engagement. Walter Hampden now acted Thomas Jefferson, Guy Sorel played Hamilton, Julie Haydon played Patsy, Marie Dow was Martha, Ken Renard was

Jupiter, and John P. Boyd was Monroe, among other changes. Cecil Humphreys was back in his role of Washington and Ross Matthew repeated his Madison, these being the only two actors from the first company.

Hampden looked too old to play the younger Jefferson, but gave a less florid performance than usual and was considered an improvement over the radio actor of the original version. The same was true of Guy Sorel's Hamilton. This version modified the picture of Hamilton to make him seem less a scoundrel and more a patriot.

As with other productions at the City Center that season, there were many complaints about the poor acoustics, and the show was one that employed, but not too successfully, an amplification system to improve audibility. The production utilized a new, streamlined touring set, so there was less to look at on the vast expanse of the stage. Lighting and drapes were much more in evidence than before.

PEEPSHOW [Comedy/Fantasy/Romance/Sex] A: Ernest Pascal; D: David Burton; S: Lemuel Ayers; C: Bianca Strook; L: Carl Kent; P: Ernest Pascal i/a/w Samuel Bronston; T: Fulton Theatre; 2/3/44 (29)

To George Freedley (*NYHT*) this effort was "pompous, pretentious, vulgar and unimaginative," therefore deserving of failure. Its story was about Jonathan Mallet (John Emery), a famous bridge player and ladies' man who has an affair with his best friend's (Dwight Weist) beautiful wife Leonie (Tamara Geva) although he is on the verge of marriage to the lovely Jessica Broome (Joan Tetzel). Whatever the elegant bon vivant does is commented on by a personified Conscience (David Wayne) who is with him everywhere, gestures and dresses similarly, and reacts to everything he experiences, but whose sardonically wise advice is usually ignored. Conscience even occasionally knocks the play itself (which endeared him to the critics). Jonathan takes the friend's wife to a New Jersey roadhouse, but she tells her spouse that she is attending a pet show with her dog. Returning, their car is in an accident and Jonathan goes to the hospital for his injuries; Leonie is unhurt. When Leonie's husband, Tommy, finds out about her lie, he seeks to discover who she was with. Meanwhile, Jessica breaks up with her fiancé. She finds herself, however, at his apartment, where the pair indulge in champagne, which releases their libidos. Just before the final curtain, Jonathan enters a bedroom with Jessica, and Conscience is abruptly kicked out on his pants.

Arthur Pollock (*BE*) dismissed the lavishly designed show as "tripe." Wilella Waldorf (*NYP*) declared that "most of it seemed as flat as stage champagne." The device of the Conscience was not as newfangled as the writer may have thought, noted several critics, who were quick to offer examples of the technique in earlier plays. Moreover, said Rosamond Gilder (*TAM*), "it proved as awkward and essentially undramatic here as it has on the various other occasions it has been used in recent years."

John Emery reminded many of John Barrymore in looks and manner, but not in natural acting talent. David Wayne as Conscience received warm reviews, as did Lionel Monagas as Jonathan's black butler.

PEG O' MY HEART [Dramatic Revival*] A: J. Hartley Manners; D: Eliza Downing; S: Robert L. Ramsey; C: Valerie Judd; P: On-Stage; T: 6 Fifth Avenue (OB); 8/24/48 (6)

New York's first revival of the-once popular 1912 (1914, the date given in volume one of this series, is incorrect) Laurette Taylor vehicle since 1921 was done in a back parlor of a brownstone on lower Fifth Avenue as part of a "Cavalcade of American Hits." The creaky play had to confront the obstacles of a tiny space and awkward direction, but it had a delightful actress in Mary V. Malone to carry Taylor's torch. Richard Watts, Jr. (*NYP*), thought that she played "Peg beguilingly, with a charming sense of comedy and a fine talent for managing sentimental pathos without going too far with it." Her good notices landed the young actress a small Broadway role in that season's *Goodbye, My Fancy*. The semipro cast included James Harwood as Alaric, the nitwit Englishman; Grace Rogers as Mrs. Chichester, the aunt; Laurie Amidon as Ethel, the haughty daughter; and Harvey Mitchell as

Jerry, the romantic juvenile.

Watts thought the sentimental Cinderella play "a mechanical, fabricated comedy that is no more a masterpiece now than it was before the First World War. Its appeal is primitive." Still, he admitted to being touched because of the life invested in the various stock characters. Jane Corby (*BE*) believed that Malone's performance demonstrated that the play could still be vastly pleasing and "strangely bright." "There is a basic honesty about the character that keeps the otherwise 1912 comedy still both touching and amusing."

PERFECT MARRIAGE, THE [Comedy/Journalism/Law/Marriage/Sex/Youth] A/D: Samson Raphaelson; S: Oliver Smith; C: (Miriam Hopkins's gowns) Valentina; P: Cheryl Crawford; T: Ethel Barrymore Theatre; 10/26/44 (92)

Not to be confused with the 1932 comedy of the same name*, this clichéd effort dealt with a marriage of much briefer duration. Whereas the former play was about a couple celebrating fifty years of marriage, the present opus concerned a couple on their tenth anniversary. This pair is Dale (Victor Jory) and Jenny Williams (Miriam Hopkins), he a designer of bombers, she a magazine editor. The well-to-do, seemingly content couple, who have a precocious nine-year-old daughter (Joyce Van Patten), realize that the sexual magic has fled their union. Lawyer friend Addison Manning (James Todd) arrives to explain divorce proceedings. Dale and Jenny bicker. Dale seeks to make Jenny jealous by reviving a thing with Gloria Endicott (Martha Sleeper), and Jenny acts similarly, dating someone else (not seen). This leads to some powerhouse jealous recriminations and finally to a sexual reawakening that brings the couple back together for the nonce.

Although it began promisingly and was peppered with clever observations, the play grew gradually duller, its characters increasingly thin, and its situations of diminished interest. Ward Morehouse (*NYS*) said, "It wanders and rambles. It is lacking in real emotion and feeling." "A muddled, verbose play," opined Robert Coleman (*NYDM*). "The only trouble with this type of formula play," commented Rosamond Gilder (*TAM*), "is that it requires consummate writing and acting, neither of which are forthcoming." Evelyn Davis played a black maid, and Helen Flint played the lawyer's wife.

Miriam Hopkins had not been on Broadway for some time, so she was nervous about her performance. When she did not show up at the first dress rehearsal, and producer Crawford called to find out the problem, Hopkins had her maid declare that the actress was sorry but she was too ill to rehearse. Crawford (according to her *One Naked Individual*) replied, "I'm sorry too. I'll call my doctor and have him there to see her in two hours." In less than an hour Hopkins appeared at the rehearsal. "The show must go on," she said. "Yes, it must," responded Crawford.

On opening night Hopkins passed out when embraced by Jory; after carrying her to the setting's bed, he ad-libbed his way through the rest of the scene. Jory later discovered, according to Peter Hay's *Broadway Anecdotes*, that the actress, even before she fainted, had cabled various columnists apologizing for having lost consciousness. "It was a little too much," Jory declared. "I have worked with actors who have upstaged their co-workers so far that they upstaged themselves. Miriam was one of those."

PETER PAN [Dramatic Revival*] A: James M. Barrie; M: Leonard Bernstein; D: John Burrell; CH: Wendy Toye; S/L: Ralph Alswang; C: Motley; P: Peter Lawrence and R. L. Stevens; T: Imperial Theatre; 4/24/50 (321)

A hit revival of the fabulous Barrie play (first seen locally in 1905 and last revived in 1928) about the boy who would never grow up. With a new--and nearly continual--score by Leonard Bernstein, including songs for various characters, and a dazzling performance by Jean Arthur as Peter and vastly amusing ones as Mr. Darling and Captain Hook by horror-movie star Boris Karloff, the show ran for nearly a year. Norman Shelly played Nana and the crocodile, Charles Taylor played Michael, Peg Hillias played Mrs. Darling, Jack Dimond played John, Marcia Henderson played Wendy, Gloria Patrice played Liza and Tiger Lily, Lee Barnett played Tootles, Charles Brill and Edward Benjamin played the twins, Buzzy Martin played Nibs, David Kurlan played Starkey, Joe E. Marks played Smee, Nehemiah Persoff played Cecco, and, among many others, William Marshall played Cookson.

Old Vic director John Burrell, making his American debut, provided a marvelous production. Louis Sheaffer (*BE*) claimed, "With a nice appreciation of the author's intentions and a feeling for peace [*sic*], [he] realizes *Peter Pan* is lightfooted or it is nothing. He has kept the action stepping through its various moods of gentle enchantment, roughhouse, free-wheeling fantasy, sweet pathos, smallfry horseplay." The production dazzled by its flying techniques (imported from England), technically adroit, picture-book sets, colorful and inventive costumes, tinkling sounds and ubiquitous blinking lights to suggest Tinker Bell, and energetically enthusiastic performances. (The flying, however, did not go up to the second balcony, as it had in Eva Le Gallienne's 1928 version.) *Peter Pan* still had the power to make children (and adults) temporarily suspend their disbelief and place their faith in elves, goblins, and magical dreams.

"As the scowling, glowering Captain Hook, Karloff is tremendous," wrote Thomas R. Dash (*WWD*), "even going into a piratical song and dance routine which thrilled last night's spectators. His burly, blustery, blood-thirsty buccaneer was a sheer delight." Instead of using a single, dull black hook, Karloff chose to wear a double pronged, very shiny one. He also sang two songs, "Drink Blood!" and "The Plank," revealing a suitable baritone. His fatiguing role involved six costume changes and three makeup changes, requiring forty pounds of makeup, according to Lindsay. Despite his fame as a horror actor, children delighted in crowding into his dressing room, and Karloff would grant them their most earnest wish--to wear his hook--only if they said "yes" when he asked if they clapped for Tinker Bell.

"Jean Arthur is the Peter," reported Arthur Pollock (*DC*), "her light hair cropped short as any boy's, her voice crackling and comical, her spirit as joyous as Peter's ever can be. She plays robustly, like a very healthy youngster, humorous and tender and gay." "Miss Arthur's rightness for the role was evident from the moment she uttered the first line and her luminous, overwhelming job never sagged or veered for a moment from the author's intentions." In accordance with tradition, Wendy was assigned to a young actress making her professional debut, and Marcia Henderson was captivating in the role.

PETRIFIED FOREST, THE [Dramatic Revival*] A: Robert E. Sherwood; D: David Alexander; S: Tom Adrian Cracraft; P: Mary Elizabeth Sherwood; T: New Amsterdam Roof Theatre (OB); 11/1/43 (8)

The first in a brief series of limited-engagement revivals of hit plays with a Broadway stock company performing at popular prices ($2.20 top). Each play was given a break-in period at the Chapel Theatre in Great Neck, Long Island. The result of the company's production of Sherwood's 1935 melodrama set in an Arizona desert lunch stop was, according to Euphemia Van Rensselaer Wyatt (*CW*), "a well directed, well rehearsed company who gave a most creditable performance."

The competent but uninspired cast could not erase the memory of the distinguished original actors, most notably Humphrey Bogart, Leslie Howard, and Peggy Conklin. In their respective roles of Duke Mantee, Alan Squier, and Gabby Maple now were Wendell K. Phillips, John McQuade, and Barbara Joyce. Of the three new principals, the most successful was McQuade, of whom Lewis Nichols (*NYT*) wrote, "Mr. McQuade is soft-spoken and leisurely, and he gives the air of being completely dangerous." Also in the company were E. G. Marshall as Gramp Maple, William Forester as Boze, Grover Burgess as Jason Maple, Robert J. Lance as Mr. Chisholm, Natalie Benish as Mrs. Chisholm, Jack Bittner as Jackie, William Toubin as Ruby, and Slim Thompson as Pyles.

Although critics like Burton Rascoe (*NYWT*) approved the choice of play ("just enough good, sure-fire hokum in it to make it stand up after eight years"), it had its detractors, too. Robert Garland (*NYJA*) said that the "melodrama has a corny and unconvincing tone. Some of the lines are practically unspeakable."

The stock company folded after two productions (the second being *Goodbye Again*). The reason, surmised George Jean Nathan (*TBY*), was the lack of any actors with personalities colorful and distinctive enough to draw the public. The choice of venue for the company was the long-disused New Amsterdam Roof Theatre, which had grown shabby and run-down, but which was thoroughly cleaned--although not renovated--for these revivals.

"PHOENIX TOO FREQUENT, A" and **"FREIGHT"** [One-Acts] D: John O'Shaughnessy; DS: Jack Landau; P: Steven H. Scheuer and Bernard Carson; T: Fulton Theatre; 4/26/50 (5)
"A Phoenix Too Frequent" [Comedy/British/Death/Military/Period/Romance/Verse] A: Christopher Fry; SC: "The Widow of Ephesus," a story Jeremy Taylor adapted from a story by Petronius; "Freight" [Dramatic Revival] A: Kenneth White

This was an uncomfortable pairing of one-acts. It included Fry's verse play, set in ancient Ephesus, with a revival of a play about Southern racial prejudice; the latter originally had been produced in 1949 by the American Negro Theatre in Harlem on a double bill with a black production of Synge's *Riders to the Sea* (see that entry).

Fry took the old Latin story of a beautiful, grief-stricken Ephesian widow, Dynamens (Nina Foch), who, accompanied by her sardonically amusing maid, Doto (Vicki Cummings), attempts to immure herself in her late husband's tomb. Along comes a handsome young centurion corporal, Tegeus-Chromis (Richard Derr), and a spark is lit in the widow's breast. When a body the soldier is supposed to be guarding is stolen, the widow allows him to substitute for it her husband's corpse, thereby saving the centurion's life while confirming herself in his affections.

Fry's play was considered often charming, and its verse, packed with similes, metaphors, and amusing colloquialisms, was at times delightful, but it was widely accused of being loquacious, overwritten, far too long, and dramatically thin. Howard Barnes (*NYHT*) declared, "The work has a degree of imagination, eloquence and wit, but it is more promising than fruitful." The story, he said, "is sometimes amusing, but it has very little dramatic substance." It "becomes a bore because of its author's inability to realize the value of brevity." Various critics, including Brooks Atkinson (*NYT*), placed a large share of the failure on direction and performances, which, by opting for too literal an approach, failed radically to capture the light and lithe style required.

In Atkinson's eyes, the powerfully performed "Freight" stole the evening's plaudits. Believing it improved from its initial presentation, he called it a "stunning, straightforward statement of a monstrous truth." But Barnes damned it as "a dull and tasteless playlet," and William Hawkins (*NYWT*) dismissed it as "a violent and unpleasant piece." Among those in the cast were many from the original showing, but Lloyd Richards was now in it and Sidney Poitier was not.

PIAF, EDITH (see *Edith Piaf*)

PICK-UP GIRL [Drama/Crime/Family/Illness/Music/Prostitution/Romance/Sex/Trial/Youth] A: Elsa Shelley; D: Roy Hargrave; S: Watson Barratt; C: Emeline Roche; P: Michael Todd; T: Forty-eighth Street Theatre; 5/3/44 (197)

This play (first titled *Elizabeth vs. You and Me*) was inspired by a current social problem concerning female adolescents who, during the war, were making themselves easily available both to servicemen on leave and to civilians. The Russian-born actress who wrote the play had hoped that the subject would inspire her playwright husband, Irving Kaye Davis, to write it himself, but he, noting the great deal of personal research into the problem that she had done, felt that she would be the perfect author. Although it seemed far from the kind of thing he was associated with, Michael Todd was set to produce it before he was called up by the navy. With his approval, and with his having granted them shares in the production, Todd's staff (James Colligan, Harry Bloomfield, and Harriet Kaplan) then proceeded to have the play mounted.

The author had intended the play as a case study, hoping to expose this aspect of the juvenile delinquency problem so that society at large could more readily confront it. The dilemma was growing so rapidly that a chief justice of Special Sessions had warned that the available facilities were being taxed to their utmost. Of the young women in public and private shelters in trouble for soliciting, ninety percent were under eighteen, fifty percent under sixteen. Still, author Shelley was criticized by some for not offering a solution of her own. In general, the critical response viewed the play as a realistic depiction of the courtroom procedures used in investigating a serious social malady. It was effective enough to prompt Burns Mantle to choose it as one of the ten best plays of the year.

The play takes the form of an afternoon's hearing at Children's Court, where Judge Bentley (William Harrigan) deals directly with the girl and her family, the latter being discouraged from employing legal counsel. The confused fifteen-year-old girl at the center of the present hearing is Elizabeth Collins (Pamela Rivers), who has been discovered in bed with a middle-aged man. The judge, a man of great kindness and sensitivity, pieces her story together as he listens to her and a string of witnesses. She is the product of a Depression family, the mother (Kathryn Grill) having had to raise three children when the father (Frank Tweddell) was thrown out of work. With the arrival of the war, the father took a shipbuilding job on the West Coast and the mother took employment as a cook for an actor and actress, forcing her to work nights and to leave Elizabeth to care for her younger siblings. For some excitement in her drab life, Elizabeth turned to a high-school friend named Ruby (Toni Favor), whose nightclub-hostess mother was away at nights and allowed her daughter to give parties. Ruby prompted Elizabeth to accompany her to Times Square to pick up sailors. An older man (Arthur Mayberry) met Elizabeth at Ruby's and later bribed a tough high-school boy (Zachary Charles) to take him to Elizabeth's home, but he was eventually discovered when a neighbor lady (Lili Valenty) complained to the district attorney, and Elizabeth was caught. Mrs. Collins, the neighbor, the boy, Ruby, and Mr. Collins, who comes home by bus for the hearing, provide the background to the girl's tragedy. A romantic interest is provided by an agitated youth (Marvin Forde), the would-be violinist son of the complaining neighbor, who is ignorant of Elizabeth's crime, but plans to elope with her if the judge decides to put her in jail. The "john" also testifies, but is excoriated by the judge. Mr. Collins now has a bungalow in California to which he wants to bring his family, but Elizabeth cannot join them because she must be hospitalized for venereal disease and will have to wait until she is cured and then released from reform school. Elizabeth accepts her fate and looks forward to when she can marry her violinist admirer.

Apart from its value as a timely treatment of an important subject exacerbated by the war, the play was appreciated by some for its absorbing dramatic effect, produced through a very restrained manner, never dissolving into violent melodramatics. Euphemia Van Rensselaer Wyatt (*CW*) called it "unusually well-written and constructed." Arthur Pollock (*BE*) dubbed it "one of the genuinely important plays of the period. . . . It is a remarkably fine and illuminating drama." Robert Garland (*NYJA*) considered it the best courtroom drama he had ever seen, "with the possible exception of *The Trial of Mary Dugan*.*" A few critics, however, pointed to structural flaws and to its sometimes monotonous question-and-answer method. Louis Kronenberger (*PM*) griped that for all its interest, the play was too didactic. "This didacticism overloads the play, and a commonplace touch and slack dramatic sense slowly undermine it." He attacked, among other things, the treacly sentiment of the love interest, saying that it "vitiates the seriousness of the main theme." George Jean Nathan (*TBY*) took issue with the entire play, which he blasted for being a sensationalistic and excessively moralizing melodrama trying to masquerade as a seriously intended problem play. He also noted the ridiculousness of the syphilis angle, since the girl's illness could easily have been treated with penicillin.

An interesting feature of the set was a scrim curtain designed by director Hargrave, showing the closed door to the courtroom painted on it, with the courtroom itself gradually disclosed as the lights behind the scrim came up, the rising layers of scrim giving the effect of a disappearing wall. This allowed the audience to gain the impression of being transported to a private hearing. William Foran played a court attendant and Doro Merande was the court stenographer.

PIE IN THE SKY [Comedy/Family/Romance] A: Bernadine Angus; D: Edgar J. MacGregor; S: Donald Oenslager; P: Edgar J. MacGregor and Lyn Logan; T:

Playhouse; 12/22/41 (6)

One of several 1941-1942 season plays that lasted a week or less on Broadway, this one led Ibee. (*V*) to write, "Not in seasons has there been any lighter or sillier play. It should go back in the box, with the lid hammered tightly."

Monte (Oscar Shaw) and Vera Trenton (Luella Gear) are impoverished socialites living on Fifth Avenue. They hope to marry their dimwitted son, Roger Montgomery Trenton III (Herbert Evers), off to Lily deLacy (Lyn Logan, the coproducer), a blond three-times divorcée with money in oil wells and a past slinging hash. Lily's interest in Roger stems purely from her desire to have some social aristocracy in her offsprings' blood. Roger actually loves brunette Susy Bransby (Barbara Arnold), daughter of similarly impoverished socialites, who takes employment as the Trenton maid in order to be close to her beloved. Because of Lily's celebrity status, Roger is courted as an executive for a perfume firm selling a scent reputed to be highly aphrodisiac, which provides some humor when people react to being sprayed with it. When Roger declines to marry Lily, his dad takes his place, with a Mexican divorce from Vera in the hopper.

Enid Markey and Herbert Corthell as poor relations provided much of the skimpy laughter. Kirk Alyn (who later played Superman in the movies) overacted as a Latin American gigolo.

PILLAR TO POST [Comedy/Military/Romance/Sex] A: Rose Simon Kohn; D: Antoinette Perry; S: John Root; P: Brock Pemberton; T: Playhouse; 12/10/43 (31)

A thoroughly predictable sex comedy that reminded some of the movie, *It Happened One Night*, and that played to nearly empty houses before shutting down. "It is neither well written nor well acted," groaned Lewis Nichols (*NYT*), "presenting the gloomy picture of a comedy which wanders with leaden feet across the stage."

A young cosmetics saleswoman named Jean Howard (Perry Wilson) can not find a room at the USO Housing Bureau near an army camp, so she talks Don Mallory (Carl Gose), a young lieutenant going on a brief leave, into driving her to a motel (or "auto court") down the road a bit. When the place has only one cabin available, she asks the soldier to sign the register as her husband so the two can share the cabin for the night. Gentleman that he is, he bypasses the double bed to sleep on the floor. This leads to all the usual complications when Don's blustering CO, Colonel Michael Otley (Franklyn Fox) and his wife (Frances Woodbury), turn up in the neighboring cabin and Jean tells them that she and Don are married. Other officer friends of Don's and their wives occupy other cabins, so the confusion grows apace. If Don's falsehood about being married is discovered, he will face a court-martial and risk losing his promotion. After three acts of struggling to extricate themselves from their difficulties, Don and Jean find themselves falling in love and anxious to get married for real.

Hamtree Harrington played a black handyman named Alabama and gave the play useful injections of humor, and Kip Good was good as a sergeant who used to be Jean's boyfriend. Producer Pemberton was ripped for his choice of such stenciled material, which seemed designed entirely for sale to the movies as a grade-B production, which is what did happen (the film was called *Pillow to Post*). Howard Barnes (*NYHT*) called the work "an obvious and labored piece that goes through the motions of a three-act drama with no more than an occasional spark of entertainment."

PIRATE, THE [Comedy/Adventure/Period/Romance/Show Business/Tropics] A: S. N. Behrman; M: Herbert Kingsley; SC: a German play, *Die Seeräuber*, by Ludwig Fulda; D: Alfred Lunt and John C. Wilson; CH: Felicia Sorel; S: Lemuel Ayers; C: Miles White; P: Playwrights' Company and the Theatre Guild; T: Martin Beck Theatre; 11/25/42 (177)

A "flamboyant and bizarre" (Lewis Nichols [*NYT*]) romantic comedy vehicle for the Lunts, based on a 1911 German play and set in the Spanish West Indies in the early nineteenth century. The idea for it came from Alfred Lunt, who, years before, had played in a translation of the German play in summer stock. It was hoped that Kurt Weill would write the score, but Weill was unavailable. The show premiered at the University of Wisconsin, Madison, before a two-month tour that brought it to Broadway.

His role gave Lunt the chance to play a juggling, tightrope-walking, conjuring, and dancing mountebank named Serafin. This brazen and handsome devil arrives with his multiracial troupe in a village whose obese and stolid mayor Pedro Vargas (Alan Reed) is actually Estramudo, a fugitive pirate with a price on his head. The mayor's lovely wife Manuela (Lynn Fontanne) dreams of the heroic pirate she has read of in adventure stories. When the mayor forbids the dashing Serafin and his troupe to present their show to the village, the actor, recognizing that the mayor is the fabled pirate, blackmails him into giving him the required license. Romantically interested in the mayor's wife, Serafin leads her to believe that he himself is Estramudo. She falls in love with him at once. Ultimately, although he is threatened with the gallows, Serafin hypnotizes Manuela during his show, and she exposes the pirate to the viceroy (Clarence Derwent), who has him arrested. The player carries Manuela off for his own.

For all its promise of vivacity and excitement, the escapist piece seemed to many out of drawing-room comedy writer S. N. Behrman's line. "His witticisms and wisecracks rub elbows uncomfortably with the romantic and orotund passages which the situations demand," argued Rosamond Gilder (*TAM*), who added, "The play is perhaps overburdened with production and sags in places."

The Lunts gave their usual superlative performances, Lunt himself doing a tour de force turn that called on numerous vaudeville skills, including the walking of a tightrope to Manuela's room with an expression of casual insouciance. None of this, however, was enough to spark the play to life except in fits and starts. It was George Jean Nathan's (*TBY*) view that "as a contribution to the art of the drama it ranks considerably less than a buck private, but though here and there haplessly halting it contrives to serve its purpose as a Luntish lark, which is something." Nevertheless, Howard Barnes (*NYHT*) declared it "an eloquent and witty farce," and George Freedley (*NYMT*) considered it "a thin but smooth and deftly written comedy."

The play was billed as being "suggested by an idea in a play by Ludwig Fulda," but in fact was pretty much an adaptation of that play, retaining its title, most of its plot, and its characters (who kept their names). The original, however, was laid in Andalusia. During its tryout period in Philadelphia, Behrman and Lunt had considerable difficulty seeing eye to eye over improvements to the script. When Lunt took issue with a line that Behrman liked, the actor would misread it during the performance so that it didn't work. Behrman noted in *People in a Diary*, "Then he would turn to me and say with impish triumph, 'See, I told you it wouldn't play.'"

Lunt and Fontanne could not not stomach people coughing during their performances, and the latter would often stop and glare at the cougher until the hacking stopped. Once, when her method failed to end a coughing attack, Lunt stepped out of character, walked downstage, and spoke directly to the cougher: "It was a cough that carried him off. It was a coffin they carried him off in" (quoted in Maurice Zolotow, *Stagestruck*). The cougher left.

In the cast were Juanita Hall, Lea Penman, Estelle Winwood (as Manuela's hoydenish mother), Muriel Rahn, Maurice Ellis, James O'Neill, Inez Matthews, and many others.

Behrman was at this point considering abandoning his membership in the Playwrights' Company. When, in order to get the Lunts, he agreed to let the Theatre Guild do *The Pirate*, it caused considerable friction among his colleagues. The situation was ironed out by the idea of a coproduction, but it foreshadowed Behrman's eventually leaving the Playwrights' Company.

(1) PIRATES OF PENZANCE, OR THE SLAVES OF DUTY, THE [Musical Revival*] B/LY: W. S. Gilbert; M: Arthur Sullivan; D: R. H. Burnside; P: Boston Comic Opera Company and Messrs. Shubert; T: St. James Theatre; 2/17/42 (11)

One in a series of Gilbert and Sullivan revivals by the Boston Comic Opera Company. Bertram Peacock was the pirate king, Frederic Persson was Samuel, Morton Bowe was Frederic, Florenz Ames was Major-General Stanley, Robert Pitkin was the sergeant of police, Kathleen Roche was Mabel, Mary Roche was

Edith, Margaret Roy was Kate, and Helen Lanvin was Ruth. On the same bill was "The Prodigal Son," a ballet by the Joos Ballet Company. Brooks Atkinson (*NYT*) considered the production "droll, mischievous and enjoyable," although the "morose" scenery annoyed him.

(2) and **"COX AND BOX"** D: Lewis Denison; P: Savoy Opera Guild; T: Cherry Lane Theatre (OB); 2/19/42

The same week that the Boston Comic Opera Company opened its *Pirates of Penzance* revival, a small company playing in the tiny Cherry Lane opened its, coupling it with the familiar "Cox and Box." Said Atkinson, "The Savoy Opera singers in their vest-pocket theatre do quite as well as the Boston Comic Opera Company in the vast spaces of the St. James. What they lack in showmanship they make up in friendliness and in love of singing."

The well-directed piece managed to maneuver its thirty cast members around the postage-stamp-sized stage without any obvious traffic jams. Seymour Penzner as the pirate king was the standout performer, and Wells Clary was admirable as the sergeant.

(3) and **"COX AND BOX"** D: R. H. Burnside; P: R. H. Burnside i/a/w the Gilbert and Sullivan Opera Company; T: Ambassador Theatre; 2/17/44 (8)

A revival by the renamed Boston Opera Company, discussed in the first entry. Florenz Ames, Robert Pitkin, and Kathleen Roche repeated their *Pirates* roles, while Robert Eckles took the pirate king, Bertram Peacock moved to Samuel, Allen Stewart was Frederic, Kathryn Reece was Edith, Marie Valdez was Kate, Mary Lundon was Isabel, and Catherine Judah was Ruth. In the old one-act, Allen Stewart played Cox, Florenz Ames acted Box, and Robert Eckles was Sergeant Bouncer.

The evening was an improvement over the company's two prior presentations. "No longer in evidence were the contrived caperings and the overstressed business. . . . Instead," wrote L. C. (*NYT*), "the emphasis has been placed on the singing of the songs and on the direction." The decor remained unprepossessing.

(4) D: Eugene Bryden; CH: Igor Schwezoff; S: H. A. Condell; P: New York City Opera Company; T: City Center of Music and Drama; 5/12/46 (4)

The New York City Opera Company, presenting a series of grand operas, relaxed for several nights with its rendition of this comic opera, showing how effective the piece could be with truly operatic voices, both principals and chorus. Despite the singing talents on display, the words of lyrics and libretto were crisply presented, and, apart from some occasional overplaying, the comic business in Eugene Bryden's stylized staging hit the spot.

The pirate king was shared by Gean Greenwell and James Pease, Samuel was played by Hubert Norville, Frederic by John Hamill, Ruth by Catherine Judah, the major-general by John Dudley, Mabel by Virginia MacWatters, and the sergeant by Emile Renan. Howard Taubman (*NYT*), while chiding the acting, noted, "Gilbert and Sullivan haven't been made to sound so good in years."

(4) and **"TRIAL BY JURY"** D: Anna Bethel; S: Charles Ricketts; C: George Sheringham; P: D'Oyly Carte Opera Company; T: Century Theatre; 1/5/48 (16)

England's famous Savoyards produced this double bill as part of their nine piece visiting repertory. In *Pirates* Martyn Green was Major-General Stanley, Darrell Fancourt was the pirate king, Richard Dunn was Samuel, Thomas Round was Frederic, Richard Walker was the sergeant of police, Helen Roberts was Mabel, Joyce Wright was Edith, Joan Gillingham was Kate, Enid Walsh was Isabel, and Ella Halman was Ruth. In "Trial by Jury" Watson was the learned judge, Charles Dorning was counsel for the plaintiff, Radley Flynn was foreman of the jury, Walker was the usher, C. William Morgan was the associate, Gwyneth Cullimore was the plaintiff, Leonard Osborn was the defendant, and Enid Walsh was the first bridesmaid.

In *Pirates* Fancourt and Green, the company's stars, stole the show, which Brooks Atkinson (*NYT*) considered a big improvement over the company's faulty presentation of *The Mikado**. "Both 'Trial by Jury' and *The Pirates of Penzance* are freshly dressed in gay and enchanting costumes," said Atkinson, "and they are played with sparkle and relish."

(6) D/P: S. M. Chartock; S/L: Ralph Alswang; C: Peggy Morrison; T: Mark Hellinger Theatre; 10/10/49 (8)

The second in a second-rate series of three Gilbert and Sullivan revivals. It featured Morton Bowe as Frederic, Joseph Macaualay as the pirate king, Robert Eckles as the sergeant, Kathleen Roche as Mabel, Jean Handzlik as Ruth, and Ralph Riggs as the major-general (the weakest performance). Brooks Atkinson (*NYT*) had to report that the production was "not very satisfactory." The uninformed spectator, he mused, would probably view this show as if it were "a romantic musical play in an obsolete style" instead of as the "satirical opera" it was meant to be.

PLACE OF OUR OWN, A [Comedy/Family/Journalism/Marriage/Period/Politics/Small Town] A/D: Elliott Nugent; S: Raymond Sovey; C: Lucinda Ballard; P: John Golden i/a/w Elliott Nugent and Robert Montgomery; T: Royale Theatre; 4/2/45 (8)

Elliott Nugent was continuing in his role in the long run *Voice of the Turtle* when he managed to find time to write, direct, and coproduce this timely but "downright feeble" (Arthur Pollock [*BE*]) one-week flop. Inspired by the coming San Francisco Conference designed to establish the United Nations, it was intended as an exposé of the type of citizens who defeated President Wilson's dream of getting America into the League of Nations; Nugent hoped that nothing would hinder our participation in a similar body after World War II. A program note quoted George Santayana, "Those who cannot remember the past are condemned to repeat it."

Nugent's father, J. C. Nugent, played Sam Reddy, grandfather of Nancy (Jeanne Cagney), and a resident of Calais, Ohio, in 1919, when the play is set. His granddaughter marries David Monroe (John Archer) when the youth returns from World War I. David wants to become a journalist in Cleveland, but his wealthy father-in-law Charles Reddy (Robert Keith) wants him to stay in Calais so his daughter can be his housekeeper. Charles therefore buys the local newspaper for David as a wedding gift. David is an idealist, believing in Wilson, the League of Nations, and a world without war. Sam is a reactionary businessman with little patience for liberal notions. David uses his paper to gain political backing for the treaty and the league, but the influential Sam does what he can to destroy the alliance that David has established. When even Nancy opposes his ideas, David walks out, taking his young cousin Mary Lorimer (Mercedes McCambridge, in her Broadway debut) with him. Wilson's plans are crushed, but David is reconciled with Nancy and leaves Calais with her.

A chief problem with the play was its inability to blend the political story with the domestic one. Lewis Nichols (*NYT*) said that it was "on the plodding side, mechanical and forced and sometimes even silly." The company included Seth Arnold, Toni Favor, Lotta Palfi, Helen Carew, and Wolfe Barzell.

PLAN M [Drama/Illness/Military/Politics/War] A: James Edward Grant; D: Marion Gering; S: Lemuel Ayers; P: Richard Aldrich and Richard Myers; T: Belasco Theatre; 2/20/42 (6)

After a week of showings, this "tiresomely unbelievable charade" (Rowland Field [*NEN*] of a wartime spy melodrama folded, leaving nothing but shell-shocked critical memories behind. A good production was totally wasted on a tale set in the War Office headquarters of General Hugh Winston (Len Doyle), British chief of staff. The general takes electric cabinet treatments for his physical ailments, but his physician, Dr. Hawes (Lumsden Hare), is really a German spy, as are his two aides. The general is poisoned while in his contraption, and a German agent who is an exact duplicate of Winston--one who not only bears a precise physical resemblance but also has the same personality and military knowledge--takes over for him and puts into operation a false Plan M, replacing the one that was designed to prevent a German invasion. England is on the brink of being invaded before the ruse is discovered by the plot device of having the phony Winston make a pass at a secretary (Anne Burr); the gimmick is that Winston was the girl's father and would never have acted this way.

No one could buy the play's premise, which seemed so implausible as to be silly. "If it were ever printed in book form, it is the sort of thing that would be done on pulp, with a lurid cover for small boys to gap [*sic*] at," wrote Burns Mantle (*NYDN*).

PLAYBOY OF NEWARK, THE [Comedy/Boarding House/Gambling/Marriage/Religion/Sex] A: Ben K. Simkhovitch; D: Sanford Meisner; P: American Actors Company; T: Provincetown Playhouse (OB); 3/19/43

A Saroyanesque (see especially *Love's Old Sweet Song**) comedy--called by its author a "fantasy," although the appellation was disputed--set in a Huntington, Long Island, boarding house near the railroad tracks, the majority of the boarders being workers in the local pickle factory. The landlord is Sam Dupree (Dwight Marfield), a naive and ineffectual fellow who dreams of travel out West, but who has barely ever been anywhere else in his life. One of the boarders has a visitor from Newark, an ex-evangelist, spreader of good cheer, and master crapshooter named Bancroft Binks (Russell Collins). Bancroft is fleeing both his creditors and a rich widow (Lillian Little) he swindled under promise of marriage. Bancroft brings light into the dull lives of the inhabitants, especially when he talks of building an ark in which a chosen few will sail into a new life. This talk fascinates Sam as well as his younger and sexually starved wife Minerva (Donna Keath), who was on the brink of running off with a drunken boarder before Bancroft arrived. The Duprees lend him the money he needs for his project. Bancroft, whose pretensions are shown up when the widow catches up to him, leaves without building his ark (although he comes back to pay off his "loan"), but he has inspired the Duprees to build their own trailer and to go off and see the world.

Burns Mantle (*NYDN*) thought the piece "woefully short on skill," but Wilella Waldorf (*NYP*) offered encouragement: "Mr. Simkhovitch has written on the whole a rather mild little play about a group of very simple souls, but he does have a flair for character and a human perception that is sometimes heartwarming and true." In the cast were Peggy Meredith (director Meisner's wife), Jane Rose, Ad Karns, and Will (William) Hare.

PLAYBOY OF THE WESTERN WORLD, THE [Dramatic Revival*] A: John Millington Synge; D: Guthrie McClintic; S/C: John Boyt; P: Theatre Incorporated; T: Booth Theatre; 10/26/46 (81)

A somewhat disappointing revival of Synge's oft-produced comedy, last seen here in 1937 in its Abbey Theatre of Dublin version. The centerpiece--and main problem--of the new production was the performance of Burgess Meredith as Christy Mahon. Supporting the star were Eithne Dunne (of Dublin's Gate Theatre) as Pegeen Mike, Dennis King, Jr., as Shawn Keogh, J. M. Kerrigan (who had appeared in the first New York production--given by the Abbey--in 1911) as Michael James Flaherty, Barry Macollum as Philly Cullen, J. C. Nugent as Jimmy Farrell, Mildred Natwick as the Widow Quin, Julie Harris as Nelly, Maureen Stapleton (in her Broadway debut) as Sara Tansey, and Fred Johnson (another Irish import) as Old Mahon.

Synge's piece about the youth who becomes a hero by presumably slaughtering his "da" still had plenty of fun in it for contemporary viewers, especially when expertly performed. There were divided opinions, though, on whether such expertness was provided. Most decided that the direction and much of the acting were off the mark. George Jean Nathan (*TBY*) took issue with McClintic's staging, declaring that the entire point of the work had been missed in the attempt to direct "it much as if it were a half naturalistic problem drama, half literal melodrama." Brooks Atkinson (*NYT*) was sorry that "the acting represents several styles that are not homogeneous," and he regretted the revival's too-literal approach and lack of imagination and charm.

The biggest hole in the production came from the normally admired Meredith.

Atkinson thought his portrayal faithful but devoid of "spontaneity and the light touch." Rosamond Gilder (*TAM*) claimed that he lacked the appropriate fire and gusto. "Burgess Meredith, sensitive to human values--the pathos of a frightened, bullied youngster running for his life--does not catch the bold epic grandeur of the picture. He is more literally, humanly correct but less poetically right." At the same time, the production as a whole and Meredith in particular were lauded by several critics. Richard Watts, Jr. (*NYP*), for example, said that this was "the finest and most striking" of the eight versions of the play he had seen, and that Meredith's was "the most completely satisfying performance of the central character." Although Eithne Dunne's authentic brogue made understanding some of her lines difficult at times, her Pegeen was far superior in many eyes.

PLAY'S THE THING, THE (**Játek a Kastélyban**) [Dramatic Revival*] A: Ferenc Molnár; AD: P. G. Wodehouse; D: Gilbert Miller; S: Oliver Messel; C: (gowns) Castillo; L: Ralph Alswang; P: Gilbert Miller i/a/w James Russo and Michael Ellis; T: Booth Theatre; 4/28/48 (244)

Molnár's popular Hungarian trifle about theatrical illusion, not seen locally since 1928, was given a "captivating revival" (Howard Barnes [*NYHT*]) in this Wodehouse adaptation starring Louis Calhern as Sandor Turai and featuring Ernest Cossart as Mansky, Richard Hylton as Albert Adam, Francis Compton as Johann Dwornitschek, Hollywood's Faye Emerson (in her Broadway debut) as Ilona Szabo, Arthur Margetson as Almady, and Claud Allister as Mell (which he had played in the New York premiere).

The play seemed, surprisingly, as fresh as ever. George Jean Nathan (*TBY*), while commenting on Molnár's use of such conventional devices as the play-within-the play, yet found much to admire in the dramatist's unusually deft technique. Ward Morehouse (*NYS*) was less impressed and argued that "the gayety . . . comes through spasmodically." But most critics sided with John Mason Brown (*SR*), who delighted in the urbane comedy's soufflé-like lightness and its ability to make one check one's morals at the door: "It is pure make-believe for make-believe's sake. It belongs to the theatre rather than to reality. . . . After a start which nowadays seems leisurely, it becomes dateless in its fooling. The evening abounds in entertainment."

Fortunately, it was accorded "a production as shimmering and gossamer as its writing," he added. "Oliver Messel's setting of a Riviera castle is regal," noted Brooks Atkinson (*NYT*), "and the gowns, tail-coats, dinner-jackets, robes and lounging suits are properly expensive."

Calhern, wrote Barnes, handled his difficult role "superbly. He picks up the somewhat tattered threads of the farce on every occasion and weaves them into a skein of laughter. The final scene, in which he gives an aging Lothario a going-over, is a brilliant piece of timing and significant gestures."

PLOUGH AND THE STARS, THE [Dramatic Revival*] A: Sean O'Casey; D: Al Saxe; S: Gerhardt Henschke; P: Theatre Today; T: Hudson Guild Theatre (OB); 2/5/50

The last time this satiric piece about the Easter Rebellion of 1916 in Ireland had been staged was in 1937, by the visiting Abbey Players. The present production included several interesting actors, such as Margaret Croyden, future theatre journalist, as Nora Clitheroe and Stefan Gierasch as Peter Flynn.

The unknown ensemble was given very high marks by Arthur Pollock (*DC*), who observed that the "young actors play it as if they had lived for the day they could step forward on a stage as Sean O'Casey's characters, as if to them nothing else in the world mattered but their becoming actors. They are very good." House. (*V*) verified that the play was "being presented with great feeling and lively movement. . . . The production has a certain professional polish without certainly the many technical aids of the Broadway companies." Both critics were willing to overlook certain infelicities in the acting, including the erratic brogues, because the overall effect was so strong. Among those chosen for mention were Sy Travers as Fluther Good, Vincent Beck as the young Covey, and Elsa Fried as Bessie Burgess.

POLONAISE [Musical/Historical-Biographical/Military/Period/Politics/Romance/War] B: Gottfried Reinhardt and Anthony Veiller; M: Frederic Chopin; ADD.M.: Bronislaw Kaper; LY: John Latouche; D: Stella Adler; CH: David Lichine; S: Howard Bay; C: Mary Grant; P: W. Horace Schmidlapp i/a/w Harry Bloomfield; T: Alvin Theatre; 10/6/45 (113)

The title of this uninspired operetta comes from the music of Chopin, which, in an adapted form with lyrics, constituted the undramatic score of this musical set in the 1780s right after the American Revolution. Its central character is Lithuanian-born Polish hero General Thaddeus Kosciusko (Jan Kiepura), who contributed importantly to the American victory. Despite his extremely active career fighting for Polish freedom, the libretto gave little indication of his heroic stature. Euphemia Van Rensselaer Wyatt (*CW*) suggested that the authors' "one idea seems to be to eliminate drama from the life of a soldier who lived a series of scenarios."

A lot of talented people were involved in "projecting a mediocre musical more notable for its return to an old-fashioned formula than for its success even in that uninspiring line," reported Wyatt. One of its greatest drawbacks was the acting of Kiepura, a fine singer whose wooden, nonmusical playing was ridiculed. The same was true of his wife, Marta Eggerth, who played Marisha, the romantic feminine lead. According to Alan Jay Lerner's *The Musical Theatre*, when Kiepura read his bad reviews, he asked his wife, "How can they say I stink when I'm better than ever?"

The "inconceivably amateurish and silly" (Burton Rascoe [*NYWT*]) book concerns Kosciusko's activity, following the Revolutionary War, in fighting for freedom in Poland, then under the thumb of Russia, Austria, and Prussia. It also treats his romantic relationship with the peasant girl Marisha, a love affair threatened unsuccessfully by a wicked countess (Rose Ingraham).

Curt Bois did his best in an unfunny comic role, Tania Riabouchinska showed balletic talent in dully choreographed routines, and Ingraham had a show-stopping song, "The Next Time I Care," written by Kaper, not Chopin. Stella Adler took over the direction out of town when the show was in trouble.

POPSY [Comedy/Family/Marriage/Romance/Small Town/Youth] A: Fred Herendeen; D: Roland G. Edwards; S: Tom Adrian Cracraft; P: Theodore Hammerstein and Denis Du-For i/a/w Hugh Skelly; T: Playhouse; 2/10/41 (4)

Despite veteran vaudevillian Al Shean's being behind the wheel of this faltering vehicle (originally called *Home, Sweet Home*), it ran out of gas almost as soon as it began to accelerate. Most critics were baffled that the play ever reached the Broadway stage. "*Popsy* is one of the worst plays ever written," spewed forth Brooks Atkinson (*NYT*).

Shean was the title character, actually Professor Henry Tibbs, a math professor in Madison, Wisconsin, who has dreamed of retirement so that he can take his wife on a long-hoped-for trip to Hawaii, where he can write a book. His three inane daughters--Jane (Natalie Thompson), Florence (Sylvia Field), and Ruth (Nancy Evans)--interrupt his plans with their romantic and marital problems, one of them arriving with two kids in tow. Two broken marriages and a broken engagement get patched, and Popsy and Momsy (Edith King) get to take their trip, but to Niagara Falls instead.

"It is amazing how long and how tediously Mr. Herendeen is able to spin out this frail, dreary little plot," wondered John Mason Brown (*NYP*). The play was filled with tired jokes such as "that fellow could sell electric fans to the Eskimos." Cast members included Eva Condon as a cook and child actress Joyce Van Patten as one of Popsy's grandchildren.

(1) **PORGY AND BESS** [Musical Revival*] B: DuBose Heyward; M: George Gershwin; LY: DuBose Heyward and Ira Gershwin; D: Robert Ross; S: Herbert Andrews; C: Paul du Pont; P: Cheryl Crawford; T: Majestic Theatre; 1/22/42 (286)

A rousing revival of the great 1935 Gershwin folk opera about the black inhabitants of Catfish Row, with Avon Long as Sportin' Life, Todd Duncan as Porgy, Warren Coleman as Crown, and Anne Brown as Bess. Of these leads, only Avon

Long was not in his role in the original production. Many others from the original production were also repeating their roles, including Edward Matthews as Jake, Ruby Elzy as Serena, and Georgette Harvey as Maria. Harriett Jackson, originally in the chorus, now was Clara. Long stopped the show with his rendition of "It Ain't Necessarily So", proving himself, said Rosamond Gilder (*TAM*), "an agile, incandescent comedian with a body built on springs and a neat comic comment."

The new version more than doubled the run of the first one. The score, the lyrics, and the story were as impressive as ever, if not more so, and the characters had taken on the aura of American icons in the fifteen years since they first had been dramatized in the 1927 play, *Porgy**. Many critics noted that they liked the revival more than they did the first production, which was saying something, considering the warmth of the work's original reception. John Mason Brown (*NYP*) pointed out, "What Mr. Gershwin's score lacks to equal the tension of the book's emotional climaxes, it more than makes up for in color, in gaiety, in the sheer loveliness of its melodies. It is a brilliant manifestation of Mr. Gershwin's maturing powers. Its pretentions may have been large, but its idiom is popular."

Musical director Alexander Smallens had made many helpful modifications in the score, especially the elimination of the recitatives (which cut the time by forty-five minutes) and the return to spoken dialogue, which better communicated the story and characters. His pit orchestra was twenty-seven strong, down from the original's forty-two.

"There is the prodigal richness that is felt in works of real genius," noted Euphemia Van Rensselaer Wyatt (*CW*), "and it leaves the American musical world the poorer for Gershwin [*sic*]. One comes away from *Porgy and Bess* full of warm vibrations--not only musical but human." The opening-night audience was so thrilled that the only way their clapping could be halted was for the orchestra to break into "The Star-Spangled Banner."

The production's management wanted the work to be considered as an opera, not a musical, which point it stressed by providing detailed synopses of the story, almost as if the audience couldn't understand the English language in which it was sung and spoken. Whether it is indeed an opera or a musical was a subject that the critics tussled with, but no one had a definitive answer, nor does anyone.

(2) [Return Engagement] P: Cheryl Crawford i/a/w John J. Wildberg; T: Forty-fourth Street Theatre; 9/13/43 (24)

A return engagement of the previous production, which closed a year earlier, and which was now being readied for a road tour. The major cast changes were in the roles of Bess, now played very well by Etta Moten (the singer whom Gershwin envisioned in the role) , and Serena, taken now by Alma Hubbard (Ruby Elzy died during the previous year's tour).

Most critics continued to rave, but George Jean Nathan (*TBY*) thought the production vastly inferior to the original in that its look had been "streamlined" and its imagination dissipated. John Chapman (*NYDN*) said, "The whole affair is over-mannered, from music to lighting. If a sudden big shadow on a wall is effective, as in the funeral scene, then it is sure to be repeated. People are forever opening and closing shutters, just long enough to pose for a picture, on the various levels of the Catfish Row dwellings."

There were also complaints from some of the deafening playing of the orchestra, which drowned out the words of the singers. Burton Rascoe (*NYWT*) called for the use of amplification if the problem could not otherwise be solved, and admitted to being of the minority who viewed the work itself as "simply a musical botch, neither an opera nor a music drama but a series of sentimental chromos . . . and for which [Gershwin] tried to supply a whole operatic background without having the slightest talent for opera."

(3) [Return Engagement] T: City Center of Music and Drama; 2/7/44 (16; 48; total: 64)

After finishing its tour, the show returned to New York to play for low prices ($2.20 top) at the City Center. It was given two engagements here, the second beginning on 2/28/44. It was the same show described in the previous entry except that William Franklin now played Porgy. "Mr. Franklin," wrote George Freedley (*NYMT*), "seems a shade too educated for the part and refuses to slur the lyrics as written, which makes Porgy a bit pedantic at times. However, he may have been afraid of the notorious acoustics at the Center." Franklin's singing was more appreciated than his acting, which was not considered as touching and engaging as Todd Duncan's.

PORTRAIT IN BLACK [Drama/Crime/Labor/Medicine/Mystery/Romance] A: Ivan Goff and Ben Roberts; D: Reginald Denham; S/L: Donald Oenslager; C: Helene Pons; P: David Lowe and Edgar F. Luckenbach; T: Booth Theatre; 5/14/47 (62)

Prior to opening on Broadway, this talky psychological melodrama had appeared in London (with Diana Wynyard in the lead) and had had two productions outside of New York. By the time it arrived on the Great White Way, the plot's three acts had been reduced to two. It deals with a set of well-tailored, elegantly mannered San Francisco sophisticates.

A tycoon married to the lethally beautiful Tanis Talbot (Clare Luce), a beautifully coiffed blond who dresses throughout in striking black ensembles, has just been put to his final rest. He had been murdered by Mrs. Talbot's physician and secret lover, Dr. Philip Graham (Donald Cook), who administered a deadly hypodermic to the elderly, ailing shipping magnate. Mrs. Talbot, accessory to the slaying, is the mother of a young boy (David Anderson). She and her lover believe that they have committed the perfect crime until a note arrives congratulating Mrs. Talbot on the success of her criminal endeavor. It is thought that the message comes from Rupert Marlowe (Sidney Blackmer), the dead man's estate lawyer, who proposes marriage to Mrs. Talbot a day after the funeral. The guilty pair also momentarily suspect the handyman (Barry Kelley) when his request for an advance on his salary is construed as blackmail. When the lawyer is killed on stage by Dr. Graham, the police believe that the shooter may be Blake Ritchie (Thomas Coley), the young union leader who is about to head the marine workers' strike against the dead man's line, and who is the beloved of the Talbot daughter (Dorothea Jackson). It turns out that the late lawyer was not the note sender, as yet another note arrives. The guilty pair plan to flee to Brazil, but the doctor discovers that the note writer is none other than the psychopathic Tanis herself (she wrote the letters to keep the doctor fearful and thus close to her); also revealed is that her son is the offspring of the estate lawyer. Dr. Graham sees no future with Tanis, and he and she contemplate suicide as an answer to their dilemma.

Several critics thought that the excellent talents of the stars, especially the striking Clare Luce, were wasted on the extremely well produced effort. Brooks Atkinson (*NYT*) said that by the time the play's five scenes were over he no longer cared about the characters. George Jean Nathan (*TBY*) poked holes in the play's plausibility, noted various stereotyped plot contrivances, mocked the artificialities of the dialogue, and argued that "a melodramatic thriller whose general tone is depressing . . . is inevitably headed for the storehouse."

POWER OF DARKNESS, THE (***Vlast Tmy***) [Dramatic Revival*/Blacks] A: Leo Tolstoy; AD/D: Abram Hill; S: Richard Brown; P: 110th Street Community Center; T: Master Institute Theatre (OB); 10/10/48

A group of actors associated with the American Negro Theatre performed in this black adaptation of Tolstoy's naturalistic Russian tragedy, last produced locally in January 1920. The action was shifted to a small Southern town, and the names were Americanized. Although Brooks Atkinson (*NYT*) commended several players, he noted, "The group performance, scattered and unsteady, conveys almost nothing of the moral fervor of Tolstoy's theme." Those he singled out included Geneva Fitch, William Dillard, Theodora Smith, Georgette Harvey, Cynthia Raglyn, and J. Lawrence Criner.

Tolstoy's dark and potent story, based on a real incident and recounted here with the names in Hill's version, tells of how an evil farm woman, Rosa (Fitch), awaits her wealthy old husband's (Criner) death so she can marry the young Casanova, Nick (Dillard), she foolishly loves. The youth's greedy mother, Matilda Akers (Harvey), convinces Rosa to poison the old man. Meanwhile, an orphaned girl the youth has made pregnant is treated coldly by him. Rosa eventually poisons her husband and takes his money, which she gives to Nick, whom she marries, although he continues an affair with the dead man's slow-witted stepdaughter, Odet (Smith), upon whom he spends much of his money and whom he gets pregnant. Disgusted with his son's dissolute ways, Nick's father repudiates him. When Odet gives birth, Rosa and Matilda cause Nick to kill the baby; the corpse is buried in the cellar. Later, the guilt-ridden Nick attempts to seduce the orphan girl, who has married someone else, but he is rebuffed. He prepares to kill himself but is prevented by someone else. He goes to Odets's wedding party and there confesses his sins and begs forgiveness. He is then led away to his punishment.

POWER WITHOUT GLORY [Drama/British/Crime/Family/Romance/Sex] A: Michael Clayton Hutton; D: Chloe Gibson; S: Charles Elson; P: John C. Wilson and the Messrs. Shubert; T: Booth Theatre; 1/13/48 (31)

An interesting and frequently suspenseful British psychological thriller, mingled with humor. It had been a London hit and received several strong notices locally, but it lasted only a month. It was played by an all-English company of superior ability, and many felt that the actors were more responsible for the play's impact than the dramatist.

The melodrama concerns a dully respectable East End working-class family, the Lords, who live near the Thames, where a girl's murder recently has taken place. The family is headed by shopkeeper John Lord (Trevor Ward) and his wife Maggie (Marjorie Rhodes). The family are doing as best they can under the strain of living in postwar London, with its rationing and queues. Eddie (Lewis Stringer) is the intellectual older son, Cliff (Peter Murray) is the temperamental younger brother (and his mother's favorite), and Flo (Joan Newell) is the rebellious young sister. While Eddie was off at war, Eddie's fiancée Anna (Hilary Liddell), who lives with the Lords, fell in love with Cliff. Eddie grins and bears it because of his affection for Anna. The girl who gets killed offstage is Flo's promiscuous friend Connie, who has been having an affair with Cliff and was killed when Cliff discovered that she was pregnant. Flo, Anna, and Maggie shortly realize that the killer is Cliff, who is also something of a thief. The dilemma arises of keeping his guilt secret or allowing him to be punished for his crime. Each of the characters' preconceptions about the others is gradually stripped away. Flo threatens to inform on Cliff. Anna and Cliff contemplate turning Eddie in to the police as the guilty party, and Eddie, because of his love for Anna, is willing to comply. But the egotistic Cliff wants to shoulder the blame and is eventually arrested after the family, led by Maggie, bands together to give him strength.

George Freedley (*NYMT*) called this "a taut and exciting English drama which held the first night audience breathless with excitement." It "appeared to grip the attention of a majority of premiereites like a vise," reported Robert Coleman (*NYDM*). "It is a deftly linked series of virulent shocks," approved William Hawkins (*NYWT*). But Ward Morehouse (*NYS*) believed that after two solid acts, the piece disintegrated in the third "as the author turns to speechmaking and nobility." Louis Kronenberger (*PM*) agreed that without the riveting performances, "the evening would surely be damned by its bad last act."

PRESENT LAUGHTER [Comedy/Business/Romance/Sex/Theatre] A: Noël Coward; D/P: John C. Wilson; S: Donald Oenslager; C: Sylvia Saal (Doris Dalton and Marta Linden's costumes: Castillo); T: Plymouth Theatre; 10/29/46 (158)

The majority of the critics found this Noël Coward offering strained, tiresome, and dull and gave it only the slightest approbation. Arthur Pollock (*BE*) considered it "palpably contrived, slow, and entertaining only by jerks." The first act, in particular, said the reviewer, was one of the dullest of the author's career. To John Beaufort (*CSM*) it was "tedious, tasteless, and rather old hat." Rowland Field (*NEN*) declared that the play "may not match up in verve or originality with certain of its memorable predecessors but it is a nimble work that seems bound to succeed, despite a lack of invention." Yet Howard Barnes (*NYHT*) conceded that despite the heavy going of act one, "the mirth is there to sustain high gayety in scene after scene." The piece had been premiered in London in 1943. Its title comes from *Twelfth Night**'s lines, "What is love? 'tis not hereafter; / Present mirth hath present laughter."

Garry Essendine (Clifton Webb in the role created in London by Coward) is a pampered, narcissistic London matinee idol of forty-two contemplating a repertory trip to Africa. Garry is much sought after and sponged on by various fawning femmes and sycophants. Among these is his estranged wife Liz (Doris Dalton), his cynically sharp-tongued secretary Monica Reed (Evelyn Varden), worshipful and eccentric young playwright Roland Maule (Cris Alexander), and Garry's business associates Morris Dixon (Gordon Mills) and Hugo Lyppiatt (Robin Craven). Liz, who wants to renew her marital relationship with Garry, has a maternal inclination toward him and is useful in disentangling his frequent amours. Figuring importantly in the action is a spare bedroom from which various women must be secretly spirited out without creating embarrassing situations for the actor or themselves. One of the room's occupants is a stagestruck blond ingenue named Daphne Stillington (Jan Sterling). Then there is Hugo's seductively attractive wife Joanna (Marta Linden), who is having an affair with Morris, but for whom Garry falls when he tries to talk her out of it. After the usual complications, Garry decides to abandon his profligate ways and return to the arms of Liz.

There were mixed feelings about the quality of the production, some lauding it and others dismissing it as ineffective and plodding. Webb's acting was considered appropriately Cowardian in certain quarters, while others thought that only Coward could have pulled the role off. The company also included Grace Mills, Aidan Turner, and Leonore Harris.

PRETTY LITTLE PARLOR [Drama/Alcoholism/Family/Marriage/Period/Sex/Small Town/Youth] A: Claiborne Foster; D: Ralph Bellamy; S: Stewart Chaney; C: Paul du Pont; P: Ralph Bellamy and John Moses; T: National Theatre; 4/17/44 (8)

Ralph Bellamy's directorial and producing debut was with this turkey by a once-popular actress. It had a cast filled with names that were or would one day be ones to reckon with, but they had to play so unpleasant an assortment of characters that no one wanted to watch them. Their combined talents could not keep the thinly plotted play, which was reminiscent of *The Little Foxes**, "from being tedious, sometimes ridiculous, and always in the mood of ten-twent'-thirt', which needed only peanuts in the balcony to be the breath of an earlier day," according to Lewis Nichols (*NYT*). The audience often laughed at the play's melodramatic excesses. "For one scene of morbid psychological power there are a dozen dreary passages in which melodramatic cliches are accompanied by painfully inept dialogue," growled Howard Barnes (*NYHT*).

The play is set in a small town in 1905. Stella Adler played the leading role, that of the bitchy Clotilde Hilyard, who has driven her harried second husband, Jefferson (Sidney Blackmer), to alcoholism. This wickedly unscrupulous, grasping stepmother keeps her stepdaughter Dora (Joan Tetzel) in a state of submission while she prompts her own sixteen-year-old daughter, Anastasia (Marilyn Erskine), over whom she has complete domination, to steal the step-daughter's fiancé, Dennis (Kip Good), although the fact that his wealthy parents make him earn his living enrages Clotilde. She uses her seductive wiles on two railroad executives (Ed Begley and Paul Parks) to gain lucrative employment for her spouse, but Jefferson's drinking loses him his job. She again tries to maneuver one of the executives on her husband's behalf, although he suggests that he will do her bidding only if she sleeps with him. She then is responsible for helping Jefferson get drunk before he goes out fishing with Anastasia, the result being that both are drowned. Dennis decides to marry Dora, who still loves him, and they leave Clotilde in disgust. She remains alone but manages to wangle $5,000 from one of the railroad men just before the curtain falls.

"Stella Adler plays Clotilde," wrote George Freedley (*NYMT*), "like a cross between Tallulah Bankhead and a peevish tigress. She overacts so outrageously and consistently that her role is never believable for an instant." Perhaps her performance had something to do with the fact that she brought her psychiatrist to each rehearsal.

PRIORITIES OF 1942 [Revue] CN/D: Clifford C. Fischer; M/CH: Marjery Fielding; P: Clifford C. Fischer i/a/w the Messrs. Shubert; T: Forty-sixth Street Theatre; 3/12/42 (353)

Despite some middling reviews, this popular-priced offering ($1 for matinees, $2 for evenings) turned out to be a hugely successful vaudeville show, one of several that opened as Broadway offerings the same season, two of them mounted by the impresario responsible for this one.

Priorities of 1942, which included fourteen numbers, made use of three great comedians, bilingual comic Lou Holtz (who emceed), double-talking Willie Howard, and accordian-playing Phil Baker. Whether they were used wisely was a question about which many had their doubts. Brooks Atkinson (*NYT*) was only one of several who claimed that their material was little more than a rehash of familiar routines, many of them heard on the radio. One of Howard's bits with Holtz, in which there was a play on words on the names "Chambers" and "Potts," was considered tasteless and recommended for the refuse heap. Baker, who used to work with a stooge named Sid Silvers, replaced him now with a woman named Flo Campbell. One of the comic routines involved Holtz and Howard making sport of other famous comedians, such as George Jessel, Danny Kaye, Eddie Cantor, and Olsen and Johnson. Baker then came on to reprimand them for their sarcasm, only to put his own two cents in at another comic's expense.

The show definitely scored bull's-eyes with the singing and piano playing of black entertainer Hazel Scott, who offered jazz renditions of Chopin and other classics among other pop offerings, and of creative dancer Paul Draper, whom the opening-night audience would not let leave the stage. This latter was a surprise, given that Draper's style of tap dancing to classical music was considered rather eccentric and not in the usual tradition of Broadway hoofing. "To listen to the staccato beat of his magic feet is to discover new beauties in musical composition from Bach to jazz," observed Euphemia Van Rensselaer Wyatt (*CW*). Also hitting the mark were Gene Sheldon, a very funny baggy-pants banjo-playing clown; and the Nonchalants, a comic tumbling team.

Following the tepid opening-night reviews, the show underwent some revamping, including a rearrangement of the numbers, an improvement in the overall pacing, and the cutting down of the amount of Yiddish joking. The comedy team of Johnny Master and Rowena Rollins was removed from the bill by the second night after having laid an egg. A subsequent show in the same vein was offered by Fischer, who called it *New Priorities of 1943*.

PRIVATE LIFE OF THE MASTER RACE, THE (***Furcht und Elend des Dritten Reiches***) [Drama/Family/German/Jews/Law/Marriage/Military/Politics/Prison/Religion/War] A: Bertolt Brecht; TR: Eric Bentley; M: Hanns Eisler; D: Berthold Viertel and George George; DS: Leo Kerz; P: Theatre of All Nations; T: Pauline Edwards Theatre (City College Auditorium; OB); 6/12/45 (6)

This Brecht play was produced during the years of the German author's exile in America from the Nazi government. It was seen at an auditorium on Twenty-third Street and Lexington Avenue in a nine-scene version of the twenty-four-scene work (more accurately known as *Fear and Misery of the Third Reich*). A fuller production had been given at the University of California. This was actually a revised version of the original play, which had had music by Paul Dessau; eight scenes from it had premiered in Paris in 1938 under the title *99%*.

It was viewed as an experimental drama and struck Lewis Nichols (*NYT*) as more interesting and adult than most conventional plays. He did feel, though, that some of the scenes were overlong, that some of the material was "obscure," and that the acting was often "florid" and the words muffled. Nichols noted that with the collapse of the German army the play lacked the topicality it would have had several years earlier. In George Jean Nathan's (*TBY*) opinion, Brecht had failed at adapting his personal style to the needs of the American theatre. "He retains some power as a dramatist, but it is more the power of lungs than of the spirit."

The episodic work presents a series of largely self-contained, bitter scenes designed to create contempt for the Nazi ideology. The scenes fit within a framework picturing a Panzer tank rolling along through Europe with its "Horst Wessel"-singing troops; raucous Nazi propaganda is heard over the amplifiers at specific moments. Among its most memorable sequences was one ("In Search of Justice") about a judge (Clarence Derwent) who can barely do his job because of his need to solve a case to the satisfaction of the Nazis; one known as "The Jewish Wife," which subsequently was given frequent performances on its own and is basically a one-woman piece about a Gentile doctor's Jewish spouse calling her friends to say goodbye as she prepares to leave Germany, where her religion has begun to cause problems for her husband; and one ("The Informer," also later produced separately) about a father (Albert Bassermann) and mother (Else Bassermann) who think that their absent child has been informing on them, and whose fears are not quelled when he returns from a seemingly innocent excursion to buy candy. Other scenes display the imprisonment of men in labor battalions, the brutalities of life in concentration camps, and other inhuman situations.

In the cast were Elaine Stritch, Dwight Marfield, Hester Sondergaard, Eda Reiss-Merin, and others.

PRIVATE LIVES [Dramatic Revival*] A: Noël Coward; D: Martin Manulis; S/L: Charles Elson; P: John S. Wilson; T: 10/4/48 (248)

Coward's popular comedy, first seen here in 1931 with himself and Gertrude Lawrence, was given its first of many subsequent New York revivals in this production starring Tallulah Bankhead as Amanda. She had played the role earlier in a 1944 summer-theatre revival. The present revival began in Westport, Connecticut, and then went on tour. It was put on hold while Bankhead ventured onto Broadway in a flop production of *The Eagle Has Two Heads* and then resumed for a major cross-country tour, which proved exhausting but highly profitable (it grossed $970,000), and during which Bankhead was often ill and suffering from neuritis. Barbara Baxley was Sibyl, Donald Cook was Elyot, William Langford (who replaced Phil Arthur) was Victor Prynne, and Therese Quadri was Louise. Nineteen-year-old Baxley, a future star, had replaced Buff Cobb, whom she had understudied, during the tour. Baxley's good looks soon attracted Cook, which made Bankhead so jealous that she made life hell for the young actress. For example, when Bankhead, who disliked acting schools, learned that Baxley, who had studied with Sanford Meisner, had decided to use the image of a hummingbird for her character, the older actress blew up and screamed, "*Hummingbird*," as she pounded her open hand on a table. "*Hummingbird!* There's a beat to this play, and you say your lines!" (quoted by Lee Israel in *Miss Tallulah Bankhead*).

Bankhead's fans went wild over her performance, but some critics had their doubts. George Freedley (*NYMT*) declared, "Miss Bankhead overacts outrageously and was encouraged by her audience who roared at every grimace, every bit of outlandish but characteristic business which she introduced." Only Cook was able to hold the stage with her, the actors playing the other leading couple fading into insignificance in colorless roles that even Laurence Olivier and Jill Esmond had trouble making interesting in the original production. John Lardner (*TS*) thought that the play's thinness had tempted Cook and Bankhead to have a thespian field day by camping it up. Their aggressively American qualities (and those of the other actors) were another reason for the approach they took to get laughs. "Making like a pair of Mayfair butterflies," wrote Lardner, "Miss Bankhead and Mr. Cook manage . . . to remain strictly cornfed." Cook, he said, "delivered his lines in a series of bleats and whinnies. Miss Bankhead alternates between seal barks and low-pitched gutterals." Bankhead was good, however, at the slugfest acrobatics required when she engaged with Cook in a lovers' wrestling match.

Many thought the play brittle, dated, and barely as sophisticated as it once seemed, but still able to garner belly laughs when played, as here, with the kind of energetic comic brio that led Otis L. Guernsey, Jr. (*NYHT*), to say of the star that she turned the piece into "a defiant one-woman show." John Mason Brown (*SR*) concluded that Bankhead was more than a volcano; she was "a volcano in a hurricane. . . . She tosses both the script and Miss Lawrence's performance right out the window. In their place, she plays Tallulah. . . . Part of the audacity, hence the fascination, of Miss Bankhead's Amanda is that she acts her not only as if Mr. Coward must have had her in mind, but as if he should have even if he didn't."

Coward is said to have forbidden Bankhead from bringing the piece to New York but to have changed his mind after seeing her do it in Chicago. While agreeing with the critics that the interpretation of Amanda was seriously off the mark, he acknowledged that her performance, with its constant gurglings and double takes on Cook's lines, was nevertheless very amusing to the audience. Still, he agreed with the critics about her misinterpretation of Amanda. "Perhaps," suggested Euphemia Van Rensselaer Wyatt (*CW*), "he realized that it was no longer the play he had acted in." Instead, she said, it was "now a medley of burlesqued French farce and Hollywood passion. . . . The translation of Coward's decadent Mayfair wit into vaudeville vernacular has proved equally tasty to the prairies, the oil lands, the corn belt and Broadway's hard-boiled associates."

PROOF THRO' THE NIGHT [Drama/Drugs/Homosexuality/Politics/Tropics/War/Women] A/D: Allan R. Kenward; S: Albert Johnson; L: Moe Hack; P: Lee Shubert; T: Morosco Theatre; 12/25/42 (11)

This drama had played in Hollywood as *Cry Havoc* and was still referred to under that title by several careless critics. The reason for the change was to allay confusion with the imminent film version using the original title. Received with considerable approval on the West Coast (where its author was a screenwriter), it was rebuffed by New York's critics.

It is an all-female war play set on the site of a converted gun emplacement adjacent to the Bataan peninsula in the Philippines in 1941, shortly before the fall of Corregidor. There are twelve young women, four regulars--including Doc (Ann Shoemaker) and her chief nurse Smitty (Katherine Emery)--and eight volunteers pressed into service as nurses when they arrive; there is also a native woman (Teresa Teves). The war provides an exciting background for their individual crises, which are brought out under the pressure of constant bombardment. The women arrive filled with the feeling that their work will be interesting and fun, but their lightheartedness soon fades when danger intrudes from the sky and the reinforcements fail to appear. Unprepared for such danger, their nerves start to go and their true natures begin to arise. There is a suspected drug user, but it turns out that she needs the drugs to kill the pain from an injury. Another, Steve (Carol Channing), is a lesbian. One of them turns out to be a German spy, and the play shifts from concern with people under enormous stress to the discovery of the traitor in their midst. Pat (Thelma Schnee), the funny former switchboard operator with a penchant for wisecracks, is suspected at first, but the spy turns out to be Connie (Katherine Locke), a character whose participation in the action until she is found out has been minimal. Holding the others off with a gun, she declaims against democracy and boasts of being Bund-trained in the United States. She kills one of the others. Her comments, of course, are abundantly rebutted by the others. Finally, the Japanese arrive, the spy is shot, and the others are marched off and machine-gunned to death.

In some views, such as Rosamond Gilder's (*TAM*), the play--which reminded many of *Journey's End**--succeeded in bringing all the characters to three-dimensional life. Others found its brutal ending one that elevated the play into importance by the severity with which it confronted the Japanese peril. More common was the opinion that the play bypassed its concern with the women to wallow in the melodramatics of its spy plot and its overly obvious propaganda for democracy. Lewis Nichols (*NYT*) thought it "shrill and hysterical." George Jean Nathan (*TBY*) ridiculed the clichéd character types, who reminded him of "a stranded one-night-stand musical comedy company." His overall impression was less that of a band of valiant nurses endangered by the terrors of battle than it was of "a lot of heterogeneous cuties spending a few days' summer vacation in a shared Atlantic City Pacific

Avenue hotel room during a boozy convention of Japanese rolling-ball game concessionaires."

The cast was considered superior, being made up of some of Broadway's finest young female talent, including Florence Rice, Margaret Phillips, Helen Trenholme, Muriel Hutchinson, Florence McMichael, and Julie Stevens. Despite the presence of a clearly lesbian character, there was little public controversy, and very few critics even mentioned her. The character was removed from the film script.

PUBLIC RELATIONS [Comedy/Family/Films/Marriage/Romance/Sex] A: Dale Eunson; D: Edward Childs Carpenter; S: Stewart Chaney; P: Robert Blake; T: Mansfield Theatre; 4/6/44 (28)

The author of this comedy about Hollywood was derelict in providing good material for his worthy actors. "His dialogue moves from one bright line to another with irritating leisureliness," groused Arthur Pollock (*BE*), "leaving the actors flat in between, and his plot, which is tiny to begin with, remains undeveloped." Ward Morehouse (*NYS*) dubbed it "incredibly laborious."

The scene is the White House, a glorious Beverly Hill mansion reminiscent of Mary Pickford and Douglas Fairbanks's Pickfair; it was built by a tremendously popular silent-movie couple (also reminiscent of Pickford and Fairbanks), Anita Sawyer (Ann Andrews) and Wallace Maxwell (Philip Merivale), who have since divorced because of his womanizing. The house, owned jointly by Wallace and Anita, has been empty, but Anita, who is now married to agent David Robinson (Bradford Hunt), reopens it for a USO lawn party. Unaware that it has been shut down, Wallace returns to it with his young South American bride, Dolores (Yolanda Ugarte). The exes meet and, as they conflict about who is going to occupy the house, slowly find themselves attracted to one another again. They have a movie-star son Maurice (Michael Ames), who is the object of a blackmail scheme by an extra girl (Lynette Brown) with whom he has dallied, but who escapes the consequences and is forgiven by his wife (Frances Henderson). They also have a daughter (Suzanne Jackson), whom Wallace has forgotten, and who has married a small-town politician. The girl has come to the White House to have her baby there (there is an offstage birth scene). Also figuring in the action is Anita's bibulous former movie-star friend Madge Torrance (Betty Blythe, onetime silent-screen star, who had not acted in twenty-three years). Stirred by the near threat to their son's marriage, Anita and Wallace team up again and go off to entertain the troops, while David and Dolores find comfort in each other's hearts.

In the cast were Mason Adams, Virginia Sherry, and Owen Coll, among others.

PYGMALION [Dramatic Revival*] A: George Bernard Shaw; D: Cedric Hardwicke; S: Donald Oenslager; C: Motley; P: Theatre Incorporated; T: Ethel Barrymore Theatre; 12/26/45 (179)

A hit revival of the great 1914 Shaw comedy that had been revived locally in 1926, 1927 (in Spanish), and 1938, the latter by the Federal Theatre Project. In the current incarnation, Henry Higgins was played by Raymond Massey, Eliza Doolittle by Gertrude Lawrence, Colonel Pickering by Cecil Humphreys, Alfred Doolittle by Melville Cooper, Clara Eynsford-Hill by Wendy Atkin, Mrs. Eynsford-Hill by Myrtle Tannehill, Freddy by John Cromwell, Mrs. Pearce by Anita Bolster, and Mrs. Higgins by Katherine Emmett.

Cedric Hardwicke's production--set in the play's original period--underlined the romantic story over the satirical elements, despite Shaw's own written attempts to suggest the reverse approach. John Mason Brown (*SR*), however, faulted the director for the stodginess of his sense of humor and his "cigarstore-Indian groupings." Some of the play's original luster had worn thin, but the piece still managed to hold its own.

The performance centerpiece was Lawrence's as the cockney flower girl. Wrote Rosamond Gilder (*TAM*), "Though she plays her first scenes for softness and pathos rather than toughness and vulgarity, Miss Lawrence's handling of the fabulous moment in Mrs. Higgins's drawing room is so witty and at the same time so winning that the weakness of the earlier passages must be forgiven her. . . . There is a delicate, almost inaudible hesitation in her carefully articulated speech--a sense of vowels and consonants being formed in the mind before they come off the tongue; a careful balance and restraint in the carriage of the body, the poise of the head, the use of gloved hands and dainty parasol that suggest the hair-trigger equilibrium of an artiste stepping out on a slack-wire." While most critics agreed with her, George Jean Nathan (*TBY*) insisted that Lawrence's "progress . . . is more a matter of costume change than change in character" and that her acting was superficial.

Shaw calls for a scene in which Eliza is to throw Higgins's slippers at him, one after the other. When Lawrence kept missing widely during the early performances, audiences were disappointed because they wanted Higgins to be struck, or almost struck. Lawrence actually had an accurate arm and costar Massey begged her to use it, but she was afraid that he would be unable to duck and might get hurt. Ultimately, however, Lawrence, without warning, decided to throw for real. According to Massey (as quoted in Richard Aldrich's *Gertrude Lawrence as Mrs. A*), "One night, when I had given up expecting anything, a whizzing slipper caught me on the nose. Gertie was as startled as I. 'Oh!' she exclaimed. 'I've hit you. . . ' She dropped the other slipper in horror." When he began to laugh and the audience did, too, "She picked up the slipper and let me have it. For a season afterwards I had to duck pinpoint pitching."

Lewis Nichols (*NYT*) wrote that Massey "gives a fine rendition, although once or twice he leaned a bit to the side of exaggeration. He is every inch the misogynist." Brown thought him lacking in charm and criticized his Canadian accent. The others did very well also, although Cooper, whose acting was on the broad side, was not quite as amusing as Doolittle should be. A magnificent series of settings was provided by Oenslager, especially the opening scene at St. Paul's.

The producing company, headed by Lawrence's husband Richard Aldrich, was a new one, established on a not-for-profit basis and dedicated to the presentation of revivals and new plays. The actors all accepted Equity minimum salaries for the venture.

Q

QUIET PLEASE [Comedy/Films/Marriage/Music/Sex] A: F. Hugh Herbert and Hans Kraly; SC: a short story by Ferdinand Reyher; D: Russell Fillmore (under supervision of Henry Duffy); S: Everett Burgess; P: Jesse L. Lasky and Henry Duffy; T: Guild Theatre; 11/8/40 (16)

Three plays about Hollywood appeared almost simultaneously on Broadway in the fall of 1940, and all were clinkers. The others were *Glamour Preferred* and *Beverly Hills*. *Quiet Please* was "an inept and unattractive tale of amorous revenge," complained Rosamond Gilder (*TAM*).

The play, which came to New York after a Los Angeles production, was an ill-assorted compilation of stock material put into service for a plot about Carol Adams (Jane Wyatt), a screen star whose husband, Roland Pierce (Donald Woods), is not only a class-B actor, but one with a roving eye. His various amours during filming drive his director (Fred Niblo)--not to mention his wife--to distraction. To even the score, Carol flirts with a handsome auto mechanic, Michael Kilmer (Gordon Jones, in his Broadway debut), who turns out to be not only musically talented but a college grad as well. He already has a girlfriend, but the film star's attentions begin to turn his head. Whether their relationship is consummated is never clearly stated. Roland returns and discovers what has been happening, but reveals that he has really been faithful all the while, only pretending to be a skirt-chaser because of the professional inferiority he feels being married to an actress of Carol's standing.

The only novel element in the production was its conceit that the audience in the theatre was actually a group of extras playing a New York audience during the filming of a movie scene set in a theatre. The theatre was actually supposed to be Sound Stage 18 at Imperial Studios, and the place was filled with all the expensive paraphernalia of movie-making. Everyone in the audience was given a page from the "film script" so they could respond on cue when required. Members of the actual cast made considerable use of the theatre's aisles in the course of the play. Most of the audience felt self-conscious about the concept. The beautiful and talented Wyatt was wasted in this turkey. The cast included Bruce MacFarlane, Anthony Kemble Cooper, and Ann Mason as a silent-screen star.

R

R.U.R. [Dramatic Revival*] A: Karel Capek; TR: Paul Selver; D: Lee Strasberg; S: Boris Aronson; P: David Silberman and L. Daniel Blank; T: Ethel Barrymore Theatre; 12/3/42 (4)

Capek's science-fiction drama with a moral, first produced here by the Theatre Guild in 1922 and shown by it again in 1930, was revived to little effect in 1942 with Gordon Oliver as Harry Domin, Lewis Wilson as Marius, Edith Atwater as Helena Glory, Horace Braham as Dr. Gall, Louis Hector as Dr. Hallemeier, Hugo Haas as Mr. Alquist, Reginald Mason as Consul Busman, Sydney Smith as Radius, and Katherine Balfour as Helena. The production was thought to bear certain parallels to contemporary conditions with its story of men against inhuman robot monsters, but it seemed "dated and not a little slow," thought Lewis Nichols (*NYT*). He declared that "the play lacks characterization, the humans being more typed than the robots, and it has dialogue that seems stilted and unpointed now," an opinion widely shared. There had been minor changes in the dialogue, but George Jean Nathan (*TBY*) felt that these did not go far enough, especially as the play was meant to be in the still distant future and lines suggesting someone's shock at a young lady's traveling alone and without a chaperone seemed ridiculous in this context.

The production was poorly directed in an inappropriately introspective mood. George Freedley (*NYMT*) commented, "Lee Strasberg has staged it portentously and has paced it slowly and pitched it so inaudibly that you can count between the lines." It also lacked--except for Czech actor Haas--distinguished acting, although it was granted three fascinating settings by Boris Aronson.

RAIN [Dramatic Revival*/Blacks] A: John Colton and Clemence Randolph; D: Ted Post; S: Roger Furman; L: George Lewis; P/T: American Negro Theatre (OB); 12/26/47 (28)

A blizzard was raging on the opening night of this black revival of the steamy 1922 drama based on a famous Somerset Maugham story. Its most recent revival had been in 1935. Produced at a theatre at 15 West 126th Street in Harlem, it included actress-writer Alice Childress as Sadie Thompson, her husband Alvin Childress as the Reverend Davidson, Maxwell Glanville as Sergeant O'Hara, Bootsie Davis as Trader Joe Horn, Geneva Fitch as Mrs. Davidson, Kenneth Mannigault as Dr. McPhail, and Clarice Taylor as Mrs. McPhail.

Brooks Atkinson (*NYT*) considered the production intelligent and professional, with a proper stress on the irony of the writing. However, he felt that there was a missing subtlety in the psychological explorations of the leading roles. A major technical problem was that the sound effects of rain and tom-toms drowned out much of the dialogue; the problem was compounded by the sloppy and rushed speech of various players.

Atkinson thought Alvin Childress's Davidson the strongest performance, marked by "thorough insight and superior skill." Of his wife's Sadie, Atkinson reported that she "acts the exuberance, the recklessness, the anger and the remorse with force and clarity that help to define the dramatic conflicts. . . . Obviously, this is good acting." He faulted her, though, on her lack of "poignancy." Vernon Rice (*NYP*), however, said that she "has a nice earthy, lusty-gusty quality."

RAMSHACKLE INN [Comedy/Crime/Hotel/Mystery/Small Town] A: George Batson; D: Arthur Sircom; S: Frederick Fox; C: Peggy Clark; P: Robert Reud; T: Royale Theatre; 1/5/44 (216)

A ramshackle "melodramatic farce" that nevertheless offered film comedienne ZaSu Pitts a tour de force opportunity in which to make her Broadway debut. Her role as a spinster librarian "in no way affected her fluttering, circular gestures or her endless wrestlings with her reticule," reported Rosamond Gilder (*TAM*). "Miss Pitts, with eyebrows perpetually at alert, hands in flight and an expression amiably moronic, has on hand a stock collection of comic devices which are applicable to all emergencies and were liberally applied to the vagaries of *Ramshackle Inn*." Some critics were worn out by her antics, though, and found her ultimately tiresome.

Her vehicle, which somehow managed to run for over 200 showings, was widely abused by the critics, Howard Barnes (*NYHT*) labeling it "a tedious bit of balderdash," and Kahn. (*V*) declaring that it "clatters all over the stage in its too frequently dull, obvious script."

The play's title refers to Ye Olde Colonial Inn, a hostelry near Gloucester, Massachusetts, purchased sight unseen with her life's savings of $3,000 by a Vermont librarian named Belinda Pryde (Pitts). There she encounters a murderous bootlegging gang running its operation from the basement. After multiple complications, including a goodly number of homicides, she uses her native wiles, including the impersonation of an FBI agent, to ensnare the criminals and earn $5,000 in reward money with which she will refurbish the ramshackle inn. All of the action is accompanied by a full panoply of special effects, with lights that flicker on and off; sound effects of thunder and lightning, as well as pistol shots; corpses that keep appearing in different places, including safes, trunks, and closets; and so on. The company included Joe Downing as the head crook, Harlan Briggs as the constable, Ruth Holden as a G-woman, and Mason Curry, Ruth Gates, Ralph Theadore, Maurine Alexander, Richard Rober, Mary Barthelmess, and Royal Dana Tracy in other roles.

RAPE OF LUCRETIA, THE [Musical/British/Marriage/Military/Period/Sex] B: Ronald Duncan; M: Benjamin Britten; D: Agnes de Mille; S/C: John Piper; L: Peggy Clark; P: Marjorie and Sherman Ewing and Giovanni Cardelli; T: Ziegfeld Theatre; 12/29/48 (23)

This "music drama" was actually a modern opera, originally staged in England at Glyndebourne, later seen elsewhere in Europe, and given its American premiere in Chicago in 1947. It was based on a story first found in Livy and later used by others, including Ovid, Shakespeare, and André Obey, whose *Lucrèce** played on Broadway in 1932. Because of the demands placed by opera on the singers' voices, there was an alternating cast for a number of roles. Broadway audiences were not accustomed to attending operas, and the out-of-place piece was removed within a month.

The story concerns the chaste Lucretia (Kitty Carlisle), described by Livy as she "within whose face Beauty and Virtue strived which of them both should underprop her fame." Ronald Duncan's plot is extremely close to that of Obey, and some were surprised that the French writer had not been credited. As in Obey, the story is told by two narrators, a man (Edward Kane) and a woman (Brenda Lewis). Here they are placed in niches, with Sibylline books in their hands, and are responsible for a large amount of the singing. The action unfolds in the year 509 B.C., in the camp at Ardea. General Collatinus (Holger Sorensen), Lucretia's husband, brags about her virtue at the expense of the other generals' wives. This so enrages General Junius (Emile Renan) that he suggests to General Sextus Tarquinus (George [Giorgio] Tozzi) that the latter's reputation as a woman's man will be greater if he seduces Lucretia. The Etruscan Tarquinus is so fired up that he rushes off to her, fording the Tiber on his way, and makes his way to her chamber, where he violates her. She later confesses to her spouse and redeems both his and her honor by stabbing herself to death at his feet.

The production was costumed in ancient Roman garb (Obey's play had been set in the Renaissance), and a very vital element in the production was the impressionistically poetic costume and scenic conceptions of painter John Piper. Also important to the total unity of aesthetic effect was the direction. Euphemia Van Rensselaer Wyatt (*CW*) wrote, "Agnes de Mille has staged the entire production with graceful grouping of the women and particularly gracious movements of their spinning wheels, while Lucretia walks in purest beauty through her sorrows."

Music critic Olin Downes (*NYT*) found the work "as revolutionary as it is exhilarating." He thought the work both "singable" and dramatically effective, and said--despite certain reservations--that it was Britten's "most mature, flexible and distinguished" composition yet. He also commended highly the excellence of the cast, whose members were physically attractive, vocally talented, and capable of fine acting. Another music critic, Robert Bagar (*NYWT*), however, thought the music uninspired.

Theatre critic Howard Barnes (*NYHT*), while approving the decor, much of the music, and most of the performances, found serious fault with the script. "Ronald Duncan's text has literary ambitions but no style or concentration. It is pompous, wandering and incredibly garrulous. . . . It is all thoroughly silly and without reality." Yet Bron. (*V*) found it "superior stuff." Among the standout performances were those of Vivian Bauer as Bianca and Marguerite Piazza as the maid Lucia.

RAPE OF THE SABINE WOMEN, THE [Comedy/German Language/Theatre] A: Franz and Paul V. Schoenthan; D: Walter Engel; C: Brooks Costume Company; P: Players from Abroad; T: Barbizon-Plaza Theatre (OB); 2/4/49

The Players from Abroad were composed of German-speaking refugee actors. In the present production--a once popular German farce--they were headed by the once-great Continental star Albert Bassermann, now in his eighties. The role of Striese, a manager of a wandering theatrical troupe, was one of Bassermann's old favorites, and he was still "uproariously comic in it," wrote Brooks Atkinson (*NYT*). "He has an imposing figure, snowy hair and a resonant voice. . . . Playing a low comedy part with whole-hearted abandon, he capers through the mechanical situations . . . with the most infectious good nature."

The action of the play centers on developments stemming from the decision of a professor (Walter Pose)--despite his distaste for the theatre--to allow Striese's troupe to produce a play called *The Rape of the Sabine Women* that the professor wrote when he was young, and that he and his maid (Else Basserman) still consider fondly.

RAT RACE, THE [Comedy-Drama/Boarding House/Crime/Music/Romance/ Show Business] A/D: Garson Kanin; S/L: Donald Oenslager; C: Lucinda Ballard and Joseph Fretwell III; P: Leland Hayward; T: Ethel Barrymore Theatre; 12/22/49 (84)

Barry Nelson had one of his earliest leading roles in this flubbed boy-meets-girl story with a "philosophy," set in a seamy New York rooming house for show-biz types run by a woman called Soda (Doro Merande). She, with the simpleminded old Mac (Joseph Sweeney), comments on the action somewhat like a Greek chorus; Soda does so from a window on one side of the stage, Mac from a tavern on the other. In this rooming house a broken-hearted, cynical taxi-dance hostess, Helen Brown (Betty Field), who has long since given up hopes of a Broadway career, befriends Gus Hammer (Nelson), a young, starry-eyed jazz saxophonist from the Midwest. Helen, abandoned by her husband, once won a rhumba contest and is the sort who lives more in the nostalgic past than in the hard-to-face present. Gus is a complete naif, committed to the future; he allows himself to be conned by other musicians, who steal his instrument. The life-toughened Helen takes Gus into her room and lets him live there for several weeks rent-free, although it takes him some time to wake up to her personal appeal. Gus and Helen have not gotten much further at the end, but they at least have decided to face the city's rat race together.

Kanin's play was pungently and toughly directed (Kanin took over from Daniel Mann) and played (especially by Field), but was little more than a diffusely told, shabby slice of life with one-dimensional characters and with profane language and surroundings barely redeemed by the central romance. "The author-director has mixed a plaintive parable about little people with ribald burlesque and incidental business so randomly that his show is meaningless and fatiguing," scowled Howard Barnes (*NYHT*). Hobe. (*V*) thought the chorus device a serious impediment because it offered no new information to the audience and also necessitated a complex scenic arrangement. Ward Morehouse (*NYS*) contended that Kanin "has tossed together a great deal of everything--gags, atmosphere, vaudeville, sentiment, melodrama . . . but he never did get around to writing himself a play."

A has-been vaudevillian boarder named Bo Kerry who believes that Irving Berlin once stole a song from him was played by Pat Harrington, and his wife by Dennie Moore. Ray Walston was a lecherous phone repairman, Rex Williams a hood, and Joe Bushkin, Georgie Auld, and Sherman Kane musician crooks.

RATS OF NORWAY, THE [Drama/Alcoholism/British/Homosexuality/Romance/School/Sex] A: Keith Winter; SC: Keith Winter's novel of the same name; D/P: James Elliott i/a/w Carl Schreuer; S/L: William De Forest; T: Booth Theatre; 4/15/48 (4)

An "inept and pretentious" (Thomas R. Dash [*WWD*]), disastrously directed, 1933 drama set in an English prep school and dealing with adultery and the impossible search for perfect love. The symbolic title refers to the Norwegian legend concerning the mass suicidal migrations of lemmings who swim south from Norway in the North Sea, presumably driven by a racial memory of migrations to an island now submerged. (George Jean Nathan [*TBY*] cited academic sources to disprove the veracity of the legend.) This title is meant to refer to the play's two pairs of doomed lovers, who, according to the program, "finally drown their spiritual selves in their quest for the impossible." A hit in London, with Laurence Olivier, Raymond Massey, and Gladys Cooper, the play joined Broadway's lemmings when it drowned after four performances.

The older of the two pairs of lovers contrasted in the action is the drunken headmaster's (Colin Keith-Johnston) wife, Jane Claydon (Jeanne Stuart), and an alcoholic teacher and war veteran, Hugh Sebastian (John Ireland), with a bad heart. Hugh wants to run off with Jane, but she hasn't the courage to risk a life of security on such recklessness. She eventually decides to go with him, but the drunken Hugh dies of a heart attack in her bed before this is possible. A younger set of lovers is new teacher Stephan Beringer (William Howell) and Tilly Shane (Rett Kitson), the piano instructor. She believes that she must accommodate his frequently shifting moods, but this only harms her own character and upsets him. Stephan and Hugh find that they are actually happier in each other's company than in that of their female companions. Chetwood (Bert Jeter), an effeminate younger teacher who wears face powder, is clearly a latent homosexual. No one finds contentment.

"A ridiculous script . . . is badly acted," scoffed Howard Barnes (*NYHT*), who decried the motiveless eccentricities of the characters and the "muddy exposition." Audiences laughed over some of the play's most serious lines.

REBECCA [Drama/Crime/Marriage/Mystery] A: Daphne Du Maurier; SC: Daphne Du Maurier's novel, *Rebecca*; D: Clarence Derwent; S: Watson Barrett; P: Victor Payne-Jennings; T: Ethel Barrymore Theatre; 1/18/45 (20)

Daphne Du Maurier's novel had already been a resounding success in its printed form, its outstanding Alfred Hitchcock-directed movie version, and its radio dramatization, but the author wanted to squeeze even more from it and turned it into a play. It did well on the road before coming to New York, but the latter city turned thumbs down on it. Reviews were divided, with the balance going to the pans. George Freedley (*NYMT*) maintained that the story no longer seemed novel, the dramatization was "unsatisfactory and inadequate," and the production was mediocre. Louis Kronenberger (*PM*) said that it was "hardly ever exciting or tense, and very indifferently produced." But Robert Garland (*NYJA*) said that the play "has color, movement, suspense and the power to raise the hair."

It is set in Manderley, the stately, ancestral Cornwall home of Maxim de Winter (Bramwell Fletcher), to which Maxim has brought his new and unsophisticated wife (Diana Barrymore), an orphan, after meeting and marrying her in the south of France. Presiding over the house is the malignant housekeeper, Mrs. Danvers (Florence Reed). The spell of the glamorous first Mrs. de Winter, Rebecca, drowned a year earlier, lingers at Manderley and, through the prodding of the baleful Mrs. Danvers, begins to make the pitiful second Mrs. de Winter feel so uncomfortable and unwanted that she begins to fear losing her mind. Eventually, Maxim confesses that he killed the beautiful Rebecca, whom he loathed and who loathed him. He murdered her when he learned that she had had an affair with her cousin. Mrs. de Winter agrees with her husband that the homicide was justifiable. Although Maxim is endangered by the accusations of the cousin (George Baxter), Rebecca's death is ultimately classed as a suicide. Only Mrs. de Winter shares the secret of the killing, and her spell is snapped.

The principal actors had to do battle with the memories of Laurence Olivier, Joan Fontaine, and Judith Anderson in the film. Although some were caustic in their responses, others approved the Broadway cast. If anyone came off poorly in the majority of the reviews, it was Diana Barrymore, although she was excused by many as the victim of faulty writing and direction. Also involved were Franklyn Fox as Major Giles Lacy, Margaret Bannerman as Maxim's sister, Claude Horton as Frank Crawley, Richard Temple as Frith, Reginald Mason as Colonel Julyan, and Edgar Kent as William Tabb.

When the play was trying out in New Haven, Bramwell Fletcher introduced something of a novelty in curtain speeches. After the actors took their calls, he stepped forward and raised his hand dramatically, bringing a hush to the house. Instead of speaking the expected thanks to the audience, he declared, "I have been asked to announce there will be no bus or trolley transportation available" (quoted in Fred Fehl, *On Broadway*).

RED GLOVES (*Les Mains Sales*) [Drama/Crime/French/Marriage/Politics/Romance] A: Jean-Paul Sartre; AD: Daniel Taradash; D: Jed Harris; S/L: Stewart Chaney; C: Emeline Roche; P: Jean Dalrymple b/a/w Gabriel Pascal; T: Mansfield Theatre; 12/4/48 (113)

During the late 1940s there was a vogue for French existentialist playwright Jean-Paul Sartre, who was responsible for this cerebral political melodrama (also known as *Dirty Hands* and *Crime Passionnel*) starring Charles Boyer, the French-born movie actor, in his Broadway debut. The play was still running in Paris, where it was a hit. It was also successful in a literal translation produced in London, but the New York producer decided to have Daniel Taradash write a new version. This adaptation--cut considerably from the original--offended Sartre, who repudiated it before the production opened, claiming that it was a distortion of his intentions.

The piece is set in a fictional Balkan nation caught between the Nazi threat and the USSR during the years 1943 to 1945. Boyer played Hoederer, the nation's Communist leader, seen by Sartre as an ideal political figure because of his total pragmatism and ability to dirty his hands in compromise to justify desired ends. Hoederer is on the brink of effecting a political alliance with enemy factions, a move that the Communist party believes morally inappropriate but that Hoederer thinks is politically sound because it will save the lives of his fellow citizens. The party wants the leader assassinated before the alliance can be made and selects to do the deed Hugo (John Dall), a young, intellectual aristocrat and somewhat muddle-headed political innocent who has turned to Marxist totalitarianism as a result of misplaced romantic impulses. Hugo takes a position as Hoederer's secretary; his wife, Jessica (Joan Tetzel), falls in love with the leader and betrays her husband's intentions. After much procrastination, Hugo concludes that he does not have the killer instinct and instead denounces Hoederer at a political meeting. He finally kills Hoederer, however, not because of political motivations, but because he believes that Hoederer is having an affair with Jessica. Hoederer forgives Hugo's deed by accepting it not as a political killing but as a crime of passion. Hugo goes to prison; when he gets out in 1945 as the Russians are entering the capital, he discovers that the party line of 1943 has been reversed, and Hoederer is viewed as a martyr. Hugo himself must now be liquidated.

Boyer's performance was deemed far more compelling than the play, which did not live up to the expectations most critics had of it. "Mechanically built, composed of long arguments about abstract political ideas, it is a tiresome piece of work, redeemed only by the acting of Charles Boyer and John Dall," grumbled Brooks Atkinson (*NYT*); he nonetheless thought its melodramatic qualities more theatrically interesting than earlier examples of Sartre's work. He also appreciated Sartre's intellectual clarity in dramatizing the weakness in totalitarian political systems. Considerable debate raged concerning whether the play was pro or anti-Communist, Sartre himself declaring that his position was neutral and that the play was neither leftist nor rightist. Atkinson and some others saw its target as being all totalitarianism. Howard Barnes (*NYHT*) viewed the work as "a garrulous and rarely provocative study of revolutionary tactics. . . . Sartre has given few of his characters honest and appealing definition." John Mason Brown (*SR*), discounting reports of alleged revisions to Sartre's play, decided that the "play was never any good; that, indeed, it is as dull and synthetic a phony as has so far been written about one of the greatest and most tantalizing themes of our time." But William Hawkins (*NYWT*) insisted that this was "a provocative sort of drama that occurs far too rarely for the theater's own good. This is a wisely stated play and a deeply ironical one."

Boyer (who abandoned his toupee for the role and reminded some of Benito Mussolini) was brilliant. Richard Watts, Jr. (*NYP*), reported that he turned "out to be a superb actor, powerful, intelligent, imaginative and resourceful, without a trace of film nonsense or pretentiousness about him." Boyer had not wanted to take the role at first, thinking the play a bore and believing Hugo to be the actual leading role (which, in the original, it is). When he soon after went to Paris and saw the play there, it put him to sleep. But the matter refused to die, and film star Madeleine Carroll, thinking Hoederer perfect for Boyer, made a concerted effort to persuade him to take it. Finally, after reading the first two acts of the American version, Boyer accepted. As he played it, of course, Hoederer became the chief character.

As mentioned previously, an altercation soon developed, however, with Sartre himself. The playwright brought suit against his agent, Louis Nagel, for having allowed the play to become a piece of anti-Communist propaganda. He was also miffed at not having been given a look at the adaptation, which he considered vulgarly melodramatic. (After learning more about the new version, he decided it was pro-Communist.) He wanted to return his advance and seek an injunction against the production, but he never did either. Meanwhile, as the play tried out in Boston, a death threat was received by producer Dalrymple, and her master script was stolen. A lot of publicity was generated, and the play was prejudged according to Sartre's charges, but the production went forward nonetheless. Producer Dalrymple, who was forced to defend the Taradash version in the press, felt that the controversy seriously damaged the play's reception. As for the missing script, Dalrymple came to believe that it ended up in Sartre's hands because the script described in a *TAM* interview as being in the playwright's hands sounded suspiciously like the one she had lost.

There was disagreement over Jed Harris's direction, but many agreed that of the supporting cast, the best performance was turned in by Francis Compton as a prince. Horace McMahon, Jesse White, Anna Karen, and Royal Beal were other well-known cast members.

RED MILL, THE [Musical Revival] B/LY: Henry Blossom; B.AD: Milton Lazarus; M: Victor Herbert; ADD.LY: Forman Brown; D: Billy Gilbert; CH: Aida Broadbent; S: Arthur Lonergan; C: Walter Israel and Emile Santiago; L: Adrian Awan; P: Paula Stone and Hunt Stromberg, Jr.; T: Ziegfeld Theatre; 10/16/45 (531)

The 1906 original version of this operetta (starring David Montgomery and Fred Stone) ran for 274 performances, while its revival managed a surprising 531, which was then a record for revivals. Victor Herbert's memorable score, including a string of familiar tunes such as "Moonbeams," "When You're Pretty and the World Is Fair," "Isle of Our Dreams," "Every Day Is Ladies Day with Me," and "Because You're You," was a large reason for the show's success, as was a heavy dollop of nostalgia.

It began as a production of the Los Angeles Civic Light Opera Company, where its book had been revised and additional lyrics had been supplied. This version proved so effective that it was moved to Broadway, with Eddie Foy, Jr., and Michael O'Shea playing the roles of Kid Conner and Con Kidder originated by Montgomery and Stone (Foy and O'Shea eventually were replaced by Jack Whiting and Jack Albertson). Stone himself was in the audience on the opening night of the revival, which was coproduced by one of his daughters and starred another of them. Lazarus's adaptation was quite faithful to the original, retaining its story and much of its comedy, but the piece had been trimmed of three songs and some of its tired humor; it was otherwise reworked to allow for additional dancing by Dorothy Stone (as Tina) and her husband Charles Collins (as Gaston).

The Sign of the Red Mill is a Dutch inn where the American comic heroes are forced to work to pay off their bill. They engage in a plot to allow the innkeeper's daughter Gretchen (Ann Andre) marry Captain Van Damm (Robert Hughes), the man she loves, instead of the governor (Edward Dew), whom her father wants her to wed. When her father locks her up, Kid and Con free her, and a search for the missing bride involves the Americans in pretending to be Sherlock Holmes and Dr. Watson, among other characters. All is happily resolved upon the discovery that Gretchen's lover is heir to a fortune.

Despite the show's ultimate hit status, most critics were lukewarm, admiring the old songs, some of the comedy, and one or two performances, notably Eddie Foy, Jr.'s, but considering the book seriously dated, much of the company undistinguished, and the production so-so. Lewis Nichols (*NYT*) did not believe that its "lavander [*sic*] and old-lace charm" was enough to rescue it, and he thought that the singers were not up to their songs. Rosamond Gilder (*TAM*) saw nothing in it "to lift the theatre from its temporary doldrums." But Euphemia Van Rensselaer Wyatt (*CW*) was delighted to find it "still good entertainment--funny, melodious and decent." Burton Rascoe (*NYWT*), its loudest drumbeater, praised everything about the show, demanding that its plan to run for eight weeks be abandoned in favor of at least a year and insisting that the revival was "insuperably better" than the original.

Foy's part allowed him many opportunities for hilarious buffoonery, while O'Shea was a valuable straight man. "Foy and O'Shea," wrote Wyatt, "are neither strident, suggestive nor oggling [*sic*]. They are just happily, uproariously foolish and they seem to want everyone else to enjoy the fun of being funny with them." The cast also included Odette Myrtle, Billy Griffith, George Meader, and Frank Jaquet.

REGINA [Musical/Blacks/Business/Crime/Family/Illness/Marriage/Small Town/Southern] B/M/LY: Marc Blitzstein; SC: Lillian Hellman's play, *The Little Foxes**; D: Robert Lewis; CH: Anna Sokolow; S/L: Horace Armistead; C: Aline Bernstein; P: Cheryl Crawford i/a/w Clinton Wilder; T: Forty-sixth Street Theatre; 10/31/49 (56)

Regina, an operatic adaptation of Hellman's powerful 1939 melodrama about the rapacious Hubbard clan of turn-of-the-century Bowden, Alabama, which had starred Tallulah Bankhead in the role of Regina Giddens, was better liked by the music critics than those covering the drama, and it closed in two months' time. It has been revived on subsequent occasions, but has never become as important a work as some thought it deserved to be.

Radio and nightclub singer Jane Pickens, formerly of a popular sister act, met with split opinions in the title role. When Bankhead heard about the show, she asked, "Who's playing me?" Told it was Pickens, she cracked, "Pickens? I didn't even like her when she was with the Andrews Sisters." Still, she offered to assist the star on delivering Regina's poisonous line to Horace, "I hope you die. I hope you die soon. I'll be waiting for you to die." Director Lewis reminded Bankhead that Pickens would be singing the words. "She's going to sing it? What the hell do you think I did?" (reported by Eric A. Gordon in *Mark the Music*, where the work is discussed in great detail). Pickens was backed by such able supporting players as Lilyn Brown as

Addie, William Warfield as Cal, Priscilla Gillette as Alexandra (Zan), Brenda Lewis as Birdie (probably the most admired performance), David Thomas as Oscar, Russell Nype as Leo, William Wilderman as Horace, and George Lipton as Ben.

Although Hellman's plot remained intact, the work was expanded to include dance and choral numbers, a jazz group called the Angel Band, and so on, but all the embellishments failed to satisfy the many who questioned the need to turn the play into an opera. (Actually, Blitzstein claimed that his work was a musical drama, not an opera, but the critics insisted on treating it as if it were the latter.) The lines were presented in a combination of straight dialogue, song, and recitative, creating an effect that turned some critics off. "On the whole the dramatic impact of a fine tragedy is vitiated in stylized situations and jangling moods," carped Howard Barnes (*NYHT*). As a work of opera, *Regina* met with some strong approval, as witness the comments of Brooks Atkinson (*NYT*), who averred that not only was the piece superbly acted, sung, designed, and directed, but that Blitzstein had composed "a tart and astringent score for ferocious characters on the foundation of a stirring orchestration." Yet he admitted that the work did not add anything of value to the Hellman drama. "In fact, the language of opera seems cumbersome in comparison with the compact, tensile, realistic drama that" Hellman had created. Similarly, John Mason Brown (*SR*), after expressing his admiration for all the talent on display, questioned why it was necessary to operatize so excellent a play. "Although Mr. Blitzstein's score seems interesting enough . . . , I found it a constant deterrent rather than an aid. . . . It interrupts the action, annihilates the tension, and destroys the suspense. . . . Its colloquial and mundane recitatives struck me as downright silly." George Jean Nathan (*TBY*) dismissed many of the criticisms leveled at the work and instead chose to fault it mainly for its musical style. Blitzstein, he argued, "very plainly mistakes freakish innovation for sound originality, and mere novelty for sound experiment."

"RESPECTFUL PROSTITUTE, THE" (see *An Evening of Two Plays*)

RESPECTFULLY YOURS [Comedy/Family/Literature/Marriage/Period/University] A: Peggy Lamson; D: Marjorie Hildreth; S: David Reppa; L: Rebecca Jennings; P: Blackfriars' Guild; T: Blackfriars' Theatre (OB); 5/13/47 (16)

The twenty-fourth play produced by Off-Broadway's semiprofessional Blackfriars' Guild during its first six years of existence was this conventional Broadway-type period comedy known in its earlier Charleston, South Carolina, incarnation (with Dorothy Gish) as *Bee In Her Bonnet*. It had been optioned for a commercial New York run with the title *Her Lord and Master*, but none of the producers, including Oscar Serlin and the Theatre Guild, who at one time or another held the option followed through. Most critics could understand why.

It is set in Cambridge, Massachusetts, in 1912 and covers what happens when Lydia Greenleaf (Anne Follman), shy young wife of bossy Harvard English professor Carl Greenleaf (Clifford West), publishes a best-seller called *How to Command Respect at Home*, instructing wives on how to assert themselves in their domiciles. Lydia herself is the opposite of the aggressive woman she describes. The controversial publication--confronting the issues of the single and double standard--shames her stuffed-shirt spouse with the campus community but brings her wide attention and even influences her own behavior. Complications force the pair to separate, but the playwright manages to have the husband see the error of his ways, and the couple are reunited for a happy ending. Along the way, the heroine lands some blows at the expense of "male fatuousness and conceit, at period prejudices, and at academic big shots," reported Louis Kronenberger (*PM*).

There were a few kind words for some of the material, but most felt that the play could not sustain its initial impetus. George Jean Nathan (*TBY*) said that the subject was old-hat and lacked the requisite "wit and humor to revitalize it." Brooks Atkinson (*NYT*) thought it "endlessly tiresome" and its few amusing notions belabored.

RETREAT TO PLEASURE [Comedy/Gambling/Labor/Politics/Romance] A: Irwin Shaw; D: Harold Clurman; P: Group Theatre; S: Donald Oenslager; C: Paul du Pont; T: Belasco Theatre; 12/17/40 (23)

Cardboard characters, an indecisive point of view, and excessive talkativeness were among the faults of this tiresome and pretentious work. John Anderson (*NYJA*) characterized it as "a mild and rather empty little comedy that seems to get nowhere very slowly in three acts." John Mason Brown (*NYP*) bemoaned the waste of talent "in a vehicle which chugs its way to an occasional laugh without ever hitting on more than one cylinder, and often goes in reverse."

It focuses on pretty Norah Galligan (Edith Atwater), a minor executive for the Works Progress Administration in Ohio who watches helplessly as the federal government removes 10,000 workers from the rolls. Trying to cope with her feelings, she contemplates marriage to Lee Tatnall (Hume Cronyn), a wealthy valve manufacturer, romance with Chester Stack (John Emery), a rich and handsome playboy, or ditto with the idealistic Peter Flower (Leif Erickson), a loquacious young socialist artist. While making up her mind, she and the manufacturer take a retreat to pleasure from life's problems in Florida, but the other men follow her there (Peter having won $1,000 in a poker game). Peter's social conscience affects everyone, and they seem to have a glimpse of a better life in the future. Peter is offered a high-paying job, Lee thinks of running for Congress, and Chester contemplates a life of usefulness. Norah decides to marry Peter, but he now believes that he needs to live some more before settling down.

A group of fine supporting actors was involved, including Helen Ford, Ruth Nelson, Florence Sundstrom, Dorothy Patten, Art Smith, George Mathews, John McGovern, and Fred Stewart; only a few were representative members of the Group Theatre, which was nearing its end. Richard Lockridge (*NYS*) said of Cronyn that he "gives a sharp, droll performance and pretty much runs away with the play."

RETURN ENGAGEMENT [Comedy/Family/Romance/Theatre] A: Lawrence Riley; P: W. Horace Schmidlapp and Joseph M. Gaites; T: John Golden Theatre; 11/1/40 (8)

A "shopworn" (John Anderson [*NYJA*]) romantic comedy teaming Bert Lytell and Mady Christians as Geoffrey Armstrong and Elizabeth Emerson in a tale about a pair of skidding middle-aged actors, now divorced, who find that they have been hired to costar in a the tryout of a new play at the Stockton Playhouse, a converted barn on the estate of the wealthy socialite, Mrs. Carlotta Faulkner (Leona Powers). Mrs. Faulkner pays the bills because she wants to see her talentless daughter Caryl Smith) play important roles. Geoffrey and Elizabeth's characters in the new play reflect their own lives and relationship. After a number of conventional complications, including a flirtation between Geoffrey and the dopey Mrs. Faulkner, the once-married couple find that they have fallen in love again and are willing to make a return engagement as man and wife.

The premise of the play gave the author a chance to make standard jokes at the expense of summer theatricals, from the acting lessons and living arrangements of the actors to the rough-hewn theatrical facilities and idiocies of the season's wealthy backer. Most critics found it hard to see in this work the author of the successful *Personal Appearance** of several seasons earlier. As Kelcey Allen (*WWD*) observed, "The action is artificial and the play is exasperatingly talky." The chief benefit for audiences was the good production, which also used such players as Audrey Christie, Augusta Dabney, and Evelyn Varden.

RHAPSODY [Musical/Music/Period/Politics/Romance/Sex] B: Leonard Levinson and Arnold Sundgaard; M: Fritz Kreisler; LY: John Latouche; ADD.LY: Russell Bennett and Blevins Davis; SC: an original story by A. N. Nagler; D/CH: David Lichine; S: Oliver Smith; C: Frank Bevan; L: Stanley McCandless; P: Blevins Davis i/a/w Lorraine Manville Dresselhuys; T: Century Theatre; 11/22/44 (13)

This lavishly produced old-fashioned operetta set in the court of Vienna's Empress Maria Theresa (Annamary Dickey) in the eighteenth century was shooed off the stage in brief order. It labored under the load of silly lyrics and a bloated and moribund libretto. "What passes for a book . . . establishes something of a low for libretto falsification," reported Howard Barnes (*NYHT*). One of the script's humorous high points came when an actress referred to Casanova as "a perpetual emotion machine."

The story concerns a court intrigue devised by persons in the employ of Madame Pompadour, who wishes to create a scandal about the empress and her emperor, Francis I (George Young), in order to establish a political crisis. The plotters are Casanova (Eddie Mayehoff) and Madame Boticini (Rosemarie Brancato), each of them aiming to seduce one of the royal figures.

The Fritz Kreisler score, though dated, was listenable and often distinctively melodious, and the sets and costumes were eye-filling. (Some of Kreisler's music was an adaptation of his older tunes, among them "Caprice Viennois" and "The Old Refrain.") Nevertheless, Louis Kronenberger (*PM*) admitted, "It has lavishness without style, and fanfare that ushers in folderol. Its choreography too often misuses talent to produce stage-show fancy business."

The cast, while replete with expert singers and dancers, was embarrassingly inept when it came to acting. The dance experts included ballet principals George Zoritch, Alexandra Denisova, Patricia Bowman, Nicolas Berizoff, and acrobatic whizz Jerry Ross. Lost in this "ponderous, pretentious, preposterous mess" (Wilella Waldorf [*NYP*]), reputed to have cost $365,000, were Bertha Belmore, John Hamill, John Cherry, and Gloria Story.

RICH FULL LIFE, THE [Comedy/Family/Illness/Marriage/Romance/Small Town/Youth] A: Vina Delmar; D/P: Gilbert Miller; S: Raymond Sovey; T: John Golden Theatre; 11/9/45 (27)

A sentimental and shallow comedy concerned with the dangers of smothering family love. It would have been "completely negligible were it not for the performance of Judith Evelyn," reported Rosamond Gilder (*TAM*).

It tells of Cynthia Fenwick (Virginia Weidler), a teenager who suffers from pernicious anemia. Cynthia's physician uncle (Frank M. Thomas) has instructed her mother, Lou (Evelyn), and father, Lawrence (Frederic Tozere), to keep the girl out of drafts and to otherwise beware of infection. Cynthia, prone to catching cold, has been raised with an unhealthy degree of overprotectiveness, but circumstances conspire to get her a date to the senior prom with her school's most popular fellow, Ricky Latham (Jonathan Braman), captain of the swimming team. Cynthia is ecstatic about the forthcoming event, but her father, uncle, and others insist that the risk to her health is too great, especially as the weather is inclement on the night of the prom. The brave Lou, however, is equally insistent on Cynthia's being given the night out so that she will always have this night to remember. Cynthia goes and catches pneumonia. Things look bad for her, but--at the instigation of Lou--a visit from Ricky, whose jokes cheer her up, helps to cure her.

The work was filled with dramaturgical clichés and loose ends. Various critics were disappointed that Evelyn did not have a vehicle worthy of her considerable talents. Lewis Nichols (*NYT*) considered the piece worthy of a matinee audience. "Two-thirds of [the play] give the air of treading water while waiting for a climax, and when the last act comes it is so heavy with sweet scent as to be incredible."

The talented cast included Ann Shoemaker, Jessie Busley, and Edith Meiser. Elizabeth Taylor played the title role when the play became a movie called *Cynthia* (1947), although it had been planned that she would make her Broadway debut in the play.

RICH UNCLE, THE [Musical/Yiddish Language] B: Louis Freiman and Isidor Friedman; M: Sholem Secunda; LY: Isidor Lillian; D: Abe Gross; CH: Lillian Shapero; P: Menasha Skulnik; S: Michael Saltzman; T: Second Avenue Theatre (OB); 2/13/43

A few sparse lines in English flavored this typical Second Avenue offering that kept its Yiddish-speaking audience in stitches. Burton Rascoe (*NYWT*) called it "a most extraordinary combination of opera, operetta, burlesque, farce comedy and serious drama, with a very complicated plot." The piece had to do with adultery and marital sacrifices, but neither of the two available reviews describe it any further.

Its stars were Menasha Skulnik, Miriam Kressyn, and Michal Michalesko, with

Jacob Susanoff in important support. Paula Lubelska, Yetta Zwerling, and Goldie Eisman were others in the large company.

RICHARD III (see *King Richard III*)

"RIDERS TO THE SEA" and **"FREIGHT"** [One-Acts/Blacks] D: John O'Shaughnessy; S: (suggested by) Ralph Alswang; L: George Lewis; P: American Negro Theatre; T: Harlem Children's Center (OB); 2/3/49
"Riders to the Sea" [Dramatic Revival*] A: John Millington Synge; C: Roger Furman; "Freight" [Drama/Blacks/Crime/Race] A: Kenneth White

A double bill of one-acts done by a black acting company in Harlem. Synge's piece proved beyond the grasp of the actors. These were Audrey Beatrice as Cathleen, Bessie Powers as Nora, Osceola Archer as Maurya, and Henry B. Scott as Bartley.

More effective was the new play, which was notable for "beautiful, hard-hitting" dialogue that made it "alive and kicking," in Robert Garland's (*NYJA*) view. It concerns a group of nine frightened black men fleeing in a boxcar from a lynching. Another fugitive, a white man (Glen Gordon), whose crime is unrelated to the lynching, joins them. Armed with a knife, he begins to act abusively, even tossing the wooden leg of a one-legged man (Maurice Thompson) out of the car. Ultimately, the blacks get the weapon away from him. By the play's end, after he has been rejected as being too low even to bother killing, he has been reduced to a cowardly mess, trying to get someone to listen to his claim that his whiteness can not be altered.

Brooks Atkinson (*NYT*) considered this "a harsh and smoldering play," although never as powerful as it might have been. "At best it is only a seething, writhing tangle of tough talk and tough behavior." It lacked a focal character to put the author's views into perspective. One of the actors in the boxcar was future star Sidney Poitier. Others included Maxwell Glanville, William Greaves, and Dots Johnson.

On 4/26/50 "Freight" was produced on Broadway, sharing a double bill with Christopher Fry's poetic drama, *A Phoenix Too Frequent*.

RIGHT NEXT TO BROADWAY [Comedy/Business/Jews/Labor/Romance/Sex] A/P: Paul K. Paley; D: William B. Friedlander; S: Karle Amend; T: Bijou Theatre; 2/21/44 (15)

This first play (originally called *Special Model*) by a certified public accountant was greeted by such a barrage of catcalls that the author returned to his regular profession for good. "Silly, with an almost morbid sense for awkwardness and cliché, it is alike badly acted and directed," protested Lewis Nichols (*NYT*). Louis Kronenberger (*PM*) said that it "managed to be almost a worse production than it was a play."

The garment district on Seventh Avenue was the locale for the action about a temperamental young designer named Lee Winston (Jeannette C. Chinley), who assumes control of her father's (Leon Schachter) dressmaking establishment when he goes bankrupt. Engaged to salesman Ben (Tom Daly), she allows herself to be attracted to a worthless gigolo (John Baragrey), who departs when the shop's finances decline. A new dress is a big seller and the shop looks like it will get back on its feet, but there is no money to pay the bills. The banks refuse to extend credit for the necessary material and the government imposes stringent regulations on the use of cloth. Lee's father elopes with one of the models. The workers want a raise for their piece work, and two radical union representatives refuse to make things easier for the management. A strike of the laborers is called. Finally, the recalcitrant shop foreman (James Russo) has a change of heart and helps Lee out of her difficulties. The fiancé, who had walked out, returns, and the union men agree to a compromise. Even the government agrees to help.

Frances Tannehill played a model with loose morals, Roger Sullivan was a comical office boy, Cleo Mayfield was a buyer with nymphomaniacal tendencies, and Jonathan Harris and Charles Cohan were union men. Joseph Leon and Norman

Rose were also involved.

RING AROUND ELIZABETH [Comedy/Family/Legacy/Marriage/Mental Illness/Romance] A: Charl Armstrong; D: William Schorr; S: Raymond Sovey; P: Allen Boretz and William Schorr i/a/w Alfred Bloomingdale; T: Playhouse; 11/17/41 (10)

Even the impetuous acting of Jane Cowl could not salvage this comedy, of which John Beaufort (*CSM*) noted, "One receives the impression that Mr. Armstrong has set down things with a stub pencil, hence the characters are heavy, and the feeling--whether comic or serious--inclines to bluntness." Brooks Atkinson (*NYT*) described Cowl by saying, "She acts like a steam-engine all evening, throwing gestures around freely, jumping up and down with great energy, thinking and pondering with nervous concentration when she is on the stage alone and registering every point as vehemently as though she were going to vote a straight ticket."

Cowl was cast as Elizabeth Cherry, the patient but much put-upon matriarchal foundation of a family that takes advantage of her good nature. She has two temperamental daughters, Mercedes (Marilyn Erskine) and Jennifer (Katharine Bard). The latter is courted by a caddish older fellow, Andy Blayne (Barry Sullivan), who doesn't seem all that sweet on her. Her mother (Katherine Emmett) is a selfish nag, her spouse (McKay Morris) is a petulant complainer, her eccentric father-in-law (Herbert Yost) insists on banging a small gong because he is a volunteer fireman, and the cook (Ruth Chorpenning) is constantly threatening to quit. When the family begins to quibble about how they might share in a $1,500 inheritance that comes to Elizabeth, she chooses to escape the pressure by pretending to have amnesia, only her memories of her youth being vivid. Her family, realizing how much for granted they have taken her, begin to treat her as a queen while she lets them know, under the ruse of her memory loss, some hard facts about themselves. Elizabeth claims that she is buying a boat to go with Andy to the West Indies, where he has business interests. The family appears to be chastened, and Elizabeth decides to remain at home.

RIP VAN WINKLE [Dramatic Revival] A: Dion Boucicault; AD/D: Herbert Berghof; M: André Singer; DS: Carl Kent (masks: Remo Bufano); P: New York City Center Company; T: City Center of Music and Drama; 7/15/47 (15)

A two-week summer showing of Herbert Berghof's adaptation of Boucicault's once enormously popular stage version of Washington Irving's nineteenth-century *Sketch Book* story, played for many years as the meal ticket of Joseph Jefferson III. Jefferson's son Thomas had been in the most recent revival of the play, in 1905.

Rip, who fell asleep for twenty years somewhere in the Catskill Mountains and awoke to find surprising changes among his family and friends, was played by Philip Bourneuf. Others in the company were Grace Coppin as Rip's wife Gretchen, Jimsey Somers as Minnie, Martin Wolfson as Nick Vedder, Byron McGrath as Derrick Van Beekman, Jack Manning as Cockles, Jack Bittner as Jacob Stein, Haila Stoddard as Katie, Frances Reid as the older Minnie, and Arthur Franz as the older Peter.

Unfortunately, the piece did not stand the test of time and seemed "languid, arch and maudlin--compounded of the absurd hokum of *The Black Crook* and the stage melodramas that are tolerable only in burlesque now," according to Brooks Atkinson (*NYT*). Atkinson appreciated the excellences of the acting, decor, and staging, but George Jean Nathan (*TBY*), who, as a child, frequently had seen Jefferson's performance, was offended by the "miserable staging and direction." The offering was supposed to be the first in a season of summer stock, to be followed by Shaw's *Arms and the Man**, but the company came to a dead end with this production.

RIVALS, THE [Dramatic Revival*] A: Richard Brinsley Sheridan; M/LY; Arthur Guiterman and Macklin Morrow; D: Eva Le Gallienne; S/C: Watson Barratt; P: Theatre Guild; T: Shubert Theatre; 1/14/42 (54)

From 1922 to 1930 there had been three revivals of this late eighteenth-century comedy classic, but this was the first to come along since then. Its claim to fame was the performance of vaudeville clown Bobby Clark (sans his painted-on eyeglasses and cigar) as the country lout, Bob Acres, in a performance that has become legend. Clark had earlier done similar honors to a role in Congreve's *Love for Love**. Other principal players involved were Haila Stoddard as Lydia Languish, Helen Ford as Lucy, Mary Boland as Mrs. Malaprop, Frances Reid as Julia, Walter Hampden as Sir Anthony Absolute, Robert Wallsten as Faulkland, Donald Burr as Captain Absolute, and Philip Bourneuf as Sir Lucius O'Trigger.

Despite the excellent lineup of actors, a new prologue (by Arthur Guiterman) in which the work was described as the "*Follies* of another age," several new songs, and lots of inventive comic business, the production never really hit the mark for several critics. These felt the play was not written to support the kind of broad and farcical humor the production seemed to stress. Rosamond Gilder (*TAM*) said that Le Gallienne "has directed for speed and high spirits rather than for style and high comedy, and in so doing has rubbed off some of the polish of Mr. Sheridan's prose." Much more antipathetic, though, was Louis Kronenberger (*PM*), who argued that "the production, with its crude underlinings, seemed more like a burlesqued revival of some absurdity of 1875 than a recreated comedy of 1775." On the other hand, when it sought to ape the manners of the eighteenth century, said the critic, the production turned coy instead of stylish. Only Clark's hilarious and sometimes scene-stealing behavior saved the evening for Kronenberger. Wilella Waldorf (*NYP*) believed that there were still scenes where one's interest lagged, but that, on the whole, "this is a very merry, sometimes sidesplitting production."

A few critics were disappointed with Boland's Malaprop, but others thought that she was just right. John Anderson (*NYJA*), for example, thought she "seems to miss the part almost completely," while John Beaufort (*CSM*) said, "She does Mrs. M. with ease, propriety, clipped precision, and not more inflective glissando than is just."

Director Le Gallienne was herself displeased with the actress. In *With a Quiet Heart* she told of when the play was trying out in Toronto and a very funny song was inserted that had comically insulting comments on Mrs. Malaprop's appearance. The actress was so offended that she refused to perform until the song was removed. Le Gallienne argued that the actress's ego took precedence over her artistry. Boland even insisted on costuming and makeup that made her look like a beautiful Dresden shepherdess instead of the "weatherbeaten old she-dragon" described by the playwright. Le Gallienne bravely faced the imposing actress about the offending song, determined not to buckle. Boland thereafter may have disliked her director, but the song remained. Later, when the show had moved to St. Louis, Boland fell ill and had to go to the hospital with a temperature of 106.50½. Le Gallienne herself valiantly stepped into the breach at that night's sold-out performance, although, apart from knowing the words, she was artistically unprepared to play the part. In the hour and a half she had to get ready, she did whatever she could to ruin her attractiveness and meet Sheridan's requirements, while simultaneously practicing her lines. Her performance was greeted with so much laughter that the audience did not hear the prompts she kept receiving from the wings. Le Gallienne continued in the role for two more weeks until Boland was well enough to return.

As for Clark, Richard Lockridge's (*NYS*) comments must suffice: "Mr. Clark comes on cracking a long whip, making faces, starting back in his own brand of terror at the explosive utterances of the highly sensitive Capt. Absolute and the highly sensitive Mr. Faulkland. He does little dances to prove this and that, and makes engaging sounds of which Mr. Sheridan never thought. He throws quill pens like darts, and suspends himself between chair and table to write his famous challenge. . . . He quakes with terror; he growls like a cat; he has his hair done up in curl papers. . . . He is as broad as he is funny, and nobody has told him 'No!'" As part of his performance Clark sang "Buxom Joan," the comic song he had performed in *Love for Love*, and it was as sidesplittingly funny now as it had been in that production.

ROBIN HOOD [Musical Revival*] B/LY: Harry B. Smith; M: Reginald De Koven; D: R. H. Burnside; S: United Studios; C: Veronica; P: R. H. Burnside and J. J.

Shubert; T: Adelphi Theatre; 11/7/44 (15)

A once extremely popular 1891 comic opera (last seen locally in 1932) given a third-rate production that George Freedley (*NYMT*) said was "one of the poorest revivals that we have seen on the American stage in a long time." In the title role was Robert Field; the Sheriff of Nottingham was played by George Lipton, Little John by Harold Patrick, Will Scarlett by Wilfred Glenn, Friar Tuck by Jerry Robinson, Allan-a-Dale by Edith Herlick, Lady Marian by Barbara Scully, Sir Guy by Frank Farrell, and Annabel by Margaret Spencer.

The music was still sound and the singing was adequate, but the stilted acting, shabby sets, lackluster costumes, embarrassing comedy, and corny staging were ready for the bonfire. It was, wailed Howard Barnes (*NYHT*), "a rather sorry exhumation of a solid show."

ROMANTIC MR. DICKENS [Comedy/Literary-Biographical/Period/Romance] A: H. H. and Marguerite Harper; D: Arthur Sircom; S: Watson Barratt; C: Ernest Schrapps; P: John Tuerk; T: Playhouse; 12/2/40 (8)

A trite biographical drama about the romantic dalliances of Charles Dickens (Robert Keith), based on the famous writer's love letters to Dora Spenlow (the source for Dora in *David Copperfield*) and other authentic historical sources. Few critics were interested in the results. "Mr. and Mrs. Harper are pedestrian writers with considerable fondness for clichés," commented Brooks Atkinson (*NYT*). "And the impression their drama creates is of a stuffy stock broker on an amorous fling out of office hours." The chief interest the play holds for theatre history is that it marked the Broadway debut of nineteen-year-old Diana Barrymore, daughter of John Barrymore and Michael Strange (Blanche Oelrich). She was the best thing in the play, showing surprising ability and excellent vocal qualities. Kelcey Allen (*WWD*) said that she "contributes a real impersonation, rich in vitality, variety and charm."

Spanning many years, the play covers the novelist's life from the age of twenty-eight to middle age and represents his various love affairs, beginning with Marianne Leigh (Mary Heberden), whom he left for his one true love, Dora Spenlow (Gertrude Flynn). Because of her father's (Marshall Bradford) opposition to her wedding someone with no money, he marries another lady (Zolya Talma), a shrew with whom he is miserable until the now-married Dora, recognizing herself in *David Copperfield*, writes to him and, after a period of correspondence, comes to visit. However, his interest wanes upon discovering that she has not only added poundage, but also is a frivolous airhead. He finds temporary happiness with the actress Caroline Bronson (Barrymore), who acted in one of his plays, but when scandal threatens and both his wife and mistress leave him, he returns to his study to focus on his books.

Cast members included Thais Lawton and Elwynne Harvey. Later in the decade, *The Ivy Green* was also biographically concerned with Dickens.

ROSALINDA (*Die Fledermaus*) [Musical Revival*] B: Karl Haffner and Richard Genee; AD: Gottfried Reinhardt and John Meehan, Jr., from Max Reinhardt's German version; M: Johann Strauss, Jr.; LY: Paul Kerby; D: Felix Brentano ("entire production under the supervision of Max Reinhardt"); CH: George Balanchine; S: Oliver Smith; C: Ladislas Czettel; L: Jean Rosenthal; P: Lodewick Vroom for the New Opera Company; T: Forty-fourth Street Theatre; 10/28/42 (521)

Johann Strauss's 1874 operetta was prone to being adapted under new titles with revised librettos, having most recently been seen locally as *Champagne, Sec* (1933). By 1942 it had also been called *The Bat*, *One Wonderful Night**, *The Merry Countess*, and *Night Birds* and was now being titled *Rosalinda* under the direction of famed regisseur Max Reinhardt, who had staged this version in Berlin in 1929. With its run of over 500 performances, it was the only commercial success the director managed during his decade or so in America.

According to Reinhardt's son Gottfried in the latter's *The Genius*, when the production--sponsored by a new company created to foster American singing talent--was initially announced, the director was listed as Felix Brentano (formerly

Felix Weissberger), who once had been an employee of Reinhardt in Europe; he owed his escape from the Nazis to Reinhardt's influence. Brentano not only remembered every detail of Reinhardt's productions, but also had promptbooks of all those he had worked on, including *Die Fledermaus*. The show's musical director, Erich Wolfgang Korngold, who equally owed his safety from the Nazis to Reinhardt, had directed the music for Reinhardt's European production, and their version was copyrighted. Upon discovering that the new production was using the Korngold-Reinhardt orchestration and staging, he threatened to walk out on it unless the New Opera Company bought the rights, hired Reinhardt, and demoted the plagiarizing Brentano. This threat worked, and Reinhardt was employed at a generous fee with a percentage of the gross. Reinhardt, whose Broadway career had not flourished, was cautioned against risking another flop with this old museum piece. To protect his reputation, Reinhardt was given the credit, "entire production under the supervision of," and Brentano remained director in name only. However, he was stung by these developments and did what he could to sabotage his mentor.

Reinhardt's son Gottfried agreed to collaborate on the writing of a new version, which--to the producer's astonishment--he promised (and delivered) within a week. Oscar Karlweis, an Austrian émigré actor, who had played his role of Prince Orlofsky in Europe, and whose English was very limited at the time, had learned his lines by rote for the version being rehearsed and was terrified of learning new ones. Very early one morning, around 5:30 A.M., while Reinhardt and his collaborator--both of whom were then in the army and had to be back at their post by six--were struggling to add finishing touches to their libretto, Karlweis burst in upon them in extreme agitation, claiming, "Hitler I have to thank for this!" He downed a proffered glass of scotch, repeated the comment, then downed another glass. Gottfried said, "Stay as long as you like, Oscar. But we've got to go now. We too've got Hitler to thank for something!" The actor hiccuped, "Hitler . . . ." "You're goddamn right!" burst out the Irish-American Meehan, who then walked out, slamming the door as he said, "You got Hitler to thank for this and I got you to thank for Hitler!" Karlweis, however, later had much to thank Hitler for, as this production made him a Broadway star. When the show first began its run, he had kept the old lines, but when he received little audience response in contrast to the rest of the cast, he changed to the new ones during the run.

The story and dialogue were Americanized and updated a few years to 1890 Vienna, and conductor Erich Korngold (who had also conducted Reinhardt's Berlin production) added to the score several numbers from other Strauss works, including "Wiener Wald" and "Wein, Weib, und Gesang." Despite its revisions, some critics despised the old-fashioned libretto.

With Dorothy Sarnoff as Rosalinda Von Eisenstein, Ralph Herbert (a last-minute replacement) as Eisenstein, Everett West as Alfredo Allevanto, José Limon as the premier dancer, Mary Ellen as the premiere danseuse, Gene Barry as Falke, Virginia MacWatters (a Philadelphia socialite in her Broadway bow) as Adele, and Shelley Winters (then Winter) as Fifi, the company was strong, but George Jean Nathan (*TBY*) disliked the performances. He said, "When the libretto . . . is treated to acting that seems persistently to be beset by the conviction that high Alt Wien spirits are best to be interpreted by comportment indistinguishable from a number of chamois frisking with an equal number of kangaroos, that deficiency [in the libretto] becomes doubly apparent." Yet others found the performances vibrant with life and talent. Olin Downes (*NYT*) insisted that "there are several fine, fresh voices in the cast, and there was some first-class singing." He pointed to Winters as, "vocally speaking, the most distinguished stylist of the evening. Her air in the second act was one of the occasions when applause momentarily held up the show."

Karlweis's portrayal of Orlofsky was outside tradition, as the role was normally played by a contralto in tights. This Austrian emigrant proved a brilliant comic actor in the role, which did not require too much singing of him.

Few disputed the outstanding score, which was outstandingly played under Korngold's supervision. Nor was there much dispute about the excellent quality of the dance numbers, especially the second act ball, staged by George Balanchine. "The ballet prepared by Balanchine with the girls in their pink tulle ballgowns is so varied and swift in pattern that it has an excitement which pink tulle doesn't suggest," reported Euphemia Van Rensselaer Wyatt (*CW*).

John Bagar's (*NYWT*) opinion sums up the event: "Given in a thoroughly workmanlke vernacular adaptation, one that didn't mind parading an occasional cliche or, perhaps, a corny line, the work teemed with color and action and spirited life. It was most intelligently staged, handsomely costumed and it boasted likeable as well as serviceable sets."

In *Shelley*, Shelley Winters told several stories about the production. In one she wrote about the night that her character awaited the entrance of Adele and Orlofsky, but neither appeared. Two thousand spectators watched her agony. "I said my four lines--NO PRINCE. I repeated the lines, paraphrasing them slightly in order to sound different. STILL NO PRINCE." Neither the chorus nor the ballet dancers, with whom she tried to strike up a period conversation, would help. She looked off for aid from the stage manager, but "NO STAGE MANAGER!" It turned out that actress MacWatters had not heard her signal in her dressing room and was writing a letter. Karlweis refused to enter alone, so the stage manager had to dash up to the third-floor dressing room to get the actress into costume. Winters, meanwhile, improvised casually about old Vienna, including its traffic, while the audience roared at her witty comments. She was on the verge of saying, "Audience, go home! I can't think of anything else to say," when the missing actors showed up. Karlweis said his usual line, "I'm sorry we're late, Fifi, but the Emperor had one of his parades, and it delayed us." Winters looked at the audience and cracked, "See, I knew it was the traffic."

ROSE IN THE WILDERNESS [Drama/Crime/Period/Religion/Romance/Sex] A: Marguerite F. Melcher; M: G. Wood; D: Gloria Monty; CH: Doris Humphrey; C: Kay Dawn; P: Robert O'Byrne and Gloria Monty for the Abbe Practical Workshop; T: Master Institute Theatre (OB); 1/4/49 (2)

This play was presented by a company of professional and student actors. It was set in a Shaker community in 1863 and illustrated many of the Shaker customs, including their religious songs and dances. The ultimate aim was to demonstrate certain inherent flaws in the sect that led to its downfall. The Shakers believed in celibacy, community property, and open confession. Despite their high ideals and belief that pure love of one's fellows is the only road to happiness, the play argued that human weakness made living up to their standards of denial nearly impossible. When love appeared, sect members found themselves abandoning the sect or suffering a trial of the will to overcome their feelings.

Elder Pletus (John Martin) leads the community. Then a girl he has employed as a medium runs off and accuses him of seducing her and of having instructed her in the visions she supposedly could see. Having obtained proof of the accusations, Elder Caleb (Frank Dudley) calls a meeting to confront Pletus, who claims that he will be saved by a sign from God. But Caleb is killed by the drunken father of a group of children Caleb has been protecting. Pletus then destroys Caleb's proof, not yet known to the community. At a last-act revival meeting, staged with ecstatic dancing and foot-stomping, Pletus openly confesses his sins, and the blow falls heavily on the believers.

The melodrama received encouraging reviews. Bron. (*V*) declared, "Well acted and staged, . . . it has suspense and mood, an essential integrity, and considerable historical interest." Vernon Rice (*NYP*) agreed, noting that the play "is not without its shortcomings, but it has honesty and integrity in its writing and its production." Good acting was offered by Richard Venture, Dorothy Patten, Lee Austin, and others.

ROSMERSHOLM [Dramatic Revival*] A: Henrik Ibsen; D: Wendell K. Phillips; S: Arthur Aronson; L: Shanon Welles; P: Equity Library Theatre; T: Hudson Park Branch of the New York Public Library (OB); 11/22/46

One of the few 1946-1947 Equity Library Theatre showcases to get some press attention was this version of Ibsen's drama, last seen locally in 1935. Rosmer was played by Phillip Sann, Rebecca West by Barbara Pond, Kroll by Charles Thompson, Brendel by Wendell K. Phillips, Mortensgard by William Major, and Madame Helseth by Mabbs Merrill.

George Freedley (*NYMT*) appreciated the production, which he thought finely acted, designed, and directed. But Brooks Atkinson (*NYT*), who thought the drama dated, (*NYT*) wrote, "This kind of acting is worse than no acting at all, because it is fraudulently genteel and has no relation to life or to art."

ROUND TRIP [Comedy/Family/Marriage/Romance/Sex/Small Town/Theatre/Youth] A: Mary Orr and Reginald Denham; D: Reginald Denham; S: Samuel Leve; C: Bianca Stroock; P: Clifford Hayman; T: Biltmore Theatre; 5/29/45 (7)

A naughty comedy on the ever-popular subject of marital infidelity, a subject then cluttering up Broadway's pristine stages. Ironville, Ohio, the locale of *Wallflower*, a previous effort by the current team, was again their background for this predictable tale of a vain small-town woman named Sarah Albright (June Walker), an actress in the Ironville Women's Club play being directed by a New York actor named Clive Delafield (Eddie Nugent). He thinks that she can help him raise the money for a new play he wants to do, so he pays her undue attention. To her delight, she is convinced that he has other things in mind. She follows the actor to New York, where she discovers him living in sin with a sexy blond stenographer named Linda Marble (Phyllis Brooks). Sarah had hoped to convince the actor to allow her to move in with him and to star with him on Broadway. Sarah's angry spouse Edgar (Sidney Blackmer) follows her to the actor's lair to bring her home. He takes a fancy to the blond, however, and returns with her to set her up as his secretary, leaving his wife with the actor. Before divorce proceedings can progress, however, the Albrights' promiscuous teenage daughter Virginia (Patricia Kirkland) manages to use the threat of scandal to get her mom and pop back together again.

In the eyes of the critics, this was a noxious piece of filth that completely wasted some fine talents. Burton Rascoe (*NYWT*) abominated it as "a crudely contrived gas bomb." "Unctuously suggestive and halting in execution, the show is not even good enough for leering laughter," spewed Howard Barnes (*NYHT*).

Actors considered besmirched by involvement in the saga included Paul Marlin, Edith Meiser, Angela Jaye, Viola Dean, and Morton L. Stevens.

RUDDIGORE [Musical Revival*] B/LY: W. S. Gilbert; M: Arthur Sullivan; D: R. H. Burnside; P: R. H. Burnside i/a/w the Gilbert and Sullivan Opera Company; T: Ambassador Theatre; 3/2/44 (3)

Ruddigore's only revival in the forties was this unimpressive outing by the former Boston Comic Opera Company. Florenz Ames was Sir Rupert Murgatroyd, Allen Stewart alternated with Roland Partridge as Richard Dauntless, Robert Pitkin was Sir Despart Murgatroyd, Robert Eckles was Old Adam, Kathleen Roche was Rose Maybud, Marjorie Hayward was Mad Margaret, Catherine Judah was Dame Hannah, Kathryn Reece was Zorah, and Mary Lundon was Ruth.

The production was "listless and lacking in spontaneity," wrote L. C. (*NYT*). The players mumbled, the acting was lifeless, the sets were hopeless, and the comedy was dead.

RUGGED PATH, THE [Drama/Business/Journalism/Marriage/Military/Politics/Sea/Tropics/War] A: Robert E. Sherwood; D: Garson Kanin; S/L: Jo Mielziner; C: (gowns) Valentina; P: Playwrights' Company; T: Plymouth Theatre; 11/10/45 (81)

Sherwood's propagandistic war play (his first play in five years), selected as one of the season's ten best, lured Spencer Tracy back to Broadway from Hollywood, where he had been for fifteen years. Some say that he was talked into making the return by Katharine Hepburn. Others insist that it stemmed from his guilty conscience over not having served in the war and having failed to fulfill promises to perform overseas for the USO. Even with his pull, the play managed only 81 showings. Tracy was never really happy with his part, the play, or his contract and even missed several performances in Boston (attributed to illness, drunkenness, or personal disgruntlement, according to different sources). After the play opened in New York, he would sometimes bad-mouth it to the press, which led to extremely strained relations with Sherwood, who believed that Tracy's attitude seriously hampered the play's success. His unhappiness with the experience kept him off the stage for the rest of his career.

The play itself had been conceived as two plays, one dealing with the response of important journalists toward the American government's positions in times of crisis, the other with a particular intelligent soldier's reaction to the war and his role in it. The former would be set in the United States, the other in an occupied country. But a trip by Sherwood to the Pacific on behalf of the Roosevelt administration convinced him to join the two plays into a single work set largely in the Philippines, with the hero a former journalist who joins the armed forces. Lewis Nichols (*NYT*) argued that the fusion was unsuccessful and that the two halves of the play remained distinct, the first half being concerned with political ideas, the second with wartime adventure.

Tracy played Morey Vinion, a disillusioned, idealistic, liberal newspaper editor in 1940. He has observed the fighting as a correspondent and is frustrated in his attempts to convince reactionary isolationists--including his paper's owner (Clinton Sundberg)--of this country's inevitable involvement. Hitler's invasion of Russia incites him to publish an editorial by a young writer (Rex Williams) supporting the Russians and advocating lend-lease to the Communists. This leads to a brouhaha with the paper's business manager (Lawrence Fletcher), who is afraid of upsetting the advertisers. Morey thereupon quits the paper and joins the navy as a cook, leaving behind the wife (Martha Sleeper) from whom he has become increasingly alienated because of her unwillingness to recognize the drift of world affairs. Aboard his destroyer in the Pacific he confronts--in the rugged individuals around him--the spirit of the America he has been seeking. His ship is sunk (in a fairly spectacular scene of lighting and sound effects that could not match what the movies could do), and Morey is the sole survivor. He soon encounters and joins up with a band of Filipino guerrillas combatting the Japanese. Here he regains his faith in the goal for which the free world is fighting, but here, too, he meets his end from an enemy bullet. His courage is celebrated posthumously by the White House's conferring on him the Medal of Honor.

The Rugged Path received mildly respectable reviews, but more because of the work's intentions than its achievement. The twelve-scene play vitiated its elements of action and drama by following them with verbose speeches thick with high-flown rhetoric. The various scene changes also slowed things down considerably. Although John Chapman (*NYDN*) thought the play "soundly written and holding" and its talk consistently interesting, Howard Barnes (*NYHT*) was representative of the wider view. He praised it for its eloquence and thoughtfulness, but had to admit that it was "a series of animated editorials rather than a challenging and absorbing play." In his opinion, it was "self-conscious, wordy and disappointing." Sherwood's play, thought George Jean Nathan (*TBY*), was "a carpentered job which belatedly plows up ground already deeply furrowed, and is without critical merit save possibly for those whom he himself in one of his play's passages ridicules for esteem of mere sincerity." And John Mason Brown (*SR*) considered the work little more than "a first draft."

The critics pondered Tracy's performance, regretting the time he had spent in making films when his talent might have served the stage. "He has power, breadth, sincerity, simplicity--all invaluable assets," wrote Rosamond Gilder (*TAM*). "He can be eloquent with words as well as with silences." In the large cast were Clay Clement, Kay Loring, Ralph Cullinan, Jan Sterling, Gordon Nelson, Vito Christi, Edward Raquello, and many others.

One of the demands that Tracy made before doing the play was that Garson Kanin direct it. Kanin was then in the army, but Playwrights' Company member Robert E. Sherwood was in a position of political strength as a confidant of President Roosevelt's. Company lawyer John F. Wharton noted in *Life among the Playwrights* that he commented to Sherwood, "To get things done surely and quickly in the army you needed a regular army general's help. Bob smiled and said, 'You're right. I've heard that, too. We have General Marshall working on it.' I suspect [said Wharton] Kanin is the only army captain who, during a war, ever had the President of the United States and his Chief of Staff cooperating to make sure of a short leave of absence for him."

RUN, LITTLE CHILLUN! [Dramatic Revival*] A: Hall Johnson; D: Clarence Muse; CH: Felicia Sorel; S/C: Perry Watkins; P: Lew Cooper i/a/w Meyer Davis and George Jessel; T: Hudson Theatre; 8/11/43 (16)

Author Hall Johnson, famed for his activity as a conductor of black spiritual singing groups, directed the chorus in this revival of his 1933 play set in the deep South and dealing with religious conflict among Baptists and worshippers of a ritualistic pagan cult. His rousing and moving choruses and Felicia Sorel's orgiastic choreography, often bordering on the erotically sensational, were the strengths of the production, the play itself holding scant interest for many in the 1943 audience.

Ward Morehouse (*NYS*) wrote, "Considered as play, [it] is hardly a play at all. It is scanty drama, clumsy of dialogue and situation." Although the great majority of the critics held similar views, Burton Rascoe (*NYWT*) went so far as to claim that the play was "one of the most beautiful, most thrilling, most touching things I ever saw or heard in my life."

The direction and the action were on the feeble side (although not without defenders). Louis Sharp was the Reverend Jones, Caleb Peterson was his son Jim, P. J. Sidney was the young pagan priest, Edna Mae Harris was Sulamai, and Helen Dowdy was Jim's wife, Ella. "Not only has the whole piece been made too sophisticated by the overdressing and overacting of the company," lamented George Freedley (*NYMT*), "but the simplicity and honesty which was originally a part of the script has been completely submerged."

Director Muse, a black film actor, had directed a more successful West Coast version of the play for the Federal Theatre Project several years earlier. Spirituals heard in the play included "Amazing Grace," "Steal Away," "Oh, Jesus, Come This Way," "Nobody Knows the Trouble I See," and others.

RUSSIAN PEOPLE, THE [Drama/Marriage/Politics/Romance/Russian/War] A: Konstantin Simonov; AD: Clifford Odets; D: Harold Clurman; S: Boris Aronson; P: Theatre Guild; T: Guild Theatre; 12/29/42 (39)

An emotional Russian propaganda play in nine scenes that was produced in Russia during the siege of Stalingrad and eventually performed by over two hundred troupes attached to the Red Army. Its story of how the Russian people bravely sacrifice themselves in the knowledge that they would eventually triumph over the Nazis was potent stuff for native audiences, if not for most New Yorkers. A program note by Russian critic K. Borisov pointed out:

> The hearts of the spectators beat faster, and no one is ashamed of his tears. . . . We are not only touched, but intent; we are not only shaken, but filled with hatred of the enemy. . . . "The motherland demands it"--this is the root of all the emotions, deeds, and actions of these people. "The motherland demands it"--this is the law to which their lives, thoughts and feelings are subordinated.

Some American critics, while pointing to occasional flaws, felt deeply moved. Rosamond Gilder (*TAM*) described the play as "a sound piece of wartime journalism, reeking with blood and terror and the clash of arms but lit with heroism and touched with the gaiety and tenderness that men can summon, even in the face of death."

It is 1941 in a town situated in an occupied portion of Russia. The town's doctor (E. A. Krumschmidt), frightened of being killed, has turned quisling and become mayor under the thumb of the Nazis. They, under the leadership of the psychopathic Rosenberg (Rudolph Anders), make his home their headquarters. Hidden in their houses, the townspeople keep in contact with the underground across the river and plan to fight back. Across the river is a bombed-out railroad station occupied by a cutoff army unit led by the idealistic Captain Safonov (Leon Ames) and by a variety of local citizen guerrillas. They wait valiantly for relief to arrive, although death may come first. Most of the action alternates between the Nazi and army headquarters, the latter displaying a cross-section of Russian types, young and old, male and female. One of them is Panin (Herbert Berghof), a war correspondent. Another is Kozlovsky (Eduard Franz), who turns out to be a traitor. Yet another is Kozlovsky's uncle (Victor Varconi), an elderly tsarist officer who fought in the Russo-Japanese War and takes up arms again in this one. When his nephew's spying is revealed, he shoots him. A romantic attachment develops between Safonov and Valya (Elisabeth Fraser), a woman reconnaissance scout who during the play swims the icy river three times, is captured, and is saved. Valya dies during the action, as does Globa (Luther Adler), a brave, life-loving surgeon who spies for his fellows and becomes a sacrificial victim. Safonov's mother (Margaret Waller), who lets her house be used by Russian agents, is caught and hanged. The mayor's Nazi-hating wife (Eleanora Mendelssohn) brings herself and her traitor husband down when she manages to poison Rosenberg, who has tortured them. More people die when the Russian forces finally arrive and drive the Germans back.

Major weaknesses included too much detail clogging the flow of the melodramatic action, a sprawling and disunified structure, an excessive use of English-language colloquialisms in the adaptation, talky scenes of exposition, too many cardboard characters mixed in with the three-dimensional ones, and several leading players (especially Ames and Fraser) who simply were too American. Lewis Nichols (*NYT*) claimed that "barring a few scenes, the play does not rise to the heights of the spirit of the people it represents, and almost all of its earlier passages are confused and sluggish." And Burton Rascoe (*NYWT*) considered the play "a libel" on the Russian people, not a tribute to them. "It is almost a burlesque of the old ten-twenty-thirty melodrama. There is nothing real, convincing, believable about it." Cast members included Peter Hobbs, Ernest Graves, Anna Minot, Joseph Shattuck, Harold Dyrenforth, Ad Karns, and Michael Strong.

(1) RUTH DRAPER [Miscellaneous/Solo] P: Sol Hurok; T: Booth Theatre; 12/26/40 (22)

Monologuist Ruth Draper appeared for the holidays in a limited engagement with her nephew, dancer Paul Draper. The unusual program consisted of the actress giving three of her standard sketches and the dancer doing his well-known specialty of tap-dance routines--he did a dozen--set to classical melodies by composers such as Scarlatti, Debussy, Handel, and Bach.

There were three acts, Paul Draper's work constituting act one, Ruth's act two, and the pair sharing act three. Ruth's selections included "At a Children's Party in Philadelphia," "On the Porch in a Maine Coast Village," and "In a Church in Philadelphia."

The idea of varying the evening with performances by two artists instead of one was deemed a good one, although the familiarity of the monologue material--seen frequently in New York--was a drawback. In fact, the unusual dances of Paul Draper actually stole the show. Hobe. (*V*) declared, "This classic-tapping (or whatever it may rightly be called) is not only completely new, it is also enormously skillful and spectacular and exciting."

(2) P: Sol Hurok; T: New York Times Hall; 12/25/42 (10)

Ruth Draper reappeared in New York repeating a program of her well-known sketches. She wore a brown gown and played against a pinkish background. The opening program was "At a Children's Party in Philadelphia," "A Dalmatian Peasant in the Hall of a New York Hospital," "A Class in Greek Poise," "On the Porch in a Maine Coast Village," and "In a Church in Italy." Other pieces, such as "Doctor and Diets," "Three Imaginary Folk Songs," "Three Generations in a Municipal Court," "Love in the Balkans," and "In a Railway Station," were chosen for different nights in the engagement.

"After almost three decades," noted Mark Schubart (*PM*), "Miss Draper's style is still, in the main, fresh and amusing, skillful and tasteful." She played at the Little Theatre, known at the time as New York Times Hall before reverting to its former name.

(3) P: John C. Wilson; T: Empire Theatre; 1/12/47 (42)

Draper's first postwar visit to New York revealed her in various of her familiar sketches. "Miss Draper's rendition of [her material] is so uncannily accurate that she seems to people the stage with other personalities among which her own is merely the most forceful," applauded Otis L. Guernsey, Jr. (*NYHT*).

There were also two new sketches. One was "The Return," concerning the preparations made for the homecoming of an English prisoner of war to his rural cottage. Draper first played the soldier's wife, nervous because the tenants have messed up the house, which she wants to look perfect for her husband's return. Then she was the village postmistress, organizing a cleaning bee among the neighbors. Brooks Atkinson (*NYT*) thought the piece (based on a true incident) too long, but agreed that literary criticism was "beside the point" when it came to the excellences of Draper's histrionic art.

The other was "Vive la France," in which all the dialogue was in French and which revealed a sad but courageous Breton wife waiting in 1940 at the Brittany seaside for the boat that will take her spouse away across the channel to England to fight for the Free French. Kneeling and sifting the sand through her fingers, she consoles her mother-in-law. Then she bids a poignant farewell to her husband. English planes fly overhead, and she cries out to them for victory.

The three older pieces on the opening-night program were "Opening a Bazaar," "Doctors and Diets," and "Three Women and Mrs. Clifford," as usual the most admired of her sketches. A new program was scheduled for the second week of the brief engagement.

The program demonstrated Draper's warmth, love of humankind, extraordinary versatility and polish, touching characterizations, and abundant sense of humor. "It is hard to believe that one woman alone can hold an audience with such intentness for two and a half hours. Miss Draper does it, and enthrallingly," wrote William Hawkins (*NYWT*).

(4) P: John C. Wilson; T: Empire Theatre; 12/28/47 (26)

Draper's fourth visit of the decade began with a program of her favorite pieces, including "Three Breakfasts," "At an Art Exhibition," "In County Kerry--1919," "A Children's Party," and "A Scottish Immigrant at Ellis Island." Her performances were given on Sunday evenings and at Tuesday, Wednesday, and Friday matinees. Several critics thought that the program's unbalanced emphasis on pieces stressing the inane banter of society ladies was not a wise one, and would have preferred more of the meaty dramatic matter suggested by the "In County Kerry" sketch, in which an aged Irishwoman grieves over her son's death. "As always," wrote Hobe. (*V*), "her character portraits cover impressive range and her performance and personality consistently hold interest. . . . She not only reveals the full dimensions of the characters she plays, including the complex pattern of their experience and emotional backgrounds, but also actually creates the illusion of a stage alive with other people." Draper's later programs offered a wide assortment of sketches, but none were new to New York.

RYAN GIRL, THE [Drama/Crime/Family/Marriage/Military/War] A/D: Edmund Goulding; S: Raymond Sovey; P: Messrs. Shubert i/a/w Albert de Courville; T: Plymouth Theatre; 9/24/45 (48)

Famous Hollywood director Edmund Goulding returned to the Great White Way to stage his energetic melodrama, a play jammed with dramatic incident, but basically disunified. The script seemed more like a film scenario than a fully crafted play, thought Lewis Nichols (*NYT*), and the scenario was old-fashioned and filled with stock characters with very little subtlety or living qualities.

Twenty-eight-year-old June Havoc played thirty-nine-year-old Venetia Ryan, a former *Ziegfeld Follies** showgirl who, at sixteen, had an illegitimate son by a gangster named Miley Gaylon (Edmund Lowe), but gave the baby to another showgirl (Doris Dalton) to bring up. The friend's marriage to a wealthy man has provided an advantageous background for the son. The latter (John Compton) has since grown up and been awarded the Congressional Medal of Honor for his valor in combat.

Miley has been spending his time as a fugitive in Venezuela, but sneaks back to New York, hoping that by revealing his relationship to this national hero (who knows nothing of his real parents) he can get a reprieve from capital punishment. Venetia, who has been living with a wealthy banker but still cares deeply for Miley, tries to dissuade him from doing something that will ruin their son's life. When he refuses, she shoots him dead. At the end, radio broadcaster Lowell Thomas is heard interviewing the brave son.

The Ryan Girl was considered straightforward melodrama in the old-fashioned tradition. George Jean Nathan (*TBY*) listed all its stereotypical situations. It had faults, said Burton Rascoe (*NYWT*), but he liked it because "the story is an unusual one; the drama is unfolded with credibility and mounting suspense; and the production is newsworthy as well as admirable." But Ward Morehouse (*NYS*) considered it "a botch" that was "clumsily written and indifferently acted." Opinions such as his carried the day.

Havoc, in her first dramatic part, had a hapless role as the noble sinner, although she had several strong critical supporters. Lowe, returning to Broadway after two decades in films, was stuck with a villainous role bearing no redeeming qualities. Among their supporting cast were Curtis Cooksey and Una O'Connor, the latter as Weavy, a former wardrobe woman who offers shrewd advice to Venetia.

S

S.S. GLENCAIRN [Dramatic Revival*] A: Eugene O'Neill; D: José Ferrer; S/L: Herbert Brodkin; C: Emeline Roche; P: New York City Center Theatre Company; T: City Center of Music and Drama; 5/20/48 (14)
"The Moon of the Caribbees"; "In the Zone"; "Bound East for Cardiff"; "The Long Voyage Home"

O'Neill's four one-acts, grouped under the title of *S.S. Glencairn*, the name of the British tramp steamer on which each of the first three plays takes place, had last been seen locally in an all-black revival given in 1937. There also had been revivals in 1924 and 1929. The present version, offered by a company organized under José Ferrer's direction at the City Center, where it did a series of limited-run revivals, was well liked for its excellent staging, set and lighting design, and acting. Several seamens' roles recur in three or all four of the plays, including Yank (Richard Coogan), Driscoll (George Mathews), Olson (Ralph Roberts), Smitty (Robert Carroll), Cocky (Kenneth Treseder), Ivan (Harold J. Stone), Davis (Ray Walston), and Scotty (Winston Ross), many of them ethnic dialect characters of one sort or another. Among the women who appear (but none in more than a single play) are Pearl (Mildred Joanne Smith), Violet (Rena Mitchell), Bella (Juanita Hall), Mag (Phyllis Hill), Kate (Philippa Bevans), and Freda (Nan McFarland). Ferrer's only role was as Fat Joe, the wicked proprietor of a waterfront dive in the fourth playlet. George Coulouris played Donkey Man in the first piece. Most came in for their share of commendation, although some critics were not amused.

In "The Moon of the Caribbees," native women rumrunners bring themselves and their brew to the ship's crew. "In the Zone," taking place as the ship passes through a submarine zone, concerns the mistaken assumption that Smitty is a German spy, only for it to be discovered that his "bomb" is really a packet of tragedy-laden love letters. "Bound East for Cardiff" is centered around the death of Yank and the recollections of his friendship with Driscoll. "The Long Voyage Home" is set in a low London waterfront saloon, where the young Swede, Olson, who plans to save his earnings and return to his farm, is shanghaied by crimps. The critics differed on which was the best produced of the quartet.

The plays retained the power to grip some reviewers, largely because of the excellence of O'Neill's sharply delineated personages. "These are some of Mr. O'Neill's most memorable characters," reported Brooks Atkinson (*NYT*), "and he has recorded their fumbling careers with comradely affection and the compassion of an artist." Howard Barnes (*NYHT*) said that "the four vignettes of sea-faring life are still filled with eloquence and dramatic excitement." But William Hawkins (*NYWT*) thought that the plays lost their special atmosphere and intimacy on the huge City Center stage and found the overall tone too solemn for so large a theatre. Rowland Field (*NEN*) concluded, "It was at best an extremely dull passage, unevenly acted, poorly directed, and hardly worth the effort."

SADIE IS A LADY [Musical/Yiddish Language] B: Louis Freiman; AD/D: Jacob Kalich; M: Joseph Rumshinsky; LY: Molly Picon; CH: Lillian Shapero; S: Michael Saltzman; P: Irving Jacobson; T: Second Avenue Theatre (OB); 1/29/50

Second Avenue's favorite gamin, Molly Picon, headed what was a virtual stock company in her production of this formula Yiddish musical. Her first entrance was befitting a star of her nature, for, dressed in jeans and sneakers, and wearing a crewcut like Mary Martin's in *South Pacific*, she appeared by zipping down a slide preceded by a great many bundles; at first, she looked like one of them. She subsequently got to dress in a fancy evening gown and as a cancan dancer and even sang "Sadie Is a Lady," a Yiddish version of the swinging "Jenny" song from *Lady in the Dark*. She also stopped the show with a nostalgic number called "My Street," singing of Second Avenue's theatrical past.

The book was a sketchy thing designed as little more than an excuse to display the hoydenish Picon. Even her husband, actor and director Jacob Kalich, appeared on stage to perform with her, although he was not a listed member of the cast. It had little to do with the book, but she offered a favorite sketch of hers, in which she was a temperamental old aunt at a wedding who has a grudge against everyone and leaves in a huff when she imagines that she is insulted.

The "corny, entertaining frolic," reported Bron. (*V*), was "an old-fashioned musical melange, derivative and familiar, for easygoing, palatable entertainment." Jeanette Wilken (*NYDN*) said that it was "fast, broad and melodious." It featured Picon as Sadie, a woman who answers an ad for a $5,000 reward to whoever claims a certain foundling discovered on the doorstep of young Rabbi Green (Muni Serebrov), who is engaged. Sadie, who comes from a money-grubbing Lower East Side family, is persuaded to pass as the mother and names Rabbi Green, whom she loves, as the father. This leads to romantic troubles with the rabbi, but all turns out for the best when the woman who offered the reward--the rabbi's fiancée--is revealed as the real mother. Sadie gets the rabbi and the fiancée gets the baby.

Musical comedy, burlesque, and revue elements figured in the telling of the story. One hilarious number was called "Monkey Business" and featured Julius Adler and Henrietta Jacobson. The fine company included Max Bozhyk, Irving Jacobson, and the Feder sisters (Sylvia and Miriam). As for Picon, Lewis Funke (*NYT*) declared, she "is a first-rate comedienne, fond of her audience and in perfect tune with what it desires and expects. She sings sentimental songs with a tear in her voice, acts the hoyden with endearing charm, bounces over the stage and gives everyone that nice intimate feeling of being played to individually."

SADIE THOMPSON [Musical/Military/Prostitution/Religion/Sex/Tropics] B: Howard Dietz and Rouben Mamoulian; M: Vernon Duke; LY: Howard Dietz; SC: John Colton and Clemence Randolph's play, *Rain**, itself an adaptation of W. Somerset Maugham's short story, "Miss Thompson"; D: Rouben Mamoulian; CH: Edward Caton; S: Boris Aronson; C: Motley and Azadia Newman; P: A. P. Waxman; T: Alvin Theatre; 11/16/44 (60)

A disappointing musical version of the sensational 1922 hit play *Rain** about a hooker's temptation of a fundamentalist preacher on the steamy South Pacific island of Pago Pago. Sadie Thompson, the part that Jeanne Eagels had made famous, was originally supposed to go to Ethel Merman, but--according to which story one accepts--Merman backed out either because the producer was not willing to use her current husband as lyricist or because she did not like Vernon Duke's music. June Havoc, then at the rise of her fine career as an actress, singer, and dancer, starred instead, but she found herself snared in a laborious show that never succeeded in making the story live in musical terms.

Havoc was dynamic (although not gifted with a strong singing voice) and the Rousseauesque jungle sets were spectacular (and included real rain effects), but the music was routine, the lyrics were innocuous, and the comedy was nonexistent, while the musical numbers kept getting in the way of the story and vice versa. The result was a mishmash of no definable genre. "*Rain* with a musical score is a hybrid; the story is too dolorous for a musical, the score not good enough for an operetta," argued Euphemia Van Rensselaer Wyatt (*CW*).

The story remained the same as in the drama. A major character removed from the musical was Dr. McPhail, the understanding medical missionary. Reverend Davidson was played by Metropolitan Opera singer Lansing Hatfield, his wife by Zolya Talma, Joe Horn by Ralph Dumke, Sergeant O'Hara by James Newill, and Horn's wife by Grazia Narciso, while other performers included Walter Burke, Doris Patston, Beatrice Kraft, Milada Mladova, and Chris Volkoff, the latter three being the chief dancers.

Songs that were singled out included "Life's a Funny Present" and "The Love I Long For," both put across by Havoc, who "performed" her numbers more than she sang them. There were three extended dance segments, one a jungle dance, another recounting Sadie's life from Kansas City to the South Seas, and one based on a famous phrase in the play, "The Mountains of Nebraska."

Robert Garland (*NYJA*) discarded the work as "a muddled and none too mettlesome what-have-you." The show was "costly, colorful--and very dull," opined Ward Morehouse (*NYS*). Louis Kronenberger (*PM*) wrote, "The music is commonplace, the choreography quite uneven and the general movement lacking in verve." Nevertheless, Wilella Waldorf (*NYP*), while pointing out various lapses, thought the production excellent and Havoc memorable. Burton Rascoe (*NYWT*), who often took strikingly different tacks from his colleagues, thought the show in a class with *Oklahoma!* and hailed almost every element of the show as brilliant.

ST. LOUIS WOMAN [Musical/Blacks/Gambling/Period/Romance/Sex/Sports] A: Arna Bontemps and Countee Cullen; M: Johnny Mercer; LY: Harold Arlen; SC: Arna Bontemps and Countee Cullen's novel, *God Sends Sunday*; D: Rouben Mamoulian; CH: Charles Walters; DS: Lemuel Ayres; P: Edward Gross; T: Majestic Theatre; 3/30/46 (113)

This promising Frankie and Johnny-type musical about black society in 1898 St. Louis failed to snare the brass ring, although it had such bright lights in it as Pearl Bailey (in her Broadway debut) and the Nicholas brothers, Harold and Fayard. The lead, played by Ruby Hill, originally was intended for Lena Horne, but she withdrew rather than play a woman of easy virtue. More bad luck came to the show when colibrettist Cullen died before rehearsals started. Various other problems arose, including the need to replace choreographer Anthony Tudor with Charles Walters.

It tells of the beautiful Della Green (Hill), who wavers in her affection for Biglow Brown (Rex Ingram) when Little Augie (Harold Nicholas) suddenly rises to prominence as a winning jockey. Brown takes out his jealousy by beating Della, and Augie seeks to take revenge, but a discarded flame (June Hawkins) of Biglow's shoots him first. Biglow places a curse on Augie as his life ebbs, and Augie finds himself losing races, which leads to Della's departure. When his luck turns, Della comes back as well.

If not remembered for much else, the show is important for having introduced the standard, "Come Rain or Come Shine," although it was not the show-stopper one might have expected. The remainder of the score was unmemorable, although Bailey, making her strong Broadway debut in the bawdy comedy role of the waitress Butterfly, had two show-stoppers with "Legalize My Name" and "A Woman's Prerogative." "It was Pearl Bailey who stole the show," commented Vernon Rice (*NYP*). "She's a comedienne with a frank admiration of sex, but she gives the impression that through her passes only the purest of thoughts."

The talky book was weak, while its dancing was strong. "It goes blandly through all the usual steps, and is so heavy the best will in the world cannot lighten it," observed Lewis Nichols (*NYT*), who considered it a hybrid between folk opera and musical comedy. John Mason Brown (*SR*) enjoyed the production values but was irate at what he deemed an insult to black people because of the show's employment of "every formula not only of the Negro-show as it has always been but of every stale idea the white man has tried to keep fresh in his thinking about the Negro." A bit more approving was George Jean Nathan (*TBY*), who thought that "it has some spirit and color, a fairly serviceable story and several pleasant songs and lyrics," although he admitted it may have seemed better than it was because of the general dreariness thus far of the season's musicals.

It was excellently designed and memorably staged with extraordinarily colorful act-ending crowd scenes created by Mamoulian. Especially notable was the cake-walk at the end of act one and the racetrack scene closing act three. Very well received were the dancing Nicholas brothers and the gorgeous Ruby Hill. Others included Juanita Hall, Lorenzo Fuller, Creighton Thompson, and Yvonne Coleman.

At one point early in rehearsals Mamoulian's staging did not sit well with the black company. It centered on some business in the scene of Biglow's funeral. June Hawkins had been directed to fall on her knees at the grave and raise her hands heavenward, followed by a similar gesture from the rest of the cast. "Well, sir," wrote Pearl Bailey in *The Raw Pearl*, "that gesture only served to make the cast angry. They felt it was too Negroid." No one spoke up about their displeasure, and Mamoulian sensed that something was wrong but could not figure out what. The director asked the company what the problem was, but everyone kept quiet. Bailey, however, disgusted with their private grumbling and public silence, spoke up. Mamoulian proceeded to gather the cast around him and then told the story of how, when he was an unknown refugee director, he had made *Porgy** (the play from which *Porgy and Bess** was created) into an American classic, spoke of the black people's great musical contributions to the country, and then dismissed them. "Out of that came some new feelings and better relationships," recalled Bailey.

SALLY [Musical Revival*] B: Guy Bolton; M: Jerome Kern; LY: P. G. Wodehouse and Clifford Grey; D: Billy Gilbert; CH: Richard Barstow; S/L: Stewart Chaney; C: Henry Mulle; P: Hunt Stromberg, Jr., and William Berney; T: Martin Beck Theatre; 5/6/48 (36)

Dancer Bambi Linn had her first starring role as the eponymous heroine in this flop revival of the 1920 musical that had starred the scintillating Marilyn Miller as the dishwasher who becomes a *Follies* dancer. The best-known player in the cast and the name-over-the-title star, however, was Willie Howard, dialect comic, in the role of the Grand Duke Constantine ("Connie"), originally played by Leon Errol. Jack Goode was cast in the important comedy-dance role of Otis Hooper, first performed by Walter Catlett.

The revival fell flat because it lacked the spectacular and colorful presentation of the original, because it seemed dated, and because it did not have Marilyn Miller. Only Howard was widely admired, his role amplified with imitations of George Jessel, Maurice Chevalier, Al Jolson, and Eddie Cantor. Still, Brooks Atkinson (*NYT*) thought that his role gave him not enough to do. Linn scored with her looks and dancing, but her small singing voice was a serious drawback. Even her dance numbers were not all they should have been. Linn's big number with sixteen chorus men in evening dress was a letdown because of the dreary choreography.

The show tried to compensate for various weaknesses by inserting a few topical jokes and borrowing some numbers from other Jerome Kern shows, so "Cleopatra" from 1915's *Leave It to Jane* provided material for a good number in Bibi Osterwald's capable hands; "The Siren Song" was also pilfered from that show. A few pieces of music from 1917's *Oh, Lady! Lady!* also invaded the score. None were as good as the show's best numbers, "Look for the Silver Lining" and "Wild Rose."

"All in all," sighed William Hawkins (*NYWT*), "this . . . is a lackadaisical entertainment. It has neither imagination nor punch." Others felt similarly, if not as strongly, but Howard Barnes (*NYHT*) thought that despite its "long-winded" book, this was a "sparkling revival" and its "songs . . . as fresh and captivating as ever." The cast included handsome baritone Robert Shackleton as Sally's love interest and Kay Buckley in a comedy-dancing role.

SARAH SIMPLE [Comedy/British/Marriage] A: A. A. Milne; D: Wallace Rooney; S: Forrest Thayer, Jr.; P: Hilltop Theatre; T: Provincetown Playhouse (OB); 11/17/40

A production sponsored by a troupe of semiprofessional summer-theatre enthusiasts from Ellicott City, Maryland, near Baltimore. They were appearing in the New York debut of Milne's innocuous 1937 comedy about Sarah Simple (Joy Harrington), a young milliner who ran away to New York with another man eight years earlier. She returns to her husband (Guy Spaull), who never divorced her, at the moment he is involved in an affair with a cleric's widow (Helen Riggs). To allow him to wed the widow, he contrives to take divorce action against his wife by pretending to be the corespondent in the case. But the divorce is never completed because he decides to take up with his wife again and travel to America.

The play was deemed unbearably cute and featherweight. John Mason Brown (*NYP*) called it a "little comedy, which is so little as to be invisible." Calling it the author's worst play, he said, "It can sound like a collection of quips rejected by *Punch*. It can mistake a play-on-words for a play. It can consist of the smallest small-talk known to the drama. . . . It can deafen the ears, dampen the spirits, and sugar the blood."

The cast of six (four of whom belonged to Equity) was at a loss to do anything but make the play's faults even more obvious. Only British actress Harrington gained substantial notice. The company was hoping to run a six-month season at the Provincetown, with each show running two weeks, followed by two weeks off. A children's theatre also was being operated by the Hilltoppers, but the venture quickly petered out.

SAVONAROLA [Drama/Historical-Biographical/Period/Politics/Religion] A: Father Urban Nagle; D: Dennis Gurney; S: Leo Kerz; P: Blackfriars' Guild; T: Blackfriars' Theatre (OB); 4/23/42

An "uninspired and inexpert" (Brooks Atkinson [*NYT*]) attempt to dramatize the life of fifteenth-century religious zealot Savonarola (Brandon Peters). Staged in the small Blackfriars' Theatre at 320 West Fifty-seventh Street, this idea-heavy drama, with its lengthy, interesting, but often undramatic speeches, tells of how the fiery and bigoted preacher Girolamo Savonarola came to be ruler of Florence and how his unusual combination of democratic beliefs and religious frenzy caused him to become a fanatical dictator believing himself the agent of God. His chief antagonists are the overreaching Medicis, whom he topples, and the corrupt Borgia Pope Alexander VI (Graham Velsey), whom he accuses of simony. Balancing Savonarola's extreme behavior is the more rational, wise, and compromising figure of Fra Ricardo (Robert Ober), who believes that there are more subtle ways of achieving one's ends. In the end, Savonarola goes too far in his methods and becomes a martyr to the Church's awesome power, being tortured, forced to abjure his beliefs, and burned at the stake in the Piazza della Signoria.

The play depended too much on the audience's familiarity with the historical events it depicted. While literate and often of much interest, it stressed talk over action, had an overly complex plot, and failed to clearly convey the development of Savonarola's career. Still, some critics showed the play much respect, finding the timeliness of its theme reason enough to recommend it. Louis Kronenberger's (*PM*) words offered clear perceptions: "*Savonarola* is anything but a good play; it is too stiff, too awkward, too verbose. . . . But it is sincere and intelligent and, on its own terms, interesting." Chief actors included Frank Gibney as Fra Domenico, Morgan Farley as Giovanni de' Medici, and Albert Carroll as Lorenzo de' Medici.

SCAPEGOAT, THE [Drama/Crime/Fantasy/Law/Romance/Trial] A: John F. Matthews; SC: Franz Kafka's novel, *The Trial*; D: Erwin Piscator; S: H. A. Condell; P: Dramatic Workshop; T: President Theatre (OB); 4/19/50

Kafka's *The Trial*, one of the greatest of modern novels, already the subject of a successful French adaptation by André Gide (*Le Procès*), was offered in another version by Erwin Piscator's Dramatic Workshop group of semiprofessionals. The adaptor, a playwriting instructor at the Dramatic Workshop, had brought the piece (written after World War I) up to date with contemporary allusions and suggestions of World War II's atrocities. Some Kafka fans were upset by this dramatic license.

The story begins by revealing a dead man whose cause of death is unstated, other than that he died after turning off the radio. The following action expresses how he may have died or have imagined that he died. It tells of Joseph K. (Scott Hale), bank executive, placed under arrest for no definite reason by the Court of Special Supervision, which invades his home with three informers. He is allowed to continue in his bank job but ponders what crime he may have committed. A secret trial is held in a courtroom filled with enemies, and he is ordered to confess to an unnamed crime. His mental state grows more and more paranoiac. He is regularly whipped by a cultured gentleman (Steve Gravers) who does it for the money. His influential uncle (Robert H. Fuller) turns out to be against him. His job is taken from him. His girl (Elaine Fiester) leaves him. Another girl (Madeleine Sherwood) who loves him pleads with him to confess. A phony priest (Richard Bull) tries to get him to make a blanket confession that will include the crimes of which he is accused. Finally, he confesses to the indifference and ignorance responsible for allowing a world in which a man can endure what he has. His execution ends the play.

Brooks Atkinson (*NYT*) commented, "Although *The Scapegoat* may seem at times a little weak or static as a drama, it is one of the most original dramas of the season--hovering between reality and insanity where so much of our life seems to be today." Piscator's excellent production managed to provide touches of nightmarish fantasy to a very realistically acted script. Arthur Pollock (*DC*) declared, "Piscator has directed it himself in his best style, odd and grotesque and fantastic and unfailingly imaginative. Its characters may appear from anywhere or nowhere or be seen only as shadows on a wall. The scenery is of the simplest sort and yet seemingly complex and of the greatest versatility."

SCHOOL FOR BRIDES, THE [Comedy/Business/Marriage/Romance/School/Sex] A: Frank Gill, Jr., and George Carleton Brown; D: Harold Morton; S: Ernest Glover; P: Howard Lang; T: Royale Theatre; 8/1/44 (375)

"A deadly dirty and stupid farce" (George Freedley [*NYMT*]) that was reviled as little more than leering smut, poorly written, acted, and directed; still, it was one of the season's biggest hits. It came to Broadway after a successful run in Chicago and starred film comedian Roscoe Karns.

It tells of a young model-agency owner named Jeff Connors (Warren Ashe) whose financial problems inspire him to raise money by turning the business into a school for brides--the curriculum focusing on how to marry a millionaire--so as to find a seventh wife for wealthy playboy Frederick M. Hasty (Karns). The latter puts up $100,000 for the enterprise and hopes to marry the "valedictorian." (The role was presumably based on the often married bon vivant, Tommy Manville). Jeff's suspicious wife Mary (Ann Turner) believes that her spouse is having a fling with the school's alleged dean of women, who calls herself Dean Baxter but is really an actress named Connie King (Bernadene Hayes). Mary enrolls in the school under her maiden name. The millionaire, who is pretending to be a professor at the school, falls for her and sets up a bedroom rendezvous. Several complications ensue when a sequence of women take the wife's place in bed, until, finally, Jeff and his wife iron out their problems and the dean removes her glasses and lets down her hair, becoming so irresistible that the millionaire marries her.

Double entendres, ten lovely girls in bathing suits and negligees, and suggestive situations were piled on in abundance, but, said Louis Kronenberger (*PM*), "the play, beyond its other shortcomings, is far oftener silly than sultry." "A trite and labored contrivance," rasped Ward Morehouse (*NYS*). Company members included John Sheehan and Yolande Donlan.

SEA GULL, THE (***Chaika***) [Dramatic Revival*] A: Anton Chekhov; TR: Stark Young; D: Zara Shakow; P: Equity Library Theatre; T: George Bruce Branch of the New York Public Library (OB); 4/3/45

One of the thirty-seven 1944-1945 productions by the fledgling showcase arm of Actors Equity, this revival of Chekhov's great play included Jeraldine Dvorak as Irina, Leonard Elliott as Trigorin, Alix Taran as Nina, Alan Shayne as Trepleff, and Pat Smith as Sorin. "The acting is uneven," said George Freedley (*NYMT*), the sole reviewer attending. The production was riddled with directorial faults as well and suffered from being produced in a cramped and tiny library auditorium. The most recent revival of the play had been in 1938, starring the Lunts.

SEARCHING WIND, THE [Drama/Family/France/Hotel/Journalism/Military/

Period/Politics/Romance/Sex/War] A: Lillian Hellman; D/P: Herman Shumlin; S: Howard Bay; C: Aline Bernstein; T: Fulton Theatre; 4/12/44 (326)

Burns Mantle chose this as one of the ten best of the season, although the reviews were not invariably favorable. Considered inferior to some of the author's previous dramas, it nevertheless made an impact because of the relative dearth of timely, effectively written, serious plays then available. Its concern is with the results of appeasement in the days when something might have been done to stop the fascist juggernaut.

The play moves back and forth through time, beginning at the tasteful home of the Hazen family in Washington, D.C., in the Spring of 1944. Visiting ex-Ambassador Alexander Hazen (Dennis King) and his wife Emily (Cornelia Otis Skinner) is their childhood friend Cassie Bowman (Barbara O'Neil), whom Emily has not seen in over twenty years. The events of the past twenty years are recounted, despite Cassie's distaste for the discussion. The Hazens' twenty-year-old soldier son Sam (Montgomery Clift), wounded in Italy, absorbs the painful information as he listens. With flashbacks to Rome in 1922, Berlin in 1923, and Paris in 1938, it is revealed that Emily stole Alexander from Cassie, whom he has always loved, and that Alexander and Cassie subsequently had an affair of which Emily knew. Compromise has marred all their social relations. More importantly, Alexander and Emily, for all their good intentions, preferred to compromise in their politics as well. Alexander, former diplomat, backpeddled when confronted by Mussolini in 1922, violent German anti-Semitism in 1923, and a later German diplomat's (Arnold Korff) attempt to strike a deal with America to keep it from messing up Germany's game with Chamberlain and Daladier. Emily, for her part, hobnobbed with all the shallow European émigré socialites who thought more of their own necks than of their own countries, which they easily betrayed by their selfish behavior. There is also Emily's father, the once-powerful newspaper publisher Moses Taney (Dudley Digges); despite his professed liberalism, he decided to retreat into a shell in 1922 and let the rest of the world take care of itself while he ineffectually shot verbal bullets at the lousy job it was doing. Sam, whose leg must be amputated because of the mess into which these people led the world, expresses shame at his parents' actions and, in a resounding final speech, expounds his love of America.

Most critics expressed appreciation for the play while registering their reservations. Many said that it was, for all its faults, the finest drama of the season. A chief drawback was seen to be the combination of the personal with the political story. Rosamond Gilder (*TAM*) argued that the play was too discursive and that Hellman had "allowed her play to wander away from its main theme, which is the blindness of men of good will who could not foresee the sinister outcome of what was happening in Europe . . . , to lose itself in an inept love story about two women and a man." Lewis Nichols (*NYT*), who considered the play "a credit to the theatre," also regretted that the love story was not as interesting as the play's political angle. George Freedley (*NYMT*) liked the play while warning about its being "frequently muddy." Howard Barnes (*NYHT*) decided that Hellman "has brought back a full measure of dignity, perception and beauty to the theater. Her new play is not all of a piece. . . . The romantic misadventures of these characters are inevitably dwarfed by the international compromises and defeats, which they obviously mirror." But Arthur Pollock (*BE*) appreciated the way the private and public stories intermingled and praised the play as "a sharp, precise and unrelenting indictment of appeasement and appeasers." Burton Rascoe (*NYWT*) thought it Hellman's best play, "a beautiful, powerful and touching drama." On the other hand, George Jean Nathan (*TBY*) dismissed all the positive commentary of his fellow critics and trashed the work as "an overwrought, often muddled and generally subordinate example of pamphleturgy."

Admiration was expressed for the clear-cut characterizations of the brilliant cast, including Mercedes Gilbert as the Hazen family's matriarchal black maid, Joseph de Santis as an Italian waiter, Alfred Hesse as a butler, Walter Kohler as a hotel manager, William F. Schoeller as a restaurant owner, and Eugene Earl as an aide to Alexander. A distinguished production, including memorably realistic sets and noteworthy costumes, helped project this work into the hit category.

SECOND BEST BED [Comedy/Literary-Biographical/Marriage/Period/Theatre] A: N. Richard Nash; D: Ruth Chatterton and N. Richard Nash; DS: Motley; P: Ruth Chatterton and John Huntington; T: Ethel Barrymore Theatre; 6/3/46 (8)

The first show of the 1946-1947 season was this pseudobiographical comedy about William Shakespeare (Barry Thomson), set--to lovely effect--in the early seventeenth century at the picture-postcard-pretty Stratford-on-Avon cottage of Anne Hathaway (Ruth Chatterton, who also codirected and coproduced, and who was Thomson's real-life wife). The play was a prizewinner for comedy writing at Stanford University and had been touring the country before arriving locally. On Broadway it "merely seemed a tired and talky comedy which tried to be bawdily outspoken and merely succeeded in being occasionally dirty," according to George Freedley (*NYMT*). Howard Barnes (*NYHT*), noting the play's unclear objectives, wondered whether it was intended as a "plausible comedy about Shakespeare's somewhat mythological married life," or whether it was supposed to be a spoof at the playwright's expense. The result, he decided, was "woefully bad, in both writing and execution." Its title derives from the Bard's will, in which he left his "second best bed" to his wife.

At the time of the action, Will Shakespeare is a rising London dramatist who, after three years, returns home to his family in Stratford, where Anne Hathaway Shakespeare, with whom he is forever squabbling, is threatening to leave him for the pompous candidate for bailiff, Lewis Poggs (Ralph Forbes). The roguish Shakespeare then buys the village inn and gets the whole town tipsy. He also rejects the local wench, Nell (Elizabeth Eustis), who has him thrown in jail. He gets himself released via his knowledge of an old paternity charge against Squire Lummle (Richard Temple). Subsequently, Will gets Poggs into hot water and provokes him to propose to Nell as a way of saving himself, which cools Anne's interest in Poggs. Shakespeare then returns to London.

Mediocre acting by the leads did not help the already-weak comedy to make an impression. Several old ballads were well sung by Richard Dyer-Bennett, though. Ralph Cullinan, John McKee, and John Gay were in the cast.

SECRET ROOM, THE [Drama/Crime/Mental Illness/Sex/Youth] A: Robert Turney; D: Moss Hart; S: Carolyn Hancock; L: Frederick Fox; P: Joseph M. Hyman and Bernard Hart i/a/w Haila Stoddard; T: Royale Theatre; 11/7/45 (21)

A flimsy psychological thriller that tells of what happens when an old psychiatrist named Dr. Jackson (Ivan Simpson) asks a younger colleague, Dr. John Beverly (Reed Brown, Jr.) to look after Leda Ferroni (Eleanora Mendelssohn), a psychopathic Italian refugee from the Dachau concentration camp, at his country home (this although Dr. Beverly has just been called up by the army). Leda, a former concert pianist, suffers from manic depressive episodes stemming from her being raped and forced into prostitution by the Nazis, one of whom fathered a child by her and then took it from her. She wants to care for small children, but when she learns that Dr. Jackson has left her case history in Dr. Beverly's possession, she fears that she will not be granted access to children if her story is known. She thereupon smothers the old man and hides the case history. The doctor's death is attributed to a heart attack, although the two Beverly children (Jane Earle and Fuzzy McQuade) have witnessed the killing from a secret room. While Dr. Beverly is off with the military, Leda cares for his youngsters, for whom she develops an unhealthy fondness that makes her insanely jealous of Mrs. Beverly (movie actress Frances Dee, in her Broadway bow), against whom she turns the kids. Leda discovers Mrs. Beverly reading the notebook; she grabs a pillow, aiming to smother her as well, but is prevented just in time. Her attempt to kidnap the children is also foiled before the depth of her insanity is finally revealed.

The Secret Room turned out to be an uncomfortable blend of sentiment and murder, was wordy to a fault, and was riddled with improbabilities such as Leda's being brought to Dr. Beverly when he is leaving for the army. It was "poor, even preposterous, melodrama on all counts," scoffed George Jean Nathan (*TBY*). "The play," noted Wilella Waldorf (*NYP*), "is so childishly contrived that it is impossible for anybody connected with the production to make it seem anything but hopelessly artificial and lacking in conviction."

SEEDS IN THE WIND [Drama/Politics/Trial/War/Youth] A: Arthur Goodman; D: Paul Tripp; P: Monroe Hack and the Experimental Theatre, Inc., of the American National Theatre and Academy; T: Lenox Hill Playhouse (OB); 4/24/48 (3)

Seeds in the Wind was first offered as the opening salvo in an "invitational" project presenting five new American plays at the Lenox Hill Playhouse, 331 East Seventieth Street. The few reviewers who visited it in this shoestring ($75) showing (no designer was credited for its bare-stage set) were strongly positive. L. B. (*NYT*) thought it "deeply felt, imaginatively conceived and frequently moving," although it lapsed into excessive verbosity. George Freedley (*NYMT*) dubbed it "a really satisfying and heart-warming play"; his suggestion that it "should promptly be shown on Broadway" was taken up, and the show, now produced by Eunice Healey and Harald Bramley and designed with skeletal settings by Ralph Alswang, moved to the Empire on 5/25/48, where it was rejected by the critics and was gone with the wind after 7 performances.

A propaganda play for peace, it tells of how, in 1942, a group of children from Lidice, Czechoslovakia, who had witnessed the Germans' slaughter of their parents and elders, were crammed into a freight train with other children from Prague; all were to be indoctrinated by the Nazis. According to the play's fiction, a number of the traumatized children escaped into the Carpathian Mountains and established a refuge there. By the time the play begins, in 1945, several have died. Their leader is Tonya (Cy Chermak Off Broadway; twenty-two-year-old Sidney Lumet on), in love with his coleader Marta (Abby Bonime). A refugee Czech partisan (Tonio Selwart) blunders into their hiding place, and his presence immediately causes chaos in the youthful community, where the children are from five to sixteen. During their three years in hiding, the youngsters had decided to create universal peace through a "world nation of children," rejecting the adult world, but the problem presented by the kindly and wise refugee soldier stirs up factional discord and doubts among them. (They also divide on whether to allow German and Japanese children into their new nation.) Ultimately, under Tonya's influence (he may also be jealous of Marta's affection for the man), they put the Czech on trial and find him guilty of the adult crime of subjecting children to the horrors of war. He leaves, presumably to hang himself.

The Broadway production was a disaster. Howard Barnes (*NYHT*) wrote, "The acting and the staging do not save this . . . offering from the worst aspects of amateurish make-believe." "This play would be more interesting if it was downright bad," scoffed William Hawkins (*NYWT*). "It is just dull. The script is pedestrian and illogical. . . . The motivation is vague and confusing." Young actors of promise were Jerry Stone, Richard Kenny, Teddy Rose, Mimi Strongin, Eeta Kinden, and Jimmy Dutton.

SENDER BLANK [Comedy/Family/Legacy/Yiddish Language] A/D: Jacob Rothbaum; SC: a story by Sholem Aleichem of the same name; M: Sholem Secunda; S: Alexander Chertov; P: Yiddish Art Theatre (OB); 12/1/40

Maurice Schwartz did well in the comic title role of this farce, but the work itself was mediocre and not up to Yiddish Art Theatre standards. Sender Blank is a wealthy Russian baker with a prodigious appetite that finally gives him a severe stomach ache. The comedy takes off from his belief that he has something more serious than indigestion and from the greedy anticipation of his kinfolk and neighbors that they will reap the profits from his will. In one of the funniest scenes, an eccentric physician diagnoses the baker and takes the family aside to whisper his findings while Sender climbs over the end of the bed to listen in. To the disappointment of the vultures, of course, he does not die after all, and he realizes the need to gain respect for his person and not his property.

Abel Gorham (*DW*), who correctly predicted the company's imminent demise, wrote that Sholem Aleichem's humor survived the dramatization, but that the characters were more stereotypes than real people: "It is also true that nearly all of the warmth of Sholem Aleichem is missing. His villains in the play are downright murderous, rather than comic." The critics took pleasure in seeing the usually somber Schwartz enjoying himself in a broad comic role with burlesque overtones. Leading members of the troupe, such as Lucy German, Muni Serebrov, Judith Abarbanell, Leon Gold, Luba Kadison, Anatol Winogradoff, Anna Appel, and Isadore Casher, had roles in the piece.

SERVANT OF TWO MASTERS, THE (***Il Servitore di Due Padroni***) [Dramatic Revival*] A: Carlo Goldoni; D: Dino Yannopolous; P: Equity Library Theatre; T: Hamilton Grange Branch of the New York Public Library (OB); 4/1/46 (4)

A shoestring-budget revival of the eighteenth-century Italian comedy that had last been seen locally in Max Reinhardt's visiting German production twenty years earlier. The best in the present company was said by George Freedley (*NYMT*), the sole critic on duty, to be Don Hirst as Truffaldino. In the role of Smeraldina was Joan Copeland, a future actress of note who also happened to be the sister of the as-yet-unsung playwright Arthur Miller. Freedley said the director did "a rather exciting, and certainly imaginative job of direction."

SET MY PEOPLE FREE [Drama/Blacks/Historical-Biographical/Period/Politics/Race/Religion] A: Dorothy Heyward; D: Martin Ritt; S/L: Ralph Alswang; C: Ernest Schrapps; P: Theatre Guild; T: Hudson Theatre; 11/3/48 (36)

An abortive racial uprising in 1822 Charleston, South Carolina, was the impetus for this highly interesting but somewhat stiff period drama. The play contrasts two slaves, George (Canada Lee), the head slave to the kindly Master Wilson (Blaine Cordner), and the discontented Denmark Vesey (Juano Hernandez), kidnapped son of an African chief, who has grown from an illiterate slave to a fervent Bible reader and free man; he believes himself to be a Moses who will lead his people out of bondage. Denmark plots for twelve years to overthrow the white society of Charleston and put the city into black hands. His conspiracy--backed by thousands of slaves--is carried out in the black church. To carry out his plan he must have absolute secrecy; even his name is known to only a tight little cadre of followers. The very hesitant George agrees at last to join the insurrection, but only on the condition that the Wilson family will be spared the massacre and allowed to flee. Unfortunately, on the night of the uprising, circumstances conspire to detain the Wilson family in Charleston, and George is torn between revealing the plan to them or seeing them slaughtered. He finally betrays the plan and tells the dreaded secret, which leads to the overthrow of the insurrection and a consequent manhunt for Vesey.

There were many strong notices for the strongly acted play, but its episodic structure and sharply varying levels of intensity were considered serious weaknesses that detracted from the play's cumulative power. The best scenes were those concerning the moral debate between the moderate George and the firebrand Denmark. George Jean Nathan (*TBY*) carped that the play, interesting as it was, was yet too similar to other dramas on like themes about black uprisings to be of importance. Robert Coleman (*NYDM*) said that the work seemed "exciting in the writing but in the acting it becomes amazingly static." Ward Morehouse (*NYS*) thought it "more oratorical than dramatic," although "frequently theatrically effective" and well worth seeing. Howard Barnes (*NYHT*) called the work "an angular and somewhat stilted historical drama." Good work was contributed by Mildred Joanne Smith, Leigh Whipper, and Frank Wilson.

This play had met with various troubles before its New York opening. Its title on the road had been *Charleston 1822*. The role of George originally was to be played by Rex Ingram, who suddenly had to drop out during the tryout period when he was arrested on a violation of the Mann Act involving a white girl. He was substituted for in New Haven by John Marriott, who had to read his lines from a script. Canada Lee eventually was cast and received excellent notices for his "dignity, restraint and deep feeling," as Euphemia Van Rensselaer Wyatt (*CW*) observed.

SEVEN LIVELY ARTS [Revue] CN/P: Billy Rose; SK: Moss Hart, George S.

Kaufman, Robert Pirosh, Joseph Schrank, Charles Sherman, and Ben Hecht; M/LY: Cole Porter (ballet music: Igor Stravinsky); D: Hassard Short and Philip Loeb; CH: Jack Donohue; S: Norman Bel Geddes; C: Mary Grant and Valentina; T: Ziegfeld Theatre; 12/7/44 (183)

Unlike the abundance of contemporary revues that were really vaudeville shows, this lavish entertainment returned to the revue formula of earlier years, with an assortment of sketches featuring outstanding comic performers, and added lavish sets and costumes to back a bevy of singers and dancers. Producer Rose boasted that the show contained not a whit of social significance and was meant entirely as wartime escapism. He said that he was suggesting the nation's strength and stability by opening the show on the third anniversary of Pearl Harbor, but a number of people found the idea offensive. The ostentatious show--which had a then-huge $500,000 advance and is reported to have cost the fabulous sum of $350,000--boasted a company including hilarious players Beatrice Lillie, Bert Lahr (coaxed back from Hollywood), Albert Carroll, and Doc Rockwell, ballet dancers Anton Dolin and Alicia Markova, swing clarinetist Benny Goodman, and songstress Dolores Gray. There also was a large singing chorus, a line of showgirls, a dancing chorus, and a sizable orchestra. Lillie was returning to Broadway after five years. Just as the show was beginning its preparations, she learned that her only son, Robert Peel, missing in action, had died on 4/5/42 when his ship was dive-bombed.

The company performed in the thoroughly renovated Ziegfeld Theatre, reclaimed from movie theatre oblivion by Billy Rose, who paid $700,000 for the privilege of owning it. The theatre boasted a gallery of Salvador Dali paintings. But for all the expense and hullabaloo, the show was a critical dud, even with such writers as Kaufman, Hart, and Hecht and with a score by Porter and Stravinsky. Its original intention of being a spoof of show business had been deflected into a sprawling, overproduced display of sequins and gaudy production numbers with barely any thematic string to tie the pieces together. Once the hefty advance sale was depleted, the show--which charged up to $7.70 a seat--folded its tents.

The show began with a tentative story about a group of art enthusiasts who come to New York to pursue their muses, but it was soon forgotten in the welter of numbers. Lillie was the show's laugh delight, although much of her material was second-rate. "Neat, trim, delectably witty, and yet capable of the rowdiest burlesque, she is a whole show in herself," applauded John Mason Brown (*SR*). She scored when singing the double-entendre-laden "When I Was a Little Cuckoo." In Moss Hart's "Heaven on Angel Street" skit, she was the worried Mrs. Manningham, so frightened of her psychopathic spouse that she tucks her teacup into her bodice, saying "You are so good to me." Coming to visit her on Angel Street were Bert Lahr as Father Day from *Life with Father** and Albert Carroll as Jeeter Lester from *Tobacco Road**, with the skit making comic sport of the Drama Critics Circle. Also amusing was Lillie's bit about a British lady at a canteen innocently trying to be friendly to American GIs by using the sexually suggestive language she found in their handbooks. She garnered laughs, too, with her sketch about standing in line to buy tickets for a ballet whose title, for all she could remember, was "S. Hurok." To demonstrate the subject matter of the work she intended to see, she did a hilarious version of "The Dying Swan."

Lillie, struggling to mask her grief about her son, often tussled with Rose as well as with director Loeb, who did not fully appreciate her inventive pieces of comic business. She also had disagreements with Cole Porter, who, apart from the Stravinsky ballet music, would allow no other songs, while Lillie wanted to sing a number she had succeeded with in London. The conflict with Porter grew so heated that she sent word from her hotel on opening night that she was too ill to go on, while Porter stubbornly refused to give in to her demands. The only way she could be persuaded to appear was if she were permitted to sing her song at the opening and Porter's on the second night, with Porter to judge which was more successful. (Bruce Laffey, who told the story in *Beatrice Lillie*, did not name the tunes, or which song was the victor. A playbill insert noted ambivalently that she would sing a song, but gave no title or composer.) It is no wonder that she privately dubbed the show "Seven Deadly Hours."

Bert Lahr was especially unhappy with his material. Some new sketches were created for him, but they did not satisfy him, although he later acknowledged that at least one, written by Moss Hart, was actually better than he thought it. Lahr also objected on grounds of taste to a Porter lyric that rhymed cinema with enema. Although most of his material was less effective than Lillie's, he was funny in "Drink, Drink, Drink," a bit in which he was dressed as an English admiral singing a drinking song on a battleship deck and getting drunk from the alcoholic lyrics alone. His sketch, "The Great Man Speaks," in which he lampooned Orson Welles's vanity, was a flop.

Scenic spectacle was the reason for such production numbers as "Fragonard in Pink" (with Lahr and Lillie in a pink arcadia, she on a swing and he in pink pantaloons and powdered wig) and "Frahngee-Pahnee," at the conclusion of which Lillie performed a risible satire on Indian dance to a jungle drum, making fun of a current theatre fad. One night, during the former number, the swing hit Lahr on the chin and decked him. Dolin and Markova danced to the music of Stravinsky, but seemed out of place amid the show-biz antics of the other entertainments. There is a story that Rose had liked Stravinsky's score at rehearsal but that he had second thoughts about it after hearing it at the Philadelphia opening. According to John Lahr's *Notes on a Cowardly Lion*, he wired the composer: "YOUR MUSIC GREAT SUCCESS STOP COULD BE SENSATIONAL STOP IF YOU WOULD AUTHORIZE ROBERT RUSSELL BENNETT RETOUCH ORCHESTRATION STOP BENNETT ORCHESTRATES EVEN COLE PORTER." To this Stravinsky replied: "SATISFIED WITH SUCCESS."

One sequence in which Benny Goodman was featured was the opulent close of the first act, "Billy Rose Buys the Manhattan Opera House," which showed what *Aida* would look like with a silver Jumbo the elephant; an all-black *Carmen* as in *Carmen Jones*; and an aquacade version of *Rheingold*.

The best-remembered Cole Porter tune in the show was "Ev'ry Time We Say Goodbye," introduced by Nan Wynne. Less well liked was an off-color physiology lecture by Hecht and delivered by Doc Rockwell, who also presented a Hecht-written running commentary on the show that could have been eliminated.

Observed Rosamond Gilder (*TAM*), "It has all the ingredients to make a superb show, but the tone, the spirit is lacking." Brown complained of a superfluity of stars, sets, routines, and so on, so that the most delicious parts were lost in an overloaded buffet that left the palate jaded. George Freedley (*NYMT*) determined that "the production in all its parts simply does not create the perfect whole which is essential to a really good revue. The songs are mediocre, though pleasing; the lyrics . . . are twisting, if not really witty. The sketches . . . have many good lines, but not a single one is a smash. The dances . . . are occasionally effective pictorially, but they lack the extra quality which comes from greatness." The large company included Jere McMahon, Billy Worth, William Tabbert, Mary Roche, Dennie Moore, Teddy Wilson, Red Norvo, and, buried in the corps de ballet, future musical comedy star Helen Gallagher, in her Broadway bow.

SEVEN MIRRORS [Drama/Religion/Women] A: students at Immaculate Heart College, Los Angeles (edited by Emmett Lavery); D: Dennis Gurney; CH: Patricia Newman; S: Edward Rutyna; P: Blackfriars' Guild; T: Blackfriars' Theatre (OB); 10/25/45 (23)

An episodic, intermissionless "experiment in social drama" created by a playwriting class at a West Coast Catholic college. It was an overly sentimental, amateurish offering that represented a step back for the semipro Catholic theatre group producing it. Its chief footnote to theatre history is the fact that its large company included future star Geraldine Page in her New York debut in the role of Sophomore.

In prologue, seven scenes, and epilogue, the play investigates themes of peace and brotherhood. The scenes, according to Euphemia Van Rensselaer Wyatt (*CW*), were meant to stand for the Seven Sorrows of Our Lady and to demonstrate how women worldwide may unite in creating the Kingdom of God. Six Madonnas, those of Warsaw, Leyte, Mexico, Lourdes, New York, and Berlin, introduce the respective scenes. The Warsaw scene shows women beating up Nazis. One in an American college suggests that women should be in combat. That in Lourdes shows late writer Franz Werfel being converted to Catholicism and receiving the inspiration for his spiritually uplifting *Song of Bernadette*.

The staging employed a large cross inclined on an angle and constituting a stage providing several levels for the action. A choir formed an important part of the presentation, and there were choreographed dances. Locales were suggested by projections on the rear wall. "The language . . . is stilted and the ideas are neither clear nor well expressed," opined Lewis Nichols (*NYT*). "What emanates from the mishmash," barked George Jean Nathan (*TBY*), "is everything but drama."

SEVENTH TRUMPET, THE [Drama/Politics/Religion/Romance/War] A/D: Charles Rann Kennedy; M: Horace Middleton; S/L: Jo Mielziner; P: Theatre Associates; T: Mansfield Theatre; 11/21/41 (11)

A floridly acted, talky anti-Nazi drama that sought to defuse the German menace through the power of religious faith. It proved too steeped in mystical and theological argument and not enough in solid theatrics to interest a Broadway audience. The play attacked both the Nazi threat and British plutocracy and imperialism, while calling for their replacement by a type of Christian Socialism and an Arthurian Round Table-like communion of men. "However noble its aim," claimed Louis Kronenberger (*PM*), "*The Seventh Trumpet* is utterly appalling in execution and less easily called a play than an interminable piece of rant and sermonizing."

Its action takes place on the lawn of a primitive chapel of St. Lazarus, near Glastonbury, England. The church has just been bombed by the Luftwaffe, and on the site of its ruins gather seven characters: an Anglo-Catholic priest, Father Bede (Ian Maclaren), who is also a reformed capitalist; an atheistic London bobby, Percival (Peter Cushing), who has been wounded in a heroic mission to defuse a bomb; an aged and testy Calvinist peasant, Sam Brodribb (A. G. Andrews); Lady Madeline (Carmen Mathews), a nurse; Deborah Broome (Leslie Bingham), the mother of two pilots killed in battle; a Greek Orthodox monk searching for the holy grail, Brother Ambrose (Thaddeus Suski); and the German bomber pilot, Bomber 666 (Alan Handley), who has been shot down after destroying the church. Lady Madeline, who loves and cares for the crippled bobby, also loves the German, whom she knew at Cambridge. The play concludes with the offstage suicide of the German after he has been forgiven by the mother whose sons he killed and those whose chapel he bombed. The others pray for forgiveness from God until they, too, are killed in an air raid.

The practically plotless play was little more than a succession of duologues and monologues, each character having his say on the subjects of religion, war, politics, and the like. A major point was Father Bede's to the effect that pacificism is a weak solution, and that Hitler, the Anti-Christ, can be defeated through the combined will of people of all faiths, as witnessed by the British people's awakening after Dunkirk.

SHADOW AND SUBSTANCE [Dramatic Revival*] A: Paul Vincent Carroll; D: Norman Fenster; P: Equity Library Theatre; T: Hudson Park Branch of the New York Public Library (OB); 6/9/44

Norman Fenster provided "sympathetic and sensitive" (George Freedley [*NYMT*]) direction for this revival of the Irish play originally seen here in 1938 with Sir Cedric Hardwicke in the role of Canon Skerritt, now played by Cyrus Staehle. Freedley thought the "deeply moving little play" worthy of consideration for a Broadway resuscitation. In the role of Brigid, played six years earlier by Julie Haydon, was Leah Elaine Easton, offering "a remarkably simple, unaffected and touching" performance. The liberal schoolmaster, Dermot Francis O'Flingsley, was played by Lawrence Arine, while other roles were played by Frederick Colecord and Peg Mayo.

SHADOW OF THE GLEN, THE (see "Fumed Oak")

SHAKE HANDS WITH THE DEVIL [Drama/Blacks/Journalism/Labor/Politics/

Race/Religion/Trial] A: Robert C. Healey; D: Dennis Gurney; S: Gregg Kane; L: Joan Tyne; P: Blackfriars' Guild; T: Blackfriars' Theatre (OB); 10/20/49

This "documentary on current affairs," as it was called, was a six-episode "living newspaper"-style play concerned with the evil influence of communism on American life. It used a recent trial of Communists presided over by Judge Harold Medina as a springboard for the discussion of a number of important, socially provocative events that discloseD the extent to which the communists had infiltrated American society. A *Daily Worker* reporter discovers the phoniness of the cause to which he has given his life. A worker's wife (Marcia Murray) convinces her spouse that a jurisdictional strike stopping war production is a ploy to serve the Communists' ends. A schoolteacher, Mme. Kasenkina (Jane Murray), tries to kill herself when hounded by the Soviets. The mother (Sadie Stockton) of a boy in the Scottsboro case reveals her disgust at the way her son and his friends were exploited for Communist purposes. A Russian clerk in the USSR's Canadian embassy struggles to expose the proof of Communist espionage he has uncovered. Cardinal Mindszenty of Hungary is duped into betraying his church on behalf of the Reds. These stories are examined to uncover their real facts as opposed to those promulgated by the Communists, who allegedly turned the events to their own advantage.

This was, said Edba. (*V*), "highly interesting and gripping little theatre," and Robert Coleman (*NYDM*) was very impressed, not only by the expressionist production, but by a new playwright who "knows how to stimulate interest and generate excitement." Several, however, agreed with William Hawkins (*NYWT*) that while the facts were made very accessible, "the issues become almost too simple and the prejudice sometimes too overbalanced for conviction." Brett O'Hollewitt was the judge, Paul Lynch the prosecuting attorney, Harry Bolden a black minister, and Vincent Gordon the defense attorney.

SHE STOOPS TO CONQUER [Dramatic Revival*] A: Oliver Goldsmith; M: William Brooks; D: Morton Da Costa; S: Peter Wolf; C: Emeline Roche; P: New York City Theatre Company; T: City Center of Music and Drama; 12/28/49 (16)

The most recent revival of this 1773 English comedy classic had been in 1928, in an "all-star" version. Another such all-star attempt was represented here with a distinguished troupe including Ezra Stone as Tony Lumpkin, Burl Ives as Hardcastle, Evelyn Varden as Mrs. Hardcastle, Carmen Mathews as Miss Neville, Celeste Holm as Kate, Brian Aherne as young Marlow, Staats Cotsworth as Hastings, Royal Dano as Roger, Jack Fletcher as Diggory, and Richard Temple as Marlow.

The play, which had a new prologue by college professor W. W. Watt, was the first in a four-play, popular-price series under the "artistic supervision" of actor Maurice Evans (aided by George Schaefer); Evans, dressed in white tie and tails, spoke the prologue. Concessions from the unions that enabled the productions to be realized at minimum costs meant that the plays could receive only two weeks of rehearsal each, which often led to critical comments about the rough-edged quality of opening-night performances. All company members earned the stock minimum of $50 a week plus $20 a week for their rehearsal period. It was hoped that the company would be an American version of London's Old Vic, but that dream never was realized.

The production was primarily in a vein of broad burlesque, with the characters played for their most obvious qualities. Several actors, such as Stone, were accused of overplaying (although Stone was some critics' favorite), and it was noted that the company played in a variety of conflicting styles. A few critics liked this "slapdash" approach, as John Chapman (*NYDN*) called it.

Reviews ranged from the mildly complimentary to downright pans. Brooks Atkinson (*NYT*), while noting infelicities in the acting, which he felt would be ironed out during the run, declared that the play "has been affectionately restored by a cast that is not afraid of horseplay and sentiment." Howard Barnes (*NYHT*) concluded, "This is not a brilliant revival, but it is a competent one. . . . It wants smoothness and a more consistent and dashing stylization." To Ward Morehouse (*NYS*) it was "brightly, if by no means brilliantly, played." But George Jean Nathan (*TBY*) pulled no punches in announcing that the play "has been staged with a miscellaneous acting troupe . . . apparently recruited by the tick-tack-toe method. Though one or two . . . are independently right enough, the majority are out of their element . . . and are additionally embarrassed by stage direction that seeks to camouflage the lack of rehearsals by" presenting the piece like a vaudeville show olio with each actor taking his turn performing an act.

SHEPPEY [Comedy/British/Death/Family/Fantasy/Gambling/Mental Illness/Prostitution/Religion] A: W. Somerset Maugham; D: Cedric Hardwicke; S: Watson Barratt; P: Jacques Chambrun; T: Playhouse; 4/18/44 (23)

Famed British actor Sir Cedric Hardwicke staged this Maugham piece, the playwright's last, on Broadway more than a decade after its London debut (1933). The local cognoscenti were of several minds about it.

A parable play, it is about a lovable barber of London's Bond Street named Sheppey (Edmund Gwenn), who wins £8,000 plus in the Irish Sweepstakes. He has a religious experience following the celebration of his coup and decrees that he will spend the money according to the principles of Christianity by giving it to the indigent. These include a prostitute (Doris Patston) and a thief (Victor Beecroft) he befriends and takes into his home, although they prefer their former existence. The immediate response of his family is to consider him mad and to have him examined by a psychiatrist (Horace Cooper). The latter opines that anyone who behaves as Sheppey does must be balmy. Sheppey's greedy daughter (Frances Heflin), who wants a cut of the winnings for herself and her snobbish fiancé (Anthony Kemble-Cooper), hopes that he will be proved insane, while his wife (Barbara Everest), although disappointed, is content to allow him his eccentricities. Death, a beautiful woman (Katherine Anderson), who has been seen only by Sheppey (who has a history of heart problems), comes to take him with her before he can be committed. The playwright does not offer an opinion on Sheppey's sanity, leaving the question open to debate.

Too much of the play was devoted to words, too little to action. The play also veered sharply from mood to mood, being spirited at some points and gloomy elsewhere, with barely a transition to prepare the way. "All in all," yawned Louis Kronenberger (*PM*), "it is a pretty tired and pretty tiring play--too pat, too static, and entirely too talky." It also borrowed many dramatic devices from other plays. In fact, said George Jean Nathan (*TBY*), "It amounts to what is basically so obvious a kleptomania in appropriating the standard ingredients of popular drama of the last fifty years as to be almost impertinent." Yet John Chapman (*NYDN*), while admitting that the play would not appeal to a Broadway crowd, thought it "a modest, warming, talkative and funny story." Alexander Clark, Vera Fuller Mellish, Gerald Savory, and Harry Sothern were among the cast members, most of them English. Gwenn's performance was one of the best of the season.

SHINING HOUR, THE [Dramatic Revival*] A: Keith Winter; D/S: Teresa Hayden; P: Equity Library Theatre; T: Hudson Park Branch of the New York Public Library (OB); 2/7/45

A revival by Equity's showcase arm of the British play that had opened on Broadway in 1934. The young actors in the new production did a competent job in a version that had been transferred from the Yorkshire countryside to the Midwest, allowing the actors to forgo English accents. "The result certainly did not help the play," wrote George Freedley (*NYMT*), the sole critic in attendance, because the idea of the extreme difference between the central female character and her new surroundings was not as easily captured in this new environment. The role of the striking Mariella was played by Mavis Freeman, who was first-rate, while Judy was taken by Rosalind Fradkin, David was played by Edward Kreisler, Leon Forbes was Henry, and Tom Grace was Micky.

SHOEMAKER'S PRODIGIOUS WIFE, THE (*La Zapatera Prodigiosa*) and **"THE STRONGER"** (***Den Starkare***) P: Studio-7; T: Provincetown Playhouse (OB); 6/14/49
The Shoemaker's Prodigious Wife [Comedy/Marriage/Show Business/Spanish] A: Federico García Lorca; D: John Stix; CH: Shirley Broughton; S: Eldon Elder; C:

Eileen Holding; "The Stronger" [Dramatic Revival/One-Act] A: August Strindberg; D: William Myers

Studio-7 was a new Off-Broadway group formed by recent Yale students. They planned "to competently present plays of critical and literary interest that conscientious theatregoers may not be able to see through regular commercial channels." Their first program held true to these convictions, providing the first New York showings of Lorca's short 1930 Spanish farce and Strindberg's 1889 three-character study.

"The Stronger," written for an intimate theatre Strindberg sought to found in Copenhagen, was the curtain raiser. Actually a monologue, it reveals two actresses, Madame X (Lila Paris) and Madame Y (Eleanor Tullman), who meet in a tea room. (A third character is the waiter [Dale Mendell].) As Madame X chatters away, commiserating with her unmarried companion for her lonely life, she comes to realize that Madame Y was once her husband's mistress and is the inspiration of his current interests in food and fashion. Madame Y also has had an effect on her own behavior toward her husband. Madame X slowly comes to the conclusion that Madame Y is a shallow, unbendingly proud, and spiteful person, and that her silence stems from stupidity and not from deeper reasons. She thereupon realizes that she, Madame X, is much the stronger of the two.

The piece is designed as a tour de force for Madame X, but also gives Madame Y many interesting opportunities for silently expressive acting. Critical enthusiasm for the play was muted. William Hawkins (*NYWT*) liked the acting, but thought that "it is too pat a piece of work to be very moving." Richard Watts, Jr. (*NYP*), called it "a reasonably dull sketch."

The commedia-like Lorca farce is about an introverted fifty-three-year-old shoemaker (Charles Kleinpeter) whose lovely, extroverted eighteen-year-old wife, (Brenda Ericson) turns out to be a virago who ruefully reminds him of his inadequacy as a spouse and of the many other men she turned down to marry him. Unable to take it any longer, he leaves her, but eventually returns, having become a goateed puppeteer. To his surprise, he finds that the local men are fighting over his wife but that she really loves only him and has been mourning his absence all the time. A highlight of the piece was its puppet show with live actors (Shirley Broughton, Dale Sehnert, and Ray Malon) as the puppets.

"Director John Styx [*sic*] handles the simple story with taste, imagination and verve," reported Barnard Rubin (*DW*), who also liked Eldon Elder's "charming little sets." But Watts found the work "slightly unexhilarating. Two acts of stylized Iberian whimsy are . . . a little hard to take, unless brightened by considerably more style, humor and invention than were" present in this presentation. The company included William Myers, Richard Tashman, Boris Sagal, Clint Atkinson, and, as the shoemaker's apprentice, future critic, educator, and director Robert Brustein.

SHOP AT SLY CORNER, THE [Drama/British/Crime/Family] A: Edward Percy (Smith); D: Margaret Perry; DS: Willis Knighton; P: Gant Gaither; T: Booth Theatre; 1/18/49 (7)

A flubbed attempt at a chilling melodrama, with Boris Karloff in the leading role. Rowland Field (*NEN*) termed it "a decidedly weak and unexciting dish of tea. . . . It is little more than a routine potboiler that rarely ever reaches more than a polite simmer." But Thomas R. Dash (*WWD*) opined that while it was "of the mechanical and synthetic school of contrived melodrama, it is a good one for this category." In London the piece had run two years. An earlier American version, called *Play with Fire*, had played out of town in 1941 with Henry Hull but had been abandoned.

Karloff played Decius Heiss, French-accented former inmate of Devil's Island, who is operating a London antique shop as a respectable front for his fencing business. He melts down the stolen jewels he fences in a secret furnace behind his fireplace. These carryings on become clear to Archie Fellowes (Jay Robinson), an effeminate employee who subsequently blackmails his boss for sums that allow him to become a regular dandy. When Archie plans to marry Heiss's daughter Margaret (Mary McLeod), Heiss murders him. A police inspector (Reginald Mason) begins to investigate the murder, and Heiss, thinking that the detective is on to him, commits suicide by poisoning, only to learn as he lies dying that the man's interest was in a suit of armor and not in Heiss after all.

The cast included Ethel Griffies as Heiss's nervous sister, Una O'Connor as a comic maid, Emmett Rogers as a thief, and Philip Saville as the juvenile. The director, making her debut, was the daughter of director Antoinette Perry. "She has discharged her assignment creditably and succeeded in distilling a mood of ominous eventualities," wrote Dash.

(1) SHOW BOAT [Musical Revival*] B/LY/P: Oscar Hammerstein II; M: Jerome Kern; D: Hassard Short and Oscar Hammerstein II; CH: Helen Tamiris; S: Howard Bay; C: Lucinda Ballard; L: Hassard Short; T: Ziegfeld Theatre; 1/5/46 (418)

A rousingly successful revival of the 1927 show, not seen on Broadway since 1932, and now presented in its original theatre. The new version included Ralph Dumke as Captain Andy, Carol Bruce as Julie, Jan Clayton as Magnolia and Kim, Charles Fredericks as Gaylord Ravenal, Ethel Owen as Parthy Ann Hawks, Kenneth Spencer as Joe, Buddy Ebsen as Frank, Colette Lyons as Ellie, Pearl Primus in several minor roles, Talley Beatty as Bora, Frank Mahoney in his original role of Rubber Face, and Max Showalter as Jake.

For George Jean Nathan (*TBY*) the show surpassed any musical then running on Broadway in the quality of its book, music, lyrics, and production values. "It is a lovely, insinuating, honestly romantic, and uncommonly tuneful show," he rhapsodized. "*Show Boat*," rejoiced Richard Watts, Jr. (*SR* [he was sitting in for John Mason Brown]), "is just as enchanting as memory has made it; in fact, if anything, it is even a more sturdy dramatic structure than I had remembered." He also thought the production as good as, if not better than, the original. Ward Morehouse (*NYS*), however, was one of those who had minor equivocations, such as that the piece occasionally seemed labored and pat.

If any performer could be said to have stood out more than others, it was Carol Bruce in the role immortalized by Helen Morgan. Her brilliant acting and singing of Julie's classic songs quickly erased Morgan's memory and gained acclaim on their own terms. Watts noted, "She possesses a grave, romantic loveliness which gives her a physical advantage over her predecessor that is not to be overlooked in such a role. . . . She captures a deeply moving and completely credible mood of lyric sadness in her playing as well as in her singing."

Jan Clayton was superb as Magnolia, and was given a new Kern song, "Nobody Else But Me," that proved, however, to be less effective than those in the 1927 score. Not quite up to the original cast were Dumke and Owen in roles created by Charles Winninger and Edna May Oliver. The long-run production grossed the hefty sum of $3,500,000, but was so expensive to operate that barely any profit remained.

(2) [Return Engagement] P: Richard Rodgers and Oscar Hammerstein II; T: City Center of Music and Drama; 9/7/48 (15)

A two-week engagement at popular prices of the same production as the previous entry (which had been on a major tour), but with a largely new cast. It was produced preparatory to another tour. One of the cast members, Sammy White, who played Frank, had been in the original 1927 show. Carol Bruce was back as Julie, but William C. Smith was Joe, Clare Alden was Ellie, Fred Brookins was Steve, Gerald Prosk was Pete, Helen Dowdy was Queenie, Ruth Gates was Parthy Ann Hawks, Billy House was Captain Andy, Gordon Alexander was Rubber Face, Norwood Smith was Gaylord, and Pamela Caveness was Magnolia. The most noted dancer was La Verne French, who played Sam.

The producers treated the "revival with care and respect," announced Bron. (*V*), "and the result is a worthy production, fresh and melodious as ever."

SHOW TIME [Revue] CN/P: Fred F. Finklehoffe, Jr.; T: Broadhurst Theatre; 9/16/42 (342)

Show Time's 342 performances were a record-breaking run for a vaudeville show. One of the reasons for its success was the excellence of its company, headed by George Jessel and Jack Haley, with Ella Logan (a singer), the De Marcos (Tony and Sally, ballroom dancers), the Berry Brothers (a trio of black acrobatic dancers), Bob Williams (a comic who worked with a hilarious dog named Red Dust who balked at doing his tricks), Con Colleano (a tightrope expert), Olsen and Shirley (a youthful acrobatic dance team), and Lucille Norman (a beautiful blond soprano) being the only other entertainers on the bill. A number of similar vaudeville shows were on Broadway during the war years as a suitable attraction for the many people flocking into the city in search of escapist entertainment. The show came to New York after five months in Los Angeles and San Francisco, which was one reason it seemed so polished. Jessel acted as MC. or conférencier for the program and was hailed for one of his best performances. He introduced all the other acts and also presented seven acts of his own between each of the others. He did his Czechoslovakian professor routine giving a slide lecture, one of his slides accidentally revealing a seminude woman. One reason he was appreciated was his more mellow and relaxed approach, toned down from his usual egocentric and hard-sell style. Haley had the audience in stitches with his bit about receiving a letter from the draft board; spoofs of popular songs; a sandwich-and-beer routine with Jessel in which they ate and drank while bemoaning the demise of vaudeville; and one in which he and Jessel spoke from phone booths, the former to his wife, the latter to his mother, ripping one another to shreds. Logan (billed as "the Glasgow grenade") scored with her various songs, especially "Strip Polka," "Something I Dreamed Last Night," "Tipperary," and "You Take the High Note and I'll Take the Low Note" (shared with Haley).

Good taste, a small and expertly selected company, and quality material were among the reasons this show clicked. Some would have liked the material pruned somewhat, as the evening tended now and then to drag, but, on the whole, it was "varied, funny and reminiscent," as Howard Barnes (*NYHT*) wrote. John Mason Brown (*NYWT*) declared, "It is a good, warm, intimate and entertaining program, friendly in its feeling, gay in its spirit, and professional in its execution."

SHOW-OFF, THE [Dramatic Revival*] A: George Kelly; D: Martin Manulis; DS: Beulah Frankel; P: David Heilweil and Derrick Lynn-Thomas; T: Arena (Edison Hotel); 5/31/50 (6)

Arena staging was very much in the air in the forties, which saw it established in various regional theatres, most notably in Seattle, Washington, and Dallas, Texas. It had been tried in New York in both the 1930s and 1940s in tiny venues of the type later to be familiar in the world of Off-Off Broadway; its first commercial use came on 5/3/50, just a month before the present venture opened, at a Lower East Side garage showing a play called *John Brown*. *The Show-Off*, however, was located on Broadway in the converted ballroom of the Edison Hotel (which was quiet because of the dearth of banquets in the summer months), where it was provided with 500 seats. The critics considered it the first Broadway production using this stage format. Soon others, at the Arena as well as elsewhere, but principally Off Broadway, would be offered, so it is fitting for the last production of the 1940-1950 decade to have been in such a then-unconventional arrangement.

Brooks Atkinson (*NYT*) described the way the play looked: "The stage is a low platform [about 14' x 18' and about 5" off the floor] in the center of a large room, and banks of seats surround it. There is no scenery, but there are the necessary props to indicate the living room of a commonplace house in North Philadelphia. The lighting comes from above. About thirty seconds after the play has begun, arena or central staging seems normal, except that it is a little more familiar than proscenium staging permits." He predicted that it would soon catch on. But Howard Barnes (*NYHT*) said that there were certain drawbacks: "It has a . . . merry-go-round effect that is definitely wearing on the neck muscles as actors troop down the aisles onto the stage and move around rather arbitrarily to allow the customers grouped around them to view the nuances of particular passages." He declared that *The Show-Off*, which he liked, was not the perfect choice for the experiment. But John Chapman (*NYDN*) wrote that "no better choice could have been made."

Kelly's 1924 play, about an incorrigible braggart, had last been seen in two

1930s productions, the second one (1937) Off Broadway with an all-black cast. Most reviewers were rather positive about the present revival, but to Atkinson, it seemed dated. Some of it, he indicated, came fitfully to life, but the satirical points of the 1920s had been blunted. Yet others praised the play and said that it was as fresh as ever. Barnes observed, "Kelly's work retains heart, flavor and humor, with or without a proscenium and curtain." Chapman noted, "It is still a shrewd, well made and funny play, and it is recognizably human enough to be called folksy."

Many praised the direction and the performances of an expert cast. Lee Tracy, in his third flop of the season, was Aubrey Piper, Jane Seymour (whom some considered the show stealer) was Mrs. Fisher, Carmen Mathews was Clara, Frances Waller was Amy, Joseph Holland was Frank Hyland, Walter Cartwright was Mr. Fisher, Archie Smith was Joe (the role Tracy had played in the original production), Howard Wendell was Mr. Gill, and Dudley Sadler was Mr. Rogers.

"SHY AND THE LONELY, THE" (see "Hello Out There," second entry)

SHYLOCK AND HIS DAUGHTER [Drama/Business/Family/Jews/Period/Religion/Romance/Trial/Yiddish Language] A: Maurice Schwartz w/Ari Ibn-Zahav; M: Joseph Rumshinsky;SC: Ari Ibn-Zahav's novel of the same name; D: Maurice Schwartz; CH: David Lison and Selma Schneider; S: James R. Hotchkiss; P/T: Yiddish Art Theatre (OB); 9/29/47

The Yiddish Art Theatre opened its twenty-sixth season with this reinterpretation of Shakespeare's *The Merchant of Venice** aimed at correcting the widespread view of Shylock as a greedy and malicious fiend. Here Shylock (Maurice Schwartz) is treated in the most sympathetic of manners; his character is explained by an understanding of the anti-Semitic ghetto background of sixteenth-century Jews. Shylock himself is responsible for rejecting the Jew-baiting Antonio's (Gustave Berger) payment of his pound-of-flesh bond because the moneylender's religion forbids the spilling of blood. Other important revisions include having Antonio borrow money for Lorenzo (Muni Serebrov) so that the latter can elope with Jessica (Charlotte Goldstein) and having the latter commit suicide at the end to express her shame at having betrayed her father.

The retelling was based on extensive historical research by Ari Ibn-Zahav. Schwartz's adaptation of Ibn-Zahav's novel retained the essence of a number of Shakespeare's famous speeches. The comedy, however, was excised, and the work became "both grim drama and protest," according to Louis Biancolli (*NYWT*).

The novelist's program note included these words: "It should finally be emphasized that Shylock's monologues, the wonderful statements which Shakespeare placed in his mouth, can be taken as indisputable proof that had Shakespeare scrutinized closely the life of the sixteenth-century Jew in Italy, he would have given us a Shylock who could have served as eternal protest against the inquisition and persecution of Jews generally."

The result, said Richard Watts, Jr. (*NYP*), was "a moving and provocative work, one of Mr. Schwartz's most striking achievements." According to John Beaufort (*CSM*), "Schwartz plays an indomitable Shylock, a man much buffeted by the injustices of the time, who endures courageously but is finally brought down amid a storm of controversies." In able support were Dinah Halpern as Portia, Isadore Casher as Launcelot, and Edmund Zayenda as Morro (a new character).

SHYLOCK '47 [Drama/Hebrew Language/Jews/Period/Theatre] A: Peter Frye; TR: Simon Halkin; SC: William Shakespeare's play, *The Merchant of Venice**; P: Pargod Theatre; T: Juilliard School of Music (OB); 5/27/47 (8)

A new play inspired by *The Merchant of Venice* and given in Hebrew by America's only Hebrew-speaking company. It presents Shakespeare's work as a play-within-a-play as given by a troupe of Jewish actors seeking to find an appropriate means of interpreting it for a modern audience and as a means of attacking anti-Semitism. This leads to three different methods of interpreting the character of Shylock.

The critics did not comment on the work. After being shown at Juilliard, the play moved to the Master Institute Theatre (OB).

SIGNATURE [Drama/Crime/Law/Legacy/Period/Romance/Rural/Southern/Trial] A: Elizabeth McFadden; SC: Melville Davisson Post's short story, "Naboth's Vineyard"; D/L: Roy Hargrave; S: Stewart Chaney; P: Richard Skinner and Dorothy Willard; T: Forrest Theatre; 2/14/45 (2)

Lost somewhere in the large number of actors (twenty-eight) who were turned out after two showings of this "most tedious" (Rowland Field [*NEN*]) psychological melodrama was young Anne Jackson, making her Broadway bow in the role of Alice Steuart, who figures prominently in the action.

Based on a 1912 short story, it tells of a violent homicide in the hills of Virginia in 1856. A hired hand named William Taylor (Bob Stevenson) is accused of the crime, but his girlfriend Alice (whose poor parents had forced her to become engaged to the wealthy victim), tries to protect him by claiming to have done the deed herself. The idealistic young attorney John Cartwright (Donald Murphy) does not believe either of them guilty and determines that the responsible party is actually Simon Kilrail, the circuit-court judge (Frederic Tozere) himself. The murder was committed so that the greedy judge could inherit his cousin's fortune. Cartwright then spends a good deal of time contriving a method of nailing the jurist within the unique constraints of Virginia law, which allows the judge to get around any attempt to indict him by holding the defense in contempt of court. To overrule the law, the town's voters, who elected Kilrail, vote to remove his legal power.

Since the guilt of the judge is made clear in the first act, and the rest of the characters know of it in the second, the third was completely lacking in suspense or surprise. Numerous atmospheric sound effects (katydids, wind, spiritual singing, mobs, shutters banging, dogs baying, and the like) were used, but none of the actors used Southern accents; moreover, their characters were inordinately dull. "The drama just couldn't shoulder its way through," grumbled John Chapman (*NYDN*). "It was set upon by too many things, including the author." Nevertheless, the play was interesting, if only in part, to a small number of reviewers. One was Rosamond Gilder (*TAM*), who thought the scene of the voters rising one by one to be counted "was extraordinarily dramatic and effective." Roles were taken by Judson Laire, John McKee, George Lessey, Nell Harrison, Lyster Chambers, Charles Francis, Marjorie Lord, Gregory Robins, and Bruce Halsey.

SILVER TASSIE, THE [Dramatic Revival*] A: Sean O'Casey; D: Al Saxe; S: David Berman; P: Interplayers; T: Carnegie Recital Hall (OB); 7/21/49

O'Casey's bitter, once-controversial antiwar drama had received its first New York showing in 1929. This low-budget, tiny-stage showing was its first local revival. Harry, the soldier who returns a cripple, was played by future star Jack (formerly Walter) Palance, with Gene Dow as Simon Norton and Henri Beckman as Sylvester Heegan. Jessie was played by Anne Meara, the future comic star, in her first local role, and Susie by Nancy Stiber. Others in the cast included Anna Berger, Else Fried, Ben M. Hammer, Stefan Gierasch, John Denny, and Louis Criss.

Critics such as William Hawkins (*NYWT*) and Richard Watts, Jr. (*NYP*), expressed admiration for the still-relevant drama, its poetic language, and its characterizations, but had reservations about the overall quality of the direction and the acting of the fledgling troupe. The company had great difficulty expressing the play's mercurial shifts of mood. Hobe. (*V*) noted that "despite an uneven performance it provides interesting and provocative theatre." But Robert Garland (*NYJA*) dismissed the piece as "a mediocre and muddled play." Hawkins said that Palance "has a fresh intensity and frustrated dynamism that gives the performance a keel."

SILVER WHISTLE, THE [Comedy/Gambling/Old Age/Religion/Romance/Sex] A: Robert E. McEnroe; D: Paul Crabtree; S/L: Herbert Brodkin; C: Ernest Schrapps; P: Theatre Guild; T: Biltmore Theatre; 11/24/48 (219)

José Ferrer scored a hit in this picaresque comedy with his brilliant portrayal of the flamboyant Oliver Erwenter, a moonstruck, Omar Khayyam-quoting tramp who carries about a cage with a fighting cock named Omar. Oliver cons his way into an old folks' home by using a found birth certificate and claiming to be seventy-seven years old; he proceeds so to charm the depressed residents with his fanciful stories that--aided as well by his bogus youth-restoring potions--they begin to shed their troubles and become rejuvenated. He also engages in a romance with Miss Tripp (Eleanor Wilson), the fiancée of the stuffy rector (Robert Carroll) in the adjoining church, but is eventually exposed by a friend (George Mathews) as a fake. However, he has helped the rector to become a more relaxed and pleasant person. The rector gains back Miss Tripp and persuades the bishop (Lawrence Fletcher) to allow the oldsters--who discover that they do not need Oliver to maintain their new vigor--to raise money for the home by holding a bazaar at which games of chance will be played.

Robert Coleman (*NYDM*) approved the whimsical play by labeling it "a rewarding, literate and heartwarming comedy hit." Richard Watts, Jr. (*NYP*), described it as "an amusing, disarming and oddly endearing little comedy."

Among those portraying the codgers were Doro Merande as a cynical old lady, William Lynn as an eternal Casanova, Frances Brandt as a constantly tippling senior citizen, Kathleen Comegys as a man-chasing geriatric, Jane Marbury, and Burton Mallory. Ferrer's reviews were outstanding. Watts said, "He brings to it such style, grace, humor, spirit and imagination that his performance becomes one of the really notable characterizations of the recent theatre." Brooks Atkinson (*NYT*) opined that "Mr. Ferrer is the most able, the most stimulating, and the most versatile actor of his generation in America."

Ferrer first had played the role in the tryout given the play--when it was called *Oliver Erwenter*--at the Westport Country Playhouse. Its author was a research worker at a United Aircraft plant when he wrote the play, his eleventh but his first to be produced. When he accepted the suggestion to change the title to *The Silver Whistle*, an item not among the props in the action, he added a couplet for Erwenter to justify the new name: "The old dog crawled away to die and hid among the thistle / Then joy and youth came back to him on the note of a silver whistle." The name Erwenter was chosen because the author, being a lefty, found it easy to type with his left hand.

SIM SALA BIM [Miscellaneous] T: Morosco Theatre; 9/9/40 (54)

A spectacular magic show (its title means "thanks to you" in Danish), billed as a "Mystery Spectacle" and starring the Danish-American illusionist Dante Harry A. Jansen, who was described by Lewis Nichols (*NYT*) as looking "like a combination of Mephistopheles and Monte Woolley, as though the magician himself had put the pair of them into separate trunks and then got tangled up somehow in getting them out." He was assisted by the pretty Moi Yo Miller.

Dante, who had been touring Europe with his thirty-five member cast, but who had had to leave because of the dangerous international situation, put on a wonderful show, much of it reminiscent of when he played in vaudeville as the Great Dante. Throughout the evening, a considerable amount of humor was inserted in the acts. A number of tricks involved the participation of audience members, who loaned the magician various personal possessions for his use. Dante's many illusions--some of them rather ordinary, others quite original--included his portrayal of a barber shaving a customer and then somehow transforming himself into the customer at the end of the routine. At other times he showed performers in a balloon on stage, only for them in a twinkling to be seen running down the aisle from the rear of the house. Similarly, a girl in a cage disappeared, only to be shown descending in a hermetically sealed box from the top of the theatre. Many were startled when he borrowed several rings from women in the house and then revealed them tied tightly to roses inside a series of locked boxes. A real puzzler was Dante's strapping a pair of transparent glass panes together with rubber bands; when he fired a revolver there immediately appeared between the panes the precise playing card called out by a spectator.

Herrick Brown (*NYS*) commented, "The fun got better and better the longer it ran and at the close he [Dante] had his audience alternating chuckles at his quips with gasps of amazement at the climax of his tricks." Several famous personalities present at the opening night were willing participants in the onstage activities, among them Milton Berle.

SIMON'S WIFE [Drama/Bible/Marriage/Period/Religion] A: Father Francis D. Alwaise; D: Dennis Gurney; S: Thomas Keary; P: Blackfriars' Guild; T: Blackfriars' Theatre (OB); 3/8/45 (15)

A Lenten play by a Dominican priest. It was an awkwardly written and unsatisfactory attempt. "The play is slight and its construction somewhat over-simplified," declared George Freedley (*NYMT*). "It is an uninspired, hackneyed and rather static drama," decided Burton Rascoe (*NYWT*).

It deals with the emotional and spiritual suffering of Leah (Ruth Fischer), the wife of Galilean fisherman Simon called Peter (W. Hussung) and daughter-in-law of Rachel (Helen Purcell), when he decides to leave his trade and womenfolk and follow Jesus to become leader of his apostles. The distraught Leah refuses to accept Jesus, whom she thinks an imposter, even after her own mother is miraculously cured. However, it is she, having finally come to believe in Jesus, who restores the shattered Peter's faith after the Crucifixion and inspires him to round up Jesus' disciples and carry on his teachings.

Actors in the semipro company included Joseph Boley as Judas, Wilson Brooks, James Kearney, Fran Lee, David Knight, and others.

SING BEFORE BREAKFAST [Comedy/Romance] A: Peter Levin and Warren McMurray; D: billy m. greene [*sic*]; P: Actors' Theatre; T: Provincetown Playhouse (OB); 5/24/41

"A singularly tasteless farce which was acted in tedious fashion by a semi-amateur group," was how George Freedley (*NYMT*) described this piece. Set in a Greenwich Village house, it deals with Tiny Van Dyck (David Sullivan), heir to an old American family, who keeps an eye out for girls wandering into his neighborhood. He is not attracted to Christine Holt, with whom he has grown up, but turns his attention to Viola Hopping. Viola proves a mistake, and Christine suddenly looms large in Tiny's eyes.

SING OUT, SWEET LAND! [Musical/Fantasy/Music/Period/Romance/War/Western] B: Walter Kerr; D: Leon Leonidoff and Walter Kerr; CH: Doris Humphrey and Charles Weidman; S/L: Albert Johnson; C: Lucinda Ballard; P: Theatre Guild; T: International Theatre; 12/27/44 (102)

Future critic Walter Kerr put together this thinly plotted cavalcade musical as a way of introducing numerous songs from the American past and thereby celebrating the nation's folk and popular music treasury, much of it anonymous. It was first produced at Catholic University in Washington, D.C., where Kerr was a professor of theatre.

The story of wandering minstrel Barnaby Goodlove (Alfred Drake), a sort of combined Johnny Appleseed and Paul Bunyan mad for song and dance, who wants to unite his fellow Americans through music, was merely a device via which to take the audience on a musical tour through American history, with luscious Currier and Ives-like period sets and costumes marking the stops along the way. The piece moves from Puritan to revolutionary times to the Illinois wilderness to the Oregon trail to a Mississippi show boat to a Civil War campfire to a Texas railroad station to various urban settings to a roaring twenties speakeasy to the deck of a World War II aircraft carrier. In each, Barnaby is reincarnated in the spirit of the times depicted, accompanying himself on fiddle, guitar, or accordian as appropriate. Appearing in multiple versions of the same role, the villain who would not allow music, was Philip Coolidge, while Bibi Osterwald was a romantic link to Barnaby in varying times and places.

The show was larded with the witty choreography of Humphrey and Weidman, Weidman himself dancing in "Camptown Races" when lead dancer Peter Hamilton's injury restricted the number of dances he could do. Howard Barnes (*NYHT*) reported, "Walter Kerr's dramatic scheme is obvious and not always too effective, but the show sings and struts with lusty comic vigor." Several reviewers noted the need for cutting, but nevertheless approved the overall package.

Alfred Drake moved from his role as Curly in *Oklahoma!* to the lead in this show with great success. "If ever an actor deserved starring after his work in a show it is Alfred Drake," recorded George Freedley (*NYMT*), "whose acting and singing are a joy to watch. His voice is singularly pleasing and flexible. He works in all moods and rhythms to excellent effect." Standout Drake pieces were "As I Was Going Along" (by Elie Siegmeister and Edward Eager, the former being the show's conductor and arranger), "Wanderin'," "More Than These," "The Devil and the Farmer's Wife," "Springfield Mountain," and, most especially, a recitation of Stephen Vincent Benét's "Mountain Whippoorwill."

Equally outstanding was burly folk singer and guitarist Burl Ives, who was praised for his comic sensibility, strong voice, and overall professionalism. Many thought that he stole the show with his renditions of such tunes as "Big Rock Candy Mountain," "Foggy, Foggy Dew," and "Blue Tail Fly." There also were expert renditions of "Casey Jones" by Osterwald (who also stopped the show with "When I Was Single"), and "Frankie and Johnnie" by Alma Kaye and Jack McCauley. A cast including Juanita Hall, Ellen Love, Monty Halpern, and James Westerfield, also got to do "My Blue Heaven," "I've Got Rhythm," and many others.

"There is nothing raucous or frenetic about this show," observed Burton Rascoe (*NYWT*), "it is a thing of beauty, dignity and taste, simple, homely and refreshing." Many reviews were in this laudatory vein, but for others, like Lewis Nichols (*NYT*), the show was "disappointing." Lewis believed that Kerr "has written a book that is coy, cute and--to come right out with it--often childish." He also took issue with the decision to present some of the material in a burlesque rather than a straight fashion. George Jean Nathan (*TBY*) ridiculed the show's humor, its selection of songs, and the quality of its singing and orchestra.

In its original form the show had had a feeling of simplicity and intimacy that was lost when Leon Leonidoff took it over for Broadway production and blew it up to grandiose proportions. Upset by what had happened to the show, the Theatre Guild's producers, Lawrence Langner and Theresa Helburn, called in director Elia Kazan to reshape it for New York, which he did without credit. Euphemia Van Rensselaer Wyatt (*CW*) said that Kazan "managed to bring continuity out of chaos and to disentangle some of Mr. Kerr's dialogue from the stage properties."

SISTER OAKES [Drama/Blacks/Race/Religion/Small Town/Southern] A: Nelise Child; D: Edward Ludlum; S: Ben Edwards; P: Invitational Series of the Experimental Theatre u/t/a/o the American National Theatre and Academy; T: Lenox Hill Settlement House (OB); 4/23/49 (4)

Fortunately, it cost spectators nothing to view this garrulous play that Hobe. (*V*) described as "a vehement, sprawling, prolix melodrama." It is set in a small Southern mill town and tells of Sister Oakes (Natalie Core), a young female evangelist who endeavors to bring a rational and useful type of worship to the townspeople, congregationalists at the storefront Ark of God Church, who are superstitiously involved with "the snake-bite and mumbo-jumbo school of revivalism," as J. P. S. (*NYT*) expressed it. Although she has serious obstacles to overcome, she manages to succeed in her quest. The play also explores elements of racial prejudice, with Earle Hyman and Pauline Myers playing black citizens who react with dignity to their demeaning treatment. Robert Garland (*NYJA*) said that the actors "slugged it out for three talky, tasteless acts of tiresome repetition."

SIX CHARACTERS IN SEARCH OF AN AUTHOR (Sei Personaggi in Cerca d'Autore) [Dramatic Revival*] A: Luigi Pirandello; D: Robert T. Eley; P: New York Repertory Group; T: Cherry Lane Theatre (OB); 6/10/48

The most recent revival of Pirandello's modern Italian classic had been in 1931. It was now given in a minor Off-Broadway revival that displayed an enthusiastic and promising young group of actors in their first company effort. The piece is a difficult one to stage successfully, but Robert T. Eley managed, despite occasional lapses, to make the piece work. A good many entrances and exits were made down the tiny theatre's center aisle, which tended to rob the play of some needed illusion.

"Their production is uneven," wrote John S. Wilson (*PM*), "occasionally a little self conscious, but the overall result is stimulating and frequently very effective." Robert Garland (*NYJA*) called the production "dizzy and delightful." Less enthusiastic was William Hawkins (*NYWT*), who chafed at the actors' tendency to bellow and at the excessive use of movement by some of the cast members. Still, he thought the piece "intensely interesting to watch." The father was played by Jack Burkhart, the mother by Beatrice Arthur, the stepdaughter by Eleanor Fitzpatrick, the director by Stephen Gray, the juvenile by George Scott, the son by Robert Herrell, and Madame Pace by Jean Wolcott.

SIX O'CLOCK THEATRE [One-Acts] P: Fred Stewart i/a/w Six O'Clock Theatre and the Experimental Theatre u/t/a/o the American National Theatre and Academy; T: Maxine Elliott's Theatre; 4/11/48 (8)
"Hope Is the Thing with Feathers" [Comedy-Drama] A: Richard Harrity; D: Joseph Kramm; "Celebration" [Drama/Alcoholism/Family/Southern] A: Horton Foote; D: Joseph Anthony; "Afternoon Storm" [Drama/Fantasy/Historical-Biographical/Romance] A: E. P. Conkle; D: John O'Shaughnessy

A noncommercial showing of three one-acts, one of which, "Hope Is the Thing with Feathers," would go on to be produced commercially in May 1948 with two other playlets by the same author on a program called *Hope's the Thing*. The title of the present program was chosen because of the hour at which the actors--part of a studio workshop group--found it most convenient to rehearse. The plays were done without sets, costumes, or special props. Fred Stewart acted as a narrator to explain whatever was left out by this bare-bones approach.

As demonstrated by its selection for a regular showing, "Hope Is the Thing with Feathers" was the most widely approved play. This "stunning sketch" (Brooks Atkinson [*NYT*]) told with tragicomic overtones the story of nine friendly tramps passing the cold night on a Central Park bench. They are hungry, so one of them, Doc (E. G. Marshall), comes up with three outlandish schemes for snaring ducks from the lake. His cynical buddy Sweeney (Will Geer) thinks he hasn't got a chance. Sweeney is right, for Doc never does catch the ducks but does capture a monkey from the zoo. They refuse to eat the animal and set it free. The play ends with the bums going to sleep. During the action, each of the various characters gets to provide commentary on the schemes of the would-be hunter.

The actors included Lou Gilbert as a punchy ex-pugilist, Daniel Reed as an old hymn singer who is an expert on sleeping conditions in the nation's parks, and George Mathews as a slow-witted roughneck. Harrity's play was appreciated for its indirect action and blend of pathos and humor. Richard Watts, Jr. (*NYP*), called this "a touching, imaginative and oddly charming little fable," and William Hawkins (*NYWT*) thought that "Harrity has written it with deep sympathy and great humor."

Horton Foote's contribution, "Celebration," concerns the disintegration of a Southern family as told through the depiction of three dissolute members meeting at the sordid home of elder sister Red (Hilda Vaughn), a drunk who would revive the family with sister Babe (Perry Wilson) and brother Sonny (Warren Stevens). They all get loaded, but Red's drink-fueled pretensions are punctured by a bitchy visitor, Ellen Belle (Sally Gracie), and Sonny dies from too much booze. "The play is intense and violent," decided Hawkins. "It is not satisfying because it has no comment to make on its subject."

"Afternoon Storm" was inspired by the marital problems of Abraham (John Morley) and Mary Lincoln (Helen Marcy). In 1840, on the day of their wedding in Springfield, Illinois, young Abe runs off, fearful of his coming dilemmas. Abe is urged to return, marry Mary, and face his destiny by the ghost of Ann Rutledge (Norma Chambers), on whose grave he falls in tears. Rowland Field (*NEN*) concluded that "this somewhat affected bit of Lincolniana is never made very arresting in spite of the players' best efforts."

SKIN OF OUR TEETH, THE [Comedy/Family/Fantasy/Marriage/Period/Sex/War/Youth] A: Thornton Wilder; D: Elia Kazan; S: Albert Johnson; C: Mary Percy Schenck; P: Michael Myerberg; T: Plymouth Theatre; 11/18/42 (355)

The Pulitzer Prize for drama in 1942-1943 was handed to this whimsical philosophical comedy that kicked up a critical and audience fuss (many perplexed spectators departed at the first intermission) because of its fantastical and purposely anachronistic method of telling an allegorical story. The play had been turned down by Jed Harris, director-producer of Wilder's *Our Town**, and when opera producer Michael Myerberg acquired it, he labored in vain to find someone to provide the necessary funds, going through thirty-seven potential investors without a penny in return. By the time the show had finished playing in several out-of-town cities, Myerberg had succeeded in selling only thirty percent of his investment, but he was encouraged enough by the response not to sell any more, although he could have done so very profitably. One of his strongest supporters was his star, Fredric March, who owned a five percent interest and had turned down $200,000 in film contracts so that he and his wife, Florence Eldridge, could stay with the play. Brilliantly cast and acted, memorably directed and designed, *The Skin of Our Teeth* (which was also selected as one of Burns Mantle's ten best of the year) represented one of Broadway's most distinguished moments in the 1940s.

At the heart of the play is the typical American family, the Antrobuses, Mr. George Antrobus (March), Mrs. Antrobus (Eldridge), their daughter Gladys (Frances Heflin), and their son Henry (Montgomery Clift), previously called Cain. All are clearly symbolic, the family name being based on the Greek for "man." Equally symbolic is the family maid, Sabina (Tallulah Bankhead), who represents the eternal Lillith-like seductress. Her character is also unusual in that she frequently comments caustically on the play itself directly to the audience. When she wants to quit, the stage manager (E. G. Marshall) talks her into staying. George, a sort of Everyman, is the eternal thinker, the inventor of the wheel, the alphabet, and the multiplication table (its invention makes him late for his first entrance) and a Babbitt-like mainstay in his New Jersey suburban community of Excelsior. Sabina, who first appears as a French farce maid with feather duster, is his conquest from the Sabine hills who has lost her domestic sway to Mrs. Antrobus. The first act is set in the ice age, when it is so cold that "the dogs are sticking to the sidewalks." When George finally appears (his arrival is announced by a singing telegraph boy [Dickie Van Patten] who reads his smoke signals), he discloses that the world is coming to an end because of the glaciers slipping down from Vermont. The dinosaur (Remo Bufano) and the mammoth (Andrew Ratousheff), the family pets, must be permitted to become extinct. He gives shelter at the fire to a group of shabby people, including a judge named Moses (Joseph Smiley); the blind Homer (Ralph Cullinan); and the three Muses (Edith Faversham, Emily Lorraine, and Eva Mudge Nelson). Henry, who previously killed his brother, kills someone else, angering his disillusioned father, but bringing out his mother's protective instincts. The audience is asked to pass up their chairs to provide fuel for restarting the fire (and thereby saving humanity) the angry George has put out. The action shifts for act two to Atlantic City where George is to present a speech on the occasion of his election to as president of the Ancient and Honorable Order of Mammals, Subdivision Humans, a group depicted as a bunch of Shriner-like conventioneers. (The convention is their six hundred thousandth, and the Antrobuses are celebrating wedding anniversary number five thousand.) Sabina, who has been selected bathing-beauty queen, tries to woo George to give up his wife and marry her instead. He agrees. Meanwhile, the children are up to no good, Gladys flaunting her sex appeal in red stockings and Cain--his forehead marked--stoning a black boy. But Mrs. Antrobus convinces George not to leave, and the family reunites to enter the ark for protection from the Deluge, their safety proclaimed by a boardwalk fortune teller (Florence Reed). In act three the world's population has been decimated by war, although the Antrobuses are still around and Sabina is dressed as a camp follower from Napoleonic times (she later appears with the feather duster she used in the beginning). After a self-consciously theatrical interruption concerning a procession of philosophers, the action reveals a Hitler-like Henry who is now a major figure for the enemy and is prepared to kill his father. They argue, both as characters in the play and as actors playing their parts. Sabina turns in her hoarded beef cubes, and the once-more disillusioned Antrobus begins again to find a purpose in life, despite the struggle it entails. The play ends in a deliberately ambiguous way, suggesting that mankind will go on and on, as Sabina speaks the closing lines to the audience and wishes them a good night.

Wilder's theme was easier to assimilate than his unconventional dramatic technique, which owed much to James Joyce's *Finnegan's Wake*, among other stylistic influences, including expressionism and epic theatre. It was, as John Anderson (*NYJA*) contended, "that humanity is as indestructible as its hopes, that from the glacial age up to right now, from the invention of the wheel to the perfection of high altitude bombing, man is forever improving himself and eternally falling in ruins, forever building and tearing down, but that somehow, through hell, high water, and, as the playbill says 'double feature movies,' he manages to survive." This panorama of mankind clinging to survival by "the skin of its teeth" from prehistory to 1942 mingles the ice age with the present, dinosaurs with contemporary folk, and figures from the Bible with Atlantic City bathing beauties. It is at one moment serious and at another farcical, sometimes down-to-earth and other times eloquent. It is funny and wise, challenging and accessible. Much of its fun comes from its awareness of its own existence as a play, with scenic practices that draw attention to themselves, characters who miss cues, and others who employ direct address while seemingly talking in the actor's own persona.

Even those critics who were confused recommended the play as a tour de force theatrical exercise that should not be missed. George Freedley (*NYMT*), for example, insisted that the play "is mad, profound, comic, tender, serious and completely baffling. The author's inventiveness puts William Saroyan to shame. It is certainly my idea of a perfect piece of theater." "On the whole," said Howard Barnes (*NYHT*), "it is a tremendously exciting and profound stage fable, which could only have attained its luminous expression in the theater." Among the play's drawbacks were mentioned its frequent superficiality, its failure to touch any deep feelings to contrast with its cosmic humor, and its often-distracting gimmickry. Most critics were willing to ignore such flaws, but George Jean Nathan (*TBY*) attacked the play with gusto. He dismissed Wilder as "a talented dilettante" and called the play embarrassingly arch. It was, he declared, little more than pure surface effect, very much like an imitation gold charm bracelet: "It is pretty and cute, but it isn't the real article, and its novelty very quickly wears off."

Although every principal gave an indelible performance, it was Bankhead's that attracted the most attention, and there were those who lost interest when she was not on. Lewis Nichols (*TAM*) wrote, "Miss Bankhead is magnificent--breezy, hard, practical by turns. She can strut and posture in broad comedy, she can be calmly serene."

There are many stories about the trouble caused during the production process by Bankhead. The following is drawn from Elia Kazan's autobiography, *Elia Kazan*. "I've hated only two people in my life," wrote the director. "One was Tallulah Bankhead." Nevertheless, it was his experiences with this tempestuous actress, he admitted, that taught him that a director, when all other diplomatic methods fail, must be as forceful as possible to get his way.

Bankhead seemed from the start of the production to want Kazan fired. She did whatever she could to further this desire, including making life miserable for her more lady-like costar, Eldridge, who warned Kazan to be on his "guard against 'that bitch.'" Kazan, however, thought that the tension generated between the two actresses was good for the production and, at first, did nothing to ameliorate the situation. Then, one day, Kazan was called to Bankhead's apartment by the producer. Bankhead declared that she was unhappy with the way she was being directed because she was asked to be part of an ensemble rather than being handled as a "star." Things like having other actors cross in front of her drove her crazy.

Thereafter, the battle was on, with Kazan stubbornly but patiently sticking to his ways and Bankhead walking out of rehearsals when she was displeased. She was especially miffed about the stylized set, which had no masking between the Antrobus house and the wings and required her to be seen before her character actually entered. She threw a fit before the out-of-town dress rehearsal and continued to loudly condemn everything about the production even when offstage during the performance. She also acted very rudely to her fellow players. After the dress, at three in the morning, with the company gone and the crew waiting on stage for instructions, Bankhead started to leave, saw Kazan, and lashed out viciously at him for not siding with her about the sets. "It was then that I became a director," Kazan writes. In front of everyone, including the ailing producer, he shouted her down, telling her "at the top of my voice and in the crudest language, how shamefully she'd behaved. I told her that I despised her and that everybody else did too. . . . I told her I wasn't going to stand for any more shit from her." His vituperation followed Bankhead as she made her way up the aisle and out of the theatre. The crew then burst into applause.

Thereafter, Kazan was the boss. He and the star did not speak to one another, except for his delivery of "mechanical instructions." However, not long after, Bankhead tried to make up with Kazan and came knocking at his hotel door after a performance. She entered and immediately dropped her skirt ("She never wore underpants," observed Kazan) and removed her sweater. She dashed for his bed, but was brought up short when she saw another woman there. "Tallulah looked at me with a terrible fury, growled like an animal, pulled on her clothes, and left."

SKIPPER NEXT TO GOD [Drama/Dutch/Jews/Politics/Religion/Sea] A: Jan de Hartog; D: Lee Strasberg; S: Boris Aronson; P: Experimental Theatre u/t/a/o the American National Theatre and Academy; T: Maxine Elliott's Theatre; 1/4/48 (6)

Dutch writer Jan de Hartog's second offering to reach Broadway was this "very fine and moving play" (Euphemia Van Rensselaer Wyatt [*CW*]) selected as one of the ten best of the season. It first was given in a noncommercial mounting that aroused enough interest for it to receive a commercial mounting at the Playhouse that opened 3/27/48 and ran for 93 performances before being closed because its star, John Garfield, had a film commitment. Author de Hartog had played the Garfield role in the play's London debut in 1945.

The leading role was Joris Kuiper, Dutch shipowner-captain of *The Young Nelly*, a tramp steamer that, in 1938, is transporting to South America a cargo of 146 Jewish refugees fleeing Hitler's terror. When he reaches port, the country decides to close its doors to the unfortunate group, and the Dutch consul (Wallace Acton) advises Kuiper to take them back to where they came from, as no one in South America will accept them. Instead, the skipper, a Christian who recently has found God, heads for Long Island with the hope that public pressure will open America to his passengers. Three times he tries to land his cargo on a beach, and three times he is rejected by the U.S Navy (Brooks Atkinson [*NYT*] suggested that it should have been the Coast Guard), which even warns that it will fire on the ship if he should try again. Meanwhile, the Jews are becoming ever more frustrated. Kuiper's native government threatens to rescind his sailing papers and commands him to leave immediately, for he is in the path of an American yacht regatta. Mutiny from the crew is in the offing, and the desperate passengers begin to commit suicide. He asks his wife by wireless what he should do, and she wires back a biblical quote, "Matthew x.37," which is "he that loveth son or daughter more than me is not worthy of Me." He places the Jews in boats, radios an SOS, decides to put his faith in God and his resolute spouse, and scuttles *The Young Nelly*. He has faith that the Jews will be rescued by the regatta and allowed to enter America.

Those who liked the play appreciated it for its depiction of the skipper's moral and religious confusion and its presentation of a strong conflict between human charity and strict legality. Almost all the positive notices, however, were mingled with reservations. George Freedley (*NYMT*) liked the play but blamed director Strasberg for making foolish cuts that made the development of the script (available in published form) cloudy. Still, he said, it was "theatrically exciting because of the dramatic and timely nature of the play." Richard Watts, Jr. (*NYP*), claimed that it was "at once provocative, arresting and disappointing." While imaginative and morally fervent, it failed "exasperatingly to approach the promise of its theme in thought or emotion." Atkinson was disturbed principally by the dramatist's decision to spare the audience the suffering of the Jews by reporting it rather than showing it. "This gives his play a studious rather than human impact." George Jean Nathan (*TBY*) disliked the play, demeaning its melodramatic conclusion and declaring that the playwright had lost "whatever may have been dramatic in the [central] idea in enough windy argument and . . . Biblical quotations to have driven the late Billy Sunday to a rest cure."

Garfield headed an all-male cast in which John Shellie was the engineer, Joseph Anthony the ship's doctor, Robert White a dishonest messboy, Wolfe Barzell a rabbi, Eugene Stuckmann a Dutch naval attaché, and Harry Irvine a clergyman. Also involved were Simon Oakland, John Becher, Peter Kass, Jabez Gray, Richard Coogan, and Nola Chilton, among others.

Garfield's acting was appreciated for its emotionality and physical vigor, but he was found wanting in certain scenes requiring the demonstration of the character's psychological quagmire. Some thought his overall performance wanting, and others blamed his fuzzily written role.

SKYDRIFT [Drama/Aviation/Death/Fantasy/Military/War] A: Harry Kleiner; D/L: Roy Hargrave; S/C: Motley; P: Rita Hassan; T: Belasco Theatre; 11/13/45 (7)

One of the few notable facts about this clichéd drama was that it marked the debut of Eli Wallach, who played the crew chief of a company of seven paratroopers killed while flying a mission over Japanese-held territory in the Pacific. The play's first part reveals the very realistically created interior of their carrier plane. Each is then given the opportunity for a last visit with his grief-stricken loved ones, ranging from a wife to a team mascot to parents. The only one whose return is of a nonsentimental nature is the crew chief, who decides to haunt his widow for her suspected adultery (although she is innocent). The living are advised that they must go on with their lives in order to serve the memory of those who have died.

The scenic effects were memorable, especially the plane's interior and the suggestion of the battle that brought it down. From a first act done in very realistic style, the production had to move to a more highly stylized method. However, "For all its good intentions," wrote Rosamond Gilder (*TAM*), "it turned out to be in the end more an adventure in scene shifting than an illumination of the hereafter." "It is long, unbelievable, unmoving, talky," noted Lewis Nichols (*NYT*).

Among the good performances were those by Alfred Ryder and Olive Deering (real-life brother and sister). Also involved were Arthur Keegan, William Chambers, Elliott Sullivan, Zachary A. Charles, Paul Crabtree, Sid Martoff, Carl Specht, Marty Miller, Wolfe Barzell, Lili Valenty, and others. Among the various earlier plays of which it reminded critics, *The Wind Is Ninety* was the most commonly mentioned.

SLEEP, MY PRETTY ONE [Drama/Crime/Family/Mental Illness/Romance] A: Charlie and Oliver Garrett; D: Roy Hargrave; S: Raymond Sovey; P: Richard W. Krakeur i/a/w Roger Clark; T: Playhouse; 11/2/44 (12)

Any new play starring veteran actress Pauline Lord raised critical expectations, but this talky example of the silver-cord theme, like too many of Lord's vehicles in the recent past, was "without the slightest critical merit," according to George Jean Nathan (*TBY*). The audience seemed to take the advice of the title too literally, as it was a soporific picture of a smothering, homicidal mother that failed overwhelmingly in its attempt to raise goose pimples. Rowland Field (*NEN*) called it "the drowsiest drama to be perpetrated hereabouts in many a moon."

Ever since she lost her husband on the *Titanic*, the elderly Alicia Sturdevant (Lord) has not been all there in the mental department; she also has been confined ever since to a wheelchair. This pathologically possessive mother resides in comfortable Gramercy Park surroundings. She has on two previous occasions prevented her middle-aged Milquetoast son Donald (Harry Ellerbe) from marrying someone; one fiancée was frightened off by the mother's horrific stories, the other was pushed out of an upstairs window. For the third time, Donald gets engaged, this time to Winifred Agate (Julie Stevens), and Alicia decides to again cut off the relationship. After a considerable amount of verbal delay and failed attempts to create sexual suspicion of the lady and then to poison her, Alicia attempts to push Winifred out of the same window she has used similarly before. When her plan is foiled and the frightened fiancée takes a powder with the young naval officer (Don Gibson) who also loves her, Alicia herself drinks the poison she prepared and dies happy, knowing that the son will not get married.

Lord's role was unpleasant and unconvincing. Little had been done to provide her with effective motivations for her evil behavior, and she could do little to make the part interesting. The critics gave her an awful hiding for her muddled work. The play itself lacked action, had boring characters, and, said Robert Garland (*NYJA*) was "sorry stuff, recited in language that is not believable." The cast included J. Colville Dunn, Norma Chambers, Theresa Dale, Audrey Ridgewell, and Ivan Simpson.

SLEEP NO MORE [Comedy/Business/Crime/Romance/Science/Sex] A: Lee Loeb and Arthur Strawn; D: Cledge Roberts; S: A. A. Ostrander; T: Clyde Elliott; P: Cort Theatre; 8/31/44 (7)

The Hollywood scriptwriters who wrote this tired farce could not keep audiences awake despite the breakneck pace at which it was played. The play was jam-packed with familiar gags, many of them sexually suggestive. Rowland Field (*NEN*) called it "a rather laborious exaggeration that harks back to stage patterns of yesteryear."

H. Clifford Gates (Robert Armstrong) is a shady promoter who tries to market phony inventions, such as an electric hair-growing machine he demonstrates to a trio of barbers (Raymond Bramley, John "Skins" Miller, and John Kane) in act one. A woman who invested money with the promoter in a machine that washes and irons in one operation demands her money back. Just before he lands in the clutches of the law, there comes to him William Jennings Brown (George Offerman, Jr.), an Indiana druggist who has invented a pill that kills sleep and allows people to keep active twenty-four hours a day without ill effects. The larcenous Gates and the trio of barbers form a company to promote the product, and it looks like they have struck it rich. Brown gets married to his sweetheart (Patricia Ryan) and wants to go off on his honeymoon, but must first prove the efficacy of the formula. He thereupon takes the pill for six days and gets no sleep at all. A mattress manufacturer (Ed Latimer) wants to buy the formula for big bucks to prevent his business from disappearing. Right in the middle of the sale, Brown nods off and cannot be aroused. He later learns that the reason he has not been getting any sleep is because of punctured eardrums. Brown provides his own money to the promoters to pay back swindled investors in order to beat a mail-fraud charge. The pills, however, turn out to be good for dogs with worms, and Brown earns $25,000. This cash, however, is diverted into yet another invention.

"*Sleep No More* has a central situation which inspires laughter, but it has been treated in a yawning manner," sighed Howard Barnes (*NYHT*). Louise Larabee, Len Hollister, G. Swayne Gordon, Doris Underwood, Gerald Martin, and Horace Cooper were in the flop.

SLEEPY HOLLOW [Musical/Period/Romance] B/LY: Russell Maloney and Miriam Battista; M: George Lessner; SC: Washington Irving's story, "The Legend of Sleepy Hollow"; D: John O'Shaughnessy and Marc Connelly; CH: Anna Sokolow; S/L: Jo Mielziner; C: David Ffolkes; P: Lorraine Lester; T: St. James Theatre; 6/3/48 (12)

The yawning critics had a field day relating the title of this musical to its soporific influence on them. George Freedley (*NYMT*) attacked the "insipid lyrics," "banal book," "uninteresting dances," and so on. William Hawkins (*NYWT*) dubbed it "a tedious, dragged out production with no visible distinction. It had the air of having been written and restaged yesterday afternoon." The work was found devoid of comedy, good songs, or appropriate Dutch-American atmosphere.

This is the story of Sleepy Hollow's (near Tarrytown, New York) timid, lanky schoolmaster Ichabod Crane (Gil Lamb) and the Headless Horseman, beloved of generations of children. As adapted here, the practical joke to have Ichabod driven out of town by someone impersonating the Headless Horseman of local legend is the brainstorm of Katrina Van Tassel (Betty Jane Watson), who became his betrothed in a moment of pique at her true love, Brom "Bones" Van Brunt (Hayes Gordon) and has to find a means to break her engagement.

The hapless Ichabod proved a poor choice for a hero, as he is little more than a worm who does not turn. Critics also were not thrilled that the frightening ride of the Headless Horseman was carried out as a ballet. "Somehow the idea of a musical comedy hero being put to flight by a pirouette had an ominous and symbolic ring to it," thought Richard Watts, Jr. (*NYP*). Among the performers enjoyed by the critics were Mary McCarty, Dorothy Bird, Kate Friedlich, James Starbuck, and Ward Garner.

SLICE IT THIN! [Comedy/Family/Journalism/Military/Small Town/Theatre/Youth] A: Lieutenant Edward Heghinian; M/LY: Al Moritz; D: Dennis Gurney; S/C: Jerry Boxhorn; P: Blackfriars' Guild; T: Blackfriars' Theatre (OB); 5/10/45 (12)

The final offering of the semiprofessional Blackfriars' 1944-1945 season was a feeble farce by an officer in the naval reserve; it included five unmusical songs.

"Herman" Coleman (Joan Field) has two children, a son (Neal Miller) who writes songs and a daughter (Miriam Craig) who wants to be an actress and is about to perform in her college play. Mrs. Coleman invites an old boyfriend, James Waverly (Wilson Brooks), now a hammy Hollywood actor, with the hope that he can give the girl's career a boost. Accompanying Waverly are a gossip columnist (Sudie Bond) and a photographer (Delmar Nuetzman). Various complications stemming from the presence of the film star in the small Maryland town ensue. These are exacerbated by a Russian film actress (Jean Emslie) in romantic pursuit of the actor and the daughter's sailor boyfriend (Sidney Welch), who objects to his sweetheart's interest in the star.

"It is silly, inept, badly acted, badly sung and badly staged," growled George Freedley (*NYMT*).

SLIGHTLY MARRIED [Comedy/Family/Marriage/Military/Sex/Small Town/Youth] A: Aleen Leslie; D/P: Melville Burke; S: Phil Raigeul; T: Cort Theatre; 10/25/43 (8)

After a considerable success in San Francisco (where it was called *Mother's Day*), this cliché-ridden, feverish farce lasted but a week on Broadway. Plays about enceinte young women were then coming fast and furious to the Great White Way, and this obstetrical obsession was beginning to seriously annoy the critics. Rosamond Gilder (*TAM*) claimed that the play "combined bad taste with undistinguished acting." "By and large," thought Howard Barnes (*NYHT*), "it is more frantic and biologically boisterous than it is funny."

A sexually ignorant seventeen-year-old girl named Margaret Quin (Patti Pope) and her equally cretinous nineteen-year-old soldier boyfriend, Keith Morehouse (Jimmie Smith), think that they are secretly married merely because they have signed a license application. Margaret gets pregnant, and her distraught mother, Audrey (Leona Maricle), wife of the harried Brian (Leon Ames), believes that she can deflect the neighbors' attention from her daughter's condition if she sends the girl to a grandmother's (Isabel O'Madigan) and pretends that she herself is the pregnant one; this forces her to strap a pillow to her belly to simulate the correct appearance and allows the playwright to pepper the lines with gynecological comments related to childbearing. Conditions at the Erie, Pennsylvania, home are exacerbated by the family's difficulty in hiring a maid; one of those interviewed tries to seduce Brian, and he, with his wife's approval, makes up to her in a desperate attempt not to lose her services. (This was a hit at the current difficulty of hiring domestics.) There is also the standard precocious younger brother (Scotty Beckett) with a cynical wit and a polysyllabic vocabulary. The premature birth of the baby in an upstairs room, where it is delivered by an ambulance driver (Bert Horton) using a medical book, and the AWOL father's announcement that he and Margaret are getting married bring the situation to a conclusion.

The cast included Mona Barrie and Tom Seidel.

SLIGHTLY SCANDALOUS [Comedy/Family/Literature/Marriage/Military/Music/Sex] A/D: Frederick Jackson; SC: an idea by Roland Bottomley; S: Harry Dworkin; C: Adrian; P: Charles Leonard i/a/w Thomas McQuillan; T: National Theatre; 6/13/44 (7)

An "incredibly feeble" (George Freedley [*NYMT*]) vehicle that marked the return to Broadway of once-popular actress Janet Beecher after a period of twelve years in Hollywood. It was inspired by Roland Bottomley's *Olivia Bows to Mrs. Grundy*, which had a tryout tour in 1932 but never reached Manhattan. The play originally was called *Are Fathers Necessary?* and then *Love and Learn*.

Beecher's role was that of Frances Stuart, noted novelist-lecturer, whose liberated principles prevented her from marrying but not from having children. She has three of them (Nino Pipitone, Jr., William Berens, and Anne Henderson), and two are preparing to get married. The prospective in-laws, however, demand some assurance about the children's father, presumably the man pictured in a portrait hung above the fireplace. The portrait is actually one that Frances purchased from an antique dealer and has told the children is a portrait of their father. Frances now must inform her brood that she has never wed and that each is the offspring of a different father, a French military officer (Jean de Briac), a Polish pianist and patriot (Gene Gary), and an English baronet (Boyd Davis). She agrees to marry one of the three, all of whom live in America and are still bachelors, and they are duly invited to Frances's Westchester home for the selection process. None of the fathers passes the test, and all agree to continue with the lie about the man in the portrait being the late Mr. Stuart.

"The piece has neither wit nor point. It bumbles through three ponderous scenes without giving players or spectators a Chinaman's chance," reported Howard Barnes (*NYHT*). Barry Macollum, Dorothy Vaughan, Paul McVey, Michael Meehan, and Frances Carson were among those involved.

SMALL WONDER [Revue] SK: Charles Spalding, Max Wilk, George Axelrod, and Louise Laun; M: Baldwin Bergersen and Albert Selden; LY: Phyllis McGinley and Billings Brown; D: Burt Shevelove; CH: Gower Champion; S: Ralph Alswang; C: John Derro; P: George Nichols III; T: Coronet Theatre; 9/15/48 (134)

A lot of very talented people, some making their Broadway debuts, were involved in this mildly successful intimate revue. Among the players, several to become future headliners, were singers Jack Cassidy, Mary McCarty, Virginia Oswald, Marilyn Day, Phyllis McGinley, and Joan Diener, dancer Tommy Rall, comic actor Tom Ewell, and chinless comedienne Alice Pearce. Ewell rambled through the entertainment in the guise of the "Normal Neurotic," commenting dryly on life.

The show, which provided Gower Champion with his debut as a Broadway choreographer, was not very encouragingly received by some critics. Brooks Atkinson's (*NYT*) response began, "Unfortunately, the wonders of *Small Wonder* are uniformly small and become uniformly monotonous. Neither the writers nor the performers have scope enough to break the mood." He did approve, however, of the satirical tone, the well-planned staging, and the tasteful decorative elements. Euphemia Van Rensselaer Wyatt (*CW*), however, said that the show was "intimate, impudent and funny." John Chapman (*NYDN*) liked the sketches but not the songs. John Lardner (*TS*) approved the fact that the show's humor had a unifying point of view and a consistently skeptical mood.

The sketches included one that satirized three different types of best-selling books (the autobiography, the psychological love story, and the historical novel). Another used tableaux to spoof the ads in the *Saturday Evening Post*, with the enactment of ads for products to relieve itches, bladder problems, and so on. Another showed how a European peasant (Pearce) responds to radio broadcasts of lessons in democracy (presented by Ewell) in the form of soap operas. A satirical bit at the expense of the film world showed a happy ending as filmed by the Russians, the British, and Hollywood. Pearce (with Mort Marshall) stood out with a number about ice-cream flavors called "Pistachio," while McCarty scored with "A Ballad for

Billionaires," about wealthy southwesterners. She also stopped the show with her Clara Bow routine in the roaring twenties number, "Flaming Youth." Rall was outstanding when he danced "The Show Off" as a young man performing before a shaving mirror and his younger sister.

SMILE OF THE WORLD, THE [Drama/Law/Marriage/Period/Politics/Romance] A/D: Garson Kanin; S: Donald Oenslager; C: Forrest Thayer (Ruth Gordon's: Mainbocher); P: Playwrights' Company; T: Lyceum Theatre; 1/12/49 (5)

Both Garson Kanin and his wife Ruth Gordon wrote flops for Broadway in the 1948-1949 season, but Kanin's, which starred his spouse, had the briefer life. It was "a rather pretentious and static play composed of polite shreds and patches," stated Brooks Atkinson (*NYT*). George Jean Nathan (*TBY*) labeled the play "grandiose twaddle." Richard Watts, Jr. (*NYP*), called it "a strangely drab and lifeless play, lacking in incisiveness and dramatic bite."

Kanin's play is set in Washington in 1923 and is about a Supreme Court justice named Reuben Boulting (Otto Kruger), formerly a firebrand who fought fiercely for his beliefs. As he has become middle-aged, however, he has become increasingly stuffy and his liberal ideals have turned reactionary (as represented by a judgment he makes in a free-speech case). He no longer seems to his younger wife Sara (Gordon) the man she married, and even Boulting's feistily outspoken mother (Laura Pierpont) finds him tiresome. But Sara sees in young law clerk Sam Fenn (Warren Stevens), new to the employ of Justice Boulting, the type of man she admired in the young Boulting. Boulting allows the affair to continue rather than fighting for his wife, but he ultimately ends up with neither wife nor clerk, although they do not depart together. The jurist will have to reconsider his philosophy.

Although some found drawbacks in the acting, especially with Gordon's mannered style, most were appreciative of the performance. The cast included Ossie Davis, Ruby Dee, Elizabeth Dewing, Sam Jackson, and Boris Marshalov. Watts regretted finding Davis, "one of the finest young actors on the American stage, . . . playing the bit part of a family retainer."

SNAFU [Comedy/Crime/Family/Military/Politics/Romance/Sex/War/Youth] A: Louis Solomon and Harold Buchman; D/P: George Abbott; S: John Root; T: Hudson Theatre; 10/25/44 (158)

Young William (Billy) Redfield came into his own as a Broadway actor in the leading role of Ronald Stevens, a sixteen-year-old boy from Pomona, California, who enlists in the armed forces at fifteen by lying about his age and makes it to the rank of sergeant. At the height of battle against the Japanese in the South Pacific, he is--to his great annoyance--sent home by his commanding officers when a message arrives declaring that his mama wants him. Mama (Elspeth Eric) only learned of Ronald's whereabouts when he sent her a postcard from the war zone. But when he comes home, he is not your average teenager; his war experiences have hardened him into a man with a mature outlook on life and with military habits that are hard to break, such as blowing his bugle at dawn. His father (Russell Hardie) and mother are baffled by his behavior. When dad finds it difficult to have a heart-to-heart with him, the latter, suspecting that his father has had an affair, proceeds to give him a moral lecture on the dangers of promiscuity. (This was the best-liked scene.) Meanwhile, Roland becomes reacquainted with his girlfriend Kate (Bethel Leslie). Danny Baker (Dort Clark), a visiting soldier buddy on furlough, gets involved in an escapade with a journalism student (Patricia Kirkland) at a local girl's college; she is trying to get an interview with Roland and mistakes Danny for him. Everyone suspects Ronald of being the soldier seen leaving the dormitory at 3:00 A.M. By the final curtain, the misunderstandings are cleared up, Ronald is awarded the Purple Heart by a colonel (Winfield Smith), and parents of returning GIs are advised to treat their boys with trust and not suspicion.

Snafu was a mildly funny comedy with peaks and valleys of effectiveness. Burton Rascoe (*NYWT*) noted its sporadic weaknesses, but called it "literate, honest and imaginative; it is acidly satirical in some spots, seriously thoughtful in others." Ward Morehouse (*NYS*) declared that the play "is loosely constructed, but it is a play of amusing characters and situations." Lewis Nichols (*NYT*) considered the play mechanically contrived and more interested in gag moments than in believable characters.

The title of the play, now fairly common in colloquial English, derives from World War II military slang for "situation normal, all fucked up," although the polite substitute of "fouled" was used for the f-word in the *Encyclopedia Britannica* definition given in the program. Cast members included Ralph Chambers as a vote-hungry senator, Enid Markey as a smut-minded school teacher, ballerina Eugenia Delarova as a comic maid from Mexico, Stefan Gierasch as an American Legionnaire, Ann Dere as a neighbor, and Eve McVeagh as a pregnant Australian.

Seventeen-year-old Redfield gave a performance that "has a winning quality at once boyish and mature, awkward and reliant," according to Rosamond Gilder (*TAM*). Redfield had himself recently enlisted in the Air Combat Crew Training Corps and was expecting to be called up when he turned eighteen.

SNARK WAS A BOOJUM, THE [Comedy/Alcoholism/Family/Legacy/Mystery/Romance/Sex] A: Owen Davis; SC: the novel of the same name by Richard Shattuck (Dora Shattuck, writing under her husband's name); D: Alexander Kirkland; S: Frederick Fox; C: Michael Paul; P: Alex Yokel i/a/w Jay Faggen; T: Forty-eighth Street Theatre; 9/1/43 (5)

One of the fastest folders of the season was this implausible attempt at a whimsical farce-melodrama by veteran Owen Davis, whose 278 plays made him one of the most prolific playwrights in American history. Its title was inspired by Lewis Carroll's poem "The Hunting of the Snark." George Jean Nathan (*TBY*) noted that "the play, which aims to achieve an air of Carroll mad-hatterism, achieves only that silliness which is blood-sister to stupidity." "Double talk, mixed styles of writing, unexplained plot action and a pat denouement are not amusing in the theater," objected George Freedley (*NYMT*).

Set in the Old Shilly Homestead in New England, it concerns three expectant mothers (Florence MacMichael, Phyllis Adams, and Joan Banks), one of them unmarried, who are hoping to have the first baby born in the house so as to inherit the fortune of their late uncle (or uncle-in-law) Mortimer Shilly. Outside, a blizzard rages as the baby sweepstakes plotline is supplemented by others that concern such characters as an escaped homicidal lunatic from a local sanatorium; the three expectant fathers, one of them (Mervyn Nelson) a swishy decorator, another a greeting card writer (Fleming Ward), and the third an alcoholic (Francis Compton); a love story between a dizzy California girl named Sandy "Golden" Gate (Jane Huszagh) and Mortimer's nephew Rodney (Frank Lovejoy); the girl's aunt (Catherine Willard), who goes around with her late husband's ashes in a briefcase; a sinister aunt (Ann Dere); a harried lawyer (Ben Lackland); a veterinarian (Frank Wilcox), who arrives to midwife a bitch's litter and ends up delivering one of the babies; and a codicil to the will that gives the ingenue--who becomes engaged to Rodney--the legacy rather than the first mother who gives birth.

In the cast were Harold Waldridge and Dick Van Patten.

SNOOKIE [Comedy/Art/Journalism/Romance/Sex] A: Thomas A. Johnstone; M/LY; Thomas A. Johnstone and William B. Friedlander; D: William B. Friedlander; S: Frederick Fox; P: John Siguard (Ole) Olsen and Harold Ogden (Chic) Johnson i/a/w Lee Shubert; T: John Golden Theatre; 6/3/41 (15)

Olsen and Johnson, the comic stage stars, produced this awful frenetic farce with music but had their names removed from the program on opening night. The piece--into which are set several songs and dances performed by John McCauley and Betty Jane Smith--is set in the comic-art department of a metropolitan newspaper, where the kooky denizens spend more time playing cards, writing songs, playing pranks, and ogling girls in the building across the way than doing their appointed journalistic duties. Joining them is hick newcomer Jim Jones (Lawrence Weber) from Ashtabula, Ohio. Quigley (William Harrigan), the editor, hates comics and would like to close down the department if he can take over the paper. However, his takeover plans will be spoiled if, before a deadline is reached, the widow of the publisher gives birth to a child who will be the legal heir to the establishment. To dash Quigley's hopes, the comic artists cook up a scheme whereby Jim is to father a test-tube baby for the widow to bear. Learning of the plot, Jim's sweetheart (Julie Stevens) walks out on him. She returns when it is learned that the newborn heir was not fathered with his assistance. What Jim actually did was contribute blood for a transfusion. Jim earns a fortune for his comic strip, "Snookie," about a baby, and Quigley decides that he loves the comics.

The play's earlier titles were *Test Tube Baby* and *Whose Baby Are You?* Sidney B. Whipple (*NYWT*) announced that the play "hits an ultimate low in adult entertainment, and since it decidedly is not suitable for clean-minded youth, there would be little profit to anybody in dwelling at length upon its puerile indecencies. For the record, it is the most embarrassing play of the season." Well-known cast members included J. C. Nugent, Eddie Nugent, and Florenz Ames.

SOJOURNER TRUTH [Drama/Blacks/Family/Historical-Biographical/Period/Race/Religion/Romance] A: Katherine Garrison Chapin; D: Osceola Archer; CH: Gertrude Shurr; S: Richard Bernstein; C: Willanna Cephas; L: George Lewis; P: American Negro Theatre; T: Theresa L. Kaufmann Auditorium, YMHA (OB); 4/22/48 (3)

First seen at the YMHA auditorium at Lexington Avenue and Ninety-Second Street, this "sprawling, loosely-knit and ragged" (Thomas R. Dash [*WWD*]) work was presented for another 19 performances at the company's home base at 15 West 126th Street. It chronicles episodically the story of the actual Northern slave woman of the title (Muriel Smith), born in Ulster County, who was a Kingston tavern worker before gaining her liberty in the 1820s and subsequently becoming an evangelist.

The play, set largely in New York, covers about twenty years in the life of Bella, who later took the name of Sojourner Truth, showing her personal sorrows--such as her unfulfilled love for another man's slave, Gillis (Ferman Phillips), her forced marriage to an elderly man, and the selling of her child--and her accomplishments, including her religious triumphs and her work on behalf of abolition. When she is finally reunited with her son (Harold G. [Harry] Belafonte, in his New York debut), he has become an unworthy derelict and an embarrassment to her religious efforts. Among the dire topics covered was the practice of interbreeding blacks to raise a more marketable variety of slaves. The hostility of Northern slave owners to the ending of slavery is also clearly shown.

The play's story was strong but its dramatization was not. The title character was never fully fleshed out in the writing and her dialogue was often hollow. Still, said Louis Kronenberger (*PM*), "Though consistently amateurish and stilted, it is not very often dull."

Smith's "extraordinary interpretation," revealing "remarkable dignity, feeling and stature" (Dash) was the chief reason for audiences to remain seated throughout. The direction of the large black and white cast was, said Brooks Atkinson (*NYT*), lacking in a "firm hand."

SOLDIER'S WIFE [Comedy/Journalism/Literature/Marriage/Military/Sex/War] A/D: Rose Franken; S: Raymond Sovey; P: William Brown Meloney; T: John Golden Theatre; 10/4/44 (253)

Rose Franken's hit comedy made Burns Mantle's list of the season's ten best, but was not highly respected by the critics. Well acted, designed, and directed, its dramaturgic flaws were concealed by a fine production.

It is set in a small apartment in an Upper West Side apartment building overlooking the Hudson. Residing here are the personable but unworldly Kate (Martha Scott) and John Rogers (Myron McCormick), he being a soldier fighting in the South Pacific. Kate has had a baby that John has never seen. Her closest companion is her sister Florence (Frieda Inescort), whose civilian husband died during the war. John arrives home, having been discharged after being wounded. The play begins to explore the problems of readjustment he must face coming back to a wife who has learned to cope without him. Compounding his problems is what happens when--through his having submitted them--Kate's letters to him are published by the father of a combat buddy who died in the hospital bed near his. The book made from the letters promises to become a best-seller titled *Soldier's Wife*. This brings into their lives a cynical, wisecracking writer named Alexander Craig (Glenn Anders), who comes to interview Kate, and Alexander's fashionable newspaper editor and former wife Peter Gray (Lili Darvas). Although there is the suggestion of a romance between John and the editor, John finds himself becoming more and more secondary in his wife's life as Kate is wooed by Alexander and begins to find life in the fast lane attractive. Hollywood wants her to write a film version of the book and the newspaper wants her to do a column on letters to soldiers' wives. There is an attempt to remake Kate into the image of a worldly sophisticate. But before things can go too far, Kate, really a simple homebody at heart, realizes that she is happier in her old lifestyle and that she does not like to write, so she and John settle in for a life of conventional domestic bliss.

This was a standard Broadway comedy with charming characters and not-too-threatening situations. It was deemed a good choice for the matinee crowd. Many thought Kate a more mature version of the eponymous heroine in the author's most popular play, *Claudia*. It set out to examine the difficulties of civilian readjustment but shifted gears to opt for stenciled plotting concerning potential infidelity and the ego problems of men whose wives make more money than they do. George Freedley (*NYMT*) felt that Franken had failed to effectively dramatize the threat to the marriage, and that there was never any real suspense as to the outcome of that important element. Ward Morehouse (*NYS*) commented, "It is a sparse and insufficient play. There is some crisp dialogue in it. . . . But the material is scanty, thinly spread over three acts." Louis Kronenberger (*PM*) asserted, "It really is not a play at all but something put together with pins to divert through its dialogue, its details, its small recognitions, its dusting of surfaces, its acting opportunities. It is quite harmless and quite aimless." Nevertheless, Wilella Waldorf (*NYP*) had no reservations about the comedy and recommended it as "an unusually entertaining play, simple, unpretentious, intelligent and full of a warm understanding of human nature and decent values." Lili Darvas, wife of playwright Ferenc Molnár and Hungarian-born star of great repute, had appeared earlier in English Off Broadway, but this was her English-language Broadway debut.

SOLITAIRE [Comedy/Crime/Family/Friendship/Religion/Youth] A: John van Druten; SC: the novel of the same name by Edwin Corle; D: Dudley Digges; S: Jo Mielziner; P: Dwight Deere Wiman; T: Plymouth Theatre; 1/27/42 (23)

A sensitive work that could not find a large-enough audience or enough strongly impressed critics to back it, although it gained considerable critical respect for a play that lasted so briefly. It tells of an eleven-year-old rich girl, Virginia Stewart (Patricia Hitchcock, film director Alfred Hitchcock's twelve-year-old daughter), living in comfortable surroundings in Pasadena, California. She befriends a kindly and intelligent bum named Ben (Victor Kilian), owner of a pet white rat, who lives in the dry arroyo beneath the Stewarts' home. Virginia's busy parents ignore her when she tries to tell them of her new friendship. She and Ben, tied together by their mutual interest in the rat, talk together of philosophy and religion, he being more of a parent to her than her flesh-and-blood ones. Virginia feeds Ben with canned goods taken from her mother's pantry. When Virginia's mother (Sally Bates) finally learns of the relationship, she grows hysterical with fear over the possible implications--another child has been killed in similar circumstances in a nearby county--and informs the cops, who threaten to burn down all the shacks in the arroyo. Afraid for Ben and the rat, Virginia makes a late-night visit to them, leading to a crisis when she confronts a dangerous, fascistic tramp named Dean (Frederic Tozere) and several other denizens of the arroyo, who beat up Ben. Thinking that they might collect a reward from Virginia's banker dad (Ben Smith), they try to make it look like they saved Virginia from Ben, but a screwup occurs and, in a melodramatic climax, the police appear in time to save the child from real harm. Virginia returns to the bosom of her family, and Ben once more hits the road.

The play was viewed by Euphemia Van Rensselaer Wyatt (*CW*) as a worthwhile exploration of a child's loneliness. Flin. (*V*) thought it a somewhat confusing but "sometimes beautiful" work suggesting that "the world in which we live is created within individual consciousness, and a change of viewpoint brings about changed circumstances." Rosamond Gilder (*TAM*) said that van Druten had "accomplished the task of transferring this tale from idea and novel to theatre with remarkable skill and sympathy." But Louis Kronenberger (*PM*) viewed it as a misalliance between elements from *The Poor Little Rich Girl, Of Mice and Men**, and *On Borrowed Time**. John Anderson (*NYJA*) had to admit that the evening, for all its good points, seemed "frail and tenuous."

Young Hitchcock, in her professional acting debut, gave a remarkably expert performance in a difficult role. Also very fine was Kilian, returning to the stage after seven years in Hollywood. Jo Mielziner, using a turntable, devised two striking settings to contrast the modern home of the Stewarts with the overgrown vegetation of the arroyo.

SOMETHING FOR THE BOYS [Musical/Aviation/Legacy/Military/Romance/Show Business/War/Western] B: Herbert and Dorothy Fields; M/LY: Cole Porter; D: Hassard Short and Herbert Fields; CH: Jack Cole; S: Howard Bay; C: Billy Livingston; L: Hassard Short; P: Michael Todd; T: Alvin Theatre; 1/7/43 (422)

Ethel Merman starred in this smash-hit musical created by a top-drawer team and produced with lavish expenditure (to the tune of $125,000, $62,500 of it from producer Todd's own pocket). It had a great cast, an excellent score, a solid book, and memorable staging and choreography (with Jack Cole making his Broadway bow in this department). Merman played former chorus girl and present defense-plant worker Blossom Hart, Paula Laurence was nightclub entertainer Chiquita Hart, and Allen Jenkins was doll and souvenir-button pitch man Harry Hart. They are three distantly related cousins who, through the "Court of Missing Heirs," a radio program, are informed that they have inherited a ranch in Texas. Lawyer Roger Calhoun (Jed Prouty) brings the trio--who dislike one another at first--together from their diverse occupations. The ranch, which turns out to be ramshackle and lacking in oil, adjoins Kelly Field, being used by the army as a training camp. The house, moreover, has been requisitioned by the army for maneuvers. In order to make some money from their inheritance, the trio decide to convert it into a boarding house for the wives of the local fliers. They also set up a factory to manufacture airplane parts. On the base is handsome Staff Sergeant Rocky Fulton (Bill Johnson), a former band leader with whom Blossom falls in love, although he is engaged to Melanie Walker (Frances Mercer), the arrogant and spoiled daughter of a senator. Danger threatens when Melanie tries to convince the base commandant (Jack Hartley) that Blossom and Chiquita are immoral women, and his investigation sees things that mislead him into believing her. He declares the ranch out of bounds and arrests the occupants. However, the tart-tongued Blossom has discovered that she can receive radio messages through the carborundum on one of her fillings, and she comes through when a plane with a dead radio is saved during a storm via her dental receiver. Blossom wins her guy, and the femme fatale is put in her place.

Rosamond Gilder (*TAM*) raved that this "is the answer to a wartime showman's--and to a wartime audience's--prayer. It is a piece of wild-eyed, zany nonsense, lovely to look at and filled to the brim with music that is by turns bold, witty and tender." Burton Rascoe (*NYWT*) declared that this was "a musical show as glamorous, kinetic, balanced and seductive as the still lamented Ziegfeld in his heyday used to stage them."

Howard Bay's sets were among his best yet and included the realistic effect of a bomber in flight roaring out over the footlights. The performances were all that could be desired, especially Merman's and Laurence's, the latter making her musical comedy debut. The contrast in the two performers' physical types--Merman stocky and buxom, Laurence tall, lanky, and angular--helped tremendously in creating the right comic effect, especially when, dressed as Indian squaws, they sang the mildly risqué, show-stopping "By the Mississinewa."

One night, Merman suddenly became ill. Art Cohn wrote in *The Nine Lives of Michael Todd* that Todd decided not to close the show but to inform the audience that they could have a refund if they desired it. (There was one such request.) Otherwise, they were told by costar Bill Johnson, "There is a little girl who has been waiting eleven months to go on. Betty Garrett appears on Broadway for the first time tonight and . . . it may be *a new star is born*." He was right about Garrett's becoming a star, but not about her debut, as she already had done four Broadway shows. She played the part for a week.

There were wonderful contributions by tap dancer Betty Bruce, Spanish dancer Anita Alvarez. Also clicking with the critics were William Lynn, Stuart Langley, Madeleine Clive, Remi Martel, Bill Callahan, and Walter Rinner. Despite the critical raves, the tunes did not last long, only "Could It Be You?" and "Hey, Good Lookin'" becoming standards.

During the show's preparation period, there was a power struggle with the star, the book and lyric writers, and the composer on one side and Todd on the other. Todd wanted a certain scene dropped; the others thought that it was a great scene and insisted that it remain. According to Cohn, the flamboyant producer said, "I'll *prove* it and let *you* have the pleasure of heaving it out. If I'm wrong I'd better go back to selling shoes." He spent $5,000 to have scenery built and costumes created for the scene. "They were used once, for the dress rehearsal. The scene was thrown out, at the request of Ethel Merman, Cole Porter and the Fieldses."

On opening night Todd ordered his ushers to prevent any critics from leaving before the show was over because he had a last-act special effect that simulated a bomber taking off that he wanted them to see. Two critics, Howard Barnes and Burns Mantle, were stopped by Todd himself. When they complained about missing their deadlines, he declared, "You'll miss my bomber!"

SONG OF BERNADETTE, THE [Drama/Family/France/Period/Religion] A: Jean Kerr and Walter Kerr; SC: Franz Werfel's novel of the same name; D: Walter Kerr; S: Willis Knighton; P: Victor Payne-Jennings and Frank McCoy; T: Belasco Theatre; 3/26/46 (3)

A dramatically ineffective, episodic version of Werfel's story of religious faith, already well known from its 1943 film version starring Jennifer Jones. The play was originally written for and produced by the theatre department at Catholic University in Washington, D.C. It suffered from excessive sentimentality and melodramatics, shapelessness, repetitiousness, length, and long-windedness. It failed to convey the appropriate holy atmosphere and, according to George Jean Nathan (*TBY*), dissolved "whimsically into something resembling a pious *Harvey*." Louis Kronenberger (*PM*) called it "rather a chronicle than a story, something with less form than content, and perhaps with content not altogether suited to the stage." Making things worse was a company of mostly inadequate performers.

Werfel's story is that of the commonplace schoolgirl of Lourdes, Bernadette Soubirous (Elizabeth Ross), who, in 1858, has seen a vision of herself and the Virgin Mary in the Grotto of Massabielle. Subsequently, a spring on the spot gushes healing waters. The story of Bernadette's miraculous vision is doubted, both by her poor parents (Whit Vernon and Pamela Rivers) and by the townspeople in general, especially the rigid Dean (Keinert Wolf). Through her complete and unwavering conviction, she overcomes their doubts, enters a convent in ill health, and is eventually sanctified by the Church.

SONG OF NORWAY [Musical/Marriage/Music/Musical-Biographical/Period/Romance] B: Milton Lazarus; M/LY: Robert Wright and George Forrest; SC: a play by Homer Curran; D: Charles K. Friedman; CH: George Balanchine; S: Lemuel Ayers; C: Robert Davison (Irra Petina's costumes: Ted Shore); L: Howard Bay; P: Edwin Lester; T: Imperial Theatre; 8/21/44 (860)

A sumptuously produced, blockbuster operetta hit based on the life of Norwegian composer Edvard Grieg (Lawrence Brooks, in his Broadway debut), whose music was effectively adapted and supplied with lyrics by the team of Wright and Forrest. It came to New York after a great success on the West Coast, but its Los Angeles and San Francisco price of $3.90 top was increased to $6 for New York. The book, unfortunately, was stenciled and dull and took dramatic liberties with

Grieg's biography, but it did include some pleasantly humorous sections to lighten the atmosphere.

The acting, often stiff in shows of this sort, was more relaxed and natural than usual. Despite the generally routine choreography with which Balanchine provided the work, the ballet performances by Alexandra Danilova, Frederick Franklin, Nathalie Krassovska, and Leon Danielen of the Ballets Russes de Monte Carlo were admired, especially in the Peer Gynt Suite number. Most important was the outstanding score, which was superbly performed, especially by Metropolitan Opera mezzo-soprano Irra Petina as Italian prima donna Louise Giovanni, a fictional character devised for plot purposes.

In 1860 Edvard Grieg leaves behind his sweetheart Nina (Helena Bliss) and his fish-selling father and mother (Walter Kingsford and Ivy Scott) in their Norwegian town of Troldhaugen to become the accompanist to Louisa Giovanni, temperamental grand opera singer and countess, who is married to her manager (Sig Arno), on a grand Continental tour. They travel from Bergen to Copenhagen, and Grieg's fame grows. Playwright Henrik Ibsen (Dudley Clements) asks him to write the Peer Gynt Suite. Before they embark for Rome, Grieg marries Nina, who now goes with him. Instead of being inspired by the Italian singer to write great music, Grieg writes only frothy compositions of no lasting value. His dream always had been to write music capturing the unique flavor of Norwegian folklore inspired by the poetry of his close friend Rykard Nordraak (Robert Shafer). When Rykard dies, Grieg rejects his newfound sophisticated world, reaffirms his commitment to Nina, from whom he nearly has been estranged, and returns with her to Norway, where he composes his famous "Song of Norway" to accompany a poem by Rykard. (The playing of this number at the end suggested to E. C. Sherburne [*CSM*] a topically symbolic purpose concerning Norway's then-awaited deliverance from the German forces.)

"There is much that is heavy and a shade dull and uninspired about this operetta," wrote George Freedley (*NYMT*), "but the good far outweighs the bad." Louis Kronenberger (*PM*) approved the music as just right for Broadway, "colorful and easy, and for the most part not so familiar as to seem hackneyed," but called the show "purely formula stuff, without style or originality." Howard Barnes (*NYHT*) castigated the book as "lamentable." "It has great vitality and is as pretty as it is melodious," was Ward Morehouse's (*NYS*) positive verdict on the show. Outstanding songs included "Anitra's Dance," "Ich Liebe Dich," "Springtide," "Nocturne," "Wedding in Troldhaugen," "Scherzo," "March of the Dwarfs," "Now," "Strange Music," and "To Spring." The music was culled from well over two hundred Grieg compositions. Petina was the show-stopping star, appreciated for her magnificent voice as well as for her comedy talents and vivacious personality.

SONG OF THE DNIEPPER [Drama/Crime/Jews/Period/Politics/Prison/Trial/Yiddish Language] A: David Licht; SC: Zalman Shneour's novel of the same name; M: Joseph Rumshinsky; D/L: Maurice Schwartz; S: Samuel Leve; P/T: Yiddish Art Theatre (OB); 10/25/46

This Yiddish drama, set in prerevolutionary Russia, was the episodic tale (in twenty scenes) of the powerfully built teamster, Noah Pandre (Maurice Schwartz) of Shklov, who becomes a hero to his people in a time of virulent anti-Semitism. On the eve of his wedding, the Samson-like Noah is framed for a crime of which he is innocent and sent to prison. There he is instructed in revolutionary ideas by Chatze the furrier (Abraham Teitelbaum). When he is released, he learns of a planned pogrom and puts an end to it by killing (in self-defense) the evil police chief (Isaac Arco) behind his imprisonment.

The play was praised as a lusty vehicle with saltily witty Yiddish dialogue. It was, however, talky and unwieldy because of its novelistic source. Louis Kronenberger (*PM*) wrote, "There are interesting and picturesque moments; but the general effect . . . is extremely slow and sprawling, and the tone is less one of period folk drama than of straight old-fashioned theater." Richard Watts, Jr. (*NYP*), considered it "a rather undistinguished work which possesses at best a modest kind of narrative interest," but thought the rich non-naturalistic acting made it easy to follow the story even without knowing Yiddish. He said that the acting was not excessively exaggerated but that the "actors enter into their assignments with such delight in the color, the sweeping gesture and the resounding phrases . . . that their work takes on a fascinating quality of vitality and relish."

Brooks Atkinson (*NYT*) had to admit that Schwartz was a bit long in the tooth and wide at the waist to be playing romantic heroes. The chief support in the very large cast came from Menachem Rubin, Ola Shlifko, Anna Appel, Jenny Casher, Jacob Rechtzeit, Luba Kadison, Isador Casher, and Frances Adler. Despite the many scenes, the action moved swiftly because of Samuel Leve's design incorporating two sets on stage simultaneously, one being acted on and the other, behind an upstage wall made of panels that could go up and down like garage doors, ready to be pushed onstage when needed and requiring only thirty seconds to be changed.

SONG OUT OF SORROW [Drama/Alcoholism/Crime/Drugs/Friendship/Illness/Literary-Biographical/Period/Prostitution] A: Felix Doherty; D: Dennis Gurney; S/L: William Schoeller; P: Blackfriars' Guild; T: Blackfriars' Theatre (OB); 12/11/41

"A deeply moving play" (B. B. [*NYT*]) produced in a small theatre two flights up on West Fifty-seventh Street. George Freedley (*NYMT*) thought that it had "real dramatic power and a fine sense of characterization."

Francis Thompson (Stacey Harris), the Victorian poet, was the subject of the biographical play, which examined the darkest year of his life (1887) when, living in London eight years after flunking out of medical school, he is struggling to stave off starvation as he writes and seeks recognition. To keep alive, he depends on laudanum. He is taken in by Flossie (Rosanna Seaborn), a streetwalker, who lives with the perpetually drunken Bill (Guy Spaull). A young doctor (Ted Erwin) whom Francis knew in school looks in on him. When Flossie is arrested for harboring stolen goods, the poet takes employment as an errand boy. In spite of the decadence of his friends, they provide the poet with the strength and love he needs to become regenerated as a human being and writer. He is dying from laudanum poisoning when his writings are discovered by a publisher (Robert Perry), and he begins to achieve recognition. Before the curtain falls, he vows to kick his drug habit, no matter how painful. (Thompson succeeded and lived another twenty years.)

Wilella Waldorf (*NYP*) went not expecting anything special and was pleasantly surprised by the "workmanlike" play and competent performances. She recommended it as a worthy experiment, adding that the author "has a feeling for dialogue that is seldom overdone, even in a play about a poet, and he manages to keep an audience interested."

SONS AND SOLDIERS [Drama/Alcoholism/Family/Fantasy/Marriage/Medicine/Period/Romance/Sex/War] A: Irwin Shaw; D: Max Reinhardt; CH: Wally Jackson; S: Norman Bel Geddes; P: Max Reinhardt, Norman Bel Geddes, and Richard Myers; T: Morosco Theatre; 5/4/43 (22)

A distinguished lineup of actors performed this serious message drama by Irwin Shaw under the direction of great European regisseur Max Reinhardt, but the result was unprepossessing. Despite some effective moments, wrote Lewis Nichols (*NYT*), the play "often appeared talky and scattered, with a good many stock situations and with pretentiousness not always absent." The issue of pretentiousness in telling what might have been more effective if simply told was one brought up by others as well.

The action begins in 1916 in a small American city when Rebecca Tadlock (Geraldine Fitzgerald), wife of John (Herbert Rudley), is about to have a baby and is told by Dr. Carnrick (Millard Mitchell) that she must decide either on going through with the birth, in which her chances of survival are one in ten, or having an abortion. The stress of Rebecca's dilemma causes her to faint, and she has a visionary dream in which she lives the next twenty-five years of her life. She sees all the joys and tragedies that life will hold in store for the two sons she foresees bearing. Her boys turn out to be ordinary fellows, her elder son, Andrew (Gregory Peck) eventually rebelling at her maternally dominating ways. He experiences typical adolescent problems, goes to college but drops out, has an affair with Dr. Carnrick's prostitute wife Catherine (Stella Adler), sees the doctor become a cynical alcoholic, loses his brother (Kenneth Tobey) in World War II, gets married to a neighbor girl, and volunteers for the army preparatory to going overseas to fight for a better world. Despite what she sees of the future, Rebecca decides to go ahead and have the child, believing that life must be lived despite the dangers of death.

To John Anderson (*NYJA*) this was "a maudlin word-stuffed drama [that] sounds like all the wild empty plays scribbled in outline on speakeasy menus during the Volstead Renaissance." Louis Kronenberger (*PM*) took issue with the dream device, claiming that as realized there was nothing dreamlike about it and that the story was presented straightforwardly. Also, he believed that Rebecca's final affirmation would have been more powerful had it grown out of actual experience rather than as the "visionary guesswork" of a young bride. But several reviewers liked the play, one of the most favorable being Burton Rascoe (*NYWT*), who declared, "Everything is very real and natural in this play; nothing is sentimentalized or falsified. It is human and very true to life as we know it."

Minor roles were well handled by Karl Malden, Edward Nannery, Jesse White, Sara Lee Harris, and Leonard Sues, the trumpet player, who acted Andrew's musician friend. Concerning Reinhardt's direction (in Bel Geddes's too-elaborate setting), there were few encomiums; George Jean Nathan (*TBY*) even said that it "was nothing for even a second-rate Broadway director to be proud of."

Fitzgerald's performance had some in raptures, proclaiming the arrival of a luminous new star. Her role required a vast variety of moods and asked her to change ages constantly. "Miss Fitzgerald turns loose all of her Irish art, her Gaelic charm, her brilliant theatrical skill on this difficult role, and proves genuinely enchanting in it," reported Wilella Waldorf (*NYP*).

Peck continued to prove himself an actor of substance and appeal, but he soon would leave for Hollywood, never to act on Broadway again. He always remembered later how director Reinhardt had unblocked him when he was having trouble conveying his character's emotional turmoil. Although the frail director normally had Lili Darvas, his assistant, give notes to the actors, on one occasion he took Peck aside himself. "Gregory--see the great advantage of being a play actor. We do not stop being children when we grow up. Play act, play act--it's all performance and imagination. You must put part of yourself into the corner just off-stage and then you must send the player--or the child, if you will--out on the stage to play act. Nothing to be afraid of. It's only playing" (quoted in Michael Freedland, *Gregory Peck*). The actor was therefore able to shed his self-consciousness and not to be afraid of making a fool of himself.

SONS O' FUN [Revue] SK: (mostly) Ole Olsen and Chic Johnson, and Hal Block; M: Sammy Fain; LY: Jack Yellen; D/L: Edward Duryea Dowling; CH: Robert Alton; C/S: Raoul Pène du Bois; P: Messrs. Shubert; T: Winter Garden; 12/1/41 (742)

A smash hit revue starring madcap comedians Olsen and Johnson. It was very much in the vein of their previous success, *Hellzapoppin'**, which had run for three years, only most critics thought it superior to that show. Euphemia Van Rensselaer Wyatt (*CW*) called it "bigger, noisier, richer and rougher."

As in the previous show, all kinds of crazy stunts were pulled in the theatre, both on stage and in the auditorium, with so many stooges planted in the seats that no one knew who the plants were and who the real spectators. Ads in the papers warned audiences to "come prepared to defend yourselves." The fun started the minute the customers walked into the Winter Garden. A cigar-smoking policeman warned patrons not to smoke. Comedian Frank Libuse ushered people to the wrong seats. Vents were built into the auditorium floor so stooges could release compressed air and flip ladies' skirts up. People were ushered to their box seats via the aid of a ladder. Throughout the show someone sat in a lookout seat placed atop a pole at the side of the proscenium. When a woman down front groaned, a stork on wires appeared to drop a baby in her lap. Guns kept going off when least expected. Chorus girls filled the aisles and pulled men--including former governor Al Smith--out of their seats to dance with them; they then borrowed the men's jackets, put them on, and forced the red-faced fellows to follow them up on the stage to retrieve their garments. An auction was held and objects and money given to the bidders. In a contest bit, three young women had to remove the undershirts of three young men, the winner being awarded $10. As in *Hellzapoppin'*, an actress kept going through the house, calling for "Oscar," and wanting to know who was going to care for the infant in her arms. Before the evening was over, the infant was replaced by a pretty girl, leading many men, including the guy in the lookout seat, to rush forward as volunteer helpers.

The headline entertainers included tiny Brazilian bombshell Carmen Miranda and legitimate singer-actress Ella Logan. Miranda wore her trademark fruit-packed turbans, thick platform shoes, and numerous pieces of costume jewelry and performed several torrid numbers backed by an octet of male musicians. Her English numbers included "Thank You North America," and she also sang several songs in her native Portuguese. At the end of one of these, a midget performer named Helen Magna appeared as a miniature Miranda. A few critics felt that she had cooled down since earlier Broadway appearances, but Richard Watts, Jr. (*NYHT*), said that she gave the "show its one touch of distinction." Logan had the show's big hit, "Happy in Love," now a standard, and also delivered "It's a New Kind of Thing," "Let's Say Goodnight with a Dance," and other tunes in the undistinguished score.

In addition to the hilarity in the auditorium, there was a full supply on stage, as when Olsen and Johnson did "A Quiet Night in the Country," "Induction Center," set in an army training camp, and "Hellzapoppin' Night in Buckeye, Arizona." Playing second banana in most of the sketches was comic Joe Besser, who was especially funny as a lisping inductee in the army scene. Olsen and Johnson were not appreciated as innately funny men, but rather for their inventive zaniness as showmen.

There were a host of dance numbers, most of them staged by Robert Alton, and several of them employing four sets of twins, the Statlers, Mullens, Crystals, and Blackburns. A specialty dance team, Rosario and Antonio, from Seville, were also standouts with their gypsy routines. Miscellaneous entertainers included the Pitchmen, who used gadgets in their mouths to imitate various musical instruments; comic juggler Ben Beri; puppeteers Walton and O'Rourke; and others.

Summing up, John Anderson (*NYJA*) reported, "*Sons O' Fun* is twin bedlam at its wildest and as crazy as they come, but a whole lot handsomer."

SOPHIE [Comedy/Family/Military/Romance/Rural/Sex/Small Town] A: George Ross and Rose C. Feld; SC: Rose C. Feld's *New Yorker* stories, "Sophie Halenczik, American"; D: Michael Gordon; S: Samuel Leve; C: Rose Bogdanoff; P: Meyer Davis and George Ross; T: Playhouse; 12/25/44 (9)

Academy Award-winning Greek actress Katina Paxinou continued to have tough luck on Broadway in the title role of this frantically staged and tedious patriotic comedy in which she played a resourceful Czech immigrant widow named Sophie Halenczik with a son in the army and two grown daughters. Sophie serves as a domestic in rural Ridgefield, Connecticut. The play, coauthored by former New York theatre critic George Ross, was an awkward piece that tried to combine several separate plot strands. One involves Sophie's attempt to tie the town's various foreign elements together as Americans by organizing a series of home-cooked dinners to be prepared by local European women, with the money raised aimed for War Relief. The plan meets the opposition of a local bigot, Chet Blanchard (John McGovern), a hundred percenter who hates foreigners. There is also a romantic interest between Sophie and the Yankee postman (Will Geer); another--of seven years' duration--between daughter Irene (Donna Keath) and a hesitant Hungarian neighbor (John Harmon); and another between daughter Annie (Ann Shepherd) and the bigot's spineless son Tom (Richard Deane), who is afraid to propose because he fears his father's reaction. Also occupying plot time is the problem of Sophie's soldier son Frankie (Donald Buka), who has fathered an illegitimate child by Marge Nelson (Marguerite Clifton), but has spurned her because of certain rumors. Sophie takes the girl in nonetheless and by the end of the play has managed to marry off all three of her children, to have won the postman as her spouse, and resoundingly to have proved her Americanism.

Ward Morehouse (*NYS*) regretted that this was "an aimless, folksy and cluttered little play" showing "a lack of dexterity in the writing and the direction." "It never quite comes off . . . because of its wordy monotony and woefully unskilled direction," lamented Rowland Field (*NEN*).

Paxinou, whose English was now practically accentless, received reviews that ranged from approbatory (George Freedley [*NYMT*]) to condemnatory (George Jean Nathan [*TBY*]). Louis Sorin played Sophie's brother from New York, and Jerry Boyar was a local brat. Eda Reiss Merin and Ronald Alexander were also in the cast.

SOUND OF HUNTING, A [Comedy-Drama/Military/War] A: Harry Brown; SC: Harry Brown's poem, "Incident on a Front Not Far from Castel de Sangro"; D: Anthony Brown; D: Samuel Leve; P: Irving L. Jacobs; T: Lyceum Theatre; 11/20/45 (23)

Burt (then called Burton) Lancaster, in the role of Sergeant Joseph Mooney, made his Broadway bow in this interesting all-male war play set in a war-torn house in Cassino, Italy. The greatly appreciated star of the event, however, was Sam Levene (returning to Broadway after five years in movies) as the hilariously wise-cracking Private Dino Colluci of New York's Bleecker Street. Taking place in January 1944, the play examines with considerable realism events surrounding eleven soldiers and an asinine war correspondent named Frederick Finley (Bruce Evans).

A clumsy, bespectacled soldier named Small has gotten lost in the zone between the Germans and the GIs, and though he is no one's particular favorite, the men in Sergeant Mooney's squad--who consider themselves lucky for having survived intact thus far--become preoccupied with his safety, refusing to accept a period of relief until he is rescued. In defiance of orders, a rescue party goes out but fails. However, Colucci, on his own, manages to silence the German machine gun nest and then to locate the missing soldier, who has been killed. The platoon now is able to move on to Naples.

Despite some very strong notices, the play failed commercially. The critics lauded the plot's simplicity, its relative lack of sentimentality, the feeling of camaraderie created among the men, the sense of gritty and slangy realism, the psychological accuracy, and the healthy admixture of humor, especially as expressed in the colorful Colucci's lines. Robert Garland (*NYJA*) claimed that it was the best play about the war yet written, praising it for its ringingly real dialogue, suspense, excellent chunks of comedy, and superb ensemble playing. John Mason Brown (*SR*) called it the finest war play since 1924's *What Price Glory?** He thought that Brown had created "the most pungent and authentic soldier dialogue to have been written by an American dramatist since Pearl Harbor." Wilella Waldorf (*NYP*) found herself considerably interested, "although there is much talk, little action and a minimum of heroics." But Lewis Nichols (*NYT*) thought it all too "glib," "repetitious," and lacking in events "which cannot be foreseen." One major drawback mentioned by several was the hard-to-swallow picture of the caricatured war correspondent. George Jean Nathan (*TBY*), who admired much of the work, suggested that its failure was a matter of timing and that the war-weary nation now wanted to forget the recently ended strife.

The fine cast included Frank Lovejoy, James McGrew, William Beal, Charles J. Flynn, George Tyne, Kenneth Brauer, Carl Frank, Ralph Brooke, and Stacy Harris.

SOUTH PACIFIC [Drama/Blacks/Military/Race/Romance/Sex/Tropics/War] A: Howard Rigsby and Dorothy Heyward; M: Paul Bowles; D: Lee Strasberg; S: Boris Aronson; P: David Lowe; T: Cort Theatre; 12/29/43 (5)

A promising drama on a vital theme of race relations that began strongly, but failed to sustain its impetus. It was set on a small Japanese-held island in the South Pacific, and Boris Aronson's lush setting gave viewers an excellent sense of what it looked like in a locale then being discussed daily in the media. To this seeming paradise come two shipwrecked and battered Americans, a black merchant seaman named Sam Johnson (Canada Lee) and the white Captain Dunlap (Wendell K. Phillips). Their ship has been torpedoed by the enemy. The natives accept them warmly, as do the village's black missionary doctor (Louis Sharp) and his pretty native fiancée (Wini Johnson). Sam, who has grown up amid racial prejudice in America, soon appreciates the ease with which he can exist in this dark-skinned community, while the captain begins to be the racial outsider. Even the Japanese do not oppress him. Sam uses his abilities to exert power in the community and to reject any interest in the war, which he comes to see as a struggle between white America and the Japanese, but not of his concern. He lords it in the village, even seducing the doctor's sweetheart, who becomes his mistress. Eventually, things happen to change his attitude. Both Daniel (Rudolph Whitaker), a native boy he has befriended, and the doctor are shot by the Japanese. Then the captain, having taken up a rifle in an attempt to attack an enemy position, is shot. Sam realizes that all men must stand together, regardless of race, and fight for freedom. He reaches for a gun and goes off to do his duty as the sounds of an offshore bombardment from the American navy are heard.

The play was approved as a serious attempt to confront a meaningful issue, but was not accepted as a work of dramatic art. Its plot devices were feeble compared with its thematic premise. It also descended from an action-oriented first half to a rhetoric-dominated second. Howard Barnes (*NYHT*) argued that "the offering never comes to grips with its fascinating thesis," and Burton Rascoe (*NYWT*) complained that "the motivation is 'literary' in the worst sense and the action is confusing and often ridiculous."

For some, Lee's performance was up to his proven standard. "Canada Lee," wrote Rosamond Gilder (*TAM*), "carried the play electrically through its first act and with remarkable skill through the heavier seas of the last two. He played with vigor and assurance and, especially in the first act, with a nice power of conveying the unspoken thought." Others thought that the role was too ill written even for Lee to make believable.

One of the native girls was played by Ruby Dee, in her Broadway debut. Frank Wilson played the local chief. Lee Strasberg's direction was approved for its use of interesting sound effects but not for the deliberateness of its pacing.

SOUTH PACIFIC [Musical/Military/Race/Romance/Tropics/War] B/LY: Oscar Hammerstein II and Joshua Logan; M: Richard Rodgers; SC: James Michener's book, *Tales of the South Pacific*; S/L: Jo Mielziner; C: Motley; P: Richard Rodgers, Oscar Hammerstein II, Leland Hayward, and Joshua Logan; T: Majestic Theatre; 4/7/49 (1,925)

The remarkable partnership of Rodgers and Hammerstein came through with yet another landmark musical in this adaptation of Pulitzer Prize-winning stories by James Michener dealing with the American presence in the South Pacific during World War II. Michener did not work on the show, although he profited handsomely from its royalties. (When he wanted to invest in the show, but was low on cash, Richard Rodgers loaned him the money, which he was quickly able to repay.) Hobe. (*V*) announced that "it's one of the most enjoyable and satisfying musicals in theatre history." The excellence of the adaptation was especially to be commended, as the original stories were linked only in the most tenuous way. Instead of the usual clichés associated with musicals set in the tropics, colibrettists Hammerstein and Logan had provided "a swift story of unusual literacy," according to Rosamond Gilder (*TAM*). So great was the word of mouth before the show reached New York that the show had the then record-breaking advance sale of $500,000.

The project had been initiated by Joshua Logan, who convinced Rodgers to read one of Michener's stories, "Fo' Dolla," concerning Lieutenant Joseph Cable's love affair with a Polynesian girl. Wishing to avoid *Madame Butterfly* comparisons, Rodgers and Hammerstein added another story, "Our Heroine," to the plot, both tales having the theme of love's smashing of racial obstacles. The chief characters in "Our Heroine" were sophisticated, middle-aged French planter Emile de Becque and the considerably younger naive navy nurse Nellie Forbush, from Otolousa, Arkansas (changed to Little Rock for the show). Ezio Pinza, the great operatic star, made a resounding Broadway debut in the role of de Becque, and Mary Martin had one of her greatest roles as Ensign Forbush. Various liberties were taken with

Michener's originals in order to unify the dramatic action. Their dramaturgic efforts were awarded the 1949 Drama Critics Circle Award for best musical, the 1950 Pulitzer Prize, and eight 1950 Tonys. However, an unacknowledged contributor was actor-playwright Emlyn Williams, who was brought in during the out-of-town period to snip ten minutes from the running time when the authors themselves were baffled. He had performed a similar service on another Logan project, *Mister Roberts*.

The show contributed numerous songs to the world's pop-classic repertoire, including "Dites-Moi Pourquoi," "A Cockeyed Optimist," "Some Enchanted Evening," "Bloody Mary," "There Is Nothing like a Dame," "Bali H'ai," "I'm Gonna Wash That Man Right Outa My Hair," "I'm in Love with a Wonderful Guy," "Younger Than Springtime," "Happy Talk," "Honey Bun," "You've Got to Be Taught," and "This Nearly Was Mine." All the songs were beautifully integrated into the story line, and each song was precisely appropriate to the character who sang it. Rodgers won a Tony for his music.

The action is set on two Pacific islands occupied by the American Seabees. Two love stories are intertwined to occupy most of the plot. One ends happily, the other tragically. In the main plot line, Nellie falls in love with Emile, the colonial planter, father of two children (Barbara Luna and Michael DeLeon [or Noel DeLeon]) by his native wife, now deceased. Her discovery that he is the parent of half-breed children nearly causes the Southern-born Nellie to end the affair, but his return from a dangerous espionage mission against the Japanese inspires a reconciliation. Cable (William Tabbert), a Marine flyer, falls in love with Liat (Betta St. John, who changed her name from Betta Streigler for the show), the daughter of Bloody Mary (Juanita Hall), an ugly, betel-chewing Tonkinese woman with entrepreneurial skills picked up from the Seabees. (Hall was exceptional when singing the haunting "Bali H'ai," about a neighboring island.) Cable's prejudices prevent him from marrying the dark-skinned girl. Unlike de Becque, Cable does not return alive from the espionage mission.

South Pacific offered a cornucopia of riches to Broadway, from Pinza's romantic stature and glorious bass voice to Martin's effervescent musical comedy antics; from the immortal music and lyrics of Rodgers and Hammerstein to the blend of raucous comedy and sensitive drama culled from Michener's book; from Logan's imaginative, insightful, energetic, staging to Mielziner's lushly tropical settings. Although there were several casual dance interludes, there was no formal choreography (an exceptional thing for a Broadway musical), the dances seeming to emerge naturally from the inventive, Tony-winning staging. Either the actors created their own dance routines (Martin, originally a dance teacher, was adept at this) or Logan staged them, as he did with the excellent "Nothing Like a Dame" sequence, practically improvised at a single rehearsal. Scene breaks were absent, a cinematic lap-dissolve technique using scrim travelers blending one scene with another.

There were also memorable supporting performances, among the most notable being Myron McCormick's Tony Award cavorting as the boastful, conniving Seabee Luther Billis. McCormick's performance at a company talent show, with a mural-like tattoo of a ship undulating on his stomach, a grass skirt, and a brassiere made of a pair of coconuts, was a comic classic of the modern musical stage. McCormick underwent a nightly ritual of having the two-colored tattoo drawn on in red and blue ball-point ink. He was also one of nine cast members who stayed with the show during the entire length of its run. Juanita Hall copped the Tony for that year's supporting actress in a musical.

Excellent supporting actors included Martin Wolfson as Captain George Brackett, Henry Slate as Stewpot, Fred Sadoff as Professor, Biff McGuire as Radio Operator Bob McCaffrey, Harvey Stephens as Commander Harbison, and Don Fellows as Lieutenant Buzz Adams.

Pinza, who also won a Tony for his performance, proved a fine dramatic actor as well as a magnificent singer, and he stopped the show with such songs as "Some Enchanted Evening." Martin also had several show-stoppers, such as "I'm Gonna Wash That Man Right Outa My Hair," which she sang while taking an actual on-stage shower with her head full of real lather. (She had a much remarked-on cropped haircut so that it would dry more quickly.) "She is cute without being coy;

sweet but not saccharine; and rowdy without being vulgar," declared John Mason Brown (*SR*). "She moves as if Terpsichore had taught her, and she can play a straight scene with the same surety that she can put over a number. Dressed in an outsized sailor's suit [for "Honeybun"] or in Motley's best, she is a figure--and a personality--of radiance and enchantment." Martin was another of the show's Tony winners, giving it a sweep in all musical performance categories.

Martin wrote in *My Heart Belongs* that at first, she was reluctant to do the show because she could not see herself playing a nurse, especially one who might have to dress in unattractive military khaki. She was also frightened of appearing on stage with an opera star. When she did sing with Pinza, the song ("Wonder How It Feels") allowed each to perform in his or her natural style, without competing. Martin took credit for inspiring the "I'm Gonna Wash That Man" number. She was taking a shower one day when the idea came to her of doing a song while taking a real onstage shower and then emerging with her hair dripping wet. The idea spread to the creative staff, the song--which also proved useful to moving the plot along--was written, and she got to wash her hair onstage eight times a week. Since she never could get all the soap out during the show, she washed it afterwards in the dressing room, and also washed it at home before leaving for the theatre. This meant between twenty-six and twenty-eight washings a week over a three-year period. Another of her memorable numbers, "Honey Bun," performed at the camp show, was inspired by a picture Logan saw of her as a child in men's clothing and a sailor's cap. Logan conjured up an egregiously oversized sailor's uniform for her and hilarious baggy-pants business to be performed in it. Martin was at first reluctant to do one piece of business he created, where she would put her leg through her sailor's tie and let the tie hold up her pants at the crotch. When she finally tried it, it brought a roar of laughter and remained a part of the number thereafter.

During the tryout period, William Tabbert was in danger of being fired because he did not seem to have the sex appeal needed for Lieutenant Cable. Martin and her husband thought that they could remedy the situation. They took the actor, bleached his too-fine hair, permed it, and restyled it until he became a stunning, curly blond. Then his costume was made as tight as possible, so that he could barely sit. The transformation was so complete, that many in the cast thought on seeing him for the first time that he was a replacement. Martin soon after became company barber, and various actors were always lining up for a cut.

Hammerstein and Logan's book was a lovingly crafted one, with fully fleshed out characters and a strong dramatic line. Brown approved of how the librettists had managed "to keep heavy materials light. If they supply pathos which is credible, they also provide humor which is enjoyable. They know how to vary their ingredients so that they emerge gay yet tender, compulsive but comic enough." "*South Pacific,*" raved Brooks Atkinson (*NYT*), "is as lively, warm, fresh and beautiful as we had all hoped that it would be." Gilder called it "one hell of a funny, moving, lyrical and absorbing play."

SPOOK SCANDALS [Revue/One-Acts] CN/P/D: Jerry Sylvon; M/LY: Sergio DeKarlo; CH: Paul Haakon, Raul Reyes, and Marta Nita; L: Sammy Lambert; P: Michael Todd Midnight Players; T: President Theatre (OB); 12/8/44 (2)
"The Gobi Curse" A: Arthur Gondra; "The Coffin Room" A: Al Henderson; "The Blind Monster" A: Jerry Sylvon

An assortment of one-acts, songs, and dances performed at midnight showings by players in the companies of *Catherine Was Great*, *Mexican Hayride*, and *Pick-up Girl*, all these shows produced by Michael Todd. The long-disused President Theatre was hired for the occasion, at which the critics looked askance and which they considered depressingly amateurish. The plays were of the Grand Guignol variety and employed screams in the dark, pistol shots, and the like. The hooded ushers were dressed like figures in Charles Addams's cartoons and told the spectators, "Fright this way; pull up a coffin and sit down."

In "The Coffin Room" a master criminal was shown trapped in a coffin. In "The Blind Monster," inspired by a Grand Guignol piece called "Kiss in the Dark," a man whose face had been disfigured by acid returned the favor on the girl who scarred him. Among the songs was "Nightly My Love," sung by someone calling herself Perdita, the Phantom. A cancan number was called "Since We Met in Paris." In "We're So Happy," the ghosts of Caruso, Pavlova, and Beethoven sang about how great they felt about being dead.

"It is a singularly tasteless horror, singing and dancing, and it is difficult to estimate which was the worst," declared George Freedley (*NYMT*). Todd had agreed to finance a two-week run, but when the show was panned, he paid everyone two weeks' wages and killed the project. Cast members included Paul Haakon, Don de Leo, Al Henderson, Eva Reyes, Kendal Bryson, Arthur Gondra, and Eddie Grove.

SPRING AGAIN [Comedy/Broadcasting/Business/Films/Hotel/Marriage/Romance] A: Isabel Leighton and Bertram Bloch; D/P: Guthrie McClintic; S: Donald Oenslager; T: Henry Miller's Theatre; 11/10/41 (241)

This hit comedy, which moved to the Playhouse on 1/12/42, was an "amiable if not exciting" (Rosamond Gilder [*TAM*]) vehicle for two veteran troupers, C. Aubrey Smith and Grace George, who played Halstead and Nell Carter, an aging couple living in genteel poverty in a residential hotel. (Donald Oenslager's set of their small flat was considered beautiful but too luxurious for their circumstances.) Between them constantly falls the shadow of Halstead's father, a famous Civil War general who died at Shiloh. The curmudgeonly Halstead has made a virtual career out of presiding at ceremonies eulogizing and memorializing his late forebear, which continually disturbs the dainty Nell, who knows what the cantankerous general really was like. The Carters' daughter, Edith (Ann Andrews), a snob married to a wealthy businessman (Richard Stevenson), is trying to break up the marriage of her own daughter (Jane Cotter, later known as Jayne Meadows; this was her Broadway debut) to a struggling radio writer (John Craven). To teach Edith a lesson and to express her own rebellion, Nell collaborates with the writer on a money-making radio serial debunking the cantankerous General Carter. This leads to civil war in the Carter household when the family feels that they are being ridiculed. More eruptions occur when William Auchinschloss (Joseph Buloff), a gregarious movie producer, appears, wanting to buy the movie rights for $60,000, and Nell refuses. Halstead is willing, however, provided Ronald Colman, not Charles Laughton, plays the general. Finally, all is put to rights, the young couple's marriage is saved, and the general's shadow vanishes from the Carters' life.

As a work of dramatic literature, this was a failure. Its only memorable material came in act three with the arrival of the Hollywood producer. The characters were deemed ineffective, the situations implausible, and the pacing lethargic. George Freedley (*NYMT*) said that the play, "as a whole, is too mild, too weak a dish of tea to stand the dousing of spirits" given it in the last act.

As a piece for talented players, it was a success. "Miss George makes every one in the audience feel pleasantly crude and awkward by the lightness of her walk, the grace of her manners, the sweetness of her voice and the wit of her acting," applauded Brooks Atkinson (*NYT*). Smith matched her moment for moment, and the comic performance of Buloff as the nervy producer practically stole the show from the distinguished leads. John Beaufort (*CSM*) wrote that when Buloff entered, "hilarity knew no bounds. I don't know how much funnier Mr. Buloff is than his part, or whether he is out of key with the proceedings. He is so uproariously funny that he leaves the impression of having walked out the door of Donald Oenslager's set with the play in his pocket."

The cast included Ben Lackland, Michael Strong, William Talman, and Robert Keith, as well as twenty-one-year-old Kirk Douglas in his Broadway debut as a singing Western Union boy. In *The Ragman's Son*, Douglas recalled his audition for Guthrie McClintic. He was given a piece of paper with several lines on it and told to learn the words to the tune of "Yankee Doodle." After an hour of practicing, he was allowed to show his stuff by entering through a door and singing his telegram. "I came in, sang as loudly as I could, and was shocked to find that I had the part." During rehearsals he stayed so close to McClintic, serving as his gofer, that he was soon made assistant stage manager. He was so ardent in his tasks that a simple call of "Kirk!" guaranteed an instant appearance. While the show was still in tryouts, he had been given four roles to understudy and promoted to stage manager. He even directed the understudy rehearsals.

SPRING PRODUCTION [Comedy-Drama/Marriage/Sex/Theatre] A: Oskar Gens; D: John F. Grahame; P: Modern Play Productions, Inc.; T: Provincetown Playhouse (OB); 5/20/44

George Freedley (*NYMT*) wrote that this "play is so completely mediocre that it is absolutely impossible to get enough of a reaction even to write a damning column about it." It is about a dramatist (Robert Feyti) living in Putnam County, New York, who is unable to draw a line between his private life and the world he dramatizes. He is being urged to complete a play by a harried producer, but complications develop when he rescues a scheming aspiring actress (Josephine Lombardo) and becomes enthralled by her intellectual abilities. His infatuation leads to his ignoring his own attractive and--unbeknownst to him--pregnant wife (Genie Conrad). The actress manages to wangle her way into the playwright's new play, nearly destroying his career and private life in the process. He makes the most of it, though, and sits down to pen a new play in which the actress leaves him for Broadway and he wins back his spouse and newborn baby.

STAR AND GARTER [Revue] D/L: Hassard Short; CH: Al White, Jr. and Albertina Rasch; S: Harry Horner; C: Irene Sharaff; P: Michael Todd; T: Music Box Theatre; 6/24/42 (605)

Wartime crowds seeking pure escapism on Broadway were lured not only by a brief resurgence of vaudeville, but by expensively produced pseudoburlesque shows such as this one starring ecdysiast Gypsy Rose Lee and classic clown Bobby Clark as her top banana. The show, ticketed at an expensive $4.40 top, seemed to be what the customers wanted, especially since real burlesque had recently been banned. New York Supreme Court Judge Aaron J. Levy called it "inartistic filth." An unnamed *V* reviewer correctly predicted, "It's bawdy and racy, lusty and sexy, an excursion into the double-entendre (sometimes it's just singleness of thought) that will draw a large clientele." Producer Todd, warned that sophisticated audiences would not tolerate this old-hat type of material, responded that it would be old-hat to audiences who saw it at forty-cent burlesque shows, but not to those able to spend $4.40, especially with the cachet of Hassard Short's name on the marquee as director.

Pulchitrude (including that of bump and grinder Georgia Sothern) triumphed over comedy, with Clark falling flat in his familiar sketches, such as "The Sacred Gherkin," "That Merry Wife of Windsor," and "In the Malamute Saloon," and coming back too late with "Robert the Roué" and "Alfred in Court." In the latter he played a judge who spat spitballs at the prosecuting attorney. When the male witness claimed, despite the presence of a sofa, not to have done anything to the pretty defendant (Lee), the judge replied, "I would have done just what you did, only I wouldn't lie about it!" He also fell off his seat whenever the defendant crossed her shapely legs.

The show had its fair share of standard variety acts, including acrobats (Wayne and Marlin; the Hudson Wonders); a dog and monkey act (trained by Gil Maison); a female singer (Marjorie Knapp with a naughty tune, "The Bunny"); a nightclub comedian (Pat Harrington); a Latin dancer (Juanita Rios); a comic xylophonist (Professor Lamberti); a drunk act (Frank and Jean Hubert); and comic-adagio dancing (Lynn, Royce, and Vanya). There was also burly burleycue queen Carrie Finnell, who could make the tassels on her breasts swing in multiple directions. The best-known song in the show was Johnny Mercer and Harold Arlen's "Blues in the Night."

Todd circumvented the ordinances against stripping, said George Jean Nathan (*TBY*), by "bringing on the girls stark naked in the first place except for small rosebuds on their nipples and miniature gilt stars on their pupenda [*sic*]." Speaking of Lee, Arthur Pollock (*BE*) deposed, "Gypsy Rose Lee, looking very pretty and wearing gorgeous clothes, turns out to be a surprisingly sweet actress, very smooth indeed. She's pleasing in the opening chorus, charming in an Irving Berlin song, 'The

Girl on the Police Gazette,' quite delectable in her strip tease, 'I Can't Strip to Brahms.'" Lee herself, whose strip was done in aloof and dignified style, wrote this last named number.

Art Cohn noted in *The Nine Lives of Michael Todd* that because there was not enough money for an out-of-town tryout shakedown, the show was going to open "cold," with only a single preview performance. That preview, however, proved so catastrophic that one backer asked for his $10,000 investment back. "I hate angels," remarked Todd. "They usually have opinions." Todd was asked to take the show to Boston, but he refused, saying that all it needed was "new songs, new skits and new scenery." "And new money," added an investor. When Todd told Lee that the show was too frail too open, she complained that it had to open, as she had bought enough body paint for two years. On hearing that the show not only required at least a week's additional work, but that a backer wanted his money back, Lee put the money up herself. Todd then began to reshape the show, with new material added. When a $25,000 bond had to be posted with Equity, the cash again came from the stripper star, who herself led the most frugal of lives and resided in a thirty-dollar-a-month apartment in an old apartment house (owned by her). Lee also provided numerous routines from burlesque that she knew intimately, and Todd touched them up with his own flavor, thereby turning the flop into a hit.

During the run there was an interesting crisis in the theatre. A pair of FBI agents took over the box office before a sold-out performance, and soon there were numerous quarrels at the box office as over sixty outraged people who had bona fide reservations for that evening's show were turned away, told that there were no tickets in their names. During the show two couples in the orchestra were, like everybody else, laughing loudly, when one of the men was tapped on the shoulder and beckoned to leave. He and the three others with him were soon making their way up the aisle. They had been surrounded until then by sixty-some-odd FBI agents and their escorts, watching from the disputed seats. It turned out that the FBI had been tipped off that these two couples would be at the show, and that the foursome headed one of the biggest Nazi espionage rings in the country.

STAR SPANGLED FAMILY [Comedy/Family/Marriage/Mental Illness/War/Youth] A: B. Harrison Orkow; D: William Castle; S: Edward Gilbert; C: Lou Eisele; P: Phil A. Waxman and Joseph Kipness; T: Biltmore Theatre; 4/10/45 (5)

Sally Jones (Frances Reid) lost her husband Mac in the war, where he was a hero pilot. Shortly after the war, this Manhattan widow falls for another man, Dr. Richard Morley (Edward [Eddie] Nugent). Mac's bitter mother Margaret (Jean Adair) and his nine-year-old son Bud (Donald Devlin) worship his memory and are indignant not only that Sally would remarry but that it would be to a man whose war responsibilities kept him at Fort Dix, New Jersey. Margaret poisons Bud against the marriage, and Bud becomes so fixated on the problem that he has to be seen by a psychiatrist, while Margaret gets so carried away by her venomous emotions that she loses her mind and is carted off to the hospital. Dr. Morley finally gains his stepson's confidence in a scene during which the boy, in a delirium, thinks that the voice he hears is that of his late father, at whose portrait he is looking.

Only two-thirds of the audience remained at the final curtain on opening night. The play was "packed with sincerity and a lot of very clumsy writing," wrote Ward Morehouse (*NYS*). James Aronson (*NYP*) called it "a plodding, pedestrian job, full of poor writing that sprouted a weedbed of cliches."

STAR TIME [Revue] P: Paul Small; T: Majestic Theatre; 9/12/44 (120)

One more attempt to revive vaudeville in the guise of a Broadway show, this one starring waggish comedian Lou Holtz, armed with his cane and cigar, as the MC. For some, he overstayed his welcome, but George Jean Nathan (*TBY*) thought that he was one of the few things in the show worth paying for. His rambling dialect stories included three new ones about his favorite character, Sam Lapidus.

The other principal performer was singer Benny Fields, whose sentimental repertoire included "Over There" and "Lullaby of Broadway." Ballroom dancers Tony and Sally De Marco glided across the stage in several numbers; black tapsters the three Berry Brothers were on hand; striking nineteen-year-old singer Shirley Dennis performed some songs, but was too dependent on a microphone that overamplified her voice; comic acrobats the Whitson Brothers flew through the air; and Jimmy and Mildred Mulcay harmonized on their numerous harmonicas.

In general, the reviewers felt that the show lacked life and originality. Holtz and the De Marcos were the only ones widely appreciated. Lewis Nichols (*NYT*) thought that the revue could have been sprightlier, with greater variety and faster pacing. "It was all faintly nostalgic and decidedly out of date," yawned Rosamond Gilder (*TAM*).

STARLIGHT [Drama/Blacks/Crime/Religion/Sex] A/D: Curtis Cooksey; S: A. A. Ostrander; P: American Negro Theatre; T: 135th Street Library Theatre (OB); 6/7/42

Curtis Cooksey, a white actor who had played leading roles on Broadway, authored and directed this play for the black actors of Harlem's American Negro Theatre. It was considered by Ralph Warner (*DW*) to be a choice "unworthy of [the company's] position and prestige. . . . It is a very bad play, amateurishly constructed, violating many simple rules of dramaturgy, wandering, incoherent, 'hooked-up' and vulgar."

Meant as an exposé of phony evangelism, it focuses on a fake preacher (Maxwell Glanville) with a penchant for young girls. He seduces two women, one of them a pleasure-starved girl named Starlight (Ruby Wallace), stepdaughter of a depraved and violent woman (Claire Leyba). Starlight loses her mind and is killed by her seducer.

STARS OF TOMORROW [Revue] P: Jules Denes; T: Malin Studio Theatre (OB); 7/19/44

An intimate Off-Broadway revue with James McGarry as MC. It employed a company entirely made up of unknowns. They remained so in the years to come. The numbers included a dog act starring Chiko the chihuahua; Ray and Gladys Royce, who danced in red flannel underwear as well as in drag; Helena Hughes, a pseudo-Spanish dancer; Maria Karolyi, a singer; Edythe Kline, who did the conga; and others. Robert Garland (*NYJA*) wondered why such shows were put on, and why performers allowed themselves to make such fools of themselves, especially as the audience was allowed to jeer those they disliked.

(1) STARS ON ICE [Revue] M: Paul McGrane and Paul Van Loan; LY: Al Stillman; D: William H. Burke and Catherine Littlefield; CH: 0Catherine Littlefield (skating direction: May Judels); S: Bruno Maine; C: Lucinda Ballard; L: Eugene Braun; P: Sonart Productions (Sonja Henie and Arthur M. Wirtz); T: Center Theatre; 7/2/42 (427)

This monster hit was a happy follow-up to the previous ice revue at Radio City's Center Theatre, *It Happens on Ice*, produced by the same people. Coproducer Henie, however, appeared in neither, although she was regularly seen in ice-skating spectaculars shown at Madison Square Garden (those shows are not covered in this work).

Stars on Ice included a wide assortment of skating specialties, such as speed skaters, ballet skaters, comic skaters, and chorus-line skaters. One production number, "The Pan-Americana," with Mayita Montez, was to a samba rhythm; others were geared to children's interests. Another suggested a fox hunt--including the hurdles--on ice. "Jack Frost Reverie" was a ballet fantasy. "Autumn Leaves" evoked a falling chrysanthemum buffeted by the winds, and "Victory Ball" smacked of patriotism. There was more than enough variety available, and it was even suggested that some of it could profitably be eliminated to tighten the show (there were nine more numbers than in its predecessor).

Carol Lynne and Lloyd "Skippy" Baxter were the leading figure skaters. Other brilliant skaters were Freddie Trenkler, the Four Bruises, Dr. A. Douglas Nelles, tiny Paul Castle, seven-year-old prodigy Twinkle Watts, the Brandt Sisters, Mary Jane Yeo, Gene Berg, Alex Hurd, Carol Lynne, and the Rookies. Several performers were not skaters, such as Vivienne Allen, who sang during a Saturday-night jukebox number (which introduced the still played "Juke Box Saturday Night") as others flew about on the ice.

Euphemia Van Rensselaer Wyatt (*CW*) welcomed the show, noting, "If not as rarely beautiful from the spectacular point of view as the first production [*It Happens on Ice*], *Stars on Ice* has more variety and hence may be even more popular." But not a few agreed with George Jean Nathan (*TBY*) that such shows, no matter how good, eventually grew monotonous: "Two hours and a quarter of precision is more than one can comfortably endure, whether in an ice rink or Walter Pater."

(2) C: Paul du Pont and Lucinda Ballard; 6/24/43 (403)

A trimmed-down second-edition revision of *Stars on Ice* that was deemed outstanding, despite the absence of several top skaters, such as Gene Berg, Lloyd "Skippy" Baxter, and half of the Four Bruises, who had been called up by the armed forces. The remaining Bruises dropped their hilarious scrub woman routine, which they had been doing since *It Happens on Ice*, and added "The Three Kilties," which was equally funny as performed to the tune of "Loch Lomond." It employed Geoffe Stevens, Monte Scott, and Rudy Van Dyke.

The show's new skaters included James Wright (Baxter's replacement), Gretle and Robert Uksila, Rudy Richards, Muriel Pack, James Caesar, and Leo Freisinger, among others, while many who were in the first edition remained intact. Many of the original numbers remained as well. One of the few new ones was "Little Miss Muffet," with child skater Twinkle Watts. Comic skater Freddie Trenkler almost stole the show with his routines, but another funny bladesman, Geoffe Stevens of the Four Bruisers, had some hilarious solos, too, including a routine about a drunk who sees pink elephants. Carol Lynne remained the featured female figure skater.

G. E. Blackford (*NYJA*) observed, "It is skilfully blended and expertly staged, gorgeously costumed in the manner that has become [*sic*] to be expected at the big Rockefeller Center Theatre. Practice is making more perfect each succeeding effort of the big cast of ice stars. This one is really quite a show." But George Jean Nathan (*TBY*) emphasized that, apart from some superficial additions, this show and its predecessor were "as alike, and in their likeness as monotonous and unstimulating, as a pair of metronomes timing the brewing of a vat of iced tea."

STATE OF THE UNION [Comedy/Business/Hotel/Journalism/Marriage/Politics/Sex] A: Howard Lindsay and Russel Crouse; D: Bretaigne Windust; S: Raymond Sovey; P: Leland Hayward; T: Hudson Theatre; 11/14/45 (765)

Burns Mantle selected this highly regarded wisecracking satire--originally called *I'd Rather Be Left*--as one of his ten best plays of the year; even more prestigiously, it won the Pulitzer Prize for drama. It was one of the most successful politically oriented works of its day, satirizing, among other targets, voter practices and corrupt campaigning. It was inspired by actress Helen Hayes asking Lindsay and Crouse if they might not like to write a political play with a hero based on Wendell Willkie, an idealistic politician who had run in the controversial 1940 presidential campaign. Hayes turned down other opportunities as she awaited the promised script, but writers' block kept the collaborators from putting pen to paper. One night, Crouse was at a party where a Ouija board was being used. He asked it when he and Lindsay would write the play. The planchette immediately spelled "tonight." Crouse immediately made a dash for Lindsay's house and began to write the piece. When the play was completed, Hayes turned it down as being too political for her. "I could smell the cigar smoke coming from the back room," she said (quoted in Cornelia Otis Skinner's *Life with Lindsay and Crouse*). Crouse, asked later if the leading character was, in fact, based on Willkie, replied, "He's not Willkie. But he's certainly Crindsay--and maybe Louse."

To keep it as up-to-the-minute as possible, certain lines were changed periodically and there was a new newspaper headline read each night to reflect the actual headline of the day. The dialogue was peppered with the names of current political figures to give the play a cachet of even greater authenticity.

The story, designed to demonstrate that political leaders are chosen not by the people but by other politicians, is about Grant Matthews (Ralph Bellamy), a well-to-do, idealistic airplane manufacturer, married to the cynically amusing Mary Matthews (movie actress Ruth Hussey, in her Broadway debut), from whom he is estranged. His view of postwar America is of a nation whose unity is becoming unraveled, and it is his desire to reunite the nation as it was during the war. His mistress is a powerful newspaper publisher, Kay Thorndyke (Kay Johnson), who seeks to ride his coattails to the White House. She uses her persuasive powers to get the Republican party interested in him as a potential 1948 presidential candidate, and Grant is himself bitten by the bug. The party bigwigs insist that he make his speaking tour with his wife, while his liaison with the publisher is discreetly hidden. Mary's jibes are a healthy tonic for keeping Grant's overweening self-esteem in perspective. But Grant's manager, the hard-boiled ex-reporter, Spike McManus (Myron McCormick), comes to see the danger in the marital relationship because Mary's uncompromising sense of truth is not the stuff of practical politics. Grant and Mary must host a dinner for various politicos, and Mary, despite her vow to keep from drinking so as to avoid saying anything untoward, finds herself sipping a potent concoction. Soon her inhibitions fly out the nearest window. Rebuked by Grant, she responds, "Personally, I'd rather be tight than president." Before long, each of the guests, including the tough party boss, James Conover (Minor Watson), is devastated by her tart remarks. Pushed to the limit, his integrity on the line, Grant realizes that to gain the nomination, he will have to make too many compromises and too many deals; he thereby loses the presidential bid. He and Mary are reconciled, and Grant promises to fight for his ideals and the "state of the union."

One major reason many enjoyed the play was its ability to provide solid entertainment while offering an appropriate lesson in morality for both those in politics and those outside it. "Cynical as it may be to demonstrate that a candidate for president can rarely preserve his personal integrity, a capitalist is exhibited who prefers to remain true to his wife and without any sticky sentiment," averred Euphemia Van Rensselaer Wyatt (*CW*). "With wonderfully funny lines and situations, the new comedy . . . also has enough sentiment to keep it from being farce, enough idea to show that its heart is in the right place," noted Lewis Nichols (*NYT*). "In spite of all its little tricks, its smartly tailored laughs, it is really a human play," wrote Louis Kronenberger (*PM*). "Its characters, as far as they go, are lifelike." Howard Barnes (*NYHT*) commented, "It tosses barbs at a great rate, but they are honeyed with good fun and persuasion." There were, however, some criticisms of its occasionally sagging action, unfocused dramatic issues, and contrived happy ending. George Jean Nathan (*TBY*) considered it a rewrite of various similar plays of fifty years before and thought its politics naive.

The performances by the leads were first-rate, and they were supported by a truly able company that included G. Albert Smith, Victor Sutherland, Aline McDermott, and Maidel Turner. In general, the production was considered virtually flawless and an excellent example of slick Broadway showmanship.

Bellamy, in *When the Smoke Hit the Fan*, remembered how adept coauthor Crouse was at coming up with important lines in an emergency. This was illustrated when it became evident that a strong curtain line was needed for the backroom political discussion that served the play as a prologue. When nothing had been provided to end the scene and the company began to grow nervous, Crouse's collaborator, Lindsay, asked him please to provide the needed tag. Crouse took a short stroll up and down the aisles and then suggested that at the climax of the political argument someone mention the difference between the Democrats and the Republicans. Minor Watson improvised, "The only difference between the two parties is: they're in and we're out!" This became the scene's all-important curtain line.

As mentioned previously, a daily headline was read in the play to keep it fresh. Bellamy had the nightly task of thinking of an appropriate one and would scan the papers and listen to the radio as part of his daily research. The line would be delivered after Mr. and Mrs. Matthews came downstairs to await a room service meal of hamburgers and martinis before he delivered a major political address. One night, when British prime minister Winston Churchill was in the audience, Bellamy, wanting to come up with something especially pertinent, concocted the headline, "After two strenuous weeks, Churchill relaxes in New York seeing plays," which precipitated a huge laugh. The following day, as Churchill prepared to embark on the ship back to England, he was asked his opinion of *State of the Union*. After a brief pause, he declared, "I don't know what kind of speech a man could make on a hamburger and only one martini."

Another story concerns the show's Pittsburgh tryout, where Crouse watched unsmilingly from the back of the house as he studied the audience's reactions in detail. The woman sitting next to him glared at his dour expression. At the end, she said to him in scolding tones, "I've been watching you, and you never laughed once during the entire show! You're the sort of person who gives Pittsburgh a bad reputation as a theatre town!"

STEP A LITTLE CLOSER [Revue] SK: Gordon Cotler, Daniel Klugherz, and Alvin S. Yudkoff; M: Albert Sherwin; LY: Richard P. Malkin; D: Daniel Klugherz; S: Albert Castro-Lopez; CH: Beatrice Seckler; P: Theatre Downtown; T: Provincetown Playhouse (OB); 5/27/48

"A soggy little revue" (Rube Dorin [*NYMT*]), that lacked imagination or talent. Among the few likable numbers were "Phyllis" as sung by Connie Dose, and "The Saturday Review," concerning a bright young woman's (Ellen Davey) advertising in a magazine for a similarly intellectual soulmate. Among less-than-mediocre pieces was a travesty of the hit play *Harvey*. John S. Wilson (*PM*) growled that the show "has practically nothing to recommend it. The songs and sketches are feeble reworkings of material that has long since been worked to death."

STEPS LEADING UP [Drama/Business/Labor/Romance] A: George Harr; D: Paul A. Foley; P: Experimental Theatre; T: Cort Theatre; 4/18/41 (1)

This was the second production of the Experimental Theatre, a group organized with the cooperation of Actors Equity and the Dramatists Guild to allow showcase productions of new authors and to give actors a chance to work in a rapidly decreasing theatrical marketplace. Single matinee performances were given of plays at regular Broadway playhouses. Unlike the usual antimanagement plays of the thirties, this work was an indictment of labor racketeering in the millinery industry. However, while frequently powerful in its message and demonstrating familiarity with its milieu, it suffered from undeveloped dramaturgy and stereotypical characters. Typical was George Freedley's (*NYMT*) response: "It is a loose and sprawling play which shows possibilities for future production, if sufficiently cut and tightened. As it stands now it is unready for hte [*sic*] public view." The play was given on a bare stage sparsely set with chairs and tables.

Its chief characters are young finishers ("slickers") in the ladies hat-making business who find that because they, unlike the senior laborers, are unprotected by a strong union, they are being burdened with an increasing workload to save money for the employers. The aggressive Dave Gordon (James Gregory) sets about organizing the other workers and goes forth to the headquarters of the blockers' union for advice. The union leaders, meanwhile, are scheming to fleece their members of more money for a trumped-up fund, the money really being intended for the leaders' pockets. Frustrated in their attempts to gain assistance, Dave and his cohorts seek aid from the National Labor Relations Board, although union leader Blackie Hymen (Sanford Bickart) tries unsuccessfully to use his connections on the board to obstruct them. The union leaders are persuaded to accept the younger workers into the union, but the leaders cook up a plan to deprive the new members of any real rights. Meanwhile, Dave is blacklisted, fired, and then beaten when he fights for his rights. Only the hard-nosed but decent trimmer (Adele Harrison) he loves revives Dave's defeated faith.

The large cast included Robert Breen, William Prince, and Will Kuluva.

STEVEDORE [Dramatic Revival*] A: Paul Peters and George Sklar; M: Joe Liebling; D: Dan Levin; P: Equity Library Theatre; T: Charles Weidman Studio (OB); 2/14/49 (8)

Reviews of Equity Library Theatre productions were rare in the late 1940s, except for projects of unusual interest. One such was this revival of the 1934 left-wing propaganda play *Stevedore*, which drew a tiny handful of critics. The production, starring Ossie Davis, was deemed interesting enough to have its brief, limited-engagement run extended for three extra performances. The production depended for its effect on a quality of raw feeling. The director, said Vernon Rice (*NYP*), "packed the show with plenty of fast action." "Its high-paced performance is superb," applauded Robert Garland (*NYJA*). And J. P. S. (*NYT*) called it "a spirited and powerful production."

As Lonnie, Ossie Davis "rises to the occasion magnificently," said J.P.S. "He makes of the dungaree-clad waterfront worker an heroic symbol of resistance to the vicious oppression that can stem from intolerance and greed." The cast included Helen Martin as Ruby, Lauri Lauria as the preacher, Roman Henderson as Blacksnake, Georgette Harvey repeating her 1934 role as Binnie, Lawrence Criner as Sam, Lloyd Richards as Jim Veal, Ted Kazanoff as Marty, Rod Steiger as Al, and Jack Klugman as Mitch. For Richards, Steiger, and Klugman it was their New York debut, making the event remarkable in introducing such an array of future greats.

STORM OPERATION [Drama/Military/Religion/Romance/Sex/War] A: Maxwell Anderson; D: Michael Gordon; S: Howard Bay; C: Rose Bogdanoff; L: Moe Hack; P: Playwrights' Company; T: Belasco Theatre; 1/11/44 (23)

Although it racked up only three weeks of showings, *Storm Operation* made it to Burns Mantle's collection of the ten best of the season. To prepare for writing this propaganda play, author Anderson received special permission from the army to observe the invasion of North Africa. After considerable effort, he received accreditation as a correspondent, General Dwight D. Eisenhower having to approve him. He managed to get to Algiers and met the general himself at Allied Headquarters. Telling Eisenhower of his interest in writing about the Anglo-American activity in North Africa, he found that the general was so enthusiastic that the latter actually suggested the very topic on which the play eventually was written. This was the Storm Operation, the code name for the North African campaign. As part of the arrangement Anderson made with the War Department, he had to submit his script for its approval. This led to a number of required changes that irked the playwright considerably. Among these were a revision that eliminated a pregnant nurse's pregnancy, a scene in which a GI kicked a praying Muslim, and one in which American soldiers abused German POWs. Anderson was further annoyed by advice he was given by fellow playwright Robert E. Sherwood, serving in the Office of War Information. Sherwood asked Anderson to remove all traces of the fact that the leading female in the play, Nurse Grey, was promiscuous. The play ultimately failed, but its importance in being the first American drama to deal with the nation's involvement in the all-important campaign was deemed significant enough to warrant it a place in Mantle's list.

As most reviewers noted, the play is actually two in one. First, there is the story of the response to the war of a group of raw recruits who are gaining their first battle experiences and who are concerned about the meaning and impact of the war. The action takes place aboard a landing barge (the prologue) off the Tunisian coast, in camp at Maknassy, in combat near Mazzouna, and again on a barge (the epilogue) as it is about to make a landing. Against regulations, a technical sergeant (Cy Howard) purchases an Arab girl (Sara Anderson), which leads to some bawdy humor when he tries to converse with her and other Arabs in double-talk. Both the soldier and the girl are eventually killed. Then there is the story of a love affair involving an Australian army nurse, Lieutenant Thomasina Grey (Gertrude Musgrove), who had deserted her top-sergeant boyfriend, Peter Moldau (Myron McCormick), for the English Captain Sutton (Bramwell Fletcher). She reencounters the sergeant when she and Sutton--a liaison officer--arrive at the front lines together. A sharp conflict is established between the green sergeant and the self-assured, militarily capable Briton, much of the friction stemming from the fact that the sergeant is temporarily in charge and the arrogant Englishman does not like taking orders from a lower-ranking and less seasoned man. After much time-consuming discussion of love-related matters, the romantic story ends as Peter and Sutton prepare to go off on a risky mission. Following the loss of some men in an advance unit, Peter has acknowledged his lack of preparation for desert warfare and has allowed Sutton to take over the command. As German Stuka aircraft dive-bomb, the officer, a former student of religion, marries the nurse to the sergeant by reading the marriage service from his Book of Common Prayer. In the epilogue on the barge, Peter gives his men their last orders before they attack an unnamed coast. His earlier philosophy of "living off the country" has been transformed into one whereby he tells his men to carry a dear one's photo when they go into danger to give them something to fight for.

The play had a documentary quality that was not matched by dramaturgic power. When it was concerned with the talk among men at war, it was often lustily funny and intriguing, and the characters were easy to get involved with. However, the play soon bogged down into soppy sentimentality. Nearly every critic was annoyed by the love story, which seemed completely out of place. The play, said Lewis Nichols (*NYT*), "is talky and slow, and some of it is maudlin." "It lacks the depth, imagination and eloquence of a fine drama," argued Howard Barnes (*NYHT*). "*Storm Operation*," said Arthur Pollock (*BE*), "is a play without body and no ideas at all." And Hobe. (*V*) excoriated the work as "turgid and confused."

McCormick--who had joined the production as an out-of-town replacement--gained kudos along with various others in the cast, but there was disagreement over the quality of the production. Director Michael Gordon replaced Rusty Lane during the out-of-town period. The latter's lackadaisical and unimaginative direction, wrote Playwrights' Company lawyer John F. Wharton in *Life among the Playwrights*, was so harmful that it resulted in "one of the greatest out-of-town debacles I ever witnessed."

In the cast were Millard Mitchell, Nick Dennis, Michael Ames, Elizabeth Inglise, Walter Kohler, and, in his Broadway debut, future star director Alan Schneider in the small role of Winkle. Schneider had been hired by Lane before the latter was fired (Lane was his former college professor) and had also been given the job of assistant stage manager. He said in *Entrances* that Michael Gordon, the new director, gave the cast a brilliantly perceptive half-hour analysis of the play's social and political background, but that his actual directing consisted of reversing the set to make a mirror image of the original and then keeping "everything else exactly as it was, spending hours talking with all the leads but changing nothing."

During the run, Schneider was blamed when a seat used by Gertrude Musgrove in a scene was not where it was supposed to be, although he himself had seen that it was in place as required. Her fellow actor in the scene covered for the lapse by giving her his seat and then sitting on a desk. When she came off, the actress was in a towering rage, threatening to hang and fire Schneider. The regular stage manager, however, had noticed that the chair had been in place and that a stagehand who disliked the actress for making antiproletarian comments had whisked the chair away just before the scene began. "So," wrote Schneider, "I had lesson number one in how to behave on Broadway: Don't antagonize the stagehands; they can kill in more ways than one."

Another contretemps involved lawyer Wharton, who noted that in the original script the comic role of the soldier who falls for the Arab girl had a line that seemed incongruously humorous at a serious point in the action. The line was "Gosh, take an *Aye*-rab girl into Detroit?" When Wharton asked Anderson why he had put such a funny line in here, the author grew indignant and insisted that the line was meant to be serious, even moving. The line drew a roar whenever it was spoken during the tryout period, so it was cut, but the sensitive Anderson, smarting over Wharton's earlier criticism, would not talk to the attorney for days.

STORY FOR STRANGERS, A [Drama/Crime/Fantasy/Gambling/Period/Prostitution/Religion/Romance/Small Town] A/D: Marc Connelly; S/L: Ralph Alswang; C: Millie Sutherland; P: Wico Company (Dwight Deere Wiman); T: Royale Theatre; 9/21/48 (15)

Marc Connelly, once a very successful Broadway playwright, was teaching playwriting at Yale University when he returned to the Great White Way with this doleful parable play about a talking horse.

In 1934 a traveling paint salesman (Edward Nannery) misses his bus and is temporarily stranded in the small Michigan town of Huntsville. Puzzled by the barber's unwillingness to accept money for a haircut, he gets the man to explain. This leads to the "story for strangers," the enactment of a series of flashbacks that recall how the once-scurvy townspeople encountered a miracle and abandoned their materialistic ways. (The dramatic device reminded critics of *Our Town**'s narrative technique.) It seems that there was a well-bred, upright, but impoverished young milkman named Norman Hunt (James Dobson), whose decrepit horse, Irving, was at death's doorstep when the beast was suddenly rejuvenated and given the gift of gab (but only to his master) by a bolt of lightning. (All that is heard by the audience of the horse is his offstage whinnying.) When Irving, breaking the rule about speaking to only one human, imparted his advice about right living to the corrupt, gambling, and dishonest townsfolk, and then died from the effect, they were so moved that they abandoned their evil ways and became decent, nonmaterialistic citizens. Criminals reformed, the town strumpet (Joann Dolan) became a manicurist, and small-mindedness vanished. Huntsville became a model of human love and charity. Norman's love for the young widow Bessie Bessie (Joan Gray) also came to a happy conclusion, despite her greedy mother's (Grace Valentine) desire to marry the girl off to a wealthy man.

"It has a few affecting moments and it offers several engaging performances, but it comes through as a singularly inept combination of realism and fantasy," declared Ward Morehouse (*NYS*). Stock characters and a confused dramatic structure were weaknesses pointed out by others. Thomas R. Dash (*WWD*) rejected the work as "listless and soporific." John McGovern, Jane Hoffman, Frank Tweddell, George Cotton, Lauren Gilbert, and Paul Huber were among those involved.

STORY OF MARY SURRATT, THE [Drama/Boarding House/Crime/Historical-Biographical/Law/Period/Politics/Prison/Trial] A/D: John Patrick; S: Samuel Leve; C: Jane Edgerton; L: Girvan Higginson; P: Russell Lewis and Howard Young; T: Henry Miller's Theatre; 2/8/47 (11)

This play--originally titled *This Gentle Host*--divided the critics and was quickly removed, but nevertheless was selected as one of the ten best of the season. It was a serious work based on an actual incident in American history in which author Patrick had long been interested. In preparing the semidocumentary script, he made much use as primary research material of such documents as the actual transcript of the trial in which his title character was found guilty of complicity in the assassination of Abraham Lincoln. It was Patrick's contention that the lady in question was railroaded under the pressure of contemporary hysteria and unjustly executed. To dramatize the story, he had to take some liberties with the chronology of events but kept his faith with the essence of the facts, and he invented at least one important character, Father Wiget (Harlan Briggs), a compendium of various priests involved in the case, as well as creating the final prison scene, of which there was no record.

Southern-born Mary Surratt (Dorothy Gish) was the Washington, D.C., boarding-house owner in whose residence the plot to kill Lincoln was hatched and whose own misguided son John (John Conway) was deeply involved in the conspiracy. The play, set in 1865, purports to demonstrate her innocence of any knowledge of the events that were transpiring under her roof. The action begins shortly before the assassination. Mary begins to suspect that something is wrong when John's roommate (Bernard Thomas) informs her of her son's strange behavior and gives her a dagger found in John's possession. (This is the dagger flashed by John Wilkes Booth [James Monks] during the assassination, and it became a crucial piece of evidence against Suratt.) Unaware of the plotting, she even tries to persuade Booth to end his friendship with her son. She is then arrested and illegally tried by the military as a conspirator in the president's killing, with the deck loaded against her by the suppression of evidence in her favor and the emphasis on damning evidence, including the testimony of perjured witnesses. Her capable but frustrated attorney--who is even denied access to President Johnson and the secretary of war--is Reverdy Johnson (Kent Smith), her childhood sweetheart. He is persuaded to take the case by Mary's daughter (Elizabeth Ross). After her sentencing, the bewildered Mary, shown in her cell, achieves the courage to meet her Maker, and a moral note is struck by the attorney on behalf of all such miscarriages of justice.

More interest was expressed in the play's historical background and revisionist viewpoint than in its dramatic capabilities. Cavils noted the lesser stature of Surratt as a dramatic heroine, the lack of ingenuity in the dramaturgy, the overly compressed and unconvincing trial scene, the stereotypically melodramatic ingredients, and other drawbacks. George Freedley (*NYMT*) called the play "an earnest and frequently moving drama" that was damaged by windy writing, and Ward Morehouse (*NYS*) termed it "a lumbering and unwieldy drama." But Rowland Field (*NEN*) called the play "a stage work of dignified substance and impelling strength." There were frequent commendations for the acting, especially of Gish and Smith.

STRANGE BEDFELLOWS [Comedy/Family/Marriage/Period/Politics/Prostitution/Sex/Women] A: Florence Ryerson and Colin Clements; D: Benno Schneider; S/L: Ralph Alswang; C: Morton Haack; P: Philip A. Waxman; T: Morosco Theatre; 1/14/48 (229)

Not to be confused with the 1924 Barry Connors farce (also known as *So This Is Politics**) of the same name, this popular, ribald comedy nevertheless shared with the earlier play the theme of women's liberation. Coauthor Ryerson, however, confided to the press that the real theme was "the war between the sexes." (Coauthor Clements died during the Philadelphia tryouts.)

The action is set in 1896 San Francisco, amid the lush trappings of wealthy Senator Cromwell's (Carl Benton Reid) grotesquely ostentatious Nob Hill mansion. (A big laugh came when the senator's wife commented on how bare the place seemed.) Senator Cromwell has worked his way up to his position of power in the Barbary Coast's Republican party with his wife Julia (Ruth Amos) at his side; she, too, has political aspirations. He is a behemoth of a conservative and a vociferous opponent of women's suffrage. The comic spark is ignited when--in the midst of an election--his son Matthew (John Archer) brings home his well-known suffragette bride, Clarissa (Joan Tetzel). The debate rages, the senator and his cronies try to thwart her, and the family rumbles--everyone, including Matthew, opposing Clarissa's views. Clarissa finally wins the women over, and they attempt to gain a victory by borrowing an Aristophanic ploy and refusing the men their favors. The plan flops when the men get drunk and troop off to a whorehouse. Then Clarissa digs up the dirt that Senator Cromwell's antisuffrage campaign is being financed with money contributed by the town's brothels, and, with blackmail power in their hands, the women's conquest is in the offing.

The critics generally had a good time but in no way were deceived into thinking this a good play. It was knocked for thin characterizations, sloppy craftsmanship, and emotional shallowness. "Critically speaking, it is all pretty shabby but," admitted George Jean Nathan (*TBY*), "like bygone burlesque, at times incorrigibly funny." Louis Kronenberger (*PM*) said, "It has very few surprises. In fact, it could almost bear the subtitle of Scenes From Old Play." "This is not a show to be analyzed," advised William Hawkins (*NYWT*), "because any stickler could find objections. It is a show with great good fun in it." But the unimpressed Brooks Atkinson (*NYT*) noted that the authors "have accomplished the remarkable feat of writing an entire comedy without writing a single witty line or coming up with anything but mechanical ideas."

Among the best performances in the raucously acted show were Doris Rich as a brothel madam, Nydia Westman as the senator's daughter, and John Craven as her spouse. Will Lee, Michael Hall, Mary Kay Jones, and Frieda Altman were also in the cast.

STRANGE FRUIT [Drama/Blacks/Crime/Race/Romance/Sex/Small Town/Southern] A: Lillian Smith and Esther Smith; SC: Lillian Smith's novel of the same name; D/P: José Ferrer; S/L: George Jenkins; C: Patricia Montgomery; T: Royale Theatre; 11/29/45 (60)

A number of important debuts occurred in this turgid, unoriginal melodrama of miscegenation and murder in the deep South, adapted by sisters from a well-known novel by one of them. It was the first Broadway play for Jane White, Ralph Meeker, and Murray Hamilton. José Ferrer made his producing debut with it. The large cast also included Earl Jones, father of actor James Earl Jones.

José Ferrer's uninspired direction (the acting was so low-keyed as to be inaudible at times) was of little assistance in making the awkward, twelve-scene dramatization come to life. Its attempt to make a statement about racial equality was a failure, and its infusion of ideas about world issues, labor, and religion only muddied the problem. Talking of the dramaturgy, George Jean Nathan (*TBY*) noted that the authors had done little more than "snip sections out of the novel and spread them upon a stage with no fusion, no direction, and no cumulation." He also criticized the play's lack of economy and failure to convey the complexity of a town's life without resorting to bloat. Lewis Nichols (*NYT*) recorded that whereas there were scenes of strength and feeling, the play as a whole "is sprawling and too much of its length is verbose."

Mel(chor) Ferrer played Tracy Deen, a feckless male Southern white drugstore proprietor of Maxwell, Georgia, in love since his boyhood with a proud mulatto girl, Nonnie Anderson (White), who gets pregnant by him. Because of his unwillingness to formally acknowledge his relationship to Nonnie, he tries to end the relationship and salve his conscience by bribing his black houseboy (Jones) to marry her and be a father to the child. Nonnie refuses to accept the arrangement. Circumstances lead to Tracy's being slain by Nonnie's brother (George B. Oliver) and to the consequent mob lynching of the houseboy, who is accused of the murder.

Important cast members were Juano Hernandez as a black doctor and Ralph Theadore as a liberal mill owner. Eugenia Rawls, Vera Allen, Steven Chase, Frank Tweddell, Dorothy Carter, and Edna Thomas were also involved. Many thought that Jones deserved the evening's acting honors.

STRANGE PLAY, A and **"ACCORDING TO LAW"** D/P: Eugene Endrey; S: Harry Bennett; T: Mansfield Theatre; 6/1/44 (4)
A Strange Play [Comedy/Marriage/Sex/Theatre] A: Patti Spears; "According to Law" [Dramatic Revival*] A: Noel Houston

This bill opened with a revival of Houston's one-act, originally produced and directed in March 1940 at the Provincetown Playhouse by the same person assuming those tasks on this occasion. The piece, about a lawyer's (Don Appell, repeating his original role) defense of a black man (Wardell Saunders) accused of raping a white woman, was considered superior to the play for which it now served as a curtain raiser. Still, it was deemed a stereotyped propaganda drama.

The characters in the main play wear white dinner jackets and drink Napoleon brandy served by a butler (Byron Russell). The plot concerns the affair of an elderly surgeon's (Richard Gordon) young wife (Alicia Parnahay) with a good-looking actor (Herbert Heyes). The old doctor's playwright friend William Douglas (Ralph Clanton) realizes what's going on and tries to use the situation as his inspiration for a play. He wonders what a man's best friend should do in such a case, tell the friend or keep it secret? As he writes down his ideas with pad and pencil, the other characters act out what he has written, requiring that some of the dialogue be repeated several times. Shown are what will happen if he tells, if he doesn't tell, and if the butler tells.

It all seemed hilariously inane to the audience, which could not refrain from bursting into laughter at the idiocy of the dialogue. Otis L. Guernsey, Jr. (*NYHT*), thought that "the dialogue is so incredibly naive and over-written that the actors appear to have wandered in by mistake, doggedly attempting to make up a play as they go along."

STRANGER, THE [Drama/Crime/Jews/Mystery/Period/Politics] A: Leslie Reade; D/P: Shepard Traube; S/L: Boris Aronson; C: Rose Bogdanoff; T: Playhouse; 2/12/45 (16)

Shepard Traube, director of the hit thriller *Angel Street*, set in Victorian London, flopped with another Victorian-period mystery play that George Freedley (*NYMT*) labeled "a dull and obvious melodrama with red herrings a dime a dozen."

Its author was a South African citizen.

All three acts are set in the meeting room of the International Workmen's Educational Club in a poor section of London 1888. It is frequented by political radicals, such as the anarchist Napoleon Micalieff (Eugene Sigaloff) and the expatriate Frenchman Jean Prunier (Alfred Hesse). A series of killings reminiscent of Jack the Ripper's are committed nearby, the victims all being tarts. Into the club wanders a young, piano-playing, Wandering Jew-like shoemaker named David Mendelsohn (Eduard Franz), whose suspicious behavior raises eyebrows among the club's members. He even carries the small black bag and large knife and wears the leather apron rumored to be connected with the murderer. A constable (Stanley Bell) asking questions provokes an accusation against the cobbler. As the evidence mounts and the cobbler behaves in his supremely egotistical way, it becomes ever more certain that he is the guilty one, although a young seamstress named Christina Thomson (Perry Wilson) believes that he is innocent. At the end, David is found guiltless and the real killer (Morton L. Stevens) is revealed.

Some rebelled against the play because all of the offstage killings were of people who were not made important to the plot, so that one could not care about their demise. Moreover, the actual villain turned out to be a character who had barely figured in the action. Very few of the actors had convincing cockney accents, which distracted from the required feeling of authenticity. George Jean Nathan (*TBY*) objected to the playwright's attempt to make his play seem worthy by infusing it with comments of a political and social significance. Ward Morehouse (*NYS*) disposed of the work as "a listless and dawdling play, badly constructed and ineptly written." "The dialogue is not sharp or real or humorous enough to keep things entertaining while the pace lags," sighed Arthur Pollock (*BE*). The cast included Kim Spalding, Stella Todd, Eva Leonard-Boyne, and Wendy Atkin.

STREET SCENE [Musical/Crime/Family/Marriage/Romance/Sex] B: Elmer Rice; M: Kurt Weill; LY: Langston Hughes; SC: Elmer Rice's play of the same name*; D: Charles Friedman; CH: Anna Sokolow; S/L: Jo Mielziner; C: Lucinda Ballard; P: Dwight Deere Wiman and the Playwrights' Company; T: Adelphi Theatre; 1/9/47 (148)

A near-operatic, $160,000 musical version of Elmer Rice's 1929 success about the life and loves of people dwelling in a New York City brownstone tenement and about the *crime passionnel* that happens there. The story--played out largely in the street before the building by a large, multiethnic cast suggesting a cross-section of local citizens--remained much the same as in the original play, largely because Rice, in the role of librettist, was again responsible for it. The original text was closely followed, although several characters were omitted and the Swedish janitor was changed to a black one in order for Langston Hughes to write a blues lyric for him.

The show suffered serious out-of-town travails and had an especially disastrous time in Philadelphia, where there was practically no demand for tickets. A number of people associated with the production were gathered together one morning when the sister-in-law of coproducer Dwight Deere Wiman, seeing everyone's depression, piped up, "Well, I like the show; I'm going again and take friends with me." Wiman's general manager responded with a straight face, "Could you use a couple of . . . hundred tickets for this afternoon's matinee?" (recounted by John F. Wharton in *Life Among the Playwrights*).

Among the unconventional touches of the show were the lack of a dancing chorus, of a leading comic character, of eye-catching set changes, and of flashy costuming. Brooks Atkinson (*NYT*) said that if you added to the Rice text "a fresh and eloquent score by Kurt Weill . . . you have a musical play of magnificence and glory." Atkinson believed that the work represented the high point in the European-born composer's career. George Jean Nathan (*TBY*) was disappointed by the first twenty minutes and had other objections, but found his overall opinion radically altered by what followed, which was "an approach to American folk opera without the slightest pretentiousness, with an affecting book resolutely handled, with appropriately simple lyrics, with--aside from two honky-tonk compromises--the most satisfactory . . . music that Kurt Weill has thus far given us, and with" an outstanding troupe of singing performers. The show was "a minor miracle," exclaimed Rosamond Gilder (*TAM*). "All the values of *Street Scene* as a play have been preserved, but they have been given a new dimension. Kurt Weill's music lifts and enlarges the mood. . . . His music reflects the hot night, the chatter of gossiping housewives, the sound of children at play, the ebb and flow of anonymous existence." Euphemia Van Rensselaer Wyatt (*CW*) concurred, "Weill's score . . . transfuses each incident with a glowing beauty that raises it from the trivial to the universal." One of the few less impressed critics was John Mason Brown (*SR*), who commented that the play as Rice wrote it was still powerful, but that its transformation into musical drama seemed uncomfortable and awkward. Some of the more Broadway-oriented music was acceptable, he felt, but when the score ascended into operatic realms, it jarred distractingly from the realism of the text and production. "It is easy to believe in its enchanting lighter numbers but hard not to question its more ambitious reachings, and particularly its recitative."

Numbers that were singled out of the seamless and seriously minded score included Anna Maurrant's (Polyna Stoska) "Somehow I Never Could Believe" and "A Boy like You"; Sam Kaplan's (Brian Sullivan) "Lonely House"; "I'm Nuts about Ice Cream," with Mr. Fiorentino (Sidney Rayner) leading the chorus; Rose Maurrant's (movie actress Anne Jeffreys, in her Broadway bow) "What Good Would the Moon Be?"; "The Woman Who Lived Up There," sung by Henry Davis (Creighton Thompson), the black janitor, and the chorus; the apachelike jitterbug dance number, "Moon-Faced, Starry-Eyed," brilliantly performed by Sheila Bond (as Mae Jones) and Danny Daniels (as Dick McGann). But the music was so well integrated with the book that the songs were not of the sort that could easily be removed. Langston Hughes's warm and human and immediately comprehensible lyrics captured the flavor of New York street life.

The company was acclaimed for the brilliance of its players, who demonstrated equal talent in their singing and their acting. Especially striking were Jeffreys, Stoska, Norman Cordon (of the Metropolitan Opera House) as Frank Maurrant, Irving Kaufman as Abraham Kaplan, Hope Emerson as Emma Jones, and others.

Jo Mielziner, designer of the original play, created a new version of his famous naturalistically detailed apartment house, although modified to suit the style of the musical version by toning down its more garish features and reproportioning its dimensions. His lighting played a vital role as well by combining realistic with poetic effects.

Reviewers who wrote for journals on the "second-night" list went to see the show on 1/11/47, viewing it at a matinee while attending the second night of *Finian's Rainbow* that evening. Rarely have critics had the chance to see two new shows of such artistic rank on the same day.

Despite the warm response and initial audience interest, ticket sales began to decline fairly soon. To stimulate the box office, Wiman took out very large ads, but this sparked a conflict with the show's authors, who subcribed to the belief that the more you advertise a show the more you are telling the public that seats are easy to obtain. "When Wiman began to run larger advertisements," reported John F. Wharton in *Life among the Playwrights*, "he was admitting that tickets were not so difficult to get; this, the authors thought, was destroying the demand. Unhappily, the reality of the situation was that the *demand was not there*; and neither the absence nor the presence of advertising had any effect." In later incarnations the work was deemed an opera and was offered locally in the repertory of the New York City Opera Company.

(1) STREETCAR NAMED DESIRE, A [Drama/Alcoholism/Homosexuality/Marriage/Mental Illness/Prostitution/Romance/Sex/Southern] A: Tennessee Williams; M: Lehman Engel; D: Elia Kazan; S/L: Jo Mielziner; C: Lucinda Ballard; P: Irene M. Selznick; T: Ethel Barrymore Theatre; 12/3/47 (855)

One of the biggest dramatic bombshells to land on Broadway during the decade was this Pulitzer Prize and New York Drama Critics Circle Award winner that was also, as would be expected, chosen as one of the ten best plays of the season. It overtopped Williams's earlier hit, *The Glass Menagerie*, in critical and commercial success, came eventually to be considered one of the greatest of American plays, and catapulted all its leading players to stardom, none more so than Marlon Brando (understudied by another future star, Jack Palance), who went to Hollywood and never appeared on the New York stage again. Brando's part originally had been intended for John Garfield, while that of Blanche DuBois (Jessica Tandy) was written for Tallulah Bankhead. Bankhead later played it in a short-lived 1953 revival. In addition to marking a notable producing debut for Hollywood's Irene M. Selznick, it added brilliant plumes to the many-feathered headdresses of director Kazan and designers Mielziner and Ballard.

Williams got the idea for the play while recuperating in a hospital from a cataract operation, where he remembered his days in New Orleans's French Quarter. Outside his door there had been streetcars passing by in opposite directions and bearing the names CEMETERY and DESIRE. The irony in the contrasting names stirred his creative juices, and he went to Chapala, Mexico, to write this masterpiece.

A Streetcar Named Desire, originally called *The Poker Night*, is set on a raffish street called Elysian Fields in the tiny, squalid French Quarter flat of Stanley (Brando) and the pregnant Stella Kowalski (Kim Hunter, in her Broadway debut), a place depicted by Mielziner with scrims so that both the inside and the outside of the tenement could be seen as needed. Also visible through a scrim when appropriately lighted were the passersby at the rear of the apartment. Stanley, a muscular, crude, young Polish-American mechanic, and Stella are deeply in love, but their lives are disrupted by the arrival of Stella's frail, neurotic, guilt-ridden, and alcoholic older sister Blanche, who moves in with the couple until she can get her confused life back on track. Blanche, formerly a Mississippi schoolteacher, is a compulsive dreamer and self-dramatizer who harks back to her youth on the now-lost family plantation of Belle Reve and seriously annoys Stanley with her refined attitudes and delusions of grandeur. Seeing through her lies, he proceeds to peel away her layers of deceit, but fails to appreciate her desperate need to cover up her descent into a world of shame by donning a mask of gentility. There is both strong hostility and a sexual attraction between the brutish but not unintelligent husband and the delicate sister-in-law. Their conflict simmers until Stanley breaks open Blanche's trunk, throws her clothing about, and blames her for having lost Belle Reve. Meanwhile, a relationship has been slowly blossoming between Blanche and Stanley's shy and awkward poker buddy, mother's boy Harold Mitchell, called Mitch (Karl Malden), who listens sympathetically to her tragic account of her marriage at sixteen to a homosexual who committed suicide when Blanche discovered him with another man. Mitch, who has held true to his faith in Blanche's purity, abandons her, however, when Stanley vindictively reveals to him that he has learned of Blanche's sordid past as a prostitute at the Flamingo Hotel. Having sunk into the mire of nymphomania, she was dismissed from her teaching job for attempting the seduction of her students. The cruelty of Mitch's dismissal of her causes Blanche to lose her mental balance, and she dresses in a seedy old satin gown and rhinestone tiara. While Stella is in the hospital giving birth, Stanley and Blanche confront one another, she fabricating a tale about an admirer she dreams of going away with to the Caribbean. The scene ends with Blanche being raped by Stanley. When Stella returns, she can not believe Blanche's story. A doctor (Richard Garrick) and matron (Ann Dere) from a mental institution come for Blanche and take her away as she speaks her now-famous line about always depending "on the kindness of strangers."

The play and its theatrical realization were landmarks in Broadway history. Williams's drama was admired for its poetic language, earthy humor, human insight, brilliant characterizations, and powerful emotions. Euphemia Van Rensselaer Wyatt (*CW*) said that the play "takes one on a trip that makes *Medea* seem like a pleasure ride." Howard Barnes (*NYHT*) thought it "a savagely arresting tragedy . . . , a work of rare discernment and craftsmanship. Although it is almost explosively theatrical at times, it is crowded with the understanding, tenderness and humor of an artist achieving maturity." "*A Streetcar Named Desire* is not a play for the squeamish. It is often coarse and harrowing and it is grequently [*sic*] somewhat jerky in its blacked-out sequences, but it is a playwriting job of enormous gusto and vitality and poignance," wrote Ward Morehouse (*NYS*). Thomas R. Dash (*WWD*) referred to "this emotion-stirring play of power and lust, of poetry and imagination and of tremendous emotional drive." Scattered through the positive reviews were occasional reservations, including comments on the play's excessive length, its fetid atmosphere, and its unconventional structure. The most serious charges were leveled by George Jean Nathan (*TBY*), for whom the play, which he considered sensationalistic, should have been called "*The Glans Menagerie*." His several arguments included one declaring that whereas the playwright had succeeded in skillfully dramatizing sordid materials, he had "scarcely contrived to distil from them any elevation and purge."

Although it is Brando's performance that later generations usually recall, the most luminous reviews went to Tandy. Each of the other principals, in their less showy roles, was also hosannaed. Speaking of Tandy, whose role was extremely long and loquacious, Brooks Atkinson (*NYT*) wrote, "This must be one of the most perfect marriages of acting and playwriting. For the acting and playwriting are perfectly blended in a limpid performance, and it is impossible to tell where Miss Tandy begins to give form and warmth to the mood Mr. Williams has created. . . . Miss Tandy is a trim, agile actress with a lovely voice and quick intelligence. Her performance is almost incredibly true."

Brando's acting of the hulking Stanley led to an entire school of T-shirted, brawny, and inarticulate naturalistic acting that figured in many films and plays in coming years. Dash commented, "Marlon Brando catches the skepticism of the brother-in-law. He is properly uncouth, unmannered and violent and can explode in a convincing fit of temper." William Hawkins (*NYWT*) contended, "Marlon Brando plays the blunt and passionate Stanley with astonishing authenticity. His stilted speech and swift rages are ingeniously spontaneous, while his deep-rooted simplicity is sustained every second."

Contributing importantly in smaller roles were Rudy Bond as Steve, Gee Gee James as the negro woman, Peg Hillias as Eunice, Nick Dennis as Pablo, Vito Christi as a young collector, and Edna Thomas as the Mexican woman whose haunting cry, "*Flores para los muertos*," now and then punctuates the action. Kazan's direction was masterful, and he was praised for the excellence of the offstage sounds he integrated into the drama, from of rattling streetcars and jazz music to the arguments of volatile neighbors.

(2) [Return Engagement] T: City Center of Music and Drama; 5/23/50 (24)

The play had run on Broadway and toured the country for the past couple of years, employing several sets of actors. One such company, most of whose members had been in the play when it closed, reopened it in New York at the cavernous City Center, where many complaints were lodged against the actors' inaudibility, the difficulty of seeing the poorly lighted stage, and the generally depressing influence of the too-large theatre on so delicate a play. Hobe. (*V*) moaned, "The present experience is a letdown. The subtlety, depth and compassion of the play is now largely missing, with greater emphasis on the brutality and coarse comedy. Since the players have to practically bellow to be heard at all . . . the performance becomes a travesty. Considering the difficulties, the acting is admirable."

The new cast included Anthony Quinn as Stanley, Uta Hagen as Blanche, Joria Curtright as Stella, and George Mathews as Mitch. Each received excellent reviews. None were considered inferior to the original actors, and some critics felt that a couple were better. A sample comment on Hagen and Quinn is William Hawkins's (*NYWT*): "As the play opens there is . . . no doubt of Blanche's sanity. Miss Hagen expresses the woman's nervous extremity and fear through a childish compulsion to nag, and a childlike bordering on the brink of tears. One feels from her querulous tones that she is older than her actual years and is begging desperately for help. . . . Anthony Quinn in many ways is a natural for . . . Stanley, and he understands the balance between crudeness and simplicity in the character. When he first accosts Blanche, in a long, appraising stare, he plants the whole progress of their scornful and lustful relationship." Still, Hawkins and others accused Quinn of mumbling.

STREETS ARE GUARDED, THE [Drama/Aviation/Military/Religion/War] A: Laurence Stallings; M: Tom Bennett; D: John Haggott; S: Lee Simonson; P: John C. Wilson; T: Henry Miller's Theatre; 11/20/44 (24)

Laurence Stallings had not been represented on Broadway since writing the book for the 1937 musical *Virginia**. In the present muddled melodramatic offering, he was concerned with the question of religious faith within the context of a story about the current war in the South Pacific.

The title derives from the last lines of the Marine Corps song: "They will find the streets are guarded / By United States Marines." The flashback technique is used, with the action beginning in a Washington naval hospital, where Chief Petty Officer Jelks (Morton L. Stevens) informs marine Colonel White (Gordon Nelson) that his marine corporal son may still be alive and not killed in action as reported. In the following scene, Jelks is seen as a wounded noncom on a tiny island in the Pacific, together with a trio of air-force men who bailed out when their plane was hit, several navy men, including a tough and racily humorous bosun's mate (George Mathews), and a nurse of Dutch parentage named Angelika (Jeanne Cagney). After Jelks prays for help, a highly resourceful character called the Marine (Phil Brown) arrives, his dead captain's helmet on his head and a carbine, the island's only weapon, in his hands. He has escaped the hell at Bataan in an open boat and traveled a number of miles before arriving. Jelks is suffering from malaria and requires quinine and sulfa drugs. Because of his helmet, the Marine is designated the ranking officer. He, the bosun's mate, and another man shove off in the tiny boat to raid the Japanese installation. Jelks believes that the Marine, reportedly killed at Bataan, is a divine savior. The foraging party kills a Japanese officer and returns with medical supplies, smokes, food, and a walkie-talkie set, which allows them to monitor the Japanese airwaves through the medium of the nurse, who understands the language. They send a message that reaches a submarine, and the vessel deposits Admiral Overhold (Len Doyle) and his men on the island. With the information gleaned from the island, an expedition is sent to wipe out the Japanese force, with the Marine an important aid to the admiral. He disappears, however, during the sub squadron's attack. In the epilogue, back in the naval hospital, the question remains as to whether the Marine was a fantasy figure or a real person. The obscurity of the writing leaves the answer vague, which several critics resented.

There was good melodramatic action and colorful lingo in the play, but many thought that it failed to deliver on its promise, growing extremely talky, lacking onstage action, and being unduly murky in the mysticism of Jelk's preoccupation with miracles. Another criticism held that the dialogue was often too technical to appreciate. Burton Rascoe (*NYWT*) assumed that the play would be of more interest to military personnel than to civilians. Arthur Pollock (*BE*) rejected the work as "fuzzy, rambling, formless." Of the few who favored the work, Rowland Field (*NEN*) called it "a distinguished achievement," the best play yet penned about World War II, and "a tense and expressive human document of emotions under stress." Cast members included Joel Marston, Paul Crabtree, Robertson White, Lewis Charles, Roderick Maybee, John Effrat, and Jack Manning.

STRINGS, MY LORD, ARE FALSE, THE [Drama/Irish/Politics/Prostitution/Religion/Romance/Sex/War] A: Paul Vincent Carroll; D: Elia Kazan; S: Howard Bay; C: Paul du Pont; P: Edward Choate i/a/w Alexander Kirkland and John Sheppard, Jr.; T: Royale Theatre; 5/19/42 (15)

Critical response toward this well-meaning but pretentious drama by a respected Irish dramatist resident in Scotland was decidedly on the cool side. The play's premiere had been in Dublin, where it was still playing.

Its many characters and subplots swirl around the liberal Scottish priest, Canon Courtenay (Walter Hampden), who, during Hitler's blitz, presides over St. Bride's Church in the Scottish steel town of Port Monica, in the Firth of Clyde. Seeking shelter from the bombs, a cross-section of citizens, cutting across religious, class, and political lines, arrives. Among them are Sadie O'Neil (Margot Grahame), a golden-hearted prostitute; Jerry Hoare (Philip Bourneuf), a young pacifist whose beliefs were molded when his father was killed in a food riot, and who--though circumstances eventually convert him to militancy--refuses to fight for a nation that is so badly in need of social reform; Iris Ryan (Ruth Gordon), a canteen worker pregnant with a baby by a man other than the honest councillor Bill Randall (Colin Keith-Johnston), who loves her; Veronica (Alice MacKenzie), a pregnant woman whose child is midwifed during the blitz by the prostitute; Maisie Gillespie (Constance Dowling), a tragically brave telephone operator; Ted Bogle (Art Smith), a widowed Communist truck driver raising his young daughter as a freethinker; Louis Liebens (Will Lee), a Jewish idealist who lost an arm at Dunkirk; Councillor McPearkie (Tom Tully), who makes money by providing inferior cement for bomb shelters and who steals food and sells it to the wealthy on the black market; a religious zealot (Hurd Hatfield); and others. The wise and saintly canon manages to handle his own problems with the church authorities who tell him to stick to religious matters and keep out of local politics, while helpfully ministering to those seeking haven in his Refuge Room and the crypt under the church.

Carroll was attempting to demonstrate how the besieged common people rise above their personal problems to unite in fighting for common ends when all are threatened by disaster, both from abroad and from corruption within their own society. When victory comes, the strings will be well tuned. His play, however, was accused of wordiness, stenciled characters, shallow and commonplace developments, sentimentality, and other faults of weak melodramaturgy. Louis Kronenberger (*PM*) called the play "hopelessly preachy" and "endlessly talky" and accused its author of having "ceased to be creative." Burns Mantle (*NYDN*) claimed that epic plays about the war could not be as effective as those treating it from a more limited perspective: "So long as [playwrights] insist on trying to reproduce on their tiny stage canvasses a sweeping confusion of action, and the utter bewilderment of large groups of people, all we will get is a realism that is unconvincingly realistic and human studies that are no more than bundles of makeup and muddled speech."

Despite a cast of outstanding players, there was little strong commendation for the performances, which employed an unconvincing assortment of accents. Moreover, Elia Kazan, while gaining scattered approval, was considered to have provided little enlightenment with his direction. Kazan had ideas for improving the show, but--despite keeping the credit--actually was fired just before the opening, with coproducer Kirkland taking over.

According to Ruth Gordon's *My Side*, after the show's poor reviews appeared, the producers came up with a plan to keep the show running. The cast was assembled on the stage, and a woman named Elsa Shroeder was introduced. She had seen the play and had ideas for improving it. According to Equity's rules, if the actors were to allow her to redirect them, they would have to vote unanimously in favor. That would allow a four weeks' run. Otherwise, the play would close quickly. The unanimous vote was to fold. Gordon asked herself why: "Was it the German accent? Was it the take-charge manner? Was it loyalty to Elia? Could she do what he couldn't? What he could have if the managers had stuck with him?"

Well-known actors involved included Ralph Cullinan, Frances Bavier, Reynolds Evans, Gordon Nelson, and Hale Norcross.

STRIP FOR ACTION [Comedy/Military/Romance/Sex/Show Business] A: Howard Lindsay and Russel Crouse; D: Bretaigne Windust; S: Raymond Sovey; P: Oscar Serlin, Howard Lindsay, and Russel Crouse; T: National Theatre; 9/30/42 (110)

Most of the critics jumped on the bandwagon to praise this zestily ribald, forty-nine-performer, Lindsay-Crouse effort produced shortly after burlesque was outlawed in New York City. It shows what might happen if a burlesque troupe were to mingle indiscriminately with the soldiers at an army camp in Maryland.

Private Nutsy Davis (Keenan Wynn), one-time straight man of the troupe, thinks that it would be a swell idea to have them put on a show for his fellow recruits, even though this is in flagrant disregard of army regulations. He gets a furlough from the guardhouse, where he has been spending his days of late, and has the willing players move into the Bijou Theatre. They begin rehearsing with their director (Billy Koud), although various soldiers keep interrupting for one reason or another. The commanding officers decide to cancel the show. Meanwhile, pretty young Squee (Eleanor Lynn), daughter of a famous but now-deceased stripper named Za-Za, appears, having run away from school, her education having been paid for by the company's performers. She has decided to be a stripper. (When she gets to do a strip, she stops midway, unable to remove her panties.) Nutsy, Squee, and Joey (Joey Faye) rush off to Washington by stealing the commanding officer's (David Kerman) car and, using wile and luck, manage to obtain an official permit from the chief of staff (Harry Bannister). One bit of hilarity here was when Joey and Nutsy did a famous burlesque bit called "Flugel Street" as a ploy to prevent an important Englishman (Leslie Barrie) from getting to the chief of staff. Finally, the show goes on and Squee and Nutsy are united.

The show had lots of backstage atmosphere, aided by the casting of several experienced burlesque troupers (including Murray Leonard, Faye, and Koud). Playing the showgirls as tired and bored gum chewers added a touch of amusing realism. The rehearsal sequences allowed for some healthy parodies of classic burlesque shtick and were especially funny when things were not going well, as when the soldier drummer couldn't match his drum beats to the bumps of Florida (Jean Carter, a veteran burlesque queen), the chief stripper. Louis Kronenberger (*PM*) thought it "remarkably fresh" and "uproariously funny" and could not remember when he had "had a better time in the theater." Howard Barnes (*NYHT*) pointed out, "While the material may be corny and the dramatic structure absurdly elastic, it is every inch a show and an exceedingly entertaining one." A few critics were less kind, finding it only spottily effective, most of the fun coming from the play-within-a-play spoof of burlesque material. "Too much of it is padding and not all of it is funny," insisted Richard Lockridge (*NYS*). "Here and there a modest laugh pried itself loose from the familiar materials," observed George Jean Nathan (*TBY*), "including several old Columbia Wheel acts, but in the aggregate the attempt to burlesque burlesque, a superhuman feat at best, did not come off." A small role among the soldiers was played by Jack Albertson.

STUDENT PRINCE, THE [Musical Revival*] B/LY: Dorothy Donnelly; M: Sigmund Romberg; D: J. J. Shubert; CH: Ruthanne Boris and Alexis Dolinoff; S: Watson Barratt; C: Stage Costumes, Inc.; P: Messrs. Shubert; T: Broadway Theatre; 6/8/43 (153)

Twelve years after its previous resuscitation in New York, this 1924 operetta was staged locally again (although it was usually playing somewhere in the country throughout the years). Despite an uneven production, it went on to have a boisterous run. Howard Barnes (*NYHT*) said that the work "was revived faithfully, decorously, and a bit ponderously." There was a virile-sounding male chorus, but the costumes and sets seemed hand-me-down. The book was tired now, but the score was as fresh as ever.

The strongest feature of this popular-priced ($2.75 top) revival was the baritone of Everett Marshall in the role of Dr. Engel, the tutor, who sings "Golden Days," among other songs. His singing far outshone the other principals, including Frank Hornaday's Prince Karl and Barbara Scully's Kathie. Nat Sack was Toni, and Detmar Poppen was dully ponderous in the comic role of Lutz. Ann Pennington, once a Broadway star, was Gretchen the waitress.

Marshall, said Lewis Nichols (*NYT*), "has a baritone which reaches out over the orchestra and fills the theatre; it is stronger and more distinct than those of most of his colleagues." In a brief scene Pennington displayed "a bit of her agile stepping style, plus those famed dimpled knees of hers, atop a table, but some of the comedy demands of the part are a bit trying," reported Rowland Field (*NEN*).

SUDS IN YOUR EYE [Comedy/Alcoholism/Friendship/Music/Orientals/ Romance] A/D: Jack Kirkland; SC: the novel of the same name by Mary Lasswell; S: Joseph B. Platt; C: Kermit Love; P: Katharine Brown and J. H. Del Bondio; T: Cort Theatre; 1/12/44 (37)

A ho-hum slapstick farce that was more a character study than a well-plotted and funny play. Jane Darwell returned from Hollywood to play an old, coarse-tongued Irishwoman named Mrs. Feeley whose late husband has left her a San Diego junkyard. She lives in a beflowered shack, Noah's Ark, on the front porch of which she keeps her husband's ashes in a beer bottle. Into the shack she takes as roommates Miss Tinkham (Brenda Forbes), a middle-aged, penniless, and genteel music teacher from Ohio, who has wandered into the yard, and Mrs. Rassmussen (Kasia Orzazewsky), an aged Polish neighbor who does the cooking and who is fleeing from an unpleasant daughter (Wanda Sponder) who tolerates her only because of her $30-a- month welfare check. Also part of the crew is a Chinese lad named Chinatown (Fredric Munn Zseto, alternating with Chueck Ming Chin), whom she has adopted. The trio, who imbibe vast quantities of beer, intend to raise the cash to pay off the taxes on the junkyard and to join in romance Mrs. Feeley's sailor nephew Danny (Will [William] Hare) and the nice young miss (Janet Tyler) who teaches Spanish to Miss Tinkham at the night school. Their efforts get them into tax and legal troubles when the tax collector (John Adair) gets roughed up for his pains, and they are hauled to court and fined. When the needed money, hidden in a wooden Indian, vanishes along with the Indian, things look bad, but the money (or enough of it) and the Indian are retrieved and all works out well.

"*Suds in Your Eye* had in it the raw materials of a pleasantly irrational farce, but it lacked imagination both in the writing and the direction," lamented Rosamond Gilder (*TAM*). George Freedley (*NYMT*) offered that "the whole evening adds up to sentiment and a few laughs which are not enough to carry a play." Yet George Jean Nathan (*TBY*), while acknowledging that "Kirkland may not have contrived much of a play in the strict critical sense," had to declare that "he has managed for the most part to contrive a pretty jolly roughhouse evening."

Bretaigne Windust offered an uncredited assist in the direction. The cast was excellent, the three drunken guzzlers providing stellar performances. Ruth Gilbert, Bruno Wick, Frank Tweddell, Tom McElhaney, and Kenneth Tobey were among others in the play.

SUMMER AND SMOKE [Drama/Medicine/Mental Illness/Prostitution/Religion/ Romance/Sex/Small Town/Southern] A: Tennessee Williams; M: Paul Bowles; D/P: Margo Jones; S/L: Jo Mielziner; C: Rose Bogdanoff; T: Music Box Theatre; 10/6/48 (102)

The fact that Tennessee Williams's *A Streetcar Named Desire* was still running when *Summer and Smoke* opened has been been suggested as a principal factor in the latter play's not having a successful run. While it shares some thematic ideas with the earlier play, *Summer and Smoke* paled in most critical eyes still dazzled by *Streetcar*'s pyrotechnics. Only a handful of critics wholeheartedly lauded the work. It would have to wait for a renowned Off-Broadway revival in 1952 starring Geraldine Page before its artistic stature was widely recognized.

The play originally had been done at Margo Jones's theatre-in-the-round in Dallas, Theatre '47, where the acting area was twenty-four by twenty feet, and had to be restaged for a Broadway proscenium theatre. Those who saw both productions appreciated the Texas version more because of its innate simplicity. The play had been pared down from fifteen to twelve scenes, and a new character, Rosa Gonzalez (Monica Boyar), had been added, replacing a more sketchily created character. The intimacy of the small Dallas playhouse version, however, was dissipated on the large Broadway stage. Still, Jo Mielziner's skeletally suggestive settings-- which placed all the locales on stage simultaneously--were an important element in capturing the play's fragile atmosphere and suggesting its conflict between the spirit and the flesh. Several actors from the Dallas version (including Tod Andrews, Marga Ann Deighton, and Raymond Van Sickle) repeated their roles on Broadway.

While still in preparation in New York, the production ran into a temporary snag when Williams, apparently influenced by agent Audrey Wood, decided that Jones--who was his close friend--was not right for the play and that he wanted to direct it himself. At one rehearsal, the playwright even jumped onto the stage to show actor Ray Walston how to play his part. According to Helen Sheehy's *Margo*, Jones shouted out, "Now, Tennessee. I am director of this play. You get yourself off the stage this minute. I am the director and you better know that. You get off the stage, Tennessee."

A number of critics insisted that the play was something Williams dragged out of the bottom of his trunk, although he went to great pains to deny such allegations, insisting that it had been conceived around the same time as his *A Streetcar Named Desire*, in 1945. For some time, he alternated between writing the two plays. The only old material of his he noted bore a relation to the present play was a short story he had written called "The Yellow Bird," which bore certain plot resemblances.

The play takes place in Glorious Hill, Mississippi, from the turn of the century to 1916. At the center of the town is the fountain statue of the Angel of Eternity. At one side of the stage is the interior of Dr. Buchanan's (Ralph Theadore) home; at the other is that of the Reverend Winemiller (Van Sickle). The action focuses on the relationship of two characters, Alma Winemiller (Margaret Phillips) and John Buchanan, Jr. (Andrews), whose strikingly contrasting natures are first represented by their childhood selves (Arlene McQuade and Donald Hastings). Alma (whose name is meant to suggest "soul") is the timorous daughter of the puritanical preacher and his mentally ill wife (Deighton). John is the handsome, hedonistic son of the doctor. Under the influence of her parents, Alma grows up to be a neurotically introverted old maid who gives singing lessons, while John becomes a morally dissolute but brilliant medical student. The idealistic Alma strives to reconcile their conflicting personalities by getting John to accept her spirituality. Although he understands her inhibitions, he rejects whatever can not be seen on his anatomy chart and opts for a life of sensual pleasure. (The angel and the huge chart--in the doctor's office--were displayed as obviously contrasting symbols.) Following a personal disaster in which his own orgiastic behavior is responsible for his father's death, John discovers spiritual values by donating his services during an epidemic, but he can give to Alma nothing other than his thanks for this newfound insight. He even marries someone else, one of her pupils named Nellie (Anne Jackson). Alma, meanwhile, her sexuality aroused by John's influence, but unable to exercise her passions with him, picks up a traveling salesman (Walston) and takes him to the very room where she earlier had rejected John's advances.

A number of reviewers took pains to note the relatively eventless play's various resemblances to Williams's previously produced dramas. These similarities--the moody musical underscoring, the preoccupation with sex, the tragically frustrated Southern belle, the conflict between morality and amorality, the symbolism, and so on--were described as if they were dramaturgic mannerisms that were growing annoyingly transparent. John Mason Brown (*SR*) detected Williams's attempt to create complex characters with multiple dimensions to them, but felt that the results were unsuccessful because the writer relied "upon over-easy outward symbols to denote interior struggles." Noting that the play was an early work only recently exhumed, he declared, "Painfully repetitious as it sometimes proves, it contains the hints of the dramatist Mr. Williams was to become." Ward Morehouse (*NYS*) averred, "It has a certain gallantry and dignity of its own, but it comes through as a blurry and indefinite play, and frequently a quite tedious one." One of the play's few significant admirers was Brooks Atkinson (*NYT*), who had seen it in Dallas as well as on Broadway. He praised the play's poetic mood (he called it a "tone poem"), its lucid character insights, its cruel truthfulness, and its outstanding performances from Phillips and Andrews. (Most critics thought their work exceptional, even brilliant.) Williams, said Atkinson, "is a writer of superb grace and allusiveness, always catching the shape and sound of ideas rather than their literal meaning." Thomas R. Dash (*WWD*) thought it less "electric" than *Streetcar*, but was gripped by "its haunting wistfulness, by its touching tenderness and by its understanding compassion. . . . Mr. Williams is still digging in the same mine, but again he comes up with gold ore instead of dross." Williams himself remained dissatisfied with the play and eventually rewrote it in 1965 under the title *The Eccentricities of a Nightingale*. The cast included Hildy Parks as a girl and Earl Montgomery as Roger Doremus.

SUN AND I, THE [Dramatic Revival*] A: Barrie Stavis; D: Boris Tumarin; S/L: Robert Grundlach; C: Grace Houston; P/T: New Stages (OB); 3/20/49 (23)

New York's most ambitious Off-Broadway group in the late 1940s was responsible for the staging of this modern retelling of the story of Joseph (Karl Weber) in Egypt. Although dressed in biblical garb, the play is infused with a contemporary spirit, and the story is meant to comment on the present-day world. The chief theme concerns the abuses of power and the danger such abuses can have for the cause of freedom. An earlier version of the play by Stavis and his late wife, Leona, had been staged by the Federal Theatre Project in 1937. The play had not been very well received in its original form, and the new version similarly elicited few approving comments. Among the positive critics was Thomas R. Dash (*WWD*), who deemed it "a searching, intelligent and provocative play." Much more common were such rejections as that of Bron. (*V*), who said, "It fails because of its confused thinking; talky rambling; and lack of humor." Howard Barnes (*NYHT*) suggested that "numerous revisions have added little clarity or dramatic force to" the play. "Since Stavis has a minimum of wit and only moderate skill at inventing characters, the work is heavy and aimless."

Leading roles in the sprawling, large-cast play were acted by Kermit Murdock as Pharaoh, Peter Capell as an elder statesman, Merrill E. Joels as a mean-spirited assistant chamberlain, Martin Tarby as Potiphar, Nancy R. Pollock as Potiphar's wife, and Florence Luriea as Asenath. Also involved were Frederic de Wilde, Joseph (Joe) Silver, John Randolph, Jack Manning, Salem Ludwig, Willard Swire, and Richard Kiley as the executioner. Kiley's only previous New York appearance had been in an unreviewed Equity Library Theatre presentation of *The Trojan Women* (1947).

SUN FIELD, THE [Comedy-Drama/Journalism/Marriage/Romance/Sex/Sports] A: Milton Lazarus; SC: the novel of the same name by Heywood Broun; D: Edward Clarke Lilley; S: Ernest Glover; C: Kenn Barr; P: Howard Lang; T: Biltmore Theatre; 12/9/42 (5)

Baseball plays aplenty had been tried on Broadway before, but all of them, like this "tedious yarn" (Howard Barnes [*NYHT*]) based on a novel of about two decades earlier, were unsuccessful. The play was sprinkled with authentic touches in its dialogue, scenes, and characters, but the overall effect was of a "machine-made" (George Freedley [*NYMT*]) work without any sense of spontaneity.

The central role is that of "Tiny" Tyler (Joel Ashley), a great home-run hitter who was kicked out of NYU and has many social vices, such as womanizing and boozing. His life takes a turn when he meets magazine writer Judith Winthrop (Claudia Morgan), who, for all her class, finds herself attracted to the uneducated but colorful athlete. They get married, and Tyler attempts to raise his intellectual abilities by reading Schopenhauer between games, although neither his amazed teammates nor his supercilious wife encourage him. As he grows in knowledge, his batting abilities decline. After Judith leaves him, his team, despite an eight-game lead, loses the pennant. Tiny consoles himself by relighting a fire with a trashy former flame (Florence Sundstrom). At the next season's spring training, Judith appears on the scene to reunite with her spouse.

The role of Judith was unpleasant and confusingly drawn, seriously harming interest in the plot, and there was far too little humor available to compensate. Ibee. (*V*) alleged, "First act is somnolent and while the performance picks up in the second and third innings, the pall of the start is never overcome." Betty Kean and Katherine Meskill played players' wives, Tom Tully was the manager, and Robert Lynn, Karl Malden, and Lewis Charles were among the athletes. The voice of famed broadcaster Bill Stern was heard during some of the action.

SUNDOWN BEACH [Drama/Marriage/Mental Illness/Military/Romance/Sex/War] A: Bessie Breuer; S: Ben Edwards; D: Elia Kazan; L: Jean Rosenthal; P: Louis J. Singer; T: Belasco Theatre; 9/7/48 (7)

Julie Harris first came to the attention of the critics in this twenty-eight-character piece staged by Elia Kazan to give an opportunity to various actors at the newly formed Actors Studio, of which he was a cofounder with Robert Lewis and Cheryl Crawford. It came to Broadway after a tryout in Westport, Connecticut. The cast list includesd many actors who would go on to achieve fame, among them

Nehemiah Persoff, Martin Balsam, Steven Hill, Joan Copeland (playwright Arthur Miller's sister), Phyllis Thaxter, and Cloris Leachman.

Sundown Beach was lauded for its sincerity but criticized for its clumsy episodic construction and inability to project its soap-opera-ish story clearly. Instead of focusing on a select few tales, the play meandered into the lives of too many characters, leaving an effect of extreme fuzziness. "With a large and confusing cast and a script which never comes into focus," lamented Howard Barnes (*NYHT*), "it is painful in more than one respect." He noted the play's missing ingredients of "eloquence, skill and heart," and its "sorry lack of dramatic craftsmanship." William Hawkins (*NYWT*) stated, "The play involves so many interesting characters that one never learns a satisfying amount about any of them." And Ward Morehouse (*NYS*) thought the piece "a cluttered and congested drama, and a play that remains singularly lifeless."

The action takes place in 1945 at the Sundown Café, near a military hospital on the Gulf coast of Florida. The hospital treats members of combat crews convalescing from wartime mental traumas and battle fatigue; the café plays host to the patients, their wives, lovers, and girlfriends. The complex play tells the story of a number of these people, such as George (Edward Binns) and his wife Muriel (Leachman), the latter being a selfish, pleasure-loving creature who can not bear to be touched by him when she is frightened by his talking in his sleep, and who asks for a divorce. Arthur (Warren Stevens) is faced with the tragic situation of being retired by the air force, which is the only place he has been able to gain respectability, but the WAC who loves him, Nancy (Thaxter), helps him to overcome his depression. Otis (Don Hanmer), clinging to an older divorcée (Anne Hegira), learns that his mother, on whom he has a fixation, is dying. Ida Mae (Harris) is a young hick wife whose husband, Thaddeus (Hill) angrily believes her to be someone else's girlfriend. She wins back his affections partly by a recitation of the first meal she will cook for him when they return home. (As delivered by Harris, this was one of the play's highlights.) These are the four principal pairs in the play, but there are many other characters who occupy the spotlight as well; one of the most significant is the major (John Sylvester), a sort of author's mouthpiece, who goes on and on about love being the cure-all for all mental ailments.

George Currie (*BE*) said, "Julie Harris is a sharp standout among the rather shadowy characters." Among others involved were Lenka Peterson, Treva Frazee, Michael Lewin, Kathleen Maguire, Lou Gilbert, and Ira Cirker.

Elia Kazan's strained direction was considered one of the important factors in the play's failure, and the piece was one of his rare failures. "The performance is mannered and self-conscious," scolded Brooks Atkinson (*NYT*). "It is full of violent physical interludes that have no particular meaning. Sometimes it seems to be ignoring the play--so lost in its own inventiveness that it renders the lines unintelligible."

SUNNY RIVER [Musical/Marriage/Period/Politics/Romance/Show Business] B/LY/D: Oscar Hammerstein II; M: Sigmund Romberg; CH: Carl Randall; S: Stewart Chaney; C: Irene Sharaff; P: Max Gordon; T: St. James Theatre; 12/4/41 (36)

New Orleans in the early nineteenth century was the colorful setting for this saccharine operetta, which represented producer Max Gordon's fourth show to be running simultaneously on Broadway. Stewart Chaney's lush settings and Irene Sharaff's vivid costumes successfully captured the appropriate romantic mood, but the show itself was standard stuff and did not make the grade.

Its journeymanlike book tells of how the lovely and talented singer Marie Sauvinet (Muriel Angelus), performing at Lolita's (Ethel Levey) Café des Oleandres, is fallen in love with by the young Creole aristocrat and lawyer Jean Gervais (Bob Lawrence). Cecilie Marshall (Helen Claire), the upper-class daughter of Jean's employer, cheats Marie out of romance and marriage by falsely telling her that she and Jean have been long-time lovers. Marie borrows $5,000 and leaves for Paris, where she becomes a renowned singing star. Five years pass. Now a famous opera star, Marie returns to New Orleans to win Jean's heart, and he is willing; however, when she realizes how much pain she will cause Cecilie, who is pregnant, she decides to give up the love of her life. Even Cecilie fails to gain Jean for good, however, as he dies a hero in the Battle of New Orleans (he has been a staunch believer in democracy), leaving both women to mourn for him.

Apart from the show's look and some of its performances, nothing in its writing or music was especially impressive. Although he selected several tunes as worthwhile listening, Brooks Atkinson (*NYT*) had to declare, "Most of Mr. Romberg's music is ponderous and pedestrian. It conveys a vast respect for the art of music without conveying emotion." John Mason Brown (*NYWT*) found himself getting depressed by the "bogus and out-moded ritual" of shows such as this. He said that he hated it when musicals "take themselves too seriously and go in for all the pretentions of grand opera with nothing but sentimentality as their motive and dullness as their means."

The show was very heavy on romance and very sparing of its humor, although Tom Ewell as Daniel Marshall, girl-chasing brother of Cecilie, added a few much-desired lighter notes. Black comedian Oscar Polk was good as George Marshall, and Joan Roberts, in her Broadway debut, stood out as a local sex pot. Dancers Jack Riano and Miriam LaVelle were memorable in a specialty number featuring Harlequin and Columbine, and Howard Freeman was an amusing drunk.

SUNRISE [Musical/Yiddish Language] B: Abraham Blum; M: Joseph Rumshinsky; LY: Isidor Lillian; D: Ludwig Satz; CH: Marietta Alva; S: Michael Saltzman; T: Yiddish Folk Theatre (OB); 10/24/40

A well-done piece of sentimental Yiddish escapist theatre, with heavy portions of humor, telling a modern-day version of a famous biblical story. Kahn. (*V*) found this one of the better examples of the Yiddish musical theatre, and Robert Coleman (*NYDM*) said, "It sets a new standard for East Side musicals."

It begins with a prologue enacting the tale of Pharaoh's edict to slay all newborn Hebrew infants, of Moses' being hidden in the bullrushes to save him, and of his being discovered by Pharaoh's daughter (Charlotte Goldstein). In the main drama, the Moses story is transmuted into that of a Hungarian countess's (Rose Greenfield) switching her idiot son for a Jewish child--that of the city's chief rabbi (Michael Wilensky), who, to prevent anti-Semitism, sacrifices his child so that the noblewoman may present him as her son to her obtuse spouse. The work proceeds to reveal what happens twenty-five years later when the children become the adult Moishele (Ludwig Satz), the imbecile Jew (really the count), and Carl (Edmund Zayenda, in his American debut), the count (really the Jew). Carl loves Tzirele (Ola Lillith), but their supposedly differing faiths prevent their marriage. The fact that Moishele also loves Tzirele brings about the revelation of the truth, and the simpleton assumes his title while Carl renounces it with pleasure so he may marry Tzirele.

Lillith, Satz, and Zayenda turned in sterling performances and were greeted with very warm reviews, as were the comical pair Abraham Lax and Tillie Rabinowitz as a lusty young rabbi and a lovelorn spinster.

SURVIVORS, THE [Drama/Family/Hotel/Period/Rural/War/Western] A: Peter Viertel and Irwin Shaw; D: Martin Gabel; S/L: Boris Aronson; C: Rose Bogdanoff; P: Bernard Hart and Martin Gabel; T: Playhouse; 1/19/48 (8)

A lot of high-powered acting talent was involved--not always in the best interest of the actors'--in this disappointing flop set in Decker City, Missouri, in the aftermath of the Civil War. It was an overproduced antiwar play that used the rural Western setting to comment on contemporary global politics and the futility of killing. This infusion of political significance into an otherwise promising melodrama annoyed many critics, such as George Freedley (*NYMT*), who remarked that it "was so fouled up with ideas and inner meanings that it became a bore in the theater."

In 1865 Steve (Richard Basehart) and Morgan Decker (Kevin McCarthy), who, for four years, had been abused Yankee prisoners of the Confederacy in Richmond, Virginia, return to their home town. They are angry at having been abandoned by their commanding officer, Tom Cameron (Anthony Ross), who locked them up in their cells after a court-martial and left them to the mercy of the enemy forces. There has been a long-standing feud between the Camerons and the Deckers. Another Decker brother, the ornery Finlay (E. G. Marshall), unable to go off to the war, has an obsessive desire to take revenge on Tom and feeds the anger of his siblings. Morgan, injured during his captivity, soon dies, and Finlay manipulates the basically fair-minded Steve into trying to kill Tom. Fatherly attorney Vincent Keyes (Louis Calhern)--the *raisonneur* character--tries to act as peacemaker, and Steve thinks it worth the trouble to see if his suspicions of Tom are correct. But others interfere, and both Tom and Steve end up dead before the play concludes.

According to Howard Barnes (*NYHT*), "The show frequently realizes its depressing blend of melodrama and the vision of a brave new world, but the net effect is definitely depressing." Brooks Atkinson (*NYT*) stood alone in his appreciation of the play and production.

The company included Neil Fitzgerald, Marc Lawrence, Russell Collins, Hume Cronyn, Jane Seymour, Marianne Stewart, and Kenneth Tobey. George S. Kaufman and Moss Hart (brother of a coproducer) are reputed to have worked on the script as play doctors.

SUSAN AND GOD [Dramatic Revival*] A: Rachel Crothers; D: Robert Burton; S: Jo Mielziner; P: John Golden; T: City Center of Music and Drama; 12/13/43 (8)

New York City took over the former Mecca Temple on West Fifty-fifth Street in order to use it as a popular-priced municipal center for the performing arts. During its first season, the City Center of Music and Drama, as it now was called, performed a series of plays and musicals in revival, as well as operas, ballets, and concerts. The first play done was *Susan and God*, Rachel Crothers's 1937 comedy-drama about a sophisticated woman who imposes her newfound religious faith on her friends and family with all sorts of unexpected consequences. Its original star, Gertrude Lawrence, returned to play Susan, and it was adorned with sets by its original designer and a production arranged by its original producer. Mayor La Guardia was on hand to host the festivities. He introduced Dame May Whitty to say a few words of greeting on behalf of the English theatre. Noël Coward, scheduled as guest speaker, was at home ill with the flu.

George Jean Nathan (*TBY*) was one of several upset that so auspicious a cultural occasion was marred by the selection of "this six-year-old Broadway box-office knickknack," which would have served better to open a commercial venture. Others, however, thought it a fine choice, one that was still stageworthy.

Lawrence gave a demonstration of animal vitality in her heavily embroidered performance, sweeping about the stage with dress, scarf, and hair flying, which gave some reviewers plenty to laugh about. Louis Kronenberger (*PM*), partly excusing her overacting by referring to the huge playhouse, wrote, "Nuances of gesture and inflection would be quite lost on the more remotely stationed customers. So Miss Lawrence has simplified her performance and gone in for strenuous pantomime. It is probably the only way out, but Miss Lawrence does seem at times like a rather desperate performer in a game of charades; there are even moments when she appears to be playing both Susan and God at the same time."

Conrad Nagel played Susan's husband Barrie, and Jean Sampson played their daughter Blossom. Others in the cast included Jeannette C. Chinley, Francis Compton, and William Weber. Douglas Gilmore repeated his role of Michael O'Hara and Eleanor Audley hers of Charlotte Marley. The production (and others that followed it) was seriously injured by the cavernous theatre's horrible sound system, which provided echoes and failed to pick up voices out of range of the microphones.

SUZANNA AND THE ELDERS [Comedy/Period/Politics/Religion/Romance/Sex] A: Lawrence Langner and Armina Marshall; D: Worthington Miner; S/C: Stewart Chaney; P: Jack Kirkland; T: Morosco Theatre; 10/29/40 (30)

There were a host of well-known actors in this well-intentioned but artificial play by Mr. and Mrs. Lawrence Langner set at Harmony Heights, a Massachusetts Christian socialistic community of 1878. The brunt of the comedy stems from the community's concern with selective breeding among its members, and the authors could not avoid their humor being "prurient," in Brooks Atkinson's (*NYT*) view: "It is an easy subject for adolescent guffawing" and makes for "a cheap and immature play." Rosamond Gilder (*TAM*) took the production to task for its "smirking bad taste." To her, this was "a poor play which tries to make up in vulgarity for its lack of dramatic content." Lawrence Langner in *The Magic Curtain* said that when the play was first done, at the Westport Country Playhouse, with Uta Hagen and Onslow Stevens, it had emphasized spiritual values; in the process of revision for Broadway, the physical element gradually became predominant and its humor was broadened.

At Harmony Heights people do not own their own property, and multiple marriage is practiced. The characters all are referred to as Sister this or Brother that. The plot circumstances circle around the various attitudes of the characters, male and female, to the process of the eugenic creation of children among certain selected members. The community is ruled by the benevolent despot, John Adam Kent (Morris Carnovsky, made up with a red beard to resemble George Bernard Shaw), and Mother Kent (Jane Seymour); their most ardent follower is the fiery Sister Suzanna Leeds (Haila Stoddard). New community member Charles Owens (Paul Ballantyne), a young inventor, is drawn to Suzanna. However, after a year's trial, when he suggests that he and she be permitted to formalize their relationship, he learns that she has been chosen to participate in a breeding experiment with a certain middle-aged brother. As the community begins to realize the drawbacks of their social philosophy, Owens leads it to revolt in favor of monogamy and capitalism. He wins Suzanna before the final curtain.

Making his Broadway debut as Brother Tom was Lloyd Bridges. Also in the large cast were Royal Beal, Theodore Newton, Hale Norcross, and Lois Hall, who received excellent notices for her performance of a frump who is transformed into a sexpot.

SWAN SONG [Drama/Crime/Mental Illness/Music/Youth] A: Ben Hecht and Charles MacArthur; SC: *Crescendo*, an unpublished play by Ramon Romero and Harriett Hinsdale; D: Joseph Pevney; S/L: Ralph Alswang; P: John Clein; T: Booth Theatre; 5/15/46 (158)

This "pretty inferior" (Lewis Nichols [*NYT*]) swan song for the once successful collaborative team of Hecht and MacArthur takes place in the Long Island living room of Stanislaus Kubin (Theo Goetz). The chief character is psychotic young Leo Pollard (David Ellin), a would-be but untalented concert pianist who has been forced to live in his more gifted sister's shadow, and who spent time in a sanatorium following her death at his hands. Kubin was his sister's "maestro," and Leo arrives at Kubin's home in order to take up his own interrupted career. However, Kubin has found another prodigy, twelve-year-old Vera Novak (Jacqueline Horner), which prompts Pollard's intense jealousy. This propels him to seek a means of poisoning his rival. His efforts are confounded and he is captured.

Among the criticisms leveled at this psychological melodrama were its tediousness and outdated quality. It was very slowly paced and verbose, lacked suspense (except for a few minutes at the end), and employed too many familiar stencils. George Jean Nathan (*TBY*) faulted it for "overwritten" dialogue and "underwritten" thrills. The result was "pompously ridiculous." "*Swan Song*," noted Louis Kronenberger (*PM*), "is a poky thriller, and more a blurred palimpsest than a play."

So upset were Hecht and MacArthur about the critical reaction that they got one of the actors to deliver curtain speeches in which he noted how much audiences liked the play, while the critics felt the opposite. Audiences were asked to talk the play up with their friends and make it so successful that it would "kill" the reviewers.

Its most interesting feature was the appearance of twelve-year-old Jacqueline Horner, herself a fine pianist who had appeared at venues such as Town Hall. Louis Sorin, Harry Sothern, Ivan Simpson, Marianne Stewart, Mary Servoss, and Scott McKay were in the cast.

The play was a rewritten version of a work that had closed in its pre-Broadway tryout period and had been seen on the West Coast in 1943. Cut-rate tickets allowed the play an inflated run on Broadway.

SWEET CHARITY [Comedy/Drugs/Women] A: Irving Brecher and Manuel Seff; D: George Abbott; S: Cirker and Robbins; P: Alfred Bloomingdale; T: Mansfield

Theatre; 12/28/42 (8)

This comedy had no connection whatsoever with the later hit musical comedy of the same name. Instead, it was an occasionally amusing, but otherwise inadequate, fast-paced farce about a Connecticut woman's club, the Helping Hand Society, whose members want to put on a children's home fund-raiser by hiring King Cole and his orchestra. The officers, Mrs. Pat Mitchell (Augusta Dabney), Mrs. Eva Ingersoll (Viola Roache), Miss Beulah Ogilvie (Jane Seymour), Mrs. Laura Brindle (Enid Markey), and Mrs. Jane Martindale (Mary Sargent) manage to collect the necessary $2,500, but the cash is attached by the sheriff (Calvin Thomas) when a town derelict (Harlan Briggs), who broke his leg in the club's building, sues them. Tickets have been sold, a program printed, and all sorts of other preparatory arrangements have been made, so it is too late to cancel. In the events that follow, as the women try to replace the money and the band's annoyingly persistent agent (Philip Loeb) insists on getting paid, they inadvertently smoke a stash of marijuana cigarettes left by a local musician (Dort Clark). They not only lose their dignity (one of them tries to crawl into the neck of a water-cooler bottle and another tries to pour tea from a watering pot), but scandalize the man from the Chamber of Com merce from whom they are trying to wrest some money. Finally, the derelict helps them out by pretending to be a government agent and thereby getting the club's landlord to contribute the needed money.

Whatever novelty the piece had lay in its substitution of "reefer" for the usual alcohol to make dignified characters act foolishly. Otherwise, the characters were caricatures, the plot outline tiresomely familiar, and the gags stale. Director George Abbott, said George Jean Nathan (*TBY*), had to rely "upon his established brand of grasshopper direction, jumping and scooting the actors all over the stage, to invest his lifeless exhibit with an aspect of inner vitality." (Abbott had taken over the reins during the play's out-of-town troubles.) Rowland Field (*NEN*) concluded that "the talents of an excellent cast have been squandered on a crude and tasteless farce." In the cast were Whit (formerly Whitner) Bissell, Mildred Todd, and others.

SWEET GENEVIEVE [Comedy/Marriage/Medicine/Period/Sex/Youth] A: M. G. Chute and Marchette Chute; D: Mina Cole; P: M. G. Chute, Marchette Chute, Joy Chute, and Mina Cole; T: President Theatre (OB); 3/20/45 (1)

Most critics chose to ignore this "experimental" offering at the President, a theatre that saw barely any action in the forties and was hired out chiefly for trivialities such as this. Otis L. Guernsey, Jr. (*NYHT*), referred to it as a "slow, nonsensical script, which doesn't belong within a day's march of Broadway." Bron. (*V*) said that the acting "was godawful."

Set in 1886, it looks at the first forty-eight hours in the married life of a young intern (Sam Banham) who has eloped with the seventeen-year-old daughter (Rosilyn Weiss) of patrician parents before he has graduated from medical school. They set up house in a shabby rooming-house flat on the Lower East Side, which is all they can afford. Recognizing their poverty, various neighbors contribute what they can. After numerous jokes about the wedding night and other commonplaces, the play concludes with the bride's mother (Nolia Trammel) deciding to accept the marriage once she realizes that a neighbor's child is not her daughter's bastard.

The three Chutes in the credits were sisters, better known for their short stories. Marchette also authored several books on Shakespeare, one of which remained popular for many years. Their show was budgeted at $5,000 and hoped to last for two weeks.

SWEETHEARTS [Musical Revival*] B: Harry B. Smith and Fred de Gresac; REV: John Cecil Holm; M: Victor Herbert; LY: Robert B. Smith; D: John Kennedy; CH: Theodore Adolphus and Catherine Littlefield; S: Peter Wolf; C: Michael Lucyk; P: Paula Stone and Michael Sloane; T: Shubert Theatre; 1/21/47 (288)

A revival of the 1913 operetta last seen in a mediocre 1929 production. Practically the sole attraction on the present occasion was the appearance of great clown Bobby Clark, for whom much of the book had been revised. Clark played the role of Mikel Mikeloviz, while the romantic leads of Sylvia and Prince Franz were taken by

Gloria Story and Mark Dawson.

The show itself was considered meagre, but Clark was toasted for his inimitable humor, which employed his stock painted-on spectacles, live cigar, walking stick, tarnished coat, and flat hat. Richard Watts, Jr. (*NYP*), reported, "He changed odd costumes, grimaced, darted about, sang, danced, commented with some asperity on the plot in which he was entangled, remembered a line from his own recent version of *The Would-Be Gentleman**, made bad lines bearable and fair ones hilarious, and refused to be let off anything. The result was a display of comic virtuosity that was nothing short of epic." "Add a smiling old-fashioned chorus, a story making remarkably little sense, scenery suitable for any Victor Herbert operetta, a second-rate Victor Herbert score and you have--? An evening of Bobby Clark," concluded Euphemia Van Rensselaer Wyatt (*CW*).

Of the dated old operetta not much was considered salvageable, apart from a few tunes such as "Pilgrims of Love" and "I Might Be Yours Once-in-a-While." The book--even though revised--seemed primitive and confusing, and there was little of interest in most of the show's formerly pleasurable Ruritanian aspects. Among the supporting actors were Marjorie Gateson, June Knight, and Anthony Kemble-Cooper.

T

TAKE A BOW [Revue] D: Wally Wanger; CH: Marjery Fielding; S: Kaj Velden; C: Ben Wallace; P: Lou Walters; T: Broadhurst Theatre; 6/15/44 (12)

The onslaught of attempts to revive vaudeville in the 1940s suffered a mild setback with this uninspired show featuring Jay C. Flippen as MC, with piano-playing Chico Marx of the Marx Brothers attempting without much success to infuse the evening with madcap zaniness. Flippen's material was musty and sometimes off-color. The acts all seemed old-hat, although several of them did momentarily enliven the evening, especially the acrobatic Whitson Brothers and a talented baggy-pants pantomime comedian and banjo player named Gene Sheldon. Among his numbers was an old poker-game skit called "Don't Play with Strangers," which he shared with Marx, and which came from the Marx Brothers' hit of many years earlier, *The Cocoanuts**.

The program was filled out with such entertainers as tap dancer Johnny Mack; white-haired soft-shoe man Pat Rooney, celebrating his fiftieth year in vaudeville; magician "Think-a-Drink" Hoffman, who made any kind of drink appear on demand from two empty shakers and a pitcher of water; comedy singers Cross and Dunn; ballroom dance experts Mary Raye and Naldi; and others.

Those who liked this sort of show felt that it was a decent example of the genre. Such was Howard Barnes (*NYHT*), who termed it "familiar, fast-paced and funny." Those who did not--the majority--thought it a dull and routine assortment of acts completely lacking in variety. This group included Burton Rascoe (*NYWT*), who claimed that the show "is thrown together haphazardly and without taste."

TAKE IT AS IT COMES [Comedy/Broadcasting/Crime/Drugs/Family/Journalism/Marriage/Politics/Small Town/Youth] A: E. B. Morris; D: Anthony Brown; S: Perry Watkins; P: Armin L. Robinson; T: Forty-eighth Street Theatre; 2/10/44 (16)

There were few takers for this "mechanical and tedious little banality about the ups and downs of a small-town family," as Burton Rascoe (*NYWT*) described it. The play was "dull, harmless, straggling," said Ward Morehouse (*NYS*). E. B. Morris was the pseudonym of a Warner Brothers attorney named Morris Ebbenstein.

In Wiltonwood, New Jersey, in the year 1939 ("the good old days," said the program), resides the all-American Bliven family, father Albert (Frank Wilcox), the decent and friendly school superintendent; his wife Cora (Louise Lorimer); their unmarried daughter (Angela Jacobs), who loves the poetic boy (Richard Basehart) who works in the library; their married daughter (Marilyn Monk) and her struggling lawyer husband (Harry Pedersen); their Boy Scout son Tommy (Jackie Ayers); and Mrs. Bliven's old-maid sister (Sara Floyd). A Swedish maid (Gloria Willis) rounds out the household. The Blivens are selected by the inspirational *Fireside* magazine, the family's favorite, as "the model American family." The magazine's quack editor (Harold Moulton) appears with his staff and with radio personnel to do a broadcast from the house, but their preparations are interrupted by the machine-gun murder of an Italian neighbor, Anthony Pasquale (Tito Vuolo), done in by fellow members of Murder, Inc., for holding out on them. Prior to his death, Pasquale had asked Tommy to hold a package for him that he said was a present for his wife (Grazia Narciso). The police suspect that Pasquale had been hiding a cache of drugs. The Blivens, hearing of this, fear that the package in their household contains those drugs. With Tommy not around, they open it and discover over $500,000 in cash. Soon, the morals of the all-American Blivens begin to crumble as they struggle over whether to keep the loot or turn it in. Greed begins to nibble at the family well-being. However, Albert, secure in his newfound wealth and high on celebratory champagne, tells off the town's corrupt mayor (Arthur Griffen), to whom he has kowtowed in the past. But he should not have been so secure, since Tommy, without telling his folks, has turned the package over to the cops, for which he is commended and presented with a medal. The Blivens are saved from corruption. But the police chief (Curtis Cooksey) takes off with half of the dough, indirectly benefiting the Blivens when Albert is backed by the corrupt politicos, wins the mayoralty, and is signed to write sanctimonious articles for the magazine at $100 a pop.

TALLEY METHOD, THE [Comedy/Family/Literature/Medicine/Politics/Romance/Youth] A: S. N. Behrman; D: Elmer Rice; S: Jo Mielziner; P: Playwrights' Company; T: Henry Miller's Theatre; 2/24/41 (56)

S. N. Behrman's thoughtful but rather bloodless and undramatic vehicle about "the nature of sympathy" (Euphemia Van Rensselaer Wyatt [*CW*]) for Ina Claire and Philip Merivale was respectfully but not enthusiastically received and did not last very long. Merivale was the widower, Dr. Axton Talley, something of a reactionary tyrant, famous for having discovered a life-saving surgical technique. He is extremely impatient with human weakness, for which he has only contempt. His relations with his son Philip (Dean Harens), whose failure in medical school disturbs him profoundly, and adopted daughter Avis (Claire Niesen) are mechanically perfunctory (the play once had been titled *The Mechanical Heart*). Even his love affair with the attractive patient he has saved, the Candida-like poetess Enid Fuller (Claire), is on the icy side. Enid, who represents the sympathetic nature so alien to Dr. Talley, soon grows conscious of the chill in his home and of the anxieties and frustrations of the doctor's children. Philip loves a fan dancer, and Avis, who rejects the perennial Columbia University student (Hiram Sherman) who pays her court, is an active member of the radical American Youth Congress. Enid tries to reconcile the father with his offspring. She herself becomes an object of affection for Manfred Geist (Ernst Deutsch), a middle-aged German poet and refugee who was a political revolutionary in his homeland. Manfred is loved as well by Avis, who now has more reason to resent Enid. Manfred, however, kills himself, and Enid, finding that Dr. Talley is not the unselfish pillar she hoped for, decides against marrying the fatuous physician.

The critics felt that Behrman was after bigger fish to fry than merely providing light theatrical entertainment, and that his portentous dramaturgy, with each character seemingly being representative of a point of view, suggested that this was "no time for comedy" (the title of one of his better plays). His play was deemed better for the armchair than the theatre seat. "After three diffuse acts," revealed Rosamond Gilder (*TAM*), "the attentive observer finds that he has come out by the same door as in he went. Mr. Behrman's idea has failed to take on flesh and blood. . . . Now and again his wit flashes with its accustomed swift, ironic assurance. But on the whole his words have a literary rather than a dramatic ring." Brooks Atkinson (*NYT*) wrote, "It is hardly possible to sit before *The Talley Method* without realizing that his magic of phrase and his agility of thought evaporate when he assumes an earnest manner. When he sticks to his comedy last, he writes with wonderful skill and radiant integrity."

The acting of Claire and Merivale in particular came in for kudos. Neither role had been easy to cast, and Katharine Cornell had been considered for the female lead. Ina Claire, then nearing the end of her active career, despite her relative youth, had trouble learning her lines, especially with the constant rewriting of the script. John Halliday had been cast in the male lead, but during the rehearsal period he was stricken with pneumonia, and Merivale replaced him. The actual director was Herman Shumlin, but when various conflicts arose late in rehearsals, Shumlin retired and Rice took over, although it was too late to do anything for the play. Many of the difficulties stemmed from Shumlin's emphasis on developing the serious themes of the play, while playwright Behrman wanted the comic values stressed. At one point, he declared, "They don't laugh as much as they did before I rewrote it" (quoted by John F. Wharton in *Life among the Playwrights*.)

TAMING OF THE SHREW, THE [Dramatic Revival*] A: William Shakespeare; D: Robert T. Eley; S: Mallory; C: Donald Finlayson; L: Day Erban; P: New York Repertory Group; T: Cherry Lane Theatre (OB); 10/10/48

"A rough uproarious reproduction" (Robert Garland [*NYJA*]) done by an Off-Broadway troupe born in 1948. Robert T. Eley staged the play to squeeze out as much slapstick fun from it as possible, while company members not on stage sold apples and apple tarts in the house. A lot of the acting also took place in the aisles. All the scenes were represented by a set suggesting a bright street scene. For Petruchio's house's interior, a simple arch and curtain did service.

Jack Burkhart was a lusty Petruchio and Beatrice Arthur was a tempestuous Kate. "They are a rough uproarious pair," noted Garland. Others involved were Jack Sorian as Baptista, Bert Neimark as Gremio, Gerold Grayson as Hortensio, Anthony Franciosa (in one of his earliest New York appearances) as Lucentio, James Winslow as Tranio, Bernard Diamond as Grumio, Jimmy McElwain as Gregory, and William Hickey (another newcomer) as Nathaniel. "The whole cast plays in the spirited fashion that manages to catch the true feeling and fast-paced humor the play requires," thought A. R. P. (*WWD*).

TANYARD STREET [Drama/Invalidism/Irish/Marriage/Religion/Sex/War] A: Louis D'Alton; D: Arthur Shields; S: Mercedes; P: Jack Kirkland; T: Little Theatre; 2/4/41 (23)

This "literate, moderately interesting, and well played" (Burns Mantle [*NYDN*]) drama's title comes from the name of a street in Annakill, Ireland, where the action is set. Here reside Hessy (Margo) and Kevin McMorna (Arthur Shields, the director), although Kevin has been off to Spain to fight on the side of Franco. Kevin returns to Tanyard Street a paraplegic, crippled from the waist down. A powerful religious faith sustains him, and he is sure he will walk again after he sees the Blessed Lady in his dreams. His interest in his bride has waned, however, to her enormous distress. Kevin's down-to-earth brother Hugh (Lloyd Gough), who holds a cynical attitude toward the Irish church and toward Franco's cause, loves Hessy, and she feels an attraction for him. When the flowers in his bedroom shrine mysteriously appear beside his pillow, Kevin is certain it is because of the agency of his visions, and his ability to walk miraculously returns. News of the miracle spreads throughout the country. Kevin now discovers his vocation for the priesthood, the church agreeing to accept him if he will remain celibate. When his wife tells him that it was she who moved the flowers, he has a relapse. The parish priest (Art Smith), hoping to sustain faith in the church even on false grounds, rebukes her. Hessy, aware of Ke vin's hatred, recants her words, ignores Hugh's importuning, and agrees to be a celibate spouse.

The play, previously done at Dublin's Abbey Theatre, opened only after several delays stemming from accidents to the cast. It was considered well intentioned but not especially dramatic fare. Kevin's character was thought unsympathetic and unconvincing. Although it was a serious drama, the best scenes were the comic ones featuring Barry Fitzgerald (brother of the director-star) as the hypochondriac boarder, Mosey Furlong, a role that had little to do with the main plot and threw the play out of focus whenever he appeared. Richard Lockridge (*NYS*) said that the evening revealed the author "fumbling wordily with a spiritually exciting situation and making almost precisely nothing of it." Hale Norcross, Zamah Cunningham, and Aideen O'Connor were also in the cast.

"TELEPHONE, THE" (see *The Medium*)

TEMPER THE WIND [Drama/Business/Military/Politics] A: Edward Mabley and Leonard Mims; D: Reginald Denham; S: Raymond Sovey; C: Anna Hill Johnstone; P: Barnard Straus and Roland V. Haas; T: Playhouse; 12/27/46 (35)

In general, the subject of this play--originally called *Drums of Peace*--was considered especially pertinent and thoughtful, but its dramatic treatment was said to leave much to be desired. Its subject was the question of whether the Allies should have been allowing the German factories that participated in the war on behalf of Hitler to resume operations right away. Brooks Atkinson (*NYT*) termed it "the most forceful and absorbing topical drama of the season" and praised it for its nonpropagandistic and restrained treatment. But George Jean Nathan (*TBY*) took the opposite view and found his taste for the play soured by the too-biased treatment of the American hero, whom he called "smug and self-satisfied." He also was offended by the authors' intention to have their work considered as serious drama rather than melodrama.

Lieutenant Colonel Richard Woodruff (Thomas Beck) has been put in charge of the occupation forces in the Bavarian manufacturing town of Reitenberg, used to make munitions during the war; his mission is to de-Nazify the local industry. Hugo Benckendorff (Reinhold Schunzel), unscrupulous owner of the town's only factory, lost his son, who went to college with Woodruff, when the Nazis hung him in 1933. He wishes to use the connection with Woodruff to gain the latter's permission to reopen the factory and even has his pretty daughter (Vilma Kurer), married to the Nazi Erich (Tonio Selwart), dress up to further influence the officer, who was once engaged to her. The industrialist argues that he will thus revivify the town's stagnant economy and take some of the pressure off the American forces, who are suffering from demoralization. Benckendorff's desires are promoted by his American house guest, Theodore Bruce (Walter Greaza), a Chicago businessman with cartel inclinations, who declares that rearming Germany will help keep Russia at bay. Woodruff does not wish to follow Benckendorff's wishes until the industry has first been cleansed of its Nazi followers, who constituted all the factory's foremen. The businessman goes over the officer's head and gains permission to reopen the factory, with the Nazis at their old jobs. Various violent acts result from the officer's policy, including a local riot. The officer arrests Benckendorff and revokes Bruce's visa, with the latter threatening to call Washington down on Woodruff when he gets home.

Euphemia Van Rensselaer Wyatt (*CW*) said that the play "is both exciting and provocative and presents a puzzling situation from different angles without too much comment." Yet John Mason Brown (*SR*) exclaimed that the play, while thankfully dealing with a subject of vital concern, was "slow and inept" and that it demonstrated how the theatre "can be stubbornly resistant to ideas."

Excellent performances were given by Blanche Yurka as Benckendorff's aristocratic Prussian sister with a distaste for both Americans and Nazis and by Herbert Berghof as a Nazi-hating Czech captain who kills the fanatical Erich. George Mathews, Martin Brandt, and Paul Tripp were also cast members.

(1) TEMPEST, THE [Dramatic Revival*] A: William Shakespeare; M: David Diamond; D: Margaret Webster; S/C: Motley; L: Moe Hack; P: Cheryl Crawford; T: Alvin Theatre; 1/25/45 (100)

Since the late 1930s there had been only one director who could time and again make Shakespeare successful on Broadway. That director was Margaret Webster, who, on the present occasion, chose for revival a play that since 1916 had received only a third-rate shoestring production in 1933 by a ragged band of second-rate Shakespeareans. Webster's innovative, "intensely theatrical" (Wilella Waldorf [*NYP*]) production, inspired by a clever scenic idea of Eva Le Gallienne's, made news not only for its inherent artistry but for some of its unusual casting choices, most notably black actor Canada Lee for Caliban, ballerina Vera Zorina for Ariel, and (in their Broadway debuts) famed Czech refugee comedians George Voskovec and Jan Werich for Trinculo and Stephano. The other principals were taken as follows: Alonso, Philip Huston; Gonzalo, Paul Leyssac; Antonio, Berry Kroeger;

Sebastian, Eugene Stuckmann; Prospero, Arnold Moss; Miranda, Frances Heflin; and Ferdinand, Vito Christi. The well-rounded company also included Joseph Anthony as the ship-master and Stephen Elliott as the boatswain. Both were to become important theatrical personages.

An enchanting score by David Diamond accompanied the presentation, which began with the shipwreck scene, as described by Euphemia Van Rensselaer Wyatt (*CW*): "A most decorative and heraldic caravel under full sail is pictured on a silver curtain and as the orchestral storm gains its crescendo, a transparency discloses the helmsman at the wheel." The play proper was set on a revolving stage with angularly shaped, multiple-leveled rocks into which stairways were built, and two pinnacles set against a dazzling blue and green horizon background. Magical, otherworldly colors bathed the scenes, and highly imaginative costumes contrasted with the stark and austere decor. Turning the revolve in full view of the audience instantly transformed the vista for continual action without scene-change pauses. For Arthur Pollock (*BE*), however, the acting space was cramped, resulting in a flatness of effect, particularly in the talkier scenes, whose movement was restricted.

Eva Le Gallienne had conceived the set and even created a three-dimensional model of it before a designer was selected. Zorina declared in *Zorina* that while a designer was being considered, she asked several she knew to consider the project. One was Eugene Berman, a hot-tempered Russian who was quick to take offense at the slightest provocation. He walked into producer Crawford's office, saw Le Gallienne's model, and heard Le Gallienne and Webster begin to discuss it. He then spoke up. "Looks like hospital, exactly like New York Hospital. If that is what you want, you don't need *me*," he said, and then walked out. The set that was realized by the firm of Motley provided no masking between the wings and the island, so Ariel and Caliban had to be onstage, hidden in tiny niches at the rear of the revolve, ready to appear when their cues came. This required considerable endurance, given the lengthy opening scenes. Zorina managed to get through the ordeal by imagining herself to be trapped electricity that would shoot out like lightning at Prospero's command. But on opening night, Canada Lee spent the opening moments sleeping. His cue approached and the stage manager, seeing him asleep, could not communicate with him by whispering; thereupon, a long stage hook was brought silently and slowly into play to prod the actor, who spoke his first lines quite naturally, as if being roused from slumber.

The script had been sharply trimmed to the proportions of two acts. Among the cuts was the masque sequence with Iris, Ceres, and others. (Despite its very expensive costumes, this scene was eliminated in Philadelphia when it stopped the play in its tracks. Webster felt justified in the omission, since she believed the masque not to have been in Shakespeare's original text, but to have been added for a royal command performance.) Some material was rearranged, most notably the "Our revels now are ended" lines, transposed here to the very end as an epilogue. As the lines were spoken, the lights faded and the actors disappeared, leaving Prospero on a height, dressed in his red robe, with the sky darkening behind him before he too "melted into air, thin air." The revision met with general approbation: "By daring to transpose them so that they now conclude the fantasy, Miss Webster has shown that in this instance she knows Shakespeare's business, if not better than he did, at least better than his editors have known it," commented John Mason Brown (*SR*).

There was poetry, spectacle, fantasy, comedy, sentiment, and philosophy in this lovely revival. Brown represented most of his colleagues in saying, "More than anyone would believe possible, and to a degree we are not likely to see excelled in our time, [Webster] has brought *The Tempest* to the stage so that its magic remains magical, and audiences are at liberty 'to sail their own seas to their own haven.'" The principal opponent to this view was George Jean Nathan (*TBY*), for whom Webster, in the interests of commercial success, had infused the mounting with too much theatrical hocus-pocus (especially the revolving set), thereby depriving the audience of the privilege of using their imaginations to conjure up the images presented in the poetry.

As Prospero, Moss, wearing a makeup that suggested "a gentle Mephisto" (Lewis Nichols [*NYT*]), gave a dignified, beautifully spoken Shakespearean performance, conventional, apart from his relative youth, but extremely satisfying. "Arnold Moss' Prospero is a serene and glowing portrayal," declared George Freedley (*NYMT*), "rich in voice, sure in detail and encompassing in its all-over effect." Voskovec and Werich were exceptionally good casting, as they were renowned comedians playing roles that are usually given to straight actors trying to be funny. Thus they made what is often amusing truly hilarious and were applauded for their comic genius. Ward Morehouse (*NYS*) even thought that there was too much of their low comedy antics, and one or two critics disparaged them for their Olsen and Johnson-like antics.

Lee wore a hideous makeup and rags to portray the man-beast. His voice was clear and resounding, and he captured much of the required animality, but his diction was not always as distinct as it should have been, and discomfort was expressed by some at his savage grunting and snorting. Zorina danced and leaped her part as much as she spoke it, giving her an aerial and musical charm that was pure delight. Waldorf noted, however, "Zorina is not a dancer here. She is an actress of infinite grace and rhythmic beauty who not only makes a most fascinating sprite but speaks her lines with distinction, charm and a genuine feeling for the frolicsome, quicksilver quality of the role. Her singing is her only weakness." A few critics, however, commented unfavorably not only on her singing but on her speaking of the poetry.

Zorina had made a valiant effort to overcome her foreign accent for her debut as a dramatic actress and had studied intensively for a six-month period with a New York University professor to train her voice and diction and to learn how to read poetry. But, as she admitted in her autobiography, she apparently drilled herself into such mechanical perfection that after impressing the director and cast at the first re hearsal, she was unable to go any further in developing her role. One day, Webster even yelled at her, "For Christ's sake, why don't you make a mistake sometimes!"

It was planned for Zorina's Ariel to do some flying, but the specialists needed to do the rigging could not be found. The show's technical personnel felt that they could work the problem out themselves, and a flying system was set up. It proved trickier than first thought. Le Gallienne, an experienced flyer from her *Peter Pan** days, volunteered to test it out, but after she was dropped several times, it was decided that the mechanism was too risky, so a more conventional disappearing trick was used to get Zorina off magically.

The Tempest was one of several shows of the decade that ran into problems with Local 802 of the musicians' union. There are slightly different versions of the situation in Webster's *Don't Put Your Daughter on the Stage* and Crawford's *One Naked Individual*, but the chief difficulty seems to have been the fact that Diamond's score was created for a smaller number of musicians than were necessary for a musical. The show hired more musicians than were needed when the Alvin housed a straight play, but nowhere near the twenty-two demanded by a musical. When the union learned that the show used a considerable amount of incidental music, as well as the settings for Ariel's songs, they insisted that twenty-two musicians be hired. The production nearly closed down as a result, but Crawford battled the union, and the result was a new category called "a play with music" that allowed an eight-man orchestra and twenty minutes of music. Some snipping of the score ensued, and one song was made a cappella.

(2) [Return Engagement] T: City Center of Music and Drama; 11/12/45 (24)

Following a road tour, the production returned to New York for popular-priced showings at $2.40 top. While some minor actors differed--including Wallace Acton as Trinculo, Benny Baker as Stephano, Bram Nossen as Alonso, Robert Harrison as Gonzalo, Joseph Hardy as Antonio, Diana Sinclair as Miranda, and Albert Hachmeister as Ferdinand--the leads remained intact. The new Trinculo and Stephano were even more farcically inclined than their predecessors, reminding Lewis Nichols (*NYT*) of Olsen and Johnson. The poetic fantasy was not well served by being offered in the cavernous, increasingly dingy environment of the City Center, wrote George Jean Nathan (*TBY*).

TEMPORARY ISLAND, A [Drama/Circus/Period/Romance/School] A/D: Halsted Welles; M: Lehman Engel, Lorenzo Fuller; S/L: Lawrence Goldwasser; C: Mildred Sutherland; P: Cheryl Crawford and T. Edward Hambleton for Experimental Theatre, Inc., u/t/a/o the American National Theatre and Academy; T: Maxine Elliott's Theatre; 3/14/48 (6)

Dotted throughout the lengthy cast list of this promising but garrulous effort (produced for a limited engagement) were the names of some important performers, from the established Vera Zorina, Philip Bourneuf, and Ernest Truex to such new talents as Rita Gam (in her Broadway debut) and Walter (Jack) Palance. The play had a provocative subject but was dramaturgically inept. "It is as short on story as it is long on words," rebuked Hobe. (*V*). "It steadily loses pace and dramatic impact until, at the final curtain, it has come to a standstill. It is indifferently directed and unevenly acted."

Mr. Fisk (Bourneuf) is the president of a drab female seminary in 1881 Massachusetts. When a circus sets up nearby, he tries to persuade the management to leave because he fears for the moral effect on his impressionable students. He falls in love, however, with Mlle. Suzette (Zorina), the circus manager, and finds in the colorful big-top life the romance and color missing from his empty life at the school. When it comes down to deciding between his conventional existence and the glamor of the circus, he follows Suzette's advice that the circus is merely a temporary island and returns to his staid career.

The cast included Hilda Vaughn, Philippa Bevans, Harrison Dowd, Jane Hoffman, Nancy Franklin, Ruth Vaughn, and Bill Dillard.

TEN LITTLE INDIANS [Drama/British/Crime/Mystery/Religion/Romance] A: Agatha Christie; SC: Agatha Cristie's novel, *And Then There Were None*; D: Albert de Courville; S: Howard Bay; P: Messrs. Shubert and Albert de Courville; T: Broadhurst Theatre; 6/27/44 (425)

Ten Little Indians was one of the most popular murder mysteries of its day and remained so for decades following, being made into several movies and TV shows, as well as being given frequent revivals in college, community, and regional theatres. In London it was acted under the title of its source novel (also known as *The Nursery Rhyme Murders*).

It concerns the gathering of eight guests, none of whom ever have met one another before, on lonely Indian Island off the coast of Devon, England, to which they have been asked by unknown hosts, Mr. and Mrs. Owen. Two servants, Rogers (Neil Fitzgerald) and Mrs. Rogers (Georgia Harvey), and a boatman (Patrick O'Connor) complete the group. Over the mantlepiece is a painting of the legend of the ten little Indians of the nursery rhyme ("Ten little Indians going out to dine . . .). Beneath the painting stand ten little statuettes of Indians. A strange recording informs them that each--including the two servants--is to be killed for having been connected at some earlier time with the death of at least one person, but sometimes more. The island is cut off from communication with the mainland because of a storm. As the play progresses, the victims are mysteriously slain, their deaths being marked by the breaking or disappearance of a statuette. The deaths are varied, including poisoning, being pushed off a cliff, a gunshot to the head, an injection, a strangling, a stabbing, and so on. Those meeting their demise include the religious zealot, Emily Brent (Estelle Winwood); the hanging judge, Sir Lawrence Wargrave (Halliwell Hobbes); the neurotic nerve specialist, Dr. Armstrong (Harry Worth); the vapid young ne'er-do-well, Anthony Marston (Anthony Kemble-Cooper); the retired general, General Mackenzie (Nicholas Joy); and the ex-Scotland Yard detective William Blore (J. Pat O'Malley). At the end, the killings are solved by the romantic pair, secretary Vera Claythorne (Claudia Morgan) and ex-soldier Philip Lombard (Michael Whalen). The boatman did them.

Mixed reviews greeted this whodunit, into which a goodly share of humor had been mixed. For those who liked it, it was a perfectly set, expertly cast and directed, and tautly written piece of escapist melodrama. Howard Barnes (*NYHT*) called it "mannerly, literate, and occasionally terrifying." To Burton Rascoe (*NYWT*) it was "top-notch escapist stuff, sheer, unmitigated, fantastic, enjoyable nonsense." Some did not like it. George Jean Nathan (*TBY*) noted the familiarity of its formula plot and the shallowness of the character depictions. Louis Kronenberger (*PM*) felt that it was "too tame." "There isn't enough of either physical or psychological excitement; there isn't drama enough in the situations or continuity enough in the suspense." Robert Garland (*NYJA*) considered it "contrived, incredible and obvious as to the outcome."

TENTING TONIGHT [Comedy/Family/Gambling/Marriage/Romance/Small Town/University] A: Frank Gould; D: Hudson Fasset; S: John Root; C: Robert Moore; P: Saul Fischbein; T: Booth Theatre; 4/2/47 (46)

A thin and drawn-out comedy dealing with the housing problems faced by ex-GIs seeking a higher education in the postwar years. "Its aim is modest and its achievement is no higher than its aim," remarked John Chapman (*NYDN*). Ward Morehouse (*NYS*) called it "a clamorous and exhausting comedy, rompish in an elephantine way." It had been under the producership of Judith Abbott and Mary Mason until shortly before its opening, when the ladies bowed out and Saul Fischbein, the principal backer, took over.

Chemistry professor Peter Roberts (Richard Clark), his wife Leonie (Jean Muir), and their niece Edna (June Dayton) reside in a small college town in California. When the school itself becomes so overcrowded that ex-GIs wishing to attend must sleep in garages and in pool halls, Edna places an ad in the town's newspaper offering room and board at the Roberts' home for a needy veteran-student. The notion leads to the house being occupied by three ex-GIs and the wife of one of them. One of the boys, Phil Alexander (Dean Harens), engages in a romance with Edna. Things get more complicated when another of the threesome, would-be bookie Joe Wolinski (Joshua Shelley), makes the residence into an office for taking race results over the phone. The third fellow is Elliot (Jackie Kelk), who is always gumming up the works. Joe interests various big-time gamblers in his plan to convert a projected nightclub and casino in an abandoned local factory into a dormitory for 200 ex-servicemen who wish to go to college. The professor, whose job has been endangered, is saved, and the stuffed-shirt chairman (William David) of the school board becomes a hero when he is convinced to subsidize the dorm.

Cast members included Michael Road, Henry Lascoe, Michael Lewin, Ethel Remey, Ralph Brooke, and others.

TEXAS, LI'L DARLIN' [Musical/Journalism/Politics/Romance/Southern] B: John Whedon and Sam Moore; M: Robert Emmet Dolan; LY: Johnny Mercer; D: Paul Crabtree; CH: Al White, Jr.; S/L: Theodore Cooper; C: Eleanor Goldsmith; P: Studio Productions and Anthony Brady Farrell Productions; T: Mark Hellinger Theatre; 11/25/49 (293)

An intermittently amusing, moderately successful, but artistically inadequate stab at a musical satire on Texas politics and on magazines like *Time* and *Life*. A large share of its fun came from the presence of comedian Kenny Delmar, famous as radio's mule-voiced Senator Claghorn (on Fred Allen's show) and here making his Broadway debut.

The homespun, rather unsophisticated show tells of a romantic duo, Easy Jones (Danny Scholl), a tall, shy young veteran, and Dallas (Mary Hatcher), his small-town Texas gal, whose theatrical aspirations in Chicago did not pan out and who has come home to the Lone Star State. Dallas's rascally, drawling, hypocritically pious dad, Hominy Smith (Delmar), is running for reelection as senator. The idealistic friends of Easy encourage him to run for the post himself because Hominy never keeps his exaggerated campaign promises and is probably crooked. Even Dallas decides to go against her father. Hominy follows instructions from higher-ups and, seeing that his local position is threatened, is willing to allow a Henry Luce-like magazine publisher (Loring Smith) to help him, instead of Thomas Dewey, aim for the presidency in the next campaign.

This was an old-fashioned show, but it had a number of virtues, including some pleasant songs with clever lyrics and an exuberant company. Most critics enjoyed themselves but also found various nits to pick. Arthur Pollock (*DC*) stated, "The show has a leisurely pace, is pleasant in humor, never strident. Not a thing in it to cheer about. . . . Nothing to be vexed about either." Joseph T. Shipley (*NL*) believed that the show "starts like a gusher but winds up more like an ooze." Richard Watts, Jr. (*NYP*), while finding much to enjoy, felt that the show failed to have the needed satirical edge because the writers were not able to create in Hominy a man who was both dishonest and sympathetic.

Hobe. (*V*) blamed his dissatisfaction not on the writing but on the "deplorable" production, which did not take full advantage of the materials available. Major performers were Kate Murtah, Fredd Wayne, Jared Reed, Ray Long, and child performer Betty Lou Keim.

One of the best-liked songs was the spoof of Western tunes, "The Big Movie Show in the Sky." Among other numbers were "They Talk a Different Language," "Take a Crank Letter," "Politics," and "Affable, Balding Me."

TEXAS TOWN [Drama/Alcoholism/Blacks/Romance/Small Town] A: Horton Foote; D: Mary Hunter; S: Joseph Anthony; P: American Actors Company; T: Weidman Studio Theatre (OB); 4/29/41

An Off-Broadway theatre at 108 West Sixteenth Street (dancer Charles Weidman's studio theatre) was the intimate venue for this first play by Horton Foote to be staged locally. Foote, a regular member of the four-year-old company, also appeared in the play, although his acting was considered second-rate. Most of the troupe's previous work had gone unreviewed. These included Euripides' *The Trojan Women* (1938), Lynn Riggs's *Sump'n like Wings* (1939), and Paul Green's *Shroud My Body Down* (1940), as well as several one-act programs.

A drugstore in a small Texas town is the locale of the action; here various characters pass the time in idle conversation. The central character is Ray Case (Foote), a young man who longs to leave the town and his domineering mother. Some think him lazy, others a dreamer. The equally restless Carrie (Loraine Stuart) is his love, but she is also loved by Maner (William [Will] Hare), the drugstore clerk and soda jerk. When Carrie declares her intention to marry Maner, Ray finds the incentive to leave the town. Carrie belatedly realizes that she has erred and that Ray is the one she wants. While thinking that she will go off after him, she receives word that he has been killed in a car wreck. Among the other characters are an impoverished cotton farmer, Digger (Dwight Marfield), close friend to the local judge (Frederick Campbell), whose mortgage is lifted, greatly to the dismay of the bullying Damon (Burrell Smith). Doc (Roland Wood), an alcoholic physician, and Hannah (Randall Steplight), a pathetic black man, are other important characters.

The play captured considerable critical enthusiasm for its deep sense of authenticity and close observation of real life. Brooks Atkinson (*NYT*) was deeply impressed with the quality of the various characterizations and with the excellence of the young company's acting: "It is something to walk in out of Sixteenth Street in New York into the waiting and idle atmosphere of a small town in Texas." Future star Wendell Corey had a role in the play.

THANK YOU, SVOBODA [Comedy/Military/Politics/Prison/Romance/War] A: H. S. Kraft; SC: John Pen's novel, *You Can't Do That to Svoboda*; D: H. S. Kraft and Moe Hack; S: Samuel Leve; L: Moe Hack; P: Milton Baron; T: Mansfield Theatre; 3/1/44 (6)

Svoboda (Sam Jaffe) is the likable, illiterate porter at the inn in a Czechoslovakian village in 1939. He is engaged to the widow Mary (Adrienne Gessner), a junk dealer, and will reside with her in her shack after they are wed. The Nazis overrun the town and loot all the houses. A watch Mary gave Svoboda is crushed by a Nazi, which so enrages Svoboda that he beats the lout up. The innocent porter then is accused of blowing up a bridge (actually, some Germans did it as a pretext for their looting) and made to swear to his guilt by affixing a cross to his confession. He goes to a concentration camp but, considered an idiot of no use, is released after two months, wearing new clothes he bought with what he earned from doing odd tasks for the other inmates. But he discovers that all his savings have been taken by the Germans. He takes his revenge by actually dynamiting a bridge as a trainload of Germans from Prague are passing over it.

Stock characters, important action that occurred mostly offstage, a lack of humor, flat and repetitious dialogue, a central character who goes from being a near-moron to a clever saboteur, and a tale completely lacking in credibility were faults cited by the critics. "It is anything but a good play," noted Louis Kronenberger (*PM*). "On almost every count, indeed, it is an extremely bad one." Lewis Nichols (*NYT*) sighed, "The saga of Svoboda . . . is tedious and talky and lacks the characterization and also the charm of the original source."

Whitford Kane as a bibulous engineer, Frank Tweddel as the innkeeper, Arnold Korff as a Czech colonel, John McGovern as a doctor, Francis Compton as a villager, John Ravold as a padre, Michael Strong as a Nazi private, and Dehl Berti as another Nazi were among the others in the cast, which had only one woman.

THAT LADY [Drama/Period/Politics/Prison/Romance] A: Kate O'Brien; SC: Kate O'Brien's novel, *For One Sweet Grape*; D: Guthrie McClintic; DS: Rolf Gérard; P: Katharine Cornell; T: Martin Beck Theatre; 11/22/49 (78)

A Katharine Cornell vehicle, set in sixteenth-century Spain, spanning the years from 1577 to 1590, and allowing the great star to sport a dashing-looking eyepatch. Her role was that of Ana de Mendoza y de Gomez, princess of Eboli, a beautiful widow living at the court of the petulant but crafty Philip II (Henry Daniell), who loves her but, seeing no political advantage in it, refuses to wed her. The princess's patch is the result of a dueling accident suffered at age fourteen. Ana, to spite the king, chooses to have an affair with Antonio Perez (Torin Thatcher), the philandering secretary of state, but the couple find themselves actually falling in love, which also has its effect on the married Perez's family. The villainous Juan de Escovedo (Joseph Wiseman) slanders the lovers and also conspires against Philip. For his troubles, he is killed, but the madly jealous monarch also has the lovers locked up in prison and puts them to the torture. If Ana were to promise never again to see Perez, she would be pardoned, but her agreement carries the condition of his freedom. Perez eventually escapes and, after a farewell scene with Ana (at the end of which he kisses her on the eyepatch), flees to Aragon. Ana is punished by being walled up in the darkness of her Madrid palace for the last few months of her life.

Cornell and her associates were lavisly praised for their excellent work, but the brocaded play was considered inadequate to their efforts. It was reckoned to be an inert romantic melodrama replete with stock characters and situations and clichéd dialogue. Not only was the author's dramatization of her own novel seriously undramatic, but the passion with which it was concerned was unable to warm the spectators. "*That Lady* never rises above situations that it contrives mechanically," wrote Brooks Atkinson (*NYT*), who found the character of Ana unmotivated and less interesting than those of Philip and Perez. "Miss O'Brien's writing is commonplace. She says the stock things with no distinction," he added. George Jean Nathan (*TBY*) concluded that the play, for all its handsome staging and accomplished acting, "remains a snail-paced spoken novel rather than a vital and active drama."

With one or two exceptions, the performances were considered superlative, but Cornell's was luminous. John Mason Brown (*SR*) remarked, "She does everything that she can within her extraordinary powers to make Ana hold the same interest for an audience that she plainly does for Miss Cornell. The patch she is condemned to wear . . . is unable to obscure her radiance. As always, Miss Cornell is lovely to look at and moves with a wonderful free-limbed grace." The distinguished cast included Henry Stephenson as the archbishop of Toledo, Esther Minciotti as Ana's duenna, Marian Seldes as her daughter, Douglass Watson as her son, and Will Kuluva and Oliver Cliff in other roles.

THAT OLD DEVIL [Comedy/Journalism/Marriage/Sex/Small Town] A/D: J. C. Nugent; S: Paul Morrison; C: Johnnie Johnstone; P: Lodewick Vroom; T: Playhouse; 6/5/44 (16)

Septuagenarian J. C. Nugent starred in, wrote, and directed this baleful effort set in Beechville, Connecticut. He played Jim Blair, an aging, retired businessman. To annoy his nagging younger wife (Luella Gear), he allows it to be known that he is the father of an illegitimate baby to be born to Lila Merrill (Agnes Doyle), an English refugee girl he and his wife have taken in. To his delight, the town is soon buzzing about his virility, especially the women who previously ignored him. His wife finally leaves home because of all the gossip, and her friends start to pursue him. She comes back and everything returns to normal when it is revealed that Lila is secretly wed to home-town boy Jerry Swift (Michael Ames), a radical journalist who had to leave town because of his muckraking articles and who is now seeking to join the armed forces. To round things out, Jim and his wife learn that they will have a child of their own.

A few critics found the play tasteless. Arthur Pollock (*BE*) thought it amateurish: "It has that amateur zeal for sauciness, the novice's lack of cohesion, and is made up of familiar comic notions." Lewis Nichols (*NYT*) claimed that the play "grows tiresome through desperate repetition of a standard joke." Ruth Gilbert, Matt Briggs, J. Colville Dunn, and Ruth Gates were some of the actors.

THEATRE [Comedy/Family/Marriage/Sex/Theatre] A: Guy Bolton and W. Somerset Maugham; SC: the novel of the same name by W. Somerset Maugham; D/P: John Golden; S: Donald Oenslager; T: Hudson Theatre; 11/12/41 (69)

An occasionally pleasing but consistently empty time-passer that suffered from an insufficient infusion of the wit of coadaptor Maugham, upon whose novel it was very thinly based. It provided a chance for famed monologist Cornelia Otis Skinner to share the stage with flesh-and-blood actors. She was considered beautiful, charming, and highly polished, but, in some eyes, missing the dimensions that were necessary to bring her role completely to life.

Theatre's subject was the familiar one of a celebrated middle-aged British actress, Julia Lambert (Skinner), who has begun to think her sex appeal on the wane. Although ostensibly married to her equally popular acting partner, Michael Gosselyn (Arthur Margetson), she seeks to seduce a younger man, accountant Tom Fennell (John Moore), to prove her appeal is not declining. The Gosselyns are actually divorced but keep up a sham domestic life to protect their reputations as well as the psychological well-being of their son Roger (Frederick Bradlee). Michael, who is not averse to other women's charms, is also being pursued by Julia's best friend, wealthy Dolly De Vries (Helen Flint), who is privy to the truth about his marital status. Jealous of Julia's affair with Fennell, he goes yachting with Dolly and even announces his imminent retirement from the stage in favor of a second marriage. Julia's heart may be breaking because of this, but she goes on alone with her production of a play called *Lola Montez*. The plot then proceeds to arrange things so that Michael and Julia rediscover their love for one another, he returns to her side for her opening, and they decide on remarriage. Julia makes her final exit after her triumphant performance by passing through the stage door on the set and down the aisle of the theatre in which the play is being performed.

Triteness and a lack of originality burdened the play, although several of its comic scenes were found effective. "Their play," lamented Brooks Atkinson (*NYT*), "is a mechanical contrivance, without characterizations or enthusiasm." Richard Lockridge (*NYS*) said, "It is difficult to feel toward it any emotion more violent than benevolent neutrality." The cast included Viola Roache, J. Colvil Dunn, Francis Compton, and Jane Gordon, among others.

THEATRE OF ANGNA ENTERS, THE [Miscellaneous/Solo] CN/D/C: Angna Enters; P: Luther Greene; T: Alvin Theatre; 12/27/42

Angna Enters, who performed unusual one-woman shows, had provided several earlier programs in New York, but this was the first produced at a Broadway house and intended for a wide audience. Her wordless program was a combination of dance, acting, piano playing, onstage painting, and mime. Each of her numbers told a story, sometimes realistically, sometimes surrealistically.

During the course of her run, she offered slightly varying programs at each performance. Her material included "Boy Cardinal"; "Moyen Age"; "My First Dance--Hungarian Routine"; "Queen of Heaven"; "Delsarte"; "Field Day"; and three pieces about prostitutes: "Hollywood Horror Story," about a girl who becomes a prostitute because she can find no work as an actress; "Aphrodisiac--Green Hour";

and "Harlot's Progress," set in Paris between 1830 and 1838. This latter told of an amoral young woman who catches a man's attention at a carnival and manages to communicate her address to him. The next morning she awakes in her garret to find gifts of fine clothing and a request for a rendezvous. She meets the man, marries him, finds happiness, and becomes an old prude. In the first scene of the piece Enters appeared in the nude, surprising at least one reviewer who expected to hear the arrival of the disapproving mayor and his commissioner of licenses. There was also "Piano Music No. 4--Commencement," about a youngster presenting her first piano recital, and "Dilly Dally--Ah Sweet Mystery of Life," intended as a spoof of artist Salvador Dali and showing a young and eccentric amateur painting, dancing, and writing in alternation as she tries feverishly to express the mystery of life. Background music was provided by Madeleine Marshall.

There was some questioning as to whether the program deserved to be called theatre, it being generally agreed that it was, but only in the widest definition of the term. Robert Lawrence (*NYHT*) accepted some of Enters's work without qualifications, but maintained that "too often . . . her sketches are short of emotional impact, lacking not only in broad dramatic impulse but in the power to stir hearty laughter. They are decadent in the classical sense of the word--a series of embroideries upon trivia." Robert Coleman (*NYDM*) found the whole thing boring, unfunny, and vastly overrated by the highbrows who had touted the performer.

THERE IS NO END [Drama/Military/Prison/Religion/War] A: Anthony Palma; D: David Alexander; S: Hal Shafer; P: Dramatic Workshop; T: President Theatre (OB); 2/16/50 (16)

An effective antiwar play, somewhat on the preachy side, but filled with sharply drawn characters and dealing with a significant subject. It had been seen earlier on the West Coast in an Actors' Lab production.

An all-male play based on the author's experiences, it is set in a German prisoner-of-war camp for American soldiers and deals with the problems of the men as they confront homesickness and approaching death from slow starvation. One key character is a hillbilly from Tennessee (Everett Chambers), another is a religious zealot (Robert O'Neil), one is a boy (John Munson) confused about war, another (John Sargent) is a ruthless individual. Under duress, the better natures of some are revealed, while others revert to self-serving cruelty.

L. C. (*NYT*) believed that the group had skillfully performed a drama that "proves at once touching, sensitive and horrifying." "It's not a pretty play, but you won't forget it," thought Vernon Rice (*NYP*).

THERESE [Drama/Art/Crime/Invalidism/Marriage/Period/Sex] A: Thomas Job; SC: Emile Zola's play, *Thérèse Raquin*; D: Margaret Webster; S/C: Raymond Sovey; P: Victor Payne-Jennings and Bernard Klawans; T: Biltmore Theatre; 10/9/45 (96)

An adaptation of 1873's *Thérèse Raquin*, one of the first naturalistic plays, based by Zola on his own 1867 novel of the same name. Thomas Job's version provided "a most sedate and conversational melodrama," regretted Lewis Nichols (*NYT*), who called it "old-fashioned and leisurely." The piece was desultory and talky, lacking in the all-important element of action, and stretched out to the point of boredom. It also made little of the characters, who were pasteboard figures, made more of greasepaint than of flesh and blood. Rosamond Gilder (*TAM*) chalked it up as "a drab and static exercise in stagecraft."

Therese (Eva Le Gallienne), a maid-of-all-work for the Raquin family, marries young clerk Camille Raquin (Berry Kroeger) and rises in social position to mistress of the household. She is adulterously entwined with Camille's painter friend Laurent (Victor Jory), who wishes to gain her at the expense of her husband. The latter becomes their victim when he is drowned in the river. Guilt soon haunts the pair, who have married at the request of Camille's mother, Madame Raquin (Dame May Whitty), but who find the flame of their love quenched. Madame Raquin suffers a stroke on overhearing Laurent and Therese talk of the murder on their wedding night. She is confined to an armchair, able to express her hateful feelings only through her eyes. Still, she regains use of one hand, but stops herself from spelling out the truth of their deed to others, choosing to watch the couple self-destruct to the point where they even consider one another's murder. She regains her physical powers at the melodramatic end when, unlike the original, Therese and Laurent do not poison themselves but are taken away by the authorities after confessing to the police inspector (Averell Harris), who plays dominoes with them.

Despite a first-rate cast, the acting was weak, save for Whitty, the director's mother. Le Gallienne was deemed especially lacking in her passionate scenes. Webster's direction also failed to capture the proper atmosphere for the chilling tale. Annette Sorel, Doris Patston, and John F. Hamilton were in the cast.

THESE ARE THE TIMES [Revue] SK/LY: Henry Myers, Edward Eliscu, Joe Darion, Norman Franklin, Ira Wallach, Les Pine, Irving Caesar, Dick Howard, Sam Locke, Lou Dropkin, Felix Leon, and Henry Foner; M: Jay Gorney; D: Edmund Morris; CH: Herbert Ross; S/C: Dick Mumms and Hal Shafer; L: Hans Sondheimer; P: Sondra and Jay Gorney u/t/a/o the Dramatic Workshop; T: President Theatre (OB); 5/10/50

Erwin Piscator's Dramatic Workshop was behind this youthful revue that came up with mixed results. Some of it fell flat, but some of it was delightful. Among the critically approved numbers were "That Mittel Europa of Mine," in which Frank Moore, Bobby Brooke, and John Di Beni nostalgically longed for the days of romance and fun in old Vienna and Budapest; a double-talk sketch, "Salamic Bimba," with the rubber-faced Philip Matthews as federal agent Jack Dalton involved in an espionage plot focusing on the secret "bimba," which is revealed to be useless without mustard; "Let's End the Beguine," with Liz Ross as a femme fatale; Ross as a salesgirl singing racily to a piece of lingerie in "Ballad to a Bra"; a spoof of existentialism in "No Sartre by Jean-Paul Exit," with Moore, Ross, Laird Brooks, James Copeland, and Lois Richards; "Simian's Rainbow," with Frank Aletter and Yolanda McKool as sophisticated monkeys in a zoo pondering the foibles of the human race; and "B-29," a meaningful thrust at atomic warfare, with one bomber wiping out the Eastern Hemisphere and another the Western, leaving the enemy pilots without hemispheres to return to.

Robert Garland (*NYJA*) termed it "a fresh, intelligent and winningly un-Broadway young revue." But Louis Sheaffer (*BE*) opined that "the musical is not important, no great shakes, pleasant in spots but trying too hard much of the time." There were frequent jibes at the less than expert voices and the somewhat shaky acting of the tyro cast (most of them students in a musical course taught by Jay Gorney).

THESE HILLS ARE SCARRED [Drama/Family/War] A: Nishan Parlkian; S: Walter L. Steinharter; P: Drama Lab; T: Master Institute Theatre (OB); 11/16/49 (4)

An "embarrassingly contrived" (*V*) drama about postwar Germany that posited the notion that Nazism had not died there. A major role was that of a woman (Patricia Sawyer) who was waiting for Germany to rise from the ashes and conquer. The company included future actor of note Pat Hingle, whose biography in *Who's Who in the Theatre* lists his first New York performance as not coming until 1953.

THESE TENDER MERCIES [Comedy-Drama/Blacks/Crime/Family/Race/Religion/Romance/Sex/Small Town/Southern] A/D: Barton Yarborough; P: Invitational Series of the Experimental Theatre, Inc.; T: Lenox Hill Playhouse (OB); 6/4/48 (4)

An antilynching melodrama that John S. Wilson (*PM*) said failed to make a happy marriage between satiric intentions and a topic of great seriousness. L. B. (*NYT*) declared that the effort proved "a disservice to the cause and an affront to good taste."

The story is set in the deep South in 1909, where a local family strongly believes in the need to protect "the honor of Southern womanhood." The boy (Elliott Reid) of the family becomes disgusted with them when his father leads a lynch mob that kills a black man suspected of a white girl's (Gloria McGhee) rape. He rebukes the so-called local "Christians" and himself becomes a fugitive. His hiding place is in the rape victim's cabin. The degree to which he believes in his principles is further tested when he hears that another black man has raped his fiancée. He is eventually captured by the same mob that also seizes the current rape suspect. First the black man is hung, and then, just as the youth is about to meet a like death, his fiancée confesses that she has not even been touched by the black man. The mob now turns against her, and the boy ends up with the other girl.

The characters included various colorful examples of Southern white trash, religious zealots, and a town idiot. It was "curiously uneven and unsatisfactory," reported Vernon Rice (*NYP*), yet he liked the vivid character depiction. In the cast were Elizabeth Jones, Nina Probette, Adele Fortin, Ed Fuller, Elmer Lehr, Louis Peterson, Urylee Leonardos, and Gordon Peters, among others.

THEY ALL WANT TO GET MARRIED [Musical/Yiddish Language] B: Julie Berns; M: Al Olshanetsky; LY: Jacob Jacobs; D/P: Judah Bleich; CH: Benjamin Zemach; S: Leo Kerz; T: Public Theatre (OB); 10/8/44 (245)

A successful Yiddish musical that incorporated the usual ingredients of colorful costumes and sets, corny situations, and enthusiastic performances. Kahn. (*V*) said that with this show, "the Yiddish theatre has the best musical it has had in several years."

Its episodic book concerns a standard Yiddish theatre character, the marriage arranger (Judah Bleich), whose problems are compounded by a war-caused shortage of men. Seeking respite from the demands of would-be brides, he goes off to the Catskills. His story is mingled with that of a young refugee woman (Nina Rochelle) who flees to America after killing several Nazis and who, after twenty years, is reunited with her mother (Lucy German).

The cast included Max Wilner, Aaron Lebedeff, Diana Goldberg, Irving Grossman, Tillie Rabinowitz, and Luba Kadison.

THEY CAME TO A CITY [Drama/Yiddish Language] A: J. B. Priestley; TR: N. Buchwald; D: Paul Mann; S: Ralph Alswang; P: Yiddish Theatre Ensemble; T: Barbizon-Plaza Theatre (OB); 1/31/50 (15)

A Yiddish version of a 1943 Priestley political play, given by a group formerly associated with the Artef Theatre, a semipro Yiddish group active in the 1930s. The sole critic attending, Arthur Pollock (*DC*), thought it a worthwhile presentation of a meaningful British play, suitable for Yiddish audiences and even of potential interest for Broadway. He thought the actors the best group of Yiddish players in New York because there was nothing flamboyant or old-fashioned about them. "The acting is . . . smooth and sensitive and eloquent."

The plot concerns an unfathomable supernatural event that places a group of British people at the gates to a city where everything is on an ideal plane. These people include a thoroughgoing capitalist (Abraham Sandroff), in love with money; a wealthy aristocratic man (Hyman Lowenstein); a titled woman (Lyuba Rymer) and her unhappy daughter (Miriam Laserson); a waitress (Zelda Lerner); a scrubwoman (Luba Eisenberg); a radical working man who has lost his faith in the revolution (Abraham Hershbein); and a miserable bank clerk (Lieb Freilich) and his wife (Goldie Russler). After spending a day in the city, they reassemble at the gates to discuss their thoughts. There are those who find in the city a utopia of human life, while there are others who are cynical about its virtues and prefer the status quo of England. A number of them wish to stay in the city, and two of them, the scrubwoman and the worker, want to spread the news of the place to the rest of mankind to give them hope.

THEY KNEW WHAT THEY WANTED [Dramatic Revival*] A: Sidney Howard; D: Robert Perry; DS: Frederick Fox; P: John Golden; T: Music Box Theatre; 2/16/49 (61)

This second Broadway revival (the first was in 1939) of Howard's 1924 Pulitzer Prize-winning play starred Paul Muni as the California grape grower, Tony, and Carol Stone as Amy, his mail-order bride. The critics differed on the staying power of the play and the quality of Muni's performance. "After a quarter of a century," wrote Howard Barnes (*NYHT*), the play "retains form, substance and feeling." William Hawkins (*NYWT*) felt that the piece "packs a real theatrical wallop" with its straightforward story and characters. But Richard Watts, Jr. (*NYP*), and several others believed that while the drama "still has atmosphere, vitality, some racy characterization, and a fine, mellow, tolerant point of view, . . . it has lost a great deal of its emotional impact and excitement."

Barnes thought that Muni was not the ideal Tony, with his overemphasis on the character's Italian dialect and overly studied approach. Watts wrote similarly, noting that the actor's portrayal "was so ornate, so filled with elaborate detail, that most of its simple emotional appeal was drained from it." Hawkins disagreed and noted that "the instant Paul Muni enters he establishes a warm, spirited simplicity, and in a few moments it is clear that this man is stubborn, passionate and clear thinking." The weight of opinion, though, was on the negative side.

Stone was lavishly praised for her excellence, but some--especially those who had seen Pauline Lord in the original presentation--felt otherwise, among them Brooks Atkinson (*NYT*) and George Jean Nathan (*TBY*). Edward Andrews turned in a plausible job as Joe. Charles Kennedy, the original Father McKee, returned to that role. The supporting cast included Francisco Salvacion as Ah Gee, John Craven as the R. F. D., and Henry Jones (billed here as Henry Burk Jones) as the doctor.

"The direction," wrote Atkinson, "is machine-made. The handling of the crowd scenes is especially perfunctory." Muni apparently did not have much faith in the young director and always seemed not to hear his suggestions. That there was nothing wrong with his hearing was proved when the actor's wife Bella was sitting with Carol Stone's understudy, Eileen Heckart, in the rear of the theatre at a rehearsal. Heckart told Jerome Lawrence (in *Actor*), "Bella leaned over and whispered softly to me, 'I wish Muni wouldn't wear those carpet slippers.' At which Muni, on stage, roared, 'What did you say, Bella?'"

THEY SHALL NOT DIE [Dramatic Revival*] A: John Wexley; D: Gene Frankel; S: Linza Ford; C: William Korff; P/T: People's Drama (OB); 6/9/49

The space at which People's Drama began its Off-Broadway career was an old church at 405 West Forty-first Street, but it would soon move to the Lower East Side to provide New York's first venture into arena staging. This socially conscious company was here reviving Wexley's 1934 antiracist propaganda play inspired by the Scottsboro case, in which a group of nine young black men were railroaded in Alabama for a sexual assault they did not commit. The play, said Arthur Pollock (*DC*), "has now exactly the same impact it had then." "It is chastening to discover that it is still a painfully timely work," agreed Richard Watts, Jr. (*NYP*). The revival reduced the number of suspects to six to correspond with a recent case in New Jersey that had that number of suspects and whose facts corresponded to the Scottsboro situation.

The acting company was very earnest but not very polished. A too-slow pace threatened to harm the production, but the players managed to communicate the play's power nonetheless. Watts averred that "the new group . . . is not always as articulate as it should be, and the acting is somewhat uneven, but it has an excellent instinct for theatrical excitement." The set was a cleverly designed "space stage" consisting of a round platform made of plain wooden boards, with several side platforms for subsidiary scenes. The two young women of the play were played by Ruth Tarson and Shirley Morris, and Lee Nemetz was the defense attorney. Others in the large company included Ted Kazanoff, Irving Pakewitz, Bill Robinson, Howard Wierum, Neil S. Polidori, Lester Cooley, and Bill Weaver.

THEY SHOULD HAVE STOOD IN BED [Comedy/Gambling/Romance/Sex/Sports] A: Leo Rifkin, Frank Tarloff, and David Shaw; D: Luther Adler; S: Samuel Leve; P: Sam H. Grisman i/a/w Alexander H. Cohen; T: Mansfield Theatre; 2/13/42 (11)

Rosamond Gilder (*TAM*), referring to its trio of playwrights, thought that this formula farce suffered because it had "too many cooks." Rowland Field (*NEN*) dismissed it as "extraordinarily dull and tasteless." Its most eye-catching feature was the appearance, in his acting debut, of thirty-three-year-old Tony Canzoneri, former featherweight, junior lightweight, junior welterweight, and lightweight boxing champion of the world. His acting was distinctly amateurish--he had only a few lines--and his physique showed signs of pudginess.

Faintly reminiscent of *Three Men on a Horse**, the plot follows the maneuverings of four Broadway wise guys, Al Hartman (Grant Richards), the ringleader; Barney Snedeker (Jack Gilford), a lawyer without any clients; Harry Driscoll (Russell Morrison), a would-be private eye; and Sam Simpkins (Sanford Meisner), a fence. They lack the wherewithal to pay their office rent. Al discovers Henry Angel (Edwin Philips), a young fellow with a culinary gift, so he convinces the others that they can raise money if they get famous fighter Killer Kane (Canzoneri) to lend his name to a restaurant that they will open. Kane agrees only when Harry blackmails him with pictures showing the pugilist with the wife (Katherine Meskill) of the boxing commissioner (Richard Irving). (Angel also gets himself involved with the wife, although his true love is Vivian Lowe [Florence Sundstrom].) Circumstances lead to the quartet of promoters presenting a fight between Kane and, of all people, the young cook, touted as a terrific boxer. With $30,000 they haven't got they bet on Kane. But the private eye comes across a dictaphone recording revealing Kane's plan to throw the fight, and the quartet go bananas trying to call off their bets with three dangerous gangsters (Norman Budd, George Mathews, and Martin Ritt, the future director). Both the cook and Kane are determined to lose because of their own financial entanglements, and the fight consists of Kane trying to get the cook to hit him so he may take his dive. When Kane knocks out the cook, he guarantees that he doesn't win by knocking out the referee (Arnold Spector). But when the commissioner must make the decision, he chooses in favor of the cook, having found his wife and Kane in a compromising situation.

THEY WALK ALONE [Drama/British/Crime/Mental Illness/Music/Sex] A: Max Catto; M: Benjamin Britten; D: Berthold Viertel; S: Lemuel Ayers; L: Wil Washcoe; P: Ben A. Boyar; T: John Golden Theatre; 3/12/41 (21)

A British psychological melodrama starring Elsa Lanchester as Emmy Baudine, an unusual young Cornish woman who takes a position as a maid with the stock-breeding Tallent family in their Lincolnshire farmhouse. Suffering from a split personality, she veers from moods of happiness and well-being to those when, stirred by the playing of organ music, she becomes so sensually attractive that one man after another falls prey to her charms and ends up being violently slain and mutilated by her during the act of love. (All the killings are offstage.) The Tallents' married daughter, Bess Stanforth (Carol Goodner, who played the same role in London), eventually suspects Emmy and has a dramatic confrontation with her. Emmy is fired but strikes back by killing the Tallent son (Martin Manulis, the future director). It is in a church's organ loft that Emmy is discovered, playing her homicidal music.

The play had been tried out several years earlier at Saratoga, New York, under the title *Alien Soil*, and that version was deemed by some to be superior to this one. In England, with Beatrix Lehmann as Emmy, the play had been a hit, but in New York it closed in three weeks' time. A few thought the subject too depressing for the time the world was living through. Rosamond Gilder (*TAM*) believed that the play "had so absurd a premise that no amount of earnest acting . . . could keep the audience from explosive giggles." It disturbed the critics to note how obtuse the other characters were to the obvious insanity of the maid.

Many panned Lanchester's overripe performance, John Anderson (*NYJA*) remarking, "She seems an improbable and tiresome maniac, haywired for sound." The fine cast included A. P. Kaye, Erford Gage, Olive Deering, and John Moore, but it was Carol Goodner who walked off with the acting honors.

THIS IS THE ARMY [Revue] CN/M/LY: Irving Berlin; SK: Private James MacColl; D: Sergeant Ezra Stone with Pvt. Joshua Logan; CH: Private Robert Sidney and Corporal Nelson Barclift; S/C: Private John Koenig; P: "Uncle Sam" (United

States Army); T: Broadway Theatre; 7/4/42 (113)

An all-soldier revue conceived by Irving Berlin to lift national morale and to raise money for the Army Emergency Relief Fund; it employed over 300 recruits from training camps all across America. Many of the performers were professional show-business veterans, and all were billed with their military rank attached to their names. A significant feature of the company--insisted upon by Berlin--was that it included black personnel as well as white, making the unit the only integrated one in the armed forces at the time.

The show--developed and rehearsed at Camp Upton--was conceived by Berlin as something of a sequel to his 1918 *Yip! Yip! Yaphank* (also developed at Camp Upton). Had the army not been interested in it, he would simply have changed the branch of the services named in the title to the one that accepted the show. Berlin donated all profits from sales of the music and rights to the relief fund. Seats ranged from $2.20 to $27.50. A down payment of $250,000 against a percentage of the profits already had been spent by Warner Brothers for the screen rights. In August Berlin presented the army with a check for $500,000. The show eventually earned over $2 million for the fund.

Originally scheduled to run only a month, the run was extended for the entire summer. During the month before the premiere, the actors rehearsed in New York while also attending military drill sessions for the army at the armory or in a park. Opening night drew the huge sum of $45,000, which may have been a Broadway record at the time. Singer Kate Smith was reported to have paid $10,000 for a pair of ducats.

One piece from the 1918 show, the classic army tune "Oh, How I Hate to Get Up in the Morning," was revived for the show, with Berlin himself appearing in World War I uniform late in the evening to sing it. He was joined by a group of aging performers from the old show, also appearing in their World War I uniforms, to dance to the tune. Most of the other material, however, was new. A minstrel show opened the proceedings, with the large, racially mixed chorus seated upstage of the principals on a grandstand. (Berlin had to be talked out of having the sequence done in blackface.) During it, "This Is the Army, Mr. Jones" was introduced, as well as "I'm Getting Tired So I Can Sleep," "I Left My Heart at the Stage Door Canteen," and other tunes. There were also jokes at the army's expense (and at the WAAC's) delivered by Private James MacColl and Private Leonard Berchman. Sergeant Ezra Stone, the director, stepped out to sing "The Army's Made a Man Out of Me," backed by Corporal Philip Truex and Private Jules Oshins (one of the continually funny performers in the show and later a comedy star). This song had replaced another one, "My Captain and I Are Buddies," inspired by the strife between Stone and his captain. One more song from 1918, "Mandy," was danced in blackface by Private Fred Kelly and others.

The show then moved into a vaudeville format, with various talented performers doing their specialty routines. These included a juggling act with KP potatoes; a tumbling and strong-man act; a takeoff on Russian ballet called "That Russian Winter," with several soldiers in drag; a fiery-paced black dance routine called "What the Well Dressed Man in Harlem Will Wear"; a first-act finale with the soldiers appearing in naval dress to salute their fellow servicemen; a Stage Door Canteen number with soldiers impersonating theatrical luminaries Jane Cowl, Zorina, Noël Coward, the Lunts, and Gypsy Rose Lee (played by Oshins); Private Joe Cook, Jr., son of the great clown, doing bits reminiscent of his father's; a comical Japanese and German chorus rendition of "Aryans under the Skin," one of the performers being Private Burl Ives; a spectacular nod to the air force in "American Eagles"; a ballet; and "A Soldier's Dream" of girls (portrayed by pretty soldiers in drag) and breakfast in bed segueing into Berlin's reprise of "Oh, How I Hate to Get Up in the Morning."

"The result," applauded Rosamond Gilder (*TAM*), "is a thoroughly vigorous and competent show, entirely valid as straight entertainment but with added values, both practical and imponderable, which its unique circumstances provide." George Jean Nathan (*TBY*) asserted that in his opinion, "There hasn't been a frankly designed patriotic spectacle that was in quieter and better taste, that had so much merit in it of its independent own, and that so strainlessly and modestly persuaded its audience into emotional response."

Among the later-famous performers in the show was Private Gary Merrill. *This Is the Army* closed on Broadway but continued to tour the country throughout the war years. The idea for the tour was Eleanor Roosevelt's. She loved the show so much that she wanted President Roosevelt to see it, too, and a tour that included Washington was the only way for the chief executive to get to view it.

As with any theatre project of these dimensions, various stories emerged concerning difficulties encountered. One had to do with Stone's singing of "The Army's Made a Man of Me." During rehearsals, Stone was unhappy about Berlin's having failed to provide a conclusive concluding couplet, so he made one up himself. When Berlin heard it, the roof caved in. According to Stone (quoted in Laurence Bergreen's *As Thousands Cheer*), "He ripped up the music and said, 'It has always been and always will be, "Words and Music by Irving Berlin." And nobody else!' The next day, he gave me his own version of the ending, which was virtually the same as the one we were using." Subsequently, relations between Stone and Berlin became increasingly strained, and Berlin brought Joshua Logan in to provide additional directorial advice. Logan was so delighted by the show as it was that his additions were minimal, although Berlin was sure that the show was in serious trouble.

THIS ROCK [Comedy/Family/Romance/War/Youth] A: Walter Livingston Faust; D/P: Eddie Dowling; S: Watson Barratt; C: (gowns) Valentina; T: Longacre Theatre; 2/18/43 (37)

"To be frank about it," observed Lewis Nichols (*NYT*) of this new play, "there are certain moments . . . which sound a good deal like a parody, when wooden figures wander about the stage expressing overwritten thoughts." Walter Livingstone Faust's play was set in 1939 at the manor home of Malcolm (Nicholas Joy) and Cecily Stanley (Billie Burke) on the river Tyne in England. The Stanleys have been asked to take on the burden of boarding ten poor and raggedy children from London's East End during the duration; the play's action develops largely from the conflict between the upper-class, stuffed-shirt Stanleys and their coarse little charges. Cecily at first resents the intrusion of the youngsters, who pretty soon make life uncomfortable for all the regular residents, especially the servants. However, circumstances are contrived to allow her to gradually change her mind, especially about an urchin named Johnny MacMasters (Alastaire Kyle), brother of the outspoken RAF mechanic Douglas (Zachary Scott), who brought the children to the house. Eventually, Douglas cures his class hatred of the Stanleys, polishes his manners, and becomes a suitable suitor for the Stanleys' heiress daughter Margaret (Jane Sterling), whom he loves despite his principles.

Billie Burke's reappearance in a Broadway play was the principal attraction, and through it all she "laughs and twinkles, bobs and flutters in her own peculiar and endearing way," claimed Rosamond Gilder (*TAM*). However, she was trapped in an unrewarding role in a comedy that Burton Rascoe (*NYWT*) called "a badly shopworn piece of theatrical shoddy, puerile in concept, dialogue and structure." Lucia Victor, Ethel Morrison, Malcolm Dunn, Victor Beecroft, and Joyce Van Patten were among the many cast members.

THIS TIME TOMORROW [Drama/Death/Dutch/Fantasy/Illness/Medicine/Romance/Science] A: Jan de Hartog; D: Paul Crabtree; S: Herbert Brodkin; C: Patricia Montgomery; P: Theatre Guild; T: Ethel Barrymore Theatre; 11/3/47 (32)

Jan de Hartog's first Broadway play was given during the same season that saw his more talked-about drama, *Skipper next to God*. He was a Dutch national, well known as a writer and actor, who had gone into exile in England in 1943 when threatened by the Nazis with arrest. *This Time Tomorrow* (originally titled *Death of a Rat*) is a symbolical four-character drama that Euphemia Van Rensselaer Wyatt (*CW*) said "is so confused and jerky as to baffle completely the efforts of a new and inexperienced director." It was, lamented George Jean Nathan (*TBY*), "gassy balderdash pretentiously offered as profundity, and with little more sense than a pack of mousehounds."

The hokey drama, filled with portentous allusions to mystical phenomena, concerns a tubercular and sex-obsessed young woman named Yolan (Ruth Ford) whose X-rays reveal that, by all accounts, she should be dead instead of volubly alive, in love with a research doctor (John Archer), and subject to prophetic visions. She wants to pass one of her visions about immortality on to mankind. Old scientist Wouterson (Sam Jaffe), puzzled by her case, puts her under hypnosis and discovers that love (he calls it "the mating instinct") is sustaining her, but that if her love is consummated with a kiss, she will die. And so it comes to pass. The other actor in the cast was Tyler Carpenter as a lab assistant.

THIS, TOO, SHALL PASS [Drama/Family/Jews/Military/Romance/Small Town] A/D: Don Appell; S: Raymond Sovey; P: Richard Krakeur and David Shay; T: Belasco Theatre; 4/30/46 (63)

Sam Wanamaker had his first major role as Mac Sorrell, a young Jewish GI who returns from World War II to meet and marry the Gentile Janet Alexander (Jan Sterling), sister of his army friend, Buddy (Walter Starkey), whose life he saved. Their engagement has been effected through correspondence, and they have known one another in the flesh for less than a week. Janet's small-town, midwestern family of Dr. (Ralph Morgan) and Mrs. Alexander (Kathryn Givney) are happy at first to see the young people married, but the anti-Semitic mother becomes violently recalcitrant on learning that Mac is Jewish. Dr. Alexander has no such qualms. Mac is ordered from the house by Mrs. Alexander and Buddy runs out after him, only to be accidentally killed by Mac's car. Mac is accused of murdering Buddy by Mrs. Alexander, but Janet runs off and marries Mac after all.

This amateurish, bathetic, five-character thesis play was reminiscent of the same season's *A Young American* and *On Whitman Avenue*, dramas about intolerance toward blacks. The present offering was "flabby and weak," wrote Lewis Nichols (*NYT*). Its writing was overemotional and predictable. "Of competent and fertile playwriting it indicated no seed," lamented George Jean Nathan (*TBY*). Wanamaker's acting was considered the best in the production.

(1) **THOSE ENDEARING YOUNG CHARMS** [Comedy/Aviation/Family/Hotel/Romance/Sex/War] A/D: Edward Chodorov; S: Frederick Fox; P: Max Gordon; T: Booth Theatre; 6/16/43 (61)

Edward Chodorov's four-character play about romance during wartime had run into many difficulties during its tryout period and underwent extensive revision, thus considerably delaying its Broadway premiere. But for all its reworking, the play could not measure up to sharp critical standards.

Jerry (Dean Harens) is a friend of Mrs. Brandt (Blanche Sweet) and her daughter Helen (film actress Virginia Gilmore, in her stage debut). Mrs. Brandt had once loved Jerry's dad but gave him up when she feared he might not return from World War I. He and his buddy, Lieutenant Hank Trosper (Zachary Scott), an aviator soon to leave for the battlefront, pay the Brandts a visit in their New York apartment. The virginal Helen is attracted to the handsome Hank, and he, cynical about the future, cold-bloodedly attempts to seduce her before he departs. He has no trouble in satisfying his desires because Helen does not wish to repeat her mother's mistake concerning Jerry's father. Before he leaves for immediate active duty, though, with a half hour remaining, he realizes that he loves her and asks her to marry him.

Critical response was mixed, most believing that the ending was a phony sop to conventional morality (and the movie censor, in case of a film version, which it received in 1945). It was argued that the play never really confronted the problem it set out to explore. Burton Rascoe (*NYWT*) thought Chodorov's treatment "not only banal but spurious." Arthur Pollock (*BE*) called it "a meagre play, thin, hard, opaque and with few charms to endear it." But a few liked the play well enough, Wilella Waldorf (*NYP*) reporting that it was "written with understanding and humor and a warm feeling for the young people involved. Without achieving any brilliance as drama, it is unusually pleasant summer entertainment." Virginia Gilmore walked off with the acting honors.

(2) [Dramatic Revival] D: Aline MacMahon; P: Equity Library Theatre; T: Muhlenberg Branch of the New York Public Library (OB); 11/28/44 (2)

A partial revival that presented only selected scenes as part of a showcase program of three pieces, the other two being William Saroyan's "Hello, Out There" and Irwin Shaw's "The Shy and the Lonely." See "Hello, Out There" for details of the latter pair. Robert Garland (*NYJA*) saw no reason for reviving Chodorov's flop, despite the presence of several of its original actors, Frieda Altman, Teresa Hayden, and Tom Grace.

THREE GIFTS [Drama/Crime/Death/Fantasy/Jews/Music/Religion/Romance/Yiddish Language] A: Melach Ravitch and Maurice Schwartz; SC: a story of the same name by I. L. Peretz; M: Joseph Rumshinsky; D: Maurice Schwartz; CH: Lillian Shapero; DS: H. A. Condell; P/T: Yiddish Art Theatre (OB); 10/1/45

A symbol-laden fantasy filled with music, dancing, melodrama, and comedy. It begins in nineteenth-century Poland and tells about the poverty-stricken Joel (Maurice Schwartz), a married violinist of extramarital amorous tendencies, who heads the town band, in which his eight sons also play. He is engaged to play at a wedding only to discover that the bride is his own mistress. Asked by her to play the dance music, he is so overcome by the sight of her in her bridal gown that he dies and goes to heaven. There the tribunal, recounting his deeds, declares that they are equally balanced between good ones and sins. It offers him a chance to redeem himself if he accomplishes the task of retrieving "the three gifts of pure virtue," soil from the Holy Land, the skullcap of a rabbi killed in an anti-Semitic pogrom, and the pins with which a Jewish girl held her clothes together while being publicly dragged by the Nazis. He goes through Europe like the Wandering Jew until he gains the items and is accepted into heaven with his wife. He requests permission to provide some alleviation of earth's misery by playing his violin with the heavenly orchestra, and his celestial music fills the spheres when God agrees.

Wilella Waldorf (*NYP*) reported, "The production sways giddily from fantasy to realism, and from opera to something approaching vaudeville with the greatest of ease and the audience obviously has not the slightest trouble adjusting itself to the quick shifts in mood." George Jean Nathan (*TBY*) was impressed by the music, unimpressed by the flamboyant acting, and had varying feelings about the uneven direction, although he liked the handling of the crowds. The play itself he dismissed as "an impenitent amalgam of *Faust*, *Liliom**, *The Fatal Wedding*, Howard Pyle, and the Hanlon Brothers' *Fantasma*." Kahn. (*V*) considered, "This may not be one of Schwartz's best productions, but there's a considerable beauty to the prose and symbolism of I. L. Peretz's work."

Of the star himself, George Freedley (*NYMT*) observed, "Maurice Schwartz . . . is always an impressive actor, with his rich and full voice, his splendid stage presence, his sense of timing and his prescient understanding of character." Major roles were played by Menachem Rubin, Victor Bergman, and Muriel Gruber, who received very warm reviews. The cast included Luba Kadison, Berta Gersten, Abraham Teitelbaum, Isadore Casher, and many others.

THREE MEN ON A HORSE [Dramatic Revival*] A: John Cecil Holm and George Abbott; D: John Cecil Holm; S: Perry Watkins; P: Alex Yokel; T: Forrest Theatre; 10/9/42 (28)

This 1935 hit farce was revived at low prices ($1.65 top) with five of its original cast members, including William Lynn in the lead as Erwin and with Teddy Hart reprising the role of Frankie. Three other players returned, they being Horace McMahon, Fleming Ward, and Richard Huey. By now the play had been made into a 1936 film as well as a 1941 musical with Eddie Cantor (*Banjo Eyes*). Despite the absence of George Abbott's driving direction (which Holm attempted to duplicate), and with a supporting cast not equal in hilarity to that of the original, the work still had some comic punch. Audrey Trowbridge was now played by Kay Loring, Harry by William Foran, Patsy by Sid Stone, and Mabel by Kay Casto.

It was suggested that one reason for the revival was Mayor La Guardia's cam paign against racetrack betting, George Freedley (*NYMT*) noting, "Some of the play's lines took on added meanings in light of the present agitation and so there were a few laughs that grew over night." "All things considered," added John Mason Brown (*NYWT*), "the play still holds its many laughs and passes the evening agreeably."

THREE SISTERS, THE (*Tri Sestry*) [Dramatic Revival*] A: Anton Chekhov; AD: Alexander Koiransky and Guthrie McClintic; D: Guthrie McClintic; DS: Motley; P: Katharine Cornell; T: Ethel Barrymore Theatre; 12/21/42 (123)

One of the most completely satisfying revivals of this play ever seen in New York. The all-star cast included Judith Anderson as Olga, Katharine Cornell as Masha, Gertrude Musgrove as Irina, Patricia Calvert as a maid, Alexander Knox as Tuzenbach, McKay Morris as Solyony, Edmund Gwenn as Chebutykin, Alice Belmore Cliffe as Anfisa, Kirk Douglas as an orderly (he carried on a samovar), Dennis King as Vershinin, Eric Dressler as Andrey, Arthur Chatterton as Ferapont, Tom Powers as Kuligin, Ruth Gordon as Natasha (she really wanted to play Masha), and Stanley Bell as Fedotik, with Walter Craig (who became film actor Tony Dexter) singing and playing the guitar, among others less well known.

Alfred Lunt had expressed an interest in playing Vershinin, but only if his wife, Lynn Fontanne, could play Masha, while Cornell would play Olga. When director McClintic would not accept this arrangement, Lunt was ready to go along, with Fontanne as Olga, but Fontanne balked. She had no qualms about playing Olga, but was sure that the audience would find it hilarious every time Lunt embraced Cornell's Masha as Olga peeked from behind a pillar.

The critics were astonished at the range of fine acting talent assembled, for which they gave producer and star Cornell great credit. Some appreciated the degree to which the company had been welded into an ensemble despite the widely varying styles of a cast composed of English and American actors; a minority, among them George Freedley (*NYMT*), argued that the production emphasized individual star performances over the ensemble. Cornell must have sought the former effect, as hers was only one of many major parts and not one geared for a star seeking a vehicle. (An obstacle to the ensemble rhythm was an opening-night performance in which each major exit was followed by a round of applause from the audience.)

Choosing whom to single out for special praise proved difficult, but most gravitated toward Ruth Gordon as the brazenly dominating peasant sister-in-law. Her combination of innocuous comedy and hateful passion was considered forceful and original. Some, like Rosamond Gilder (*TAM*), however, thought that Gordon's conception, interesting as it was, threw off the ensemble effect somewhat. "She plays Natasha in a vein all her own, giving play to the flutter of hands, the bridling and tossing, the eccentricities of voice and gesture that have marked, and somewhat marred, her recent performances. The result is often amusing, making for laughter if not for harmony."

Cornell was her usual brilliant self. Howard Barnes (*NYHT*) mused, "Miss Cornell is completely charming and poignant in expressing the longing of troubled Masha, bringing into play all the gleaming luster of those quiet, persuasive gifts of an incomparable actress. In the scene wherein she confesses her love for the colonel she is truly magnificent."

Among the men, the finest performance was generally conceded to be that of Edmund Gwenn as the lonely old army doctor who takes to drink. His tour de force drunk scene was noted by many, although some suggested that it might have gone a bit too far. Dennis King's Vershinin was technically appropriate, although there was a feeling that he was not as successful as he might have been in evoking the character's deepest feelings.

The tone of the production was lightly satiric, but the comedy was allowed to grow organically out of the characters rather than being imposed by directorial whim. The new adaptation, which compressed acts one and two into a single act, sounded very natural and unstilted and was deemed a major advance over the then-standard version by Constance Garnett. There were, however, several cuts, one of them rather disturbing, although George Jean Nathan (*TBY*) was the only critic to point it out. This was the excision of the last three speeches in the play, from Olga's entire speech about time passing and the sisters being forgotten to Chebutykin's humming of "Ta-ra-ra-boom-de-ay" and his subsequent few words as he reads the newspaper to Olga's curtain line, "If we only knew, if we only knew."

As a play *The Three Sisters* continued to appeal with its vivid character studies and prophetic indications of the Russian future, but it was clear that because of its thin plot and slow movement, respect for it as a stageworthy modern classic demanded performances on a level with the present one. Burton Rascoe (*NYWT*), however, claimed that "never did a play seem more like a museum piece" with its story of "three completely uninteresting females whose aspirations are trivial and whose fate is unimportant." The play's datedness seemed especially vivid against the contemporary backdrop of World War II.

The great number of stars in the play necessitated very diplomatic maneuvering in order to provide suitable dressing rooms for them all. The theatre had only a large star dressing room on the stage floor, traditionally given over to the most important star. The others were on the second and third floors. To offset problems, Cornell took a dressing room on the second floor, giving the stage level room to Gordon and Anderson. King was assigned a room on the second floor. When his dresser arrived and noticed the room assignment, he declared, "Mr. King does not go upstairs," but had to eat his words on seeing Cornell's amenities being placed in an equally "upstairs" chamber (quoted in Tod Mosel, *Leading Lady*).

Shortly after the play opened, Edmund Gwenn became very ill and had to leave the cast to recuperate. At first, his understudy could not be found; when he was, it was too late to coach him in all the changes the part had undertaken recently. Director McClintic, who had not acted in many years, decided to go on in his stead, while the rest of the cast quaked. He reported in *Me and Kit* that he did the part for a month and thought himself "very good indeed."

THREE TO MAKE READY [Revue] SK/LY: Nancy Hamilton; M: Morgan Lewis; D: Margaret Webster and John Murray Anderson; CH: Robert Sidney; S: Donald Oenslager; C: Audré; P: Stanley Gilkey and Barbara Payne; T: Adelphi Theatre; 3/7/46 (327)

This ambitious revue, which marked Shakespearean director Webster's first attempt at the genre, was by the sketch writer and lyricist who previously had provided the less successful revues, *One for the Money** and *Two for the Show**. The talented cast in the present offering was headlined by dancer-comedian Ray Bolger and also featured such people as comediennes Brenda Forbes and Bibi Osterwald, singers Gordon MacRae (in his Broadway debut) and Rose Inghram, dancers Jane Deering and Harold Lang, and radio's Arthur Godfrey (acting as an MC in his Broadway debut), as well as Meg Mundy, Carleton Carpenter, and others.

Howard Barnes (*NYHT*) informed his readers that this was "a stunning revue" with "pace, excitement and wit." However, like most others, the disappointed Lewis Nichols (*NYT*) decided that the show bogged down without Bolger because of its "indifferent material." Robert Garland (*NYJA*) even accused the show of amateurism in its non-Bolger aspects. In general, the reviews were of the thumbs-down variety.

The long-legged Bolger's amusing antics and remarkable dancing highlighted the show. Among the sketches was "Wisconsin" or "Kenosha Canoe," which spoofed Theodore Dreiser's *An American Tragedy* by suggesting how it might appear if staged as a musical in the Rodgers and Hammerstein tradition of *Oklahoma!* and *Carousel*, with folk songs and ballets. Other sketches included "The Russian Lesson," with Forbes one of a group of Upper Montclair suburban women tackling the language, and then, in "The Story of the Opera," offering her gesticulatory description at a dinner party of Wagner's *Walköre.* (The last was inserted in the show three days before the opening, although the piece originally had been performed by Hamilton in *One for the Money*.)

George Jean Nathan (*TBY*) argued that the sketches might have been greatly improved if they had each been five minutes shorter. Hamilton "simply does not know when there is too much of a good thing," he wrote. The sets and costumes were charmingly distinctive, and Donald Oenslager even provided a shimmering white velvet curtain commemorating Hamilton's two previous revues in imaginatively graphic blue script.

Bolger was brilliant in the pantomimic vaudeville-type routine, "The Old Soft Shoe." He parodied ballroom dancing teams to hilarious effect in "If It's Love"; was a charming scarecrow in "A Lovely Lazy Kind of Day," the lyrics sung by Godfrey; garnered yocks in "Cold Water Flat," although its bathroom-fixture humor was offensive to some; and clowned around delightfully in "The Sad Sack," based on Bill Mauldin's cartoon character. Morgan Lewis's music was not highly considered, its best contribution being "Barnaby Beach," for a prettily staged scene using a silhouette technique and showing young folk taking a vacation.

(1) **THREE'S A FAMILY** [Comedy/Blacks/Family/Marriage/Medicine] A: Phoebe and Henry Ephron; D: Henry Ephron; S: Stewart Chaney; P: John Golden i/a/w John Pollock and Max Siegel; T: Longacre Theatre; 5/5/43 (497)

The Ephrons, ultimately best known as a screenwriting duo, made their Broadway bow with this popular but innocuous comedy that just missed hitting the 500-performance mark. Despite its commercial success, it did not tickle the palate of too many important reviewers. Lewis Nichols (*NYT*), for example, said that it was "some distance from being hilarious."

The action occurs in the smallish West 110th Street flat of Sam (Robert Burton) and Frances Whitaker (Ruth Weston). She has a job and he cares for the house. Residing with them is Frances's acidulous old-maid sister, Irma (Ethel Owen). To the abode return their married daughter, Kitty (Katharine Bard), and her four-month-old infant. Aunt Irma must now sleep on a sofa bed, the mastering of whose intricacies provided some amusement. Dad Eugene (Francis De Sales), with whom Kitty has quarreled, has joined the army. This precipitates various comic situations concerning the care and feeding of the toddler. Soon son Archie (Edwin Philips) comes home as well, bearing in tow Hazel (Dorothy Gilchrist), his pregnant wife, who has been unable to find an available local hospital in which to give birth to her overdue baby. Things are getting as crowded as can be. Next to appear is Eugene, home on leave with presents for his kid, but he soon is arguing with Kitty again and threatening divorce. Meanwhile, the baby has vanished with the drunken black maid (Gee Gee James). (There is also a white maid, Adelaide [Doro Merande], who contributes to the mayhem). Finally, because military needs have created a shortage of physicians, a doddering, deaf, and half-blind octogenarian obstetrician, Dr. Bartell (William Wadsworth, fifty year stage veteran who stole the show), is called into service to deliver Hazel's infant, although he initially mistakes the old maid and the black maid for the prospective mother. The baby is born, Eugene and Kitty make up, and all is put to rights.

The play mirrored contemporary concerns, such as the shortage of maternity beds (there was a baby boom going on) and a similar shortage of doctors, so its premise of making comedy out of the difficulties of being pregnant in such a situation was a valid one. Major criticisms were that the humor was flat, that the comedy did not start to get interesting until too late in the proceedings, that the humor about diapers was too repetitive, and that the characters were neither interesting nor sufficiently separated from one another by their dialogue. Even the moderately positive notices offered reservations. George Freedley (*NYMT*) said that it was "so replete with stock situations and gags that it is bound to offend the purist and bore some of the captious. Still it is funny in a rowdy family way." "There are gags galore and a lot of genuine laughs," commented Otis L. Guernsey, Jr. (*NYHT*), "but there is not enough breadth or complexity . . . to hold its high spots together." The most memorable part of the play was at the end when the old doctor appeared and garnered more belly laughs than the show in its entirety had hitherto accumulated. Earlier titles by which the play was known included *Three-Cornered Pants* and *The Wife Takes a Child*.

(2) [Dramatic Revival/Blacks] D: Abram Hill; S: Geraldine Preillerman; P: American Negro Theatre; T: 135th Street Public Library Theatre (OB); 11/18/43

While still running on Broadway, the play was produced by a semiprofessional Harlem theatre group (producer John Golden had released the rights to them) with an all-black cast. It did a decent job within the rather awkward and limiting environment of the library theatre it employed, although the pace loped along too slowly, and the dragging was exacerbated by lengthy waits between scenes. The best-liked actors were Jacqueline André as the old maid sister, Frederick O'Neal (later a major figure in the American theatre) as the father, and Howard Augusta as the old doctor, although he was nowhere near as funny as the actor on Broadway.

Few critics attended. L. C. (*NYT*) claimed that the mounting was "competent," and Louis Kronenberger (*PM*) said that the company "has some very good comedy actors, whose timing and inflections stir up a lot of laughs."

THUMBNAIL THEATRE [Miscellaneous/Solo] A/D: Mary Hutchinson; T: Times Hall; 12/5/48

Mary Hutchinson was a very attractive actress who brought her evening of one-woman sketches to New York for a brief run. She was best in comedy and offered a broad range of amusing styles. Her show was a bit thin for Broadway, but she demonstrated physical appeal, theatrical intelligence, and versatility. Among the sketches she performed were "A Case of Mistaken Identity," in which a scatter-brained Park Avenue hostess entertains at a cocktail party; "Mountain Idyll," in which she was a moonshine-swilling hillbilly; and "East Lynne," a parody of the famous old melodrama.

"Her material is not geared to a sophisticated audience," reported William Hawkins (*NYWT*), "but her intimate method of presentation is perfectly suited to simple and direct ideas." An onstage screen allowed her to change her costumes behind it while preparing the audience verbally for the coming scene.

THUNDER ON THE LEFT [Dramatic Revival*] A: Jean Ferguson Black; D: Jasper Deeter; P: Hedgerow Theatre; T: Cherry Lane Theatre (OB); 1/21/46

The Hedgerow Theatre was a company from Moylan-Rose Valley, Pennsylvania, near Philadelphia. One of the country's first "regional" theatres, it had been operating under Jasper Deeter's leadership for about twenty years when it arrived for a one-month repertory season at Off-Broadway's Cherry Lane in January 1940. Its work was barely reviewed, but Lewis Nichols (*NYT*) did write a Sunday piece (1/28/46) about it. Only Otis L. Guernsey, Jr. (*NYHT*), reviewed its revival of this 1933 fantasy--based on a Christopher Morley story--about a boy (Dan Christman) who goes two decades into the future to see how his childhood friends turned out. "Obscure though certain of its points may be, it cuts across the usual story conventions and therefore does not demand the usual Broadway treatment." Thus it was done with extreme simplicity, against a simple cyclorama on a nearly bare stage with only a few chairs scattered about. The cast, which had a fine performance by Audrey Ward as a summer housekeeper, was merely adequate, but managed "to create the weird atmosphere which is all important to the fantasy."

TICKETS, PLEASE! [Revue] SK: Harry Herman, Edmund Rice, Jack Roche, and Ted Luce; M/LY: Lyn Duddy, Joan Edwards, Mel Tolkin, Lucille Kallen, and Clay Warnick; ADD.M: Phil Ingalls and Hal Hastings; D: Mervyn Nelson; CH: Joan Mann; S/L: Ralph Alswang; C: Peggy Morrison; P: Arthur Klein; T: Coronet Theatre; 4/27/50 (245)

An "amiable and diverting" (Thomas R. Dash [*WWD*]) intimate revue headlined by the comic dance team the Hartmans, Grace and Paul, and featuring versatile comic-dancer-singer Jack Albertson, eccentric dancer Dorothy Jarnac, West Virginia funnyman Roger Price, singer-comedienne Patricia Bright, hoofer Tommy Wonder, and others, including Larry Kert in his Broadway bow. The unpretentious show featured more of the Hartmans' comedy than it did their dancing, but the reviews were generally congratulatory because there was enough humor available to keep funny bones tickled. Some of the material had been tried out by the Hartmans during a summer theatre tour in a revue called *Up to Now*. There was no chorus line in the show, but the tired businessman, whose eyes might otherwise have tired of ogling a bevy of chorines, was granted a single long-stemmed beauty (Mildred Hughes) to stare at.

The Hartmans made their first entrance from the audience and sat downstage close to the audience as they began to amuse the crowd by delivering a witty prologue (actually, the mock-innocent Grace did, while the plodding Paul tried to get a word in edgewise). It explained the reason for the title, which came to them while standing on line for *South Pacific* and hearing others crying "Tickets, please," a phrase apparently much in vogue at the moment. They appeared in a good many of the evening's routines. One was a satire on a congressional investigation, with Paul as a scientist being grilled for not having created a new bomb and answering that he does not know how, and then being lectured by a senator on American know-how. He also was a cookbook author delivering a lecture on cooking to a ladies' group and then botching up his preparation of dumplings. Grace symbolized fire in a song about fire in which the fire department figured. She also did a satirical striptease that parodied the Parisian Ballet's staging of *Carmen*. In a roller-derby spoof she was an aggressive spectator annoying a broadcaster. With Price, the Hartmans played in a sketch about the similarity of all dramatic plots down through the ages. The Hartmans did a bit in which he was a magician and she a lady in the audience. Price, dryly comic and famed for his doodles, illustrated his family tree with them; he showed how certain genes traveled through the family to create, after many generations, a final monstrosity. Jarnac offered a delightfully surrealistic sketch in which she illustrated in dance a Greenwich Village art lecture concerning an abstract painting. To explain the various isms, she used a large, white, elastic band that she reshaped as required, using her arms and feet. Albertson scored with his nostalgic soft-shoe dances and old Palace vaudeville bits, while also having one of the show's best songs in "Spring Has Come."

Most, but not all, reviews were kind. Arthur Pollock (*DC*) was happy to note, "It's lean and tidy, funny in an adult way, graceful, expert. . . . There is smart organization, smart writing, knowing direction that cuts each scene off before it has started to run down." Louis Sheaffer (*BE*) applauded because "the Hartmans are back. Grace with her humorous aplomb, Paul with his outrageously broad mugging and hilarious look of pained confusion." But Richard Watts, Jr. (*NYP*), while laughing "like a maniac" at all the Hartman japeries, nevertheless felt that they, Price, and Albertson aside, the show was "pretty dismal."

TIDBITS OF 1946 [Revue] SK/D: Sam Locke; D: Arthur Klein; P: Arthur Klein i/a/w Henry Schumer; T: Plymouth Theatre; 7/8/46 (8)

An intimate summertime revue emceed by Lee Trent. It was quickly rejected as being too meagre for Broadway audiences. The show had originated Off Broadway at the Barbizon-Plaza Hotel under the auspices of the Youth Theatre Alumni, an amateur group. Those who had been in the original version were gone now, replaced by more experienced troupers, such as burlesque comic Joey Faye, comedian Joshua Shelley, straight man Jack Diamond, harmonica player Eddy Manson, satirical singer Josephine Boyer, Latin dancers Carmen and Rolando, black singer Muriel Gaines, South African folk singers Josef Marais and Miranda, tenor Robert Marshall, the harmonizing Mack Triplets, the tap-dancing Debonairs, and others.

The "long-drawn and pointless" (Robert Garland [*NYJA*]) sketches included "Psychiatry in Technicolor," a spoof of the Alfred Hitchcock movie *Spellbound*, and "Meet Me on Flugle Street," a tired, old burlesque routine. George Jean Nathan (*TBY*) thought it "wholly devoid of merit," and George Freedley (*NYMT*) said that it was "two and a half hours of dullness with nary a laugh."

TIME FOR ELIZABETH [Comedy/Business/Marriage/Southern] A: Norman Krasna and Groucho Marx; D: Norman Krasna; S/L: George Jenkins; P: Russell Lewis and Howard Young; T: Fulton Theatre; 9/27/48 (8)

Otto Kruger and Katherine Alexander were highly effective in the leading roles of this otherwise woeful flop coauthored by great comedian Groucho Marx. Kruger's role was Ed Davis, a successful executive of the Snowdrift Washing Machine Company, who is told by a company employee (Leonard Mudie) that it is time for him (the employee) to retire to Elizabeth, New Jersey. When Ed's boss (John Arthur) fires him, Ed impulsively believes it his time for Elizabeth, only he chooses to retire to Florida. Soon, though, he finds himself getting bored out of his mind from idleness, despite a lovely apartment a mile from the ocean. The whole scene of palm trees and too-friendly neighbors gets on his and his wife's (Alexander) nerves. Things get even more irksome when Ed's money is lost in several foolish investments. But when Ed's old boss agrees to let him return, the Davises sail north on the boss's yacht.

The play had been written a few years earlier by Marx alone (under the title *April Fool*) and was then revised by Krasna. It tried out in California and underwent many revisions and cast changes. Joseph T. Shipley (*NL*) believed that the "play has a good initial idea, and a trite banal development. As the characters in Florida grow bored, so do the persons watching them." Hobe. (*V*) said that it "has only occasionally effective scenes of funny dialog. It lacks either the propulsion or emotional grip necessary for success."

Kruger's actual daughter Ottilie played Ed's daughter Anne. Various friendly Floridians were played by Harlan Briggs, Edward Clark, John Arthur, Sheila Bromley, and Theresa Lyon. Also involved were Russell Hicks, Leila Bliss, and Dick Hogan.

TIME, THE PLACE AND THE GIRL, THE [Musical Revival] B: Will Morrissey and John Neff; M: Joe Howard; LY/D: William B. Friedlander; SC: the show of the same name by Will M. Hough, Frank R. Adams, and Joe Howard; CH: Carl Randall; S: Karl Amend; C: Paul du Pont; P: Georges D. Gersene; T: Mansfield Theatre; 10/21/42 (13)

This was an eccentric revival of a 1906 work provided with light book and lyric revisions, but essentially the same as the original, which had been a hit in Chicago but a flop in New York (where it played in 1907). Among its novelties was the appearance of the elderly Joe Howard as himself, singing with jaunty ebullience some of his old standards (including "Hello, My Baby" and "I Wonder Who's Kissing Her Now," neither in the original show). He was in far better shape at seventy-five than the show was at thirty-six. Its dialogue having been termed dull by a 1907 reviewer, it appeared to Brooks Atkinson (*NYT*) in 1942 that "the dullness seems now to have permeated the entire production and has at last overtaken the dancing and scenery." Richard Lockridge (*NYS*) transcribed, "The lyrics have a tendency to remind one of all the other lyrics in the world, without quite attaining the stature of burlesque. The whole thing is very odd, and discouraging."

The vintage plot was laid in the Keely Institute, a sanatorium for alcoholics, which is invaded by a group of schoolgirls who are then quarantined there when measles breaks out. There are supposedly comical characters with the d.t.'s, and there are also some romantic situations. The play's cast included Vicki Cummings, Red Marshall, Rolfe Sedan, Irene Hilda, and others.

TIN TOP VALLEY [Drama/Blacks/Crime/Family/Friendship/Race/Southern/Youth] A: Walter Carroll; D: Abram Hill; M: Hattie King-Reavis; S: Roger Furman; P/T: American Negro Theatre (OB); 2/28/47 (43)

A weakly performed and only partly effective drama produced in the 126th Street playhouse of the American Negro Theatre. It is set in a deep South mill town where a "white trash" youth named Greg Talbot (Charles Nolte) lives in a shack with his ignorant mother, Ruth (Lillian Adams). Greg befriends a black boy, Willie Turner (James Jackson), with whom he plans on going to college in the North. The relationship so disturbs Greg's racially biased mother that she murders her son to protect the "family honor." Despite her confession, the black friend is held for the murder, and his lynching seems likely.

"For all its knowledge of a corner of the South," responded Brooks Atkinson (*NYT*), "Mr. Carroll's drama is loosely strung and not very original." Even worse, he said, was "the limp, generalized performance" accorded the play. The story, said George Jean Nathan (*TBY*), is "dramatized with no feeling for dramaturgy or for the critical acumen of an audience." Frederick O'Neal and Owen Tolbert-Hewitt alternated in the role of a garrulous character named Buck Price, played in whiteface and reminiscent of Jeeter Lester in *Tobacco Road**.

TINKER'S DAM [Comedy/Death/Fantasy/Journalism/Military/Nightlcub/Religion/Romance/Science/War] A: Andrew Hawkes; M: Thomas H. F. Padian; D: Dennis Gurney; CH: Jane MacLean; P: Blackfriars' Guild; T: Blackfriars' Theatre (OB); 1/28/43 (16)

A limited-appeal, Off-Broadway presentation of a morality play with a sermon-like message about heaven, employing an incidental musical background and choreographic scenes. The critics suspected that it was pseudonymously written to disguise its priestly author (the Blackfriars was a Catholic society). "For the most part the script is over-literary and drearily repetitous," grumbled George Freedley (*NYMT*).

New York is being bombed, and a diverse group has taken cover in an air-raid shelter. The allegorical types represent all ranges of the philosophical spectrum, from the idealist to the hedonist to the cynic. George Brown (Lawrence Fletcher) is a disillusioned journalist whose wife died in childbirth. Some of the others are an Irish tinker (Gerald Buckley) who believes in the reality of dreams, a skeptical scientist (H. E. Currier) who thinks that death is simply the end of life and that there is no soul, a doctor (Robert Hayward) who still has his faith, a hedonistic soldier (James Gannon) about to be sent overseas, and a girl (Peggy Wynne) in love with the soldier. They discuss one another's ideas about the meaning of life and the value of religious faith. The journalist is seriously wounded and, while lingering between life and death, dreams about his soul taking a journey through the way stations of the afterworld. This begins with the Land of No Reason for Things, then moves to the Land of Vicious Circles (a sleazy nightclub), and finally comes to the Land of Heart's Desire. There he learns that he can be reunited with his wife and child if he regains his faith. He does, and with his death he enters the pearly gates.

John Anderson (*NYJA*) emphasized that the author "has not been able to translate his evident fervor into dramatic terms, or to convert the old morality play symbols into human characters. The play's simplicity turns naive, its humor becomes labored, and its statement not so much spiritually exalted in its searching definition and emotional values as literal and uninspired." In the role of Mrs. Cow, which required some Mae West-type behavior, Eileen Heckart (then spelled Heckert) made her New York debut. Burton Rascoe (*NYWT*) thought her "very amusing." Also involved was Dort Clark.

'TIS OF THEE [Revue] CN/D/P: Nat Lichtman; SK: Sam Locke; M: Alex North and Al Moss; LY: Alfred Hayes; ADD. MTL: David Greggory, Peter Barry, and Richard Lewine; CH: Esther Junger; S: Carl Kent; T: Maxine Elliott's Theatre; 10/26/40 (1)

An "ill-advised" (Richard Watts, Jr. [*NYHT*]) intimate revue created at Camp Unity, an adult summer camp for members of the International Ladies' Garment Workers Union, in Bushkill, Pennsylvania; it died the night it opened on Broadway. Most of the entertainers were more amateur than not, but comic George Lloyd and dancers Cappella and Beatrice were pros who had not been involved at Bushkill. Lloyd failed to impress with his routines, including one in which he talked about the uses of a piece of string and then finished by hanging himself. In another, he was a mental patient just released from the sanatorium. "This new show is filled with dull and futile numbers done without any particular skill," noted Watts.

TO KILL A CAT [Comedy-Drama/British/Crime/Family/Mystery/Romance] A: Roland Pertwee and Harold Dearden; D/P: Alexander Ivo; T: Barbizon-Plaza Theatre (OB); 4/18/43 (2)

A tryout performance of a 1938 British mystery play that smacked of J. B. Priestley's *Dangerous Corner** and Alec Coppel's *I Killed the Count*. It takes place in 1937 in London at the home of the wealthy Proust family. Mark Proust (Stiano Braggiotti) is married to Lillian (Cherry Hardy), his second wife. She is a demanding hypochondriac and an interfering person who breaks up the love affair of her stepson (Clement Brace) and his fiancée (June Brehm). When her secretary (Julie Mars) becomes her husband's love interest, she exposes the fact that the girl's father is an embezzler. The gardener's (John Roland) child dies because she refuses to let the boozy Dr. Raikes (John Clarke), who is in her debt, leave in the middle of a bridge game to care for her. Only her brother-in-law (Brent Sargent), a charming parasite who is planning a robbery with the maid (Rosanna Seaborn), has no apparent motive for killing Lillian. Her corpse is discovered with a bottle of cyanide--bought to kill the cat--nearby. Whodunit?

"If the producer were to ask my advice," remarked George Freedley (*NYMT*), "I should suggest that he leave his play on Lexington Avenue and forget the crosstown bus."

TO TELL YOU THE TRUTH [Comedy/Bible/Fantasy/Period/Sex] A: Eva Wolas; M: George Karlin; D: Ezra Stone; S/L: Ralph Alswang; P/T: New Stages (OB); 4/18/48 (15)

At its intimate theatre on Bleecker Street, the young New Stages troupe followed up its production of Sartre's "The Respectful Prostitute" with this archly campy but only sporadically amusing philosophical comedy set in the Garden of Eden, but imbued with contemporary overtones, including many hopefully cute anachronisms. Its author was the adaptor of the Sartre play. Howard Barnes (*NYHT*) thought it "woefully lacking in either talent or taste."

It tells the biblical tale of Adam (Anthony [Tony] Randall) and Eve (Jean Gillespie), called Woman here, and of the Tallulah Bankhead-like serpent dressed in black lace, named Zilah (Judy Somerside). The scenic environment is chicly modern, including drapes, a terrace, a tea wagon, and a painting easel. Until Woman appears in his life, Adam is bored. When she arrives, she becomes a nuisance with her desire to rearrange the furniture and her nagging. Adam's dream of a perfect companion is ruined. He seeks advice from the sexy serpent and learns how to pleasure himself and Woman sexually. When this is exposed as sinful behavior, paradise is lost and the lovebirds depart to make love and quarrel forever. Also figuring importantly in the tale is the Archangel Michael (Raymond E. Johnson).

The play, said Richard Watts, Jr. (*NYP*), "is not merely a singularly lugubrious striving after laughter. . . . It is fatuous, tasteless and of a depressing kind of smart-aleck whimsy that tends to leave the spectator limp with frustrated impatience." Few critics admired any of the performances, but it is interesting to note that George Freedley (*NYMT*) thought that Tony Randall looked like writer Truman Capote. Brooks Atkinson (*NYT*) did say of Randall that "his voice is melodically masculine; he moves with the grace of a dancer and he acts . . . with humor."

(1) TOBACCO ROAD [Dramatic Revival*] A/P: Jack Kirkland; D: Anthony Brown; S: Robert Redington Sharpe; T: Forrest Theatre; 9/5/42 (34)

Sixteen months after this record-breaking long run 1933 play closed, it was revived for another month of showings with John Barton as Jeeter, Norman Budd as Dude, Sara Perry as Ada, Sheila Brent as Ellie May (her neat permanent wave a jarring note), Vinnie Phillips as Sister Bessie (her role since 1936), Edwin Walter as George Payne (his role in the original production), Sondra Johnson as Pearl, Lillian Ardell as Grandma, Joe Silver as Lov, and Harry Townes as Captain Tim, among others. When the run ended, it took to the road.

The play was still outlawed in Rhode Island and was forbidden in many states of the deep South. K. S. (*NYT*), however, claimed that the piece "strikes one, at this date, as neither dirty nor daring. It is just good hokum." John Barton, uncle of long-time Jeeter James Barton, had been playing Jeeter on the road for five years, but this was his Broadway debut in it. He was the sixth to essay it on the Main Stem. "Although he does not play Jeeter Lester with the same loving kindness that others have given the role," K. S. wrote, "he performs with reasonable assurance. . . . He consumes far less turnips than his predecessors and doesn't seem quite as afflicted with pellagra as some."

(2) [Return Engagement] T: Ritz Theatre; 9/4/43 (66)

Almost a year to the day later, the previously described revival returned to Broadway after its tour. Some cast changes had been made, including Dan Denton's assuming the role of Dude, Barbara Joyce's that of Ellie May, Kim Spalding's that of Lov, and Michael King's that of Captain Tim, but John Barton, Sara Perry, Edwin Walter, Vinnie Phillips, and Lillian Ardell were still around.

George Freedley (*NYMT*), not having seen the play since 1934, said, "I was agreeably surprised to find that the play was quite as good as I had remembered its being and that the present company is giving, on the whole, a good performance." Most critics noted, though, that the play had lost its serious edge and that the profanity and slovenly conditions of the characters were now played farcically for every laugh they could get.

(3) [Blacks] D: Evelyn Ellis; P: Negro Drama Group i/a/w Jack Kirkland; T: Forty-eighth Street Theatre; 3/6/50 (7)

A nearly all-black revival of the play. Jimmy Wright was Dude, Evelyn Ellis (who directed) was Ada, Powell Lindsay was Jeeter, Baby Joyce was Ellie May, Estelle Hemsley was Grandma, John Tate was Lov, Cherokee Thornton was Henry Peabody, Mercedes Gilbert was Sister Bessie, Delores Mack was Pearl, John Mark was Captain Tim, and John Bouie was George Payne.

A distracting low-comedy approach was taken to the play, and the result proved seriously deficient, especially because the acting company, apart from Ellis and Tate, was widely thought inferior. Most critics distanced themselves from the project, feeling that the conversion to a black cast had not brought any illumination to the play. George Jean Nathan (*TBY*), who questioned the concept of converting the play's poor white trash into "even poorer and more miserable Georgia colored trash," declined the work because it "was so smellily directed and acted and the original infected play so distorted that the audience . . . was sure that it had acquired . . . something it didn't have when it entered the theatre." But a small percentage liked the revival, among them Robert Coleman (*NYDM*), who called it "a first-rate production . . . equal to those played for so many years by white actors."

TOBIAS AND THE ANGEL [Dramatic Revival*] A: James Bridie (Dr. Osborne Henry Mavor); M: Nat Sokoloff; D/S: Robert Ramsey; C: Valerie Judd; P: On-Stage; T: Bleecker Street Playhouse (OB); 4/25/50

This fanciful 1930 morality play, based on a story in the Apocrypha, had been given here in a free admission production in 1937 under Federal Theatre Project auspices at Off-Broadway's Provincetown Theatre. Now, a few blocks away, it was being revived by an intrepid Off-Broadway group. A turntable setting was employed, and the fantasy elements were better represented than the comic. The production, however, lacked "acute direction and acting," wrote Joe Pihodna (*NYHT*). "The substitute for dramatic power is shouting and strutting." J. P. S. (*NYT*), who did not care for the play, said that the company "has done nothing to improve the quality of the offering." Because of the relatively undraped harem girls, the play reminded the critic of *Ladies Night at a Turkish Bath*, and Thomas R. Dash (*WWD*) observed, "In one or two instances bulging wads of flesh almost flapped over the exposed navels." The cast included Jack Burkhart, Michael Egan, Al Croce, Stephen Gattoni, Anna Berger, and Sara by Barbara Long.

TOMORROW THE WORLD [Drama/Family/Jews/Politics/Science/War] A: James Gow and Arnaud d'Usseau; D: Elliott Nugent; S: Raymond Sovey; P: Theron Bamberger; T: Ethel Barrymore Theatre; 4/14/43 (500)

"Today we rule Germany, Tomorrow the world," runs a line in the Nazi's "Horst Wessel" song, which gave this arresting anti-Nazi melodrama its title. The propagandistic play, later made into a memorable film, was delayed in getting to Broadway because of the need to summon sufficient production funds; a then-considerable number of twenty-eight backers eventually signed up to invest in it. The movie-writer authors sent the play to a New York agent who ran into producer Bamberger in a bank and casually suggested that the latter might want a look at the new work, which several others already had rejected. Bamberger liked it enough to produce it, although the critical reaction both on the pre-Broadway tryout tour and in New York was mixed. It scored powerfully with audiences, though, and made redheaded "Skippy" Homeier (a radio actor making his Broadway debut) into a twelve-year-old star in a villainous role with which he was ever after identified (he also played it in the movie). The play further benefited from another brilliant performance by a child, Joyce Van Patten, and from the acting of its distinguished adult stars, Shirley Booth and Ralph Bellamy. It was chosen as one of the ten best plays of the season.

Emil Bruckner (Homeier), a German child whose father, a liberal philosopher, was killed at Dachau, has been brainwashed to believe in Hitler's evil philosophy of force, treachery, and racial superiority. He is taken in by his American uncle, a widowed midwestern professor, Michael Frame (Bellamy), brother of the boy's late mother. His arrival is eagerly anticipated. However, no sooner does he arrive than he shocks the German-born but Americanized maid (Edit Angold) by donning his Hitler Youth uniform, adorned with its swastika armband. He behaves like a robot and declaims against democracy, denounces his father as a coward, and calls Frame's fiancée, Leona Richards (Booth), a Jewish bitch. He also ferments dissension between Frame's spinster sister (Dorothy Sands) and Leona. He gets a good smack in the face for that. Professor Frame being a scientist, Emil plans to sneak into his laboratory and steal his secrets on behalf of the Gestapo. Frame's ten-year-old daughter Patricia (Van Patten, who alternated with Nancy Nugent, the director's daughter), the only one who has befriended Emil, spots him stealing the laboratory key, and he tries to kill her by slamming her in the head with a metal bookend. Michael--to his own ultimate amazement at this blow to his idealism--nearly strangles the boy in revenge, but is stopped by Leona, a teacher, who realizes that the boy must be cured by more gentle means. She (and the guileless Patricia) succeeds in breaking through and begins the boy's regeneration and enlightenment.

Tomorrow the World pondered the question of what to do with twelve million indoctrinated and twisted German youths after the United States won the war. The solution was broached of liquidating them as completely uncorrectable, but the play opted for a belief that with the proper methods these youngsters could be reformed. (In actuality, the case upon which the play was based was a failure; the child involved had been so deeply indoctrinated that nothing could be done with him, and he was sent back to Germany.) As a drama, *Tomorrow the World* proved extremely compelling, although it began slowly and later raised serious questions over the relative ease with which kind treatment reforms the previously intractable Emil. Despite its flaws, the drama successfully presented in simple and immediate--if somewhat obvious--terms a provocative contemporary problem of considerable importance. It was, indeed, more as a discussion starter than as a drama that it was respected. As George Jean Nathan (*TBY*) observed, "The play rests for audience response solely on the spontaneous combustible under present circumstances inherent in its theme, since the writing is without trace of subtlety." There were, however, critics who acclaimed the drama as excellently written. Burton Rascoe (*NYWT*) was one, calling it "a highly original and ingenious drama written with great concision and skill."

Homeier was treated as a prodigy by the reviewers, who found his performance remarkable for the depths of evil it conveyed. "His tight-cropped head, his hard, high voice with its well-trained German accent, his cold and aggressive manner are convincing throughout," claimed Rosamond Gilder (*TAM*). Richard Taber was also in the cast.

In *When the Smoke Hit the Fan*, Ralph Bellamy recalled how impressed he was during certain performances by the tears that would well up in Dorothy Sands's eyes when they acted a dramatic scene. He believed that she must have been barricading herself in her dressing room to prepare for the moment, unwilling to allow anyone to intrude on her privacy. When he finally mentioned to her the emotional depth he had noted in her acting in this scene, she told him that the effect was caused by her new contact lenses, the wetting liquid for which would leak out after she reapplied the lenses between the acts.

TONIGHT AT 8:30 [Dramatic Revival*] A/D: Noël Coward; CH: Richard Barstow;

S: George Jenkins; C: (gowns) Hattie Carnegie; P: Homer Curran, Russell Lewis, and Howard Young; T: National Theatre; 2/20/48 (26)
First Group: "Ways and Means"; "Family Album"; "Red Peppers"
Second Group: "Hands across the Sea"; "Fumed Oak"; "Shadow Play"

Two programs of Coward one-acts that originally had been seen locally in 1936 starring the author and Gertrude Lawrence. The original nine plays were now reduced to six, and many lamented the absence of "Still Life," famous as the source of the excellent movie, *Brief Encounter*. Lawrence returned to her old roles in this revival, but Coward allocated his own parts to Graham Payn. Once both programs were seen (the second one opening on 2/23/48), the programs were produced in a repertory system.

Despite Payn's abler singing talents, Coward's sparklingly sophisticated presence and unique rapid-fire delivery were sorely missed. As Euphemia Van Rensselaer Wyatt (*CW*) observed, "Graham Payn . . . has all the proper attributes of a musical comedy hero and it is these very amiable qualities which forestall his achieving the vindictiveness of Coward's wit." George Jean Nathan (*TBY*) asserted that Payn's "unmistakable masculinity" was at variance with "the falsetto tone" required by the roles. The only Coward part not taken by Payn was the husband in "Fumed Oak," assumed by Philip Tonge. The brilliant Lawrence did her best to hold the fort, but it was not sufficient. Richard Watts, Jr. (*NYP*), described her as "just as magnificent as ever, if not a little more so. Assuredly she has never looked more beautiful or played with more wonderful vitality." Most of the plays no longer seemed as charming as they had a dozen years earlier, and the presentation as a whole was widely considered a letdown.

On the first bill, "Red Peppers," largely for its delicious insult humor, was the most popular attraction in what was otherwise "a slow and decorous evening," according to Brooks Atkinson (*NYT*). Louis Kronenberger (*PM*) asserted that apart from "Red Peppers," "the evening has a harsh high-styled nastiness, and a tired tinkly jauntiness, that are very little fun." Company members included William Roerick, Sarah Burton, Valerie Cossart, Norah Howard, Booth Colman, and Rhoderick Walker.

To Atkinson, the second program proved "no better than the first. . . . Although Gertrude Lawrence is a superwoman, she cannot restore a world that has been lost, and none of us can recapture the enchantments or the values that seemed to fill the theatre with magic twelve years ago." Several others, however, found the bill a slight improvement. "Fumed Oak" was the favorite of some, "Hands across the Sea" that of others.

TONONA [Drama/Romance/Sex/Spanish Language] A/D: Rolando Barrera; P: Helen Rubens; T: New York Times Hall; 5/31/43 (1)

Rolando Barrera, a Dominican author, was responsible for this Spanish-language presentation at the playhouse better known as the Little Theatre. It is set in Havana and concerns the family of Don Luis, an older man married to a younger woman named Linda. Riccardo, the son of the family, arrives, and it becomes apparent that he and Linda have known each other intimately in the past. She is also loved by the jealous and tubercular Julian (Barrera, the author and director). Don Luis finally gives in and allows Riccardo and Linda to go off to New York, while he turns to the matronly housekeeper, Tonona (Mary Reid), and Julian commits suicide.

"Senor Barrera's play seems highly dramatic and amusing, to judge from the amount of delighted laughter in the audience," reported George Freedley (*TAM*).

TOO HOT FOR MANEUVERS [Comedy/Military/Romance/School/Sex/Youth] A/D: Les White and Bud Pearson; S: Wolfgang Roth; C: Lou Eisele; P: James S. Elliott; T: Broadhurst Theatre; 5/2/45 (5)

An "aesthetic misdemeanor" (Burton Rascoe [*NYWT*]) loaded with double entendres. The farce begins in Hadley's Military Academy, in upstate New York, run by Colonel Steve Hadley (movie actor Richard Arlen, in his Broadway bow), just returned from three years in the service. During his absence the place has gone downhill. When it is learned that a colonel (Lawrence Fletcher) is arriving from the War Department to inspect the school, the staff attempts to bring it up to snuff. One of the problems faced is what to do about a nearby fancy massage parlor and reducing salon named--after its proprietor--Countess Rosini's (Ellen Andrews). Two cadets have gone there to get in shape for the basketball team. The team needs all the help it can get since the gym was burned down by the senile Major Peters (Jed Prouty), whose dismissal provides a sentimental interlude. The presence of the boys at the parlor is misunderstood because the authorities believe it to be a brothel. The final scene takes place at the countess's establishment, where the school's authorities make asses of themselves when it turns out not only that the place is aboveboard but that the inspecting colonel and the countess are old and close acquaintances.

"The piece has no more fragrance than a cigar butt in a smoking compartment," coughed Howard Barnes (*NYHT*). "When it is not downright tasteless it is dreary."

Helene Reynolds as Steve's faithful girlfriend supplied some romantic interest. Dick Van Patten, Michael Dreyfuss, Alastair Kyle, and Billy Nevard were cadets, while other important roles were taken by Arthur Hunnicutt, Ronald Telfer, Harry Antrim, Fleming Ward, Agnes Heron Miller, and Eve McVeagh.

TOO MANY THUMBS [Comedy/Fantasy/Religion/Romance/Science/University] A: Robert Hivnor; D: Curt Conway; DS: Charles Hyman and William Sherman; P: Off Broadway, Inc.; T: Cherry Lane Theatre (OB); 7/27/49

A sporadically funny farce satirizing science and theology and featuring future star Kim Stanley in one of her first local appearances (she does not list the production in her credits). The title refers to the name of an amazing, jungle-bred chimpanzee (Nehemiah Persoff) who is brought into a college science lab to inspire progress in Psyche (Sadie Long), a Bronx Zoo-born simian. He makes amazing evolutionary progress within a couple of weeks, eventually turning into a normal man named Tom. He falls in love with the science professor's (Dick Robbins) girlfriend, Jennie Macklebee (Stanley), and becomes concerned with equal rights. By the end, thinking himself God, he walks off on his own.

Most of the funny stuff derived from the scenes of the monkey's criticizing human civilization with Psyche or outsmarting a fanatical theology professor (Gene Saks), who can not bring himself to accept what his eyes see. While often diverting, the play was bogged down in some overweighted poetic dialogue, needed cutting, and lost its impetus when it moved from comedy to philosophizing. "The fantasy had its uproarious moments," thought George Currie (*BE*), "and clever lines were interpolated to keep the action on the move." The unnamed *V* reviewer said that it "starts off weakly but builds into an amusing and fanciful comedy." Stanley, said the critic, "has little to do but lend charm to the proceedings." And Richard Watts, Jr. (*NYP*), conceded, "Whatever its weaknesses, this is a play that was worth doing. It has the rare gift of freshness and imagination." The play had been given earlier stagings by the theatre departments at the University of Minnesota and at Stevens College.

TOPAZE [Dramatic Revival*] A: Marcel Pagnol; AD: Benn W. Levy; D: Leo Mittler; S: Oliver Smith; C: Audré; L: Peggy Clark; P: Yolanda Mero-Irion for the New Opera Company; T: Morosco Theatre; 12/27/47 (1)

Last seen locally in a 1931 revival, this French comedy was revived again with Viennese actor Oscar Karlweis in the title role first played on Broadway by Frank Morgan. Karlweis's too self-conscious approach seemed wrong for the role and was a major reason for critical dissatisfaction. Brooks Atkinson (*NYT*) argued that his performance was one of many elements in the production that lacked spontaneity and that the play--a satire on the corruptibility of all human institutions--was sunk by the weight of so heavy-handed an interpretation. George Jean Nathan (*TBY*) insisted that the play itself was not at fault, that it had not aged at all and remained "a humorous and diverting satirical comedy," but that the direction and most of the acting were responsible for the failure. All in all, "Pretty feeble entertainment," groaned Richard Watts, Jr. (*NYP*). The one-performance flop wasted the services of Clarence Derwent (whose resumption of his 1930 role of Regis Castel-Benac many thought the best thing in the production), Robert Chisholm, Joe E. Marks, Tilly Losch, Helen Bonfils, Jean (Gene) Saks, Lucille Patton, and many others.

TOPLITZKY OF NOTRE DAME [Musical/Fantasy/Jews/Romance/Sports] B/LY: George Marion, Jr.; M: Sammy Fain; ADD.LY (and dialogue): Jack Barnett; D: José Ruben; CH: Robert Sidney; S: Edward Gilbert; C: Kenn Barr; P: William Cahn; T: Century Theatre; 12/26/46 (60)

There was a noticeable lack of funniness in this $230,000 musical comedy that sought to combine Jewish and Irish charm in the same piece. The only acceptable tune in the show was "Love Is a Random Thing."

Although he was not a singer, J. Edward Bromberg was tapped to play the title role, that of a New York City Jewish tavern keeper who is an ardent fan of Notre Dame's football team (he prays for them in the synagogue), although he has never seen them play in the flesh. His business is across the street from St. Patrick's Cathedral and is a popular watering hole for visiting Notre Dame players and fans. With the big game against Army coming up, the angels in heaven decide to send to earth an athletic angel named Angelo (Warde Donovan) to give Notre Dame the edge. Toplitzky adopts the angelic backfield player, who subsequently falls in love with the tavern keeper's adopted daughter (Betty Jane Watson). She was raised on Toplitzky's money by a family who led the tavern keeper to think that she was a boy and was being groomed for football at Notre Dame. After being warned by the angels, Angelo gives up the girl and Toplitzky, but is eventually allowed to remain on earth as a human, albeit without his supernatural powers. Then the angels take pity on him and he manages to win the big game for the Fighting Irish at Yankee Stadium with a miraculous 105-yard drop kick. He settles down on earth with his future bride.

The show was very colorful, lavishly staged, and vigorously choreographed, but it had no knockout performances or songs, and the book left much to be desired. Aside from a few decent notices, most critics were displeased. Hy Hollinger (*NYMT*) said, "It reaches the 20-yard line but doesn't score a touchdown." Vernon Rice (*NYP*) thought it "a routine and indifferent" show. Among the better reviews was Lee Mortimer's (*NYDM*), which called it "a very gay musical comedy with a pleasing score, many laughs, some terrific dancing, and one great moment." The company included Gus Van, Frank Marlowe, Marion Colby, Walter Long, Estelle Sloan, Doris Patston, Harry Fleer, and Robert Bay.

TOP-NOTCHERS [Revue] CN: Clifford C. Fischer; P: Clifford C. Fischer and Messrs. Shubert; T: Forty-fourth Street Theatre; 5/29/42 (48)

The immediate successor to *Keep 'Em Laughing*, which took the new title after its seventy-seventh performance. It played twice a day and three times on Sunday. In effect, Clifford C. Fischer simply replaced one lineup of vaudeville performers with another. It ran too long on opening night, which was common for such shows, but was considered "superior" (Louis Kronenberger [*PM*]) to its predecessor.

An international cast was headed by Spanish dancer Argentinita and Britain's blond music-hall comedienne-singer Gracie Fields. Entering in an ermine wrap in the show's second half, the Lancashire lass sang "The Sweetest Song in the World," dropped the wrap with a joke about social classes, offered the comic "Turn Herbert's Face to the Wall, Mother," added "Scotch Boy's Birthday," and then sang several others. Her highlights were "Biggest Aspidistra in the World" and a hilarious impression of a stuffy concert artiste almost strangling on her pearls. When she sang the "Aspidistra" song with its lyric about 'anging old 'itler from the highest bough of the biggest aspidistra in the world, British sailors in the gallery kicked up a rumpus and were joined by similarly patriotic Americans elsewhere in the house.

Argentinita was supported by her dancer sister Pilar Lopez and slender Frederico Rey. Their numbers included "Malaguena," "El Huayno," and others. They were good but went on too long. Spanish classical guitarist Carlos Montoya was on the bill as well. Also of memorable entertainment value were the juggling sextet, the Six Willys; political humorist (and the evening's host), Walter O'Keefe, with some unfunny jokes at the expense of Mayor La Guardia and Eleanor Roosevelt; the hilarious dog act called the Bricklayers, held over from the other show; clown A. Robins, who seemed to have thousands of bananas hidden in his coat; a brilliant turn by Zero Mostel (another holdover), spoofing such things as Jimmy Durante, a U.S. senator, and jitterbug dancing; Paul and Grace Hartman, popular comic dancers (also holdovers); a chorus line of sixteen (which some felt slowed the show down); singers Evelyn Brooks and Jack Stanton; comedian Al Trahan and a pretty brunette partner, Marguerite Adams; "Think-a-Drink" Hoffman, who could make water into whisky of any type; and others.

Speaking of Fields, John Anderson (*NYJA*) confided, "Miss Fields held me entranced by her comic songs sung in a voice that seemed part goddess and part banshee. As long as there are people like Miss Fields there will probably be something like vaudeville. She works wonders with an audience, and an audience plainly inspires Miss Fields to her most glorious fooling. Here we have contagion, warmth, hilarity. Here we have the sheer power of personality present and alive, and the per fection of its expression."

TOUCH AND GO [Revue] SK/LY: Jean and Walter Kerr; M: Jay Gorney; D: Walter Kerr; CH: Helen Tamiris; DS: John Robert Lloyd; P: George Abbott; T: Broadhurst Theatre; 10/13/49 (176)

This show, originally called, *Thank You, Just Looking*, was first produced at Washington, D.C.'s, Catholic University, where the Kerrs were on the faculty. It was a youth-oriented revue (making it right up producer George Abbott's alley) that met with mixed responses. The unnamed *TAM* reviewer believed it to be "entirely devoid" of "inventiveness and originality." "The first act overture gives the impression of all one's favorite show tunes rolled into one--but not too expertly. Two big dance numbers are stuffy and pretentious. Sketches start off brightly but run steadily downhill." Herrick Brown (*NYS*) thought it "an uneven and slight bit of theatrical fare." But Brooks Atkinson (*NYT*) designated the show "a capital light revue . . . put on with skill and wit." The score and choreography, he opined, were first-rate, and he added that the show was "good-humored, bright, original and intelligent." William Hawkins (*NYWT*) claimed, "It is energetic without being frantic, has more respect for all-around talent than starry names, and is up to the minute with its spoofing."

The company included singer-comedienne Nancy Andrews, beautiful blond singer Kyle MacDonnell, dancers Pearl Lang and Daniel Nagrin, varitalented performers Helen Gallagher, George Hall, Dick Sykes, Ray Page, Larry Robins, and Jonathan Lucas, and, in her Broadway bow, comedienne Peggy Cass. Future star Ray Walston was fired from the show out of town because Walter Kerr wanted to replace him with one of his university sophomores. When the show's press agent questioned the student's qualifications for the demanding role, producer Abbott responded, "You don't understand. He's been a sophomore for five years" (quoted in Richard Maney, *Fanfare*).

Outstanding numbers included "Gorilla Girl," spoofing the movies, with the gorilla in the scene being rehearsed revealed as smarter than the star actress; a sketch set at the scene of combat in which the enlisted men and the brass are all writing their memoirs, one of them called *The Bloody and the Sweaty*; a musical comedy version of *Hamlet** (called "Great Dane a-Comin") in the vein of Rodgers and Hammerstein and with Polonius played like Bobby Clark; "Be a Mess," a song parody of the unattractive characters played by recent Oscar-winning actresses, with Cass, Andrews, and MacDonnell spoofing Olivia de Havilland (in *The Snake Pit*), Barbara Stanwyck (in *Sorry, Wrong Number*), and Jane Wyman (in *Johnny Belinda*) as stars who regained their popularity by looking like a mess; "Miss Platt Selects Mate," which was a show-stopper for Andrews; "Wish Me a Luck," another Andrews number, in which she sang about her lack of matrimonial success; the somewhat more serious "American Primitive," inspired by the paintings of Grandma Moses; and, for a conclusion, a company performance of "Cinderella" as if directed by Elia Kazan and written by Tennessee Williams and Arthur Miller. When the prince came looking for Cinderella, who was in the bathroom, he was told by the stepmother and sisters that she was not at home. A huge laugh came when Cinderella flushed the toilet and the prince realized that she was indeed home. Director Abbott revealed in *"Mister Abbott"* that he had wanted to cut this bit because he thought it vulgar, but on hearing the audience response realized that he had almost made one of his "worst judgements about a theatrical effect."

TOWN HOUSE [Comedy/Business/Family/Journalism/Marriage/Science/Youth] A: Gertrude Tonkonogy; SC: John Cheever's *New Yorker* stories; D: George S. Kaufman; S/L: Donald Oenslager; C: John Derro; P: Max Gordon; T: National Theatre; 9/23/48 (12)

This play's title was inspired by the locale of the action, a former mansion on New York's Upper East Side in which three couples, unable to find suitable living quarters because of the postwar housing shortage, decide to live cooperatively. A snooty Baltimore couple is the intolerant Jack (James Monks) Tremaine, a would-be broker, and his spoiled wife Lucille (June Duprez), both of them inept at practical matters; another pair is an ambitious magazine editor, Larry Hyler (Reed Brown, Jr.), trying to finance a new magazine, and his wife, Carol (Peggy French); the third duo, prone to malapropisms, consists of former Clevelanders, scientist Pete (Hiram Sherman) Murray and his gawky wife Esther (Mary Wickes). Accompanying the latter is their bratty daughter (Roberta Field), a student at a progressive school. Eventually, they run into various problems as their temperaments and circumstances interact and clash. Each couple wants to make the most of a wealthy neighbor, Mr. Phelps (Edwin Jerome), and their competition in getting his money leads to frequent squabbles. Finally, they agree to split up, but before the final curtain, they realize how much they enjoy living together and decide to reconcile and remain united.

The piece suffered from an exceedingly loose construction and the lack of a strong central action and fully fleshed-out characters. "So little honest dramatic development is there that scenes could have been transposed without seriously marring the entertainment," observed Howard Barnes (*NYHT*). "The comedy element is labored and obvious and never compensates for the constant wrangling," thought William Hawkins (*NYWT*).

During the writing period, director Kaufman had practically collaborated on the script with Tonkonogy. She later declared that she was not happy with the process, as he wanted to punch everything up for comedy and farce, and she wanted to explore the characters more deeply.

Production values were first rate. Donald Oenslager provided a handsome set consisting of two levels, a living room and two upstairs bedrooms. The set led to very high cost, because a hole had to be cut in the stage floor to allow a staircase to look as if it were going to the basement. The height of the upper level also caused difficulty for those down front, who had to strain their necks to see the action up there. According to Malcolm Goldstein's *George S. Kaufman*, Kaufman responded to the problem with a crack about people having pestered him for front-row seats for years and that now he would be able to give them what they wanted. At any rate, Kaufman's direction took good advantage of the arrangement, sometimes by having action going on in three rooms at once. To his job he brought "a mastery of stage mechanics, an exactness of timing, an uncanny manipulation of entrances and exits," wrote Ward Morehouse (*NYS*). The cast included Esther Dale, Henry Jones, and Vera Fuller Mellish.

TRAITOR, THE [Drama/Military/Politics/Science] A: Herman Wouk; D/P: Jed Harris; S/L: Raymond Sovey; C: Joseph Fretwell III; T: Forty-eighth Street Theatre; 4/4/49 (67)

Cold war preoccupation with atomic bomb secrets sparked this ambitious but unsuccessful espionage melodrama. Its subject matter included communism, loyalty, academic freedom, nationalism, and Soviet-U.S. relations. It was riddled with flaws but had a strong inherent interest. The playwright's methods seemed dated, and the play's ideas were open to question, but, said Hobe. (*V*), in one of the more positive responses, "It is tautly written, superbly produced, and convincingly performed, so it tends to lull an audience into temporarily overlooking its shortcomings."

Professor Allen Carr (Wesley Addy), engaged to a smart young woman (Louise Platt) of sound ethical standards, is an idealistic young physicist who believes it appropriate to hand over atomic materials to the Russians because he feels that if both sides have the bomb it will produce an arms stalemate that will effectively prevent nuclear war. He is a protégé of the old and upstanding philosopher, Professor Emanuel (Walter Hampden), who expresses moral anguish over the problems faced by Carr. Agents of naval intelligence, led by Captain Gallagher (Lee Tracy), suspects Carr of espionage activities with a Russian spy (John Wengraf) and attempts to get the goods on him, which they do by using a Geiger counter to detect his recent exposure to radioactivity. With their assistance, Carr realizes that he has made an error and attempts to rectify it by trapping the spy. Although the spy is caught, Carr is himself killed by a pistol equipped with a silencer.

Various critics noted that despite the topicality and importance of the topic, the play's chief interest lay in its melodramatic trappings. Rosamond Gilder (*TAM*) turned thumbs down as a result: "*The Traitor*, for all its bogus timeliness, is an unthrilling thriller." "The writing is trivial and the melodrama opportunistic," insisted Brooks Atkinson (*NYT*). But John Mason Brown (*SR*) and George Jean Nathan (*TBY*) went on at length about how much pleasure the play's melodramatic devices gave them, especially as masterfully handled by director Harris. "Although *The Traitor* may be far from a perfect melodrama, it is an exciting one," noted Brown. He also (as did several others) made much of the fact that a real Geiger counter was used in the play, this being an invention about which there was then considerable curiosity. Jean Hagen and Richard Derr were in the large cast.

TREAD THE GREEN GRASS [Drama/Fantasy/Religion/Rural/Sex/Southern/Youth] A: Paul Green; AD/D: Herbert V. Gellendre; M: Eugene Broadnax; P: Abbe Practical Workshop; T: Master Institute Theatre (OB); 4/20/50 (3)

The first professional staging of a twenty-year-old "folk fantasy with music," first produced in 1932 at the University of Iowa. The production demonstrated why it had been avoided by producers over the years. L. C. (*NYT*) said that it was "old-fashioned and devoid of action," *V*'s unnamed reviewer declared that "spasmodic moments of captivating drama are bogged down by a talky script," and Richard Watts, Jr. (*NYP*), concluded that the work "strives for difficult and important things and accomplishes only an evening of tedium and confusion."

Basically a morality play, it is set in a primitive rural community in the South and tells of the raging internal conflicts between good and evil within Tina (Deirdre Owens), an innocent adolescent girl who is prevented by repressive forces from unabashedly enjoying her natural human impulses with the Pan-like Davie (Marc Raven). Davie, a symbol of the Devil, fights for her soul against the forces of the local church, represented by a half-dozen zealots, who shout about salvation. These struggles are enacted in dream sequences in which the Devil fires the town church and spreads moral corruption among the young folk. The struggle over Tina ends in her death, despite the efforts of a mountaineer and a minister (Douglass Parkhurst) to save her.

TRIAL BY FIRE [Drama/Blacks/Crime/Family/Race/Rural] A: George H. Dunne; D: Albert McCleery; S: William Riva; P: Blackfriars' Guild; T: Blackfriars' Theatre (OB); 12/4/47 (20)

A Jesuit priest wrote this six-scene, noncommercial, documentary drama, based on a true incident, about the tragic deaths in 1945 of a black couple, the Johnsons (Will Marshall and Paula Mayer), and their children (Clarence Rock and Charlynn Q. Wright). Despite being warned by a vigilantes committee of the possible consequences, the family accepted the reassurances of an FBI agent and bravely moved into a chicken farm in a bigoted white community in the rural outskirts of Los Angeles. The author included in his text some of the actual coroner's findings as well as material based on his talks with those familiar with the victims. Dunne had written up the story in *Commonweal* in 1945 and based his play on his earlier account. It was first staged in Los Angeles in 1946.

The play takes the form of the coroner's (Marc Snow) inquest, with flashbacks used to introduce the scenes leading up to the explosion that caused the fire. The seemingly prejudiced district attorney (Thomas Roberts) uses the words he took from the dying Johnson to prove that the deaths were accidental, which is what the jury decides to believe. The audience is assumed to be in attendance at the inquest, and witnesses are mixed in with the spectators. Instead of preaching a message, the playwright presents the facts straightforwardly and allows the audience to decide on the merits of the case.

To Edba. (*V*) and George Jean Nathan (*TBY*), among others, the material was strong but the treatment second-rate theatrical art. Robert Coleman (*NYDM*), though, thought it superior to the recent *On Whitman Avenue*, which had treated a similar subject. He considered the direction by McCleery (director of Fordham University's theatre program) of Broadway quality, and the acting of many very good, including Thomas Roberts as the district attorney. Vernon Rice (*NYP*) thought the play "an earnest and sincere piece of writing," although, as Nathan noted, the subject was familiar and had been better handled previously.

"TRIAL BY JURY" (see *H.M.S. Pinafore* and *The Pirates of Penzance*)

TRIAL HONEYMOON [Comedy/Hotel/Marriage/Sex] A: Conrad S. Smith; D: Edward Ludlum; S/L: Philip Kessler; L: Chester Manzer; P: Harry Rosen; T: Royale Theatre; 11/3/47 (8)

Eileen Heckart made her Broadway debut in this "amateurish bit of dramaturgy" (Vernon Rice [*NYP*]) that originated at the Greenbush Theatre (on the strawhat circuit) in Blauvelt, New York. She played the acidulous friend of the heroine, a wisecracking type of role she would play countless times in later shows. The action occurs in a hotel's bungalow (actually a canvas tent) in Los Angeles and tells the old story of a young couple, George Willoughby (Jack Fletcher) and Linda Melton (Ellen Fenwick), about to be wed, who discover that because of regulations concerning the time lapsed between application for marriage and the actual wedding, California law requires them to delay their nuptials, even though they are already sharing a bedroom together. Since family and friends have gathered, and there are no separate bedrooms, they talk the clergyman (Stapleton Kent) into performing a make-believe ceremony, and they intend to have the real one a day later in Mexico. The groom's interfering sister (Helen Waters), however, creates various complications. George and Linda end up sleeping together, but without any sinful effects, because he dozes off. The next day, Linda decides that George's best man (Ed Moroney) is the man for her anyway, so her failure to marry George is a blessing in disguise.

"All this is quite innocent, a bit desperate, and utterly futile," wrote Hobe. (*V*). "It's not merely trivial and immature, but silly and embarraswsingly inept." The humor was based on cracks about effeminate men, bird droppings, female pulchritude, and toilets. A sample one-liner: She: (referring to a wolf) "The only reason he joined the Army was that he hoped they'd send him to the Virgin Islands."

TRIO [Drama/Homosexuality/Literature/Romance/University/Youth] A: Dorothy and Howard Baker; SC: Dorothy Baker's novel of the same name; D: Bretaigne Windust; S: Stewart Chaney; P: Lee Sabinson; T: Belasco Theatre; 12/29/44 (67)

Trio was one of the most controversial plays of the forties, creating a storm of contention because of its treatment of the theme of lesbianism. The play had an extremely hard time finding a theatre it could rent, the Shuberts being particularly adamant against offering one of theirs to the producer because their Ambassador Theatre had been shut down after it housed the allegedly salacious *Wine, Women, and Song*. *Trio*, however, proved to have treated its sensitive material with restraint and integrity and to be anything but the scandal that was expected. Nevertheless, despite good reviews and an interested public, the play was closed down by the pressures put upon the theatre owner by License Commissioner Moss, who considered the play a "morally offensive exhibit" and threatened to invoke the Wales Padlock Law against the theatre. Interestingly, the play had not caused a similar outcry in Philadelphia or Boston. The incident reminded many of a similar controversy over Edouard Bourdet's *The Captive** in 1926. (A detailed discussion of the controversy is in Kaier Curtin, *We Can Always Call Them Bulgarians*.)

The story recounts how a sophisticated and charming older woman, Pauline Maury (Lydia St. Clair), a professor of French civilization at a midwestern university, gains sexual and mental control over young Janet Logan (Lois Wheeler), who resides with her. The professor believes that genius is the result of perversion. Pauline is challenged by Janet's boyfriend, student Ray McKenzie (Richard Widmark), when, to his shock, he discovers the nature of the relationship. He brings all his anger to an argument with Janet. After calming down, he manages to win Janet away from Pauline, who needs the girl for ego support, to assist her in the writing of a book, and to help defend her against charges of plagiarism over an earlier book for which she was acclaimed, but which was cribbed from a previous student's thesis. When she loses Janet, Pauline hangs herself.

The reviewers saw nothing to be ashamed of in terms of treatment or theme. In fact, the play was deemed a highly moral diatribe against "degeneracy." What quarrels they had were with the work's dramaturgy. "It is without sensationalism, and without any deliberate intent to catch the ear of prurient groundlings," reported George Jean Nathan (*TBY*). "Compared with Bourdet's excellent play it is third-rate; it out-talks its subject matter, it engages at two points in extrinsic melodrama, and it in one instance, that of the young man's character, neglects to support his stubborn blindness to the young girl's sexual abnormality with any . . . hintful psychological explanation." But Nathan considered it a better-than-average play with an especially strong scene between the boy and the girl in the second act where they struggle to come to grips with their situation. Lewis Nichols (*NYT*) had slightly similar feelings, noting, "*Trio* has only moments that are moving or tragic; it has long stretches that are talky, repetitious and sometimes not well acted." Rosamond Gilder (*TAM*) declared, "It varies between dullness and melodrama, with emphasis on the first." Louis Kronenberger (*PM*), who found various strengths and weaknesses, noted, "Though the dialogue is neat and literary at times, it is at other times powerful, sharp and adult."

In spite of Nichols's comment about the acting, many critics thought that the three leads were excellent, particularly Wheeler and Widmark. Howard Barnes (*NYHT*) wrote, "Richard Widmark does a remarkable job. . . . His tense underplaying sustains the most faltering moments of the play." Widmark was replaced by Kirk Douglas in the middle of the run. According to his *The Ragman's Son*, Douglas learned the part in three days, but at his first performance, when he made his big entrance in the scene where he discovers Janet in the teacher's apartment, he acted with such force that the audience burst into laughter. Unable to sleep because of this humiliation, he realized in his dressing room the next night that "all my tensions had erupted as I banged onto the stage, and it became funny. This time, when the climactic moment came, I slowly walked into the room and very calmly looked at the two of them. There was an intake of breath from the audience, and complete silence."

Harry Irvine, Kenneth Williams, and Sara Perry were among the cast members.

TROJAN WOMEN, THE [Dramatic Revival] A: Euripides (prologue: Robert Turney); AD: Gilbert Murray; M: Lehman Engel; D: Margaret Webster; CH: Felicia Sorel; P: Experimental Theatre, Inc.; T: Cort Theatre; 4/8/41 (3)

The Experimental Theatre was founded with the cooperation of Actors Equity and the Dramatists Guild "to give actors and playwrights an opportunity to practice their respective arts and exhibit their wares and to create activity which might stimulate production." No one was paid, and the plays were produced for a miniscule number of performances at matinees or on Sunday evenings on the stages of theatres currently being used for other presentations. Makeshift settings were employed. The Experimental Theatre was the inception of the idea that eventually led to the Equity Library Theatre.

Despite its avowed aim to present new plays, the company opened with this revival of Murray's version of *The Trojan Women*, one of the great antiwar plays of all time. To placate the Dramatists Guild, the production used a new prologue by Robert Turney. This prologue established the connection of the production to contemporary world events, displaying the tragedy of Rotterdam refugees on a road in northern France fleeing a bombardment. At its conclusion, as smoke rose and bombs crashed, Poseidon's voice could be heard, "How are ye blind, ye treaders down of cities, / Ye that cast temples to desolation . . . / Yourselves so soon to die," followed by the shapes of the regular dramatis personae materializing in the smoke. Some thought its presence totally unnecessary, as Euripides' viewpoint needed no additional underlining. John Mason Brown (*NYP*) said that it was "as superfluous as a caption under a picture of the Crucifixion."

As an opportunity for new actors, the production also had to be faulted. The role of Hecuba was played by Dame May Whitty, mother of the director, while the director herself played Andromache. A number of people were upset about this apparent "vanity" casting, although Webster attempted to defend it in *Don't Put Your Daughter on the Stage*. There was even more of a to-do made by Equity because Whitty was an alien. Frederic Tozere was Talthybius, Walter Slezak played Menelaus, Florence Williams was Cassandra, Joanna Roos was a young mother, and Helen was acted by Tamara Geva. Unknowns performed the slightly characterized choral roles.

"Miss Webster's Andromache," noted Euphemia Van Rensselaer Wyatt (*CW*) "remains the feature of the experiment, commanding and fiery as it was tender." None of the others equalled her performance and some were plain bad. There was difficulty understanding the foreign-born Geva, and the German-accented Slezak played his scene with Helen as an obese, comical weakling to her cunning whore. The chorus was awkwardly choreographed, and some said that it was unpleasant to listen to.

Webster, working on a zero budget, dressed the cast in a combination of modern military garb resembling Nazi uniforms for the men and timeless, soft-colored, robelike costumes for the women. The set (hiding that of *Charley's Aunt**, which was the regular attraction at the Cort) consisted of black drapes, a draped platform, and some smoke effects. A traditional style informed the staging, with original touches only rarely being apparent. What stood out were the scenes of anguish surrounding the death of Andromache's child (Lorna Lynn), largely because of Webster's dignified acting.

One of the strongest criticisms of the production was of the choice of Murray's verse adaptation, which was scored as verbose and undramatic. "This distended, emasculated verse makes *The Trojan Women* terribly slow-moving and garrulous," growled Louis Kronenberger (*PM*). Despite some kind words, the production proved a critical failure.

TROUBLE IN JULY [Drama/Blacks/Crime/Politics/Race/Small Town/Southern] A: Owen Steele; SC: Erskine Caldwell's novel of the same name; D: James Dyas; S: Karl Hueglin; P: The Troupers; T: 6 Fifth Avenue (OB); 12/1/49 (10)

A strong drama about a Southern lynching that some thought might do well on Broadway. Like so many similar plays, it concerns the reactions of a small town's populace to the news that a white female citizen (Tommie Tompkins) has been raped by a black youth, here named Sonny (Greg Hunter). Actually, though, the white girl grabbed the black man as he was passing her, and his struggle to free himself was misinterpreted by an eccentric woman who reported having seen a rape. The sheriff (Ben M. Hammer), a fairly tolerant man, does not want to get involved for fear of losing votes in the coming election, so he tries to vanish on a fishing trip. The innocent Sonny is hunted down. When the girl is questioned, she tries to save the alleged rapist and has her head bashed in for her troubles. A sympathetic but cowardly white man turns the fugitive over to the posse and Sonny is hanged.

The theatre used was an anteroom on the first floor of a four-story brownstone, with seats for eighty. Critics attending had considerable praise for the staging in this tiny environment and thought the play a powerful piece of social propaganda. Especially effective was the depiction of the racist mob, each character well delineated. "*Trouble* travels at a rapid pace and is sparked with an abundance of action," declared the unnamed *V* critic. The cast included Lloyd Richards as a black overseer, Alice de Loache, June Fraser, James Winslow, and Sheppard Kerman.

TRUCKLINE CAFÉ [Comedy-Drama/Alcoholism/Crime/Marriage/Military/Sex] A: Maxwell Anderson; D: Harold Clurman; S: Boris Aronson; C: Millia Davenport; P: Elia Kazan and Harold Clurman i/a/w the Playwrights' Company; T: Belasco Theatre; 2/27/46 (13)

Although this work about the problems faced by veterans returning to a peacetime society was a quick failure, it is historically interesting on several accounts. Anderson had gone ahead with the production despite the attempts of his Playwrights' Company colleagues to dissuade him. Even a poor tryout in Baltimore failed to change his mind. When the play opened on Broadway, it was stoned unmercifully by the critics. The coproducers (one of whom, Kazan, was making his debut in this capacity) took out a newspaper ad declaring their decision to close the play, but also using the opportunity to express their anger over the damage being done to the New York theatre by such critical vituperation, especially when the critics were ill prepared for their tasks. This was followed by a blast from playwright Anderson himself, in which he retaliated against the severity of the critics' attacks and called the critics "a sort of Jukes family of journalism" (see the Introduction to this volume, p. xxvi). A heated controversy soon ensued in the press.

In his autobiography, *Elia Kazan*, Kazan acknowledged his great disappointment in the play and faulted director Clurman for not having forced Anderson to make needed improvements. He declared that Clurman, informed by Kazan of the latter's impatience with the scantiness of Anderson's revisions, replied fatalistically, "That's the play. You can't do anything about it. It will succeed or fail, but that's it."

Another significant element in the play's otherwise sorry history was the opportunity it gave to the young Marlon Brando to provide a performance that brought him to public attention. Brando (whose fictional *Playbill* bio said that he was born in Bangkok, where his father was doing zoological research) had impressed neither Kazan nor Clurman at his audition (they had wanted Burgess Meredith), but was urged on them by Clurman's wife, actress Stella Adler. During rehearsals, Brando had to be forced to emote and to project by Clurman, who resorted to unorthodox methods, including forcing the actor to roll on the floor and then kicking him to get him mad. The muscular actor took his preparation so seriously that he dropped to 135 pounds to have the right look of gauntness for the role, but Clurman ordered him to regain his weight because he wanted Brando to look appropriately attractive for an entrance in a bathing suit. During the performance, Brando had to appear shivering and wet after having thrown his wife's body into the ocean. Two men were stationed offstage to douse him with cold water just before his entrance, and he delivered his lines with his teeth chattering, making a powerful impression.

Mort (Richard Waring) is a British RAF flyer whose wife, Anne (Virginia Gilmore), believes him to have died in a Nazi prison camp. Lonely and desperate, she has taken to drink and other men and, having had an abortion, works as a waitress in Kip (Ralph Theadore) and Min's (June Walker) eponymous roadside diner, situated between Los Angeles and San Francisco. Cabins are available to interested travelers. Mort has not died, however, and he turns up, revealing that he escaped from the camp, had an affair with a Polish slave girl, and fathered a child (Eugene Steiner) by her, although she died in childbirth. He strives to reunite with Anne, who refuses. The play's parallel plot concerns Sage McCrae (Brando), who suspects that his wife Tory (Ann Shepherd) has had an affair with his friend. When he finds out that his fears are justified, he murders her and deposits her corpse in the sea. This prompts Anne to change her mind and to take Mort back and rebuild their relationship. Various subplots and minor characters--most related to the idea of servicemen readjusting to peacetime life--swarm around this nucleus.

The play was considered scattershot and formless, unfocused, and essentially undramatic. Its characters were not convincing and its style was artistically jumbled. Lewis Nichols (*NYT*) accused the work of "causing an occasional choppy wave but more often a ripple, and never building up to the even breeze of good drama." Ward Morehouse (*NYS*) viewed it as "hopelessly artificial and muddled . . . , a curious and lumbering mixture of comedy, melodrama and philosophy." One of the least negative comments came from Rosamond Gilder (*TAM*), who noted that the play was "not a masterpiece," but that "it dealt sympathetically if not profoundly with a poignant, immediate problem, it held its audience in continuous interest and it had several striking and unforgettable scenes."

Gilder said that Brando gave his role "a signal intensity and pathos." Among the other fine performances was one by Karl Malden as a drunken sailor seeking to rent a cabin for himself and two girls. Also on hand in the large cast were Kevin McCarthy, David Manners, Irene Dailey, Kenneth Tobey, Jutta Wolf, and Lou Gilbert, among others.

TRY AND GET IT [Comedy/Romance/Sex] A: Sheldon Davis; D: Frank Merlin; C: Norman Edwards; P: A. H. Woods; T: Cort Theatre; 8/2/43 (8)

Veteran producer A. H. Woods assembled a cast of unknowns for this turkey (originally titled *The Key to Vivy's Room*, which became the subtitle) that was directly in the outdated bedroom farce tradition for which he was known. The only performance that glittered was that of young movie actress Margaret Early (in her Broadway bow) as Sarah Smith.

While her married sugar-daddy lover, Thomas Barton (Albert Bergh), is out of town, naughty Vivienne Gordon (Iris Hall) pays nice but naive Southern gal Sarah to impersonate her when a Southern friend of Thomas calls, expecting to be entertained. Vivy wants to be off partying in the Adirondacks with her girlfriend Evelyn (Virginia Smith) and with some football hunks. The peaches-and-cream lass, who is engaged to a delicatessen clerk (Raymond Rand), must act the part of a siren to make her three-day job convincing. The fellow who arrives turns out to be the handsome soldier son (Donald Murphy) of the expected visitor, which leads to various mistaken-identity crises because the fellow has been led to expect a hot time. After various frustrations stemming from Sarah's refusal to lose her virtue (for protection, she makes the fat comic maid [Hattie Noel] sleep with her), the boy discovers the deception and falls in love with her. Barton is killed in a train wreck, and a messenger (Charles Knight) delivers an envelope containing $5,000 for Vivy. Vivy gives Sarah $500 to keep the ruse secret. Barton's widow (Claire Meade) turns up and, thinking that Sarah is Vivy, pays her $20,000 because she thinks that her husband did not give the girl enough. The soldier and Sarah become engaged.

Rowland Field (*NEN*) admitted, "The incumbent farce is utterly lacking in entertainment value." Charles A. Siegferth (*BC*) announced, "*Try and Get It* is a wooden little comedy; creaks with old age; amateurish in many spots, and as funny as Hitler trying to be 'boss man' of this little world of ours." The management used a publicity ploy of giving every male spectator a key and presenting the one whose key fit the door to Vivy's room with a $25 war bond. This idea was forbidden by the authorities, however, as being an illegal lottery.

(1) **TWELFTH NIGHT** [Dramatic Revival*] A: William Shakespeare; D: Margaret Webster; M: Paul Bowles; S/C: Stewart Chaney; P: Theatre Guild and Gilbert Miller; T: St. James Theatre; 11/19/40 (129)

Helen Hayes as Viola (her first Shakespearean role) and Maurice Evans as Malvolio headed the cast of this highly successful revival of Shakespeare's lovely comedy; its last important revival--starring Jane Cowl--had been in 1930, although there were lesser ones in 1931 and 1932. While it enjoyed a long run and gained many kudos (John Mason Brown [*NYP*] deemed it of "uncommon charm"), it did have its drawbacks. As Brooks Atkinson (*NYT*) noted, it was a presentation of "mixed blessings--good in spots, very good in spots, but unable to achieve the full gayety that it strives to evoke." The chief problem he pointed to was the "desire to be funny at any cost," an approach that overlooked the poetic and more romantic elements of the work. And Rosamond Gilder (*TAM*) felt that for all its joy and color, "it never coheres around a central mood; it lacks intention except the obvious one of achieving a smooth-running, vigorous performance."

The major interpretive adjustment of the production was in Evans's performance, which he chose to deliver in a solemn cockney accent while dressed in a manner--goateed chin, white shirt with great flared collar, oversized shoes suggesting fallen arches, black tie, and tails--that suggested the image of a very proper British butler (although a fantastical touch was added by a hat adorned with cocksfeathers). The idea was to suggest a commoner trying to become even more lofty than his noble masters. Gilder said, "The accent makes Malvolio's dream of Olivia's favor more ridiculous than ever and it adds yet another note to the chorus of colloquial speech with which American productions of Shakespeare are afflicted, but it is justified by Mr. Evans' use of it as a comic device." Several critics noted how effectively he garnered laughs without strain, especially when Olivia commanded him to "Run after that same peevish messenger / The County's man: he left this ring behind him," and he interpolated the word "Run!?" with a polite superciliousness. "It is only one word," observed Atkinson. "But somehow Mr. Evans puts into it the disdain, the fastidiousness, the vanity and alarm of a fatuous underling." (Evans confessed in *All This . . . and Evans Too* that the word had emerged involuntarily during a rehearsal and had broken up the company. Bets were laid that if it were kept in, none of the critics would spot it.) Brown wrote that Evans played the role "as a time-pleaser, sick of self-love; a pathetic, quiet, entirely human being who is more ridiculous inside than out." Gilder's only quibble with the performance was Evans's failure to mine the character's full measure of dignity, when he must garner a touch of sympathy after being mistreated by the others.

"Miss Hayes's Viola is not so much a lovelorn maid as a delightful urchin," avowed Euphemia Van Rensselaer Wyatt (*CW*). "So heartily and bravely does she assume the boy that the audience almost shares Olivia's mystification. As the boy has all of Miss Hayes's sensitive honesty, he is the nicest boy imaginable, and, in her neat gray breeches, forsaking majesty, Miss Hayes affects the easy postures but never the swagger of young manhood. She is really funny in her first scene with Olivia and very, very funny in the duel but equally real is her solicitude for the Duke and Olivia." She added, though, "The strength of her passion for the Duke is less convincing." George Freedley (*NYMT*) loved Hayes's ability to combine lyricism with comic technique. "She is buoyant, boyish and never coy." Brown believed that her performance "has dash and spirit without losing its sentimental self-pity." To Atkinson, however, Hayes had overstressed the boyish charm of the role, missing out on "breeding and even sophistication of character, grace of motion, music of verse." Gilder, despite appreciating the "integrity" of the actress's performance, found that "many of her attitudes, positions, gestures, movements seem the result of direction, not the outgrowth of situation. Her performance lacks spontaneity, as it lacks real poetry. . . . Only once or twice . . . does she release the full lyric loveliness of the part."

Early in the rehearsals Hayes had taken Evans aside to ask him his secret for speaking iambic pentameter. They were interrupted before he could proffer any advice, but Evans revealed in his autobiography that he "hadn't the faintest idea of any magic formula." He was soon impressed by how quickly Hayes picked up the skill herself, sans tips from anyone.

Others in the cast included English actress Sophie Stewart as an elegant Olivia (who was accompanied by a tiny blackamoor); Mark Smith as an unimaginative Toby Belch, lacking in aristocratic bearing; Wallace Acton as a competent but too-effeminate Sir Andrew; multitalented Donald Burr of the musical theatre as an outstanding Feste, singing with great charm; Wesley Addy as a merely adequate Orsino; and June Walker as a vivacious, captivating Maria. Anthony Ross had two small roles, as the sea captain and a soldier.

Stewart Chaney's lovely Stuart masquelike setting made use of a false proscenium decorated with billowing painted curtains framing an inner stage within which perspective settings were employed. The actors played in front of the false proscenium on a modified apron while set changes were going on upstage. The costumes were an imaginative re-creation of Elizabethan silhouettes. Essences of Scarlatti and Purcell haunted the lovely melodies provided by composer Paul Bowles.

Freedley paid director Webster many compliments: "She has combined pace, gaiety, gravity and pause in such relation as to make her production extremely effective." Webster divided the play into two acts and fifteen scenes. "It all flows freely through a theatrical never-never land where candelabra hang on curves of sky, where conspirators hide behind realistic bushes half their size, where all the make-believe of yesterday and today meets in a merry jumble," declared Gilder.

(2) D: Michael Chekhov and George Shdanoff; M: Joseph R. Wood, Jr.; S/C: Michael Chekhov; P: Chekhov Theatre Players; T: Little Theatre; 12/2/41 (15)

A stylized, low-comedy interpretation of the play that seriously overlooked its poetic qualities. There was a decidedly improvisational quality to the production, said several critics, some of whom noted the considerable cuts and occasional ad libs. A result of the swiftly moving performances was to blur the details of the plot for those who would like to have paid more attention to it. "Much of the direction," wrote John Anderson (*NYJA*), "seemed more horseplay than truly spirited." Several critics noted a decidedly Russian quality to the cavortings.

More than in typical productions, Sir Toby Belch (Ford Rainey) became the center of attention. Sam Schatz played Malvolio in a manner that Euphemia Van Rensselaer Wyatt (*CW*) called "rather El Greco in elongated melancholy and too sensitive not to arouse sympathy in his baiting." Richard Lockridge (*NYS*) pointed out that Schatz's Malvolio was played "fully and amusingly, but in his interpretation the butt of the play is not so much a pompous ass as an avowed idiot."

Beatrice Straight, although still somewhat unformed as an an artist, was a charming Viola. Hurd Hatfield (in chalk-white makeup) was Aguecheek, Mary Haynsworth was Maria, John Flynn was Orsino, Mary Lou Taylor was Olivia, Alan Harkness was Feste, and Youl Bryner (later spelled Yul Brynner) was Fabian. Most were adequate, a few, such as Haynsworth, Rainey, and Straight, quite good. George Freedley (*NYMT*) said, "The actors . . . seem more like students undertaking a task with hope and enthusiasm than actors playing their parts. Yet at the same time there is a fresh approach to playing which is both amusing and heartening."

All set changes were done by costumed actors (playing servants) in full view of the audience, the actors coming on to make the changes as if they had been eavesdropping on the previous scene. Occasionally they moved actors about as well as scenery. The scene changes, which gained considerable attention in the press, proved more time-consuming than was to be desired, and Rosamond Gilder (*TAM*), for one, would have preferred blackouts and mechanical scene-shifting techniques. Lockridge, however, said that the method "sounds a little precious, but in performance amounts to unassuming simplicity."

It was widely agreed that the company was not of Broadway quality, and that it took a good deal of nerve to play there so soon after the outstanding production starring Helen Hayes and Maurice Evans. The Chekhov Theatre Players, founded by Straight, had their home base in Ridgefield, Connecticut, to which they recently had moved from Devonshire, England, and normally performed by touring around the country in trucks and playing in schools and colleges against simple backgrounds with gaily colored screens that were flexible enough in their use to suggest almost any locale or shape. The present production came to New York in the midst of a fifteen-state tour.

(3) [Dramatic Revival] D: Chouteau Dyer; P: Equity Library Theatre; T: Hudson Park Branch of the New York Public Library (OB); 4/17/45

Chouteau Dyer, who had staged *Twelfth Night* for the New School's Dramatic Workshop the previous season with a company of students (one of them Marlon Brando, who had played Sebastian), repeated her expressive staging for the Equity Library Theatre. With its cast now consisting of professionals, the production seemed even better, at least to the one reviewer attending, George Freedley (*NYMT*). He thought it the best revival of the play he had ever seen in the United States. "Certainly it is more imaginative and genuinely light-hearted than the pompous" Theatre Guild revival, he suggested. Dyer "is concerned with putting the play across rather than with maintaining a tradition."

Lee Truhill played Viola excellently and was backed by outstanding interpretations of Olivia by Margretta Ramsey, Aguecheek by Jerry Holman, Sir Toby by John Regan, Maria by Patricia Hosley, and Feste by Marc Spinelli. Van Grona repeated

(4) D: Valentine Windt; DS: Louis Kennel; P: Roger Stevens; T: Empire Theatre; 10/3/49 (48)

This nonstar revival, staged in Elizabethan dress, was first offered at the Ann Arbor Drama Festival. It employed several excellent actors. Nina Foch was Olivia, Frances Reid was Viola, Arnold Moss was Malvolio, Henry Brandon was Orsino, Carl Benton Reid was Toby Belch, Philip Tonge was Aguecheek, Ruth Enders was Maria, and Harry Townes was Feste.

For some, like George Jean Nathan (*TBY*), it was an ordeal to sit through. Rosamond Gilder (*TAM*) complained that the production failed because director Windt had given equal stress to each of the play's three major elements, the Belch-Aguecheek-Feste drolleries, the anti-Malvolio prank, and the mixed-identity love story. Ward Morehouse (*NYS*) deemed the production not a complete letdown but generally unimpressive and "routine." Not all agreed with these and other nay-sayers. For example, Brooks Atkinson (*NYT*) judged the production "light and joyous," with Moss "giving us the best Malvolio of our time." "Mr. Windt's production has captured the buoyant spirit of the comedy. It has been put together out of attractive curtains . . . , a vast expanse of lovely sky, some catches of music and entrancing costumes." John Mason Brown (*SR*) submitted that "there is little wrong and almost everything right about the production. . . . Windt's direction is sprightly, swift-moving, and charming in touch and quality."

Unlike Nathan, who scored many of the actors for archness and artificiality, Brown thought the actors vital and believable and praised their speaking and moving graces. "Frances Reid . . . is an ingratiating Viola. Although lacking the full-throated voice which would grant her lovelier speeches their final melody, and sometimes unmindful of the laughter latent in the double-meanings of her scenes with Olivia and Orsino, she is none the less gay and captivating." Morehouse singled out Foch's Olivia as the best performance. "She is an enchanting Olivia, radiant in appearance, speaks the verse clearly, and is definitely a young woman who has improved as an actress." Almost every leading player, however, found himself or herself blessed by some and damned by others.

TWO BLIND MICE [Comedy/Journalism/Military/Old Age/Politics/Romance] A/D: Samuel Spewack; S/L: Albert Johnson; C: Natalie Barth Walker; P: Archer King and Harrison Woodhull; T: Cort Theatre; 3/2/49 (157)

Kiss Me, Kate, for which Spewack was colibrettist with his wife Bella, was already a season hit when the author provided 1948-1949 Broadway with another success, this one being a political satire starring Melvyn Douglas in his first Broadway role in fourteen years. The subject of the comedy was a Washington agency known as the Office of Seeds and Standards a.k.a. the Office of Medicinal Herbs. Although voted out of existence by Congress four years earlier, the place, run by two charming old biddies, Mrs. Letitia Turnbull (Laura Pierpont) and Mrs. Crystal Hower (Mabel Paige), has remained open for business as if nothing had ever happened. To keep the place operating without costing the taxpayers anything, the old ladies purchase their own stamps and stationary, refuse to answer calls, and burn their salary checks. They also help make ends meet by renting space to a rhumba instructor (Roland Wood), a black pants presser (Alonzo Bosan) who rehearses his choir in the basement, and a young married couple expecting a baby. A smart-alec reporter, Tommy Thurston (Douglas), who married and then divorced Karen Norwood (Jan Sterling), a niece of one of the old ladies, sees what is going on and learns that they are threatened with eviction. A practical joker, he creates a plan to fool the army, navy, air force, and State Department into thinking that a top secret operation regarding "herbological warfare" is going on in the agency and that he is in charge of the mission. The farcical plot gets more and more complicated until the reporter, using an incriminating photo, blackmails a cost-cutting politician, Senator Kruger (Frank Tweddell), into passing a law that will put the agency back in business. There is also a reconciliation between Karen, engaged to a stuffy doctor (Richard Kendrick), and Tommy, with whom she engages in frequent badinage.

The critics enjoyed the performances, but not many were overly enthused about

The critics enjoyed the performances, but not many were overly enthused about the play, most thinking that it had a clever premise that ran out of steam. Hobe. (*V*) found it "strained, synthetic and never more than mildly funny." Rowland Field (*NEN*) thought it "a strident farce in which a gay basic idea is stretched almost to the breaking point by far-fetched exaggerations." Thomas R. Dash (*WWD*) wrote, "*Two Blind Mice* in its amiable arraignment of the cockeyed doings in Washington generates considerable merriment," but found a good deal to cavil about. Robert Coleman (*NYDM*), however, said, "It is going to make a lot of customers howl gleefully." The piece was selected as one of the ten best of the season. Actors in the play included Geoffrey Lumb as a statesman, Howard St. John as a journalist, and Elliott Reid as a comically puzzled ensign.

TWO MRS. CARROLLS, THE [Drama/Art/British/Crime/France/Marriage/Mystery/Romance] A: Martin Vale (Mrs. Bayard Veiller); D: Reginald Denham; S: Frederick Fox; P: Robert Reud and Paul Czinner; T: Booth Theatre; 8/3/43 (585)

A 1935 British comedy-melodrama that received tepid reviews but went on to become a major hit. It was expertly cast, with leading roles played by Victor Jory, Viennese actress Elisabeth Bergner, and, in her Broadway debut, Irene Worth.

The central role was that of Sally, the second Mrs. Carroll, played by Bergner and originated in London by Elena Miramova. Many thought her performance so able that it single-handedly carried the play. Euphemia Van Rensselaer Wyatt (*CW*) even argued that her colleagues should now and then attend a play and forget about its dramaturgic flaws when in the presence of a performance that used the script as a vehicle for such thoroughly absorbing acting. Reported Rosamond Gilder (*TAM*), "She swings from the gay, the tender, the troubled, to the terrified, the horror-stricken with an ease that delights the dazzled observer. Miss Bergner knows her business. She provides the profound, almost physical satisfaction of perfect timing and superb craftsmanship. She can hold a gesture to the exact breaking-point. She can suffuse her whole body with the mood of the moment." But Gilder noted one weakness: "She does not win you to any sympathy with the character she is so expertly portraying; she lacks the gift of sharing an experience."

Set in a villa on the French Riviera over a two-month period, the action examines the behavior of a handsome, idealistic, beauty-worshipping artist named Geoffrey Carroll (Jory), who is married to his ecstatically happy second wife, Sally. Living next door is the glamorous Cecily Harden (Worth). Mrs. Harden is said to have been the cause of the villa's previous tenant's having shot herself when she feared that her spouse and Mrs. Harden were having an affair. Geoffrey asks Cecily--who would not mind becoming the third Mrs. Carroll--to pose for a picture of the Angel of Death, his idea being that death can be more beautiful than life. He decides to kill his wife because that is easier than getting a divorce. The unattractive first Mrs. Carroll, Harriet (Vera Allen), arrives to inform her successor that Geoffrey is trying to slowly poison her via her nightly glass of milk, as he tried with her, but the devoted Sally, despite feeling wobbly, refuses to credit this. When her health begins to slip, however, Sally begins to fight for her survival. As the plot thickens, she nearly loses her life. The villain is foiled at the last minute when he attempts to kill her by making her death look like the work of an intruder, and he takes the poison himself. (Although the poison is supposedly slow-acting, he dies at once.)

Problems were found with the play's failure to maintain suspense, its uninspired dialogue, patches of inaction, predictability, the length of time it took for the murderous plot to be unveiled, and the failure to fully explore Geoffrey's psychological aberration while favoring the character of Sally instead. George Freedley (*NYMT*) dubbed it "a somewhat loosely constructed melodrama" that was "a dud which promised but never delivered." Howard Barnes (*NYHT*) caviled that "it packs quite a jolt in its final scenes, but it takes an unconscionable time in arriving at its climax and the motivation for an attempted murder does not even have a base of credible insanity."

Philip Tonge played a doctor who attributes Sally's weakness to a change in climate, Margery Maude played Cecily's mother, Stiano Braggiotti was Sally's former suitor, and Michelette Burani was a maid. Of newcomer Worth, Wilella

Waldorf (*NYP*) said that she was "a striking young woman . . . who comes to the theatre from the movies and makes a splendid sophisticated foil for Miss Bergner's appealing personality."

U

UNCLE HARRY [Drama/Crime/Family/Legacy/Mystery/Period/Prison/Small Town] A: Thomas Job; D: Lem Ward; S/L: Howard Bay; C: Peggy Clark; P: Clifford Hayman i/a/w Lennie Hatten; T: Broadhurst Theatre; 5/20/42 (430)

Toward the end of what had proved to be an uninspiring season arrived this effective murder mystery that turned into a major hit and was also selected as one of Burns Mantle's ten best of the year. Written by a Yale University professor, the play previously had had an unsuccessful road tryout with Russell Collins. The playwright, however, disagreed with the casting of Joseph Schildkraut, a slender Continental, believing that the role required "a sandy-haired, blue-eyed, slightly pot-bellied Welshman," as Schildkraut wrote in *My Father and I*. He talked the writer into perceiving the role in a new way and even persuaded him to move the action from Wales to French Canada and to change the period. Schildkraut, moreover, convinced the producer to cast his close friend and former costar, Eva Le Gallienne, instead of Pauline Lord, in the female lead.

Schildkraut and his wife raised the money for the show themselves, but were barely able to raise enough to open. There was no money for an out-of-town tryout, so they opened "cold." Playwright Job was dissatisfied with the interpretation because the melodramatic elements had been toned down in favor of the romantic and comical. Then, just before the opening, Schildkraut's wife said, "I wouldn't give you a dollar fifty for the whole play. The end was terribly anticlimactic. For heaven's sake, cut out the epilogue." The furious actor argued that it was this scene that had inspired him to do the play in the first place. But the epilogue was cut, the prologue was rewritten, and the play was a hit.

Using a flashback device, the play begins in the back room of a tavern in a small Quebec town with middle-aged Harry Quincy (Schildkraut) telling a stranger (Guy Sampsel) about a killing he committed and quoting from Thomas De Quincey's *Murder as One of the Fine Arts*. The scene moves back in time to 1909 and the home in which the gentle and repressed bachelor lives with his domineering spinster sisters, Hester (Adelaide Klein) and Lettie (Le Gallienne), and where his ex-fiancée, Lucy (Beverly Roberts), has come to declare that she is going to marry someone else. Harry's sisters have interfered in his love life because the terms of their father's legacy decreed that all three siblings share equally in the estate. Harry blames his jealous sisters for his having lost Lucy and begins to plan the perfect crime to get rid of them. His scheme involves tricking Lettie into purchasing prussic acid (presumably to kill their dog) and then having her serve a cup of poisoned cocoa to Hester. The evidence having been concocted to make Lettie appear guilty (a maid [Leona Roberts] is a crucial witness), she is accused, convicted, and sentenced to hang. When Harry learns that Lucy will never wed him, even with his sisters out of the way, his conscience begins to bother him so badly that he writes out a confession, and gives it to the prison warden. But when Lettie is shown the confession she refuses to acknowledge it, preferring to punish her brother by going to her death and letting him suffer the resultant guilt. Harry must suffer further from his failure to get anyone to believe his tale.

Because the murderer was known from the start, the usual suspense did not hold true in this melodrama. This served, however, to heighten audience interest even more, and the gloomy proceedings were balanced by fresh infusions of humor every now and then. There was little of thematic importance in the piece, but it was considered an immensely entertaining example of its genre. *Uncle Harry* was recommended to those interested in a literate murder mystery and not those seeking more overt dramatic excitement. Some felt, though, that the ironic ending was too much of an artificial contrivance and that a more melodramatic climax was called for. "Mr. Job's study is done in terms more nearly related to theatricalism than to dramatic literature," thought John Beaufort (*CSM*). "But, while that affects the stature of the play, it does not detract from the shrewdness of its execution." Rowland Field (*NEN*) claimed that the play was "a lethal escapade brimming with suspense and full-strength chills." On the more negative side was Louis Kronenberger (*PM*), who opined, "The plot is interesting, but over-extended. The characters are interesting, but rather inconsistent. The author has the virtue of relentlessness, but pushes it so far that it becomes a fault--and a trick. The writing is skillful, but the construction is clumsy." John Mason Brown (*NYWT*) thought that it would have been improved if it had moved more quickly and if it had had some judicious pruning.

In addition to relishing the dark moods of this psychological thriller, most critics took considerable pleasure in the meticulously realistic direction and the compelling acting, particularly that of the leads. Supporting players included Wauna Paul, Ralph Theadore, Karl Malden, John McGovern, Bruce Adams, and A. P. Kaye.

UNCLE VANYA (***Dyadya Vanya***) [Dramatic Revival*] A: Anton Chekhov; TR: Constance Garnett; D: John Burrell; S/C: Tanya Moiseiwitsch; L: John Sullivan; P: Theatre Incorporated i/a/w the Old Vic Company; T: Century Theatre; 5/13/46 (5)

One of the five plays produced in repertory by the visiting Old Vic company of London on its first American tour, with artistic directors Ralph Richardson and Laurence Olivier demonstrating their range in a wide variety of roles. Olivier was Astrov in *Uncle Vanya*, and Richardson was the title character, also known as Voynitsky. Ena Burrill was Marina, Nicholas Hannen was the professor, Margaret Leighton was Yelena, Joyce Redman was Sonya, George Relph was Telyegin or "Waffles," Byrony Chapman was Marya Voynitsky, and William Monk was Yefim.

This first New York showing of the play since 1930 came as a bit of a disappointment to the critics after the company's excellent productions of *Henry IV, Part I** and *Part II*. According to Lewis Nichols (*NYT*), the play seemed too gloomy and lacking in action for sustained audience interest, and the company did not seem to have fully fleshed out all the details of its characters. He also felt that the somberness of the play had been marred by some extraneous comic infusions. One such instance was the farcelike treatment of the attempted shooting of the professor by Uncle Vanya. This undue comedy also disturbed others, such as John Mason Brown (*SR*), who thought that there was room for laughter in the melancholy play, but that which was evoked on this occasion was inappropriate, seeming to be parodistic of the playwright's familiar dark moods. Brown considered the play less important than several other Chekhov dramas, but "extraordinary" nonetheless.

The best performance was that of Olivier as the forestry-loving doctor. "He has a fine flair for comedy," wrote Brown, "an inventive sense of business, a wonderfully accurate eye for character, and a charming personality." However, Louis Kronenberger (*PM*) faulted him for not being completely convincing and suggested that he might have been better as the professor. Also well liked was Leighton, but there were mixed opinions about most of the others, including Richardson, whose Uncle Vanya was too redolent of his brilliant work as Falstaff.

There were also critical comments aimed at the stiff translation, the stock company decor, and the portentously dull direction. Those who had seen Jed Harris's 1930 version felt that the Old Vic's was inferior.

UNDER THE COUNTER [Musical/British/Military/Romance/Theatre] B: Arthur Macrae; M: Manning Sherwin; LY: Harold Purcell; D: Jack Hulbert; CH: Jack Hulbert and John Gregory; DS: Clifford Pember; P: Lee Ephraim i/a/w the Messrs. Shubert; T: Shubert Theatre; 10/3/47 (27)

This British musical comedy import, advertised as "a comedy with music," employed the considerable talents of British musical comedy star Cicely Courtneidge (not seen locally since 1925) in the leading role of aging British musical comedy star Jo Fox. The show, rebuked as "a sickly bit of would-be funny stuff" by Robert Garland (*NYJA*), was little more than a vehicle for Courtneidge's music-hall antics. Euphemia Van Rensselaer Wyatt (*CW*) said that "for sheer exuberance of spirits, [she] seems to outspring Beatrice Lillie."

Jo is in love with director Mike Kenderdine (Ballard Berkeley), whom she has not seen in five years because he has been serving as a major in the war. Her attempt to marry him years ago went awry because he was irritated by her manipulative methods. Even now she occupies herself in similar behavior, being a wheeler-dealer on the black market. Mike, on leave from the army, shows up in London but is stationed in Paris. Jo uses all her clever wiles to arrange for him to be transferred home so that he can direct her new production and marry her. Her efforts prove successful.

The show was considered tedious and too topically British (especially its satire on the black market), and Courtneidge, onstage almost throughout, was appreciated by those who found her knockabout style their cup of tea. Howard Barnes (*NYHT*), wondering why it had been a London hit, said that it had three acts, "and the last two are deplorable." He added that the zany star lacked witty dialogue and funny situations on which to expend her talents.

Wilfred Hyde-White played Sir Alex Dunne, a Labour lord in the British cabinet. Other cast members included John Gregory, Thorley Walters, and Glen Alyn. Songs included "The Moment I Saw You" and "Everywhere."

UNDER THIS ROOF [Drama/Business/Marriage/Period/Politics/Romance/Rural/War] A: Herbert B. Ehrmann; D: Russell Lewis; S: Perry Watkins; C: Ernest R. Schrapps; P: Russell Lewis and Rita Hassan; P: Windsor Theatre; 2/22/42 (17)

A period chronicle drama set in the midnineteenth century, but with topical relevance for 1942. Written by a Boston attorney who had studied playwriting under George Pierce Baker, this was a seriously intended effort that moved on leaden feet through the years from 1846 to 1873 to tell a tale too bogged down with dramatic contrivances to keep an audience consistently attentive.

It is set in an eighteenth-century farmhouse near Wachusett, outside of Boston. Here young Cornelia (Barbara O'Neil) chooses not to marry Gibeon Warren (Peter Hobbs), whom she loves, because she does not wish to face the uncertainties of life as the spouse of an Abolitionist radical. His more conservative brother Ezra (Russell Hardie), who wants to earn money in business, seems far the wiser, more stable choice. Years pass and in 1864, to her confusion, her son David (John Draper), an idealist like his uncle, chooses to fight for the cause of freedom at a time when others are buying substitutes to fight for them. He subsequently is slain in the Battle of the Wilderness. After the war, during the Panic of 1873, Ezra's fortune and reputation are ruined by his involvement in a corrupt, unpatriotic scheme concerning the transcontinental railroad. Cornelia's erroneous choice in 1846 has led to the subsequent disasters that she has faced.

The play had decent ideas in its contrast of complacency and idealism but was burdened by dreary dramaturgy. It lacked suspense, strong dramatic conflict, and rounded characters. Norton Mockridge (*NYWT*) stated that the "play . . . is confused, poorly written, badly constructed and . . . as leisurely as a churchless Sunday morning." It also suffered from mediocre direction. There were a few good performances, especially O'Neil's. In the cast were actors such as James O'Neill, Harlan Briggs, Louise Galloway, and Howard St. John.

UNIFORM OF FLESH [Drama/Crime/Law/Military/Period/Sea/Trial/Verse] A: Louis O. Coxe and Robert H. Chapman; SC: Herman Melville's novel, *Billy Budd,*

Foretopman; D: Norris Houghton; DS: Paul Morrison; P: Invitational Series of the Experimental Theatre; T: Lenox Hill Playhouse (OB); 1/29/49 (7)

An all-male, blank-verse play based on a great nineteenth-century novel about the sea and a saintly young man sacrificed to the necessities of a brutal naval law. The play would reemerge in a revised 1951 version under Melville's original title and would become a frequently staged work in many theatres. Hobe. (*V*), in the minority, thought that the 1949 version--shown only to invited audiences--was "a ponderous drama with insufficient point." But George Freedley (*NYMT*) called it "an absorbing drama," and Richard Watts, Jr. (*NYP*), thought it "a work of exceptional interest both emotionally and intellectually." Brooks Atkinson (*NYT*) opined that it was "a thoroughly engrossing piece of work, well directed and well acted and well worth mulling over for the comment it makes on good and evil." His minor cavils included the "too gaudy" title, the sometimes "ridiculously archaic" language, the obscurity of some of the ideas, and the failure to fully dramatize Claggart's sadism toward the men.

The episodic play, presenting an allegorical conflict between pure good and evil, is set on a British battleship, H.M.S. *Indomitable*, in 1799 and tells of how the physically and spiritually beautiful, but stammering, sailor Billy (Charles Nolte) is tormented by the sadistic Master-at-Arms Claggart (Peter Hobbs). In the presence of Captain Vere (Tom McDermott), his hesitant speech so frustrates him on being falsely accused by Claggart of attempted mutiny that he lashes out and kills the bully. Billy subsequently is court-martialed and hung. Although various officers defend Billy, his death is used by the captain as an example to the men, whose discipline must be maintained because of fear of subversion following the French Revolution and reports of a British mutiny.

Although produced for only $500, the play was imaginatively set and costumed and used an expressive score of sea chanties arranged by Lehman Engel and sung by a quartet of sailors between the acts. Houghton's staging received kudos for "capturing color, credibility and strength" (Watts). The cast of twenty-five's acting was highly thought of, including performances by Preston Hanson, Robert McQueeny, Martin Brandt, Anthony Carr, Paul Anderson, Winston Ross, John Fisher, and Sherman Lloyd. Lee Marvin as Payne was making one of his few New York appearances.

The story of how director Houghton got the piece produced on Broadway two years later (2/10/51) is told in his *Entrances and Exits*.

UNQUIET SPIRIT, THE (*L'Ame en Peine*) [Drama/Drugs/French/Marriage/Sex] A: Jean-Jacques Bernard; D: Juel Rodack; P: "Q" Productions; T: Little Theatre (Hotel Sutton); 5/30/50

An interesting metaphysical endeavor about how one's success or failure is determined by the chance associations one makes in life. It was staged in an East Fifty-sixth Street hotel auditorium. The premise is that two promising individuals, Marceline (Carey Calvert) and Antoine (Kevin Gillespie), never meet and therefore waste both their lives. They now and then cross one another's paths, never closely enough to meet but enough somehow to affect each other's feelings. The wealthy Marceline marries a sensitive engineer (William Malkin), whom she does not really love, ultimately becomes unfaithful with many men, and turns to drugs in her quest for new excitement. Antoine, a social misfit, remains single, can not remain on a job, and fails to establish permanent relationships. Marceline determines to divorce her husband and tries to justify her behavior to him (behavior presumably influenced by Antoine).

"This is a delicate play, with no great point to prove, but rather stands as an expert illustration of a perfectly feasible idea," noted William Hawkins (*NYWT*). J. P. S. (*NYT*) thought the play "an absorbing study of some confused and unhappy people," given an excellent performance by Calvert, but an inept one by the rest of the company.

(1) UP IN CENTRAL PARK [Musical/Hotel/Journalism/Music/Period/Politics/Romance] B: Herbert and Dorothy Fields; M: Sigmund Romberg; LY: Dorothy

Fields; D: John Kennedy; CH: Helen Tamiris; S: Howard Bay; C: Grace Houston and Ernest Schrapps; P: Michael Todd; T: Century Theatre; 1/27/45 (504)

Producer Mike Todd parlayed some of the most outstanding creative talents in the musical theatre into a substantial hit show that, for all its claims to be a "musical play," was really an old-fashioned piece verging on operetta. Todd had recently read Dennis Lynch's *Boss Tweed and His Gang* and was gazing out on Boston Commons when he got the idea of doing a show about Central Park, with the rapacious Tweed as a central figure.

The notion of a musical set in the 1870s, when the *New York Times* was crusading against the corrupt politician "Boss" William Marcy Tweed (Noah Beery, Sr.), who was stealing from the tax levies for his own pocket, proved a worthwhile one. The soon-discovered fact that among Tweed's activities was his involvement in graft connected with the park's development (Tweed's contractors charged the city government $800,000 for benches alone) further demonstrated the viability of the concept. The park was definitely developed, but at outrageous costs to the taxpayers. The *Times* lambasted Tweed in the editorials of Lewis Jennings, while the acid-dipped cartoons of Thomas Nast were being published in *Harper's Weekly*, both publications allegedly being offered bribes from the Tweed faction to cease and desist from their mudslinging. Tweed was eventually convicted of larceny and imprisoned on Blackwell's Island.

These facts form the background to the semifictionalized libretto of *Up in Central Park*, where the *Times* journalist is named John Matthews (Wilbur Evans) and is only partly based on Jennings. John and Rosie Moore (Maureen Cannon, who assumed the role at the last minute), daughter of Tweed ward heeler Timothy Moore (Charles Irwin), fall in love. She, however, chooses to marry Richard Connolly (George Lane), New York's comptroller and a Tammany crony of Tweed's, when she is promised aid in becoming a famous singer. She also seeks revenge on John for his exposés of her father. Rosie learns to regret her choice when Tweed's corruption is exposed through the efforts of the press. Her husband turns out to be a bigamist whose marriage to her is illegal. A year later, while in New York to study music, she meets John at a park concert, and they are happily reunited.

The show's lavish expenditure provided lovely costumes suggestive of Godey's *Lady Book* and one gorgeous set after the other, each with a Currier and Ives lithograph atmosphere. "It is a souvenir album of picture postcards," approved John Chapman (*NYDN*). There were vibrant scenes in the Stetson Hotel, Central Park Gardens, the Zoo, and the Mall, among others. The most memorable show-stopping number began with a character named Joe Stewart (Fred Barry) showing his gal (Elaine Barry) a series of Currier and Ives etchings, each of which came to resplendent tableau life, climaxing with a ballet simulating ice skating ("April Snow") in Central Park that used one hundred pounds of expensive stage snow nightly.

The lugubriously paced, dullish book was excoriated by many for slowing down the show and for not taking sufficient advantage of Tweed's colorful presence. Some, however, thought it a literate and intelligent, if not especially funny, effort. The songs did not become standards, but were highly praised, among them being "Close as Pages in a Book," "Carousel in the Park," "The Big Back Yard," "When She Walks in the Room," "It Doesn't Cost You Anything to Dream," and "The Fireman's Bride." George Freedley (*NYMT*) called the score "melodious and richly rewarding."

In Burton Rascoe's (*NYWT*) opinion, "This is one of the most charming musicals ever staged and doubtless will become a classic." Euphemia Van Rensselaer Wyatt (*CW*) pointed out, "Mr. Todd has contributed an operetta rich in local color and in flawless taste but with not quite enough politics!" Yet Lewis Nichols (*NYT*) regretted that the show "plods along where it should dance, it talks where it should laugh; it is long and . . . is pretty dull."

Thomas Nast was played by Maurice Burke, and Betty Bruce scored in the soubrette role of Bessie O'Cahane, Rosie's friend, although her tap dancing was superior to her comedy. Also involved were Walter Burke, Guy Standing, Jr., Daniel Nagrin, and Robert Field, among others.

On opening night Todd provided a lavish, $10,000 champagne supper dance at Central Park's Tavern-on-the-Green restaurant; continuing the nineteenth-century theme of the show, the critics were brought to the affair in broughams pulled by horses, which were also employed to get the critics to the theatre in the first place. (It was a Saturday night, so the critics did not have to worry about deadlines.)

(2) [Return Engagement] T: City Center of Music and Drama; 5/19/47 (16)

Following an exhausting but very profitable tour, the show returned to New York to play a limited engagement at the City Center at popular prices. Earle MacVeigh was now playing John Matthews, Guy Standing, Jr., was Nast, and Malcolm Lee Beggs was Tweed.

In George Freedley's (*NYMT*) view, the show had greatly deteriorated, becoming "tired and tawdry." Some expressed disdain for the show, new or old, among them Brooks Atkinson (*NYT*), who had not reviewed the original. He thought that most of the work fell "into the general spirit of cliché. . . . It contains nearly everything that the musical stage has tossed into the discard and declared surplus property." Most others did not object strongly and welcomed the show as a worthwhile bargain.

UP THE REBELS! [Drama/Family/Military/Period/Politics/Romance/War] A: Sean Vincent (Father Larnen, O.P.); D: Dennis Gurney; S: Edward Rutyna; P: Blackfriars' Guild; T: Blackfriars' Theatre (OB); 10/30/41 (4)

An uneven but occasionally forceful nine-scene chronicle play covering a quarter of a century and concentrating on the Irish uprisings between 1916 and 1922, with historical background on the travails of the Irish Republican Army and the establishment of the Irish Free State. The plight of two families, the Boyces and the Dunnings, is shown as they conflict politically and emotionally over a span of two generations. For example, Kathleen Boyce (Barbara Barton) is engaged to one of the rebel Dunnings (William Hollenbeck) although her brother (Paul Wendel) holds a British army commission. The latter eventually sacrifices his commission to fight on Ireland's side following his disgust at the British army's atrocities during the Black and Tan events.

Author Vincent (a priest's pen name), while holding a disparaging view of England, nevertheless called for a humane and peaceful approach to world events wherein he detected a worse menace than the neighboring island. The production was respectfully welcomed, the acting and writing being better than expected. Robert Francis (*BE*) commented that the playwright "has drawn an interesting and sometimes moving picture of events. He has touched it with humor. But his craftsmanship is not equal to the task he has set himself."

This was the first performance by a new group producing plays Off Broadway, the Blackfriars, sponsored by the Dominican order, which already had dramatic outlets in eleven other cities nationwide. They had begun in 1931 in Washington, D.C., where they had been founded by the Reverend Urban Nagle and the Reverend Thomas Carey. Their offerings were intended to reflect Catholic ideals and beliefs. The company consisted of professionals, although none of them in this first production were especially well known.

V

VAGABOND KING, THE [Musical Revival*] B/LY: Brian Hooker and Russell Janney; M: Rudolf Friml; D: George Ermoloff; CH: Igor Schwezoff; S: Raymond Sovey; C: James Reynolds; P: Russell Janney; T: Shubert Theatre; 6/29/43 (56)

This first New York revival of the romantic 1925 operetta hit had a mixed reception. Instead of getting a lush new treatment, wrote George Jean Nathan (*TBY*), "the manner suggested a fancy dress party of haberdashery clerks and their ladies." The new Villon was Metropolitan Opera singer John Brownlee, whose diction, said Nathan, turned a line like "Would it not be a pity, sweet lady?" into "Would ut nut be pity, sweat lady?" His Katherine de Vaucelles was played by beauteous Frances McCann, who departed the cast of *Rosalinda* to take the role.

Some critics defended the stars, but most approved their singing more than their histrionics. Brownlee especially seemed a wooden reminder of Dennis King's Villon. Also in the cast were José Ruben as a spidery Louis XI (one of the better performances), Will H. Philbrick as the comical Guy Tabarie, Arline Thomson as Huguette, Douglas Gilmore as Tristan l'Hermite, Ben Roberts as Thibaut D'Aussigny, Teri Keane as Lady Mary, Betty Berry as the queen, and Curtis Cooksey as the effeminate Oliver le Dain, among others.

On the whole, the reviewers thought the book mildewed and creaky and its attempts at humor labored, but the score melodious and worth listening to again. "All in all," went Howard Barnes's (*NYHT*) middling verdict, "the present revival of a second-rate musical play is on the sorry side." But apart from his distress at Brownlee's casting and the staging of one of the numbers, Burton Rascoe (*NYWT*) applauded the show as "far more sumptuous and exhilarating than the original." The songs that stood out were "Drinking Song," "Only a Rose," "Love Me Tonight," "Song of the Vagabonds," and "Serenade."

VELVET GLOVE, THE [Comedy/Journalism/Religion/Old Age/Politics/University] A: Rosemary Casey; D/P: Guthrie McClintic; S/L: Donald Oenslager; T: Booth Theatre; 12/26/49 (152)

Veteran Broadway star Grace George was the chief draw in this comically mild defense of freedom of speech set within the office of a mother superior at a convent in northern New York. Ten days after the opening, on a Friday, George's husband, long-time producer William A. Brady, passed away, but George and her granddaughter Barbara Brady (making her Broadway debut in the play) went on with the show like troupers and did not miss a performance.

The Velvet Glove pictured George as the kindly Mother-General Hildebrand, celebrating her silver anniversary in God's service when she encounters a serious problem that she overcomes by using her native wit and good sense. The archconservative Bishop Gregor (John Williams) has decided to dismiss progressive, young, lay history professor Tom Pearson (James Noble) from his teaching position at the Catholic girls' university. The reason is Pearson's expression of liberal sentiments, distortedly reported in a newspaper article that calls them communistic. Although the newspaper publisher (Ben Lackland) apologizes for the article, the bishop refuses to budge. Pearson, who explains that his misquoted comments were actually from a pope's encyclical, also happens to be involved in a touch-and-go romance with Mother Hildebrand's secretary (Brady). The saintly but pragmatic Mother Hildebrand must exercise all her ingenuity to get the bishop to reverse his decision. Her campaign--aided by the aged Monsignor Burke (Walter Hampden)--involves church politics, sources providing endowment funds, and arguments concerning freedom of the press. Only when the bishop learns that fund-raising efforts on behalf of a new seminary are to be canceled does he back off. Despite all her efforts, Mother Hildebrand never compromises her religious beliefs in her ultimately successful path toward gaining the righftul conclusion.

Despite a wispy plot and a lack of inspiration, the play was widely considered "a literate, cleverly devised" (Louis Sheaffer [*BE*]) comedy on a worthwhile and significant theme. Disregarding its thinness, Rowland Field (*NEN*) felt that "it has been so affectingly presented in writing and performance that the charm is constantly maintained." But Arthur Pollock (*DC*) and a few others dismissed it as a trifle, too lightweight, sugary, and contrived for its own good.

George gave a highly adept performance. "Her character etching . . . is magnificent," reported Thomas R. Dash (*WWD*). Good acting was displayed by Jean Dixon as Sister Monica, Naomi Riordan as Sister Lucy, and Will Davis as Father Benton.

A similar theme had been the subject of plays such as *The Male Animal** and *Goodbye, My Fancy*. *The Velvet Glove* won the first annual Christopher award ($5,000) for a drama that promoted Christian ideals in American life.

VICKIE [Comedy/Marriage/Military/Science/Sex/War/Women] A: S. M. Herzig; D: José Ferrer and Frank Mandel; S: Ernest Glover; P: Frank Mandel; T: Plymouth Theatre; 9/22/42 (48)

Actor José Ferrer, who shared his duties with Frank Mandel, made his Broadway directing debut with this breathlessly paced but mindless farce that costarred him with his then wife, Uta Hagen. The play was a satire on the dangers represented by overzealous women wartime volunteers.

Set in a New York suburb during a September weekend, this "undistinguished, heavy-handed romp" (Brooks Atkinson [*NYT*]) pictures the domestic affairs of George (Ferrer) and Vickie Roberts (Hagen). George is a henpecked engineer who has invented a machine in which the War Production Board has shown an interest. Vickie belongs to one of the women's volunteer uniformed services, the AWCS (American Women's Camp Service), which, commanded by the flinty Mrs. Dunne (Mildred Dunnock), provides sandwiches to the armed forces. The empty-headed women make peanut butter sandwiches for the Canteen, but these are inadvertantly wrapped in the plans for George's invention and are retrieved only after various mix-ups. A pair of girl-hungry rookie soldiers (Red Buttons, in his Broadway debut, and Edmund Glover) are billeted at the house (Vickie also belongs to the EGS or Emergency Godmother Services) for the weekend and run after two sexy women (Colette Lyons and Gerry Carr) living next door. There is also an intrusive old man (Frank Conlan) on the balcony working as a plane spotter. The usually patient George is going nuts because of all the distractions from his work on the invention. Things get too hectic for the cook (Evelyn Davis), so she leaves, her replacement being the enormous ex-Metropolitan Opera star Greta (Margarete Matzenauer, a famous Wagnerian soprano), who cannot stop warbling opera tunes. When a WPB representative (Charles Halton) comes to inspect George's inventive contribution, Vickie and her cohorts suspect that he is a spy and tie him up. When they realize their error, they blackmail their captor into accepting George's invention, since he turns out to be the sugar daddy of one of the women quartered in the house.

"Call it farce of the second flight, spottily funny, often goofy and amusing, but almost as often childishly far-fetched," summarized Richard Lockridge (*NYS*). The acting was not what it should have been, Hagen finding the farcical style out of her line. "Her voice with its curious note of suppressed anguish, its lilt and sob is more adapted to serious or pathetic roles," suggested Rosamond Gilder (*TAM*). Ferrer's farce talents were strained to their utmost in trying to make unfunny material laughworthy. One of the few to garner genuine approval for his comic gifts was former burlesque comic Red Buttons, whose name caused several critics to do a doubletake. Veteran Taylor Holmes was in the cast, playing Mildred Dunnock's silly husband.

VICTORS, THE (*Morts sans Sépulture*) [Drama/French/Politics/Sex/War/Youth] A: Jean-Paul Sartre; AD: Thornton Wilder; D: Mary Hunter; S/L: Robert Gundlach; P/T: New Stages (OB); 12/26/48 (31)

The first play given during its second season by the Off-Broadway cooperative group called New Stages was this 1946 naturalistic Sartre work also known in English as *The Unburied Dead* and *Men without Shadows*. The company had scored highly during its first season with Sartre's "The Respectful Prostitute."

The play is a philosophical melodrama in which ideas take precedence over action. Some of its most memorable scenes involve torture, and these made a powerful impact on viewers. To several critics it seemed garrulous and didactic, to others gripping and tense with important ideas. Similarly, some thought Mary Hunter's direction and the work of the ensemble distinguished, while others found the production limp.

The drama is set in southern France during the summer of the American invasion. Five resistance fighters (called Maquis) have been captured and imprisoned in a village schoolhouse attic following an aborted sortie. The five, who are being interrogated concerning the identity of their leader (John Larkin), include a sole woman (Florida Friebus), who becomes a rape victim; a Greek underground fighter (Boris Tumarin); the woman's frightened fifteen-year-old brother (Larry Robinson), who is strangled by his mates to prevent him from blabbing; a former medical student (Alexander Scourby); and a weakling (Ernest Stone) who finds the courage to kill himself rather than give in to his tormentors. The Vichy police leader (Leon Janney) uses physical and mental torture on his captives, but to little avail. The situation evolves into a great psychological battle of wills, each side determined to be the "victors." The situation allows for development of Sartre's existentialist ideas on man's need to take an active part in events and make choices--even under great duress--that determine his existence. A man's acts are seen to be the measure of his worth. The information finally provided by the captives turns out to be a ruse that leads the enemy into an ambush. The three remaining captives emerge triumphant.

One of the negative responses came from Thomas R. Dash (*WWD*), to whom the play was "a gloomy, depressing work which is a combination of long passages of static theatre and spurts of Grand Guignol. . . . *The Victors* is singularly unmoving and sometimes downright monotonous." Brooks Atkinson (*NYT*) disapproved of the character drawing and the "mechanical unreality" of the dramaturgy. Euphemia Van Rensselaer Wyatt (*CW*) was too squeamish to sit through it all. More approbatory was Ward Morehouse (*NYS*): "Notwithstanding a certain repetitiousness and a frequent garrulity, *The Victors* emerges as a play of dramatic values. . . . You will listen to it at every moment." And Richard Watts, Jr. (*NYP*), while cautioning weak-stomached playgoers, asserted that "it is . . . arresting and steadily absorbing drama for those who can stand its sadism. It is a work that is provocative to both the mind and the emotions."

VICTORY BELLES [Comedy/Family/Military/Romance/Sex/War] A: Alice Gerstenberg; D/P: Henry Adrian; S: Edward de Forrest; T: Mansfield Theatre; 10/26/43 (87)

Spectators left this "embarrassing" (K. S. [*NYT*]) play in droves during its performance, and it received some of the most scathing reviews ever printed. The fact that it managed to hold on for nearly three months was owing to the producer's vain attempt to give the show a feeling of prosperity by papering the house. K. S. said that "a group of actors and actresses, but one or two of whom could be understood, screamed their way through as dull and dreary and ineptly written a script as has been foisted upon the public in many a sad moon." "It has to be seen to be depreciated," scoffed Robert Garland (*NYJA*).

Several good actors were trapped in this tasteless stew about the husband shortage expected when the war concluded. It is set in Tarrytown, New York, and concerns the discovery of a local matron, Mrs. Grace Stewart (Mabel Taliaferro), that when the war ends there will be four and a half men to every seven women. She decides to guarantee a mate for her daughter Ann (Ellen Merrill) before the soldiers at a neighboring army camp are sent overseas. Her method is to invite eligible soldiers over for weekend parties, hoping that one will prove ideal. When this approach doesn't seem to be producing results for Ann and her friends, a thrice divorced family friend with worldly ways named Flo Hilliard (Barbara Bennett) agrees to instruct the damsels in how to seduce a man. To this end, she organizes them into what she calls Victory Belles. Soon the soldiers are chasing the girls up and down, in and around, with one girl's dress coming off in a romantic tussle. Mixed in with this story is one about a pistol-packing butler (Addison Randall) working for the family; he is actually an FBI man in disguise seeking a Nazi spy who turns out to be an army colonel (Raymond Van Sickle). When he spots the officer trying to remove a ring from a lady's finger, the butler bops him on the head with a telephone. He gets his man and the Victory Belles get theirs.

Robert Ober, Marie Gale, Sally Gracie, Ralph Clanton, Stanley Phillips, and Burton Mallory were among those in the play. The critics took note of the fact that Barbara Bennett was the sister of film stars Constance and Joan Bennett and was making her return to Broadway after many years in other media. She was married to the actor who played the butler.

VIE PARISIENNE, LA [Musical Revival] B: Henri Meilhac and Ludovic Halévy; M: Jacques Offenbach; D: Felix Brentano; S/C: Marco Montedoro; P: New Opera Company; T: Forty-fourth Street Theatre; 11/5/41

This 1866 French operetta had its ups and downs in the 1940s. When it was first revived in 1941 it gained some notice because it had been done over into English. Nevertheless, it was treated as a musical event and not a theatrical one.

Olin Downes (*NYT*) declared that the production came off like "an American musical comedy, done in a rather inferior American way, though with much muscularity and a tremendous display of energy." Only the performance of a virtually uncut score, supplemented by songs from other Offenbach works, made the event worthwhile. The text, however, while retaining the 1860s period and place, had suffered from thoughtless revisions, including the substitution of an American millionaire for the character of Baron Gondremark. None of the performers was considered worthy of notice, apart from comedian George Rasely. The show had a return engagement at the Broadway Theatre on 11/10/42, but was unreviewed.

(2) B: Felix Brentano and Louis Verneuil; LY: Marian Farquhar; D: Ralph Herbert; CH: Leonid Massine; S: Richard Rychtarik; C: Ladislas Czettel; P: Yolanda Mero-Irion for the New Opera Company; T: City Center of Music and Drama; 1/12/45 (37)

This was the first 1940s revival of the operetta to gain widespread attention as a theatrical event. Produced as a tryout before a long road tour, it was coadapted by the director of the previous versions, who did not direct it now, but it remained a production of the New Opera Company. On its third try the company seems to have gotten it right, partly because the score was considerably adapted by Antal Dorati, the conductor, and partly because it used good new singers. There were also excellent new sets and costumes, as well as effective choreography (particularly of the cancan). The new book modernized the story by setting it in the 1880s and making it about an American millionaire and his family on a Parisian spree, with a couple of French aristocrats attempting to trick the millionaire into getting rid of a valuable racehorse.

George Freedley (*NYMT*) called it "fresh, colorful and altogether delightful." Ward Morehouse (*NYS*) wrote that the show "provides an evening of lovely music, colorful stage groupings, fetching costumes and settings and the rhythms of the famous Can Can." But Howard Barnes (*NYHT*) observed, "The piece still remains a rather bombastic trifle, with a minimum of comedy and melodic eloquence." The leading performers were Marion Carter as Metella, Lillian Anderson as Evelyn, Frances Watkins as Gabrielle, Brian Lawrence as Comte Raoul de Gardefeu, Edward Roecker as Baron Bobinet, David Morris as Jackson, Arthur Newman as Hutchinson, and dancers Anna Istomina, Elena Kramarr, and James Lyons.

VIGIL, THE [Drama/Bible/Crime/Death/Religion/Small Town/Trial] A: Ladislas Fodor; D: Alexander Markey; DS: Nicholas Yellenti; P: Alexander Markey b/a/w George Jessel; T: Royale Theatre; 5/21/48 (11)

A trick "miracle play" based on the Resurrection of Jesus Christ and cast in the guise of a modern-dress courtroom trial with the actual audience cast as the jury (a device used in Ayn Rand's *Night of January 16** [1935]). The time of the action is the nights between Good Friday and Easter Sunday and the locale is a small-town courtroom anywhere in the United States. Various witnesses are called to the stand to testify on the events surrounding the Resurrection. The central question is whether the Gardener (Tom Fadden), working for the powerful Jew, Joseph of Arimathea (Lauren Gilbert), stole Jesus' body from the tomb and buried it behind an irrigation canal in order to substantiate Jesus' promise to return from the dead. Several witnesses raise doubts, others confirm the story.

Some found this dramatized struggle between skepticism and faith interesting and occasionally quite absorbing, but its parade of witnesses grew tedious and the dramatic impact gradually was weakened. "The play has a pervading literary quality," remarked William Hawkins (*NYWT*), "and entirely lacks pictorial action." "The craftsmanship is so untidy," added Howard Barnes (*NYHT*), "that much of the exposition takes the form of mere sermonizing." Brooks Atkinson (*NYT*) simply dismissed it as "cheap, plodding and wordy."

It was considered well acted by a large cast including Henry Wilcoxon as the Prosecutor (suggestive of the Devil), Ian MacDonald as the Counsel for the Defense, Maria Palmer as Mary, Milton Parsons as Saul, Ann Pearce as Susanna, Dan Reed as a professor of "angelology," King Donovan as a phony private eye, Helen Seamon as a barmaid, Joe E. Marks as a Jewish textile manufacturer, Guy Spaull and Muriel Hutchinson as the socialite Pilate and his wife, Walter (Jack) Palance as Simon, and, among others, Edward Van Sloan as the judge.

VILLAGE GREEN [Comedy/Art/Family/Politics/Romance/Small Town] A: Carl Allensworth; D: Felix Jacoves; S: Raymond Sovey; P: Dorothy and Julian Olney and Felix Jacoves; T: Henry Miller's Theatre; 9/3/41 (30)

A modest vehicle for homespun actor Frank Craven, this piece focused on the character of Judge Homer Peabody (Craven), a Democrat who has been trying for sixteen years to get elected to the state legislature from his Republican small town of North Oxford, New Hampshire. Onto the scene arrives Jeremiah Benton (John Craven, the star's son), a young artist who paints a mural for the town hall. On the mural is the symbolically depicted figure of a nude suckling her baby. This upsets the town's prudes, starting with the Reverend Horace Shurtleff (Calvin Thomas). When Jeremiah learns that the judge's daughter (Perry Wilson) may wed the callow Hubert Carter (Henry Jones), his dismay causes him to add the girl's face to his mural. Despite this potential blow to his current campaign, Judge Peabody, spurred by a visiting *Life* photographer (Norman Lloyd) and a liberal minister (Frank Wilcox), comes valiantly to the artist's defense. The judge's political aspirations are enhanced when the local liberals stand by his anticensorship platform, especially after an opposition member inadvertently sets fire to the town hall. The Republican boss (Matt Briggs) tries to buy him off and, this failing, does his best to ruin the judge's reputation. Although the election seems at one point to be going against him, the judge pulls through and wins the coveted office. The artist gains national acclaim as another Grant Wood or Thomas Hart Benton, and the nation's Constitution is upheld.

Most critics considered this a well-meaning but unimportant comedy, despite its pro-civil liberties stand. It was viewed as worthwhile theatregoing principally for Craven's acting. Still, a few critics had nice words to say about the writing. Ralph Warner (*DW*) thought it "an amusing, pleasant offering plentifully sprinkled with laughs" and with a point "worth saying." Richard Lockridge (*NYS*) declared, "It is as blandly transparent as a glass clock striking 12, with all the works outlined in Neon lights, but it is amiable, folksy, shirtsleeve comedy that does exactly what is expected from moment to moment."

Craven "was as benign and expert as ever," noted Rosamond Gilder (*TAM*). "He beamed over his eyeglasses at the audience, rehearsed his speeches for its benefit, exuded folksy charm." It was impossible for the actor to shake loose the aura of his stage manager character from *Our Town**, as there really was not that much difference between that role and Judge Peabody. One night, Craven blew his lines and began to ad-lib, impressing his fellow actors, Lloyd and Briggs. Briggs, however, afraid that Craven might not give him his cue, interrupted. "Wait a minute! Wait a minute!" said the now-inspired Craven, "Let me finish!" (reported by Tony Randall in *Which Reminds Me*). There were good supporting performances from Laura Pierpont as the judge's spouse and Joseph Allen as the town drunk, as well as by Maida Reade and John Ravold.

VIOLET [Comedy/Art/Family/Romance/Rural/Youth] A/D: Whitfield Cook; SC: Whitfield Cook's *Red Book Magazine* stories; S: Howard Bay; C: Grace Houston; P: Albert Margolies; T: Belasco Theatre; 10/24/44 (23)

Whitfield Cook's first theatrical endeavor was "old stuff and rather dull and monotonous at times," thought Edgar Price (*BC*). It is set in a Vermont farmhouse to which twice-married Pete Granden (Harvey Stephens), a would-be artist, has brought his potential third wife, Lily Foster (Helen Claire), a would-be singer, in order to spend a New Year's weekend and propose marriage. Each falsely claims to be an artistic success. Lily, his sweetheart of fifteen years earlier, does not know of his first two marriages, and he wants her to think that he has had no other woman on his mind all these years. Pete's designs are obstructed, however, by the arrival of his sister (Paula Trueman), his five obstreperous offspring by his marriages, and a sixth child, born to his first wife and her second husband. The thirteen-year-old daughter after whom the play is named (Patricia Hitchcock), a precocious little Miss Fix-It who thinks Lily an unsuitable third wife, sends telegrams to the first two wives, Crystal (Fay Baker) and Charlotte (Joan Vitez), bringing them to the farmhouse by claiming that one of the kids has measles. The wives arrive, but Lily wins Pete in the end, by which time their previous deceptions have been cleared up.

"What might have been an appealing little stage fable is severely hampered by inexpert writing and direction plus a generally poor performance," crabbed Rowland Field (*NEN*). Patricia Hitchcock, daughter of movie director Alfred Hitchcock, was aided by such players as Doro Merande, John Cherry, Len Hollister, Billy Nevard, Mason Adams, and Russell Gaige.

VIRGINIA REEL [Drama/Alcoholism/Family/Prostitution/Rural/Southern] A: John Weaver and Harriet Weaver; D: Gerald Savory; S: Richard Bernstein; L: Herbert Brodkin; P: Leonard Field i/a/w the American National Theatre and Academy and the Experimental Theatre; T: Princess Theatre; 4/13/47 (5)

A poorly received work offered for a limited run by the Experimental Theatre, devoted to showcasing new works. Edba. (*V*) thought it "the most tedious" of the five plays shown in 1946-1947. He said that the play often "slows up to a walk." George Freedley (*NYMT*) ripped the play for its formless structure, and Otis L. Guernsey, Jr. (*NYHT*), wrote, "It flares up only intermittently in the midst of a tiresome, dull gray absence of poignancy."

In the Blue Ridge country, near Royalton, Virginia, is the run-down rural post office and country store operated by alcoholic old Henry Haskins (Alan MacAteer). Creed (Barbara Leeds), the postmistress, is his chief prop, keeping him from debt and putting off her marriage to the lazy, harmonica-playing town playboy (James Daly). Another daughter, named May Belle (Jetti Preminger), returns after an eight-year absence spent as a prostitute in factory towns. She is the only character whose head is not lost in dreams, but her outraged sister tries to drive her away. The residents of the community, excited about a factory opening up locally, invest their savings in land, and the old man spruces up the store, but the investment advice proves to be false. A happy ending is rigged up, however, and Creed marries her boyfriend.

Cast members included Reta Shaw, Richard Shanklard, Robert Emhardt, and Don MacLaughlin.

VISITOR, THE [Drama/Crime/Family/Legacy/Mystery/Small Town/Youth] A: Kenneth White; SC: the novel of the same name by Leane Zugsmith and Carl Randau; D/P: Herman Shumlin; S: Howard Bay; T: Henry Miller's Theatre; 10/17/44 (23)

Herman Shumlin fell below his usual high standard in play selection when he chose this melodramatic folderol that took a promising situation and failed to satisfactorily dramatize it. It deals with a boy (Richard Hylton) who was thought drowned at the age of fourteen by his friend (William [Will] Hare), although his body was never recovered. An ex-police chief (Thomas Chalmers), seeking a $10,000 reward, finds the boy, now seventeen, in Baltimore and returns him to his wealthy mother (Frances Carson) and not wealthy father (Walter N. Greaza). The boy's puzzling behavior leads everyone, including his mother, to begin to doubt his identity, it being suspected that he is an imposter after a family inheritance. Eventually the mystery is cleared up, the boy turns out to be authentic, and a stepfather is found responsible for all the previous confusion.

The play was "random and soporific where it might have been truly terrifying," maintained Howard Barnes (*NYHT*). "It is diffuse, cluttered and exhausting--and very badly acted," commented Ward Morehouse (*NYS*). Anna Minot, Dorrit Kelton, and Ralph Forbes as the most likely suspect could do little to salvage the play.

VIVA O'BRIEN [Musical/Fantasy/Mexico/Romance] B: William K. and Eleanor Wells; M: Maria Grever; LY: Raymond Leveen; D: Robert Milton (comedy scenes: William K. Wells); CH: Chester Hale; S: Clark Robinson; C: John N. Booth, Jr.; P: John J. Hickey, Chester Hale, and Clark Robinson; T: Majestic Theatre; 10/9/41 (20)

A twenty-foot-long, nine-foot-deep pool, constituting part of the set for this elaborate "aquamusical," was deemed by many its most outstanding feature (there was also a waterfall, but its "water" was made of tons of sugar), which does not say much for the quality of the show. The best part came when Olympic champion Peter Desjardins demonstrated some fancy low- and high-board diving in company with a pair of other divers. As Rosamond Gilder (*TAM*) observed, the show "brought out all the old jokes, the old routines, the old tune-formulas and plot-absurdities of the duller musicals of twenty years ago."

The almost totally laughless flop, which allegedly was backed to the tune of nearly $100,000 by a wealthy Mexican hoping to promote his native land, was very colorfully designed and had several strong chorus numbers, but otherwise was immediately consigned to oblivion by the reviewers. Rowland Field (*NEN*) wrote, "Seldom has there been anything so painfully inept served up as alleged amusement."

A second-rate cast made up largely of nightclub and vaudeville performers enacted the trite story about a band of Miami Beach revellers who meet at the home of Professor J. Foster Adams (Edgar Mason), where American Don José O'Brien (Russ Brown) falls for a Mexican lass (Victoria Cordova), and a Mexican guy (Milton Watson) falls for an American girl (Marie Nash). All go on an archaeological expedition for a wishing stone said to lie at the bottom of a sacred pool somewhere south of the border. They find it in a Yucatan jungle and make use of its properties, which allow whoever tosses it to be transported to a dream environment (such as the Floating Gardens of Xochimilco and the bullring in Mexico City). After several scenes allowing for scenic changes, the party returns to Miami (where the diving scenes occur), and the several romantic attachments are finalized before the curtain falls.

The hapless company included Ann Dere, John Cherry, the Diamond Boys, and many others.

VOICE OF ISRAEL, THE [Drama/Family/Jews/Journalism/Military/Politics/War/Yiddish Language] A: Elias Gilner; M: Simon Tenowsky; D: Maurice Schwartz; S/L: Leo Kerz; P/T: Yiddish Art Theatre (OB); 10/25/48

An anti-British Yiddish drama about Israel's fight for survival. The piece met with a warm, sometimes tearful reception from those who found its topical subject matter and the travails of its characters deeply moving, but it did not score highly in most critical eyes. Too much of its impact depended on ready-made means for stimulating a positive reaction. In addition, the Yiddish Art Theatre's production was widely considered pedestrian and overwrought. Wrote Seymour Peck (*TS*), "*The Voice of Israel* is a rather shapeless editorial on Israel, a series of speeches put into the mouths of characters who are little more than the expressions of a point of view." "It's amazing that the tragic history of the Jews can be developed into a plot so lacking in vitality, in believable action, or characters that breathe and live," complained Jeanette Wilken (*NYDN*). John Beaufort (*CSM*) said that the play "gives the impression of being an argument rather than a drama." But a few critics sided with the drama. Thomas R. Dash (*WWD*) called it "a stirring and blistering battle cry and a paean to" Israel's brave freedom fighters and pioneers.

The play proper begins after a series of lantern slides depicting the history of the oppression of the Jews, with a special blow aimed at British policy over Israel. Maurice Schwartz played Nathan Ometz, who has given up his textile factory in New Jersey and moved to Palestine to help smuggle Jewish settlers into the country. Here, where he has become mayor of a small community, he has lost two sons in the fighting. Another son, Gavriel (Muni Serebrov), has saved the life of a British major named Henderson (Anatole Winogradoff), who has subsequently befriended Nathan. The friendship becomes problematical because of the pro-Arab British policy against Jewish refugees emigrating to the Holy Land and Nathan's practice of helping them run the blockade. Nathan has made peace with the Arabs, but the British foment distrust between the Arabs and the Jews. The villain of the piece is Colonel Howler (Mischa Fishzon), head of the British Office of Criminal Investigation, who works with a Polish spy named Captain Galski (Boris Auerbach) to destroy the Haganah and prevent the Zionists from establishing a Jewish homeland. A major conflict erupts concerning the British attempt to get the Jews to hand over their hidden cache of guns. At the end, the British are thwarted by the creation of a free Israel.

The large cast included Charlotte Goldstein as the beloved of one of the sons, Gustave Berger as a son, Evelyn Shiner as a waif separated from her brother in a concentration camp, Jacob Mestel as an old Jew who elicited tears in a scene when he kissed the ground on his arrival in Israel, Rosetta Bialis as a woman driven mad by her experiences in the camps, and Sara Gingold as an American journalist.

VOICE OF THE TURTLE, THE [Comedy/Military/Romance/Sex/Theatre/War] A/D: John van Druten; S: Stewart Chaney; P: Alfred de Liagre, Jr.; T: Morosco Theatre; 12/8/43 (1,557)

The fact that this comedy hit went on to run for over 1,500 performances was partly because of its having only three actors on its payroll and a single setting, but mostly because it was a beautifully crafted play that just happened to hit the public in the right spot at the right time. The three superb actors employed were Elliott Nugent as Bill Page, Margaret Sullavan as Sally Middleton, and Audrey Christie as Olive Lashbrooke. The play easily made Burns Mantle's selection of the season's ten best. Its title comes from the Song of Solomon in the Old Testament: "The flowers appear on the earth; the time of the singing of birds is come; and the voice of the turtle is heard in our land." Before the show opened, producer de Liagre expressed doubts about the title. When Nugent's wife Norma said that she thought it intriguing, despite its ambiguity, van Druten declared, "There, you see, the women like it. The title stays!" (quoted in Nugent's *Events Leading Up to the Comedy*).

All the action takes place in Sally's three-room apartment in Manhattan's East Sixties, near Third Avenue. The simple story concerns Sergeant Bill Page, on leave for a weekend in New York before going to the front and scheduled to meet worldly actress Olive Lashbrooke at the apartment of her friend Sally, an aspiring young actress so far confined to bit parts. In contrast to the hard-boiled Olive, with whom Bill already has had a casual fling, Sally is refined, inhibited, and still smarting from an unhappy love affair, an experience she seeks carefully to avoid repeating. Bill, too, has been unlucky in love. Olive leaves Bill and Sally together when a more interesting prospect--a second lieutenant--turns up in town. Most of the remainder of the play is a duologue between Sally and Bill as they gradually overcome their emotional distance, which is more difficult for Sally than Bill to accomplish; find themselves drawn to one another; have sex; and contemplate a deeper love for the future. Before the final curtain, Olive returns, her date having been a disappointment, but she is further disappointed to discover that Bill and Sally have decided to get married.

Standout features of the piece were its buoyant dialogue; humane humor; expert use of physical business, especially that involving the phone; Chaney's fascinatingly realistic set showing a cross-section of the apartment, complete with working refrigerator and stove; ability to sustain dramatic interest in the small cast without resorting to dramaturgic tricks; and scintillating performances. The dialogue was replete with theatrical references but with barely any to the war. Three-character plays were still extremely rare on Broadway, although many playwrights learned from this piece that the feat was not only possible but profitable as well.

"Mr. van Druten has written the best light comedy of his career," cheered Louis Kronenberger (*PM*), "as winningly gay in spirit as it is superlatively adroit in craftsmanship, and what goes for the play goes equally for the production." "It is light, sophisticated and frank," noted Kelcey Allen (*WWD*). "The dialog is always sprightly, but touched here and there with sentiment. The piece also has charm, humor and fine characterization." "It's a lively and literate masterpiece that has everything to recommend it," praised Robert Garland (*NYJA*). He said that it was "a brilliant comedy, brilliantly conceived, brilliantly written, brilliantly produced and brilliantly acted." Wilella Waldorf (*NYP*) commended van Druten for taking a simple and obvious plot and making it seem continually interesting and original. Even the usually acidulous George Jean Nathan (*TBY*) approved the play, saying "that for smoothness, wit, humorous understanding and all-around satisfaction [this comedy] has not been surpassed on the local stage in several seasons." He also expressed his approval of the fact that despite what he deemed the play's complete immorality, barely a soul complained of it because of the author's deftness in dealing with his theme. One of those who did complain was Euphemia Van Rensselaer Wyatt (*CW*), who thought it "the most subversive and anti-social play which could well have been written," a play that, by its enormous charm, covered up what was essentially an invitation for young people to engage in premarital sex without responsibility. She even wondered if the play would have been a hit if the producer had titled the play *The Voice of the Turtle, or The Pleasures of Fornication.*

As the naive thespian from Joplin, Missouri, Sullavan showed why she was one of her generation's most charming actresses. Looking young enough to pass for twenty (she was really thirty-three and the mother of three), she dazzled Broadway audiences. "She has a gift of youth," explained Rosamond Gilder (*TAM*), "a something shining and lustrous, which fits perfectly the character" drawn by the playwright. "She moves well; she has variety and a sense of line like a dancer. . . . Her voice is still husky, sounding dangerously near the vanishing point, but carrying that implication of passion which, combined with her virginal allure, is part of her individual charm." The actress, for all her acclaim, was unhappy doing a long-run play and pinned a calendar near the door to the set. At the end of each performance she would check off another day bringing her closer to the expiration of her contract. Nugent was praised for his complete naturalness and perfect comic timing, and Christie was in her element in the role of the brassy, wisecracking friend.

(1) VOLPONE [Dramatic Revival*] A: Ben Jonson; M: Rosabel Watson; D: Donald Wolfit and Christopher Ede; S: Donald Wolfit; P: Hall Shelton b/a/w Advance Players Association, Ltd., of London; T: Century Theatre; 2/24/47 (3)

England's Donald Wolfit Repertory Company, visiting here with four Shakespeare plays (*King Lear**, *As You Like It**, *Hamlet**, and *The Merchant of Venice**) and one by Jonson, scored its highest marks with the latter. Most of its other offerings were riddled with problems stemming from inadequate and uninspired direction, unattractive touring settings, and a second-rate supporting company, among other things. Despite the usual complaints about the direction, its *Volpone* was generally appreciated, however, and the company's faults were far less obvious. Wolfit had streamlined the text by eliminating its subplot. The revival also had some historical importance, as it seems to have been the first local showing of the actual Jonson play as opposed to an adaptation, such as the English translation of Stefan Zweig's German version shown by the Theatre Guild in 1928. Wolfit played Volpone, John Wynyard was Mosca, Frederick Horrey was Voltore, Eric Maxon was Corbaccio, Alexander Gauge was Corvino, Rosalind Iden was Corvino's wife, Celia, and the three magistrates were Josef Shear, George Bradford, and Malcolm Watson.

Jonson's virulent satire on greed was given a mounting that Brooks Atkinson (*NYT*) said "is generally satisfactory as a rendering of an Elizabethan classic; and when Jonson is most outrageously sardonic it is very amusing indeed." "The play is wildly and poetically ribald," noted Ward Morehouse (*NYS*), "turning frequently into a low-comedy romp, and the visitors give their best show to date." Reservations were expressed, though, by William Hawkins (*NYWT*), for whom the production was uneven.

Especially worthwhile for most was Wolfit's characterization, for which he dressed in vivid yellow tights. Robert Garland (*NYJA*) reported, "Donald Wolfit's Venetian magnifico was rough and rowdy. With tongue in cheek, his feet were firmly planted on the playwright's ground." But Hawkins thought him too flamboyant and lacking the correct lightness of approach, and Louis Kronenberger (*PM*) stated, "He makes the part fun rather than fascinating, gives it spirit rather than size--the big scene with Corvino's wife . . . he cannot . . . compass." Both Wynyard and Gauge gave fine performances in support, some thinking their well-rounded and vigorous characterizations the best of the production.

(2) AD: José Ferrer, Richard Whorf, and Richard Barr; D: Richard Barr; S/L: Herbert Brodkin; C: Emeline Roche; P: New York City Center Theatre Company; T: City Center of Music and Drama; 1/8/48 (14)

One of a series of popular-priced plays produced by a company headed by José Ferrer at the City Center. Ferrer, padded to make him look grossly fat, played the title role, emphasizing his lechery and the fun of his tricks rather than the character's foxy guile. He was ably abetted by Richard Whorf as a graceful, dancerlike Mosca; John Carradine as a hammily bizarre, coarse and unrefined Voltore; Fred Stewart as a blind and deaf Corbaccio; Le Roi Operti as Corvino; Leonardo Cimino as Nano; Phyllis Hill as Celia; Walter Coy as Bonario; Paula Laurence as Lady Politic Wouldbe; and, among others, Lou Gilbert as the court clerk. A pair of court officers were played by Earl Jones and Frank Campanella.

The production, trimmed to two hours' running time, was suggestive of commedia dell'arte; it was played as mad and ribald farce with all the stops pulled out and with every double entendre doubly underlined. Some critics were upset that the sourness of satire was exchanged for the fun of Ferrer, whose antics they considered overdone, but others found the gaiety infectious. "In this melee of roaring voices, Bronx cheers and fanny-kicking, the satire of animalistic human being [*sic*] clawing away at each other gives way almost completely to burlesque," reported Howard Barnes (*NYHT*). "It is all in key and a lot of it is funny, but it is about as blunt as Punch's cudgel." Richard Watts, Jr. (*NYP*), believed that this interpretation so completely robbed the play of its savage thrust and crafty humor that it seemed like little more than "a high school dramatic society having a romp." He also was appalled at the total loss of the play's occasional poetic values. But William Hawkins (*NYWT*) sided with those who found the results "colorful, bawdy and sly." Costumes and makeup were highly stylized, but the settings were fairly simple, being a parody of Elizabethan trappings, including a curtained alcove that allowed for rapid shifts and nonstop action.

The most remarked-on and admired performance was Carradine's. Euphemia Van Rensselaer Wyatt (*CW*) observed, "With his interminably lengthy form in dusty black, his nose prolonged into a rubber beak, with stringy black hair, cadaverous face and sepulchral poses he is the boisterous acme of melancholy."

(1) **WALK HARD** [Drama/Blacks/Family/Gambling/Race/Romance/Sports] A/D: Abram Hill; SC: Len Zinberg's novel, *Walk Hard--Talk Loud*; S: John Proctor; P: American Negro Theatre; T: 135th Street Library Theatre (OB); 11/30/44 (42)

The black theatre group that had recently produced *Anna Lucasta* before it became a Broadway hit in a revised version offered this less successful play that was awkwardly staged but showed dramaturgical promise. For seventy-five cents one saw a drama concerning a bitter black shoeshine boy named Andy Whitman (Roy Allen) who resents feeling alienated because of his skin color and whose natural fighting ability leads him to become a professional boxer, despite his family's desire that he go to college. He encounters racial prejudice in the fight racket and floors a powerful white gambler (Joseph Kamm), which leads the other to buy up his contract so that he cannot get any bouts. His outspoken grandmother (Jacqueline Andre) advises him to walk hard and talk loud if he wants to make a mark for himself in this world.

The play is an episodic work with locales in various states. It gave Ruby Dee one of her first important roles as Andy's girlfriend. Leonard Yorr was Andy's white manager and .pn1391Howard Augusta a punchdrunk pal. "Set *Walk Hard* down as an honest attempt to write of a difficult racial problem, but its weakness of structure and slightness of characterization robbed it of much of the power the theme possesses," reported George Freedley (*NYMT*).
Lewis Nichols (*NYT*) took issue with Hill's introduction "of extraneous scenes and people which slow his play and cloud his story." Burton Rascoe (*NYWT*) rejected the vague conclusion but enjoyed the excellent characterizations, "so natural, so easy, so unfeigned, so unactorish, so right in timing and inflection."

(2) [Dramatic Revival] D: Gustav Blum; S: John Wenger; P: Gustav Blum and Gilbert Weiss; T: Chanin Auditorium (OB); 3/27/46 (7)

One of the chief features of this unsuccessful revival in a skyscraper auditorium on the East Side was the appearance of erstwhile welterweight and middleweight champion Mickey Walker (the "Toy Bulldog") in the role of fighter Larry Batcheller, the hero's friend. He came off surprisingly well, outclassing some of his more theatrically trained stagemates. Leonard Yorr, Jacqueline Andre, and Joseph Kamm repeated their roles of 1944, but, among other changes, Andy was now played by Maxwell Glanville.

The slightly revised play, not well reviewed its first time out, was even less well liked on this occasion. "Uptown it had a semi-amateurish zest for life, with the accompanying spirit," lamented Lewis Nichols (*NYT*). "Now it is just a bad play rather tediously performed." George Jean Nathan (*TBY*) thought that the revisions had "further lamed an already crippled script."

WALK INTO MY PARLOR [Drama/Business/Crime/Family/Labor/Marriage/

Romance/Sex] A: Alexander Greendale; D: Alexander Greendale and Luther Greene; S: Paul Morrison; P: Luther Greene; T: Forrest Theatre; 11/19/41 (29)

Alexander Greendale, a young playwright who had won a Rockefeller Foundation Playwrighting Award, wrote this drama of a Chicago Italian-American immigrant family in a manner that was too overtly reminiscent of Clifford Odets's *Awake and Sing!* and thereby impressed few important reviewers. The tenement-dwelling family here is the Sarellis, whose head, Ilio (Silvio Minciotti), is struggling to make a living selling produce off a truck with his son Salvatore (Duane McKinney). Daughter Grace (Helen Waren) is supporting an unemployed spouse, Luigi (Joseph De Santis). She decides to leave him because she is a zealous trade unionist and he takes a job as a scab. Son Gino (Nicholas [Richard] Conte) has a yen for his sultry and pregnant sister-in-law Carmella (Rita Piazza), Salvatore's wife. Gino, a sharply dressed petty mobster, is doing all right financially, if not legally and morally, with his counterfeiting racket. When he feels guilty for coming on to Carmella, he punishes himself by grasping a red-hot coal in his palm. At other times, he casually drops live goldfish down his throat. Desperate for money to keep the family together (she wants to put Luigi into business by buying him a stable), Mrs. Sarelli (Rosina Galli) gets involved in passing Gino's phony money. This outrages the family, although they had known all along of Gino's wrongdoing. Family disintegration sets in. The federal authorities are hot on Gino's track, and he departs. Mrs. Sarelli repents her deeds and the family glue starts to hold once again, although Grace and Luigi decide to call it quits.

There was some strong, often-profane, colloquial dialogue and a few decent scenes of passion and sentiment, but on the whole, this was "an arrestingly bad play," according to Richard Lockridge (*NYS*). Wilella Waldorf (*NYP*) wrote that most of the "dialogue is commonplace, even inept and silly at times, and the play in general lacks the luminous, exciting quality a more inspired dramatist might have given it." Most critics felt, however, that for all the play's weaknesses, the playwright showed considerable promise for the future.

Good performances from all the principals, including Lou Polan as Gino's counterfeit money engraver, were wasted on the unripe drama. Conte's performance reminded spectators of Elia Kazan and John Garfield.

WALKING GENTLEMAN, THE [Drama/Crime/Mental Illness/Mystery/Romance/Theatre] A: Grace Perkins and Fulton Oursler; D: Marion Gering; S: Harry Horner; L: A. H. Feder; P: Albert Lewis and Marion Gering; T: Belasco Theatre; 5/7/42 (6)

An elaborate, expensively produced murder mystery that proved a lugubrious bore, being boringly written and boringly played. Victor Francen, a French actor, made his American stage debut in the role of a famous actor, Basil Forrest, whose ex-wife and former leading lady, Doris (Arlene Francis), is planning to marry the renowned psychiatrist Dr. Gerald Blake (Richard Gaines). Basil, however, is still carrying a torch for Doris. Following a series of strangulations of women in different American cities, a detective begins to suspect Basil because the killings coincided with the actor's appearance in the cities where they occurred. He is scheduled to open in New York in *Dr. Jekyll and Mr. Hyde* when his leading lady's hanged corpse is discovered in her dressing room. Basil gets Doris to take over the part. However, the perspicacious Dr. Blake helps the police to pin the homicides on Basil, who has been carrying out his romantic disappointment with Doris by slaying other women. Had he not been stopped, Doris would have been his next victim. But Basil evades the law by smoking a poison-laced cigarette and dying.

Arthur Pollock (*BE*) observed of the authors that "while trying to make their murderer a pathological case in accord with the latest custom in the writing of thrillers, they forgot to give their play anything like credibility. It is a phoney all the way through." Louis Kronenberger (*PM*) said, "It is hard to understand how it can be so talky, slow-moving and dull." George Jean Nathan (*TBY*) reported several years later that the play had undergone irreparably damaging revisions at the hands of the egotistical French star, Francen, in order to make his role more sympathetic and attractive to the female spectators. Cast members included Oscar Polk, Clay Clement, Clarence Derwent, Toni Gilman, Margery Maude, Arnold Korff, and Lew Hearn.

WALLFLOWER [Comedy/Family/Politics/Romance/Sex/Youth] A: Mary Orr and Reginald Denham; D: Reginald Denham; S: Samuel Leve; C: (gowns) Bianca Stroock; P: Meyer Davis; T: Cort Theatre; 1/26/44 (192)

A number of reviewers took offense at what they considered the indecency of this ribald sex farce, but the piece was effective enough with the general public to run for half a year. "There may have been more badly written plays but never one in worse taste," sniffed Euphemia Van Rensselaer Wyatt (*CW*), who could not understand why the audience laughed so much at it.

Two young stepsisters in Ironville, Ohio, are the dazzling blond Joy Linnet (Sunnie O'Dea), very popular with the boys, and the plainer, but still pretty, Jackie Linnet (Mary Rolfe), the eponymous heroine whom the boys neglect. Their bickering parents are Jessamine (Kathryn Givney) and Andrew Linnet (Walter N. Greaza), the latter an irate judge concerned about the problems of juvenile delinquency. Jackie cares for one of her sister's boyfriends, Princetonian Warren James (Joel Marston), who ignores her to have joy with Joy. But when Joy disposes of him and he imbibes too much of Mr. Linnet's whisky, Jackie takes off with him for a drive that ends up at a roadhouse. The joint is raided and all hell breaks out when Jackie and Warren are discovered in flagrante delicto. Mr. Linnet's political standing plummets, but Jackie's sexual standing with the local swains skyrockets, as the phone keeps jingling with requests for dates. Everything is cooled off, however, when it is disclosed that Jackie and Warren had taken the trouble to get married before plunging into carnal bliss.

Those who condoned other comedies about sex among the young folk, such as *Kiss and Tell*, pointed out that those plays had a delicacy and charm that were absent from what they viewed here as a more overt, unsubtle example of the genre. Rosamond Gilder (*TAM*) labeled it "a sort of debased Cinderella plot, with emphasis on cheapness and vulgarity and with every possible variation on the double entendre." Louis Kronenberger (*PM*) "found it thoroughly offensive." Others appreciated the show for its comical ideas and excellent performances, and some thought it one of the funniest shows around. Robert Coleman (*NYDM*) believed that "some of the . . . dialogue seems stilted and a few of the situations might be described as arbitrary . . . but it moves with such speed and so many robust howls that these seem minor points over which to squabble." Arthur Pollock (*BE*) dubbed it "dynamite, the most obvious hit of the season."

A number of laughs were gained by Vilma Kurer as a Viennese maid who uses adolescent slang taught to her by the girls. To arriving guests she says, "Park your fannies." To departing ones, she declares, "So long, you bums!" Leona Powers, Fred Irving Lewis, Ann Dere, and coauthor Orr were also in the play.

WALRUS AND THE CARPENTER, THE [Comedy/Family/Marriage/Romance/Youth] A: A. N. Langley; D/P: Alfred de Liagre, Jr.; S: Raymond Sovey; T: Cort Theatre; 11/8/41 (9)

Another in a string of ill-chosen plays for leading actress Pauline Lord, whose career continued to tumble for lack of suitable material. This "singularly unfunny" (Louis Kronenberger [*PM*]), frantically paced, cartoonlike comedy (earlier titled *The Mulberry Bush*) was considered a cross between *You Can't Take It with You** and *Hellzapoppin'**. John Beaufort (*CSM*) opined that this was "a noisy, overwrought, and bewilderingly untidy comedy."

Presiding over the helter-skelter well-being of East Eighty-eighth Street's Stuyvesant family is the scatterbrained Essie (Lord), a widow with a trio of daughters and a passel of debts. Against a background largely preoccupied with the birth of a baby to Essie's oldest daughter in an upstairs room, the play depicts the stormy love affair of the adolescent daughter (Frances Heflin, in her first major role) with a starving twenty-one-year-old actor (Harold Landon); the marital unhappiness of Gerda (Karen Morley), the sensible middle daughter, and her caddish author hus band (Alan Hewitt), who thinks everyone but himself a moron; and the addle-brained behavior of the nervously expectant father (Frank Albertson). Meanwhile, a villainous butler (Ivan Triesault), not having been paid his salary for three months, steals a valuable ring. The family is also under the gun for non-payment of their rent, but they are saved from eviction when (1) the real-estate agent (Gordon Oliver), having accepted Essie's supposedly worthless stock in lieu of her $800 back rent, discovers that it has considerable value, and (2) the family doctor (Nicholas Joy), who has long loved Essie, decides to cement their relationship. The agent also becomes bonded to the rebounding Gerda.

On opening night, Lord consistently fluffed her lines, and, for many, her performance never fulfilled its comic potential. However, some critics raved about her acting. John Anderson (*NYJA*) declared, "Even when you see quite plainly how Miss Lord gets her effects--the helpless hands, the trailing voice, broken sentences, and wandering smile--there is no escaping the effect. With all her familiar mannerisms she does create out of the skimpiest materials a masterly sketch of mental confusion and sheer goofiness."

WANDERING STARS [Comedy/Jews/Period/Romance/Theatre/Yiddish Language] A: Maurice Schwartz; SC: Sholem Aleichem's novel of the same name; M: Abraham Goldfaden and Joseph Rumshinsky; D: Maurice Schwartz; S: Alexander Chertov; P/T: Yiddish Art Theatre (OB); 12/13/46

Maurice Schwartz provided a tour de force role for himself in his adaptation of a Sholem Aleichem backstage story loosely based on the life of actor-composer Abraham Goldfaden, considered the founder of the Yiddish theatre. Several of his songs were interpolated into the production. Schwartz played actor Bernard Holtzman, leader of a turn-of-the-century troupe of wandering actors touring the villages of central Europe, where he discovers a talented young pair of players (Jacob Rechtzeit and Beatrice Kessler) and, after various obstacles are overcome, convinces them to join his company. Plot circumstances contrive to separate the youngsters, but after many hardships, they find one another on the Lower East Side, where he has become a tragic star and she an operatic diva.

During his performance Schwartz got to do a comic bit in drag, playing with surprising energy "an aging coquette in a piebald costume topped with ostrich plumes" (L. B. [*NYT*]). "His devoted followers seemed to enjoy him as much in this as in tragic roles," declared George Freedley (*NYMT*). "Evidently on Second Avenue A [*sic*] Schwartz can do no wrong." Like so many Yiddish opuses, this one mixed large dollops of broad comedy with others of poignant sentimentality. Outstanding character turns were offered by Ola Shlitko, Gustave Berger, Anna Appel, Charles Cohan, and Menachem Rubin.

WANHOPE BUILDING, THE [Drama/Barroom/Broadcasting/Fantasy/Politics/Romance/Science] A: John Finch; M: Arthur Kreutz; D: Brett Warren; S/L: Wolfgang Roth; P: Theatre Incorporated and the American National Theatre and Academy i/a/w theExperimental Theatre; T: Princess Theatre; 2/9/47 (5)

The first of five "experimental" plays given for five showings each under the general auspices of the Experimental Theatre during the 1946-1947 season. Like most of the others in the present series, this drama met with disapproval, although it did have promising features. The episodic, didactic piece was intended to rouse contemporary man out of a state of laisser-faire and to make him work actively for a better world.

It begins in Michael's Bar at a time when it is revealed over the radio that John B. Sherman (Ford Rainey), a potential dictator, has invented a W-bomb, which has the power to destroy man's will. (The bomb is intended as a symbol of great world events.) People respond to the danger apathetically, asking what they can possibly do about it, as if any attempt to do something were impossible. This disturbs Flashy Page (John Jordan), a sailor, who goes to Sherman's lair at the top of the 500-story Wanhope Building to solve the problem. His journey is a fantastical one, beset with many symbolic obstacles in the form of temptations and moral dilemmas. He learns that the bomb is a hoax and, using a radio with a nationwide hookup, attempts to inform his fellow citizens of it, telling them that they can overcome such weapons by the power of thinking for themselves and acting with responsibility. He discovers, upon returning to the bar, that all he gets is more indifference, except for the girl who loves and understands him.

"The dramaturgy through which the allegory is filtered is generally so ill-contrived that confusion piles on confusion to the frequent point of absurdity," scoffed George Jean Nathan (*TBY*). Louis Kronenberger (*PM*) noted the play's occasionally satirical intelligence but argued that it was not "outwardly dramatic enough. Nor is it . . . inwardly dynamic enough." It also "makes the old mistake . . . of projecting symbols without first making them people, of giving social commentary no personal impress, of being too bloodless and fleshless." Actors involved included Beatrice Straight as Felina the masseuse, Margaret Barker, Frieda Altman, Robert Wark, Walter Craig, Martin Balsam (in his Broadway debut in the role of Eddie), Courtney Burr, Jr., Winifred Cushing, and Will Kuluva, among others.

WAR AND PEACE [Drama/Family/Marriage/Period/Romance/War] A: Alfred Neumann, Erwin Piscator, Harold L. Anderson, and Maurice Kurtz; SC: the novel of the same name by Leo Tolstoy; D/P: Erwin Piscator; S: H. A. Condell; C: Rose Bogdanoff; L: Hans Sondheimer; T: Studio Theatre of the New School for Social Research (OB); 5/20/42

An "epic" adaptation by four writers of the classic Tolstoy novel. Although this experimental version--staged with experienced professionals and young student actors--was not deemed stageworthy, some of the original's force and thematic interest seeped through nonetheless. Of particular interest was the relation between the story of Napoleon's devastating warfare--including the burning of Moscow--and that of Adolf Hitler.

Done in the confines of the New School's small theatre, the sprawling work was given an adventurous, often-striking presentation, but the credit went more to the designers than to the director or the writers. The stage was divided into two levels, with a separate platform at the side. Gauze curtains, screens, panels, and projections suggested the varying locales, aided by excellent lighting. Holding the episodic action together was the figure of a commentator or narrator, assumed by the character of the humane Pierre Besuchov (Hugo Haas), who becomes disillusioned by the actions of Napoleon, whom he had believed would create a United States of Europe; Pierre moves through the play from pacificism to a militant position. To suggest the battlefield of Borodino, Napoleon and Kutuzov, the generals, were depicted as toy figures in the commentator's hands as he loomed like a giant over the scene.

Because of the broad canvas of the novel, not enough of the tale of the Bolkonsky and Besuchov families and the many friends, enemies, and servants who surround them came across to make the story compelling or even clear. The play focuses on the love of Prince Andrei (Warner Anderson) and the faithless Countess Natasha (Dolly Haas), with the sensitive and peace-loving Pierre acting as confidant, although he too loves Natasha. Natasha's love affair with Anatol Kuragin (Paul Mann), however, is skimpily portrayed.

The military and political background never came sufficiently to the fore for some critics, and unevenness marred the writing, based as it was on a 1,300-page novel. Consequently, while there were some excellent scenes, much of it seemed to Brooks Atkinson (*NYT*) "dull, old-fashioned and slow." Louis Kronenberger (*PM*) argued that "this most spacious and multiple of all novels . . . becomes deformed and empty when squeezed into another mold and compressed into three hours." On the other hand, Robert Francis (*BE*) believed that a bridge between the novel and the stage had been built "with understanding and craftsmanship."

Excellent performances were offered by those mentioned, as well as Edwin Cooper as Andrei's reactionary father, Prince Bolkonsky; Fay Baker as Pierre's unpleasant wife, Countess Helena; and Mildred Dunnock as Andrei's sister, Princess Maria, in a company of many actors.

Piscator's version of *War and Peace* was first devised in 1938, had been known in New York theatre circles for a couple of years, and had been considered for Broadway production under Gilbert Miller's management before it was decided to be too risky an undertaking in the commercial milieu. The Broadway version would have been far more elaborate, making use of such trademark Piscator devices as a treadmill to move the action along. A good description of the production as originally conceived is in Maria Ley-Piscator's *The Piscator Experiment*, which also relates the development of the workshop production, which met with a combination of confused resistance and growing fascination from the company. She noted that Piscator went ahead, despite the technical drawbacks, because the recent outbreak of war had demonstrated the pertinence of Tolstoy's themes (especially the evolution of Pierre from pacifist idealist to fighter) to the current crisis, and also to provide a basis for the director's teaching of his epic theatre principles to his student actors.

WAR PRESIDENT [Drama/Historical-Biographical/Military/Period/Politics/War] A: Nat Sherman; D: Wendell K. Phillips; S/C: Rose Bogdanoff; L: Jack Landau; P: the Escholiers for the Experimental Theatre; T: Shubert Theatre; 4/24/44 (2)

An Equity-approved showcase for invited matinee audiences about problems faced by Abraham Lincoln during the Civil War. It was staged with a minimum of means, the actors using pantomime to suggest doors and similar business. Central to the drama is the conflict between Lincoln (Joel Ashley) and the dawdling, arrogant General McClellan (Alexander Scourby), who later became a presidential rival. McClellan is desirous of accepting a stalemate with the South in exchange for the promise of the Democratic nomination. McClellan's solution would have allowed the South to keep its slaves.

Some found the play to have some fascinating scenes, but were convinced that it did not hold together consistently. The pictures of McClellan and Lincoln were judged effective, as were those of their colleagues and relations. Louis Kronenberger (*PM*) thought that it too frequently sounded like its sources rather than re-creating them, but felt that it occasionally had "liveliness" and "force." *V*'s unnamed reviewer evaluated it as "a pedestrian play, passable but undistinguished. . . . Its faults lie in its static, bookish quality, matter-of-fact writing, and sometimes too-pat parallels." These parallels meant to suggest that President Roosevelt had had problems with General MacArthur similar to those of Lincoln with McClellan.

Joanna Roos was Mary Lincoln, Donald Rose was Tad Lincoln, Teddy Rose was Willie Lincoln, William Marceau was Edwin M. Stanton, Russell Collins was Senator Wade, Paul Ford was Senator Chandler, Morton Da Costa was General Smith, Gregory Morton was Fernando Wood, Joseph Leon was General Hooker, and Graham Velsey was Horace Greeley. This was the second play dealing with Lincoln staged by the Experimental Theatre, *Yours, A. Lincoln* having been on its agenda the previous season.

WATCH ON THE RHINE [Drama/Family/Marriage/Politics/Romance/War] A: Lillian Hellman; D/P: Herman Shumlin; S: Jo Mielziner; C: Helen Pons; T: Martin Beck Theatre; 4/1/41 (378)

For many years this stood as one of the most potent anti-Nazi dramas ever penned by an American. It was one of the ten best plays of the year and the winner of the Drama Critics Circle Award.

The play is set in the spring of 1940 in the living room of Farrelly Country House in a suburb of Washington, D.C. This is the comfortable residence of a wealthy, witty dowager in her sixties, Fanny Farrelly (Lucile Watson), who lives in security removed from a world going up in flames. Her well-to-do lawyer son David (John Lodge) lives with her, as do Joseph (Frank Wilson), a black butler, and a French maid, Anise (Eda Heinemann). She has been growing weary of a couple of constantly bickering guests, the unscrupulous Rumanian Count Teck de Brancovis (George Coulouris) and his American wife, Marthe (Helen Trenholme), with whom David is in love. Arriving to seek sanctuary at the house are Mrs. Farrelly's daughter Sara (Mady Christians), gone for twenty years, Sara's expatriate German husband Kurt Mueller (Paul Lukas), an engineer, and the Mueller children, Joshua (Peter Fernandez), Bodo (Eric Roberts), and Babette (Anne Blyth, in her Broadway debut). They have been in exile since 1933, fleeing from nation to nation and working with an underground organization to overthrow the fascist leadership of Germany. The sensitive but rabidly anti-Nazi Kurt is planning to go back to Germany with $23,000 in bribe money to help free from the Gestapo prison some persons with whom he was involved in the underground movement. Aware of Kurt's plans, de Brancovis, who has connections in the German embassy, attempts to blackmail the Farrelly family for $10,000, which leads to Kurt's overcoming his dread of violence and killing him. Following a tearful farewell, in which he condemns his own act of violence and expresses hope for a better future, Kurt leaves for Germany to carry out his mission, it being understood that he probably will never return.

The play succeeded despite its lack of overtly jingoistic sloganeering or propagandizing against the Nazis (fascism was the evil force referred to, not Nazism). Even the villain was not a Nazi, but a maritally troubled nobleman on his uppers seeking self-preservation at any cost. Hellman stressed not so much Hitler's evil as Kurt Mueller's idealistic heroics. A strong sense of sympathy was evoked for the German people not in Hitler's camp. That war was not offered as an answer to the problem of Hitlerism pleased leftist critic Ralph Warner (*DW*), who was, however, disturbed by the lack of clarity concerning whether or not Kurt was meant as a Communist radical.

Watch on the Rhine had an overwhelming effect on its auditors. It was appreciated for its strong anti-Nazi stance and its exciting melodramatic action, culminating in Mueller's slaying of the count and becoming the man of action needed by the melodramatic times. "In the suspense and force with which its original plot and characters are developed, in the vigor of its dialog, it easily takes rank with some of the best dramas seen on our stage," reported Kelcey Allen (*WWD*). And Richard Watts, Jr. (*NYHT*), said, "*Watch on the Rhine* is a moving and beautiful play, filled with eloquence and a heroic spirit." On the other hand, some critics had definite reservations, finding it faulty in construction, in need of editing, burdened with a clumsy subplot, thematically confused, and burdened by an excessively long, sentimental, and anticlimactic final curtain. John Anderson (*NYJA*), for example, commented that despite this being a "deeply moving work," it "falters badly in its craftsmanship and loses its most vivid and vigorous points in over-writing."

The acting of all was highly lauded, but most especially praised was Paul Lukas, a Hungarian actor already established here as a film star. "He *is* Kurt Mueller--and I am not given to throwing that kind of phrase around," stated Louis Kronenberger (*PM*). "He plays the part with terrific inner passion, and with not one ounce of surface theatricality."

WATCHED POT, THE [Dramatic Revival] A: Saki (H. H. Munro); D: Walter Mullen; S: Bob Ramsey; P: On-Stage; T: Cherry Lane Theatre (OB); 10/28/47 (27)

British author Saki, who died in 1916, was better known for his short stories than his plays, but this example of the latter, never seen before in New York, proved "a skillfully written comic escapade" to Brooks Atkinson (*NYT*), one of the few critics in attendance. He called it "stylized nonsense about . . . engagingly worthless people" with "dialogue that turns logic upside down and applies fastidious diction to inconsequential topics." The ill-equipped actors in this version, however, apart from Jean (Gene) Saks as René St. Gall and Kchast Sayers as Ludovic, were not up to Saki's demands for "a dry and lacquered performance in impeccable style."

WAY, THE [Drama/Religion/School/War] A: Martha Cabanne (Martha Kayser); SC: Martha Cabanne's novel, *Faith*; D: Wendell Phillips Dodge and Frank Lea Short; P: Olive Productions; T: Cherry Lane Theatre (OB); 10/11/40

A little-regarded Off-Broadway production of a play with an inspirational message but an awful plot and dialogue. The author expressed a belief in the power of positive thinking as demonstrated in a story about one Faith Morton (Eve Casanova), head of a school in Naples at a time just prior to Italy's entry into World War II. Here Faith teaches her idea that faith in right thinking can cure mankind's ills. Her students then go off to open branches of the school in other nations. The fetching Faith, known as the Siren of the Mediterranean, demonstrates her powers of thought when she overcomes by mental effort a jealous pistol-packing wife who believes Faith to have been dallying with her spouse. She also helps a disciple headed for Stockholm survive a plane crash. Her work on behalf of peace lands her in trouble when Italy goes to war and she is arrested; a few moments later, however, she has managed to effect her release.

L. H. (*NYT*) noted, "During the first act the audience was reasonably attentive, but during the second it began to participate vocally in the proceedings, which must have made it even harder for the cast."

WE WILL LIVE [Drama/Yiddish Language] A: David Bergelson; M: Sholem Secunda; D: Jacob Rothbaum; S: H. A. Condell; P: Joseph Green; T: Jewish Folk Theatre (OB); 12/19/44

An overly subjective, emotional depiction of what happened to the Jews in a Soviet community in the Ukraine overrun by the Nazis in 1941. Numerous characters and plot strands figure in the action, which centers on the house of Abraham Ber Levitt (Jacob Ben-Ami), superintendent of a laboratory that has perfected a chemical for making barren earth fertile. The Nazis use every means at their disposal to get the formula from the citizenry, including rape, torture, and murder, but the people keep their silence until the enemy is finally driven out by partisan fighters.

There were several truly powerful scenes, but the play did not hold together well, being too sprawling and diffuse and providing too much detail for the audience to easily comprehend. Good work was provided by Ben-Ami, Isadore Casher as a lab director, and Menachem Rubin as a ruthless Nazi major. Other roles in the large company were played by Muriel Gruber, Abraham Teitelbaum, Michael Gibson, Dora Weissman, and Dinah Halpern.

WEDDING IN JAPAN [Drama/Military/Orientals/Race/Romance/Trial] A: Ted Pollack; P: Dramatic Workshop; T: President Theatre (OB); 11/13/49

This was the first play to attempt to confront the problem of postwar romances between Japanese citizens and members of the American occupation forces. The action is set in Yokohama. Making it even more provocative is the fact that the American sergeant (Duke Williams) who loves the Japanese girl (Michi Okomoto) is a black man. A bigoted Southern lieutenant (John Munson) represents the chief obstacle to the relationship because he wants the girl for himself. To get rid of his rival, the officer frames him on an attempted murder charge, with himself the presumed victim. The sergeant--befriended by another lieutenant (George Smith)--is then subjected to a court-martial for his alleged crime. Just as he is about to be declared guilty, the Japanese girl reveals that on the night of the supposed attack the sergeant was with her. This immediately clears the sergeant's name.

William Hawkins (*NYWT*) appreciated that despite the writer's occasional lapses into melodrama, he was able to provide an entertaining evening of theatre. A chief flaw was the sharp contrast between the lighter mood of the first half and the somber one of the second (the court-martial). Robert Fuller and Michael St. John were in the play.

WHAT A GUY (***Der Emmiser Bucher***) [Musical/Yiddish Language] B: Isidor Friedman; M: Abe Ellstein; LY: Isidor Lillian and Jacob Jacobs; D/P: Menasha Skulnik w/Isidor Goldstein; CH: Lillian Shapero; DS: Michael Saltzman; T: Second Avenue Theatre (OB); 10/17/48

Menasha Skulnik continued to present his shy, bumbling persona--the type called a *nebichel* in Yiddish--in this pleasurable, if formulaic, musical comedy, but he now added a bit of stupidity to the characterization. Also on hand was his usual comic partner, Yetta Zwerling, who always played the widow in mad pursuit of the tiny Skulnik; as usual, she got to sing with him, as she often did, a parody medley of hit American songs, with the selections--spiced with Yiddish gags--related to their characters in the production. A good deal of English was inserted into the dialogue for those without Yiddish.

The unimportant book tells of how Skulnik's character, Tsoozik, has been given a month to live by his doctor. A young woman (Lilly Lilliana) is heiress to an uncle's will that requires that she be widowed before she can inherit the deceased's half-million, so she proposes to the supposedly dying Skulnik, only to find that he does not die after they are married. He declares that vitamin "she" is definitely proving an elixer. The doctor seems to have made a mistake, and it is he who drops dead instead. The wife wants out of this unfortunate marriage because she already has a fellow (Leon Liebgold) she loves. Finally, all works out well; Tsoozik makes it seem as though he has drowned so the woman can gain her inheritance, and he elopes to Florida with Gracie Goldwasser (Zwerling).

"It all adds up to an evening of merry frolic and antic capers with a rare comic spirit," chuckled Thomas R. Dash (*WWD*). Kahn. (*V*) noted the "trite book" and the "merely workmanlike" score, but said that these were secondary, as the real attraction was the delightful Skulnik, especially when he appeared, for no clear reason, as a Yiddish-speaking Indian. One of his songs, in fact, was titled "Galizianer Indianer" (The Galician Indian). Seymour Peck (*TS*) wrote, "The proscenium arch does not inhibit Menasha; he gives out energetically with his songs, he socks across every joke, he reaches the last row of the second balcony with a broad, low comedy style that is slightly reminiscent of Groucho Marx and Bobby Clark, but is individual enough to be uniquely Menasha."

WHAT BIG EARS! [Comedy/Films/Gambling/Hotel/Show Business] A: Jo Eisinger and Judson O'Donnell; D: Arthur Pierson; S: Horace Armistead; C: Kenn Barr; P: L. Daniel Blank and David Silberman; T: Windsor Theatre; 4/20/42 (8)

"An overpoweringly dull" (Brooks Atkinson [*NYT*]) farce about a carnival pitchman named Gabby Martin (Taylor Holmes) who, with his wife Jean (Ruth Weston), is stranded without a penny or a job in Hollywood. With them is thick-witted young Joey Smithers (Edwin Philips), who worked for Gabby's medicine-show pitch as a shill by dressing up as an old lady. Sent by Gabby and Jean to seek employment as a movie extra, Joey is hired for the title role in a movie called *Whistler's Mother*. Gabby and Jean do their best to keep Joey's true sex a secret. This becomes a major problem when Joey--who would rather raise rabbits than be a movie star--is summoned to New York to be examined by a doctor preparatory to being insured by the movie company's bankers, who don't want to take chances on their new star dying on them. A series of *Charley's Aunt**-like plot complications ensue in a New York hotel room, with lots of doors being slammed and people running in and out. Mingled in all of this is a romance between Joey and a movie stenographer (Marilyn Erskine) and the attempt of some tough bookmakers to collect $15,000 owed them by the compulsively gambling Gabby. Finally, the truth about Joey is revealed, and the movie people get out of their predicament by advertising the sensational fact that Whistler's mother is played by a young man.

Ethel Morrison as a bibulous maid was the only funny thing in this play that most critics thought the worst of the year.

WHAT EVERY WOMAN KNOWS [Dramatic Revival*] A: James M. Barrie; D: Margaret Webster; S: Paul Morrison; C: David Ffolkes; P: American Repertory Theatre; T: International Theatre; 11/8/46 (21)

The second offering of the new but short-lived American Repertory Theatre founded by Eva Le Gallienne and Margaret Webster was this revival of Barrie's "amiable Scotch valentine" (Rosamond Gilder [*TAM*]), last seen locally in 1926 with Helen Hayes as Maggie Wylie. This old political comedy was a striking change from the company's opening presentation of *King Henry VIII* and was clearly designed to demonstrate the possibilities of a versatile repertory troupe. June Duprez acted Maggie, Ernest Truex was Alick, Arthur Keegan was James, Philip Bourneuf was David, Richard Waring was John Shand, Le Gallienne was the Countess de la Brière, Mary Alice Moore was Lady Sybil Tenterden, Cavada Humphrey was a maid, Walter Hampden was Charles Venables, and Efrem Zimbalist, Jr., was a butler. The rest of the large company played the crowd roles of the electors of Glasgow and members of the Cowcaddens; they included Eli Wallach, Anne Jackson, and William Windom, all then at the start of their careers.

The reviewers deemed the play a pleasant period piece that was still amusing in its quiet and mellow way. Gilder said that it "remains a lighthearted and agreeable diversion, its basic humanity and truthfulness saving it from the bathos into which it sometimes threatens to fall." Brooks Atkinson (*NYT*), however, while admitting to enjoying it in general, did think that it became annoyingly cloying at times, and George Jean Nathan (*NYJA*) dismissed it as "simply a pleasant if oversentimentalized little comedy."

Most critics found the performances fine, although they differed on the relative merits of the performers. But John Mason Brown (*SR*), so bored he left halfway through, rejected the entire production as "stock company stuff, on an off day, by an off stock company," an opinion shared by Nathan. A mild approver of the play, he "could not bear to see what was being done to it, especially by June Duprez as a charmless Maggie." Yet many clearly approved of Duprez, despite her being too classically beautiful for the role. George Freedley (*NYMT*), for instance, wrote that Duprez had in no way imitated her famed predecessors as Maggie (Hayes and Maude Adams), "but she has achieved a charm of her own which flows from the character. . . . Duprez gives a warm and understanding performance." Despite several dissenters, there was also a consensus that Waring's John Shand was a noteworthy performance.

WHAT'S UP? [Musical/Aviation/Illness/Orientals/Politics/Romance/School/War/Youth] B: Alan Jay Lerner and Arthur Pierson; M: Frederick Loewe; LY: Alan Jay Lerner; D: Robert H. Gordon; CH: George Balanchine; S: Boris Aronson; C: Grace Houston; P: Mark Warnow; T: National Theatre; 11/11/43 (63)

Lerner and Loewe, eventually to be Broadway legends, got off on the wrong foot with their first collaboration, a routine but expensive musical starring baggy-pants comic Jimmy Savo as an Eastern potentate with a yen for full-bodied women. Major problem number one was the embarrassingly clumsy book; number two was the lack of good material for the pantomimic Savo to handle. An enthusiastic and attractive young cast, colorful sets and costumes, and expert dancers and dance routines--including jazz, tap, jitterbug, and ballet (two dream sequences)--were not enough to elevate this show.

The war situation has prompted Washington to fly the Rawa of Tanglinia (Savo) from his Indian homeland to confer with the president and other bigwigs. An important mineral has been discovered in his country, and he has offered it to America to help in the war. Accompanying the frock-coated, fezzed, and lorgnetted Rawa, who speaks no English, is an interpreter, Virginia Miller (Gloria Warren, in her Broadway debut), a rare American who speaks Tanglinian. Virginia is in love with Sergeant Dick Benham (William Tabbert), one of the air-force crew assigned to bring the monarch to these shores. The plane, unfortunately, is forced to land near the posh Miss Langley's School for Girls in Virginia. No sooner do the Rawa, the interpreter, and the crew arrive at the school than a case of measles breaks out, and all are quarantined there for eight days. The plot then proceeds to mix and match the boy-starved students and the girl-hungry fliers as the prim housemistress (Claire Meade)--who keeps a closet full of liquor--struggles to keep order. A climax of sorts is reached when the mousy Virginia calls President Roosevelt for advice on winning back the boy she craves. He advises her to spruce up her clothes and her looks, a ploy that works wonders. All the boys and all the girls find love by the end.

"The authors," disclosed Arthur Pollock (*BE*), "bulging with nice ambitions and dubious talent, offer only second-rate inventions." Wilella Waldorf (*NYP*) called the show "as pretty and sweet and self-consciously cute as a movie starlet, and just as vapid." Among the songs singled out for praise were "How Time Flies," "Joshua," and "You've Got a Hold on Me." The comic highlight was Savo's dream-sequence ballet with Phyllis Hill, a large-sized toe dancer whom the pint-sized comic pursued with risible results. The other dream sequence had the fliers in pajamas dancing with the schoolgirls in their nightgowns. Among the noticed performers were Don Weismuller (an outstanding tap dancer), comic actor Johnny Morgan, dancers Jack Baker, Sondra Barrett, Kenneth Buffett, Honey Murray, and singer Mary Roche.

WHEN DIFFERENCES DISAPPEAR [Drama/War] A/D: Leonard Black; P: Leonard Black and Ed Hussey; S: Edna Mundson; T: Provincetown Playhouse

(OB); 6/2/41

A terrible vanity production with the author producing, directing, and starring in the leading role, Lenny, presumably as himself. Brooks Atkinson (*NYT*) hated every minute, "especially when the author forgot his lines and had to duck out to prompt himself." Most critics were gone before the final curtain.

The play was about the customers and management of a Lenny's Mole-in-the-Wall luncheonette, where the philosophical Lenny dispenses his anti-Hitler advice and reminds everyone to forget their individual differences and unite to fight the common enemy. In the final act an American ship is sunk, precipitating our entry into the war to fight the Nazis.

Communist critic Ralph Warner (*DW*) decried the play's jingoistic efforts to get America into combat. He accused the author of "being out of step with his times. There are, it happens, many people as confused and as easily misled as Mr. Black's characters" about the need to make war, which the critic characterized as an imperialistic and capitalistic endeavor. "The acting, on the whole, was as bad as the writing and direction," commented George Freedley (*NYMT*).

WHEN THE BOUGH BREAKS [Drama/Marriage/Medicine] A: Robert S. Scott and John L. Gerstad; D: George Schaefer; S/L: Peter Wolf; P: Abbe Practical Workshop; T: Master Institute Theatre (OB); 3/8/50 (3)

This play has no connection with the 1937 work called *The Bough Breaks**. Like its similarly titled predecessor, it was a dud, although far more promising.

It takes place entirely within a maternity hospital where a troubled young couple (Toni Darnay and William Windom) are awaiting the woman's childbirth. The husband is a reclusive being who lives within a self-protective shell, but the birth of the child, which is abnormal, serves to break his shell and to bring the couple together again.

The subject promised a poignant drama, but the product--although very well acted--was superficial, the characters simplistic, the constant technical allusions intrusive, and the comic intrusions clumsy. Bob Francis (*BB*) rejected it as "emotional claptrap." Brooks Atkinson (*NYT*) asserted, "The characterization of the husband is pinched and spare. The play is loosely flung together. The second act is maudlin." Still, he said that he found the material intrinsically dramatic and interesting. Priscilla Morrill was a sympathetic nurse, and others in the cast included John C. Becher, Al Thaler, John Boruff, and Anne Dougherty.

WHEN WE DEAD AWAKEN [Dramatic Revival*] A: Henrik Ibsen; D: Jain Staw; P: Equity Library Theatre; T: George Bruce Branch of the New York Public Library (OB); 4/23/45

George Freedley (*NYMT*) was wrong when he stated in his review that this was the play's first local revival in forty years, for there had been a production of it in 1926, done Off Broadway, just as this one was. Freedley said that the play was directed "in a rather static fashion, getting very little movement into a play which needs a good deal to enliven it." Part of the problem stemmed from the cramped space of the performance.

Ulfheim was played by Val Valentinoff, Maja was played by Dulce Fox, Rubek was played by Joseph Hardy, and Isene was played by Sala Staw. Hardy, who was deemed too young for his role, went on to have a successful theatre career.

WHERE STARS WALK [Comedy/Fantasy/Irish/Journalism/Romance/Theatre] A: Micheal MacLiammoir; D: Hilton Edwards; S: Molly MacEwen; P: Dublin Gate Theatre u/t/a/o Richard Aldrich and Richard Myers i/a/w Brian Doherty; T: Mansfield Theatre; 2/24/48 (14)

The third and last play in the repertoire brought here by Dublin's Gate Theatre, run by Hilton Edwards and Micheal MacLiammoir, the author and star of the piece. Taking its title from a famous passage in W. B. Yeats's *Land of Heart's Desire*, it is a somewhat talky comic fantasy mingled with a drawing room comedy. Like many other Irish plays, it attempts to contrast contemporary Irish realities with an idealistic and romantic past. Herm. (*V*) said that it had "considerable charm and occasional moments of dramatic power," but suffered from dramaturgical inconsistency and a thin story. Louis Kronenberger (*PM*) considered it mildly charming, but said that it "too often goes slack or runs thin--or just seems straight-out tedious." Most critics raved about the acting, but Brooks Atkinson (*NYT*) and George Jean Nathan (*TBY*) were not among them.

The material is based on an ancient Irish legend about a pair of doomed lovers, Princess Edain and King Midhir. The pair are reborn as moonstruck servants named Martin (MacLiammoir) and Eileen (Helena Hughes) in a modern Dublin home owned by retired actress Sophia Sheridan (Meriel Moore). Sophia and her sophisticated and bored friends are engaged in rehearsing a charity production of a play (based on Yeats's version of the legend) when Eileen feels strange stirrings at the mention of her equivalent; she grows disturbed as well at Sophia's practice of spirit writing. Martin shows up as a manservant in search of employment. The couple are drawn to one another by their shared dreams. They speak in poetic phrases that contrast with the up to date modernisms of their mistress and her companions. Eileen watches the play but finds it lacking in any sense of the actual pain she once felt on being forced to choose between earthly and immortal love. She and Martin then go off to where the stars walk, and Sophia watches two swans flying off toward the stars. The satire is thickened by the burlesqued character of an obtuse English journalist (Norman Barrs) who is patronizingly fond of everything Irish.

WHERE'S CHARLEY? [Musical/Period/Romance/University/Youth] B/D: George Abbott; M/LY: Frank Loesser; SC: Brandon Thomas's play, *Charley's Aunt**; CH: George Balanchine w/Fred Danielli; DS: David Ffolkes; P: Cy Feuer and Ernest H. Martin i/a/w Gwen Rickard; T: St. James Theatre; 10/11/48 (792)

George Abbott, who had not had a hit recently, had one this time out with his adaptation of Brandon Thomas's classic 1892 British farce, *Charley's Aunt*, which Abbott retitled *Where's Charley?* (He later expressed distaste for the new title.) The play had had its last local revival in 1940 with José Ferrer. By 1948 the play had had twenty-nine London revivals, three movie versions, and countless stock productions, so it was inevitable that it would turn up one day as a musical comedy. Although the show was a smash hit (its advance sale was over $250,000), it was subject to many critical reservations.

Heading the cast--and the chief reason for the show's success--was the lanky comic dancer Ray Bolger in the role of Charley Wykeham. The character of Lord Fancourt Babberly had been excised, and it was Charley who now got to impersonate his own aunt from Brazil ("where the nuts come from") in order for him and his friend Jack Chesney (Byron Palmer) to be able to spend time in their room with their girlfriends sans a chaperone. The show even had a satirical "where the nuts come from" calypso ballet (actually titled "Pernambuco"). The Victorian period was preserved, as were all of the other characters, but there were also some new--and unimportant--figures inserted into the plot. Of the standard characters, Brassett was played by John Lynds, Doretta Morrow was Kitty Verdon, Allyn Ann McLerie was Amy Spettigue, Paul England was Sir Francis Chesney, Horace Cooper was Mr. Spettigue, and Jane Lawrence was Donna Lucia d'Alvadorez (the real aunt).

In many eyes, the blend of farce and musical did not always work, as the songs tended to slow down the action. "Every time the orchestra tunes up . . . ; every time a chorus enters or a singer sings, whatever farcical mood may have been established . . . is cruelly interrupted," criticized John Mason Brown (*SR*). There were several charming songs included, but the biggest hit was "Once in Love with Amy," which, danced in soft-shoe style, eventually became a Bolger trademark. Other important tunes were "The New Ashmolean Marching Society and Students' Conservatory Band," "My Darling, My Darling," and "Make a Miracle."

Regardless of such matters, various critics thought that the show simply was not as funny as it should have been, despite the brilliant efforts of Bolger to make it so. Howard Barnes (*NYHT*) thought the work "a heavy-handed and witless entertainment," rescued only by Bolger's slapstick and dancing. Much of the blame was placed by Brown on George Abbott's direction, which seemed ill at ease in the Oxonian surroundings of the script. Among other problems, "He does not seem to have made up his mind whether to stage the book as a period piece or to enliven it by employing a more contemporary idiom." As usual, there were opposing viewpoints, although they were in the minority. George Freedley (*NYMT*), for instance, thought it "one of the most delightful musical comedies of several seasons," and William Hawkins (*NYWT*) observed, "*Where's Charley?* is a sublimely satisfactory evening. With its taste, its beauty and its vigor, it is the sort of show you fall in love with and go back to see over and over again." He praised Abbott's book and direction highly: "It is humorous and concise, constructed in a form that lets every production number become an integral progression of the show, and he has directed the whole thing with fine pace."

Few critics quarreled about the ravishing costumes or sets or about the performances, especially that of Bolger, who was delightful whether singing, mugging, making one quick change after the other, or dancing in a variety of styles ranging from soft shoe to adagio and rhumba. "An eminent hoofer of the bucolic breed, he pushes the show aside now and then to spin rhapsodically through his mocking dances, grinning like a country gawk and translating love into leaps, whirls and comic staggers," wrote Brooks Atkinson (*NYT*). There is a well-known story that Bolger's most famous number, "Once in Love with Amy," was enormously enhanced when, at one performance, the star noticed a little girl in the audience singing along with him. Bolger then turned the song into a sing-along, feeding the lines to the audience one by one. As they happily followed him through the song, he developed it into a comical tour de force.

In *"Mister Abbott"* Abbott recalled that the production process was quite harmonious, but that one altercation did erupt during the Philadelphia tryouts. Abbott and the composer had given several solo assignments to chorus members, but the young, inexperienced producers felt that the singers were not good enough to sing these parts. As the argument grew hotter, coproducer Martin shouted, "We haven't won an argument with you two yet and we're going to win this one." Abbott commented, "This seemed a rather poor reason for making a decision, but it also seemed a trivial matter for such a clash of wills and so they won this argument."

After the show had been running about a year, twenty-two-year-old dancer Beverly Bozeman joined it; she was thrilled to be in a show with the dancer who had played the Scarecrow in *The Wizard of Oz* movie. She was warned, however, to be careful of Bolger because of his tendency to blame others when something went wrong in the performance. One night, after she had been given a new costume by the designer, Bolger was so upset at seeing it that he purposely tripped her in a big dance number and she landed on her rear end. Determined to get even, she began to make arm movements from her position on the floor as Bolger danced around and whispered more and more urgently for her to get up. Only when Bolger had to help her up himself did she rise. "When he looked at me I said: 'Don't you ever do that again to me, you sonofabitch.' He didn't even blink. From then on we were fine" (quoted in Peter Hay, *Broadway Anecdotes*).

WHILE THE SUN SHINES [Comedy/British/Gambling/Military/Romance/War] A: Terence Rattigan; D: George S. Kaufman; S: Edward Gilbert; P: Max Gordon; T: Lyceum Theatre; 9/19/44 (39)

By the time the last third of Rattigan's often witty British drawing room farce came into sight, most of its charm and sprightliness had been depleted, and the reserves were on empty. The thinly plotted, one-set play takes place in the sitting room of wealthy young Lord Harpenden's (Stanley Bell) home in London. Lord Harpenden holds the rank of ordinary seaman, his intelligence not having been up to acquiring an officer's rating. His fiancée Lady Elizabeth Randall (Anne Burr) is a British WAAF, daughter of an impecunious duke (Melville Cooper) with a penchant for gambling and shady speculations. A couple of days before they are to be wed, he meets the drunken, loutish American bombardier Lieutenant Mulvaney (Lewis Howard) when the latter is bounced from a nightclub. Lady Elizabeth, for her part, meets a Free French officer, Lieutenant Colbert (Alexander Ivo), in a railway carriage. The British nobleman wants to unload his former girlfriend, the trollopy Mabel Crum (Cathleen Cordell), on the Yank, who is happy to oblige. Mulvaney, however, mistakes Lady Elizabeth for Mabel, and both he and the Frenchman pursue her with ardor. After some passionate wooing from the American, Lady Elizabeth breaks her engagement with the sailor, and he, in turn, becomes engaged to Mabel. Finally, the American and the British noblewoman decide that they are not really in love, and she goes back to Harpenden, while he will return to his gal Gertie in the States. Mabel, meanwhile, graciously steps out of the picture (with a fat check for her troubles), sure that she could not remain faithful to one man.

This was a frequently diverting and extremely well played piece, but one that simply did not have the staying power for a Broadway audience. (It had been a hit abroad.) As Louis Kronenberger (*PM*), who scored the play for veering uncomfortably between farce and comedy, noted, "Mr. Rattigan's comedy starts wobbling after the first act, and completely wilts after the second." Wilella Waldorf (*NYP*) called it "a not too adroit bit of hack work made up of gags about London in wartime." Howard Barnes (*NYHT*), however, liked the piece for being "literate, amusing and smartly turned out." J. P. Wilson played a butler.

(1) WHITE STEED, THE [Dramatic Revival*] A: Paul Vincent Carroll; D: J. Augustus Keogh; P: Irish Repertory Players; T: Blackfriars' Theatre (OB); 4/9/42 (5)

A semiprofessional little theatre group located in Greenwich Village moved up to West Fifty-seventh Street to find a venue for its revival of Carroll's Irish play, originally done here in 1939. Director Keogh played the leading role of liberal priest Canon Matt Lavelle. The production was considered worthwhile by the few critics who saw it. It also was thought timely because its criticism of clerics who mingle too freely in secular affairs (represented by Father Shaughnessy [Paul Nemoek]) mirrored the contemporary hubbub over the reactionary priest, Father Coughlin, who sought to interfere in American politics. Ralph Warner (*DW*) thought the performance spotty, although Keogh's performance (he was an Abbey Theatre veteran) was outstanding.

(2) D: Anita Grannis; P: Equity Library Theatre; T: Muhlenberg Branch of the New York Public Library (OB); 5/29/44

A barely noticed revival by the showcase arm of Actors Equity. Respected actor Whitford Kane played Canon Matt Lavelle and was "lovable, likable and true," according to Robert Garland (*NYJA*). Nora was played by Gertrude Flynn, and Lester Fletcher was Denis Dillon. Garland wrote, "Here was a thoughtful, timely and far from unimportant play, in a thoughtful, timely and far from unimportant resuscitation."

WHOLE WORLD OVER, THE (***Tak i Budet***) [Comedy/Family/Romance/Russian] A: Konstantin Simonov; AD: Thelma Schnee; D: Harold Clurman; S/C: Ralph Alswang; P: Walter Fried and Paul F. Moss; T: Biltmore Theatre; 3/27/47 (100)

Some of the finest acting talents of the day were employed in this adaptation of a romantic Russian comedy set in Moscow shortly after the war. The current housing shortage was the presumed inspiration for the slightly plotted play's production.

Professor Feodor Vorontsov (Joseph Buloff), a crotchety army engineer whose wife died during a bombing raid in the war, is assigned with his depressed daughter Olya (Uta Hagen) to the sizable apartment formerly occupied by a military officer named Dmitri (Stephen Bekassy), who lost his wife and child during the fighting. Olya, whose fiancé also died in the war, is now engaged to Sergei (Sanford Meisner), a sycophantic young city planner, who is more interested in the professor's ideas, which he freely steals, than he is in Olya. The professor would like to get rid of him. Opportunity knocks in the person of the widowed and embittered officer, who returns to the apartment with various friends from the front. The girl's cleverly manipulative father succeeds in kindling a romantic relationship between his daughter and the officer, who decide to stop mourning and make the most of their lives while they can.

This was Joseph Buloff's first role since his long-continuing performance of the peddler in *Oklahoma!*, and he scored a terrific success as the eccentric engineer that practically carried the evening. As for the play itself, the critics were divided. Some were delighted to learn that the play had no propagandistic overtones and was decidedly unpolitical. William Hawkins (*NYJA*) thought it "rambling" but liked it because "it is simply human and amusing, and has a pleasant flavor that stays with you." But Ward Morehouse (*NYS*), who liked the early portions, declared, "It's a play that sags and lags; it doesn't hold together for a full evening." George Jean Nathan (*NYJA*) thought it a conventional boy-meets-girl tale given a veneer of interest by its topical aspects.

Brooks Atkinson (*NYT*), who had mixed feelings about the writing, declared that "the performance under Harold Clurman's direction has the subtlety of a Tammany clambake." George Bartenieff debuted on Broadway as a teenage corporal, Lou Polan was a Red Army officer, Jo Van Fleet played an army surgeon with designs on the officer, Michael Strong played a bad actor, Elizabeth Neumann was a maid, Fred Stewart was a janitor, and Beatrice de Neergaard acted his wife. The play also is known as *And So It Will Be*.

(1) **WILD DUCK, THE** (***Vildanden***) [Dramatic Revival*] A: Henrik Ibsen; TR: John L. Gerstad; D: Jack DeShay; S: Ronald Bishop; P: Library Theatre Project; T: George Bruce Branch of the New York Public Library (OB); 4/29/44 (3)

A library auditorium at 518 West 125th Street in Harlem was the site of this addition to the first season of the Library Theatre Project's (later the Equity Library Theatre) offerings. The translation was by an actor from the Norwegian National Theatre then playing a small role in *Othello* on Broadway. The most recent revival of the play had been in 1938.

"This is a lively, friendly and frequently effective revival," said George Freedley (*NYMT*), the only critic to attend. The direction downplayed the symbolism of the play and emphasized its human qualities as well as its melodrama. Hedwige was played by young Edythe Ward, who gave a memorable performance. William Woodson was Hjalmar, Barbara Coburn was Gina, for which she was a bit too young, and Al Hachmeister was Gregers, a part that defeated him.

(2) TR: Frances Archer; D: Alvin Kronacher; S: Roderich Winchell; P: Equity Library Theatre; T: Fort Washington Branch of the New York Public Library (OB); 5/24/45

A year after the previous revival, the same group, now called by what would be its permanent name, produced the play again, but in a somewhat stiff new translation. It was the thirty-fifth of thirty-seven works staged by the busy showcase company during the season.

The reason for the revival was to demonstrate the powers of refugee actor Albert Bassermann and his wife Else in the roles of Hjalmar and Gina. Bassermann, an octogenarian, had been a famous Hjalmar in Europe years earlier. Said George Freedley (*NYMT*), "His makeup and acting are a tour de force, for he has many more years now than are usually granted to Hjalmar Ekdal." Freedley observed that Bassermann kept talking all the time, which may have annoyed his fellow players. Else Bassermann was fine, but the most touching acting came from Millicent Brower as Hedwige, said Freedley. Old Werle was acted by Arnold Emanuel, old Ekdal by Mischa Tonken.

WILLOW AND I, THE [Drama/Art/Family/Medicine/Mental Illness/Period/Romance/Small Town] A: John Patrick; D: Donald Blackwell; S: Lemuel Ayers; C: Aline Bernstein; L: Girvan G. Higginson; P: Donald Blackwell and Raymond Curtis i/a/w David Merrick; T: Windsor Theatre; 12/10/42 (28)

Author John Patrick was at war in North Africa when his psychological drama opened on Broadway; had he been in New York, he might have attended to some necessary dramaturgical revisions to make his play more critically acceptable. A major objection was to the play's excessive talkiness and its inability to sustain attention to its developing action. Moreover, George Jean Nathan (*TBY*) took serious issue with Patrick's psychological portraiture, declaring that in his examination of his characters' mental problems "he so makes himself up like a medicine-show pitchman and employs so many of the pitchman's sales tricks that what you get for your good money, theatrically speaking, is a bottle labeled *Psychoanalysis* but containing only an ounce of the stuff to a gallon of tincture of melodramatic potassium nitrate."

The central role in this chronicle drama, which begins in 1900 and covers many years (requiring several characters to age visibly), is the fragile Mara Sutro (Martha Scott), whose drunkard father (Edward Pawley), a former artist, planted a willow in her honor when she was born. She has a willful, grasping younger sister, Bessie (Barbara O'Neil), who falls in love with the same man as she, young Dr. Robin Todd (Gregory Peck). Robin and Mara are to be married, and the jealous Bessie decides to shoot herself on their wedding day. But Mara finds the gun. When she struggles with her sister over it, it discharges. Mara thinks that she has killed Bessie, which causes her to lose her mind. Bessie, who was only wounded, eventually marries Robin and takes Mara as her lifetime charge. Over three decades later, the doctor has passed away and the sisters are getting on. Mara, sitting at the window gazing at her willow tree, is so shocked by a flash of lightning and a blast of thunder that her sanity returns, although she cannot recall anything of the period when her mind was unbalanced. Seeing Robin and Bessie's son Kirkland (also Peck), she thinks that it is Robin. Slowly, as her memory returns, she is aided by a doctor (Francis Compton) to piece together the puzzle of her life. She and Bessie argue over who Robin really loved, and she learns that it was herself. As the curtain falls, Kirkland, an artist, sketches her now-luminous face, which is just what he has been seeking for a mural he will call Fulfillment.

The play contained a considerable amount of discussion by doctors about the reasons for Mara's mental problems, but some were not easily convinced. Rosamond Gilder (*TAM*) indicated that this was "partly due to an overly literary style, a lack of sound theatre speech, and partly to the fact that the plot, for all its murder and madness, lacks substance." Although most reviews were on the down side, there were several upbeat ones. Richard Lockridge (*NYS*), for example, thought that the play was composed with "subtlety and cunning. The best of it has a shuddery intensity which leaves you sitting on the edges of your emotions." Good acting was in abundance. Cora Witherspoon and Alec Englander were among those in the cast. Young attorney David Merrick was making his bow as a producer.

WIND IS NINETY, THE [Drama/Aviation/Death/Family/Fantasy/Marriage/War/Youth] A: Ralph Nelson; D: Albert de Courville; S: Frederick Fox; P: Messrs. Shubert i/a/w Albert de Courville; T: Booth Theatre; 6/21/45 (108)

On opening night, playwright Ralph Nelson (then a captain in the air force and later a successful film director) gave a curtain speech in which he dedicated his drama to the next of kin of those who died in the war. Unfortunately, the sincerely intended play--winner of the National Theatre Conference playwriting contest--was mawkishly sentimental, overwritten in preachy and often flowery language, and contrived; it failed to meet the noble purpose for which it had been conceived. Still, Lee Shubert, considered the crassest of commercial producers, believed deeply in it and surprised many, especially Blanche Yurka (who reported it in *Bohemian Girl*) with the speech he delivered on opening night: "My friends, I want to tell you now, before there are any notices to be read, that this play is going to run in this theatre--my theatre--for at least four months. It's an important play with an important message. It is going to be kept alive for at least that long. I just wanted you all to know this before the curtain went up. Good night--and good luck!"

As Shubert may have suspected, the notices were not approving. Louis Kronenberger (*PM*) argued that the playwright had failed in his depiction of the ghost character as well as in his portrayal of the "living characters, who are sadly one-dimensional." He also said that the work was not a play. "It is only a relentless, evening-long gnawing away at a single situation; a situation, moreover, that involves very personal emotion rather than human drama." George Jean Nathan (*TBY*) noted the play's obvious resemblances to a 1929 turkey called *Thunder in the Air** and thought it just as bad. But some critics, such as Robert Garland (*NYJA*), John Chapman (*NYDN*), and Burton Rascoe (*NYWT*), were powerfully moved. The play eked out its existence at cut-rate prices and lost $75,000.

The family of Don Ritchie (Wendell Corey), a fighter pilot, read his final letter, anxiously await further word from him, and ponder his eventual return. He has been shot down, however, and in order to soften the blow that news of his death will bring, comes home in the form of a spirit the night before the War Department's telegram arrives. With him is the spirit of World War I's Unknown Soldier (Kirk Douglas). They cannot be seen by the family. After the family learns of his passing, each remembers him in his or her own way, his wife (Frances Reid) recalling their courtship and his proposal, his mother (Blanche Yurka) her little boy with a black eye, his father (Bert Lytell) his college freshman son, and so on. After failing to communicate with them, Don manages to telepathically convey to them the message that whenever they feel that the wind is ninety, meaning coming from the northeast, he will be there at their sides whenever he is needed.

Kirk Douglas received the best reviews of his young career for his work. Lewis Nichols (*NYT*) said that his character "is honest, frank, amusing, and Kirk Douglas plays him well." In *The Ragman's Son*, Douglas recounted his difficulty in acting with Wendell Corey, another future film star. Corey refused to look at Douglas when sharing a scene, ignoring him as if they were not on stage together. Whenever Douglas tried to discuss the matter Corey verbally abused him (and, according to Douglas, thought of him as "a dirty Jew"). (He was wrong, however, when he noted that the critics also ignored him while praising Corey.) Douglas got around his acting problem by playing his speeches as soliloquies instead of dialogues, as if in a self-contained world of mystery. Ironically, when Corey died in 1968, Douglas, who had continued to dislike the man, was prevailed upon by Corey's wife to speak his eulogy. Also in the cast were child actors Dick and Joyce Van Patten.

WINE, WOMEN, AND SONG [Revue] P: Izzy Herk, Max Liebman, and Messrs. Shubert; CH: Truly McGee; S: Frederic Fox; T: Ambassador Theatre; 9/28/42 (150)

Burlesque, which usually cost $.40 a seat, and which recently had been outlawed in New York, was somehow made legitimate by its being shown in a Broadway house for $1.65 top in this self-styled "revue-vaudeville-burlesque." Compared with the Broadway Theatre's current semiburlesque show, *Star and Garter*, which charged a $4.40 top, *Wine, Women, and Song* seemed cheesy and forgettable. Scho. (*V*) called it "a tired, slow-moving succession of girl numbers, spaced by blackouts and specialties." The show was performed two times a day and thrice on Saturday.

Among the specialty acts were the Wesson Brothers, impersonators; dancer Evelyn Farney; and jitterbuggers Billy and Buster Burnell. The girl acts included fleshy "Queen of Quiver" Marian Miller; muscular bump-and-grinder Isabel Brown, who wore a rosebud G-string painted to glow in the dark and a pair of similarly painted hands on her derriere that she suggestively manipulated on turning around; and Chinese fan dancer Noel Toy, who showed more epidermis than the rest. Chief stripper was flame-tressed Margie Hart, who appeared in a variety of skintight costumes, but performed only one strip, accompanied by an Irv Graham tune with simpleminded lyrics. John Anderson (*NYJA*) wrote, "Though her structure seems sound and handsomely shaped, the disrobing stunt has about the allurement of a tired salesclerk taking off a mannequin in a Fifth Avenue window." In the blackouts, comics Herbie Faye, Pinky Lee, Jimmy Savo, Murray Briscoe, and Murray White, the latter two straight men, figured prominently. Best (and most famous) was Savo, whose routines included his famous "River, Stay Away from My Door" number.

"Whether you choose to call it vaudeville or burlesque, it drops into last place for shoddiness, poor showmanship, and the ability to be dull," groaned Louis Kronenberger (*PM*). Because License Commissioner Moss deemed the show to be salacious, it came to an early end, and the Ambassador Theatre was padlocked for a year.

WINGED VICTORY [Drama/Aviation/Family/Friendship/Hotel/Marriage/Military/Romance/Small Town/Tropics/War] A/D: Moss Hart; M: Sergeant David Rose; S: Sergeant Harry Horner; C: Sergeant Howard Shoup; L: Sergeant A. H. Feder; P: United States Army Air Forces for the Army Emergency Relief Fund; T:

Forty-fourth Street Theatre; 11/20/43 (212)

Moss Hart was inspired to create this play (one of the season's ten best) when a young air-force officer stopped by his seat in the Oak Room of New York's Plaza Hotel and asked if he would be interested in writing about the air force. Hart's project caught the interest of certain important officers, and he was allowed to travel over 28,000 miles in a bomber (despite his aversion to flying) as he visited many camps and gathered material for his saga. The play was completed in three weeks and staged in two and a half despite a cast numbering eighty-six speaking roles, all the males of which were servicemen. Many were rising young actors who one day would be stars, and a few were making their Broadway debuts. Most of the players, drawn from a pool of 7,000 applicants, were then unknown. The reason Hart gave for his ability to stage the play so quickly with so large a company was that all the players took orders without discussion, being forced to by their military situation. The show was an instant hit and, with Hart magnanimously waiving his royalties, earned at least $1 million for the Army Emergency Relief Fund.

Considered more a great production than a great play (although some were moved enough to put it in the latter category), the work was nevertheless completely gripping and served its purpose as a piece of unfailingly consistent, rousing propaganda. The multiscened, epic-scoped drama begins on an all-American lawn in Mapleton, Ohio (a town that figures in several Moss Hart works), where three civilian friends, Allan Ross (Corporal Mark Daniels), Frankie Davis (Private Dick Hogan), and "Pinky" Scariano (Private Don Taylor) are anxiously awaiting word of their acceptance into air-force flight-training school. Allan is married to Dorothy (Phyllis Avery) and is the son of an air-force colonel (Private Damian O'Flynn). They all receive their call-up notices, and the next scene occurs on a barracks street at the induction training field. As other recruits razz them about camp hardships, Allan, Frankie (just wed to Jane [Jean McCoy]), and "Pinky" are teamed up with three other potential fliers, Texas's Dave (Sergeant Rune Hultman), Brooklyn's Irving (Private Edmond O'Brien), and Oregon's Bobby (Private Barry Nelson). In the examination room the men learn from Major Halper (Private Alan Baxter) that they will be classified as pilots, bombardiers, or navigators, depending on their progress in camp; everyone wants to make pilot. A washroom displays "Pinky" as the standout candidate thus far, the only one who finds the grueling training fun. Frankie is on the verge of breaking. In the Faculty Board Meeting Room "Pinky" learns that he has been disqualified from becoming a pilot because of depth-perception problems. Distraught, he is comforted by his buddies. He bucks up and sings the air-force song when he is alone. Soon he will be in gunnery school. The classifications are handed out in a lecture hall, and Allan and Frankie make pilot. Those who do not are dejected. Allan and Dorothy and Frankie and Jane (pregnant, but not to Frankie's knowledge) say farewell before the men ship out, but the women will follow their husbands to their next assignment. In the next scene, the men have become pilots but Frankie is killed in a training flight. Shortly the boys are celebrating their graduation from flight school, and a ceremony is held with speeches by the brass, Allan receiving honors from his dad. While awaiting orders for combat duty, the boys attend Bobby's wedding on his Oregon farm. While there, they receive word to report immediately. Bobby has to skip his honeymoon in order to catch the train. At a California flying field, pilot Allan and copilot Irving reunite with "Pinky," who is coincidentally on their Flying Fortress crew. The plane is dubbed "Winged Victory." In the barracks, Allan and Irving write their last letters home before going to fight in the Pacific. Their wives, meanwhile, comfort one another in a tawdry hotel room. Months later, on a lush island in the Pacific, the men celebrate Christmas with a show, "The Yuletide Follies," including several acts in drag (one fellow imitates Carmen Miranda). Now a hospital tent is shown, and "Pinky" is brought in wounded. "Pinky" will live, the doctor (Private Lee J. Cobb) says. A letter from Dorothy reveals that she has had a son. Allan writes a letter to his new boy with the hope that the world will be better for his and other kids after the war.

Actors in the cast included, to mention only the noteworthy names, Private Red Buttons, Sergeant Kevin McCarthy, Private Whitner Bissell, Private Anthony Ross, Corporal Gary Merrill, Private Philip Bourneuf, Sergeant George Reeves, Sergeant

Zeke Manners, Corporal Jerry Adler, Sergeant Ray Middleton, Private Alfred Ryder, Sergeant Daniel Scholl, Private Karl Malden, Private Peter Lind Hayes, Private Martin Ritt, and Lieutenant Don Beddoe. Among the many women--who were all civilians--were Olive Deering (Alfred Ryder's sister) and Elisabeth Fraser. Most had only a couple of lines. Together with those doing walk-ons, singing in the choruses (directed by Lieutenant Leonard de Paur), and playing in the orchestra, they totaled well over 300 performers. The casting was done by Lieutenants Ben Landis and Irving P. Lazar, the latter eventually famed as "Swifty" Lazar, one of the most powerful agents in Hollywood.

Most critics soared into the wild blue yonder in ecstasy over the production. It was reckoned outstanding for its individualistic characterizations, its lack of stump-thumping rhetoric, its boiling down of the true experiences of many men into a basic and affecting tale of great universality and appeal, its honest and integral humor, its effective incorporation of martial music at key points, and its incorporation of air-force ritual and spirit. This was, said Lewis Nichols (*NYT*), "a stirring, moving and, what is more important, a most human play about the boy next door." Rosamond Gilder (*TAM*) considered it "a remarkable achievement, for it succeeds in making articulate the modern miracle of which one of the officers in it speaks--the miracle of the creation, almost overnight, of one of the world's greatest air forces, the rising up of an easy-going, careless and carefree generation in defense of an ideal." "Here is a thrilling show, a combination of play and spectacle," reported Ward Morehouse (*NYS*), "that dwarfs all else of the current season and beside which the majority productions of the present decade and century shrink to mediocrity." Howard Barnes (*NYHT*) judged it "a great and profoundly moving war play. . . . The author has taken a huge canvas for his work, but he has written with such simplicity, passion and artistry that its effect is always immediate and personal." However, George Freedley (*NYMT*) thought that the show began well but bogged down in wordiness in the second of its two acts. He found it "only incompletely moving" and was sorely disappointed by what he deemed flat characters, pat direction, and not always convincing action and dialogue. Much nastier was George Jean Nathan (*TBY*), who lambasted the piece on many fronts and said that it was "an unimaginative, a juvenile, and an oversentimentalized job."

To keep the show moving smoothly, Harry Horner designed five revolving stages so that the sixteen scenes could seamlessly blend with one another. The speed and efficiency with which the kaleidoscopic work proceeded was one of its best features. Hart's direction was exceptional in its marshalling of the huge company and its attention to the details of individual performances.

On opening night, Hart was brought forth at the end to address the audience. He stepped out very nervously as the entire company joined the audience in applause. He said, "Thank you, ladies and gentlemen. Tonight I heard over the radio that we were bombing Berlin again. This is what this play is about." The national anthem was played, and the emotionally drained audience departed from what many thought a unique event in the annals of American theatre history. At the opening-night party, held on the Astor Hotel Roof, a thirty-minute takeoff on the show was done by various participants. It was called "Singed Victory" and featured Hart and Peter Lind Hayes.

WINNERS AND LOSERS [Drama/Military/Politics/Trial] A: Nicholas Biel; D/S: Edward R. Mitchell; P: Associated Playwrights, Inc.; T: Henry Street Playhouse (OB); 2/26/47 (5)

The first showcase venture by an Off-Broadway group made up of Theatre Guild actors-in-training was this sprawling, large-cast effort about the problems of the occupying forces in Germany. The time is right after V-E Day and the place is the town of Hellesradt. There are Nazis to be uncovered in the town, but the American commanding officer does nothing about them. The clearheaded and clever Corporal Gilbert Wanstead (Gaylord Mason), despite opposition, takes on the job himself and succeeds; however, he is court-martialed for his troubles. Before the play concludes, the Germans discover that their territory has been placed in the hands of the Russians, who will not treat them as lackadaisically as the fishing, hunting, and girl-chasing GIs.

Joe Pihodna (*NYHT*) said that the drama offered "a story without shade or penetration," and that it came off more as the work of a reporter than a dramatic artist. There was a clear anti-officer and anti-German bias, while the enlisted men were depicted very favorably. Still, the dialogue and atmosphere were sufficiently authentic to suggest the author's own experiences overseas. Brooks Atkinson (*NYT*) thought the play "amateurish in craftsmanship and acting."

WINSLOW BOY, THE [Drama/British/Family/Labor/Law/Period/Politics/School/Trial/Women/Youth] A: Terence Rattigan; D: Glen Byam Shaw; DS: Michael Weight; P: Atlantis Productions, the Theatre Guild, H. M. Tennent, Ltd., and John C. Wilson); T: Empire Theatre; 10/29/47 (215)

A solid British drama that ran out the season and was selected as one of the season's ten best as well as winning the Drama Critics Circle Award as best foreign play. Its story is based on a real-life incident in the life of George Archer-Shee, who died at Ypres in the first year of World War I. The David and Goliath case, with its little man pitted against the giant establishment represented by the British Crown, and with its symbolic representation of the rights of average citizens, gained international attention.

The central figure is thirteen-year-old Ronnie Winslow (Michael Newell), who, shortly before World War I, has been kicked out of the Royal Naval College for stealing a five-shilling postal order, although the evidence is circumstantial; the school is sustained by the Lords of the Admiralty. His father, Arthur Winslow (Alan Webb), convinced of Ronnie's guiltlessness, struggles to no avail to get the case reopened. The family then turns to Sir Robert Morton (Frank Allenby in the role created in London by Emlyn Williams), a brilliant attorney, who upsets them by his merciless questioning of the boy before he agrees to accept the case. Two years of grueling legal battles ensue, including the attorney's clever maneuvering to get the king to sign a petition of right--necessary to permit a public trial--with the words, "Let right be done." Meanwhile, Arthur's health suffers, and he experiences financial hardship. He even is forced to withdraw another son, Dickie (Owen Holder), from college because of his financial straits. The much-publicized case goads others into treating the obsessed Winslows with scorn for having the audacity to fight the establishment on so trivial a matter. Even Mrs. Winslow (Madge Compton) attempts to have Arthur cease his efforts. Another blow comes when suffragette and trade unionist daughter Catherine (Valerie White) is abandoned by her priggish fiancé (Michael Kingsley), although Catherine is willing to make the sacrifice in the name of justice and democracy. It turns out that her suspicions of the supposedly reactionary attorney are unfounded, and that he has made major sacrifices on behalf of the case. The case eventually is won, the postmistress's weak testimony being demolished, although the actual courtroom scenes are offstage. The Conservative party attorney and the Labour suffragette join hands as friends. It turns out, though, that while the trial was reaching its climax, Ronnie was asleep, and when the verdict came in he was in a theatre watching a film.

The tautly composed drama followed the historical case rather closely while taking various liberties with such things as the actual years involved, the names of the personages, the city of their residence, and various other details. A few were as moved by the message of the play as they were by its dramatic quality. Some felt that the play might have been even more potent if the trial scenes had been enacted, rather than keeping the entire action in the Winslows' home and requiring Greek messenger-type speeches to bring on the offstage events. Still, said Euphemia Van Rensselaer Wyatt (*CW*), "The careful characterization and skillful arrangement of the scenes sustain the suspense in the action." Howard Barnes (*NYHT*) called it "richly satisfying drama," created "with deep feeling, humor and passion." William Hawkins (*NYWT*) wrote, "It is a shrewd play, compelling, suspenseful and inspiring." Not all were so positive. George Jean Nathan (*TBY*) grudgingly agreed that it was "very fair theatrical goods," but insisted that it was contrived and an example of "journeyman box-office style." Even less impressed was John Chapman (*NYDN*), for whom it was "frightfully genteel and more than faintly tedious."

The all-English cast was considered outstanding. Those who had seen the London version thought the acting even better on Broadway.

WINTER SOLDIERS [Drama/Broadcasting/Military/Politics/Prostitution/War] A: Dan James; D: Shepard Traube; S: H. A. Condell; L: Hans Sondheimer; P: Erwin Piscator; T: Studio Theatre of the New School for Social Research (OB); 11/29/42 (30)

This was the first Off-Broadway play that did not ultimately go on to a Broadway production ever selected by Burns Mantle for his best plays of the year series. A Broadway production had been considered, but even after its warm reception at its theatre on West Twelfth Street (where the most expensive seat was $1.65), the expense of putting on such a large-cast drama (there were forty-two actors in it) in the commercial mainstream was too great, and the idea was abandoned. The epic play won the second Sidney Howard Memorial Award, a $1,500 prize granted by the Playwrights' Company (the money was sunk in the production), and also was praised highly by many of the critics.

Dan James's eleven-scene play, aided in shifting its locales by a clever setting employing a revolving stage, concerned the underground soldiers--the courageous little people--in occupied Europe who fight the Nazi terror not only in the winter of snow and cold but in the winter of their adversity. Set in November 1941, it begins with the Nazis prepared to occupy Moscow under Marshal von Falken (Ronald Alexander), whose battle plan has been meticulously prepared. His subordinates (including the cynical Gestapo agent, Tieck [Herbert Berghof]) protest, but he orders the Death's Head Regiment in Yugoslavia to join the Russian assault. In a hut in Zagreb, Yugoslavia, a Nazi colonel (Alfred L. Linder) is slain by a deaf and mute underground peasant fighter (Vaughn George), who obtains the plans and hands them over to his superiors. The information is then broadcast to Austria and Poland over a freedom station by a former professor (Paul Marx) hiding in a mountain cave. The action then follows the route of the troop train as it moves to Moscow. On the way it encounters railroad sabotage in Vienna, where a track is loosened while an Austrian sergeant (Paul Wagner) whose sympathies are not with the Nazis allows himself to be distracted by a girl (Dolly Haas) who turns prostitute for the purpose; a railroad strike in Prerau, Czechoslovakia, where the workers--despite the dissolution of their union--hold up the train for four hours; the blowing up of a bridge by a frightened telegraph operator when he presses a key he has rigged; and, in Russia, the killing of a number of Germans by guerrilla fighters from a collective farm. Marshal von Falken's carefully laid plans to attack at dawn come to naught when faced by the bravery and patriotism of freedom fighters throughout Eastern Europe. The Nazis are forced to retreat and suffer their first major defeat.

A principle drawback to the play was its lack of a single hero on whom to focus, the only consistently recurring characters being the Nazis. Its rhetorical "messages" were kept to a blessed minimum, but these too might have been omitted. It could have used more suspense as well, although this may have been a fault of the production. Although several critics pointed to shortcomings in the presentation, the cast--consisting of a number of refugees from Hitler--provided a highly absorbing and coherent evening. Despite the limits of the small theatre, the production made excellent use of special lighting and sound effects and side stages for action that could not be contained on the main stage.

Among the strong critical responses was that of George Jean Nathan (*TBY*): "Here, for a welcome change, is a good, honest, full-fisted, intelligent war melodrama." George Freedley (*NYMT*) insisted, "This is adult entertainment and is a play into which you can set your teeth and feel that there is real body. It is moving and exciting." More ambivalent was Howard Barnes (*NYHT*), who considered it "a singularly provocative and prodigal piece of theater," written "with considerable eloquence and dramatic power," but lacking in "the knowing craftsmanship that might have resulted in a taut and moving war melodrama rather than a repetitious and contrived entertainment." Not appreciative at all was Burton Rascoe (*NYWT*), to whom the play was "a series of cartoons. . . . Mr. James has given us instead of a play a series of stereopticon views."

There were many fine performances, Berghof's as the vicious Gestapo man being one of the best. Other valuable contributions were made by Ross Matthew as a German general, Boris Marshalov as Nikolai, Paula Bauersmith as a brave Russian woman who is killed, R. Ben Ari as the religious peasant Grigori, Miriam Goldina as Marya, Boris Tumarin as Karel, Guy Sorel as Stefan, and David Alexander as a Russian commissar. Mason Adams made his New York debut in a small role.

The attention brought to the Dramatic Workshop by this and preceding productions led to demands by the unions that their members all be paid at scale for their services. When, despite energetic fund-raising attempts, the moneys needed for such an increased budget could not be found, the Dramatic Workshop's connection with the Studio Theatre at the New School was severed. The Dramatic Workshop thereupon moved to the intimate old Broadway theatre, the President, for its subsequent productions, where the casts were invariably composed of student actors.

WINTER'S TALE, THE [Dramatic Revival] A: William Shakespeare; M: Anthony Bernard and Leo Russotto; D: B. Iden Payne and Romney Brent; CH: William Bales; S/C: Stewart Chaney; P: Theatre Guild Shakespearean Repertory Company; T: Cort Theatre; 1/15/46 (39)

This was the first major New York revival of Shakespeare's comedy-drama since 1910, when it had been given at the ill-fated New Theatre with Edith Wynne Matthison as Hermione and Henry Kolker as Leontes. It was produced for the then-hefty sum of $100,000 by the Theatre Guild, which offered another lesser example of Shakespeare the same season with *The Merry Wives of Windsor*, but chose to show it only on the road and not in New York. Some think that the venture into Shakespearean repertory floundered because the plays chosen were from the Bard's less well known oeuvre.

Despite some highly respected players in the cast, the production received mixed reviews. Henry Daniell played Leontes, Florence Reed was Paulina, Romney Brent was Autolycus, Colin Keith-Johnston was Camillo, David Powell was Polixenes, Jessie Royce Landis was Hermione, Philip Huston was Dion and Time, Whitford Kane was the old shepherd, Jo Van Fleet was Dorcas, Robert Duke was Florizel, and Geraldine Stroock was Perdita. The presentation originally had been under the direction of B. Iden Payne, but actor Brent was called on to take over during the sixteen-week pre-Broadway tour because Payne's approach was considered too stodgy.

It was a straightforward revival with unexceptionable settings suggestive of the classical ruins associated with Piranesi's designs. The work was edited to fit into two acts with a single intermission. Plot inconsistencies were smoothed over, and the play was made to seem more coherent than usual. The acting was noticeably nonrhetorical and the lines spoken with naturalness, but none of the performances was especially noteworthy. No interesting method of solving Leontes' sudden jealousy was found, however, and his behavior remained incomprehensible.

"At its best," noted Euphemia Van Rensselaer Wyatt (*CW*), "it has moments of tenderest beauty; at its worst it at least proves to young playwrights that even a genius may falter." Lewis Nichols (*NYT*) discovered that the "production makes interesting and generally alive a play which normally reclines only on the library shelf." George Jean Nathan (*TBY*) believed that the play "remains as confused and disturbing to actors, directors, and audiences as it seemingly was to its creator." On the other hand, Robert Garland (*NYJA*) gave the play and production a rave, and Burton Rascoe (*NYWT*) called the work "a thing of utter magnificence."

WINTERSET [Dramatic Revival*] A: Maxwell Anderson; D: Moe Hack; S/C: Bob Dozier and Al Conrad; P: Equity Library Theatre; T: Hudson Park Branch of the New York Public Library (OB); 3/22/45

Capacity audiences of seventy attended the tiny theatre in which this revival of Anderson's 1935 drama was produced by Equity's showcase arm. The designers successfully met the challenge of the cramped playhouse by attaching steps from the stage to the auditorium so that acting could go on in both locations. George Freedley (*NYMT*) believed that "this poetic tragedy . . . stands up beautifully after the 10 eventful years which have passed." Kurt Richards was Mio, Sydna Scott was Miriamne, Harrison Dowd was Judge Gaunt, Michael Everett was Garth, Joe Martell was Trock, and Kenneth Cook was Shadow.

WISH ME LUCK [Musical/Yiddish Language] B: Isidor Friedman and Israel Rosenberg; M: Abe Ellstein; LY: Jacob Jacobs and Isidor Lillian; D/P: Menasha Skulnik; CH: Valentina Belova; S: Edward Sundquist; C: Gropper; T: Second Avenue Theatre (OB); 10/11/45

No one really minded that much that Menasha Skulnik's Yiddish theatre vehicles were cut from the same cloth (the same people were almost always responsible for writing them) as long as he was his typical shnook of a character. His "mere appearance on the stage with his bashful shuffle and sheepish grin is enough to draw a roar of merriment," wrote Bernard R. Rachmel (*WWD*).

In the present case, the story was about Rachelle (Miriam Kressyn), who meets and falls in love with David (Muni Serebrov) while he is visiting her native country in Europe. The war comes along and he joins the U.S. Air Force, leaving Rachelle behind. He comes to believe that she has died in a concentration camp, so he marries someone else. He meets Rachelle again by chance in Paris, however, and seeks to get her into America by marrying her to his friend Sheike (Skulnik). The usual complexities arise, but both couples divorce so that they can all marry whom they really love. Skulnik ends up with Yetta Zwerling, his usual romantic foil.

Jose. (*V*) observed, "A perfunctory melodramatic book acted to the hilt by a capable cast only serves to point up Skulnik's laugh-provoking abilities."

WISTERIA TREES, THE [Drama/Blacks/Business/Family/Period/Romance/Rural/Southern] A/D: Joshua Logan; SC: Anton Chekhov's Russian play, *The Cherry Orchard**; M: Lehman Engel; S/L: Jo Mielziner; C: Lucinda Ballard; P: Leland Hayward and Joshua Logan; T: Martin Beck Theatre; 3/29/50 (165)

With this play, Joshua Logan fulfilled a dream he had had since attending Princeton University. The dream was that of taking Chekhov's *The Cherry Orchard* and transplanting it to the American soil of the deep South, where he himself was raised. He knew that Helen Hayes's secret ambition was to act in Chekhov's play, which he had loved ever since seeing Stanislavsky's Moscow production. Having seen Hayes use a perfect Southern accent years before in *Coquette**, he knew that she would be perfect for his version. It placed the story on the decaying Wisteria Plantation in Louisiana in the 1890s, where the serving class is entirely black. The title was derived from the huge oak trees entwined with the ubiquitous wisteria vines that he remembered seeing on Southern plantations. Logan and a young Russian acquaintance first translated the original play verbatim, a chief goal being to capture much of the Chekhovian humor that was so often omitted from English-language translations.

Hayes enjoyed the play on hearing it, but did not commit herself to it. Logan put the play away and nearly forgot about it, taking on the job of directing *The Member of the Wedding*. But Hayes's young daughter died of polio, and at the request of Charles MacArthur, Hayes's husband, *The Wisteria Trees* project was resurrected to take her mind off the tragedy. Logan reluctantly gave up *Member* and set about revising his script. Because of Hayes's gloom, a pre-Broadway tour was not planned, and the play opened at a period late in the season considered unfavorable for dramatic works. Because of Logan's fondness for his alma mater, the play was premiered at Princeton.

It took considerable revisions during the out-of-town tryout period to prepare the piece for Broadway. One major change from Chekhov was the elimination of the abandonment of the old servant at the end; instead, the play concluded solely with the sound of axes chopping down the oaks. What Logan considered a wise piece of advice came from S. N. Behrman, who told him to forget Chekhov in making his revisions and to write his play from scratch. But many problems remained, among them Hayes's behavior, usually exemplary, but now strained by her sorrow and that of her husband. In Philadelphia, Logan gave her a note about creating a certain mood by slowing down the pace of her opening scene, and she became so offended that she slowed down not only that scene but her whole performance to the point that the performance was ruined. Logan then angrily told the actress to play the piece however she liked and never to let him make any suggestions again. He was thereupon advised by others to close the show because Hayes was destroying it. But the next night, Hayes was a different person and insisted that everything possible be done to improve the show, so it remained alive, revivified by the star's determination.

The play opened to split opinions, with the emphasis on the negative (it eventually was ribbed as being "Southern fried Chekhov"), although the lustrous performance of Hayes as the flighty, impractical former belle, Lucy Andrée Ransdell, was lauded almost unanimously. Still, the drama was selected as one of the season's ten best. In some eyes, Logan's effort was considered a new play and not a straight copy; others felt that it was an interesting adaptation, but surely not a new work. While the Chekhov plot was retained in most particulars, the romantic alliances were slightly altered, so that (coupling Logan's dramatis personae here with Chekhov's) Yancy Loper/Yermolai Lopakhin (Kent Smith) woos Lucy/Lyubov instead of being interested in the spinster cousin Martha/Varya (Peggy Conklin), although the latter is in love with him, and Peter Whitfield/Pyotr Trofimov (Douglass Watson) and Antoinette/Anya (Bethel Leslie) end up with a happy future before them.

Brooks Atkinson (*NYT*) agreed that Logan fell far short of Chekhov's "philosophical spirit and . . . literary texture," but found his loosely structured drama engrossing and touching in its picture of an old family slowly going to seed in a world that has passed them by. Howard Barnes (*NYHT*) represented the majority faction that felt that this was a clever but contrived exercise. "There are affecting moments," he admitted, "but it is a laggard show," redeemed only by the luminescence of Hayes. William Hawkins (*NYWT*) believed that Logan had abandoned Chekhov's astringency and "over and over substituted a romantic method of highlighting ideas, but has not bolstered the narrative so it will support his artifice." Hobe. (*V*) complained that the piece was static and remained "curiously untheatrical. . . . It seems a bit anemic, ineffectual and, in the end, disappointing."

John Chapman (*NYDN*) said that Hayes was "superb, wonderful, gallant, brilliant, heartbreaking--all or any of the things that anyone could wish an extraordinary actress could be." Her performance was abetted by an expert cast that included the Gavin Leon Andrée/Leonid Gayev of Walter Abel, the Scott/Firs of Alonzo Bosan, the Jacques/Yasha of Ossie Davis, the Henry Arthur Henry/Epihodov of Maurice Ellis, the Dolly Mae/Dunyasha of Vinie Burrows, the Cassie/Charlotta of Georgia Burke, and others.

With the play doing good business, Hayes decided that it would be best to close for a summer vacation and to reopen in the fall, but Logan thought this a crazy idea, knowing that the momentum now building would never be regained. His fears proved justified.

WITH A SILK THREAD [Drama/Family/Marriage/Medicine/Sex/Theatre] A/D: Elsa Shelley; DS: Watson Barratt; P: Irving Kaye Davis; T: Lyceum Theatre; 4/12/50 (13)

An old-fashioned, "singularly unseemly" (Howard Barnes [*NYHT*]) drama of marital infidelity about Rose Raymond (Clare Luce), a beautiful, egotistical, and restless former actress married for two decades to a successful surgeon, Dr. Walter Lucas (Philip Huston), a jealous type whose dealings with Rose border on the cruel. All the action takes place at the Lucases' beach house (real sand was part of the decor). The unhappy Rose, mother of a nineteen-year-old son (William Duff), wants to return to the theatre in a summer production of *Candida** (whose theme inspires the action, which employs it with a twist). Rose is attracted to the handsome young actor playing Marchbanks, Tony Fern (Phil Arthur), who went to college with her son. Tony is interested in Rose as a boost to his career. When she leaves her home for him, he rejects her, and she returns to the bosom of her forgiving family.

Mediocrity ruled in acting, direction, and dramaturgy. "The authoress's story-plotting, characterizations and dialog are inept," barked Hobe. (*V*). "The script sounds as though it had been fashioned by a novice with a meat-axe," wrote Barnes. Lilia Skala played a maid. Producer Davis was playwright Shelley's husband.

WITHIN THE GATES [Dramatic Revival*] A: Sean O'Casey; P: Interplayers; T: Provincetown Playhouse (OB); 7/8/48

O'Casey's play, which had had a 100-performance run here in 1934, was misused in this Off-Broadway company's presentation, which freely eliminated dialogue and characters it felt were repetitious. For this it was sharply castigated by several critics, including Richard Watts, Jr. (*NYP*), who also took it to task for "oversimplifying everything and making the narrative as conventional as possible." He added that the necessary exuberance and poetic style demanded by the piece were completely beyond the grasp of the young players and that this modern masterpiece was "reduced to pygmy status by an uncomprehending production." "This group seems quite simply to have bitten off more than it can chew," insisted William Hawkins (*NYWT*). None of the reviewers deigned to mention the actors or other creative personnel.

WITHOUT LOVE [Comedy/Marriage/Politics/Romance/Sex/War] A: Philip Barry; M: Richard E. Myers; D: Robert B. Sinclair (with the assistance of Arthur Hopkins); S/L: Robert Edmond Jones; C: (gowns) Valentina; P: Theatre Guild; T: St. James Theatre; 11/10/42 (113)

The combination of a Barry comedy and a star performance by Katharine Hepburn, so successful in the late thirties on Broadway and in movies, did not make for scintillating theatre in this effort because neither Barry nor the actress was in tip-top form. "In both the writing and the acting," argued Brooks Atkinson (*NYT*), "*Without Love* is theatre on the surface of a vacuum."

The play had been given a spring tryout tour, but it was decided not to bring it into New York at the time because the piece needed more work. The male lead might have gone to Spencer Tracy, Hepburn's lover, but his drinking problem cooled the Theatre Guild management. For some reason, they were not as worried about using another alcoholic, Elliott Nugent, in the role. The actress often overacted to compensate for his lack of stage fire and sexual appeal. Possibly some other problems were related to director Sinclair's having joined the armed forces following the tour. When the production was revived for a limited run in the fall, the directorial chores were in the hands of Arthur Hopkins, fading and near the end of his career. Euphemia Van Rensselaer Wyatt (*CW*) pointed out, for example, that "the whole direction seemed to lack determination." Despite its weak reviews, the show was doing good business when Hepburn, contracted for only fourteen weeks, chose not to extend the run. The production marked the inauspicious opening of the twenty-fifth subscription season of the Theatre Guild. Fortunately, the Guild was revived soon after with its conspicuously successful mounting of *Oklahoma!*

The play was directly in the vein that Barry had mined so well before, high comedy played in the residence of a member of the upper classes, in this case Jamie Coe Rowan (Hepburn), widowed and wealthy, New England Puritan-descended daughter of a U.S. senator. Patrick Jamieson (Nugent), ex-foreign correspondent son of a foreign diplomat, is actively engaged in getting the Irish Republic to abandon neutrality, provide naval bases for America, and unite Ireland and England in fighting the war as partners. Assuming the guise of an Irishman, he takes employment as a butler at Jamie's home, but she soon discovers his true identity. The lonely Jamie--who has vowed never to remarry because her late spouse was so perfect that she knows she can never find another like him--greatly respects Pat's mind and wants to do what she can to help him, such as by introducing him to the right persons while he is in Washington. He has had an unhappy love affair with a Frenchwoman and is in no mood for a new romance, but he agrees to her suggestion that, with the housing shortage in Washington, they marry for convenience, he move in, and they keep separate bedrooms and private lives. Although a carnal relationship develops by the end of act two, by act three, their marriage becomes truly more than a matter of convenience. (There is a symbolic suggestion that Pat and Jamie represent England and Ireland and that their permanent union is the natural evolution of a decision to unite in name only.)

Among the comedy's problems were a lack of consistently amusing dialogue, the burdensome intrusion of political arguments into the obviously stenciled plot, the failure of those issues to provoke interest, and the foregone conclusion as to how it would all work out. "It is all placid, polished and polite. It is as light and even, as shiny as a bubble, and about as empty," noted John Anderson (*NYJA*). Comparing it to *The Philadelphia Story**, the great Barry-Hepburn hit of 1939, which she found "second-rate," Wilella Waldorf (*NYP*) declared *Without Love* to be "longer, duller and sillier." Louis Kronenberger (*PM*) maintained that Barry's "old touches of insight, the old gift of preserving the proper tone for social comedy has been replaced by cuteness, fancifulness and snob appeal."

Rosamond Gilder (*TAM*) left a good picture of Hepburn, who wore a succession of smashing Valentina creations: "Her mannerisms--the striding walk, the swinging shoulders, the trick of leaning stiffly against furniture, the monotonous voice with its deliberately misplaced pauses--all these are more in evidence than ever; yet there are happy moments . . . when these weaknesses are overcome and her peculiar gift of creating a fragile, tender, almost poignant mood is at its best."

As with Hepburn, there were those who thought Nugent outstanding and those who thought him ineffective. More uniformly admired was Audrey Christie as Kitty Trimble, Pat's hard-boiled loyal secretary. Sherling Oliver, Robert Chisholm, Royal Beal, Tony Bickley, and Neil Fitzgerald were among others in the cast.

WOMAN BITES DOG [Comedy/Hotel/Journalism/Politics/Romance/Small Town] A: Bella and Samuel Spewack; D: Coby Ruskin; S: Howard Bay; C: Mary Grant; P: Kermit Bloomgarden; T: Belasco Theatre; 4/17/46 (5)

Future stars Kirk Douglas, Frank Lovejoy, Mercedes McCambridge (who replaced Elaine Stritch during tryouts), and E. G. Marshall were bitten by this innocuous satirical farce on the newspaper business. At its heart are three reactionary newspaper owners and relatives, the childishly egomaniacal Commander Southworth (Taylor Holmes); his cynical brother, Major Southworth (Royal Beal), a onetime liberal turned Republican; and their egotistical cousin, Lizzie Southworth (Ann Shoemaker), who is preoccupied with gaining a new society editor. The first owns a paper in Chicago, the second in New York, and the third in Washington, D.C. The isolationist commander's crusading journalistic diatribes against communism, the New Deal, Roosevelt, Britain, and other targets so incense a liberal-minded army veteran and former small-town newspaper editor named Hopkins (Douglas) that he contrives a plan to convince the newspaper owner of the subversion by the Communists of his (Hopkins's) hometown, Danville, Illinois. The commander sends his crack reporter, Betty Lord (McCambridge), to investigate, but she finds no evidence to support the charges. She is prepared to expose the hoax, but a disappointed romance with the commander's editor, Tony Flynn (Frank Lovejoy), leads to her getting drunk and writing an article attacking the town's alleged radicalism. The story spreads nationwide and becomes a cause célèbre. By the time the publisher discovers the truth, he is unable to quiet the reactionary forces that have been unleashed. Meanwhile, the girl reporter falls for the ex-soldier. To extract himself from his embarrassing dilemma, the commander must forgo punitive measures against Hopkins and the reporter. Hopkins even sells the story of the deception to *PM*.

Credibility was overlooked in the play's headlong and mechanical rush to garner laughs. A few good laughs were scattered through an otherwise uneventful comedy. It was acted and written too broadly for general consumption, and the inevitable love affair only served as padding that bogged the play down. Louis Kronenberger (*PM*) noted that the authors' "panting farce plot and burlesque characters . . . add up to too little as either commentary or comedy." Robert Garland (*NYJA*) lambasted it as "a jerrybuilt contraption in which puppets pretend to be people."

In the cast were Maury Tuckerman, Boris Kogan, Dudley Sadler, Sam Bonnell, Edward F. Nannery, Eda Heinemann, Harold Grau, and others. The play contained a disclaimer that the leading characters "are fictional, of course," but it was widely known that the three publishers satirized were Colonel Robert McCormick of the *Chicago Tribune*, Cissy Patterson of the *Washington Times-Herald*, and Joseph Patterson of the *New York Daily News*.

WONDERFUL JOURNEY [Comedy/Crime/Death/Fantasy/Romance/Sports] A: Harry Segall; D: Frank Emmons Brown; S: Raymond Sovey; C: Bianca Stroock; P: Theron Bamberger i/a/w Richard Skinner; T: Coronet Theatre; 12/25/46 (9)

This flop play originally had been known as *Heaven Can Wait*; it was the source of the popular 1941 movie *Here Comes Mr. Jordan*. Now, under a new title, it was being given its first Broadway showing, although it had had a considerable success in Pasadena, Indianapolis, and at the Bucks County Playhouse, at which latter venue it had played the previous summer with much the same cast as now was acting it. Another movie, 1943's *Heaven Can Wait*, had nothing to do with the present play. The piece was good for a few intermittent laughs but was vastly inferior to its Hollywood incarnation.

Joe Pendleton (Donald Murphy) is a young boxer-pilot who dies fifty years too soon as the result of a divine error by an overeager celestial messenger (Wallace Acton), who snatched him before he actually had been killed in a plane crash. The heavenly agent, Mr. Jordan (Sidney Blackmer), is in the midst of rectifying things and sending Joe back to earth when Max Levene (Philip Loeb), the boxer's manager, has the body cremated. This necessitates the location of a new physical entity for Joe's soul to occupy. The choices lie among those on the verge of death. Joe selects playboy financier J. F. Farnsworth, about to be murdered by his wife and her lover. Joe inhabits the Farnsworth flesh for a month and falls for Bette Logan (Frances Waller). With Farnsworth's body, he is about to resume his boxing career, but the late tycoon, in hell, objects. Joe finds a more appropriate physique into which to transmigrate, that of K. O. Murdock, a champion prizefighter who has been murdered by gangsters. He and Bette--who recognizes the soul inside through his eyes--happily face the next fifty years together, and Joe forgets his previous existence.

The critics found that the dully directed material was "hard to swallow and makes one wonder how the pug's friends can be such dopes as not to recognize him in his new body despite the fact that he acts and talks exactly as he did when he was Joe Pendleton" (Herb. [*V*]). Louis Kronenberger (*PM*) called it "a sort of harmless, but not quite painless, bore." The acting honors went hands down to Loeb. Among others in the cast were Michael Lewin, Fay Baker, Barry Kelley, Stephen Elliott, and Hal Conklin.

WOOKEY, THE [Comedy-Drama/Family/Politics/Romance/Sea/War] A: Frederick Hazlitt Brennan; D: Robert B. Sinclair; S: Jo Mielziner; P: Edgar Selwyn; T: Plymouth Theatre; 9/10/41 (134)

One of the best anti-Nazi plays of the year was this offering starring British veteran Edmund Gwenn as Mr. Wookey, self-styled "the Wookey," a representative of the gallant "little people" of Great Britain. It was written by an American screenwriter and begins on the day before England's entry into World War II.

The Wookey is a middle-aged cockney tugboat captain living with his family, which worships him, near the London docks. Although he served in the BEF during World War I, the gruff skipper disapproves of Churchill's handling of the present crisis, preferring for England to keep its nose out of Europe's mess. He refuses to participate in air-raid drills and in various ways snubs his nose at those in power. However, when his stripteaser sister-in-law's (Carol Goodner) husband (who eventually dies) is in danger at Dunkirk, the war becomes personal to him, and he steers his ferry over there to help in the evacuation, repeating his heroic efforts seventeen times, for which he is awarded a medal by the government. Still opposed to British participation in the fighting, he dictates a virulent letter to the prime minister, his bomb-wary daughter (Heather Angel) being his amanuensis. As an air raid threatens, he claims his disgust at his ferry's having been publicly smeared by a refueling company after he failed to pay fuel charges for a mission that should have been paid for by the government. (The scene offered Gwenn a brilliant opportunity for first-class acting.) But when his own home is bombed, his wife (Norah Howard) killed, and his young son (George Sturgeon) crushed under a beam, he realizes the path he must take. He sends his daughter, sister-in-law, and son to safety and takes shelter in the basement of his home, although warned to leave by the military. An air raid starts and, as a German voice comes over a loudspeaker telling the people to surrender or be wiped out, the indomitable Wookey climbs the steps carrying a tommy gun too big for him, prepared to give his life to fight the Nazi Luftwaffe.

It was reported that $15,000 had been spent on sound effects recorded by the British Ministry of Information during the London blitz. Rosamond Gilder (*TAM*) declared, "The all-too-realistic sounds of screaming bombs, crashing buildings, roaring planes, anti-aircraft guns deafen the ear and stun the imagination." The effect gave audiences as close as possible a rendition of how it would feel if they were themselves subject to an air raid. The scenic effects, too, were unique, particularly the bombed out, still smoking shell of the Wookey's home.

Some critics found the Wookey more a caricature than a character, but were compelled to belief in him by Gwenn's wonderfully rounded performance. Beginning as comedy, the play moved deeper and deeper into darker waters. It was recognized as being an essentially shallow and sentimental melodrama, its dialogue decidedly on the hokey side, but a work that, with its powerful appeal to the emotions, its mingling of the sad and comic, and its delightful characters, was impossible not to get caught up in. Richard Lockridge (*NYS*) was willing to overlook its flaws and said, "It is an absorbing, moving play, and sporadically rather more." But John Beaufort (*CSM*) reasoned, "Mr. Brennan has written a play which possesses moments of both humor and pathos. But by seeming to write for effect rather than from conviction, by stressing melodramatic and sentimental elements, by allowing physical assets to become the main show, . . . by digressing from even the main theme, Mr. Brennan had trifled with a subject of deep concern to the world." Excellent work was offered by all the actors, including Horace McNally (as the daughter's Irish suitor), Henry Mowbray, Everett Ripley, and Olive Reeves-Smith.

WORLDS APART [Drama/Family/Jews/Yiddish Language] A: Benjamin Ressler; M: Sholem Secunda; D: Maurice Schwartz; S: Alexander Chertov; P/T: Yiddish Art Theatre (OB); 1/22/41

In its third production of the 1940-1941 season, Maurice Schwartz's Yiddish Art Theatre scored strongly with this timely play that promised to refill the company's empty coffers. Schwartz starred as a refugee rabbi who arrives at the Upper West Side home of his son (Samuel Goldenburg), whom he has not seen for twenty-eight years, to drum up support for the Jews being persecuted by Hitler. He discovers that the immigrant Jews of America also have problems of their own to confront. The old rabbi must moreover be concerned with his social-climbing daughter-in-law (Lucy German) when she objects to the changes the bearded cleric tries to bring about in her up-to-date household. A happy ending is effected.

"Benjamin Ressler's excellent script is rich in comedy, while underneath runs a deep current of pathos," wrote D. H. (*WWD*). L. B. (*NYT*), though, felt that a weak second act was overloaded with problems to solve because the author "compromised reality with wishful thinking and violated the consistency of a few splendid characterizations." Cast members included Isadore Casher, Leon Gold, Anna Appel, Muni Serebrov, Luba Kadison, Lazar Freed, and Judith Abarbanell. The play is also known as *Three Generations*, *Strange Worlds*, and *Three Wishes*.

WORLD'S FULL OF GIRLS, THE [Comedy/Family/Military/Romance/Sex/War] A: Nunnally Johnson; SC: Thomas Bell's novel, *I'll Come Back to You*; D/P: Jed Harris; S: Stewart Chaney; T: Royale Theatre; 12/6/43 (9)

Set in Brooklyn for two acts and Greenwich Village for one, this first play by a well-known screenwriter dealt with a theme of growing frequency, the last-minute fling of lovers before the guy goes off to war. A play that opened two nights later, *The Voice of the Turtle*, handled the idea so much better that lesser competition such as this pasteboard effort was quickly exiled to the rubbish heap. Johnson stuck to Hollywood thereafter.

This is a two-ply story, dealing with a Brooklyn Irish family on the one hand, and with a romance between a young man who has enlisted in the marines and his estranged girlfriend. Mr. and Mrs. Bridges (Thomas W. Ross and Eva Condon) are an aging couple who want to leave Brooklyn and retire to a small farm. Their sluttish daughter Florrie (Gloria Hallward) is going with a draft-dodging, anti-Semitic fascist (Charles Lang) who gets her pregnant, which leads her to try to force him into marriage. Another daughter, Adele (Frances Heflin), is unhappily married to and the mother of a baby (a real one was used) by a dim-witted war worker (Walter Burke) whose low IQ has cost him his job. Daughter-in-law Hannah (Julie Stevens) is married to son Dave (Thomas Hume), but they have no kids, although she longs for one. Non-family members are Miley (Berry Kroeger), the marine enlistee, and Sally (Virginia Gilmore), who have been separated because he was not ready to marry when she asked him to. Another plot strand is introduced by the arrival of a heroic soldier (Harry Bellaver), who killed a Japanese soldier during a struggle in which two of his fingers were bitten off. His story of the incident is compelling, although barely related to the rest of the action. He does, however, get into an argument with the fascist and knocks him out with one blow. In the last act, Sally and Miley, having finally been reconciled, retire to his Greenwich Village flat before he leaves for the marines and, following a blackout, embrace for a night of love together without benefit of clergy.

The stories never meshed comfortably, Howard Barnes (*NYHT*) noting that "the piece has no more dramatic contour than a radio soap opera." Burton Rascoe (*NYWT*) characterized the comedy as a "feeble and pointless piece of nothing." Famed producer-director Jed Harris's direction was considered a negative, although a few of the performances were thought of highly.

(1) WOULD-BE GENTLEMAN, THE (***The Bourgeois Gentleman***; ***Le Bourgeois Gentilhomme***) [Dramatic Revival*] A: Molière; D: Chaim Brisman; P: Equity Library Theatre; T: 115th Street Branch of the New York Public Library; 5/23/45

This was "a better than competent revival" (George Freedley [*NYMT*]) of the Molière comedy, called here *The Bourgeois Gentleman* and last been seen locally as *The Would-Be Gentleman* in the Civic Repertory production of 1931. A lack of male actors forced the director to cast half the roles with women, but the play was broad enough to support this decision. Ray Lanning played M. Jourdain and Jane Dillon was his maid Nicole, while Jacqueline Soans took M. Jourdain's daughter and Nora Whille his wife. Cleonte and his valet were in the hands of Harold Miller and Bob Lenn, respectively.

(2) AD: Bobby Clark; M: Jerome Moross (adapted from Jean-Baptiste Lully); D: John Kennedy; S: Howard Bay; C: Irene Sharaff; P: Michael Todd; T: Booth Theatre; 1/9/46 (77)

A freewheeling, lowbrow adaptation of the Moliére classic (titled *The Would-be Gentleman* in this version) made especially palatable by the burlesque extravagances of its adaptor and comic star, Bobby Clark, who--without his trademark cigar and painted-on spectacles--played the parvenu M. Jourdain. A number of critical pundits deplored Clark's liberties, which involved considerable ad libbing, oldtime show-biz shtick, and the use of lines culled from other Molière plays. Clark admitted to stealing most of his additional comments from *The Precious Young Ladies*. One of his biggest laughs was his own invention. It came when he was being taught how to pronounce words properly and discovered that the alphabet is composed of two classifications, vowels and consonants. Said Clark, "Hmmm. That's only fair." Clark took special pleasure in breaking up the line of footmen who had to stand there with poker faces. He would appear without his wig, with his hat at a funny angle, or some such thing to make them laugh. One night, as Clark's character stood talking to his daughter on one side of the stage, one of the footmen was trying to blow a dustball from the bowl of soup soon to be eaten by M. Jourdain. Although he tried to do this surreptitiously, the audience began to laugh. When he looked up, Clark, who was standing there watching, tore the house down with his ad-lib, "Marcel, I thank you to let me blow on my own soup" (quoted in Peter Hay, *Broadway Anecdotes*).

Clark and producer Todd also agreed to add female characters to the first act, where they do not appear in the original. Art Cohn reported in *The Nine Lives of Michael Todd* that the producer claimed, "There wasn't a dame in the whole first act of Molière, and you can't get away with that."

Representing the nay-sayers was Lewis Nichols (*NYT*), who complained that seventeenth-century satire was not Clark's cup of tea and that the disparity between player and playwright was too great to bridge. He dubbed the production "simply a series of vaudeville incidents." To George Jean Nathan (*TBY*), however, the only parts that did not drag a bit were those in which Clark appeared, at which he laughed uproariously. Rosamond Gilder (*TAM*) felt that Clark's performance rescued the presentation "from inanity." "When Bobby Clark prances out on the stage," she reported, "paws the earth with his foot, tosses his head back with loud, anguished howls, climbs up the door jamb in an ecstasy of absurd, lascivious glee, only the most ungrateful of theatregoers would fail to be amused." John Mason Brown (*SR*), expecting to tire quickly, found that the only thing that fatigued him was too much laughing at Clark's antics. The troupe included Donald Burr as the music master, Alex Fisher as the dancing master, Eleanore Whitney as Lucille, Earle MacVeigh as the fencing master, Frederic Persson as the philosopher, June Knight as Marquise Dorimene, Gene Barry as Count Dorante, and Ann Thomas, Albert Henderson, Ruth Harrison, and Leonard Elliott in other roles.

(3) D: Sidney Lumet; P: Off Broadway, Inc.; T: Cherry Lane Theatre (OB); 8/30/49

Sidney Lumet, future film directing giant, staged this barely known Off-Broadway revival in the style of the commedia dell'arte. It, too, was titled *The Bourgeois Gentleman*. To Vernon Rice (*NYP*), "Last evening's concoction was like saying you have French pastry only it's shortenin' bread." The result of the farced-up treatment led to "tediousness," said Rice. None of the participants was listed.

Y

YANKEE POINT [Comedy-Drama/Family/Marriage/Politics/War] A: Gladys Hurlbut; D: John Cromwell; S: Frederick Fox; P: Edward Choate and Marie Louise Elkins; T: Longacre Theatre; 11/23/42 (24)

A headline story in the summer of 1942 concerned a group of enemy saboteurs who had landed at Amagansett, Long Island, but were then captured. This event inspired Gladys Hurlbut's play about a family, the Adamses, who have a summer home on the New England coast at Yankee Point, which is a convenient place to search the sky for enemy planes. This task is undertaken by Mary Adams (Edna Best), a dedicated civilian defense worker whose husband Bob (John Cromwell, stepping in at the last minute for Dean Jagger) holds down a desk job in Washington. Bob, a World War I veteran turned pacifist, has chucked those beliefs because he now is convinced that he must fight for his country in the present difficulties. The Adamses have two daughters, the ebullient Jeremy (Dorothy Gilchrist), concerned with getting married to a young flier stationed in Texas, and her older sister Sandy (K. T. Stevens), a pacifist upset by her father's change of convictions. She is pregnant, and her husband is going to be drafted. A Scottie dog belonging to a Miss Higgins (Ann Dere), another CD observer, uncovers evidence of a German spy's presence in the dunes. The spy is turned over to a Coast Guard officer (John Forsythe, in his Broadway debut), but it is learned from the spy (never seen) that an air raid is imminent. The raid occupies the latter part of the action, providing an opportunity for plenty of special effects. During the attack, the best in everybody is brought out. Sandy recognizes the justice of her father's decision in fighting for a better world into which she can bring her child.

The flag-waving *Mrs. Miniver*-like play was intended as a tribute to the patient civilian skywatchers, mainly female, who served so importantly during the war effort at home. To arouse interest in their job required the creation of a melodramatic and basically implausible plot (the well-bred response to the invasion at the end was only one of several things that were hard to swallow). Critical opinion held that the play should not have divided its interest between the personal problems of the family and that represented by the foreign threat. "There are moments of incisive human drama," contended Howard Barnes (*NYHT*). "Unfortunately, the play wavers between martial pyrotechnics and an account of brave, disturbed people facing a crisis. In the doing it bogs down rather badly." Richard Lockridge (*NYS*) appreciated the honesty of the character depictions, but was put off by the "unconvincing melodrama which surrounds them."

The play contained a couple of good performances, among them that of Elizabeth Patterson as an old New England retainer of the Adamses and that of Arthur Aylsworth as another old retainer, who hunts Germans on the beach with an old muzzle loader. Margaret Mullen and James Todd also proved useful.

YEARS AGO [Comedy/Family/Marriage/Period/Romance/Small Town/Theatre/

Youth] A: Ruth Gordon; SC: Ruth Gordon's *Atlantic Monthly* stories, based on her high-school diary; D: Garson Kanin; S: Donald Oenslager; C: John Boyt; P: Max Gordon; T: Mansfield Theatre; 12/3/46 (206)

Leading character actress Ruth Gordon penned (and her husband directed) this charmingly unpretentious autobiographical account of her growing-up years in small-town Massachusetts. The principal character in the account is not so much Gordon herself, however, but her good-naturedly blustering father. Though regarded as a slender piece of nostalgia-laden period comedy, it was heartwarming and amusing enough to enjoy a decent run and to be selected as one of the ten best of the season. The play was inspired by an evening Gordon had spent ten years earlier as the dinner companion of the paralyzed and blind playwright, Edward Sheldon. Feeling strangely depressed, Gordon was wondering what she might talk to Sheldon about when she considered reading to him her high school diary from 1913, which she had come across several days before. The diary seemed to her an especially lively depiction of the times it recorded when she was a girl at Quincy High School. Sheldon thought that the material deserved to be published and got critic Alexander Woollcott excited about the project. Gordon then reworked the diaries into four stories that were published in the *Atlantic Monthly*. She soon realized that a play could be formed from the stories, and this led her to write *Years Ago* (originally called *Miss Jones*).

The central role is stage-struck sixteen-year-old Ruth Gordon Jones (Patricia Kirkland), of Wollaston, Massachusetts, a Boston suburb. Her financially strapped parents ($37.50 a week) are Clinton (Fredric March) and Annie (Florence Eldridge). The central issue is young Ruth's burning ambition to become an actress in the face of her confused and reluctant parents. The choleric Mr. Jones wants Ruth to finish school and become a teacher of "physical culture." Her mother is devoted to keeping the family peace. A Harvard man (Richard Simon) proposes to her and tempts her with a life of respectable security and ease. Ruth wins a hearing from a stock-company manager, which her father forbids her to attend. When she does anyway and is turned down, Clinton is furious at the rejection. He agrees to let her try her luck in the theatre after she finishes out the school year. At the end, the glowingly self-confident Ruth leaves with her trunk, an heirloom from her father's seafaring days, and $2.40 in her purse. She is headed for New York, where she has paid two weeks board in advance at the Three Arts Club.

The piece was crammed with meticulously realistic period bric-a-brac and memorabilia, from *McClure's Magazine* and *The Saturday Evening Post* to frequent nostalgic references in the dialogue, gas-logs, and Grand Rapids furniture. Life in 1913 was seen tenderly through the "pathos of distance" and allowed the play to be greatly enjoyed by "those who can take their weak tea with a great deal of sugar," wrote Rosamond Gilder (*TAM*). George Jean Nathan (*NYJA*) observed that it was "a mildly agreeable and mildly pleasant little thing, never quite interesting enough though never really dull, and on the whole the kind that amiable criticism pats lightly on the head in passing." William Hawkins (*NYWT*) noted, "It is atmospheric rather than eventful. The characters are lovable and uncomplicated. The conflict is brief and the suspense is briefer. This tale . . . is nostalgic and warm and unexciting."

March's acting as the thickly mustached, stern, but kindly father won him the first Antoinette Perry (Tony) award for a male actor. He also had won the Oscar the same year for his role in the movie *The Best Years of Our Lives*. Euphemia Van Rensselaer Wyatt (*CW*) wrote, "Fredric March gives a study of Clinton Jones so perfect in detail, so convincing and delightful in extremes of simplicity and wisdom, kindliness and irascibility that it raises the whole production to a distinguished category." Seeing it several weeks after its opening, John Mason Brown (*SR*) was deeply impressed by the performance. "He had explored the part fully, mastered its shadings, and was acting it from within. The slight stoop of the shoulders; the hint of an accent; the suggestion of a sailor's walk, remembered from youth and persisting years afterwards on dry land; the manual dexterity shown in tying knots and handling a knife when doing up a package; the indications of an old codger's temper ever-ready to erupt; and the pathos of the 'little man,' gallant at heart but hard-driven economically--all of these were admirably established by Mr. March." Yet

Richard Watts, Jr. (*NYP*), thought, "There are occasions when his rages seem too loud and studied for entire credibility." The ensemble included Bethel Leslie, Jennifer Bunker, Seth Arnold, Frederic Persson, and Judith Cargill.

YEARS BETWEEN, THE [Comedy/Art/Business/Family/Literature/Military/Romance/Sex/Small Town/War] A: Edward Burbage; D: Dennis Gurney; S: William Schoeller; P: Blackfriars' Guild; T: Blackfriars' Theatre (OB); 2/6/42 (5)

A fairly amusing comedy about small-town family life, focused on the Taylors of New England, the patriarch (Donald Cornwall) of which is on the brink of bankruptcy because of his conservative business methods. There are two Taylor daughters, the brainy Anne (Shirley Gregory), involved with social causes and her own efforts to paint and write, and the younger, "hep-cat" Betty (Joann Dolan), mad about the opposite sex. Son Bill (Dort Clark) wants to be a football star. Mrs. Taylor (Barbara Shure) is on the dizzy side, and she has a resident brother, Peter O'Rourke (Robert E. Perry), who keeps putting his benignly philosophical two cents into all the family problems. Various romantic complications intrude, Betty liking Bill's friend Don (John Campbell), who, in turn, likes the cynical Anne, who ignores him and is wooed--at Peter's suggestion--by a sociology professor named Tommy Paine (Jim Hines). When war comes, Bill and Don join up and Tommy is drafted, but is turned down by Anne when he proposes. Anne takes over her dad's failing business when a nervous breakdown threatens. With the help of Uncle Peter she revives the business, dad resumes his headship of it, Bill's military experience matures him, Betty lands Don, and Tommy wins Anne.

George Freedley (*NYMT*) thought that the play was for undemanding audiences only, and Wilella Waldorf (*NYP*) called it "hopeless stuff," but Robert Francis (*BE*) considered it to be "endowed with wit and insight," and Burns Mantle thought it "an intelligent, timely, clean comedy about decent, likable humans."

(1) YELLOW JACK [Dramatic Revival*] A: Sidney Howard; D: Private Martin Ritt; S: Private Robert Rowe Paddock; P: members of *Winged Victory* cast; T: Forty-fourth Street Theatre; 4/6/44 (1)

A number of professional actors then appearing in *Winged Victory*, the all-serviceman show on Broadway, rehearsed in their limited spare time for this revival of Howard's 1934 drama about Walter Reed's search for the yellow fever microbe. An invited audience of soldiers, friends, and press viewed it prior to its being shown to soldiers at various army camps. A practically bare stage was used for the intermissionless matinee production, which also eliminated the prologue and epilogue. The running time was thus reduced to two hours.

It featured Private Alfred Ryder as Jesse W. Lazear, Private Philip Bourneuf as Dr. Carlos Finlay, Sergeant George Reeves as James Carroll, Corporal Gary Merrill as Walter Reed, Olive Deering as Miss Blake, Private Whit Bissell as Brinkerhof, and Private John Forsythe as O'Hara, to name those who, if not already theatrically important, one day would be. Most of them played only minor roles in *Winged Victory*, so this was an opportunity for them to strut their stuff. Few were singled out for special praise, but Otis L. Guernsey, Jr. (*NYHT*), noticed Forsythe as being "especially good" in his human guinea pig role.

The play was still considered a worthy and absorbing work, and the performance was a creditable one. Louis Kronenberger (*PM*) stated that Howard's drama was "simple yet dramatic. His doctors are human beings--spirited, hot-headed, sharp-tongued. His dialogue has naturalness. . . . Whether a genuine play or not, *Yellow Jack* is effective theatre."

(2) M: Lehman Engel; D: Martin Ritt; S: Wolfgang Roth; P: American Repertory Theatre; T: International Theatre; 2/27/47 (21)

The American Repertory Theatre, after failing to generate the required electricity with its offerings of *King Henry VIII*, *Androcles and the Lion**, *John Gabriel Borkman**, and *What Every Woman Knows**, abandoned its repertory schedule and turned for economic salvation to the thirteen-year-old *Yellow Jack*, which originally had been a critical but not a commercial success. Thus hopes of its bailing out the failing troupe were sorely misplaced, and it did not even fulfill the leadership's hopes that it would run at least a month. Production funds had been raised from various well-wishers in the profession, including Actors Equity and the United Scenic Artists.

Its direction was in the hands of Martin Ritt, who had staged the revival described in the previous entry. George Jean Nathan (*TBY*), who severely castigated the ART's management for its entire season and its shortsightedness in play and actor selection, took Ritt to task for violating the playwright's antiheroic approach by causing "the characters to strike such poses in spotlight baths that they frequently assumed the appearance of the holy figures in the religious dramas of the last century." However, most felt more positively, Brooks Atkinson (*NYT*), for one, declaring, "Well acted with a minimum of heroics, it emerges as a refreshing and engrossing production." "There can be no question," averred Euphemia Van Rensselaer Wyatt (*CW*), "that the current production is a thoroughly fine one, simple in its setting and direct in its impact."

Although a number of secondary ART members were involved, only two of the leading players appeared, Philip Bourneuf (who had played the part in 1944) as Dr. Carlos Finlay and Victor Jory as James Carroll. In other important roles there were Alfred Ryder as Dr. Lazear (also repeating his 1944 role), Efrem Zimbalist, Jr., as Dr. Agramonte, Arthur Keegan as O'Hara, William Windom as McClelland, Raymond Greenleaf as Walter Reed, Eli Wallach as Busch, and Anne Jackson as Miss Blake.

(1) YEOMEN OF THE GUARD, OR THE MERRYMAN AND HIS MAID, THE [Musical Revival*] B/L: W. S. Gilbert; M: Arthur Sullivan; D: Lewis Denison; P: Savoy Opera Guild; T: Cherry Lane Theatre (OB); 12/18/41

In the confines of the tiny Cherry Lane on Commerce Street, a company of hardy Savoyards produced this Gilbert and Sullivan standby. Although it had been doing the Gilbert and Sullivan repertory for about eight months, it was unreviewed until this presentation, which received only a single notice by an unnamed *NYT* reviewer. A short time afterwards, its version of *The Pirates of Penzance** also was noticed by the *NYT*. The performers sang, said the critic, "with gusto and feeling."

Sylvia Clyde played Elsie Maynard, Bernard O'Brien was Colonel Fairfax, Vivian Denison was Sergeant Meryll's daughter, and Wilfred Shadbolt was ably sung by Wells Clary. A single piano provided the entire accompaniment.

(2) D: R. H. Burnside; P: R. H. Burnside i/a/w the Gilbert and Sullivan Opera Company; T: Ambassador Theatre; 3/3/44 (1)

The final offering in the series given by the company previously known as the Boston Comic Opera Company. Bertram Peacock was Sir Richard Cholmondeley, James Gerard was Colonel Fairfax, Robert Eckles was Sergeant Meryll, Allen Stewart was Leonard Meryll, Florenz Ames was Jack Point, Robert Pitkin was Wilfred Shadbolt, Kathleen Roche was Elsie Maynard, Kathryn Reece was Phoebe Meryll, Catherine Judah was Dame Carruthers, and Marie Valdez was Kate.

The voices were not up the score's demands, the principals were as lacking as the supporting players, and only Pitkin, Ames, and Gerard attracted praise. "The bright moments are few and far between," observed L. C. (*NYT*).

(3) D: Anna Bethell; DS: Peter Goffin; P: D'Oyly Carte Opera Company; T: Century Theatre; 2/2/48 (16)

Among the 136 performances of Gilbert and Sullivan offered by Britain's famed comic opera troupe during its nine piece visiting repertory was the decade's third revival of *Yeomen*. The outstanding feature of the event was the discarding of the traditional scenery and costumes in favor of newly designed and executed ones. Surprised at seeing such daring innovation in so staid a company, audience members were unsure how to respond. George Jean Nathan (*TBY*) had no such problem, however. Hoping to see an interesting new conception, he was vastly disappointed. "No longer did the Tower of London look like the old August Düpschnitz brewery; it resembled much more impressively the new wing to the old Schlitz brewery in

Milwaukee." As for the costumes, they resembled nothing so much as "oversize museum strawberry shortcakes." Brooks Atkinson (*NYT*) thought that the first-act set was "a dismal monstrosity." The performances were highly acceptable, with Martyn Green as Jack Point, Helen Roberts as Elsie Maynard, Leonard Osborn as Colonel Fairfax, Richard Walker as Wilfred Shadbolt, Ella Halman as Dame Carruthers, and Denise Findlay as Phoebe.

YERMA [Drama/Marriage/Sex/Spanish] A: Federico García Lorca; TR: Richard O'Connell and James Graham Lujan; D: Alan Harper; CH: Bert Prensky; S/L: Bob Ramsey; C: Frances Ellison and Edna Mobley; P: On-Stage; T: Cherry Lane Theatre (OB); 12/47

This practically unknown production of Lorca's 1934 tragedy was its first in New York, although there would be several revivals in later years. It was given by a valiant group of semipros as part of their season on Commerce Street. George Freedley (*NYMT*), seemingly the only critic present, thought it their best presentation: "There are several exciting moments which were much better acted than usual by a very handsome company." The title role was played by Beatrice Arthur, who was a regular in the company (she married fellow company member Gene Saks). She gave "quite a satisfactory interpretation," said Freedley.

Yerma (which means "barren") takes place in the Spanish countryside and concerns a woman who passionately desires a child, while her husband, Juan (Paul Stevens), is more preoccupied with making a living from his farm. News of a friend's pregnancy only makes her obsession stronger. An old woman tells her that if she enjoyed sex more she would be able to conceive. The relationship with Juan festers and he restricts her freedom, placing his sisters as guards to watch her. She fights her physical attraction to a shepherd, who Juan gets to leave, but she continues to be sexually repressed with Juan. Yerma prays for a baby in the cemetery after midnight and the angry Juan finds her there, mad at her late night absence. He treats her cruelly when she pleads for his help. At a fertility rite, she rejects the advice given her to have sex with another man. Juan appears to tell her that he loves her but wants no children. He begins to take her sexually, but Yerma, crazed, strangles him, ending any chance she may have for a child.

YES IS FOR A VERY YOUNG MAN [Drama/France/Politics/War] A: Gertrude Stein; D: Lamont Johnson; DS: Edwin Wittstein; P: Off Broadway, Inc.; T: Cherry Lane Theatre (OB); 7/6/49

Gertrude Stein's play about the French resistance, first called *In Savoy*, is set in German-occupied Savoy, France, and covers the years from 1940 to 1944. It had premiered at the Pasadena Playhouse in 1946 and was Stein's first play produced without music. Its language and style are in Stein's idiosyncratic tautological manner, repeating things frequently and occasionally using a nursery-school locution.

The subject matter is the attitude of the French people toward the facts of their occupation, a subject close to the author, who lived in a French village at the time depicted. Stein, influenced by childhood stories she had heard of divided loyalties among Civil War families, used a similar premise here. She employed her unique prose manner to artfully suggest the psychological reactions of the French villagers and an American woman to the situation.

Brooks Atkinson (*NYT*) cautioned that while a certain effort was necessary to appreciate Stein's method in "this thin, sketchy drama," the patient viewer would be rewarded by "a certain freshness of truth [that] does come through it in some elusive fashion." "In her clipped, reiterative style," declared Howard Barnes (*NYHT*), "the author has written a work of complete lucidity and considerable fascination. . . . The plot structure is simple, the dialogue lean and strong, and the characters somewhat undefined." Arthur Pollock (*DC*) discovered that it "proves surprisingly intelligible, a good deal more like the work of a conventional dramatist that [*sic*] might have been expected and altogether a gratifying experience." But Thomas R. Dash (*WWD*) refused to praise the play simply because it was more straightforward than other Stein works and observed that at bottom the play was "comparatively shallow . . . , in addition to being extremely garrulous, static and pulseless."

Stein's plot tells of the divided feelings in Savoy. Some accept Petain's Vichy government, others want to fight and overthrow the Germans. The chief characters are the aristocratic but harebrained young wife Denise (Kim Stanley), who is a collaborationist ready to accept any ruling power, and who wants her young brother-in-law Ferdinand (Anthony Franciosa) to come over to her side, although he prefers to remain neutral; her violently anti-German husband Henri (Michael Vincente Gazzo), whose Maqui resistance activities are secret; and a visiting American Francophile spinster (Beatrice Arthur), who is loved by Ferdinand and who supports the Maquis. Ferdinand at first joins Petain's side and goes to work in a German labor camp. But he returns, takes revenge for the killing of his father by the Germans, and joins his brother in the underground. He can now say "no," whereas when he was very young he could only say "yes." Liberation arrives at the end, but Ferdinand resolves to go on fighting.

The production was competent and not inspired enough to do full justice to the writing, but it did provide jobs for some of the bright theatre figures of the new generation, several of them products of the Actors Studio. One was Stanley. Atkinson said that she was "a talented actress with temperament, craft and, if there is any justice on Broadway, a future." To some, the best performance was that of Franciosa. Dash noted that Arthur had stage presence and poise but that "her performance is pitched in one key of placid coolness and tends to grow into a monotone." Gene Saks acted the part of a German. The designer, Edwin Wittstein, later to shorten his name to Ed, also became a distinguished theatre figure. He was praised for the ingenuity of his sets on the postage-stamp-sized stage.

YES, M'LORD [Comedy/British/Marriage/Old Age/Politics/Romance] A: William Douglas Home; D: Colin Chandler; DS: Edward Gilbert; P: Lee and J. J. Shubert; T: Booth Theatre; 10/4/49 (87)

A "trifling" (Brooks Atkinson [*NYHT*]) import known as *The Chiltern Hundreds* in London, where it was still running under that name. It starred aged British actor A. E. Matthews (whose eightieth birthday was celebrated during the run) as the desiccated, absentminded Earl of Lister, who has retired from politics to his huge ancestral castle with his wife (Mary Hinton). He is attended by his class-conscious man, Beecham (George Curzon), and spends his time rabbit and fox hunting. His son, Lord Pym (Hugh Kelly), whose aggressive American fiancée, June Farrell (Elaine Stritch), has insisted that he get a job, tries to run for Parliament but is defeated in the general elections on the Conservative ticket. He joins Labor, which so shocks Beecham that the latter runs against him, jumping from Labour to Conservative to do so. Beecham, of course, is the victor, but he decides to resign his seat for marital happiness.

The best that Home had achieved, said Atkinson, was "a languid parlor charade," although the subject offered promise of some delicious satirical comedy. Ward Morehouse (*NYS*) evaluated the work as "a slack and placid comedy, gabby and leisurely," but given an entertaining performance by its polished, mostly British company.

Matthews, who was a dry and very contained comic actor, noted for the way he could gain effects by a simple growl or raised eyebrow, gave a masterful comic performance that was much more attractive than his vehicle. "Matthews," wrote Robert Coleman (*NYDM*), "is magnificent at underplaying, at knowing when to wham over a line and when to toss one away. He makes vacuity seem immensely charming and almost important." Curzon's performance was a perfect match.

YESTERDAY'S MAGIC [Drama/Alcoholism/Boarding House/British/Family/Invalidism/Romance/Theatre] A: Emlyn Williams; D: Reginald Denham; S: Watson Barratt; P: Theatre Guild; T: Guild Theatre; 4/14/42 (55)

Emlyn Williams's first play since his great success with *The Corn Is Green* was this tedious work that Brooks Atkinson (*NYT*) said "is an actor's joint piece, written cleverly without much drive and no real conviction." Richard Watts, Jr. (*NYHT*), labeled it "a dull, futile and lugubrious play." First staged in London, where it ran for 700 performances, as *The Light of Heart*, with Godfrey Tearle (followed by Williams), it starred American great Paul Muni and Jessica Tandy as Cattrin, his crippled daughter. Muni's performance was uninspired, however, and did not give the play the boost it needed.

His role was that of Welshman Maddoc Thomas, once an important Shakespearean actor, who has slipped because of alcohol from a life of glamour into one of squalor. Reduced to playing Santa Claus in a department store, he gets the chance to renew his reputation when he is offered a small role in a London musical. His devoted daughter does her best to see that he makes his mark. Top producer C. B. Cochran, convinced that Thomas is back to his old form, produces *King Lear** at Covent Garden as a vehicle in which the old actor may make a triumphant comeback. As he is preparing to open, Thomas learns that his daughter is on the brink of getting married to a songwriter (Alfred Drake) from their rooming house, but has not told him because she did not wish to disturb him while he was in the throes of preparing for Lear. The news comes as a blow, and he falls off the wagon, becoming too soused to go on. Cattrin decides to sacrifice her happiness to care for him, but he chooses defenestration for himself as a way of ending her problems.

Drake and Tandy gave strong performances, as did Brenda Forbes in the low comedy role of the rooming house landlady. Drake was hired after French actor Louis Jourdan walked out following his second rehearsal because the author's wife, serving as his proxy, asked him to eliminate his French accent. Muni was widely considered too heavyhanded in his role, which required a lighter touch. According to Hobe. (*V*), "Paul Muni gives a thoughtfully conceived and carefully detailed performance, but he lacks the personal magnetism, the inherent gaiety and the sense of humor for which the part, and the play itself, cry aloud."

George Freedley (*NYMT*) said of Tandy, "She is incredibly lovely to look upon, her voice is clear, her response warm and touching. It is clearly the best performance she has given in New York." Also effective were Margaret Douglass, Cathleen Cordell, James Monks, and Patrick O'Moore.

YOSELE, THE NIGHTINGALE [Comedy-Drama/Jews/Literature/Music/Period/Religion/Romance/Yiddish Language] A/D: Maurice Schwartz; SC: Sholem Aleichem's story of the same name; M: Sholem Secunda; CH: Belle Didjah; S: Leon Foch; P/T: Yiddish Art Theatre (OB); 10/10/49

Down at his theatre on Second Avenue and Fourth Street, Maurice Schwartz launched his company's thirty-first season of first-class Yiddish theatre, this time with his adaptation of a comic folk tale by Sholem Aleichem (who appears as a character in the piece). Even those without Yiddish could savor the richly detailed Jewish customs and folkways of the piece as realized in Schwartz's skillful directorial hands. Schwartz also played to outstanding comedic effect the role of choirmaster Gedalye Bass, which gave him a chance to exploit his multicolored voice, including some singing in his distinctive baritone.

The play, a mingling of broad comedy and pathos, takes place in the nineteenth-century Russian village of Mazepevke and concerns a mournful young cantor named Yosele (Moshe Zamar). Sholem Aleichem (Yudel Dubinsky) comes to the town and decides to write about the brilliant cantor and to do something to advance his career. But the cheerily disreputable Bass gets in the way and, seeking to make money from Yosele's talent, maneuvers him into marrying the wealthy and seductive widow Perele (Ola Shlifko), despite Yosele's love for childhood sweetheart Esther (Charlotte Goldstein). Bass also convinces him to give up religious music for opera. Esther spites him by marrying the obese rich man (Jacob Zanger). Yosele faints and Esther collapses in despair, and it seems likely both will die of broken hearts.

Yosele was a welcome change from the Yiddish Art Theatre's predisposition toward preachy message plays. It was appreciated for its folksy atmosphere, picturesque characters, splashily colorful sets and costumes, and vigorous performances, especially Schwartz's. Jeanette Wilken (*NYDN*) reported that the play "picks itself up after a talky start and goes on to become one of the most warmly humorous plays the" company ever produced. Arthur Pollock (*DC*) observed, "The acting is in the familiar Yiddish Art Theater style, broad and skillful with an old style skill exhibited by actors long familiar with their trade and equipped with a full repertory of speaking gestures less eloquent than they would be if they were not taken so readily out of the actors' stock, but always effective nonetheless." The actors included Jenny Casher, Anatole Winogradoff, Berta Gersten, Jacob Mestel, Lucy Gehrman, Gustave Berger, and Julius Adler.

YOU CAN'T SLEEP HERE [Revue] SK: Joe Darion, Ned Lehack, S. David, and others; M: Alex North, Earl Robinson, and others; LY: Harry Schachter and others; D: David Pressman; P: American Youth Theatre; T: Barbizon-Plaza Theatre (OB); 5/10/41

A poor excuse for an intimate revue, characterized by L. B. (*NYT*) as "an entertainment generally possessed of an absence of invention and a lack of organization." The show seemed promising in its mingling of modern dance, vaudeville routines, and poetry, but the result was dampened by inadequate material and performing talent. The humor was partly of the topical kind, with laughs garnered at the expense of Brooklyn Dodger fans, the radio, burlesque nightclubs, and movies.

Some names that one day would be important figured in the performances, among them modern dancer Anna Sokolow, who did fairly well with a number called "Exile" about the plight of Jewish refugees. Singer Betty Garrett also showed her stuff to good effect.

YOU CAN'T TAKE IT WITH YOU [Dramatic Revival*] A: George S. Kaufman and Moss Hart; D/P: Frank McCoy; S: Harry Gordon Bennett; T: City Center of Music and Drama; 3/26/45 (17)

Old-time comic actor Fred Stone returned to Broadway at age seventy to play the role of Grandpa Vanderhof in the limited-engagement revival of this Pulitzer Prize-winning 1936 comedy. The production, unfortunately, was of the "slap-dash stock company level" (Wilella Waldorf [*NYP*]), which was a shame, considering the high-flown goals the City Center had set when it opened as a cultural mecca. "They threw away more of the delightful lines than they delivered," groused Richard P. Cooke (*WSJ*), "and all-in-all the present version is a threadbare replica of the original." One example of the skimpy production was the lack of anything more than a muffled pop or two for the sound of the firecrackers exploding in the basement.

Stone's daughter Dorothy played Essie, the would-be dancer, while her offstage husband Charles Collins essayed Boris Kolenkhov, the Russian dancing master. Others included Daisy Atherton as Penelope, Eula Belle Moore as Rheba, John Souther as Paul, Charles Benjamin as Donald, Richard Maloy as Tony, and Ulla Kazanova as Olga. After the final curtain Stone came on to reminisce with the audience about his vaudeville days and did a song and dance using the ropes for which he was famous. Dorothy Stone and Collins performed a "Hot Gavotte."

YOU NEVER CAN TELL [Dramatic Revival*] A: George Bernard Shaw; D: Peter Ashmore; DS: Stewart Chaney; P: Theatre Guild i/a/w Alfred Fischer; T: Martin Beck Theatre; 3/16/48 (39)

This was the first local showing of Shaw's lesser and only mildly appealing 1898 comedy since its premiere New York production with Arnold Daly in 1905. Shaw had written it "to show that drama can humanize" such things as "fun, . . . fashionable dresses, . . . a pretty scene or two, a little music, and even . . . a great ordering of drinks," the very stuff of which commercial plays were concocted. The play was entertaining and mildly enlightening to a minority, but most thought it on the garrulous and worn-out side. "It is not very good," insisted Brooks Atkinson (*NYT*). "The humor is arch and stylized; the artifices are coy." "It is as dated as a hansom cab and not nearly as expeditious at getting from one point to another," believed Howard Barnes (*NYHT*), although he thought that the production had done right by the play.

The play opens at Devon, England, a seaside resort, where the young dentist Valentine (Tom Helmore) extracts his first tooth, the patient being the recently arrived adolescent Dolly (Patricia Kirkland). Dolly and her twin brother Philip (Nigel Stock) invite Valentine to lunch. A love affair soon develops between Valentine and the twins' older sister Gloria (Faith Brook), who advocates the social reform positions about which their feminist mother, Mrs. Clandon (Frieda Inescort), writes. Secretively using an anesthetic, Valentine painlessly extracts a tooth from his hot-tempered landlord Fergus Crampton (Ralph Forbes), thereby being relieved of the arrears on his rent. The wealthy Crampton is soon revealed to Mrs. Clandon's children as their father, from whom she separated eighteen years earlier, bringing up her brood on Madeira. Crampton's unhappiness at finding his family at the luncheon leads to the possibility of a disaster, but everyone's feelings are calmed down by the diplomatic behavior of the waiter, William (Leo G. Carroll), the most memorable character in the assemblage, who talks of his son Mr. Bohun (William Devlin), the queen's counsel. Soon after, Valentine begins to break down the extremely rational Gloria's defenses with his "scientific" wooing methods.

Leo G. Carroll, wearing a silver wig, performed deliciously as the "perfect waiter," giving this production "deftness and direction," according to Euphemia Van Rensselaer Wyatt (*CW*). Tom Helmore was equally admired. The production itself tended to bore the critics, most of whom went along with John Mason Brown's (*SR*) view that "this revival is a strangely unsatisfactory and pedestrian affair. It lacks confidence, style, and distinction. . . . It is dull in most of its acting; above all, in its director's desperate attempts to be gay." (One reason for the desultory performance may have been the fact that director Ashmore returned to England two weeks before the opening.)

YOU TOUCHED ME! [Comedy/Alcoholism/Family/Military/Romance/Sex] A: Tennessee Williams and Donald Windham; SC: D. H. Lawrence's short story of the same name; D: Guthrie McClintic; S: Motley; P: Guthrie McClintic i/a/w Lee Shubert; T: Booth Theatre; 9/25/45 (109)

Tennessee Williams's first play on Broadway after his striking debut with *The Glass Menagerie* was this collaborative effort at a "romantic comedy" "suggested" by a D. H. Lawrence story. (It had been produced in Cleveland and Pasadena before *The Glass Menagerie*'s Broadway opening.) It represented a surprising setback for the promising author, for a number of critics agreed with Lewis Nichols (*NYT*) that it was--apart from some felicitious passages--verbose, speechifying, disunified, and unevenly acted.

The theme, according to the Lawrence quote in the program, concerns "Life and Growth amid all this mass of destruction and disintegration." A considerable amount of symbolism--mostly sexual--was interlarded in the dialogue and action, which tells of Cornelius Rockley (Edmund Gwenn), a likably irascible retired sea captain in his cups, who lives in rural England. The set representing his home--called Pottery House because it was once part of a pottery plant--is divided into a conventional provincial living room and a pseudo-ship's cabin where the captain downs his daily rum. With him is his straitlaced, life-denying, spinster sister Emmie (Catherine Willard); Hadrian (Montgomery Clift), the youth he adopted from an orphanage, who is now a fighter pilot in the Canadian air force; and his repressed daughter Matilda (Marianne Stewart), a mirror of her frigid aunt, who does not wish to see her married. Hadrian returns home on leave and tries to "touch" Matilda, to free her from Emmie's unhealthy influence. His attempts to persuade the girl to elope with him are assisted by the amiable captain, who wants his daughter to conquer life, not be defeated by it like himself. In the end Hadrian succeeds in marrying the girl.

George Jean Nathan (*TBY*) drew many parallels between *The Glass Menagerie* and this work and wondered whether Lawrence's story had not inspired the other play, for all the playwright's admission of autobiographical inspiration. He dismissed the present work, largely because of his belief that it had been inadequately directed: "The result is an exhibit that hovers ineffectually between realism and foggy fancy." Louis Kronenberger (*PM*) thought that the play's message was "decidedly damaged by the broad strokes, the black-and-whiteness, the conscious or unconscious buffoonery of [the] playwriting." Still, several reviewers appreciated the work, among them Rosamond Gilder (*TAM*), who was touched despite its being "halting and occasionally flat." She found in it "moments of tenderness and intensity that lift it above the average." She enjoyed, too, Williams's language, "a diction that is fresh and arresting; his people speak with the licence granted the poet, not in the idiom of the dictaphone."

Most critics agreed that the acting veered from one style to the other, with too much emphasis on farce. Clift's sensitive performance was outstanding, although his habit of running his words together in emotional moments was a drawback. The character of Hadrian and many of his idealistic ideas were too close, though, to the roles that Clift had played in *Foxhole in the Parlor* and *The Searching Wind*.

Neil Fitzgerald, who played a prissy rector, told Robert LaGuardia, author of *Monty*, that Clift's onstage behavior sometimes disturbed his fellow actors. When he was unhappy with his direction, he would revise it to make himself more comfortable. This included altering his blocking or changing the arrangement of furniture and props. There was a scene in this play where three actors were seated around a table, with Clift apart from and slightly downstage of them. Disliking this position, Clift would gradually move upstage, forcing the others to turn to face him. Veteran actor Gwenn, not in the scene, told the others, "Well, you fellows talk to the spot where he's supposed to be. Let him go wherever he likes." They followed the hint, and Clift soon was forced to return to his directed position.

YOU WITH ME [Miscellaneous/Solo] A/DS: Raymond Duncan; DS: Raymond Duncan; T: Shubert Theatre; 2/23/47

Raymond Duncan, seventy-two-year-old eccentric painter, poet, and teacher, starred in his own one-man play in which he "held his audience as if by magic when he told the story of his life complete with dramatic gestures and interlarded with philosophy," according to Joe Pihodna (*NYHT*). Brother of famed dancer Isadora Duncan and actor Augustin Duncan, he was born in San Francisco, took part in five wars, and, with his wife Penelope, lived in Greece, where they constructed their own home and raised goats. His life in Paris during the German occupation was also described. Dressed in his daily garb of a Roman toga and sandals, with a headband circling his brow, he offered moral commentary and controversial ideas, such as when he warned against book learning because a man must be mature enough to discern which books are good to read and which to burn for warmth. His belief in free love was also given a hearing. He spent much time cautioning against the wearing of shoes, which he dubbed "hooves." Duncan's acting leaned toward dance, particularly his expressive gestures. At his rear was a beautiful hand-painted silk backdrop he himself created.

YOU'LL SEE STARS [Musical/Historical-Biographical/Period/Show Business] B: Herman Timberg; M: Leo Edwards; D: Herman Timberg and Dave Kramer; CH: Eric Victor; S: Perry Watkins; P: Dave Kramer; T: Maxine Elliott's Theatre; 12/31/42 (4)

This show, which opened on New Year's Eve, did not contribute to the gaiety of that event. George Freedley (*NYMT*) attested that "it is the poorest show I've ever seen on the New York stage, the worst rehearsed, the least prepared cast, the poorest dancing, the corniest book." Howard Barnes (*NYHT*) said that it plunged "right down to the lowest depths of dramatic ineptitude." The show did not begin until 9:20 P.M. (it was advertised for 8), and by 10:30 most of the critics departed for more joyous festivities.

It purported to be a musical comedy biography of Gus Edwards (Alan Lester), song writer and vaudeville developer--via a sketch called "School Days"--of many famous child performers early in the century. (Edwards was still alive when the show opened and insisted that the show was not authorized by him.) Some of those pictured in their youth in the show were Walter Winchell (Irving Freeman), Eddie Cantor (Jackie Green), George Jessel (Jackie Michaels), Groucho Marx (Lou Dahlman), Herman Timberg (Fene Bayliss; Timberg was the book writer); Harpo Marx (George Lyons), Lila Lee (Phyllis Baker), and Georgie Price (Buddy Simon). In addition to Timberg, director-producer Dave Kramer was a former protegé of Edwards, while composer Leo Edwards was the impressario's brother.

YOUNG AMERICAN, A [Drama/Blacks/Family/Music/Race] A: Edwin Bronner; D: Dennis Gurney; P: Blackfriars' Guild; T: Blackfriars' Theatre (OB);

1/17/46 (26)

This occasionally interesting but predictable and platitudinous play tells of what happens when a famous American conductor (Alex Wilson) receives a symphony in the mail and invites the composer (Louis Peterson, Jr.) to stay with the conductor's family while the composition is being worked on. The young composer turns out to be black, which leads to various revelations about racial prejudice within the musician's white household. The composer's bitterness emerges from his discoveries, but he is persuaded that the answer to his dilemma lies in education and understanding, not revenge.

The play received mixed reviews. "One or two of the scenes are fairly well handled," argued George Jean Nathan (*TBY*), "but the whole suffers from the fact that the workings of the theme are obvious in advance." But L. C. (*NYT*) declared that the play, although not of Broadway quality, was "a work of fine dramatic unity, containing enough signs of life to hold the eye." Liam Dunn, Joan Field, Murray Stewart, and Harry Bolden were in the cast.

YOUNG AND FAIR, THE [Drama/Crime/Mental Illness/School/Youth] A: N. Richard Nash; D: Harold Clurman; S/L: Paul Morrison; C: Eleanor Goldsmith; P: Vinton Freedley i/a/w Richard W. Krakeur; T: Fulton Theatre; 11/22/48 (48)

Julie Harris had been one of the bright lights in the otherwise dismal *Sundown Beach*, which had played a bit earlier in the season. In the all-female *The Young and Fair* she came into her own and elicited a storm of applause following her big dramatic speech. Alongside her were the outstanding performances of an array of talented actresses, including old-time leading lady Frances Starr, making a return to Broadway after many years. The play itself--about the deceit and chicanery at an exclusive girls' school--had been worked on previously at the Actors' Lab in Hollywood, but had not reached production there. It was seen instead at the theatre in Falmouth, Massachusetts, in the summer of 1948.

Brook Valley Academy is a fancy women's junior college near Boston run by servile head mistress Sara Cantry (Starr), a would-be liberal who compromises her ideals in order to guarantee a sound financial base for the school. To Brook Valley comes alumnus Frances Morritt (Mercedes McCambridge), hired to be the personnel director. She too finds herself making compromises with conditions of which she disapproves. When a wave of thefts hits the school, she prefers to use tactful methods to root out the culprit, but comes into conflict with student Drucilla Eldridge (Doe Avedon), daughter of a trustee, and an incipient fascist. Drucilla heads a power-hungry vigilante committee that seeks to find the culprit. The committee is voted out of existence by the student council, but Drucilla and her friends want to have it reinstated and to rid the school of the personnel director. Thus, Drucilla plants stolen items in the room of Frances's younger sister Patty (Patricia Kirkland), who is then accused of theft. It turns out, however, that mousy Nancy Gear (Harris), who has been bullied by Drucilla into accusing Patty, is actually the kleptomaniacal thief. In a climactic scene the neurotic girl breaks down and confesses her wrongdoing. At the end, the head mistress sadly admits that she is no longer equal to her burden.

Among the characters is a Jewish girl, Lee Barron (Lois Wheeler), who fakes her religion in order to get into the school and becomes the victim of anti-Semitism. Other important roles in the twenty-one-character play were acted by Frieda Alt man, Betty Morrissey, and Lenka Peterson.

A few critics appreciated the play's treatment of the theme of moral compromise versus principle, but others thought it a mechanical melodrama with formula action and dramatis personae. Few disputed the excellence of Clurman's staging. "Contrived situations and trite structure prove this merely a pedestrian play whose chances are limited," prognosticated Bron. (*V*). Rowland Field (*NEN*) thought the action predictable from the first act on. Ward Morehouse (*NYS*) declared it "overwrought and cluttered," despite "some effective scenes." One of those was the confession scene, with Harris turning in "an extraordinary bit of acting."

YOUNG MAN'S FANCY, A [Comedy/Romance/Rural/Sex/Youth] A: Harry

Thurschwell and Alfred Golden; D: Robert E. Perry; S/L: Ralph Alswang; C: Lou Eisele; P: Henry Adrian; T: Plymouth Theatre; 4/29/47 (335)

Although various critics thought this noisy farce (produced earlier in summer stock as *S'Wonderful*) dramatically clumsy and on the tastelessly smutty side, it survived to become a considerable hit. John Chapman (*NYDN*) hated the play and called it "a witless comedy." Howard Barnes (*NYHT*) said, "It is as dull as it is disappointing. . . . There is too little wit in the writing, too little imagination in the plotting, and too little taste in the jokes." Some critics, like Brooks Atkinson (*NYT*), liked the farcical situations, but frowned on the romantic complications.

It is set in a boy's bunkhouse at a Connecticut coed summer camp, Camp Freedom, run by counselor-owners Harold Greenley (Bill Talman) and his sister Helen (Lenore Lonergan). A plot thread concerns the mortgage hanging over the fate of the place. One of the campers is a precociously bright mama's boy named Dickie Crandell (Ronnie Jacoby), spoiled child of smothering parents (Raymond Bramley and Lee Carney). The boy is more interested in reading than in the rough-and-tumble life of camping, so he becomes the hazing victim of the more aggressive boys. A sympathetic female counselor named Sylvia (Margaret Langley, replacing the ill Lynne Carter), in love with Harold, advises Dickie on how to take revenge on his tormentors. He manages to disrupt their beds, dismantle the lights, and invent other booby traps and embarrassments. There is also the attempt of the boys to devise a way to bring Sylvia and Harold together, which--inspired by the theft of the camp doctor's books--involves various gags revolving around sex and parenthood; it also creates a scandal that threatens to close down the camp. At the end, Dickie's discovery of the practical worth of the baseball guide, which helps win the big game, brings the play to a happy conclusion when he gains the approval of the other boys.

The cast of energetic youngsters--most of them very good--included Roy Sterling, Donald Hastings, Richard Leone, Bart Roe, and Joan Shepard.

YOUR LOVING SON [Comedy/Family/Marriage/Romance/Sex/Youth] A: Abby Merchant; D: Arthur Sircom; S: Raymond Sovey; P: Jay Richard Kennedy i/a/w Alfred Bloomingdale and Joseph F. Loew; T: Little Theatre; 4/4/41 (3)

"A mechanical little farce" (George Ross [NYWT]) about Joshua Winslow, Jr. (Frankie Thomas), a teenager who returns to his Upper East Side duplex apartment from summer camp to find his parents, Joshua (Jay Fassett) and Dorcas (Jessie Royce Landis) in the midst of divorce proceedings. Each of them is involved in outside affairs, his mother with a young artist (Eddie Nugent), his father with the married lady upstairs (Ruth Lee). He thereupon steps in to patch things up, doing what he can to interfere in each parent'ws extramarital carryings on. These devices proving fruitless, he and his sweetheart, Rosamond (Charita Bauer), the daughter of his father's amour, pretend to have eloped, a ruse that brings about the desired reconciliation.

"The reason that *Your Loving Son* is plodding and not funny . . . is simply that Miss Merchant doesn't write well. Her efforts at wit are unskillful. Her dialogue is flat. Her contrivances are at once intricate and hackneyed," commented Richard Lockridge (*NYS*).

YOURS, A. LINCOLN [Drama/Historical-Biographical/Period/Politics] A: Paul Horgan; SC: a book by Otto Eisenschiml, *Why Was Lincoln Murdered?*; D: Robert Ross; P: Experimental Theatre, Inc.; T: Shubert Theatre; 7/9/42 (2)

One of the plays in the Experimental Theatre series, founded with the approval of the Dramatists Guild and Actors Equity, to produce plays as a showcase for new theatre talent. It also, as now, occasionally gave established stars a chance to play roles that they might not otherwise have had a chance to perform. Performance number one was for an invited audience of professionals, number two for the public, with the money taken in donated to the Stage Relief Fund and Actors' Fund. In the early productions, performances were only given at special matinees.

Rising star Vincent Price (then acting in *Angel Street*) was given the chance to don the familiar chin whiskers and cheek mole of the title character. The play was based on a book of five years earlier that propounded the idea that Secretary of War

Stanton (Sherman A. MacGregor) and the Radical Republicans had planned the president's assassination for political reasons of their own. George Jean Nathan (*TBY*), startled by what he deemed Price's eccentric portrayal, sarcastically suggested that the present production interpreted the killing as being the result of thespian John Wilkes Booth's (Donald Randolph) contempt for acting of so vile a nature.

The nine-scene drama was undramatic, remaining too close to the book that provided its substance. Covering the events of the month just prior to Lincoln's death, it shows him as a man of great compassion who would make whatever concessions were necessary to bring the war to an end and stop the bloodshed. Unfortunately, Stanton stands in the way of Lincoln's desires. The scenes show Lincoln comforting a dying Union soldier in a Washington military hospital; the ruthless Stanton in his office plotting with his South-hating cronies against the president he despises; Booth on the stage of Ford's Theatre, plotting against Lincoln; Lincoln with his son Tad (Robert Lee) on the yacht *River Queen*, where the president soon asks Generals Sherman (Bill Johnson) and Grant (Harry Bellaver) to show mercy toward the South; the White House porch, where Lincoln asks that the band celebrating the North's victory play "Dixie"; Booth in a boarding house engaged in further plotting; the door to the president's bedroom, with Lincoln upset by a prophetic dream; the president's box at Ford's Theatre, with Booth rehearsing the shooting; and, finally, the sitting room at the White House, shortly before the assassination (not shown), where the president sentimentally remembers the dying soldier from the first scene with that soldier's father (Parker Fennelly).

Played on a bare stage with only a few pieces of furniture to suggest locales, the piece proved only sporadically effective. Herrick Brown (*NYS*) contended that "Mr. Horgan's play proves too episodic and meandering to furnish a historical picture that is stirring." He suggested that the source was too closely followed, "for there are long stretches where the audience has the feeling of hearing something read aloud rather than seeing a play acted out."

Price's Lincoln was not at all effective. Lewis Nichols (*NYT*) said, "He has the height, but he gives a faintly mincing, posturing Lincoln with an accent at times like that of a settler along *Tobacco Road**; he often fails to suggest the warm humor and the equally warm dignity which were the President's." In the cast were Mary Michael as Mrs. Lincoln and Harry Townes and Wendell K. Phillips in small parts.

YOURS IS MY HEART (***Das Land des Lachelns***) [Musical/China/Orientals/Prison/Romance] B/LY: Harry Graham, Ira Cobb, and Karl Farkas; M: Franz Lehár; SC: Franz Lehár's operetta, *The Land of Smiles*; D: Theodore Basche and Monroe Manning; CH: Henry Schwarze; S/C: H. A. Condell; L: Milton Lowe; P: Arthur Spitz; T: Shubert Theatre; 9/5/46 (36)

A gauchely written, directed, and designed operetta, Broadwayized from a famous one of 1928 by Viennese composer Franz Lehár. It had been tried out several times a decade earlier under the title *Prince Chu Chan* and under its original name. The operetta provided a New York showcase for the outstanding Viennese singer but inadequate actor Richard Tauber, who had played it 2,500 times in other cities. His part allowed the overweight, fifty-six-year-old tenor to play a romantic hero and to sing the work's renowned central number, "Yours Is My Heart Alone," which he encored ad nauseam, with versions in English, French, Italian, and German. His voice problems in midrun forced the early cancellation of the show.

Tauber played Prince Sou Chong of China, who falls in love in Paris with the prima donna Claudette Vernay (Stella Andrevna), but who must return to China because of political unrest. Claudette follows the prince to Peiping (Beijing), but their marriage is barred for diplomatic reasons, and he must take a Chinese bride to save Claudette's life. Then, to keep Claudette from leaving, he puts her in prison, but lets her go when she tries to escape.

"A dated story, limp humor and stodgy direction make something bizarre out of this production, to nix any Broadway success," prognosticated Bron. (*V*). Robert Garland (*NYJA*) dubbed it "an unhappy hodge-podge." Robert Coleman (*NYDM*) said that the libretto was "deplorable--old fashioned, dismal, unfunny and corny." Chief supporting roles, none of them ably played, were in the hands of comedian

Sammy White, magician Fred Keating, Lillian Held, and Alexander D'Arcy.

Z

ZIEGFELD FOLLIES [Revue] SK: Jerry Seelen, Lester Lee, Bud Pearson, Les White, Charles Sherman, Harry Young, Baldwin Bergersen, Buddy Burston, Dan White, Ray Golden, Sid Kuller, Lester Lawrence, Joseph Erens, William Wells, and Harold J. Rome; M: Ray Henderson and Dan White; LY: Jack Yellen and Buddy Burston; D: John Murray Anderson, Arthur Pierson, and Fred De Cordova; CH: Robert Alton; S: Watson Barratt; C: Miles White; P: Messrs. Shubert i/a/w Alfred Bloomingdale and Lou Walters; T: Winter Garden; 4/1/43 (553)

The original *Ziegfeld Follies**, which was produced almost annually from 1907 to 1931, with sporadic attempts to revive the format in 1934 and 1936, provided the inspiration for this new version of the spectacular revue. A large company of entertainers, including headliners Milton Berle, Arthur Treacher, and Ilona Massey parlayed their talents into a smash hit that ran for many months. Opening-night tickets cost up to $8.80, but even regular performances were expensive, costing a top of $5.50 on Friday and Saturday nights. At the opening, Billie Burke, Florenz Ziegfeld's widow, watched from a stage box. This proved to be the longest-running of any show with the *Ziegfeld Follies* title, including those produced during Ziegfeld's life.

Although some critics, such as George Jean Nathan (*TBY*), felt that the show was not up to Ziegfeld's standards, it did not stint on gorgeous numbers designed to glorify beautiful American girls, with lavish costumes and excellent choreography. The costumes, the dances, and Berle's humor were the three most memorable elements. Berle, on and off throughout, hit many funny bones in "Merchant of Venison," about wealthy butcher J. Pierswift Armour (he sang "Meat for Sale") and food rationing. With bodyguards on either side holding tommy guns, he opened a safe to deposit a porterhouse steak. His other routines included a tribute to comics Olsen and Johnson, "Loves-a-Poppin'" (with Treacher and Massey). Treacher, the British gentleman's gentleman comedian, did not have outstanding material, his best being a skit called "Good God Godfrey." The blond, Hungarian-born Massey, in her Broadway debut, sang songs titled "35 Summers Ago" and "Love Songs Are Made in the Night." Massey impressed more by her beauty than her stage presence or vocal talent.

Unlike the *Follies* of old, this one included barely any takeoffs on contemporary shows, the only remnant of that kind of sketch being a Noël Coward satire--with Berle doing Coward--*Private Lives* in the style of *Hellzapoppin'**. Among the notable specialty performers were comedienne-singer Sue Ryan, scoring highly with Buddy Burston and Dan White's "Carmen in Zoot," a jive version of Bizet's music, among other pieces. Eccentric dancer Jack Cole did his "Wedding of a Solid Sender" dance, accompanied by seven female dancers. Later in the show he did "Hindu Serenade." Dancers Tommy Wonder and Nadine Gae were singled out, as were terpsichoreans Ray Long and long-legged Christine Ayres. Mimic Dean Murphy--with impersonations of politicos such as Wendell Willkie and Franklin Delano and Eleanor Roosevelt--was noticed, along with puppeteers Bil and Cora Baird, who came on too late for some (opening night ended at 11:40). One of the Bairds' most impressive marionettes was able to tap dance. Singer-pianist Imogen Carpenter was on the bill; Katherine Meskill and Jack McCauley acted in the sketches; the male sextet called Ben Yost's Vi-Kings vocalized, with Berle mixing in with hilariously effeminate shtick at one point (he also mingled amusingly with an acrobatic act, the Jansleys); and the singing quartet, the Rhythmaires, performing. These are only a sampling of the diverse entertainment offered in this expensively produced revue.

Ziegfeld Follies moved smoothly, alternating musical numbers with sketches, and offered an effectively varied program. None of the songs was truly outstanding. It was standard material, but of a high standard. Dominating all was Berle. Rosamond Gilder (*TAM*) commented: "His explosive sentences that break down in the middle and then ride off in all directions, his burbling, luscious style, his inexhaustible bounce have their particular appeal to the risibles. His material is vintage and some of it has not kept well, but his ebullience is contagious and he knows where the laughter of his particular audience resides."

APPENDIXES

Appendix 1
Calendar of Productions

This is a chronological calendar of all productions with entries in the text. There were a good many other productions offered during the decade, but those not listed here were all in tiny Off-Broadway venues, were generally amateur, and were either not attended by the press or were accorded an amount of coverage too insubstantial to warrant inclusion. Even such relatively important Off-Broadway groups as On-Stage were occasionally overlooked by reviewers. Titles and scraps of information concerning additional works may be gleaned from the Off-Broadway sections (also incomplete) in the *Best Plays of the Year* series. For listings of the numerous productions of Equity Library Theatre, the majority of which were unreviewed, see the *Best Plays* series and the *Theatre World* series, edited during the decade by Daniel Blum. When the number of performances for a run is not known, a dash (--) is entered instead. Wherever such a lack of data exists, it is for an Off-Broadway presentation, although the number of performances of many Off-Broadway works is known. For a few classical revivals, mainly Shakespearean, the name of an important star has been provided to help distinguish one production from another of the same play. Several abbreviations have been used to make the list more useful:

(RE) return engagements (as distinguished from revivals); by a return engagements is meant the presentation of a recent work in a manner as close as possible to the original, and with the same production personnel (directors, designers, producers, etc.), although the cast may be different.
(R) revivals; new productions of previously produced works, usually with new creative personnel and a new interpretation. In this list, the only revivals indicated are of works given their initial production during the decade.
(FRL) French language
(GEL) German language
(YL) Yiddish language

Selected organizations responsible for productions are designated by the following abbreviations:

(ANT) American Negro Theatre
(ART) American Repertory Theatre
(BG) Blackfriars' Guild
(DGT) Dublin Gate Theatre
(DW) Dramatic Workshop
(ET) Experimental Theatre
(HT) Habimah Theatre
(NS) New Stages

(NYCC) New York City Center Theatre Company
(NYRG) New York Repertory Group
(OS) On-Stage
(OV) Old Vic
(TG) Theatre Guild (some productions were coproduced with other individuals or groups)
(YAT) Yiddish Art Theatre

This list contains several return engagements of plays that opened before 6/16/40 but were brought back for brief runs in the 1940-1941 season. Such return engagements, however, do not have entries in the text. Shows that continued their runs after summer vacations are not listed twice here, and the initial figure for length of run covers both the original run and the run following the layoff period. Where the opening date is not definitely known, the production is given with its opening month only. In the case of a few Off-Broadway productions, there are disparities between the opening dates provided in different sources; sometimes even the available contemporary documentation does not make it clear precisely when a play opened. The dates given here are as close to the actual openings as could be ascertained.

Date	Title	Run
9/3/40	*Kind Lady*	107
9/9/40	*Jupiter Laughs*	24
	Sim Sala Bim	54
9/11/40	*Hold on to Your Hats*	158
9/18/40	*Johnny Belinda*	321
9/30/40	*The Gondoliers*	24
10/1/40	*Boys and Girls Together*	191
10/5/40	*Journey to Jerusalem*	17
10/10/40	*It Happens on Ice*	180
10/11/40	*Boyd's Daughter*	3
	The Way	--
10/15/40	*Blind Alley*	63
10/17/40	*Charley's Aunt*	233
	Ester'ke (YL; YAT)	--
10/18/40	*George Washington Slept Here*	173
	The Glass Slipper	--
10/22/40	*Big White Fog*	64
10/23/40	*Injury Sustained*	--
10/24/40	*Sunrise* (YL)	--
10/25/40	*Cabin in the Sky*	156
10/26/40	*'Tis of Thee*	1
10/29/40	*Suzanna and the Elders*	30
10/30/40	*Panama Hattie*	501
11/1/40	*Return Engagement*	8
11/7/40	*Beverly Hills*	28
11/8/40	*Quiet Please*	16
11/15/40	*Glamour Preferred*	11
11/17/40	*Sarah Simple*	--
11/19/40	*Twelfth Night* (TG)	129
11/23/40	*Horse Fever*	25
11/26/40	*The Corn Is Green*	477
11/27/40	*Fledgling*	13
12/1/40	*Sender Blank* (YL; YAT)	--
12/2/40	*Romantic Mr. Dickens*	8
12/3/40	*Four Short Plays*	--

Date	Title	Run
12/4/40	*Delicate Story*	29
12/5/40	*Mum's the Word*	12
12/9/40	*Every Man for Himself*	3
12/11/40	*Blow Bugle Blow*	--
12/15/40	*King Lear* (DW)	--
12/17/40	*Retreat to Pleasure*	23
12/19/40	*Cue for Passion*	12
12/20/40	*The Old Foolishness*	3
12/23/40	*Old Acquaintance*	170
12/25/40	*Meet the People*	160
	Men in White (YL)	--
	Pal Joey	374
12/26/40	*My Sister Eileen*	866
	Ruth Draper	22
12/27/40	*All in Fun*	3
12/29/40	*The Flying Gerardos*	24
12/30/40	*Flight to the West*	136
1/2/41	*The Lady Who Came to Stay*	4
1/5/41	*First Stop to Heaven*	8
	No for an Answer	3
1/6/41	*Eight O'Clock Tuesday*	16
1/7/41	*Night of Love*	7
1/10/41	*Arsenic and Old Lace*	1,444
1/12/41	*Mr. and Mrs. North*	163
1/14/41	*Crazy with the Heat*	7
1/20/41	*The Cream in the Well*	24
1/22/41	*Worlds Apart* (YL; YAT)	--
1/23/41	*Lady in the Dark*	467
1/30/41	*Crazy with the Heat* (revised)	92
2/4/41	*Tanyard Street*	23
2/5/41	*Liberty Jones* (TG)	22
2/7/41	*Boudoir*	11
2/10/41	*Popsy*	4
2/11/41	*Out of the Frying Pan*	104
2/12/41	*Claudia*	722
2/24/41	*The Talley Method*	56
2/27/41	*Brooklyn Biarritz*	4
3/11/41	*The Doctor's Dilemma*	121
3/12/41	*They Walk Alone*	21
3/13/41	*Five Alarm Waltz*	4
3/23/41	*My Fair Ladies*	32
3/24/41	*Fiv'ke, the Slave* (YL)	--
	Native Son	114
3/25/41	*Gabrielle*	2
3/26/41	*The Circle of Chalk*	--
3/27/41	*The Fiddler's House*	--
3/28/41	*Escape into Glory*	--
4/1/41	*Watch on the Rhine*	378
4/4/41	*It Happens on Ice* (2d ed.)	180
	Your Loving Son	3
4/8/41	*The Trojan Women* (ET)	3
4/10/41	*The Night before Christmas*	22
4/18/41	*Steps Leading Up* (ET)	1
4/21/41	*The Beautiful People*	120
4/25/41	*Not in Our Stars* (ET)	1
4/29/41	*Texas Town*	--

Date	Title	Run
5/3/41	*Johnny Johnson*	--
5/7/41	*Natural Man* (ANT)	--
5/8/41	*Everyman*	2
5/10/41	*You Can't Sleep Here*	--
5/11/41	*American Legend*	--
5/13/41	*The Happy Days*	23
5/20/41	*L'Annonce Fait á Marie* (FRL)	1
5/24/41	*Sing before Breakfast*	--
5/27/41	*4 Saints in 3 Acts*	--
6/2/41	*When Differences Disappear*	--
6/3/41	*Snookie*	15
6/9/41	*Any Day Now*	--
7/16/41	*It Happens on Ice* (3d ed.)	386
9/3/41	*Village Green*	30
9/10/41	*The Wookey*	134
9/12/41	*Brother Cain*	19
9/15/41	*The More the Merrier*	16
9/16/41	*Cuckoos on the Hearth*	129
9/22/41	*The Distant City*	2
9/29/41	*Ghost for Sale*	6
9/30/41	*Mr. Big*	7
10/1/41	*Best Foot Forward*	326
10/2/41	*Ah, Wilderness!* (TG)	29
10/6/41	*All Men Are Alike*	32
	The Day of Judgment (YL; YAT)	--
10/7/41	*Anne of England*	7
	Live and Laugh (YL)	--
10/9/41	*Viva O'Brien*	20
10/20/41	*As You Like It*	8
10/21/41	*Good Neighbor*	1
10/22/41	*Candle in the Wind* (TG)	95
10/28/41	*The Land Is Bright*	79
10/29/41	*Let's Face It*	547
10/30/41	*Up the Rebels!* (BG)	4
10/31/41	*High Kickers*	171
11/4/41	*The Man With Blond Hair*	7
11/5/41	*Blithe Spirit*	657
	La Vie Parisienne	--
11/8/41	*The Walrus and the Carpenter*	9
11/10/41	*Spring Again*	241
11/11/41	*Macbeth*	131
11/12/41	*Theatre*	69
11/16/41	*Little Dark Horse*	9
11/17/41	*Ring around Elizabeth*	10
11/18/41	*Junior Miss*	710
11/19/41	*Walk into My Parlor*	29
11/21/41	*The Seventh Trumpet*	11
11/26/41	*Hope for a Harvest* (TG)	38
11/28/41	*The Days of Our Youth* (DW)	--
12/1/41	*Sons o'Fun*	742
12/2/41	*Twelfth Night*	15
12/4/41	*Sunny River*	36
12/5/41	*Angel Street*	1,293
12/8/41	*Golden Wings*	6
12/11/41	*Song out of Sorrow* (BG)	--
12/18/41	*The Yeomen of the Guard*	--

Date	Title	Run
12/20/41	*The Criminals*	15
12/21/41	*Brooklyn, U.S.A.*	57
12/22/41	*Pie in the Sky*	6
12/23/41	*Letters to Lucerne*	23
12/25/41	*Banjo Eyes*	126
12/27/41	*Clash by Night*	49
12/28/41	*In Time to Come*	40
1/2/41	*The First Crocus*	5
1/6/42	*Papa Is All* (TG)	63
1/7/42	*Out of My House*	--
1/8/42	*Johnny on a Spot*	4
1/9/42	*The Lady Comes Across*	3
1/14/42	*The Rivals* (TG)	54
1/20/42	*All in Favor*	7
1/21/42	*H.M.S. Pinafore*	18
	Jason	125
1/22/42	*Porgy and Bess*	286
1/23/42	*Café Crown*	141
1/26/42	*Lily of the Valley*	8
1/27/42	*Solitaire*	23
1/29/42	*Hedda Gabler*	12
1/30/42	*Food for Midas*	--
2/3/42	*The Mikado*	19
2/5/42	*The Flowers of Virtue*	4
2/6/42	*The Years Between* (BG)	5
2/11/42	*Of V We Sing*	76
2/12/42	*Heart of a City*	28
2/13/42	*They Should Have Stood in Bed*	11
2/17/42	*The Pirates of Penzance*	11
2/20/42	*Plan M*	6
2/22/42	*Under This Roof*	17
	Iolanthe	5
2/24/42	*Guest in the House*	153
2/28/42	*One-Woman Theatre*	--
3/3/42	*The Gondoliers*	3
3/10/42	*A Kiss for Cinderella*	48
3/11/42	*Nathan the Wise*	11
3/12/42	*Priorities of 1942*	353
3/16/42	*Johnny 2 X 4*	65
3/18/42	*Johnny Doodle*	6
3/20/42	"Across the Board on Tomorrow Morning" and "Theatre of the Soul"	--
3/23/42	*Arlene*	4
3/30/42	*It's about Time*	4
4/2/42	*Me and Harry*	--
4/3/42	*Nathan the Wise* (moves to Broadway)	28
4/7/42	*The Moon Is Down*	71
4/9/42	*The White Steed*	5
4/13/42	*Autumn Hill*	8
4/14/42	*Yesterday's Magic* (TG)	55
4/20/42	*What Big Ears!*	8
4/23/42	*Savonarola* (BG)	--
4/24/42	*Keep 'Em Laughing*	77
4/26/42	*Mexican Mural*	4
4/27/42	*Candida*	27
4/29/42	*The Life of Reilly*	5

Date	Title	Run
5/1/42	*Harlem Cavalcade*	49
5/7/42	*The Walking Gentleman*	6
5/19/42	*The Strings, My Lord, Are False*	15
5/20/42	*Uncle Harry*	430
	War and Peace (DW)	--
5/24/42	*Claudia* (RE)	24
5/25/42	*All the Comforts of Home*	8
5/26/42	*Comes the Revelation*	2
5/29/42	*Top-Notchers*	37
6/3/42	*By Jupiter*	427
6/7/42	*Starlight* (ANT)	--
6/15/42	*The Goldfish Bowl*	--
6/16/42	*The Cat Screams*	5
6/22/42	*Laugh, Town, Laugh*	65
6/23/42	*Broken Journey*	23
	The Chocolate Soldier	24
6/24/42	*Star and Garter*	605
7/2/42	*Stars on Ice*	427
7/4/42	*This Is the Army*	113
7/9/42	*Yours, A. Lincoln* (ET)	2
7/15/42	*The Merry Widow*	39
8/17/42	"Across the Board on Tomorrow Morning" and "Talking to You"	8
8/18/42	*The New Moon*	24
8/31/42	*I Killed the Count*	29
9/5/42	*Tobacco Road*	34
9/8/42	*The Canteen Show*	--
9/10/42	*Janie*	642
9/14/42	*The Morning Star*	24
9/15/42	*New Priorities of 1943*	54
9/16/42	*Show Time*	342
9/22/42	*Vickie*	48
9/26/42	*Anton Chekhov Sketches*	--
9/28/42	*Wine, Women, and Song*	150
9/29/42	"Hello Out There" and *Magic*	47
9/30/42	*Strip for Action*	110
10/5/42	*Let Freedom Sing*	8
10/7/42	*The Eve of St. Mark*	306
10/8/42	*Count Me In*	61
10/9/42	*Three Men on a Horse*	28
10/11/42	*Be Happy* (YL)	--
10/12/42	*Oy, Is Dus a Leben!* (YL)	139
10/14/42	*Beat the Band*	68
10/19/42	*Bird in Hand*	8
10/21/42	*The Time, the Place, and the Girl*	13
10/22/42	*The Damask Cheek*	93
10/23/42	*Native Son* (R)	84
10/27/42	*Little Darling*	23
10/28/42	*Rosalinda*	521
10/29/42	*Inside Story* (BG)	--
10/30/42	*Deliver Us from Evil*	--
11/10/42	*La Vie Parisienne*	19
	Without Love	113
11/13/42	*Mr. Sycamore* (TG)	19
11/16/42	*Homecoming*	12
11/18/42	*The Skin of Our Teeth*	355

Date	Title	Run
11/19/42	*La Leyenda del Besso*	--
	Once Over Lightly	6
11/23/42	*Yankee Point*	24
11/24/42	*Counsellor-at-Law*	258
11/25/42	*The Pirate* (TG)	177
11/26/42	*The Great Big Doorstep*	28
11/29/42	*Winter Soldiers* (DW)	30
11/30/42	*Lifeline*	8
12/3/42	*R.U.R.*	4
12/5/42	*Only the Heart*	--
12/9/42	*The Sun Field*	5
12/10/42	*The Willow and I*	28
12/15/42	*The Last Generation*	2
12/21/42	*The Three Sisters*	123
12/22/42	*New Faces of 1943*	94
12/23/42	*Flare Path*	14
12/25/42	*Proof thro' the Night*	11
	Ruth Draper	10
12/27/42	*The Theatre of Angna Enters*	--
12/28/42	*Sweet Charity*	8
12/29/42	*The Russian People* (TG)	39
	You'll See Stars	4
12/30/42	*The Doughgirls*	671
1/4/43	*Night Watch in Syria*	7
1/7/43	*Something for the Boys*	422
1/13/43	*Nine Girls*	5
1/14/43	*Dark Eyes*	230
1/28/43	*Tinker's Dam* (TG)	16
1/29/43	*The Patriots*	172
2/1/43	*The Barber Had Two Sons*	24
2/3/43	*Counterattack*	85
2/4/43	*Ask My Friend Sandy*	12
2/5/43	*For Your Pleasure*	11
2/11/43	*The Moon Vine*	20
2/13/43	*The Rich Uncle* (YL)	--
2/18/43	*This Rock*	37
2/26/43	*God Strikes Back*	5
2/27/43	*Lady in the Dark* (RE)	83
3/43	*Johnny Belinda* (R; YL)	--
3/3/43	*Harriet*	377
3/10/43	*Men in Shadow*	21
3/15/43	*Love Is No Heaven*	--
3/17/43	*Kiss and Tell*	962
3/19/43	*The Playboy of Newark*	--
3/22/43	*Apology*	8
3/24/43	*King Richard III* (Coulouris)	11
3/30/43	*The Family*	7
	It's up to You	1
3/31/43	*Oklahoma!* (TG)	2,248
4/1/43	*A Man's House* (BG)	16
	Ziegfeld Follies	553
4/14/43	*Tomorrow the World*	500
4/18/43	*To Kill a Cat*	2
4/28/43	*The First Million*	5
5/3/43	*The Corn Is Green* (RE)	56
5/4/43	*Sons and Soldiers*	22

Date	Title	Run
5/5/43	*Three's a Family*	497
5/31/43	*Moment Musical* (BG)	10
	Tonona	1
6/8/43	*The Student Prince*	153
6/9/43	*The Milky Way*	16
6/14/43	*The Army Play-by-Play*	1
6/16/43	*Those Endearing Young Charms*	61
6/17/43	*Early to Bed*	382
6/22/43	*Boy Meets Girl*	15
6/23/43	*The Merry Duchess*	2
6/24/43	*Stars on Ice* (2d ed.)	403
6/29/43	*The Vagabond King*	55
7/22/43	*Bridge to the Sun*	--
8/2/43	*Try and Get It*	8
	The Army Play-by-Play (RE)	40
	Try and Get It	8
8/4/43	*The Merry Widow*	322
8/11/43	*Run, Little Chillun*	16
8/12/43	*Chauve-Souris 1943*	12
8/18/43	*Murder without Crime*	37
9/1/43	*The Snark Was a Boojum*	5
9/2/43	*The Familiar Pattern*	--
9/4/43	*Blossom Time*	47
	Tobacco Road	66
9/6/43	*Blithe Spirit* (RE)	32
9/8/43	*Laugh Time*	126
9/9/43	*My Dear Public*	44
9/13/43	*Porgy and Bess* (RE)	24
9/15/43	*A New Life*	70
9/16/43	*Bright Lights of 1944*	4
9/21/43	*Land of Fame*	6
9/29/43	*All for All*	85
10/1/43	*Hairpin Harmony*	3
10/7/43	*One Touch of Venus*	567
10/12/43	*Another Love Story*	104
10/15/43	*Lucky Days* (YL)	--
10/17/43	*The Golden Land* (YL)	--
10/18/43	*The Family Carnovsky* (YL; YAT)	--
10/19/43	*Othello* (TG)	295
10/21/43	*The Naked Genius*	36
10/25/43	*Slightly Married*	8
10/26/43	*Manhattan Nocturne*	23
	Victory Belles	87
10/28/43	*Career*	7
11/1/43	*The Petrified Forest*	8
11/3/43	*Outrageous Fortune*	77
11/5/43	*Artists and Models*	28
11/9/43	*Goodbye Again*	8
	Hotel Universe	--
	I'll Take the High Road	7
11/11/43	*What's Up?*	63
11/15/43	*The Innocent Voyage* (TG)	40
11/16/43	*Lady, Behave*	23
11/17/43	*A Connecticut Yankee*	135
11/18/43	*Career Angel* (BG)	--

Date	Title	Run
	Three's a Family (ANT)	--
11/20/43	*Winged Victory*	212
11/24/43	*Get Away Old Man*	13
11/29/43	*Lovers and Friends*	168
12/2/43	*Carmen Jones*	502
12/6/43	*The World's Full of Girls*	9
12/8/43	*The Voice of the Turtle*	1,557
12/10/43	*Pillar to Post*	31
12/13/43	*Susan and God*	8
12/20/43	*The Patriots* (RE)	8
12/21/43	*Feathers in a Gale*	7
12/22/43	*Listen, Professor!*	29
12/28/43	*Doctors Disagree*	23
12/29/43	*South Pacific*	5
1/3/44	*Over 21*	221
1/5/44	*Ramshackle Inn*	216
1/10/44	*Our Town*	24
1/11/44	*Storm Operation*	23
1/12/44	*Suds in Your Eye*	37
1/13/44	*Jackpot*	69
1/24/44	*The Duke in Darkness*	24
1/25/44	*The Cherry Orchard*	96
1/26/44	*Wallflower*	192
1/28/44	*Mexican Hayride*	481
2/2/44	*Decision*	158
2/3/44	*Peepshow*	29
2/7/44	*Porgy and Bess* (RE)	16
2/10/44	*Take It As It Comes*	16
2/11/44	*The Mikado*	6
2/14/44	*H.M.S. Pinafore* and "Trial by Jury"	7
2/17/44	*Caukey* (BG)	22
	The Pirates of Penzance and "Cox and Box"	8
2/20/44	"Ile," "In the Zone," *The Man Who Came to Dinner*,	--
	"Fumed Oak" and "The Shadow of the Glen"	--
2/21/44	*The Gondoliers*	4
	Nathan the Wise	--
	Right next to Broadway	15
2/22/44	*Iolanthe*	6
2/25/44	*Patience*	4
2/28/44	*Porgy and Bess* (RE)	48
2/29/44	*Mrs. Kimball Presents*	7
3/1/44	*Thank You, Svoboda*	6
3/2/44	*Bright Boy*	16
	Ruddigore	3
3/3/44	*My Friend Yossel* (YL)	--
	The Yeomen of the Guard	1
3/14/44	*Jacobowsky and the Colonel* (TG)	415
3/20/44	*The House in Paris*	16
3/31/44	*Mrs. January and Mr. X*	43
4/4/44	*Only the Heart* (R)	47
4/5/44	*Chicken Every Sunday*	317
4/6/44	*Public Relations*	28
	Yellow Jack	1
4/8/44	*Follow the Girls*	882
4/11/44	*--But Not Goodbye*	23
4/12/44	*The Searching Wind*	326

Date	Title	Run
4/17/44	*Pretty Little Parlor*	8
4/18/44	*Sheppey*	23
4/20/44	*Allah Be Praised!*	20
4/22/44	*He Who Gets Slapped*	--
4/24/44	*Helen Goes to Troy*	96
	War President (ET)	2
4/27/44	*Earth Journey* (BG)	16
4/28/44	*A Highland Fling*	28
4/29/44	*The Wild Duck*	3
5/3/44	*Pick-up Girl*	197
5/8/44	*Hickory Stick*	8
5/14/44	*Africapers*	1
5/17/44	*The New Moon*	45
5/18/44	*Dream With Music*	28
5/20/44	*Spring Production*	--
5/23/44	*Career Angel* (moves to Broadway)	22
5/29/44	*The White Steed*	--
6/1/44	*A Strange Play* and "According to Law"	4
6/5/44	*That Old Devil*	16
6/9/44	*Shadow and Substance*	--
6/12/44	*Broken Hearts of Broadway*	14
6/13/44	*Slightly Scandalous*	7
6/14/44	*For Keeps*	29
6/15/44	*Take a Bow*	12
6/16/44	*Anna Lucasta* (ANT)	19
6/20/44	*Love on Leave*	7
6/22/44	*Hats Off to Ice*	890
6/27/44	*Ten Little Indians*	425
7/3/44	*Hamlet*	--
7/19/44	*Stars of Tomorrow*	--
8/1/44	*The School for Brides*	375
8/2/44	*Catherine Was Great*	191
8/8/44	*Good Morning, Corporal*	13
8/14/44	*The Two Mrs. Carrolls*	585
8/21/44	*Song of Norway*	860
8/25/44	*Lower North*	11
8/30/44	*Anna Lucasta* (moves to Broadway)	957
8/31/44	*Sleep No More*	7
9/5/44	*Last Stop*	23
9/7/44	*The Day Will Come*	20
9/11/44	*Down to Miami*	8
9/12/44	*Star Time*	120
9/19/44	*While the Sun Shines*	39
9/20/44	*Korb'n*	24
9/27/44	*Good News* (YL)	200
	Harriet (RE)	11
10/2/44	*The Odds on Mrs. Oakley*	24
10/3/44	*Men to the Sea*	23
10/4/44	*Soldier's Wife*	253
10/5/44	*Bloomer Girl*	654
10/7/44	*The Merry Widow*	32
10/8/44	*They All Want to Get Married* (YL)	245
10/10/44	*The Miracle of a Ghetto* (YL)	--
10/16/44	*Meet a Body*	24
10/17/44	*The Visitor*	23
10/19/44	*I Remember Mama*	714

Date	Title	Run
10/24/44	*Violet*	23
10/25/44	*Snafu*	158
10/26/44	*The Perfect Marriage*	92
10/30/44	*No Way Out*	8
10/31/44	*Embezzled Heaven* (TG)	52
11/1/44	*Harvey*	1,775
11/2/44	*Don't, George* (BG)	22
	Sleep, My Pretty One	12
11/7/44	*Robin Hood*	15
11/14/44	*In Bed We Cry*	47
11/16/44	*Sadie Thompson*	60
11/20/44	*The Streets Are Guarded*	24
11/21/44	*The Late George Apley*	384
11/22/44	*Rhapsody*	13
11/23/44	*The Man Who Had All the Luck*	4
11/28/44	"Hello Out There", *Those Endearing Young Charms*, and "The Shy and the Lonely"	2
	Mary Rose	2
11/29/44	*Design for Laughter*	--
11/30/44	*Walk Hard* (ANT)	42
12/4/44	*Hand in Glove*	40
12/6/44	*A Bell for Adano*	296
12/7/44	*Seven Lively Arts*	183
12/8/44	*Spook Scandals*	2
12/11/44	*Dark Hammock*	2
12/12/44	*Little Women*	23
12/13/44	*Dear Ruth*	683
12/19/44	*We Will Live* (YL)	--
12/23/44	*Laffing Room Only*	233
12/25/44	*Sophie*	9
12/27/44	*Sing Out, Sweet Land* (TG)	102
12/28/44	*On the Town*	462
12/29/44	*Trio*	67
1/3/45	*The Hasty Heart*	204
1/5/45	*Many Happy Returns*	3
1/10/45	*A Lady Says Yes*	87
1/12/45	*La Vie Parisienne*	37
1/16/45	*The Emperor Jones*	--
1/17/45	*Good Night, Ladies*	78
1/18/45	*Home Is the Hero* (BG)	23
	Rebecca	20
1/23/45	*A Goose for the Gander*	15
	"The Happy Journey" and *The Merchant of Venice*	3
1/25/45	*The Tempest*	100
1/27/45	*Up in Central Park*	504
1/30/45	*As You Desire Me*	--
1/31/45	*Alice in Arms*	5
2/6/45	*The Overtons*	175
2/7/45	*Hope for the Best*	117
	No More Ladies	--
	The Shining Hour	--
2/8/45	*One-Man Show*	36
2/12/45	*The Stranger*	16
2/14/45	*Signature*	2
2/21/45	*And Be My Love*	14
2/28/45	*Maedchen in Uniform*	--

Date	Title	Run
3/7/45	*Calico Wedding*	5
	Garden of Time (ANT)	30
3/8/45	*Simon's Wife* (BG)	15
3/12/45	*It's a Gift*	47
3/13/45	*Foolish Notion* (TG)	104
3/14/45	*Dark of the Moon*	318
3/15/45	*Happily Ever After*	12
3/19/45	*The Deep Mrs. Sykes*	72
3/20/45	*Kiss Them for Me*	110
	Sweet Genevieve	1
3/21/45	*Eternal Cage*	10
3/22/45	*The Firebrand of Florence*	43
	Winterset	--
3/26/45	*The Barretts of Wimpole Street*	87
	You Can't Take It with You	17
3/28/45	*Death Takes a Holiday*	4
3/29/45	*Lady in Danger*	12
3/31/45	*The Glass Menagerie*	561
4/2/45	*A Place of Our Own*	8
4/3/45	*The Sea Gull*	--
4/10/45	*Star Spangled Family*	5
4/17/45	*Twelfth Night*	--
4/19/45	*Carousel* (TG)	890
4/23/45	*When We Dead Awaken*	--
4/25/45	*Common Ground*	69
5/1/45	*The Late Christopher Bean*	2
5/2/45	*Carmen Jones* (RE)	21
	Too Hot for Maneuvers	5
5/7/45	*The Moon in the Yellow River*	--
5/10/45	*Slice It Thin!* (BG)	12
5/17/45	*The Animal Kingdom*	--
5/21/45	*Blue Holiday*	8
5/22/45	*Othello* (RE; TG)	24
5/23/45	*The Bourgeois Gentleman*	--
	The Children's Hour	--
	Foxhole in the Parlor	45
5/24/45	*Memphis Bound!*	36
	The Wild Duck	--
5/29/45	*Round Trip*	7
5/31/45	*Hollywood Pinafore*	53
6/1/45	*Concert Varieties*	36
6/6/45	*Henri Christophe* (ANT)	25
6/12/45	*The Private Life of the Master Race*	6
6/19/45	*Oh, Brother!*	23
6/21/45	*The Wind Is Ninety*	108
7/3/45	*As You Like It*	7
7/18/45	*Marinka*	165
9/6/45	*Mr. Strauss Goes to Boston*	12
9/11/45	*A Boy Who Lived Twice*	15
9/12/45	*Devils Galore*	5
9/13/45	*Make Yourself at Home*	4
9/24/45	*The Ryan Girl*	48
9/25/45	*You Touched Me!*	109
9/26/45	*Deep Are the Roots*	477
9/27/45	*Carib Song*	36
9/29/45	*Live Life Again*	2

Date	Title	Run
10/1/45	*Three Gifts* (YL; YAT)	--
10/6/45	*Polonaise*	113
10/9/45	*Therese*	96
10/11/45	*Wish Me Luck* (YL)	--
10/16/45	*The Red Mill*	531
10/17/45	*The Assassin*	13
10/25/45	*Seven Mirrors* (BG)	23
10/27/45	*Beggars Are Coming to Town*	25
10/29/45	*The Next Half Hour*	8
11/7/45	*The Secret Room*	21
11/8/45	*The Girl from Nantucket*	12
11/9/45	*The Rich Full Life*	27
11/10/45	*Are You with It?*	266
	The Rugged Path	81
11/11/45	*The Importance of Being Earnest*	4
11/12/45	*The Tempest* (RE)	24
11/13/45	*Skydrift*	7
11/14/45	*State of the Union*	765
11/20/45	*A Sound of Hunting*	23
11/21/45	*Marriage Is for Single People*	6
11/22/45	*The Day before Spring*	165
11/27/45	*The First Wife*	12
11/28/45	*The Mermaids Singing*	53
11/29/45	*Strange Fruit*	60
12/4/45	*The Good Hope*	4
12/8/45	*The French Touch*	33
12/12/45	*Brighten the Corner*	29
12/13/45	*Hamlet* (Evans)	131
12/14/45	*Dream Girl*	348
12/16/45	*Oedipus Rex*	2
12/20/45	*Dr. Herzl* (YL; YAT)	--
	Home Is the Hunter (ANT)	18
12/21/45	*Billion Dollar Baby*	220
12/23/45	*Little Women*	16
12/25/45	*A New Way to Pay Old Debts*	4
12/26/45	*Dunnigan's Daughter* (TG)	38
	Pygmalion	179
12/27/45	*Home of the Brave*	69
1/5/46	*Show Boat*	418
1/7/46	*A Joy Forever*	16
1/8/46	*The Desert Song*	45
1/9/46	*The Would-Be Gentleman*	77
1/15/46	*The Winter's Tale* (TG)	39
1/17/46	*A Young American* (BG)	26
1/19/46	*My Wedding Night* (YL)	--
1/21/46	*Nellie Bly*	16
	Thunder on the Left	--
1/22/46	*The Magnificent Yankee*	160
1/23/46	*O Mistress Mine* (TG)	452
1/27/46	*The Mayor of Zalamea*	2
1/29/46	*Faust*	4
2/4/46	*Born Yesterday*	1,642
	January Thaw	48
2/5/46	*Apple of His Eye*	118
2/6/46	*Lute Song*	142
2/13/46	*The Duchess Misbehaves*	5

Date	Title	Run
2/18/46	*Antigone*	64
2/21/46	*Jeb*	9
2/27/46	*Truckline Café*	13
2/28/46	*On Strivers Row* (ANT)	27
3/6/46	*Little Brown Jug*	5
3/7/46	*Three to Make Ready*	327
3/19/46	*Flamingo Road*	7
3/20/46	*He Who Gets Slapped* (TG)	46
3/22/46	*I Like It Here*	52
3/25/46	*Mary of Magdala* (BG)	25
3/26/46	*The Song of Bernadette*	3
3/27/46	*Walk Hard* (R; ANT)	7
3/30/46	*St. Louis Woman*	113
4/1/46	*The Servant of Two Masters*	4
4/3/46	*Candida*	24
4/7/46	*Carmen Jones* (RE)	32
4/8/46	*Mandragola*	4
4/17/46	*Woman Bites Dog*	5
4/18/46	*Call Me Mister*	734
4/30/46	*This, Too, Shall Pass*	63
5/6/46	*Henry IV, Part I* (OV)	14
5/7/46	*Henry IV, Part II* (OV)	6
5/8/46	*On Whitman Avenue*	150
5/12/46	*Pirates of Penzance*	4
5/13/46	*Uncle Vanya* (OV)	5
5/15/46	*Swan Song*	158
5/16/46	*Annie Get Your Gun*	1,147
5/18/46	*Come Marching Home* (BG)	23
5/20/46	*Oedipus* and *The Critic* (OV)	8
5/27/46	*All for Love*	4
5/31/46	*Around the World*	75
6/3/46	*Hamlet* (RE; Evans)	16
	Second Best Bed	8
6/5/46	*The Affairs of Anatol*	4
	The Dancer	5
6/20/46	*Icetime*	405
7/8/46	*Tidbits of 1946*	8
7/10/46	*Molehills*	--
7/15/46	*Maid in the Ozarks*	103
9/4/46	*The Front Page*	79
9/5/46	*A Flag Is Born*	120
	Yours Is My Heart	36
9/17/46	*Gypsy Lady*	79
9/19/46	*Hidden Horizon*	12
9/26/46	*The Bees and the Flowers*	28
10/1/46	*Obsession*	31
10/7/46	*Hear That Trumpet*	8
10/8/46	*Cyrano de Bergerac*	193
10/9/46	*The Iceman Cometh* (TG)	136
10/10/46	*Mr. Peebles and Mr. Hooker*	4
10/14/46	*Lady Windermere's Fan*	228
10/15/46	*The Duchess of Malfi*	38
10/16/46	*Loco*	37
10/17/46	*Lysistrata*	4
10/19/46	*Naughty Naught ('00)*	17
10/24/46	*Made in Heaven!*	92

Date	Title	Run
10/25/46	*Song of the Dniepper* (YL; YAT)	--
10/26/46	*The Playboy of the Western World*	81
10/28/46	*Derryowen* (BG)	24
10/29/46	*Present Laughter*	158
10/31/46	*Happy Birthday*	564
11/4/46	*Park Avenue*	72
11/6/46	*King Henry VIII* (ART)	40
11/7/46	*Bal Negre*	52
11/8/46	*What Every Woman Knows* (ART)	21
11/12/46	*John Gabriel Borkman* (ART)	21
11/13/46	*The Haven*	5
11/18/46	*Joan of Lorraine*	199
11/19/46	*The Fatal Weakness* (TG)	119
11/20/46	*Another Part of the Forest*	182
	I'm in Love (YL)	--
11/22/46	*Rosmersholm*	--
11/26/46	*No Exit*	31
11/27/46	*A Family Affair*	6
11/30/46	*Christopher Blake*	114
12/3/46	*Years Ago*	206
12/5/46	*If the Shoe Fits*	21
12/11/46	*Land's End*	5
12/13/46	*Wandering Stars* (YL; YAT)	--
12/19/46	*Androcles and the Lion* and "Pound on Demand" (ART)	40
12/25/46	*Burlesque*	439
	Lovely Me	37
	Wonderful Journey	9
12/26/46	*Toplitzky of Notre Dame*	60
	Beggar's Holiday	108
	Toplitzky of Notre Dame	60
12/27/46	*Temper the Wind*	35
1/1/47	*Love Goes to Press*	5
1/6/47	*Bloomer Girl* (RE)	48
1/8/47	*The Big Two*	21
1/9/47	*Street Scene*	148
1/10/47	*Finian's Rainbow*	725
1/12/47	*Ruth Draper*	42
1/15/47	*Little A*	21
1/16/47	*If in the Greenwood* (BG)	28
1/21/47	*Sweethearts*	288
1/29/47	*All My Sons*	328
2/3/47	*It Takes Two*	8
2/4/47	*John Loves Mary*	423
2/8/47	*The Story of Mary Surratt*	11
2/9/47	*The Wanhope Building* (ET)	5
2/12/47	*Craig's Wife*	69
2/18/47	*King Lear* (Wolfit)	8
2/20/47	*As You Like It* (Wolfit)	4
2/22/47	*The Merchant of Venice* (Wolfit)	6
2/23/47	*O'Daniel* (ET)	5
	You with Me	--
2/24/47	*Volpone* (Wolfit)	3
2/26/47	*Hamlet* (Wolfit)	2
	Winners and Losers	5
2/27/47	*Tin Top Valley* (ANT)	45
	Yellow Jack (ART)	21

Date	Title	Run
3/3/47	*The Importance of Being Earnest* (TG)	81
3/4/47	*Parlor Story*	23
3/6/47	*On the Seventh Day* (BG)	25
3/9/47	*As We Forgive Our Debtors* (ET)	5
3/10/47	*Maurice Chevalier*	46
3/12/47	*The Chocolate Soldier*	70
3/13/47	*Brigadoon*	581
3/19/47	*The Eagle Has Two Heads*	29
3/21/47	*The Deputy of Paris*	8
3/26/47	*Bathsheba*	29
3/27/47	*The Whole World Over*	100
3/30/47	*The Great Campaign* (ET)	5
4/2/47	*Tenting Tonight*	46
4/3/47	*Barefoot Boy with Cheek*	108
4/5/47	*Alice in Wonderland* (ART)	100
4/13/47	*Virginia Reel* (ET)	5
4/16/47	*Message for Margaret*	5
4/17/47	*The Flies*	21
4/19/47	*Our Lan'*	12
4/25/47	*Miracle in the Mountains*	3
4/29/47	*A Young Man's Fancy*	335
5/47	*Henry IV* (ELT)	--
5/1/47	*The Medium* and "The Telephone"	212
5/2/47	*The Dybbuk* (HL; HT)	8
	Heads or Tails	35
5/13/47	*Respectfully Yours* (BG)	16
5/14/47	*Portrait in Black*	62
5/19/47	*Up in Central Park* (RE)	16
5/26/47	*Love for Love* (TG)	48
5/27/47	*Shylock '47* (HL)	8
5/28/47	*Icetime of 1948*	422
6/2/47	*Louisiana Lady*	4
6/3/47	*Open House*	7
6/9/47	*No Exit* (OS)	38
6/26/47	*Laura*	44
7/15/47	*Rip Van Winkle* (NYCC)	15
7/21/47	*The Dog Beneath the Skin* (OS)	27
8/18/47	*Gas* (OS)	--
9/3/47	*The Magic Touch*	12
9/22/47	*Anna Lucasta* (RE)	32
9/25/47	*I Gotta Get Out*	4
9/27/47	*Just My Luck* (YL)	--
	Our Lan' (moves to Broadway)	41
9/29/47	*The Heiress*	410
	Shylock and His Daughter (YL; YAT)	--
9/30/47	*How I Wonder*	63
10/1/47	*Command Decision*	409
10/2/47	*Music in My Heart*	125
10/3/47	*Under the Counter*	27
10/5/47	*Dear Judas*	17
10/7/47	*Duet for Two Hands*	7
	Life Sentence (OS)	--
10/8/47	*Man and Superman*	294
10/9/47	*High Button Shoes*	727
10/10/47	*Allegro* (TG)	315
10/20/47	*Medea*	214

Date	Title	Run
10/21/47	*An Inspector Calls*	95
10/22/47	*The Druid Circle*	70
10/23/47	*Hoboes in Heaven* (BG)	26
10/28/47	*The Watched Pot* (OS)	27
10/29/47	*The Winslow Boy* (TG)	215
10/30/47	*Edith Piaf*	44
11/3/47	*This Time Tomorrow* (TG)	32
	Trial Honeymoon	8
11/4/47	*For Love or Money*	263
11/5/47	*The First Mrs. Fraser*	38
11/18/47	*Eastward in Eden*	15
11/21/47	*A House Possessed*	--
11/24/47	*The Cradle Will Rock*	2
11/26/47	*Antony and Cleopatra*	126
11/27/47	*Faust* (GEL)	--
11/28/47	*The Family Reunion* (OS)	--
11/30/47	*Nights of Wrath* (DW)	26
12/47	*Yerma* (OS)	--
	Anna Christie (ELT)	--
12/3/47	*A Streetcar Named Desire*	855
12/4/47	*Trial by Fire* (BG)	20
12/5/47	*Caribbean Carnival*	11
12/7/47	*Galileo* (ET)	6
12/9/47	*The Gentleman from Athens*	7
12/10/47	*Henry IV* (OS)	--
12/11/47	*Angel in the Wings*	308
12/21/47	*Lamp at Midnight* (NS)	51
12/22/47	*Crime and Punishment*	64
12/26/47	*The Cradle Will Rock* (moves to Broadway)	21
	Rain (ANT)	28
12/27/47	*Topaze*	1
12/28/47	*Ruth Draper*	27
12/29/47	*The Mikado*	40
1/4/48	*Skipper Next to God* (ET)	6
1/5/48	*The Pirates of Penzance* & "Trial by Jury"	16
1/7/48	*Four Flights Up*	--
1/8/48	*Volpone* (NYCC)	14
1/12/48	*Harvest of Years*	16
	Iolanthe	16
1/13/48	*Power without Glory*	31
1/14/48	*Strange Bedfellows*	229
1/15/48	*Make Mine Manhattan*	429
1/16/48	*The Big Shot* (YL)	67
	The Men We Marry	3
1/18/48	*All the King's Men* (DW)	21
1/19/48	*H.M.S. Pinafore* and "Cox and Box"	16
	The Survivors	8
1/22/48	*Angel Street* (R; NYCC)	14
1/26/48	*The Gondoliers*	16
1/27/48	*The Last Dance*	7
1/29/48	*Look, Ma, I'm Dancin'*	188
2/2/48	*The Yeomen of the Guard*	16
2/3/48	*Kathleen*	2
2/5/48	*Four One-Act Comedies* ("A Tragedian in Spite of Himself," "The Bear," "On the Harmfulness of Tobacco," and "The Wedding") (NYCC)	14

Date	Title	Run
2/8/48	*A Long Way from Home* (ET)	6
2/9/48	*An Evening of Two Plays* ("The Respectful Prostitute" & "Church Street"; NS)	40
	Patience	16
2/10/48	*John Bull's Other Island* (DGT)	8
2/11/48	*Doctor Social*	5
2/12/48	*Lady of Fatima* (BG)	41
2/16/48	*Ghosts* (ART)	10
2/17/48	*The Old Lady Says "No!"* (DGT)	8
2/18/48	*Mister Roberts*	1,157
2/20/48	*Tonight at 8:30* (first series)	26*
2/23/48	*Tonight at 8:30* (second series)	
2/24/48	*Hedda Gabler* (ART)	15
	Where Stars Walk (DGT)	14
2/26/48	*Me and Molly*	158
2/29/48	*Maurice Chevalier*	33
3/2/48	*The Linden Tree*	7
3/4/48	*The Hallams*	12
3/14/48	*A Temporary Island* (ET)	6
3/16/48	*You Never Can Tell* (TG)	39
	"The Respectful Prostitute" and "The Happy Journey to Trenton and Camden" (moves to Broadway; NS)	318
3/17/48	*Chaff* (DW)	10
3/18/48	*Joy to the World*	124
3/25/48	*The Golden Falcon*	--
3/27/48	*Skipper next to God* (moves to Broadway)	93
3/31/48	*Macbeth* (Redgrave)	29
4/11/48	*Six O'Clock Theatre* ("Hope Is the Thing with Feathers," "Celebration," and "Afternoon Storm")	8
4/15/48	*The Rats of Norway*	4
4/18/48	*To Tell You the Truth* (NS)	15
4/20/48	*The Cup of Trembling*	31
4/22/48	*Sojourner Truth* (ANT)	3
4/24/48	*Seeds in the Wind* (ET)	3
4/27/48	*Holiday on Broadway*	6
4/28/48	*The Play's the Thing*	244
4/30/48	*Inside U.S.A.*	339
5/5/48	*Hold It!*	46
5/6/48	*The Alchemist* (NYCC)	14
	Sally	36
5/9/48	*Ballet Ballads* ("Susanna and the Elders," "Willie the Weeper," and "The Eccentricities of Davy Crockett") (ET)	69
	David's Crown (HL; HT)	8
5/11/48	*Hope's the Thing* ("Hope Is the Thing with Feathers" [moves to Broadway], "Gone Tomorrow," and "Home Life of a Buffalo"	7
5/16/48	*The Golem* (HL; HT)	16
5/17/48	*Battle for Heaven* (ET)	4
5/20/48	*S.S. Glencairn* (NYCC)	14
5/21/48	*The Vigil*	11
5/22/48	*Oedipus Rex* (HL; HT)	8
5/25/48	*Seeds in the Wind* (moves to Broadway)	7
5/27/48	*G-II*	--
	Step a Little Closer	--
6/3/48	*The Insect Comedy* (NYCC)	14
	Sleepy Hollow	12

Date	Title	Run
6/4/48	*"Almost Faithful"* (ANT)	--
	These Tender Mercies (ET)	4
6/10/48	*Six Characters in Search of an Author* (NYRG)	--
6/15/48	$E=MC^2$ (ET)	3
6/16/48	*The Infernal Machine*	--
6/24/48	*Howdy, Mr. Ice!*	406
7/6/48	*No Exit* (NYRG)	--
7/8/48	*Within the Gates*	--
7/22/48	*The Contrast* (OS)	6
7/26/48	*him*	--
7/28/48	*The Moon in the Yellow River*	--
7/31/48	*The Owl and the Pussycat* (NYRG)	--
8/4/48	*Billy the Kid* (OS)	8
8/17/48	*The New York Idea* (OS)	--
8/24/48	*Peg O' My Heart* (OS)	6
8/28/48	*East Lynne* (OS)	6
9/1/48	*The Bat* (OS)	--
9/7/48	*Show Boat* (RE)	15
	Sundown Beach	7
9/9/48	*Hilarities*	14
9/15/48	*Small Wonder*	134
9/20/48	*Magdalena*	88
9/21/48	*A Story for Strangers*	15
9/22/48	*Grandma's Diary*	6
9/23/48	*Town House*	12
9/27/48	*Time for Elizabeth*	8
9/30/48	*Edward, My Son*	260
10/4/48	*Private Lives*	248
10/6/48	*Summer and Smoke*	102
10/7/48	*Love Life*	252
10/10/48	*The Power of Darkness*	--
	The Taming of the Shrew	--
10/11/48	*Where's Charley?*	792
10/14/48	*The Minstrel Boy* (BG)	--
10/17/48	*What a Guy* (YL)	--
10/18/48	*The Leading Lady*	8
10/19/48	*My Romance*	95
10/20/48	*Life with Mother*	265
10/25/48	*The Voice of Israel* (YL; YAT)	--
10/27/48	*Minnie and Mr. Williams*	5
10/28/48	*Partition*	--
11/48	*The Adding Machine* (NYRG)	--
11/3/48	*Set My People Free* (TG)	36
11/11/48	*Bravo!*	44
11/13/48	*As the Girls Go*	414
	The Heeple Steeple	2
11/16/48	*For Heaven's Sake, Mother!*	7
11/17/48	*Goodbye, My Fancy*	446
11/18/48	*Light Up the Sky*	214
11/21/48	*Hippolytus* (ET)	4
11/22/48	*The Young and Fair*	48
11/24/48	*The Silver Whistle* (TG)	219
12/48	*The Dog beneath the Skin*	--
12/4/48	*Red Gloves*	113
12/5/48	*Thumbnail Theatre*	--
12/6/48	*From Morn to Midnight*	--

Date	Title	Run
12/7/48	*The Medium* and "The Telephone" (RE)	40
12/8/48	*Anne of the Thousand Days*	288
12/12/48	*Herschel the Jester* (YL; YAT)	--
12/16/48	*Lend an Ear*	460
12/22/48	*Make Way for Lucia* (TG)	29
12/23/48	*Jenny Kissed Me*	20
12/26/48	*Oh, Mr. Meadowbrook!*	64
	The Victors (NS)	31
12/27/48	*The Madwoman of Chaillot*	368
12/28/48	*Don't Listen, Ladies*	15
12/29/48	*The Rape of Lucretia*	23
12/30/48	*Kiss Me, Kate*	1,077
1/4/49	*Rose in the Wilderness*	2
1/12/49	*The Smile of the World*	5
1/13/49	*Along Fifth Avenue*	180
1/18/49	*The Shop at Sly Corner*	7
1/21/49	*Leaf and Bough*	3
1/22/49	*All for Love*	141
1/25/49	*Carousel* (RE; TG)	48
1/28/49	*Forward the Heart*	19
1/29/49	*Uniform of Flesh* (ET)	7
2/3/49	"Riders to the Sea" and "Freight" (ANT)	--
2/4/49	*The Rape of the Sabine Women* (GEL)	--
2/5/49	*Diamond Lil*	181
2/6/49	*Blood Wedding* (NS)	35
2/8/49	*King Richard III* (Whorf)	23
2/9/49	*My Name Is Aquilon*	31
2/10/49	*Death of a Salesman*	742
2/13/49	*Leave It to Charley* (YL)	--
2/14/49	*Madame Is Served*	4
	Stevedore	8
2/16/49	*They Knew What They Wanted*	61
2/17/49	*Nine Month Midnight*	2
2/19/49	*City of Kings* (BG)	--
2/24/49	*The Big Knife*	108
2/25/49	*Anybody Home*	5
2/27/49	*Cock-a-Doodle-Do* (ET)	6
3/1/49	*Outside the Door* (DW)	--
3/2/49	*Two Blind Mice*	157
3/8/49	*At War with the Army*	151
3/20/49	*The Sun and I* (NS)	23
3/23/49	*Detective Story*	581
3/27/49	*The Nineteenth Hole of Europe* (ET)	4
3/30/49	*The Biggest Thief in Town*	13
4/4/49	*The Traitor*	67
4/5/49	*The Ivy Green*	7
4/6/49	*The Millionairess*	13
4/7/49	*South Pacific*	1,925
4/8/49	*Iphigenia in Tauris* (GEL)	--
4/9/49	*Fifty*	3
4/18/49	*Magnolia Alley*	8
4/23/49	*Sister Oakes* (ET)	4
4/25/49	*The Happiest Years*	8
5/2/49	*Medea* (RE)	16
5/3/49	*Bruno and Sidney* (NS)	6
5/4/49	*Mrs. Gibbons' Boys*	5

Date	Title	Run
5/9/49	*Concerto for Fun*	16
	Don't Go Away Mad	2
5/10/49	*Gayden*	7
5/14/49	*Me, the Sleeper* (ET)	4
5/16/49	*Man and Superman* (RE)	16
5/25/49	*Mr. Adam*	5
5/26/49	*Howdy, Mr. Ice of 1950*	430
6/4/49	*The Millionairess*	3
6/9/49	*They Shall Not Die*	--
6/13/49	*The Fifth Horseman* (ET)	--
6/14/49	*The Shoemaker's Prodigious Wife* and "The Stronger"	--
6/21/49	*The Journey of Simon McKeever* and "I've Got the Tune"	1
6/30/49	*Funzapoppin'*	31
	Out of the Picture	--
7/49	*The Ascent of F-6* (OS)	--
7/6/49	*Yes Is for a Very Young Man*	--
7/7/49	*Cabalgata*	76
7/15/49	*Miss Liberty*	308
7/20/49	*The Father*	95
7/21/49	*The Silver Tassie*	--
7/26/49	*A Dream of Love*	--
7/27/49	*Too Many Thumbs*	--
7/28/49	*H.M.S. Pinafore*	--
8/30/49	*The Bourgeois Gentleman*	--
9/6/49	*[Ken Murray's] Blackouts of 1949*	51
?	*The Ascent of F-6* (RE)	--
9/16/49	*Heaven on Earth*	12
10/3/49	*Twelfth Night*	48
10/4/49	*The Mikado*	8
	Yes, M'Lord	87
10/8/49	*Abi Gezunt* (YL)	--
10/10/49	*The Pirates of Penzance*	8
	Yosele, the Nightingale (YL; YAT)	--
10/12/49	"The Browning Version" and "Harlequinade"	69
10/13/49	*Touch and Go*	176
10/17/49	*H.M.S. Pinafore* and "Trial by Jury"	8
10/20/49	*Shake Hands with the Devil* (BG)	--
10/21/49	*Double Trouble* (YL)	--
10/29/49	*Montserrat*	65
10/30/49	*Lost in the Stars*	281
10/31/49	*Regina*	56
11/2/49	*I Know My Love* (TG)	246
11/7/49	*Love Me Long*	16
11/10/49	*The Edge of the Sword*	3
11/13/49	*Wedding in Japan* (DW)	--
11/16/49	*The Father* (Massey)	69
	These Hills Are Scarred	4
11/21/49	*Creditors* (OS)	108
11/22/49	*That Lady*	78
11/25/49	*Texas, Li'l Darlin'*	293
12/1/49	*The Closing Door*	22
	Trouble in July	10
12/3/49	*Clutterbuck*	218
	Hamlet (NYRG)	--
12/6/49	*Metropole*	2
12/8/49	*Gentlemen Prefer Blondes*	740

Date	Title	Run
12/14/49	*Deirdre of the Sorrows*	3
12/16/49	*The Burning Bush* (DW)	--
12/21/49	*Caesar and Cleopatra*	149
12/22/49	*The Rat Race*	84
12/26/49	*Holiday in Paris*	--
	The Velvet Glove	152
12/27/49	*How Long till Summer?*	7
12/28/49	*She Stoops to Conquer* (NYCC)	16
1/5/50	*The Member of the Wedding*	501
1/6/50	*Happy as Larry*	3
1/11/50	*The Corn Is Green* (R; NYCC)	16
1/17/50	*Alive and Kicking*	46
1/19/50	*The Man*	92
1/18/50	*The Enchanted*	45
1/20/50	*Dance Me a Song*	35
1/21/50	*The Cocktail Party*	409
1/23/50	*Design for a Stained Glass Window*	8
1/24/50	*The Happy Time*	614
1/25/50	*The Devil's Disciple* (NYCC)	127
1/26/50	*As You Like It* (TG)	145
1/29/50	*Sadie Is a Lady* (YL)	--
1/30/50	*Mistress of the House*	4
1/31/50	*Mr. Barry's Etchings*	31
	They Came to a City	15
2/1/50	*The Innocents*	141
2/2/50	*Arms and the Girl* (TG)	134
	The Clandestine Marriage	--
2/4/50	*Building 222*	3
2/5/50	*The Plough and the Stars*	--
2/8/50	*The Heiress* (R: NCC)	16
2/9/50	*All You Need Is One Good Break*	4
2/14/50	*Macbeth*	--
2/15/50	*Come Back, Little Sheba* (TG)	190
2/16/50	*There Is No End*	16
2/20/50	*All You Need Is One Good Break* (revised)	32
2/21/50	*The Devil's Disciple* (moves to commercial Broadway production)	111
2/22/50	*The Bird Cage*	21
2/23/50	*Armor of Light* (BG)	--
3/2/50	*Now I Lay Me Down to Sleep*	44
3/6/50	*Tobacco Road*	7
3/8/50	*When the Bough Breaks*	3
3/15/50	*The Consul*	269
3/21/50	*Heartbreak House* (OS)	--
3/23/50	*Great to Be Alive!*	52
3/26/50	*The Miser*	--
3/29/50	*The Wisteria Trees*	165
4/4/50	*The Greener Grass*	--
4/11/50	*Cry of the Peacock*	2
4/12/50	*With a Silk Thread*	13
4/13/50	*The Dybbuk*	4
4/17/50	*And So They Perish*	14
4/19/50	*Katherine Dunham and Her Company*	37
	The Scapegoat (DW)	--
4/20/50	*Tread the Green Grass*	3
4/24/50	*Peter Pan*	321

Date	Title	Run
4/25/50	*Tobias and the Angel* (OS)	--
4/26/50	"A Phoenix Too Frequent" and "Freight"	5
4/27/50	*Tickets, Please!*	245
5/50	*Longitude*	--
5/2/50	*Brigadoon* (RE)	24
5/3/50	*John Brown*	--
5/10/50	*These Are the Times* (DW)	--
5/18/50	*The Liar*	12
5/23/50	*A Streetcar Named Desire* (RE)	24
5/24/50	*The House of Bernarda Alba*	3
5/25/50	*Master Builder Solness*	--
5/30/50	*The Unquiet Spirit*	--
5/31/50	*The Show-Off*	6

* This sum includes both the first and second series.

Appendix 2
Play Categories

This appendix provides category listings for every *full-length* play covered by the entries in the text. Productions mentioned in the text, but not given full entries because of a lack of information, are also included, as are several plays that, while technically in one act, were offered as the only piece on the program. Shorter one-acts, including such important works as "The Browning Version" and "The Respectful Prostitute," are not listed here, although a list of one-acts is provided that includes the name of the programs on which they appeared. (The title of the play sometimes coincides with that of the program.) Although admittedly imperfect, these listings should prove of value to those seeking to discern patterns in playwriting and production. The lists are based on the category breakdowns printed next to the titles in the text. A small number of categories proved too common to make a listing of them here worthwhile. Most of these categories are retained in the play entries, however. Reference to them is also made in the lists that follow by the use of the following symbols: F (Family), MA (Marriage), RM (Romance, that is, plays containing one or more love interests), SX (Sex). Plays that conform only to one or more of these symbols will not be found in the listings. The categories of Comedy, Comedy-Drama, and Drama have not been repeated. Most of the remaining categories are self-explanatory, but a few words of clarification have been added where it was deemed appropriate. The lists are subsumed under several groupings: Nature of the Production; National Origin; Subject Matter; Background Locales; Foreign-Language Productions; Ethnic Groups; and Miscellaneous. Categorization applies principally to new plays (plays not produced previously in New York). Plays identified as "Dramatic Revivals" or "Musical Revivals" will have no further identifying symbols unless a specific production was given in a foreign language or a play originally intended for white actors was revived with blacks; in these cases the appropriate symbols will follow the title. In some cases a play that was new when first produced in the decade was revived again during the same period. Such a play will be found in both the revival listings and in those for new plays. Titles given are those under which the plays are listed in the entries.

Alphabetical List of Categories and Their Symbols

AD Adventure
AL Alcoholism
A Art
AU Australian
AV Aviation
BA Barroom
BC Broadcasting
BH Boarding House
BI Bible
BL Blacks
BR British
BS Business
CH China
CI Circus
CR Crime
DE Death

DRG	Drugs
DU	Dutch
F	Family
FA	Fantasy
FI	Films
FL	Flemish
FNC	France
FR	French
FRL	French Language
FS	Friendship
GA	Gambling
GE	German
GEL	German Language
HEL	Hebrew Language
HIB	Historical-Biographical
HO	Homosexuality
HT	Hotel
HU	Hungarian
IC	Ice Show
IL	Illness
IN	Invalidism
IR	Irish
JE	Jews
JO	Journalism
L	Labor
LA	Law
LE	Legacy
LIB	Literary-Biographical
LT	Literature
M	Musical
MA	Marriage
MD	Medicine
ME	Mental Illness
MEX	Mexico
MI	Military
MS	Miscellaneous
MU	Music
MUB	Musical-Biographical
MU	Music
MUB	Musical-Biographical
MY	Mystery
NC	Night Club
OA	Old Age
OR	Orientals
PE	Period
PN	Prison
POL	Politics
PS	Prostitution
RC	Race
REL	Religion
REV	Revue
RM	Romance
RR	Rural
RSM	Russian
S	School
SC	Science
SE	Sea
SH	Show Business
SM	Small Town
SO	Southern
SP	Spanish
SPL	Spanish Language
SPR	Spiritualism
SPT	Sports
SX	Sex
TH	Theatre
TR	Trial
TRP	Tropics
UN	University
V	Verse
W	War
WE	Western
WO	Women
YL	Yiddish Language
YO	Youth

NATURE OF THE PRODUCTION

Dramatic Revivals

Dramatic revivals are considered to be (1) nonmusical plays previously performed in New York, even if the original performance was in a language other than English; (2) plays at least twenty years old originally performed elsewhere than in New York. The numbers in parentheses next to some titles signify the number of revivals given the play during the decade. An asterisk (*) is used to denote plays that were revived after making their New York debut earlier in the decade. The list does not include return engagements, that is, productions that were repeated in the same or subsequent seasons by the same company, although sometimes with new actors.

Adding Machine, The
Affairs of Anatol, The
Ah, Wilderness!
Alchemist, The
Alice in Wonderland

All for Love
All the Comforts of Home
Androcles and the Lion
*Angel Street**
Animal Kingdom, The
Anna Christie
*Anna Lucasta**
Annonce Fait á *Marie, L'* FRL
Anton Chekhov Sketches
Antony and Cleopatra
As You Desire Me
As You Like It (4)
Ascent of F-6, The
Barretts of Wimpole Street, The
Bat, The
Billy the Kid
Bird in Hand
Blind Alley
Blood Wedding
Bourgeois Gentleman, The (also called *The Would-be Gentleman*) (3)
Boy Meets Girl
Burlesque
Caesar and Cleopatra
Candida (2)
*Career Angel**
Charley's Aunt
Cherry Orchard, The
Children's Hour, The
Circle of Chalk, The
Clandestine Marriage, The
Contrast, The
*Corn Is Green, The**
Counsellor-at-Law
Craig's Wife
Creditors
Critic, The
Cyrano de Bergerac
David's Crown HEL
Death Takes a Holiday
Deirdre of the Sorrows
Devil's Disciple, The
Diamond Lil
Doctor's Dilemma, The
Duchess of Malfi, The
Dybbuk, The (2) HL
East Lynne
Emperor Jones, The
Everyman
Father, The (2)
Faust (2; #2 in GEL)
Fiddler's House, The
Four One-Act Comedies
From Morn to Midnight
The Front Page
Gas
Ghosts
Glass Slipper, The
Golem, The HEL
Good Hope, The

Good Night, Ladies
Goodbye Again
Hamlet (4)
He Who Gets Slapped (2)
Heartbreak House
Hedda Gabler (2)
*Heiress, The**
"Hello Out There"*
Henry IV, Part I
Henry IV, Part II
him
Hippolytus
Hotel Universe
"Ile"
Importance of Being Earnest, The (2)
Infernal Machine, The
Insect Comedy, The
Iphegenia in Tauris GEL
John Bull's Other Island
John Gabriel Borkman
Johnny Johnson
*Johnny Belinda** YL
Kind Lady
King Henry VIII
King Lear (2)
King Richard III (2)
Kiss for Cinderella, A
Lady Windermere's Fan
Last Dance, The
Late Christopher Bean, The
Little Women (2)
Love for Love
Lysistrata
Macbeth (3)
Maedchen in Uniform
Man and Superman
Mandragola
Mary Rose
Master Builder Solness
Mayor of Zalamea, The
Medea
Men in White YL
Merchant of Venice, The
Milky Way, The
Millionairess, The
Minnie and Mr. Williams
Miser, The
Mistress of the House
Moon in the Yellow River, The (2)
Nathan the Wise
*Native Son**
New Way to Pay Old Debts, A
New York Idea, The
No Exit (2)
No More Ladies
Obsession
Oedipus Rex (3; #3 in HL)
On Strivers Row
*Only the Heart**

Othello
Our Town
Peg O' My Heart
Peter Pan
Petrified Forest, The
Playboy of the Western World, The
Play's the Thing, The
Plough and the Stars, The
Power of Darkness, The
Private Lives
Pygmalion
R.U.R.
Rain
Rip Van Winkle
Rivals, The
Rosmersholm
Run, Little Chillun
S.S. Glencairn
Sea Gull, The
Servant of Two Masters, The
Shadow and Substance
She Stoops to Conquer
Shining Hour, The
Show-Off, The
Silver Tassie, The
Six Characters in Search of an Author
Stevedore
Sun and I, The
Susan and God
Taming of the Shrew, The
Tempest, The
They Knew What They Wanted
They Shall Not Die
*Those Endearing Young Charms**
Three Men on a Horse
Three Sisters, The
*Three's a Family**
Thunder on the Left
Tobacco Road (2)
Tobias and the Angel
Tonight at 8:30
Topaze
Trojan Women, The
Twelfth Night (4)
Uncle Vanya
Volpone (2)
*Walk Hard**
Watched Pot, The
What Every Woman Knows
When We Dead Awaken
White Steed, The (2)
Wild Duck, The (2)
Winter's Tale, The
Winterset
Within the Gates
Would-Be Gentleman, The
Yellow Jack (2)
You Can't Take It with You
You Never Can Tell

Musical Revivals

The same basic criteria used to determine "dramatic revivals" apply for musical revivals. Musicals are here considered to be any show combining a libretto or book telling a consistent story from beginning to end with a substantial quantity of accompanying music in the form of songs and/or dance numbers; operettas, comic operas, and the like are thus considered as musicals for purposes of categorization.

Blossom Time
*Brigadoon**
Chocolate Soldier, The (2)
Connecticut Yankee, A
Cradle Will Rock, The
Desert Song, The
4 Saints in 3 Acts
Gondoliers, The (4)
H.M.S. Pinafore (5)
Iolanthe (3)
Merry Duchess, The
Merry Widow, The (2)
Mikado, The (4)
Naughty Naught ('00)
New Moon, The (2)
Once Over Lightly
Patience (2)
Pirates of Penzance, The (6)
Porgy and Bess
Red Mill, The
Robin Hood
Rosalinda
Ruddigore
Sally
Show Boat
Student Prince, The
Sweethearts
Time, the Place, and the Girl, The
Vagabond King, The
Vie Parisienne, La (2)
Yeomen of the Guard, The (3)

Musicals

See "Musical Revivals" for definition of "Musicals."

Abi Gezunt YL
Allah Be Praised! POL/RM/SX
Allegro F/MA/MD/RM/SM/SX
Annie Get Your Gun HIB/PE/RM/SH/WE
Are You With It? BA/BH/RM/SH/SX
Arms and the Girl MI/PE/RM/W
Around the World AD/GA/PE/SE
As the Girls Go F/MA/POL/SX/WO
Ballet Ballads
Banjo Eyes BA/FA/GA/SPT
Barefoot Boy with Cheek POL/RM/SX/UN/YO
Be Happy YL
Beat the Band HT/NC/RM/SH

Beggar's Holiday BL/CR/PN/POL/PS/RM/SX
Best Foot Forward FI/RM/S/YO
Big Shot, The YL
Billion Dollar Baby CR/NC/PE/RM/SH/SX
Bloomer Girl BL/BS/F/HIB/PE/POL/RC/RM/SM/SO/W/WO
Brigadoon BA/FA/PE/RM
By Jupiter MA/MI/PE/RM/SX/W
Cabin in the Sky BL/DE/FA/GA/MA/REL/RR/SO
Carib Song BL/MA/SX/TRP
Carmen Jones BL/CR/MI/RM/SO/SPT/SX/W
Carousel CR/DE/FA/MA/PE/RM/SM
Consul, The MA/POL
Count Me In F/MI/W
Day before Spring, The MA/LT/RM/UN
Double Trouble YL
Dream with Music BC/FA/JO/PE/RM/SX
Duchess Misbehaves, The A/FA/PE/SX
Early to Bed PS/RM/S/SPT/SX/TRP/YO
Finian's Rainbow BL/F/FA/L/POL/RC/RM/RR/SO
Firebrand of Florence, The A/PE/RM/SX
Follow the Girls MI/RM/SH/W
Gentlemen Prefer Blondes FNC/HT/PE/RM/SE
Girl from Nantucket, The A/RM/SM
Golden Land, The YL
Good News YL
Great to Be Alive! CR/DE/FA/MY/RM/SX
Gypsy Lady PE/RM/TH
Hairpin Harmony BC/BS/MU/RM
Happy as Larry CR/FA/MA/PE/RM/SX
Heaven on Earth FA/PN/RM
Helen Goes to Troy FA/PE/POL/RM/SX
Herschel the Jester JE/PE/REL/RM/YL
High Button Shoes BS/CR/GA/PE/SPT/UN/YO
High Kickers HT/LE/RM/SH/TR
Hold It! FI/RM/UN/YO
Hold on to Your Hats BC/CR/RM/SH/WE
Hollywood Pinafore FI/JO/RM
If the Shoe Fits FA/PE/RM
I'm in Love YL
Jackpot GA/MI/RM/W
Johnny Doodle FA/PE/POL/W
Just My Luck YL
Kiss Me, Kate CR/GA/MA/PE/TH
Lady Comes Across, The AD/FA/HT/RM
Lady in the Dark M/FA/JO/ME/RM/SX
Lady Says Yes, The CH/FA/MI/PE/SX
Leave It to Charley YL
Let's Face It MA/MI/RM/SX/W
Leyenda del Besso, La RM/SP/SPL
Liar, The PE/RM/SX
Live and Laugh YL
Look, Ma, I'm Dancin' LE/RM/SH
Lost in the Stars BL/CR/PN/POL/RC/REL/SX/TR
Louisiana Lady PE/PS/RM/SO/SX
Love Life BS/F/FA/MA/PE/POL/SH/TR/WO/YO
Lucky Days YL
Lute Song CH/F/MA/OR/PE
Magdalena L/MI/PE/POL/REL/RM
Marinka PE/POL/RM

Medium, The CR/DE/F/ME/RM
Memphis Bound! BL/RM/SH/TR
Mexican Hayride CR/GA/HT/MEX/RM/SPT
Miss Liberty A/FNC/HT/JO/PE/RM/SE
Mr. Strauss Goes to Boston HT/MA/MU/PE/POL/RM
Music in My Heart HIB/MI/MU/MUB/PE/RM
My Dear Public BS/RM/TH
My Friend Yossel YL
My Romance MU/PE/REL/RM
My Wedding YL
Nellie Bly AD/BA/JO/PE/RM
Night of Love MU/RM/SX
No for an Answer AL/L/POL/RM
Oklahoma! RM/RR/SX/WE
On the Town MI/RM
One Touch of Venus A/BH/CR/FA/HT/PN/RM/SX
Oy, is Dus a Leben! HIB/JE/TH/YL
Pal Joey NC/RM/SH/SX
Panama Hattie MI/POL/PS/RM/SX/TRP/YO
Park Avenue F/MA/RM
Polonaise HIB/MI/PE/POL/RM/W
Rape of Lucretia, The BR/MA/MI/PE/SX
Regina BL/BS/CR/F/IL/MA/SM/SO
Rhapsody MU/PE/POL/RM/SX
Rich Uncle, The YL
Sadie Is a Lady YL
Sadie Thompson MI/PS/REL/SX/TRP
St. Louis Woman BL/GA/PE/RM/SPT/SX
Sing Out, Sweet Land! FA/MU/PE/RM/W/WE
Sleepy Hollow PE/RM
Something for the Boys AV/LE/MI/RM/SH/W/WE
Song of Norway MA/MU/MUB/PE/RM
South Pacific MI/RC/RM/TRP/W
Street Scene CR/F/MA/RM/SX
Sunny River MA/PE/POL/RM/SH
Sunrise YL
Texas, Li'l Darlin' JO/POL/RM/SO
They All Want to Get Married YL
Toplitzky of Notre Dame FA/JE/RM/SPT
Under the Counter BR/MI/RM/TH
Up in Central Park HT/JO/MU/PE/POL/RM
Viva O'Brien FA/MEX/RM
What a Guy YL
What's Up? AV/IL/OR/POL/RM/S/W/YO
Where's Charley? PE/RM/UN/YO
Wish Me Luck YL
You'll See Stars HIB/PE/SH
Yours Is My Heart CH/OR/PN/RM

Revues

Those shows classified here as "revues" are works that concentrated mainly on presenting a succession of separate numbers, often, but not always, unconnected by a general theme or story. The numbers were normally a variety of songs, dances, and comedy sketches. In the more lavish revues, spectacle was an important ingredient. Several shows were actually showcases for a single star performer. Others were performed on ice skates. A number of shows listed here as revues were actually attempts to revive the vaudeville form, which is even more lacking in thematic continuity than most revues. Revues whose casts were predominantly made up of black performers bear the letters BL at their side.

Africapers BL
Alive and Kicking
All for Love
All in Fun
Along Fifth Avenue
American Legend
Angel in the Wings
Artists and Models
Bal Negre BL
Blackouts of 1949
Blue Holiday
Boys and Girls Together
Bright Lights of 1944
Cabalgata
Call Me Mister
Canteen Show, The
Caribbean Carnival BL
Chauve-Souris 1943
Concert Varieties
Crazy with the Heat (2)
Dance Me a Song
Design for Laughter
Edith Piaf FRL
For Your Pleasure
Funzapoppin'
Harlem Cavalcade BL
Hats Off to Ice IC
Hilarities
Holiday in Paris
Holiday on Broadway BL
Howdy, Mr. Ice! IC
Howdy, Mr. Ice of 1950 IC
Icetime IC
Icetime of 1948 IC
Inside U.S.A.
It Happens on Ice (3) IC
It's about Time
Katherine Dunham and Her Company BL
Keep 'Em Laughing
Laffing Room Only
Laugh Time
Laugh, Town, Laugh
Lend an Ear
Let Freedom Sing
Make Mine Manhattan
Maurice Chevalier
Meet the People
New Faces of 1943
New Priorities of 1943
Of V We Sing
Priorities of 1942
Seven Lively Arts
Show Time
Small Wonder
Sons O' Fun
Spook Scandals

Star and Garter
Star Time
Stars of Tomorrow
Stars on Ice IC (2)
Step a Little Closer
Take a Bow
These Are the Times
This Is the Army
Three to Make Ready
Tickets, Please!
Tidbits of 1946
'Tis of Thee
Top-Notchers
Touch and Go
Wine, Women, and Song
You Can't Sleep Here
Ziegfeld Follies of 1943

NATIONAL ORIGIN

The listings that follow offer the titles of plays arranged according to the nation from which their authors come. Yiddish plays by authors living in America can be found under the "Yiddish Language" listing below (see "Foreign-Language Prodcutions"). In several cases British plays premiered in New York before being seen in England; for purposes of categorization, however, these works are considered British.

Australian

Lady in Danger CR/JO/LT/MY/POL

British

All Men Are Alike MA/MI/SX/W
Angel Street CR/MA/ME/MY/PE
Anne of England HIB/PE/POL/WO
Another Love Song F/MA/RM/SX
Ascent of F-6, The F/FA/POL
Blithe Spirit DE/FA/LT/MA/SX/SPR
Clutterbuck HT/MA/SE/SX/TRP
Cocktail Party, The FI/MA/REL/SX/V
Corn Is Green, The S/SX/YO
Crime and Punishment AL/BH/CR/F/ME/PE/PS/REL
Dog beneath the Skin, The AD/DRG/FA/HT/IL/ME/POL/PS/RM/V/W
Duet for Two Hands CR/LT/MD/PE/RM
Duke in Darkness, The FNC/ME/PE/PN/POL
Edward, My Son AL/BS/CR/F/MA/PE/POL/SX
Flare Path AV/HT/MA/MI/RM/TH/W
Ghost for Sale MY/RM
Hidden Horizon CR/MY/TRP
I Killed the Count CR/MY
Inspector Calls, An CR/F/MY/PE/RM/SX
Jupiter Laughs MD/REL/RM/SC/SX
Lifeline SE/W
Linden Tree, The BS/F/MA/MD/MU/REL/OA/SC/UN/YO
Lovers and Friends F/MA/RM/TH
Man's House, A BI/F/IN/JE/PE/REL/RM
Men in Shadow AV/MI/W
Message for Margaret MA/SX

Millionairess, The BS/MD/RM
Morning Star, The LT/MA/MD/SX/W
Murder without Crime CR/MA/MY/SX
O Mistress Mine F/POL/RM/SX/YO*Out of the Picture* A/POL/RM/W
Power without Glory CR/F/RM/SX
Rape of Lucretia, The M/MA/MI/PE/SX
Rats of Norway, The AL/HO/RM/S/SX
Sarah Simple MA
Sheppey DE/F/FA/GA/ME/REL/PS
Shop at Sly Corner, The CR/F
Skipper Next to God JE/POL/REL/SE
Ten Little Indians CR/MY/REL/RM
They Walk Alone CR/ME/MU/SX
To Kill a Cat CR/F/MY/RM
Two Mrs. Carrolls, The A/CR/FNC/MA/MY/RM
Under the Counter M/MI/RM/TH
While the Sun Shines GA/MI/RM/W
Winslow Boy, The F/L/LA/PE/POL/S/TR/WO/YO
Yes, M'Lord MA/OA/POL/RM
Yesterday's Magic AL/BH/F/IN/RM/TH

Dutch

Skipper Next to God JE/POL/REL/SE
This Time Tomorrow DE/FA/IL/MD/RM/SC

Flemish

Hoboes in Heaven AL/BA/DE/FA/REL

French

Antigone FR/POL/RM
Cry of the Peacock F/MA/ME/PE/RM/SX
Don't Listen Ladies A/BS/MA/SX/WO
Eagle Has Two Heads, The LT/PE/POL/RM/SX
Enchanted, The DE/FA/POL/RM/YO
Flies, The CR/F/PE/REL
Happy Days, The AV/RM/SX/YO
Little Dark Horse BL/F/IL/RC/SX/YO
Madwoman of Chaillot, The BS/FA/ME/POL/TR
Montserrat A/FR/MI/PE/POL/SX/TH/YO
My Name Is Aquilon CR/RM
Nights of Wrath POL/W
No Exit DE/FA/HO/HT/JO/POL/RM/SX
Red Gloves CR/MA/POL/RM
Unquiet Spirit, The DRG/MA/SX
Victors, The POL/SX/W/YO

German

Burning Bush, The JE/LA/PE/REL/TR
Criminals, The CR/LA/POL/RM/SX/TR
Galileo F/HIB/PE/POL/REL/SC
Jacobowsky and the Colonel JE/MI/POL/RM/W
Outside the Door DE/FA/MI/W
Private Life of the Master Race, The F/JE/LA/MA/MI/PN/POL/REL/W
Rape of the Sabine Women, The GEL/TH

Hungarian

Delicate Story MA/MI/RM/SX/W

Irish

Boyd's Daughter BS/REL/RM
Derryowen BA/GA/IR/J0/POL/RM/W
Kathleen F/MD/REL/RM/SX/YO
Nineteenth Hole of Europe, The LT/POL/PS/REL/RM/SX/W
Old Foolishness, The F/POL/REL/RM
Old Lady Says "No!," The FA/HIB/PE/POL/TH
Strings, My Lord, Are False, The POL/PS/REL/RM/SX/W
Tanyard Street IN/MA/REL/SX/W
Where Stars Walk FA/JO/RM/TH

Russian

Counterattack MI/POL/SX/W
Listen, Professor! F/RM/YO
Russian People, The MA/POL/RM/W
Whole World Over, The F/RM

Spanish

House of Bernarda Alba, The F/RM/SX/WO
Leyenda del Besso, La M/RM/SPL
Shoemaker's Prodigious Wife, The MA/SH
Yerma MA/SX

SUBJECT MATTER

The listings in this section attempt to present general areas related to the content of the decade's shows. The relative importance of an identified area in a play's structure is not considered, provided its treatment was deemed of sufficient note to warrant its inclusion here. A few of the listings (for example, Bible, Mystery, Period) are not actually "subjects" so much as areas suggesting source material, style, and background, but they are included here for the sake of convenience.

Adventure

These are plays of derring-do, usually in an exotic locale, and depending on action for much of their effect.

Around the World M/GA/PE/SE
Dog beneath the Skin, The BR/DRG/FA/HT/IL/ME/POL/PS/RM/V/W
Golden Falcon, The PE/POL/W
Innocent Voyage, The CR/ME/PE/SE/SX/YO
Lady Comes Across, The M/FA/HT/RM
Nellie Bly M/BA/JO/PE/RM
Pirate, The PE/RM/SH/TRP

Alcoholism

Plays in this listing either treat the subject of alcoholism directly or, as is more common, include one or more alcoholic characters.

Anna Lucasta BL/F/PS/SM
Big Knife, The BS/CR/FI/MA/SX

Biggest Thief in Town, The DE/F/JO/RM/SH/SM
Bird Cage, The BS/CR/F/MA/NC/RM/SH/SX
Boudoir CR/MA/MU/PE/SX
Bruno and Sidney RM/SC
Come Back, Little Sheba MA/SX/YO
Cream in the Well, The F/RM/RR/SX/WE
Crime and Punishment BH/BR/CR/F/ME/PE/PS/REL
Cup of Trembling, The F/JO/MA/ME/SX
Dancer, The A/CR/F/FNC/HO/ME/PS/SH
Deep Mrs. Sykes, The F/MA/MU
Edward, My Son BR/BS/CR/F/MA/PE/POL/SX
Every Man for Himself FI/RM/SX
Family, The BH/CH/F/OR/POL/RM/W
Happy Birthday BA/RM
Happy Time, The FA/MA/OA/PE/RM/SX/YO
Harvest of Years F/MA/RM/RR/WE
Harvey F/FA/ME
Hear That Trumpet BL/CR/MA/MU/RC/RM
Heart of a City MI/RM/TH/W
Highland Fling, A DE/FA/GA/RM/SX/YO
Hoboes in Heaven BA/DE/FA/FL/REL
How Long Till Summer? BL/CR/FA/LA/POL/RC/YO
Iceman Cometh, The BA/CR/JO/ME/PE/POL/PS
Johnny on a Spot CR/JO/POL/PS/RM/SO/SX
Joy Forever, A A/BS/RM/SX
Leaf and Bough F/RM/RR/SM/SX
Long Way from Home, A BL/CR/GA/MA/REL/SO/SX
No for an Answer M/L/POL/RM
Out of My House BL/F/LE/REL/SM/WE
Pretty Little Parlor F/MA/PE/SM/SX/YO
Rats of Norway, The BR/HO/RM/S/SX
Snark Was a Boojum, The F/LE/MY/RM/SX
Song Out of Sorrow CR/DRG/FS/IL/LIB/PE/PS
Sons and Soldiers F/FA/MA/MD/PE/RM/SX/W
Streetcar Named Desire, A HO/MA/ME/PS/RM/SO/SX
Suds in Your Eyes FS/MU/OR/RM
Texas Town BL/RM/SM
Truckline Cafè CR/MA/MI/SX
Virginia Reel F/PS/RR/SO
Yesterday's Magic BH/BR/F/IN/RM/TH
You Touched Me! F/MI/RM/SX

Art

In these plays the subject of art or the work of an artist character is important.

Barber Had Two Sons, The CR/F/POL/RM/SX/W
Brooklyn Biarritz CR/F/JE/RM/SX/YO
Dancer, The AL/CR/F/FNC/HO/ME/PS/SH
Don't Listen, Ladies BS/FR/MA/SX/WO
Duchess Misbehaves, The M/FA/PE/SX
Dunnigan's Daughter BS/MA/MEX/PL/RM
Firebrand of Florence, The M/PE/RM/SX
Foxhole in the Parlor FS/ME/MU/POL/RM/SX/W
Gayden CR/F/ME/RM/SX
Girl from Nantucket, The M/RM/SM
Guest in the House F/IL/RM/RR/YO
House in Paris, The FNC/PE/RM/SX
Joy Forever, A AL/BS/RM/SX

Maid in the Ozarks RM/RR/SO/SX
Miss Liberty M/FNC/HT/JO/PE/RM/SE
Mr. Barry's Etchings CR/HT/JO/POL/RM
Montserrat FR/MI/PE/POL/SX/TH/YO
My Sister Eileen F/JO/LT/MI/PS/RM/SPT/SX/TH
Oh, Brother! CR/LE/RM
One Touch of Venus M/BH/CR/FA/HT/PN/RM/SX
One-Man Show BS/F/RM/SX
Out of the Picture BR/POL/RM/W
Snookie JO/RM/SX
Therese CR/IN/MA/PE/SX
Two Mrs. Carrolls, The BR/CR/FNC/MA/MY/RM
Village Green F/POL/RM/SM
Violet F/RM/RR/YO
Willow and I, The F/MD/ME/PE/RM/SM
Years Between, The BS/F/LT/M/RM/SM/SX/W

Aviation

Plays about flyers, airplanes, and the like.

Command Decision MI/POL/W
Fifty MI/RM/W
Flare Path BR/HT/MA/MI/RM/TH/W
Flight to the West F/JE/JO/MA/POL/W
Golden Wings MI/POL/RM/SX/W
Happy Days, The FR/RM/SX/YO
Kiss Them for Me BS/HT/MD/MI/RM/SX/W
Men in Shadow BR/MI/W
New Life, A BS/F/MA/MD/POL/SH/W
Over 21 FI/JO/LT/MA/MI/W
Skydrift DE/FA/MI/W
Something for the Boys M/LE/MI/SH/RM/W/WE
Streets Are Guarded, The MI/REL/W
Those Endearing Young Charms F/HT/RM/SX/W
What's Up? M/IL/OR/POL/RM/S/W/YO
Wind Is Ninety, The DE/F/FA/MA/W/YO
Winged Victory F/FS/HT/MA/MI/RM/SM/TRP/W

Bible

Plays derived or adapted from biblical sources.

Armor of Light PE/REL
Bathsheba MI/PE/SX/W
Dear Judas PE/POL/REL
Journey to Jerusalem PE/POL/REL
Man's House, A BR/F/IN/JE/PE/REL/RM
Mary of Magdala PE/REL/RM
Night Watch in Syria PE/REL
Simon's Wife MA/PE/REL
To Tell You the Truth FA/PE/SX
Vigil, The CR/DE/REL/SM/TR

Broadcasting

Works touching on the broadcast industries of radio and/or television.

Broken Journey JO/RM/W

Dream with Music M/FA/JO/PE/RM/SX
Grandma's Diary MA/MI/RM/SX
Hairpin Harmony M/BS/MU/RM
Hallams, The F/IL/MA/OA
On the Seventh Day F/FA/JO/ME/W
Spring Again BS/FI/HT/MA/RM
Take It As It Comes CR/DRG/F/JO/MA/POL/SM/YO
Wanhope Building, The BA/FA/POL/RM/SC
Winter Soldiers MI/POL/PS/W

Business

Plays about business, businessmen, and businesswomen; plays about the advertising industry are also listed here.

All for All FS/L/RM
All My Sons CR/F/MA/SM/W
Another Part of the Forest BL/F/MA/ME/PE/PS/REL/RM/SO/SX
Any Day Now F/GA/RM/SC
Apology F/FA/PE/REL/RM/SM/W
Ask My Friend Sandy LT/MA/MI/RM
Beggars Are Coming to Town CR/NC/RM
Big Knife, The AL/CR/FI/MA/SX
Bird Cage, The AL/CR/F/MA/NC/RM/SH/SX
Bloomer Girl M/BL/F/HIB/PE/POL/RC/RM/SM/SO/W/WO
Blow Bugle Blow
Born Yesterday CR/JO/LA/POL/RM/SX
Broken Hearts of Broadway PE/RM
--But Not Goodbye DE/F/FA/PE/SM
Calico Wedding MA/SX
Chicken Every Sunday BH/F/MA/PE/RM/SX/WE
Death of a Salesman F/HT/MA/ME/SX
Don't Listen, Ladies A/FR/MA/SX/WO
Down to Miami F/HT/MI/REL/RM/SO
Dunnigan's Daughter A/MA/MEX/POL/RM
Edward, My Son AL/BR/CR/F/MA/PE/POL/SX
Food for Midas TR
Hairpin Harmony M/BC/MU/RM
High Button Shoes M/CR/GA/PE/SPT/UN/YO
Home Is the Hunter BL/CR/L/MA/POL/W
I'll Take the High Road F/FI/POL/RM/SM/W
In Bed We Cry MA/RM/SC/SX/W
Joy Forever, A A/AL/RM/SX
Joy to the World FI/L/RM/SX
Kiss Them for Me AV/HT/MD/MI/RM/SX/W
Land Is Bright, The CR/F/MI/OA/PE/POL/RM/W/YO
Last Stop CR/OA
Life with Mother F/MA/PE/RM/YO
Linden Tree, The BR/F/MA/MD/MU/OA/REL/SC/UN/YO
Loco F/IL/MA/SX
Love Life M/F/FA/MA/PE/POL/SH/TR/WO/YO
Madwoman of Chaillot, The FA/FR/ME/POL/TR
Man Who Had All the Luck, The F/RM/SM/SPT
Me and Molly F/JE/MA/MU/REL/RM/S/YO
Metropole JO/RM
Millionairess, The BR/MD/RM
My Dear Public M/RM/TH
My Fair Ladies RM/W
New Life, A AV/F/MA/MD/POL/SH/W

Night before Christmas, The CR/RM
Not in Our Stars F/POL/RM
No Way Out CR/GA/LE/MA/MD
One-Man Show A/F/RM/SX
Only the Heart BL/F/MA/SM/SX
Present Laughter F/MA/RM/SM/SX
Regina M/BL/CR/F/IL/MA/SM/SO
Right next to Broadway JE/L/RM/SX
Rugged Path, The JO/MA/MI/POL/SE/TRP/W
School for Brides, The MA/RM/S/SX
Shylock and His Daughter F/JE/PE/REL/RM/TR/YL
Sleep No More CR/RM/SC/SX
Spring Again BC/FI/RM
State of the Union HT/JO/MA/POL/SX
Steps Leading Up L/RM
Temper the Wind MI/POL
Time for Elizabeth MA/SO
Town House F/JO/MA/SC/YO
Under this Roof MA/PE/POL/RM/RR/W
Walk into My Parlor CR/F/L/MA/RM/SX
Wisteria Trees, The BL/F/PE/RM/RR/SO
Years Between, The A/F/LT/MI/RM/SM/SX/W

Circuses

Flying Gerardos, The F/RM
Heeple Steeple, The RM/SX
Temporary Island, A PE/RM/S

Crime

Plays about crimes and criminals. A wide range of crimes are included, such as murder, theft, fraud, graft, rape, and kidnapping.

All My Sons BS/F/MA/SM/W
All the King's Men JO/MA/POL/SO/SX
Angel Street BR/MA/ME/MY/PE
Arsenic and Old Lace ME/OA/RM/TH
Assassin, The MI/PN/POL/RM/W
Autumn Hill LE/REL/RM/RR
Barber Had Two Sons, The A/F/POL/RM/SX/W
Beggars Are Coming to Town BS/NC/RM
Beggar's Holiday M/BL/PN/POL/PS/RM/SX
Big Knife, The AL/BS/FI/MA/SX
Billion Dollar Baby M/NC/PE/RM/SH/SX
Bird Cage, The AL/BS/F/MA/NC/RM/SH/SX
Born Yesterday BS/JO/LA/POL/RM/SX
Boudoir AL/MA/MU/PE/SX
Bridge to the Sun ME/MY
Bright Boy POL/RM/S/YO
Brooklyn Biarritz A/F/JE/RM/SX/YO
Brooklyn, U.S.A. L/PN/RM
Carmen Jones M/BL/MI/RM/SO/SPT/SX/W
Carousel M/DE/FA/MA/PE/RM/SM
Cat Screams, The DE/DRG/LT/MEX/MY/RM/SX
Chaff AU/MA/RR/SX
Clash by Night MA/REL/RM/SX
Crime and Punishment AL/BH/BR/F/ME/PE/PS/REL
Criminals, The GE/LA/POL/RM/SX/TR

Cuckoos on the Hearth LT/ME/MY/RR/SC
Cue for Passion HT/JO/LT/MA/MY/POL/SX/TH
Dancer, The A/AL/F/FNC/HO/ME/PS/SH
Dark Hammock LE/MA/PE/RR/SC/SO
Decision BL/JO/L/MI/POL/RC/RM/SM/SX/W
Deep Are the Roots BL/F/POL/RC/RM/S/SM/SO
Deliver Us from Evil DE/FA/PE/REL/RM
Detective Story JO/LA/MA/MD/RM
Distant City, The F/PN/PS/REL/RM/SX
Duet for Two Hands BR/LT/MD/PE/RM
Edward, My Son AL/BR/BS/F/MA/PE/POL/SX
Eight O'Clock Tuesday MY/SX
Embezzled Heaven PE/REL
Family Carnovsky, The F/JE/MA/MD/POL/YL
First Crocus, The F/RM/SM/YO
First Million, The F/RR/SX
Fledgling F/IL/LT/ME/REL/SX
Flies, The F/FR/PE/REL
Flowers of Virtue, The IL/L/LT/MEX/MI/POL/REL/RM
Four Flights Up MY
Gayden A/F/ME/RM/SX
Good Neighbor F/IN/JE/MA/RM/YO
Great to Be Alive! DE/FA/MY/RM/SX
Hand in Glove BH/ME/MY/SX
Happy as Larry FA/MA/PE/RM/SX
Haven, The LT/MA/MY
Hear That Trumpet AL/BL/MA/MU/RC/RM
Hidden Horizon BR/MY/TRP
High Button Shoes M/BS/GA/PE/SPT/UN/YO
Hold on to Your Hats M/BC/RM/SH/WE
Home Is the Hunter BL/L/MA/POL/W
How Long till Summer? AL/BL/FA/LA/POL/RC/YO
I Killed the Count BR/MY
Iceman Cometh, The AL/BA/JO/ME/PE/POL/PS
Innocent Voyage, The AD/ME/PE/SE/SX/YO
Inspector Calls, An BR/F/MY/PE/RM/SX
Johnny Belinda CR/IN/MD/RM/RR/SX/TR
Johnny on a Spot AL/JO/POL/PS/RM/SO/SX
Johnny 2 X 4 MU/NC/PS/SH
Kiss Me, Kate M/GA/MA/PE/TH
Lady in Danger AUS/JO/LT/MY/POL
Land Is Bright, The BS/F/MI/OA/PE/POL/RM/W/YO
Last Stop BS/OA
Laura MY/RM/SX
Life of Reilly, The GA/HT/SPT
Lily of the Valley DE/FA/PS/REL
Little Brown Jug F/MY
Long Way from Home, A AL/BL/GA/MA/REL/SO/SX
Longitude 49 BL/SE
Lost in the Stars M/BL/CR/PN/POL/RC/REL/SX/TR
Love Is No Heaven MA/SH/SM/SX/W
Man, The ME
Man with Blond Hair, The JE/POL/W
Me and Harry ME/RM/SPT
Medium, The M/DE/F/ME/RM/SPR
Meet a Body DE/JO/MY/RM
Mexican Hayride M/GA/HT/MEX/RM/SPT
Miracle in the Mountains FA/PE/POL/REL/SX/TR
Mr. and Mrs. North MA/MY

Mr. Barry's Etchings A/HT/JO/POL/RM
Mr. Big MY/POL/RM/TH
Mrs. Gibbons' Boys F/POL
Mrs. Kimball Presents RM/TH
Moon Vine, The PE/REL/RM/SM/SO/TH/YO
More the Merrier, The POL/RM
Murder without Crime BR/MA/MY/SX
My Name Is Aquilon FR/RM
Naked Genius, The LT/RM/SX/SH
Native Son BL/F/JO/LA/PN/POL/RC/RM/TR
Natural Man BL/FA/GA/L/PE/PN/RC/REL/SO
Night Before Christmas, The BS/RM
Nine Girls MD/POL/SPT/TH/UN/WE/WO/YO
No Way Out BS/GA/MA/MD
Oh, Brother! A/LE/RM
One Touch of Venus M/A/BH/FA/HT/PN/RM/SX
Pick-up Girl F/IL/MU/PS/RM/SX/TR/YO
Portrait in Black L/MD/MY/RM
Present Laughter RM/SX/TH
Power without Glory BR/F/RM/SX
Ramshackle Inn HT/MY/SM
Rat Race, The BH/MU/RM/SH
Rebecca MA/MY
Red Gloves FR/MA/POL/RM
Regina M/BL/BS/F/IL/MA/SM/SO
Rose in the Wilderness PE/REL/RM/SX
Ryan Girl, The F/MA/MI/W
Scapegoat, The FA/LA/RM/TR
Secret Room, The ME/SX/YO
Shop at Sly Corner, The BR/F
Signature LA/LE/PE/RM/RR/SO/TR
Sleep, My Pretty One F/ME/RM
Sleep No More BS/RM/SC/SX
Snafu F/MI/POL/RM/SX/W/YO
Solitaire F/FS/REL/YO
Song of the Dniepper JE/PE/PN/POL/TR/YL
Song out of Sorrow AL/DRG/FS/IL/LIB/PE/PS
Starlight BL/REL/SX
Story for Strangers, A FA/GA/PE/PS/REL/RM/SM
Story of Mary Surratt, The BH/HIB/LA/PE/PN/POL/TR
Strange Fruit BL/RC/RM/SM/SO/SX
Stranger, The JE/MY/PE/POL
Street Scene M/F/MA/RM/SX
Swan Song ME/MU/YO
Take It As It Comes BC/DRG/F/JO/MA/POL/SM/YO
Ten Little Indians BR/MY/REL/RM
Therese A/IN/MA/PE/SX
These Tender Mercies BL/F/RC/REL/RM/SM/SO/SX
They Walk Alone BR/ME/MU/SX
Three Gifts DE/FA/JE/MU/REL/RM/YL
Tin Top Valley BL/F/FS/RC/SO/YO
To Kill a Cat BR/F/MY/RM
Trial by Fire BL/F/RC/RR
Trouble in July BL/POL/RC/SM/SO
Truckline Café AL/MA/MI/SX
Two Mrs. Carrolls, The A/BR/FNC/MA/MY/RM
Uncle Harry F/LE/MY/PE/PN/SM
Uniform of Flesh LA/MI/PE/SE/TR/V
Vigil, The BI/DE/REL/SM/TR

Visitor, The F/LE/MY/SM/YO
Walk into My Parlor BS/F/L/MA/RM/SX
Walking Gentleman, The ME/MY/RM/TH
Wonderful Journey DE/FA/RM/SPT
Young and Fair, The ME/S/YO

Death

In these plays death is a thematic concern, not merely a plot element in which characters pass away. Most of these works hinge on the author's views of the afterlife and frequently border on the fantastical.

Biggest Thief in Town, The AL/F/JO/RM/SH/SM
Blithe Spirit BR/FA/LT/MA/SX/SPR
Boy Who Lived Twice, A F/FA/RM/Y
--But Not Goodbye BS/F/FA/PE/SM
Cabin in the Sky M/BL/FA/GA/MA/REL/RR/SO
Carousel M/CR/FA/MA/PE/RM/SM
Cat Screams, The CR/DRG/LT/MEX/MY/RM/SX
Deliver Us from Evil CR/FA/PE/REL/RM
Devils Galore FA/LT/RM/SX
Don't Go Away Mad BL/IL/MA
Enchanted, The FA/FR/POL/RM/YO
G-II FA/IL/SC/W
Great to Be Alive CR/FA/MY/RM/SX
Hasty Heart, The FS/IL/MI/RM/TRP/W
Highland Fling, A AL/FA/GA/RM/SX/YO
Hoboes in Heaven AL/BA/FA/FL/REL
Innocents, The FA/MY/YO
Lady in the Dark M/JO/ME/RM/SX
Lady Who Came to Stay F/FA/ME/MY/RM/SX/YO
Lily of the Valley CR/FA/PS/REL
Live Life Again F/FA/PE/RM/RR/SM/V
Medium, The M/CR/F/ME/RM/SPR
Meet a Body CR/JO/MY/RM
Next Half Hour, The F/FA/PE/SX/YO
No Exit FA/FR/HO/HT/JO/POL/RM/SX
Outside the Door FA/GE/MI/W
Sheppey BR/F/FA/GA/ME/REL/PS
Skydrift AV/FA/MI/W
This Time Tomorrow DU/FA/IL/MD/RM/SC
Three Gifts CR/FA/JE/MU/REL/RM/YL
Tinker's Dam FA/JO/MI/NC/REL/RM/SC/W
Vigil, The BI/CR/REL/SM/TR
Wind Is Ninety, The AV/F/FA/MA/W/YO
Wonderful Journey CR/FA/RM/SPT

Drugs

Plays in which drug use or trafficking has a part.

Cat Screams, The CR/DE/LT/MY/RM/SX
Dog beneath the Skin, The AD/BR/FA/HT/IL/ME/POL/PS/RM/V/W
Proof 'thro the Night HO/POL/TRP/W/WO
Song out of Sorrow AL/CR/FS/IL/LIB/PE/PS
Sweet Charity WO
Take It As It Comes BC/CR/F/JO/MA/POL/SM/YO
Unquiet Spirit, The FR/MA/SX

Fantasy

Plays treating of a wide variety of fantastical materials; among them are those that depend on dream sequences. A few plays might be considered "science fiction."

Apology BS/F/PE/REL/RM/SM/W
Ascent of F-6, The BR/F/POL
Banjo Eyes M/BA/GA/SPT
Blithe Spirit BR/DE/LT/MA/SPR/SX
Boy Who Lived Twice, A DE/F/RM/YO
Brigadoon M/BA/PE/RM
--But Not Goodbye BS/DE/F/PE/SM
Cabin in the Sky M/BL/DE/GA/MA/REL/RR/SO
Career Angel REL/SO/YO
Carousel M/CR/DE/MA/PE/RM/SM
Christopher Blake F/LA/MA/POL/TH/TR/YO
Cock-a-Doodle-Do RM/RR/SX
Dark of the Moon REL/RM/RR/SO/SX
Day Will Come, The JE/ME/MI/POL/REL/W
Deliver Us from Evil CR/DE/PE/REL/RM
Devils Galore DE/LT/RM/SX
Dog beneath the Skin, The AD/BR/DRG/HT/IL/ME/POL/PS/RM/V/W
Dream Girl BA/JO/LT/MEX/PS/RM/SX/TH/TR
Dream of Love, A LT/MA/MD/SX
Dream with Music M/BC/JO/PE/RM/SX
Duchess Misbehaves, The M/A/PE/SX
Earth Journey CH/OR/REL/RM
Enchanted, The DE/FR/POL/RM/YO
Eternal Cage, The IL/MA/MD
Eve of St. Mark, The F/GA/IL/MI/RM/SX/TRP/RR/W
Fifth Horseman, The REL/SX/W
Finian's Rainbow M/BL/F/L/POL/RC/RM/RR/SO
Flag Is Born, A JE/OA/PE/POL/REL
Foolish Notion MA/MI/RM/TH/W/YO
G-II DE/IL/SC/W
Garden of Time BL/PE/RR
Great to Be Alive! CR/DE/MY/RM/SX
Happy as Larry CR/MA/PE/RM/SX
Harvey AL/F/ME
Heaven on Earth M/PN/RM
Helen Goes to Troy M/PE/POL/RM/SX
Highland Fling, A AL/DE/GA/RM/SX/YO
Hoboes in Heaven DE/F
Homecoming F/REL/SO/W
How I Wonder BL/F/L/RC/SC/UN/W
How Long Till Summer? AL/BL/CR/LA/POL/RC/YO
If the Shoe Fits M/PE/RM
Innocents, The DE/MY/YO
Johnny Doodle PE/POL/W
Lady Comes Across, The M/AD/HT/RM
Lady of Fatima PE/REL/YO
Lady Says Yes, A M/CH/MI/PE/SX
Lady Who Came to Stay, The DE/F/ME/MY/RM/SX/YO
Liberty Jones IL/MI/POL/RM
Lily of the Valley CR/DE/PS/REL
Live Life Again DE/F/PE/RM/RR/SM/V
Love Life M/BS/F/MA/PE/POL/SH/TR/WO/YO
Madwoman of Chaillot, The BS/FR/ME/POL/TR

Mexican Mural IN/MEX/POL/REL/PS/RM/SX
Miracle in the Mountains CR/PE/POL/REL/SX/TR
Mr. Sycamore LT/MA/REL/SM
Natural Man BL/CR/GA/L/PE/PN/RC/REL/SO
Next Half Hour, The DE/F/PE/SX/YO
No Exit DE/FR/HO/HT/JO/POL/RM/SX
Old Lady Says "No!," The HIB/IR/PE/POL/TH
On the Seventh Day BC/F/JO/ME/W
One Touch of Venus M/A/BH/CR/HT/PN/RM/SX
Outside the Door DE/GE/MI/W
Peepshow RM/SX
Scapegoat, The CR/LA/RM/TR
Sheppey BR/DE/F/GA/ME/REL/PS
Sing Out, Sweet Land! M/MU/PE/RM/W/WE
Skin of Our Teeth, The F/MA/PE/SX/W/YO
Skydrift AV/DE/MI/W
Sons and Soldiers AL/F/MA/MD/PE/RM/SX/W
Story for Strangers, A CR/GA/PE/PS/REL/RM/SM
This Time Tomorrow DE/DU/IL/MD/RM/SC
Three Gifts CR/DE/FA/MU/REL/RM/YL
Tinker's Dam DE/JO/MI/NC/REL/RM/SC/W
To Tell You the Truth BI/PE/SX
Too Many Thumbs REL/RM/SC/UN
Toplitzky of Notre Dame M/JE/RM/SPT
Tread the Green Grass REL/RR/SO/SX/YO
Viva O'Brien M/MEX/RM
Wanhope Building, The BA/BC/POL/RM/SC
Where Stars Walk IR/JO/RM/TH
Wind Is Ninety, The AV/DE/F/MA/W/YO
Wonderful Journey CR/DE/RM/SPT

Films

Plays that deal with Hollywood, the film industry, film personalities, and those who aspire to work in films.

Best Foot Forward M/RM/S/YO
Beverly Hills MA/SX
Big Knife, The AL/BS/CR/MA/SX
Candle in the Wind FNC/JO/MI/PN/RM/W
Cocktail Party, The BR/MA/REL/SX/V
Every Man for Himself AL/RM/SX
Five Alarm Waltz LT/MA/TH/YO
Get Away Old Man RM
Glamour Preferred M/SX
Greener Grass, The BL/RC
Hold It! M/RM/UN/YO
Hollywood Pinafore M/JO/RM
I'll Take the High Road BS/F/POL/RM/SM/W
Joy to the World BS/L/RM/SX
Marriage Is for Single People F/NC/RM/TH
Over 21 AV/JO/LT/MA/MI/W
Public Relations F/MA/RM/SX
Quiet Please MA/MU/SX
Spring Again BC/BS/RM
What Big Ears! GA/HT/SH

Friendship

Plays in which the friendship of the principal characters is a crucial factor.

All for All BS/L/RM
Dark Eyes RM/TH
Foxhole in the Parlor A/ME/MU/POL/RM/SX/W
Hasty Heart, The DE/IL/MI/RM/TRP/W
John Loves Mary HT/MA/MI/POL/RM
Land's End HT/RM/SX
Letters to Lucerne RM/S/W/YO
Life Sentence F/HO/RM/SX
Old Acquaintance LT/RM/SX
Solitaire CR/F/REL/YO
Song out of Sorrow AL/CR/DRG/IL/LIB/PE/PS
Suds in Your Eye AL/MU/OR/RM
Tin Top Valley BL/CR/F/RC/SO/YO
Winged Victory AV/F/HT/MA/MI/RM/SM/TRP/W

Gambling

All You Need Is One Good Break F/IL/JE/ME/PN/RM
Any Day Now BS/F/RM/SC
Around the World M/AD/PE/SE
Banjo Eyes M/BA/FA/SPT
Cabin in the Sky M/BL/DE/FA/MA/REL/RR/SO
Derryowen BA/IR/JO/POL/RM/W
Eve of St. Mark, The F/FA/IL/MI/RM/RR/SX/TRP/W
High Button Shoes M/BS/CR/PE/SPT/UN/YO
Highland Fling, A AL/DE/FA/RM/SX/YO
Horse Fever F/HT/SC/SPT
I Gotta Get Out SC/SPT
Jackpot MI/RM/W
Kiss Me, Kate M/CR/MA/PE/TH
Life of Reilly, The CR/HT/SPT
Long Way from Home, A AL/BL/CR/MA/REL/SO/SX
Mexican Hayride M/CR/HT/MEX/RM/SPT
Natural Man BL/CR/FA/L/PE/PN/RC/REL/SO
No Way Out BS/CR/LE/MA/MD
Odds on Mrs. Oakley, The JO/MA/SPT/SX
Overtons, The MA/SX/TH
Playboy of Newark, The BH/MA/REL/SX
Retreat to Pleasure L/POL/RM
St. Louis Woman M/BL/GA/PE/RM/SPT/SX
Sheppey BR/DE/F/FA/ME/PS/REL
Silver Whistle, The OA/REL/RM/SX
Story for Strangers, A CR/FA/PE/PS/REL/RM/SM
Tenting Tonight F/MA/RM/SM/UN
They Should Have Stood in Bed RM/SPT/SX
Walk Hard BL/F/RC/RM/SPT
What Big Ears! FI/HT/SH
While the Sun Shines BR/MI/RM/W

Historical-Biographical

Plays purporting to present episodes in the lives of actual persons of the past. See also "Bible," "Literary-Biographical," and "Musical-Biographical."

Anne of England BR/PE/POL/WO
Anne of the Thousand Days MA/PE/POL/REL/SX/TR/V
Annie Get Your Gun M/PE/RM/SH/WE

Battle for Heaven OA/REL
Bloomer Girl M/BL/BS/F/PE/POL/RC/RM/SM/SO/W/WO
Deputy of Paris, The FNC/PE/POL
Design for a Stained Glass Window PE/POL
Dr. Herzl JE/JO/POL/REL/YL
Galileo F/GE/PE/POL/REL/SC
In Time to Come FNC/PE/POL/W
Joan of Lorraine PE/PN/POL/REL/TH/TR
John Brown F/PE/RC
Lamp at Midnight PE/POL/REL/SC
Magnificent Yankee, The LA/MA/OA/PE/POL
Old Lady Says, "No!," The FA/IR/PE/POL/TH
Oy, Is Dus a Leben! M/JE/TH/YL
Patriots, The PE/POL/SX*Polonaise* M/MI/PE/POL/RM/W
Savonarola PE/POL/REL
Set My People Free BL/PE/POL/RC/REL
Sojourner Truth BL/F/PE/RC/REL/RM
Story of Mary Surratt, The BH/CR/LA/PE/PN/POL/TR
War President, The MI/PE/POL/W
You'll See Stars M/PE/SH
Yours, A. Lincoln PE/POL

Homosexuality

Plays with homosexual characters or that touch on the subject in a significant way. Plays with overtly effeminate characters, such as *Lady in the Dark*, are not included unless such effeminacy is specifically linked to homosexuality. In some works the homosexuality is merely alluded to, but not represented by an onstage character.

Building 222 ME/MI/REL/W
Dancer, The A/AL/CR/F/FNC/ME/PS/SH
Life Sentence F/FS/RM/SX
No Exit DE/FA/FR/HT/JO/POL/RM/SX
Outrageous Fortune F/JE/MD/MU/RC/RM/SX
Proof thro' the Night DRG/POL/TRP/W/WO
Rats of Norway, The AL/BR/RM/S/SX
Streetcar Named Desire, A AL/MA/ME/PS/RM/SO/SX
Trio LT/RM/UN/YO

Illness

Plays in which one or more characters are suffering from a serious illness or disease.

All You Need Is One Good Break F/GA/JE/ME/PN/RM
Claudia F/MA/RR/SX
Doctor Social MD/RM/SC
Doctors Disagree MD/RM/SX/WO
Dog beneath the Skin, The AD/BR/DRG/FA/HT/ME/POL/PS/RM/V/W
Don't Go Away Mad BL/DE/MA
Eternal Cage, The FA/MA/MD
Eve of St. Mark, The F/FA/GA/MI/RM/RR/SX/TRP/W
Fledgling CR/F/LT/ME/REL/SX
Flowers of Virtue, The CR/L/LT/MEX/MI/POL/REL/RM
G-II DE/FA/SC/W
Gabrielle LT/MA/MD/MU/RM
Guest in the House A/F/RM/RR/YO
Hallams, The BC/F/MA/OA

Hasty Heart, The DE/FS/MI/RM/TRP/W
I Remember Mama F/IN/LT/PE/YO
Liberty Jones FA/MI/POL/RM
Little Dark Horse BL/F/FR/RC/SX/YO
Loco BS/F/MA/SX
Pick-up Girl CR/F/MU/PS/RM/SX/TR/YO
Plan M MI/POL/W
Regina M/BL/BS/CR/F/MA/SM/SO
Rich Full Life, The F/MA/RM/SM/YO
Song out of Sorrow AL/CR/DRG/FS/LIB/PE/PS
This Time Tomorrow DE/DU/FA/MD/RM/SC
What's Up? M/AV/OR/POL/RM/S/W/YO

Invalidism

Plays in which one or more principal characters suffer from being physically handicapped in some way.

Forward the Heart BL/F/RC/RM/W
Glass Menagerie, The F/LT/RM
God Strikes Back F/MI/POL/W
Good Neighbor CR/F/JE/MA/RM/YO
I Remember Mama F/IL/LT/PE/YO
Johnny Belinda CR/MD/RM/RR/SX/TR
Journey of Simon McKeever, The MD/OA
Man's House, A BI/BR/F/JE/PE/REL/RM
Mexican Mural FA/MEX/POL/REL/PS/RM/SX
Tanyard Street IR/MA/REL/SX/W
Therese A/CR/MA/PE/SX
Yesterday's Magic AL/BH/BR/F/RM/TH

Journalism

Plays that feature one or more journalists or that deal with the job of reporting or publishing/editing the news.

All the King's Men CR/MA/POL/SO/SX
Big Two, The HT/JE/MI/MY/POL/RM
Biggest Thief in Town, The AL/DE/F/RM/SH/SM
Born Yesterday BS/CR/LA/POL/RM/SX
Broken Journey BC/RM/W
Candle in the Wind FI/FNC/MI/PN/RM/W
Common Ground JE/MI/POL/SH
Cue for Passion CR/HT/LT/MA/MY/POL/SX/TH
Cup of Trembling, The AL/F/MA/ME/SX
Decision BL/CR/L/MI/POL/RC/RM/SM/SX/W
Derryowen BA/GA/IR/POL/RM/W
Detective Story CR/LA/MA/MD/RM
Dr. Herzl HIB/JE/POL/REL/YL
Dream Girl BA/FA/LT/MEX/PS/RM/SX/TH/TR
Dream with Music M/BC/FA/PE/RM/SX
First Wife, The CH/F/MA/OR/POL/YO
Flamingo Road P0L/PN/PS/RM/SX/SO
Flight to the West AV/F/JE/MA/POL/W
Goldfish Bowl, The F/POL
Goodbye, My Fancy POL/RM/UN/YO
Happily Ever After MA/POL/REL/RM/SM
Hollywood Pinafore M/FI/RM
Hope for the Best POL/RM/W

Iceman Cometh, The AL/BA/CR/ME/PE/POL/PS
If in the Greenwood POL/SX/V
Inside Story, The F/MI/RM/TH/W/YO
Janie F/MI/RM/SM/W/YO
Johnny on a Spot AL/CR/POL/PS/RM/SO/SX
Lady in Danger AUS/CR/LT/MY/POL
Lady in the Dark M/FA/ME/RM/SX
Love Goes to Press MI/RM/SH/SX/W/WO
Meet a Body CR/DE/MY/RM
Metropole BS/RM
Miss Liberty M/A/FNC/HT/PE/RM/SE
Mr. Barry's Etchings A/CR/HT/POL/RM
My Sister Eileen A/F/LT/MI/PS/RM/SPT/SX/TH
Native Son BL/CR/F/LA/PN/POL/RC/RM/TR
Nellie Bly M/AD/BA/PE/RM
No Exit DE/FA/FR/HO/HT/POL/RM/SX
O'Daniel MI/POL/RM/W
Odds on Mrs. Oakley, The GA/MA/SPT/SX
On the Seventh Day BC/F/FA/JO/ME/W
Over 21 AV/FI/LT/MA/MI/W
Parlor Story MA/POL/SX/UN/YO
Perfect Marriage, The LA/MA/SX/YO
Place of Our Own, A F/MA/PE/POL/SM
Rugged Path, The BS/MA/MI/POL/SE/TRP/W
Searching Wind, The F/FNC/HT/MI/PE/POL/RM/SX/W
Shake Hands with the Devil BL/L/POL/RC/RE/TR
Slice it Thin! F/MI/SM/TH/YO
Snookie A/RM/SX
Soldier's Wife LT/MA/MI/SX/W
State of the Union BS/HT/MA/POL/SX
Sun Field, The MA/RM/SPT/SX
Take It As It Comes BC/CR/DRG/F/MA/POL/SM/YO
Texas, Li'l Darlin' M/POL/RM/SO
That Old Devil MA/SM/SX
Tinker's Dam DE/FA/MI/NC/REL/RM/SC/W
Town House BS/F/MA/SC/YO
Two Blind Mice MI/OA/POL/RM
Up in Central Park M/HT/MU/PE/POL/RM
Velvet Glove, The OA/POL/REL/UN
Voice of Israel, The F/JE/MI/POL/W/YL
Where Stars Walk FA/IR/RM/TH
Woman Bites Dog HT/POL/RM/SM

Labor

Plays concerned with the problems of workers; many deal with unions, strikes, and problems with management.

All for All BS/FS/RM
And So They Perish
Brooklyn, U.S.A. CR/PN/RM
Brother Cain F/LA/RM
Decision BL/CR/JO/MI/POL/RC/RM/SM/SX/W
Finian's Rainbow M/BL/F/FA/POL/RC/RM/RR/SO
Flowers of Virtue, The CR/IL/LT/MEX/MI/POL/REL/RM
Home Is the Hunter BL/BS/CR/MA/POL/W
How I Wonder BL/F/FA/RC/SC/UN/W
Joy to the World BS/FI/RM/SX
Korb'n F/JE/POL/REL/RM

Magdalena M/MI/PE/POL/REL/RM
Mr. Peebles and Mr. Hooker BL/RC/REL/RR/SM/SO/SX
Natural Man BL/CR/FA/GA/PE/PN/RC/REL/SO
No for an Answer M/AL/POL/RM
Portrait in Black CR/MD/MY/RM
Retreat to Pleasure GA/POL/RM
Right next to Broadway BS/JE/RM/SX
Shake Hands with the Devil BL/JO/POL/RC/REL/TR
Steps Leading Up BS/RM
Walk into My Parlor BS/CR/F/MA/RM/SX
Winslow Boy, The BR/F/LA/PE/POL/S/TR/WO/YO

Law

Plays about lawyers and legal problems. See also "Trials."

Anybody Home MA/RM/SX
Born Yesterday BS/CR/JO/POL/RM/SX
Brother Cain F/L/RM
Christopher Blake F/FA/MA/POL/TH/TR/YO
Criminals, The CR/GE/POL/RM/SX/TR
Detective Story CR/JO/MA/MD/RM
Familiar Pattern, The JE/MA/SX
George Washington Slept Here F/LE/RM/RR/TH/YO
House Possessed, A F/ME/PE/RM
How Long till Summer? AL/BL/CR/FA/POL/RC/YO
Magnificent Yankee, The HIB/MA/OA/PE/POL
Native Son BL/CR/F/JO/LA/PN/POL/RC/RM/TR
Perfect Marriage, The JO/MA/SX/YO
Private Life of the Master Race, The F/GE/JE/MA/MI/PN/POL/REL/W
Scapegoat, The CR/FA/RM/TR
Signature CR/LE/PE/RM/RR/SO/TR
Smile of the World, The MA/PE/POL/RM
Story of Mary Surratt, The BH/CR/HIB/PE/PN/POL/TR
Uniform of Flesh CR/MI/PE/SE/TR
Winslow Boy, The BR/F/L/POL/S/TR/WO/YO

Legacy

Plays in which wills and inheritances form a crucial plot element.

As We Forgive Our Debtors F/RR/SX
Autumn Hill CR/REL/RM/RR
Dark Hammock CR/MA/PE/RR/SC/SO
George Washington Slept Here F/LA/RM/RR/TH/YO
Heiress, The F/PE/RM
High Kickers M/HT/RM/SH/TR
It's a Gift F/PE/REL/RM/S/SM/SX/YO
January Thaw F/RR/SX
Look, Ma, I'm Dancin' M/RM/SH
Madame Is Served MA/SX
Oh, Brother! A/CR/RM
Out of My House AL/BL/F/REL/SM/WE
Ring around Elizabeth F/MA/ME/RM
Sender Blank F/YL
Signature CR/LA/PE/RM/RR/SO/TR
Snark Was a Boojum, The AL/F/MY/RM/SX
Something for the Boys M/AV/MI/RM/SH/W/WE
Uncle Harry CR/F/MY/PE/PN/SM

Visitor, The CR/F/MY/SM/YO

Literature

Plays in which writers are principal characters. Playwrights as characters figure in plays found under "Theatre." See also "Literary-Biographical."

Ask My Friend Sandy BS/MA/MI/RM
Blithe Spirit BR/DE/FA/MA/SX/SPR
Cat Screams, The CR/DE/DRG/MEX/MY/RM/SX
Cuckoos on the Hearth CR/ME/MY/RR/SC
Cue for Passion CR/HT/JO/MA/MY/POL/SX/TH
Day before Spring, The M/MA/RM/UN
Devils Galore DE/FA/RM/SX
Dream Girl BA/FA/JO/MEX/PS/RM/SX/TH/TR
Dream of Love, A FA/MA/MD/SX
Duet for Two Hands BR/CR/MD/PE/RM
Eagle Has Two Heads, The FR/PE/POL/RM/SX
First Stop to Heaven BH/MA/RM
Five Alarm Waltz FI/MA/TH/YO
Fledgling CR/F/IL/ME/REL/SX
Flowers of Virtue, The CR/IL/MEX/MI/POL/REL/RM
Gabrielle IL/MA/MD/MU/RM
Glass Menagerie, The F/IN/RM
Haven, The CR/MA/MY
I Remember Mama F/IL/IN/PE/YO
Lady in Danger AUS/CR/JO/MY/POL
Little Darling F/RM/SX/TH
Magic Touch, The MA
Manhattan Nocturne MA/ME/PS/SX/TR
Men We Marry, The MA/RM/RR
Mr. Sycamore FA/MA/REL/SM
Morning Star, The BR/MA/MD/SX/W
My Sister Eileen A/F/JO/MI/PS/RM/SPT/SX/TH
Naked Genius, The CR/RM/SH/SX
Nineteenth Hole of Europe, The IR/POL/PS/REL/RM/SX/W
Old Acquaintance FS/RM/SX
Over 21 AV/FI/JO/MA/MI/W
Respectfully Yours F/MA/PE/UN
Slightly Scandalous F/MA/MI/SX
Soldier's Wife JO/MA/MI/SX/W
Talley Method, The F/MD/POL/RM/YO*Trio* HO/RM/UN/YO
Years Between, The A/BS/F/MI/RM/SM/SX/W
Yosele, the Nightingale JE/MU/PE/REL/RM/YL

Literary-Biographical

Eastward in Eden PE/REL/RM
Escape into Glory F/PE/RM
Harriet BL/F/MA/PE/POL/RM/W
Ivy Green, The F/MA/PE/RM/SX
Minstrel Boy, The OA/PE/POL/RM/W
Romantic Mr. Dickens PE/RM
Second Best Bed MA/PE/TH
Song out of Sorrow AL/CR/DRG/FS/IL/PE/PS

Medicine

Plays in which medical doctors and dentists and their work figure. See also

"Illness," "Invalidism," and "Science."

Allegro M/F/MA/RM/SM/SX
City of Kings BL/PE/RC/REL
Detective Story CR/JO/LA/MA/RM
Doctor Social IL/MD/RM/SC
Doctors Disagree IL/MD/RM/SX/WO
Dream of Love, A FA/LT/MA/SX
Duet for Two Hands BR/CR/LT/PE/RM
Eternal Cage, The FA/IL/MA
Family Carnovsky, The CR/F/JE/MA/POL/YL
Gabrielle IL/MA/MU/RM
Injury Sustained F/POL
Johnny Belinda CR/IN/RM/RR/SX/TR
Journey of Simon McKeever, The IN/OA
Jupiter Laughs BR/REL/RM/SC/SX
Kathleen F/IR/REL/RM/SX/YO
Kiss and Tell F/MI/RM/SX/W/YO
Kiss Them for Me AV/BS/HT/MI/RM/SX/W
Linden Tree, The BR/BS/F/MA/MU/OA/REL/SC/UN/YO
Millionairess, The BR/BS/RM
Morning Star, The BR/LT/MA/SX/W
New Life, A AV/BS/F/MA/SH/W
Nine Girls CR/POL/SPT/TH/UN/WE/WO/YO
No Way Out CR/GA/MA
Outrageous Fortune F/HO/JE/MU/RC/RM/SX
Portrait in Black CR/L/MY/RM
Sons and Soldiers AL/F/FA/MA/PE/RM/SX/W
Summer and Smoke ME/PS/REL/RM/SM/SO/SX
Sweet Genevieve MA/PE/SX/YO
Talley Method, The F/LT/POL/RM/YO
This Time Tomorrow DE/DU/FA/IL/RM/SC
Three's a Family BL/F/MA
When the Bough Breaks MA
Willow and I, The A/F/ME/PE/RM/SM
With a Silk Thread F/MA/SX/TH

Mental Illness

Plays dealing with characters who suffer from various psychological aberrations; the handling of these characters may be serious or comic.

All You Need Is One Good Break F/GA/IL/JE/PN/RM
Angel Street BR/CR/MA/MY/PE
Another Part of the Forest BL/BS/F/MA/PE/PS/REL/RM/SO/SX
Arsenic and Old Lace CR/OA/RM/TH
Bravo! RM/SC/TH
Bridge to the Sun CR/MY
Building 222 HO/MI/REL/W
Closing Door, The F/MA
Crime and Punishment AL/BH/BR/CR/F/PE/PS/REL
Cry of the Peacock F/FR/MA/PE/RM/SX
Cuckoos on the Hearth CR/LT/MY/RR/SC
Cup of Trembling, The AL/F/JO/MA/SX
Dancer, The A/AL/CR/F/FNC/HO/PS/SH
Day Will Come, The FA/JE/MI/POL/REL/W
Death of a Salesman BS/F/HT/MA/SX
Dog beneath the Skin, The AD/BR/DRG/FA/HT/IL/POL/PS/RM/V/W
Duke in Darkness, The BR/FNC/PE/PN/POL

Family Reunion, The F/OA/REL/V
Fledgling CR/F/IL/LT/REL/SX
Foxhole in the Parlor A/FS/MU/POL/RM/SX/W
Gayden A/CR/F/RM/SX
Hand in Glove BH/CR/MY/SX
Harvey AL/F/FA
Home of the Brave JE/ME/MI/REL/TRP/W
House Possessed, A F/LA/PE/RM
Iceman Cometh, The AL/BA/CR/JO/PE/POL/PS
Innocent Voyage, The AD/CR/PE/SE/SX/YO
Lady, Behave! RM/SX/TH
Lady in the Dark M/FA/JO/RM/SX
Lady Who Came to Stay, The DE/F/MY/RM/SX/YO
Madwoman of Chaillot, The BS/FA/FR/POL/TR
Man, The CR
Manhattan Nocturne LT/MA/PS/SX/TR
Me and Harry CR/RM/SPT
Me, the Sleeper F/MA/SPT
Medium, The M/CR/DE/F/RM/SPR
Men to the Sea BH/BL/MA/MI/REL/SE/SX/W
On the Seventh Day BC/F/FA/JO/W
Ring around Elizabeth F/LE/MA/RM
Secret Room, The CR/SX/YO
Sheppey BR/DE/F/FA/GA/REL/PS
Sleep, My Pretty One CR/F/RM
Star Spangled Family F/MA/W/YO
Streetcar Named Desire, A AL/HO/MA/PS/RM/SO/SX
Summer and Smoke MD/PS/REL/RM/SM/SO/SX
Sundown Beach MA/MI/RM/SX/W
Swan Song CR/MU/YO
They Walk Alone BR/CR/MU/SX
Walking Gentleman, The CR/MY/RM/TH
Willow and I, The A/F/MD/PE/RM/SM
Young and the Fair, The CR/S/YO

Military

Plays featuring military personnel in key roles. These are not necessarily war plays, but, because the period coincided with World War II, the number of plays that are greatly inflate the statistics. See also "War."

Alice in Arms RM/SM/SX
All Men Are Alike BR/MA/SX/W
Arlene RM/SX/YO
Arms and the Girl M/PE/RM/W
Ask My Friend Sandy BS/LT/MA/RM
Assassin, The CR/PN/POL/RM/W
At War with the Army RM/SX/W
Bathsheba BI/PE/SX/W
Bell for Adano, A POL/RM/W
Big Two, The HT/JE/JO/MY/POL/RM
Building 222 HO/ME/REL/W
By Jupiter M/MA/PE/RM/SX/W
Candle in the Wind FI/FNC/JO/PN/RM/W
Carmen Jones M/BL/CR/R/SO/SPT/SX/W
Catherine Was Great PE/POL/SX/W
Command Decision AV/POL/W
Common Ground JE/JO/POL/SH
Count Me In M/F/W

Counterattack POL/RSN/SX/W
Day Will Come, The FA/JE/ME/POL/REL/W
Dear Ruth F/POL/RM/W/YO
Decision BL/CR/JO/L/POL/RC/RM/SM/SX/W
Delicate Story HU/MA/RM/SX/W
Doughgirls, The HT/POL/RM/SX/W
Down to Miami BS/F/HT/REL/RM/SO
Eve of St. Mark, The F/FA/GA/IL/RM/RR/SX/TRP/W
Fifty AV/RM/W
Flare Path AV/BR/HT/MA/RM/TH/W
Flowers of Virtue, The CR/IL/L/LT/MEX/POL/REL/RM
Follow the Girls M/RM/SH/W
Foolish Notion FA/MA/RM/TH/W/YO
God Strikes Back F/IN/POL/W
Golden Wings AV/POL/RM/SX/W
Good Morning, Corporal MA/SX/W
Grandma's Diary BC/MA/RM/SX
Hasty Heart, The DE/FS/IL/RM/TRP/W
Heart of a City AL/RM/TH/W
Home of the Brave JE/ME/REL/TRP/W
Inside Story F/JO/RM/TH/W/YO
Jackpot GA/RM/W
Jacobowsky and the Colonel GE/JE/POL/RM/W
Janie F/JO/RM/SM/W/YO
John Loves Mary FS/HT/MA/POL/RM
Kiss and Tell F/MD/RM/SX/W/YO
Kiss Them for Me AV/BS/HT/MD/RM/SX/W
Lady Says Yes, A M/CH/FA/PE/SX
Land Is Bright, The BS/CR/F/OA/PE/POL/RM/W/YO
Land of Fame POL/RM/W
Let's Face It M/MA/RM/SX/W
Liberty Jones FA/IL/POL/RM
Love Goes to Press JO/RM/SH/SX/W/WO
Love on Leave F/HT/RM/SX/Y0
Lovers and Friends BR/F/MA/RM/TH
Lower North BA/MA/S/SX/W
Magdalena M/L/PE/POL/REL/RM
Men in Shadow AV/BR/W
Men to the Sea BH/BL/MA/ME/REL/SE/SX/W
Mermaids Singing, The BA/F/HT/RM/SX/TH
Mr. Adam MA/POL/SC/SX
Mister Roberts SE/W
Moment Musical MA/RM/SX/W
Montserrat A/FR/PE/POL/SX/TH/YO
Moon Is Down, The POL/SX/W
Music in My Heart M/MU/MUB/PE/RM
My Sister Eileen A/F/JO/LT/PS/RM/SPT/SX/TH
O'Daniel JO/POL/RM/W
On the Town M/RM
Outside the Door DE/FA/GE/W
Over 21 AV/FI/JO/LT/MA/W
Panama Hattie M/POL/PS/RM/SX/TRP/YO
Pillar to Post RM/SX
Plan M IL/POL/W
Polonaise M/HIB/PE/POL/RM/W
Private Life of the Master Race, The F/GE/JE/LA/MA/PN/POL/REL/W
Rape of Lucretia, The M/BR/MA/PE/SX
Rugged Path, The BS/JO/MA/POL/SE/TRP/W
Ryan Girl, The CR/F/MA/W

Sadie Thompson M/PS/REL/SX/TRP
Searching Wind, The F/FNC/HT/JO/PE/POL/RM/SX/W
Skydrift AV/DE/FA/W
Slice It Thin! F/JO/SM/TH/YO
Slightly Married F/MA/SM/SX/YO
Slightly Scandalous F/LT/MA/SX
Snafu CR/F/POL/RM/SX/W/YO
Soldier's Wife JO/LT/MA/SX/W
Something for the Boys M/AV/LE/SH/RM/W/WE
Sophie F/RM/RR/SM/SX
Sound of Hunting W
South Pacific BL/RC/RM/SX/TRP/W
South Pacific M/RC/RM/TRP/W
Storm Operation REL/RM/SX/W
Streets Are Guarded, The AV/REL/W
Strip for Action RM/SH/SX
Sundown Beach MA/ME/RM/SX/W
Temper the Wind BS/POL
Thank You, Svoboda PN/POL/RM/W
There Is No End PN/REL/W
This, Too, Shall Pass F/JE/RM/SM
Tinker's Dam DE/FA/JO/NC/REL/RM/SC/W
Too Hot for Maneuvers RM/S/SX/YO
Traitor, The POL/SC
Truckline Café AL/CR/MA/SX
Two Blind Mice JO/OA/POL/RM
Under the Counter M/BR/RM/TH
Uniform of Flesh CR/LA/PE/SE/TR/V
Up the Rebels! F/PE/POL/RM/W
Vickie MA/SC/SX/W/WO
Victory Belles F/RM/SX/W
Voice of Israel, The F/JE/JO/POL/W/YL
Voice of the Turtle, The RM/SX/TH/W
War President HIB/PE/POL/W
Wedding in Japan OR/RC/RM/TR
While the Sun Shines BR/GA/RM/W
Winged Victory AV/F/FS/HT/MA/RM/SM/TRP/W
Winners and Losers POL/TR
Winter Soldiers BC/POL/PS/W
World's Full of Girls, The F/RM/SX/W
Years Between, The A/BS/F/LT/RM/SM/SX/W
You Touched Me! AL/F/RM/SX

Music

Plays about music, singers, composers, and musicians. These are not musicals unless so indicated. See also "Musical-Biographical" and "Show Business."

Beautiful People, The F/REL/YO
Boudoir AL/CR/MA/PE/SX
Career MA
Day of Judgment, The JE/PE/RM/YL/YO
Deep Mrs. Sykes, The AL/F/MA
Foxhole in the Parlor A/FS/ME/POL/RM/SX/W
Gabrielle IL/LT/MA/MD/RM
Hairpin Harmony M/BC/BS/RM
Hear That Trumpet AL/BL/CR/MA/RC/RM
Johnny 2 X 4 CR/NC/PS/SH
Linden Tree, The BR/BS/F/MA/MD/OA/REL/SC/UN/YO

Little A MA/SM/SX
Me and Molly BS/F/JE/MA/REL/RM/S/YO
Mr. Strauss Goes to Boston M/HT/MA/PE/POL/RM
Music in My Heart M/MI/PE/RM
My Romance M/PE/REL/RM
Night of Love M/RM/SX
Outrageous Fortune F/HO/JE/MD/RC/RM/SX
Pick-up Girl CR/F/IL/PS/RM/SX/TR/YO
Quiet Please FI/MA/SX
Rat Race, The BH/CR/RM/SH
Rhapsody M/PE/POL/RM/SX
Sing Out, Sweet Land! M/FA/PE/RM/W/WE
Slightly Scandalous F/LT/MA/MI/SX
Song of Norway M/MA/MUB/PE/RM
Suds in Your Eye AL/FS/OR/RM
Swan Song CR/ME/YO
They Walk Alone BR/CR/ME/SX
Three Gifts CR/DE/FA/JE/REL/RM/YL
Up in Central Park M/HT/JO/PE/POL/RM
Yosele, the Nightingale JE/LT/PE/REL/RM/YL
Young American, A BL/F/RC

Musical-Biographical

Music in My Heart M/MI/MU/PE/RM
Song of Norway M/MA/MU/PE/RM

Mystery

For purposes of this list, mystery dramas are those in which there is either a strong element of suspense, usually associated with the commission of a crime, or horrific scenes designed to frighten the audience.

Angel Street BR/CR/MA/ME/PE
Big Two, The HT/JE/JO/MI/POL/RM
Bridge to the Sun CR/ME
Cat Screams, The CR/DE/DRG/LT/MEX/RM/SX
Cuckoos on the Hearth CR/LT/ME/RR/SC
Cue for Passion CR/HT/JO/LT/MA/POL/SX/TH
Eight O'Clock Tuesday CR/SX
Four Flights Up CR
Ghost for Sale BR/RM
Great to Be Alive! CR/DE/FA/RM/SX
Hand in Glove BH/CR/ME/SX
Haven, The CR/LT/MA
Hidden Horizon BR/CR/TRP
I Killed the Count BR/CR
Innocents, The DE/FA/YO
Inspector Calls, An BR/CR/F/PE/RM/SX
Lady in Danger AUS/CR/JO/LT/POL
Lady Who Came to Stay, The DE/F/ME/RM/SX/YO
Laura CR/RM/SX
Little Brown Jug CR/F
Meet a Body CR/DE/JO/RM
Mr. and Mrs. North CR/MA
Mr. Big CR/POL/RM/TH
Murder without Crime BR/CR/MA/SX
Portrait in Black CR/L/MD/RM
Ramshackle Inn CR/HT/SM

Rebecca CR/MA
Snark Was a Boojum, The AL/F/LE/RM/SX
Stranger, The CR/JE/PE/POL
Ten Little Indians BR/CR/REL/RM
To Kill a Cat BR/CR/F/RM
Two Mrs. Carrolls, The A/BR/CR/FNC/MA/RM
Uncle Harry CR/F/LE/PE/PN/SM
Visitor, The CR/F/LE/SM/YO
Walking Gentleman, The CR/ME/RM/TH

Old Age

Plays in which the advanced age of one or more characters is a plot element.

Arsenic and Old Lace CR/ME/RM/TH
Battle for Heaven HIB/OA/REL
Family Reunion, The F/ME/REL/V
Flag Is Born, A FA/JE/PE/POL/REL
Hallams, The BC/F/IL/MA
Happy Time, The AL/F/MA/PE/RM/SX/YO
I Know My Love F/MA/PE/SX
Journey of Simon McKeever, The IN/MD
Land Is Bright, The BS/CR/F/MI/PE/POL/RM/W/YO
Last Stop BS/CR
Linden Tree, The BR/BS/F/MA/MD/MU/REL/SC/UN/YO
Magnificent Yankee, The HIB/LA/MA/PE/POL
Minstrel Boy, The LIB/PE/POL/RM/W
Silver Whistle, The GA/REL/RM/SX
Two Blind Mice JO/MI/POL/RM
Velvet Glove, The JO/POL/REL/UN
Yes, M'Lord BR/MA/POL/RM

Period

These are works that are set, in full or part, at least twenty years before the year in which the play was produced, thus making them "period" plays.

Angel Street BR/CR/MA/ME/MY
Anne of England BR/HIB/POL/WO
Anne of the Thousand Days HIB/MA/POL/REL/SX/TR/V
Annie Get Your Gun M/HIB/RM/SH/WE
Another Part of the Forest BL/BS/F/MA/ME/PS/REL/RM/SO/SX
Apology BS/F/FA/REL/RM/SM/W
Armor of Light BI/REL
Arms and the Girl M/MI/RM/W
Around the World M/AD/GA/SE
Bathsheba BI/MI/SX/W
Billion Dollar Baby M/CR/NC/RM/SH/SX
Bloomer Girl M/BL/BS/F/HIB/POL/RC/RM/SM/SO/W/WO
Boudoir AL/CR/MA/MU/SX
Brigadoon M/BA/FA/RM
Broken Hearts of Broadway BS/RM
Burning Bush, The GE/JE/L/REL/TR
--But Not Goodbye BS/DE/F/FA/SM
By Jupiter M/MA/MI/RM/SX/W
Carousel M/CR/DE/FA/MA/RM/SM
Catherine Was Great MI/POL/SX/W
Chicken Every Sunday BH/BS/F/MA/RM/SX/WE
City of Kings BL/MD/RC/REL

Comes the Revelation REL/RR/SX
Crime and Punishment AL/BH/BR/F/ME/PS/REL
Cry of the Peacock F/FR/MA/ME/RM/SX
Damask Cheek, The F/RM
Dark Hammock CR/LE/MA/RR/SC/SO
Day of Judgment, The JE/MU/RM/YL/YO
Dear Judas BI/POL/REL
Deliver Us from Evil CR/DE/FA/REL/RM
Deputy of Paris, The FNC/HIB/POL
Design for a Stained Glass Window HIB/REL
Don't, George F/MA/RM
Dream with Music M/BC/FA/JO/RM/SX
Druid Circle, The MA/RM/SX/UN/YO
Duchess Misbehaves, The A/FA/SX
Duet for Two Hands BR/CR/LT/MD/RM
Duke in Darkness, The BR/FNC/ME/PN/POL
Eagle Has Two Heads, The FR/LT/POL/RM/SX
Eastward in Eden LIB/REL/RM
Edward, My Son AL/BR/BS/CR/F/MA/POL/SX
Embezzled Heaven CR/REL
Escape into Glory F/LIB/RM
Ester'ke JE/POL/REL/RM/SX/YL
Feathers in a Gale RM
Firebrand of Florence, The M/A/RM/SX
Flag Is Born, A FA/JE/OA/POL/REL
Flies, The CR/F/FR/REL
Galileo F/GE/HIB/POL/REL/SC
Garden of Time BL/FA/RR
Gentlemen Prefer Blondes M/FNC/HT/RM/SE
Golden Falcon, The AD/POL/W
Gypsy Lady M/RM/TH
Happy as Larry CR/FA/MA/RM/SX
Happy Time, The AL/F/MA/RM/OA/SX/YO
Harriet BL/F/LIB/MA/POL/RM/W
Heiress, The F/LE/RM
Helen Goes to Troy M/FA/POL/RM/SX
Henri Christophe BL/POL/REL/TRP
Herschel the Jester M/JE/REL/RM/YL
High Button Shoes M/BS/CR/GA/SPT/UN/YO
House in Paris, The A/FNC/RM/SX
House Possessed, A F/LA/ME/RM
I Know My Love F/MA/OA/SX
I Remember Mama F/IL/IN/LT/YO
Iceman Cometh, The AL/BA/CR/JO/ME/POL/PS
If the Shoe Fits M/FA/RM
In Time to Come FNC/HIB/POL/W
Innocent Voyage, The AD/CR/ME/SE/SX/YO
Inspector Calls, An BR/CR/F/MY/RM/SX
It's a Gift F/LE/REL/RM/S/SM/SX/YO
Ivy Green, The F/LIB/MA/RM/SX
Joan of Lorraine HIB/PN/POL/REL/TH
John Brown F/HIB/RC
Johnny Doodle FA/POL/W
Journey to Jerusalem BI/PE/POL/REL
Kiss Me, Kate M/CR/GA/MA/TH
Lady of Fatima FA/REL/YO
Lady Says Yes, A M/CH/FA/MI/SX
Lamp at Midnight HIB/POL/REL/SC
Land Is Bright, The BS/CR/F/MI/OA/POL/RM/W/YO

Late George Apley, The F/RM/YO
Leading Lady, The MA/RM/TH
Liar, The M/RM/SX
Life with Mother BS/F/MA/RM/YO
Live Life Again DE/F/FA/RM/RR/SM/V
Louisiana Lady M/PS/RM/SO/SX
Love Life M/BS/F/FA/MA/POL/SH/TR/WO/YO
Lute Song M/CH/F/MA/OR
Magdalena M/L/MI/POL/REL/RM
Magnificent Yankee, The HIB/LA/MA/OA/POL
Make Way for Lucia WO
Man's House, A BI/BR/F/IN/JE/REL/RM
Marinka M/POL/RM
Mary of Magdala BI/REL/RM
Minstrel Boy, The LIB/OA/POL/RM/W
Miracle in the Mountains CR/FA/POL/REL/SX/TR
Miss Liberty M/A/FNC/HT/JO/RM/SE
Mr. Strauss Goes to Boston M/HT/MA/MU/POL/RM
Montserrat A/FR/MI/POL/SX/TH/YO
Moon Vine, The CR/REL/RM/SM/SO/TH/YO
Music in My Heart M/HIB/MI/MU/RM
My Romance M/MU/REL/RM
Natural Man BL/CR/FA/GA/L/PN/RC/REL/SO
Nellie Bly M/AD/BA/JO/RM
Next Half Hour, The DE/F/FA/SX/YO
Night Watch in Syria BI/REL
Old Lady Says "No!," The FA/HIB/IR/POL/TH
Our Lan' BL/POL/RC/RM/RR/SO
Owl and the Pussycat, The POL/PS/SH
Patriots, The HIB/POL/SX
Pirate, The AD/RM/SH/TRP
Place of Our Own, A F/JO/MA/POL/SM
Polonaise M/HIB/MI/POL/RM/W
Pretty Little Parlor AL/F/MA/SM/SX/YO
Rape of Lucretia, The M/BR/MA/MI/SX
Respectfully Yours F/LT/MA/UN
Rhapsody M/MU/POL/RM/SX
Romantic Mr. Dickens LIB/RM
Rose in the Wilderness CR/REL/RM/SX
St. Louis Woman M/BL/GA/RM/SPT/SX
Savonarola HIB/POL/REL
Searching Wind, The F/FNC/HT/JO/MI/POL/RM/SX/W
Second Best Bed LIB/MA/TH
Set My People Free BL/HIB/POL/RC/REL
Shylock '47 HEL/JE/TH
Shylock and His Daughter BS/F/JE/REL/RM/TR/YL
Signature CR/LA/LE/RM/RR/SO/TR
Simon's Wife BI/MA/REL
Sing Out, Sweet Land! M/FA/MU/RM/W/WE
Skin of Our Teeth, The F/FA/MA/SX/W/YO
Sleepy Hollow M/RM
Smile of the World, The LA/MA/POL/RM
Sojourner Truth BL/F/HIB/RC/REL/RM
Song of Bernadette, The F/FNC/REL
Song of Norway M/MA/MUB/RM
Song of the Dniepper CR/JE/PN/POL/TR/YL
Song out of Sorrow AL/CR/DRG/FS/IL/LIB/PS
Sons and Soldiers AL/F/FA/MA/MD/RM/SX/W
Story for Strangers, A CR/FA/GA/PS/REL/RM/SM

Story of Mary Surratt, The BH/CR/HIB/LA/PN/POL/TR
Strange Bedfellows F/MA/POL/PS/SX/WO
Stranger, The CR/JE/MY/POL
Sunny River M/MA/POL/RM/SH
Survivors, The F/HT/RR/W/WE
Suzanna and the Elders POL/REL/RM/SX
Sweet Genevieve MA/MD/SX/YO
Temporary Island, A CI/RM/S/SX
That Lady PN/POL/RM
Therese A/CR/IN/MA/SX
To Tell You the Truth BI/FA/SX
Uncle Harry CR/F/LE/MY/PN/SM
Under This Roof BS/MA/POL/RM/RR/W
Uniform of Flesh CR/LA/MI/SE/TR/V
Up in Central Park M/HT/JO/MU/POL/RM
Up the Rebels! F/MI/POL/RM/W
Wandering Stars JE/RM/TH/YL
War and Peace F/MA/RM/W
War President HIB/MI/POL/W
Where's Charley? M/RM/UN/YO
Willow and I, The A/F/MD/ME/RM/SM
Winslow Boy, The BR/F/L/LA/POL/S/TR/WO/YO
Wisteria Trees, The BL/BS/F/RM/RR/SO
Years Ago F/MA/RM/SM/TH/YO
Yosele, the Nightingale JE/LT/MU/REL/RM/YL
You'll See Stars M/HIB/SH
Yours, A. Lincoln HIB/POL

Politics

"Politics" is used here in a fairly broad sense to encompass plays dealing with political figures, events, and ideologies in the contemporary world and in the past. Many of the plays listed were concerned with the problems of fascism and Nazism.

All the King's Men CR/JO/MA/SO/SX
Allah Be Praised! RM/SX
Anne of England BR/HIB/PE/WO
Anne of the Thousand Days HIB/MA/PE/REL/SX/TR/V
Antigone FR/RM
As the Girls Go M/F/MA/SX/WO
Ascent of F-6, The BR/F/FA
Assassin, The CR/MI/PN/RM/W
Barber Had Two Sons, The A/CR/F/RM/SX/W
Barefoot Boy with Cheek M/RM/SX/UN/YO
Beggar's Holiday M/BL/CR/PN/PS/RM/SX
Bell for Adano, A MI/RM/W
Big Two, The HT/JE/JO/MI/MY/RM
Big White Fog, The BL/F/JE/PS/RC
Bloomer Girl M/BL/BS/F/HIB/PE/RC/RM/SM/SO/W/WO
Born Yesterday BS/CR/JO/LA/RM/SX
Bright Boy CR/RM/S/YO
Catherine Was Great MI/PE/SX/W
Caukey BL/F/RC/RM
Christopher Blake F/FA/LA/MA/TH/TR/YO
Criminals, The CR/GE/LA/RM/SX/TR
Come Marching Home
Command Decision AV/MI/W
Common Ground JE/JO/MI/SH

Consul, The M/MA
Counterattack MI/RSN/SX/W
Cue for Passion CR/HT/JO/LT/MA/MY/SX/TH
Day Will Come, The FA/JE/ME/MI/REL/W
Days of Our Youth, The RM/SPT/SX/UN/YO
Dear Judas BI/PE/REL
Dear Ruth F/MI/RM/W/YO
Decision BL/CR/JO/L/MI/RC/RM/SM/SX/W
Deep Are the Roots BL/CR/F/RC/RM/S/SM/SO
Deputy of Paris, The FNC/HIB/PE
Derryowen BA/GA/JO/IR/RM/W
Dr. Herzl HIB/JE/JO/REL/YL
Dog beneath the Skin, The AD/BR/DRG/FA/HT/IL/ME/PS/RM/V/W
Doughgirls, The HT/MI/RM/SX/W
Duke in Darkness, The BR/FNC/ME/PE/PN
Dunnigan's Daughter A/BS/MA/MEX/RM
Eagle Has Two Heads, The F/MA/PS/SX
Edge of the Sword, The FR/LT/PE/PS/RM/SX
Edward, My Son AL/BR/BS/CR/F/MA/PE/SX
Enchanted, The FA/DE/FR/POL/RM/YO
Ester'ke JE/PE/REL/RM/SX/YL
Family, The AL/BH/CH/F/OR/RM/W
Family Carnovsky, The CR/F/JE/MA/MD/YL
Finian's Rainbow M/BL/F/FA/L/RC/RM/RR/SO
First Wife, The CH/F/JO/MA/YO
Flag Is Born, A FA/JE/OA/PE/REL
Flamingo Road JO/PN/PS/RM/SO/SX
Flight to the West AV/F/JE/JO/MA/W
Flowers of Virtue, The CR/IL/L/LT/MEX/MI/REL/RM
Foxhole in the Parlor A/FS/ME/MU/RM/SX/W
French Touch, The FNC/MA/TH
Galileo F/GE/HIB/PE/REL/SC
Gentleman from Athens, The RM/SO
God Strikes Back F/IN/MI/W
Golden Falcon, The AD/PE/W
Golden Wings AV/MI/RM/SX/W
Goldfish Bowl, The F/JO
Goodbye, My Fancy JO/RM/UN/YO
Great Campaign, The REL/RR
Happily Ever After JO/MA/REL/RM/SM
Harriet BL/F/LIB/MA/PE/RM/W
Heads or Tails MA/RM
Helen Goes to Troy M/FA/PE/RM/SX
Henri Christophe BL/PE/REL/TRP
Home Is the Hunter BL/BS/CR/L/MA/W
Hope for the Best JO/RM/W
How Long till Summer? AL/BL/CR/FA/LA/RC/YO
I Like It Here F/RM/SM
Iceman Cometh, The AL/BA/CR/JO/ME/PE/PS
If in the Greenwood JO/SX/V
I'll Take the High Road BS/F/FI/RM/SM/W
In Time to Come FNC/HIB/PE/W
Injury Sustained F/MD
Jacobowsky and the Colonel GE/JE/MI/RM/W
Joan of Lorraine HIB/PE/PN/REL/TH/TR
John Loves Mary FS/HT/MA/MI/RM
Johnny Doodle FA/PE/W
Johnny on a Spot AL/CR/JO/PS/RM/SO/SX
Journey to Jerusalem BI/PE/REL

Korb'n
Lady in Danger AUS/CR/JO/LT/MY
Lamp at Midnight HIB/PE/REL/SC
Land Is Bright, The BS/CR/F/MI/OA/PE/RM/W/YO
Land of Fame MI/RM/W
Last Generation, The F/W
Liberty Jones FA/IL/MI/RM
Lost in the Stars M/BL/CR/PN/RC/REL/SX/TR
Love Life M/BS/F/FA/MA/PE/SH/TR/WO/YO
Madwoman of Chaillot, The BS/FA/FR/ME/TR
Magdalena L/MI/PE/RM/REL
Magnificent Yankee, The HIB/LA/MA/OA/PE
Man with Blond Hair, The CR/JE/W
Marinka M/PE/RM
Mexican Mural FA/IN/MEX/PS/REL/RM/SX
Minstrel Boy, The LIB/OA/PE/RM/W
Miracle in the Mountains CR/FA/PE/REL/SX/TR
Mr. Adam MA/MI/SC/SX
Mr. Barry's Etchings A/CR/HT/JO/RM
Mr. Big CR/MY/RM/TH
Mr. Strauss Goes to Boston M/HT/MA/MU/PE/RM
Mrs. Gibbon's Boys CR/F
Mrs. January and Mr. X F/RM/SM
Montserrat A/FR/MI/PE/SX/TH/YO
Moon Is Down, The MI/SX/W
More the Merrier, The CR/RM
Native Son BL/CR/F/JO/LA/PN/RC/RM/TR
New Life, A AV/BS/F/MA/MD/SH/W
Nights of Wrath FR/W
Nine Girls CR/MD/SPT/TH/UN/WE/WO/YO
Nineteenth Hole of Europe, The IR/LT/PS/REL/RM/SX/W
No Exit DE/FA/FR/HO/HT/JO/RM/SX
No for an Answer M/AL/L/RM
Not in Our Stars BS/F/RM
O Mistress Mine BR/F/RM/SX/YO
O'Daniel JO/MI/RM/W
Old Foolishness, The F/IR/REL/RM
Old Lady Says "No!," The FA/HIB/IR/PE/TH
Our Lan' BL/PE/RC/RM/RR/SO
Out of the Frying Pan MA/TH
Out of the Picture A/BR/RM/W
Owl and the Pussycat, The PE/PS/SH
Panama Hattie M/MI/PS/RM/SX/TRP/YO
Parlor Story JO/MA/SX/UN/YO
Partition OR
Patriots, The HIB/PE/SX
Place of Our Own, A F/JO/MA/PE/SM
Plan M IL/MI/W
Polonaise M/HIB/MI/PE/RM/W
Private Life of the Master Race, The F/GE/JE/LA/MA/MI/PN/REL/W
Proof thro' the Night DRG/HO/TRP/W/WO
Red Gloves CR/FR/MA/RM
Retreat to Pleasure GA/L/RM
Rhapsody M/MU/PE/RM/SX
Rugged Path, The BS/JO/MA/MI/SE/TRP/W
Russian People, The MA/RM/RSN/W
Savonarola HIB/PE/REL
Searching Wind, The F/FNC/HT/JO/MI/PE/RM/SX/W
Seeds in the Wind TR/W/YO

Set My People Free BL/HIB/PE/RC/REL
Seventh Trumpet, The REL/RM/W
Shake Hands with the Devil BL/JO/L/RC/REL/TR
Skipper next to God BR/DU/JE/REL/SE
Smile of the World, The L/MA/PE/RM
Snafu CR/F/MI/RM/SX/W/YO
Song of the Dniepper CR/JE/PE/PN/TR/YL
State of the Union BS/HT/JO/MA/SX
Story of Mary Surratt, The BH/CR/HIB/LA/PE/PN/TR
Strange Bedfellows F/MA/PE/PS/SX/WO
Stranger, The CR/JE/MY/PE
Strings, My Lord, Are False, The IR/PS/REL/RM/SX/W
Sunny River M/MA/PE/RM/SH
Suzanna and the Elders PE/REL/RM/SX
Take It As It Comes BC/CR/DRG/F/JO/MA/SM/YO
Talley Method, The F/LT/MD/RM/YO
Temper the Wind BS/MI
Texas, Li'l Darlin' M/JO/RM/SO
Thank You, Svoboda MI/PN/RM/W
That Lady PE/PN/RM
Tomorrow the World F/JE/SC/W
Traitor, The MI/SC
Trouble in July BL/CR/RC/SM/SO
Two Blind Mice JO/MI/OA/RM
Under this Roof BS/MA/PE/RM/RR/W
Up in Central Park M/HT/JO/MU/PE/RM
Up the Rebels! F/MI/PE/RM/W
Velvet Glove, The JO/OA/REL/UN
Victors, The FR/SX/W/YO
Village Green, The A/F/RM/SM
Voice of Israel, The F/JE/JO/MI/W/YL
Wallflower F/RM/SX/YO
Wanhope Building, The BA/BC/FA/RM/SC
War President HIB/MI/PE/W
Watch on the Rhine F/MA/RM/W
What's Up? M/AV/IL/OR/RM/S/W/YO
Winners and Losers MI/TR
Winslow Boy, The BR/F/L/LA/PE/S/TR/WO/YO
Winter Soldiers BC/MI/L/PS/W
Without Love MA/RM/SX/W
Woman Bites Dog HT/JO/RM/SM
Wookey, The F/RM/SE/W
Yankee Point F/MA/W
Yes Is for a Very Young Man FNC/W
Yes, M'Lord BR/MA/OA/RM
Yours, A. Lincoln HIB/PE

Prostitution

Plays in which the profession of prostitution figures or in which there are characters who are prostitutes.

Anna Lucasta AL/BL/F/SM
Another Part of the Forest BL/BS/F/MA/ME/PE/REL/RM/SO/SX
Beggar's Holiday M/BL/CR/PN/POL/RM/SX
Big White Fog, The BL/F/JE/POL/RC
Crime and Punishment AL/BH/BR/CR/F/ME/PE/REL
Dancer, The A/AL/CR/F/FNC/HO/ME/SH
Distant City, The CR/F/PN/RE/RM/SX

Dog beneath the Skin, The AD/BR/DRG/FA/HT/IL/ME/POL/RM/V/W
Dream Girl BA/FA/JO/LT/MEX/RM/SX/TH/TR
Early to Bed M/RM/S/SPT/SX/TRP/YO
Edge of the Sword, The FR/LT/PE/RM/SX
Flamingo Road JO/PN/POL/RM/SO/SX
Iceman Cometh, The AL/BA/CR/JO/ME/PE/POL
Johnny on a Spot AL/CR/JO/POL/RM/SO/SX
Johnny 2 X 4 CR/MU/NC/SH
Lily of the Valley CR/DE/FA/REL
Louisiana Lady M/PE/RM/SO/SX
Magnolia Alley BH/MA/REL/SO/SPT/SX
Manhattan Nocturne LT/MA/ME/SX/TR
Mexican Mural FA/IN/MEX/POL/REL/RM/SX
My Sister Eileen A/F/JO/LT/MI/RM/SPT/SX/TH
Nineteenth Hole of Europe, The IR/LT/POL/REL/RM/SX/W
Open House RM/SX
Owl and the Pussycat, The PE/POL/SH
Panama Hattie M/MI/POL/RM/SX/TRP/YO
Pick-up Girl CR/F/IL/MU/RM/SX/TR/YO
Sadie Thompson M/MI/REL/SX/TRP
Sheppey BR/DE/F/FA/GA/ME/REL
Song out of Sorrow AL/CR/DRG/FS/IL/LIB/PE
Story for Strangers, A CR/FA/GA/PE/REL/RM/SM
Strange Bedfellows F/MA/PE/POL/SX/WO
Streetcar Named Desire, A AL/HO/MA/ME/RM/SO/SX
Strings, My Lord, Are False, The IR/POL/REL/RM/SX/W
Summer and Smoke MD/ME/REL/RM/SM/SO/SX
Virginia Reel AL/F/RR/SO
Winter Soldiers BC/MI/POL/W

Race

Plays in which racial issues are significant. The principle racial minority represented is black. See also "Blacks." The subject of anti-Semitism is found in some plays listed under "Jews."

Big White Fog, The BL/F/JE/POL/PS
Bloomer Girl M/BL/BS/F/HIB/PE/POL/RM/SM/SO/W/WO
Caukey BL/F/POL/RM
City of Kings BL/MD/PE/REL
Decision BL/CR/JO/L/MI/POL/RM/SM/SX/W
Deep Are the Roots BL/CR/F/POL/RM/S/SM/SO
Finian's Rainbow M/BL/F/FA/L/PL/RM/RR/SO
Forward the Heart BL/F/IN/RM/W
Greener Grass, The BL/FI
Hear That Trumpet AL/BL/CR/MA/MU/RM
Hope for a Harvest RM/RR/WE
How I Wonder BL/F/FA/L/SC/UN/W
How Long till Summer? AL/BL/CR/FA/LA/POL/YO
Jeb BL/SO
John Brown F/HIB/PE
Little Dark Horse BL/F/FR/IL/SX/YO
Lost in the Stars M/BL/CR/POL/PN/REL/SX/TR
Mr. Peebles and Mr. Hooker BL/L/REL/RR/SM/SO/SX
Native Son BL/CR/F/JO/LA/PN/POL/RM/TR
Natural Man BL/CR/FA/GA/L/PE/PN/REL/SO
On Whitman Avenue BL/F
Our Lan' BL/PE/POL/RM/RR/SO
Outrageous Fortune F/HO/JE/MD/MU/RM/SX

Set My People Free BL/HIB/PE/POL/REL
Shake Hands with the Devil BL/JO/L/REL/TR
Sister Oakes BL/REL/SM/SO
Sojourner Truth BL/F/HIB/PE/REL/RM
South Pacific BL/MI/RM/SX/TRP/W
South Pacific M/MI/RM/TRP/W
Strange Fruit BL/CR/RM/SM/SO/SX
These Tender Mercies BL/CR/F/REL/RM/SM/SO/SX
Tin Top Valley BL/CR/F/FS/SO/YO
Trial by Fire BL/CR/F/RR
Trouble in July BL/CR/POL/SM/SO
Walk Hard BL/F/GA/RM/SPT
Wedding in Japan MI/OR/RM/TR
Young American, A BL/F/MU

Religion

Anne of the Thousand Days HIB/MA/PE/POL/SX/TR/V
Another Part of the Forest BL/BS/F/MA/ME/PE/PS/RM/SO/SX
Apology BS/F/FA/PE/RM/SM/W
Armor of Light BI/PE
Autumn Hill CR/LE/RM/RR
Battle for Heaven HIB/OA
Beautiful People, The F/MU/YO
Boyd's Daughter IR/RM
Building 222 HO/ME/MI/W
Burning Bush, The GE/JE/L/PE/TR
Cabin in the Sky M/BL/DE/FA/GA/MA/RR/SO
Career Angel FA/SO/YO
City of Kings BL/MD/PE/RC
Clash by Night CR/MA/RM/SX
Cocktail Party, The BR/FI/MA/SX/V
Comes the Revelation PE/RR/SX
Crime and Punishment AL/BH/BR/CR/F/ME/PE/PS
Dark of the Moon FA/RM/RR/SO/SX
Day Will Come, The FA/JE/ME/MI/POL/W
Dear Judas BI/PE/POL
Deliver Us from Evil CR/DE/FA/PE/RM
Design for a Stained Glass Window HIB/PE
Distant City, The CR/F/PN/PS/RM/SX
Dr. Herzl HIB/JE/JO/PO/YL
Down to Miami BS/F/HT/MI/RM/SO
Earth Journey CH/FA/OR/RM
Eastward in Eden LIB/PE/RM
Embezzled Heaven CR/PE
Ester'ke JE/PE/POL/RM/SX/YL
Family Reunion, The F/ME/OA/V
Fifth Horseman, The FA/SX/W
Flag Is Born, A FA/JE/OA/PE/POL
Fledgling CR/F/IL/LT/ME/SX
Flies, The CR/F/FR/PE
Flowers of Virtue, The CR/IL/L/LT/MEX/MI/POL/RM
Galileo F/GE/HIB/PE/POL/SC
Great Big Doorstep, The F/RM/RR/SO/YO
Great Campaign, The POL/RR
Happily Ever After JO/MA/POL/RM/SM
Henri Christophe BL/PE/POL/TRP
Herschel the Jester M/JE/PE/RM/YL
Hoboes in Heaven AL/BA/DE/FA/FL

Home of the Brave JE/ME/MI/TRP/W
Homecoming F/FA/SO/W
It's a Gift F/LE/PE/RM/S/SM/SX/YO
Jenny Kissed Me RM/YO
Joan of Lorraine HIB/PE/PN/POL/TH/TR
Journey to Jerusalem BI/PE/POL
Jupiter Laughs BR/MD/RM/SC/SX
Kathleen F/IR/MD/RM/SX/YO
Korb'n F/JE/L/POL/RM
Lady of Fatima FA/PE/YO
Lamp at Midnight HIB/PE/POL/SC
Lily of the Valley CR/DE/FA/PS
Linden Tree, The BR/BS/F/MA/MD/MU/OA/SC/UN/YO
Long Way from Home, A AL/BL/CR/GA/MA/SO/SX
Magdalena L/MI/PE/POL/RM
Magnolia Alley BH/MA/PS/SO/SPT/SX
Man's House, A BI/BR/F/IN/JE/PE/RM
Mary of Magdalena BI/PE/RM
Me and Molly BS/F/JE/MA/MU/RM/S/YO
Men to the Sea BH/BL/MA/ME/MI/SE/SX/W
Mexican Mural FA/IN/MEX/POL/PS/RM/SX
Miracle in the Mountains CR/FA/PE/POL/SX/TR
Mr. Peebles and Mr. Hooker BL/L/RC/RR/SM/SO/SX
Mr. Sycamore FA/LT/MA/SM
Moon Vine, The CR/PE/RM/SM/SO/TH/YO
My Romance M/MU/PE/RM
Natural Man BL/CR/FA/GA/L/PE/PN/RC/SO
Night Watch in Syria BI/PE/REL
Nineteenth Hole of Europe, The IR/LT/POL/PS/RM/SX/W
Old Foolishness, The F/IR/POL/RM
Out of My House AL/BL/F/LE/SM/WE
Papa Is All F/MA/RM/RR
Playboy of Newark, The BH/GA/MA/SX
Private Life of the Master Race, The F/GE/JE/LA/MA/MI/PN/POL/W
Rose in the Wilderness CR/PE/RM/SX
Sadie Thompson M/MI/PS/SX/TRP
Savonarola HIB/PE/POL
Set My People Free BL/HIB/PE/POL/RC
Seven Mirrors WO
Seventh Trumpet, The POL/RM/W
Shake Hands with the Devil BL/JO/L/POL/RC/TR
Sheppey BR/DE/F/FA/GA/ME/PS
Shylock and His Daughter BS/F/JE/PE/RM/TR/YL
Silver Whistle, The GA/OA/RM/SX
Simon's Wife BI/MA/PE
Sister Oakes BL/RC/SM/SO
Skipper next to God BR/DU/JE/POL/SE
Sojourner Truth BL/F/PE/RC/RM
Solitaire CR/F/FS/YO
Song of Bernadette, The F/FNC/PE
Starlight BL/CR/SX
Storm Operation MI/RM/SX/W
Story for Strangers, A CR/FA/GA/PE/PS/RM/SM
Streets Are Guarded, The AV/MI/W
Strings, My Lord, Are False, The IR/POL/PS/RM/SX/W
Summer and Smoke MD/ME/PS/RM/SM/SO/SX
Suzanna and the Elders PE/POL/RM/SX
Tanyard Street IN/IR/MA/SX/W
Ten Little Indians BR/CR/MY/RM

There Is No End MI/PN/W
These Tender Mercies BL/CR/F/RC/RM/SM/SO/SX
Three Gifts CR/DE/FA/JE/MU/RM/YL
Tinker's Dam DE/FA/JO/MI/NC/RM/SC/W
Too Many Thumbs FA/RM/SC/UN
Tread the Green Grass FA/RR/SO/SX/YO
Velvet Glove, The JO/OA/POL/UN
Vigil, The BI/CR/DE/SM/TR
Way, The S/W
Yosele, the Nightingale JE/LT/MU/PE/RM/YL

Science

And Be My Love F/RM/SX/TH
Any Day Now BS/F/GA/RM
Bravo! ME/RM/TH
Bruno and Sidney AL/RM
Cuckoos on the Hearth CR/LT/ME/MY/RR
Dark Hammock CR/LE/MA/PE/RR/SO
Doctor Social IL/MD/RM
E=MC²
G-II DE/FA/IL/W
Galileo F/GE/HIB/PE/POL/REL
Happiest Years, The F/MA/SM/UN/YO
Horse Fever F/GA/HT/SPT
How I Wonder BL/F/FA/L/RC/UN/W
In Bed We Cry BS/MA/RM/SX/W
Jupiter Laughs BR/MD/REL/RM/SX
Lamp at Midnight HIB/PE/POL/REL
Mr. Adam MA/MI/POL/SX
Sleep No More BS/CR/RM/SX
This Time Tomorrow DE/DU/FA/IL/MD/RM
Tinker's Dam DE/FA/JO/MI/NC/REL/RM/W
Tomorrow the World F/JE/POL/W
Too Many Thumbs FA/REL/RM/UN
Town House BS/F/JO/MA/YO
Traitor, The MI/POL
Vickie MA/MI/SX/W/WO
Wanhope Building, The BA/BC/FA/POL/RM

Show Business

Plays about persons and activities concerned with the various worlds of show business, from songwriting to performing, exclusive of the legitimate stage, for which see "Theatre." Nightclub entertainment, vaudeville, burlesque, carnivals, musical theatre, and dance are among the worlds explored. For circus life, see "Circus." See also "Music."

"Almost Faithful" BL/FA/MA/SX
Annie Get Your Gun M/HIB/PE/RM/WE
Are You with It? M/BA/BH/RM/SX
Beat the Band M/HT/NC/RM
Biggest Thief in Town, The AL/DE/F/JO/RM/SM
Billion Dollar Baby M/CR/NC/PE/RM/SX
Bird Cage, The AL/BS/CR/F/MA/NC/RM/SX
Common Ground JE/JO/MI/POL
Dancer, The A/AL/CR/F/FNC/HO/ME/PS
Follow the Girls M/MI/RM/W
High Kickers M/HT/LE/RM/TR

Hold on to Your Hats M/BC/CR/RM/WE
Johnny 2 X 4 CR/MU/NC/PS
Look, Ma, I'm Dancin' M/LE/RM
Love Goes to Press JO/MI/RM/SX/W/WO
Love Is No Heaven CR/MA/SM/SX/W
Love Life M/BS/F/FA/MA/PE/POL/TR/WO/YO
Lovely Me F/HT/RM/YO
Memphis Bound! M/BL/RM/TR
Naked Genius, The CR/LT/RM/SX
New Life, A AV/BS/F/MA/MD/POL/W
Owl and the Pussycat, The PE/POL/PS
Pal Joey M/NC/RM/SX
Pirate, The AD/PE/RM/TRP
Rat Race, The BH/CR/MU/RM
Shoemaker's Prodigious Wife, The MA/SP
Something for the Boys M/AV/LE/MI/RM/W/WE
Strip for Action MI/RM/SX
Sunny River M/MA/PE/POL/RM
What Big Ears! FI/GA/HT
You'll See Stars M/HIB/PE

Spiritualism

Plays about psychic phenomena, mediums, séances, and the like.

Blithe Spirit BR/DE/FA/LT/MA/SX
Medium, The M/CR/DE/F/ME/RM

Sports

Horse racing, boxing, bullfighting, baseball, and football are among the sports that figure in the plays listed.

Banjo Eyes M/BA/FA/GA
Carmen Jones M/BL/CR/MI/RM/SO/SX/W
Days of Our Youth, The POL/RM/SX/UN/YO
Early to Bed M/PS/RM/S/SX/TRP/YO
High Button Shoes M/BS/CR/GA/PE/UN/YO
Horse Fever
I Gotta Get Out GA/RM
Life of Reilly, The CR/GA/HT*Magnolia Alley* BH/MA/PS/REL/SO/SX
Man Who Had All the Luck, The BS/F/RM/SM
Me and Harry CR/ME/RM
Mexican Hayride M/CR/GA/HT/MEX/RM
My Sister Eileen A/F/JO/LT/MI/PS/RM/SX/TH
Nine Girls CR/MD/POL/TH/UN/WE/WO/YO
Odds on Mrs. Oakley, The GA/JO/MA/SX
St. Louis Woman M/BL/GA/PE/RM/SX
Sun Field, The JO/MA/RM/SPT/SX
They Should Have Stood in Bed GA/RM/SX
Toplitzky of Notre Dame M/FA/JE/RM
Walk Hard BL/F/GA/RC/RM
Wonderful Journey CR/DE/FA/RM

Theatre

Plays about the people and life of the legitimate theatre. See also "Circus," "Music," and "Show Business."

And Be My Love F/RM/SC/SX
Arsenic and Old Lace CR/ME/OA/RM
Bravo! ME/RM/SC
Café Crown JE/MA/RM
Christopher Blake F/FA/LA/MA/POL/TR/YO
Cue for Passion CR/HT/JO/LT/MA/MY/POL/SX
Dark Eyes FS/RM
Dream Girl BA/FA/JO/LT/MEX/PS/RM/SX/TR
Family Affair, A F/SX
Five Alarm Waltz FI/LT/MA/YO
Flare Path AV/BR/HT/MA/MI/RM/W
Foolish Notion FA/MA/MI/RM/W/YO
For Heaven's Sake, Mother! F/JE/MA/SX
For Love or Money RM/SX
French Touch, The FNC/MA/POL
George Washington Slept Here F/LA/LE/RM/RR/YO
Gypsy Lady M/PE/RM
Heart of a City AL/MI/RM/W
Inside Story F/JO/MI/RM/W/YO
Jason MA/SX
Joan of Lorraine HIB/PE/PN/POL/REL/TR
Kiss Me, Kate M/CR/GA/MA/PE
Lady, Behave! ME/RM/SX
Leading Lady, The MA/PE/RM
Light Up the Sky HT/MA
Little Darling F/LT/RM/SX
Lovers and Friends BR/F/MA/MI/RM
Make Yourself at Home RM
Marriage Is for Single People F/FI/NC/RM
Mermaids Singing, The BA/F/HT/MI/RM/SX
Mr. Big CR/MY/POL/RM
Mrs. Kimball Presents CR/RM
Montserrat A/FR/MI/PE/POL/SX/YO
Moon Vine, The CR/PE/REL/RM/SM/SO/YO
My Dear Public M/BS/RM
My Sister Eileen A/F/JO/LT/MI/PS/RM/SPT/SX
Nine Girls CR/MD/POL/SPT/UN/WE/WO/YO
Oh, Mr. Meadowbrook! MA/RM/SX
Old Lady Says "No!," The FA/HIB/IR/PE/POL
Out of the Frying Pan MA/POL
Overtons, The GA/MA/SX
Oy, Is Dus a Leben! M/HIB/JE/YL
Present Laughter BS/RM/SX
Rape of the Sabine Women, The GEL
Return Engagement F/RM
Round Trip F/MA/RM/SM/SX/YO
Second Best Bed LIB/MA/PE
Shylock '47 HEL/JE/PE/TH
Slice It Thin! F/JO/MI/SM/YO
Spring Production MA/SX
Strange Play, A MA/SX
Theatre F/MA/SX
Under the Counter M/BR/MI/RM
Voice of the Turtle, The MI/RM/SX/W
Walking Gentleman, The CR/ME/MY/RM
Wandering Stars JE/PE/RM/YL
Where Stars Walk FA/IR/JO/RM
With a Silk Thread F/MA/MD/SX
Years Ago F/MA/PE/RM/SM/YO

Yesterday's Magic AL/BH/BR/F/IN/RM

Trials

Plays in which a courtroom trial is an important part of the plot.

Anne of the Thousand Days HIB/MA/PE/POL/REL/SX/V
Burning Bush, The GE/JE/LA/PE/REL
Christopher Blake F/FA/LA/MA/POL/TH/YO
Criminals, The CR/GE/LA/POL/RM/SX
Dream Girl BA/FA/JO/LT/MEX/PS/RM/SX/TH
Food for Midas BS
High Kickers M/HT/LE/RM/SH
Joan of Lorraine HIB/PE/PN/POL/REL/TH
Johnny Belinda CR/IN/MD/RM/RR/SX
Lost in the Stars M/BL/CR/PN/POL/RC/REL/SX
Love Life M/BS/F/FA/MA/PE/POL/SH/WO/YO
Madwoman of Chaillot, The BS/FA/FR/ME/POL
Manhattan Nocturne LT/M/ME/PS/SX
Memphis Bound! M/BL/RM/SH
Miracle in the Mountains CR/FA/PE/POL/REL/SX
Native Son BL/CR/F/JO/LA/PN/POL/RC/RM
Pick-up Girl CR/F/IL/MU/PS/RM/SX/YO
Scapegoat, The CR/FA/LA/RM
Seeds in the Wind POL/W/YO
Shake Hands with the Devil BL/JO/L/POL/RC/REL
Shylock and His Daughter BS/F/JE/PE/REL/RM/YL
Signature CR/LA/LE/PE/RM/RR/SO
Song of the Dniepper CR/JE/PE/PN/POL/YL
Story of Mary Surratt, The BH/CR/HIB/LA/PE/PN/POL
Uniform of Flesh CR/LA/MI/PE/SE/V
Vigil, The BI/CR/DE/REL/SM
Wedding in Japan MI/OR/RC/RM
Winners and Losers MI/POL
Winslow Boy, The BR/F/L/LA/PE/POL/S/WO/YO

War

War plays included here are mostly concerned with the behavior of people in actual or potential wartime situations, but some treat of a war's effect on postwar life. All periods of history are represented, but there are many plays here that deal with World War II, which was contemporaneous with the decade. See also "Military."

All Men Are Alike BR/MA/MI/SX
All My Sons BS/CR/F/MA/SM
Apology BS/F/FA/PE/REL/RM/SM
Arms and the Girl M/MI/PE/RM
Assassin, The CR/MI/PN/POL/RM
At War with the Army MI/RM/SX
Barber Had Two Sons, The A/CR/F/POL/RM/SX
Bathsheba BI/MI/PE/SX
Bell for Adano, A MI/POL/RM
Bloomer Girl M/BL/BS/F/HIB/PE/POL/RC/RM/SM/SO/WO
Broken Journey BC/JO/RM
Building 222 HO/ME/MI/REL
By Jupiter M/MA/MI/PE/RM/SX
Candle in the Wind FI/FNC/JO/MI/PN/RM
Carmen Jones M/BL/CR/MI/RM/SO/SPT/SX

Catherine Was Great MI/PE/POL/SX
Command Decision AV/MI/POL
Count Me In M/F/MI
Counterattack MI/POL/RSN/SX
Day Will Come, The FA/JE/ME/MI/POL/REL
Dear Ruth F/MI/POL/RM/YO
Decision BL/CR/JO/L/MI/POL/RC/RM/SM/SX
Delicate Story HU/MA/MI/RM/SX
Derryowen BA/GA/IR/JO/POL/RM
Dog beneath the Skin, The AD/BR/DRG/FA/HT/IL/ME/POL/PS/RM/V
Doughgirls, The HT/MI/POL/RM/SX
Eve of St. Mark, The F/FA/GA/IL/MI/RM/RR/SX/TRP
Family, The AL/BH/CH/F/OR/POL/RM
Fifth Horseman, The FA/REL/SX
Fifty AV/MI/RM
Flare Path AV/BR/HT/MA/MI/RM/TH
Flight to the West AV/F/JE/JO/MA/POL
Follow the Girls M/MI/RM/SH
Foolish Notion FA/MA/MI/RM/TH/YO
Forward the Heart BL/F/IN/RC/RM
Foxhole in the Parlor A/FS/ME/MU/POL/RM/SX
G-II DE/FA/IL/SC
God Strikes Back F/IN/MI/POL
Golden Falcon, The AD/PE/POL
Golden Wings AV/MI/POL/RM/SX
Good Morning, Corporal MA/MI/SX
Harriet BL/F/LIB/MA/PE/POL/RM
Hasty Heart, The DE/FS/IL/MI/RM/TRP
Heart of a City AL/MI/RM/TH
Home Is the Hero MA
Home Is the Hunter BL/BS/CR/L/MA/POL
Home of the Brave JE/ME/MI/REL/TRP
Homecoming F/FA/REL/SO
Hope for the Best JO/POL/RM
How I Wonder BL/F/FA/L/RC/SC/UN
I'll Take the High Road BS/F/FI/POL/RM/SM
In Bed We Cry BS/MA/RM/SC/SX
In Time to Come FNC/HIB/PE/POL
Inside Story F/JO/MI/RM/TH/YO
Jackpot GA/MI/RM
Jacobowsky and the Colonel GE/JE/MI/POL/RM
Janie F/JO/MI/RM/SM/YO
Johnny Doodle FA/PE/POL
Kiss and Tell F/MD/MI/RM/SX/YO
Kiss Them for Me AV/BS/HT/MD/MI/RM/SX
Land Is Bright, The BS/CR/F/MI/OA/PE/POL/RM/YO
Land of Fame MI/POL/RM
Last Generation, The F/POL
Let's Face It M/MA/MI/RM/SX
Letters to Lucerne FS/RM/S/YO
Lifeline BR/SE
Love Goes to Press JO/MI/RM/SX/SH/WO
Love Is No Heaven CR/MA/SH/SM/SX
Lower North BA/MA/MI/S/SX
Man with Blond Hair, The CR/JE/POL
Men in Shadow AV/BR/MI
Men to the Sea BH/BL/MA/ME/MI/REL/SE/SX
Minstrel Boy, The LIB/OA/PE/POL/RM
Mister Roberts MI/SE

Moment Musical MA/MI/RM/SX
Moon Is Down, The MI/POL/SX
Morning Star, The BR/LT/MA/MD/SX
My Fair Ladies BS/RM
New Life, A AV/BS/F/MA/MD/POL/SH
Nights of Wrath FR/POL
Nineteenth Hole of Europe, The IR/LT/POL/REL/PS/RM/SX
Now I Lay Me Down to Sleep RM/SE/SX
O'Daniel JO/MI/POL/RM
On the Seventh Day BC/F/FA/JO/ME
Out of the Picture A/BR/POL/RM
Outside the Door DE/FA/GE/MI
Over 21 AV/FI/JO/LT/MA/MI
Plan M IL/MI/POL
Polonaise M/HIB/MI/PE/POL/RM
Private Life of the Master Race, The F/GE/JE/LA/MA/MI/PN/POL/REL
Proof thro' the Night DRG/HO/POL/TRP/WO
Rugged Path, The BS/JO/MA/MI/POL/SE/TRP
Russian People, The MA/POL/RM/RSN
Ryan Girl, The CR/F/MA/MI
Searching Wind, The F/FNC/HT/JO/MI/PE/POL/RM/SX
Seeds in the Wind POL/TR/YO
Seventh Trumpet, The POL/REL/RM
Sing Out, Sweet Land! M/FA/MU/PE/RM/WE
Skin of Our Teeth, The F/FA/MA/PE/SX/YO
Skydrift AV/DE/FA/MI
Snafu CR/F/MI/POL/RM/SX/YO
Soldier's Wife JO/LT/MA/MI/SX
Something for the Boys M/AV/LE/MI/RM/SH/WE
Sons and Soldiers AL/F/FA/MA/MD/PE/RM/SX
Sound of Hunting MI
South Pacific BL/MI/RC/RM/SX/TRP
South Pacific M/MI/RC/RM/TRP
Star Spangled Family F/MA/ME/YO
Storm Operation MI/REL/RM/SX
Streets Are Guarded, The AV/MI/REL
Strings, My Lord, Are False, The IR/POL/PS/REL/RM/SX
Sundown Beach MA/ME/MI/RM/SX
Survivors, The F/HT/PE/RR/WE
Tanyard Street IN/IR/MA/REL/SX
Thank You, Svoboda MI/PN/POL/RM
There Is No End MI/PN/REL
These Hills Are Scarred F
Those Endearing Young Charms AV/F/HT/RM/SX
This Rock F/RM/YO
Tinker's Dam DE/FA/JO/MI/NC/REL/RM/SC
Tomorrow the World F/JE/POL/SC
Under This Roof BS/MA/PE/POL/RM/RR
Up the Rebels! F/MI/PE/POL/RM
Vickie MA/MI/SC/SX/WO
Victors, The FR/POL/SX/YO
Voice of Israel, The F/JE/JO/MI/POL/YL
Victory Belles F/MI/RM/SX
Voice of the Turtle, The MI/RM/SX/TH
War and Peace F/MA/PE/RM
War President HIB/MI/PE/POL
Watch on the Rhine F/MA/POL/RM
Way, The REL/S
What's Up? M/AV/IL/OR/POL/RM/S/YO

When Differences Disappear
While the Sun Shines BR/GA/MI/RM
Wind Is Ninety, The AV/DE/F/FA/MA/W/YO
Winged Victory AV/F/FS/HT/MA/MI/RM/SM/TRP
Winter Soldiers BC/MI/POL/PS
Without Love MA/POL/RM/SX
Wookey, The F/POL/RM/SE
World's Full of Girls, The F/MI/RM/SX
Yankee Point F/MA/POL
Years Between, The A/BS/F/LT/MI/RM/SM/SX
Yes Is for a Very Young Man FNC/POL

Women

Plays that deal primarily with female characters or with feminist issues.

Anne of England BR/HIB/PE/POL
As the Girls Go M/F/MA/POL/SX
Bloomer Girl M/BL/BS/F/HIB/PE/POL/RC/RM/SM/SO/W
Doctors Disagree IL/MD/RM/SX
Don't Listen, Ladies A/BS/FR/MA/SX
House of Bernarda Alba, The F/RM/SP/SX
Love Goes to Press JO/MI/RM/SH/SX/W
Love Life M/BS/F/FA/MA/PE/POL/SH/TR/YO
Make Way for Lucia PE
Nine Girls CR/MD/POL/SPT/TH/UN/WE/YO
Proof thro' the Night DRG/HO/POL/TRP/W
Seven Mirrors REL
Strange Bedfellows F/MA/PE/POL/PS/SX
Sweet Charity DRG
Vickie MA/MI/SC/SX/W
Winslow Boy, The BR/F/L/LA/PE/POL/S/TR/YO

Youth

Plays in which children or adolescents figure importantly.

All in Favor RM/SX
Arlene MI/RM/SX
Barefoot Boy with Cheek M/POL/RM/SX/UN
Beautiful People, The F/MU/REL
Best Foot Forward M/FI/RM/S
Boy Who Lived Twice, A DE/F/FA/RM
Bright Boy CR/POL/RM/S
Brooklyn Biarritz A/CR/F/JE/RM/SX
Career Angel FA/REL/SO
Christopher Blake F/FA/LA/MA/POL/TH/TR
Come Back, Little Sheba AL/MA/SX
Corn Is Green, The BR/S/SX
Day of Judgment, The JE/MU/PE/RM/YL
Days of Our Youth, The POL/RM/SPT/SX/UN
Dear Ruth F/MI/POL/RM/W
Druid Circle, The MA/PE/RM/SX/UN
Early to Bed M/PS/RM/S/SPT/SX/TRP
Enchanted, The FA/DE/FR/POL/RM/YO
First Crocus, The CR/F/RM/SM
First Wife, The CH/F/JO/MA/OR/POL
Five Alarm Waltz FI/LT/MA/TH
Foolish Notion FA/MA/MI/RM/TH/W

For Keeps F/RM/SX
George Washington Slept Here F/LA/LE/RM/RR/TH
Good Neighbor CR/F/IN/JE/MA/RM
Goodbye, My Fancy JO/POL/RM/UN
Great Big Doorstep, The F/REL/RM/RR/SO
Guest in the House A/F/IL/RM/RR
Happiest Years, The F/MA/SC/SM/UN
Happy Days, The AV/FR/RM/SX
Happy Time, The AL/F/MA/PE/RM/OA/SX
Hickory Stick RM/S
High Button Shoes M/BS/CR/GA/PE/SPT/UN
Highland Fling, A AL/DE/FA/GA/RM/SX
Hold It! M/FI/RM/UN
How Long till Summer? AL/BL/CR/FA/LA/POL/RC
I Remember Mama F/IL/IN/LT/PE
Innocent Voyage, The AD/CR/ME/PE/SE/SX
Innocents, The DE/FA/MY
Inside Story F/JO/MI/RM/TH/W
It's a Gift F/LE/PE/REL/RM/S/SM/SX
Janie F/JO/MI/RM/SM/W
Jenny Kissed Me REL/RM
Junior Miss F/RM/SX
Kathleen F/IR/MD/REL/RM/SX
Kiss and Tell F/MD/MI/RM/SX/W
Lady of Fatima FA/PE/REL
Lady Who Came to Stay, The DE/F/ME/MY/RM/SX
Land Is Bright, The BS/CR/F/MI/OA/PE/POL/RM/W
Late George Apley, The F/PE/RM
Letters to Lucerne FS/RM/S/W
Life with Mother BS/F/MA/PE/RM
Linden Tree, The BR/BS/F/MA/MD/MU/OA/REL/SC/UN
Listen, Professor! F/RM/RSN
Little Dark Horse BL/F/FR/IL/RC/SX
Love Life M/BS/F/FA/MA/PE/POL/SH/TR/WO
Love on Leave F/GA/HT/SCF/HT/MI/RM/SX
Me and Molly BS/F/JE/MA/MU/REL/RM/S
Member of the Wedding, The BL/F/RR/SO
Montserrat A/FR/MI/PE/POL/SX/TH
Moon Vine, The CR/PE/REL/RM/SM/SO/TH
Next Half Hour, The DE/F/FA/PE/SX
Nine Girls CR/MD/POL/SPT/TH/UN/WE/WO
O Mistress Mine BR/F/POL/RM/SX
Panama Hattie M/MI/POL/PS/RM/SX/TRP
Parlor Story JO/MA/POL/SX/UN
Perfect Marriage, The JO/LA/MA/SX
Pick-up Girl CR/F/IL/MU/PS/RM/SX/TR
Popsy F/MA/RM/SM
Pretty Little Parlor AL/F/MA/PE/SM/SX
Rich Full Life, The F/IL/MA/RM/SM
Round Trip F/MA/RM/SM/SX/TH
Secret Room, The CR/ME/SX
Seeds in the Wind POL/TR/W
Skin of Our Teeth, The F/FA/MA/PE/SX/W
Slice It Thin! F/JO/MI/SM/TH
Slightly Married F/MA/MI/SX/SM
Snafu CR/F/MI/POL/RM/SX/W
Solitaire CR/F/FS/REL
Star Spangled Family F/MA/ME/W
Swan Song CR/ME/MU

Sweet Genevieve MA/MD/PE/SX
Take It As It Comes BC/CR/DRG/F/JO/MA/POL/SM
Talley Method, The F/LT/MD/POL/RM
This Rock F/RM/W
Tin Top Valley BL/CR/F/FS/RC/SO
Too Hot for Maneuvers MI/RM/S/SX
Town House BS/F/JO/MA/SC
Tread the Green Grass FA/REL/RR/SO/SX
Trio HO/LT/RM/UN
Victors, The FR/POL/SX/W
Violet A/F/RM/RR
Visitor, The CR/F/LE/MY/SM
Wallflower F/POL/RM/SX
Walrus and the Carpenter, The F/MA/RM
What's Up? M/AV/IL/OR/POL/RM/S/W
Where's Charley? M/PE/RM/UN
Wind Is Ninety, The AV/DE/F/FA/MA/W
Winslow Boy, The BR/F/L/LA/PE/POL/S/TR/WO
Years Ago F/MA/PE/RM/SM/TH
Young and Fair, The CR/ME/S
Young Man's Fancy, A RM/RR/SX
Your Loving Son F/MA/RM/SX

BACKGROUND LOCALES

Playwrights of the period were particularly fond of certain environments for the setting of their plays. The most common of them are categorized in the listings that follow. Among them is a group of listings for plays set (wholly or partly) in foreign nations; such plays are either American or British. Although English-language plays of the era were set in many far-flung locales, those most frequently employed were China and France. Among specific, nonnational settings, the most popular were barrooms, boarding houses, hotels, nightclubs, prisons, schools, and universities. More general backgrounds used frequently were rural areas (in cabins, on farms and ranches, in the mountains, and so on), ships at sea, American small towns, tropical climes, and the American South and West.

China

Earth Journey FA/OR/REL/RM
Family, The AL/BH/F/OR/POL/RM/W
First Wife, The F/JO/MA/OR/POL/YO
Lady Says Yes, A M/FA/MI/PE/SX
Lute Song M/F/MA/OR/PE
Yours Is My Heart OR/PN/RM

France

Candle in the Wind FI/JO/MI/PN/RM
Dancer, The AL/AL/CR/F/HO/ME/PS/SH
Deputy of Paris, The HIB/PE/POL
Duke in Darkness, The BR/ME/PE/POL/PN
French Touch, The MA/POL/TH
Gentlemen Prefer Blondes M/HT/PE/RM/SE
House in Paris, The A/PE/RM/SX
In Time to Come HIB/PE/POL/W
Miss Liberty M/A/HT/JO/PE/RM/SE
Searching Wind, The F/HT/JO/MI/PE/POL/RM/SX/W
Song of Bernadette, The F/PE/REL
Two Mrs. Carrolls, The A/BR/CR/MA/MY/RM

Yes Is for a Very Young Man POL/W

Mexico

Cat Screams, The CR/DE/DRG/LT/MY/RM/SX
Dunnigan's Daughter A/BS/MA/PL/RM
Dream Girl BA/FA/JO/LT/PS/RM/SX/TH/TR
Flowers of Virtue CR/IL/L/LT/MI/OL/REL/RM
Mexican Hayride M/CR/GA/HT/RM/SPT
Mexican Mural FA/IN/POL/REL/PS/RM/SX

Barrooms

Are You with It? M/BH/RM/SX/SH
Banjo Eyes M/FA/GA/SPT
Brigadoon M/FA/PE/RM
Derryowen GA/IR/JO/POL/RM/W
Dream Girl FA/JO/LT/MEX/PS/RM/SX/TH/TR
Happy Birthday AL/RM
Hoboes in Heaven AL/DE/FA/FL/REL
Iceman Cometh, The AL/CR/JO/ME/PE/POL/PS
Lower North MA/MI/S/SX/W
Mermaids Singing, The F/HT/MI/RM/SX/TH
Nellie Bly M/AD/JO/PE/RM
Wanhope Building, The BC/FA/POL/RM/SC

Boarding Houses

Are You with It? M/BA/RM/SH/SX
Chicken Every Sunday BS/F/MA/PE/RM/SX/W
Crime and Punishment AL/BR/CR/F/ME/PE/PS/REL
Family, The AL/CH/F/OR/POL/RM/W
First Stop to Heaven LT/MA/RM
Hand in Glove CR/ME/MY/SX
Magnolia Alley MA/PS/REL/SO/SPT/SX
Men to the Sea BL/MA/ME/MI/REL/SE/SX/W
One Touch of Venus M/A/CR/FA/HT/PN/RM/SX
Playboy of Newark, The GA/MA/REL/SX
Rat Race, The CR/MU/RM/SH
Story of Mary Surratt, The CR/HIB/LA/PE/PN/POL/TR
Yesterday's Magic AL/BR/F/IN/RM/TH

Hotels

Beat the Band M/NC/RM/SH
Big Two, The JE/JO/MI/MY/POL/RM
Clutterbuck BR/MA/SE/SX/TRP
Cue for Passion CR/JO/LT/MA/MY/POL/SX/TH
Death of a Salesman BS/F/MA/ME/SX
Dog beneath the Skin, The AD/BR/DRG/FA/IL/ME/POL/PS/RM/V/W
Doughgirls, The MI/POL/RM/SX/W
Down to Miami BS/F/MI/REL/RM/SO
Flare Path AV/BR/MA/MI/RM/TH/W
Gentlemen Prefer Blondes M/FNC/PE/RM/SE
High Kickers M/LE/RM/SH/TR
Horse Fever F/GA/SC/SPT
John Loves Mary FS/MA/MI/POL/RM
Kiss Them for Me AV/BS/MD/MI/RM/SX/W
Lady Comes Across, The M/AD/FA/RM

Land's End FS/RM/SX
Life of Reilly, The CR/GA/SPT
Light Up the Sky MA/TH
Love on Leave F/GA/HT/SCF/MI/RM/SX/YO
Lovely Me F/RM/SH/YO
Made in Heaven! MA/SX
Mermaids Singing, The BA/F/MI/RM/SX/TH
Mexican Hayride M/CR/GA/MEX/RM/SPT
Miss Liberty M/A/FNC/JO/PE/RM/SE
Mr. Barry's Etchings A/CR/JO/POL/RM
Mr. Strauss Goes to Boston M/MA/MU/PE/POL/RM
No Exit DE/FA/FR/HO/JO/POL/RM/SX
One Touch of Venus M/A/BH/CR/FA/PN/RM/SX
Ramshackle Inn CR/MY/SM
Searching Wind, The F/FNC/JO/MI/PE/POL/RM/SX/W
Spring Again BC/BS/FI/RM
State of the Union BS/JO/MA/POL/SX
Survivors, The F/PE/RR/W/WE
Those Endearing Young Charms AV/F/RM/SX/W
Trial Honeymoon MA/SX
Up in Central Park M/JO/MU/PE/POL/RM
What Big Ears! F/GA/SH
Winged Victory AV/F/FS/MA/MI/RM/SM/TRP/W
Woman Bites Dog JO/POL/RM/SM

Nightclubs

Beat the Band M/HT/RM/SH
Beggars Are Coming to Town BS/CR/RM
Billion Dollar Baby M/CR/PE/RM/SH/SX
Bird Cage, The AL/BS/CR/F/MA/RM/SH/SX
Johnny 2 X 4 CR/MU/PS/SH
Marriage Is for Single People F/FI/RM/TH
Pal Joey M/RM/SH/SX
Tinker's Dam DE/FA/JO/MI/REL/RM/SC/W

Prisons

All You Need Is One Good Break F/GA/IL/JE/ME/RM
Assassin, The CR/MI/POL/RM/W
Beggar's Holiday M/BL/CR/POL/PS/RM/SX
Brooklyn, U.S.A. CR/L/RM
Candle in the Wind FI/FNC/JO/MI/RM/W
Distant City, The CR/F/PS/REL/RM/SX
Duke in Darkness, The BR/FNC/ME/PE/POL
Flamingo Road JO/POL/PS/RM/SO/SX
Heaven on Earth M/FA/RM
Joan of Lorraine HIB/PE/POL/REL/TH/TR
Lost in the Stars M/BL/CR/POL/RC/REL/SX/TR
Native Son BL/CR/F/JO/LA/POL/RC/RM/TR
Natural Man BL/CR/FA/GA/L/PE/RC/REL/SO
One Touch of Venus M/A/BH/CR/FA/HT/RM/SX
Private Life of the Master Race, The F/GE/JE/LA/MA/MI/POL/REL/W
Song of the Dniepper CR/JE/PE/POL/TR/YL
Story of Mary Surratt, The BH/CR/HIB/LA/PE/POL/TR
Thank You, Svoboda MI/POL/RM/W
That Lady PE/POL/RM
There Is No End MI/REL/W
Uncle Harry CR/F/LE/MY/PE/SM

Yours Is My Heart CH/OR/RM

Schools

Elementary through high-school levels are represented.

Best Foot Forward M/FI/RM/YO
Bright Boy CR/POL/RM/YO
Corn Is Green, The BR/SX/YO
Deep Are the Roots BL/CR/F/POL/RC/RM/SM/SO
Early to Bed M/PS/RM/SPT/SX/TRP/YO
Hickory Stick RM/YO
It's a Gift F/LE/PE/REL/RM/SM/SX/YO
Letters to Lucerne FS/RM/W/YO
Lower North BA/MA/MI/SX/W
Me and Molly BS/F/JE/MA/MU/REL/RM/YO
Rats of Norway, The AL/BR/HO/RM/SX
School for Brides, The BS/MA/RM/SX
Temporary Island, A CI/PE/RM/SX
Too Hot for Maneuvers MI/RM/SX/YO
Way, The REL/W
What's Up? M/AV/IL/OR/POL/RM/W/YO
Winslow Boy, The BR/F/L/LA/PE/POL/TR/WO/YO
Young and Fair, The CR/ME/YO

Universities

Barefoot Boy with Cheek M/POL/RM/SX/YO
Day before Spring, The M/LT/MA/RM
Days of Our Youth, The POL/RM/SPT/SX/YO
Druid Circle, The MA/PE/RM/SX/YO
Goodbye, My Fancy JO/POL/RM/YO
Happiest Years, The F/MA/SC/SM/YO
High Button Shoes M/BS/CR/GA/PE/SPT/YO
Hold It! M/FI/RM/YO
How I Wonder BL/F/FA/L/RC/SC/W
Linden Tree, The BR/BS/F/MA/MD/MU/OA/REL/SC/YO
Nine Girls CR/MD/POL/SPT/TH/WE/WO/YO
Parlor Story JO/MA/POL/SX/YO
Respectfully Yours F/LT/MA/PE
Tenting Tonight F/GA/MA/RM/SM
Too Many Thumbs FA/REL/RM/SC
Trio HO/LT/RM/YO
Velvet Glove, The JO/OA/POL/REL
Where's Charley? M/PE/RM/YO

Rural

This list is restricted to American plays. It includes plays set wholly or partly in rural environments, including country homes.

Apple of His Eye RM
As We Forgive Our Debtors F/LE/SX
Autumn Hill CR/LE/REL/RM
Cabin in the Sky M/BL/DE/FA/GA/MA/REL/SO
Chaff AU/CR/MA/SX
Claudia F/IL/MA/SX
Cock-a-Doodle-Do FA/RM/SX
Comes the Revelation PE/REL/SX

Cream in the Well, The AL/F/RM/SX/WE
Cuckoos on the Hearth CR/LT/ME/MY/SC
Dark Hammock CR/LE/MA/PE/SC/SO
Dark of the Moon FA/REL/RM/SX/SO
Eve of St. Mark, The F/FA/GA/IL/MI/RM/SX/TRP/W
Finian's Rainbow M/BL/F/FA/L/POL/RC/RM/SO
First Million, The CR/F/SX
Garden of Time BL/FA/PE
George Washington Slept Here F/LA/LE/RM/TH/YO
Great Big Doorstep, The F/REL/RM/SO/YO
Great Campaign, The POL/REL
Guest in the House A/F/IL/RM/YO
Gypsy Lady M/PE/RM/TH
Harvest of Years AL/F/MA/RM/WE
Hope for a Harvest RC/RM/WE
January Thaw F/LE/SX
Johnny Belinda CR/IN/MD/RM/SX/TR
Leaf and Bough AL/F/RM/SM/SX
Live Life Again DE/F/FA/P/RM/SM/V
Maid in the Ozarks A/RM/SO/SX
Member of the Wedding, The BL/F/SO/YO
Men We Marry, The LT/MA/RM
Mr. Peebles and Mr. Hooker BL/L/RC/REL/SM/SO/SX
Oklahoma! M/RM/SX/WE
Our Lan' BL/PE/POL/RC/RM/SO
Papa Is All F/MA/REL/RM
Signature CR/LA/LE/PE/RM/SO/TR
Sophie F/MI/RM/SM/SX
Survivors, The F/HT/PE/W/WE
Tread the Green Grass FA/REL/SO/SX/YO
Trial by Fire BL/CR/F/RC
Under This Roof BS/MA/PE/POL/RM/W
Violet A/F/RM/YO
Virginia Reel AL/F/PS/SO
Wisteria Trees, The BL/BS/F/PE/RM/SO
Young Man's Fancy, A RM/SX/YO

Sea

Plays that deal with seafaring characters or that take place, to some extent, on boats or ships.

Around the World M/AD/GA/PE
Clutterbuck BR/HT/MA/SX/TRP
Gentlemen Prefer Blondes M/FNC/HT/PE/RM
Innocent Voyage, The AD/CR/ME/PE/SX/YO
Lifeline BR/W
Longitude 49 BL/CR
Men to the Sea BH/BL/MA/ME/MI/REL/SX/W
Miss Liberty M/A/FNC/HT/JO/PE/RM
Mister Roberts MI/W
Now I Lay Me Down to Sleep RM/SX/W
Rugged Path, The BS/JO/MA/MI/POL/TRP/W
Skipper next to God BR/DU/JE/POL/REL
Uniform of Flesh CR/LA/MI/PE/TR/V
Wookey, The F/POL/RM/W

Small Town

Alice in Arms MI/RM/SX
All My Sons BS/CR/F/MA/W
Allegro M/F/MA/MD/RM/SX
Anna Lucasta AL/BL/F/PS
Apology BS/F/FA/PE/REL/RM/W
Biggest Thief in Town, The AL/DE/F/JO/RM/SH
Bloomer Girl M/BL/BS/F/HIB/PE/POL/RC/RM/SO/W/WO
--But Not Goodbye BS/DE/F/FA/PE
Carousel M/CR/DE/FA/MA/PE/RM
Decision BL/CR/JO/L/MI/POL/RC/RM/SX/W
Deep Are the Roots BL/CR/F/POL/RC/RM/S/SO
First Crocus, The CR/F/RM/YO
Girl from Nantucket, The M/A/RM
Happiest Years, The F/MA/SC/UN/YO
Happily Ever After JO/MA/POL/REL/RM
I Like It Here F/POL/RM
I'll Take the High Road BS/F/FI/POL/RM/W
It's a Gift F/LE/PE/REL/RM/S/SX/YO
Janie F/JO/MI/RM/W/YO
Leaf and Bough AL/F/RM/RR/SX
Little A MA/MU/SX
Live Life Again DE/F/FA/PE/RM/RR/V
Love Is No Heaven CR/MA/SH/SX/W
Man Who Had All the Luck, The BS/F/RM/SPT
Mr. Peebles and Mr. Hooker BL/L/RC/REL/RR/SO/SX
Mr. Sycamore FA/LT/MA/REL
Mrs. January and Mr. X F/POL/RM
Moon Vine, The CR/PE/REL/RM/SO/TH/YO
Only the Heart BL/BS/F/MA/SX
Out of My House AL/BL/F/LE/REL/WE
Place of Our Own, A F/JO/MA/PE/POL
Popsy F/MA/RM/YO
Pretty Little Parlor AL/F/MA/PE/SX/YO
Ramshackle Inn CR/HT/MY
Regina M/BL/BS/CR/F/IL/MA/YO
Rich Full Life, The F/IL/MA/RM/YO
Round Trip F/MA/RM/SX/TH/YO
Sister Oakes BL/RC/REL/SO
Slice It Thin! F/JO/MI/TH/YO
Slightly Married F/MA/MI/SX/YO
Sophie F/MI/RM/RR/SX
Story for Strangers, A CR/FA/GA/PE/PS/REL/RM
Strange Fruit BL/CR/RC/RM/SO/SX
Summer and Smoke MD/ME/PS/REL/RM/SO/SX
Take It As It Comes BC/CR/DRG/F/JO/MA/POL/YO
Tenting Tonight F/GA/MA/RM/UN
Texas Town AL/BL/RM
That Old Devil JO/MA/SX
These Tender Mercies BL/CR/F/RC/REL/RM/SO/SX
This, Too, Shall Pass F/JE/MI/RM
Trouble in July BL/CR/POL/RC/SO
Uncle Harry CR/F/LE/MY/PE/PN
Vigil, The BI/CR/DE/REL/TR
Village Green A/F/POL/RM
Visitor, The CR/F/LE/MY/YO
Willow and I, The A/F/MD/ME/PE/RM
Winged Victory AV/F/FS/HT/MA/MI/RM/TRP/W
Woman Bites Dog HT/JO/POL/RM
Years Ago F/MA/PE/RM/TH/YO

Years Between, The A/BS/F/LT/MI/RM/SX/W

Southern

All the King's Men CR/JO/MA/POL/SX
Another Part of the Forest BL/BS/F/MA/ME/PE/PS/REL/RM/SX
Bloomer Girl M/BL/BS/F/HIB/PE/POL/RC/RM/SM/W/WO
Cabin in the Sky M/BL/DE/FA/GA/MA/REL/RR
Career Angel FA/REL/YO
Carmen Jones M/BL/CR/MI/RM/SPT/SX/W
Dark Hammock CR/LE/MA/PE/RR/SC
Dark of the Moon FA/REL/RM/RR/SX
Deep Are the Roots BL/CR/F/POL/RC/RM/S/SM/SO
Down to Miami BS/F/HT/MI/REL/RM
Finian's Rainbow M/BL/F/FA/L/POL/RC/RM/RR
Flamingo Road JO/PN/POL/PS/RM/SX
Gentleman from Athens, The POL/RM
Great Big Doorstep, The F/REL/RM/RR/YO
Homecoming F/FA/REL/W
Jeb BL/RC
Johnny on a Spot AL/CR/JO/POL/PS/RM/SX
Long Way from Home, A AL/BL/CR/GA/MA/REL/SX
Louisiana Lady M/PE/PS/RM/SX
Magnolia Alley BH/MA/PS/REL/SPT/SX
Maid in the Ozarks A/RM/RR/SX
Member of the Wedding, The BL/F/RR/YO
Mr. Peebles and Mr. Hooker BL/L/RC/REL/RR/SM/SX
Moon Vine CR/PE/REL/RM/SM/TH/YO
Natural Man BL/CR/FA/GA/L/PE/PN/RC/REL
Our Lan' BL/PE/POL/RC/RM/RR
Regina M/BL/BS/CR/F/IL/MA/SM
Signature CR/LA/LE/PE/RM/RR/TR
Sister Oakes BL/RC/REL/SM
Strange Fruit BL/CR/RC/RM/SM/SX
Streetcar Named Desire, A AL/HO/MA/ME/PS/RM/SX
Summer and Smoke MD/ME/PS/REL/RM/SM/SX
Texas, Li'l Darlin' M/JO/POL/RM
These Tender Mercies BL/CR/F/RC/REL/RM/SM/SX
Time for Elizabeth BS/MA
Tin Type Valley BL/CR/F/FS/RC/YO
Tread the Green Grass FA/REL/RR/SX/YO
Trouble in July BL/CR/POL/RC/SM
Virginia Reel AL/F/PS/RR
Wisteria Trees, The BL/BS/F/PE/RM/RR

Tropics

Carib Song M/BL/MA/SX
Clutterbuck BR/HT/MA/SE/SX
Early to Bed M/PS/RM/S/SPT/SX/YO
Eve of St. Mark, The F/FA/GA/I/MI/RM/RR/SX/W
Hasty Heart, The DE/FS/IL/MI/RM/W
Henri Christophe BL/PE/POL/REL
Hidden Horizon BR/CR/MY
Home of the Brave JE/ME/MI/REL/W
Panama Hattie M/MI/POL/PS/RM/SX/YO
Pirate, The AD/PE/RM/SH
Proof thro' the Night DRG/HO/POL/W/WO
Rugged Path, The BS/JO/MA/MI/POL/SE/W

Sadie Thompson M/MI/PS/REL/SX
South Pacific BL/MI/RC/RM/SX/W
South Pacific M/MI/RC/RM/W
Winged Victory AV/F/FS/HT/MA/MI/RM/SM/W

Western

The American West (and Southwest) offered a vivid setting for plays and musicals; the works listed here are primarily rural in character or deal with urban life in a period setting.

Annie Get Your Gun M/HIB/PE/RM/SH
Chicken Every Sunday BH/BS/F/MA/PE/RM/SX
Cream in the Well, The AL/F/RM/RR/SX
Harvest of Years AL/F/MA/RM/RR
Hold on to Your Hats M/CR/RM/SH
Hope for a Harvest RC/RM/RR
Nine Girls CR/MD/POL/SPT/TH/UN/WO/YO
Oklahoma! M/RM/RR/SX
Out of My House AL/BL/F/LE/REL/SM
Sing Out, Sweet Land! M/FA/MU/PE/RM/W
Something for the Boys M/AV/LE/MI/RM/SH/W
Survivors, The F/HT/PE/RR/W

FOREIGN LANGUAGE PRODUCTIONS

The number of foreign-language productions was down from that given in the previous decade. The only such presentations covered by the English-language press were those given in French, German, Hebrew, Spanish, and Yiddish, and even these do not represent complete coverage.

French Language

Annonce Fait á Marie, L' DR
Edith Piaf RV

German Language

Faust DR
Iphigenia in Tauris DR
Rape of the Sabine Women, The TH

Hebrew Language

David's Crown DR
Dybbuk, The DR
Golem, The DR
Oedipus Rex DR
Shylock '47 JE/PE/TH

Spanish Language

Leyenda del Besso, La M/SP
Tonona RM/SX

Yiddish Language

Abi Gezunt M
Be Happy M

Big Shot, The M
Day of Judgment, The JE/MU/PE/RM/YO
Dr. Herzl HIB/JE/JO/POL/REL
Double Trouble M
Ester'ke JE/PE/POL/REL/RM/SX
Family Carnovsky, The CR/F/JE/MA/MD/POL
Five'ke, the Slave
Golden Land, The M
Good News M
Herschel the Jester M/JE/PE/REL/RM/YL
I'm in Love M
Johnny Belinda DR
Just My Luck M
Leave It to Charley M
Live and Laugh M
Lucky Days M
Men in White DR
Miracle of a Ghetto
My Friend Yossel M
My Wedding Night M
Oy, Is Dus a Leben! M/HIB/JE/TH
Rich Uncle, The M
Sadie Is a Lady M
Sender Blank F/LE
Shylock and His Daughter BS/F/JE/PE/REL/RM/TR
Song of the Dniepper CR/JE/PE/PN/POL/TR
Sunrise M
They All Want to Get Married M
They Came to a City
Three Gifts CR/DE/FA/JE/MU/REL/RM
Voice of Israel, The F/JE/JO/POL/W
Wandering Stars JE/PE/RM/TH
We Will Live
What a Guy M
Wish Me Luck M
Worlds Apart F/JE
Yosele, the Nightingale JE/LT/MU/PE/REL/RM

ETHNIC GROUPS

The ethnic groups most consistently visible in plays of the period were blacks and Jews. A smaller number of plays concerned orientals.

Blacks

This list includes plays in which most of the characters are black, plays in which the chief characters are black, and mostly white plays in which one or more important black roles figure. Plays originally produced with white actors but revived with blacks are also given.

Africapers RV
"Almost Faithful" FA/MA/SH/SX
Anna Lucasta AL/F/PS/SM
Another Part of the Forest BS/F/MA/ME/PE/PS/REL/RM/SO/SX
Bal Negre RV
Beggar's Holiday M/CR/PN/POL/PS/RM/SX
Big White Fog, The F/JE/POL/PS/RC
Bloomer Girl M/BS/F/HIB/PE/POL/RC/RM/SM/SO/W/WO
Cabin in the Sky M/DE/FA/GA/MA/REL/RR/SO

Carib Song M/MA/SX/TRP
Carmen Jones M/CR/MI/RM/SO/SPT/SX/W
Caukey F/POL/RC/RM
City of Kings ME/PE/RC/REL
Decision CR/JO/L/MI/POL/RC/RM/SM/SX/W
Deep Are the Roots CR/F/POL/RC/RM/S/SM
Don't Go Away Mad DE/IL/MA
Finian's Rainbow M/F/FA/L/POL/RC/RM/RR/SO
Forward the Heart F/IN/RC/RM/W
Garden of Time FA/PE/RR
Greener Grass, The FI/RC
Harlem Cavalcade RV
Harriet F/LIB/MA/PE/POL/RM/W
Hear That Trumpet AL/CR/MA/MU/RC/RM
Henri Christophe PE/POL/REL/TRP
Holiday on Broadway RV
Home Is the Hunter BS/CR/L/MA/POL/W
How I Wonder F/FA/L/RC/SC/UN/W
How Long till Summer? AL/CR/FA/LA/POL/RC/YO
Jeb RC/SO
Katherine Dunham and Her Company RV
Little Dark Horse F/FR/IL/RC/SX/YO
Long Way from Home, A AL/CR/GA/MA/REL/SO/SX
Longitude 49 CR/SE
Lost in the Stars M/CR/PN/POL/RC/REL/SX/TR
Lysistrata DR
Member of the Wedding, The F/RR/SO/YO
Memphis Bound! M/RM/SH/TR
Men to the Sea BH/MA/ME/MI/REL/SE/SX/W
Mr. Peebles and Mr. Hooker L/RC/REL/RR/SM/SO/SX
Native Son CR/F/JO/LA/PN/POL/RC/RM/TR
Natural Man CR/FA/GA/L/PE/PN/RC/REL/SO
On Whitman Avenue F/RC
Only the Heart BS/F/MA/SM/SX
Our Lan' PE/POL/RC/RM/RR/SO
Out of My House AL/F/LE/REL/SM/WE
Power of Darkness, The DR
Rain DR
Regina M/BS/CR/F/IL/MA/SM/SO
St. Louis Woman M/GA/PE/RM/SPT/SX
Set My People Free HIB/PE/POL/RC/REL
Shake Hands with the Devil JO/L/POL/RC/REL/TR
Sister Oakes RC/REL/SM/SO
Sojourner Truth F/HIB/PE/RC/REL/RM
South Pacific M/MI/RC/RM/TRP/W
Starlight CR/REL/SX
Strange Fruit CR/RC/RM/SM/SO/SX
Texas Town AL/RM/SM
These Tender Mercies CR/F/RC/REL/RM/SM/SO/SX
Three's a Family F/MA/MD
Tin Top Valley CR/F/FS/RC/SO/YO
Tobacco Road DR
Trial by Fire CR/F/RC/RR
Trouble in July CR/POL/RC/SM/SO
Walk Hard F/GA/RC/RM/SPT
Wisteria Trees, The BS/F/PE/RM/RR/SO
Young American F/MU/RC

Jews

This list covers both plays in which most characters are Jewish and those in which at least one Jewish character's ethnicity is important to the plot. Yiddish-language plays are not included here. See "Yiddish Language."

Big Two, The HT/JO/MI/MY/POL/RM
Big White Fog, The BL/F/POL/PS/RC
Brooklyn Biarritz A/CR/F/RM/SX/YO
Burning Bush, The GE/LA/PE/REL/TR
Café Crown MA/RM/TH
Common Ground JO/MI/POL/SH
Day Will Come, The FA/ME/MI/POL/REL/W
Familiar Pattern, The LA/MA/SX
Flag Is Born, A FA/OA/PE/POL/REL
Flight to the West AV/F/JO/MA/POL/W
For Heaven's Sake, Mother! F/MA/SX/TH
Good Neighbor CR/F/IN/MA/RM/YO
Home of the Brave ME/MI/REL/TRP/W
Jacobowsky and the Colonel GE/MI/POL/RM/W
Korb'n F/L/POL/REL/RM
Man with Blond Hair, The CR/POL/W
Man's House, A BI/BR/F/IN/PE/REL/RM
Me and Molly BS/F/MA/MU/REL/RM/S/YO
Outrageous Fortune F/HO/MD/MU/RC/RM/SX
Private Life of the Master Race, The F/GE/LA/MA/MI/PN/POL/REL/W
Right next to Broadway BS/L/RM/SX
Shylock '47 HEL/PE/TH
Skipper next to God BR/DU/POL/REL/SE
Stranger, The CR/MY/PE/POL
This, Too, Shall Pass F/MI/RM/SM
Tomorrow the World F/POL/SC/W
Toplitzky of Notre Dame M/FA/RM/SPT

Orientals

Earth Journey CH/FA/REL/RM
Family, The AL/BH/CH/F/POL/RM/W
First Wife, The CH/F/JO/MA/POL/YO
Lute Song M/CH/F/MA/PE
Partition POL
Suds in Your Eye AL/FS/MU/RM
Wedding in Japan MI/RC/RM/TR
What's Up? M/AV/IL/POL/RM/S/W/YO
Yours Is My Heart CH/PN/RM

MISCELLANEOUS

Productions that do not fit into normal categories. They are listed as one-acts, solo presentations, and verse plays. Ice shows are indicated by the letters IC in the "Revue" listing above. Two shows do not fall into any definite category:

It's up to You
Sim Sala Bim

One-Act Plays

This listing gives the titles of the several one-act programs produced during the decade. Titles in quotation marks are of single plays that were presented on a bill with plays in more than one act, with other one-acts, or alone. Plays of more than one act on the same bills are given in italics. Other titles were used for an evening of two or more one-acts. The titles are given without accompanying categories, which can be found under the specific entries.

"According to Law" and *A Strange Play*
"Across the Board on Tomorrow Morning" and "Theatre of the Soul"
"Across the Board on Tomorrow Morning" and "Talking to You"
Anton Chekhov Sketches
Army Play-by-Play, The
Ballet Ballads
"Browning Version, The" and "Harlequinade"
Evening of Two Plays, An
Four One-Act Comedies
Four Short Plays
"Fumed Oak" and "The Shadow of the Glen"
"Happy Journey, The" and *The Merchant of Venice*
"Hello Out There" and *Magic*
"Hello Out There," "The Shy and the Lonely," and *Those Endearing Young Charms*
Hope's the Thing
"Ile," "In the Zone," and *The Man Who Came to Dinner*
Medium, The and "The Telephone"
"Phoenix Too Frequent, A" and "Freight"
"Respectful Prostitute, The" and "The Happy Journey to Trenton and Camden"
"Riders to the Sea" and "Freight"
Shoemaker's Prodigious Wife and "The Stronger"
Six O'Clock Theatre
Spook Scandals

Solo

Concerto for Fun
Maurice Chevalier (2)
Mum's the Word
One-Woman Theatre
Ruth Draper (4)
Theatre of Angna Enters, The
Thumbnail Theatre
You with Me

Verse

Anne of the Thousand Days HIB/MA/PE/REL/SX/TR
Cocktail Party, The BR/FI/REL/SX
Dog beneath the Skin, The AD/BR/DRG/FA/HT/IL/ME/POL/PS/RM/W
Family Reunion, The F/ME/OA/REL
If in the Greenwood JO/POL/SX
Life Again DE/F/FA/PE/RM/RR/SM
Uniform of Flesh CR/LA/MI/PE/SE/TR

Appendix 3
Awards

The five most significant signs of recognition for theatre in the 1940s were the Pulitzer Prize; the New York Drama Critics Circle Award; the Antoinette Perry Award (the Tony), inaugurated in 1947; the Clarence Derwent Award (inaugurated in 1945); and selection as one of the ten best plays of the year (actually, the season) in the annual Burns Mantle *Best Plays* collection (its editorship was taken over in 1948 by John Chapman, following Mantle's death). Other important awards and lists included the Theatre World Award (from 1945); the Barter Theatre Award; the Drama League Award; the Donaldson Awards; the *Variety* polls; and, among others, the George Jean Nathan selections in his annual *Theatre Book of the Year* series.

PULITZER PRIZES

1940-1941 *There Shall Be No Night** by Robert E. Sherwood
1941-1942 no award
1942-1943 *The Skin of Our Teeth* by Thornton Wilder
1943-1944 no award
1944-1945 *Harvey* by Mary Coyle Chase
1945-1946 *State of the Union* by Howard Lindsay and Russel Crouse
1946-1947 no award
1947-1948 *A Streetcar Named Desire* by Tennessee Williams
1948-1949 *Death of a Salesman* by Arthur Miller
1949-1950 *South Pacific* by Oscar Hammerstein II, Joshua Logan, and Richard Rodgers

THE BEST PLAYS

1940-1941

Arsenic and Old Lace by Joseph Kesselring
Claudia by Rose Franken
The Corn Is Green by Emlyn Williams
Flight to the West by Elmer Rice
George Washington Slept Here by George S. Kaufman and Moss Hart
Lady in the Dark by Moss Hart and Kurt Weill
Mr. and Mrs. North by Owen Davis
My Sister Eileen by Joseph Fields and Jerome Chodorov

---

*This play, which opened 4/29/40, is covered in the 1939-1940 volume, but because of factors related to award deadlines it is listed here.

Native Son by Paul Green and Richard Wright
Watch on the Rhine by Lillian Hellman

1941-1942

Angel Street by Patrick Hamilton
Blithe Spirit by Noël Coward
Candle in the Wind by Maxwell Anderson
Hope for a Harvest by Sophie Treadwell
In Time to Come by Howard Koch and John Huston
Jason by Samson Raphaelson
Junior Miss by Jerome Chodorov and Joseph Fields
Letters to Lucerne by Fritz Rotter and Allen Vincent
The Moon Is Down by John Steinbeck
Uncle Harry by Thomas Job

1942-1943

The Damask Cheek by John van Druten and Lloyd Morris
The Doughgirls by Joseph Fields
The Eve of St. Mark by Maxwell Anderson
Harriet by Florence Ryerson and Colin Clements
Kiss and Tell by F. Hugh Herbert
Oklahoma! by Richard Rodgers and Oscar Hammerstein II
The Patriots by Sidney Kingsley
The Skin of Our Teeth by Thornton Wilder
Tomorrow the World by James Gow and Arnaud d'Usseau
Winter Soldiers by Dan James

1943-1944

Decision by Edward Chodorov
The Innocent Voyage by Paul Osborn
Jacobowsky and the Colonel by Franz Werfel; adapted by S. N. Behrman
Outrageous Fortune by Rose Franken
Over 21 by Ruth Gordon
Pick-up Girl by Elsa Shelley
The Searching Wind by Lillian Hellman
Storm Operation by Maxwell Anderson
The Voice of the Turtle by John van Druten
Winged Victory by Moss Hart

1944-1945

Anna Lucasta by Philip Yordan
A Bell for Adano by Paul Osborn
Dear Ruth by Norman Krasna
Foolish Notion by Philip Barry
The Glass Menagerie by Tennessee Williams
Harvey by Mary Coyle Chase
The Hasty Heart by John Patrick
I Remember Mama by John van Druten
The Late George Apley by John P. Marquand and George S. Kaufman
Soldier's Wife by Rose Franken

1945-1946

Antigone by Jean Anouilh

Born Yesterday by Garson Kanin
Deep Are the Roots by Arnaud d'Usseau and James Gow
Dream Girl by Elmer Rice
Home of the Brave by Arthur Laurents
Lute Song by Sidney Howard and Will Irwin
The Magnificent Yankee by Emmet Lavery
O Mistress Mine by Terence Rattigan
The Rugged Path by Robert E. Sherwood
State of the Union by Howard Lindsay and Russel Crouse

1946-1947

All My Sons by Arthur Miller
Another Part of the Forest by Lillian Hellman
Brigadoon by Alan Jay Lerner and Frederick Loewe
Christopher Blake by Moss Hart
The Fatal Weakness by George Kelly
The Iceman Cometh by Eugene O'Neill
Joan of Lorraine by Maxwell Anderson
John Loves Mary by Norman Krasna
The Story of Mary Surratt by John Patrick
Years Ago by Ruth Gordon

1947-1948

Allegro by Richard Rodgers and Oscar Hammerstein II
Command Decision by William Wister Haines
Eastward in Eden by Dorothy Gardner
The Heiress by Ruth and Augustus Goetz
An Inspector Calls by J. B. Priestley
Me and Molly by Gertrude Berg
Mister Roberts by Thomas Heggen and Joshua Logan
Skipper next to God by Jan de Hartog
A Streetcar Named Desire by Tennessee Williams
The Winslow Boy by Terence Rattigan

1948-1949

Anne of the Thousand Days by Maxwell Anderson
Death of a Salesman by Arthur Miller
Detective Story by Sidney Kingsley
Edward, My Son by Robert Morley and Noel Langley
Goodbye, My Fancy by Fay Kanin
Life with Mother by Howard Lindsay and Russel Crouse
Light Up the Sky by Moss Hart
The Madwoman of Chaillot by Jean Giraudoux
The Silver Whistle by Robert Edward McEnroe
Two Blind Mice by Samuel Spewack

1949-1950

Clutterbuck by Benn W. Levy
The Cocktail Party by T. S. Eliot
Come Back, Little Sheba by William Inge
The Enchanted by Jean Giraudoux
The Happy Time by Samuel Taylor
I Know My Love by S. N. Behrman
The Innocents by William Archibald
Lost in the Stars by Maxwell Anderson and Kurt Weill

The Member of the Wedding by Carson McCullers
The Wisteria Trees by Joshua Logan

NEW YORK DRAMA CRITICS CIRCLE AWARDS

1940-1941 *Watch on the Rhine* by Lillian Hellman (American); *The Corn Is Green* by Emlyn Williams (foreign)
1941-1942 no American award; *Blithe Spirit* by Noël Coward (foreign)
1942-1943 *The Patriots* by Sidney Kingsley (American); no foreign award
1943-1944 no American award; *Jacobowsky and the Colonel* by Franz Werfel and S. N. Behrman (foreign)
1944-1945 *The Glass Menagerie* by Tennessee Williams; no foreign award
1945-1946 no American or foreign award; *Carousel* by Benjamin Glazer, Richard Rodgers, and Oscar Hammerstein II (musical)
1946-1947 *All My Sons* by Arthur Miller (American); *No Exit* by Jean-Paul Sartre (foreign); *Brigadoon* by Alan Jay Lerner and Frederick Loewe (musical)
1947-1948 *A Streetcar Named Desire* by Tennessee Williams (American); *The Winslow Boy* (foreign); no musical award
1948-1949 *Death of a Salesman* by Arthur Miller (American); *The Madwoman of Chaillot* by Jean Giraudoux (foreign); *South Pacific* by Oscar Hammerstein II, Joshua Logan, and Richard Rodgers (musical)
1949-1950 *The Member of the Wedding* by Carson McCullers (American); *The Cocktail Party* by T. S. Eliot (foreign); *The Consul* by Gian-Carlo Menotti (musical)

TONY AWARDS

(Award designations are given as listed in Isabelle Stevenson's *The Tony Award*; dates are actually for inclusive seasons, 1948, for example, referring to 1947-1948. Special awards for noncreative theatrical activity are not listed here.)

1947

Actors (Dramatic)	José Ferrer, *Cyrano de Bergerac* Fredric March, *Years Ago*
Actresses (Dramatic)	Ingrid Bergman, *Joan of Lorraine* Helen Hayes, *Happy Birthday*
Actress, Supporting or Featured (Dramatic)	Patricia Neal, *Another Part of the Forest*
Actor, Supporting or Featured (Musical)	David Wayne, *Finian's Rainbow*
Director	Elia Kazan, *All My Sons*
Costumes	Lucinda Ballard, *Happy Birthday*, *Another Part of the Forest*, *Street Scene*, *John Loves Mary*, *The Chocolate Soldier*
Choreographers	Agnes de Mille, *Brigadoon* Michael Kidd, *Finian's Rainbow*

1948

Actors (Dramatic)	Henry Fonda, *Mister Roberts* Paul Kelly, *Command Decision* Basil Rathbone, *The Heiress*
Actresses (Dramatic)	Judith Anderson, *Medea* Katharine Cornell, *Antony and Cleopatra* Jessica Tandy, *A Streetcar Named Desire*
Actor (Musical)	Paul Hartman, *Angel in the Wings*
Actress (Musical)	Grace Hartman, *Angel in the Wings*
Director	Joshua Logan, *Mister Roberts*

Play	*Mister Roberts* by Thomas Heggen and Joshua Logan
Producer	Leland Hayward, *Mister Roberts*
Authors	Thomas Heggen and Joshua Logan, *Mister Roberts*
Costumes	Mary Percy Schenck, *The Heiress*
Scenic Designer	Horace Armistead, *The Medium*
Choreographer	Jerome Robbins, *High Button Shoes*

1949

Actor (Dramatic)	Rex Harrison, *Anne of the Thousand Days*
Actress (Dramatic)	Martita Hunt, *The Madwoman of Chaillot*
Actor, Supporting or Featured (Dramatic)	Arthur Kennedy, *Death of a Salesman*
Actress, Supporting or Featured (Dramatic)	Shirley Booth, *Goodbye, My Fancy*
Actor (Musical)	Ray Bolger, *Where's Charley?*
Actress (Musical)	Nanette Fabray, *Love Life*
Play	*Death of a Salesman* by Arthur Miller
Producers (Dramatic)	Kermit Bloomgarden and Walter Fried, *Death of a Salesman*
Author	Arthur Miller, *Death of a Salesman*
Director	Elia Kazan, *Death of a Salesman*
Musical	*Kiss Me, Kate*, music and lyrics by Cole Porter, book by Bella and Samuel Spewack
Producers (Musical)	Arnold Saint-Subber and Lemuel Ayers, *Kiss Me, Kate*
Authors (Musical)	Bella and Samuel Spewack, *Kiss Me, Kate*
Composer and Lyricist	Cole Porter, *Kiss Me, Kate*
Costumes	Lemuel Ayers, *Kiss Me, Kate*
Scenic Designer	Jo Mielziner, *Sleepy Hollow*, *Summer and Smoke*, *Anne of the Thousand Days*, *Death of a Salesman*, *South Pacific* (the latter was mentioned in the award although it was officially part of the 1950 season's award eligibility)
Choreographer	Gower Champion, *Lend an Ear*
Conductor/Musical Director	Max Meth, *As the Girls Go*

1950

Actor (Dramatic)	Sidney Blackmer, *Come Back, Little Sheba*
Actress (Dramatic)	Shirley Booth, *Come Back, Little Sheba*
Actor (Musical)	Ezio Pinza, *South Pacific*
Actress (Musical)	Mary Martin, *South Pacific*
Actor, Supporting or Featured (Musical)	Myron McCormick, *South Pacific*
Actress, Supporting or Featured (Musical)	Juanita Hall, *South Pacific*
Play	*The Cocktail Party* by T. S. Eliot
Producer (Dramatic)	Gilbert Miller, *The Cocktail Party*
Author (Dramatic)	T.S. Eliot, *The Cocktail Party*
Director	Joshua Logan, *South Pacific*
Musical	*South Pacific*, music by Richard Rodgers, lyrics by Oscar Hammerstein II, book by Oscar Hammerstein II and Joshua Logan
Producers (Musical)	Richard Rodgers, Oscar Hammerstein II,

	Leland Hayward, and Joshua Logan, *South Pacific*
Authors (Musical)	Oscar Hammerstein II and Joshua Logan, *South Pacific*
Costumes	Aline Bernstein, *Regina*
Scenic Designer	Jo Mielziner, *The Innocents*
Choreographer	Helen Tamiris, *Touch and Go*
Conductor/Musical Director	Maurice Abravanel, *Regina*

CLARENCE DERWENT AWARDS

Awarded for the best supporting male and female performances of the season in non-starred and nonfeatured roles.

1945 Judy Holliday in *Kiss Them for Me*; Frederick O'Neal in *Anna Lucasta*
1946 Barbara Bel Geddes in *Deep Are the Roots*; Paul Douglas in *Born Yesterday*
1947 Margaret Phillips in *Another Part of the Forest*; Tom Ewell in *John Loves Mary*
1948 Catherine Ayers in *A Long Way from Home*; Lou Gilbert in *Hope's the Thing*
1949 Leora Dana in *The Madwoman of Chaillot*; Ray Walston in *Summer and Smoke*
1950 Gloria Lane in *The Consul*; Douglass Watson in *The Wisteria Trees*

Appendix 4
Sources of Plays

Novels, both current and established, served as source material for dozens of straight plays of the period, and straight plays provided the creators of musicals with a fertile source of inspiration for their librettos. The first list that follows offers the titles of all known 1940s straight plays based on novels; the second lists all musicals taken from plays, including unproduced or unpublished ones. Many other sources were also responsible for inspiring the decade's works; they include short stories (the *New Yorker Magazine* was an especially productive source), poems, fairy tales, and works of nonfiction, such as biographies, diaries, and so on. Such sources are not given here. Sources for works listed as revivals are not provided here or in the specific entries. Although several musicals were based on novels, there numbers are very small and are therefore not listed here.

PLAY	**NOVEL**
All the King's Men	*All the King's Men*
Barefoot Boy with Cheek	*Barefoot Boy with Cheek*
A Bell for Adano	*A Bell for Adano*
The Cat Screams	*The Cat Screams*
Chicken Every Sunday	*Chicken Every Sunday*
Crime and Punishment	*Crime and Punishment*
The Cup of Trembling	*Breakdown*
The Day of Judgment	*The Day of Judgment*
Edward, My Son	*Edward, My Son*
Eight O'Clock Tuesday	*Fair Warning*
Embezzled Heaven	*Embezzled Heaven*
Ester'ke	*Ester'ke*
The Family	*The Family*
The Family Carnovsky	*The Family Carnovsky*
Flamingo Road	*Flamingo Road*
Fledgling	*Follow the Furies*
Gentlemen Prefer Blondes	*Gentlemen Prefer Blondes*
The Great Big Doorstep	*The Great Big Doorstep*
Guest in the House	*Guest in the House*
Hand in Glove	*Hughie Roddis*
The Happy Time	*The Happy Time*
The Haven	*The Haven*
The Heiress	*Washington Square*
Hidden Horizon	*Death on the Nile*

The House in Paris	*The House in Paris*
I Remember Mama	*Mama's Bank Account*
In Bed We Cry	*In Bed We Cry*
The Innocent Voyage	*A High Wind in Jamaica*
The Innocents	*The Turn of the Screw*
Janie	*Janie*
January Thaw	*January Thaw*
The Journey of Simon McKeever	*The Journey of Simon McKeever*
Kiss Them for Me	*Shore Leave*
The Lady Who Came to Stay	*The Lady Who Came to Stay*
Land's End	*Dawn in Lyonesse*
The Late George Apley	*The Late George Apley*
Laura	*Laura*
Make Way for Lucia	the *Lucia* novels
The Member of the Wedding	*The Member of the Wedding*
Mr. Adam	*Mr. Adam*
Mr. and Mrs. North	*The Norths Meet Murder*
Mr. Peebles and Mr. Hooker	*Mr. Peebles and Mr. Hooker*
Mister Roberts	*Mister Roberts*
The Moon Is Down	*The Moon Is Down*
Native Son	*Native Son*
Now I Lay Me Down to Sleep	*Now I Lay Me Down to Sleep*
The Rats of Norway	*The Rats of Norway*
Rebecca	*Rebecca*
The Scapegoat	*The Trial*
Shylock and His Daughter	*Shylock and His Daughter*
The Snark Was a Boojum	*The Snark Was a Boojum*
Solitaire	*Solitaire*
The Song of Bernadette	*The Song of Bernadette*
Song of the Dniepper	*Song of the Dniepper*
Strange Fruit	*Strange Fruit*
Suds in Your Eye	*Suds in Your Eye*
The Sun Field	*The Sun Field*
Ten Little Indians	*And Then There Were None*
Thank You, Svoboda	*You Can't Do That to Svoboda*
That Lady	*For One Sweet Grape*
Theatre	*Theatre*
Trio	*Trio*
Trouble in July	*Trouble in July*
Uniform of Flesh	*Billy Budd, Foretopman*
The Visitor	*The Visitor*
Walk Hard	*Walk Hard--Talk Loud*
Wandering Stars	*Wandering Stars*
War and Peace	*War and Peace*
The Way	*Faith*
The World's Full of Girls	*I'll Come Back to You*

MUSICAL	**PLAY**
Arms and the Girl	*The Pursuit of Happiness*
Banjo Eyes	*Three Men on a Horse*
Beggar's Holiday	*The Beggar's Opera*
Bloomer Girl	unproduced, untitled play
By Jupiter	*The Warrior's Husband*
Carousel	*Liliom*
The Firebrand of Florence	*The Firebrand*

Kiss Me, Kate	*The Taming of the Shrew*
Let's Face It	*The Cradle Snatchers*
The Liar	*The Liar*
Louisiana Lady	*Creoles*
Lute Song	*Pi-Pa-Ki* (also called *Pi-Pa-Ji*)
My Romance	*Romance*
Night of Love	*Tonight or Never*
Oklahoma!	*Green Grow the Lilacs*
Regina	*The Little Foxes*
Sadie Thompson	*Rain*
Song of Norway	unproduced, untitled play
Street Scene	*Street Scene*
Where's Charley?	*Charley's Aunt*

Appendix 5
Institutional Theatres

The institutions listed here range from repertory companies such as the American Repertory Theatre to such organizations as the Theatre Guild, which used a new company for each production. The list of companies is selective. A couple of known productions that were not reviewed are placed in brackets. Otherwise, only productions with entries are listed. (The Off-Broadway companies were responsible for several unreviewed productions.) Appendix 6 contains visiting foreign companies. Names in parentheses are of companies and individuals with whom plays were coproduced.

ABBE PRACTICAL WORKSHOP

Building 222
Deirdre of the Sorrows
Don't Go Away Mad
The Edge of the Sword
Fifty
The Heeple Steeple
Nine Month Midnight
Rose in the Wilderness
Tread the Green Grass
When the Bough Breaks

AMERICAN ACTORS COMPANY (or **THEATRE**)

American Legend
Only the Heart
Out of My House
The Playboy of Newark
Texas Town

AMERICAN NEGRO THEATRE

"Almost Faithful"
Anna Lucasta
Garden of Time
Henri Christophe
Home is the Hunter
Natural Man
On Strivers Row

[The Peacemaker]
Rain
"Riders to the Sea" and "Freight"
Sojourner Truth
Starlight
Three's a Family
Tin Top Valley
Walk Hard

AMERICAN REPERTORY THEATRE

Alice in Wonderland
Androcles and the Lion and "Pound on Demand"
Ghosts
John Gabriel Borkman
King Henry VIII
What Every Woman Knows
Yellow Jack

BLACKFRIARS' GUILD

Armor of Light
Career Angel
Caukey
City of Kings
Come Marching Home
Derryowen
Don't, George
Earth Journey
Hoboes in Heaven
Home Is the Hero
If in the Greenwood
Inside Story
Lady of Fatima
A Man's House
Mary of Magdala
The Minstrel Boy
Moment Musical
On the Seventh Day
Respectfully Yours
Savonarola
Seven Mirrors
Shake Hands with the Devil
Simon's Wife
Slice It Thin!
Song out of Sorrow
Tinker's Dam
Trial by Fire
Up the Rebels!
The Years Between
A Young American

DRAMATIC WORKSHOP (of THE NEW SCHOOL FOR SOCIAL RESEARCH)

All the King's Men
The Burning Bush
Chaff
The Days of Our Youth
The Flies

King Lear
The Millionairess
Nights of Wrath
Outside the Door
The Scapegoat
There Is No End
These Are the Times
War and Peace
Wedding in Japan
Winter Soldiers

EXPERIMENTAL THEATRE

As We Forgive Our Debtors
Ballet Ballads
Battle for Heaven
Cock-A-Doodle-Do
[Danny Larkin]
$E=MC^2$
The Fifth Horseman
Galileo
The Great Campaign
Hippolytus
A Long Way from Home
Me, the Sleeper
The Nineteenth Hole of Europe
Not in Our Stars
O'Daniel
Seeds in the Wind
Sister Oakes
Six O'Clock Theatre
Skipper next to God
A Temporary Island
These Tender Mercies
The Trojan Women
Uniform of Flesh
Virginia Reel
The Wanhope Building
The War President
Yours, A. Lincoln

INTERPLAYERS

him
The Infernal Machine
Out of the Picture
The Silver Tassie
Within the Gates

NEW STAGES

Blood Wedding
Bruno and Sidney
An Evening of Two Plays ("The Respectful Prostitute" and "Church Street"; the latter replaced by "The Happy Journey to Trenton and Camden")
Lamp at Midnight
The Sun and I
To Tell You the Truth
The Victors

NEW YORK CITY [CENTER] THEATRE COMPANY

The Alchemist
Angel Street
The Corn Is Green
The Devil's Disciple
Four One-Act Comedies
The Heiress
The Insect Comedy
Rip Van Winkle
S.S. Glencairn
She Stoops to Conquer
Volpone

NEW YORK REPERTORY GROUP

The Adding Machine
Hamlet
No Exit
The Owl and the Pussycat
Six Characters in Search of an Author
The Taming of the Shrew

ON-STAGE

The Ascent of F-6
The Bat
Billy the Kid
The Contrast
Creditors
The Dog beneath the Skin
East Lynne
The Family Reunion
Gas
Heartbreak House
Henry IV
Life Sentence
The New York Idea
No Exit
Peg O' My Heart
Tobias and the Angel
The Watched Pot
Yerma

PLAYERS FROM ABROAD

Faust
Iphigenia in Tauris
The Rape of the Sabine Women

PLAYWRIGHTS' PRODUCING COMPANY

Anne of the Thousand Days (with Leland Hayward)
Candle in the Wind (with Theatre Guild)
Dream Girl
The Eve of St. Mark
Flight to the West
Joan of Lorraine

Journey to Jerusalem
Lost in the Stars
A New Life
The Patriots (with Rowland Stebbins)
The Pirate (with Theatre Guild)
The Rugged Path
The Smile of the World
Storm Operation
Street Scene (with Dwight Deere Wiman)
The Talley Method
Truckline Café (with Harold Clurman and Elia Kazan)

STUDIO-7

The Father
The Shoemaker's Prodigious Wife and "The Stronger"

THEATRE GUILD

Ah, Wilderness!
Allegro
As You Like It
Candle in the Wind (with Playwrights' Producing Company)
Carousel
Come Back, Little Sheba
Dunnigan's Daughter
Embezzled Heaven
The Fatal Weakness
Foolish Notion
He Who Gets Slapped
Hope for a Harvest
I Know My Love (with John C. Wilson)
The Iceman Cometh (with Armina Marshall)
The Importance of Being Earnest (with John C. Wilson and H. M. Tennent, Ltd.)
The Innocent Voyage
Jacobowsky and the Colonel (with John H. Skirball)
Liberty Jones
Love for Love (with John C. Wilson and H.M. Tennent, Ltd.)
Make Way for Lucia
Mr. Sycamore
My Name Is Aquilon
O Mistress Mine (with John C. Wilson)
Oklahoma!
Othello (with John Haggott)
Papa Is All
The Pirate (with Playwrights' Producing Company)
The Rivals
The Russian People
Set My People Free
The Silver Whistle
Sing Out, Sweet Land!
This Time Tomorrow
Twelfth Night (with Gilbert Miller)
The Winslow Boy (with Atlantis Productions, H. M. Tennent, Ltd., and John C. Wilson)
The Winter's Tale
Without Love
Yesterday's Magic
You Never Can Tell (with Alfred Fischer)

THEATRE INCORPORATED

Macbeth
The Playboy of the Western World
Pygmalion
The Wanhope Building (for the Experimental Theatre)
(for Old Vic Company offerings sponsored by Theatre Incorporated, see Old Vic listings in appendix 6)

YIDDISH ART THEATRE

The Day of Judgment
Dr. Herzl
The Family Carnovsky
Herschel the Jester
Sender Blank
Shylock and His Daughter
Song of the Dniepper
Three Gifts
The Voice of Israel
Wandering Stars
Worlds Apart
Yosele, the Nightingale

Appendix 6
Foreign Companies and Stars

DONALD WOLFIT REPERTORY COMPANY (ADVANCE PLAYERS)

As You Like It
Hamlet
King Lear
The Merchant of Venice
Volpone

D'OYLY CARTE OPERA COMPANY

The Gondoliers
H.M.S. Pinafore and "Cox and Box"
Iolanthe
The Mikado
Patience
The Pirates of Penzance and "Trial by Jury"
The Yeomen of the Guard

DUBLIN GATE THEATRE COMPANY

John Bull's Other Island
The Old Lady Says "No!"
Where Stars Walk

HABIMAH THEATRE

David's Crown
The Dybbuk
The Golem
Oedipus Rex

OLD VIC COMPANY

Henry IV, Part I
Henry IV, Part II
Oedipus and *The Critic*
Uncle Vanya

Appendix 7
Longest-Running Shows of the 1940s

The following shows attained runs of at least 500 performances.

Oklahoma!	2,245
South Pacific	1,925
Harvey	1,775
Born Yesterday	1,642
The Voice of the Turtle	1,557
Arsenic and Old Lace	1,444
Angel Street	1,293
Mister Roberts	1,157
Annie Get Your Gun	1,147
Kiss Me, Kate	1,077
Kiss and Tell	962
Anna Lucasta	957
Carousel	890
Hats Off to Ice	890
Follow the Girls	882
My Sister Eileen	866
Song of Norway	860
A Streetcar Named Desire	855
Where's Charley?	792
State of the Union	765
Death of a Salesman	742
Sons O' Fun	742
Gentlemen Prefer Blondes	740
Call Me Mister	734
High Button Shoes	727
Finian's Rainbow	725
Claudia	722
I Remember Mama	714
Junior Miss	710
Dear Ruth	683
The Doughgirls	671
Blithe Spirit	657
Bloomer Girl	654
Janie	642
The Happy Time	614
Star and Garter	605
The Two Mrs. Carrolls	585

Detective Story	581
Brigadoon	581
One Touch of Venus	567
Happy Birthday	564
The Glass Menagerie	561
Ziegfeld Follies of 1943	553
Let's Face It	547
The Red Mill	531
Rosalinda	521
Up in Central Park	504
Carmen Jones	502
The Member of the Wedding	501
Panama Hattie	501
Tomorrow the World	500

Appendix 8
List of Review Source Abbreviations

This list provides the abbreviations and full names of all newspapers and periodicals from which reviews cited in the text are drawn. The reference to *Theatre Book of the Year* is to an annual (1942-1943 to 1951-1952) compilation (and expansion) by George Jean Nathan of his reviews, published mainly in the *New York Journal-American*.

AC	*Actors' Cues*
BB	*Billboard*
BC	*Brooklyn Citizen*
BE	*Brooklyn Daily Eagle*
CSM	*Christian Science Monitor*
CW	*Catholic World*
DC	*Daily Compass*
DW	*Daily Worker*
NEN	*Newark Evening News*
NL	*New Leader*
NYDM	*New York Daily Mirror*
NYDN	*New York Daily News*
NYHT	*New York Herald-Tribune*
NYJA	*New York Journal-American*
NYMT	*New York Morning Telegraph*
NYP	*New York Post*
NYS	*New York Sun*
NYT	*New York Times*
NYWT	*New York World-Telegram*
PM	*PM*
SR	*Saturday Review*
TAM	*Theatre Arts [Monthly]*
TBY	*Theatre Book of the Year*
TS	*The Star*
V	*Variety*
WSJ	*Wall Street Journal*
WWD	*Women's Wear Daily*

Appendix 9
Seasonal Statistics

This appendix provides annual statistics concerning the total number of productions covered by this volume. It should be remembered that the figures given in the Introduction on page xxi refer to Broadway alone, while those presented here cover both Broadway and Off Broadway. Shows that moved from one venue to another during the same season are not counted twice. (Season = S)

1. Straight plays (P): Full-length (more than one act) comedies, dramas, and comedy-dramas written after 1920 and given their initial production in New York; this applies to foreign-language productions as well as English versions.

2. Musicals (M): Operettas, musical comedies, and comic operas produced in the legitimate theatre (generally, on Broadway) as opposed to those produced by opera companies.

3. Revues (RV): Nonbook musicals, extravaganzas, and ice shows; included are shows centered around a famous musical performer, such as Maurice Chevalier.

4. Dramatic Revivals (DR): Straight plays that had previously been produced in New York or plays never before produced in New York, provided that they were written before 1920.

5. Musical Revivals (MR): Same as no. 4, except for musicals, operettas, and the like.

6. Miscellaneous (MS): Presentations that do not fit in the previous categories, including solo performances.

7. Return Engagements (RE): See the explanation in appendix 9 of the previous volume.

8. Foreign Language (FL): Productions given in foreign languages. The number of foreign language productions are not included in the final totals, although the productions themselves are subsumed under the other categories.

9. One-Act (OA): Programs made up of or including one-act plays.

S	P	M	RV	DR	MR	MS	RE	FL	OA	Total
1940-1941	68	8	7	12	2	2		7	1	93
1941-1942	73	8	8	9	8	1	1	2	1	109
1942-1943	60	9	12	9	7	3	2	5	3	109
1943-1944	63	15	5	16	15		5	4	2	120
1944-1945	75	14	9	12	1		3	4		118
1945-1946	58	15	4	21	4		1	4		103
1946-1947	61	13	5	26	3	1	2	5		111
1947-1948	64	9	7	26	9	1	1	6	3	120
1948-1949	69	10	7	28		1	5	5	1	121
1949-1950	55	13	9	29	4		3	4	2	116

Appendix 10
Theatres

This is an alphabetical listing of the theatres engaged in production during the 1940s. The list is in two parts, Broadway and Off Broadway. Other names by which Broadway playhouses and selected Off-Broadway ones were known during the period are indicated in parentheses. Many Off-Broadway theatres were created from nontheatrical spaces or were simply halls or auditoriums borrowed for the occasion. If a play was produced there, it is listed. Names by which theatres still active were known in 1992 are *italicized* if such names were taken subsequent to the 1940s. An asterisk (*) denotes theatres no longer in legitimate theatre use or demolished. A few theatres listed here under Broadway were, by the 1940s, on the borderline between being classed as Broadway or Off Broadway. For example, while the President was technically a Broadway house, it housed for much of the decade a troupe consisting of the students of Erwin Piscator's Dramatic Workshop, and their work was generally considered in the same category as most Off-Broadway companies. Another small Broadway house that might fall in this indeterminate area was the Princess, here classed--with some reservations--as an Off-Broadway theatre. Madison Square Garden was (and still is) a sports arena, but was used at one point for the comedy show, *Funzapoppin'*, thereby turning it into a Broadway venue. And the City Center was a large, nonprofit house in the Broadway vicinity, so it had Broadway status while operating on a separate contract from Broadway theatres. The list does not present every name by which Broadway theatres were known during their history.

BROADWAY

Adelphi Theatre*
Alvin Theatre (*Neil Simon Theatre*)
Ambassador Theatre
ANTA Theatre (Guild Theatre; *Virginia Theatre*)
Arena Theatre (Edison Hotel ballroom)
Belasco Theatre
Bijou Theatre
Biltmore Theatre
Booth Theatre
Broadhurst Theatre
Broadway Theatre
Center Theatre*
Century Theatre* (Jolson Theatre; Molly Picon Theatre; New Century Theatre; Yiddish Art Theatre)
City Center of Music and Drama (Mecca Temple)

Columbus Circle Theatre* (International Theatre)
Concert Theatre* (John Golden Theatre [on Fifty-eighth Street])
Coronet Theatre (Forrest Theatre; *Eugene O'Neill Theatre*)
Cort Theatre
Empire Theatre*
Ethel Barrymore Theatre
Forrest Theatre (Coronet Theatre; *Eugene O'Neill Theatre*)
Forty-eighth Street Theatre* (Windsor Theatre)
Forty-fourth Street Theatre*
Forty-sixth Street Theatre (*Richard Rodgers Theatre*)
Fulton Theatre*
Guild Theatre (ANTA Theatre; *Virginia Theatre*)
Henry Miller's Theatre*
Hollywood Theatre (Mark Hellinger Theatre)
Hudson Theatre*
Imperial Theatre
International Theatre* (Columbus Circle Theatre)
John Golden Theatre (on Forty-fifth Street)
Jolson Theatre* (Century Theatre; Molly Picon Theatre; Yiddish Art Theatre)
Little Theatre (New York Times Hall; *Helen Hayes Theatre*)
Longacre Theatre
Lyceum Theatre
Madison Square Garden
Majestic Theatre
Mansfield Theatre (*Brooks Atkinson Theatre*)
Mark Hellinger Theatre (Hollywood Theatre)
Martin Beck Theatre
Maxine Elliott's Theatre*
Mecca Temple (City Center of Music and Drama)
Molly Picon Theatre* (Century Theatre; New Century Theatre; Jolson Theatre; Yiddish Art Theatre)
Morosco Theatre*
Music Box Theatre
National Theatre (*Nederlander Theatre*)
New Century Theatre* (Century Theatre; Jolson Theatre; Molly Picon Theatre; Yiddish Art Theatre)
New York Times Hall (Little Theatre; *Helen Hayes Theatre*)
Playhouse*
Plymouth Theatre
President Theatre
Ritz Theatre (*Walter Kerr Theatre*)
Royale Theatre
St. James Theatre
Shubert Theatre
Windsor Theatre* (Forty-eighth Street Theatre)
Winter Garden Theatre
Yiddish Art Theatre (Jolson Theatre)
Ziegfeld Theatre*

OFF BROADWAY

Academy of Music
Actors Studio
American Actors Company
American Negro Theatre Playhouse
Barbizon-Plaza Theatre (or Concert Hall)
Belmont Theatre
Blackfriars' Theatre
Bleecker Street Playhouse

Brander Matthews Hall
Carnegie Hall
Chanin Auditorium
Charles Weidman Studio (also Humphrey-Weidman Studio; Theatre of the American Scene)
Cherry Lane Theatre
Clinton Theatre
Cosmopolitan Opera House
Czechoslovak Hall
Daly's Theatre
Educational Alliance
Fourth Street Playhouse
Friendship House Church
Grand Street Playhouse
Greenwich Mews Playhouse
Harlem Children's Center
Henry Street Playhouse
Hudson Guild Theatre
Humphrey-Weidman Studio (Charles Weidman Studio; Theatre of the American Scene)
Interplayers Theatre (in Carnegie Hall)
Jewish Guild for the Blind (also called Guild for the Jewish Blind)
Juilliard School of Music
Lenox Hill Playhouse (Lenox Hill Settlement House)
Lenox Hill Settlement House (Lenox Hill Playhouse)
Lincoln Theatre
Malin Theatre (also Malin Studio)
Master Institute of the United Arts (Roerich Theatre)
National Arts Club
New Amsterdam Roof Theatre
New Jewish Folk Theatre
New Stages Theatre
New York Music Hall
New York Public Library (various branches)
Neighborhood Playhouse
Old Knickerbocker Music Hall
On-Stage Theatre
135th Street Library Theatre
Pauline Edwards Theatre (CCNY Auditorium)
People's Drama
Popular Theatre
Princess Theatre
Provincetown Playhouse
Public Theatre
Roerich Theatre (Master Institute)
Rooftop Theatre
Second Avenue Theatre
6 Fifth Avenue
Stage Door Canteen
Studio Theatre of the New School for Social Research
Theatre of the American Scene (Charles Weidman Studio; Humphrey-Weidman Studio)
Theatre Showcase
Theatre Workshop
Theresa L. Kaufman Auditorium (YMHA)
Town Hall
Walt Whitman School
Yiddish Art Theatre
Yiddish Folks Theatre

Selected Bibliography

Abbott, George. *"Mister Abbott."* New York: Random House, 1963.

Abramson, Doris. *Negro Playwrights in the American Theatre, 1925-1959*. New York: Columbia University Press, 1969.

Adams, Cindy. *Lee Strasberg: The Imperfect Genius of the Actors Studio*. Garden City, N.Y.: Doubleday, 1980.

Aherne, Brian. *A Proper Job*. Boston: Houghton Mifflin, 1969.

Aldrich, Richard Stoddard. *Gertrude Lawrence as Mrs. A: An Intimate Biography of the Great Star*. New York: Greystone Press, 1954.

Alpert, Hollis. *The Barrymores*. New York: Dial Press, 1964.

American Theatre. Stratford-Upon-Avon Studies No. 10. London: Edward Arnold, 1967.

Anderson, John Murray, and Hugh Abercrombie Anderson. *Out Without My Rubbers*. New York: Library Publishers, 1954.

Archer, Stephen, ed. *American Actors and Actresses*. Detroit: Gale Research, 1983.

Arden, Eve. *Three Phases of Eve*. New York: St. Martin's, 1985.

Asher, Don. *The Eminent Yachtsman and the Whorehouse Piano Player*. New York: Coward, McCann and Geoghegan, 1973.

Atkinson, Brooks. *Broadway Scrapbook*. New York: Theatre Arts, 1947.

_______. *Broadway*. New York: Macmillan, 1970.

Atkinson, Brooks, and Al Hirschfeld. *The Lively Years, 1929-1973*. New York: Association Press, 1973.

Aumont, Jean-Pierre. *Sun and Shadow*. Translated by Bruce Benderson. New York: W. W. Norton, 1977.

Bacon, James. *How Sweet It Is: The Jackie Gleason Story*. New York: St. Martin's Press, 1985.

Bailey, Pearl. *The Raw Pearl*. New York: Harcourt Brace and World, 1968.

Bankhead, Tallulah. *Tallulah: My Autobiography*. New York: Harper and Bros., 1952.

Baral, Robert. *Revue*. New York: Fleet, 1962.

Barker, Felix. *The Oliviers*. London: Hamish Hamilton, 1953.

Barrow, Kenneth. *Flora* [Robson]. London: Heinemann, 1981.

Barrymore, Ethel. *Memories: An Autobiography*. New York: Harper and Bros., 1955.

Bauland, Peter. *The Hooded Eagle: Modern German Drama on the New York Stage*. Syracuse: Syracuse University Press, 1968.

Behrman, S. N. *People in a Diary: A Memoir*. Boston: Little, Brown, 1972.

Bellamy, Ralph. *When the Smoke Hit the Fan*. Garden City, N.Y.: Doubleday, 1979.

Bergman, Ingrid, and Alan Burgess. *Ingrid Bergman: My Story*. New York: Delacorte, 1980.

Bergreen, Laurence. *As Thousands Cheer: The Life of Irving Berlin*. New York: Viking, 1990.

Berle, Milton, with Haskel Frankel. *Milton Berle*. New York: Delacorte Press, 1974.

Billington, Michael. *Peggy Ashcroft*. London: John Murray, 1988.
Bloom, Ken. *Broadway: An Encyclopedic Guide to the History, People, and Places of Times Square*. New York: Facts on File, 1991.
Blum, Daniel, ed. *Theatre World* [annually from 1944-1945]. New York: Crown, 1945-1951.
Bogard, Travis, Richard Moody, and Walter J. Meserve. *The Revels History of Drama in English*. Vol. 8, *American Drama*. New York: Barnes and Noble, 1977.
Bordman, Gerald. *American Musical Theatre: A Chronicle*. New York: Oxford University Press, 1978.
———. *American Operetta: From H.M.S. Pinafore to Sweeney Todd*. New York: Oxford University Press, 1981.
———. *The Oxford Companion to the American Theatre*. New York: Oxford University Press, 1984.
Bosworth, Patricia. *Montgomery Clift*. New York and London: Harcourt Brace Jovanovich, 1978.
Botto, Louis. *At This Theatre*. New York: Dodd, Mead, 1984.
Bradshaw, Jon. *Dreams That Money Can Buy: The Tragic Life of Libby Holman*. New York: William Morrow, 1985.
Brian, Dennis. *Tallulah, Darling*. New York: Macmillan, 1980.
Brockett, Oscar, and Robert R. Findlay. *Century of Innovation: A History of Euro pean and American Theatre and Drama since 1870*. Englewood Cliffs, N.J.: Prentice-Hall, 1973.
Bronner, Edwin J. *The Encyclopedia of the American Theatre, 1900-1975*. New York: A. S. Barnes, 1980.
Brough, James. *The Fabulous Fondas*. New York: David McKay, 1973.
Broussard, Louis. *American Drama: Contemporary Allegory from Eugene O'Neill to Tennessee Williams*. Norman: University of Oklahoma Press, 1962.
Brown, Jared. *The Fabulous Lunts*. New York: Atheneum, 1986.
———. *Zero Mostel*. New York: Atheneum, 1989.
Brown, John Mason. *Dramatis Personae*. New York: Viking, 1963.
———. *The Ordeal of a Playwright: Robert E. Sherwood and the Challenge of War*. New York: Harper and Row, 1970.
Brynner, Rock. *Yul: The Man Who Would Be King*. New York: Simon and Schuster, 1989.
Burke, Billie. *With a Feather on My Nose*. New York: Appleton-Century-Crofts, 1949.
Caesar, Sid, with Bill Davidson. *Where Have I Been?* New York: Crown, 1982.
Callow, Simon. *Charles Laughton: A Difficult Actor*. London: Methuen, 1987.
Carey, Gary. *Judy Holliday: An Intimate Life Story*. New York: Seaview, 1982.
———. *Anita Loos*. New York: Alfred A. Knopf, 1988.
Carson, William G. B. *Dear Josephine: The Theatrical Career of Josephine Hull*. Norman: University of Oklahoma Press, 1963.
Chapman, John, ed. *The Burns Mantle Best Plays of* [date]. Annual series. New York: Dodd, Mead, 1947-1948 to 1949-1950. (See also Burns Mantle, ed. *Best Plays* series.)
Chinoy, Helen Krich, and Linda Walsh Jenkins. *Women in American Theatre*. New York: Crown, 1981. Rev. ed. 1987.
Clark, Barrett H., and George Freedley, eds. *A History of Modern Drama*. New York: Appleton-Century, 1947.
Clurman, Harold. *Lies like Truth*. New York: Grove Press, 1958.
———. *All People Are Famous*. New York: Harcourt Brace Jovanovich, 1974.
Cohn, Art. *The Nine Lives of Michael Todd*. New York: Random House, 1958.
Collier, Richard. *Make-Believe: The Magic of International Theatre*. New York: Dodd, Mead, 1986.
Connelly, Marc. *Voices Offstage: A Book of Memoirs*. New York: Holt, Rinehart and Winston, 1968.
Conrad, Earl. *Billy Rose: Manhattan Primitive*. Cleveland, Ohio: World, 1968.
Cook, Bruce. *Brecht in Exile*. New York: Holt, Rinehart and Winston, 1982.

Corsaro, Frank. *Maverick*. New York: Vanguard Press, 1978.
Cottrell, John. *Laurence Olivier*. Englewood Cliffs, N.J.: Prentice-Hall, 1975.
Courtney, Marguerite. *Laurette*. New York: Rinehart, 1955.
Crawford, Cheryl. *One Naked Individual: My Fifty Years in the Theatre*. New York: Bobbs-Merrill, 1977.
Curtin, Kaier. *We Can Always Call them Bulgarians*. Boston: Alyson Publications, 1987.
Davidson, Bill. *Spencer Tracy: Tragic Idol*. New York: E. P. Dutton, 1987.
de Mille, Agnes. *Dance to the Piper*. Boston: Little, Brown, 1952.
Derwent, Clarence. *The Derwent Story*. New York: Henry Schuman, 1953.
Dingwell, Wilbur, ed. *The Handbook Annual of the Theatre*. New York: Coward McCann, 1941.
Douglas, Kirk. *The Ragman's Son*. New York: Pocket Books, 1989.
Douglas, Melvyn, and Tom Arthur. *See You at the Movies: The Autobiography of Melvyn Douglas*. Lanham, Md.: University Press of America, 1986.
Downer, Alan S. *Fifty Years of American Drama, 1900-1950*. Chicago: Henry Regnery, 1951.
———. *The American Theatre*. N.p.: Voice of America Forum Lectures, 1967.
Drutman, Irving. *Good Company*. Boston: Little, Brown, 1976.
Druxman, Michael B. *Basil Rathbone*. New York: A. S. Barnes, 1975.
Duberman, Martin Bauml. *Paul Robeson*. New York: Alfred A. Knopf, 1988.
Duke, Vernon. *Passport to Paris*. Boston: Little, Brown, 1955.
Edwards, Anne. *A Remarkable Woman: A Biography of Katharine Hepburn*. New York: William Morrow, 1985.
Eells, George. *The Life That Late He Led: A Biography of Cole Porter*. New York: G. P. Putnam's Sons, 1967.
Eells, George, and Stanley Musgrove. *Mae West: A Biography*. New York: William Morrow, 1982.
Engel, Lehman. *This Bright Day: An Autobiography*. New York: Macmillan, 1974.
Evans, Maurice. *All This . . . and Evans Too!* Columbia: University of South Carolina Press, 1987.
Ewen, David. *The Story of Irving Berlin*. New York: Henry Holt, 1950.
———. *The Story of America's Musical Theater*. Philadelphia: Chilton, 1961.
———. *New Complete Book of the Musical Theater*. New York: Henry Holt, 1976.
Eyles, Allen. *Rex Harrison*. London: W. H. Allen, 1985.
Fehl, Fred, with William Stott and Jane Stott. *On Broadway*. Austin: University of Texas Press, 1978.
Fonda, Henry, as told to Howard Teichman. *Fonda: My Life*. New York: New American Library, 1981.
Fordin, Hugh. *Getting to Know Him: A Biography of Oscar Hammerstein II*. New York: Random House, 1977.
Forsythe, James. *Tyrone Guthrie*. London: Hamish Hamilton, 1976.
France, Richard. *The Theatre of Orson Welles*. Lewisburg, Pa.: Bucknell University Press, 1977.
Francis, Arlene, with Florence Rome. *Arlene Francis: A Memoir*. New York: Simon and Schuster, 1978.
Freedland, Michael. *Irving Berlin*. New York: Stein and Day, 1974.
———. *Gregory Peck*. New York: William Morrow, 1980.
———. *The Secret Life of Danny Kaye*. New York: St. Martin's Press, 1985.
Freedley, George. *The Lunts*. New York: Macmillan, 1958.
Freedley, George, and John R. Reeves. *A History of the Theatre*. 3d ed. rev. New York: Crown, 1968.
Garfield, David. *A Player's Place: The Story of the Actors Studio*. New York: Macmillan, 1980.
Gassner, John. *The Theatre in Our Times*. New York: Crown, 1954.
———, and Edward Quinn. *The Reader's Encyclopedia of World Drama*. New York: Thomas Y. Crowell, 1967.

Gaver, Jack. *Curtain Calls*. New York: Dodd, Mead, 1949.
Gelb, Arthur, and Barbara Gelb. *O'Neill*. New York: Harper and Bros., 1962.
Geva, Tamara. *Split Seconds*. New York: Harper and Row, 1972.
Gielgud, John. *Early Stages: An Autobiography*. Rev. ed. London: Heinemann, 1974.
Gielgud, John, with John Miller and John Powell. *Gielgud: An Actor and His Time*. New York: Clarkson N. Potter, 1980.
Gill, Brendan. *Tallulah*. London: Michael Joseph, 1973.
Gish, Lillian, with Ann Pinchot. *The Movies, Mr. Griffith, and Me*. Englewood Cliffs, N.J.: Prentice-Hall, 1969.
Goldman, Herbert G. *Jolson: The Legend Comes to Life*. New York: Oxford Univer sity Press, 1988.
Goldstein, Malcolm. *George S. Kaufman*. New York: Oxford University Press, 1979.
Goldstone, Richard. *Thornton Wilder: An Intimate Portrait*. New York: Saturday Review Press, 1975.
Gordon, Eric A. *Mark the Music: The Life and Work of Marc Blitzstein*. New York: St. Martin's Press, 1989.
Gordon, Max, with Lewis Funke. *"Max Gordon Presents."* New York: Bernard Geis, 1963.
Gordon, Ruth. *Myself among Others*. New York: Atheneum, 1971.
_______. *My Side: The Autobiography of Ruth Gordon*. New York: Harper and Row, 1976.
Gottfried, Martin. *Broadway Musicals*. New York: Harry N. Abrams, 1979.
_______. *Jed Harris: The Curse of Genius*. Boston: Little, Brown, 1984.
Gottlieb, Polly Rose. *The Nine Lives of Billy Rose*. New York: Crown, 1968.
Grebanier, Bernard. *Then Came Each Actor*. New York: David McKay, 1975.
Green, Abel, and Joe Laurie, Jr. *Show Biz, from Vaude to Video*. New York: Henry Holt, 1951.
Green, Stanley. *The World of Musical Comedy*. 3d ed. Cranbury, N.J.: A. S. Barnes, 1974.
_______. *Encyclopaedia of the Musical Theatre*. New York: Da Capo, 1976.
Guernsey, Otis L., Jr, ed. *Playwrights/Lyricists/Composers on Theater*. New York: Dodd, Mead, 1974.
_______, ed. *Broadway Song and Story*. New York: Dodd, Mead, 1985.
Guinness, Alec. *Blessings in Disguise*. New York: Alfred A. Knopf, 1986.
Guthrie, Tyrone. *A Life in the Theatre*. London: Hamish Hamilton, 1960.
Hardwicke, Cecil, with James Brough. *A Victorian in Orbit*. London: Methuen, 1961.
Harris, Jed. *Watchman, What of the Night?*. Garden City, N.Y.: Doubleday, 1963.
_______. *A Dance on the High Wire*. New York: Crown, 1979.
Harrison, Gilbert. *The Enthusiast: A Life of Thornton Wilder*. New Haven, Conn.: Ticknor and Fields, 1983.
Harrison, Rex. *Rex*. Boston: G. K. Hall, 1976.
Havoc, June. *More Havoc*. New York: Harper and Row, 1980.
Hay, Peter. *Theatrical Anecdotes*. New York: Oxford University Press, 1987.
_______. *Broadway Anecdotes*. New York: Oxford University Press, 1989.
Hayes, Helen, with Katherine Hatch. *My Life in Three Acts*. New York: Harcourt Brace Jovanovich, 1990.
Hayman, Ronald. *John Gielgud*. London: Heinemann, 1971.
Helburn, Theresa. *A Wayward Quest*. Boston: Little, Brown, 1960.
Hellman, Lillian. *Pentimento*. Boston: Little, Brown, 1973.
Henderson, Mary C. *The City and the Theatre: New York Playhouses from Bowling Green to Times Square*. Clifton, N.J.: James T. White, 1973.
_______. *Theater in America: 200 Years of Plays, Players, and Productions*. New York: Harry N. Abrams, 1986.
Henreid, Paul, with Julius Fast. *Ladies Man*. New York: St. Martin's Press, 1984.
Herron, Ima Honaker. *The Small Town in American Drama*. Dallas: Southern Methodist University Press, 1969.
Hewitt, Barnard. *Theatre U.S.A. 1665-1957*. New York: McGraw-Hill, 1959.
Higham, Charles. *Kate: The Life of Katharine Hepburn*. New York: W. W. Norton, 1975.

———. *Charles Laughton: An Intimate Biography*. Garden City, N.Y.: Doubleday, 1976.
———. *Orson Welles: The Rise and Fall of an American Genius*. New York: St. Martin's Press, 1985.
———. *Brando: The Unauthorized Biography*. New York: New American Library, 1987.
Hirsch, Foster. *George Kelly*. Boston: Twayne, 1975.
———. *A Method to Their Madness: The History of the Actors Studio*. New York: W. W. Norton, 1984.
Hirschfeld, Al. *Show Business Is No Business*. New York: Curtis, 1951.
Hirschhorn, Clive. *Gene Kelly*. New York: St. Martin's Press, 1984.
Holden, Anthony. *Laurence Olivier*. New York: Atheneum, 1988.
Hopkins, Arthur. *Reference Point*. New York: Samuel French, 1948.
Houghton, Norris. *Entrances and Exits: A Life in and out of the Theatre*. New York: Limelight, 1991.
Houseman, John. *Run-through*. New York: Simon and Schuster, 1972.
———. *Front and Center*. New York: Simon and Schuster, 1979.
———. *Entertainers and the Entertained: Essays on Theater, Film, and Television*. New York: Simon and Schuster, 1986.
Hughes, Glenn. *A History of the American Theatre: 1700-1950*. New York: Samuel French, 1951.
Hughes, Langston, and Milton Meltzer. *Black Magic: A Pictorial History of the Negro in American Entertainment*. Englewood Cliffs, N.J.: Prentice-Hall, 1967.
Hunter, Allan. *Walter Matthau*. London: W. H. Allen, 1984.
Isaacs, Edith J. R. *The Negro in the American Theatre*. New York: Theatre Arts, 1947.
Israel, Lee. *Miss Tallulah Bankhead*. New York: G. P. Putnam's Sons, 1972.
Jablonski, Edward. *Harold Arlen: Happy with the Blues*. Garden City, N.Y.: Double day, 1961.
Jackson, Arthur. *The Best Musicals: From Show Boat to A Chorus Line*. New York: Crown, 1979.
Kasha, Al, and Joel Hirschhorn. *Notes on Broadway: Conversations with the Great Songwriters*. Chicago: Contemporary Books, 1985.
Kazan, Elia. *Elia Kazan: A Life*. New York: Alfred A. Knopf, 1988.
Kennedy, Harold J. *No Pickle, No Performance*. New York: Berkley, 1979.
Kieran, Thomas. *Olivier*. London: Sidgwick and Jackson, 1981.
Kislan, Richard. *Hoofing on Broadway: A History of Show Dancing*. New York: Pren tice-Hall, 1987.
Kitt, Eartha. *I'm Still Here*. London: Sidgwick and Jackson, 1989.
Kotsilibas-Davis, James. *The Barrymores: The Royal Family in Hollywood*. New York: Crown, 1981.
Kraft, Hy. *On My Way to the Theater*. New York: Macmillan, 1971.
Krutch, Joseph Wood. *American Drama since 1918: An Informal History*. Rev. ed. New York: George Brazillier, 1957.
LaGuardia, Robert. *Monty: A Biography of Montgomery Clift*. New York: Avon, 1977.
Laffey, Bruce. *Beatrice Lillie: The Funniest Woman in the World*. New York: Wynwood Press, 1989.
Lahr, John. *Notes on a Cowardly Lion: The Biography of Bert Lahr*. New York: Alfred A. Knopf, 1969.
Lanchester, Elsa. *Elsa Lanchester Herself*. New York: St. Martin's Press, 1983.
Landis, Jessie Royce. *You Won't Be So Pretty (But You'll Know More)* London: W. H. Allen, 1954.
Langner, Lawrence. *The Magic Curtain*. New York: E. P. Dutton, 1951.
Laufe, Abe. *Anatomy of a Hit*. New York: Hawthorn, 1966.
———. *Broadway's Greatest Musicals*. Rev. ed. New York: Funk and Wagnalls, 1977.
———. *The Wicked Stage: A History of Theatre Censorship and Harassment in the United States*. New York: Frederick Ungar, 1978.

Lawrence, Gertrude. *A Star Danced*. Garden City, N.Y.: Doubleday, Doran, 1945.

Lawrence, Jerome. *Actor: The Life and Times of Paul Muni*. New York: G. P. Putnam's Sons, 1974.

Le Gallienne, Eva. *With a Quiet Heart*. New York: Viking, 1953.

Leamer, Laurence. *As Time Goes By: The Life of Ingrid Bergman*. New York: Harper and Row, 1986.

Lee, Lawrence, and Barry Gifford. *Saroyan: A Biography*. New York: Harper and Row, 1984.

Lees, Gene. *Inventing Champagne: The Worlds of Lerner and Loewe*. New York: St. Martin's Press, 1990.

Leonard, William Torbert. *Once Was Enough*. Metuchen, N.J.: Scarecrow Press, 1986.

Leiter, Samuel L. *From Belasco to Brook: Representative Directors of the English-speaking Stage*. Westport, Conn.: Greenwood Press, 1991.

Lerner, Alan Jay. *The Street Where I Live*. New York and London: W. W. Norton, 1978.

________. *The Musical Theatre: A Celebration*. London: Collins, 1986.

Lesley, Cole. *The Life of Noël Coward*. London: Jonathan Cape, 1976.

Lesley, Cole, Graham Payne, and Sheridan Morley. *Noël Coward and His Friends*. New York: William Morrow, 1979.

Lewis, Emory. *Stages: The Fifty-Year Childhood of the American Theatre*. Englewood Cliffs, N.J.: Prentice-Hall, 1969.

Lewis, Robert. *Slings and Arrows: Theater in My Life*. New York: Stein and Day, 1984.

Ley-Piscator, Maria. *The Piscator Experiment: The Political Theatre*. Carbondale: Southern Illinois University Press, 1970.

Lifson, David. *The Yiddish Theatre in America*. New York: Thomas Yoseloff, 1965.

Lillie, Beatrice, with James Brough. *Every Other Inch a Lady*. Garden City, N.Y.: Doubleday, 1972.

Lindsay, Cynthia. *Dear Boris: The Life of William Henry Pratt a.k.a. Boris Karloff*. New York: Alfred A. Knopf, 1975.

Little, Stuart. *Off-Broadway: The Prophetic Theater*. New York: Coward, McCann and Geoghegan, 1972.

Logan, Joshua. *Josh: My Up and Down, In and Out Life*. London: W. H. Allen, 1977.

Loney, Glenn. *Twentieth Century Theatre*. 2 vols. New York: Facts on File, 1983.

________. *Unsung Genius: The Passion of Dancer-Choreographer Jack Cole*. New York: Franklin Watts, 1984.

Lyon, James K. *Bertolt Brecht in America*. Princeton, N.J.: Princeton University Press, 1980.

McBride, Joseph. *Orson Welles, Actor and Director*. New York: Harvest, 1977.

McCambridge, Mercedes. *The Quality of Mercy*. New York: Times Books, 1981.

McClintic, Guthrie. *Me and Kit*. Boston: Little, Brown, 1955.

McNamara, Brooks. *The Shuberts of Broadway*. New York: Oxford University Press, 1990.

MacNicholas, John. *Twentieth-Century American Dramatists*. Detroit: Gale Re search, 1981.

Maney, Richard. *Fanfare: The Confessions of a Press Agent*. New York: Harper's, 1957.

Mantle, Burns, ed. *Best Plays of* [date]. Annual series. New York: Dodd, Mead, 1940-1941 to 1946-1947. (See also John Chapman, ed. *The Burns Mantle Best Plays of* series)

Martin, Mary. *My Heart Belongs*. New York: William Morrow, 1976.

Marx, Samuel, and Jan Clayton. *Rodgers and Hart: Bewitched, Bothered, and Bedev iled.* New York: G. P. Putnam's Sons, 1976.

Massey, Raymond. *A Hundred Different Lives*. London: Robson, 1979.

Mates, Julian. *America's Musical Stage: Two Hundred Years of Musical Theatre*. Westport, Conn.: Greenwood Press, 1985.

Matlaw, Myron. *Modern World Drama: An Encyclopedia*. New York: E. P. Dutton,

1972.
Meredith, Scott. *George S. Kaufman and His Friends*. Garden City, N.Y.: Doubleday, 1974.
Merman, Ethel, and George Eells. *Merman: An Autobiography*. New York: Simon and Schuster, 1978.
———, and Pete Martin. *Who Could Ask for Anything More?* Garden City, N.Y.: Doubleday, 1955.
Mersand, Joseph L. *The American Drama since 1930*. Port Washington, N.Y.: Kennikat Press, 1968.
Meserve, Walter J. *An Outline History of American Drama*. Totowa, N.J.: Littlefield, Adams, 1965.
———, ed. *Discussions of Modern American Drama*. Boston: D. C. Heath, 1965.
Mielziner, Jo. *Designing for the Theatre: A Memoir and a Portfolio*. New York: Atheneum, 1965.
Miller, Arthur. *Timebends: A Life*. New York: Grove Press, 1987.
Miller, Jordan. *American Dramatic Literature*. New York: McGraw-Hill, 1961.
Milne, Tom. *Rouben Mamoulian*. Bloomington: Indiana University Press, 1969.
Mitchell, Loften. *Black Drama: The Story of the American Negro in the Theatre*. New York:Hawthorn, 1967.
———. *Voices of the Black Theatre*. Clifton, N.J.: James T. White, 1975.
Mordden, Ethan. *The American Theatre*. New York: Oxford University Press, 1981.
———. *Broadway Babies: The People Who Made the American Musical*. New York: Oxford University Press, 1983.
Morehouse, Ward. *Matinee Tomorrow*. New York: Whittlesey House, 1949.
Morley, Margaret. *Larger Than Life: The Biography of Robert Morley*. London: Robson, 1979.
Morley, Robert. *Robert Morley: A Reluctant Autobiography*. New York: Simon and Schuster, 1967.
Morley, Sheridan. *A Talent to Amuse: A Biography of Noël Coward*. London: Heine mann, 1969.
———. *Gertrude Lawrence: A Biography*. New York: Weidenfeld and Nicolson, 1981.
———. *James Mason: Odd Man Out*. New York: Harper and Row, 1989.
Morris, Lloyd. *Curtain Time: The Story of the American Theater*. New York: Random House, 1953.
Morrow, Lee Alan. *The Tony Award Book: Four Decades of Great American Theater*. New York: Abbeville Press, 1987.
Mosel, Tad, with Gertrude Macy. *Leading Lady: The World and Theatre of Katharine Cornell*. Boston: Little, Brown, 1978.
Moseley, Roy, with Philip Masheter and Martin Masheter. *Rex Harrison: A Biogra phy*. New York: St. Martin's Press, 1987.
Mostel, Kate, and Madeline Gilford, with Jack Gilford and Zero Mostel. *170 Years of Show Business*. New York: Random House, 1978.
Munn, Michael. *Kirk Douglas*. New York: St. Martin's Press, 1985.
Nadel, Norman. *A Pictorial History of the Theatre Guild*. New York: Crown, 1969.
Nannes, Casper. *Politics in the American Theater*. Washington, D.C.: Catholic Uni versity Press, 1960.
Neal, Patricia. *As I Am*. New York: Pocket Books, 1988.
The New York Times Directory of the Theatre. New York: Arno Press, 1973.
Noble, Peter. *The Fabulous Orson Welles*. London: Hutchinson, 1956.
Notable Names in the American Theatre. Clifton, N.J.: James T. White, 1976.
Nugent, Elliott. *Events Leading up to the Comedy*. New York: Trident, 1965.
Oberfirst, Robert. *Al Jolson: You Ain't Heard Nothin' Yet*. San Diego: A. S. Barnes, 1981.
O'Connor, Garry. *Ralph Richardson*. London: Hodder and Stoughton, 1982.
Oenslager, Donald. *The Theatre of Donald Oenslager*. Middletown, Conn.: Wesleyan University Press, 1978.
Olivier, Laurence. *Confessions of an Actor*. London: Weidenfeld and Nicolson, 1982.
Oppenheimer, George. *The Passionate Playgoer*. New York: Viking, 1958.

Palmer, Lilli. *Change Lobsters and Dance*. New York: Macmillan, 1975.
Parish, James Robert, with Steven Whitney. *Vincent Price Unmasked*. New York: Drake, 1974.
Pendleton, Ralph. *The Theatre of Robert Edmond Jones*. Middletown, Conn.: Wes leyan University Press, 1959.
Peyser, Joan. *Bernstein: A Biography*. New York: Beech Tree Press, 1987.
Picon, Molly, with Jean Bergantini Grillo. *Molly! An Autobiography*. New York: Simon and Schuster, 1980.
Poggi, Jack. *Theater in America: The Impact of Economic Forces, 1870-1967*. Ithaca, N.Y.: Cornell University Press, 1968.
Poitier, Sidney. *This Life*. New York: Alfred A. Knopf, 1980.
Porter, Cole, with Richard G. Hubler. *The Cole Porter Story*. Cleveland: World, 1965.
Preminger, Erik Lee. *Gypsy and Me: At Home and on the Road with Gypsy Rose Lee*. Boston: Little, Brown, 1984.
Preminger, Otto. *Preminger: An Autobiography*. Garden City, N.Y.: Doubleday, 1977.
Price, Julia S. *The Off-Broadway Theatre*. New York: Scarecrow Press, 1962.
Price, Vincent. *Vincent Price: His Movies, His Plays, and His Life*. Garden City, N.Y.: Doubleday, 1978.
Quinn, Arthur Hobson. *A History of the American Drama*. Vol 2. *From the Civil War to the Present Day*. New York: Appleton-Century-Croft, rev. ed., 1964.
Quirk, Lawrence J. *Margaret Sullavan: Child of Fate*. New York: St. Martin's Press, 1986.
Randall, Tony, with Michael Mindlin. *Which Reminds Me*. New York: Delacorte Press, 1989.
Rathbone, Basil. *In and out of Character*. Garden City, N.Y.: Doubleday, 1962.
Redgrave, Michael. *In My Mind's Eye: An Actor's Autobiography*. New York: Viking, 1983.
Reinhardt, Gottfried. *The Genius: A Memoir of Max Reinhardt*. New York: Alfred A. Knopf, 1979.
Rice, Elmer. *Minority Report*. New York: Simon and Schuster, 1963.
Rich, Frank, with Lisa Aronson. *The Theatre Art of Boris Aronson*. New York: Alfred A. Knopf, 1987.
Robbins, Jhan. *Yul Brynner: The Inscrutable King*. New York: Dodd, Mead, 1987.
Rodgers, Richard. *Musical Stages*. New York: Random House, 1975.
Roppolo, Joseph P. *Philip Barry*. New York: Twayne, 1965.
Ross, Lillian, and Helen Ross. *The Player: A Profile of an Art*. New York: Simon and Schuster, 1961.
Schildkraut, Joseph. *My Father and I*. New York: Viking, 1959.
Schneider, Alan. *Entrances: An American Director's Journey*. New York: Viking, 1986.
Schwartz, Charles. *Cole Porter: A Biography*. New York: Dial Press, 1977.
Seldes, Marian. *The Bright Lights: A Theatre Life*. Boston: Houghton Mifflin, 1978.
Seaman, Barbara. *Lovely Me: The Life of Jacqueline Susann*. New York: William Morrow, 1987.
Sheaffer, Louis. *O'Neill: Son and Playwright*. Boston: Little, Brown, 1968.
________. *O'Neill: Son and Artist*. Boston: Little, Brown, 1973.
Sheehy, Helen. *Margo: The Life and Theatre of Margo Jones*. Dallas: Southern Methodist University Press, 1989.
Shivers, Alfred. *The Life of Maxwell Anderson*. New York: Stein and Day, 1983.
Sieben, Pearl. *The Immortal Jolson*. New York: Frederick Fell, 1962.
Sievers, W. David. *Freud on Broadway: A History of Psychoanalyis and the American Drama*. New York: Cooper Square, rev. ed. 1970.
Sillman, Leonard. *Here Lies Leonard Sillman, Straightened Out at Last*. New York: Citadel, 1959.
Silvers, Phil, and Robert Saffron. *This Laugh Is on Me: The Phil Silvers Story*. Engle wood Cliffs, N.J.: Prentice-Hall, 1973.
Simon, Linda. *Thornton Wilder: His World*. Garden City, N.Y.: Doubleday, 1979.
Singer, Kurt. *The Laughton Story: An Intimate Biography of Charles Laughton*. Phila-

delphia: J. C. Winston, 1954.
Skinner, Cornelia Otis. *Life with Lindsay and Crouse*. Boston: Houghton Mifflin, 1976.
Smith, Cecil. *Musical Comedy in America*. New York: Theatre Arts, 1950.
Sobel, Bernard. *Broadway Heartbeat*. New York: Hermitage House, 1953.
Sobol, Louis. *The Longest Street*. New York: Crown, 1968.
Sorell, Walter. *Hanya Holm: The Biography of an Artist*. Middletown, Conn.: Wes leyan University Press, 1969.
Spoto, Donald. *Lenya: A Life*. Boston: Little, Brown, 1989.
Stagg, Jerry. *The Brothers Shubert*. New York: Random House, 1968.
Stevenson, Isabelle, ed. *The Tony Award*. New York: Arno Press, 1975.
Stickney, Dorothy. *Openings and Closings*. Garden City, N.Y.: Doubleday, 1979.
Swindell, Larry. *Body and Soul: The Story of John Garfield*. New York: William Morrow, 1975.
Taubman, Howard. *The Making of the American Theatre*. New York: Coward, McCann, 1965.
Taylor, John Russell. *Alec Guinness: A Celebration*. Boston: Little Brown, 1984.
Taylor, Theodore. *Jule: The Story of Composer Jule Styne*. New York: Random House, 1979.
Teichman, Howard. *George S. Kaufman: An Intimate Portrait*. New York: Atheneum, 1972.
Todd, Michael, Jr., and Susan McCarthy Todd. *A Valuable Property: The Life Story of Michael Todd*. New York: Arbor House, 1983.
Toohey, John L. *A History of the Pulitzer Prize Plays*. New York: Citadel, 1967.
Tunney, Kieran. *Tallulah: Darling of the Gods*. New York: E. P. Dutton, 1973.
Vickers, Hugo. *Cecil Beaton*. Boston: Little, Brown, 1985.
Waters, Ethel, with Charles Samuels. *His Eye Is on the Sparrow*. Garden City, N.Y.: Doubleday, 1951.
Weales, Gerald. *American Drama since World War II*. New York: Harcourt, Brace and World, 1962.
———. *Odets: The Playwright*. London: Methuen, 1985.
Webster, Margaret. *Don't Put Your Daughter on the Stage*. New York: Alfred A. Knopf, 1972.
West, Mae. *Goodness Had Nothing to Do with It*. Englewood Cliffs, N.J.: Prentice-Hall, 1959.
Wharton, John F. *Life among the Playwrights*. New York: Quadrangle, 1974.
Williams, Dakin, and Shepherd Mead. *Tennessee Williams: An Intimate Biography*. New York: Arbor House, 1983.
Williams, Henry B., ed. *The American Theatre: A Sum of Its Parts*. New York: Samuel French, 1971.
Williams, Tennessee. *Memoirs*. Garden City, N.Y.: Doubleday, 1975.
Wilson, Garff. *A History of American Acting*. Bloomington: Indiana University Press, 1966.
———. *Three Hundred Years of American Drama and Theatre*. Englewood Cliffs, N.J.: Prentice-Hall, 1973.
Winters, Shelley. *Shelley, Also Known as Shirley*. New York: William Morrow, 1980.
Woll, Alan. *Dictionary of the Black Theatre: Broadway, Off-Broadway, and Selected Harlem Theatres*. Westport, Conn.: Greenwood Press, 1983.
———. *Black Musical Theatre: From "Coontown" to "Dreamgirls."* Baton Rouge: Louisiana State University Press, 1989.
Wright, William. *Lillian Hellman: The Image, the Woman*. New York: Simon and Schuster, 1986.
Wynn, Keenan, with James Brough. *Ed Wynn's Son*. Garden City, N.Y.: Doubleday, 1959.
Young, B. A. *The Rattigan Version: The Theatre of Character*. New York: Atheneum, 1988.
Young, Stark. *Immortal Shadows*. New York: Charles Scribner's Sons, 1948.
Yurka, Blanche. *Bohemian Girl*. Athens: Ohio University Press, 1970.
Zabel, Morton. *The Art of Ruth Draper*. Garden City, N.Y.: Doubleday, 1960.

Zolotow, Maurice. *No People like Show People*. New York: Random House, 1951.
———. *Stagestruck: The Romance of Alfred Lunt and Lynn Fontanne*. New York: Harcourt, Brace and World, 1964.
Zorina, Vera. *Zorina*. New York: Farrar Straus Giroux, 1986.

Index of Proper Names

This index includes names of individuals, theatres, and production companies mentioned in the entries.

Index of Titles

This index contains the titles of plays, songs, sketches, and books mentioned in the entries.

About the Author

SAMUEL L. LEITER is Professor of Theatre at Brooklyn College, City University of New York. His earlier works include *The Art of Kabuki: Famous Plays in Performance* (1979), *Kabuki Encyclopedia: An English-Language Adaptation of Kabuki Jiten, Ten Seasons: New York Theatre in the Seventies, From Belasco to Brook: Representative Directors of the English-Speaking Stage, From Stanislavsky to Barrault: Representative Directors of the European Stage, Encyclopedia of the New York Stage, 1920-1930, Encyclopedia of the New York Stage, 1930-1940* (Greenwood Press, 1979, 1986, 1991, 1991, 1985, 1989), and numerous articles in journals such as the *Educational Theatre Journal, Literature East and West, Drama Survey, Players, Theatre History Studies*, and the *Asian Theatre Journal*. He is the editor of *Shakespeare Around the Globe: A Guide to Notable Postwar Revivals* (Greenwood Press, 1986). He also is the editor of the *Asian Theatre Journal*.